# THE OXFORD HANDBOOK OF

FEMINISM AND LAW IN THE UNITED STATES

THE OXFORD HANDBOOK OF

FEMINISM AND LAW IN THE UNITED STATES

Edited by
DEBORAH L. BRAKE, MARTHA CHAMALLAS,
and VERNA L. WILLIAMS

OXFORD
UNIVERSITY PRESS

Oxford University Press is a department of the University of Oxford. It furthers
the University's objective of excellence in research, scholarship, and education
by publishing worldwide. Oxford is a registered trade mark of Oxford University
Press in the UK and certain other countries.

Published in the United States of America by Oxford University Press
198 Madison Avenue, New York, NY 10016, United States of America.

© Oxford University Press 2023

All rights reserved. No part of this publication may be reproduced, stored in
a retrieval system, or transmitted, in any form or by any means, without the
prior permission in writing of Oxford University Press, or as expressly permitted
by law, by license, or under terms agreed with the appropriate reproduction
rights organization. Inquiries concerning reproduction outside the scope of the
above should be sent to the Rights Department, Oxford University Press, at the
address above.

You must not circulate this work in any other form
and you must impose this same condition on any acquirer.

Library of Congress Cataloging-in-Publication Data
Names: Brake, Deborah L., editor. | Chamallas, Martha, editor. | Williams, Verna L., editor.
Title: The Oxford handbook of feminism and law in the United States /
edited by Deborah L. Brake, Martha Chamallas, and Verna L. Williams.
Description: New York : Oxford University Press, [2023] |
Series: Oxford handbooks series |
Includes bibliographical references and index. |
Identifiers: LCCN 2022049852 (print) | LCCN 2022049853 (ebook) |
ISBN 9780197519998 (hardback) | ISBN 9780197520024 (online) | ISBN 9780197520017 (epub)
Subjects: LCSH: Feminist jurisprudence—United States. |
Women—Legal status, laws, etc.—United States—History.
Classification: LCC KF478 .O94 2023 (print) | LCC KF478 (ebook) |
DDC 342.7308/78—dc23/eng/20230105
LC record available at https://lccn.loc.gov/2022049852
LC ebook record available at https://lccn.loc.gov/2022049853

DOI: 10.1093/oxfordhb/9780197519998.001.0001

Printed by Integrated Books International, United States of America

Contents

Contributors	xi
Introduction	xix
Deborah L. Brake, Martha Chamallas, and Verna L. Williams	

PART I: THEORY, CONNECTIONS, AND CRITICISMS

Historical Perspectives

1. The Long History of Feminist Legal Theory Tracy A. Thomas	1

A. Prominent Strands of Feminist Legal Theory

Liberal Feminism

2. Liberal Feminist Jurisprudence: Foundational, Enduring, Adaptive Linda C. McClain and Brittany K. Hacker	19

Dominance Feminism

3. Dominance Feminism: Placing Sexualized Power at the Center Kathryn Abrams	39

Relational Feminism

4. A Relational Approach to Law and Its Core Concepts Jennifer Nedelsky	57

Intersectional Feminism

5. A Genealogy of Intersectionality Emily Houh	75

Sex-Positive Feminism

6. Sex-Positive Feminism's Values in Search of the Law of Pleasure — 94
   SUSAN FRELICH APPLETON

Postmodern Feminism

7. Feminism is Dead, Long Live Feminisms: A Postmodern Take on The Road to Gender Equality — 112
   CAMILLE GEAR RICH

Comparative Perspectives

8. Gender Disruption, Amelioration, and Transformation: A Comparative Perspective — 131
   ROSALIND DIXON AND AMELIA LOUGHLAND

B. Connections to Adjacent Theoretical Discourses

Queer Theory

9. When Queer Theory Goes to Law School — 150
   BRENDA COSSMAN

Masculinities Theory

10. Masculinities Theory as Impetus for Change in Feminism and Law — 169
    ANN C. MCGINLEY

Distributional Theory

11. Governance Feminism and Distributional Analysis — 187
    AZIZA AHMED

C. Connections to Feminist Activism and Movements

The ERA Movement

12. The Equal Rights Amendment, Then and Now — 201
    JULIE C. SUK

The Movements to End Rape and Domestic Violence

13. The Anti-Rape and Battered Women's Movements of the 1970s and 1980s — 220
    LEIGH GOODMARK

The Campus Sexual Assault Movement

14. The Title IX Movement Against Campus Sexual Harassment: How a Civil Rights Law and a Feminist Movement Inspired Each Other — 240
    NANCY CHI CANTALUPO

The #MeToo Movement

15. Feminism and #MeToo: The Power of the Collective — 259
    TRISTIN K. GREEN

The Reproductive Justice Movement

16. From Reproductive Rights to Reproductive Justice: Abortion in Constitutional Law and Politics — 276
    MARY ZIEGLER

D. Backlash and Critics of Feminism

Economic Critiques

17. Law and Economics Against Feminism — 294
    MARTHA T. MCCLUSKEY

Conservative and Religious Critiques

18. Backlash Against Feminism: Rethinking a Loaded Concept — 313
    SALLY J. KENNEY

PART II: FEMINIST INFLUENCE ON LAW

A. Legal Claims and Doctrines

Sexual Harassment

19. Sexual Harassment: The Promise and Limits of a Feminist Cause of Action — 332
    THERESA M. BEINER

Gender Stereotyping

20. Degendering the Law Through Stereotype Theory — 350
    STEPHANIE BORNSTEIN

The Battered Women's Defense

21. Beyond Battered Women's Syndrome — 370
    SARAH M. BUEL

Title IX and Gender Equity in Sports

22. Title IX: Separate but Equal for Girls and Women in Athletics — 388
    ERIN E. BUZUVIS

B. Legal Understandings

Consent in Sexual Encounters

23. Consent, Rape, and the Criminal Law — 406
    KATHARINE K. BAKER AND MICHELLE OBERMAN

Pregnancy Discrimination

24. Pregnancy and Work: 50 Years of Legal Theory, Litigation, and Legislation — 423
    DEBORAH A. WIDISS

Reproductive Rights

25. Constitutionalizing Reproductive Rights (and Justice) — 442
    MELISSA MURRAY AND HILARIE MEYERS

Motherhood

26. Disputed Conceptions of Motherhood — 461
    JENNIFER S. HENDRICKS

Gender, Human Rights, and International Law

27. Applying International Feminist Insights to Gendered Violence in the United States — 478
    TRACY E. HIGGINS

C. Pedagogy and Judging

Feminist Pedagogy in Legal Education

28. Feminism's Transformation of Legal Education and Unfinished Agenda — 496
    JAMIE R. ABRAMS

Gender, Social Justice and Judging

29. Feminist Judging: Theories and Practices ... 515
    KRISTIN KALSEM

D. Emerging Areas

Contract Law

30. Contract's Influence on Feminism and Vice Versa ... 532
    MARTHA M. ERTMAN

Digital Privacy

31. Feminism, Privacy, and Law in Cyberspace ... 552
    MICHELE ESTRIN GILMAN

Environmental Law

32. Environmental Law and Feminism ... 573
    CINNAMON P. CARLARNE

Immigration Law

33. Reconceptualizing the Terms and Conditions of Entry to the United States: A Feminist Reimagining of Immigration Law ... 592
    MARIA L. ONTIVEROS

Intellectual Property

34. Invisible Women and Intangible Property: A Feminist Consciousness Raising for Authors and Inventors ... 610
    ANN BARTOW

Tax Law

35. A Taxing Feminism ... 630
    ANTHONY C. INFANTI AND BRIDGET J. CRAWFORD

Tort Law

36. Tort Law and Feminism ... 648
    SARAH L. SWAN

Index ... 667

Contributors

Jamie R. Abrams is Professor of Law and Director of the Legal Rhetoric Program at American University's Washington College of Law. She writes in the areas of reproductive decisionmaking, gendered violence, and legal education pedagogy. She has authored torts and family law volumes in the West Academic Bridge to Practice Series and has won numerous awards for her inclusive and innovative teaching techniques.

Kathryn Abrams is Herma Hill Kay Distinguished Professor of Law at UC-Berkeley Law School. She writes in the areas of feminist theory, law and emotions, and social movements. Her scholarship has appeared in journals such as *Yale Law Journal*, *Columbia Law Review*, and *California Law Review*.

Aziza Ahmed is Professor of Law at Boston University School of Law. She writes in the area of public health law, science and technology studies, and feminist legal theory, and her scholarship has appeared in journals such as *Boston University Law Review*, *Journal of Law and Biosciences*, and the *Wisconsin Law Review*.

Susan Frelich Appleton is the Lemma Barkeloo & Phoebe Couzins Professor of Law at Washington University in St. Louis. She writes in the areas of family law, sex, gender, reproduction, and feminist legal theory, and her scholarship has appeared in journals such as the *Yale Journal of Law & Feminism*, the *Dukeminier Awards Journal*, and *Columbia Law Review*.

Katharine K. Baker is a University Distinguished Professor of Law at the Illinois Institute of Technology's Chicago-Kent School of Law. Her scholarship focuses on the intersection of women's intimate lives and the law, particularly in the areas of sexual violence and family law. Her articles have appeared in *Harvard Law Review*, *Yale Law Journal*, and *University of Chicago Law Review*.

Ann Bartow is a Professor of Law at the University of New Hampshire School of Law. She writes in the areas of intellectual property law, privacy law, and feminist legal theory. She is a coeditor of *The Jurisprudential Legacy of Justice Ruth Bader Ginsburg* (NYU Press, 2023) (with Ryan Vacca), including a coauthored chapter on Justice Ginsburg's copyright jurisprudence (with Ryan Vacca).

Theresa M. Beiner is the Dean and Nadine Baum Distinguished Professor of Law at the University of Arkansas at Little Rock William H. Bowen School of Law. She writes in the areas of women in the legal profession, employment discrimination, federal judicial appointments, and constitutional law, and is the author of *Gender Myths v. Working*

Realities: Using Social Science to Reformulate Sexual Harassment Law (NYU Press, 2005) and a coauthor of *Civil Procedure: A Context and Practice Textbook*.

Stephanie Bornstein is Professor of Law at the University of Florida Levin College of Law. She writes in the areas of antidiscrimination law, employment and labor law, and civil procedure. Her scholarship has appeared in numerous journals including the *California Law Review, Boston University Law Review*, and *Minnesota Law Review*, and she is coauthor of the casebook *Cases and Materials on Employment Discrimination* (Aspen, 10th ed., 2021) (with Charles A. Sullivan and Michael J. Zimmer).

Deborah L. Brake is Professor of Law, John E. Murray Faculty Scholar, and Associate Dean for Research and Faculty Development at the University of Pittsburgh. Her scholarship on law and gender has appeared in journals such as *Georgetown Law Journal, Minnesota Law Review, Harvard Journal of Gender Law*, and *William & Mary Law Review*. She is the author of *Getting in the Game: Title IX and the Women's Sports Revolution* (NYU Press, 2010) and coauthor of the casebook, *Gender and Law: Theory, Doctrine, Commentary* (9th ed., Wolters Kluwer, 2023) (with Katharine T. Bartlett, Joanna L. Grossman and Frank Rudy Cooper).

Sarah M. Buel is a retired Clinical Professor of Law at Arizona State University Sandra Day O'Connor College of Law. Her almost forty years' scholarship, pedagogy, and practice focused on the juxtaposition of gender violence, poverty, criminal, and human rights law. She has authored more than thirty articles, book chapters, and amicus briefs to the U.S. Supreme Court and the Inter-American Commission on Human Rights.

Erin E. Buzuvis is Associate Dean for Academic Affairs and Professor of Law at Western New England University School of Law. She writes in the areas of gender, education, and sport, and her scholarship has appeared in journals such as the *Journal of College and University Law, Marquette Sports Law Review*, and the *Oklahoma Law Review*.

Nancy Chi Cantalupo is Associate Professor of Law at Wayne State University. Her scholarship seeks to combat gender-based and other discriminatory violence through the use of civil rights laws and has appeared in journals such as *Harvard Journal of Law & Gender, Wake Forest Law Review*, and *Yale Law Journal Forum*.

Cinnamon P. Carlarne is the Associate Dean for Faculty & Intellectual Life and the Robert J. Lynn Chair in Law at The Ohio State University Moritz College of Law. She writes in the areas of domestic and international environmental law and is the author of *Climate Change Law & Policy: EU & US Perspectives* (Oxford University Press, 2010) and *Climate Change Law* (Foundation Press, 2018) (with Daniel A. Farber).

Martha Chamallas is the Distinguished University Professor and Robert J. Lynn Chair in Law Emerita at the Moritz College of Law, The Ohio State University. She writes on feminist legal theory, employment discrimination law, and gender and race bias in tort law. She is the author of *Introduction to Feminist Legal Theory* (3d ed., Wolters Kluwer, 2013), *The Measure of Injury: Race, Gender and Tort Law* (NYU Press, 2010) (with

Jennifer B. Wriggins), and *Feminist Judgments: Rewritten Tort Opinions* (Cambridge University Press, 2020) (with Lucinda M. Finley).

Brenda Cossman is the Goodman-Schipper Chair and Professor of Law at the University of Toronto. She writes in the area of gender, sexuality, and law and is the author of *The New Sex Wars: Sexual Harm in the #MeToo Era* (NYU Press, 2021).

Bridget J. Crawford is a University Distinguished Professor of Law at Pace University. She writes in the areas of taxation, wills and trusts, and feminist legal theory and is the coeditor (with Anthony C. Infanti) of *Feminist Judgments: Rewritten Tax Opinions* (Cambridge University Press, 2017), and *Critical Tax Theory: An Introduction* (Cambridge University Press, 2017).

Rosalind Dixon is a Professor of Law at the University of New South Wales, Faculty of Law, and works in the fields of comparative constitutional law and design, socioeconomic rights and economic policy, and law and gender. She is the author of *Abusive Borrowing: Legal Globalization and the Subversion of Liberal Democracy* (Oxford University Press, 2021) (with David Landau), *From Free to Fair Markets: Liberalism After COVID-19* (Oxford University Press, 2022) (with Richard Holden), and *Responsive Judicial Review: Democracy and Dysfunction in the Modern Age* (Oxford University Press, 2023).

Martha M. Ertman is Carole & Hanan Sibel Research Professor at the University of Maryland Carey Law School. She writes in the areas of commodification —focusing on the upside of contracts for have-nots in contexts such as family law and racial justice— as well as contracts and transactional skills. Her scholarship has appeared in journals such as *Texas Law Review* and *Columbia Journal of Gender & Law*, and she is the author of *Love's Promises: How Contracts and Deals Shape All Kinds of Families* (Beacon Press, 2015).

Michele Estrin Gilman is the Venable Professor of Law and Associate Dean for Faculty Research and Development at the University of Baltimore School of Law. She writes in the areas of data privacy and gender equity, and her scholarship has appeared in journals such as *California Law Review*, *Vanderbilt Law Review*, and *Washington University Law Review*.

Leigh Goodmark is the Marjorie Cook Professor of Law at the University of Maryland Carey School of Law. She writes in the area of gender violence and is the author of *Decriminalizing Domestic Violence: A Balanced Policy Approach to Intimate Partner Violence* (University of California Press, 2018) and *Imperfect Victims: Criminalized Survivors and the Promise of Abolition Feminism* (University of California Press, 2023).

Tristin K. Green is Professor of Law, Dean's Circle Scholar, and Co-Director of the Work Law and Justice Program at the University of San Francisco School of Law. She writes in the areas of race and sex inequality and discrimination and is the author of *Discrimination Laundering: The Rise of Organizational Innocence and the Crisis of*

Equal Opportunity Law (Cambridge University Press, 2017) and *Racial Emotion at Work: Dismantling and Building Racial Justice in the Workplace* (California University Press, 2023).

Brittany K. Hacker is a VOCA Staff Attorney at Legal Services of Northern Virginia. She specializes in representing survivors of domestic violence in family law litigation.

Jennifer S. Hendricks is Professor of Law and Co-Director of the Juvenile and Family Law Program at the University of Colorado, Boulder. She writes in the areas of sex differences, equality, and constitutional family law and is the author of *Essentially a Mother: A Feminist Approach to the Law of Pregnancy and Motherhood* (University of California Press, 2023).

Tracy E. Higgins is Professor of Law and Founding Director of the Leitner Center for International Law and Justice at Fordham Law School. She writes in the areas of feminist theory and international human rights and her scholarship has appeared in journals such as *Harvard Law Review*, *Cornell Law Review*, and *Yale Journal of Law and Feminism*.

Emily Houh is the Gustavus Henry Wald Professor of the Law and Contracts and co-founder of the Nathaniel R. Jones Center for Race, Gender, and Social Justice at the University of Cincinnati College of Law. Much of her scholarship focuses on the interplay between contract law and critical race theory. An active member for many years of the Association of American University Professors (AAUP), she serves on the AAUP's Committee A on Academic Freedom and Tenure, Committee on Historically Black Institutions and Scholars of Color, and Litigation Committee.

Anthony C. Infanti is the Christopher C. Walthour, Sr. Professor of Law at the University of Pittsburgh School of Law. He writes in the area of tax law and policy from both critical and comparative perspectives and is the author of *Our Selfish Tax Laws: Toward Tax Reform That Mirrors Our Better Selves* (MIT Press, 2018) and *Tax and Time: On the Use and Misuse of Legal Imagination* (NYU Press, 2022).

Kristin Kalsem is the Charles Hartsock Professor of Law and co-founder of the Nathaniel R. Jones Center for Race, Gender, and Social Justice at the University of Cincinnati College of Law. She writes in the areas of critical race/feminist legal theory, law and literature, commercial law, and participatory action research and is the author of *In Contempt: Nineteenth-Century Women, Law, and Literature* (Ohio State University Press, 2012).

Sally J. Kenney holds the Newcomb College endowed chair and is a faculty member in the Political Science Department at Tulane University. She served as the Executive Director of the Newcomb Institute from 2010–2022. Her research interests include sexual assault, gender and judging, judicial selection, feminist social movements, and pregnancy discrimination. She is the author of *Gender and Justice: Why Women in the Judiciary Really Matter* (Routledge, 2013).

Amelia Loughland is a Judicial Associate at the Federal Court of Australia and was previously a commercial litigator at Herbert Smith Freehills. She writes in the areas of constitutional law and feminist theory, and her scholarship has appeared in journals such as *Federal Law Review*, *Melbourne University Law Review*, and *International Journal of Constitutional Law*.

Linda C. McClain is the Robert Kent Professor of Law at Boston University School of Law. She writes and teaches in the areas of feminist legal theory, gender and law, family law, and civil rights. The author of several books, including *Who's the Bigot?: Learning from Conflicts over Marriage and Civil Rights* (Oxford University Press, 2020) and *The Place of Families* (Harvard University Press, 2006), she is currently working on the forthcoming *Routledge Companion to Gender and COVID-19* (with coeditor Aziza Ahmed).

Martha T. McCluskey, Professor Emerita and Senior Research Scholar at the University at Buffalo School of law, State University of New York, writes in the areas of feminist legal theory, political economy, and social welfare policy. She is the author (with Martha A. Fineman) of *Feminism, Media and the Law* (Oxford University Press, 1997) and serves as a member scholar for the Center for Progressive Reform and on the Boards of Directors for ClassCrits and APPEAL (Association for Promotion of Political Economy and Law).

Ann C. McGinley is the William S. Boyd Professor of Law at the University of Nevada, Las Vegas, Boyd School of Law. She writes in the areas of employment discrimination and gender and is the author of *Masculinity at Work: Employment Discrimination through a Different Lens* (NYU Press, 2016), and the coeditor of *Masculinities and the Law: A Multidimensional Approach* (NYU Press, 2012) (with Frank Rudy Cooper).

Hilarie Meyers received her J. D., *cum laude*, from NYU School of Law in 2021, where she was an Arthur T. Vanderbilt Scholar and served on the executive boards of OUTLaw and Moot Court Board, participated in the Reproductive Justice Clinic, and worked as a research assistant to Professor Melissa Murray. She is currently working to improve access to reproductive health care as an NYU Reproductive Justice and Women's Rights Fellow.

Melissa Murray is the Frederick I. and Grace Stokes Professor of Law and Faculty Director of the Birnbaum Women's Leadership Network at New York University School of Law. She writes in the areas of constitutional law, family law, and reproductive rights and justice and her scholarship has appeared in journals such as *Harvard Law Review*, *Yale Law Journal*, and *Columbia Law Review*. She is a coauthor, with Kristin Luker, of *Cases on Reproductive Rights and Justice*, the first casebook in this field.

Jennifer Nedelsky is a Professor of Law at Osgoode Hall Law School, York University, Toronto, Canada. She writes on feminist legal theory, restructuring work and care, judgment, and property. She is the author of *Law's Relations: A Relational Theory of Self Autonomy and Law* (Oxford University Press, 2011) and *Part Time for All: A Care Manifesto*, coauthored with Tom Malleson.

Michelle Oberman is the Katharine & George Alexander Professor of Law at Santa Clara University. She writes about legal issues arising at the intersection of sex, reproduction, and the law, focusing on the areas of abortion, infanticide, and statutory rape. Her books include *Her Body, Our Laws: On the Frontlines of the Abortion War from El Salvador to Oklahoma* (Beacon Press, 2018), and *When Mothers Kill: Interviews from Prison* (NYU Press, 2008).

Maria L. Ontiveros is Professor of Law and co-director of the Work Law and Justice Program at the University of San Francisco. She writes in the areas of workplace harassment of women of color, organizing immigrant workers, and modern-day applications of the Thirteenth Amendment. She is lead author of the casebook *Employment Discrimination Law: Cases and Materials on Equality in the Workplace*.

Camille Gear Rich is the Dorothy Nelson Chair of Law and Professor of Law and Sociology at USC Gould School of Law. She writes in the areas of the First Amendment, race and the law, and feminist legal theory, and her scholarship has appeared in journals such as *California Law Review*, *Harvard Law Review*, and *Georgetown Law Journal*.

Julie C. Suk is Professor of Law at Fordham University School of Law. She writes in the areas of comparative constitutional law, antidiscrimination law, employment law, and procedure and is the author of *We the Women: The Unstoppable Mothers of the Equal Rights Amendment* (Skyhorse, 2020).

Sarah L. Swan is an Associate Professor at Rutgers Law School. She writes in the areas of torts, local government law, and family law, and her scholarship has appeared in journals such as *Harvard Law Review*, *Duke Law Journal*, and *UCLA Law Review* and *Michigan Law Review*.

Tracy A. Thomas is the Seiberling Chair of Constitutional Law at The University of Akron School of Law. She writes in the areas of constitutional gender equality and women's legal history and is the author of *Elizabeth Cady Stanton and the Feminist Foundations of Family Law* (NYU Press, 2016) and coeditor of *Feminist Legal History: Essays on Women and Law* (NYU Press, 2011) (with Tracey Boisseau).

Deborah A. Widiss is Professor of Law and Associate Dean for Research at Indiana University Maurer School of Law. She writes in the areas of employment law, family law, and statutory interpretation, and her scholarship has appeared in journals such as *Minnesota Law Review*, *Texas Law Review*, and *Yale Law Journal Forum*.

Verna L. Williams is the Chief Executive Officer of Equal Justice Works. She was Dean and Nippert Professor of Law at University of Cincinnati College of Law from 2019–2022, and a member of the College of Law faculty from 2001–2022. She is a critical race feminist scholar whose work examines the intersection of race, gender, and class in such areas as education law and policy. Her scholarship has appeared in journals such as *Michigan Journal of Race and Law*, *William & Mary Journal of Women and Law*, and *Wisconsin Law Review*.

Mary Ziegler is the Martin Luther King Professor of Law at the University of California, Davis. She is the author of three books on social movement struggles around abortion, including the award-winning *After Roe: The Lost History of the Abortion Debate* (Harvard University Press, 2015), *Abortion and the Law in America: Roe v. Wade to the Present* (Cambridge University Press, 2020) and *Dollars for Life: The Anti-Abortion Movement and the Fall of the Republican Establishment* (Yale University Press, 2022).

Introduction

DEBORAH L. BRAKE, MARTHA CHAMALLAS, AND VERNA L. WILLIAMS

Few fields of law have been as dynamic as the field of legal feminism as it has played out in the United States over the past half century. It is a field marked by constant contestation and negotiation over its boundaries and scope, the terminology used to define its animating principles and commitments, and its relationship to other critical discourses. During this period, the meaning of feminism itself has expanded and de-stabilized, from its early association with promoting the rights and status of women (understood as a distinct biological class), to newer approaches that challenge the strict male/female binary and focus on gender as a social construct embedded in systems of multiple and interacting identities.

Reflecting the complexity and diversity of the field, the contributors to this *Handbook* employ differing understandings of feminism and often speak in somewhat different languages. As editors we have embraced these variations of feminism, whether tied to women, gender, or intersecting identities, and have not attempted to impose a uniform definition of feminism (or feminists) throughout the volume. In keeping with our expansive definition of feminism, we have also not attempted to draw sharp demarcation lines between feminism and other critical discourses. Thus, many of the feminist approaches represented in this volume overlap with other critical discourses, such as critical race theory or scholarship grounded in LGBTQ perspectives. To give a more complete picture of legal feminism's intellectual terrain, we include chapters on adjacent theoretical discourses that reveal their similarity and divergence from more distinctively feminist approaches.

As the title of the *Handbook* indicates, however, we have generally limited our scope to feminism and the law in the United States, tracking theoretical, doctrinal, and political developments in the U.S. only. This "domestic" focus is a matter of feasibility, not philosophy, and we note that a few of our authors are from outside the U.S. and several incorporate international and comparative perspectives into their analyses, tracing how

U.S. legal feminism has been or could be influenced by scholarship and developments outside of the United States.

The main purpose of the *Handbook* is to examine the influence that feminist legal theory and feminist social movements have already exerted on U.S. law and to explore emerging areas of law in which feminist approaches to law have the potential to shape future developments. The framing of the volume reflects our broad understanding of the multiple ways in which feminism engages with law, not only manifesting in litigation and legal doctrine, but also inspiring and impacting social movements that radiate throughout the culture and leave their mark on the law. Our "law and society" understanding of law's relationship to feminism captures a broad array of scholarly methodologies, often interdisciplinary in character, ranging from a close reading of legal cases to explorations of more general societal trends and discursive shifts. The *Handbook* embodies a widely held tenet of feminism that theory and practice are intricately linked, and that practice (including feminist activism and feminist movements) often informs and shapes theory. To complement the chapters devoted to feminist theory, for example, the *Handbook* includes chapters examining key periods of feminist activism in the U.S., from campaigns in the 1970s to pass the Equal Rights Amendment to the contemporary #MeToo and reproductive justice movements.

Scholars usually date the origin of feminist legal theory (or legal feminism) as a field of law to the early 1970s, when women's rights advocates of the Second Wave of feminism in the U.S. first mounted an organized legal campaign in the courts against sex discrimination.[1] For the most part, the contributions in the volume share a similar starting point, although some look back at the longer history of legal feminism. In the nearly 50 years since its inception, legal feminism has become an established feature in U.S. law schools, generating a rich variety of law school courses, an outpouring of scholarship, and providing impetus for legal reforms, big and small. However, to a certain degree, the field remains marginalized, as critics proliferate and efforts to mainstream feminist approaches have met with only limited success. The *Handbook* catalogues these developments and interrogates (and sometimes resists) the "established yet marginal" status of the field. Overall, the *Handbook* is designed to provide a relatively compact survey of U.S. legal feminism that takes stock of the field and showcases the latest scholarly thinking about possible new directions.

Although it has undoubtedly been said many times before, feminism in the U.S. is at a crossroads. In recent years, legal feminism has gained a new urgency, particularly as younger generations become impatient with the slow pace of change and the persistent disparities and lack of inclusion in U.S. society. In some respects, the recent feminist mobilizations resemble "old school" feminist campaigns to end violence and discrimination against women and eliminate women's subordination and marginalization. Contemporary feminist activism, however, also includes demands to rethink feminism's tie to the rights of "women," calling for upending the gender binary and insisting that feminists think and act intersectionally by fully attending to injustices and disparities linked to race, ethnicity, sexual orientation and gender identity, disability, immigration status and class. This pressure to move beyond "women" coexists uncomfortably with a reality in which many hard-fought rights important to women are under attack and short-term prospects of achieving meaningful protection through courts and legislatures appear dim.

Cultural and Political Context

To gain a sense of the milieu in which legal feminism presently operates it is useful to juxtapose a few of the more significant cultural and political moments of the last few years—surely one of the most tumultuous periods in U.S. history—starting with the election of a blatantly anti-feminist president. The calamitous events that arose on the heels of Donald Trump's campaign and election in 2016 brought gender injustice to the forefront, once again, after a somewhat dormant period in the early part of the twenty-first century. Feminists around the world marched against Trump and all he stood for—a record of sexual abuse and misogyny that underscored the fragility of the gains that women had made in areas like sexual violence, reproductive rights, and access to high-ranking positions. Trump's toxic masculinity was on display and licensed virulent forms of bigotry, targeting immigrants, racial minorities (particularly women of color), people with disabilities, and progressives generally. His nearly all-white, all-male administration and judicial appointments threatened a return to the naturalization of white male elites in government. Culminating in the violent insurgency of January 6, 2021, the Trump era dramatized the lesson that feminism could not afford to be narrowly focused on women but must also attempt to understand and engage with men and masculinities and to form progressive alliances with the many marginalized groups who were on the receiving end of Trump's harshest policies.

Beginning in March 2020, the politically induced traumas of the Trump administration were soon rivaled by the cumulative shocks of the COVID-19 pandemic, with its fear, chaos, lockdowns, and school closings. COVID laid bare the depressing state of the U.S. social safety net, marked by longstanding inadequacies in employee protections, day care, and public education. Stark gendered divisions in caregiving came to light, as women bore the brunt of homeschooling children, performing "essential" and dangerous labor in places like hospitals and supermarkets and caring for ill family members. The pandemic also exacerbated gendered violence as abuse victims found themselves isolated and vulnerable, unable to exit or escape to safe shelters and largely at the mercy of an unresponsive state. Even valiant attempts by the new Biden administration could barely begin to address the extent of COVID's dislocations.

On the legal front, the death of Ruth Bader Ginsburg in September 2020 and replacement by a conservative anti-feminist woman was a particularly harsh blow to feminists of all stripes. Ginsburg had become the face of feminism for many and represented the promise that law could propel the nation closer to gender equality. Trump's success in cementing a right-wing majority on the U.S. Supreme Court deepened the wound caused by the confirmation of Brett Kavanaugh and sent a clear signal that feminism was under siege and that basic constitutional rights, like the right to abortion, were hanging by a thread, if not already unraveling.

To be sure, the strong anti-feminist and reactionary forces that emerged in the Trump era were matched by increased mobilization by feminists and progressives. Emerging in its current hashtag form in 2017,[2] the #MeToo movement mounted a mass campaign driven by social media against widespread sexual assault and harassment, leading to the forced resignation of several high-profile harassers. Countless #MeToo stories revealed the complicity of corporate America in turning a blind eye to sexual abuse and in covering up misconduct and protecting those in power. The U.S. also witnessed what some have called a long overdue "reckoning" with white supremacy and racism. The #BlackLivesMatter movement reached an apex in 2020 after the killing of George Floyd and galvanized the nation's attention not only to police shootings but also to the lack of racial diversity and inclusion throughout society.

As in the past, these mass campaigns were followed by intense backlash and countermobilizations, including charges that the #MeToo movement trampled the rights of men and violated fundamental notions of due process. Even more prominently, critical race theory and intersectionality—distorted by its opponents to encompass virtually any examination of race or gender privilege in the U.S. —became favorite targets of the Right, with well-funded campaigns aimed at school boards and state legislatures. The intertwining of theory and practice was evident, as critical discourses spilled out from academia to fuel larger cultural struggles. The contributions to this volume were written during this challenging period as scholars stretched to find time and energy to reflect on feminism's place in this volatile environment.

THE CURRENT STATE OF U.S. FEMINIST LEGAL THEORY

The backbone of this *Handbook* is its many descriptions and interrogations of the various brands or strands of feminist legal theory, discussed not only in the beginning chapters but throughout the volume. We intentionally organized the volume around the now-familiar "brands" or "strands" of feminism rather than adopting a structure that mapped the successive waves of feminism (e.g., Second Wave, Third Wave, and Fourth Wave), as many in the field and some of our authors do. Our design is meant to showcase the diversity of feminist thought and to emphasize that legal feminism has not followed a linear, timebound progression. As the various theoretical contributions make clear, there has been quite a bit of historical overlap among the various brands, even if certain brands have seemed more prominent at certain time periods. The "brands" framing also has the virtue of highlighting what is potentially distinctive about an approach, although here too there is considerable overlap between and among the various brands of feminist legal theories.

The contributions in this volume document that feminist legal theory remains a heterogeneous enterprise, best described as a loose collection of approaches, with some commonalities but also many tensions. Perhaps the most fundamental commonality among the six brands of feminism examined in the *Handbook* is that they each expose the ubiquity of gender and grapple with its significance—revealing what is often unseen—even in settings in which women may be absent, as masculinities scholars have so successfully pointed out. Together, they eloquently refute the mainstream view that gender is relevant only in certain obvious contexts and can be ignored elsewhere. Among the tensions that surface, the brands often display different levels of ambivalence in turning to the state, including the legal system, to address gendered harms. Some feminists are quite willing to advocate legal intervention to combat gender violence and discrimination, viewing the law as just another unstable social system that can be turned to feminist ends. Others, however, have grown increasingly wary of the carceral and punitive tendencies of the state, and warn that turning to the state inevitably grows the power of the state, carrying with it a grave risk of worsening racial bias and racial disparities and producing other harmful unintended consequences that end up hurting rather than helping marginalized populations. This tension about the role of the state often drives a wedge between feminists that cannot always be mended.

From our vantage point as editors of this *Handbook*, what is most striking about the six brands of feminist legal theory is that, remarkably, none of the brands has become obsolete, even if their relative visibility and acceptance has waxed and waned. At the same time, there is little doubt that we have witnessed the ascendancy of *intersectional feminism*. Feminists of all stripes now aspire to be intersectional and likely would agree that other aspects of identity (including race, ethnicity, sexual orientation, gender identity, disability, immigration status, and class) must be taken into account in feminist theorizing, policy making, and activism. Although many feminists fall short of this aspiration—and there is a complicated relationship between intersectionality and feminism—much has changed since intersectional feminism burst on the legal scene in the 1990s.

Despite trenchant criticism from many quarters, there has also been a revival of *dominance feminism*. The #MeToo spotlight on sexual abuse and harassment has taken a page from Catharine MacKinnon and energized new voices that condemn not only behavior that violates the law, but also the institutions that fail to sanction harmful sexually exploitative behavior. Although commonly associated with state intervention, dominance feminist theory has proven remarkably successful in sparking extra-legal pressure campaigns with real consequences for offending individuals and complicit organizations.

Meanwhile, *liberal feminism* endures. Its emphasis on autonomy and consent has new relevance in many ongoing feminist struggles, as in the push to gain acceptance of "affirmative consent" as the measure of the lawful and ethical standard of sexual conduct. It has proven malleable enough to accommodate newly disruptive meanings of "gender" that encompass a diversity of gender identities based on individual choice and has managed to generate richer understandings of gender stereotyping that, if imported into legal doctrine, would go well beyond the hollow formal equality once associated with the brand. As reproductive rights have come under fierce attack, feminists find themselves returning to liberal feminism to articulate new understandings of autonomy and agency that can withstand the onslaught.

At the same time, *sex-positive feminism* has entered the mainstream. Sparked mostly by younger women who insist on their right to sexual pleasure and recoil against sexual shaming, sex-positive feminism has produced a willingness to reassess formerly taboo sexual practices like the use of pornography when used to express women's positive sexual desires. The sex-positive leaning has also promoted a greater acceptance of sex work and sex workers, with a focus on decriminalization and eradication of stigma.

The two remaining brands of feminism—*relational feminism* and *postmodern feminism*—have had somewhat lower profiles but remain relevant and continue to attract new feminist scholars. The COVID-19 pandemic has brought a new visibility to the classic relational feminist emphasis on the value of caregiving, interdependency in human relationships, and collective responsibility for vulnerable populations. Particularly outside the U.S., relational feminism has broadened its scope, reaching beyond intimate human relationships to encompass relationships to the physical environment and to future generations. For its part, postmodern feminism has done much to shift the meaning of personal identity (including gender identity) from static notions based on biology and socialization to more fluid discursive understandings linked to identity performance, greatly accelerating the destabilization of the gender binary. It has also proven useful to explain the complexities of a digital world where feminist interventions often backfire and are appropriated by reactionary forces, requiring feminists to keep up with abrupt shifts in discursive meanings and be ready to form new alliances.

Although we limit our discussion to six of the more prominent strands of feminist legal theory, we recognize that the list is ever-changing and contested. Moreover, as feminist legal theories have matured and proliferated, adjacent intellectual discourses have sprung up, sometimes complementing and adding new dimensions to legal feminism, but also challenging and departing from some of the values and strategies attached to established feminist theories. The *Handbook* highlights three very different adjacent discourses that each address feminist concerns. One of these, *masculinities theory*, has a very close connection to feminism, augmenting feminist critiques of women's subordination through deconstruction of multiple masculinities and their impacts on marginalized men as well as women. *Queer theory* has kept more of a critical distance from legal feminism, generally abjuring statist responses and regulation (feminist or otherwise), but also complicating and enriching feminist understandings of sexuality. A third emergent discourse, *distributional theory*, is grounded on a critique of what has become known as "governance feminism" and sees a pressing need to investigate feminist sites of power and feminist-inspired reforms to detect where the costs of feminism fall and whether those costs outweigh its benefits. Although it often casts particular feminist reforms and approaches as misguided in their exercise of power, its critique tracks some of the newer brands of feminism that have disavowed reliance on the state (particularly the criminal law) to achieve feminist ends.

Connection to Feminist Activism and Movements

The current state of feminist legal theory also reflects the dialectical relationship between theory and practice that has characterized legal feminism since its inception. Although sometimes quite academic in style, feminist legal theory has deep connections to feminist activism and has often developed in tandem with feminist movements. This close connection reflects feminists' recognition of the importance of changing structures and institutions, beyond modification of the law on the books or legal theory.

We can see the imprint of feminist movements on many of the prominent brands of feminist legal theory. The long (and still unsuccessful) campaign to pass the Equal Rights Amendment to the U.S. Constitution propelled liberal feminism into law and eroded many bastions of gender segregation. The early anti-rape and battered women's movements of the 1970s and 1980s shaped dominance feminism and gave rise to a network of state and private institutions dedicated to curbing gender violence. The more contemporary campus sexual assault and #MeToo movements responded to the failure of law to make good on the promise of dominance feminism, lashing out at a culture of impunity and silence and pressuring universities, employers, and other organizations to hold offenders accountable and take proactive measures to transform institutional cultures. Campus activists and #MeToo stories often invoked and disseminated sex-positive visions of sexuality that assumed a right to be sexual without being exploited or victimized. Finally, intersectional feminism found expression in the reproductive justice movement that centered the needs of women of color, going beyond abortion rights to encompass support for maternal health and welfare. The intersectional character of the #BlackLivesMatter movement has also drawn in women of color and LGBTQ activists, deepening feminist ties to social justice movements and social justice theories aimed at ending mass incarceration and racialized violence and poverty.

In complex ways, legal feminism has also been affected and altered by counter-mobilizations and backlash that has accompanied each of these movements, as they gathered force and blunted some of their progressive effects, sometimes at breakneck speed. To make sense of the dizzying developments, legal feminists have been compelled to theorize backlash, tracing the money and people behind backlash campaigns, and questioning whether such virulent responses to feminist activism are a distinctive "backlash" or simply a continuation of pre-existing forms of misogyny and white supremacy.

Feminist Influence on Law

Unquestionably, feminism has influenced law in the U.S. in profound ways. Feminists (and other critical scholars) have exposed the non-neutrality of law and have made visible harms that in earlier eras went unnamed and unnoticed or were thought to bear little connection to women or gender. Sexual harassment, domestic violence, stalking, date rape, sexual stereotyping, sterilization abuse, and so many other gendered injustices have been brought to light by legal feminism, through theory and practice, that it is now difficult to envision or remember a world where such practices had no feminist valence or words to describe them. To a much greater extent than before feminism's interventions, the masculine hold on law has loosened its grasp, if ever so slightly.

We can see the footprints of legal feminism not only in specific legal claims and defenses but also in new understandings of important legal concepts. Not all the strands of legal feminism are as easily incorporated into existing legal doctrine. Two brands especially—liberal feminism and dominance feminism—have been the most generative in creating new claims to address gendered injuries and injustices. But other strands have been taken up selectively. Overall, however, the 50-year experience of feminist intervention in law has not altered feminists' ambivalence about using law to effect social change, and some would argue that contemporary feminists are even more disillusioned than in preceding decades about the power of law to make lasting change, given the reversal of women's reproductive freedoms under the current conservative Supreme Court, as well as longstanding entanglements with a racist and carceral state.

The maturation of feminist claims and defenses has revealed that feminist influence cannot be measured in blunt assessments of success or failure. The impact and meaning of feminist interventions constantly change, requiring resets, revisions and sometimes retreats. Context—including legal context—matters, with some areas more impervious to change than others. In some instances, legal feminists have fruitfully borrowed from other disciplines, like psychology and sociology, to broaden the meaning of "sex" and of "discrimination," in order to capture contemporary forms of implicit bias and generate new protections for sexual minorities. The transformative potential of certain feminist claims, however, has been whittled down by courts which have imposed doctrinal restrictions and other barriers to recovery, pushing feminists toward extralegal activism. The U.S. Supreme Court, in particular, has progressively narrowed the scope of constitutional rights affecting reproduction and childbearing, leading many feminists to pivot to a reproductive justice framing that is sensitive to race and class and encompasses positive rights. However, in other cases, law has been a powerful catalyst for change in the larger society and has significantly altered mainstream behavior. At times these changes have produced splits within the feminist community and prompted critics to oppose feminist-driven legal efforts.

Beyond inspiring new claims and defenses, feminism has altered—and in some instances transformed—the understanding of basic legal concepts. These feminist interventions can be cross-cutting and leave their imprint on different areas of law, as when a change in the definition of consent affects not only criminal law, but legal duties in civil rights law, education law, and tort law. At times, feminist disruption of basic legal categories, such as motherhood, has produced contradictory results, such as expanding opportunities for some women but failing to provide essential material support for caregivers more generally. The challenge to address these unmet needs has led feminists to reach beyond the traditional anti-discrimination approach to advocate for accommodation models and endorse universalist policies that reach the most marginalized. Inspired by human rights law, feminists have been moved to find new ways to confront the violence associated with the carceral state and the failure of the U.S. to ensure basic economic, social, and cultural rights.

Feminist influence has not been restricted to direct efforts to change substantive law. Over the past half century, feminism has also infiltrated legal institutions and sought to influence the legal actors responsible for shaping and implementing the law. While the push for gender integration of legal education and the judiciary continues, feminist "insiders" have developed models of feminist pedagogy and feminist judging aimed at resisting hierarchies and giving voice to those governed by law. This growing cadre of feminist law professors and judges alters the terrain, even if these actors often still feel marginalized and outside the inner circle.

As we take stock of the landscape of feminist legal activity, there is little sign that interest in feminist scholarship or feminist activism has declined or dissipated, particularly as compared to pronouncements at the turn of this century that legal feminism had become stale, that feminism had lost its allure among the young, and that feminist academics were decamping to other quarters. Instead, we expect the volume of feminist scholarship to only increase in the near future. It is impossible, however, to predict those areas of law where feminism will have the most impact in the next decade, let alone half century. Our canvas of emerging areas of feminist legal scholarship reveals that feminist approaches are popular not just in new fields, such as digital privacy law, but in foundational areas as well, like contracts, torts, and tax law, where feminism has made inroads in narrow pockets of legal doctrine even if it has yet to penetrate general legal principles or mainstream theory. Although still very much a work in progress, the infusion of intersectional feminism and social justice perspectives into high stakes areas of the law—such as immigration law and environmental law—carries the potential to have a major impact not only within U.S. borders but globally. In this emerging scholarship, we see great value in the heterogeneity of feminist approaches to law that has proven deep enough to nourish the intellectual and political work of successive generations of feminists.

Organization and Contents of the Volume

The *Handbook* is divided into two major parts. Part I (Theory, Connections and Criticisms) provides the foundation for examining feminism's impacts on law, explaining the various brands of feminist legal theory and some prominent adjacent intellectual discourses. It also discusses influential feminist movements, as well as counter-mobilizations and backlash forces. Part II (Feminist Influence on Law) is devoted to identifying and analyzing several specific inroads feminism has made into U.S. law, including the creation of feminist-inspired claims and defenses. It also discusses some of the more subtle interventions that have resulted in altered understandings of traditional concepts and in re-orientations of traditional fields. Beyond legal feminism's effect on substantive law, this Part examines the impact of feminism on law school pedagogy and on judicial decision making. The final chapters of the *Handbook* are devoted to emerging areas of law that are ripe for feminist analysis but have not yet been as significantly changed by feminist interventions or inroads.

Prominent Strands of Feminist Legal Theory

The *Handbook* begins with an examination of six prominent strands of feminist legal theory, flanked by two reflective chapters—one that places the theoretical developments in a longer historical context and one that make sense of the big picture from a comparative perspective. In a chapter narrating the "long history" of feminist legal theory, *Tracy A. Thomas*[3] traces the trajectory of legal feminism covering a 150-year span, from suffragists' emphasis on maternalism, to Progressive-era ideas of global peace, market work, and birth control, through to the modern "equal protection" era of formal equality.

The three older established brands of feminist legal theory—liberal feminism, dominance feminism, and relational feminism—are explored next, with authors examining key tenets and commitments of the brands and their continuing relevance. The liberal feminism chapter by *Linda C. McClain & Brittany K. Hacker*[4] uncovers its roots in 19th and early 20th century liberal and feminist political theory and in women's rights advocacy and traces its evolution and adaptation, emphasizing Ruth Bader Ginsburg's constitutional litigation campaign and the theory's capacity to generate robust conceptions of autonomy, liberty, privacy, and gender equality. In her chapter, *Kathryn Abrams*[5] discusses the growth, development, and trenchant critiques of dominance feminism, showcasing Catharine MacKinnon's foundational work and contemporary iterations of dominance theory in #MeToo stories of sexualized violence and coercion. The relational feminism chapter by *Jennifer Nedelsky*[6] takes us beyond that theory's early focus on intimate gendered relationships to articulate a broader relational approach to law which reconceptualizes values like security and autonomy and explores questions of hierarchy, racism, property, mental health, and environmental harm.

Following the established brands, the three newer brands of feminism—intersectional feminism, sex-positive feminism, and postmodern feminism—are discussed by authors who describe their fluid, complex features, and connections to other related critical discourses. In a chapter on intersectional feminism that also discusses critical race theory, *Emily Houh*[7] presents a genealogy of intersectionality theory, canvassing its ties to Black feminist thought and Third World feminism, and showing how different social justice movements have put intersectionality theory into practice and anchored it to contemporary activist struggles. The chapter on sex-positive feminism by *Susan Frelich Appleton*[8] unearths the sex-positive threads in different eras of feminism that challenged stereotypes of female sexualities centered on passivity, subordination, harm, and repronormativity, and explores that theory's capacity to chart a supportive and affirmative course for law and legal institutions grounded in feminist notions of women's sexual pleasure. In her chapter on postmodern feminism, *Camille Gear Rich*[9] examines the fractured feminist gains of the 20th century, theorizes how certain postmodern concepts have been underutilized in contemporary feminist theory, and illustrates how postmodern tools can allow for greater insights in a digital era of competing and conflicting information and political claims. The final chapter in this Part—a comparative perspectives reflection piece by *Rosalind Dixon & Amelia Loughland*[10]—develops a framework to enhance understanding of the various brands of U.S. feminist theory and make them more accessible to feminists within and outside the United States, centered on the organizing principles of "disruption," "amelioration," and "transformation."

Adjacent Theoretical Discourses

To round out the discussion of the various brands of legal feminism, the *Handbook* includes three chapters on adjacent theoretical discourses that bear a close connection to feminism but also diverge in important ways. *Brenda Cossman's*[11] chapter on queer theory explores how that critical discourse de-naturalizes the assumed connections between sex, gender, and desire and differs from the more rights-based mainstream approach to LGBT issues. In her chapter, *Ann C. McGinley*[12] describes the insights masculinities theory has brought to feminism, with its focus on masculine practices that maintain the power of men as a group over women as a group, while creating competition and division among men. The trio concludes with a chapter by *Aziza Ahmed*[13] on distributional theory which situates it (along with governance feminism) as a descendant to critical legal theory, highlighting Janet Halley's step-by-step analysis of the allocation of costs and benefits of feminist interventions along distributional lines.

Feminist Movements and Backlash

Following the chapters on theory, the *Handbook* turns to examine some key feminist movements that have informed the development of feminist legal theory, starting in the 19th century to the present. *Julie Suk's*[14] chapter on the ERA movement takes us along a 100-year, yet-unfinished path to ratify the amendment, shedding light on the processes of feminist constitutional change and the evolution of substantive feminist legal aspirations. *Leigh Goodmark's*[15] chapter on the anti-rape and battered women's movements of the 1970s and 1980s charts the movements' beginnings in community-based organizing and strategies (such as shelters and safe houses) to increased state intervention through the criminal justice system, a policy choice criticized by anti-carceral feminists.

Three contemporary feminist movements which have had significant influence on legal and cultural understandings of sexual violence and reproduction are explored by authors who trace the movements' impacts on institutions, regulation, and litigation. *Nancy Chi Cantalupo's*[16] chapter tells the story of the grassroots movement against campus sexual assault led by feminist college students that stimulated new Title IX policies and regulations during the Obama administration but generated backlash and retrenchment during the Trump era. The #MeToo movement is dissected by *Tristin K. Green*,[17] who discusses the power of collective action to challenge entrenched institutional sexism in employment and other settings, in the face of countermobilizations aimed at minimizing and individualizing the harm and producing anti-feminist competing counter-narratives. *Mary Ziegler*[18] tackles the complex and fraught relationship between the parallel movements for reproductive justice and the narrower push for reproductive rights, contrasting the broader calls for government support of childbirth, reproductive health, and sustainable communities by justice advocates with the privacy-based framework of rights activists who focused on the U.S. Supreme Court.

Part I concludes with two chapters exploring prominent criticisms of legal feminism and theorizing the phenomenon of backlash. *Martha McCluskey*[19] takes on the powerful law and economics movement, maintaining that law and economics undermines feminism by constructing economics as a sphere insulated from morality and politics, and naturalizes a gendered baseline that makes feminist reforms appear costly, unfair, or ineffective. *Sally Kenney's*[20] contribution contends that perceived backlash to progressive social change often fails to distinguish measurable setbacks from countermobilizations of pre-existing opponents who fear they are losing ground. Kenney urges theorists to think about gender inequality intersectionally and re-examine the loaded concept of backlash.

Feminism's Impact on the Law: New Legal Claims and Defenses

Part II of the *Handbook* focuses on the ways in which feminism has impacted the law and the legal system. Feminism's influence on law can be seen most tangibly in the development of new legal claims for recognizing and redressing previously unremedied harms or, in one instance, a new theory for defending against crimes by survivors of battering and abuse. Perhaps the most well-known of these is the claim for sexual harassment, which *Theresa M. Beiner*[21] explores in her chapter, tracing the origins of the claim in grassroots activism and feminist theory. Beiner credits the claim with important legal victories and an emerging awareness of legally recognizable harm, extending beyond the workplace to such settings as housing and education, but also details the ways in which the claim has fallen short, including its cooptation by employers and its doctrinal shortcomings. Another doctrinal development, while not always styled as a distinct cause of action, is the use of gender stereotyping theory to advance discrimination claims. *Stephanie Bornstein's*[22] chapter delves deeply into the theory of gender stereotyping, which she contends has developed from an anti-classification strategy to a more robust principle informed by social science and animated by the key values of anti-subordination, individual liberty, and gender inclusivity.

Other legal developments sparked by feminism have been more controversial, including within feminist circles. Such is the case with the defense to homicide and other violent crime known as the battered women's syndrome (BWS) defense. *Sara M. Buel*[23] criticizes the development of BWS and its application by courts and advocates a more nuanced approach that considers the role of battering and its effects to understand and contextualize crime committed by survivors. One of the most popular feminist-inspired claims, at least at a general level, is Title IX's application to women's sports. Yet here, too, controversy brews. *Erin E. Buzuvis*[24] traces the history of Title IX's distinctive approach to sex equality in sports and complicates the law's premise that sex-separate competition best promotes girls' and women's equal opportunity in sports, elaborating the shortcomings of the law's "separate but equal" regime.

Changed Legal Understandings

Beyond individual legal claims and select doctrines, feminism has also made inroads in revising conventional understandings of crosscutting legal constructs and relationships. In the criminal law, no concept has felt the pressure of feminist influence more than that of "consent." The chapter on consent by *Katharine K. Baker and Michelle Oberman*[25] details the feminist reforms that redefined rape as sex without consent and explores the cultural and legal significance of that shift, along with its limitations.

On the civil side, feminism has had a long and protracted engagement with the law's treatment of pregnancy, reproduction, and motherhood—an entanglement that was fraught from the beginning. *Deborah Widiss*[26] explores the ongoing tensions and debates over how law should treat the singular condition of pregnancy and criticizes the neoliberal approach privatizing the costs of pregnancy under U.S. law. Feminist engagement with conventional legal frames for analyzing rights relating to reproduction is carried forward by *Melissa Murray and Hilarie Meyers*,[27] whose chapter showcases the growing influence of the reproductive justice movement to replace a limited "privacy" rights framework with an intersectional approach to reproductive justice. From pregnancy and reproduction to motherhood, *Jennifer S. Hendricks*[28] analyzes feminism's progress in disentangling the biological, social, and relational dimensions of motherhood, and argues that future feminist work should move beyond gender neutrality in law to account for the ways in which biological and social motherhood overlap (as in surrogacy, parental rights, and some reproductive technologies).

Finally, this section looks beyond U.S. borders to consider how feminism has changed, and been changed by, international human rights law. In her chapter, *Tracy E. Higgins*[29] considers how the experience of other nations' legal systems and insights from international human rights law might enrich U.S. feminist thought and practice, particularly in theorizing the role of the state in addressing gender violence.

Legal Education and the Legal System

Not just law but legal institutions bear the mark of feminist influence. Law schools, legal pedagogy, the judiciary, and judging have all been changed—albeit, not wholly transformed—by feminist activism and feminist-inspired reforms. *Jamie R. Abrams*[30] canvasses the unfinished work of feminists to release the masculine grip on law schools, from the influx of women students and professors, to changes in the curriculum and institutional culture, and the ongoing critiques of the traditional model of legal education.

Judges and judging have also come under the feminist gaze. In her contribution, *Kristin Kalsem*[31] breaks down the rationales for diversifying the bench with "outsider" identities and examines two feminist projects aimed at incorporating feminist methods into the process of judging.

Emerging Areas of Influence

Even areas of law not typically associated with feminism are increasingly understood by feminist scholars to have relevance for the study of gender and to be rich sites for feminist analysis. We style these "emerging areas" in the *Handbook* and include contributions on feminism's engagement with contract law, digital privacy, environmental law, immigration law, intellectual property, tax law, and torts.

One staple of the common law that occupies first-year law students, contract law, has long interested feminist scholars, even if their influence on the development of the law has not yet substantially altered the field. *Martha M. Ertman's*[32] chapter on the synergistic relationship between feminism and contract law explores the utility of contractual analysis to feminist projects, like advancing women's equality in the family, and considers how feminist analysis of contract doctrines (focusing on good faith, debtor rights, unconscionability, and duress) might reshape the law.

A more recent area of law, digital privacy, raises issues surrounding the meaning and value of "privacy" that have long drawn feminist scrutiny, as *Michele Gilman*[33] reveals in her analysis of how privacy, cyberspace, and big data map onto the public/private divide that has so often subordinated women's interests. Gilman exposes the failure of current law to address gendered harms in cyberspace and charts a path forward for feminist activism and interventions.

Feminism and environmentalism might be considered a natural pairing, as the evolution of ecofeminism, which links the subordination of women and the subordination of nature, recognizes. In her chapter, *Cinnamon Piñon Carlane*[34] explains how the existential threat of climate change draws new urgency to the need for greater convergence of legal feminism and environmental law and highlights the opportunities for stronger coalition-building between feminists and environmentalists.

Turning to immigration law, *Maria L. Ontiveros*[35] conducts a feminist reimagining of U.S. immigration law and policy, rethinking the three main grounds for entry: employment, humanitarian, and family ties. Ontiveros shows how the legacies of chattel slavery and coverture shape the current approach and critiques the law's failure to address the gendered harms specific to female immigrants.

Turning the feminist gaze on intellectual property, *Ann Bartow*[36] shows the myriad ways in which intellectual property law has displaced, marginalized, and ignored women as creators, while surreptitiously treating gender itself as a form of property. By revealing the presence of gender where it has been invisible, Bartow's chapter demonstrates how feminist methods can generate new insights even in fields traditionally understood to have no relevance to the study of gender.

Feminist scholars have confronted a similar baseline assumption about the irrelevance of gender in tax law, as *Bridget Crawford* and *Anthony Infanti*[37] take up in their chapter on feminism and tax law. Exploring a long trajectory of feminist tax scholarship dating back to the 1970s, they show that legal feminism's burgeoning critique of tax law is beginning to bear fruit, as mainstream tax scholars are forced to reckon with feminist analysis and advocacy groups, and policy makers more seriously examine the gender equity implications of tax policy.

The final chapter by *Sarah Swan*[38] returns to the common law to consider feminism's growing influence on the field of torts. Swan details feminist challenges to purportedly "objective" measures of compensation and allocation of risk, identifies some discrete areas where feminist interventions have taken root and sparked limited statutory reforms, and advocates for a more sweeping feminist reconsideration of such foundational tort concepts as the duty of care, third party liability, injury, and damage awards.

With the *Handbook's* triple focus on theory, doctrine, and social movements, it is our hope that this volume will be a valuable resource for scholars and students—in law schools and in other fields—and will be of interest to lawyers, judges, policy makers and journalists. It was written to meet the needs of those new to legal feminism who seek an introduction to and a thorough statement of the field, and to give more established scholars a sense of recent developments, a broader feel for the range of views within the feminist umbrella, and new directions for research. It is our wish that the contributions will be used as background for news stories, legal decisions and briefs, and policy initiatives related to gender. As the first *Oxford Handbook* devoted to feminism and law, it is a milestone for a field that has brought inspiration and enlightenment to so many.

Notes

1. The First Wave of feminism typically refers to the women's suffrage movement, beginning in earnest in the latter half of the 19th century and culminating in the passage of the Nineteenth Amendment to the U.S. Constitution in 1920.

2. For a critique of the current #MeToo movement for ignoring or underplaying the role of Black feminist activist Tarana Burke, who originated the MeToo movement a decade earlier as a healing force for sexually abused girls and women of color, see Angela Onwuachi-Willig, *What About #UsToo?: The Invisibility of Race in the #MeToo Movement*, 128 Yale L.J. F. 105 (2018).
3. Tracy A. Thomas, *The Long History of Feminist Legal Theory*.
4. Linda C. McClain & Brittany K. Hacker, *Liberal Feminist Jurisprudence: Foundational, Enduring, Adaptive*.
5. Kathyrn Abrams, *Dominance Feminism: Placing Sexualized Power at the Center*.
6. Jennifer Nedelsky, *A Relational Approach to Law and Its Core Concepts*.
7. Emily Houh, *A Genealogy of Intersectionality*.
8. Susan Appleton, *Sex Positive Feminism's Values in Search of the Law of Pleasure*.
9. Camille Gear Rich, *Feminism is Dead, Long Live Feminism: A Postmodern Take On The Road To Gender Equality*.
10. Rosalind Dixon & Amelia Loughland, *Gender Disruption, Amelioration and Transformation: A Comparative Perspective*.
11. Brenda Cossman, *Queer Theory Goes to Law School*.
12. Ann C. McGinley, *Masculinities Theory as an Impetus for Change in Feminism and Law*.
13. Aziza Ahmed, *Governance Feminism and Distributional Analysis*.
14. Julie Suk, *The Equal Rights Amendment: Then and Now*.
15. Leigh Goodmark, *The Anti-Rape and Battered Women's Movements of the 1970s and 80s*.
16. Nancy Chi Cantalupo, *The Title IX Movement Against Campus Sexual Harassment: How a Civil Rights Law and a Feminist Movement Inspired Each Other*.
17. Tristin A. Green, *Feminism and #MeToo: The Power of the Collective*.
18. Mary Ziegler, *From Reproductive Rights to Reproductive Justice: Abortion in Constitutional Law and Politics*.
19. Martha McCluskey, *Law and Economics Against Feminism*.
20. Sally Kenney, *Backlash Against Feminism: Rethinking a Loaded Concept*.
21. Theresa M. Beiner, *Sexual Harassment: The Promise and Limits of a Feminist Cause of Action*.
22. Stephanie Bornstein, *Degendering the Law Through Stereotype Theory*.
23. Sarah M. Buel, *Beyond Battered Women's Syndrome*.
24. Erin E. Buzuvis, *Title IX: Separate But Equal for Girls and Women in Athletics*.
25. Katharine K. Baker & Michelle Oberman, *Consent, Rape, and the Criminal Law*.
26. Deborah Widiss, *Pregnancy and Work—50 Years of Legal Theory, Litigation, and Legislation*.
27. Melissa Murray & Hilarie Meyers, *Constitutionalizing Reproductive Rights (and Justice)*.
28. Jennifer S. Hendricks, *Disputed Conceptions of Motherhood*.
29. Tracy E. Higgins, *Applying International Feminist Insights to Gendered Violence in the United States*.
30. Jamie R. Abrams, *Feminism's Transformation of Legal Education and Unfinished Agenda*.
31. Kristin Kalsem, *Feminist Judging: Theories and Practices*.
32. Martha M. Ertman, *Contract's Influence on Feminism and Vice Versa*.
33. Michele Gilman, *Feminism, Privacy, and Law in Cyberspace*.
34. Cinnamon Piñon Carlane, *Re-Attaching Environmental Law to Its Intersectional Roots*.

35. Maria L. Ontiveros, *Reconceptualizing the Terms and Conditions of Entry to the United States: A Feminist Reimagining of Immigration Law.*
36. Ann Bartow, *Invisible Women and Intangible Property: A Feminist Consciousness for Authors and Inventors.*
37. Bridget Crawford & Anthony Infanti, *A Taxing Feminism.*
38. Sarah Swan, *Imagining Feminist Tort Law.*

CHAPTER 1

THE LONG HISTORY OF FEMINIST LEGAL THEORY

TRACY A. THOMAS

Scholars typically date the beginning of feminist legal theory to the 1970s.[1] The conventional story places the advent of feminist legal theory in the second-wave feminist movement of the 1960s and 1970s, birthed by the political activism of the women's liberation movement and nurtured by the intellectual leadership of women newly entering legal academia. Yet legal feminism has a much longer history, conceptualized more than a century earlier.[2] The foundations of feminist legal theory were first established in 1848 and developed over the course of the next 150 years. The theoretical precepts were grounded in the comprehensive philosophy of the nineteenth century's first women's rights movement, advanced by the political activism of the women's suffrage movement, expanded by the global and intellectual work of progressive feminism in the early twentieth century, and consolidated in the formal equality legalism of the Equal Rights Amendment and equal protection jurisprudence.

In the beginning, theorists of women's legal rights did not use the label "feminist." Instead, they used terms like "strong minded," "true woman," or the singular "woman's rights" to describe the new ideology and its adherents. Progressives first used the word "feminist" in the United States in the 1910s to identify a person committed to principles of social revolution for women's liberation and equality.[3] It derived from the French word "feminisme" coined in 1882 by French suffrage leader and newspaper editor Hubertine Auclert. Initially employed by detractors to criticize the movement as radical, destructive, and anti-male, feminists soon claimed the word as their own, embracing the broad and radical nature of its meaning. Regardless of terminology, early women's rights advocates and thinkers talked about the key antidiscrimination principles of feminism, identifying subjugation and degradation based on sex as the core of injustice and the need for liberty and freedom to rectify such oppression.

Conventional thinking about legal feminism describes its development as linear, moving from a simplistic origin of a "first wave" to a more modern "second wave" and then to a sophisticated contemporary school of thought. This evolutionary framework, however, does not accurately reflect the richness of the early first-wave feminism which set feminist theory on its path. Early legal feminism was a comprehensive, holistic feminism. It simultaneously embraced multiple strands of feminist legal thought, including women's "sameness" of ability and opportunity, women's "difference" with respect to biology and maternal experience, the systemic role of institutions in reproducing gender inequality, and the integrated nature of the private and public spheres. Early legal feminism also developed and applied feminist legal methods, questioning the status quo, deconstructing laws to reveal male bias and misogyny, and reconstructing alternative visions of inclusive systems. Rather than following a linear trajectory, feminist legal theory evolved more like a universal theory of politics or sociology, starting with a broad ideology and then developing strands of that ideology that rose to prominence over different periods of time. Throughout each of these periods of feminist legal thought, however, there were two imperatives: the need to ask "the woman question"—an inquiry that places women at the center of analysis—and the recognition of law as both a fundamental agent in women's inequality and a powerful vehicle for change.

I. Comprehensive Legal Feminism from the Beginning (1848–1880)

Legal feminism emerged from what was called the first movement dedicated to "the Social, Civil, and Religious condition of woman."[4] At the first women's rights convention held in Seneca Falls, New York in July 1848, the movement initiated activism and devised a cohesive agenda for social and legal reform of the state, family, church, and market.[5] The "woman's rights movement" grew out of the abolition movement against slavery where social reformers like Lucretia Mott also addressed women's rights and abolitionists like Angelina and Sarah Grimké raised the "woman question" of allowing women to speak in public. It was at Seneca Falls that abolitionists like Mott, her Quaker colleagues, and noted former slave Frederick Douglass joined to endorse the nascent women's movement.[6] The Seneca Falls convention in turn spawned annual grass-roots women's rights conventions where women like Lucy Stone, Susan B. Anthony, and former slave Sojourner Truth continued to advocate for women's rights.

Credit for being the guiding force behind a theory of legal feminism belongs to organizer Elizabeth Cady Stanton.[7] Stanton has been identified as the "original feminist thinker," and the women's movement's "principal philosopher," who "singlehandedly invented standalone feminism."[8] Then a thirty-two year-old mother of three children under the age of four and wife of a leading abolitionist, Stanton joined her mentor, Mott, at Seneca Falls to organize the convention. She was responsible for drafting the convention's founding document, the Declaration of Sentiments, and articulating its now-famous claims of women's wrongs and demands for women's rights. The

Declaration of Sentiments provided an agenda that became a roadmap for women's rights, calling for eighteen specific reforms, including the equal right to vote and changes in laws and customs governing divorce, marital property, child custody, guardianship, employment, education, pay, entry into the professions, church governance, and freedom from domestic violence.[9] It also denounced the entrenched social norms that fostered male privilege, female inferiority, religious subjugation, and double standards of morality and sexuality.

Stanton was uniquely positioned to argue the legal case for women's equality, having received de facto legal education and training from her father, New York judge and lawyer Daniel Cady.[10] This was at a time when women were not formally trained in law—the first women lawyers and students would not appear until thirty-five years later, hindered by the U.S. Supreme Court's decision in 1875 in *Bradwell v. Illinois* that denied married women the right to practice law.[11] Considering that most male lawyers of the time trained through one-year apprenticeships, Stanton's training was extensive. As a child, she developed an interest in the law, spending her days in her father's office attached to the family home as he met with clients, observing his arguments in court, and debating his apprentices at the nightly dinner table. As a young adult, she clerked for her father while he traveled the judicial circuit and she read law under the tutelage of her brother-in-law. She learned to think like a lawyer, locate and cite case law, and master the craft of constructing legal arguments and articulating alternatives and supporting rationale. The brilliant and well-read Stanton integrated this legal training into her knowledge of political theory, theology, and the emerging fields of anthropology and sociology. Her intellectual approach blended multiple theories with the three philosophical traditions animating the women's movement generally: political liberalism, Protestant theology, and utopianism.[12]

Stanton's legal training gave her pioneering insights and understandings of the role of law in society. Moving beyond the moral suasion of reformers, Stanton appreciated the need to develop an agenda and philosophy to deconstruct the law of subjugation and to use that law in securing women's rights. Her legal analysis bears the hallmarks of what we now identify as feminist methodology.[13] Drawing on the work of the few preexisting feminist thinkers, including transcendentalist Margaret Fuller whom Stanton knew in Boston, abolitionist Sarah Grimké and her work *Letters on the Equality of the Sexes* (1837), socialist utopian Frances Wright, and English political theorist Mary Wollstonecraft,[14] Stanton relentlessly asked "the woman question," focusing the public debate on women's issues and demanding the inclusion of those issues into the mainstream public discourse. She also grounded the movement in women's experience, through her own personal experiences and those of her neighbors, friends, family, and employees and relayed these experiences through the conventions of narrative and what is now called consciousness raising. Stanton criticized the masculine jurisprudence, deconstructing the laws to refute their supposed objectivity and to uncover male bias. She decried what she termed "man marriage," an institution created by and for men to their own advantage, and denounced marriage and custody laws treating women as imbeciles and slaves.

More fundamentally, Stanton established the foundational principle of gender as a unified class.[15] Politically, this idea helped organize women by raising their awareness of gendered oppression and encouraging them to reach across class lines based on shared domestic experiences. This unification, however, generally ignored race, although some made arguments to include Black women, explaining that even after the elimination of slavery, Black women would continue to be bound by the chains of marriage and coverture. Universalism as a political strategy had the advantage of countering the common refrain of women who refused to join the movement, claiming "I have all the rights I want"—a belief that Karl Marx would later identify as the "false consciousness" of an oppressed class of people who failed to appreciate their membership in a subjugated class.[16] Legally, the unified class idea framed the problem of gender discrimination, exposing how women were grouped together because of sex and then treated similarly based on bias and stereotypes of weakness, inferiority, and incompetence. Universalizing women at this juncture helped expose the systemic injustices of law and power, showing how protection and coverture of women was in fact oppression.

The comprehensiveness of the first legal feminism encompassed the key strands that would later be identified as separate genres of feminist theory: formal equality, relational difference, and systemic oppression. This holistic feminism, however, was "unfettered by the modern demarcations that have circumscribed feminist theory," instead embracing multiple notions of feminism simultaneously, viewing them all as instructive to understanding and challenging women's subjugation rather than seeing them as competing ideas.[17]

A. Formal Equality

The first principle embedded in Stanton's philosophy was that of formal legal equality. Early feminism embraced an ideology of individualism and entitlement, holding that women were fully autonomous individuals deserving the same rights, freedoms, and opportunities as men.[18] This tenet derived in part from political theories of liberalism, including those of John Locke's natural and equal rights of the social contract and John Stuart Mill's liberal feminist theory of equality. As Stanton explained, women's rights were demanded "simply on the ground that the rights of every human being are the same and identical."[19]

Women, however, had been historically excluded from this social contract and republican theories of political citizenship. Instead, they were relegated to community agents of "Republican Motherhood," defining women's citizenship role as confined to the private, domestic sphere, with the responsibility of raising and morally guiding the next generation of male citizens.[20] Under this ideology, women were portrayed as different from men—weaker, emotional, and intellectually inferior, yet sentimentalized as selfless, benevolent, and morally virtuous. The problem, Stanton explained, was that people could not "take in the idea that men and women are alike; and so long as the mass rest in this delusion, the public mind will not be so much startled by the revelations made of the injustice and degradation of woman's position."[21] Thus, she said, it was important to establish the "identity of the race in capabilities and responsibilities" in order to achieve "the equality of human rights."[22]

B. Women's Difference

Formal equality, however, was only the first part of Stanton's feminist theory. As she explained, "I have wrought heretofore mainly in behalf of the equality of the sexes because it has seemed to me that the recognition of that equality was, as I still think it is, the first requisite, the first step on the road to social emancipation and social happiness."[23] However, she continued, "I perceive more and more clearly every day that the recognition of the equality of woman with man in all the senses in which it is possible that they should be equal is not enough, that it is only a first step and nothing more."[24] The second step, she explained, was to integrate considerations of women's biological and social difference, pointing out that "[t]he advocates of woman's rights do not deny a difference in sex, but on the contrary, based their strongest arguments for equal rights on this very principle, because of its mutually protecting, elevating, invigorating power over the sexes."[25] Both were important to feminist advocacy because "[t]he resemblances of sex," Stanton said, "are as great as their differences," and so from the start, she included gender difference in her theory.[26]

This acceptance of what we now regard as relational feminism was in part expedient, embracing the growing conservative and religious supporters of women's suffrage like those from the Woman's Christian Temperance Union (WCTU), which emphasized women's moral and biological difference.[27] However, incorporation of difference was also normative. Feminist understanding of difference recognized and responded to women's lived experiences of maternity and caregiving and translated into legal rights of maternal child custody, joint ownership of marital property, reproductive control, and jury service as a voice of mercy.

The difficulty with emphasizing women's difference, however, was that to law and society, gender difference meant inferiority. The new science of Darwinism and similar evolutionary theories claimed they proved that women were intellectually and physically inferior to men. As Supreme Court Justice Bradley explained concurring in *Bradwell v. Illinois*, "the civil law, as well as nature herself, has always recognized a wide difference in the respective spheres and destinies of man and woman. . . . The natural and proper timidity and delicacy which belongs to the female sex evidently unfits it for many of the occupations of civil life."[28] Accordingly, he concluded, "the paramount destiny and mission of woman are to fulfill the noble and benign offices of wife and mother. This is the law of the Creator."[29]

Feminists like Stanton subverted this difference of inferiority by proclaiming gender difference as an attribute of power. She asserted, "if a difference in sex involves superiority, then we claim it for woman; for as she is more complicated in her physical organization, fills more offices than man, she must be more exalted and varied in her mental capacities and endowments."[30] Emerging theories of sociology and positivism supported this theory of women's superiority, identifying a "feminine element" essential to the ordering of a cooperative and harmonious society free from war, colonialism, and class conflict. Stanton co-opted this idea, ignoring its conclusion of women's separate sphere, and argued that such a peaceful and caring feminine element was needed as a governing power to counteract the selfish and destructive male force.

C. Systemic Oppression

The third key component of early feminist legal thought was its radical understanding of the operation of systems of law, religion, and society that created and perpetuated a patriarchy to subordinate women. The patriarchy was erected by the legal system of coverture, under which a married woman was "covered" or "protected" by her husband and simultaneously denied a separate legal existence and individual civil rights of property, contract, child custody, and the right to sue in courts of law.[31] The patriarchy was created and endorsed by the Church, which taught women's moral inferiority in the story of Eve and her original sin and God's alleged punishment of women for this sin by the pain of childbirth. It was reinforced by sexualized cultural norms which viewed a woman as a "toy of man," an object solely for man's desire, endorsing male sexual prerogatives in and out of marriage. Under this more radical lens, women's inequality could be understood as the result of systemic effects, requiring the dismantling of laws, coverture, and religious subordination.

What was missing, however, from early legal feminism was an appreciation of the significance of race. With ties to the abolition movement, women's rights activists initially worked alongside Black reformers, aligned on a platform of antislavery and universal suffrage.[32] However, the Fourteenth and Fifteenth Amendments, which segregated Black and women's suffrage, broke this allegiance, and women's rights activists splintered into different organizations in which race and sex were viewed in opposition.[33] Stanton's willingness to resort to racist statements to advance women's suffrage, such as expressing outrage that "lower orders" of uneducated men like "Patrick and Sambo and Hans and Yung Tung" would legislate for white women, further alienated her former abolitionist colleagues and served to privilege white women's rights, regardless of Stanton's personal support for the rights of Black women.[34] For their part, Black women independently worked for women's suffrage through church and club organizations, and a few notable women, such as Mary Church Terrell and Mary Ann Shadd Cary, joined and contributed to the efforts of national suffrage organizations including Stanton's. Yet Black, Native, and Asian women were segregated in action and leadership, and concerns affecting women of color at the intersection of race and gender were dismissed, leaving early legal feminism with a legacy of essentialism and exclusion.[35]

II. Narrowing Legal Feminism in the Women's Suffrage Movement (1880–1920)

Despite the promise of first-wave legal feminism, political factors drove the movement to narrow its energies to the single issue of the vote. The unity women previously gained organizing around women's domestic and maternal experience intensified as significant numbers of women with diverse political and religious views came together for the cause of suffrage. However, the consensus on suffrage proved detrimental to legal feminism in the long run. The broad association of women's groups tended to work together only at the lowest common denominator of the vote, sacrificing the development of feminist theory and larger legal reforms.

Notably, Stanton and others in the early woman's rights movement viewed winning the vote as only one tool, as one piece of a comprehensive agenda for feminist reform. It was not meant to be all about the vote. Indeed, Stanton's inclusion of the vote, at the time, was controversial, as most of her Quaker and religious colleagues rejected political activism as morally corrupt and instead advocated for moral persuasion of the public citizenry. Women's demand for the vote had been raised in a few petitions in New York several years prior, and women had voted for several decades in colonial New Jersey.[36] Before the Civil War, reformers from the abolitionist movement agreed on universal suffrage for all, regardless of race or sex. However, after the war, reformers split, segregating Black (male) suffrage from women's suffrage and advocating only for ratification of the Fifteenth Amendment. The Fourteenth Amendment had previously set the constitutional parameters for the franchise voters by counting only "male voters" in determining sanctions for a state's denial of the right to vote. This established what Stanton called a constitutional "aristocracy of sex."[37] Feeling betrayed by her colleagues, Stanton and Susan B. Anthony established the National Woman Suffrage Association, which proposed a Sixteenth Amendment for the women's vote and continued the broad agenda of Seneca Falls. Other women, led by Lucy Stone and her husband Henry Blackwell, split off into the American Woman Suffrage Association and dedicated themselves first to Black suffrage and the Fifteenth Amendment.[38]

As the vote became the hallmark of citizenship under the Reconstruction Amendments, the women's movement evolved into a single-issue feminism aimed at suffrage. The national suffrage organization devised a strategy whereby they sought to claim women's citizenship under the new constitutionalism of suffrage. In a campaign called the "New Departure," which departed from prior political strategies for state law reform or constitutional amendment, they claimed that the Fourteenth Amendment's Privileges or Immunities Clause guaranteed women's right to vote.[39] They asserted that a simple, textual analysis of the clause protecting against state abridgment of "the privileges or immunities of the citizens of the United States" applied to women, who were U.S. citizens, and to voting, which was assumed to be a defining privilege of citizenship. Under this claimed authority, many women went to the polls to attempt to vote.

One of these women was Susan B. Anthony, famously convicted for illegal voting, but denied the right to appeal when the trial court refused to enforce the penalty. Virginia Minor's challenge then became the test case. In *Minor v. Happersett*, the U.S. Supreme Court stated that women were indeed citizens, going to some lengths to explain that "there is no doubt that women may be citizens," that "they are persons," that "women have always been considered as citizens the same as men" and "that sex has never been made one of the elements of citizenship in the United States."[40] Although this finding of women's public citizenship overturned older notions of women's limited citizenship under a conception of Republican Motherhood in the private family, it did not serve to gain women the right to vote. Instead, the Court held that federal citizenship does not include the right to vote because the vote is a right of *state* citizenship. Thus, the Court declared that voting is a privilege to be granted only by each state, and it is not a privilege of federal citizenship protected by the Privileges or Immunities Clause.[41]

The vote also emerged as the key proxy for women's rights because the political consensus among women reached out into new groups of supporters, but only on this limited ground. Beginning in 1880, a conservative prohibition group, the WCTU, joined the suffrage movement, bringing with it huge numbers of members, visibility, and grassroots support. Social reformers, club women, labor women, trade women, and professional groups such as teachers and journalists similarly endorsed and actively joined the suffrage movement. Black women, though nominally affiliated, were still segregated and kept on the outskirts of the movement. In 1890, the splintered women's suffrage organizations merged back into one National American Woman Suffrage Association (NAWSA) focused on the vote.

This new coalition of women reformers reached a feminist consensus only on difference feminism. Most of the new groups viewed women as different from men, different with respect to motherhood and different in morality. Women needed the vote, these maternalists argued, to contribute a unique perspective grounded in family and children and intended to improve the morality of the corrupt political process and resulting laws. Society was said to be a giant family, and women were ideally situated to care for that domestic home. Under these maternalist views, women had a moral duty to add their voice to the governance of the country. Such arguments amounted to a reassertion of Republican Motherhood, with women's duty as virtuous citizens to contribute to the common good, this time with the power of the vote. Prior feminist supporters of women's right to vote agreed on women's difference stemming from motherhood. However, they viewed motherhood as a source of individual entitlement and empowerment under political liberal theories of equality.

The woman's suffrage movement thus proceeded on the theoretical duality of both liberal and relational feminism. "The vote harmonized the two strands in ... women's rights advocacy; it was an equal rights goal that enabled women to make special contributions; it sought to give women the same capacity as men so they could express their differences."[42] Women's sameness and difference from men were seen as two alternative arguments bolstering women's demand for the vote. As Stanton explained, the women's movement pragmatically started out on the equality ground "because we thought, from that standpoint, we could draw the strongest arguments for woman's enfranchisement.... until we saw that stronger arguments could be drawn from a difference in sex, in mind as well as body."[43] This seeming acceptance of women's difference quieted some of the most vocal women's rights opponents, who cast their most constant and loudest criticism of suffrage and feminist legal reform as a threat to the destruction of the family.[44]

The unified movement for suffrage spent the next three decades in the trenches advocating and petitioning for women's right to vote. NAWSA concentrated on state strategies, demoting Stanton's idea of a federal constitutional amendment and focusing instead on a state level grass-roots strategy of securing voting rights piecemeal. Women had some limited successes here, securing in some states municipal suffrage, school board suffrage, and presidential elector suffrage as well as full suffrage in a handful of Western states. Then, in the early 1910s, Alice Paul led a splinter group within NAWSA, later breaking off into her own National Woman's Party (NWP), which utilized militant tactics to sway public and political support for a federal constitutional amendment.[45] Adopting tactics of the British women suffragists, learned from Irish nationalists, Paul organized the famous women's suffrage parades and pickets of the White House, leading to the jailing of the picketers under inhumane conditions that ultimately tipped public opinion. Black women were still dismissed, as Paul relegated Black and Asian suffrage women to the back of parades.

Race continued to be a barrier to women's suffrage as Southern legislators feared that ratification of the Nineteenth Amendment would strengthen the enforcement of the Fifteenth Amendment—at the time weakened by Jim Crow laws—and serve to increase Black voting power. The fear harkened back to concerns that had shaped the Fourteenth and Fifteenth Amendments and led to the exclusion of Black women who outnumbered freedmen in every state of the Confederacy. The post-Reconstruction era saw the escalation of racism and Jim Crow laws, and "as the nation's racial politics descended, so did those of leading white suffragists" as they recognized that a constitutional amendment would never pass without the support of white Southern politicians.[46] Suffragists responded to the opposition by asserting white privilege, going along with the assumption that Black women's suffrage, like that of Black men under the Fifteenth Amendment, could be restricted through state literacy laws and poll tax voting requirements.

In 1918, the Nineteenth Amendment "hung by a thread in Congress."[47] The Spanish flu pandemic shut down gatherings and ordered people to stay home, activists and legislators fell ill, and World War I continued to ravage. Persuaded by NAWSA's persistent lobbying and women's patriotic support of his war effort, President Woodrow Wilson finally helped push the amendment through in his speech to Congress in September 1918, publicly shifting from his prior opposition to suffrage.[48] Midterm elections in November put the Republicans in power, and Congress quickly passed the Nineteenth Amendment in June 1919, now supported by both political parties. The amendment was ratified by the final state, Tennessee, in August 1920, after seventy-two years of feminist advocacy.[49] However, many laws continued to restrict minority women's voting rights. Native American women were denied the vote until the Indian Citizenship Act of 1924, Asian American women were denied until the 1943 Chinese Exclusion Repeal Act and the 1952 Immigration and Nationality Act, and Black women until the Voting Rights Act of 1965 and its prohibition of Jim Crow poll taxes and literacy tests.

Once the Nineteenth Amendment was ratified, the feminist consensus quickly evaporated. Women splintered into an alphabet soup of various organizations, segregated by issues and race, and often working in opposition to one another. NAWSA became the League of Women Voters and adopted a goal of enrolling, educating, and protecting women voters. Social feminists like Florence Kelley and her National Consumers League concentrated on labor issues of maximum hours, minimum wages, and protective worker legislation. The NWP turned to formal equality and an equal rights amendment. When Black women leaders like Ida B. Wells-Barnett and Mary Church Terrell sought to forge a coalition with Paul's national organization to fight continued voting restrictions on minority women, Paul insisted that the disfranchisement of Black women was "a race, not a sex matter and of no interest to the NWP."[50] Black women formed their own organizations, oftentimes working within existing clubs and church groups, but they were excluded from the history of women's suffrage and intersectional issues of race were ignored.[51]

For a brief time following passage of suffrage, a coalition formed in the Women's Joint Congressional Committee was able to force national attention to women's issues. Built around the suffrage consensus on women's maternal difference, the Joint Committee expanded the issues debated in the U.S. Congress to include matters of marriage, motherhood, and children. It succeeded in efforts to secure passage of the Cable Act, reinstating national citizenship for American women expatriated when they married non-American men.[52] The committee also achieved success in passing the Sheppard-Towner Act, designating federal money for maternal and child healthcare and remedying high infant and maternal mortality rates.[53] Additionally, they were able to move forward the constitutional amendment against child labor, although it was never ratified.[54] This early congressional bipartisan support of women's legislation was, however, short-lived. It quickly dissipated as lawmakers realized that women voters would not vote as a collective block and thus the support of women and women's issues was not politically required.

III. Progressive Feminism (1890–1930)

While women's suffrage dominated mainstream politics with its narrow focus on the vote, a more radical vein of feminism emerged. During the late Progressive Era, "feminism" emerged as an expressly recognized term and ideology. The appearance of the word in the 1910s signaled a new phase in women's rights, distinguishing the new more radical movement from moderate suffragism. As one proponent explained, "All feminists are suffragists, but not all suffragists are feminists."[55] The new feminism was "both broader and narrower: broader in intent, proclaiming revolution in all the relations of the sexes, and narrower in the range of its willing adherents. As an *ism* (an ideology) it presupposed a set of principles not necessarily belonging to every woman— nor limited to women."[56] Like early legal feminism, progressive feminists embraced a broad agenda beyond the vote: "The real goal was a 'complete social revolution': freedom for all forms of women's active expression, elimination of all structural and psychological handicaps to women's economic independence ... release from constraining sexual stereotypes, and opportunity to shine in every civic and professional capacity."[57]

Progressive feminists severed the ties of conservatism and its affiliation with Christianity and conventional respectability and became associated with politically left ideologies and socialism. They "embedded their critique of gender hierarchy in a critique of the social system," drawing on theories of socialism and the new field of sociology.[58] Their expanded political and social theories integrated issues of class and economics and broadened the feminist agenda to global issues like pacifism and international peace. For example, the Feminist Alliance, organized in 1914, held "Feminist Mass Meetings" on topics such as "What Is Feminism?" and "What Feminism Means to Me," which included issues of labor, professions, housekeeping, married women's names, and pacifism.[59] Other organizations like the Alliance, such as Heterodoxy, sprung up in New York City's Greenwich Village to gather together feminists and discuss feminist goals. To these progressives, "[f]eminism needed to bring more than equality to women: it also needed to extend their power and agency to secure the much-needed 'human world.'"[60]

Advancing this broad agenda, two key ideas dominated and distinguished the progressive feminist movement: women's economic interests and sex rights.[61] The first issue, home economics, reenvisioned women's confinement in the isolated domestic sphere and advocated for women's right to market work. Charlotte Perkins Gilman was a strong influence, labeled by global newspapers as the "preeminent feminist intellectual theorist" of the time, although she disavowed the label, preferring the term "humanist."[62] Gilman located the source of women's oppression in biological differences, drawing on social Darwinist theory. "Androcentric culture," she maintained, promoted male culture and its hallmarks of prostitution, intemperance, and war, while relegating women to the home. Her classic work, *Women and Economics: A Study of the Economic Relation Between Men and Women as a Factor in Social Evolution* (1898), argued for the outsourcing of women's private domestic work to professionals who would perform the childcare, cooking, cleaning, and organizing of the home in more efficient ways, complete with apartments, and co-op kitchens and nurseries.[63] Such organization would then allow all women, domestic and professional, to obtain paid market work and be economically self-sustaining. In Gilman's feminism, women were extracted from their "sex work" of domestic housekeeping and repositioned in "race work" (i.e., important political and market work for the good of the human race). By grounding feminist claims in economics and sociology, Gilman transformed feminism from a privileged individualism into a theory of social evolution.

The second dominant issue marking progressive feminism was its conception of "sex rights." Former nineteenth-century notions of "voluntary motherhood" and women's control of reproduction through choosing abstinence during marriage gave way to the birth control movement.[64] During the 1920s and 1930s, the movement to legalize birth control saw feminists articulating different supporting theories, from protecting working-class women to embracing women's sexual freedom to eugenic notions of population control. Margaret Sanger based her original defense of birth control on radical feminist ideals of women's emancipation, moved by the desperate conditions of women she met as a public health nurse. But shifting alliances, brought on by obscenity laws, physician allegiances, and the eugenics movement, allowed Sanger's work to be used as a tool for the social control and regulation of poor and Black women.[65]

Progressive feminism, with its idealism and promise, was quickly lost. It was doomed in part by its association with socialism, which became a prime target in the post-World War I era. Following the Russian communist revolution, anticommunist sentiment was high. Feminists moved to distance themselves from the negative implications of communism, and from its more radical ideologies. Progressive feminism was also done in partly by its success: The home economics arguments had resulted in significant gains in women's access to employment and education, which seemed to lessen the need to challenge a sex-segregated patriarchy.

IV. Liberal Formalism as the Dominant Theory (1920–1970)

By the early twentieth century, both narrow and progressive forms of legal feminism became dormant. Only Alice Paul's NWP continued to embrace the label of feminism.[66] Paul still believed that law was the fundamental cause of women's oppression, and the key avenue for its reform. This time, she focused on an equal rights amendment.

As one of the new priorities for her organization after the suffrage success, Paul chose Burnita Shelton Matthews to lead a committee of thirteen women attorneys charged with studying the discriminatory laws of each state.[67] They examined laws relating to women's property rights, child custody, divorce and marital rights, jury duty, education, employment, and national citizenship rights—most of which paralleled those issues identified in the Declaration of Sentiments. The committee's purpose "was to expose legal inequalities between men and women that were embedded in all facets of law" and to propose new legislation to counteract these inequalities.[68]

The results of the study convinced Paul that Stanton's first step of formal equality had not yet been achieved. Women's inequality and inferiority were still embedded in the formal law. Rather than take on each issue individually, Paul decided on a national, blanket law to redress all issues at once. In 1921, one year after the Nineteenth Amendment, Paul and socialist lawyer Crystal Eastman drafted and proposed the first

Equal Rights Amendment. "The work of the National Woman's Party," Paul said, "is to take sex out of law—to give women the equality in law they have won at the polls."[69] Paul had also learned the political lesson of the suffrage campaign—that a single, concrete feminist issue was more expedient than an amorphous ideology.

Paul's formal equality approach, however, immediately garnered opposition from feminist leaders in the labor movement focused on women's difference. Progressive and left-leaning feminists opposed an equal rights amendment for its perceived threat to protective labor legislation regulating wages, hours, and working conditions of working-class women.[70] Their advocacy was based on women's differences—women's biological weaknesses of size, stamina, and maternity and the social differences of family and housekeeping demands. Such difference arguments were persuasive in the famous Brandeis brief of sociological data submitted in the *Muller v. Oregon* case, filed by then-lawyer Louis Brandeis but written and researched by his sister-in-law, Josephine Goldmark, and consumer advocate Florence Kelley.[71] Their strategy was to emphasize women's difference and weakness as a starting point for protective workplace legislation, which would have been prohibited under an equal rights law that treated all workers the same.

The battle among the feminist reformers was evident in the U.S. Supreme Court, where the Court vacillated between equality and difference feminism. In 1908, in *Muller*, the Court first embraced the legal feminism of difference guided by social feminists and upheld a maximum-hours law for women only, even though it had overturned such a law for men in the infamous case of *Lochner v. New York*.[72] However, fifteen years later, the Court in *Adkins v. D.C. Children's Hospital* embraced liberal equality feminism based on the intervening Nineteenth Amendment, which the Court interpreted as a command for broad sex equality and structural change overturning coverture and sex protection laws.[73] It struck down a minimum wage law for women only. However, that same year, the Court returned to women-protective ideals in *Radice v. New York*, upholding prohibitions on women's night work.[74] A little over a decade later, the Court reaffirmed *Adkins* in *Morehead v. New York ex rel. Tipaldo*, invalidating a New York minimum wage law for women and minors, but one year later it definitively overruled *Adkins* and in *West Coast Hotel Co. v. Parrish* upheld a women-only minimum wage law.[75] The struggle over feminisms in the context of the workplace laws was ultimately resolved by Congress in 1938 when it passed the Fair Labor Standards Act endorsing minimum wage and maximum-hours laws for all workers.

Yet old animosities and alliances persisted. Equality feminists like Paul, and many professional women who had recently entered careers, aligned with business interests. Social feminists, including Franklin Delano Roosevelt's first female cabinet member, Frances Perkins, and Florence Allen, the first federal appellate judge, sided with the American Civil Liberties Union and labor against an equal rights amendment. Feminism thus became imbued with connotations of classism and conservatism, associated with the business class and opposed by the working class.

Legal feminists continued to advocate for formal equality based on their core belief that law was fundamental to women's oppression as well as their freedom. Formal equality was easy to grasp, was objective and concrete, and blanketed all areas of civic life. It was theoretically grounded in Aristotelian ideals and the intuitive fairness of treating persons similarly situated the same. Moreover, it could be achieved practically at the individual level by women joining the professional ranks in law, medicine, and politics.

This return to formalism came despite the contrary vision of the legal realism school that emerged in the 1930s and 1940s. Legal realism was a theory of jurisprudence that rejected a conception of law as formal, absolute truth and instead saw law as influenced by political, social, and moral factors.[76] It deconstructed so-called objective legal norms and emphasized that legal interpretation had practical consequences such that law can be used as a means to achieve just ends. However, legal realism failed to live up to its social promise and, ironically, became stuck in academia rather than translating into transformative change in people's lived experience. It did, however, influence the law and society movement of the 1950s and the critical legal studies movement of the 1970s, which both led to the development of contemporary feminist legal theory.

V. Conclusion

Feminist legal theory has thus expanded and contracted over time. Starting with the broad comprehensive agenda and methodology of the first woman's rights movement, it narrowed in on a consensus of maternalism. Progressive feminism stretched the theory and agenda back again, with its focus on radical systemic change to laws, structures, and global conflict. In the twentieth century, however, a narrower formal legal equality feminism dominated, buoyed by pervasive formal gender inequality leading to a challenge to the use of women's difference as subordination. Formal legal equality proved to be a successful strategy for feminists. From securing the vote to the U.S. Supreme Court's equal protection jurisprudence beginning in the 1970s, equality provided a useful analytical vehicle for protecting women's rights. This success was facilitated by the efforts of Black lawyer Pauli Murray, who analogized sex to race discrimination to bridge the legal and political gap between racial and gender civil rights.[77] The success of equality theory was also fostered by Justice Ruth Bader Ginsburg, as an advocate and a judge, using formalism to dismantle historical gender stereotypes of women's domesticity and inferiority.[78] However, the persistence of pregnancy discrimination, workplace conflicts, and sexual harassment, among other injustices, show that women's lived difference cannot be ignored, and that larger systems of public and private institutions and sexualized norms demand attention and radical change. In particular, intersectional understandings of women's subordination are now integral to rectifying gender injustice as feminists move forward with a more holistic and integrated theory of legal feminism.

Notes

1. ANN SCALES, LEGAL FEMINISM: ACTIVISM, LAWYERING, AND LEGAL THEORY 1 (2006); MARTHA CHAMALLAS, INTRODUCTION TO FEMINIST LEGAL THEORY 31–32 (3d ed. 2010).
2. NANCY LEVIT & ROBERT R. M. VERCHICK, FEMINIST LEGAL THEORY 3 (2d ed. 2016). The terms "legal feminism" and "feminist legal theory" are used interchangeably in this chapter.
3. NANCY COTT, THE GROUNDING OF MODERN FEMINISM 13–14 (1987); Karen Offen, *Defining Feminism: A Comparative Historical Approach*, 14 SIGNS 119, 125 (1988).
4. Report of the Woman's Rights Convention, Held at Seneca Falls, July 19–20, 1848, *in* THE SELECTED PAPERS OF ELIZABETH CADY STANTON AND SUSAN B. ANTHONY, VOL. I, IN THE SCHOOL OF ANTI-SLAVERY, 1840-1866, 75, 76–79 (Ann D. Gordon ed., 1998).
5. *Id.*; NANCY ISENBERG, SEX AND CITIZENSHIP IN ANTEBELLUM AMERICA xviii (1998).
6. JUDITH WELLMAN, THE ROAD TO SENECA FALLS: ELIZABETH CADY STANTON AND THE FIRST WOMAN'S RIGHTS CONVENTION 36 (2004).
7. TRACY A. THOMAS, ELIZABETH CADY STANTON AND THE FEMINIST FOUNDATIONS OF FAMILY LAW 19 (2016); SUE DAVIS, THE POLITICAL THOUGHT OF ELIZABETH CADY STANTON 1 (2008); ELLEN CAROL DUBOIS, FEMINISM & SUFFRAGE: THE EMERGENCE OF AN INDEPENDENT WOMEN'S MOVEMENT IN AMERICA, 1848-1869, 60 (1978).
8. THOMAS, *supra* note 7, at 19; DAVIS, *supra* note 7, at 1.
9. Tracy A. Thomas, *More Than the Vote: The Nineteenth Amendment as Proxy for Gender Equality*, 15 STAN. J. C.R. & C.L. 349, 350, 355–58 (2020); *see* Reva B. Siegel, "THE RULE OF LOVE": WIFE BEATING AS PREROGATIVE AND PRIVACY, 105 YALE L.J. 2117, 2128 (1996); Reva B. Siegel, "HOME AS WORK": THE FIRST WOMAN'S RIGHTS CLAIMS CONCERNING WIVES' HOUSEHOLD LABOR, 1850-1880, 103 YALE L.J. 1073, 1107 n.188 (1994).
10. LORI D. GINZBERG, ELIZABETH CADY STANTON: AN AMERICAN LIFE 19–21 (2009); ELISABETH GRIFFITH, IN HER OWN RIGHT: THE LIFE OF ELIZABETH CADY STANTON 8–11 (1985).
11. 83 U.S. 142 (1873); *see* VIRGINIA C. DRACHMAN, SISTERS IN LAW: WOMEN LAWYERS IN MODERN AMERICAN HISTORY 5–6, 15–20, 37 (1998).
12. *See* COTT, *supra* note 3, at 16–17; DAVIS, *supra* note 7, at 2–4; ELIZABETH CADY STANTON: FEMINIST AS THINKER 9 (Ellen Carol DuBois & Richard Cándida Smith eds., 2007) [hereinafter FEMINIST AS THINKER]; Elizabeth B. Clark, *Religion, Rights and Difference in the Early Woman's Rights Movement*, 3 WIS. WOMEN'S L.J. 29, 30 (1987); Elizabeth B. Clark, *Self-Ownership and the Political Theory of Elizabeth Cady Stanton*, 21 CONN. L. REV. 905, 905–06 (1988).
13. THOMAS, *supra* note 7, at 22–23.
14. *See* ELIZABETH ANN BARTLETT, LIBERTY, EQUALITY, SORORITY: THE ORIGINS AND INTERPRETATIONS OF AMERICAN FEMINIST THOUGHT: FRANCES WRIGHT, SARAH GRIMKE, AND MARGARET FULLER (1994); Barbara Caine, *Elizabeth Cady Stanton, John Stuart Mill, and the Nature of Feminist Thought*, *in* FEMINIST AS THINKER, *supra* note 12, at 51, 62; Charles J. Reid, Jr., *The Journey to Seneca Falls: Mary Wollstonecraft, Elizabeth Cady Stanton, and the Legal Emancipation of Women*, 10 U. ST. THOMAS L.J. 1123 (2013); Eileen Hunt Botting & Christina Carey, *Wollstonecraft's Philosophical Impact on Nineteenth-Century American Women's Rights Advocates*, 48 AM. J. POL. SCI. 707 (2004); Phyllis Cole, *Stanton, Fuller, and the Grammar of Romanticism*, 73 NEW ENG. Q. 553, 553–54 (2000); Molly Abel Travis, *Francis Wright: The Other Woman of Early American Feminism*, 22 J. WOMEN'S STUD. 389 (1993).

15. Tracy A. Thomas, *Elizabeth Cady Stanton and the Notion of a Legal Class of Gender*, in Feminist Legal History 139, 140–41 (Tracy A. Thomas & Tracey Jean Boisseau eds., 2011) [hereinafter Feminist Legal History].
16. Davis, *supra* note 7, at 111, 220.
17. *Id.* at 29–33, 219–21.
18. Suzanne M. Marilley, Woman Suffrage and the Origins of Liberal Feminism in the United States, 1820-1920, 2–3, 43 (1996).
19. Elizabeth Cady Stanton, Address to the Legislature of New York (Feb. 14, 1854).
20. Linda Kerber, Women of the Republic: Intellect and Ideology in Revolutionary America 185–220 (1986); Nancy Cott, The Bonds of Womanhood 1–2, 63–64 (1982); Barbara Welter, *The Cult of True Womanhood: 1820-1860*, 18 Am. Q. 151 (1966).
21. Address to the Legislature of New York, *supra* note 19, at 17–18.
22. Report of Woman's Rights Convention, *supra* note 4, at 77.
23. Elizabeth Cady Stanton, Free Love Speech (ms.) ¶ 2 [ca. 1871], *microformed on* The Papers of Elizabeth Cady Stanton and Susan B. Anthony (Patricia G. Holland & Ann D. Gordon eds., 1991) (Scholarly Research).
24. *Id.*
25. Elizabeth Cady Stanton, *The Other Side of the Woman Question*, 129 N. Amer. Rev. 432 (1879).
26. Elizabeth Cady Stanton, *Miss Becker on the Difference in Sex*, Revolution, Sept. 24, 1868.
27. Naomi Mezey & Cornelia T.L. Pillard, *Against the New Maternalism*, 18 Mich. J. Gender & L. 229, 239–40 (2012); *see* Richard H. Chused, Courts and Temperance "Ladies," 21 Yale J. L. & Feminism 339, 368–69 (2010); *see generally* Ruth Bordin, Woman and Temperance: The Quest for Power and Liberty, 1873-1900 (1990).
28. 83 U.S. 130, 141 (1873) (Bradley, J. concurring).
29. *Id.*
30. Stanton, *Miss Becker*, *supra* note 26.
31. Norma Basch, In the Eyes of the Law: Women, Marriage, and Property in Nineteenth-Century New York 17 (1982).
32. *See generally* Martha S. Jones, All Bound Up Together: The Woman Question in African American Public Culture, 1830-1900 (2007).
33. *See* Lauren E. Free, Suffrage Reconstructed: Gender, Race, and Voting Rights in the Civil War Era 2–3, 5 (2015); Catherine Powell & Camille Gear Rich, *The "Welfare Queen" Goes to the Polls: Race-Based Fractures in Gender Politics and Opportunities for Intersectional Coalitions*, 108 Geo. L.J. 105, 131–32 (2020).
34. Elizabeth Cady Stanton, *Manhood Suffrage*, Revolution, Dec. 24, 1868; Anniversary of American Equal Rights Association, Address of Elizabeth Cady Stanton, Revolution, May 13, 1869; Elizabeth Cady Stanton, *Equal Rights to All!*, Revolution, Feb. 12, 1868; Ann Gordon, *Stanton and the Right to Vote: On Account of Race or Sex*, in Feminist as Thinker, *supra* note 12, at 124; Michele Mitchell, *"Lower Orders," Racial Hierarchies, and Rights Rhetoric*, in Feminist as Thinker, *supra* note 12, at 128, 137.
35. *See* Louise Michele Newman, White Women's Rights: The Racial Origins of Feminism in the United States 8 (1999); Roslyn Terborg Penn, African American Women in the Struggle for the Vote, 1850-1920, 2 (1998); Angela Y. Davis, Women, Race & Class ch. 4 (1981); Christine Stansell, *Missed Connections: Abolitionist Feminism in the Nineteenth Century*, in Feminist as Thinker, *supra* note 12, at 32; Angela P. Harris, *Race and Essentialism in Feminist Legal Theory*, 42 Stan. L. Rev. 581, 585–90 (1990).

36. RICHARD CHUSED & WENDY WILLIAMS, GENDERED LAW IN AMERICAN HISTORY 37–43 (2016).
37. FREE, *supra* note 33, at 2–3, 158; *Introduction, in* THE SELECTED PAPERS OF ELIZABETH CADY STANTON AND SUSAN B. ANTHONY, VOL. II, AGAINST AN ARISTOCRACY OF SEX xxiii–iv (Ann D. Gordon ed., 2000).
38. LISA TETRAULT, THE MYTH OF SENECA FALLS: MEMORY AND THE WOMEN'S SUFFRAGE MOVEMENT, 1848-1898, 34 (2014); Andrea Moore Kerr, *White Women's Rights, Black Men's Wrongs, Free Love, Blackmail, and the Formation of the American Woman Suffrage Association, in* ONE WOMAN, ONE VOTE: REDISCOVERING THE WOMAN SUFFRAGE MOVEMENT 61–78 (Marjorie Spruill Wheeler ed., 1995).
39. ELLEN CAROL DuBOIS, SUFFRAGE: WOMEN'S LONG BATTLE FOR THE VOTE 85 (2020).
40. 88 U.S. 162, 165, 169–70 (1874).
41. *Id.* at 170.
42. COTT, *supra* note 3, at 30.
43. Stanton, *Miss Becker, supra* note 26.
44. Reva B. Siegel, *The Nineteenth Amendment and the Democratization of the Family*, 129 YALE L.J. F. 450, 452 (2020); Reva B. Siegel, *She the People: The Nineteenth Amendment, Sex Equality, Federalism, and the Family*, 115 HARV. L. REV. 947, 978–79, 1000 (2002).
45. Lynda Dodd, *Sisterhood of Struggle: Leadership and Strategy in the Campaign for the Nineteenth Amendment, in* FEMINIST LEGAL HISTORY, *supra* note 15, at 189; *see generally* BERNADETTE CAHILL & ALICE PAUL, THE NATIONAL WOMAN'S PARTY AND THE VOTE (2015).
46. DuBOIS, SUFFRAGE, *supra* note 39, at 151.
47. Alisha Haridasani Gupta, *How the Spanish Flu Almost Upended Women's Suffrage*, N.Y. TIMES, Apr. 28, 2020.
48. TINA CASSIDY, MR. PRESIDENT, HOW LONG MUST WE WAIT?: ALICE PAUL, WOODROW WILSON, AND THE FIGHT FOR THE RIGHT TO VOTE 215 (2019); KIMBERLY A. HAMLIN, FREE THINKER: THE EXTRAORDINARY LIFE OF HELEN HAMILTON GARDENER 237, 254 (2020).
49. ELAINE WEISS, THE WOMAN'S HOUR: THE GREAT FIGHT TO WIN THE VOTE 1–4 (2019).
50. DuBOIS, SUFFRAGE, *supra* note 39, at 289; *see* MARTHA S. JONES, VANGUARD: HOW BLACK WOMEN BROKE BARRIERS, WON THE VOTE, AND INSISTED ON EQUALITY FOR ALL 8-9, 175–76, 179 (2020); Paula A. Monopoli, CONSTITUTIONAL ORPHAN: GENDER EQUALITY AND THE NINETEENTH AMENDMENT 2–3, 5 n.5 (2020); Liette Gidlow, MORE THAN DOUBLE: AFRICAN AMERICAN WOMEN AND THE RISE OF A "WOMAN'S VOTE," 32 J. WOMEN'S HIST. 52, 58 (2020).
51. JONES, VANGUARD, *supra* note 50, at 164–65; Barbara Young Welke, *"When All the Women Were White, and All the Blacks Were Men: Gender, Class, Race, and the Road to* Plessy, *1855-1914*, 13 LAW & HIST. REV. 261, 265–66 (1995).
52. *See* LINDA KERBER, NO CONSTITUTIONAL RIGHT TO BE LADIES 3 (1998); Felice Batlan, *"SHE WAS SURPRISED AND FURIOUS": EXPATRIATION, SUFFRAGE, IMMIGRATION, AND THE FRAGILITY OF WOMEN'S CITIZENSHIP, 1907-1940*, 15 STAN. J. C.R. & C.L. 315 (2020); Leti Volpp, *Expatriation by Marriage: The Case of Asian American Women, in* FEMINIST LEGAL HISTORY, *supra* note 15, at 68.
53. *See* JAN DOOLITTLE WILSON, THE WOMEN'S JOINT CONGRESSIONAL COMMITTEE AND THE POLITICS OF MATERNALISM, 1920-30, 27 (2007); Susan L. Waysdorf, *Fighting for Their Lives: Women, Poverty, and the Historical Role of United States Law in Shaping Access*

to Women's Health Care, 84 Ky. L.J. 745, 771–91 (1996); J. Stanley Lemons, *The Sheppard-Towner Act: Progressivism in the 1920s*, 55 J. Am. Hist. 776, 778 (1968).
54. Wilson, *supra* note 53, at 66.
55. Cott, *supra* note 3, at 3.
56. *Id.*
57. *Id.* at 35–36.
58. *Id.*
59. *Id.* at 12.
60. Judith A. Allen, The Feminism of Charlotte Perkins Gilman: Sexualities, Histories, Progressivism 176 (2009).
61. Cott, *supra* note 3, at 44, 49.
62. Allen, *supra* note 60, at xiii, 2, 5, 163, 165.
63. *Id.* at 116–17.
64. Linda Gordon, The Moral Property of Women of Women: A History of Birth Control Politics in America 57–59 (2002).
65. Dorothy Roberts, Killing the Black Body: Race, Reproduction, and the Meaning of Liberty 57–58 (1997); Ellen Chesler, Woman of Valor: Margaret Sanger and the Birth Control Movement in America 88, 231 (1992).
66. Cott, *supra* note 3, at 135.
67. Matthews would become the first woman judge on a federal district court, appointed in 1949 to the U.S. District Court for the District of Columbia. Linda Greenhouse, Burnita S. Matthews Dies at 93; First Woman on U.S. Trial Courts, N.Y. Times, Apr. 28, 1988, at D27.
68. Cott, *supra* note 3, at 227, 232.
69. Tracey Jean Boisseau & Tracy A. Thomas, *After Suffrage Comes Equal Rights? ERA as the Next Logical Step*, in 100 Years of The Nineteenth Amendment 227, 227 (Holly J. McCammon & Lee Ann Banaszak eds., 2018).
70. Nancy Woloch, A Class by Herself: Protective Laws for Women Workers, 1890s–1990s, 62, 64–68 (2015).
71. 208 U.S. 412, 421–22 (1908); Nancy Woloch, *Muller v. Oregon*: A Brief History with Documents 2–3 (1996).
72. 208 U.S. 412 (1908); Lochner v. New York, 198 U.S. 45 (1905); *but see* Bunting v. Oregon, 243 U.S. 426 (1917) (upholding maximum hours law for all workers).
73. 261 U.S. 525 (1923); Monopoli, *supra* note 50, at 187.
74. 264 U.S. 292 (1923).
75. Morehead v. New York *ex rel.* Tipaldo, 298 U.S. 587 (1936); West Coast Hotel Co. v. Parrish, 300 U.S. 379 (1937).
76. Mae C. Quinn, *Feminist Legal Realism*, 35 Harv. J. L. & Gender 1, 6 (2012).
77. *See generally* Rosalind Rosenberg, Jane Crow: The Life of Pauli Murray (2017); Serena Mayeri, Reasoning from Race: Feminism, Law, and the Civil Rights Revolution (2011).
78. Ruth Bader Ginsburg & Barbara Flagg, *Some Thoughts on the Feminist Legal Theory of the 1970s*, 1989 U. Chi. Legal F. 16.

CHAPTER 2

LIBERAL FEMINIST JURISPRUDENCE

Foundational, Enduring, Adaptive

LINDA C. MCCLAIN AND BRITTANY K. HACKER

LIBERAL feminism is a significant strand of feminist jurisprudence (or feminist legal theory) in the United States and elsewhere. The relationship between liberalism and feminism, however, is complex. As an historical matter, there is little doubt that liberal political philosophy serves as an important foundation for feminist political and legal thought. Feminists have divided, however, between viewing liberalism and feminism as "incompatible" and its doctrines as best relegated to the past and arguing that the better feminist response is to "reconfigure, rather than reject, liberalism."[1]

Any assessment of liberal feminism as a strand of feminist legal theory starts with the liberal and liberal feminist concepts of individual liberty, autonomy, dignity, and equality and recognition of the injustice of gender-based restrictions based on men's and women's proper spheres and roles.[2] A prominent example of the influence of these concepts and commitments is the sex equality litigation of the 1970s undertaken by Justice Ruth Bader Ginsburg and the ACLU's Women's Rights Project, which challenged the pervasive sex-based discrimination in law and society's basic institutions.[3] These gender-based challenges transformed the U.S. Supreme Court's interpretation of the Equal Protection Clause of the Fourteenth Amendment and ushered in a more skeptical judicial review of gender-based classifications, known as intermediate scrutiny.

Under intermediate scrutiny, legislatures may not rely on "fixed notions" about "the sexes" and must offer an "exceedingly persuasive justification" for using sex-based classifications.[4] This gender revolution continues to shape understandings of constitutional equality and the interpretation of statutory civil rights laws, such as Title VII.[5] Within "liberal feminism," there are feminist legal scholars who, similar to Ginsburg, argue for symmetry or "formal equality" in law, even when dealing with evident differences between women and men—such as pregnancy—because of the risk of protectionism and a return of harmful gender ideology.[6]

Another body of liberal feminist legal theory builds upon liberal legal and political theory and liberal feminist political philosophy, ranging from John Stuart Mill and Harriet Taylor Mill, in the nineteenth century to John Rawls and Susan Moller Okin in the twentieth century. These scholars have explored the tension between liberal ideals and gender injustice in marriage and family law and argued for governmental obligation to foster the preconditions for and address the obstacles to meaningful personal and political self-government.[7] Such theorists have also advocated law reform to advance values such as dignity, self-expression, and sexual privacy, particularly as newer technologies, such as the Internet, bring both new possibilities and new forms of gendered injury.[8]

This chapter begins with liberal feminism's historical roots in liberal and feminist political philosophy. It then considers the role of liberal feminism in law and legal thought and its relationship to other strands of feminist legal theory. It addresses how liberal feminism responds to internal feminist and external critiques and suggests the generative role of key liberal feminist tenets in ongoing struggles over sex equality.

According to one view, the contribution of liberal feminism is mostly of historical interest in light of subsequent generations of feminist legal thought. According to another, however, liberal feminism continues to inform feminist legal thought and legal advocacy, although its present-day exemplars engage in a more complex and nuanced discourse about sex, gender, and the gender binary than their forebears did a half century ago. This chapter concludes that the latter view is the more persuasive one. Liberal feminism can offer an inclusive and adaptive theory that provides insight in such diverse contexts as articulating the meaning of liberty and determining the scope of discrimination based on "sex," including transgender rights. Because liberal feminism aims at "disrupting—or bursting asunder" historical and rigid links between "biological sex and particular roles or ways of thinking associated with particular genders," liberal feminism has the potential to adapt as ideas about sex, gender, and identity continue to evolve.[9]

I. Defining Liberal Feminism

A commonplace criticism of liberalism is the slipperiness of the concept and the difficulty of defining it. The broad "family of positions" described as "liberalism" includes positions "profoundly different" from each other, such as Kantian or Rawlsian liberalism, on the one hand, and, on the other, classical utilitarianism liberalism and present-day neoliberalism.[10] For this reason, feminist defenders of liberalism have argued that feminist critics often attack a caricatured or oversimplified picture of liberalism.[11] What, then, is "liberal" in liberal feminism and what makes it "feminist"? Answering these questions begins with visiting the roots of liberal feminism and tracking its emergence as a distinct strand of feminist legal thought through to its current relevance.

A. Historical Roots: Nineteenth-Century Liberal Feminists

Liberal legal feminism has roots in both liberal and feminist political theory. "Modern Western feminism," Ruth Abbey asserts, "grew up as a sister doctrine to liberalism."[12] Classic liberal political theory, such as that of John Locke, challenged patriarchal authority with respect to political power. Pioneering "feminist liberals," including Mary Wollstonecraft, Harriet Taylor Mill, and John Stuart Mill, extended Locke's critique to private power. Such early feminists, including American feminists such as Elizabeth Cady Stanton and Lucretia Mott, applied "liberal commitments to women" as a "matter of justice."[13] Those "liberal commitments" include such values as

> individual freedom; equality before the law; equal opportunity; moral equality; personal autonomy; being rewarded (or punished) on the basis of merit rather than birth; the rejection of arbitrary and unearned power and hierarchy and its replacement with the idea that the exercise of power by one individual over another must be rationally defended; consent to rule by those ruled; and freedom of conscience.[14]

Such liberal ideals are evident in Abigail Adams's famous plea to her husband John Adams, in 1776, to "Remember the Ladies, and be more generous and favourable to them than your ancestors," as he and other male politicians constructed a "new Code of Laws." Abigail Adams urged: "Do not put such unlimited power into the hands of the Husbands. Remember that all men would be tyrants if they could."[15] John Adams responded that he "cannot but laugh" at her "extraordinary Code of Laws" and "saucy" letter. But the answer, in any case, was no: "Depend upon it. We know better than to repeal our Masculine systems."[16] John Adams asserted that men held such power more in theory than practice, and would "dare not exert" it in "its full Latitude;" nonetheless, to yield their power would subject men to "the Despotism of the Petticoat."[17]

Rather than abolishing coverture marriage (the gender hierarchical common law model of marriage that traveled from England to the colonies), the revolutionary-era political leaders enlisted marriage as an emblem or "analogue to the legitimate polity."[18] They drew on Locke's idea that political legitimacy rested on individual consent to be governed; marriage, they reasoned, was a social contract to which women freely consented.[19]

In the nineteenth century, women's rights advocates continued to challenge coverture and called for full civil and political rights. They employed liberal political ideals of individual self-determination and being "free . . . from the constraints of an ascribed status and separate sphere" to shape feminist demands.[20]

Many activists in the movement for women's rights began as "ardent abolitionists" and their experience in the antislavery movement—including gender discrimination within the movement—led them to draw parallels between abolition and women's rights.[21] Such women's rights reformers "contended that both institutions, slavery and marriage, harbored inequalities inconsistent with American principles of liberty and equality."[22] The reformers applied Locke's theory that each person had a property in his own person to argue that because both the slave and the wife under coverture lacked such self-possession, they were denied the natural right to self-ownership.[23] Abolitionist sisters Angelina and Sarah Grimké, for example, pointed out parallels between the master/slave and husband/wife relationship but disclaimed an exact comparison between "free women" and enslaved persons, given enslaved women's greater "suffering," "degradation," and denial of any legal status.[24]

Defenders of slavery, in turn, appealed to the parallels between slavery and marriage to justify both systems of white men's "mastership over their households."[25] In the pre-Civil War constitutional order, states' primary responsibility to regulate their "domestic institutions" referred "simultaneously to family and to slavery."[26]

The campaign for women's suffrage enlisted liberal principles to attack both the unjust structure of family governance and the exclusion of women from the franchise as inconsistent with democratic and constitutional ideals.[27] Illustrative is the Declaration of Rights and Sentiments, which emanated from the Seneca Falls Convention of 1848. It invoked the "liberal premises" of the Declaration of Independence: "created equal," women had "certain inalienable rights," which were "usurped" by "man" claiming the "right to "assign" women a "sphere of action," when that right belonged to "her conscience and her God."[28] To arguments that gender hierarchy and the separate roles of men and women derived from "nature" and the "Creator," feminists responded with their own appeals to divine order.

The Declaration of Sentiments foreshadowed twentieth-century liberal feminism by stressing the equal capabilities of women and men as a basis for equal rights and by condemning the legal disabilities imposed on women.[29] While radical for its time in some respects, the Declaration also "reflected its time"; some of its arguments for women's rights "elevated white women above male immigrants, free black men and women, and the destitute who lacked the advantages many middle-class women possessed."[30]

The appeal to women's equal capacities also featured in arguments that separate spheres ideology denied women the right to choose their own "proper sphere."[31] Such critiques of sex inequality invoked the influential work of John Stuart Mill and Harriet Taylor Mill.[32] In *The Subjection of Women* (1869), John Stuart Mill wrote that "the legal subordination of one sex to the other" as an organizing principle was "wrong" and should be replaced by "a principle of perfect equality, admitting no power of privilege on the one side nor disability on the other."[33]

Mill's *On Liberty* (1859) supported liberal feminist arguments about the value of personal and political self-government and antipaternalism. Further, in explaining *misunderstandings* of liberty, Mill criticized the "almost despotic power of husbands over wives," arguing that "wives should have the same rights, and should receive the protection of law in the same manner, as all other persons."[34]

While liberalism was a dominant influence on nineteenth-century feminism, another prominent strand of feminism used "the rhetoric of natural roles" to argue for including women in public life.[35] This appeal to gender differences stressed that "women's special attributes" as mothers and housekeepers would improve public life.[36] After ratification of the Nineteenth Amendment, these tensions over how best to secure women's full civil, political, and social rights recurred in disagreements over the Equal Rights Amendment, first written in 1923, and over sex-specific protective labor legislation.[37] At issue was the question of whether formal equality (or gender neutral laws) as a constitutional mandate was a better path to "true" equality than an approach that considered the "actual biological, social, and occupational differences between men and women."[38]

B. Feminists Engage Twentieth-Century Liberalism

In the twentieth century, liberal political philosopher John Rawls reinvigorated liberal thought for many political and legal theorists, including liberal feminists. *A Theory of Justice* (1971) and *Political Liberalism* (1993) offered, respectively, an argument about "justice as fairness" that distilled key liberal social contract traditions and a conception of a "political" liberalism that could support a "stable and just society of free and equal citizens profoundly divided by reasonable religious, philosophical, and moral doctrines."[39] Rawls posited that free and equal citizens have two moral powers relating to self-government: (1) the capacity for a conception of justice, which allows democratic self-government (or "deliberative democracy"), and (2) the capacity to form, act on, and revise a conception of a good life, which allows personal self-government (or "deliberative autonomy").[40]

Feminist political philosophers and legal theorists took up and critiqued Rawls's work.[41] In *Justice, Gender, and the Family*, liberal feminist Susan Moller Okin highlighted the inattention to gender and family in prominent theories of justice.[42] Rawls, she observed, assumed that, as a basic institution in a well-ordered society, families were just and could form children into self-governing members of such a society. Contradicting that assumption, however, were forms of injustice within "gendered marriage," such as domination and family violence, an unequal division of labor between husbands/fathers and wives/mothers during marriage, and divorce law that failed to recognize that inequality.[43] But Okin also argued that aspects of Rawls's theory—such as his construct of the "original position" in which people (behind a "veil of ignorance") determine what is a just outcome without knowing their social position in the society, including their sex—could be a powerful tool for feminist criticism of contemporary institutions.[44] Okin proposed that government could promote—but not compel—egalitarian marriage and adopt family law reforms so that marriage no longer contributed to women's "socially created vulnerability."[45] Responding to Okin and other feminist critique, Rawls clarified that, according to his account, the family was not a space exempt from justice but instead "the equal rights of women and the basic rights of children as future citizens are inalienable and protect them wherever they are."[46]

Gender injustice within the family was also a central concern of philosopher and law professor Martha Nussbaum's "human capabilities approach" to human development, which she characterized as reflecting both a form of political liberalism (akin to Rawls's) and a universalist feminism.[47] Nussbaum attempted to address feminist critiques of liberalism for inattention to the moral virtues linked to care as well as the practical reality that the family has been a "major site of the oppression of women."[48] To value care, her approach accorded the capabilities for love and care a prominent place in a political conception of justice and made them "important goals of social planning."[49] To guard against risks that women will not be treated as ends in themselves but as instrumental beings (e.g., as "reproducers and caregivers"), she insisted that, within the family, the focus should be on "each person," akin to the liberal tradition's focus "on the individual as the basic political subject."[50]

II. Liberal Legal Feminism in the Second Wave

The political roots of twentieth-century liberal feminism are often situated in the organized women's movement (the "second wave") that focused on "achieving equality through litigation and legislative reform."[51] In 1966, Betty Friedan (author of *The Feminine Mystique*) and civil rights activist and feminist lawyer Pauli Murray were instrumental in forming the National Organization for Women (NOW), born out of frustration over the Equal Employment Opportunity Commission's failure to enforce Title VII's prohibition against sex-based employment discrimination. NOW's purpose (famously scribbled by Friedan on a napkin) was "to take action to bring women into full participation in the mainstream of American society now, assuming all the privileges and responsibilities thereof in truly equal partnership with men."[52] That equal partnership reached beyond the "public world" to include the conventionally "private" realm of marriage, entailing "an equitable sharing of the responsibilities of the home and children and of the economic burdens of their support."[53] NOW's purposes were liberal feminist in arguing that because sexism and gender stereotypes harmed women *and* men, both had a stake in restructuring work, family, and other basic social institutions and in ratifying the Equal Rights Amendment.[54]

A. Ruth Bader Ginsburg Helms the Women's Rights Project

A similar premise about the harms of gender inequality and sexism informed Ruth Bader Ginsburg's constitutional litigation conducted with the ACLU's Women's Rights Project (WRP) while she was a professor at Rutgers.[55] Frequently described as a leading example of "early liberal feminist theorists in America,"[56] Ginsburg does not seem to have used the label "liberal feminist" to describe herself. However, she drew on the liberal philosophy discussed above to dismantle legally enforced sex inequality.

For example, in speaking of "the unfinished business of equality for women," Ginsburg quoted Mill's argument that "the legal subordination of one sex to the other" should be replaced by "a principle of perfect equality, admitting no power of privilege on the one side, nor disability on the other."[57]

Ginsburg's approach to equality is "liberal" because it insisted that people should not be disadvantaged based on membership in a group and instead should be evaluated based on their individual capacity. As Ginsburg explained the "fundamental premise" of the 1970s cases she litigated: "the law's differential treatment of men and women, typically rationalized as reflecting 'natural' differences between the sexes, historically had tended to contribute to women's subordination—their confined 'place' in man's world—even when conceived as protective of the fairer, but weaker and dependent-prone sex."[58] Ginsburg's strategy exemplified liberal feminism in identifying how sex role stereotypes and "fixed notions" about the sexes rationalized women's legal subordination. Ginsburg sought to help the Supreme Court perceive this inequity and move it toward a "constitutional principle that would provide for heightened, thoughtful review of gender classifications."[59] The challenge was formidable. To use Ginsburg's memorable image about constitutional interpretation at the time the WRP began: "Except for the vote [the Nineteenth Amendment], the Constitution remained an empty cupboard for people seeking to promote the equal stature of women and men as individuals under the law."[60]

The full story of Ginsburg's successful constitutional litigation challenging gender discrimination is amply told elsewhere.[61] This chapter briefly reviews a few cases in that campaign to highlight what they reveal about the contours of liberal feminism.[62] The tale usually begins with *Reed v. Reed*, in which Ginsburg coauthored the plaintiff's brief, and, for the first time, the U.S. Supreme Court held that a law using a gender-based classification violated the Equal Protection Clause.[63] An important prequel that shaped the winning argument in *Reed*, however, was *Moritz v. Commissioner of Internal Revenue*, which Ginsburg successfully argued with her husband, tax lawyer Marty Ginsburg, before the Court of Appeals for the Tenth Circuit.[64] *Moritz* illustrates a striking feature of Ginsburg's litigation strategy: bringing claims by male plaintiffs to show how a sex-based classification violated the Equal Protection Clause. The plaintiff in that case, Charles E. Moritz, lived with his eighty-nine-year old mother and paid someone to care for her when he could not. The Internal Revenue Service (IRS) denied him a dependent care deduction because he was a never married man; he would have received the deduction had he been a daughter, widower, or a husband to a woman in need of care. This strange scheme suggested that "the idea that a man on his own might be responsible somehow for caregiving apparently never crossed the government's mind."[65] The Tenth Circuit unanimously held that the IRS rule violated principles of equal protection because the classification, "premised primarily on sex," lacked any justification: Congress could have achieved its evident purpose of giving relief to persons "in low income brackets and bearing special burdens of dependents" without resorting to "invidious discrimination based solely on sex."[66]

Fortunately, when Solicitor General Erwin Griswold urged the U.S. Supreme Court to overrule the Tenth Circuit, he unwittingly provided Ginsburg a roadmap for attacking discriminatory laws. Included in his filing was a computer-generated list of hundreds of federal "laws and regulations that treated men and women differently, and, thus, were at risk of being found unconstitutional if the Court did not reverse.[67]

In *Reed v. Reed*, the first of Ginsburg and the WRP's cases brought before the U.S. Supreme Court, the gender-based law at issue was an Idaho statute giving preference to men as administrators of estates when more than one qualified person was available. Sally Reed sought to administer her deceased son's estate, but, under that statutory preference, the child's father (an abusive husband from whom she was separated) received the appointment.[68] Ginsburg's brief argued that "the sex line drawn by [Idaho's law], mandating subordination of women to men without regard to individual capacity, created a 'suspect classification' requiring close judicial scrutiny."[69] The brief drew analogies to race, already a suspect classification, arguing that, in both instances, an "unalterable trait of birth" should not be the basis for legislative discrimination.[70]

Liberal feminist emphases on the individual, on biology not determining a woman or man's societal roles, and on removing gender-based obstacles to full participation in society were evident in Ginsburg's brief:

> Laws which disable women from full participation in the political, business and economic arenas are often characterized as "protective" and beneficial. Those same laws applied to racial or ethnic minorities would readily be recognized as invidious and impermissible. The pedestal upon which women have been placed has all too often, upon close inspection, been revealed as a cage.[71]

In comparing race and gender discrimination, Ginsburg drew on the insights of Pauli Murray, who, as a Black woman, experienced both race and sex discrimination and theorized their connection.[72] In *Jane Crow and the Law*, Murray had argued: "That manifestations of racial prejudice have been more brutal than the more subtle manifestations of prejudice by reason of sex in no way diminishes the force of the equally obvious fact that the rights of women and the rights of Negroes are only different phases of the fundamental and indivisible issues of human rights."[73] To acknowledge that Ginsburg stood "on [the] shoulders" of Murray and Dorothy Kenyon (with whom Murray had successfully litigated civil rights cases that "put their theories of the parallels and intersections of race and gender into practice"), Ginsburg listed their names on the *Reed* brief.[74]

The Burger Court unanimously held the Idaho statute was unconstitutional under the Equal Protection Clause of the Fourteenth Amendment because it treated similarly situated applicants differently. The Court, however, did not embrace the heightened standard of review that Ginsburg sought; instead, it claimed merely to be applying a rational basis standard.[75]

Two years later, in *Frontiero v. Richardson*, argued by Ginsburg for *amicus* ACLU, the Court came within one vote of adopting strict scrutiny for classifications based on sex when it struck down a federal statute that automatically gave men in the military an allowance for healthcare and housing for their wives but allowed women that allowance only if they proved their spouse was financially dependent on them.[76] Justice Brennan's plurality opinion recognized the close relationship between sex-role stereotypes and discrimination diagnosed by liberal feminism. He also invoked the pedestal/cage imagery first used in Ginsburg's *Reed* brief to declare that, "traditionally," sex discrimination "was rationalized by an attitude of 'romantic paternalism,' which, in practical effect, put women, not on a pedestal, but in a cage."[77] Referring to "our Nation['s]... long and unfortunate history of sex discrimination," Justice Brennan observed how notions about women's proper place led to "our statute books gradually [becoming] laden with gross, stereotyped distinctions between the sexes," drawing parallels between such laws and "pre-Civil War slave codes."[78] Applying suspect classification criteria, his opinion characterized sex, like race, as immutable and determined by an "accident of birth." Declaring that "the sex characteristic frequently bears no relation to ability to perform or contribute to society," Brennan concluded that individuals must be judged on their capacity, not group membership.[79] While powerful, Brennan's race/sex comparisons came to illustrate the problem of treating "woman" and "black" as mutually exclusive categories, thus omitting Black women.[80]

In 1976, the Court finally settled on a new test for sex-based classifications: "intermediate scrutiny." Ginsburg briefed and argued *Craig v. Boren*, in which Justice Brennan— this time writing for a majority—interpreted *Reed* and other cases to establish that "classifications by gender must serve important governmental objections and must be substantially related to achievement of those objectives."[81] Under that test, as the Court subsequently elaborated, government must offer an "exceedingly persuasive justification" for such classifications.[82]

Ginsburg would bring and win more equal protection cases challenging gender-based classifications, often featuring male plaintiffs.[83] As Irin Carmon and Shana Knizhnik summed it up: Ginsburg "firmly believed that for women to be equal, men had to be free."[84] On this liberal, egalitarian view, equal treatment of men and women in law was the best path to freedom *and* equality.

B. Justice Ginsburg on the Supreme Court

After she was elevated to the U.S. Supreme Court in 1993, Justice Ginsburg had the extraordinary opportunity to explain the gender revolution in the Court's equal protection jurisprudence that she helped to launch. In 1996, in *United States v. Virginia*, Ginsburg declared that "[s]ince *Reed*, the Court has repeatedly recognized that neither federal nor state government acts compatibly with the equal protection principle when a law or official policy denies to women, simply because they are women, full citizenship stature— equal opportunity to aspire, achieve, participate in and contribute to society based on their individual talents and capacities."[85] Her majority opinion's emphasis on individual capacity, equal opportunity, and antistereotyping marked her approach as liberal feminist. Ginsburg explained that sex-based classifications "may not be used, as they once were, to create or perpetuate the legal, social, and economic inferiority of women," but may be used "to compensate women 'for particular economic disabilities [they have] suffered, to 'promot[e] equal employment opportunity,' [and] to advance full development of the talent and capacities of our nation's people."[86]

The Court struck down the Virginia Military Institute's (VMI) male-only admissions policy and concluded that its proposed remedy of offering young women a chance to attend the newly created Virginia Women's Institute of Leadership (VWIL) did not cure the constitutional violation. Ginsburg concluded that Virginia offered no "exceedingly persuasive justification for excluding all women" from VMI's "citizen-soldier training,"[87] insisting that "generalizations about 'the way women are,' [and] estimates of what is appropriate for most women, no longer justify denying opportunity to women whose talent and capacity place them outside the average description."[88]

Noting the long history of excluding women from central societal institutions based on assumptions about their capacities, Ginsburg wrote: "State actors controlling gates to opportunity, we have instructed, may not exclude qualified individuals based on 'fixed notions concerning the roles and abilities of males and females.'"[89] Accordingly, for those women who "want a VMI education and can make the grade," VWIL was not a sufficient constitutional remedy.[90]

Two decades later, in *Sessions v. Morales-Santana*, Justice Ginsburg drew on *VMI*'s antistereotyping premises to hold unconstitutional a gender-based difference in a 1940 citizenship law that favored "unwed U.S.-citizen mothers" over "unwed U.S.-citizen fathers," based on "stunningly anachronistic" gender role assumptions that only unwed mothers will care for their children.[91] Ginsburg's opinion stressed the dynamic nature of constitutional interpretation: "'new insights and societal understandings can reveal unjustified inequality . . . that once passed unnoticed and unchallenged.'"[92] This case illustrates Ginsburg's liberal feminist conviction that women *and men* benefited from freedom from "fixed notions" about gender roles continued throughout her judicial career.

Bostock v. Clayton County (2020) also suggests the capacity of liberal feminism's commitment to antistereotyping to extend to newer understandings of gender. At issue in *Bostock* was whether an adverse employment action based on an employee's gender identity or sexual orientation was discrimination on the basis of "sex" under Title VII.[93] The employer who fired Aimee Stevens, a transgender woman, stated, in misgendering language, that he did so because "he" wanted to "represent himself" and "dress like a woman."[94] In finding for Stevens, the Sixth Circuit reasoned: "a person is defined as transgender precisely because of the perception that his or her behavior transgresses gender stereotypes."[95] At oral argument before the Supreme Court, Justice Ginsburg observed that "the [precedential] cases have said that the object of Title VII was to get at *the entire spectrum of sex stereotypes.*"[96] While conservative Justice Gorsuch, writing for the majority, did not elaborate a robust gender stereotyping theory, he readily perceived the problem as sex discrimination: "it is impossible to discriminate against a person for being [gay] or transgender without discriminating against that individual based on sex."[97] The Court's ready perception that gender identity and sexual orientation discrimination are sex discrimination testifies to the success of the liberal feminist project of shaking loose fixed notions about "the sexes."

C. The Limits of Formal Equality Through Courts

Even as Ginsburg's constitutional litigation campaign enjoyed success in the courts, liberal legal feminists debated the limits of formal equality and the respective capacities of courts versus legislatures to further substantive equality. One prominent example was the sameness/difference—or equal treatment/special treatment—debate over how to accommodate pregnancy in the workplace.[98] Accounts of this debate use the term "liberal" or "liberal feminist" to characterize the equal treatment or formal equality position taken by such scholars as Wendy Webster Williams or Nadine Taub who, similar to Ginsburg, warned of the risks of judicial protectionism and of reinforcing, rather than challenging, gender stereotypes.[99] Williams related this formal equality approach and its skepticism about "gender-based" or "formally asymmetrical laws"—even if designed to benefit women—to her generation coming of age when gender-based laws "sort[ed] the world by gender in ways that defined us into the single role of wife/mother/dependent and which overtly and explicitly privileged men in the public and private spheres."[100]

In the face of critiques by "special treatment" and other feminists that formal equality required women to assimilate into a "pre-existing, predominantly male world" and left untouched a legal status quo that expressed "white male middle-class interests and values," liberal feminists made an institutional argument.[101] Formal equality as a constitutional principle, Williams argued, was what courts were best equipped to deliver; it was "a necessary, although not sufficient, condition for substantive equality of the sexes."[102] As did Ginsburg, Williams believed that legislatures were the best place for feminists to pursue substantive equality in pregnancy, work/family issues, and a wide range of areas.[103]

III. Defending and Reconstructing Liberalism

Justice Ginsburg and "symmetrists" like Williams did not explicitly describe themselves as liberal feminists. Other feminist legal theorists expressly have done so, locating their theories and law reform proposals as growing out of critical conversation with, and feminist reconstruction of, liberal commitments and principles. Although liberalism "became a suspect doctrine" for many feminist theorists "in the second half of the twentieth century," liberal feminist political theorists continued to engage in constructive critique of liberal political theory.[104] Rather than discard liberalism, they argued that the problem was the failure to extend and realize key liberal principles in the context of modern gender equality.

A. Reconstructing the Value of Autonomy and Privacy

Contemporary liberal legal feminists have developed robust conceptions of autonomy, liberty, and privacy and theorized foundations for reproductive rights. They have emphasized governmental obligations to promote gender equality and to address inequality in the family. For example, one of the authors (McClain) has drawn on Rawls and Okin to argue that gender equality, including within and among families, is a public value that government should promote. She has argued that a feminist reading of Rawls supports recognizing care as a public value that is part of a formative project of fostering capacity for democratic and personal self-government.[105] On the other hand, some liberal feminist legal scholars, such as Maxine Eichner, find Rawlsian liberalism inadequate to ground a robust argument for government's responsibility to support families.[106] Notably, both McClain and Eichner enlist liberal principles, but they also argue for an expanded list of liberal goods to "facilitate caretaking and human development."[107] Such liberal feminists disagree with perfectionist feminist theorists who argue that liberalism's commitment to "neutrality," toleration, and a conception of negative rights prevents government from taking measures necessary to further women's meaningful liberty and substantive equality.[108]

In the face of feminist skepticism about privacy, liberal legal feminists have also articulated how privacy, rightly understood, is necessary to protect women's autonomy, self-determination, and individual personhood.[109] In her pioneering book, *Uneasy Access*, philosopher and legal scholar Anita Allen acknowledged that privacy, in many instances, historically isolated and oppressed women, but she made a normative argument that women need forms of privacy that foster women's capacities and ability to "participate as equals."[110] While privacy once meant "confinement of women in the private household as subservient caretakers," Allen and other liberal feminists deployed the value of privacy to empower women's "decisional privacy," and in turn enable "legal autonomy concerning sexuality, marriage, and the family."[111] Thus, Allen argued, "privacy and private choice have survived appropriately strenuous feminist critique, re-emerging in beneficially reconstructed forms."[112] Through bodily and decisional privacy, privacy becomes a means for gender equality.[113]

Liberal feminists have articulated the importance of sexual privacy in the wake of new forms of technology, such as the Internet and social media. Danielle Citron builds on Allen and McClain's work to advance a conception of sexual privacy as "egalitarian, liberal feminist."[114] Citron defines sexual privacy as the ability to "manage the boundaries around our bodies and intimate activities" and control information about the human body, sex, sexuality, gender, and intimate activities.[115] The values of sexual privacy include securing autonomy, enabling intimacy, and protecting equality.[116] Citron explains that, on the one hand, the Internet can foster these values, including for women, LGBTQ persons, and people of color; on the other, because these groups disproportionately experience privacy violations on the Internet, the Internet can hinder their agency and autonomy.[117] Citron proposes remedies for the gendered and intersectional harms caused by "revenge porn," "deep fakes," and other online abuses.[118]

Liberal feminists have also theorized how decisional privacy in the sense of autonomy is critical to reproductive choice and reproductive justice. The pivotal case of *Planned Parenthood v. Casey* stated that "the ability of women to participate equally in the economic and social life of the Nation has been facilitated by their ability to control their reproductive lives."[119] Liberal feminists have related reproductive autonomy to an individual's personhood, liberty of conscience, self-determination, and individual identity.[120] They have elaborated a conception of privacy that is liberal in its aspiration for informed, morally autonomous choice, and egalitarian and feminist in its insistence that educational, economic, and sexual equality are a requirement for meaningful choice.[121]

B. Responses to Dominance and Relational Feminism

These liberal feminist theorists have sought to address two distinct critiques from other legal feminists. Through reconstructing conceptions of privacy, they respond to dominance feminists arguments that "the private" is a site of inequality for women, such that, in the words of Catharine MacKinnon, "the right of privacy is a right for men 'to be let alone' to oppress women one at a time."[122] They also counter dominance feminists' contention that autonomy is an illusion for women under conditions of subordination. Similar to MacKinnon, liberal feminists recognize how private power distorts the development of autonomy, but they argue that government has a responsibility to secure the preconditions for developing human capacity or human capabilities.[123] For liberal feminists, government must play an affirmative role in addressing forms of private power that hinder this development of autonomy.

Liberal feminists also engage relational, or difference, feminists' arguments that construe autonomy as atomistic and contend that liberal models of the self and of self-government fail to recognize care, interdependency, and connection.[124] Liberal feminists respond that when they emphasize *liberty*, the value of individual autonomy, or self-government and self-determination, they do not mean atomism or an unrealistic self-sufficiency. They offer notions of autonomy that mirror feminist models of "relational autonomy" in recognizing that "it is by virtue of a person's participation in relationships of nurture and care, initially within families and eventually in other forms of association, that he or she is able to develop the capacity for autonomy."[125] Thus, relationships in families and other parts of civil society—as well as the broader social structure—play a formative role in shaping a person's identity and cultivating and enabling the self.

C. Responses to Antiessentialist and Intersectional Critiques

By the late 1980s, feminist legal theory, including liberal feminism, faced internal criticism for a lack of inclusivity. The "essentialism" critique, prominently associated with Angela Harris, centered on feminism's assumed claim "that a unitary, 'essential' women's experience can be isolated and described independently of race, class, sexual orientation and other realities of experience." She contended that such accounts of women's experiences ignored the experiences of Black women and many others, silencing the voices of minority women in an effort to craft a unified message of what "feminism" is.[126]

Similarly, Kimberlé Crenshaw's intersectionality critique faulted feminist discourse for leaving out the experiences of Black women, emphasizing that individuals may face discrimination or disempowerment on multiple fronts, such as race, age, class, sexual orientation, or gender identity. She argued that the intersection of various harms based on these identities can create unique and serious disadvantages. Like Harris, Crenshaw critiqued feminism that "purports to speak for women of color through its invocation of the term 'woman,'" while excluding "women of color because it is based on the experiences and interests of a certain subset of women."[127]

Liberal feminism is compatible with, and strengthened by, these critiques, given its attentiveness to individual capacity and the rejection of stereotypes. Notably, such critiques have largely targeted dominance and relational feminism rather than liberal feminist theory.[128] Liberal feminism is flexible enough to admit and accept the essentialism critique and to develop intersectionally to support an inclusive and antiracist conception of gender equality. Decades ago, Anne Dailey predicted that, informed by such critiques, a "renewed feminist liberalism" could utilize the power of narratives to destabilize "prevailing legal discourse" and develop a richer understanding of diversity based on empathetic listening.[129] This prediction remains apt: liberal feminism embraces the individuality of each person and their choices and stands stronger as it evolves to include people of all races, ethnicities, and gender identities in their full diversity.

IV. Conclusion

Liberal feminism's project aims at "disrupting—or bursting asunder—the historical linkage between sex and gender, or between biological sex and particular roles or ways of thinking associated with particular genders."[130] This theme of disruption offers a point of continuity with newer forms of feminism, even as those newer forms address a "much broader range of linkages and identity categories."[131] Further, evolving understandings of gender can extend that promise beyond the gender binary itself, deepening the capacity of liberal feminism to adapt to new demands for liberty, inclusion, and equality.

Notes

1. Amy R. Baehr, *Introduction*, in Varieties of Feminist Liberalism 1 (Amy R. Baehr ed., 2004) (arguing that the incompatibility of liberalism and feminism has been "arguably the *dominant* view among feminist scholars over the past thirty years"); Ruth Abbey, The Return of Feminist Liberalism 2, 4 (2011) ("reconfigure").We generally use the term "liberal feminist political philosophy" to distinguish it from liberal feminist *legal* thought, but at times simply the term "liberal feminism" or "feminism liberalism" when the context makes our meaning clear.
2. *See* Allison M. Jaggar, Feminist Politics and Human Nature 47–48, 173–84 (1988 ed.).
3. Ruth Bader Ginsburg & Barbara Flagg, *Some Reflections on the Feminist Legal Thought of the 1970's*, 1989 U. Chi. Legal F. 9, 11 (1989).
4. Mississippi Univ. for Women v. Hogan, 458 U.S. 718, 724–25 (1982).
5. 78 Stat. 255, 42 U.S.C. § 2000e-2(a)(1).
6. Wendy W. Williams, *Notes from a First Generation*, 1989 U. Chi. L. F. 99 (1989).
7. *See, e.g.*, Linda C. McClain, The Place of Families: Fostering Capacity, Equality, and Responsibility (2006).
8. *See, e.g.*, Anita L. Allen, *Coercing Privacy*, 40 Wm. & Mary L. Rev. 723 (1999); Danielle Keats Citron, *Sexual Privacy*, 128 Yale L.J. 1870 (2019).
9. Rosalind Dixon, *Feminist Disagreement Comparatively Recast*, 31 Harv. J. L. & Gender 277, 315 (2008).
10. Martha C. Nussbaum, Sex and Social Justice 57 (1999).
11. Linda C. McClain, *"Atomistic Man" Revisited: Liberalism, Connection, and Feminist Jurisprudence*, 65 S. Calif. L. Rev. 1171 (1992); Nussbaum, *supra* note 10, at 57.
12. Abbey, *supra* note 1, at 1.
13. *Id.*; *see also* Deborah Rhode, Gender and Justice 12 (1989) (liberalism was the "most dominant influence" on "American feminism").
14. Abbey, *supra* note 1, at 1.
15. *Abigail and John Adams Converse on Women's Rights, 1776*, Am. Yawp Reader, https://www.americanyawp.com/reader/the-american-revolution/abigail-and-john-adams-converse-on-womens-rights-1776/#:~:text=The%20American%20Revolution%20invited%20a,the%20limits%20of%20revolutionary%20liberty (last visited June 30, 2021).
16. *Id.*
17. *Id.*
18. Nancy Cott, Public Vows: A History of Marriage and the Nation 16 (1999).
19. *Id.* at 14.
20. Rhode, *supra* note 13, at 12.
21. *See* Sally G. McMillen, Seneca Falls and the Origins of the Women's Rights Movement 35–70 (2008); Rhode, *supra* note 13, at 12.
22. Cott, *supra* note 18, at 63.
23. *Id.* at 64.
24. *Id.* at 60–66; *see also* Lisa Pace Vetter, The Political Thought of America's Founding Feminists 128, 132, 139–41 (2017) (explicating Sarah Grimké's "Quaker liberalism").
25. Cott, *supra* note 18, at 63.

26. Mark E. Brandon, States of Union: Family and Change in the American Constitutional Order 83 (2013).
27. *See* Reva B. Siegel, *The Nineteenth Amendment and the Democratization of the Family*, Yale L.J. F. 450 (Jan. 21, 2020).
28. Declaration of Right and Sentiments, reproduced as Appendix A *in* McMillen, *supra* note 21, at 237–38; Rhode, *supra* note 13, at 12.
29. Declaration of Right and Sentiments, *supra* note 28, at 237–41.
30. McMillen, *supra* note 21, at 91 (quoting the Declaration's argument "that men withheld rights from women but gave the same rights 'to the most ignorant and degraded men—both natives and foreigners'"). Susan B. Anthony's angry, racist criticisms of the Fifteenth Amendment's extending the franchise only to African American men drew on "ethnic and racial stereotypes and negative views about immigrants [and women] that were common currency in late nineteenth-century America." Virginia Sapiro, *The Power and Fragility of Social Movement Coalitions: The Woman Suffrage Movement to 1870*, 100 B.U. L. Rev. 1557, 1604–06 (2020)(giving example of Frederick Douglass's criticism of opponents of Black male suffrage as "drunken Irishmen and ignorant Dutchmen").
31. Wendell Phillips, Speeches, Lectures, and Letters (1884) ("Woman's Rights," speech made at Convention held in Worcester, Massachusetts, on October 15 and 16, 1851).
32. *Id.* at 12 (praising John Stuart Mill).
33. John Stuart Mill, *The Subjection of Women* (1869), *in* John Stuart Mill & Harriet Taylor Mill, Essays on Sex Equality (Alice S. Rossi ed., 1970).
34. John Stuart Mill, On Liberty 97 (1859) (David Spitz ed., 1975).
35. Rhode, *supra* note 13, at 14.
36. *Id.* at 14. On Jane Addams's idea of civic, or municipal, housekeeping, *see* Jean Bethke Elshtain, Jane Addams and the Dream of American Democracy 161–68 (2002).
37. Rhode, *supra* note 13, at 34–50. *See* Julie C. Suk, "The Equal Rights Amendment, Then and Now," chapter 12, in this volume.
38. Rhode, *supra* note 13, at 36–37.
39. John Rawls, Political Liberalism xxv (1993). Rawls distinguished this "political liberalism" from a "comprehensive liberalism" that would rest on or seek agreement on such doctrines.
40. *Id.* at 19; McClain, *supra* note 7, at 17 (citing James E. Fleming, Securing Constitutional Democracy 1 (2006)).
41. *See generally* Baehr, *supra* note 1; Abbey, supra note 1; Amy Baehr, *Liberal Feminism*, *in* Stanford Encyclopedia of Philosophy (Sept. 30, 2013), https://plato.stanford.edu/entries/feminism-liberal.
42. Susan Moller Okin, Justice, Gender, and the Family (1989).
43. *Id.* at 93–97.
44. *Id.* at 101.
45. *Id.* at 168–86.
46. John Rawls, *The Idea of Public Reason Revisited*, 64 U. Chi. L. Rev. 765, 791 (1997).
47. Martha C. Nussbaum, Women and Human Development: The Capabilities Approach 4–8 (2000).
48. *Id.* at 242–43.
49. *Id.* at 245.
50. *Id.* at 245–46.

51. RHODE, *supra* note 13, at 59; *see also* Patricia A. Cain, *Feminism and the Limits of Equality*, 24 GA. L. REV. 803, 829 (1990); JAGGAR, *supra* note 2, at 188–89 (describing NOW's liberal feminist focus on "equality of opportunity" and rational capacity).
52. Founding: Setting the Stage, NOW, https://now.org/about/history/founding-2/ (last visited July 4, 2020); PAULI MURRAY, SONG IN A WEARY THROAT: MEMOIR OF AN AMERICAN PILGRIMAGE 468–80 (2018 ed.).
53. JANE MANSBRIDGE, WHY WE LOST THE ERA 99 (1986)(quoting NOW's 1966 founding statement of purpose).
54. RHODE, *supra* note 13, at 59–60.
55. Ginsburg & Flagg, *supra* note 3, at 11. Ginsburg cofounded the WRP with attorney Brenda Feigen.
56. Dixon, *supra* note 9, at 298; Cain, *supra* note 51, at 829 (associating liberal feminism in legal academy with Ginsburg, Herma Hill Kay, Wendy Williams, and Nadine Taub).
57. *See* RUTH BADER GINSBURG (WITH MARY HARTNETT & WENDY W. WILLIAMS), MY OWN WORDS 119 (quoting Mill in an epigraph to Ruth Bader Ginsburg, *Women and the Law: A Symposium Introduction*, 25 RUTGERS L. REV. 1 (1971)).
58. Ginsburg & Flagg, *supra* note 3, at 11.
59. *Id.*
60. *Id.* at 13.
61. *See id.*; IRIN CARMON & SHANA KNIZHNIK, NOTORIOUS RBG 51 (2015); RBG (CNN Films 2018); ON THE BASIS OF SEX (Focus Features 2018); Linda Greenhouse, *Ruth Bader Ginsburg, Supreme Court's Feminist Icon, Is Dead at 87*, N.Y. TIMES (Sept. 18, 2020).
62. Ginsburg authored the briefs for Reed v. Reed, 404 U.S. 71 (1971); Struck v. Secretary of Defense, *cert. granted*, 409 U.S. 947, *judgment vacated*, 409 U.S 1071 (1972); Turner v. Dep't of Emp't Sec., 423 U.S. 44 (1975). She authored the brief and presented oral argument for Frontiero v. Richardson, 411 U.S. 677 (1973); Kahn v. Shevin, 416 U.S. 351 (1947); Weinberger v. Wiesenfeld, 420 U.S. 636 (1975); Edwards v. Healy, 421 U.S. 772 (1975); Califano v. Goldfarb, 430 U.S. 199 (1977); and Duren v. Missouri, 439 U.S. 357 (1979). She also wrote amicus briefs for numerous other cases in this time period. Ruth Bader Ginsburg, *The Progression of Women in the Law*, 28 VAL. U. L. REV. 1161 (1994).
63. *Reed*, 404 U.S. 71.
64. Moritz v. Comm'r of Internal Revenue, 469 F.2d 466 (10th Cir. 1972). In April 1971, Ginsburg sent the brief she and Martin Ginsburg wrote in *Moritz* to Mel Wulf, at the ACLU, who was then working on Sally Reed's appeal to the U.S. Supreme Court, commenting: "Some of this should be useful for *Reed v. Reed*." Wulf solicited her help on *Reed*. CARMON & KNIZHNIK, *supra* note 61, at 52.
65. CARMON & KNIZHNIK, *supra* note 61, at 1.
66. *Moritz*, 469 F.2d at 470. The Tenth Circuit relied on *Reed* for the need to subject sex-based classifications to "scrutiny under equal protection principles." *Id.* at 470.
67. CARMON & KNIZHNIK, *supra* note 61, at 58–59.
68. *Id.* at 52.
69. *Id.* at 56 (quoting the brief).
70. *Id.*
71. *Id.* at 57.
72. *See* Pauli Murray & Mary O. Eastwood, *Jane Crow and the Law: Sex Discrimination and Title VII*, 34 GEO. WASH. L. REV. 232 (1965–66). On Murray's contributions, see Serena

Mayeri, *Pauli Murray and the Twentieth-Century Quest for Legal and Social Equality*, 2 IND. J. L. & SOC. EQUALITY 85 (2014); MY NAME IS PAULI MURRAY (Participant 2021).
73. Murray & Eastwood, *supra* note 72, at 235.
74. CARMON & KNIZHNIK, *supra* note 61, at 54–55.
75. *Reed*, 404 U.S. at 76–77.
76. *Frontiero*, 411 U.S. at 678, 682.
77. *Id.* at 684.
78. *Id.* at 685.
79. *Id.* at 686.
80. For example, Justice Brennan stated: "although blacks were guaranteed the right to vote in 1870 [the Fifteenth Amendment], women were denied even that right . . . until the adoption of the Nineteenth Amendment half a century later." *Id.* at 686. For legal feminist critique of this problem with categories, *see* Kimberlé Crenshaw, *Mapping the Margins: Intersectionality, Identity Politics, and Violence Against Women of Color*, 43 STAN. L. REV. 1241, 1244 n.8 (1991).
81. Craig v. Boren, 429 U.S. 190, 197 (1976) (holding that Oklahoma could not justify higher age for males to drink 3.2 percent beer (21) than for females (18)).
82. *Mississippi University for Women*, 458 U.S. at 724.
83. *See, e.g., Weinberger*, 420 U.S. 636 (holding unconstitutional rule not giving widowers same Social Security benefits as widows); *Califano*, 430 U.S. 199 (holding unconstitutional Social Security provision giving survivor benefits under Social Security Act only to widows).
84. CARMON & KNIZHNIK, *supra* note 61, at 71–72.
85. United States v. Virginia, 518 U.S. 515, 532 (1996) [hereinafter *VMI*].
86. *Id.* at 533 (emphasis added).
87. *Id.* at 534.
88. *Id.* at 572 n. 2.
89. *Id.* at 541.
90. *Id.* at 555.
91. 137 S. Ct. 1678, 1693 (2017).
92. *Id.* at 1690 (quoting Obergefell v. Hodges, 576 U.S. 644, 673 (2015)).
93. Bostock v. Clayton Cty., 140 S. Ct. 1731 (2020).
94. EEOC v. R.G. & G.R. Harris Funeral Homes, Inc., 884 F.3d 560, 569 (6th Cir. 2018) (drawing on Price Waterhouse v. Hopkins, 490 U.S. 228 (1989)).
95. *Id.* at 577.
96. Transcript of Oral Argument at 50–51, R.G. & G.R. Harris Funeral Homes, Inc., v. EEOC, (No. 18-107) (argued Oct. 8, 2019) (emphasis added).
97. *Bostock*, 140 S. Ct. at 1741.
98. For example, they debated the best interpretation of the Pregnancy Discrimination Act, Congress's 1978 amendment to Title VII. *See* Deborah A. Widiss, "Pregnancy and Work—50 Years of Legal Theory, Litigation and Legislation," chapter 24, in this volume.
99. Anne Dailey, *Feminism's Return to Liberalism*, 102 YALE L.J. 1265, 1267–68 (1993); *see, e.g.,* Williams, *supra* note 6, at 99–100 (for "symmetrist/asymmetrist" terms to describe equal treatment/special treatment positions, crediting Christine Littleton, *Reconstructing Sexual Equality*, 75 CALIF. L. REV. 1279 (1987)).
100. Williams, *supra* note 6, at 110–11.

101. Wendy W. Williams, *The Equality Crisis: Some Reflections on Culture, Courts, and Feminism*, 7 WOMEN'S RTS. L. REP. 175 (1982).
102. Williams, *supra* note 6, at 110.
103. *Id.* at 99–100; *see also* Ginsburg & Flagg, *supra* note 3, at 18.
104. ABBEY, *supra* note 1, at 1–2.
105. MCCLAIN, *supra* note 7.
106. MAXINE EICHNER, THE SUPPORTIVE STATE: FAMILIES, GOVERNMENT, AND AMERICA'S POLITICAL IDEALS (2010).
107. *Id.* at 70.
108. *See, e.g.*, Kimberly Yuracko, *Toward Feminist Perfectionism: A Radical Critique of Rawlsian Liberalism*, 6 UCLA WOMEN'S L.J. 1, 47–48 (1995); Robin West, *Foreword: Taking Freedom Seriously*, 104 HARV. L. REV. 43 (1990); CATHARINE A. MACKINNON, FEMINISM UNMODIFIED 93–102 (1987). For a liberal feminist response, *see* Linda C. McClain, *Toleration, Autonomy, and Governmental Promotion of Good Lives: Beyond "Empty" Toleration to Toleration as Respect*, 59 OHIO ST. L.J. 19 (1998).
109. Linda C. McClain, *The Poverty of Privacy*, 3 COLUM. J. GENDER & L. 119, 124 (1992); Allen, *supra* note 8, at 754.
110. ANITA L. ALLEN, UNEASY ACCESS: PRIVACY FOR WOMEN IN A FREE SOCIETY 180–81 (1988).
111. Anita L. Allen & Erin Mack, *How Privacy Got Its Gender*, 10 N. ILL. U. L. REV. 441, 446 (1990).
112. Allen, *supra* note 8, at 728.
113. *See* ALLEN, *supra* note 110, at 180–81.
114. Citron, *supra* note 8, at 1876 n. 17 (2019) (referring to work of Allen and McClain). *See* Anita L. Allen, *Gender and Privacy in Cyberspace*, 52 STAN. L. REV.1175 (2000); Linda C. McClain, *Reconstructive Tasks for a Liberal Feminist Conception of Privacy*, 40 WM. & MARY L. REV. 759, 790 (1999).
115. Citron, *supra* note 8, at 1870.
116. *Id.* at 1874, 1878.
117. *Id.* at 1874–75.
118. *Id.* at 1908–28, 1944–54. *See also* DANIELLE KEATS CITRON, HATE CRIMES IN CYBERSPACE (2014); Danielle Keats Citron & Mary Anne Franks, *Criminalizing Revenge Porn*, 49 WAKE FOREST L. REV. 345, 346 (2014).
119. Planned Parenthood v. Casey, 505 U.S. 833, 856 (1992). The language from *Casey* quoted in text, as well as the argument that reproductive autonomy is crucial to the goals of reproductive justice, featured prominently in amicus briefs submitted by reproductive justice scholars and organizations in *Dobbs v. Jackson Women's Health Organization*, in which Mississippi—in defending its ban on abortion after the fifteenth week of pregnancy—has argued that the Supreme Court should overrule both Roe v. Wade, 410 U.S. 113 (1973), and *Casey*. Amici argued that the impact of overruling such cases and denying women's right to "bodily autonomy and reproductive agency" would fall disproportionately on Black women. Brief of *Amici Curiae* Reproductive Justice Scholars Supporting Respondents at 6, Dobbs v. Jackson Women's Health Organization, No. 19-1392; *see id.* at 28–30 (explaining how *Casey* recognized two key prongs of reproductive justice: the right not to have a child and the right to have a child).
120. McClain, *supra* note 109; MCCLAIN, *supra* note 7, at 223–55; Allen, *supra* note 8.
121. Allen, *supra* note 8, at 754.

122. MACKINNON, *supra* note 108, at 102.
123. NUSSBAUM, *supra* note 47; MCCLAIN, *supra* note 7.
124. An important influence on relational, or cultural, feminism was CAROL GILLIGAN, IN A DIFFERENT VOICE (1982). For an overview of relational feminist critiques of liberalism and a liberal feminist response, *see* McClain, *supra* note 11. For a feminist argument that "autonomy" obscures dependency, *see* Martha Albertson Fineman, THE AUTONOMY MYTH: A THEORY OF DEPENDENCY (2004).
125. MCCLAIN, *supra* note 7, at 18.
126. Angela P. Harris, *Race and Essentialism in Feminist Legal Theory*, 42 STAN. L. REV. 581, 585, 598 (1990) (calling MacKinnon's approach "essentialist" and "'color-blind'"). For MacKinnon's response, *see* Catharine A. MacKinnon, *Keeping It Real: On Anti-"Essentialism," in* WOMEN'S LIVES, MEN'S LAWS 84 (2005).
127. Crenshaw, *supra* note 80, at 1244 n.8 (1991). Notably, Crenshaw and MacKinnon have proposed an "Equality Amendment" embracing an intersectional and substantive approach to equality. *See* Catharine A. MacKinnon & Kimberlé W. Crenshaw, *Reconstituting the Future: An Equality Amendment*, YALE L. FORUM. 343, 363 (Dec. 26, 2019).
128. Harris, *supra* note 126, at 585 (critiquing construction of "women" in work by MacKinnon and Robin West).
129. Dailey, *supra* note 99, at 1284–85.
130. Dixon, *supra* note 9, 315.
131. *Id.*

CHAPTER 3

DOMINANCE FEMINISM
Placing Sexualized Power at the Center

KATHRYN ABRAMS

DOMINANCE feminism is a theory that describes sex and gender inequality as arising from the sexualized subordination of women by men. In legal scholarship, this theory is associated most strongly with the work of Catharine MacKinnon,[1] although MacKinnon's frequent collaborator, Andrea Dworkin, advanced similar ideas through her political organizing, essays, and fiction.[2] Dominance feminism has been influential, both for its theorization of the dynamics that produce gender inequality and for its legal efforts to address specific injuries, particularly sexual harassment and pornography. And MacKinnon, a forceful and vivid figure who lectures widely and campaigns actively for legislative change, has become prominent far beyond legal circles, a role different from that of many leading feminist legal theorists.

Dominance feminism has also been the target of powerful critiques. Feminists of color have argued that it fails to center or even describe the qualitative differences in their experiences of coercive sexuality, treating race primarily as an amplifier of severity or incidence. "Sex radical" feminists—and their more recent intellectual heirs—have argued that its vision of sexuality as an arena of systematic subordination obscures women's capacity for agency, sexual or otherwise, and neglects the role of erotic pleasure in animating women's creativity or political action. The power of these critiques and the limitations of MacKinnon's response blunted enthusiasm for the theory, although its central insight—which framed gender inequality as the product of power exercised through sexuality—continued to reverberate in feminist thought. The #MeToo movement—by exposing the pervasiveness of women's sexualized subordination in wide-ranging professional contexts—has brought renewed attention to the claims of dominance feminism. It has augmented that vision, however, by highlighting women's solidarity and their capacity to act collectively on their own behalf. It remains to be seen, though, whether this new beginning will pluralize and extend the reach of dominance feminist ideas or replicate its errors.

I. Dominance Feminism: Its Central Features

Dominance theory challenged a legal landscape in which both theoretical and practical debates about gender inequality hinged on women's similarity to, or difference from, men. This framework was shaped by the doctrinal framework of equal protection law, which required that those similarly situated should be treated the same,[3] yet occasionally acknowledged differences as the ground for compensatory, equalizing treatment.[4] MacKinnon argued that these ostensibly opposed approaches were, in fact, two sides of the same coin. Both viewed women—identifying their "sameness" or "differences"—according to an implicit but ubiquitous male referent.[5] And both assumed that the difference, where it emerged, was a biological or social fact: a reasonable basis or an unjust cause of women's inequality, depending on one's view, but not a product of that inequality.

A. Sexualized Domination

MacKinnon offered a contrasting claim: that questions of gender inequality were, at root, "questions of the distribution of power . . . of male supremacy and female subordination."[6] This unequal distribution of power was achieved and perpetuated through the sexualized domination of women by men. "Sexuality," in MacKinnon's view, was "a social construct of male power, defined by men, forced on women, and constitutive of the meaning of gender."[7] The hierarchy or inequality that this imposition of sexual power produced is the cause of what appear, socially, as gender-based differences.[8] "As power succeeds in constructing social perception and social reality, [hierarchy] derivatively becomes a categorical distinction, a difference," MacKinnon explained, "can you imagine elevating one half of a population and denigrating the other half and producing a population in which everyone is the same?"[9] If dominance theory offers a different interpretation of gender-based differences, it also offers a new view of the deepest harms of gender inequality.

Whereas cases under the equality/difference framework focused on differential opportunity in the workplace, or differential government benefits, MacKinnon sought to shift the focus to "the extent and intractability of sex segregation into poverty, which has been known before, [and] the range of issues termed violence against women, which has not been." These harms

> combine[] women's material desperation, through being relegated to categories of jobs that pay nil, with the massive amount of rape and attempted rape—44% of all women—about which virtually nothing is done, the sexual assault of children—38% of girls and 10% of boys—which is apparently endemic to the patriarchal family, the battery of women that is systematic in 1/4 to 1/3 of our homes, prostitution, women's fundamental economic condition, what we do when all else fails, and for many in this

country, all else fails often, and pornography, an industry that traffics in female flesh, making sex inequality into sex to the tune of eight billion dollars a year in profits.[10]

These injuries, rarely reachable through the "differences" framework because there is no male comparator, describe the "social reality" to which feminists are called to respond.

Two additional elements define MacKinnon's approach to gender-based injury. First, unlike many forms of "outsider jurisprudence," dominance theory does not ground its account of women's injuries in experiential narratives. The absence of first-person accounts of sexualized, or gendered, injury—particularly their subjective manifestations—distinguishes her work from many examples of feminist legal theory that aim to characterize gendered oppression. Although MacKinnon's earliest work[11] draws in part on interviews with women in pink-collar and other employment settings, her documentation of women's unequal position tends to be more sociological than experiential. She relies, as she puts it, on "aggregate indices"[12]: statistics about the society-wide incidence of particular harms. Second, the injuries MacKinnon describes are not simply material, they are also ideational: this is the "social perception" she references. The sex segregation of women into poverty and their violent sexualization through child and domestic abuse, rape, pornography, and prostitution elaborately depict who women are: not only men (including those not actively involved in the sexualized subordination of women) but women themselves internalize these images. They come to view the male gaze as what defines them, and sex as what they are good for. As MacKinnon notes, "[a]ll women live in sexual objectification the way fish live in water. Given the statistical realities ... what can life as a woman mean, what can sex mean, to targeted survivors in a rape culture?"[13] Women's self-perceptions are shaped not only in the domain of sexuality but in public-facing contexts such as market employment. "Women cope with objectification through trying to meet the male standard," MacKinnon observes, and they "measure their self-worth by the degree to which they succeed."[14]

B. Law as the Remedy of Choice

Having exposed this pervasive pattern of inequality, MacKinnon finds a remedy in law. Her recourse to law is paradoxical, because she also contends that law—in the forms in which we most regularly encounter it—"sees and treats women as men see and treat women."[15] The "differences" approach illustrates this perspective: its use of an often-implicit male referent "adopts the point of view of male supremacy on the status of the sexes."[16] So does a doctrinal approach to rape law that presumes consent and requires the prosecution to demonstrate such additional elements as "utmost resistance" on the part of the victim.[17] But, for MacKinnon, the implicit masculinist frame of law does not disqualify it as a central remedial tool. The question, she explains,

> [is] not whether one trusts the law to behave in a feminist way. We do not trust medicine yet we insist that it respond to women's needs.... We do not abdicate the control of technology

because it was not invented by women.... If women are to restrict our demands for change to spheres we can trust, spheres we already control, there will not be any.[18]

C. Legal Claims for Sexual Harassment and Pornography

Because law is one of the few social forces potent enough to reshape institutions and realign expectations, the goal is to create legal claims that address the most problematic instances of women's inequality. These claims—undertaken at the instigation of individual women—are structured by a feminist perspective on the interactions in question. For example, MacKinnon's most influential legal intervention has been the claim for sexual harassment. This claim frames harassment not in the ways in which it has traditionally been perceived, as workplace jocularity or a natural expression of masculine appreciation or desire, but as an oppressive practice that violates equal employment opportunity under Title VII. As MacKinnon proposed,[19] and the Court affirmed in *Meritor Savings Bank v. Vinson*,[20] either demands for sexual performance as a condition of employment (quid pro quo harassment) or pervasive, unwelcome treatment of a sex-based character (hostile environment sexual harassment) can form the basis for a claim.

A more controversial intervention was a local ordinance, providing civil damages for injury arising from the making or use of, or trafficking in, pornography.[21] This claim frames pornography not as harmless entertainment or the fuel for benign sexual fantasies but as an activity that socializes men to sexualized domination and injures both the women involved in making it and those whose lives, sexual and otherwise, are shaped by the often-violent objectification of women it projects and normalizes.[22] Here too, the claim is the basis for a civil action, by a woman victimized either as a participant in the production of pornography or as a participant in sexual or other encounters shaped by its circulation.

The antipornography ordinance met with fierce opposition on two grounds. First, "feminist sex radicals" or "pro-sex feminists"—a group of lesbians and other sexual dissidents who worked as scholars and activists—opposed the ordinance on the ground that it presented sexuality as pervasively problematic: an ostensibly progressive parallel to a repressive, judgmental imperative that had stigmatized sexuality, particularly nonconforming forms such as LGBTQ sexuality.[23] The sex radicals also argued that dominance feminists, and the antipornography ordinance in particular, portrayed women as sexually passive or sexually injured, denying the sexual agency that women possessed—notwithstanding gender inequality—and that could be a generative force in feminist politics. A second group of opponents argued that the antipornography ordinance, by imposing a content-based restriction on speech related to the vital, political topic of women's sexuality and equality, violated the First Amendment. This position, espoused by First Amendment advocates both inside and outside legal feminism, was sometimes accompanied by the feminist gloss that feminists and sexual dissidents could best counter pornographic speech with "more speech," specifically embodying pro-sex, feminist perspectives.[24] The Anti-Pornography Civil Rights Ordinance, which was enacted by the city of Indianapolis, Indiana—proceeding farther than any other iteration of the MacKinnon–Dworkin antipornography ordinance—was ultimately struck down on First Amendment grounds in *American Booksellers Association, Inc. v. Hudnut*.[25]

Dominance feminism has largely succeeded in breaking the exclusive hold of the "differences" framework on the legal conceptualization of gender inequality. Its focus on sexual coercion as a primary driver of women's inequality has become an influential frame for both feminist legal scholars[26] and members of a broader public.[27] The sexual harassment claim, endorsed by the Supreme Court in an ongoing line of cases,[28] has transformed the understanding of sexualized treatment in the workplace.[29] The claim has been unevenly enforced in practice. Perhaps because it has been appended to a statute grounded in "equality" theory, courts have not always seen it as structured by a view that makes sexualized subordination the linchpin of sex-based inequality.[30] It has also been implemented within workplaces, through forms of managerial control that have rendered its effects largely symbolic,[31] a pattern that has been reinforced through recent Supreme Court opinions on employer liability.[32] Yet sexual harassment has become a cultural mainstay, naming a phenomenon that was not previously viewed as an injury, and achieving wide visibility through Anita Hill's allegations against then Supreme Court nominee Clarence Thomas.[33] As a legal claim, it has offered at least the possibility of recourse for a generation of American women who have been impeded in their professional progress by sexualized treatment.[34]

II. Critiques of Dominance Feminism

Despite this influence, dominance feminism has been the focus of vigorous critique within legal feminism itself. The totalizing character of its indictment has sometimes spurred skepticism among those seeking more carefully differentiated feminist accounts; this concern has been complicated by MacKinnon's predilection for "aggregate indices," which can make it difficult to know precisely whose lives are being described.[35] These features have sparked two, interrelated lines of objection: in the first, critics claim that dominance feminism fails to depict crucial variation in women's experiences of sexualized violation, implicitly assimilating all women to a frame that reflects white women's experience; in the second, critics argue that its portrait of complete subjection fails accurately to describe the agency in their lives, sexual and otherwise.

Critical race feminists, such as Angela Harris,[36] argued that MacKinnon implicitly placed white women at the core of her analysis, neglecting qualitative differences in the sexualized injury of Black women and other women of color. MacKinnon's effort to describe a dynamic that affects all women, Harris contends, leads her to bracket differences and describe them as matters of context or degree.[37] In a hierarchical society structured by racism, such generalizations are likely to reflect the experience of the most powerful women: those who are white.[38] This is particularly true when the sexualized domination described elides central features of Black or Brown women's experience.[39] Slavery, for example, created a context in which the paradigmatic dynamics of rape involved not strangers but familiars, with whom enslaved women were held in a relationship of dangerous and inescapable servitude. The Jim Crow period created sexual danger for both Black women and Black men: the latter because they were vulnerable to charges of rape by white women—charges which often led to lynching—and the former because their accusations against white men almost always failed, as they were viewed as "promiscuous by nature."[40] Even in the contemporary period, invidious, racially differential stereotypes of women's sexuality continue to support white women who charge Black men with rape or other sexual violations, and to impede the credibility of women of color who claim sexualized injury.[41] A theory that fails to center this legacy installs white women as its focal victims, poses an ongoing threat to Black men, and perpetuates the marginalization of women of color.

Martha Mahoney shared Harris's view of MacKinnon's essentialism but offered a different emphasis.[42] Who you are, according to dominance theory, is based on "what is done to you."[43] This is, Mahoney argued, a departure from the Marxism that MacKinnon takes as her model, because workers, though oppressed, remain nonetheless capable of creating and producing.[44] MacKinnon's view of women as exclusively "the objects of constructive male force" not only fails to grasp their generative potential but "has crucial consequences when she turns to race."[45] MacKinnon's laser focus on dispossession through sexuality prevents her from seeing white women as simultaneously subordinated by their gender and privileged by their race.[46] It obscures the power that white women can exercise in the sexual domain when, for example, they raise accusations against Black men,[47] but it also obscures the unequal power that has shaped relationships between white women and women of color, in vital areas such as domestic labor.[48] This critique of characterizing women as "what is done to [us]" pointed to a second critique of dominance feminism: that it understates women's agency, in sexuality or other arenas of life.

The agency critique was previewed by the "sex wars" of the early 1980s, between antipornography feminists (a group that included MacKinnon but predated the antipornography ordinance) and "sex radical feminists," who saw sexuality as a source not simply of danger but of pleasure.[49] Associating sexuality with women's subordination by men, sex radical feminists argued, could short-circuit nascent explorations of women's sexuality, further exile sexual dissidents already marginalized by mainstream society, and chill erotic energies that could fuel political struggle.[50]

As dominance theory gained prominence, this critique reemerged to charge that dominance theory obscured and even undermined women's agency, in sexuality as in other arenas of their lives. The several variants of this argument included objections from individual women—and later from self-identified "third-wave"[51] feminists—who argued that dominance feminism left no room for the joy, satisfaction, or even empowerment that they drew from sexual experience.[52] It included challenges from feminists of color—from Harris[53] to Patricia Hill Collins[54]—who argued that the focus on systematic sexualized subjection obscured the agency and resistance that Black and other women of color have been able to marshal through collective action and vision. This focus on the possibilities of women's sexual agency was taken in other directions by queer legal theorist Janet Halley.[55] Halley argued that the primary recourse to law risked projecting an image of women as sexually passive, vulnerable, and in need of paternalistic legal rescue.[56] It also threatened to extinguish the liberatory potential of exploring one's own sexual subjectivity[57] and challenging socially normative conceptions of sexuality, including the idea that people generally know what sexual acts or overtures they view as "welcome."[58]

MacKinnon engaged these critics, in academic journals[59] and, more spontaneously, in the many venues in which she presented talks.[60] Whereas she made the credible point that her work, which moved from practice to theory, was grounded in the experience of the Black women who were the early sexual harassment plaintiffs, and that the critique of pornography she originated with Dworkin highlighted the racially differentiated imagery used to debase women,[61] other aspects of her response were less satisfying to critics. Her rejoinders to women who asserted their sexual agency ranged from dismissive sarcasm[62] to more nuanced responses that nonetheless questioned either women's understanding of their own experience or the relevance of that experience given broader social patterns.[63] The caustic way in which MacKinnon suggested that highlighting white women's privilege denied or discounted their (simultaneous) subordination[64] made it more difficult for dominance feminism and its critics to find common ground. As legal feminists leaned toward more intersectional[65] or postmodern accounts of gender inequality,[66] and MacKinnon shifted her focus to the international criminal courts, dominance feminism receded as a lightning rod for controversy and assumed a place as one among several influential theories of women's inequality.[67]

If disputes over intersectionality and agency tempered feminist enthusiasm for dominance theory—or at least the "unmodified" version MacKinnon advanced—they did not curtail the extension of dominance-based ideas to many corners of the legal feminist landscape. Ruth Colker, a feminist scholar, used the ideas of MacKinnon and other progressive constitutional theorists to construct an "antisubordination" theory of race and gender discrimination under the Fourteenth Amendment.[68] Two decades later, Colker extended the reach of the concept, by advocating an "antisubordination" framework as an alternative to long-standing "integrationist" approaches to disability.[69] Mary Anne Franks, a younger exponent of dominance theory, brought MacKinnon's insights from the areas of sexual harassment and pornography into the contemporary domain of cyberspace.[70] Other legal feminists sought not so much to extend as to "modify" MacKinnon's work, offering accounts that combined a dominance-based appreciation of the power inequalities established and perpetuated through sexual coercion with a greater emphasis on—or more nuanced appreciation of—the agency and resistance mobilized by women and other targets of its structural and individual manifestations.[71]

III. #MeToo and Dominance Theory

The advent of #MeToo has returned key tenets of dominance feminism to the center of national conversation.[72] The widening chorus of voices raised against sexual abuse demonstrated in an experiential vein what MacKinnon had argued more sociologically: the scope and pervasiveness of sexualized injury as a practice that demeaned and disempowered women as it constrained the extent of their employment opportunity. MacKinnon herself, writing in the pages of the *New York Times*,[73] described the legal feminism she had introduced as both the scaffolding for, and the possible beneficiary of, this emerging movement against the sexualized abuse of women. Yet, in another sense, #MeToo provided brought new and different resources to bear on the question of women's sexualized injury.

First, as the hashtag and its origins in Tarana Burke's organizing among survivors of color[74] suggest, the new movement was fueled by women's solidarity.[75] A torrent of online and in-person testimonials demonstrated the strength that women drew from hearing others voice a shared experience. Dominance feminism, which had presented women with aggregate data and channeled their voices through individual legal claims, could not draw on either the power of experiential stories[76] or the affective bonds or collective voice #MeToo created among those who had experienced sexualized injury. This collective voice soon began to articulate demands for change. Online campaigns sought to expose perpetrators[77] and focus public pressure on their employers or audiences.[78] And contention over injuries that might not rise to the level of the legally or professionally actionable (e.g., the debate over the private conduct of comedian Aziz Ansari[79]) sought to reshape cultural understandings of sexual coercion.

Second, #MeToo has not predominantly been a legal movement. In its earliest days, #MeToo used social and mainstream media to pressure employers, sponsors, and audiences of offending entertainment figures. But even in the years that followed, proponents have proven ambivalent about a resort to law. Some #MeToo feminists have engaged legal or regulatory frameworks to address sexualized violence—by pursuing criminal charges against Harvey Weinstein, for example, or advocating for an affirmative consent standard on some college campuses.[80] Yet others have rejected MacKinnon's paradoxical optimism, noting that given the gendered stereotypes that persist among judges, juries, and prosecutors, the courtroom is an unlikely place for women to prevail. Still others have raised probing questions about the role of punitive, often carceral justice in responding to sexualized injuries.

To be sure, a carceral focus is not an innovation, or even an emphasis, of dominance feminism. Notably, the sexual harassment claim, and the proposed antipornography ordinance, both create *civil* actions, which—as MacKinnon has noted[81]—keep decisionmaking about whether and how to move forward in the hands of the woman rather than the state. Yet dominance feminism's exposure of the pervasive, corrosive effects of sexualized violence on women's subjectivity has reinforced the societal inclination to view offending sexual acts, however those come to be defined, through a punitive lens. Moreover, the logic of dominance feminism, which takes a more encompassing view of offenses such as rape, domestic violence, and child sexual abuse, could extend the reach of a deeply racialized criminal justice system,[82] or could be vulnerable to forms of conservative appropriation,[83] particularly as conservative judges increasingly populate the federal courts. #MeToo has prompted calls to reconsider this carceral orientation[84] and to explore remedies that reflect principles of restorative or transformative justice,[85] particularly in small-scale settings.[86] Although some commentators have questioned whether this focus demands that women forgive before offenders have taken responsibility for their actions,[87] some #MeToo femininists—at the very least—aim to be part a larger reassessment of the mass incarceration of men of color.

Proponents of #MeToo have sought to avoid some of the missteps of their dominance feminist predecessors. This has been particularly true in the area of women's agency. Some feminist scholars have framed #MeToo as a recapitulation of the dominance position in a renewed staging of the "sex wars": Janet Halley argued, in particular, that the increasingly robust administration of Title IX on university campuses projected an image of women as injured and vulnerable.[88] Yet many, particularly younger, opponents of sexualized violence appear to have learned from the earlier contention over women's agency and pleasure. Controversies like Katie Way's encounter with Aziz Ansari imply that sexual coercion is a problem not simply because it injures women and curtails employment opportunity but because it impedes the kind of pleasure and autonomy women seek for themselves in their sexual lives. #MeToo feminists' support of sex-positive interventions, like the "Slutwalks,"[89] suggests a view that women can place responsibility for sexual violation on perpetrators, without having to renounce their own sexual expression. Although recent campaigns for affirmative consent rules[90] have been stymied by due process objections,[91] they demonstrate the desire of at least some #MeToo feminists to advance an enthusiastic, affirmative vision of women's sexual satisfaction.

If the view of agency articulated by #MeToo reflects a maturation of the dominance vision, progress on the pluralism and inclusion of the feminist effort—its willingness to embrace intersectionality as a hallmark of feminist analysis—has been more equivocal. The concrete victories of #MeToo—the conviction of Harvey Weinstein and the public exposure and condemnation of Louis C. K., Kevin Spacey, or James Levine—have come in cases where complainants were white cisgender women (or white gay men) in the relatively privileged category of established or aspiring actors, musicians, or academics. Beyond their unwitting tendency to reinforce an individualist focus that runs counter to the more systematic indictments of #MeToo itself, these highly visible cases have delivered the fruits of the movement to a small and comparatively privileged group of women and (a smaller group of) gay men. Progress in other areas has been considerably slower.

Some feminist scholars and organizers have challenged these limitations, using #MeToo's insights to address less visible and more challenging contexts. Scholars have argued that women of color who suffer the same kinds of workplace sexual violation exposed by #MeToo have garnered less visibility than their white counterparts.[92] Working-class women have asked when they will have their "#MeToo moment," decrying the pervasiveness of sexualized treatment in restaurant, hotel, or janitorial work.[93] Trans advocates and Black feminists have argued that the (private) employment focus obscures the many contexts in which sexualized or gendered violence is perpetrated by agents of the state, such as law enforcement officers.[94] Although there have been some discrete victories,[95] and proponents of #MeToo have affirmed this broader and more plural agenda, a concerted effort to center these contexts of greater vulnerability has not yet emerged.

As legal feminists fighting to end women's vulnerability to sexual injury, we are all—in larger or smaller ways—living in the house that dominance feminism built. The shift from the androcentric, ontological focus on women's sameness or difference to the power-infused dynamic of dominance and subordination created a new conceptual vocabulary for legal feminists, however imperfect its fit with conventional equality doctrine. The theory's focus on sexuality, sexual objectification, and sexual violation has exposed systematic abuses that had been obscured under previous frameworks. And its ambivalent view of law—as marred by reflexively masculinist perspectives yet capable of feminist revision, and as powerful enough to reshape culture and institutions, yet too often reduced to symbolism in its practical effects—has issued a challenge to those feminists eager to wield this tool. This potent vehicle has achieved limited success thus far in addressing intersecting systems of oppression, particularly those that implicate race. Whether #MeToo, with its solidaristic impetus, growing appreciation of partial agency, and pluralistic remedial approach will improve upon the mixed record of dominance feminism may depend on how well it speaks to the perspectives, and improves the lives, of those at the many intersections of gender, sexuality, race, and class.

Notes

1. *See, e.g.*, CATHARINE MACKINNON, TOWARD A FEMINIST THEORY OF THE STATE (1989)[hereinafter MACKINNON, TOWARD A FEMINIST THEORY]; CATHARINE MACKINNON, FEMINISM UNMODIFIED: DISCOURSES ON LIFE AND LAW (1987).
2. *See, e.g.*, ANDREA DWORKIN, PORNOGRAPHY: MEN POSSESSING WOMEN (1981); ANDREA DWORKIN, INTERCOURSE (1987); ANDREA DWORKIN, MERCY (1993)(autobiographical novel).
3. Frontiero v. Richardson, 411 U.S. 677 (1973); Reed v. Reed, 404 U.S. 71 (1971).
4. Kahn v. Shevin, 416 U.S. 351 (1974) (upholding differences in property tax exemption for widows and widowers).
5. MacKinnon observed: "Gender neutrality is simply the male standard and the special protection rule is simply the female standard, but do not be deceived: maleness, or masculinity is the referent for both.... Approaching sex discrimination in this way ... provides two ways for the law to hold women to a male standard, and call that sex equality." CATHARINE MACKINNON, *Difference and Dominance, in* FEMINISM UNMODIFIED: DISCOURSES ON LIFE AND LAW 32, 34 (1987) [hereinafter MACKINNON, *Difference and Dominance*].

6. *Id.* at 40.
7. MacKinnon, Toward a Feminist Theory, *supra* note 1, at 128.
8. MacKinnon uses a pithy biblical metaphor to make this point:

   Here, on the first day that matters, dominance was achieved, probably by force. By the second day, division along the same lines had to be relatively firmly in place. On the third day, if not sooner, differences were demarcated, along with social systems to exaggerate them in perception and fact, *because* the systematically differential delivery of benefits and deprivations required making no mistake about who was who. Comparatively speaking, man has been resting ever since.

   MacKinnon, *Difference and Dominance, supra* note 5, at 40.
9. *Id.* at 37.
10. *Id.* at 41.
11. Catharine MacKinnon, The Sexual Harassment of Working Women (1979) [hereinafter MacKinnon, Sexual Harassment of Working Women].
12. *Afterword, in* MacKinnon, Feminism Unmodified, *supra* note 1, at 217.
13. MacKinnon, Toward a Feminist Theory, *supra* note 1, at 149. Chapter 7, in this volume, describes in variety and detail the ways that women assimilate this message and accommodate themselves to sexualized domination by men. It illustrates the perspective that prompts the agency critique below, and the kind of problematization of women's self-understanding that has sometimes made it difficult for MacKinnon to find common ground with her critics.
14. *Id.*
15. Catharine MacKinnon, *Feminism, Marxism, Method, and the State: Toward Feminist Jurisprudence*, 8 Signs 635, 644 (1983).
16. MacKinnon, *Difference and Dominance, supra* note 5, at 42–43.
17. *See* Catharine MacKinnon, *Reflections on Sex Equality Under Law*, 100 Yale L.J. 1281 (1991).
18. *Afterword, in* MacKinnon, Feminism Unmodified, *supra* note 1, at 228.
19. MacKinnon, Sexual Harassment of Working Women, *supra* note 11.
20. 477 U.S. 57 (1986).
21. Andrea Dworkin & Catharine MacKinnon, Pornography and Civil Rights: A New Day for Women's Equality (1988).
22. "Pornography" under the ordinance is defined as "the graphic sexually explicit subordination of women, whether in pictures or in words, that also includes one or more of the following:
    1. Women are presented as sexual objects who enjoy pain or humiliation; or
    2. Women are presented as sexual objects who experience sexual pleasure in being raped; or
    3. Women are presented as sexual objects tied up or cut up or mutilated or bruised or physically hurt, or as dismembered or truncated or fragmented or severed into body parts; or
    4. Women are presented as being penetrated by objects or animals; or
    5. Women are presented in scenarios of degradation, injury, abasement, torture, shown as filthy or inferior, bleeding, bruised, or hurt in a context that makes these conditions sexual; or
    6. Women are presented as sexual objects for domination, conquest, violation, exploitation, possession, or use, or through postures or positions of servility or submission or display."

    See, e.g., Anti-Pornography Civil Rights Ordinance, Indianapolis, Indiana, Indianapolis Code §16-3(q).

23. This critique predated the formulation of the ordinance itself; rather, it emerged in response to the earliest critiques of pornography by Dworkin and MacKinnon. This basis of opposition was vividly framed at the Scholar and Feminist IX conference, "Toward a Politics of Sexuality," held at Barnard College in April 1982, and is captured in two edited collections: PLEASURE AND DANGER: EXPLORING FEMALE SEXUALITY (Carole Vance ed., 1984), and THE POWERS OF DESIRE (Ann Snitow, Christine Stansell, & Sharon Thompson eds., 1983).
24. For an example of this approach, *see* Brief Amici Curiae of Feminist Anti-Censorship Task Force, et al. American Booksellers Ass'n v. Hudnut, 771 F.2d 323 (7th Cir. 1985) (No. 84-3147), *reprinted in* 21 U. MICH. L.J. REFORM 76 (1987–88). For an argument that the making, the viewing, and the "doing" of pornography all function according to different logics, rendering pornography subject to multiple interpretations and capable of being both a site of oppressive sexual formation and a site of resistance, *see* Susan E. Keller, *Viewing and Doing: Complicating Pornography's Meaning*, 81 GEO. L.J. 2195 (1993).
25. 771 F.2d 323 (7th Cir. 1985), *aff'd mem.*, 475 U.S. 1001 (1986). In the years following *Hudnut*, MacKinnon shifted the locus of her work to the international sphere, where she argued, for example, in international tribunals, for a dominance feminist definition of rape as an instrument of genocide. *See* MARTHA CHAMALLAS, INTRODUCTION TO FEMINIST LEGAL THEORY 288–89 (3d ed., 2013). *See generally* CATHARINE MACKINNON, ARE WOMEN HUMAN? AND OTHER INTERNATIONAL DIALOGUES (2006).
26. *See, e.g.*, CHAMALLAS, *supra* note 25 (treating dominance feminism as a theory within the "Difference Generation," but identifying "subordination" as a part of the "enemies list" for feminists, and "sexual subordination" as an applied feminist theoretical frame through which to analyze injuries from rape and sexual harassment to domestic violence and prostitution).
27. *See, e.g.*, Fred Strebeigh, *Defining Law on the Feminist Frontier*, N.Y. TIMES, Oct. 6, 1991.
28. Oncale v. Sundowner Offshore Serv., 523 U.S. 75 (1998); Harris v. Forklift Sys., 510 U.S. 17 (1993), Vinson v. Meritor Sav. Bank, 477 U.S. 57 (1986).
29. Vicki Schultz's work, which critiques elements of that transformation, for curtailing attention to nonsexualized forms of derogation and discrimination and producing a stringent aversion to all forms of romantic, or erotic, engagement among coworkers, nonetheless testifies to the influence of the claim on contemporary workplaces. *See* Vicki Schultz, *The Sanitized Workplace*, 112 YALE L.J. 2061 (2003); Vicki Schultz, *Reconceptualizing Sexual Harassment*, 107 YALE L.J. 1683 (1998).
30. Because of this, they have sometimes been ambivalent about why sexual harassment is in fact a wrong, creating an inconsistent and incompletely grounded claim. *See* Katherine Franke, *What's Wrong With Sexual Harassment?*, 49 STAN. L. REV. 691 (1997).
31. *See, e.g.*, LAUREN EDELMAN, WORKING LAW: COURTS, CORPORATIONS, AND SYMBOLIC CIVIL RIGHTS (2016).
32. *See, e.g.*, Faragher v. City of Boca Raton, 524 U.S. 775 (1998); Burlington Indus. v. Ellerth, 524 U.S. 742 (1998).
33. Working as a television commentator during those hearings, MacKinnon played an active role in educating the American public about the phenomenon of, and claim for, sexual harassment.
34. Even MacKinnon, who is notoriously critical of the legal system's response to women's claims, has registered a qualified optimism in assessing its early performance, *see, e.g.*, *The Sexual Harassment Claim: Its First Decade in Court*, in MACKINNON, FEMINISM

UNMODIFIED, *supra* note 1, at 103, and a modestly positive assessment of its longer-term cultural contributions at the outset of the #MeToo movement. *See* Catharine MacKinnon, *#MeToo Has Done What the Law Could Not*, N.Y. TIMES, Feb. 4, 2018 (arguing that the sexual harassment law "created the preconditions" for the #MeToo movement by "conceiving sexual violation in inequality terms").

35. In a review of *Feminism Unmodified*, for example, Katharine Bartlett argued that the broad claims of dominance theory arrogated to MacKinnon herself the power to define women's experience. Katharine Bartlett, *MacKinnon's Feminism: Power on Whose Terms?*, 75 CALIF. L. REV. 1559 (1987).
36. Angela Harris, *Race and Essentialism in Feminist Legal Theory*, 42 STAN. L. REV. 58l, 581–601 (1990). *See also* Marlee Kline, *Race, Racism, and Feminist Legal Theory*, 12 HARV. WOMEN'S L.J. 115 (1989).
37. *See* Harris, *supra* note 36, at 588–89.
38. *See id.* at 589.
39. *See generally id.* at 598–601.
40. *See id.* at 599.
41. For example, the Innocence Project notes that Black men are twice as likely to be arrested for a sex offense and three times as likely to be accused of rape as white men, and sanctions (up to and including the death penalty) are more likely to be severe when a Black man's accuser is white. Danielle Selby, *From Emmet Till to Pervis Payne—Black Men in America Are Still Killed for Crimes They Didn't Commit*, Innocence Project (July 25, 2020), https://innocenceproject.org/emmett-till-birthday-pervis-payne-innocent-black-men-slavery-racism/. The National Organization of Women also reports that Black women who report crimes of violence are less likely to be believed than their white counterparts, and men found guilty of raping Black women are likely to receive lighter sentences. *See Black Women and Sexual Violence* (Feb. 2018), https://now.org/wp-content/uploads/2018/02/Black-Women-and-Sexual-Violence-6.pdf. *See generally* COLOR OF VIOLENCE: THE INCITE! ANTHOLOGY (Incite! Women of Color Against Violence ed., 2016).
42. Martha Mahoney, *Whiteness and Women, In Practice and Theory: A Reply to Catharine MacKinnon*, 5 YALE J.L. & FEMINISM 217, 221–51(1993).
43. Mahoney, *supra* note 42, at 222.
44. *Id.* at 223–24.
45. *Id.* at 222.
46. *Id.* at 234–35.
47. This power is referenced, for example, in an analysis of MacKinnon's discussion of a quote from Amiri Baraka, where Mahoney refers to "the rape image that is an important part of American racism." *Id.* at 229.
48. *Id.* at 239–41.
49. *See* PLEASURE AND DANGER: EXPLORING WOMEN'S SEXUALITY (Carole Vance ed., 1984).
50. *See* Kathryn Abrams, *Sex Wars Redux, Agency and Coercion in Feminist Legal Theory*, 95 COLUM. L. REV. 304, 310–14 (1995).
51. *See, e.g.*, Bridget Crawford, *Toward a Third-Wave Feminist Legal Theory*, 14 MICH. J. GENDER & L. 99 (2007). This strand of the contemporary agency critique echoes some aspects of the complaint of the sex radicals but also encompasses a more mainstream set of sexual identities and preferences, thereby blunting some of its dissident or resistant impetus. Although this critique often had an individualist focus, it was also expressed in a more solidaristic vein, through political protest, by organizers of the "Slutwalks" in the

early 2010s. *See, e.g.*, Deborah Tuerkheimer, *Slutwalking in the Shadow of the Law*, 98 MINN. L. REV. 1453 (2014).
52. *See Afterword, in* MACKINNON, FEMINISM UNMODIFIED, *supra* note 1.
53. Harris, *supra* note 36, at 612–15.
54. PATRICIA HILL COLLINS, BLACK FEMINIST THOUGHT 95–99 (1990).
55. Janet Halley, *Sexuality Harassment*, in LEFT LEGALISM, LEFT CRITIQUE (Wendy Brown & Janet Halley eds., 2002) [hereinafter Halley, *Sexuality Harassment*].
56. *See id.* Halley's emphasis on a potential confluence between dominance feminism and culturally conservative views of women—as vulnerable beings whose purity requires protection—emerges even more strongly in her recent critiques. *See* Emily Bazelon, *The Return of the Sex Wars*, N.Y. TIMES MAGAZINE (Sept. 10, 2015), https://www.nytimes.com/2015/09/13/magazine/the-return-of-the-sex-wars.html (describing Halley's more recent iteration of this view, in the context of Harvard's Title IX policy).
57. *See* Halley, *Sexuality Harassment*, *supra* note 55. Halley's emphasis on the need to preserve sexual exploration and individuality echoes some of the earliest critiques of dominance feminism by the "feminist sex radicals" who opposed proregulatory feminist views of pornography during the 1980s "sex wars." *See* Abrams, *Sex Wars Redux*, *supra* note 50.
58. *See* Halley, *Sexuality Harassment*, *supra* note 55. Halley argues in particular that ambiguity about the "wantedness" of any particular sexual gesture or encounter can be a source of sexual vitality and interest that can be extinguished by the requirement of the sexual harassment claim that a prospective claimant reach a conclusion about the "wantedness" of specific sexual acts in the workplace.
59. *See, e.g.*, Catharine MacKinnon, *From Practice to Theory, or What Is a White Woman Anyway?*, 4 YALE J.L. & FEMINISM 13 (1991) [hereinafter MacKinnon, *From Practice to Theory*]; Catharine A. MacKinnon, *Points Against Postmodernism*, 75 CHI.-KENT L. REV. 687 (2000).
60. A number of these responses are detailed at length in *Afterword, in* MACKINNON, FEMINISM UNMODIFIED, *supra* note 1, at 215–28.
61. *See* MacKinnon, *From Practice to Theory*, *supra* note 59.
62. *Afterword, in* MACKINNON, FEMINISM UNMODIFIED, *supra* note 1, at 219 ("those who believe that women can fuck our way to freedom have limited horizons").
63. Responding, for example, to the recurrent claim that a listener's experience of sexuality was more pleasurable or liberatory than MacKinnon's account suggested, she declared:

Sex feeling good may mean that one is enjoying one's subordination; it would not be the first time. Or it may mean that one has glimpsed freedom, a rare and valuable and contradictory event. Under existing conditions, what else would freedom be? The point is, the possible varieties of interpersonal engagement, including the pleasure of sensation or the experience of intimacy, does not, things being as they are, make sex empowering for women.

Afterword, in MACKINNON, FEMINISM UNMODIFIED, *supra* note 1, at 218.
64. *See* MacKinnon, *From Practice to Theory*, *supra* note 59, at 18–19. Following a long, sarcastic exposition of stereotypes concerning white women—whose origins, as well as whose relation to the work of her feminist critics, are often difficult to determine—MacKinnon describes her critics' view of white women as "woman discounted by white, meaning that she would be oppressed but for her privilege" and concludes that "this image seldom comes face to face with the rest of her reality." *Id.* at 19. Although the

conclusion that white women's reality often includes poverty and sexual violence is likely one MacKinnon's critics would endorse, its positioning at the tail end of a long and caustic passage complicates the process of establishing common ground.

65. *See, e.g.*, Kimberlé Crenshaw, *Whose Story Is It, Anyway? Feminist and Antiracist Appropriations of Anita Hill*, in RACE-ING JUSTICE, ENGENDERING POWER (Toni Morrison ed., 1992).

66. *See, e.g.*, Franke, *supra* note 30; Vicki Schultz, *Women "Before" the Law: Judicial Stories About Women, Work, and Sex Segregation on the Job*, in FEMINISTS THEORIZE THE POLITICAL 297–338 (Judith Butler & Joan Scott eds., 1992).

67. It may also be the case, that during this period, feminist accounts occupied a less prominent place in legal theory as a whole. For a version of this argument, *see* Kathryn Abrams, INTRODUCTION: THE DISTINCTIVE ENERGIES OF "NORMAL SCIENCE," 9(1) ISSUES IN LEGAL SCHOLARSHIP (SPECIAL ISSUE) Article 1 (2011). *See also* JANET HALLEY, SPLIT DECISIONS: HOW AND WHY TO TAKE A BREAK FROM FEMINISM (2008).

68. *See* Ruth Colker, *Anti-Subordination Above All: Gender, Race, and Equal Protection*, 61 N.Y.U L. REV. 1003 (1986).

69. Ruth Colker: *Anti-Subordination Above All: A Disability Perspective*, 82 NOTRE DAME L. REV. 1415 (2007).

70. Mary Anne Franks, *Revenge Porn: A View From the Front Lines*, 69 FLA. L. REV. 1251 (2018); Mary Anne Franks, 71 MD. L. REV. 655 (2012).

71. For an effort to stake out this kind of a feminist position relying on the notion of partial agency within (gender-based) constraint, see Abrams, *supra* note 50. I also see Mahoney, *supra* note 42, and Harris, *supra* note 36, as embracing more complex or "partial" views of women's agency. *See also* Kathryn Abrams, *Subordination and Agency in Sexual Harassment Law*, in DIRECTIONS IN SEXUAL HARASSMENT LAW (Catharine A. MacKinnon & Reva B. Siegel eds., 2004) (applying "partial agency" perspective to claim for sexual harassment).

72. Interestingly, one consequence of #MeToo has been to spark a renaissance of interest in Andrea Dworkin's work. *See* Lauren Oyler, *The Radical Style of Andrea Dworkin*, THE NEW YORKER, Mar. 25, 2019 ("since Donald Trump was elected and #MeToo made it fashionable to express skepticism or hatred of men, a positive, if qualified consensus has coalesced around her work").

73. Catharine MacKinnon, *#MeToo Has Done What the Law Could Not*, N.Y. TIMES, Feb. 4, 2018.

74. Tarana Burke, *MeToo Is a Movement, Not a Moment*, TED TALK (Nov. 2018), https://www.ted.com/talks/tarana_burke_me_too_is_a_movement_not_a_moment?language=en.

75. *See* Tristin K. Green, *Feminism and #MeToo: The Power of the Collective*, in Chapter 15 of this volume. While MacKinnon, personally, attests to her inspiration by women—such as Linda Marchiano, a pornography survivor, or Mechelle Vinson, the plaintiff in the Court's first sexual harassment case—who acknowledge and resist sexualized oppression, the force of women's solidarity may in fact be diffused by the dominance approach because their resistance is ultimately mediated by lawyers and by law.

76. Even as dominance theory was achieving visibility through the sexual harassment claim and MacKinnon's published work, feminists and critical race theorists—some of whom endorsed elements of its systematic critique—had argued for the importance

of experiential stories in demonstrating pervasive patterns of inequality and offering counternarratives to dominant understandings. *See, e.g.*, PATRICIA WILLIAMS, THE ALCHEMY OF RACE AND RIGHTS: THE DIARY OF A LAW PROFESSOR (1991); William Eskridge, *Gaylegal Narratives*, 46 STAN. L. REV. 607 (1994); Kathryn Abrams, *Hearing the Call of Stories*, 79 CALIF. L. REV. 971 (1991); Richard Delgado, *Storytelling for Oppositionists and Others: A Plea for Narrative* 87 MICH. L. REV. 2411 (1989).

77. Moira Donegan, *I Started the Media Men List*, THE CUT: NEW YORK MAGAZINE (Jan. 10, 2018), https://www.thecut.com/2018/01/moira-donegan-i-started-the-media-men-list.html.
78. *See, e.g.*, Katie Thomson, *Social Media Activism and the #MeToo Movement*, THE MEDIUM (June 12, 2018), https://medium.com/@kmthomson.11/social-media-activism-and-the-metoo-movement-166f452d7fd2;
79. Katie Way, *I Went on a Date With Aziz Ansari. It Turned Into the Worst Night of My Life*, BABE. NET (Jan. 13, 2018), https://babe.net/2018/01/13/aziz-ansari-28355.
80. The creation of "Time's Up," which funds legal assistance to #MeToo survivors to bring employment actions against perpetrators, is a related example.
81. *See* DWORKIN & MACKINNON, *supra* note 21.
82. MacKinnon's reluctance to acknowledge the way that claims of sexualized injury—particularly when raised by white women—bear disproportionately on men of color may make dominance feminism more vulnerable to such criticism. *See* Mahoney, *supra* note 42.
83. As scholars such as Janet Halley have argued, it is not difficult for institutional actors to conflate dominance accounts that emphasize women's sexual subordination through rape, sexual harassment, or pornography with conservative views that frame sexual violence as an assault on women's vulnerability or sexual purity, or pornography as a threat to public morality rather than to women's equality. *See* COLLINS, *supra* note 54.
84. *See, e.g.*, Lara Bazelon & Aya Gruber, *#MeToo Doesn't Always Have to Mean Prison*, N.Y. TIMES (Mar. 2, 2020), https://www.nytimes.com/2020/03/02/opinion/metoo-doesnt-always-have-to-mean-prison.html.
85. *See, e.g.*, Lesley Wexler & Jennifer Robbennolt, *#MeToo and Restorative Justice: Realizing Restoration for Victims and Offenders*, 25 DISP. RESOL. MAGAZINE 16 (2019); Donna Coker, *Crime Logic, Campus Sexual Assault, and Restorative Justice*, 49 TEX. TECH. L. REV. 1 (2016).
86. Anna North, *What's Next for #MeToo? This College Might Have the Answer*, VOX (Oct. 10, 2019), https://www.vox.com/identities/2019/10/10/20885824/me-too-movement-sexual-assault-college-campus.
87. Roxane Gay, *Louis C.K. and Men Who Think Justice Takes as Long as They Want It To*, N.Y. TIMES (Aug. 29, 2018), https://www.nytimes.com/2018/08/29/opinion/louis-ck-comeback-justice.html.
88. Emily Bazelon, *The Return of the Sex Wars*, N.Y. TIMES MAGAZINE (Sept. 10, 2015), https://www.nytimes.com/2015/09/13/magazine/the-return-of-the-sex-wars.html. *See also* Vicki Shultz, *Reconceptualizing Sexual Harassment, Again*, 128 YALE L.F. (2018) (arguing that #MeToo reintroduces the "sanitizing" focus of extirpating sexuality from the workplace, rather than addressing more varied dynamics contributing to women's inequality). Indeed, Brenda Cossman's formulation of the current debates as Sex Wars 2.0, *see* Brenda Cossman, *#MeToo, Sex Wars 2.0, and the Power of Law*, ASIAN Y.B. OF HUM. RTS. & HUMANITARIAN L. (Sept. 2018), appears to suggest this recapitulation; and recent discussions of the case of Avital Ronnell sometimes suggest tensions between #MeToo

feminists and an alleged perpetrator who might be classified as a "sex radical." For a lucid and nuanced analysis of the challenges presented by the charges against Prof. Ronnell, *see* Masha Gessen, *An NYU Sexual Harassment Case Has Spurred a Necessary Conversation About #MeToo*, THE NEW YORKER (Aug.25, 2018), https://www.newyorker.com/news/our-columnists/an-nyu-sexual-harassment-case-has-spurred-a-necessary-conversation-about-metoo.
89. *See, e.g.*, Amanda Marcotte, *Slutwalk, #MeToo and Donald Trump: A Grim but Hopeful Season for Feminism*, SALON (Oct. 3, 2018), https://www.salon.com/2018/10/03/slutwalk-metoo-and-donald-trump-a-grim-but-hopeful-season-for-feminism/ (arguing that Slutwalks helped to lay groundwork for #metoo). *See also* Nishita Jha, *The 2010's Was the Decade That Women's Rage Moved Front and Center*, BUZZFEED (Dec. 19, 2019), https://www.buzzfeednews.com/article/nishitajha/slutwalk-metoo-the-decade-in-womens-rights.
90. *Cf.* Michelle Anderson, *Campus Sexual Assault Adjudication and Resistance to Reform*, 125 YALE L.J. 1940 (2016) (advocating affirmative consent standard for campus sexual assault regulation). *See also* Nancy Chi Cantalupo, *For the Title IX Civil Rights Movement: Congratulations and Cautions*, 125 YALE L.J. F. 281 (2016)(discussing such proposals in a more equivocal light).
91. In 2016, the American Law Institute (ALI) debated and rejected a proposed change in the definition of consent in the Model Penal Code that reflected a version of affirmative consent ("'consent' means a person's positive agreement, communicated by either words or actions, to engage in sexual intercourse or sexual contact."). *See* Jennifer Morinigo, *The Evolution of the Model Penal Code 'Consent' Definition*, THE ALI ADVISOR (Sept. 6, 2016), http://www.thealiadviser.org/sexual-assault/evolution-of-model-penal-code-consent-definition/. In 2019, the Criminal Law section of the American Bar Association (ABA) proposed an affirmative consent standard. After coming under fire from the defense bar, which raised due process objections, the proposal was ultimately defeated. Jeremy Bauer-Wolf, *Lawyers' Group Disagrees on College Model of "Affirmative Consent,"* INSIDE HIGHER ED (Aug. 14, 2019), https://www.insidehighered.com/news/2019/08/14/american-bar-association-tables-new-definition-consent-criminal-sex-assault-cases.
92. Angela Onwuachi-Willig, *What About #UsToo? The Invisibility of Race in the #MeToo Movement*, 128 YALE L.J. F. 105 (2018).
93. Clare Malone, *Will Low-Wage Workers Get Their #MeToo Moment?* FIVETHIRTYEIGHT (Dec. 14, 2017), https://fivethirtyeight.com/features/the-metoo-moment-hasnt-reached-women-in-low-wage-jobs-will-it/. *See also* SARU JAYARAMAN, FORKED: A NEW STANDARD FOR AMERICAN DINING (2016) (written before #metoo but often described as "bringing #metoo to the restaurant industry").
94. *See* Jo Hsu, *(Trans)Forming #MeToo: Toward a Networked Response to Gender Violence*, 42 WOMEN'S STUD. IN COMM. 269 (2019). *See also* Kimberlé Crenshaw, *The Urgency of Intersectionality*, TED TALK (Oct. 2016), https://www.ted.com/talks/kimberle_crenshaw_the_urgency_of_intersectionality/transcript?language=en. Although Crenshaw's efforts to spotlight the Black women who have been victims of police violence predates #metoo, in her characteristic intersectional critique she has used these instances of violence to critique the Black Lives Matter movement from a feminist perspective, and the #MeToo movement from an antiracist perspective.
95. Sean Fabian, *Panic Button Laws Make Their Way Across the U.S.*, LABOREMPLOYMENTLAWBLOG.COM (May 8, 2019), https://www.laboremploymentlawblog.com/2019/05/articles/califor

nia-employment-legislation/panic-button-laws/ (describing passage of "panic button" laws to protect women hotel workers from sexual assault by hotel patrons during work). *See also* Bernice Yeung, *A Group of Janitors Started a Movement to Stop Sexual Abuse*, PBS.ORG (Jan. 16, 2018), https://www.pbs.org/wgbh/frontline/article/a-group-of-janitors-started-a-movement-to-stop-sexual-abuse/ (movement by women janitors, shortly preceding but in the spirit of #MeToo, led to California's adoption of Property Services Workers' Protection Act).

CHAPTER 4

A RELATIONAL APPROACH TO LAW AND ITS CORE CONCEPTS

JENNIFER NEDELSKY

RELATIONSHIPS are central to people's lives—to who we are, to the capacities we are able to develop, to what we value, what we suffer, and what we are able to enjoy. Relational feminism makes that relational dimension of human experience central to law and thus to the concepts and institutions by which we organize our collective lives. Particularly in the United States, relational feminism is often linked to a genre of feminist scholarship—starting with Carol Gilligan's influential book, *In a Different Voice*[1]—which emphasized the importance of intimate human relationships and the positive values of caring, nurturing, empathy, and connection. Theorists tied this "different voice" to an ethic of care used in moral decisionmaking and criticized the ways in which "feminine" roles and modes of thinking were devalued, particularly with respect to the value placed on women's labor, inside and outside the workplace.[2] Another vein of the early relational literature, found in Martha Minow's scholarship, widened the lens to critique the mainstream tendency to view any difference as a mark of inferiority and a failure to find ways to accommodate difference.[3]

In the late 1980s and early 1990s, some feminist critics pushed back against the relational turn in scholarship, worried that it would reinforce a vision of women as emotional, maternal beings—a "domesticated" portrait liberal feminists had fought to disrupt.[4] They drew a sharp contrast between the relational approaches that focused on women's difference and Catharine MacKinnon's brand of dominance feminism (focusing on power and hierarchy), which was rapidly gaining ascendancy in the United States.

In my view, the relational scholars often provided a more nuanced discussion of the link between gender and relational approaches than was ascribed to them. For example, Gilligan reported her empirical findings on (white, middle class) gender differences in modes of reasoning, but she did not ascribe these differences to biology or other forms of gender essentialism. Particularly outside the United States, relational feminism has flourished and has evolved into a broad theoretical approach that grapples with hierarchy, power, and identity, beyond and including gender.

I begin this chapter with an introduction to my version of a relational approach to law[5] and then offer a variety of other examples, which illuminate shared concepts and give a sense of the scope of the approach.

My own work on relational feminism began by developing a relational conception of autonomy, inspired by feminist critiques of individualism and the limits of the dominant individualistic framework for constitutional law. From the beginning, I saw a relational approach as important for understanding forms of gender dominance and as relevant to broad legal issues like administrative law as a vehicle for constraining state power (and advancing relational autonomy). Although I shared other feminists' sense of the importance of recognizing the value of care and relational modes of thinking associated with the feminine, my position was always that relationships are central to *all* humans, and that a relational approach is important for all legal questions. The examples I note in this chapter show the many contexts in which a relational approach is valuable. I identify my work as feminist because I see my project of reconceptualizing core concepts like autonomy as part of the central contribution of feminist theory, and because I consistently look to feminist theorists for new ways of understanding human nature and human values. In addition, I see issues such as violence against women as urgently in need of a relational analysis. More broadly, gender relations play a role in almost all forms of inequality. And, as Martha Minow identified early on, a relational approach is crucial for understanding how exclusion works.

Having begun with relational autonomy, I saw that the idea of "autonomy" presumed a particular understanding of the self, which also needed a relational reformulation. And since part of the purpose of relational *legal* theory was to enable a better analysis of law and rights, the approach needed to spell out the connections: conceptions of the human "self" shape the understanding of values like autonomy, and those values take form as rights in law. The basic claim of relational feminism is that both clear legal analysis and projects of transformation need to see how relationships make values like autonomy possible, and how law structures relationships.

The self, autonomy, and law form a "constellation," an interactive set of ideas, practices, and institutions. In the prevailing Anglo-American version, human beings are seen as essentially separate from each other. Relationships exist, of course, but they are not treated as fundamental or "constitutive." Let us turn now to what a relational approach to each part of the "constellation" looks like.

I. The Relational Self

All political and legal theorists and all institutions of law and government recognize that human beings live together. But a relational approach to human life is something more than this recognition. Humans are not best thought of as free-standing individuals who need protection from one another. People's interactions with one another matter not simply because their interests may conflict. Instead, each individual is in basic ways constituted by networks of relationships of which they are a part—networks that range from intimate ones with parents, friends, or lovers to institutional relationships between student and teacher, employer and employee, and citizen and state. All these relationships are, in turn, shaped by a global economy, with migrants driven by war and gross economic inequality, and alarming increases in global warming.

What does it mean to be *constituted* by relationships? The most familiar example is that of children being shaped by their families. This widespread recognition of the constitutive nature of relationships somehow seems to disappear for people over the age of twenty-one. It is as though once people are seen as "rational agents," relationships are things they simply have or choose. The idea of adults as autonomous actors seems in tension with, even to contradict, the idea that people continue to be profoundly shaped by relationships. Indeed, I think some find the relational approach offputting because it seems both infantilizing and feminizing: to them, it treats mature adults as the relationally dependent creatures we know children to be and seems to grant too much importance to relationships associated with women.

In fact, however, it is not hard to think of formative adult relationships. Teachers, mentors, and fellow students are common examples. Neighborhood relations may shape the kinds of employment opportunities young adults are able to envision and access. Relational norms at a workplace—hierarchy, arbitrary authority, cooperation, autonomy, trust, consultation, prejudice—may shape how one sees the world. And all these relations, and their formative effects, are affected by larger structures of economic relations, such as unemployment levels and employers' power to fire at will. Many people will see their personal relations with friends and intimate partners as formative. These relations, in turn, are shaped by wider patterns such as heterosexual norms and gender norms, including the gendered division of care and work. And these patterns intersect with institutions such as family law (which defines marriage and stipulates spousal and parental obligations), a market economy, the absence of state-supported child care, and the absence of a "family wage" (and thus norms of dual-income families). These national (or regional) institutions interact with global markets and institutions such as the World Bank, as well as with relations of economic and political power generated over centuries. And, of course, all these relationships are affected by—and affect—still larger patterns such as global warming (severe weather patterns causing migration, disruption of families, and increased conflict over natural resources).

In sum, a relational perspective will allow people to see how these nested relational patterns—from intimate to global—have shaped who they have become. For example, they marry because of gender norms; they choose their work based on family expectations and neighborhood experience; they lose their job because of a rise in unemployment; they move to another, richer country where there are more jobs; but they suffer from discrimination as immigrants. Their identities, values, and beliefs are shaped by layers of relationship they participate in.

Our embeddedness in these layers of relations makes us both vulnerable to harm we did not cause or choose and complicit in such harm. Examples abound, from racism to homelessness to intimate partner violence to child poverty. Reenvisioning the nature of responsibility (legal as well as moral) in full recognition of human interdependence is a challenge. But simplistic notions of individual agency will be inadequate.

I should note briefly what I do *not* mean by relational selves. First, as noted above, I do not mean that it is really only women who are relational. I do not refer only to intimate relationships (as opposed to the nested, intersecting relationships earlier noted). I do not mean that humans are determined by their relationships. The very concept of relational autonomy presupposes that autonomy is possible for relational selves—which precludes determinism. People are not simply passive recipients of the effects of the relationships they are a part of; relational autonomy means that people affect, and can transform, those relationships. I do not presume that relationships are benign. Part of the point of a relational approach is to understand which relationships foster—and which undermine—core values such as autonomy or security. Evaluating, not "maintaining," relationships must be the objective. To insist on the centrality of relationship is not to deny the values of privacy or solitude, and it is not to claim primacy for collective over individual values. Both collective values, such as environmental sustainability, and individual values, like privacy, are best advanced with relational requirements in mind. And, of course, some values that matter greatly to individuals, like freedom of speech, require collective norms in which to flourish. They are thus both individual rights and collective goods.

II. Relational Autonomy

Below (S. IV. B, C) I will be presenting others' work on the importance of relational autonomy for law. Here I just note the main claim that autonomy is made possible by constructive relationship. This means that "independence" cannot be a good synonym for autonomy, or even a good way of characterizing one of the basic characteristics of autonomy. The idea of autonomy as independence intersects with the American preoccupation with the idea that freedom is to be achieved and protected by keeping the state out of peoples' lives. This may be why there are more scholars using a relational framework outside the United States than within.[6] But the reality is that in all modern states, people are enmeshed within state regulation and provision of services in virtually every aspect of their lives—from education to healthcare to workplace health and safety regulation. Law in the modern state must find ways of protecting liberty and enabling democracy when people are *already within* the scope of state power. This is (in principle) one of the key tasks of administrative law.[7] A relational approach to autonomy always asks how relations can be structured to enhance rather than undermine autonomy—whether those are the relations of bureaucrat to client, employer to employee, or teacher to student. Norms and laws developed through a relational lens are needed to navigate the puzzles of autonomy—and other core values—in the modern bureaucratic state (as well as within the bureaucratic structures of corporations, universities, hospitals, law firms, and churches).

The broad point is that if a legal system tacitly relies on an understanding of autonomy as independence, it is not likely to do a very good job of fostering it. One can see this in debates about "welfare." A good system enhances autonomy as it provides needed support. But if welfare is understood as "dependency," and thus the opposite of autonomy, it is not surprising that its design, including surveillance, undermines rather than enhances autonomy. A helpful framework turns attention to law's role in the relations currently undermining autonomy and to changing the law so that it shapes relations that foster autonomy.

III. Law and Rights

Relational feminism offers a lens of analysis that highlights context and turns the analyst's attention to how relationships give lived reality to the abstractions of rights and to how law structures relationships. Law is an important focus for transformation not just because one might want the law to intervene on behalf of equality but also because the law creates unequal access to the values a society (ostensibly) treats as basic human entitlements. For example, most of the kinds of legal changes feminists advocate are not calling for an increased role of law and the state but a *different* role. Law is currently structuring relations in ways that undermine equality, and changes in the law could structure more equal relations.

In addition to revealing law's direct role in sustaining hierarchy, relational feminism is good at highlighting when the legal system has been tacitly providing impunity for what is properly illegal behavior. When advocacy starts to remove that impunity, it often appears that the scope and power of the state have increased. Those who become subject to law's constraints object strenuously, often denouncing it as inappropriate interference. Examples are the continuing evolution of law and policy with respect to intimate partner violence (IPV) (which was always illegal assault, but rarely prosecuted) and sexual harassment (which became recognized as illegal). A different example is the success of Black Lives Matter in bringing to public attention the widespread illegal violence of police officers when dealing with people of color. The ability to perpetrate illegal violence with impunity (in the cases of both IPV and police violence) serves to sustain power—not just of immediate perpetrators (e.g., husbands or cops) but whole structures of gender and race subordination held in place through violence. A relational approach helps make this role of law clearer and helps identify the fierce resistance to change as, in fact, opposition to restructuring unjust power relations.

A relational lens can be used to interpret cases, regulations, or legislation and, more broadly, public policy agendas and practices. Often hierarchies are fostered by the joint forces of law and norms, which, again, can be revealed by careful analysis of what keeps relations of inequality in place. For example, consider the ways the distribution of care (who does it, where, how, and for what remuneration, if any) is organized around categories of hierarchy such as gender, race, class, and immigration status.[8] The denigration of care reinforces and is reinforced by the denigration of those who do it. In a recent book, legal scholar Adelle Blackett shows how that dynamic works in the context of racialization and paid domestic work.[9] The book looks at the long history of exclusion of domestic workers from labor law protections and the successful advocacy for international labor standards covering domestic workers.[10] Blackett traces the way law[11] relating to domestic workers builds in subordination and often the particular subordination of racialization, showing how domestic work retains its history of servitude and slavery. She demonstrates that ethnographic studies of domestic labor establish that "race, class, and gender" are not simply factors of identity[12] but "structuring factors that mark the bodies of Indigenous, postcolonial, and Black women as those who undertake domestic work."[13] The book helps us see how the denigrated status of these women "makes sense" of the denigration of the work, and vice versa. The puzzle of the low status of care (given how obviously important it is) is obscured by the apparent "naturalness" of the subordination of the people and the work they are seen as fit for. And even as some of this subordination is increasingly challenged, Blackett offers a warning to reformers to be alert to the power of hierarchical relations: "The risk is that recurring hierarchies will continue to reassert themselves, inscribed on historically subordinated bodies or on newly emerging ones. Regulatory frameworks must look specifically at how to correct inequality."[14]

Let me now turn to some of the specifics of rights. Rights structure relations of power, trust, responsibility, and care. This is as true of property and contract rights as it is of rights created under family law.[15] All claims of rights involve interpretations and contestation. Analyzing these inevitable debates in relational terms clarifies what is really at stake. In my work, I have proposed four questions in such an analysis: (1) How has existing law helped construct the problem being addressed? What patterns and structures of relations have shaped it, and how has law helped shape those relations? (2) What values (e.g., freedom or security) are at stake in the problem? (3) What kinds of relations promote such values? In particular, what kind of shift in the existing relations would enhance rather than undermine the values at stake? (There may, of course, be more than one value at stake and they may compete with one another. For example, the relations that enhance the freedom and autonomy of a renter may decrease the security and freedom of the landlord.) (4) What interpretation or change in the existing law would help restructure the relations in the ways that would promote the values at stake?[16]

To set up a useful frame of analysis is not, of course, to offer a determinate outcome for any given rights puzzle. Values will always be contested, as will the judgments at each step of the analysis. Indeed, one of the virtues of the contextual nature of relational feminism is that it embraces contingency. For example, the laws that give effect to freedom of speech or bodily integrity in one context may not work in another. What fosters autonomy in one economy may not do so in another. In particular, the background conditions of social and economic hierarchy must always be considered.

A relational approach to rights can overcome some of the limitations ascribed to individual rights. For example, a relational approach to equality often reveals relevant contexts when an individual(istic) approach, to, say, a right to basic needs, might obscure them. For example, ending poverty is always an important goal, but it may not be sufficient to enable full democratic participation for those at the bottom of a steep economic hierarchy. A relational approach helps people see that when there is huge wealth in the top 1 percent, ending poverty at the bottom cannot provide political equality. For example, compared to the 1970s, the United States now has less poverty but more inequality and less social mobility. Similarly, for cross-national global comparisons, poverty has decreased and inequality increased. Some have argued that a rights framework created an undue preoccupation with poverty alone, thus ignoring the dangers of rising inequality. But a relational approach to rights will always keep in view the inherently relational dimensions of equality.[17]

These claims for relational equality are one instance of the wider claim that a relational approach is not in tension with core values of individual rights frameworks, such as autonomy, security, or privacy. What can actually foster these values will be better understood in a relational framework and law will be better able to implement and protect them through a relational lens.

In sum, law needs a relational framework to do its work optimally, and new concepts (such as relational autonomy) need to be given life in the law. If relational autonomy remains a philosophical concept only, which is not used in cases (or policies) where autonomy is at stake, it will not take hold as part of our shared culture and it will not actually help people who need it. And if legal analysis ignores a relational approach, it will make mistakes about what actually threatens or advances autonomy.

IV. Relational Feminism at Work

This section continues to use the interacting categories discussed in section III—self, autonomy, law, and rights—to discuss the scholarship of contemporary feminist theorists who have built upon the relational frameworks just described. In a variety of new works, we see scholars using a relational approach that is increasingly interdisciplinary and intersectional, and one that expands the scope of relations under examination. We begin with examples of broad relational approaches to law and hierarchy, then turn to how scholars have used relational conceptions of self and of autonomy, and finally look at further examples of the benefits of a relational approach to rights through a reconceptualization of property.

A. Relational Insights on Law and Hierarchy

Several new scholarly works reveal the value of a relational approach for understanding intersecting hierarchies of gender, Indigeneity, and race. They cover diverse contexts of inequality and subordination, from resource extraction on Indigenous lands to the oppressive legacy of residential schools to violence and subordination in the criminal justice and policing systems. The relational approach allows scholars in different nations to comprehend the complexities of embedded systems of hierarchy and subordination in the struggle to address racialized and gendered violence affecting marginalized communities.

The first example points to the deep connection between the relational approaches developed by Western feminist thinkers and the relational framework that underlies so many Indigenous traditions around the world.[18] In *Restructuring Relations*,[19] Finnish scholar Rauna Kuokkanen looks at the way gender relations are central to achieving Indigenous self-determination. In the context of the dispossession of Indigenous lands, she examines the failures to protect Indigenous women from violence or to ensure their equal access to political and economic roles in their own governance practices. Relying on extensive interviews, she brings the voices of Indigenous women to the fore. Her focus on structures of relations allows her to connect challenges of self-government to the gendered aspects of violence and to tensions between concern with care (including care for culture) and focus on control over resource extraction. As the title suggests, both the analysis and the aspirations of the project are framed in relational terms.

Many scholars looking to reveal the ongoing structures of oppression in the law of settler states have highlighted the intergenerational trauma of residential schools. (The United States also had residential schools, but they have not yet drawn much public attention.) Only by looking at the deep relational consequences for families, for child-rearing, and for mental health across generations can the harms of colonial practices be recognized and redressed. For example, Claire Loughnan addresses the presence of colonial violence in contemporary Australian "child protection" plans for Northern Indigenous communities and in the criminal justice system. She situates them in the context of a "long history of Indigenous children being stolen from their families by government agencies from the late 1800s and into the twentieth century, in pursuit of the assimilation of 'mixed race' children."[20] Such policies embody "a structure of unequal relations between settlers and First Nations peoples that continues to underpin contemporary sovereignty in Australia."[21] As in Canada, it is coming to be recognized that state sovereignty rests on a claim to the land as state territory, a claim that has, in turn, rested on the denigration of the Indigenous inhabitants.[22] To overcome enduring structures of hierarchy and denigration, Indigenous youth have simultaneously called for alternatives to the criminal justice system and prevailing legal regimes governing Indigenous lands, urging: "care for land and culture as a source of connection to elders, to family, to community."[23] Arguing that for Indigenous people, reforms related to land are inseparable from empowerment and safety of the individual, Loughnan explains that "[i]t is the law of the land, the relation with land and others that might bring him into relation, offer healing and assure him that he is not alone."[24] Loughnan concludes that "Australia's punitive past and present are a negation of what it means to be in relation, and to exercise responsibility to and for others."[25] But she does not despair of law as such. She invites us to imagine "a retrieval of lawful relations founded upon love as respect for human dignity, [which] offers a way of articulating lawful possibilities."[26]

In so many nations, including the United States, the violence of criminal "justice" systems plays an important role in maintaining structures of hierarchy. There are therefore many forms of critique that highlight the ways that practices of policing, of prosecutorial discretion, of sentencing, and of running prisons rely on and maintain relations of subordination. Many of these are relationally sensitive analyses of the way law reinforces and upholds unequal relations of gender, race, ethnicity, Indigeneity, and immigration status. These identities take their meaning from complex interactions between law, history, culture, and norms. A relational approach identifies law as a necessary part of transformation precisely because it reveals law as part of deeply embedded hierarchies.

For example, critical race feminist Angela Harris uses a relationally informed masculinities lens to unpack the interplay between gender, violence, race, and criminal justice.[27] She offers an expanded view of "gender violence" that goes substantially beyond (but includes) male violence against women. She argues "that violent acts committed by men, whether these acts break the law or are designed to uphold it, are often a way of demonstrating the perpetrator's manhood."[28] In this expanded view, "traditional practices of law enforcement incorporate or facilitate gender violence, whether it is directed at [men], women, sexual minorities, or racial-ethnic minorities."[29] Harris argues that although violence within policing is "widely deplored," it has not been effectively challenged,[30] demonstrating that the law works together with norms, and embrace of power, to make it seem in men's interest to enact forms of masculinity that entail hierarchy, dominance, and violence.

Harris's article exemplifies the ability of relational feminism to focus on patterns of relations and what sustains them, in ways that shift away from placing blame on individuals, or categories of people—such as men. For example, she movingly comments that no one suggested psychiatric help for the police perpetrator of the sexualized torture of Abner Louima, a Haitian immigrant.[31] This focus on relational structure raises complex questions of assigning legal and moral responsibility to individuals embedded in such unjust hierarchies. It takes concrete form in relational critiques of sentencing practices that fill jails with people from subordinated, racialized populations.[32] For example, concepts of responsibility and "risk to the community" used in sentencing practices and guidelines reinforce patterns of discrimination.[33] While developing a relational reconceptualization of responsibility remains a major challenge, a relational approach reveals that if the primary job of a criminal justice system were healing and reintegration, then the focus on blame and the need for a corresponding understanding of responsibility would diminish. Figuring out how to foster responsible autonomy under conditions of oppression (while trying to transform them) would replace blame as the focus in thinking through the inevitable mix of individual and collective responsibility for harm.

B. The Relational Self: Intergenerational Justice

Beyond uncovering embedded relationships that sustain hierarchy, many new relational scholars are interrogating new and expanded meanings of the relational self. In all areas of law, there are assumptions about the nature of the human self.[34] A relational approach helps to reveal what those assumptions are, challenge them, articulate alternatives, and see how the law could change. As Sara Seck puts it:

> Diverse relational approaches to legal analysis share a desire to shine the spotlight away from the bounded autonomous individual of liberal thought and towards interdependent relationships existing among people and the material world, including relationships in the international sphere. Attention to relational law enables us to align our concerns for local and global environmental and climate justice, including gender justice, with respect for Indigenous laws and institutions and the implementation of the United Nations Declaration on the Rights of Indigenous Peoples. Ultimately, we must guard against unconscious acceptance of legal structures that invoke the bounded autonomous individual and, instead, actively seek relational laws and practices, whether in international law, human rights law, business law, and even environmental law.[35]

One of the most important and radical shifts generated by these newer conceptions of a relational self is the recognition of relations beyond those with other humans, constructing a picture of a porous self that further challenges presumptions of a bounded (rather than relationally connected) self.[36] For example, in a recent study of "everyday toxics," relational scholars have embraced an intergenerational view of justice that asserts that "contemporary inequalities will be infused... into future persons and communities—into their physical environments, their social worlds, and in their very flesh."[37]

This study explains that toxics are ubiquitous in the Global North and are routinely (but not uniformly) found in human tissue. Racialized communities and those with lower levels of income and education often have higher levels of toxics. For reasons often shaped by law, not only is regulation inadequate, but there is also a scarcity of information about the consequences of the toxics. Studies of exposure to brominated flame retardants (BFR), for example, suggest effects on cancer, reproductive health, and neurobehavioral and developmental outcomes in children, including effects from *in utero* exposure. The picture that emerges is that our "selves" now include an array of chemicals that affect us in complex ways and "intergenerationally."[38]

The authors argue that "any legal theory capable of grounding meaningful policy prescription in this area must be attentive to the complex matrix of social, ecological, and material relations that shapes and constrains autonomy."[39] The expanded relational self emerges as we realize that "human subjects are not just embedded in a set of personal and structural social relations but are also immersed ecologically in a material world beyond their control, [which] can... condition the agencies and capacities of people."[40] They conclude that "any valid conception of justice for 'future generations' must embrace the inevitable relationship between contemporary inequalities and future harms."[41] In sum, this scientifically detailed essay lets us see what it looks like to bring together multiple relational approaches to reimagine the human self that is subject to and responsible for harm.

Legal scholars working in this expanded relational framework have also taken up the importance of transforming human-animal relations so that they express respect, care, and compassion rather than exploitation, cruelty, or indifference.[42] As people come to see human beings embedded in a vast network of relations with the entire Earth community, relationships with land and all aspects of this community are brought back into focus as foundational relations for law. Such expansions of the scope of the relational self are essential to the human capacity (including legal capacity) to respond to climate change.

C. Relational Autonomy: Mental Health and Supported Decisionmaking

The law, and feminist concerns in particular, repeatedly confront an apparent conflict between respecting autonomy and providing protection or support of some kind.[43] This conflict goes back to women's historical exclusion from contract and property rights and to controversies over "protective" labor laws (e.g., maximum-hours legislation). The tension continues today in complex issues around determining capacity for people with mental health problems who do not want to be institutionalized or forced to take medication.[44] It shows up in debates over contract pregnancy ("surrogacy"),[45] sex work, and prenuptial agreements.[46] In all these contexts, the idea of legal capacity is foundational for areas of law from contract to criminal law, and such capacity is closely linked to autonomy as the basis for responsibility. Increasingly, however, sociological and psychological research shows that people's capacities are shaped by conditions (poverty, racism, childhood abuse, toxins) over which they have no control. What happens to responsibility then? Relational feminism offers a path through many of these conundrums.

In the relational view, autonomy is conceived as arising out of constructive relations and harmed or undermined by destructive ones—whether intimate familial (abusive families) or social structural (racism, poor education, and low economic mobility for the poor). Thus, posing a *conflict* between protecting autonomy and shaping social relations through protective/supportive legislation misconceives the nature of autonomy. The focus from a relational perspective should be on interrogating the exercise of power (e.g., by the state, corporations, and schools) for its compatibility with autonomy. The relational task is to try to figure out how to construct relations so that they foster autonomy and the role of law in shaping those relations.

One example of a relational reconceptualization of autonomy is the idea of "supported decisionmaking," a replacement for a system of substitute decisionmaking (e.g., through guardianship) in which the guardian substitutes their decision for the person deemed incapable.[47] Supported decisionmaking functions as a tool that allows people with disabilities to retain decisionmaking capacity by permitting them to choose supporters to help them make choices. A person with disabilities using supported decisionmaking, for example, would select trusted advisors, such as family members, friends, or professionals, to serve as their supporters without displacing the choice of the individual with disabilities. Such a system shows that instead of treating autonomy or capacity as an "on/off" quality, law can be used to enable it.[48] This approach connects to many different contexts in which a relational approach is used to highlight the need to enable voices to be heard that have long been silenced.[49] In this way, relational feminism fosters democracy as well as protecting—and redefining—rights.

Healthcare offers many other examples of how traditionally individualist conceptions of autonomy do not serve patients well. Scholars have demonstrated the value of relational autonomy for "self-management of chronic illness,"[50] the harms of "ageism,"[51] end-of-life care,[52] and dementia.[53] The recurring theme is that support is essential for true autonomy, a point that can be obscured when autonomy is seen as incompatible with "dependency."

D. Rethinking Rights: Relational Property

In addition to reconceptualizing the self and autonomy, relational scholars have sought to reexamine rights. The relational view of rights moves away "from an imaginary based on boundaries, self-containment and control, to a consciousness which is relational, contextual, and deeply social."[54] An important example of such a revision is the idea of relational property, a view that looks to "the underlying human values that property serves and the social relationships it shapes and reflects."[55]

Property rights are foundational in Anglo-American law, tied to individual values of freedom and highly amenable to, and urgently in need of, relational reconstruction. Property is both an icon of individual rights and obviously implicated in family relations and structures of economic power. These "obvious" relations often become cemented by existing distributions of property and by dominant forms (such as the corporation) taken for granted as the natural order of things, not the construction of law and norms. A relational analysis reveals those constructions.

Property law expresses, authorizes, and enforces deeply held beliefs about the justice of economic inequality and the most basic of hierarchies: humans above all other life forms. An expanded relational approach can bring into the picture the relationship between humans and the Earth itself.[56] Property law shapes (and articulates) relationships not just between people but between people and the land they own (or are excluded from). Bringing land in as a partner in relationship, not just an object of transaction or extraction, shifts our collective understanding of the meaning of "place" in human lives.[57] This relational dimension invites a deep rethinking of the meaning of property. It also connects state law to important Indigenous legal traditions, which have so much to offer in this time of climate crisis. Rethinking property thus offers a pathway toward building just and respectful relations between settler communities and Indigenous peoples.

Estair Van Wagner's analysis of disputes over large-scale quarries provides a detailed example of the benefits of a relational approach to property. She highlights the "complex web of legal, social and ecological relationship engaged by contemporary land use disputes."[58] She specifically includes relationships between people and place, which, like relationships among people, are "structured by formal law and by cultural constructions of property, rights, and the non-human environment."[59] She also highlights the role of nonowners in these cases, and the importance of their relationship to the land.

Her relational analysis illuminates the dangers of a conception of property (still the dominant one), in which "[t]he exclusive legal relationship to the land and the resulting right to use it, even in ways that will fundamentally transform or destroy it, ultimately shapes the relationship of the owner to all other parties, human and non-human."[60] Using the steps of the rights analysis outlined above, Van Wagner first identifies exclusivity as one of the ways law structures the relations that have generated conflicts around quarries (step 1).[61] She then identifies the values at stake (i.e., freedom to use property for private profit and benefit) and, for nonowners, the importance of recognizing "the capacities and limits of land and ecological systems" (step 2).[62] For step 3, she reflects on what (change in) relationships might foster the values, noting that the governing law privileges the ownership relationship over nonowner parties, and that this owner-applicant-driven process means that the owner's information base sets the terms for the debate.[63] A relational analysis goes on to highlight how different legal priorities could foster "conceptualizing relationships that foster respect for the capacities and limits of land."[64] Here, the restructuring of relations changes the values at stake by "[r]eorienting people-place relations away from ownership as exclusion and commodification, and towards responsibility, requir[ing] acknowledgment of the human dependence on, and role in, ecological systems" (step 4).[65] As we see the human-place relationship differently, we see land differently, and we see new kinds of responsibilities built into these relationships, more specifically:

> [T]he resource is understood to have functions and relationships as it exists in an ecological system and not only as an abstract extracted commodity. Similarly, owners and non-owners are understood as part of an interconnected ecological system that constitutes a specific place. An owner's relationships of dependence and responsibility to other people, other species, and the land itself are acknowledged and made visible through a shift away from fixed exclusive rights to the more limited and contextual forms of property relations.[66]

Noting two other important scholars who offer relational approaches to property—Margarite Davies[67] and Nicole Graham[68]—Van Wagner argues for seeing these kinds of relationships to land as "stewardship" and "custodianship." Reorienting land use law away from the ownership model of property could facilitate a conceptualization and implementation of new forms of environmental rights for a range of parties, including non-human species.

Thus, Van Wagner allows us to see how traditional concepts of property shape relations of decisionmaking power between owners and nonowners and limit the scope of relationships taken into account. At the same time, she identifies points of promise that can be used to advance a conception of property suited to a wider range of respectful relations. She offers a framework suitable for restructuring relations in the direction of sustainability. Her analysis thus also expands the values at stake far beyond a simple model of competing uses.

V. Conclusion

Relational feminism reveals what is really at stake in legal contests and offers guidance for interpretation and a framework for assessing the kinds of changes that could allow law to advance autonomy, equality, and other core values. A relational approach reveals law's complicity in existing harms and invites attention to the full context of those harms. At the same time, it makes it easier to envision alternatives. Sometimes a relational approach reveals that the problem is with the understanding of the value itself, as in equating autonomy with independence. Sometimes it focuses attention on relations—of exclusion or dominance—that work against the value in question. Sometimes the key contribution is to find a solution in a change in law, like building a responsibility to the land itself into property definitions. Attention to relational context often invites both intersectional and interdisciplinary approaches, necessary for a full understanding of both problems and solutions. In short, relational conceptions of self, autonomy, and law can incorporate an expansive vision of relations suitable to our contemporary challenges.

Notes

1. Carol Gilligan, In a Different Voice: Psychological Theory and Women's Development (1982).
2. See, e.g., Robin West, *Jurisprudence and Gender*, 55 U. Chi. L. Rev. 1 (1988); Carrie Menkel-Meadow, *Portia in a Different Voice: Speculations on a Women's Lawyering Process*, 1 Berkeley Women's L.J. 39 (1985).
3. Martha Minow, Making All the Difference: Inclusion, Exclusion and American Law (1990).
4. See, e.g., Joan C. Williams, *Deconstructing Gender*, 87 Mich. L. Rev. 797, 807 (1989).
5. This introduction is drawn largely from Jennifer Nedelsky, Law's Relations: A Relational Theory of Self, Autonomy, and Law (2012) [hereinafter Nedelsky, Law's Relations]. My approach is widely shared by other relational scholars, but for this general introduction I mostly make claims for my particular version of relational feminism. In addition to the particular examples I offer, I want to note some core texts here: Relational Autonomy: Feminist Perspectives on Autonomy, Agency, and the Social Self (Catriona Mackenzie & Natalie Stoljar eds., 2000); Being Relational: Reflections on Relational Theory and Health Law (Jennifer J. Llewellyn & Jocelyn Grant Downie eds., 2012); The Politics of Women's Health: Exploring Agency and Autonomy

(Susan Sherwin ed., 1998); Marilyn Friedman, *Autonomy, Social Disruption, and Women*, in AUTONOMY, GENDER, POLITICS (2003). Also closely related is Fineman's work on vulnerability and autonomy. *See, e.g.*, Martha Fineman, *The Vulnerable Subject: Anchoring Equality in the Human Condition*, 20 YALE J. L. & FEMINISM 1 (2008).

6. *See* NEDELSKY, LAW'S RELATIONS, *supra* note 5. *See especially* Jennifer Nedelsky, *Law, Boundaries, and the Bounded Self*, in LAW'S RELATIONS, *supra* note 5 [hereinafter Nedelsky, *Law, Boundaries, and the Bounded Self*]; JENNIFER NEDELSKY, PRIVATE PROPERTY AND THE LIMITS OF AMERICAN CONSTITUTIONALISM: THE MADISONIAN FRAMEWORK AND ITS LEGACY (1994) [hereinafter NEDELSKY, PRIVATE PROPERTY].

7. *See* Genevieve Cartier, *Administrative Discretion as Dialogue: A Response to John Willis (or: from Theology to Secularization)*, 55 U. TORONTO L.J. 629 (2005); Genevieve Cartier, Reconceiving Discretion: From Discretion as Power to Discretion as Dialogue (Sept. 2004) (unpublished Ph.D. dissertation, University of Toronto) (on file with the author). *Also see* Jennifer Nedelsky, *Reconceiving Autonomy*, in LAW'S RELATIONS, *supra* note 5.

8. JENNIFER NEDELSKY & TOM MALLESON, PART TIME FOR ALL: A CARE MANIFESTO (2021).

9. ADELLE BLACKETT, EVERYDAY TRANSGRESSIONS: DOMESTIC WORKERS' TRANSNATIONAL CHALLENGE TO INTERNATIONAL LABOR LAW (2019). *See also* Terri Nilliasca, *Some Women's Work: Domestic Work, Class, Race, Heteropatriarchy, and the Limits of Legal Reform*, 16 MICH. J. RACE & L. 377, 406 (2011).

10. International Labour Organization, Decent Work for Domestic Workers Convention No. 189 (June 16, 2011); International Labour Organization, Domestic Workers Recommendation No. 201 (June 16, 2011).

11. An important dimension of "legal pluralism" theories of law (to which Blackett subscribes) is to insist that "law" consists of more than state law of legislation, regulation, and court rulings.

12. BLACKETT, *supra* note 9, at 78.

13. *Id.*

14. *Id.* at 79.

15. For an explicitly relational approach to family law, *see* ROBERT LECKEY, CONTEXTUAL SUBJECTS: FAMILY, STATE AND RELATIONAL THEORY (2008).

16. As can be seen in my phrasing of the questions, I make a distinction between rights and values. I treat rights as rhetorical and institutional means for implementing core values, such as security, liberty, autonomy, and equality. I prefer this language to simply defining such core values as rights. Usually when people do this, they mean these core values are moral rights. But my focus is on legal rights, and I want to emphasize that it is a certain kind of choice to describe a value as a legal right and construct institutions for implementing that right.

17. *See* Jennifer Nedelsky, *The Relational Self as the Subject of Human Rights*, in THE SUBJECT OF HUMAN RIGHTS (Danielle Celermajer & Alexandre Lefebvre eds., 2020). *See also* NEDELSKY, LAW'S RELATIONS, *supra* note 5 (particularly ch. 6).

18. For a beautiful U.S. example, *see* ROBIN WALL KIMMERER, BRAIDING SWEETGRASS: INDIGENOUS WISDOM, SCIENTIFIC KNOWLEDGE AND THE TEACHINGS OF PLANTS (2015) (describing the book as "a braid of stories meant to heal our relationship with the world" which is "woven from three strands: indigenous ways of knowing, scientific knowledge, and the story of an Anishinabekwe scientist trying to bring them together in service to what matters most.... old stories and new ones that can be medicine for our broken relationship with earth.").

19. Rauna Johanna Kuokkanen, Restructuring Relations: Indigenous Self-Determination, Governance, and Gender (2019) (comparing Canada, Greenland, and the Nordic countries with Sami populations (with her own origin in Finland)).
20. Claire Loughnan, *Law, Love and Being in Relation*, 17 Globalizations 1194, 1195 (2020).
21. *Id.*; Philip Zylberberg, *Who Should Make Child Protection Decisions for the Native Community*, 11 Windsor Y.B. Access Just. 74 (1991)(comparing American and Canadian approaches).
22. Joshua Nichols, A Reconciliation Without Recollection? An Investigation of the Foundations of Aboriginal Law in Canada (2019).
23. Loughnan, *supra* note 20, at 1205.
24. *Id.*
25. *Id.* at 1208.
26. *Id.* at 1209. *See also* Mary Graham, *Some Thoughts About the Philosophical Underpinnings of Aboriginal Worldviews*, 45 Austl. Human. Rev. 181 (2008); Dylan Voller, *Kids on Country, Not in Custody*, The Saturday Paper (Nov. 17, 2018), https://www.thesaturdaypaper.com.au/opinion/topic/2018/11/17/kids-country-not-custody/15423732007147#hrd
27. Angela P. Harris, *Gender, Violence, Race, and Criminal Justice*, 52 Stan. L. Rev. 777 (2000). Harris's article reminds us that activists and scholars have long been trying to get attention for arguments that Black Lives Matter are now making visible.
28. *Id.* at 780.
29. *Id.*
30. *Id.*
31. *Id.* at 778.
32. Sentencing can highlight the problem of assigning individual responsibility in the context of systemic injustice. A relational conception of autonomy and responsibility can reframe the problem. For Canadian perspectives on discriminatory sentencing and conceptions of responsibility in the context of systemic racism, *see* Elspeth Kaiser-Derrick, Implicating the System: Judicial Discourses in the Sentencing of Indigenous Women (2019); Marie-Eve Sylvestre, *Rethinking Criminal Responsibility for Poor Offenders: Choice, Monstrosity, and the Logic of Practice*, 55 McGill L.J. 771 (2010); Carmela Murdocca, *Ethics of Accountability: Gladue, Race, and the Limits of Reparative Justice*, 30 Can. J. Women & L. 522 (2018).
33. Sarah-Jane Nussbaum, Responsibility, Risk, and Social Accountability: Tensions and Connections in Canadian Criminal Law 34 (2021) (unpublished Ph.D. dissertation, Osgoode Hall Law School, York University) (on file with author) ("Criminal law is, in essence, highly individualizing and highly reluctant to confront the roles of social and political structures within criminalization processes").
34. One example is copyright law. *See* Carys J. Craig, *Reconstructing the Author-Self: Some Feminist Lessons for Copyright Law*, 15 J. Gender Soc. Pol'y & L. 207 (2007) ("Copyright's construction of authorship and its focus upon the abstract, individual rights-bearer... threatens to obscure the social purposes of the copyright system and to undermine its attempts to encourage cultural creativity.").
35. Sara L. Seck, *Relational Law and the Reimagining of Tools for Environmental and Climate Justice*, 31 Can. J. Women & L. 151, 152 (2019).
36. Nedelsky, *Law, Boundaries, and the Bounded Self, supra* note 6.
37. Jessica Eisen et al., *Constituting Bodies into the Future: Toward a Relational Theory of Intergenerational Justice*, 51 U.B.C. L. Rev. 1, 53 (2018).

38. *Id.* at 18–19.
39. *Id.* at 49.
40. *Id.*
41. *Id.* at 50–51.
42. Maneesha Deckha, Animals as Legal Beings: Contesting Anthropocentric Legal Orders (2021); Maneesha Deckha, *Unsettling Anthropocentric Legal Systems: Reconciliation, Indigenous Laws, and Animal Personhood*, 41 J. Intercultural Stud. 77 (2020); Jessica Eisen, *Beyond Rights and Welfare: Democracy, Dialogue, and the Animal Welfare Act*, 51 U. Mich. J. L. Reform 469 (2018); Steven M. Wise, Rattling the Cage: Toward Legal Rights for Animals (2000).
43. Sharon Thompson, *Feminist Relational Contract Theory: A New Model for Family Property Agreements*, 45 J.L. & Soc'y 617 (2018)("Feminists have often found themselves trying to get power dynamics recognized and being accused of advocating for paternalism, thus undermining feminists' demand for recognition of female autonomy. In many cases, a relational understanding of autonomy—of the relations that enable it and those that undermine it—can highlight how power relations play themselves out in various forms of contracts. Relational feminism can then advocate for appropriate protections and regulations without falling prey to paternalism (even if it will be a long time before they stop being accused of it)").
44. Sophie Nunnelley, *Involuntary Hospitalization and Treatment: Themes and Controversies*, in Law and Mind: Mental Health Law and Policy in Canada 113, 136–38 (Colleen M. Flood & Jennifer A. Chandler eds., 2016).
45. Roxana Banu, *A Relational Feminist Approach to Conflict of Laws*, 24 Mich. J. Gender & L. 1 (2017)("I develop a relational feminist approach to Conflict of Laws and apply it to a pressing contemporary issue, namely transnational surrogacy arrangements.").
46. Lucy-Ann Buckley, *Autonomy and Prenuptial Agreements in Ireland: A Relational Analysis*, 38 Legal Stud. 164 (2018)(Irish courts dealing with spousal agreements have tacitly accepted liberal conceptualizations of autonomy, which may lead to injustice.).
47. Committee on the Rights of Persons with Disabilities, *General Comment No. 1 (2014) Article 12: Equal Recognition Before the Law*, U.N. Doc. No. CRPD/C/GC/1 (May 19, 2014); Anna Arstein-Kerslake, Restoring Voice to People with Cognitive Disabilities: Realizing the Right to Equal Recognition Before the Law (2017); Michael Bach & Lana Kerzner, Law Commission of Ontario, A New Paradigm for Protecting Autonomy and the Right to Legal Capacity (2010), http://www.lco-cdo.org/wp-content/uploads/2010/11/disabilities-commissioned-paper-bach-kerzner.pdf; Piers Gooding, *Supported Decision-Making: A Rights-Based Disability Concept and Its Implications for Mental Health Law*, 20 Psychiatry, Psych. & L. 431 (2013).
48. *See* Camillia Kong, Mental Capacity in Relationship: Decision-Making, Dialogue, and Autonomy 49 (2017)("[A] relational analysis of legal rights,... provides a key interpretive prism through which a more relational concept of mental capacity becomes possible. This analysis helps expose ways that the law can structure relationships in normatively questionable ways. It likewise brings to the forefront much-needed debate about the underlying values that these rights seek to advance.").
49. *See* Laura Davy, *Between an Ethic of Care and an Ethic of Autonomy: Negotiating Relational Autonomy, Disability, and Dependency*, 24 Angelaki J. Theoretical Human. 101 (2019).
50. Lydia Ould Brahim, *Reconsidering the 'Self' in Self-Management of Chronic Illness: Lessons from Relational Autonomy*, 26 Nursing Inquiry (2019).

51. Laura Pritchard-Jones, *Ageism and Autonomy in Health Care: Explorations Through a Relational Lens*, 25 HEALTH CARE ANAL. 72 (2017).
52. Carlos Gómez-Vírseda et al., *Relational Autonomy in End-of-Life Care Ethics: A Contextualized Approach to Real-Life Complexities*, 21 BMC MED. ETHICS 1 (2020).
53. Terry Carney, *People with Dementia and Other Cognitive Disabilities: Relationally Vulnerable or a Source of Agency and Care*, 12 ELDER L. REV. 1 (2019).
54. Margaret Davies, *Persons, Property and Community*, 2 FEMINISTS@LAW 1, 17 (2012).
55. Gregory S. Alexander et al., *A Statement of Progressive Property*, 94 CORNELL L. REV. 743, 743 (2009).
56. Helena R. Howe, *Making Wild Law Work—The Role of "Connection with Nature" and Education in Developing an Ecocentric Property Law*, 29 J. ENVTL. L. 19 (2017) ("[C]onnection with nature—and specifically, with land—underpins any transformation of property law from an anthropocentric, individualist concept to a more ecocentric and relational one.").
57. Ozlem Aslan, RESISTANCES AGAINST HYDROPOWER PROJECTS AS PLACE-BASED STRUGGLES: THE CASE OF ARTVIN, TURKEY (June 2019) (unpublished Ph.D. dissertation, University of Toronto) (on file with author), https://hdl.handle.net/1807/96926. *See also* MARTI KHEEL, NATURE ETHICS: AN ECOFEMINIST PERSPECTIVE (2007); THOMAS BERRY, THE DREAM OF THE EARTH (1988).
58. Estair Van Wagner, *Putting Property in Its Place: Relational Theory, Environmental Rights and Land Use Planning*, 43 REVUE GÉNÉRALE DE DROIT 275, 275 (2013).
59. *Id.* at 277.
60. *Id.* at 308.
61. *Id.*
62. *Id.*
63. *Id.* at 309.
64. *Id.* at 310.
65. *Id.*
66. *Id.*
67. Davies, *supra* note 54, at 2, 5 (claiming that "property-person thematic is entirely about layers and layers of highly dynamic relationships" which "implicate people, communities, ideas, politics, and the physical world" and highlighting Van Wagner's point that the distribution of power that comes with definitions of property involve "everyday crossovers of private power into the political sphere.").
68. NICOLE GRAHAM, LAWSCAPE: PROPERTY, ENVIRONMENT, LAW (2010).

CHAPTER 5

A GENEALOGY OF INTERSECTIONALITY

EMILY HOUH

THE words "intersectionality" and "intersectional feminism" have become almost commonplace. A quick Google search of "intersectional feminism" yields 1.34 million results;[1] a Boolean search of "intersectionality/5 theory" yields four million results.[2] Since the 2016 U.S. presidential election, "intersectionality" has, in the words of journalist Jane Coaston, "gone viral"—especially among the conservative right. Coaston writes:

> To many conservatives, intersectionality means "because you're a minority, you get special standards, special treatment in the eyes of some." It "promotes solipsism at the personal level and division at the social level." It represents a form of feminism that "puts a label on you. It tells you how oppressed you are. It tells you what you're allowed to say, what you're allowed to think." Intersectionality is thus "really dangerous" or a "conspiracy theory of victimization."[3]

To those of us who have studied intersectionality and intersectional feminism even before the term was coined by Kimberlé Crenshaw in the legal context in the 1980s,[4] these mischaracterizations of intersectionality and intersectional feminism so miss the mark they seem intellectually dishonest, even if they come as no surprise.

As one of Crenshaw's former students, Kevin Minofou, put it, intersectionality is not particularly concerned with "shallow questions of identity and representation" but, rather, provides us with a framework for exploring "deep structural and systemic questions about discrimination and inequality."[5] It is a theory of liberation meant to advance the goals of race, gender, and sex equality in a continually evolving and multiracial democracy. In my usage, "intersectionality" is largely synonymous with "intersectional feminism," although some individual scholars may prefer not to label their work as a brand or strand of feminism.

This chapter's genealogy of intersectionality theory traces its roots in diverse intellectual traditions, most prominently in critical race theory (CRT), Black feminist thought, and Third World/women-of-color feminisms. To set the stage for the development of intersectionality, it starts with an overview of CRT's origins and its intellectual foregrounding in critical legal studies. It then describes intersectionality's dual origins in and relationship to CRT, as well as to woman-of-color–centered feminisms. Turning from history to theory, it identifies and explores some key substantive insights that have come to characterize intersectional analysis. The genealogy concludes with intersectionality theory as it has recently been enacted on the ground through an approach known as social justice feminism and discusses how it continues to inform activist struggles against fierce backlash forces.

I. Origins of Critical Race Theory

Critical race theory, from which intersectionality emerged, began to take shape in the legal academy during the late 1970s and early 1980s, partly as a response to the earlier critical legal studies (CLS) movement. As a critical theory, CRT built upon CLS insights, even as it broke away to form its own field of study. CLS scholars ("legal crits") understood that law, while appearing "natural" and "neutral," was, in fact, neither.[6] They were dedicated to exposing the ways in which the "neutral" and "objective" technicalities of legal doctrine had been used to mask the inherently political nature of the law and the law's role in maintaining and legitimizing a stratified social order in the liberal state. They further claimed that the inherently political nature of the law made it indeterminate in its application of rules and principles, representing not "blind justice" applied equally to all but an exercise of power by the powerful.

The civil rights that had been gained by Black and other marginalized Americans over the course of decades of struggle did not escape the legal crits' indeterminacy critique. In early writings, they contested the conventional wisdom and demonstrated the ways in which antidiscrimination law *legitimated* racial discrimination. For example, one early influential article, analyzing major U.S. Supreme Court antidiscrimination cases from 1953 to 1974, showed how, in the wake of *Brown*, the Court had significantly restricted the reach of antidiscrimination law by emphasizing the intent of the "perpetrators" of discrimination, as opposed to the impact on their "victims."[7]

During this time, Derrick Bell, later identified as a "founder" of CRT, had also begun critiquing liberal civil rights discourse. In his 1976 article, *Serving Two Masters*,[8] Bell argued that by focusing so singularly on the remedy of integration in litigating *Brown v. Board*, the NAACP Legal Defense Fund had disregarded the interests of its clients, many of whom were more concerned with the material inequities and inequalities of segregated schools. These clients, he argued, were not convinced that busing and racial integration of schools would lead to racial equality; they simply wanted greater resources and substantively better schools for their children, especially given the persistence of residential segregation. In addition to questioning integration as a remedy, *Serving Two Masters* disrupted the dominant understanding of *Brown v. Board*'s role in furthering racial progress in the United States and critiqued the liberal underpinnings and strategies behind that progress. Although CRT did not yet exist as an identifiable school of thought when Bell's article was published, his analysis exemplifies critical race analysis and remains a bedrock of the CRT canon.

As a Black law professor writing critically about the inadequacies of civil rights law, Bell set the stage for CRT's organized "emergence" from CLS. Although his writings throughout the 1970s coincided with the rise of CLS, Bell did not consider himself a legal crit. Meanwhile, by the mid-1980s, a handful of law professors of color who had initially aligned with CLS—including Richard Delgado, Mari Matsuda, Patricia Williams, and Harlon Dalton—became profoundly dissatisfied with what they saw as the failure of the legal crits (made up of mostly white male professors from elite institutions) to contend with or account for race in their critiques of social power and hierarchy as legitimated by law.[9] They wanted a theory that would address the primary role of race in the organization of American social, political, and economic life and the overwhelming fact of racial inequality and subordination in the United States.

In particular, many of these scholars of color contested the CLS critique of legal rights discourse and the view that rights had no value in the struggle toward a more equal and communitarian society. While sympathetic to the legal crits' indeterminacy critique, these scholars of color did not share the crits' rejection of rights discourse as a tool of liberation, pointing out that Black Americans had only recently, historically speaking, been granted full rights by the state. For these scholars, the legal crits' failure to comprehend the transformative nature of rights in the lives of Black Americans demonstrated a tension between the crits' theorizing of a more just society and their own race privilege. Thus, the "race crits" distanced and distinguished themselves from CLS by placing race at the center of their critical discourse, and by acknowledging the law's liberatory potential as necessarily coexistent with the law's subordinating tendencies.

This race intervention into CLS coincided with student organizing at elite law schools around the failure to hire faculty of color in anything beyond token numbers.[10] In 1980, when Derrick Bell left his position on the Harvard Law School (HLS) faculty to take up a deanship at another law school, HLS did not hire a professor of color to teach his courses in constitutional law and race and the law. HLS students organized to protest the failure to replace Bell but were told by the HLS administration that there were no "qualified" minority faculty to hire. Such a response by a liberal legal institution like HLS sparked a burst of activity that ended in several HLS students organizing a new course inspired by Bell's work. The course focused on racial critiques and analyses of American law and was taught by a group of professors of color who the students brought in from other law schools to teach various topics in the course. Many of the participants in this "alternative course"—both the teachers and the students—went on to become central figures in the establishment of CRT as its own field.[11]

Bell returned to the HLS faculty in 1986, only to find that HLS as an institution had not diversified; its large tenured faculty included only three white women and three

Black male professors. Despite the sustained organizing efforts of the Coalition for Civil Rights, which HLS students had formed to advocate for faculty diversification, things had not improved much by 1990.[12] In spring of that year, Bell began an unpaid "leave of conscience" to protest the lack of faculty diversity and, more specifically, the lack of not even one tenured or tenure-track Black female professor to represent the 107 Black women students attending HLS at the time.[13] In 1992, Harvard declined to extend Bell's leave beyond two years, thus ending his tenure and career there. It would be six more years before HLS hired its first Black woman (and woman of color)—Lani Guinier—for a tenure-track position in 1998.[14]

The story of Derrick Bell's "leave of conscience" from Harvard Law School, his subsequent dismissal, and the student activism around HLS's failure to respond adequately to their concerns encapsulated the representational, material, and interconnected aspects of institutional racism *and* sexism. In this way, the activism around Bell's "boycott" demonstrated how the CRT movement at that time had come into its own and how CRT had begun to internalize and incorporate feminist values and insights.

II. Intersectionality's Roots in CRT

One of the key organizers of the "alternative course" at HLS—Kimberlé Crenshaw—is best known as the person who introduced "intersectionality" into legal scholarship. In a pair of law review articles published in 1989 and 1991, respectively, *Demarginalizing the Intersection of Race and Sex: A Black Feminist Critique of Antidiscrimination Doctrine, Feminist Theory and Antiracist Politics*[15] and *Mapping the Margins: Intersectionality, Identity Politics, and Violence Against Women of Color*,[16] Crenshaw set out to "explore … various ways in which race and gender intersect in shaping structural, political, and representational aspects of violence [and discrimination] against women of color."[17]

In *Demarginalizing*, Crenshaw led readers through a meticulous analysis of three Title VII cases—*DeGraffenreid v. General Motors*,[18] *Moore v. Hughes Helicopter*,[19] and *Payne v. Travenol*[20]—to demonstrate how discrimination against Black women had been rendered invisible and noncognizable in judicial interpretations of antidiscrimination law. In *DeGraffenreid*, five Black women sued GM asserting that one of its seniority policies operated to discriminate exclusively and specifically against Black women; the court rejected their claims, asserting that while Title VII allowed for claims based on race *or* sex, it did *not* allow for more specific claims based on race *and* sex. Both *Moore* and *Payne* involved class action lawsuits for race and sex discrimination in which the courts refused to certify the plaintiffs as the respective class representatives on behalf of all women because they were *Black* women. Crenshaw's central contention with regard to these cases was that courts, in determining which cases would go forward, inaccurately but instinctively conceived of plaintiffs in race discrimination cases as Black men, and plaintiffs in gender discrimination cases as white women. Centering Black women in her analysis, Crenshaw set out "to contrast the multidimensionality of Black women's experience with the single-axis analysis that distorts these experiences." As she explained it:

> Not only will this juxtaposition reveal how Black women are theoretically erased, but it will also illustrate how this framework imports its own theoretical limitations that undermine efforts to broaden feminist and antiracist analyses. With Black women as the starting point, it becomes more apparent how dominant conceptions of discrimination condition us to think about subordination as disadvantage occurring along a single categorical axis.[21]

At a practical level, according to Crenshaw, antidiscrimination law functioned to leave without remedy those plaintiffs who asserted claims specifically as, for example, Black women, because courts dictated that they choose one identity or the other—race *or* gender—to advance their claims within the existing legal frameworks. Moreover, at the level of discourse, this single-axis thinking functioned to render women of color invisible and voiceless, and always subordinate to men of color and white women.

In *Mapping the Margins*, Crenshaw applied intersectional analysis to her field research on the experiences of immigrant women of color in battered women's shelters in Los Angeles who had attempted to seek protection against their abusers. Based on her observations and analysis, Crenshaw demonstrated how "the location of women of color at the intersection of race and gender makes our actual experience of domestic violence, rape, and remedial reform qualitatively different than that of white women."[22] Crenshaw's intersectional analysis first revealed how women of color were excluded, at the level of policy and legal reform, from the political work of addressing domestic violence and rape, or protecting and assisting white victims; she then showed how the physical and sexual abuse of women of color often remained unaddressed due to misguided attempts to "maintain the [patriarchal] integrity" of communities of color. Finally, Crenshaw analyzed the 1990 Florida obscenity prosecution of the Black rap group 2 Live Crew and the controversy it created both within and outside communities of color to demonstrate how the "cultural construction" of Black women as objects of violence and sexual domination constitutes yet another method of disempowerment of women of color.[23]

Crenshaw's work in these two articles, along with several pieces written by women of color race and feminist legal scholars like Mari Matsuda,[24] Patricia Williams,[25] and Margaret Montoya,[26] effected paradigm-shifting interventions into both critical race theory and feminist legal theory. Matsuda famously called for left and progressive legal theorists, and specifically those engaged in CLS, to "look to the bottom." In her words, "[T]hose who have experienced discrimination speak with a special voice to which we should listen. Looking to the bottom—adopting the perspective of those who have seen and felt the falsity of the liberal promise—can assist critical scholars in the task of fathoming the phenomenology of law and defining the elements of justice."[27] Patricia Williams departed from "law review" writing conventions and began one of her most influential pieces with a "meta-story."[28] In this compelling personal essay, she explained her unease with the legal crits' rejection of rights, invoking real-life stories of her slaveholding great-great-grandfather Austin Miller, a lawyer, and his rape of his slave and Williams's great-great-grandmother Sophie. Through her narrative, Williams illustrated how the jurisprudence of rights had empowered her to "give voice to those whose voice had been suppressed" by arguing that "they had no voice."[29] Margaret Montoya also used narrative methodology,[30] drawing in part from Chicano/a studies and activism, to provide an account of how legal discourse and culture constructs and subordinates "Outsider" others.[31] Many of the hallmarks of these works—the use of narrative, bringing those at the margins to the center, and "looking to the bottom"—would later become defining aspects of CRT and intersectionality.

As important as Crenshaw was to the emergence of intersectionality as a cross-cutting applied theory, she did not invent the concept itself. Around the same time, contemporary Black feminist legal scholars were employing other closely related theories and similar language in their own critiques. In the early 1990s, for example, Angela Harris drew from both Black feminist thought and postmodernist literary criticism to critique Catharine MacKinnon's dominance feminism and Robin West's version of difference feminism, as being "essentialist" in how they internalized and universalized the perspectives and experiences of "race- and class-privileged" women.[32]

None of the foregoing, of course, diminishes the importance of Crenshaw's contribution or her influence on intersectionality theory as she conceived it. It simply highlights how intersectionality theory is a product of multiple scholars, deeply informed and influenced by various intellectual movements and traditions. The intersectional work of women of color in the legal academy would soon become an important part of an already flourishing body of postliberal feminist writing and theory and has given rise to a rich and continually growing body of intersectional legal scholarship.[33] The next section delves into this literature, examining intersectionality's roots in a body of work I call "women-of-color–centered feminisms" that encompasses both Third world feminism and Black feminist thought.

III. INTERSECTIONALITY'S ROOTS IN WOMEN-OF-COLOR–CENTERED FEMINISMS

Intersectionality theory's connection to feminism reaches all the way back to nineteenth-century political struggles with white American suffragettes and birth control advocates, which drove formerly enslaved Black women to articulate and employ racial and class critiques of the exclusively white, middle-class "women's liberation movement." These Black feminists, to use a more contemporary term, took their trenchant critiques to the streets—perhaps most compellingly stated in Sojourner Truth's *Ain't I A Woman* speech at the Ohio Women's Rights Convention in 1851[34]— and dedicated their lives to activism in both the white-centered feminist and male-centered antislavery movements. Over the next 150 years, the work of these early Black feminists—along with that of their white counterparts—would provide the foundation for the many strands of feminism to come, including two intersectional schools centered on women of color—Third World feminism and Black feminist thought.

Throughout the 1980s and 1990s, a generation of future activists, advocates, teachers, and/or scholars of color (and I count myself among them) were introduced to the work of Cherríe Moraga, Gloria Anzaldúa, and other Third World, and women-of-color feminists. This group of writers brought new scholarly voices—the voices of Chicanas, lesbians, and other diverse women—that opened up and upended feminist discourse. Moraga and Anzaldúa's 1981 anthology, *This Bridge Called My Back: Writings by Radical Women of Color*,[35] resonated deeply with those of us who considered ourselves young feminists but were put off by the race and class essentialism of liberal feminism. In their "Introduction" to *This Bridge*, Moraga and Anzaldúa stated clearly what so many of us felt but could not adequately articulate:

> We want to express to all women—especially to white middle-class women—the experiences which divide us as feminists; we want to examine incidents of intolerance, prejudice and denial of differences within the feminist movement. We intend to explore the causes and sources of, and solutions to these divisions. We want to create a definition that expand what "feminist" means to us.[36]

Even now, forty years after its first publication, the essays, stories, personal narratives, and poetry that comprise *This Bridge* powerfully convey how and why the experiences and analyses of women of color must be accounted for in any theory or movement that aspires to liberation and the end of oppression. Put another way, Third World and women of color feminists were creating their *own* feminism—one that was multi-, inter-, and cross-disciplinary and that prioritized the lived experiences of women of color and their own intellectual interpretations of those experiences.

Many of the feminists who contributed to *This Bridge* were also deeply involved with and adherents of Black feminist thought, a new interdisciplinary genre that included well-known Black feminist intellectuals like Audre Lorde,[37] Angela Davis,[38] bell hooks,[39] Gloria Hull,[40] Barbara Smith,[41] and Patricia Hill Collins.[42] As Collins points out in her classic book, *Black Feminist Thought: Knowledge, Consciousness, and the Politics of Empowerment*,[43] "African-American women's social location as a collectivity has fostered distinctive albeit heterogeneous Black feminist intellectual traditions." Generally speaking, however, these "intellectual traditions," according to Hill Collins, emphasized the dialectical nature of Black women's "oppression and activism," the institutional and intersecting nature of those oppressions, and the inseparability of "experience and consciousness" (or, "what one does and what one thinks") in the lives of Black women[44]—all toward the goal of empowering Black women to resist oppression on their own terms.

One can see the influence of Third World feminism and Black feminist thought in many of the foundational texts of intersectional legal scholars. For example: Crenshaw's development of a theory to expose antidiscrimination law's erasure of woman of color and Black women in particular;[45] Matsuda's call to scholars and advocates to "look to the bottom" in crafting their theories and strategies for change;[46] and Montoya's deployment of narrative and both Spanish and English language to argue for a more contextualized and historically contingent approach to achieving justice through law.[47] All these works demonstrate the "inseparability of experience and conscience" and heterogeneous nature of analysis and argument in the work of intersectional legal scholars, as well as how and why women of color must be included in intersectional efforts and theorizing to end oppression.

IV. Characteristic Features of Intersectional Analysis

As an intellectual descendant of feminism and CRT, intersectionality theory has embraced many concepts and methods associated with both these discourses. These commonalities made intersectionality theory possible, even as intersectional feminists have uniquely internalized them to produce a distinctive scholarship that not only centers women of color but strives to take account of multiple axes of subordination and disempowerment. The next section provides a partial list of intersectionality's characteristic features, showing linkages to allied discourses.

A. Social Constructionism: Race, Gender, and Sex

One of the most important tenets of CRT is that race is socially constructed, an insight that itself was derived from other disciplines, among them sociology, ethnic studies, and feminist studies. In the mid-1980s, sociologists and ethnic studies scholars Michael Omi and Howard Winant theorized an explicitly social constructionist approach to race that would prove to be highly influential. In their theory of "racial formation," they stressed that "race is a social construction and not a fixed, static category rooted in some notion of innate biological differences." They went to explain that "[t]he construction of race and racial meanings can be understood as part of a universal phenomenon of classifying people on the basis of real or imagined attributes."[48] In other words, Omi and Winant believed that "[r]ace is a way of 'making up people.'"[49]

Social constructionism also is deeply embedded in feminist thought. Decades earlier in 1949—Simone de Beauvoir famously declared, "one is not born, but rather becomes a woman,"[50] distinguishing sex as a biological and anatomical fact from gender as an acquired identity. Following de Beauvoir's insight, Catharine MacKinnon built her dominance brand of feminist theory around the contention that male-dominated society, aided by male-dominated laws, socially constructed women as sexual objects.[51]

While these race crits and feminists rejected the biological determinism of race, gender, and/or sex, at the same time, they sought to demonstrate how social constructs based on those categories create and maintain an ideology of oppression based on white supremacy and patriarchy. For these scholars, what mattered is that race, gender, and sex are *real* in terms of lived realities and the perpetuation of social and structural inequalities.[52] Accordingly, their critiques of the law tended to focus not on individual acts of racism and discriminatory intent but on how the law itself—its rules and doctrines—construct and maintain racial and gender hierarchies. Importantly, Crenshaw's intersectional analysis of Title VII cases, discussed above, employed this social constructionist framework to show us how the legal construction of Black women, in particular, can marginalize and even erase the ways in which the "multiply burdened" experience discrimination.

B. Narrative as Methodology

CRT rejects the premise that there is or should be a singular methodology for "doing" CRT. This is not to say that CRT does not engage in or that it devalues conventional modes of legal discourse—but rather that CRT values and encourages additional and different methods of inquiry because their use and inclusion helps create a more complete and accurate body of research and scholarship. Likewise, Black and Third World feminists eschew singular approaches to doing theory and instead embrace and promote heterogeneous and diverse intellectual traditions.

One of the most effective of these cross-disciplinary intellectual traditions is the use of narrative and storytelling to perform analysis and critique.[53] Both CRT and intersectional scholars have used narrative to create understanding and empathy and illuminate the distinctive experiences of their subjects. The narrative intervention, itself not uniform in how it has been executed, remains controversial within the legal academy.[54] But whether one is talking about the intent requirement of constitutional equal protection claims,[55] antidiscrimination laws that dictate how Black women can wear their hair,[56] or the sociopathy of a criminal statute that requires determination of whether a baby born in secret, wrapped in newspaper, and hidden under the bathtub was "born alive," such that the baby's mother could be charged with manslaughter[57]—narrative methodology reminds us that storytelling already plays a central role in law and how it is made and developed. CRT and intersectional scholars appreciate that each party in every case presents their own story to the court. Consequently, it is the court's adaptation of the contested stories being told that determines the legal issues and outcomes in the case, and ultimately how the law changes and develops over time.

C. Disparate Effects and Substantive Equality

As discussed earlier, CRT arose out of a deep disillusionment and dissatisfaction with the state of U.S. civil rights jurisprudence and discourse in the post-*Brown v. Board of Education* era. In the 1970s and 1980s, CRT scholars expressed deep reservations about the ways in which the courts in civil rights cases were then shaping antidiscrimination doctrine, notwithstanding the fact that many of those courts had ruled in favor of minority plaintiffs.[58]

Early race crits argued that civil rights jurisprudence of the time had become overly concerned with the positionality and intentionality of the alleged defendants—termed "perpetrators" by legal crit Alan David Freeman[59]—while paying too little attention to the conditions and experiences of plaintiffs who had allegedly suffered as a result of it. Plaintiffs in both constitutional (equal protection) and statutory (Title VII) discrimination lawsuits were required to prove the defendant's intent to discriminate, a high hurdle that made it exceedingly difficult for plaintiffs to prevail. In a famous article, "The Id, The Ego, and Equal Protection: Reckoning with Unconscious Racism,"[60] CRT theorist Charles Lawrence made the case that such intent-based doctrines unjustifiably ignored the existence and role of unconscious bias in creating disparate effects and perpetuating subordination.

Without some type of correction, CRT scholars predicted, courts would continue to center antidiscrimination doctrine and its developing doctrinal frameworks around the nucleus of intent, totally missing the unconscious (and therefore more insidious and durable) nature of bias, racism, sexism, and misogyny. There is now almost universal agreement that these early CRT scholars were right: the intent requirement in discrimination lawsuits, particularly under the federal statutory antidiscrimination burden-of-proof frameworks, has become not only increasingly onerous and difficult for plaintiffs to overcome but now anchors everyday commonsense understandings of what discrimination means.[61] The conventional wisdom is that if one does not *intend* to offend or discriminate by some specific action, then there is no (cognizable) discrimination—regardless of the impact such actions have on the person—who is usually of color, female, and or LGBTQI+—directly impacted by the action.

The critique of the intent requirement in antidiscrimination jurisprudence is linked to another legitimating legal principle that is centrally and deeply revered in liberal discourse, that is, the principle of "formal" equality, often presented as the primary "neutral" principle on which civil rights and discrimination cases should be analyzed and decided. Here, formal equality stands in stark contrast to "substantive" equality. For race crits, substantive equality is concerned primarily with outcomes, that is, with the elimination of the conditions of social subordination, whereas formal equality is concerned primarily with facial legal classifications and equality of opportunity.[62] Accordingly, formal (Aristotelian) equality, which remains the reigning equality principle in American jurisprudence, looks to treat "likes alike" and "unalikes unalike." It attempts to resolve institutionalized and systemic forms of discrimination simply by recategorizing the "likes" and the "unalikes." Under a formal equality regime, it is sufficient, for example, that legal doctrine on its face treats men and women as "likes" or white and Black people as "likes," where once the law treated them as "unalikes." Feminist and CRT scholars maintain that such formal abstractions—promoting illusions of color-blindness and gender neutrality—tell us little about the lived experience of marginalized groups.[63]

For CRT and feminist legal scholars, formal equality itself is not necessarily the problem; most would agree that formal equality principles are necessary to create and develop just laws and a just society. However, given the persistent and undeniable fact of racial and gender disparities in health, wealth, and almost every other material measure of well-being in fully industrialized societies—as well as the complex architectures of subordination that created and shore up these disparities—formal equality simply is not enough. Not only does the formal equality paradigm severely constrict legal intervention, but it also fails to allow for an adequate consideration of context, that is, the specific conditions under which both individual and collective experiences of discrimination and status-based oppression occur. That history and context must be considered in addressing material and cultural inequality through law is an important tenet of both CRT and feminist legal theory, and one that requires revision of traditional paradigms such as formal equality. For these reasons, intersectional scholars have embraced ideals of substantive equality that are broad enough to counteract implicit bias and other structures that produce and reproduce widespread disparate effects.

V. Looking Ahead: Intersectional Activism

The history of intersectionality and CRT reveals that they have always been grounded in the experience of subordinated people and tied to social movements and activism. This fusion of theory with praxis has intensified in this decade, as crises mount and demands for transformation become more pressing. In quite a literal sense, intersectionality theory has been "taken to the streets" by a new generation of activists and organizers who employ intersectionality to assess and prioritize the needs and wants of the most marginalized among us; to describe and analyze the systemic, institutional, and cultural dimensions of inequities and disparities that are clearly correlated to race, gender, sex, and class; to strategize about how to eradicate these oppressions and move toward a more just society; to organize national and local actions to press for change at various levels and in various contexts; and to build sustained movements that will continue to grow and strengthen far into the future.

Pulling this off among and within hugely diverse progressive communities, however, is no easy task. Undoubtedly, theory will continue to anchor the values and goals of intersectional activism and guide young activists' analyses of structural subordination and their movement strategizing. But the history of CRT and intersectionality also teaches us that mastery and facility related to intellectual framing of a social movement is insufficient unless accompanied by intersectional methodologies that successfully bridge theory to practice, and vice versa.

One recent offshoot of intersectional feminism that holds much promise in this regard is social justice feminism (SJF),[64] a theory built for social activists. Introduced by critical race and feminist scholars Kristin Kalsem and Verna Williams, SJF, like its predecessors, draws from the histories and intellectual traditions of women-of-color scholars and activists. To make SJF work on the ground, it calls on all of us, whether engaging as intersectionality activists and/or theorists, to follow three guideposts to align what we actually do with what we think and say we are trying to do. First, SJF instructs us to "look to history" so that we can better "understand and then dismantle the bases of societal institutions that perpetuate hierarchies and inequities."[65] Second, it requires us to examine "the inter-relationships between interlocking oppressions" by always asking and interrogating how "race, gender, class, and other categories of identity and experiences work together to create social injustice"[66]—or, as Matsuda puts it, to "ask the other question."[67] And, finally, SJF demands that we focus on "bottom-up strategies in fashioning remedies."[68] As a methodology, SJF clearly and succinctly identifies and distills CRT's and intersectional feminism's key intellectual insights. By supplying guideposts that keep our "eyes on the prize," SJF makes what might otherwise seem overwhelming—doing intersectional feminism—practicable and within reach.

A recital of recent historical events shows the urgent need for inclusive and workable approaches such as SJF: the election of Donald Trump as president of the United States; the reemergence of white nationalism from the underground to mainstream politics; the death of George Floyd and many other unarmed Black and brown men and women at the hands of police; the COVID-19 pandemic and its undeniably disparate impact on Black, brown, and/or poor communities; the continuous and increasing violence committed against Middle Eastern and Asian American citizens and residents; the January 6, 2021, right-wing insurrection at the Capitol; and most recently, the legislative attempts to restrict teaching about "divisive concepts" (i.e., race, gender, and sex) in primary, secondary, and postsecondary education, to name only a few.

To take one example, we can see each of the three SJF guideposts at play in the work being done by the #BlackLivesMatter movement (#BLM). In its naming, strategizing, and organizing, #BLM consistently frames issues along historical trajectories of oppression and liberation, making explicit how the many injustices it identifies are interconnected and interlocking. Its activations and protests are focused squarely on providing for and empowering those most vulnerable to and impacted by such interlocking and systemic injustices. From the outset, the Black Lives Matter movement has been committed to intersectionality and social justice, broadly defined.

The Black Lives Matter network began as a hashtag call-to-action campaign to protest police brutality against Black Americans following the acquittal of George Zimmerman for the murder of Trayvon Martin.[69] The three Black organizers who originated the BLM hashtag—Patrice Cullers, Alicia Garza, and Opal Tometi—were trained and seasoned organizers within Black liberation, LGBTQI+, and immigrant rights movements and had intellectual training in various fields including Black liberation studies, transnational feminism, postcolonial studies, Black feminist thought, and queer theory.[70] As a result, intersectionality, in both principle and practice, became an anchor of the #BLM movement's approach to organizing, even though the word itself does not come up in how #BLM describes itself. The official website states:

Black liberation movements in this country have created room, space, and leadership mostly for Black heterosexual, cisgender men—leaving women, queer and transgender people, and others either out of the movement or in the background to move the work forward with little or no recognition. As a network, we have always recognized the need to center the leadership of women and queer and trans people. To maximize our movement muscle, and to be intentional about not replicating harmful practices that excluded so many in past movements for liberation, we made a commitment to placing those at the margins closer to the center.[71]

Although #BLM began as a movement aimed at the eradication of police violence against Black and Brown Americans, its mission has expanded beyond the United States and more broadly "to eradicate white supremacy and build local power to intervene in violence inflicted on Black communities by the state and vigilantes."[72] #BLM also explicitly "affirm[s] the lives of Black queer and trans folks, disabled folks, undocumented folks, folks with records, women, and all Black lives along the gender spectrum."[73] Indeed, in part due to the leadership of #BLM, the mass protests of Summer 2020— sparked by George Floyd's death at the hands of Minneapolis police officers, as well as the deaths of many other Black Americans, including Brionna Taylor and Ahmaud Arbery—often explicitly connected police violence against Black and Brown people to broader systems of state control and violence against not only Black men like George Floyd, but Black and Brown people of all genders, people of color more generally, queer communities of all races and genders, religious "outsiders" vilified as threats to American safety and democracy, and non-white migrant workers and (undocumented) immigrants.

Intersectional feminism and SJF methods are also ingrained in the work of the African American Policy Forum (AAPF), a think tank that was cofounded in 1996 by political scientist Luke Harris and none other than Kimberlé Crenshaw, who continues to serve as its executive director.[74] As stated on its homepage, the AAPF's mission is to

> connect [...] academics, activists and policymakers to promote efforts to dismantle structural inequality. We utilize new ideas and innovative perspectives to transform public discourse and policy. We promote frameworks and strategies that address a vision of racial justice that embraces the intersections of race, gender, class, and the array of barriers that disempower those who are marginalized in society. AAPF is dedicated to advancing and expanding racial justice, gender equality, and the indivisibility of all human rights, both in the U.S. and internationally.[75]

Two of the AAPF's greatest successes to date are its #SayHerName campaign and its "Under the Blacklight" initiative. The former was initiated in 2014 to raise awareness about "the often invisible names and stories of Black women and girls who have been victimized by racist police violence, and provides support to their families."[76] The latter is a panel series that began in the midst of the recent global pandemic to connect experts, advocates, and activists in various related fields, who could shed light on "the intersectional vulnerabilities that COVID lays bare."[77]

These successes, however, have been countered and threaten to be overshadowed by well-organized reactionary efforts at retrenchment and retreat to a patriarchal and white supremacist state. Specifically, in late 2020, the AAPF launched its #TruthBeTold campaign to respond to then-President Donald Trump's "Equity Gag Order," which prohibited federal agencies and others doing business with or receiving money from the federal government, from conducting diversity trainings that incorporated concepts of "systemic" racism and sexism. Although the Equity Gag Order was rescinded by President Joe Biden in early 2021, the Order "has since metastasized at the state and local level" through a proliferation of state legislative efforts (twenty-nine, as of this date) to ban the teaching of materials influenced by CRT and other similarly "divisive concepts," such as feminism and queer and transgender theory.

While profoundly disturbing and distressing, these legislative efforts in some sense reflect a long-in-coming shift in how we, in the larger society, think about freedom and equality, as applying not only to an elite class of race-, gender-, and sex-privileged Americans, but to all of us. I believe that CRT, feminism, intersectionality— each of these intellectual movements, collectively and individually—has played a significant role in wearing down the edifices of white supremacy, patriarchy, heteronormativity, and class dominance. Despite the massive backlash by those who are desperate to halt change and uphold the status quo, with intersectionality theory firmly in our "hearts and minds" and SJF methods firmly in hand, intersectional activists and scholars can continue to move us toward the promise of a multiracial democracy and just society.

Notes

1. Google search of the term "intersectional feminism" conducted on September 11, 2021, 11:02 AM.
2. Google search (using Boolean operator) "intersectionality/5 theory" conducted on September 11, 2021, 3:52 PM.
3. Joan Coaston, *The Intersectionality Wars*, Vox, https://www.vox.com/the-highlight/2019/5/20/18542843/intersectionality-conservatism-law-race-gender-discrimination (May 28, 2019, 9 AM EDT).
4. Kimberlé Crenshaw, *Demarginalizing the Intersection of Race and Sex: A Black Feminist Critique of Antidiscrimination Doctrine, Feminist Theory and Antiracist Politics*, 1989 U. CHI. LEGAL F. 139 (1989).
5. Coaston, *supra* note 3.
6. *See, e.g.*, Roberto Mangabeira Unger, *The Critical Legal Studies Movement*, 96 HARV. L. REV. 563, 567–70 (1983) (describing the CLS critique of "objectivism" in "legal-historical" and "legal-doctrinal" contexts); Robert Gordon, *Critical Legal Studies*, 10 LEGAL STUD. F. 335, 338 (1986) (describing one emphasis of CLS as "ideological masking: you take a system of legal rules or practices that pretends to be neutral and even-handed, and simply show that in operation it has been differently applied with a tilt favoring some interests over others").
7. Alan David Freeman, *Legitimizing Racial Discrimination Through Antidiscrimination Law: A Critical Review of Supreme Court Doctrine*, 62 MINN. L. REV. 1049 (1978).

8. Derrick A. Bell, Jr., *Serving Two Masters: Integration Ideals and Client Interests in School Desegregation Litigation*, 85 YALE L.J. 470 (1976).
9. Papers presented at the tenth National Critical Legal Studies Conference at Harvard Law School, titled *Minority Critiques of the Critical Legal Studies Movement*, were published in the Spring 1987 issue of the *Harvard Civil Rights-Civil Liberties Law Review*. The issue includes several now-classic CRT texts: Richard Delgado, *The Ethereal Scholar: Does Critical Legal Studies Have What Minorities Want*, 22 HARV. C.R.-C.L. L. REV. 301 (1987); Mari J. Matsuda, *Looking to the Bottom: Critical Legal Studies and Reparations*, 22 HARV. C.R.-C.L. L. REV. 323 (1987); Patricia J. Williams, *Alchemical Notes: Reconstructing Ideals from Deconstructed Rights*, 22 HARV. C.R.-C.L. L. REV. 401 (1987); Harlon L. Dalton, *The Clouded Prism*, 22 HARV. C.R.-C.L. L. REV. 435 (1987).
10. This portion draws from the accounts of several of CRT's founders and key figures, as documented in two essential critical race theory readers, both of which were edited by some of CRT's central figures and published in 1995. CRITICAL RACE THEORY: THE KEY WRITINGS THAT FORMED THE MOVEMENT (Kimberlé Crenshaw et al. eds., 1995) [hereinafter KEY WRITINGS]; CRITICAL RACE THEORY: THE CUTTING EDGE (Richard Delgado eds., 1995). In particular, *Key Writings* provides an insightful account of the founding of CRT that is, consistent with its basic philosophical tenets, deliberately explicit about the political nature of the "race intervention" into CLS.
11. KEY WRITINGS, *supra* note 10.
12. Caroline M. McKay, *Derrick Bell's Legacy: The story of Harvard Law School's first tenured African-American professor is hardly black and white*, THE HARVARD CRIMSON (May 24, 2012), https://www.thecrimson.com/article/2012/5/24/derrick-bell-harvard-law/.
13. Claire E. Parker, *Students Carry On Tradition of Race Activism at the Law School*, THE HARVARD CRIMSON (May 24, 2016), https://www.thecrimson.com/article/2016/5/24/HLS-activism-revival/ (stating that in spring of 1991, the sixty-five tenured and tenure-track faculty at HLS in 1991 included only five Black men and five white women; the remaining fifty-five faculty members were white men).
14. See Natasha H. Leland, *President to Deny Bell Extension of Leave: Professor Likely to End Tenure at Harvard; Blasts lack of Faculty Diversity*, THE HARVARD CRIMSON (Mar. 5, 1992), https://www.thecrimson.com/article/1992/3/5/president-to-deny-bell-extension-of/; McKay, *supra* note 12; Parker, *supra*, note 13.
15. Crenshaw, *supra* note 4.
16. Kimberlé Crenshaw, *Mapping the Margins: Intersectionality, Identify Politics, and Violence Against Women of Color*, 43 STAN. L. REV. 1241 (1991) [hereinafter *Mapping the Margins*].
17. *Id.* at 1244.
18. DeGraffenreid v. General Motors, 413 F. Supp. 142 (E.D. Mo. 1976).
19. Moore v. Hughes Helicopter, 708 F.2d 475 (9th Cir. 1983).
20. Payne v. Travenol, 673 F.2d 798 (5th Cir. 1982).
21. Crenshaw, *supra* note 4, at 139–40.
22. *Mapping the Margins*, *supra* note 16, at 1245.
23. *Id.* at 1244.
24. See, e.g., Matsuda, supra note 9; Mari J. Matsuda, *Beside My Sister, Facing the Enemy: Legal Theory Out of Coalition*, 43 STAN. L. REV. 1183 (1991).
25. See, e.g., Williams, *supra* note 9.
26. See, e.g., Margaret E. Montoya, *Mascaras, Trenzas, y Greñas: Un/Masking the Self While Un/Braiding Latina Stories and Legal Discourse*, 15 CHICANO-LATINO L. REV. 1 (1994).

27. Matsuda, *supra* note 9, at 323, 324.
28. Williams, *supra* note 9.
29. *Id.* at 420.
30. Montoya, *supra* note 26.
31. Montoya's use of the term "outsiders" includes "people of color, women, gays and lesbians, and the poor; in other words, members of groups who have been discriminated against historically." *Id.* at 1, n.1.
32. Angela P. Harris, *Race and Essentialism in Feminist Legal Theory*, 42 STAN. L. REV. 581, 585–607 (1990). In discussing her methodology of critiquing both MacKinnon and West, Harris writes:

    > I argue that [MacKinnon's and West's] work, though brilliant in many ways, relies on what I call gender essentialism—the notion that a unitary, "essential" women's experience can be isolated and described independently of race, class, sexual orientation, and other realities of experience. The result of this tendency toward gender essentialism, I argue, is not only that some voices are silenced in order to privilege others . . ., but that the voices that are silenced turn out to be the same voices silenced by the mainstream legal voice of "We the People"—among them, the voices of black women.

    Id. at 585.
33. The following exemplify the rich and diverse range of works that use intersectional theory to frame their analyses: CRITICAL RACE FEMINISM: A READER (Adrien Katherine Wing ed., 2d ed. 2003) (anthology of CRT and intersectionality writings by women of color); Khiara M. Bridges, *Race, Pregnancy, and the Opioid Epidemic: White Privilege and the Criminalization of Opioid Use During Pregnancy*, 133 HARV. L. REV. 770 (2020) (using an intersectional approach to examine the criminalization of opioid use during pregnancy); Devon W. Carbado and Mitu Gulati, *The Fifth Black Woman*, 11 J. CONTEMP. LEGAL ISSUES 2001) (discussing the future of intersectionality vis-à-vis performativity theory); Sumi K. Cho, *Converging Stereotypes in Racialized Sexual Harassment: Where the Model Minority Meets Suzie Wong*, 1 J. GENDER, RACE & JUSTICE 177 (1997) (using intersectionality to theorize "racialized (hetero)sexual harassment"); Russell Robinson, *Marriage Equality and Postracialism*, 61 UCLA L. REV. 1010 (2014) (identifying and critiquing the use of "postracial narratives at the heart of marriage equality argumentation").
34. In her 1994 article *Representing Truth: Sojourner Truth's Knowing and Becoming Known*, 81 J. AM. HIST. 461 (1994), Nell Irvin Painter explores the life of Sojourner Truth (born a slave around 1797 in New York, as Isabella Van Wagener) and the inaccurate reporting on her legendary *Ain't I a Woman* speech. In the article, which previewed her book SOJOURNER TRUTH: A LIFE, A SYMBOL (1996), Painter brings to light that Truth's famous oratory included neither the words "ain't I a woman" nor "arn't I a woman" (as was sometimes transcribed and published). Rather, Truth's speech, as transcribed by her friend and colleague Marius Robinson and published in the June 21, 1851, edition of the SALEM [Ohio] ANTI-SLAVERY BUGLE, reads:

    > May I say a few words? I want to say a few words about this matter. I am a woman's rights [sic]. I have as much muscle as any man, and can do as much work as any man. I have plowed and reaped and husked and chopped and mowed, and can any man do more than that? I have heard much about the sexes being equal; I can carry as much as any man, and can eat as much too, if I can get it. I am as strong as any man that is now. As for intellect,

all I can say is, if a woman have a pint and a man a quart—why cant she have her little pint full? You need not be afraid to give us our rights for fear we will take too much,-for we cant take more than our pint'll hold. The poor men seem to be all in confusion, and dont know what to do. Why children, if you have woman's rights give it to her and you will feel better. You will have your own rights, and they wont be so much trouble. I cant read, but I can hear. I have heard the bible and have learned that Eve caused man to sin. Well if woman upset the world, do give her a chance to set it right side up again. The Lady has spoken about Jesus, how he never spurned woman from him, and she was right. When Lazarus died, Mary and Martha came to him with faith and love and besought him to raise their brother. And Jesus wept—and Lazarus came forth. And how came Jesus into the world? Through God who created him and woman who bore him. Man, where is your part? But the women are coming up blessed be God and a few of the men are coming up with them. But man is in a tight place, the poor slave is on him, woman is coming on him, and he is surely between a hawk and a buzzard.

35. Cherríe Moraga & Gloria Anzaldúa, This Bridge Called My Back: Writings by Radical Women of Color (2d ed. 1983).
36. *Id.* at xxiii.
37. Audre Lorde, Sister Outsider: Essays and Speeches (1984) (collection of essays and speeches written by Lorde from 1976 to 1984, addressing issues of oppression based on race, gender, sexual identity/orientation, class, and/or age).
38. Angela Y. Davis, Women, Race & Class (1983). Davis spoke about Women, Race & Class in 2019 with New York Times writer Nelson George: "That book represents a number of positions of people who had a broader, more—the term we use now is 'intersectional'—analysis of what it means to struggle for gender equality.... At the time that I wrote it, I was interested in pointing out that gender did not have to be seen in competition with race. That women's issues did not belong to middle-class white women. In many ways, that research was about uncovering the contributions of women who were completely marginalized by histories of the women's movement, especially Black women, but also Latino women and working-class women." Nelson George, *The Greats: Angela Davis*, N.Y. Times Style Mag. (Oct. 20, 2019), https://www.nytimes.com/interactive/2020/10/19/t-magazine/angela-davis.html.
39. bell hooks, Talking Back: Thinking Feminist, Thinking Black (1989) (collection of personal and theoretical essays on racism, feminism, politics, and pedagogy).
40. All the Women Are White, All the Blacks Are Men, But Some of Us Are Brave: Black Women's Studies xxiii (Akasha Hull et al. eds., 2d ed. 1982) (anthology of writings that "illuminates and provides examples of... research and teaching about Black women").
41. *Id.*
42. Patricia Hill Collins, Black Feminist Thought: Knowledge, Consciousness, and the Politics of Empowerment (1990) (exploring and interpreting the work of Black feminist traditions and authors).
43. Patricia Hill Collins, Black Feminist Thought: Knowledge, Consciousness, and the Politics of Empowerment 17 (2d ed. 2008).
44. *Id.* at 22–25.
45. Crenshaw, *supra* note 4.
46. Matsuda, *supra* note 9.

47. Montoya, *supra* note 26.
48. Michael Omi & Howard Winant, Racial Formation in the United States 12 (3d ed. 2014).
49. *Id.* at 105. The term "making up people" originated with Canadian philosopher Ian Hacking, in the context of "how the sciences operate." *Id.* at 132.
50. Simone de Beauvoir, The Second Sex 309 (1973).
51. Catharine A. MacKinnon, *Feminism, Marxism, Method and the State: An Agenda for Theory*, 7 Signs J. Women in Culture & Soc'y 530–31 (1982).
52. *See, e.g.*, Ian Haney Lopez, White by Law: The Legal Construction of Race (10th anniv. ed. 2006).
53. Richard Delgado, *Storytelling for Oppositionist and Others: A Plea for Narrative*, 87 Mich. L. Rev. 2411 (1989).
54. *See*, Daniel A. Farber & Suzanna Sherry, Beyond All Reason: The Radical Assault on Truth in American Law (1997).
55. Charles R. Lawrence III, *The Id, the Ego, and Equal Protection: Reckoning with Unconscious Racism*, 39 Stan. L. Rev. 317 (1987).
56. Paulette Caldwell, *A Hair Piece: Perspectives on the Intersection of Race and Gender*, 1991 Duke L.J. 365.
57. Montoya, *supra* note 26.
58. *See* Crenshaw, *supra* note 4; Freeman, *supra* note 7.
59. *See* Freeman, *supra* note 7.
60. Lawrence, *supra* note 55.
61. Sandra F. Sperino and Suja A. Thomas, Unequal: How America's Courts Undermine Discrimination Law (2017).
62. Kimberlé Williams Crenshaw, *Race, Reform, and Retrenchment: Transformation and Legitimation in Antidiscrimination Law*, 101 Harv. L. Rev. 1331 (1988).
63. *See*, Catharine A. MacKinnon, *Difference and Dominance: On Sex Discrimination* (1984) in Feminism Unmodified: Discourses on Life and Law 40 (1987); Charles R. Lawrence, III, *Multiculturalism and the Jurisprudence of Transformation*, 47 Stan. L. Rev. 819,838 (1995).
64. Kristin Kalsem & Verna L. Williams, *Social Justice Feminism*, 18 UCLA Women's L.J. 131 (2010).
65. *Id.* at 175–81.
66. *Id.* at 181–83.
67. Mari J. Matsuda, *Beside My Sister, Facing the Enemy: Legal Theory Out of Coalition*, 43 Stan. L. Rev. 1183 (1991).
68. Kalsem & Williams, *supra* note 64, at 183–84.
69. Black Lives Matter, https://blacklivesmatter.com/about/ (last visited Sept. 12, 2021). *See also* Jelani Cobb, *The Matter of Black Lives: A New Kind of Movement Found Its Moment. What Will Its Future Be?* The New Yorker, Mar. 14, 2016, at 34.
70. Cobb, *supra* note 69.
71. *Herstory*, Black Lives Matter, https://blacklivesmatter.com/herstory/ (last visited Sept. 12, 2021).
72. *About*, Black Lives Matter, https://blacklivesmatter.com/about/ (last visited Sept. 12, 20201).
73. *Id.*

74. *About*, African American Policy Forum, https://www.aapf.org/about (last visited Sept. 12, 2021).
75. African American Policy Forum, https://www.aapf.org/ (last visited Sept. 12, 2021).
76. *#SayHerName Campaign*, African American Policy Forum, https://www.aapf.org/sayhername (last visited Sept. 12, 2021).
77. *Under the Blacklight*, African American Policy Forum, https://www.aapf.org/aapfcovid (last visited Sept. 12, 2021).

CHAPTER 6

SEX-POSITIVE FEMINISM'S VALUES IN SEARCH OF THE LAW OF PLEASURE

SUSAN FRELICH APPLETON

SEX-POSITIVE feminism challenges traditional stereotypes of female sexualities centered on passivity, subordination, harm, and repronormativity. It criticizes legal feminism generally for undervaluing women's pleasure, which it celebrates. Yet its proponents often struggle with charting a supportive and affirmative course for law and legal institutions, which have long fostered sex negativity.

This chapter proceeds in three parts. Part I identifies sex positivity not as a distinct theory but, rather, as a thread that runs through multiple iterations and eras of feminisms, sometimes expressly and at other times latently, as a potential answer to criticisms and problems. Along the way, the analysis demonstrates the importance of power and power disparities in sex-positive feminism and of the role of gender. Part II turns to the place of law and legal institutions in sex-positive feminism, juxtaposing prevailing critiques of law's sex negativity with promising opportunities for change. Part III continues on this note of optimism, consulting popular culture for possibilities to support a more fully developed sex-positive and feminist legal regime.

I. FUNDAMENTALS AND FOCAL POINTS

A. Identifying and Situating Sex-Positive Feminism's Values

Sex-positive feminism is less a free-standing theory than a set of values emphasizing women's agency and their access to erotic pleasure for its own sake and without shame. This set of values developed partly in opposition to long-held normative understandings of women's sexuality that were rooted in patriarchy. These understandings include the double standard which long expected men to be sexually active but respectable women to be chaste, at least until marriage;[1] the marital rape exception, which constructed heterosexual penetration of one's wife as legitimate without regard to her desires or lack thereof;[2] the erasure of the clitoris in mainstream views of what counts as sexual pleasure; and the normalization of the gendered orgasm gap.[3] In the "sexual revolution" of the 1960s and 1970s, women began to resist these norms and their underlying stereotypes.[4]

Other feminist concerns stole the limelight, however. In particular, the omnipresence of sexual violence not only presented a pressing case for reform but also gave rise to an encompassing theoretical framework called dominance feminism.[5] In this theory, men's sexual penetration of women serves as a prototype for ubiquitous gender-based oppression inherent in relationships, society, and law.[6] In addition, in their campaigns for reproductive self-determination and equality in employment, many feminists became preoccupied with pregnancy and its regulation, as well as the impact of motherhood on women's lives, relegating to the margins any preceding sexual activity.[7]

The devotion of so much feminist energy to nonconsensual sex and repronormativity left little room to consider sex purely for women's own pleasure.[8] Sex-positive feminism emerged to fill this gap. In doing so, it has pushed back not only against patriarchy and general second-class citizenship for women but also against feminist theorizing focused on dominance and on reproduction.

A rudimentary map of feminist theories might well locate the values undergirding sex-positive feminism at the crossroads of autonomy or agency feminism,[9] on one hand, and queer theory, on the other.[10] Similarly, a basic timeline might well historicize these values as part of a contemporary "third wave."[11] Yet such effort to pinpoint where sex-positive feminism's values belong oversimplifies because they are much more versatile and their relevance is much more pervasive than any neat classification might allow.

Autonomy feminism and the larger frames of equality feminism and liberal feminism that include it do provide one useful point of departure.[12] The core unifying idea is agency or self-determination. Sexual autonomy fits well on the list of aspirations for liberating women to control their own bodies and direct their own lives, free from stereotypes and socially constructed limits, at least to the same extent that men enjoy. One could certainly challenge unequal access to sex and its benefits, just as one could challenge the rule that men should always be preferred over women as administrators of decedents' estates—to cite one of the first liberal feminist victories in the U.S. Supreme Court as it began to apply the Fourteenth Amendment's Equal Protection Clause to gender-based discrimination.[13] The Court's early rulings striking down state restrictions on contraception and abortion took meaningful steps toward autonomy and gender equality but fell short of full charters for women's sexual freedom, leaving many limits in place[14] and using an analysis that consigned gender to unspoken subtext.[15] Indeed, feminist critics have taken the Court to task for grounding cases about reproductive capacity in privacy or liberty instead of gender equality.[16]

A simplistic notion of autonomy, however, cannot do all the work necessary to provide a foundation for sex-positive feminism for two reasons. First, Catharine MacKinnon's elucidation of dominance feminism necessarily raises questions about how much autonomy women can exercise at all, especially in the sexual realm, presented as ground zero of their subordination.[17] It will not do simply to feel confident about one's own autonomy, given that false consciousness can distort perceptions of the oppressed, fooling us into believing that we have some measure of free choice.[18]

Second, even without the baggage of all-out subordination and false consciousness, feminists have long recognized that sex presents dangers as well as pleasures. Feminists continue to decry the fact that rape and other sexual assaults, by intimate partners and strangers alike, have been all too frequent occurrences through the ages, with the contemporary #MeToo movement making such perils part of almost daily conversation and media coverage.[19] The famous 1982 conference at Barnard College brought feminists together to grapple with sexuality as a site of both pleasure and danger.[20] This conference and the papers it produced remain important because they show that sexual pleasure and danger not only coexist but also interact; in addition, they show that pleasure and the sexual freedom necessary for it to flourish have occupied prominent, if contested, positions on feminist agendas for many years,[21] upsetting any timeline that treats sexual pleasure as simply a "third-wave" feminist interest. Indeed, Patrick Califia was writing about lesbian sadomasochism and leather fetishes in 1979,[22] and historians have called attention to "pro-sex" feminist voices in still earlier eras, even if concerns about sexual danger marked those periods as well.[23]

Where to find a more unadulterated emphasis on pleasure? Enter queer theory. As Martha Chamallas explains, queer theory challenges identities (such as those based on sex, gender, or sexual orientation) as "entirely socially constructed, shifting, and fluid"; it values transgression of dominant norms, and it "celebrate[s] sex and a wide diversity of sexual performances, even varieties of sex some feminists regard as harmful or exploitative."[24] In debates about the relation between feminist theory and queer theory, some authorities place the two in opposition to one another,[25] others classify them as allied critical movements,[26] and still others see the feminist umbrella as sufficiently capacious to include insights from queer theory.[27] This last view allows us to reject any claim that "legal feminists have ceded to queer theorists the job of imagining the female body as a site of pleasure, intimacy, and erotic possibility."[28] Instead, we can call on queer legal theory to enrich feminist jurisprudence, complementing autonomy feminism as a foundation for a sex-positive legal approach.

Even if autonomy feminism and queer theory provide obvious coordinates for situating sex-positive feminism, however, it cannot and should not be so confined. It has influenced, and been influenced by, other varieties of legal feminism.

For example, proponents of relational or cultural feminism[29] have woven sex positivity into their analyses, in part to emphasize the difference between unwanted and wanted sex. Unwanted sex, which includes both rape and consensual but undesired sex (sometimes known as "sex against desire"),[30] causes harm, according to Robin West, a prominent standard bearer for relational feminism.[31] By contrast, and especially when fending off accusations of general sex negativity, West makes clear that she does not have desired sex of any flavor in her crosshairs. Sex is good, but only when desired.[32]

Likewise, sex positivity has purchase in postmodern feminism.[33] Informed by such ideas as Judith Butler's "gender performativity" and her exploration of its connection to sex,[34] postmodern feminism unsettles sexual pleasure itself, making it contingent and open to "multiple new constructions."[35]

Finally, intersectional feminism,[36] which became prominent beginning in the 1990s, provides yet another example of the far-reaching dissemination of sex-positive feminism's values. Consider the work, albeit outside the legal realm, of the sexuality educator and activist Ericka Hart. Self-identifying as a queer person of color with a body marked by breast cancer surgery,[37] Hart calls for "radical sex positivity," asserting that authentic and genuine pleasure requires dismantling multiple conditions of oppression, including those based on race, sexual orientation, gender identity, class, disability, chronic illness, and many more characteristics.[38] The relation between the two sets of ideas is dynamic: In Hart's hands, intersectionality augments sex-positive feminism, and sex-positive feminism brings a new dimension to intersectionality.

B. Power and the BDSM Test

Hart's project, like some of the other approaches already discussed, makes explicit the central role of power (and power disparities) in excavating sex-positive feminism and pursuing its goals. In fact, the concept of power looms large in a wide range of theoretical treatments of sexualities and sexual expression, in feminism and beyond, making it a vital part of any conversation about sex-positive feminism.[39] This prominence derives in significant part from the contributions of Michel Foucault, Jeffrey Weeks, and Ken Plummer, who have used the critical lenses of social constructionism and symbolic interactionism to debunk traditional understandings of sex as a natural drive and to reveal it, instead, as a set of scripts produced by particular cultures, reflecting each culture's values and power structures.[40] As we have seen, queer theory embraces such notions, and they are embedded as well in the classic feminist slogan "the personal is political,"[41] which envisions the quintessentially personal realm of sex as a site of political contest and, thus, of potential change. Other scholars have illuminated the connection between the quality of women's sexual lives and the power they enjoy or lack under the governing political regime.[42]

Power and pleasure take many shapes in sex-positive feminism. The poet and activist Audre Lorde writes about "the erotic as power":

> There are many kinds of power, used and unused, acknowledged or otherwise. The erotic is a resource within each of us that lies in a deeply female and spiritual plane, firmly rooted in the power of our unexpressed or unrecognized feeling. In order to perpetuate itself, every oppression must corrupt or distort those various sources of power within the culture of the oppressed that can provide energy for change. For

women, this has meant a suppression of the erotic as a considered source of power and information within our lives.[43]

Laura Rosenbury and Jennifer Rothman offer an expansive view of sexual pleasure that can complement Lorde's conceptualization of the erotic and its power:

> Individuals can experience sexual sensation and pleasure, including but not limited to orgasm, when engaging in the stimulating exchange of ideas, driving, horseback riding, listening to or playing music, mastering a new skill, gardening, discovering the answer to a knotty problem, looking at or creating art, or eating ice cream or chocolate.[44]

Given the repeated emphasis on power, sex-positive legal feminists must confront vexing questions about what to privilege when agency and the opportunity for pleasure might clash. For example, how far should law go in protecting individuals with cognitive impairment? Won't prohibiting others from engaging sexually with them, in the name of protection, also deprive them of valuable pleasures?[45]

Sexual practices that might include bondage and discipline, domination and submission, and sadism and masochism[46] (BDSM, sometimes just called SM) once posed similarly difficult questions, with Nan Hunter describing such practices as "a flashpoint and symbol of the collision among feminists over the politics of sexuality."[47] Today, however, positions have solidified, and one's take on the acceptability of such practices has become a litmus test for feminists, separating bona fide proponents of sexual freedom and pleasure from everyone else. Committed sex-positive feminists support BDSM for women who choose and enjoy it, even as it enacts their subordination and apparent powerlessness, so the thinking goes.[48] (If it turns you on and feels good, do it—so long as all participants want it.) Of course, the stakes mount when we factor in additional histories and bases of oppression, as Amber Musser's examination of "race, power, and masochism" demonstrates.[49] Regardless, BDSM plays an outsized role in feminist theorists' ongoing "sex wars"[50]—itself a distinctively masculine moniker for important disagreements and debates.

C. Beyond the Gender Binary

This introduction to sex-positive feminism might have been complete several years ago. Today, however, it requires grappling with complications that disruptions of the gender binary pose for a perspective developed to prioritize women's sexual pleasure. Activists and theorists increasingly question identities that feminists once took for granted— even beyond queer theory's destabilizing moves. According to this newer approach, for example, abortion discourse, a feminist staple, should avoid such terms as "women" in favor of "pregnant persons" or "people with uteruses" in order to include transmen and nonbinary or genderqueer individuals who might seek such healthcare.[51]

What might such considerations mean for sex-positive feminism? Surely, inclusivity will bring some gains for, at the risk of generalizing, feminists often favor inclusivity. Will it also bring losses? As we advance into the future, will inclusivity and the decentering of women obscure historical touchstones that make sex-positive feminism vibrant, defiant, and—from some perspectives—revolutionary? These historical touchstones include the host of gendered rules and patriarchal norms that sex-positive feminism explicitly sought to reject, from the double standard to the orgasm gap.[52] How would we understand the arc from sexual subordination and erotic suppression to sexual autonomy and pleasure if we changed the discourse from one about women to one about "people with clitorises"? The challenge will be to preserve sex-positive feminism's historical context while resisting its historical boundaries.

II. In Search of the Law of Pleasure

A. Law's Sex Negativity

Sex-positive feminism generally does not put much faith in law, legal institutions, or feminist jurisprudence writ large to reflect its values or advance its goals.[53] As Katherine Franke famously asked, "Is there something intrinsic to a legal approach to sexuality that deprives us of the tools, authority, or expertise to address desire head on? Can law protect pleasure? Should it?"[54]

The literature is replete with critiques of law's overall "sex negativity"[55] and the "sex exceptionalism" by which law singles out matters of sex for uniquely negative treatment.[56] For example, in addition to garden-variety criminal sentences such as incarceration, sex offenders (but not murderers or perpetrators of hate crimes) must have their names on a public registry, typically for the rest of their lives, with devastating impacts on housing and employment opportunities.[57] Even the oft-glorified legal institution of marriage, which operates as a regulatory system for sexual relationships while it purports to celebrate them, emerges from the literature as not only fundamentally repronormative[58] and artificially confining[59] but also downright punitive.[60]

B. Inroads via Liberty and Privacy

Despite the critiques, the prospects for making law more sex-positive are not entirely bleak. Certainly, in recent years, law has loosened its restrictive grip on sex. For example, in *Lawrence v. Texas*, the Supreme Court held unconstitutional a criminal prohibition on adult same-sex sexual activities in private.[61] This ruling, along with earlier cases decriminalizing some abortions and easing access to contraception, put a dent in law's longstanding repronormativity. Nonetheless, *Lawrence* falls well short of full sex positivity, in which sex would be valued purely for its own sake. The majority Justices "adopted a sex-in-service-to-intimacy approach,"[62] and they ultimately made *Lawrence* a stepping stone to the constitutionalization of same-sex marriage.[63]

Lawrence's deregulatory move has created a more hospitable legal environment for sex toys, undermining remaining prohibitions on their distribution.[64] As such pleasuring devices have come out of criminality's shadows, they have also gone mainstream. Who needs to visit specialty stores such as Good Vibrations now that Walmart and Amazon offer such products?[65]

Consistent with this deregulatory approach and emerging respect for the value of sexual agency and pleasure, the American Law Institute's revision of the Model Penal Code's sections on sexual assault and related offenses includes potential decriminalization of BDSM activities when the participants follow specific statutory requirements. Proposed section 213.10, "Permission to Use Force," with some exceptions, gives an actor an affirmative defense if the actor

> reasonably believed that in connection with the charged act of sexual penetration, oral sex, or sexual contact, the other party personally gave the actor explicit prior permission to use or threaten to use physical force or restraint, or to inflict or threaten to inflict any harm otherwise proscribed ... or to ignore the lack of consent otherwise proscribed.[66]

The Reporters' Notes indicate that this proposed section contemplates BDSM practices specifically and reflects effective advocacy by the National Coalition for Sexual Freedom.[67]

Certainly, additional pursuits such as obscenity or pornography and sex work might well merit a lighter regulatory touch in the name of liberty and sex-positive feminism.[68] Even if *Lawrence* does not go far enough, however, its doctrine—reinforced by the contemporary treatment of sex toys and the proposed BDSM defense for the Model Penal Code—demonstrates how negative rights, specifically liberty and privacy, can make room for pleasure by eliminating state-imposed obstacles and restrictions.

Yet it does not follow that, once so liberated, women's sexual pleasure will flourish unassisted. Keeping sex as a private matter only serves to protect a status quo that never gave women their sexual due.[69] In other words, given that sexual conduct and experiences follow scripts shaped by particular cultures and societies and these scripts tend to marginalize female enjoyment, realizing sex positivity requires affirmative interventions, not merely a hands-off approach, to revise the scripts. How might that be accomplished?

C. Toward Affirmative Legal Support for Sex Positivity

1. *Tort and Anti-Discrimination Law*

Recognizing law's expressive function, one reform would engage existing doctrines and remedies in ways that accord explicit value to sexual pleasure, especially in defiance of traditional norms and stereotypes. Tort law affords a setting for such progress to unfold,[70] as illustrated by a case from the European Court of Human Rights (ECHR). In *Carvalho Pinto de Sousa Morais v. Portugal*,[71] plaintiff, a woman of fifty with two children, had won damages for medical malpractice that, among other problems, accentuated pain resulting from a gynecological condition and impaired her ability to enjoy sex. On appeal by defendant hospital, the Supreme Administrative Court of Portugal reduced the award, in part because plaintiff "was already 50 years old and had two children, that is, an age when sex is not as important as in younger years."[72]

Before the ECHR, plaintiff argued that the reduction of damages constituted illegal age and sex discrimination. The ECHR agreed, finding violations of the European Convention on Human Rights, that is, the Convention for the Protection of Human Rights and Fundamental Freedoms, specifically Article 14 (anti-discrimination provision), read together with Article 8 (protecting the right to respect for private and family life).[73] According to the majority, the reduction of the award below rested on an "assumption [that] reflects a traditional idea of female sexuality as being essentially linked to child-bearing purposes and thus ignores its physical and psychological relevance for the self-fulfilment of women as people."[74] Here, age and sex had intersected to create compound disadvantages, but the ECHR's approach, sounding in sex-positive feminism, repudiated the discrimination(s) and underlying stereotypes.

Although the case stands out as a sex-positive feminist legal development, one can rightly question how far tort law in tandem with anti-discrimination measures can go in revising hegemonic sexual scripts, especially in the United States. American tort law has long devalued the claims of women generally,[75] with reported cases paying little attention to their sexual impairment.[76] Further, in the United States, at most, sex-based discrimination is prohibited, without the affirmative government obligations to eliminate it that apply in Europe pursuant to the United Nations Convention on the Elimination of All Forms of Discrimination Against Women.[77] The quest for a law of pleasure must persist.

2. *Sex Education*

By comparison to tort and anti-discrimination law, the legal regime of sex education provides more promising possibilities for ambitious, systemic change. Of course, sex education has long been a battleground in the "culture wars," with conservative voices urging that such learning should take place exclusively in the home or, if not, that it should promote nonmarital abstinence.[78] Since 1981 the United States Congress has provided to states funding for sex education programs—specifically programs promoting sexual abstinence until marriage.[79] According to one report published in 2018, more than two billion federal dollars have been spent on such programs since 1996.[80]

Thus, a legal structure exists for affirmative support for sex education, which *could be* transformative, feminist, and sex positive. The problem is that the content of existing federally funded programs is, at worst, misguided and damaging, and at best, inadequate. Although funded abstinence-centered programs purport to reduce student pregnancies and sexually transmitted diseases, data gathered over the years have shown them to be so ineffective that experts have called them "ethically flawed."[81] Moreover, such programs rely on gender stereotypes, for example, associating girls' sexual activities with contamination and presuming that girls should act as gatekeepers, policing boys and their uncontrollable sexual urges.[82] In 2010 Congress left abstinence-only grants in place but, as part of health care reform, also made funds available to the states for "personal responsibility education," which covers abstinence, contraception, and sexually transmitted diseases and is sometimes called "comprehensive sex education."[83]

More recently, Congress has renamed abstinence-only programs as "sexual risk avoidance education," but—despite the new name—the funding stream requires recipients to "ensure that the unambiguous and primary emphasis and context for each [prescribed topic] is a message to youth that normalizes the optimal health behavior of avoiding nonmarital sexual activity."[84] According to critics, the rebranding has misused the rhetoric that public health experts employ for inherently dangerous activities, "co-opted . . . terms such as 'evidence-based' and 'medically accurate and complete,' and embraced language on 'healthy relationships' and 'youth empowerment,' all of which are typically associated with programs that respect young people's decision making"—but are entirely inappropriate for programs centered on abstinence.[85]

Neither of the current funding streams, sexual risk avoidance education or personal responsibility education, is truly comprehensive. Both omit the topic of pleasure, embodying a sex-negative approach that Judith Levine has condemned as "harmful to minors."[86] Using the insights about female sexuality and orgasm offered by the philosopher Nancy Tuana, we can understand such omissions in prevailing sex education programs as "an active production" that maintains power and oppression, because "[i]gnorance is frequently constructed and actively preserved, and is linked to issues of cognitive authority, doubt, trust, silencing, and uncertainty."[87]

The United Nations Educational, Scientific, and Cultural Organization (UNESCO) has spelled out a contrasting model that defines access to sexuality education as a basic human right, lists curricular objectives for different age groups beginning with children five to eight years old, teaches that our understandings of sexuality and gender are socially constructed, and explicitly includes coverage of sexual pleasure, fantasies, and desires, to name just a few of the key elements.[88] American sex-positive feminists long for an alternative reality in which the billions of federal dollars devoted to sex education would instead support programs following models such as UNESCO's.

Because of the stunted sex education that many American students receive in elementary and secondary schools, colleges and universities have become sites for remedial learning, at least for those with access to higher education. Through initiatives prompted by the interpretation of Title IX's prohibition of sex-based discrimination in programs receiving federal funds to cover failures to address sexual harassment and violence,[89] campus sexual conduct has become a focus of not only investigatory and disciplinary mechanisms but also educational efforts designed to teach students how say "no" to unwelcome sexual activities, how to say "yes" to those that are welcome, and how to make sex an experience of mutual respect and egalitarian enjoyment. True, such measures have elicited both criticism and praise,[90] and changes in the executive branch have produced very different prescriptions for implementing Title IX's requirements in recent years.[91] Yet whether formally required by the Title IX regime or not, actively supplying young persons with the tools, information, and support necessary to negotiate "enthusiastic" consent to safe, respectful, and pleasurable sex belongs on the agenda for sex-positive feminist reform. Knowledge enables power.

Understood as a form of sex education designed to curb nonconsensual and unwanted sex and to cultivate the knowledge and self-awareness needed for wanted and pleasurable sex, this type of Title IX-inspired intervention goes far toward showing how law can attempt both to halt danger and promote pleasure, defying the classic binary. Sex education of this sort, like the UNESCO model, offers a "both/and" opportunity. Put differently, contrary to those who see modern rape reform and sex-positive feminism as in conflict with one another,[92] education has the potential to harmonize them, nurturing sexual agency and furthering social justice.[93]

III. Epilogue: A Turn to Popular Culture

Law and its limits should not end the analysis because law need not do all the work alone. Although law shapes culture and social practices, the arts and even contemporary media and entertainment can push law beyond familiar confines and help unsettle prevailing sexual scripts. As one star of popular culture, the film and television actor and producer Cate Blanchett, puts it: "[A]rt . . . is a social investigation, with the results contributing to the advancement of society. It is one of the key ways we work out, as a group, what makes sense to us and how best to communicate that awareness."[94] This part briefly turns to a few especially relevant examples from contemporary popular culture and the arts to show how such contributions to "the advancement of society" can interact with law in pursuit of sex-positive feminist objectives.

First, revisit the issue of sex education. Given the many associations of sex with shame and the many depictions of sex and information about it accessible online, young persons interested in acquiring knowledge often turn to self-help instead of relying on what their parents or schools might or might not offer. For youth, social media and electronic sources no doubt eclipse other approaches to acquiring knowledge about the world, accurate or not. On the troubling side of self-help, consider Peggy Orenstein's extensive interviews first with girls and then with boys, exposing the detrimental influence of Internet porn on their expectations and experiences of sex.[95] On the more encouraging side, consider *Teen Vogue*'s series of articles on masturbation; they introduce and validate commonplace and safe (but often unacknowledged) activities while emphasizing pleasure and its omission from most existing sex education curricula.[96] Law can facilitate (or restrict) young persons' access to do-it-yourself sex education.

Sex Education, a British television comedy series available in the United States, offers a different vision, with its cast of diverse and mostly endearing characters (students at a high school, the sex therapist parents of one, and assorted additional personalities); abundant sex talk and play; and various infatuations, some doomed and others frustratingly unrealized.[97] If one theme stands out, it is curiosity, and the show makes the students, although often awkward, refreshingly open with their curiosity about sex and their interest in finding answers to their myriad colorful questions. Although the characters often assume they should follow traditional scripts, they manage to extricate themselves, thanks to their curiosity and willingness to cross conventional boundaries in the pursuit of pleasure. One reviewer observes that the creator developed the show "in part because sex wasn't discussed in her schools growing up,"[98] and another writes that the series "explores sex as a learning experience about who you are, what you want and how you relate to other people."[99] Though presented in an amusing way, *Sex Education* could teach lawmakers and educators how candid and responsive sex education that acknowledges the place of pleasure can promote social justice.

Next, return to BDSM, an oft-visited topic in sex-positive feminism that occupies an increasingly salient place in literature and popular culture.[100] Even so, the Broadway stage production of Jeremy O. Harris's *Slave Play* broke new ground because of its frank, provocative, and vivid engagement with race, subordination, trauma, identity, and sexual pleasure—pushing all the buttons that have made BDSM so contentious.[101] Three interracial couples, straight and gay, portray for an uncomfortable, disoriented, and quite possibly "triggered" audience scenes of domination and humiliation (as master/mistress and enslaved person) while dressed in antebellum attire in a setting said to be the MacGregor Plantation. For example, Kaneisha (an African-American woman speaking in dialect) spends the opening scene twerking to Rihanna's "Work" and then moving rhythmically on the ground for her "Massa" Jim (a white man with a faux southern accent and a whip), who tries to order her to do her chores.[102]

A palpable release of tension occurs when the *Slave Play* audience learns later, in a very humorous scene, that the couples are role-playing in the name of treatment orchestrated by their oh-so-educated sex therapists, Teá and Patricia, also an interracial couple. According to one reviewer,

> Each of the black partners has been inexplicably losing sexual interest, experiencing what Teá insists is a racial-romantic "anhedonia," the inability to feel pleasure. What ensues is not only a deft exploration of what happens when love and power (acknowledged or not) collide but also an excavation of a newly common kind of political-academic talk.[103]

The denouement returns to Kaneisha and Jim, in their bedroom, with Kaneisha entreating Jim to listen to her wish, indeed, her need, for more role playing, despite Jim's initial reluctance to subject one he loves and respects to what he sees as denigrating mistreatment. Even the playwright, the director, and the actors do not agree on what this final scene portends for the future of the relationship.[104]

It should come as no surprise that critical acclaim, sold-out seats, and Harris's own identity as Black (and queer) did not save the work from backlash, including petitions from members of the Black community to shut the play down.[105] In fact, sex *is* complicated, messy, and fraught with power asymmetries.

Beyond the outcry, however, *Slave Play* boldly makes visible the individuality and the value of sexual pleasure, whether for maintaining self-regard or fostering intimate relationships. An optimistic perspective would view the play and other portrayals of BDSM in popular culture as evolving social context that could help gain legal acceptance for the Model Penal Code's proposed affirmative defense and for sex-positive feminist values and policies more generally.

Notes

1. *See, e.g.*, Susan Frelich Appleton, *The Forgotten Family Law of Eisenstadt v. Baird*, 28 Yale J.L. & Feminism 1, 22 (2016); Laura A. Rosenbury & Jennifer E. Rothman, *Sex in and out of Intimacy*, 59 Emory L.J. 809, 840 (2010).
2. *See, e.g.*, Jill Elaine Hasday, *Contest and Consent: A Legal History of Marital Rape*, 88 Calif. L. Rev. 1373 (2000).
3. *See* Susan Ekberg Stiritz, *Cultural Cliteracy: Exposing the Contexts of Women's Not Coming*, 23 Berkeley J. Gender L. & Just. 243 (2008); Nancy Tuana, *Coming to Understand: Orgasm and the Epistemology of Ignorance*, 19 Hypatia 194, 218 (2004).
4. *See* Robert O. Self, All in the Family: The Realignment of American Democracy Since the 1960s 190–98 (2012). *But see* Kristin Luker, When Sex Goes to School: Warring Views on Sex—and Sex Education—Since the Sixties 44 (2006) ("[S]ome scholars even argue that the period from roughly 1880 to 1920 saw the *only* real sexual revolution in American history, and that the cultural changes in sexuality during the 1960s and 1970s were mere aftershocks").
5. For one definition of dominance feminism, *see* Kathryn Abrams, *Sex Wars Redux: Agency and Coercion in Feminist Legal Theory*, 95 Colum. L. Rev. 304, 304 n.1 (1995) ("I use the term 'dominance feminism' to describe that strand of feminist (legal) theory that locates gender oppression in the sexualized domination of women by men and the eroticization of that dominance through pornography and other elements of popular culture").
6. Catharine MacKinnon introduced these ideas in the early 1980s. *See* Catharine A. MacKinnon, *Feminism, Marxism, Method, and the State: An Agenda for Theory*, 7 Signs 515, 541 (1982) ("Man fucks woman; subject verb object.").
7. *Compare, e.g.*, Wendy W. Williams, *Equality's Riddle: Pregnancy and the Equal Treatment/Special Treatment Debate*, 13 N.Y.U. Rev. L. & Soc. Change 325 (1984) (opposing special treatment for pregnancy), *with, e.g.*, Herma Hill Kay, *Equality and Difference: The Case of Pregnancy*, 1 Berkeley Women's L.J. 1 (1985) (advocating different treatment based on a given reproductive episode and its impact).
8. *See* Katherine M. Franke, *Theorizing Yes: An Essay on Feminism, Law, and Desire*, 101 Colum. L. Rev. 181 (2001); Mary Joe Frug, Commentary, *A Postmodern Feminist Legal Manifesto (An Unfinished Draft)*, 105 Harv. L. Rev. 1045 (1992) (examining law's sexualization, terrorization, and maternalization of the female body).
9. *See* Abrams, *Sex Wars Redux, supra* note 5, at 350–51.

10. *See* Franke, *supra* note 8, *Theorizing Yes*, at 182.
11. *See, e.g.*, Bridget J. Crawford, *Toward a Third-Wave Feminist Legal Theory: Young Women, Pornography, and the Praxis of Pleasure*, 14 MICH. J. GENDER & L. 99, 116, 122 (2007).
12. *See* MARTHA CHAMALLAS, INTRODUCTION TO FEMINIST LEGAL THEORY 25 (3d ed. 2013).
13. Reed v. Reed, 404 U.S. 71 (1971). *See generally* Cary Franklin, *The Anti-Stereotyping Principle in Constitutional Sex Discrimination Law*, 85 N.Y.U. L. REV. 83 (2010).
14. *See* Eisenstadt v. Baird, 405 U.S. 438 (1972) (invalidating a prohibition on the distribution of contraception to unmarried individuals, although fornication remained a crime); Roe v. Wade, 410 U.S. 113 (1973) (invalidating bans on most abortions while allowing postviability restrictions).
15. *See, e.g.*, Appleton, *supra* note 1, *Forgotten Family Law*, at 19–23; Ruth Bader Ginsburg, *Some Thoughts on Autonomy and Equality in Relation to Roe v. Wade*, 63 N.C. L. REV. 375 (1985).
16. *See, e.g.*, Sylvia A. Law, *Rethinking Sex and the Constitution*, 132 U. PA. L. REV. 955 (1984). Later cases about LGBTQ rights demonstrate how liberty and equality can work synergistically. *See, e.g.*, Obergefell v. Hodges, 576 U.S. 644, 672–73 (2015).
17. *See supra* note 6, MacKinnon, *Feminism, Marxism, Method, and the State*.
18. *See, e.g.*, Mari J. Matsuda, *Pragmatism Modified and the False Consciousness Problem*, 63 S. CAL. L. REV. 1763, 1777–80 (1990).
19. *See, e.g.*, Deborah Tuerkheimer, *Beyond #MeToo*, 94 N.Y.U. L. REV. 1146 (2019).
20. PLEASURE AND DANGER: EXPLORING FEMALE SEXUALITY (Carole S. Vance ed., 1984).
21. *See* Carole S. Vance, *Pleasure and Danger: Toward a Politics of Sexuality*, in PLEASURE AND DANGER, at 1; Gayle Rubin, *Thinking Sex: Notes for a Radical Theory of the Politics of Sexuality*, in PLEASURE AND DANGER, at 267. For a retrospective contextualizing this conference, *see* Nan D. Hunter, *Feminism, Sexuality and the Law*, in RESEARCH HANDBOOK ON FEMINIST JURISPRUDENCE 138, 143–44 (Robin West & Cynthia Grant Bowman eds., 2019).
22. *See* PAT CALIFIA, *A Secret Side of Lesbian Sexuality (1979)*, in PUBLIC SEX: THE CULTURE OF RADICAL SEX 157, 157–58 (1994).
23. *See, e.g.*, GEOFFREY R. STONE, SEX AND THE CONSTITUTION: SEX, RELIGION, AND LAW FROM AMERICA'S ORIGINS TO THE TWENTY-FIRST CENTURY 204–5 (2017) (discussing the 1920s); Ellen Carol Dubois & Linda Gordon, *Seeking Ecstasy on the Battlefield: Danger and Pleasure in Nineteenth-Century Feminist Sexual Thought*, 9 FEMINIST STUD. 7, 16–18 (Spring 1983) (discussing the nineteenth century).
24. CHAMALLAS, INTRODUCTION TO FEMINIST LEGAL THEORY, *supra* note 12, at 224–25.
25. *See, e.g.*, FEMINIST AND QUEER LEGAL THEORY: INTIMATE ENCOUNTERS, UNCOMFORTABLE CONVERSATIONS (Martha Albertson Fineman et al. eds., 2009); JANET HALLEY, SPLIT DECISIONS: HOW AND WHY TO TAKE A BREAK FROM FEMINISM (2006).
26. *See* CHAMALLAS, INTRODUCTION TO FEMINIST LEGAL THEORY, *supra* note 12, at 167–68, 223–27.
27. *See, e.g.*, Brenda Cossman, *Sexuality, Queer Theory, and "Feminism After": Reading and Rereading the Sexual Subject*, 49 MCGILL L.J. 847 (2004).
28. Franke, *Theorizing Yes*, *supra* note 8, at 182 (arguing that legal feminists have ceded this job).
29. Robin West, Introduction to RESEARCH HANDBOOK ON FEMINIST JURISPRUDENCE, *supra* note 21, at 1, 17.
30. *See* MARCIA DOUGLASS & LISA DOUGLASS, THE SEX YOU WANT: A LOVERS' GUIDE TO WOMEN'S SEXUAL PLEASURE 148 (Marlowe & Company 2002) (1997) (originally published under the title ARE WE HAVING FUN YET?).

31. *See, e.g.*, Robin West, *Desperately Seeking a Moralist*, 29 HARV. J.L. & GENDER 1, 23–25 (2006).
32. *See* Robin West, *Consensual Sexual Dysphoria: A Challenge for Campus Life*, 66 J. LEGAL EDUC. 804, 808, 814 (2017). *Cf.* Robin L. West, *Law's Nobility*, 17 YALE J.L. & FEMINISM 385, 388–89 (2005).
33. Laura A. Rosenbury, *Postmodern Feminist Legal Theory*, in RESEARCH HANDBOOK ON FEMINIST JURISPRUDENCE, *supra* note 21, at 127, 136.
34. JUDITH BUTLER, BODIES THAT MATTER: ON THE DISCURSIVE LIMITS OF SEX xi–xii (Routledge Classics 2011) (1993).
35. Rosenbury, *Postmodern Feminist Legal Theory*, *supra* note 21, at 136.
36. Intersectional feminism, sometimes called intersectionality, challenges the tendency of earlier feminist approaches to universalize—to generalize that all women face the same problems and challenges. At one time, the focus was principally on how race and gender intersect. *See* Kimberlé Crenshaw, *Demarginalizing the Intersection of Race and Sex: A Black Feminist Critique of Antidiscrimination Doctrine, Feminist Theory and Antiracist Politics*, 1989 U. CHI. LEGAL F. 139 (1989); Angela P. Harris, *Race and Essentialism in Feminist Legal Theory*, 42 STAN. L. REV. 581 (1990).
37. *See* Molly Sprayregen, *Sexuality Educator Ericka Hart Talks Dismantling Oppressive Systems in Sex-Ed and Beyond*, FORBESWOMEN (Mar. 24, 2020, 5:00 PM), https://www.forbes.com/sites/mollysprayregen/2020/03/24/sexuality-educator-and-activist-ericka-hart-talks-dismantling-oppressive-systems-in-sex-ed-and-beyond/#4993febb136c.
38. *See* The Annual Masters & Johnson Lecture, Radical Sex Positivity, Ericka Hart, Washington University, Nov. 12, 2019 (poster on file with the author); *Ericka Hart*, WASH. U. ASSEMBLY SERIES, https://assemblyseries.wustl.edu/people/ericka-hart/ (last visited Oct. 20, 2020) (lecture announcement).
39. Occasionally, critics claim that sex-positive feminism does not engage enough with questions of power, e.g., Elisa Glick, *Sex Positive: Feminism, Queer Theory, and the Politics of Transgression*, 64 FEMINIST REV. 19 (2000).
40. *See* 1 MICHEL FOUCAULT, THE HISTORY OF SEXUALITY: AN INTRODUCTION (Robert Hurley trans. 1988) (translating work originally published in 1976); Ken Plummer, *Symbolic Interactionism and Sexual Conduct: An Emergent Perspective*, in SEXUALITY AND GENDER 20, 26 (Christine L. Williams & Arlene Stein eds., 2002); JEFFREY WEEKS, SEXUALITY 22 (4th ed. 2017). *See also* BUTLER, BODIES THAT MATTER, *supra* note 34.
41. Carol Hanisch, *The Personal Is Political*, in NOTES FROM THE SECOND YEAR: WOMEN'S LIBERATION 76, 76–77 (Shulamith Firestone & Anne Koedt eds., 1970).
42. *See, e.g.*, KRISTEN R. GHODSEE, WHY WOMEN HAVE BETTER SEX UNDER SOCIALISM: AND OTHER ARGUMENTS FOR ECONOMIC INDEPENDENCE 1 (2018).
43. Audre Lorde, *Uses of the Erotic: The Erotic as Power*, in BLACK FEMINIST CULTURAL CRITICISM 285, 285 (Jacqueline Bobo ed., 2001).
44. Rosenbury & Rothman, *Sex in and out of Intimacy*, *supra* note 1, at 855.
45. *See* Alexander A. Boni-Saenz, *Sexuality and Incapacity*, 76 OHIO ST. L.J. 1201 (2015). *See also* Alexander A. Boni-Saenz, *Sexual Advance Directives*, 68 ALA. L. REV. 1 (2016) (proposing prospective consent to sex, in anticipation of legal incapacity).
46. Ali Hébert & Angela Weaver, *An Examination of Personality Characteristics Associated with BDSM Orientations*, 23 CANADIAN J. HUM. SEXUALITY 106, 106 (2014).
47. Hunter, *Feminism, Sexuality and the Law*, *supra* note 21, at 152. *See also* PAT CALIFIA, *Feminism and Sadomasochism (1980)*, in PUBLIC SEX, at 165 (providing a personal account of a conflict within feminism).

48. *Compare*, e.g., Margo Kaplan, *Sex-Positive Law*, 89 N.Y.U. L. REV. 89, 115–41 (2014), *with* Cheryl Hanna, *Sex Is Not a Sport: Consent and Violence in Criminal Law*, 42 B.C. L. REV. 239 (2001).
49. *See* AMBER JAMILLA MUSSER, SENSATIONAL FLESH: RACE, POWER, AND MASOCHISM (2014).
50. *See*, e.g., Abrams, *Sex Wars Redux*, *supra* note 5.
51. *See*, e.g., Alanna Vagianos, *Women Aren't the Only People Who Get Abortions*, HUFFPOST (June 7, 2019, 10:37 AM), https://www.huffpost.com/entry/women-arent-the-only-people-who-get-abortions_n_5cf55540e4b0e346ce8286d3 ("Transgender men and other gender-nonconforming folks get abortions, too. But no one's discussing how the recent abortion bans will affect them"). *See generally* Jessica A. Clarke, *They, Them, and Theirs*, 132 HARV. L. REV. 894 (2019).
52. *See* section I titled "Identifying and Situating Sex-Positive Feminism" *supra*.
53. *See*, e.g., Rosalind Dixon, *Feminist Disagreement (Comparatively) Recast*, 31 HARV. J.L. & GENDER 277, 301 (2008) ("In most instances, sex-positive feminists thus reject treating law as a direct vehicle for achieving sex-positive aims and approach questions relating to the regulation of sex and sexuality in strongly libertarian terms").
54. Franke, *Theorizing Yes*, *supra* note 8, at 182–83.
55. *See*, e.g., Rosenbury & Rothman, *Sex in and out of Intimacy*, *supra* note 1, at 812–23 (surveying the "sex-negative landscape").
56. As Jennifer Rothman explains, the term "sex exceptionalism" refers to the way in which laws "treat sex differently from other activities. This sex exceptionalism often exhibits a negative view of sex that either dismisses the value of sex or, worse yet, treats it as something harmful. This sex negativity can also manifest as sex normativity in which the state channels sex into preferred forms while excluding or penalizing other forms of sex." Jennifer E. Rothman, *Sex Exceptionalism in Intellectual Property*, 23 STAN. L. & POL'Y REV. 119, 120 (2012).
57. *E.g.*, Smith v. Doe, 538 U.S. 84 (2003); Connecticut Dept. of Pub. Safety v. Doe, 538 U.S. 1 (2003). *See* Ira Mark Ellman & Tara Ellman, "FRIGHTENING AND HIGH": THE SUPREME COURT'S CRUCIAL MISTAKE ABOUT SEX CRIME STATISTICS, 30 CONST. COMMENT. 495 (2015) (exposing an error underlying public registration for sex offenders).
58. *Cf.* Dixon, *Feminist Disagreement*, *supra* note 53, at 301.
59. *See* Elizabeth F. Emens, *Monogamy's Law: Compulsory Monogamy and Polyamorous Existence*, 29 N.Y.U. REV. L. & SOC. CHANGE 277 (2004).
60. *See* Melissa Murray, *Marriage as Punishment*, 112 COLUM. L. REV. 1 (2012).
61. 539 U.S. 558 (2003).
62. Rosenbury & Rothman, *Sex in and out of Intimacy*, *supra* note 1, at 823.
63. *See* Katherine M. Franke, Commentary, *The Domesticated Liberty* of Lawrence v. Texas, 104 COLUM. L. REV. 1399, 1414–16 (2004); Melissa Murray, *Rights and Regulation: The Evolution of Sexual Regulation*, 116 COLUM. L. REV. 573, 574–76 (2016).
64. Reliable Consultants, Inc. v. Earle, 517 F.3d 738 (5th Cir. 2008). *See also* Tokyo Gwinnett, LLC v. Gwinnett Cty., 940 F.3d 1254 (11th Cir. 2019) (ongoing litigation challenging a ban on selling sexual devices).
65. *Compare* LYNN COMELLA, VIBRATOR NATION: HOW FEMINIST SEX-TOY STORES CHANGED THE BUSINESS OF PLEASURE (2017), *with* Katie Van Syckle, *Sex Sells. Walmart Buys In*, N.Y. TIMES, July 4, 2019, at B1. *See also Invisible Wearable Wireless Remote Control*

Adult Toy-Style 9-Fequency Silent Rechargeable Massager—You Can Enjoy Different Modes With Your Partner to Suit Your Needs, AMAZON, https://www.amazon.com/Invisible-Toy-Style-9-Frequency-Rechargeable-Massager-You/dp/B0867HX9R4/ref=sr_1_2?dchild=1&keywords=sex+toy+stores&qid=1590176013&sr=8-2 (last visited Oct. 16, 2020) (showing availability of sex toys for purchase on amazon.com). Public advertising persists as a point of contention, however. *See* Jackie Rotman, *Vaginas Deserve Giant Ads, Too*, N.Y. Times, June 25, 2019, at A31.

66. MODEL PENAL CODE § 213.10 (AM. LAW INST., Tentative Draft No. 4, 2020).
67. *See id.* at 336–41.
68. *See, e.g.*, Adrienne D. Davis, *Regulating Sex Work: Erotic Assimilationism, Erotic Exceptionalism, and the Challenge of Intimate Labor*, 103 CALIF. L. REV. 1195 (2015); Frug, Commentary, at 1052–59; Kaplan, *Sex-Positive Law, supra* note 48, at 99–115.
69. *See* Frances E. Olsen, *The Myth of State Intervention in the Family*, 18 U. MICH. J.L. REFORM 835, 857 n.57 (1985) ("Privatizing sex reduces discussion that might lead to change. Sex is private in part because the state makes it private and because keeping sex private seems to serve the interests of those with power").
70. *See, e.g.*, Susan Frelich Appleton, *Toward a "Culturally Cliterate" Family Law?*, 23 BERKELEY J. GENDER L. & JUST. 267, 323–26 (2008).
71. Carvalho Pinto de Sousa Morais v. Portugal, 17484/15 Eur. Ct. H.R. (2017).
72. *See id.* at ¶ 16 (quoting the Supreme Administrative Court). This court also reduced the award in part because plaintiff did not need to hire a housekeeper given that her children's ages meant she "only needed to take care of her husband." *Id.*
73. *Id.* (holding).
74. *Id.* at ¶ 52. The majority proceeded to cite previous cases with male plaintiffs in their fiftiess in which courts had found that the inability to have "normal sexual relations had affected their self-esteem and resulted in a 'tremendous blow' and 'severe mental trauma.'" *Id.* at ¶ 55.
75. *See generally* MARTHA CHAMALLAS & JENNIFER B. WRIGGINS, THE MEASURE OF INJURY: RACE, GENDER, AND TORT LAW (2010).
76. *See* Appleton, *Toward a "Culturally Cliterate" Family Law?, supra* note 70, at 323–26; *see also* Hugh v. Ofodile, 929 N.Y.S.2d 122, 126 (App. Div. 2011) (Richter, J., dissenting in part) (criticizing reduction in damages because "[i]t was entirely reasonable for the jury to conclude that painful sexual relations for someone aged 40 [here, a woman] could cause significant future pain and suffering").
77. *See* Carvalho Pinto de Sousa Morais, 17484/15 Eur. Ct. H.R. at ¶¶ 25–26 (noting how the Convention requires "State Parties [to] condemn discrimination against women in all its forms, agree to pursue by all appropriate means and without delay a policy of eliminating discrimination against women" and welcomes "efforts to combat gender stereotypes"). Although President Jimmy Carter signed this treaty, the United States never ratified it.
78. *See generally* LUKER, WHEN SEX GOES TO SCHOOL, *supra* note 4.
79. Soc'y for Adolescent Health & Med., *Abstinence-Only-Until-Marriage Policies and Programs: An Updated Position Paper of the Society for Adolescent Health and Medicine*, 61 J. ADOLESCENT HEALTH 400, 401 (2017).
80. Jesseca Boyer, *New Name, Same Harm: Rebranding of Federal Abstinence-Only Programs*, 21 GUTTMACHER POL'Y REV. 11, 11 (2018).
81. *See* Soc'y for Adolescent Health & Med., *Abstinence-Only-Until-Marriage Policies*, *supra* note 79, at 401.

82. *See, e.g.*, Jennifer S. Hendricks & Dawn Marie Howerton, *Teaching Values, Teaching Stereotypes: Sex Education and Indoctrination in Public Schools*, 13 U. PA. J. CONST. L. 587, 597–98 (2011).
83. 42 U.S.C. § 713.
84. 42 U.S.C. § 710(b)(2)(A).
85. Boyer, *New Name, Same Harm*, *supra* note 80, at 11–12.
86. JUDITH LEVINE, HARMFUL TO MINORS: THE PERILS OF PROTECTING CHILDREN FROM SEX (2002).
87. Tuana, *Coming to Understand*, *supra* note 3, at 195.
88. UNITED NATIONS EDUCATIONAL, SCIENTIFIC AND CULTURAL ORGANIZATION, INTERNATIONAL TECHNICAL GUIDANCE ON SEXUALITY EDUCATION: AN EVIDENCE-INFORMED APPROACH 16, 34, 48, 50, 70 (rev. ed. 2018).
89. 20 U.S.C. § 1681(a). Title IX was enacted in 1972. Its use to combat sexual misconduct on campus intensified in 2011, when the Office of Civil Rights wrote to colleges and universities with guidance on such application. Letter from Russlynn Ali, Assistant Sec'y, Office for Civil Rights, U.S. Dep't of Educ., to Colleague 1–2 (Apr. 4, 2011) [hereinafter Dear Colleague letter], http://www2.ed.gov/about/offices/list/ocr/letters/colleague-201104.pdf (rescinded).
90. *Compare, e.g.*, Jacob Gersen & Jeannie Suk, *The Sex Bureaucracy*, 104 CALIF. L. REV. 881 (2016), *with, e.g.*, Susan Frelich Appleton & Susan Ekberg Stiritz, *The Joy of Sex Bureaucracy*, 7 CALIF. L. REV. ONLINE 49, 58–59 (2016), http://www.californialawreview.org/the-joy-of-sex-bureaucracy/.
91. *Compare* Dear Colleague letter *with* Press Release, U.S. Department of Education, SECRETARY DEVOS TAKES HISTORIC ACTION TO STRENGTHEN TITLE IX PROTECTIONS FOR ALL STUDENTS (May 6, 2020), https://www.ed.gov/news/press-releases/secretary-devos-takes-historic-action-strengthen-title-ix-protections-all-students (discussing 2020 regulations). *See also* PRINCIPLES OF THE LAW, STUDENT SEXUAL MISCONDUCT: PROCEDURAL FRAMEWORKS FOR COLLEGES AND UNIVERSITIES xvii–xviii (AM. LAW INST., Council Draft no. 4 2020) (noting changes in the federal approach over the years).
92. *See, e.g.*, Aya Gruber, *Anti-Rape Culture*, 64 U. KAN. L. REV. 1027 (2016); Aya Gruber, *Rape, Feminism, and the War on Crime*, 84 WASH. L. REV. 581 (2009).
93. Other contemporary projects have similar goals. *See, e.g.*, Deborah Tuerkheimer, *Slutwalking in the Shadow of the Law*, 98 MINN. L. REV. 1453, 1455–56 (2014) ("By taking aim at rape while expressly promoting the virtues of female sexuality, SlutWalk situates itself where anti-rape and pro-sex norms converge").
94. Cate Blanchett, *I'm Not "Mrs. America." That's the Point.*, N.Y. TIMES (May 21, 2020), https://www.nytimes.com/2020/05/21/opinion/cate-blanchett-art-mrs-america.html?searchResultPosition=4 (opinion piece on "The Big Ideas: Why Does Art Matter?"). *See also* Susan Frelich Appleton & Susan Ekberg Stiritz, *Going Wild: Law and Literature and Sex*, 69 STUDIES IN LAW, POLITICS, AND SOCIETY (SPECIAL ISSUE: FEMINIST LEGAL THEORY) 11, 16–17 (2016) (explaining the benefits of studying law through sex and sex through literature, specifically four works of fiction that illuminate the legal regulation of sex).
95. PEGGY ORENSTEIN, GIRLS AND SEX: NAVIGATING THE COMPLICATED NEW LANDSCAPE 32–43 (2016); PEGGY ORENSTEIN, BOYS AND SEX: YOUNG MEN ON HOOKUPS, LOVE, PORN, CONSENT, AND NAVIGATING THE NEW MASCULINITY 39–71 (2020).

96. Gigi Engle, *How to Masturbate if You Have a Vagina: Fingers and Toys Tips*, TEENVOGUE (Nov. 1, 2019), https://www.teenvogue.com/story/how-to-masturbate-if-you-have-a-vagina; Gigi Engle, *How to Masturbate if You Have a Penis: 9 Tips and Techniques*, TEENVOGUE (Nov. 12, 2019), https://www.teenvogue.com/story/how-to-masturbate-if-you-have-a-penis. *See* Nona Willis Aronowitz, *How to Masturbate Without Porn*, TEENVOGUE (Mar. 4, 2020), https://www.teenvogue.com/story/how-to-masturbate-without-porn; Sammy Nickalls, *Health Benefits of Masturbation*, TEENVOGUE (Apr. 1, 2020), https://www.teenvogue.com/story/health-benefits-of-masturbation. Recall that United States Surgeon General Joycelyn Elders was forced to resign her position in 1994 because she condoned teaching schoolchildren to masturbate as a way to avoid HIV/AIDS. *See* Douglas Jehl, *Surgeon General Forced to Resign by White House*, N.Y. TIMES, Dec. 10, 1994, §1, at 1.
97. *Sex Education* (Netflix 2019).
98. Sarah Larson, "SEX EDUCATION," SEASON 2: THE DOCTOR IS IN, THE NEW YORKER (Jan. 18, 2020), https://www.newyorker.com/culture/on-television/sex-education-season-2-the-doctor-is-in.
99. James Poniewozik, *A Sweet Teen Comedy of Modern Lust*, N.Y TIMES, Jan. 10, 2019, at C1.
100. *See*, e.g., Cossman, *Sexuality, Queer Theory, and "Feminism After,"* supra note 27, at 868–74 (analyzing the BDSM-themed film *Secretary*); Amber Jamilla Musser, *BDSM and the Boundaries of Criticism: Feminism and Neoliberalism in* Fifty Shades of Grey *and* The Story of O, 16 FEMINIST THEORY 121 (2015).
101. JEREMY O. HARRIS, SLAVE PLAY (2019). *See* Elizabeth A. Harris & Reggie Ugwu, *Was Broadway Ready for "Slave Play"?*, N.Y. TIMES, Feb. 2, 2020, at AR4.
102. HARRIS, SLAVE PLAY, *supra* note 101, at 9–28.
103. Vinson Cunningham, BLACK AND WHITE IN "SLAVE PLAY" AND "TO KILL A MOCKINGBIRD," THE NEW YORKER (Dec. 17, 2018), https://www.newyorker.com/magazine/2018/12/24/black-and-white-in-slave-play-and-to-kill-a-mockingbird.
104. *See* Harris & Ugwu, *Was Broadway Ready for "Slave Play"?*, *supra* note 101.
105. *See* Karu F. Daniels, *Rising Playwright Jeremy O. Harris Addresses Backlash Over Controversial* Slave Play, THE ROOT (Jan. 7, 2019, 3:13 PM), https://www.theroot.com/rising-playwright-jeremy-o-harris-addresses-backlash-o-1831545447; Juan Michael Porter II, DESPITE THE HYPE, I HATED "SLAVE PLAY," COLORLINES (Oct. 15, 2019, 10:11 AM), https://www.colorlines.com/articles/despite-hype-i-hated-slave-play-op-ed (op-ed). The controversy is reminiscent of that surrounding Kara Walker's provocative silhouettes depicting sexual performances in enslavement. *See* Adrienne D. Davis, *Bad Girls of Art and Law: Abjection, Power, and Sexuality Exceptionalism in (Kara Walker's) Art and (Janet Halley's) Law*, 23 YALE J.L. & FEMINISM 1 (2011).

CHAPTER 7

FEMINISM IS DEAD, LONG LIVE FEMINISMS

A Postmodern Take on the Road to Gender Equality

CAMILLE GEAR RICH

The King is Dead, Long Live the King. Centuries ago this cryptic phrase echoed loudly through stone castle halls, announcing the smooth transfer of power between male hands.[1] The call was used to mark the death of one patriarchal ruler and the immediate installment of another. The governing view was, when the King passed away there was a need to communicate order, peace, and stability. These values were served by the announcement that a new king stood ready immediately to take the old leader's place. The refrain crushed revolutionaries and nobles scheming for the Crown, dropping a curtain of silence in front of any would-be upstarts.[2] Given the purpose of this antiquated refrain, it may seem strange to title a chapter on postmodern feminist legal theory as a riff on this patriarchal pronouncement. Yet the refrain *Feminism Is Dead, Long Live Feminisms* perfectly captures the postmodern ironies of the present moment. For feminists are in a period of transition, facing a sea of changes—ones that could merely represent a change of the guard between generations or, alternatively, suggest the rise of new forms of power with multiple feminist voices reflecting growth within the field. In this extended period of transition, the first and the second waves—the earlier iterations of feminism, have been asked to contend with a discordant contemporary third wave of feminist legal theory. Postmodern feminists are uniquely positioned to assist all feminists as they make sense of this transition, to map the frictions between feminisms and find greater meaning. The postmodern feminist looks at the instant moment and asks, what does this transition of power between generations, variations, and waves of feminism mean? Postmodern feminists also take seriously those voices critical of feminism's "will to power," its desire to have determinative force within certain legal domains. For this concern as well, postmodern feminism provides some tentative answers, modeling how we can maintain a critical, engaged stance—one that resists making any one voice of feminism king or queen, and instead ensures that feminist understandings that govern certain areas of law are responsive to the ever-growing field of different feminist voices.[3]

This chapter provides a historical account of the emergence of postmodern legal feminism and a map for future growth of this field. While postmodern feminism has been represented as part of the third wave, it has not fully been integrated within this wave of scholarship. Its analytic tools are selectively borrowed by scholars, and often misunderstood. Therefore, section I offers a narrative of postmodern theory's emergence and partial absorption into feminism. In the discussion I offer insights to demonstrate why postmodernism was initially resisted by many feminists, and I review common critiques and concerns raised about postmodernism's role in complicating feminist politics and legal reform. Section II offers a closer examination of postmodern concepts and tools that have been underutilized in feminist legal theory. I suggest that if postmodern tools were more fully integrated, we could produce more meaningful conversations within and between second and third-wave feminism. Specifically, I identify those the areas of postmodern theory feminists have left relatively unexplored and demonstrate how full employment of postmodern tools better positions feminists to meet the challenges of the day. This discussion is critical, as the incomplete integration of postmodern theory has created key blockages in contemporary feminist theorizing and activism. Feminists still struggle to see how a new multivocal field of feminisms can be harmonized for collective action purposes. Section III provides illustrations, demonstrating how postmodern legal feminist analysis provides a much-needed burst of explanatory power to contemporary discussions in the field. For postmodernism calls on us to ask necessary questions about feminism's selective uptake in contemporary law and discourse, and to ask who benefits from its selective incorporation and use. These questions are critical in understanding the partial and fractured feminist gains of the twentieth and twenty-first century.

I. Feminism Meets Postmodernism—The Early Years

Our story begins in the late 1990s, when feminism was entering into a period of transition that later became known as the third wave.[4] As others have explained, feminists use a wave metaphor to denote particular historical periods within feminism. Each historical period features different versions of feminist theory in ascendance, distinct political struggles between feminisms, and key legal innovations and interventions that are hallmarks of the gender equality struggles of that period. Additionally, each historical wave is understood to build a foundation and spark conversations that influence subsequent waves. Authors within the field historicize and constitute the various "waves" of feminism differently.[5] For the purposes of this discussion, I characterize the first wave of feminism as the period covering the nineteenth century through the mid-twentieth century, a period of advocacy stretching over 100 years in which women fought to secure basic citizenship rights for women. The early movement focused on the right to vote, the right to hold property, and the right to keep one's wages and secure employment in one's profession. Key figures included Elizabeth Cady Stanton and Susan B. Anthony.[6] Key political events include the Declaration of Sentiments at the Seneca Falls Convention in 1848. First-wave feminists challenged all legal and cultural barriers that led to the systematic exclusion of white women from social and political life.[7] This group later evolved into what today is recognized as liberal feminist theory in the second wave of feminism.[8]

The second wave of legal feminism grew out of a period of feminist activism in the 1960s and 1970s and continued through the late twentieth century. This wave featured three distinct strands of feminism: (1) liberal feminism, (2) cultural/relational or difference feminism, and (3) radical/dominance feminism.[9] As explained above, liberal feminism is the heir of first-wave feminism. Liberal feminists focused on ensuring women were offered the same opportunities on the same terms as men in the workplace (pay, benefits, and promotions), political life (election to office), and features of economic life (taxes, inheritance, and property division).[10] Liberal feminists also forwarded claims of sexual and reproductive freedom that cast off feminine modesty norms and assumptions about the inevitability of motherhood.[11] Specifically, sexual freedom, in the form of access to abortion and birth control, were key in liberal feminists' view to women being able to secure valuable employment opportunities and enjoy their private lives on the same terms as men. Liberal feminist reforms led to a broad array of legal cases providing redress for gender bias, including constitutional cases under the Fourteenth Amendment and statutes addressing gender inequality such as Title VII and Title IX.[12] Ruth Bader Ginsburg has become a key symbol of liberal feminist thought given her decades-long litigation career addressing these issues, and her role on the Court recognizing women's struggle for equal rights. This brand of feminism, arguably, has had the most transformative effects on society.

Cultural feminism, also referred to as difference feminism or relational feminism, was a separate strand of theory in the second wave. This version of feminism posited that women were fundamentally different from men (whether as a cultural or biological matter) and as a consequence stressed different values such as collective work, mutual respect, nonaggression, and nonviolence.[13] Key figures writing from a cultural perspective include Carol Gilligan, outside the law,[14] and legal theorists Robin West, Adrienne Rich, and Clare Dalton. Cultural feminism posited that men, and patriarchal culture more generally, needed to be changed by women and influenced by feminine values for society to evolve. Although this school of thought produced a rich array of scholarship, and it played some role in transforming understandings about the characteristics required for leadership and the norms of geopolitics, it also represented certain dangers for feminists. Some felt difference arguments naturalized and justified the containment of women in the domestic and mothering sphere; consequently, it proved a less attractive model for parties seeking legal reform.[15] Innovations like the Family and Medical Leave Act of 1993[16] and other parenting policies that offered both men and women opportunities to devote themselves to parenting and family care are the clearest part of its legal legacy.

Dominance or "radical" feminism is the last school of feminism associated with the second wave. Although it attracted many adherents, it was most closely associated with legal scholar Catharine MacKinnon. Radical feminists charged male domination and patriarchy with fundamentally shaping all governmental and social institutions. They explained that unless norms that routinized and normalized male norms were challenged, women would be unable to claim space to reimagine their lives outside such domination.[17] Consequently, they were critical of liberal feminists' attempts to gain access to rights and privileges under existing regimes, claiming this only reinvested in the norms of patriarchy. They also were critical of cultural feminists' claims about women's special voice, arguing instead that this perspective was the product of women's systematic subordination and therefore should not be romanticized. Radical feminists' legal legacy came in the form of legal initiatives to address marital rape and date rape, as well as an attempt to impose stricter restrictions on pornography.[18]

Third-wave feminism crested in the 1990s, with the leading voices coming from Mari Matsuda and Angela Harris, intersectional feminists within critical race theory (CRT).[19] These feminists challenged the ways in which second-wave feminism bracketed or ignored race, class, and sexuality in its account of gender. They demonstrated that the universal experience, grand theory approach of the second-wave feminists was flawed and incomplete, as it failed to accurately represent the experiences of large classes of women. CRT feminists' analyses revealed that many feminists writing from a liberal, cultural, or dominance perspective were actually speaking about the interests of a narrow slice of wealthy, privileged, white women who had claimed center stage in feminist theorizing.[20] Criticism came from other quarters as well. Queer theorists like Janet Halley also raised questions about whose interests were served by the grand, totalizing accounts of liberal, cultural, and dominance feminism. Halley additionally wondered whether it was time for theorists to step back from these second-wave accounts to take stock of the ways in which feminist legal advances actually played a role in some forms of women's domination.[21] Third-wave scholars revealed the ways in which earlier feminists fell prey to heterosexism and questioned the second-wave decision to solely privilege the feminine gender in understanding the destructive effects of patriarchy. Third-wave theorists sought space to interrogate how gender constructions *writ large* subordinated men as well.[22] Finally, the later stages of the third wave of feminism also surfaced generational critiques of feminism, with younger feminists expressing a strong interest in exploring sex positivity and connecting gender oppression to a larger array of crosscutting political issues.[23] Importantly, as feminism moved from its second wave into the third wave, there was some anxiety as the number of critical feminisms grew. Many worried that there was no workable strategy for reintegrating or connecting all the new distinct feminist voices that had emerged.

Despite the great range of internal variation, some unifying themes in third-wave feminists' perspectives became clear. Third-wave feminists challenged the grand theorizing of second-wave feminists and the attempts these earlier feminists made to speak for all women.[24] Specifically, they complained that "grand theorizing" privileged white, female, cisgender, wealthy feminists' interests in an uncritical fashion.[25] Third-wave feminists also borrowed tools and methodology from a school of philosophical thought called postmodernism.[26] Strictly speaking, these engagements were selected and limited, concentrating primarily on a strand of postmodern analysis called "discursive analysis," as well as postmodern models of identity construction that stressed positionality—the idea that race, sex, and other identity features shape perspectives in ways that must be accounted for in theory. Specifically, CRT feminists were primarily interested in recognizing the intersectional and multidimensional nature of identity, and how identity categories change and shift in response to social conditions. Their goal was to establish that until feminist legal theory recognized that its grand theory account was merely a partial, positionally located account of knowledge, it would not be able to engage substantial portions of the constituency that claimed womanhood as an identity.[27] Some, like Patricia Williams, did this by employing a style that illustrated how a partial, shifting identity perspective, one that harmonized multiple, competing personal identity claims, could produce unique, powerful forms of knowledge.[28] CRT feminists, however, did not purport to take on the philosophical commitments of poststructuralism more broadly. Indeed, most third-wave feminists rarely claimed the label "postmodernist," and they declined to discuss large areas of postmodern theory. Second-wave feminists, therefore, needed another source to test the merits and liabilities of postmodern thought from a feminist perspective.[29] Mary Joe Frug's draft article, *A Postmodern Legal Feminist Manifesto,* seemed to offer this opportunity by directly engaging with the promise and the threat postmodern theory posed for feminist theorizing.

Fate prevented Mary Joe Frug from fully introducing postmodernism to legal feminism, as she was violently murdered before she finished her article on the topic. *A Postmodern Legal Manifesto* was ultimately published as a draft in the *Harvard Law Review.* Even in its unfinished form, the article became a seminal piece in feminist circles. In the article, Frug primarily focused on the liberatory potential of "discursive" analysis.[30] Specifically, she wanted feminists to understand that "human experience [i]s inescapably [filtered] through language."[31] Consequently, she explained, when we look to law for reform, we should also recognize that the law has naturalized and seeks to further establish certain understandings about the female body that feminism, by contrast, seeks to challenge.[32] She identified three ways law has constituted the female body: maternalization, terrorization (as a body that knows fear), and sexualization. Frug noted that feminist legal interventions designed to address the problems women faced as a result of these gender constructions were equally implicated and typically further built on these constructions. As she explained, feminist legal scholars must struggle to disrupt certain naturalized fundamental understandings about women. To be successful, Frug argued, feminists must understand that legal language itself is a site for struggle, as how bodies are legally positioned and described is also a method of control.[33]

Frug's second goal was to make feminists more comfortable with intersectionality and the multiple ways in which other identity categories complicate our understanding of the category of women. She recognized that complicating the category of woman was seen as a threat to future feminist organizing, but she hoped to reassure feminists that finding a common core of interests was still possible as long as we understood that these commonalities were often socially (and legally) constructed. As she explained:

> [W]omen stand in a multitude of places, depending on time and geographical location, on age, sexual preference, health, class status, religion and other factors. Despite these significant changes, there remains a common residue of meaning that seems affixed, as if by nature, to the female body. Law participates in creating that meaning.[34]

In order to embrace this more complicated understanding of women, feminists needed to become more comfortable with theorizing from a place of partiality and incompleteness, and they should expect to discover moments of critique and claims of erasure. She explained that, like intersectional/CRT feminist scholars, she was "in favor of localized disruptions and against totalizing theory," yet her draft did not address how one might reintegrate or harmonize newly emerging dissenting feminist voices.[35]

Most of the subsequent work that explicitly adopts a stance of engagement with postmodern legal feminism tends to explore Frug's primary themes.[36] For example, Laura Rosenbury, ten years later after the *Manifesto*, distills postmodern feminism into three general principles based on Frug's understandings: (1) the law constitutes and subordinates women as it describes them, (2) language constructs and discourse play a key role in this process, and (3) feminists must not only be anti-essentialist but must also challenge and disrupt the so-called sex/gender binary.[37] The sex/gender binary posits that the only two natural categories of gender are men and women, and typically each gender possesses traits that make it fundamentally different from the other.[38] Over the years, even when feminist scholars explicitly embraced Frug's ideas, they also remained deeply concerned about postmodernism's deconstructive impulse. Specifically, they worried that dissecting the category of women into competing political claims would compromise future feminist theory and political activism.[39]

On the ten-year anniversary of Frug's piece, Maxine Eichner summarized second-wave feminists continuing concerns, explaining that: (1) postmodernism's antiessentialist commitments would prevent broader claims from being made about women's experiences of subordination, (2) postmodernists naiveté about the workings of power made them reject and critique the gains achieved through feminist projects, and (3) postmodernism's relativism and critique of reforms could result in nihilism.[40] Regina Austin and Elizabeth Schneider similarly in their ten-year anniversary review of Frug's piece view postmodernism with a respectful, but wary, eye were concerned about the challenges it created for general theorizing and political activity.[41]

Concerns about postmodern nihilism seemed to come to a head when queer theorist Janet Halley announced in her book *Split Decisions* that it might be time to take a break from feminism and engage in a broader deconstructive project that analyzed how particular strands of Second-wave feminism, wittingly or unwittingly, played a role in various forms of social marginalization and domination.[42] Second-wave feminists began to feel that their concerns about postmodern inquiries were solidly warranted. However, a small group of scholars continued to offer hope that postmodern feminist approaches could be made responsive to some of the traditional concerns framed by second- and third-wave scholars. For example, Ben Golder argued that postmodern legal feminism could engage in reform projects while preserving its deconstruction-based ends. He suggested that feminists must perpetually engage with and deconstruct what we mean by "woman"—the subject of feminist legal theory—and what we mean by "law"—charting the multiple ways law manifests outside formal legal structures.[43] Directing our eye to the reform of both of these sites, he explained, provides feminism with the affirmative reform project feminist legal theory demands.

Frug certainly recognized that understandings from poststructuralism were deeply troubling to feminists, in particular the "decentered, polymorphous, and contingent ... understanding of the subject,"[44] as well as the need to "challenge singular, dominant interpretations."[45] However, she perhaps underestimated the degree that concerns about fractures within the category of women would play in discouraging interest in postmodern feminism.[46] At the time the piece was published, Martha Minow worried that "postmodernism risks a relativism that conflicts with feminist commitments to political engagement, and with a continuing ability to name authoritatively, and to fight against, effectively, what is oppressive."[47] The same concerns endured fifteen years later. As Ann Bartow opined, deconstruction was a threat to efforts at legal reform. She explained, "[y]ou can't theorize your way into an abortion, or out of a rape. You... have to rely on a legal system that may fail you, in which case you can work to improve it so that others don't suffer as you did."[48] Yet Frug was convinced that no matter how many legal papers were written deconstructing women, it would not be possible to eliminate the category of women from reform projects.[49] This perhaps was shortsighted, as deconstruction of the concept of woman has had successively more impact over the years on activist politics. Gender fluidity has become more a part of feminist conversations, as well as specific discussions about the role of transgender women and cisgender women in framing feminist concerns. Feminists have been presented with the claims of transgender women about unique forms of misogyny and domination in their lives. Cisgender women have been challenged on their social privilege; Cisgender women, in turn, have asked whether transwomen have the same insights about lifelong gender marginalization as cisgender feminists do.[50] Some of the seemingly abstract questions about womanhood have taken on flesh and critical importance as we move through the twenty-first century.[51]

Readers will encounter different accounts of the various waves of feminism; however, the critical point missed in most other narratives is that postmodern legal tools were introduced in feminist circles in the midst of a separate process of disaggregation in feminist legal theory *that preceded postmodernism*. Intersectional theorists and queer theorists raised issues about partiality and exclusion within feminist theory, but these issues were separate from the larger theoretical project of poststructuralism. Because poststructuralism seemed a vehicle to further advance and accelerate these already apparent disaggregating forces, second-wave feminists saw little value in embracing it fully.

As a consequence, they did not look far beyond Frug's essay in thinking about whether postmodernism has something to offer in addressing contemporary gender questions. This was unfortunate. For, as we will see in section II, although Frug started an important conversation about postmodern thought, key parts of postmodernism remain largely unexplored in feminist legal theory. Ironically, many of the unexplored aspects of postmodern thought are directly responsive to the challenges of the present moment for a disaggregated and potentially discordant third wave of feminist legal theory.[52]

II. Long Live Feminisms: The Role of Poststructuralism in a Feminist Future

Postmodern feminists are right to wonder, what might have happened had Fate granted Frug more time to continue with her ideas, or if another author picked up the mantle and the responsibility for fully educating the feminist community about the value of postmodern theory. In the thirty years that have passed, postmodern scholars have moved forward, sometimes misunderstood, primarily devoted to the task of establishing the value of discursive theory. In this section, I take up the remaining project of further fleshing out postmodern thought, offering four additional analytic tools that should be included in feminists' understanding of the scope of the postmodern toolkit. These tools include (1) an understanding of the power of hegemony, (2) the value of strategic essentialism,[53] (3) the critical role of genealogy in understanding social conditions, and (4) the importance of dialectics in understanding rights and reform. Again, some of these tools promise to help feminists negotiate our current historical moment which is shaped by contradiction and multiplicity. A foundation in postmodern theory would provide scholars with stronger, firmer ground for future theorizing.

A. Feminism by Any Other Name Is Just as Sweet: The Power of Hegemony

The postmodern feminist understands that true power rarely announces itself.[54] Rather, the more influential a perspective is on our social understandings, the more it fades into the backdrop. These ideas have reached what we call "hegemony." They are so culturally central that their relevance is no longer seen as a point of debate or question. Stated differently, hegemony is achieved when an idea is so integral to social understandings that people feel compelled to frame their thoughts around this idea instead of questioning whether they "agree" with the proposition offered. For example, the idea that children should be protected from sexual abuse is hegemonic. It is no longer seen as an issue of debate; instead, we question how to achieve this goal. Similarly, the idea that pets have feelings has achieved hegemonic status. One might debate how deeply these feelings are held or when they are triggered, but these are questions of degree and kind, rather than challenges to the proposition of an animal's capacity to feel. The ability to direct people's attention to a particular theme or set of conversations inevitably advances a particular set of interests. Most feminists would agree that the basic propositions of feminism, such as "women deserve equal rights," are so deeply ingrained in American society that they are hegemonic. We focus on strategies for achieving equality, or questioning what true equality means, rather than being forced to defend the basic idea that women deserve equal esteem in social life. Importantly, when ideas achieve hegemonic status, the strategies for further advancing those ideas are transformed. Opposition in the face of hegemony looks and feels different. Feminists would benefit from reflecting on this understanding as they face today's obstacles to feminist goals. For example, an understanding of hegemony provides a different perspective on how we manage opponents of feminism. Typically, these figures claim they are not feminist, but, when asked in substance about their values, they agree that women deserve fair and equal treatment.[55] Opposition to the label "feminist" continues, but the heart and soul of the feminist project can be carried forward, even by those who disavow the movement.[56]

Similarly, Janet Halley's allegation that feminists face a brain drain, as scholars are more attracted to schools of critique outside feminism, takes on a different valence.[57] Should feminists care whether a particular scholar calls herself a feminist or works in masculinity studies, critical race theory, or queer theory? Postmodern feminists recognize that scholars doing the work of feminism can call themselves whatever they like, as long as they in substance are forwarding key conversations about gender equality. The slow, steady and regular progress from seminal feminist work may not proceed in the same fashion, but feminists can, through radical recombination and reclaiming of scholars in other fields, allow feminist theory to proceed in a new form.[58] If the goal, in all of these respective domains—critical race theory, queer theory, masculinity studies and critical whiteness studies—is to disrupt, trouble, and critique the operation of patriarchal power and the instantiation of white male privilege, postmodern feminists would advise that we should claim, cite, and incorporate this work into a feminist canon to keep conversations moving forward.[59]

B. Strategic Essentialism

Feminist scholars would also benefit from a more active and purposeful engagement with the concept of "strategic essentialism." Created by literary critic and philosopher Gayatri Spivak, *strategic essentialism* posits that we can unite for activism or legal reform by identifying certain features of gender as sites that can be used to understand patterns of marginalization and to address structures that instantiate gender subordination and inequality.[60] Scholars employing this tool are careful to acknowledge that the generalizations they make about women, or any other category, are limited, contingent, capable of reevaluation, and only to be used for a specific purpose.[61] They recognize that claiming a standard, homogenized position for legal or theoretical claims is an act of power; generalizations always silence certain voices. Consequently, any feminist position that purports to speak for women should be contingent, used for a limited purpose, open for revision, and employed in a responsible way. This concept is explored in greater detail in section III.

C. Dialectics

Postmodern feminism has much to offer if feminists embrace an understanding of dialectics as well. Although there is some feminist work in which scholars suggest there is a dialectical relationship between various feminist voices of critique, the foundational work to establish the value of this concept has not been done.[62] This problem is corrected here.

There are two distinct ways of employing an understanding of dialectics in feminist legal theory. The first approach posits that in any dialogue about a set of interests, certain oppositions or dualities will surface. If these dualities are analyzed properly, one sees that these contrasts are only made possible because of the respective, *socially constructed* positions/locations of the two parties involved.[63] The relationships between the two conflicting parties are the product of a particular historical and social context; consequently, we learn important lessons by studying the friction between these opposing forces over time—including gradual changes, advances, and improvements that are produced through dialogue between the opposing positions. Each exchange between two opposing groups provides an incremental understanding about the framing of particular social movements and identities, and what it means for larger society. The second insight from dialectics is the understanding that advances are always followed by a period of containment and an undermining of the solutions created.[64] This proposition is a central part of CRT, as CRT posits that advances in rights should be expected to suffer a period in which the new exercise of rights faces resistance as these rights are captured or limited by social practices or new rules. In the end, rights are stalled in various ways and prevented from achieving their full liberatory potential.[65]

Once applied, these two approaches to dialectics allow us to gain great insight about the future of feminism after the third wave. Specifically, the strand of dialectics exploring learning through dialogue provides guidance for how to structure engagement with the multivocal third wave of feminism. Instead of seeking integration, learning is produced by *examining areas of friction*. These areas of friction between different schools teach us something about where feminism is at in a particular historical and cultural moment. Taken together, as different feminist voices speak out, the collective story of feminist progress will become more complicated. It will include stories where the concept of woman articulated is experienced as inclusive—welcoming in new women to the conversation, and yet, the same concept of woman will be revealed at another moment to inflict a kind of violent erasure for other communities. No definition will be perfect or complete—the frictions instead guide us. Mapping these multiple voices is complicated, but it is the only way to chart a nuanced path forward.

The separate strand of dialectics (on the containment and retrenchment of rights) will also help feminists unify for common cause. An understanding of retrenchment allows feminist scholars who are proud of prior rights campaigns to embrace the critiques of new schools of feminism as they analyze the limitations of current rights models. Perspectives must change. Feminists must expect that with any rights regime, the tools created will be limited or exploited by antifeminist forces. This is why we must remain vigilant for new opportunities and listen to voices of critique. Indeed, an understanding of dialectics helps feminist contextualize past gains and understand why many feminist innovations often end up serving the interests of men. This is the nature of dialectics—there is always one step forward and possibly one or two steps back. As structures are created to empower vulnerable groups, these structures become recognized as sources of power and institutionally vested interests find ways to resist the changes or convert these structures to their own needs. Also, facts on the ground may change such that originally imagined solutions are an ill fit with the changing nature of cultural realities and material conditions. In short, liberal feminists may have won many victories, but they will learn a lot from listening to third-wave feminists' concerns about how these reforms have been redeployed and turned against women.

In summary, postmodernism teaches that feminists must build with the understanding that we must be prepared to revise or even destroy what we have created as more marginalized voices come to the table seeking representation through the feminist movement. As more women's voices are included in feminist conversations, we can craft reforms that speak to the oppositions that have been surfaced through dialogue and aim through gradual steps, as well as comprehensive reforms, to give all women a voice.

D. Genealogy

Finally, feminist legal theory should more forthrightly explore the insights from a postmodern study of genealogy. Genealogical studies ask us to consider why certain feminist voices are recognized and given more sway than others. Indeed, the study of genealogy forces important questions for second-wave feminism. What did we learn from the contests in the 1980s and 1990s between difference feminism, liberal feminism, and dominance feminism? What accounts for the larger influence of liberal feminism in certain spaces, and the influence of dominance feminism in others? Are there ways in which all of these accounts are taken up by a larger system of difference-making and discipline to serve privileged interests?

Janet Halley has been one of the most vocal critics calling for attention to these kind of questions. As she explains, one must study the "real world proliferation of forms of organized power that break the bounds of the classically imagined state," which can be referred to as the study of "governance" structures—a broad term that encompasses "the expansion of institutional forms and the social practices they govern."[66] Indeed, if we surface how and why particular forms of feminism are taken up by social movements and government authorities, and identify the value choices that guide this selective uptake, feminist activists and scholars can make better decisions that serve an ever growing field of feminist interests.

III. The Fourth Wave of Feminisms: Long May They Rule

Examples help illustrate how a fuller embrace of postmodern legal feminism will improve discussions in feminist legal theory, allowing for full engagement with a broader range of voices.

A. The #MeToo Movement

The #MeToo movement, perhaps more than any other gender-centered contemporary movement, enables us to see how poststructuralist understandings allow us to potentially meaningfully integrate different intersectional feminist voices. Originally, "MeToo" was conceptualized as a movement for service workers and Black and brown women in public spaces subject to conditions of sexual harassment as part of paid labor.[67] It was the ultimate expression of BIPOC (Black, indigenous, women of color) intersectional feminism and deeply valuable to the BIPOC women whose lives it described. However, as it bubbled up in social media circles and turned into the #MeToo movement, it was more often associated with economically privileged women in society, mostly white Hollywood actresses.[68]

This transformation and pivot in the movement's history is given greater depth with an understanding of genealogy—an approach which traces which feminist voices get heard, why, and how feminist initiatives can become allied with existing power structures. For example, the #MeToo movement could be perceived as being in lockstep with the carceral state, as the ideal proposed feminist solution to workplace sexual abuse was to incarcerate men who had raped and assaulted privileged (mostly white) women in the past with impunity. This approach worked well with existing feminist reforms to extend statutes of limitation for rape—reforms entirely consistent with familiar players like dominance feminism and liberal feminism. But none of the fundamental understandings about how sexual harassment plays out in the workplace were shaken up when the #MeToo movement allowed discussion of workplace sexual abuse to play out in this form. Importantly, debate had ceased to speak to an equally monumental and intractable problem: the economic and sexual exploitation of working-class women of color.[69]

Yet #MeToo also gives us an opportunity to see how an understanding of dialectics provides new pathways to political activism. By dialoguing with Black and brown women, many of the privileged white women in the #MeToo movement recognized the silencing and marginalization of BIPOC voices as time went on. Consequently, they used their social privilege to redirect attention back to the original injuries of working-class Black and brown women that were the original progenitors of the MeToo conversation. The two groups of women could have understood their duality and opposition as forcing them into "conflict"; instead, they understood themselves as related, representing a broader range of economic interests frustrated and sexually taxed by a patriarchal system. In the course of this redirection, strategic essentialism (recognizing that the construct of woman is contingent, temporary, and used to surface issues) was important, as disempowered men also were given space to discuss the ways in which they had been coerced into providing sexual services in the workplace in service of patriarchal power. The conversation also refocused attention on materialist feminist understandings, as we began to explore how the tipping wage forces Black and brown women in the service industry to suffer systematic sexual and economic exploitation.[70] The conversation continues to extend, as we have begun a larger examination of the sexual and emotional labor Black and brown people are forced to shoulder because of the ways wages are structured in the service industry. Specifically, we have learned how tipped employees (who earn less than the minimum wage) are forced by economic necessity to uncomplainingly endure sexual and racial harassment as part of their jobs.

Additionally, an understanding of dialectics presupposes that once we identify and dismantle exploitative cultural practices like tipping culture, new spaces, places, and cultural practices for demanding sexual favors from "desired" bodies will emerge. The concept of hegemony completes the picture, explaining why opposition forces, organizing to prevent social and political advances in addressing sexual harassment, felt it necessary to represent themselves as allies in the struggle. Sexual harassment harms occupy a hegemonic, foundational space—this hegemony requires people to treat sexual overtures backed with economic force as a form of economic harm. Consequently, opposition by conservatives today is framed as though they are merely calling for moderation in addressing sexual harassment; they request individuals be given second chances or absolution for harms committed in the past, rather than claiming no harm occurred. This understanding of hegemony helps us understand that would-be conservative "allies" that call for restraint are really just finding ways to articulate hard core resistance in a more culturally palatable form.

B. Reproductive Rights

Reproductive rights provide another space in which we can see the value added by the application of postmodern legal feminism's tools. Recently, the reproductive rights field has faced a racial reckoning, a potential crisis initiated by intersectional/CRT feminists raising essential questions about the ethics of reproductive rights movement heroines and their role in systemic and cultural racism. Margaret Sanger has been cited for her embrace and advocacy of eugenicist ideas that discouraged reproduction by Blacks and the disabled.[71] Similarly James Marion Sims, the so-called father of modern gynecology, is regarded as far more sinister when we acknowledge that most of his discoveries resulted from experimenting and torturing unanesthetized Black slaves in his "care."[72] Reproductive rights organizations that ignored this history have attempted to take steps to correct course, but prior masking of this history prevented feminists from recognizing the connections between current welfare law policies that discourage Black and brown mothers from reproducing, and failing to provide financial support for mostly BIPOC mothers of poor children. The postmodern feminist's interest in genealogy helps us understand how the erasure of these issues has shaped feminist rights arguments in the present.

Additionally, postmodern feminists would sound the alarm about the language drift in reproductive rights conversations. Much of the debate centers on abortion and contraception concerns. These issues, on the one hand, do serve the interest of socially privileged women who need child-free years of academic study and career advancement to achieve their goals. However, we must also be aware that this framing simultaneously serves the established interests of capital and employers, as these forces want to ensure easy access to young female, child-free labor.[73] Postmodern feminists remind us to use discursive tools to chart how certain interests are erased. We must ask whose interests are served when reproductive rights are described as the interest in "controlled fertility," the freedom to (1) not reproduce, (2) schedule one's reproduction, or (3) revive one's reproductive capacity when fertility wanes. This framing renders invisible the interest of poor mothers eager to start a family early in an organic matter with the assistance of the state. Scholars such as Dorothy Roberts have long called upon us to shift the conversation to include these women's voices,[74] to understand that reproductive rights must also cover accidental or planned early exercise of one's capacity to reproduce. Harmonizing these different feminist perspectives creates opportunities for coalition and results in a different kind of activism. As we move forward, reproductive rights advocates will also need to think about forming temporary contingent coalitions including trans and cis gender "women" interested in maximizing women's choices, broadly construed, around childbearing.

IV. Conclusion

My hope is that my original call at the start of the chapter, *Feminism Is Dead, Long Live Feminisms* seems even more compelling to the reader. The statement is a provocation to old and new students of feminist legal theory. Feminism, of course, is not dying. Rather, it is everywhere, but this creates a new set of problems. Certainly, older feminist dialogues have ceded ground to make room for new iterations. Additionally, the path to aggregating perspectives, negotiating tensions, and learning from them is much harder than the grand theorizing of the past. However, poststructuralist theory provides us with tools that help us understand how and why we must harmonize these multiple strands of feminism and take insight from discordance as well. As the chapter shows, charting a *genealogical* course among feminisms and tracing prior constructs, dialogues, and histories are essential to understand new emerging voices. Additionally, a proper understanding of dialectics and conflict will help us anticipate and make good use of new conflicts as they emerge.

The next wave of feminism will be filled with promise once we recognize that feminism, because of prior partial gains, must now adopt a more self-critical and reflective approach to exercising power and influence. Gone are the days of one grand, singular theory that can be offered to unite women. Thankfully, women (and men) today feel free to explore their full selves within feminism, and feminism now must lean into the insights offered by the multiple perspectives of various feminist camps in all their specificity. Some comfort should come from knowing that this multivocal approach to feminism will extend the reach and influence of feminist ideas, as well as increase activism. But we cannot make sense of today's conflict-ridden, internally fractured but generative field of feminist voices without an understanding of postmodernism. Postmodern feminists know we must chart emerging conflicts, weather cycles of rights retrenchment and reform, and rely on tentative models that we are willing to revise when newly emerging feminist perspectives teach us something new. The fourth wave of feminism will be The Era of Feminisms. Long may the chorus flourish. Long may these various feminist voices rule.

Notes

1. Philip Graham Ryken, King Solomon: The Temptations of Money, Sex, and Power 18 (2011).
2. *See, e.g.,* Daniel H. Sexton, The Struggle for Power in Early Modern Europe: Religious Conflict, Dynastic Empires, and International Change 8 (2009).
3. Janet Halley asks us to consider where in the current legal order have feminist ideas gained inclusion, and to be critical of these "selective engagements" and incorporation of feminist theory into governance structures. She refers to this as the study of "governance." Janet Halley, *Preface: Introducing Governance Feminism, in* Janet Halley et al., Governance Feminism x, xi (2018).
4. Bridget J. Crawford, *Toward a Third-Wave Feminist Legal Theory: Young Women, Pornography and the Praxis of Pleasure*, 14 Mich. Gender & L. 99, 101–103 (2007); *see also* Claire Snyder, *What Is Third Wave Feminism: A New Directions Essay*, 34 Signs 175, 175 (2008).
5. Martha Chamallas, Introduction to Feminist Legal Theory 15 (2d ed., 2003) (discussing three stages of feminist theory as liberal, cultural and dominance feminism).
6. *See generally* Andy Bowers & Katherine Lee, The Selected Papers of Elizabeth Cady Stanton and Susan B. Anthony: An Awful Hush, 1895 to 1906 (Ann D. Gordon et al. eds., 2013). The racially restricted nature of these early suffrage campaigns are discussed elsewhere, but here we note that many white suffragists firmly believed that white women should be granted the right to vote before Black men, as well as sidelined and marginalized many Black women suffragists during this period.

7. E.g., Rachel F. Moran, *How Second Wave Feminism Forgot the Single Woman*, 33 HOFSTRA L. REV. 223, 228 (2004)(explaining that first wave feminist activism helped secure women's suffrage).
8. CHAMALLAS, *supra* note 5, at 32 (discussing continuation of traditions and pursuit of basic equal rights by early feminists in the 1800s with liberal feminists in the 1970s).
9. *Id.* at 15–22.
10. Moran, *supra* note 7, at 262.
11. *Id.*
12. *E.g.*, Roe v. Wade, 410 U.S. 113 (1973).
13. CAROL GILLIGAN, IN A DIFFERENT VOICE (1982).
14. CHAMALLAS, *supra* note 5, at 53
15. *Id.* at 61–63.
16. 29 U.S.C. §§ 2601–2654 (2006).
17. Catharine A. MacKinnon, *Difference and Dominance: On Sex Discrimination*, in FEMINISM UNMODIFIED: DISCOURSES ON LIFE AND LAW 32 (1987).
18. CATHARINE A. MACKINNON, TOWARDS A FEMINIST THEORY OF STATE 196 (1989) (discussing pornography's contribution to the normalization of violence against women).
19. *Id.*
20. *E.g.*, Mari J. Matsuda, *Love, Change*, 17 YALE J.L. & FEMINISM 185, 186 (2005)
21. JANET HALLEY, SPLIT DECISIONS: HOW AND WHY TO TAKE A BREAK FROM FEMINISM 4–10 (2006).
22. J. JACK HALBERSTAM, GAGA FEMINISM: SEX, GENDER, AND THE END OF NORMAL (2012) (explaining how sexual politics has upended traditional feminism by, in part, questioning and decentering the concept of womanhood, as well as the female body); Ki Namaste, *The Politics of Inside/Out: Queer Theory, Poststructuralism, and a Sociological Approach to Sexuality*, 12 SOC. THEORY 220, 227 (1994)("[A] poststructuralist structure would make sense of the manner in which heterosexuality is itself a social construct.").
23. Crawford, *supra* note 4, at 101. Crawford argued that this earlier group of feminist conversations did not attract younger third wave feminists and that "third-wave feminists bemoan the older generation's perceived monopoly on feminist leadership and its failure to articulate a broadly inclusive (or even relevant) feminist movement." She noted these third wave feminists were outside the legal academy and "approach problems of gender inequality as organizers, activists, writers, or scholars in disciplines other than law."
24. AUDRE LORDE, SISTER OUTSIDER 117 (1984)("To allow women of color to step out of stereotypes is too guilt provoking, for it threatens the complacency of women who view oppression only in terms of sex.").
25. Although second wave feminism had occasionally mentioned queer and/or women of color's concerns, there was a tendency to treat these groups as a footnote problem—using their experiences as particularly egregious examples of sexism or homophobia without questioning the larger cultural context of these conversations. *E.g.*, Catharine A. MacKinnon, *From Practice to Theory, What Is a White Woman, Anyway?*, 4 YALE J.L. & FEMINISM 13, 17 (1991)(explaining that women of color experience a heightened form of sexism) ("The problem here ... does not begin with a failure to take account of race or class, but with the failure to take account of gender.").
26. Helene Shugart, Catherine Egley Waggoner, D. Lynn O'Brien Hallstein, *Mediating Third Wave Feminism: Appropriation as Postmodern Media Practice*, 18 CRITICAL STUD. IN

MEDIA COMMC'N 194, 196 (2001) (discussing postmodern, third wave feminism in popular culture).
27. *E.g.*, Angela Harris, *Race and Essentialism in Feminist Legal Theory*, 42 STAN. L. REV. 581, 581–584 (1990).
28. PATRICIA WILLIAMS, THE ALCHEMY OF RACE AND RIGHTS (1991).
29. Postmodern theory was regarded as being a more masculine iteration as it appeared in Critical Legal Studies and was not treated as part of the third wave.
30. Mary Joe Frug, *A Postmodern Legal Manifesto (An Unfinished Draft)*, 105 HARV. L. REV. 1045 (1992).
31. *Id.* at 1046.
32. *Id.* at 1040–1050. As Frug explained, "legal rules permit and sometimes mandate the terrorization of the female body"; "permit and sometimes mandate the maternalization of the female body"; and "permit and sometimes mandate the sexualization of the female body."
33. *See id.*
34. *Id.* at 1049.
35. *Id.* at 1046.
36. Ruth Colker, *The Example of Lesbians: A Posthumous Reply to Mary Joe Frug*, 105 HARV. L. REV. 1084 (1992); Martha Minow, *An Incomplete Correspondence: An Unsent Letter to Mary Joe Frug*, 105 HARV. L. REV. 1097 (1992).
37. For further discussion, *see* Laura A. Rosenbury, *Channeling Mary Joe Frug*, 50 NEW ENG. L. REV. 305 (2016).
38. Laura A. Rosenbury, *Postmodern Feminist Legal Theory*, in RESEARCH HANDBOOK ON FEMINIST JURISPRUDENCE 127 (2019).
39. Maxine Eichner, *On Postmodernist Feminist Legal Theory*, 36 HARV. C.R.-C.L. L. REV. 1, 24 (2001).
40. *Id.* at 4–7.
41. Elizabeth Schneider worries that "pushing postmodern feminism's antiessentialist critique to its limits threatens self-destruction. We are left standing at the edge of an "epistemological abyss," where the infinity of difference defies defining woman, thereby rendering feminism an intellectual impossibility." Regina Austin & Elizabeth M. Schneider, *Mary Joe Frug's Postmodern Feminist Legal Manifesto Ten Years Later: Reactions on the State of Feminism Today*, 36 NEW ENG. L. REV. 1 (2010).
42. HALLEY, *supra* note 21.
43. Ben Golder, *Rethinking the Subject of Postmodern Feminist Legal Theory: Towards a Feminist Foucaultian Jurisprudence*, 8 S. CROSS U. L. REV. 73, 74 (2004).
44. Frug, *supra* note 30, at 1046.
45. *Id.* at 1048.
46. *Id.* at 1051.
47. Minow, *supra* note 36, at 1104 (discussing Sandra Harding, *The Instability of the Analytical Categories of Feminist Theory*, in FEMINIST THEORY IN PRACTICE AND PROCESS I, 4–5 (Micheline R. Malson et al. eds., 1989).
48. Ann Bartow, *Review Essay: Janet Halley, Split Decisions: How and Why to Take a Break From Feminism*, 26 WINDSOR Y.B. ACCESS JUST. 391, 391 (2008).
49. Frug, *supra* note 30, at 1051–1052.
50. Kathleen Stock, *Why Self-Identification Should Not Legally Make You a Woman*, The Conversation (Oct. 1, 2018), https://theconversation.com/why-self-identification-sho

uld-not-legally-make-you-a-woman-103372 (objecting to trans women identifying as women because of the author's belief that doing so displaces cis women).
51. *Compare* SHEILA JEFFREYS, GENDER HURTS: A FEMINIST ANALYSIS OF THE POLITICS OF TRANSGENDERISM 7 (2014) (arguing that trans women's identification as women is tantamount to men asserting their power over cis women to define what womanhood is) *with* ANDREA DWORKIN, WOMAN HATING 185–186 (1974) (arguing that the hatred of transgender people must end; implying that it is not inconsistent with feminist goals).
52. Linda Alcoff, *Introduction, in* THE SECOND WAVE: A READER IN FEMINIST THEORY 4 (Linda Nicolson ed., 1997) (describing poststructuralist-intervention as focusing on the work of Lacan and Derrida and attempting to avoid the traps of essentializing the category of women, as was common in some forms of second-wave feminism).
53. Gayatri Spivak, *In a Word, in* THE SECOND WAVE: A READER IN FEMINIST THEORY (Linda Nicolson ed., 1997).
54. Throughout postmodern feminism's short history, there have been multiple feminists who, while not declaring themselves proponents of postmodernism, have conducted analyses shaped by poststructualist tools and understandings. *See* DRUCILLA CORNELL, BEYOND ACCOMMODATION: ETHICAL FEMINISM, DECONSTRUCTION, AND THE LAW (1991); Drucilla Cornell, *The Doubly-Prized World: Myth, Allegory and the Feminine*, 75 CORNELL L. REV. 644 (1990); Martha Minow, *Justice Engendered*, 101 HARV. L. REV. 10 (1987); Martha Minow & Elizabeth V. Spelman, *In Context*, 63 S. CALIF. L. REV. 1597 (1990). Joan Chalmers Williams, *Dissolving the Sameness/Difference Debate: A Post-Modern Path Beyond Essentialism in Feminism and Critical Race Theory*, 1991 DUKE L.J. 296 (1991). Even Reva Siegel's analysis in *Why Equal Protection No Longer Protects* is a discursive analysis. Reva Siegel, *Why Equal Protection No Longer Protects: The Evolving Forms of Status-Enforcing State Action*, 49 STAN. L. REV. 1111 (1996). Some of those recognized as part of the field also were not writing in law. Indeed, the number of scholars who explicitly describe themselves as poststructuralist feminists is relatively small. *E.g.*, Marie Ashe, *Mind's Opportunity: Birthing a Poststructuralist Feminist Jurisprudence*, 38 SYRACUSE L. REV 1129 (1987). Other feminist scholars used principles from poststructuralist theory but did not declare themselves postmodern legal feminists.
55. Austin & Schneider, *supra* note 41, at 25.
56. For examples of scholars doing postfeminist work, *see* Aya Gruber, *A "Neo-Feminist" Assessment of Rape and Domestic Violence Law Reform*, 15 J. OF GENDER RACE & JUST. 583 (2012) (using novel antisubordination arguments to critique policing and prosecutorial reforms dedicated to the feminist aims that the author embraces).
57. Janet Halley, *Which Forms of Feminism Have Gained Inclusion?, in* Janet Halley et al., GOVERNANCE FEMINISM 23, 45 (2018).
58. Angela Harris, *Transgender Rights, and Whipping Girl: A Transsexual Woman on Sexism and the Scapegoating of Femininity*, 36 WOMEN'S STUD. Q. 315 (2008) (book review); Jessica Knouse, *Using Postmodern Feminist Legal Theory to Interrupt the Reinscription of Sex Stereotypes through the Institution of Marriage*, 16 HASTING'S WOMEN'S L.J. 159 (2005).
59. Roland Barthes, *The Death of the Author in* IMAGE, MUSIC, TEXT 142, 148 (Stephen Heath trans., 1977).
60. RANAJIT GUHA & GAYATRI CHAKRAVORTY SPIVAK, SELECTED SUBALTERN STUDIES 13 (1988).
61. *E.g.*, Jijian Voronka, *The Politics of "People with Lived Experience" Experiential Authority and the Risks of Strategic Essentialism*, 23 PHIL., PSYCHIATRY, & PSYCHOL. 189 (2016).

62. Alcoff, *supra* note 52, at 5 ("the political meaning of feminism cannot be derived from any pre-given concept of 'womanhood' but must evolve as different political actors, men as well as women, struggle over how gender is to be understood."). Although Alcoff does not explicitly mention dialectics, this understanding is loosely based on ideas accessed through this concept.
63. Madan Sarup, An Introductory Guide to Post Structuralism and Postmodernism 91 (1993) (discussing Nietzche's concept of dialectics).
64. Blake Emerson, *Dialectic of Color Blindness*, 39 Phil. & Soc. Criticism 693, 693 (2013) (discussing how the term "color blind" was first used to promote integration and then appropriated by proponents of segregation).
65. Sarup, *supra* note 63, at 91 (discussing Hegel's conception of dialectics).
66. Janet Halley, *Where in the Legal Order Have Feminists Gained Inclusion?*, in Janet Halley et al., Governance Feminism 3 (2018).
67. Tarana Burke, *#MeToo Was Started for Black and Brown Women and Girls. They're Still Being Ignored.*, Wash. Post (Nov. 9, 2017, 8:04 PM), https://www.washingtonpost.com/news/post-nation/wp/2017/11/09/the-waitress-who-works-in-the-diner-needs-to-know-that-the-issue-of-sexual-harassment-is-about-her-too/; Laura Brunell & Elinor Burkett, *Feminism*, Encyclopedia Britannica (Mar. 24, 2021) https://www.britannica.com/topic/feminism.
68. *See* Stephanie Zacharek, Eliana Dockterman & Haley Sweetland Edwards, *TIME Person of the Year 2017: The Silence Breakers*, TIME (Dec. 6, 2017), https://time.com/time-person-of-the-year-2017-silence-breakers/.
69. *See id.*
70. *See* Gurvinder Gill & Imran Rahman-Jones, *Me Too Founder Tarana Burke: Movement Is Not Over*, BBC News (July 9, 2020), https://www.bbc.com/news/newsbeat-53269751. *See also* At Liberty, *Tarana Burke and Alyssa Milano on the Future of #Metoo*, (podcast), ACLU (Oct. 25, 2018), https://www.aclu.org/podcast/tarana-burke-and-alyssa-milano-future-metoo-ep-19.
71. Margaret Sanger, *Women and Birth Control*, 227 N. Am. Rev. 529 (1929).
72. *See, e.g.*, Nikita Stewart, *Planned Parenthood in N.Y. Disavows Margaret Sanger over Eugenics*, N.Y. Times (July 21, 2020), https://www.nytimes.com/2020/07/21/nyregion/planned-parenthood-margaret-sanger-eugenics.html;. Hidden Brain, *Remembering Anarcha, Lucy, and Betsey: The Mothers of Modern Gynecology*, NPR (Feb. 16, 2016), https://www.npr.org/transcripts/466942135.
73. Dorothy Roberts, *Race, Gender, and Genetic Technologies: A New Reproductive Dystopia*, 34 Signs 783 (2009).
74. *E.g., id.*

CHAPTER 8

GENDER DISRUPTION, AMELIORATION, AND TRANSFORMATION
A Comparative Perspective

ROSALIND DIXON AND AMELIA LOUGHLAND

AMERICAN legal feminism is an increasingly rich body of thought: no other country today has the same depth and breadth of feminist writing and thinking as the United States. And feminists elsewhere have been strongly influenced by leading U.S. feminist legal theories in developing their own distinctive approaches to a postcolonial or subaltern feminist project.[1] Such feminist projects have extended the range of transformational feminist goals, for example, to include different axes of oppression against women in postcolonial contexts.

This complexity, however, is both a strength and potential weakness to American feminist legal thought: the complexity allows us better to understand the full range of women's experiences, and the different ways in which law and social practice must change if we are to achieve gender justice for all. The various brands and strands of feminism that have emerged in the past half century, taken together, capture the diverse challenges and aspirations of generations of feminist activists and scholars.

Yet the dizzying array of competing feminist visions also runs the risk of creating a form of feminist "information overload," or of key audiences for legal feminist arguments—inside and outside the United States—tuning out to the contributions of legal feminist thought. This risk may be especially great for newer more sex-positive, intersectional, and postmodern/poststructural feminist theories. Here, especially, a sense of information overload may mean that the core message(s) of legal feminism—about the origins and potential approaches to overcoming gender injustice—are overlooked, or at the very least, only partially and incompletely understood.

As one of us has noted previously (RD),[2] some feminists have attempted to address the problem of tuning out—and the kind of pluralism or information overload that seems to lie behind it—by attempting to bracket disagreement among feminists in particular contexts and to adopt a form of "strategic essentialism" that emphasizes feminists' shared concern for "f," whether women, females or feminine roles, styles, and ways of thinking.[3] The difficulty with this kind of approach, however, is that it tends to ignore the contribution of intersectional and poststructural/postmodern feminisms to feminist theorizing and, in particular, to ignore the arguments they make about the enduring effects of essentialist practices. One of our tasks as feminist legal scholars, therefore, is to find ways to reduce this danger of tuning out to the multiple strands and richness of the feminist theoretical corpus without distorting or erasing the differences among feminists and feminist approaches.

In prior work, one of us (RD) offered one such a roadmap, drawing on her own reading of feminist legal theory and insights from a process of "reflective" constitutional comparison.[4] In this context, reflective comparison refers to the process of studying the constitutional systems of different jurisdictions in order to critically compare them to one's own constitutional model, both to better understand them and to see them in a more critical light.

The value of a comparison of this kind is that it allows us to gain new insights about our own existing legal practices, ideas, and understandings. It can give us newly critical ways of seeing those practices, or help reaffirm their normative importance, or their importance to national constitutional identity. It can also offer new ways of understanding or describing those practices. Indeed, this is one of the great virtues of studying and researching law through a comparative lens. Certainly, Dixon's experiences of studying and teaching in both Australia and the United States for an extended period has provided invaluable insights into both Australian and U.S. constitutional practices;[5] and engaging with global practices from a U.S.-Australian vantage point has offered distinctive insights about the scope and stability of different models of constitutional rights protection and constitutional "abuse proofing" (i.e., the protection of liberal democratic norms from misuse for antidemocratic ends).[6] This is also how Dixon arrived at a roadmap for understanding feminist disagreement, this time by engaging with U.S. and South African constitutional equality jurisprudence. This comparative process made it easier to see the three broad frames in which claims of gender justice could be understood in both nations, forming the backbone for the roadmap.[7]

That roadmap consisted of, first, a division of feminism into two broad waves or generations: "older" dominance, cultural, and liberal feminist understandings dating from at least the 1970s and a "newer" set of feminist ideas developed from the 1990s onward, consisting of partial agency (or sex-positive) feminism, intersectional (or antiessentialist) feminism, and postmodern/poststructural feminism.[8] Second, Dixon offered a three-part model for understanding overlap and continuity—but also divergence—in the theoretical underpinnings and aspirations of these different feminisms. The key insight was that the different legal feminisms placed greater or lesser weight on feminist goals of amelioration, transformation, and disruption of current gender norms, systems, and hierarchies. Mapping each brand of feminism along these three goals reduces complexity by providing a common vocabulary to discuss the various feminisms but still permits theorists and activists to see and debate points of disagreements.

Dixon's roadmap has stimulated theorizing about the contours of legal feminisms. Some scholars have adapted and applied key aspects of the roadmap, finding it useful to understanding and explaining their own takes on the internal complexity within feminist legal thought.[9] Others have suggested alternative ways of achieving the same ends, including the idea of a "feminist legal realist" turn, or "universal contextualism,"[10] without, however, seeking to fundamentally challenge or supplant Dixon's theory as a roadmap for understanding the richness and internal complexity to modern U.S. legal feminist debates.[11] This suggests that the roadmap may be most useful in helping scholars outside the United States discuss and organize around particular feminist initiatives.

In this chapter, we reprise both aspects of this roadmap as a guide to understanding contemporary American feminist legal theory and broader feminist debates both within the United States and elsewhere. Specifically, we show how this roadmap can clarify the stakes—or areas of disagreement—in a vast and increasing literature on the gendered impact of the COVID-19 pandemic, and possible legal and policy responses to it, inside and outside the United States.

The remainder of the chapter is divided into four sections following this introduction. Section I summarizes the rich array of existing feminist theories in U.S. legal thought, providing a condensed version of the contributions on feminist legal theory made in this volume. Section II explains the broad approaches to feminist legal theory and approaches for finding common ground among older and newer brands of legal feminism. Section III outlines Dixon's three categories of disruptive, ameliorative, and transformative feminism(s), as categories derived inductively from comparative constitutional inquiry, that help map areas of similarity and difference among different feminisms. Section IV sketches how this applies in practice, by reference to debates over the global response to COVID-19.

I. Feminist Theoretical Disagreement: Old(er) and New(er) Feminist Legal Voices

As the contributions in this volume suggest, today, feminist legal theory in the United States can be divided into six broad schools of thought or theories: liberal, cultural, dominance, sex-positive, intersectional, and poststructural/postmodern feminism. Of these theories, the first three represent an older generation of feminist legal scholarship, which first developed in the late 1970s to early 1980s,[12] while the latter three represent a newer generation of scholarship that developed between the mid-to late 1980s and the early 1990s.[13] Often individual feminists have come to embrace elements of more than one school of thought.[14] As theories, however, the six schools remain distinct and offer quite different insights about the nature and sources of gender injustice.

In liberal feminist theory,[15] the primary source of gender injustice in American social life lies in the way in which those in positions of power tend to link a person's biological sex with particular gender roles, without attention to individual capacities to perform such roles, or individual preferences in respect of these roles.[16] Liberal feminists recognize that they must challenge stereotypical associations of this kind by directly addressing the linkage of biology with particular social domains or spheres. A central aim of liberal feminist scholarship has thus been to challenge society's "separate spheres" ideology,[17] or the way in which jurisdictional boundaries have traditionally been drawn to demarcate certain harms as of private, local, or domestic concern, rather than public, national, or international concern.[18]

In a cultural (or relational) feminist account,[19] the key source of gender injustice is understood to be the way in which "feminine" roles and modes of thinking are devalued, compared to roles and ways of thinking that are identified as masculine.[20] Cultural feminists suggest that this devaluation has two key costs. First and most immediately, they argue that it has serious distributional consequences for women when it comes to the value placed on their labor.[21] Second, they argue that it can result in a broader loss to society because of its tendency to lead to an underemphasis on feminine values, especially in contexts where such values—or ways of thinking and interacting—could be extremely valuable.[22]

Dominance feminists directly contest both of these understandings.[23] They argue that liberal feminist attempts to empower individual women and cultural feminist attempts to revalue the feminine are both misguided. In the dominance feminist account, female identity and the feminine as we know it are the products of a system of sexual subordination in which men have defined themselves as subjects and women as objects, via pornography and other systematic practices of male-to-female rape, prostitution, battering, and harassment.[24] For dominance feminists such as Catharine MacKinnon and Andrea Dworkin, pornography (as well as rape, prostitution, and sexual harassment) is the essence of this sexist social order because it socializes males to regard masculinity, sex, and sexual desire in terms of the objectification and sexual subordination of their opposite type, namely, females, or to equate masculinity with being on top of a female, bound and gagged.[25]

From the 1980s onward, newer feminisms moved away from the traditional focus of female empowerment and toward challenging the social norms and expectations around gender itself. For example, sex-positive feminism challenges the premises of dominance feminism.[26] Sex-positive feminists argue that while sex might in some cases be a source of danger for women, it is also a potentially important site of pleasure, fulfillment, and even power.[27] In this sense, they share the approach of other "partial agency" feminist theorists who emphasize the possibilities for, rather than simply constraints on, female agency.[28] A key source of injustice, for sex-positive feminists, is the way in which women's sexual agency is limited by prevailing ideologies, particularly "repronormative" ideologies (i.e., those that valorize reproduction over other socially productive activities and casts nonreproductive sex for women as dangerous and illegitimate).[29]

In intersectional feminist theory, it is impossible to make even these more limited generalizations about the nature or sources of gender injustice.[30] In an intersectional feminist account, both sex and gender hierarchies circulate and intersect with other hierarchies in ways that make gender injustice deeply contextual in nature. Both the sources and nature of gender injustice must therefore always be considered with close attention to the way in which sex and gender intersect with race and class and other axes such as religion, age, disability, sexual orientation, and immigrant status.[31] Intersectional feminists also argue that feminists should be extremely cautious about attempting to identify sources of commonality across women's diverse experiences, understanding the act of foregrounding sex or gender as axes of subordination as an exercise of power that depends upon and reflects the race and class privilege of the speaker.[32]

Poststructural and postmodern feminists take yet another approach to the nature of gender injustice in America.[33] Rather than focusing on sex and gender stereotypes or hierarchies, poststructural/postmodern feminists focus on sex-based categories as a key source of gender injustice. They argue that our understandings of sex-based differences are highly contingent and that sex as we know it is entirely "performatively produced" rather than real.[34] Poststructural feminists argue that heterosexuality produces sex-based binaries because it conditions individuals to perform their sex/gender identity in a strictly binary and univocal way.[35]

II. Finding Commonality and Convergence

In this section, we introduce three broad ideas or concepts—the idea of a disruptive, ameliorative, and transformative approach to gender justice—to highlight potential areas of overlap and convergence between older and newer feminisms. We borrow the definitions of these three concepts from the *Oxford English Dictionary* to show the different emphasis of each broad goal, realizing that in practice, the goals may intersect and strategies based on one goal may resemble those pursued from a different objective.

For this roadmap, *disruption* refers to "the action of rending or bursting asunder; violent dissolution of continuity; forcible severance." *Amelioration* refers to "the action of making better; or the condition of being made better; improvement." *Transformation* refers to "a complete change in character, condition, etc."

A. Feminist Disruption: Connecting Liberal and Newer Feminisms

As mentioned earlier, liberal feminism, on its face, has little in common with newer feminisms. In a liberal feminist account, the primary source of gender injustice in the current social order lies in individual stereotyping, or the way in which those in positions of power tend to assign gendered roles to individuals based on biological sex without attending to individuals' actual capacities or preferences in respect to these roles. In newer feminist accounts, broader social structures of subordination and ideological constraints are the key source of gender injustice.

By focusing on the concept of disruption, however, it becomes possible to identify connections between liberal feminism and these newer feminisms. In a liberal feminist account, the feminist project is aimed at disrupting—or bursting asunder—the historical linkage between sex and gender, or between biological sex and particular roles or ways of thinking associated with particular genders. In newer feminist accounts, the focus of concern is on a much broader range of linkages and identity categories. For example, intersectional feminists are concerned with disrupting both stereotypical and hierarchical linkages between sex, gender, race, and class, while sex-positive feminists seek to disrupt the linkage between biological sex, gender, and sexuality, or between femaleness, women's role as mother, and women's limited sexual and political agency. For their part, poststructural/postmodern feminists work to disrupt sex and gender categories themselves, through acts such as literary parody and cross-dressing. In each case, however, the same concern with disrupting—or bursting asunder—various identity linkages and categories can be found.

As a conception of gender justice, the idea of disruption thus provides a way of reexplaining newer feminisms to broader legal actors as simply involving a broadening and deepening of the liberal feminist commitment to unsettling current expectations and understandings about gender. Sex-positive feminism broadens the focus of liberal feminism to include a focus on the link between sex, gender, *and* sexuality, while intersectional feminism expands the feminist focus further still, to interrogate the link between sex, gender, and other identity axes. Finally, poststructural/postmodern feminism deepens the commitment of liberal feminists to disruption by turning it against the very identity categories with which liberal feminists start their analysis. In this sense, feminist disruption tends to involve longer-term or structural commitments to gender justice, as opposed to ameliorative approaches which focus on shorter-term manifestations of that injustice.

B. Feminist Amelioration and Transformation: Connecting Cultural, Dominance, and Intersectional Feminism

As many feminist theorists have observed, there are potentially vast differences between cultural and dominance feminists, on the one hand, and intersectional feminists on the other. Feminists in these different schools strongly disagree about the nature and source of gender injustice and are also directly critical of the approach taken by each other's schools of thought. Dominance feminists, for example, have been sharply critical of attempts to celebrate or revalue "the feminine" in the face of a system of sexual subordination which itself defines and sharply limits the feminine as we know it,[36] while intersectional feminists have criticized both cultural and dominance feminists for their failure to take proper account of race and other identity factors.[37]

Even in the face of these differences, however, the concepts of amelioration and transformation help point to some continuity between these different feminisms in their underlying conception of the feminist project. Admittedly, when it comes to concerns about amelioration, the three different feminisms tend to adopt somewhat different approaches to defining the benchmark for amelioration or the particular gap to be narrowed. In a cultural feminist account, the focus will be on the gap between men and women when it comes to the rewards they enjoy for their different forms of labor or, alternatively, on the gap between the symbolic and practical value placed on masculine versus feminine gender roles. In a dominance feminist account, the focus will be on the gap between men and women in terms of the sexual and political agency they enjoy. In an intersectional feminist account, the focus will be on narrowing the gap between a wider range of more and less privileged groups such as white, privileged women and poor women and women of color. All three feminisms, however, treat the gap between the benefits enjoyed by the subordinating and the subordinated groups as the benchmark for change, or at least as a useful first step in a longer-term feminist project. It thus becomes possible to reexplain intersectional feminism to a broader group of legal actors as simply a building out or adapting of these older feminists' concerns about hierarchy-based inequality to a wider range of hierarchies.

Similarly, when it comes to commitments to transformation, each feminism tends to adopt a somewhat different vision of the long-term goal to be realized. For cultural feminists, the project of feminist transformation will focus on the equal valuation of the feminine and masculine or the integration of feminine approaches into areas traditionally dominated by the masculine. For dominance feminists, transformation will involve creating a world in which men and women enjoy equal power, sexual agency, and bodily integrity and security.[38] For intersectional feminists, it will involve creating a world in which all forms of structural subordination and supremacist ideology are eliminated.[39] All three feminisms, however, adopt an approach that attempts to define what a world with gender justice would look like, and what (potentially radical) steps would be necessary to create and sustain such a world.

The concept of transformation thus helps reexplain the more radical dimensions of intersectional feminism to broader legal actors as a profound, but also logical, broadening of both the antisubordination commitments of dominance feminism and the commitment to the ultimate "integration" or revaluation of both masculine and feminine in cultural feminism. It thus also broadens its accessibility to a range of legal actors in both the United States and elsewhere. By enabling feminists of different "camps" to find convergences between their various projects, the roadmap thus provides opportunities for feminists to better address systemic and cross-jurisdictional problems, such as climate change or global pandemics.

III. The Framework in Practice: COVID-19

To illustrate how these different ideas work in practice, it is useful to consider scholarship and debates in both the United States and elsewhere about the gendered impact of the COVID-19 pandemic, and various government responses to it. Divergent feminist responses to the impacts of COVID-19 and its policy responses have nonetheless served to highlight an underlying commonality in goals for gender-based justice around the world.

No one has doubted the profound effects COVID-19 has had—and continues to have—on social, economic, and political life worldwide. Many of these impacts are also profoundly gendered, and in ways that have disproportionately affected women and communities of color.[40] But there is also disagreement among scholars and commentators about these effects: have they been unremittingly negative, or effectively created a form of "patriarchal pandemic?"[41] Or have they instead begun to shift how we see work and care, and their relationship, in ways that may have lasting benefits for feminist aims?[42]

At the center of these debates lie potential disagreements among liberal, cultural, and intersectional feminists.[43] However, the concepts of amelioration, disruption, and transformation still provide a useful theoretical roadmap to understand both areas of convergence and divergence among scholars, and how different feminists have or are likely to respond to proposals for reform in this context.

A. Intensifying the Need for Amelioration

The overwhelming conclusion from social scientists and feminists alike is that COVID-19 has been bad for women and has increased the gender gap in a range of key social and economic areas. Whether we focus on health, employment, accumulation of wealth, and so on, one set of feminist responses to the pandemic focuses on these adverse impacts on women—as implicitly a threat to the goal of gender-based amelioration.

In most countries, women have died at slightly lower rates than men of COVID-19 but have been more likely to suffer mental health effects as a result of the virus.[44] Women have been overrepresented in essential service roles, especially healthcare, where the risks of infection and mortality have been greater.[45] Interruptions in access to key health services have had a particular impact on women, especially pregnant women.[46]

Women have also been more likely to lose their jobs, have their hours cut, or be forced to reduce their working hours in order to respond to increased caring or home-school responsibilities.[47] In most households, both men and women have increased the time they have spent on child care, but women have continued to bear far more of the "second shift" or responsibility for household work, child care, and elder care.[48] These impacts have been even greater for women of color. In the United States especially, women of color have been overrepresented among those unemployed as a result the pandemic[49] but are also overrepresented in front-line roles that increase their exposure to the virus.[50]

The long-term adverse impact of these changes is also likely to be large.[51] Time out of the workforce has lasting effects on lifetime earnings.[52] So too do reduced hours or rates of pay. Current changes, therefore, are likely to have adverse impacts on gender and racial pay equity for many years after the pandemic is over.[53]

Family violence has also increased during the pandemic for obvious reasons, as households have dealt with increased economic and psychological stress, and those at risk have been "locked down" with past or potential abusers.[54] Being "locked down" has also disproportionately affected women, with a British study finding that more women left their jobs during the pandemic due to the impossibility of full-time caring and domestic work along with high-pressure jobs.[55]

The pandemic has also sharpened the line between the experiences of girls and boys as members of their households. During lockdown, several studies found that girls were more likely than boys to shoulder an increase in household chores and responsibilities, at the expense of their education.[56] This disparity also intersected with the significant educational disadvantage of homeschooling for children from lower socioeconomic backgrounds.[57]

Women and girls have also been underrepresented in the decision-making structures that have shaped the policy response to the pandemic in most countries.[58] For example, a recent study of WHO Expert Advisory Panels found that only 34 percent of members were women.[59]

Many feminist responses to these gendered impacts have focused on policies that can reduce or ameliorate these gendered effects and their negative effect on the goal of closing various gender-based gaps.[60] In Australia, for example, there have been calls for the government to make child care free and broadly accessible during the pandemic, even while schools and workplaces have been closed.[61] There are also calls to increase resources for services that provide support to those experiencing family violence.[62] In the U.K., local governments have moved to exempt eligible child care centers from tax from 2020 to 2021, a move supported by a range of women's groups.[63] And countries such as Albania, Georgia, Turkey, and Serbia created welfare schemes targeted specifically to women: Turkey and Serbia created cash payments targeted for women, while Albania and Georgia provided programs of food distribution as well as medical products and other services, specifically focusing on women-headed households and other vulnerable groups.

Feminist scholars have praised these schemes as "a crucial feature of the gendered response to COVID-19 and offer positive guidance for other governments," implicitly based on a form of gender amelioration-based logic.[64] The intensification of the gender gaps produced by the pandemic have created models for ameliorations which feminists hope will carry into a postpandemic future.

B. Disruption of Prior Work-Household Practices

When the focus is on ameliorating gender gaps, the pandemic is largely bad news for feminist reformers who see the growing disparities as cause for alarm. However, some feminists view COVID-19 as having greater benefits, or at least a silver lining, for gender justice. They note how crises such as COVID-19 can "bring to light many of the systemic and structural barriers that had held back the advancement of gender equality."[65] And in doing so, they have tended to focus on the *disruptive* effect of the pandemic on existing gender norms and structures—and the ways in which law and policy may exploit the ongoing changes brought about by this disruption.[66]

The pandemic has certainly disrupted people's lives at almost every level—in how they work, shop, travel, socialize, and move around their cities and localities.[67] This disruption has also extended to how households manage child care and combine work and care and has led to more men performing care work or domestic labor, often while working from home. For example, research from academics at Canadian universities found that a substantial number of families had divided the housework more equally—with more than 40 percent of fathers saying they were cooking more, and around 30 percent reporting that they had increased the amount of time they spent on laundry and cleaning.[68]

While COVID-19 has generally worsened the gender gap in paid work and increased the "second shift" burden on many women, there have been some exceptions: families that already had some degree of intrahousehold sharing of these responsibilities seem to have become more egalitarian.[69] And men who lost their own jobs, or who were able to work from home (WFH) while their female partners were not, took on a larger share of child-care responsibilities than previously.[70]

This disruption has arguably helped shift the gender coding of some care roles, and especially the model of combining work and care, in a flexible way. As Canadian scholar Tania King and her colleagues note, "the COVID-19 pandemic has temporarily reshaped our domestic and working lives and could sow the seeds for change to advance gender equality."[71] Indeed, there is evidence from "policy changes that engineer a similar change" in male caring roles and responsibilities that even quite temporary changes can have "persistent effects on gender roles and the division of labor."[72]

The call, by those who focus on the benefits of this disruption, has been to find ways to promote these kinds of persistent effects. One way to do so, for example, would be for more countries to enact laws making flexible work—including WFH—a presumptive legal right for all employees, both male and female.[73] Or private companies could adopt an "all roles flex" policy, which makes WFH a continued entitlement.[74]

Underneath these ideas, of course, is a fairly classically liberal feminist conception of the value of disrupting stereotypical assumptions about male and female roles. But some scholars also link the disruption of COVID-19 to a broader rethinking of the value of care work—or a disruption in people's thinking about the work-care nexus in ways that are at least partially consistent with cultural and intersectional feminist understandings. The pandemic, for example, might cause us to rethink a work culture that only sees face time and "full-time" work as contributing to productivity, in favor of a willingness to focus on outputs over inputs in the employment context, or to experiment with radical new models of team-based production or job-sharing.[75]

C. COVID as the Impetus for Transformation

Those who see the greatest potential for COVID-19 to lead to lasting gendered change, however, are feminists and social policymakers who explicitly see gender justice through a transformative lens. For these feminists, the opportunity created by the pandemic is for societies to rethink the relationship between paid and unpaid work, or market and household forms of labor, and to find more sustainable ways for men and women to share in both forms of work.

COVID has highlighted a crisis of care, which many feminist scholars argue must be understood structurally.[76] As Carlson and coauthors note, it has also "eliminated some of the *structural* barriers to sharing domestic work—particularly for men—as many adults are now working from home."[77] And with the elimination of these barriers, has come the possibility of transforming the work-care relationship.

Beyond policies that can encourage and promote sharing of care work, cultural feminists also suggest that COVID may help encourage a broader rethinking in society's approach to the *value* of care work, or current modes of production and reproduction. Feminist sociologist Lynn Craig from Australia, for example, suggests that "the fact that care is an essential bedrock to the economy has become more obvious" in many countries during the pandemic, and in the process helped clarify the significant economic value of both paid and unpaid care work.[78] Feminists Kate Bahn, Jennifer Cohen, and Yana van der Meulen Rodgers in the United States likewise suggest that any "comprehensive response to the COVID-19 crisis [must] emphasiz[e] social reproduction as an integral part of the economic system and judge the success of policy responses by how they promote human wellbeing for all."[79]

Similarly, intersectional feminists suggest a meaningful response to the pandemic may help contribute to broader economic and political transformation—including in the domain of racial justice. By serving as a "miner's canary" for what is wrong with liberal democratic structures, Catherine Powell suggests, both the COVID-19 pandemic and Black Lives Matter movement in the United States create the possibility of a form of "viral convergence—or political moment that encourages mobilization on issues such as "living wage laws, an essential worker bill of rights, and improved, universal access to health care."[80]

Many feminist and other critical scholars in the United States and elsewhere also emphasize that transformational thinking is exactly what is required in order to achieve justice during and after the pandemic.[81] Scholars emphasize that the fallout from the pandemic allows us to see the connections between physical violence and economic exploitation. In Argentina, for example, Polischuk and Fay have argued that part of the response to COVID and its disproportionate impact on women should be for governments to do more to address the structural causes of gender violence, including the unequal distribution of unpaid labor.[82]

These feminists may disagree on the precise policies likely to lead to transformative outcomes and which among several strategies are more likely to lead to long-term change—for example, investing more in access to paid child care, or doing more to support those providing unpaid care. They may disagree about the best way to ensure economic justice within as well as across countries—that is, how best to promote better-paying jobs within a country while also paying attention to questions of global welfare and economic and racial justice. But while these various feminists may disagree, or adopt different foci for their critiques, the concept of transformation usefully highlights areas of conceptual and practical convergence in their response.

IV. Conclusion

The insights provided by U.S. feminist legal theory are rich and complex. They include the insights provided by the "first wave" of liberal, cultural, and dominance feminist legal theorists, as well as those of a later wave of intersectional, sex positive/agency, and poststructural/postmodern feminist legal thinkers. And together, these various waves or schools of feminist legal thought draw attention to the many different forms of gender injustice experienced by women in the United States today—and the ways in which sex, gender, race, sexuality, and other forms of disadvantage intersect to produce constraints and disadvantage for women and men of different backgrounds. They can likewise help us understand the experiences of women worldwide and their search for gender justice.

The difficulty we suggest, however, is that this internal complexity or richness may lead to broader legal audiences "tuning out" to the full range of insights provided by American feminist legal thought—and especially the newer, more complex insights provided by intersectional, sex positive/agency, and poststructural/postmodern feminist legal thinkers.

By comparison, the approach we propose—of mapping different feminist insights onto goals of gender-based amelioration, disruption, and transformation—goes a long way toward avoiding those dangers. While inevitably simplifying and reducing the nuance and complexity of feminist legal insights, our approach is broad enough to encompass the key insights of all major feminist legal theoretic approaches in the United States today, including both older and newer feminisms.

It also provides a roadmap for understanding the nature and reasons for differences among feminists, as well as areas of commonality: the goal of amelioration can sometimes work in tandem with more radical goals of disruption or transformation, but often the two sets of goals will be in conflict. Similarly, disruption may in some cases help pave the way for transformation but in others produce too much uncertainty as to future change to be embraced by those seeking to pursue predefined transformative goals.

It is also a roadmap that comes from a process of reflective engagement with, and can assist in, understanding legal feminist claims beyond the United States. We illustrate this in the chapter by reference to transnational accounts of the gendered impact of the COVID-19 pandemic, and government responses to it. Although these debates are ongoing, and will no doubt evolve in the future, the basic contours of the debate to date show the value of understanding feminist and gender justice claims through the lens of the goals of amelioration, disruption, and transformation in gender justice.

Ultimately, "mapping" the debates according to these goals helps to illuminate continuities between different schools of thought, as well as differences, and thus clarify the conceptual and political stakes for efforts at feminist collaboration and coalition formation. Feminist disagreement will live on even after this mapping is done. Indeed, it is arguably essential to our ability to capture the multiplicity of women's experiences. But it need not stand in the way of coalition-driven efforts at feminist legal change in the United States or elsewhere. Gender amelioration, disruption, and transformation are all goals that feminists can recognize as sources of common ground, even as we continue to understand them and their priority in quite different ways.

Notes

1. *See, e.g.*, Anupama Rao, Gender & Caste (2003); Fuminobu Murakami, Postmodern, Feminist and Postcolonial Currents in Contemporary Japanese Culture: A Reading of Murakami Haruki, Yoshimoto Banana, Yoshimoto Takaaki and Karatani Kojin (2005); South Asian Feminisms (Ania Loomba & Ritty. A. Lukose eds. 2012); Ritu Menon & Kamla Bhasin, Borders & Boundaries: Women in India's Partition (1998).
2. Rosalind Dixon, *Feminist Disagreement (Comparatively) Recast*, 31 Harv. J. L. & Gender 277, 286 (2008).
3. *See* Janet Halley, Split Decisions: How and Why to Take a Break from Feminism 16–26 (2006).
4. On reflective comparison, *see, e.g.*, Frank Michelman, *Reflection: Symposium: Comparative Avenues in Constitutional Law—Borrowing*, 82 Tex. L. Rev. 1737 (2004); Vicki C. Jackson, *Constitutional Comparisons: Convergence, Resistance, Engagement*, 119 Harv. L. Rev. 109 (2005); Sujit Choudhry, *Globalization in Search of Justification: Toward a Theory of Comparative Constitutional Interpretation*, 74 Ind. L.J. 819, 838–39 (1999); Rosalind Dixon, *A Democratic Theory of Constitutional Comparison*, 56 Am. J. Comp. L. 947 (2008); Guido Calabresi et al., *In Tribute: Frank I. Michelman*, 125 Harv. L. Rev. 879 (2012).
5. *See, e.g.*, Rosalind Dixon, *Amending Constitutional Identity*, 33 Cardozo L. Rev. 1847 (2012).
6. *See, e.g.*, Rosalind Dixon, *An Australian (Partial) Bill of Rights*, 14 Int'l J. Const. L. 80 (2016); Rosalind Dixon & Anika Gauja, *Australia's Non-populist Democracy? The Role of Structure and Policy, in* Constitutional Democracy in Crisis (Mark Graber et al. eds., 2018). On the concept of constitutional abuse proofing, *see* Rosalind Dixon & David Landau, Abusive Constitutional Borrowing 193 (2021).

7. Dixon, *supra* note 2.
8. *Compare id. with* Martha Chamallas, *Past and Prologue: Old and New Feminisms*, 17 MICH. J. GENDER & L. 157, 158 (2010).
9. *See, e.g.*, Chamallas, *supra* note 8, at 158. *See also* Aya Gruber, *Rap, Feminism and the War on Crime*, 84 WASH. L. REV. 581, 603–06 (2009); Douaa Hussein, *Legal Reform as a Way to Women's Rights: The Case of Personal Status Law in Yemen*, 2 OIDA 21, 27–29 (2012); Nahid Sorooshyari, *The Tensions Between Feminism and Libertarianism: A Focus on Prostitution*, 3 WASH. U. JURIS. REV. 167, 168 (2011).
10. *See, e.g.*, Mae C. Quinn, *Feminist Legal Realism*, 35 HARV. J. L. & GENDER 1 (2012); Helen Irving, *Where Have All the Women Gone? Gender and the Literature on Constitutional Design*, 4 CONTEMP. READINGS IN LAW & SOC. JUST. 89, 109 (2012) (on universal contextualism).
11. Quinn, *supra* note 10, at 54 (noting Dixon's roadmap as an "alternative" approach to understanding feminist legal pluralism and feminist ideals of transformation); Irving, *supra* note 10, at 109 (suggesting that the roadmap or scheme Dixon provides is "valuable in conceptual design-work" but still potentially too complex in ways that call for further simplification in certain contexts).
12. For early liberal, cultural, and dominance feminist work, *see, e.g.*, Ruth Bader Ginsburg, *Sex Equality and the Constitution*, 52 TUL. L. REV. 451 (1978) (liberal feminism); CAROL GILLIGAN, IN A DIFFERENT VOICE: PSYCHOLOGICAL THEORY AND WOMEN'S DEVELOPMENT (1982) (cultural feminism); Catharine MacKinnon, *Feminism, Marxism, Method and the State: An Agenda for Theory*, 7 SIGNS: J. WOMEN CULTURE & SOC'Y 515 (1982) (dominance feminism).
13. For early statements of sex-positive, intersectional, and poststructural/postmodern feminist work, *see, e.g.*, Sylvia A. Law, *Rethinking Sex and the Constitution*, 132 U. PA. L. REV. 955, 1019 (1984) [hereinafter Law, *Rethinking Sex and the Constitution*] (sex-positive feminism); Martha Minow, *The Supreme Court Term 1986, Foreword: Justice Engendered*, 101 HARV. L. REV. 10 (1987) [hereinafter Minow, *Foreword*] (intersectional feminism); JUDITH BUTLER, GENDER TROUBLE: FEMINISM AND THE SUBVERSION OF IDENTITY (1990) (poststructural/postmodern feminism).
14. *See, e.g.*, ROBIN WEST, CARING FOR JUSTICE (1997) (combining cultural and dominance feminist arguments); Christine Littleton, *Reconstructing Sexual Equality*, 75 CALIF. L. REV. 1279, 1296 (1987) (combining cultural and dominance feminist arguments).
15. *See* Linda C. McClain & Brittany K. Hacker, "Liberal Feminist Jurisprudence: Foundational, Enduring, Adaptive," chapter 2, in this volume.
16. *See generally* Ruth Bader Ginsburg, *Some Thoughts on the 1980's Debate over Special Versus Equal Treatment for Women*, 4 J. LAW & INEQ. 143 (1986); Ruth Bader Ginsburg & Barbara Flagg, *Some Reflections on the Feminist Legal Thought of the 1970's*, 1989 U. CHI. LEGAL F. 9; Wendy W. Williams, *The Equality Crisis: Some Reflections on Culture, Courts, and Feminism*, 7 WOMEN'S RTS. L. REP. 175 (1982).
17. Ginsburg & Flagg, *supra* note 16, at 15, 17.
18. For a summary of the liberal feminist challenge to the public/private divide, *see* Frances Olsen, *Constitutional Law: Feminist Critiques of the Public/Private Distinction*, 10 CONST. COMMENT. 319, 319–27 (1993).
19. *See* Jennifer Nedelsky, "A Relational Approach to Law and Its Core Concepts," chapter 4, in this volume.
20. For leading cultural feminist works, *see, e.g.*, GILLIGAN, *supra* note 12; WEST, *supra* note 14.

21. *See, e.g.*, WEST, *supra* note 14, at 100–38.
22. *See, e.g.*, GILLIGAN, *supra* note 12, at 174; WEST, *supra* note 14, at 88.
23. For the leading statement of dominance feminism, *see* CATHARINE A. MACKINNON, TOWARD A FEMINIST THEORY OF THE STATE (1989); *see also* Kathryn Abrams, "Dominance Feminism: Placing Sexualized Power at the Center," Chapter 3, this volume.
24. MACKINNON, *supra* note 23, at 161.
25. *Id.* at 204 (describing pornography as the "essence of a sexist social order, [and] its quintessential social act"); ANDREA DWORKIN, PORNOGRAPHY: MEN POSSESSING WOMEN (1981).
26. *See* Susan Appleton, "Sex-Positive Feminism's Values in Search of the Law of Pleasure," chapter 6, in this volume. Kathryn Abrams, *Sex Wars Redux: Agency and Coercion in Feminist Legal Theory*, 95 COLUM. L. REV. 304 (1995).
27. *See, e.g.*, Law, *Rethinking Sex and the Constitution*, *supra* note 13 (confronting biological differences between the sexes and identifying women's reproductive abilities as a source of power); Vicki Schultz, *The Sanitized Workplace*, 112 YALE L.J. 2061, 2087 (2003) (disputing an essentialist view of sex and sexuality as being always harmful to women in the workplace).
28. *See* Abrams, *supra* note 26, at 348–76 (discussing such approaches, and coining the term "partial agency" feminism); *see also* Tracy E. Higgins, *Democracy and Feminism*, 110 HARV. L. REV. 1657 (1997) (urging democratic theorists to incorporate the insights of feminist theorists about the real but bounded nature of individual agency).
29. *See* Katherine M. Franke, *Theorizing Yes: An Essay on Feminism, Law, and Desire*, 101 COLUM. L. REV. 181, 205 (2001).
30. *See* Emily Houh, "A Genealogy of Intersectionality," Chapter 5, in this volume. *See also* Angela P. Harris, *Race and Essentialism in Feminist Legal Theory*, 42 STAN. L. REV. 598 (1990) (accusing MacKinnon's dominance feminist understanding of rape, which focuses on a generalized male/female hierarchy, as "shelv[ing] racism").
31. *See* Minow, *Foreword*, *supra* note 13; Martha L. Minow & Elizabeth V. Spelman, *In Context*, 63 S. CALIF. L. REV. 1597, 1632–33 (1990); Martha Minow, *Not Only for Myself: Identity, Politics, and Law*, 75 OR. L. REV. 647, 656 (1996).
32. ELIZABETH V. SPELMAN, INESSENTIAL WOMAN: PROBLEMS OF EXCLUSION IN FEMINIST THOUGHT 133–59 (1988).
33. *See* Camille Gear Rich, "Feminism Is Dead, Long Live Feminisms: A Postmodern Take on the Road to Gender Equality," chapter 7, in this volume; *see also* Butler, *supra* note 13; Mary Joe Frug, *A Postmodern Feminist Legal Manifesto (An Unfinished Draft)*, 105 HARV. L. REV. 1045 (1992).
34. Butler, *supra* note 13, at 33.
35. *Id.* at 30.
36. *See, e.g.*, CATHARINE MACKINNON, FEMINISM UNMODIFIED: DISCOURSES ON LIFE AND LAW 53 (1988).
37. *See, e.g.*, Harris, *supra* note 30, at 592–96.
38. *See* MACKINNON, *supra* note 23, at 247–49.
39. Kimberlé Crenshaw, *Race, Reform, and Retrenchment: Transformation and Legitimation in Antidiscrimination Law*, 101 HARV. L. REV. 1331, 1383 (1988).
40. *See, e.g.*, Catherine Powell, *The Color and Gender of COVID: Essential Workers, Not Disposable People*, Think Global Health (June 4, 2020), https://www.thinkg

lobalhealth.org/article/color-and-gender-covid-essential-workers-not-disposable-people?utm_medium=social_owned&utm_source=tw_wfp; Naomi Cahn, *COVID-19's Impact on Women of Color*, FORBES (May 10, 2020, 6:01 PM), https://www.forbes.com/sites/naomicahn/2020/05/10/mothers-day-and-covid-19s-impact-on-women-of-color/?utm_source=Fordham+Master+List&utm_campaign=c748434591-EMAIL_CAMPAIGN_2020_05_15_06_23&utm_medium=email&utm_term=0_808eb3c98f-c748434591-172900181#6fbff50f41ac; Kimberlé Crenshaw, *Under the Blacklight*, AAPF (2020), https://www.aapf.org/aapfcovid.

41. *See, e.g.*, Soraya Chemaly, *Coronavirus Could Hurt Women the Most. Here's How to Prevent a Patriarchal Pandemic*, NBC NEWS (Apr. 20, 2020, 7:13 PM), https://www.nbcnews.com/think/opinion/coronavirus-could-hurt-women-most-here-s-how-prevent-patriarchal-ncna1186581.

42. *See, e.g.*, Maddy Savage, *How COVID-19 Is Changing Women's Lives*, BBC (June 30, 2020),https://www.bbc.com/worklife/article/20200630-how-covid-19-is-changing-womens-lives#:~:text=The%20absence%20of%20commuting%20time,Covid%2D19%2C%20says%20Milkie.

43. So far, sex-positive/agency feminists and postmodern/poststructural feminists have had less to say on these questions.

44. *See, e.g.*, Hannah Briggs & Thoai Ngo, *The Health, Economic, and Social Effect of COVID-19 and Its Response on Gender and Sex: A Literature Review*, POPULATION COUNCIL (June 3, 2020), https://knowledgecommons.popcouncil.org/departments_sbsr-pgy/1006/; Fleury Heyworth & Tiphaine Di Ruscio, *COVID-19: What Does This Mean for Gender*, Gender Champions (Mar. 23, 2020), https://genderchampions.com/news/covid-19-what-does-this-mean-for-gender; Regan M. Johnston et al., *Evidence of Exacerbated Gender Inequality in Child Care Obligations in Canada and Australia During the COVID-19 Pandemic*, 16 POL. & GEN. 1131 (2020); Muzhi Zhou et al., Gender Inequalities: Changes in Income, Time Use and Well-Being Before and During the UK COVID-19 Lockdown (2020) (unpublished manuscript).

45. On women's overrepresentation in these roles more generally, *see also* Sulzhan Bali et al., *Off the Back Burner: Diverse and Gender-Inclusive Decision-making for COVID-19 Response and Recovery*, 5 BMJ GLOBAL HEALTH 1, 1 (2020); Richard Blundell et al., COVID-19 AND INEQUALITIES, 41 FISC. STUD. 291, 302 (2020); Clare Wenham, *Women Have Been Largely Ignored in the COVID-19 Response. This Must Change*, LSE (May 12, 2020), https://blogs.lse.ac.uk/covid19/2020/05/12/women-have-been-largely-ignored-in-the-covid-19-response-this-must-change/; WORLD BANK, GENDER DIMENSIONS OF THE COVID-19 PANDEMIC (2020).

46. Wenham, *supra* note 45; World Bank, *supra* note 45.

47. Gina Adams & Margaret Todd, Meeting the School-Age Child Care Needs of Working Parents Facing COVID-19 Distance Learning: Policy Options to Consider 11 (2020) (unpublished manuscript); Melanie Antz et al., *Working from Home and COVID-19: The Chances and Risks for Gender Gaps* 6, LEIBNIZ INFORMATION CENTRE FOR ECONOMICS (2020), https://link.springer.com/content/pdf/10.1007/s10272-020-0938-5; Caitlyn Collins et al., *COVID-19 and the Gender Gap in Work Hours*, 28 GEN. WORK & ORG. 101,101–02 (2020) (on work hours); Sou-Jie Brunnersum, *COVID-19 Childcare Burden "Destroying" Mothers Careers*, DW (Jul. 25, 2020), https://www.dw.com/en/covid-19-childcare-burden-destroying-mothers-careers/

a-54318258; Helen Jaqueline McLaren et al., *COVID-19 and Women's Triple Burden: Vignettes from Sri Lanka, Malaysia, Vietnam and Australia*, 9 Soc. Sci. 87 (2020); Janet Paskin, *Women Are Bearing the Brunt of Coronavirus Disruption*, BLOOMBERG (Mar. 12, 2020, 12:00 PM), https://www.bloomberg.com/news/articles/2020-03-11/coronavirus-will-make-gender-inequality-worse; Tania King et al., *Reordering Gender Systems: Can COVID-19 Lead to Improved Gender Equality and Health?*, 396 LANCET 80, 80 (2020); *US COVID: Child Care Closures Disproportionality Affect Women*, AL JAZEERA (July 31, 2020), https://www.aljazeera.com/economy/2020/7/31/us-covid-child-care-closures-disproportionally-affect-women; Savage, *supra* note 42; Gema Zamarro et al., Gender Differences in the Impact of COVID-19 (2020) (unpublished manuscript).

48. *See, e.g.*, ALISON ANDREW ET AL., THE GENDERED DIVISION OF PAID AND DOMESTIC WORK UNDER LOCKDOWN 3 (IZA Institute of Labor Economics 2020); Daniel L. Carlson et al., US Couples' Divisions of Housework and Childcare During COVID-19 Pandemic (2020) (unpublished manuscript); Daniela Del Boca et al., *Women's Work, Housework and Childcare, Before and During COVID-19* (CESifo Working Paper No. 8403, 2020) (on Italy); Lidia Farre et al., HOW THE COVID-19 LOCKDOWN AFFECTED GENDER INEQUALITY IN PAID AND UNPAID WORK IN SPAIN (IZA Discussion Paper No. 13434, 2020) (on Spain).

49. Powell, *supra* note 40.

50. *Id.*; Savage, *supra* note 42.

51. UNITED NATIONS, POLICY BRIEF: THE IMPACT OF COVID-19 ON WOMEN (2020); Savage, *supra* note 42.

52. Pietro Biroli et al., FAMILY LIFE IN LOCKDOWN (HCEO Working Paper No. 2020-051, 2020).

53. *See* UNITED NATIONS, *supra* note 51, at 4; Blundell et al., *supra* note 45, at 313–17.

54. Heyworth & Di Ruscio, *supra* note 44, at 3; Cristina Enguita-Fernandez et al., *The COVID-19 Epidemic Through a Gender Lens: What If a Gender Approach Had Been Applied to Inform Public Health Measures to Fight the COVID-19 Epidemic?*, 28 Soc. ANTHROPOLOGY 263 (2020); Jenny Fisher et al., *Community, Work, and Family in Times of COVID-19*, 23 COMM., WORK & FAM. 247 (2020); Wenham, *supra* note 45.

55. Savage, *supra* note 42.

56. Katarzyna Burzynska & Gabriela Contreras, *Gendered Effects of School Closures During the COVID-19 Pandemic*, 395 LANCET 1968 (2020).

57. Blundell et al., *supra* note 45.

58. Bali et al., *supra* note 45.

59. *Id.* at 1.

60. *See, e.g., id.*; World Bank, *supra* note 45; UN, *supra* note 51; King et al., *supra* note 47.

61. MATT GRUDNOFF & RICHARD DENNISS, PARTICIPATING IN GROWTH: FREE CHILDCARE AND INCREASED PARTICIPATION (Nordic Policy Centre & The Australia Institute, 2020).

62. Kate Fitz-Gibbon et al., *More Help Required: The Crisis in Family Violence During the Coronavirus Pandemic*, THE CONVERSATION (Aug. 17, 2020, 4:13 PM), https://theconversation.com/more-help-required-the-crisis-in-family-violence-during-the-coronavirus-pandemic-144126.

63. Sonia Elks, *Lack of Childcare Found "Destroying" UK Mothers' Careers Amid COVID-19*, REUTERS (July 25, 2020, 1:59 PM), https://www.reuters.com/article/us-hea

lth-coronavirus-women-careers-idUSKCN24Q0OY; HC Deb (25 June 2020) (677) col. 1535 (UK).
64. Blerta Cela, *Expert's Take: The Gendered Impact of COVID-19 Requires Transformative Changes in Economics Policies*, PreventionWeb (Sept. 9, 2020),https://www.prevention web.net/news/view/74074.
65. Savage, *supra* note 42.
66. *See, e.g.*, Titan M. Alon et al., The Impact of COVID-19 on Gender Equality 3 (NBER Working Paper No. 26947, 2020); Antz et al., *supra* note 47, at 4; Blundell et al., *supra* note 45, at 293; Victoria Costoya et al., The Impact of COVID-19 in the Allocation of Time Within Couples: Evidence for Argentina (2020) (unpublished manuscript); Savage, *supra* note 42.
67. *Cf.* Carlson et al., *supra* note 48, at 1.
68. Savage, *supra* note 42.
69. *Id.*; Karsten Hank & Anja Steinbach, *The Virus Changed Everything, Didn't It? Couples' Division of Housework and Children Before and During the Corona Crisis*, 33 J. Fam. Res. 99 (2020). This, for example, might explain why findings in Canada, which has more equitable ingoing divisions, have been slightly different: *see, e.g.*, Kevin Shafer et al., *The Division of Domestic Labour Before and During the COVID-19 Pandemic in Canada*, 57 Can. Rev. Soc. 523 (2020).
70. *See* Alon et al., *supra* note 66, at 3; Andrew et al., *supra* note 48, at 3; Costoya, *supra* note 66, at 28 (reporting data from Argentina); Claudia Hupkau & Barbara Petrongolo, *Work, Care and Gender During the COVID-19 Crisis*, 41 Fiscal Stud. 623 (2020); Almudena Sevilla & Sarah Smith, *Baby Steps: The Gender Division of Childcare During the COVID-19 Pandemic*, 36 Oxford Rev. Econ. Pol. 169 (2020).
71. King et al., *supra* note 47, at 2.
72. Alon et al., *supra* note 66, at 3.
73. *See, e.g.*, OECD, Be Flexible! Background Brief on How Workplace Flexibility Can Help European Employees to Balance Work and Family 12 (2016); Ariane Hegewisch, Flexible Working Policies: A Comparative Review 4–5, 9–10 (Equality and Human Rights Commission, 2009); Rae Cooper & Marian Baird, *Bringing the "Right to Request" Flexible Working Arrangements to Life: From Policies to Practices*, 37 Emp. Rel. 568 (2015).
74. *See, e.g.*, Dana Brownlee, *Twitter, Square Announce Work From Home Forever Option: What Are the Risks?*, Forbes (May 18, 2020, 8:08 PM), https://www.forbes.com/sites/ danabrownlee/2020/05/18/twitter-square-announce-work-from-home-forever-opt ionwhat-are-the-risks/#533df6eb2565; Rosalind Dixon & Richard Holden, Liberalism After COVID: Toward a New Democratic Economics and Politics (2020) (unpublished manuscript); *Our Approach to Flexibility*, Telstra, https://careers.telstra.com/allro lesflex.
75. *Cf.* Rosalind Dixon et al., *Reimagining Job Sharing* (2020), https://apo.org.au/node/ 277446.
76. Lidia Katia C. Manzo & Alessandra Minello, *Mothers, Childcare Duties, and Remote Working Under COVID-19 Lockdown in Italy: Cultivating Communities of Care*, 10 Dialogues in Hum. Geo. 120, 123 (2020).
77. Carlson et al., *supra* note 48, at 1 (emphasis added).

78. Lyn Craig, *COVID-19 Has Laid Bare How Much We Value Women's Work, and How Much We Pay for It*, Conversation (Apr. 20, 2020, 10:56 PM), https://theconversation.com/covid-19-has-laid-bare-how-much-we-value-womens-work-and-how-little-we-pay-for-it-136042.

79. Kate Bahn et al., A Feminist Perspective on COVID-19 and the Value of Care Work Globally, Gender Work Organ 695, 698 (2020); *cf.* Kate Power, *The COVID-19 Pandemic Has Increased the Care Burden of Women and Families*, 16 Sustainability 67 (2020).

80. Powell, *supra* note 40, at 17–19 (citing Lani Guinier & Gerald Torres, The Miner's Canary: Enlisting Race, Resisting Power, Transforming Democracy (2002)) (on the miner's canary effect).

81. *See, e.g.*, Shai Davidai et al., COVID-90 Provides a Rare Opportunity to Create a Stronger, More Equitable Society (2020) (unpublished manuscript).

82. Luciana Polischuk & Daniel L Fay, *Administrative Response to Consequences of COVID-19 Emergency Responses: Observations and Implications from Gender-Based Violence in Argentina* 50 Am. Rev. of Pub. Admin. 675 (2020).

CHAPTER 9

WHEN QUEER THEORY GOES TO LAW SCHOOL

BRENDA COSSMAN

QUEER theory is a tough thing to pin down. Lauren Berlant and Michael Warner wrote, over twenty-five years ago, that "queer theory is not the theory *of* anything in particular."[1] More recently, Sarah Lamble observes that "it has become almost customary to begin any introduction to queer theory by noting the impossibility of defining queer and the inherent paradox in doing so. If there is anything that encapsulates queer, it is the refusal of categorization."[2] Despite queer theory's disavowal of categories and boundaries, and its preference for subversion and transgression, it is possible to identify basic themes and critical dispositions, particularly in some of its foundational texts.[3] Queer theory has developed as an interrogation and deconstruction of the multiple discursive productions of sexuality, seeking to denaturalize the assumed connections between sex, gender, and desire. It did so in part as a break from what were the prevailing analytic frameworks for theorizing around sexuality. This chapter outlines the emergence of queer theory, and some of its distinctive themes and critical sensibilities. We will consider what queer theory is against, what it is for and what it has to say about law.

I. QUEER THEORY

A. Development of Queer Theory

Queer theory's genesis can perhaps be seen to lie with Foucault's argument that sexuality is a discursive production rather than a natural condition.[4] In *The History of Sexuality Volume 1*, he argued that modern discourses around sexuality were deeply implicated in power relations and the governance of individuals. However, like his work on discipline and criminality more generally, he argued that power did not operate primarily as repressive but rather productive. In his repudiation of the "repressive hypothesis," Foucault argued against what had been a prevailing belief that sexuality in the Victorian era was repressed and its discourses silenced. He argued instead that discourses about sexuality proliferated during this era, as sexuality became the object of multiple medical, juridical, and psychological discourses. These discourses produced new scientific truths about sexuality that produced sexual subjectivities; that is, power operated not through the repression of individuals as objects but through the internalization of these norms in their own experiences of sexuality. Through the eighteenth and nineteenth centuries, these discourses took increasing interest in the "world of perversion," that is, sexualities that did not fit the marital norm: children, the mentally ill, homosexuals. Same-sex sexuality—sodomy—previously conceived as an activity and a sin was, during this time, reconfigured as identity; the homosexual emerged as a pathologized, all-encompassing identity. In the final chapter, Foucault connected these scientific discourses around sexuality to the rise of a new modality of governance over populations: biopower. Foucault argued that mechanisms of power and knowledge over bodies, including discourses of sexuality, operate not through repression and the threat of death but by taking charge of lives. Foucault's *History of Sexuality* marked a groundbreaking shift in the understanding of sexuality, away from both more essentialist and biological conceptions, as well as those that focused on sexuality as primarily as a form of repression. Scholars who would become foundational to queer theory picked up on Foucault's ideas around sexuality, power, and knowledge and deployed them to break with prevailing approaches to sexuality.

B. Connections to Feminism

Foucault was not alone in approaching sexuality as a site of power; feminists in the 1970s had begun to theorize the ways in which sexuality operated as a site of oppression for women. Radical feminism in particular focused on male sexual violence and heterosexuality as an oppressive institution for women. Groundbreaking books—Susan Brownmiller's *Against Our Will*,[5] Andrea Dworkin's *Woman Hating*[6] and Diana Russell's *The Politics of Rape*[7]—focused feminist attention on the link between sexuality, sexual violence, and women's oppression. But queer theory would emerge as a break from this feminism, and from its focus on gender. Gayle Rubin in her ground breaking essay, *Thinking Sex* in 1984, argued that sex and sexuality should be examined independently from gender.[8] She challenged feminism's claim on the sexuality field, and argued that it was essential "to separate gender and sexuality analytically to more accurately reflect their separate social existence."[9] It was time, she claimed in 1984, to develop an "autonomous theory and politics specific to sexuality."[10] But Rubin's intervention was one born of feminism, and of the intense splits within feminism during the sex wars. She was an important interlocutor in the sex wars as a sex-positive feminist, opposing the radical feminist position on pornography in particular and sexuality in general. The beginnings of queer theory's break from feminism are ones that actually demonstrated the shared genealogies of both.[11]

A few years later, in what would become a foundation text of queer theory, Eve Sedgwick argued that "the study of sexuality is not coextensive with the study of gender; correspondingly, antihomophobic inquiry is not coextensive with feminist inquiry."[12] For Sedgwick, sexuality and gender represent two distinct analytic axes. She argued: "[T]he question of gender and the question of sexuality, inextricable from one another though they are . . . are nonetheless not the same question, that in twentieth-century Western culture, gender and sexuality represent two analytic axes that may productively be imagined as being distinct from one another."[13] The emerging body of queer theory demarcated the study of sex and sexuality, without gender or feminism, producing a sophisticated body of work that troubled heteronormativity, independent of feminism's focus on male/female relationships. Queer theoretical work could investigate sex and sexuality hierarchies irreducible to gender as the axis of power.

But the relationship between queer and feminism would remain ambivalent and contested. Rubin's and Sedgwick's scholarship were both influenced by feminism. Indeed, Judith Butler's foundational texts, discussed in the next section, were as much an intervention in feminist theory as they were in a nascent field of sexuality studies. Butler would come to argue against "proper objects," that is, against the idea that feminism's proper object of study was gender and queer theory's, sexuality. Butler argued for greater intellectual trespass between the two. Rubin herself, in arguing for an autonomous field of study, gestured toward a rapprochement: "In the long run, feminism's critique of gender hierarchy must be incorporated into a radical theory of sex, and the critique of sexual oppression should enrich feminism."[14] Much queer theory would develop on a trajectory entirely separate from feminism; indeed, some queer theory would come to be criticized for its gay male gaze and its erasure of lesbian specificity, while others would seek more intellectual trespass.

C. Break from Gay and Lesbian Studies

Queer theory also emerged as a break from gay and lesbian studies, and its focus on gay and lesbian identity. Teresa de Lauretis coined the term "queer theory" in 1990, as a provocation, to unsettle the complacency of "gay and lesbian studies," with queer denoting "a certain critical distance" from the terms "lesbian and gay."[15] She argued that it signaled a "refusal of heterosexuality as the benchmark for all sexual formulations." It was to "recast or reinvent the terms of our sexualities, to construct another discursive horizon, another way of thinking the sexual."[16] De Lauretis argued that it was intended to challenge the idea of gay and lesbian studies as a single entity, pointing to the differences that were elided and the silences that were constructed within this "established and often convenient formula."[17] While de Lauretis would within a few years denounce the term, queer theory took on a life of its own. Two foundational texts of queer theory, Eve Sedgwick's *The Epistemology of the Closet* and Judith Butler's *Gender Trouble* (which David Halperin notes were both written well before anyone had heard of queer theory[18]), picked up on this break, particularly in its critique of identity. Both rejected essentialist constructions of gender and sexuality, although they did so in different ways, with different starting points and emphases.

Sedgwick also sought to deconstruct the homosexual/heterosexual dichotomy on which gay and lesbian studies and identity were premised. Building on Foucault's work on the discursive production of the homosexual in the nineteenth century, as well as the construction of sexuality as a privileged site of truth and identity, Sedgwick would explore and deconstruct the heterosexual/homosexual distinction, which she argued was a central narrative of contemporary Western culture. For Sedgwick, the privileging of sexuality in identity, truth and knowledge and of the gender object of choice as the defining dimension of "sexual orientation" produced this homo/hetero distinction as a presiding narrative, which in turn marked a series of structuring binaries: public/private, secrecy/disclosure, feminine/masculine, majority/minority, passive/active, knowledge/ignorance, to name but a few. Sedgwick set out a series of axioms that would have a profound impact on the development of queer theory. The first—a seemingly simple proposition that "people are different from each other"—would disrupt the idea that the homo/hetero distinction was the only distinction relevant to sexualities; that many other dimensions of identity, practice, and subordination shaped sexuality. Sedgwick argued that gay and lesbian identity has been premised on a minoritizing discourse that operates to reinforce the heterosexual/homosexual distinction, which is itself premised on the superiority of the former and the homophobic subordination of the latter. It is an argument that is deeply anti-identitarian, that argues that gay and lesbian identity operates not to disrupt homophobia but to reinforce it.

In *Gender Trouble*, Judith Butler set out to disrupt the pervasive understanding of gender as the cultural interpretation of sex, arguing that the underlying category of sex is neither natural nor biologically determined but, rather, is itself discursively produced in and through gender.[19] She argued that gender is performative—a doing and constituting of the identity that it is purported to be: "As in other ritual social dramas, the action of gender requires a performance that is *repeated*. This repetition is at once a reenactment and a reexperiencing of a set of meanings already socially established; and it is the mundane and ritualized form of their legitimation."[20] Gender should "not to be constructed as a stable identity or locus of agency" but, rather, should be understood as "an identity tenuously constituted in time, instituted in an exterior space through a *stylized repetition of acts*."[21] Gender produces the very binaries of male and female sex that it is said to reflect, binaries produced in and through a dominant heterosexual matrix. The bodies that make sense are those presented as reflecting a stable sex, expressed through a stable gender that is oppositional and hierarchical, defined in and through the practice of heterosexuality.

It too was anti-identitarian, challenging the very category of "woman" on which feminism had been based, and disrupting the binaries of sex/gender, male/female, gay/straight. While it was an intervention in feminist debates about gender (and her feminism once again lays bare queer theory's feminist foundations), its implications were far ranging for sexual identities more generally. Her critique of the gender binary and her theory of gender performance also gestured to a rejection of essentialist gay and lesbian identities. *Gender Trouble* sought to denaturalize the female/male distinction on which heterosexuality was premised and normalized. But so too did it trouble any simply gay or lesbian identity, which were also premised on ideas of stable gender.

Through these foundational works, queer theory took aim at the dichotomy between gay and straight, homosexual and heterosexual, suggesting that these dichotomies were themselves part of the problem. The homo/hetero distinction normalized heterosexuality and reinforced the very static and essentialist conceptions of sex, sexuality, gender, and desire. It was a critique of identity—specifically, gay and lesbian identity claims—problematizing the essentialization of gay identity against a heterosexual norm. In these original stories, queer theory was decidedly anti-identitarian; it was not synonymous with gay and lesbian subjects, or LGBT subjects but, rather, explicitly sought to complicate and disrupt identity.

D. Critique of the "Normal"

Queer theory also emerged as a critique of the normal, and by extension, of normative sexuality. David Halperin described queer as whatever is "at odds with the normal, the legitimate, the dominant."[22] He elaborated: "Queer demarcates not a positivity but a positionality vis-à-vis the normative—a positionality that is not restricted to lesbians and gay men but is in fact available to anyone who is or who feels marginalized because of her or his sexual practices."[23] Or as Kathryn Stockton Bond puts it, "It's the strange we like, if we're for the queer."[24] Cathy Cohen similarly argued, "queer theory stands in direct contrast to the normalizing tendencies of hegemonic sexuality rooted in ideas of static, stable sexual identities and behaviors."[25] But, Cohen sought to push queer theory and politics beyond its exclusive focus on heteronormativity. She argued that queer's critique of the normal needed to extend beyond the queer/straight dichotomy to include the multiple axes of oppression of "non-queer" identified sexually marginalized subjects. Cohen argued for an intersectional queer politics that built alliances with a host of sexual marginalized subjects, as her title suggested, including punks, bulldaggers and welfare queens; subjects who have been oppressed because of their nonnormative sexualities, beyond the queer/straight distinction. Queer theory emerged as a critique of and resistance to sexual regimes of normalization, including but also beyond the operation of heteronormativity.

But queer did not emerge exclusively in the academy. Queer was also a politics, and queer theory the product of a deeply political moment: the AIDS crisis of the 1980s. It had an urgent political impulse, with activist organizations like ActUp and Queer Nation challenging the intense homophobia fueled by the AIDS crisis. Rallying around slogans like Silence = Death, it was an anti-assimilationist, in-your-face politics of survival. Douglas Crimp argued that it was "within this new political conjuncture that the word queer has been reclaimed to designate new political identities."[26] The political origins of queer theory are important: queer politics was a call for things to be otherwise; a call for life; for a sexual life in the face of the devastation of the AIDS crisis and stigma of a "gay" disease.

E. Queer Theory's Travels

Queer theory would travel a long way from its origins. Some would declare it dead. Others would critique it for its silences, omissions, and oppressions. The Queer of Color Critique would challenge and explode the whiteness of queer theory. While Roderick Ferguson coined the term in *Aberrations in Black*[27] as a method for challenging the discourses that conceal the intersections of race, class, gender, sexuality, and nation, he was in part giving name to a critique that emerged in earlier work by Barbara Smith, Cathy Cohen and Jose Munoz, among others. Not unlike queer theory's initial rejection of the singular axis of gender, scholars of color rejected the exclusive focus on sexuality. Queer theory would develop in many directions. Some took a temporal turn, exploring questions of queer time and queer futures.[28] Some turned to affect, exploring precognitive feelings, often with a focus on the more negative ones. Queer theory has explored feelings associated with social exclusion, from shame to despair to regret.[29] Some questioned the antinormativity of queer theory and whether it was always positioned against.[30] Some would move to nonhumanism, others to the transnational, yet others to critiques of homonationalism.[31] Queer theory would develop in a complicated relationship with its subject, with many arguing that it had no proper object or subject. Yet much of it would continue to swirl around issues of sexuality, desire, the erotic; some interested in same-sex desire, others in nonnormative desire, yet others as a way of exploring and disrupting normative sexualities.

II. Queer Theory and Law

What then has queer theory had to say about law? Admittedly, queer theory has not made the kind of inroads into law and legal scholarship that feminism has, but it has nonetheless made its mark.[32] Despite broader critiques about queer theory not having a proper object, that it is not a theory about anything in particular, in the legal context, it has tended to focus on the role of law in constituting and regulating sex and sexuality. As Sarah Lamble writes, "Queer theory as applied to socio-legal studies has been particularly attentive to the role that law plays in governing sex and sexualities, both overtly and more insidiously; and demonstrating how policing of sexual and gender identities and practices are central forms of governance and control in contemporary societies."[33] Noa Ben-Asher similarly describes: "[q]ueer legal studies investigates how sex, gender and sexuality are produced through legal discourses and other forms of knowledge."[34]

A. Anti-Identitarian Turn in Law

As with queer theory more generally, queer legal studies does not focus on gay and lesbian identities and rights per se but explores the judicial discourses that both constitutes these and other nonnormative sexualities. Some of the earliest queer legal studies works followed queer theory's vision of sexuality as an independent object of study and its deconstructive, anti-identaritarian approach to the homosexual/heterosexual binary. Janet Halley, for example, in her critical analysis of sodomy and the Supreme Court decision in *Bowers v. Hardwick*, upholding its criminalization, followed Rubin and Sedgwick in exploring sexuality independently from gender, and in refusing the homo/hetero distinction.[35] Halley explored how despite the fact that most sodomy statutes are facially neutral—they apply to same and opposite sex alike—sodomy as an act and as an identity have come to be identified with homosexuality. "Sodomy in these formulations is such an intrinsic characteristic of homosexuals, and so exclusive to us, that it constitutes a rhetorical proxy for us. It is our metonym."[36] Halley reveals the deeply unstable relationship between act and identity that underlies the *Hardwick* decision, and the ways in which the distinction has been deployed by the Court to collapse act and identity for homosexuals, while rendering heterosexual sodomy invisible. Ultimately, Halley suggests strategically less emphasis on identity, and more on acts; notwithstanding the deep instability, a greater emphasis on acts may help forge alliances with heterosexuals, and "expos[e] the immunity which invisibly gives heterosexuality its rationale."[37] Halley's analysis is one that not only refuses a fixed gay and lesbian identity but demonstrates how this identitarian approach both constitutes and reinforces the "subordination of homosexual identity and the superordination of heterosexual identity."[38]

B. Beyond LGBT Wins

1. *Sodomy Challenge*

Many of these early critiques focused on legal losses for gay and lesbian rights, though they did so in ways that were distinct from other gay and lesbian scholars. One way to bring the critical sensibilities of a queer theory approach to law into sharper relief—and its departure from LGBT legal scholarship—is through the kind of analysis it brings to gay and lesbian rights "wins," from the decriminalization of sodomy in *Lawrence* to same-sex marriage in *Obergefell*. In *Lawrence v. Texas*, the U.S. Supreme Court found that the criminal prohibitions on sodomy were unconstitutional.[39] The Court, in a 5–4 decision, overruled its previous ruling in *Bowers v. Hardwick*, which had upheld a Georgia sodomy law, finding that there was no violation of the constitutional right to privacy. In *Lawrence*, Justice Kennedy, writing for the majority, concluded that the constitutional right to privacy included the right to make private choices about intimate matters, including those matters "touching upon the most private human conduct, sexual behavior, and in the most private of places, the home."[40] In his view, the decision to enter into a homosexual sexual relationship in the privacy of one's own home was such a matter: "adults may choose to enter upon this relationship in the confines of their home and their own private lives and still retain their dignity as free persons. . . . The liberty protected by the Constitution allows homosexual persons the right to make this choice."[41]

Gay and lesbian advocates, and gay and lesbian legal scholarship, celebrated the decision, decriminalizing homosexual sexual activity. Queer legal analyses were somewhat more circumspect. On the one hand, queer theory has an antiregulatory and prosex impulse; it would welcome the decriminalization of homosexuality and sodomy. But queer legal analysis also looks at the judicial text, at the discursive terms of the right to privacy in the decision, and the way in which legal discourse constitutes the gay subject that it regulates. Katherine Franke, for example, argued that the Court in *Lawrence* recognized a highly domesticated liberty right—"the liberty interest at stake is one that is tethered to the domestic private."[42] She argues that gay men are "portrayed as domesticated creatures, settling down into marital-like relationships in which they can both cultivate and nurture desires for exclusivity, fidelity, and longevity in place of other more explicitly erotic desires."[43] This is made all the more ironic, as a number of commentators have pointed out, given that Lawrence was not in fact in a long-term relationship; the sexual encounter that resulted in the criminal changes was a casual, one-night stand. For Franke, the gay subject whose privacy rights are protected is a highly domesticated one. Her concern is that "*Lawrence* and the gay rights organizing that has taken place around it have created a path dependency that privileges privatized and domesticated rights and legal liabilities, while rendering less viable projects that advance nonnormative notions of kindship, intimacy and sexuality."[44] Franke, then, is concerned with the terms on which sodomy was decriminalized and gay subjects recognized, terms within which only certain gay subjects will be recognized, and other nonnormative sexualities once again cast aside.

Along similar lines, Teemu Ruskola, specifically asks, "[f]rom the perspective of queer theory, how should we view this victory of gay rights."[45] While welcoming the overruling of *Hardwick*, Ruskola takes a closer look at the judicial text, arguing that the terms of decriminalization within *Lawrence* comes with its own limitations.[46] Ruskola observes how the Court reframed the question away from sodomy and toward intimacy, arguing that "the problem with the Court's rhetorical formulation is not what it permits—intimate sexual association—but what it leaves out, beyond the sphere of sexual legitimacy. Being in an intimate personal relationship should not be a *requirement* for having a constitutionally protected sex life."[47] He argues, building on Halley, that while *Hardwick* focused on acts (specifically, the act of homosexual sodomy), *Lawrence* by contrast, focused on identity: "In *Lawrence*, in contrast, identity is the major rhetorical mode, as the Court seeks to justify sexual conduct by the actors' identities: capable of intimacy and hence deserving of respect, homosexuals should be permitted to engage in the acts that define them in the first place."[48] For Ruskola, respectability is the price of liberty.[49]

2. Same-Sex Marriage Challenges

A similar disjuncture between gay and lesbian constitutional wins and queer critique can be seen in the context of same-sex marriage. Indeed, there has been a long-standing debate about the desirability of same-sex marriage within LGBT communities. Gay and lesbian rights equality advocates long argued that inclusion within the institution of marriage was fundamental to full gay and lesbian citizenship; both the material and symbolic significance of marriage in the distribution of rights, benefits and recognition demand marriage equality. But there was a critique, that marriage was deeply heteronormative; that gay men and lesbians should not be seeking assimilation into such an oppressive institution. Some of the argument built on earlier feminist critiques of marriage as patriarchal, premised on the subordination of women, and that progressives should seek to dismantle rather than assimilate into it.[50] Queer activists and scholars took up a specifically queer critique of marriage, arguing that it was normalizing and domesticating, undermining the more subversive dimensions of queer identities.[51]

These debates would play out as the courts considered the multiple constitutional challenges to the exclusion of same-sex couples from marriage. The challenges would extend over more than a decade, beginning in Hawaii, through the recognition of civil unions in Vermont, of same-sex marriage in Massachusetts, ultimately culminating in *Obergefell v. Hodges*, in which the Supreme Court found a constitutional right to marry for same-sex couples. Same-sex marriage advocates would argue for the fundamental importance of equality rights and equal marriage rights for gay men and lesbians. But queer critics were far less sanguine and worried instead about how the campaign for equal marriage obscured a multiplicity of other issues facing LGBT Americans, from poverty to sexual liberation, as well as how equal marriage would create a hierarchy of socially approved relationships, marginalizing the diversity of relationships within queer communities. Katherine Franke, for example, in *Wedlocked*[52] (published the same year as *Obergefell*), warned of the costs of marriage equality to gay men and lesbians. Marriage would become a new form of state governance, reinforcing heteronormativity, and other nonmarital innovative relationships would continue to be cast as inferior and lacking respectability. Franke argued that same-sex marriage advocates, instead of seeking a "right to nonnormative sex and sexuality," pursued a strategy of respectability, wherein gays gain dignity through marriage. For Franke, these legal strategies, and legal texts that they engendered, are themselves constitutive of the legal subject: "rights-bearing subjects are almost inevitably shaped by the very rights they bear."[53] She argues that "[t]his remaking of gay and lesbian subjectivity and the turn toward respectability ... entailed carefully crafting a revised conception of gayness organized around a status or stable identity rather than sexual acts, and substituting love and familial devotion as the operative forms of affect that bound same-sex couples together rather than sodomy or sexual attraction."[54]

In 2015, the Supreme Court in *Obergefell v. Hodges*,[55] held that the fundamental right to marry for same-sex couples is guaranteed by both the due process and the equal protection clauses of the Fourteenth Amendment. Justice Kennedy, writing for the majority, emphasized the "centrality of marriage to the human condition."[56] He underscored that marriage involves a right to personal choice inherent in individual autonomy; to decide to marry is among the most intimate decisions a person can make, and this decision allows one to shape their own destiny.[57] Moreover, marriage is a keystone of our social order, and "a building block of our national community" through which a society supports a couple and protects their union through recognition and material benefits.[58] Overall, marriage embodies the highest human ideals such as love and family; "no union is more profound than marriage."[59] Kennedy's central point was that to exclude LGBTQ people from this institution is to deprive them from a choice that is fundamental to human life and dignity.

Same-sex marriage advocates were elated, and much of the mainstream media celebrated the decision as an unadulterated victory for gay and lesbian couples.[60] But the decision and its discourse around marriage has been subject to extensive queer critique. Scholars have pointed out—in an almost "we told you so" sort of way—how Kennedy reverence's for the institution of marriage in American life marginalizes alternative familial formations and relationships.[61] Cyril Ghosh, for example, has argued that the privileging of "marriage, romantic love, monogamy, parenting, and the nuclear family as a standard to which all Americans ought to aspire" demeans those—queer and straight alike—who do not seek assimilation.[62] Kendall Thomas, picking up on various queer critiques of marriage, provides a queer reading of *Obergefell* that goes beyond the focus on rights discourse as constitutive of gay subjects.[63] Thomas explores how Kennedy's decision and its articulation of the meaning of marriage is also constitutive of the state, that is, contributes to how "the state's identity gets imagined, elaborated and expressed."[64] The ruling in *Obergefell*, rather than relying on the idea of marriage as a private area of intimate life, emphasizes "a vision of civil marriage that emphasizes its constitutive role in our national public life."[65] He argues that the decision—and the gay and lesbian rights strategies behind it—brings into view several dimensions of "the American marital state and American conjugal nationalism."[66] Thomas explores *Obergefell* and same-sex marriage through the lens of conjugal state power, that is, the ways in which the state governs through marriage.[67] He argues that civil marriage laws are themselves constitutive of state conjugal power, a power that has expanded in the post-*Obergefell* world.

Queer legal critiques then can be seen to go beyond legal outcomes—whether a particular law is struck down and/or a particular right vindicated—to explore the ways in which legal discourse is itself constitutive of the subjects it regulates, of respectable modes of sexuality and intimacy, and reinforcing of state power itself. The question is not whether a particular law or ruling is good or bad for gay men and lesbians; this is not a question that queer legal studies would consider to even be answerable. It is rather to explore the multiple discursive and distributional implications of a particular law or ruling. While the tone of some queer legal analyses borders on the unequivocally normative—same-sex marriage is actually bad for the gays—arguably, a queer legal sensibility would adopt a more ambivalent stance. Noa Ben-Asher has argued that "the work of queer legal studies embraces, rather than rejects, paradox. Queer legal theorists seek and elaborate the paradox."[68] In much of my own work, I have sought to reveal the ambivalences, contradictions and paradoxes of legal strategies and discourses. For example, I have argued that same-sex marriage ought to be approached as a zone of ambivalence, something which the for-or-against debates have been unable to do.[69] Rather than arguing, for example, that same-sex marriage changes gays for the bad (the radical/queer antiassimilationist critique) or marriage for the good (the pro-marriage assimilationist argument), I have suggested that we consider the possibilities that same-sex marriage has done both—and more. We need to explore the multiple discursive and distributional implications of the legal recognition of same-sex marriage; implications that cannot be captured without embracing paradox and contradiction.

C. Beyond the LGBT Subject in Law

Although much queer legal theory has tracked issues of sexual identity and LGBT rights (and reflects the ambivalent relationship between queer legal theory and the LGBT subject), it is not exclusively tied to those subjects/objects. Following queer theory's anti-identitarian impulse, queer legal scholars have tended to adopt a critical eye toward the legal regulation of sexual orientation, seeking to destabililize the essentialized identities on which much of it is based. But queer legal scholars have also deployed these critical approaches to other nonnormative sexualities; yet others, to more normative sexualities. Janet Halley, for example, has explored the ways in which queer theory might illuminate legal reasoning and regulation in more heterosexual, if not entirely normative, contexts. Halley's work on taking a break from feminism is part of the queer tradition begun by Rubin and Sedgwick, of exploring sexual harms and their regulation in ways that are not reducible to gender oppression and allow for an exploration of the intersections of sexuality, sex and gender in ways that are not reduced to the male/female divide.[70] Both Halley and I have explored what critical insight a queer legal studies lens could bring to bear on court rulings. One case that we both explored was *Twyman v. Twyman*, a family law case of some notoriety, in which a wife sought damages for emotional injuries that she claimed she suffered because her husband induced her to engage in sadomasochistic (S/M) bondage.[71] A feminist reading would read the case through a lens of male domination and female subordination, of Sheila Twyman the victim of her husband's sexual desires, and of her "consent" as illusory. Halley proposes several alternative readings, which bracket feminism's focus on gender, on male oppression and female subordination. She suggests a Foucauldian reading in which power is more complex and ambivalent, in which the facts in Twyman can be viewed through the lens of biopolitical regulation and micropolitical deployments.[72] One reading would focus on marital monogamy: "marriage provides spouses with an amazing power over each other: the power to perform (and inflict), and to prohibit (and punish), infidelity."[73] In this reading, it would be Sheila, "the wronged wife, the enforcer of marriage vows," who has the power to "[restore] the fidelity rule to its proper place, with the avid assistance of almost every judge."[74]

I have offered a similar, if slightly different reading of *Twyman*, but one that also brackets (in my case only temporarily) feminism and its focus on gender as an axis of power, arguing that the case can be seen as performance of heteronormativity, with both Sheila Twyman and the court policing the boundaries of stable heterosexual sexuality. The BDSM encounter represented a moment of sexual excess, with the performance of deviant desire violating heteronormativity. It was this violation that both Sheila Twyman and the court sought to discipline by marking the husband as the deviant. Such a reading is more interested in the regulation of sex and sexuality as an (if not the) axis of power, the role of marriage in producing the heteronormative matrix, and the hetero/homo binary than it is with gender.[75]

Other scholars have taken queer legal sensibilities further afield. Teemu Ruskola, for example, deploys queer theory in a very different direction, operating outside of "proper objects."[76] Ruskola describes his use of queer theory as "a commitment to a mode of analysis, not to the study of a given subject or set of subjects."[77] He uses queer theory as a set of propositions through which he examines the rhetoric of colonial international law in relation to China, arguing that "a queer analysis suggests that the homoerotic violation of non-Western states is a condition of possibility of fully realized (Western) sovereignty."[78] He elaborates:

> I use the word queer to refer to a range of non-normative subject positions. These positions are at once sexual, social, and political. Thus defined, queer positions are occupied by all subjects at some point (whether they wish to acknowledge it or not) and by no subject at all times (even if they so desire). To be completely antinormative would be to be mad, and to be perfectly normative would be no less psychotic. Queer theory provides a method for analyzing how queer and normative subject positions are constituted in relation to one another and how they are secured, but also how they remain necessarily unstable and provisional. In short, it is a method for analyzing the discursive dynamics by which subjects are made and unmade, maintained and destabilized.[79]

Ruskola's is a queer analysis, with clear Sedgwickian and Butlerian influences, applied beyond the traditional sexual subjects seen in much queer legal scholarship, in this case to China as a queer subject.[80]

D. Queer of Color Critique in Law

A queer of color critique (QOCC) has, at least by name, made very little appearance in legal scholarship. References to QOCC and specifically to Ferguson's groundbreaking work has largely been relegated to footnotes. A notable exception is a recent article by Antron Mahoney and Heather Brydie Harris, who explored developments in anti-trans policy and legislation through an explicitly QOCC.[81] They build on Roderick Ferguson's QOCC to analyze the racial framing of anti-LGBT law and policy, and specifically anti-trans bathroom bills. Mahoney and Harris use QOCC to rethink how the state has memorialized Martin Luther King Jr.—particularly how the memorializing has relied on religion in ways that normalize gender and sexuality to oppose trans rights. They explain how anti-trans logic "predicated on religion... aligns the state and the Civil Rights Movement in a commemorative fashion to demonstrate a popular will for anti-LGBT policies and practices."[82] For Mahoney and Harris, QOCC is a way to center but not essentialize the black queer subject, "revealing the often-obscured interconnected logics of race, gender, sexuality and class in cultural formations to map and remap the contours of power propagated by state forces."[83] As a way to counter the state's anti-trans logic, they point to a public dance protest by a black transwoman activist which exemplifies Jose Esteban Munoz's conception of dissidentification.[84] As Ferguson describes it:

> to disidentify means to "[recycle] and [rethink] encoded meaning" and "to use the code [of the majority] as raw material for representing a disempowered politics of positionality that has been rendered unthinkable by the dominate culture"... Queer of color analysis disidentifies with historical materialism to *rethink* its categories and how they might conceal the materiality of race, gender, and sexuality. In this instance, to disidentify in no way means to discard.[85]

This limited inroad that QOCC has so far made into law is not to suggest that there is not a literature of sexuality and race; there is in fact a robust literature influenced by critical race theory and black feminism that explores the unique intersections of race and sexuality, and that seeks to reveal the racial biases and omissions of gay and lesbian legal scholarship. Darren Hutchinson, for example, is a leading legal scholar of race and sexuality, exploring LGBT issues from critical race perspectives.[86] We can certainly find queer sensibilities in Hutchinson's work, for example, its antiessentialist approach to identity, his deployment of concepts like heteronormativity and his citation to queer works. However, I am reluctant to label it "queer" since Hutchinson himself does not do so. Rather, he has described his work as influenced and shaped by critical race and black feminist theory. The same might be said of Russell Robinson, whose work explores a critical race perspective to sexuality and LGBT legal issues.[87] Robinson explores the intersectionalities of race and sexuality, processes of sexual racism and the racialized nature of masculinities. There are strong queer sensibilities to the work, but it is not self reflexively queer; it is self reflexively critical race theory.

Indeed, the work of Hutchinson and Robinson raises broader questions of labeling and claiming in seeking to provide a taxonomy of queer legal works. What works qualify and why? I have argued that there is in some legal scholarship a kind of "no-name queerness"; a kind of queer approach to law that is "a more opaque one that does not announce itself under the banner of Queer Theory."[88] It is scholarship influenced by some of the central ideas of queer theory, "of sexuality and sexual subject positions as discursively constituted, unstable, fluid"; ideas that have become deeply ingrained in much critical legal scholarship on issues of sex and sexuality. These ideas permeate Hutchinson's and Robinson's work, yet there is an ethicality in both claiming and not claiming the work as queer. Their work develops an intersectional analysis of race and sexuality that exceeds anything found in self reflexively queer work and raises questions of the boundaries and overlaps between different critical traditions.

E. Trans Legal Studies ... More Than a Postscript

Trans legal studies has emerged as its own distinct critical perspective. Although some of the influences are similar—Foucault and Butler, for example, on the construction of sexuality and gender—trans studies, and trans legal studies in particular, is not simply derivative of queer theory. In some senses, it represents a break from queer studies, much like queer theory was a break from feminism and gay and lesbian studies. But it has also developed in conversation with critical race theory, Black and women of color feminism, critical disability studies and other critical scholarships. From Dean Spade's groundbreaking work to the proliferation of younger legal scholars engaging with trans issues,[89] trans legal studies has emerged as an exciting critical field of interrogation of genders. Like queer theory and critical race theory. for example, critical trans studies breaks from rights advocacy and formal legal equality to explore the broader disciplinary and governance mechanisms of gender. Ido Katri and Samuel Singer, for example, describe critical trans legal studies as putting the lives of trans people, including the most marginalized, at the center of the analysis. They write:

> trans studies have invested in deconstructing theory by bringing forth the worldviews of its subjects of inquiry. Inspired by Dean Spade's call to stop believing that "what the law says about itself is true and what the law says about us is what matters," ... [it] is attuned to ways the law contributes to everyday experiences of exclusions, while acknowledging the protections it may grant in some circumstances.

It is impossible to do trans legal studies justice in a chapter on queer theory, yet it would be remiss to fail to mention its critical interventions in debates around genders and sexualities.

III. Conclusion

Queer theory itself is not one thing. Just as "queer theory is not the theory *of* anything in particular," queer legal theory cannot be the theory of anything legal in particular. I have suggested that it might be better described as a sensibility. And as a sensibility, we need to refuse its rigidification as a theory of law about *x*. In asking "how do we do queer things in law," we need to remain open to multiple possibilities. Just as queer theory has moved in many directions, so too will future legal scholarship be influenced by queer sensibilities. Legal histories might benefit from the creative possibilities of feeling backward and the multiplicities of queer temporalities. Legal geographies could lean into inquiries of queer spaces. For my own scholarship, queer theory continues to offer a powerful, anti-identitarian lens to explore sex, sexuality and desire. It helps me think about normative and nonnormative sexualities alike as socially constituted and fluid. It is always in conversation with other critical traditions and methodologies, from feminism to critical race theory. And it is always in state of change; it is a "category in constant formation."

Notes

1. Lauren Berlant & Michael Warner, *What Does Queer Theory Teach Us About X?*, 110 PMLA 343, 344 (1995).
2. Sarah Lamble, *Queer Theory and Socio-legal Studies*, in THE ROUTLEDGE HANDBOOK OF LAW AND SOCIETY 53, 53 (Mariana Valverde et al., eds., 2021).
3. JUDITH BUTLER, GENDER TROUBLE: FEMINISM AND THE SUBVERSION OF IDENTITY (2d ed. 1999)[hereineafter GENDER TROUBLE]; JUDITH BUTLER, BODIES THAT MATTER: ON THE DISCURSIVE LIMITS OF "SEX" (1993); Gayle Rubin, *Thinking Sex: Notes for a Radical Theory of the Politics of Sexuality*, in PLEASURE AND DANGER: EXPLORING FEMALE SEXUALITY (Carole S. Vance ed., 1984).
4. MICHEL FOUCAULT, THE HISTORY OF SEXUALITY VOLUME I: AN INTRODUCTION (Robert Hurley trans., 1978).
5. SUSAN BROWNMILLER, AGAINST OUR WILL: MEN, WOMEN AND RAPE (1975).
6. ANDREA DWORKIN, WOMAN HATING (1974).
7. DIANA RUSSELL, THE POLITICS OF RAPE: THE VICTIM'S PERSPECTIVE (1975).
8. Rubin, *supra* note 3, at 308–09.
9. *Id.* at 308.
10. *Id.* at 308.
11. *See* LYNNE HUFFER, MAD FOR FOUCAULT: RETHINKING THE FOUNDATIONS OF QUEER THEORY 45 (2009) (points to "queer theory's feminist birth"); *see also* LYNNE HUFFER, ARE THE LIPS A GRAVE? A QUEER FEMINIST ON THE ETHICS OF SEX (2013) (exploring the shared genealogies of queer and feminist theory).
12. EVE KOSOFSKY SEDGWICK, EPISTEMOLOGY OF THE CLOSET 27 (1990).
13. *Id.* at 30.
14. Rubin, *supra* note 3, at 308.
15. Teresa de Lauretis, *Queer Theory: Lesbian and Gay Sexualities: An Introduction*, 3 DIFFERENCES: J. FEMINIST CULTURAL STUD. iv (1991).
16. *Id.* at iv.
17. *Id.*
18. David Halperin, *The Normalization of Queer Theory*, 45 J. HOMOSEXUALITY 339 (2003).
19. BUTLER, GENDER TROUBLE, *supra* note 3.
20. *Id.* at 140.
21. *Id.*
22. DAVID HALPERIN, SAINT FOUCAULT: TOWARDS A GAY HABIOGRAPHY 62 (1997).
23. *Id.*
24. Kathryn Bond Stockton, *Queer Theory*, 24 THE YEAR'S WORK IN CRITICAL & CULTURAL THEORY 85, 85 (2016).
25. Cathy Cohen, *Punks, Bulldaggers, and Welfare Queens: The Radical Potential of Queer Politics?*, 3 GLQ 437 (1997).

26. Douglas Crimp, *Right On, Girlfriend*, 33 SOCIAL TEXT 14 (1992; *See also* MICHAEL WARNER, FEAR OF A QUEER PLANET: QUEER POLITICS AND SOCIAL THEORY (1993).
27. RODERICK FERGUSON, ABERRATIONS IN BLACK: TOWARD A QUEER OF COLOR CRITIQUE (2003).
28. *See, e.g.*, LEE EDELMAN, NO FUTURE: QUEER THEORY AND THE DEATH DRIVE (Michèle Aina Barale et al., eds., 2004); J. JACK HALBERSTAM, IN A QUEER TIME AND PLACE: TRANSGENDER BODIES, SUBCULTURAL LIVES (2005); JOSÉ ESTEBAN MUÑOZ, CRUISING UTOPIA: THE THEN AND THERE OF QUEER FUTURITY (2009); ELIZABETH FREEMAN, TIME BINDS: QUEER TEMPORALITIES, QUEER HISTORIES (2010); JUANA MARÍA RODRÍGUEZ, SEXUAL FUTURES, QUEER GESTURES, AND OTHER LATINA LONGINGS (2014).
29. *See, e.g.*, ANN CVETKOVICH, AN ARCHIVE OF FEELINGS: TRAUMA, SEXUALITY, AND LESBIAN PUBLIC CULTURES (2003); HEATHER LOVE, FEELING BACKWARDS: LOSS AND THE POLITICS OF QUEER HISTORY (2007).
30. Robyn Wiegman & Elizabeth A. Wilson, *Introduction: Anti-Normativity's Queer Conventions*, 26 DIFFERENCES: J. FEMINIST CULTURAL STUD. 1, 3 (2015) (arguing that "Antinormativity not only collectivizes the diverse work of such foundational figures as Leo Bersani, Judith Butler, Michel Foucault, Gayle Rubin, Eve Kosofsky Sedgwick, and Michael Warner, but it also underwrites the critical analyses and political activisms of the field's most important interlocutors."). *Contra* Lisa Duggan, *Queer Complacency Without Empire*, Bully Bloggers (Sept. 22, 2015), https://bullybloggers.wordpress.com/2015/09/22/queer-comp lacency-without-empire/; *See also* Jack Halberstam, *Straight Eye for the Queer Theorist: A Review of "Queer Theory Without Normativity,"* BULLY BLOGGERS (Sept. 12, 2015), https://bullybloggers.wordpress.com/2015/09/12/straight-eye-for-the-queer-theorist-a-review-of-queer-theory-without-antinormativity-by-jack-halberstam/.
31. JASBIR PUAR, TERRORIST ASSEMBLAGES: HOMONATIONALISM IN QUEER TIMES (2007).
32. *See* Brenda Cossman, *Queering Queer Legal Studies: An Unreconstructed Ode to Eve Sedgwick (and Others)*, 6 CRITICAL ANALYSIS L. 23 (2019) (noting that scholarship on queer legal theory often argues that there is very little queer theory in law).
33. Lamble, *supra* note 2, at 57.
34. Noa Ben-Asher, *Laws of Sex, Changed*, in THE OXFORD HANDBOOK OF LAW AND HUMANITIES (Simon Stern, Maksymilian Del Mar & Bernadette Meyler eds., 2019).
35. Janet Halley, *Reasoning About Sodomy: Act and Identity in and After* Bowers v. Hardwick, 79 VA. L. REV. 1721 (1993).
36. *Id.* at 1737.
37. *Id.* at 1772.
38. *Id. See also* Kendall Thomas, *Corpus Juris (Hetero)Sexualis: Doctrine, Discourse, and Desire in* Bowers v. Hardwick, 1 GLQ 33 (1993) (critique of *Hardwick* also relied on queer theoretical insights to deconstruct the homosexual/heterosexual divide).
39. 539 U.S. 558 (2003).
40. *Id.* at 558.
41. *Id.* at 567.
42. Katherine Franke, *The Domesticated Liberty of* Lawrence v. Texas, 104 COLUM. L. REV. 1399, 1403 (2004).
43. *Id.* at 1408–09.
44. *Id.* at 1414.
45. Teemu Ruskola, *Gay Rights Versus Queer Theory: What Is Left of Sodomy After* Lawrence v. Texas?, 23 SOC. TEXT 235, 236 (2005).
46. *Id.*

47. *Id.* at 238.
48. *Id.* at 244.
49. Many other scholars have mounted queer critiques of the gay rights win in *Lawrence*. *See, e.g.,* Libby Adler, *The Future of Sodomy*, 32 FORDHAM URB. L.J. 197 (2005) (analyzes the ruling in *Lawrence* for its "danger signs" while celebrating the advance in civil rights from the striking down of the criminalization of sodomy). Adler highlights dangers in the judicial text to both prosex and anti-identarian positions associated with queer critical sensibilities. *See also* Laura Rosenbury & Jennifer Rothman, *Sex In and Out of Intimacy*, 59 EMORY L.J. 809 (2010) (critiquing the sex negativity underlying *Lawrence* in only valuing sex within emotionally intimate relationships). Rosenbury and Rothman illustrate the deeply gendered and heteronormative nature of the sex-in-service-of-intimacy frame implicit in *Lawrence* and imagine alternative constructions of the relationship between sex and intimacy.
50. *See, e.g.,* MICHÈLE BARRETT & MARY MCINTOSH, THE ANTI-SOCIAL FAMILY (1982) on the oppressive nature of the family, and MARTHA FINEMAN, THE NEUTERED MOTHER, THE SEXUAL FAMILY AND OTHER TWENTIETH CENTURY TRAGEDIES (1995) on the feminist critique of marriage. On feminist inspired critiques of same-sex marriage, *see* Paula Ettelbrick, *Since When Is Marriage a Path to Liberation?*, 6 OUT/LOOK 9 (1989); Mary Anne Case, *What Feminists Have to Lose in Same-Sex Marriage Litigation*, 57 UCLA L. REV. 1199 (2010); NICOLA BARKER, NOT THE MARRYING KIND: A FEMINIST CRITIQUE OF SAME-SEX MARRIAGE (2012).
51. *See, e.g.,* MICHAEL WARNER, THE TROUBLE WITH NORMAL: SEX, POLITICS, AND THE ETHICS OF QUEER LIFE (1999); Katherine Franke, *The Politics of Same-Sex Marriage Politics*, 15 COLUM. J. GENDER & L. 236 (2006).
52. KATHERINE FRANKE, WEDLOCKED: THE PERILS OF MARRIAGE EQUALITY (2015).
53. *Id.* at 13.
54. *Id.* at 61.
55. Obergefell v. Hodges, 576 U.S. 644 (2015).
56. *Id.* at 657.
57. *Id.* at 665–66.
58. *Id.* at 669.
59. *Id.* at 861.
60. *See, e.g.,* Adam Liptak, *Supreme Court Ruling Makes Same-Sex Marriage a Right Nationwide*, N.Y. TIMES, June 26, 2015, https://www.nytimes.com/2015/06/27/us/supreme-court-same-sex-marriage.html ("The decision . . . set off jubilation and tearful embraces across the country, the first same-sex marriages in several states, and resistance—or at least stalling—in others. It came against the backdrop of fast-moving changes in public opinion, with polls indicating that most Americans now approve of the unions."); *US: Supreme Court Upholds Same-Sex Marriage*, HUMAN RIGHTS WATCH (June 26, 2015), https://www.hrw.org/news/2015/06/26/us-supreme-court-upholds-same-sex-marriage ("The United States Supreme Court decision on June 26, 2015, that the US Constitution grants same-sex couples the right to marry is a landmark win for marriage equality in the US that could foster change around the globe."); Amy Davidson Sorkin, *The Supreme Court Reaffirms Marriage Vows*, NEW YORKER (June 26, 2015), https://www.newyorker.com/news/amy-davidson/supreme-court-same-sex-marriage-kennedy ("The opinion is . . . probably the strongest manifesto in favor of marriage—anybody's marriage—a Court could produce.").

61. *See* Melissa Murray, Obergefell v. Hodges *and Nonmarriage Inequality*, 104 CALIF. L. REV. 1207 (2016); Courtenay W. Daum, *Marriage Equality: Assimilationist Victory or Pluralist Defeat?*, *in* LGBTQ POLITICS: A CRITICAL READER (Marla Brettschneider, Susan Burgess & Christine Keating eds., 2017).
62. Cyril Ghosh, *Marriage Equality and the Injunction to Assimilate: Romantic Love, Children, Monogamy, and Parenting in* Obergefell v. Hodges, 50 POLITY 275, 276 (2018).
63. Kendall Thomas, *Practicing Queer Legal Theory Critically*, 6 CRITICAL ANALYSIS L. 8 (2019).
64. *Id.* at 16.
65. *Id.* at 17.
66. *Id.*
67. Thomas argues that the decision illustrates how the new public realm of same-sex marriage expands the space "for American state to practice the art of conjugal government in a new, distinctively homonationalist register," as well as illustrates the ways in which the state actively participates in marriage, arguing that "when two people get married by the State they always also get married to the State, in ways both material and symbolic." Rather than reflecting the marriage as a choice/marriage as contract rhetoric, Thomas argues that the "freedom to marry movement," as reflected in *Obergefell,* has reinforced an older vision of marriage as status.
68. Ben-Asher, *supra* note 34, at 614.
69. BRENDA COSSMAN, SEXUAL CITIZENS: THE LEGAL AND CULTURAL REGULATION OF SEX AND BELONGING (2007).
70. JANET HALLEY, SPLIT DECISIONS: HOW AND WHY TO TAKE A BREAK FROM FEMINISM (2008).
71. The majority opinion of the Texas Supreme Court described the bondage as "deviate sexual acts," although one of the dissenting opinions in the case described the encounter in more consensual terms. Justice Hecht described it as two or three occasions in which "the couple engaged in what they referred to as 'light bondage.'" The encounters ceased when the wife told her husband that she associated the activities with the trauma of being raped. But the husband subsequently pursued his S/M desires elsewhere and had an affair with another woman who shared his interests.
72. HALLEY, SPLIT DECISIONS, *supra* note 70, at 362.
73. *Id.*
74. *Id.*
75. Though my own reading is one that then seeks to reincorporate a feminist reading that asks what feminism might add. For example, a queer reading of Sheila as a normalizing agent might be supplemented by asking whether gendered assumptions about women as victims of male sexual violence facilitated her in a way that would not have worked if she had been the aggressor? *See* Brenda Cossman, *Sexuality, Queer Theory and "Feminism After,"* 49 MCGILL L.J. 847 (2004).
76. Teemu Ruskola, *Raping Like a State*, 57 UCLA L. Rev. 1477 (2010); *see also* Teemu Ruskola, *Notes on the Neutered Mother, or Toward a Queer Socialist Matriarchy*, 67 EMORY L.J. 1165 (2018).
77. Ruskola, *Raping Like a State*, *supra* note 76, at 1481.
78. *Id.* at 1480.
79. *Id.* at 1481.
80. *See also* Aziza Ahmed, *When Men Are Harmed: Feminism, Queer Theory, and Torture at Abu Ghraib*, 11 UCLA J. ISLAMIC & NEAR E. L. 1 (2011) (deploying Ruskola's queer

theoretical frame to analyze the photographs of torture at Abu Ghraib). Ahmed argues that bracketing the focus on women as sexual victims allows a shift in the frame to male harm, female soldiers participation in it, and homonationalist discourses that position "Islam as homophobic and Muslims as highly sensitive to sexual harm resulting in the U.S. military portrayed as tolerant, accepting and encouraging of sexual diversity all while engaging in homophobic and racist acts." *Id.* at 18.

81. Antron D. Mahoney & Heather Brydie Harris, *When the Spirit Says Dance: A Queer of Color Critique of Black Justice Discourse in Anti-Transgender Policy Rhetoric*, 19 U. MD. L.J. RACE, RELIGION, GENDER & CLASS 7 (2019).
82. *Id.* at 8.
83. *Id.* at 9.
84. JOSÉ ESTEBAN MUÑOZ, DISIDENTIFACTIONS: QUEERS OF COLOR AND THE PERFORMANCE OF POLITICS 1–5 (1999).
85. FERGUSON, supra note 27, at 5.
86. *See, e.g.*, Darren Lenard Hutchinson, *Ignoring the Sexualization of Race: Heteronormativity, Critical Race Theory and Anti-Racist Politics*, 47 BUFF. L. REV. 1 (1999); Darren Lenard Hutchinson, IDENTITY CRISIS: *"Intersectionality," "Multidimensionality," and the Development of An Adequate Theory of Subordination*, 6 MICH. J. RACE & L. 285 (2001); Darren Lenard Hutchinson, *"Gay Rights" for "Gay Whites"?: Race, Sexual Identity, and Equal Protection Discourse*, 85 CORNELL L. REV. 1358 (2000); Darren Lenard Hutchinson, *"Closet Case": Boy Scouts of America v. Dale and the Reinforcement of Gay, Lesbian, Bisexual, and Transgender Invisibility*, 76 TUL. L. REV. 81 (2001); Darren Lenard Hutchinson, *Sexual Politics and Social Change*, 41 CONN. L. REV. 1523 (2009); Darren Lenard Hutchinson, *"Not Without Political Power": Gays and Lesbians, Equal Protection, and the Suspect Class Doctrine*, 65 ALA. L. REV. 975 (2014). Hutchinson's corpus of work sometimes cites some specifically queer identified work, such as MICHAEL WARNER, FEAR OF A QUEER PLANET (1993), and Cohen, *Punks, Bulldaggers, and Welfare Queens*, supra note 25.
87. *See, e.g.*, Russell Robinson, *Masculinity as Prison: Sexual Identity, Race, and Incarceration*, 99 CALIF. L. REV. 1309 (2011); Russell Robinson, *Mayor Pete, Obergefell Gays, and White Male Privilege*, 69 BUFF. L. REV. 295 (2021); Russell Robinson, RACING THE CLOSET, 61 STAN. L. REV. 1463 (2009); Russell Robinson & David Frost, *LGBT Equality and Sexual Racism*, 86 FORDHAM L. REV. 2739 (2018).
88. Cossman, *Queering Queer Legal Studies*, supra note 32, at 36.
89. *See, e.g.*, DEAN SPADE, NORMAL LIFE: ADMINISTRATIVE VIOLENCE, CRITICAL TRANS POLITICS, & THE LIMITS OF LAW (2011); Dean Spade, *Laws as Tactics*, 21 COLUM. J. GENDER & L. 40 (2011); Ido Katri, *Transgender Intrasectionality: Rethinking Anti-Discrimination Law and Litigation*, 20 U. PA. J.L. & SOC. CHANGE 51 (2017); 35 CANADIAN J. LAW & SOC'Y (Special Issue: On the Margins of Trans Legal Change) (Ido Katri & Samuel Singer eds., 2020); Florence Ashley, *Genderfucking Non-Disclosure: Sexual Fraud, Transgender Bodies, and Messy Identities* 41 DALHOUSIE L. J. 339, 339–37 (2018); Florence Ashley, *Don't Be So Hateful: The Insufficiency of Anti-Discrimination and Hate Crime Laws in Improving Trans Well-being*, 68 U. TORONTO L.J. 1 (2018).

CHAPTER 10

MASCULINITIES THEORY AS IMPETUS FOR CHANGE IN FEMINISM AND LAW

ANN C. MCGINLEY

According to masculinities scholars, men, too, suffer constraints and expectations due to their gender. Men must constantly engage in performances to prove their masculinity to other men. Although agreeing with feminists that men as a group are powerful, masculinities scholars assert that individual men, because of the pressures to compete with other men to prove their masculinity, often do not feel powerful, at least in relation to one another.[1] They conclude that men achieve conformity to masculinity at a price that includes denial of their emotions, acceptance of health and safety hazards to demonstrate strength, and relinquishment of fruitful relationships with their children. One major principle of masculinities theory is that masculinities are plural and changeable. In essence, masculinity is a performance, and performances change depending on the identities of the individuals performing masculinity and the social context.

Feminist legal scholars have found much in the field of masculinities to deepen and enrich the feminist analysis of law. In drawing on and incorporating masculinities theories into legal feminism, feminist scholars have added their own insights into the meaning of "masculinities." As Nancy Dowd, Nancy Levit, and I explain:

> "Masculinities" has multiple meanings. First, it is a structure that gives men as a group power over women as a group. Second it is a set of practices, designed to maintain group power, that are considered "masculine." Third, it is the engagement in or "doing" of these masculine practices by men or women. Finally, the term refers to a body of theory and scholarship by gender experts in various fields of social science.[2]

Although masculinities originated in fields outside of law, legal scholars have adopted insights raised by masculinities scholars, combined with those of feminist theory, queer theory, and critical race theory to develop a legal theory of masculinities that proposes new legal interpretations and policies that better correspond to the lived experiences of persons of different genders, races, and classes. This chapter explores how masculinities research has influenced legal feminism in the United States.

I. Importing Masculinities into Feminist Legal Theory

Masculinities theory has become a major force in feminist legal theory, complicating and expanding its understanding of gender in law, culture, and society. Yet it came late to critical legal theory, having originated as a distinct, interdisciplinary field situated outside of law.

A. Masculinities' Origins Outside of Law

Masculinities scholarship, which was itself heavily influenced by feminism and feminist theory in fields apart from law, emerged in the 1970s within the disciplines of sociology, social psychology, and psychology in the United States, Australia, and Great Britain.[3] A group of mostly male social science scholars during this era extended feminist analysis of patriarchy to examine how concepts of masculinity affected men. These masculinities scholars viewed gender as socially constructed and hierarchical and focused on the harms gender constructs created for men.[4] Some of the earliest concepts of masculinity appeared in psychologist Joseph Pleck's studies of the male sex role from the 1970s.[5] Later work by other scholars extended the insights of masculinities into a variety of different fields and contexts. James Messerschmidt analyzed criminology through the lens of masculinities theory[6] and demonstrated that, for some men, crime was a means of performing and proving their masculinity.[7] Sociologists Raewyn Connell and Michael Kimmel challenged the concept that masculinity is a biological trait rather than a socially constructed creation of a gender structure.[8] Sociologist Jeff Hearn and Professor of Leadership and Organization, David Collinson, studied men, masculinities, and management, critically examining how men exert and experience power in workplaces.[9] Sociologist Patricia Yancy Martin did qualitative empirical studies in organizations to study how men "do" masculinities by unconsciously engaging in masculine behaviors that harm others.[10] All this work contributed to an understanding of masculinities as a distinct field with unifying concepts, while highlighting the importance of studying masculinity in particular social and institutional settings.

For the most part, the early masculinities scholars who launched the field in the 1970s saw themselves as feminists who study the gender order's effects on men; they believed that masculinities studies complemented feminist theory by introducing the study of men as gender subjects rather than seeing men as "the norm." "Gender" did not apply exclusively to women; it applied also to men.[11] Moreover, these scholars were concerned that feminist analysis saw all men as powerful and did not deal with how the important variations in men's positioning affected the relationships among men. The biggest difference between feminist and masculinities theorists, as they saw it, was one of focus: Feminist theorists focused on how men's power as a group harmed women; masculinities theorists acknowledged that, as a group, men are powerful, but they studied the harm that trying to attain and maintain the accepted "masculinity" did to men.

Soon, however, a split emerged. Although most masculinities theorists continued to see themselves as feminists, some of the early masculinities scholars left the discipline in the early 1990s to become men's rights activists. They came to see men as the victims of feminism, which, they believed, blames men unjustly for sexual abuse, harassment, and domestic violence.[12] Masculinities scholars Bethany Coston and Michael Kimmel, describing these members of the men's rights movement, explained, "Somewhere along the way, the critique of the oppressive male sex role, and the desire to free men from it, morphed into a celebration of all things masculine, and a near-infatuation with the traditional masculine role itself."[13] The heirs of this movement today, men's rights supporters, emphasize a stereotypical vision of masculinity that masculinities scholars condemn as a cause of men's pain.[14]

It is not the men's rights activists who have influenced feminist legal scholars in the United States and abroad but, rather, the masculinities (also known as "men's studies") scholars who publish theoretical and empirical work on gender's effect on men. These masculinities theorists, who align themselves with feminists, but who believe that feminism often portrays men in a unidimensional fashion, have had significant influence on feminist legal scholars.

B. Masculinities Meets Feminist Legal Theory

Masculinities theory began to attract and influence legal scholars in the 1990s. Even without explicitly referencing masculinities, much legal scholarship from that decade analyzed gender and men in a way that makes their scholarship a precursor to the movement of masculinities theorists.[15] In one of the earliest works on law and masculinity, British legal scholar and sociologist Richard Collier explicitly drew on masculinities theory in an article published in 1995 to argue that the law has constructed fatherhood.[16] One year later, feminist legal scholar Nancy Dowd also took a critical look at fatherhood, examining the law's influence on fathers' relationships with their children.[17] That same year, Nancy Levit became the first feminist legal academic in the United States to overtly draw from masculinities theory and bring it into dialogue with legal feminism.[18] Levit argued that feminism had neglected and essentialized men, and that for feminism to be successful, feminism needed men, and men must be feminists.[19]

Taking up the call, feminist legal scholars soon embarked upon a deep engagement with masculinities theory. A foundational move was to identify the key insights from the field of masculinities that are of particular significance for legal feminism. Nancy Dowd, in *The Man Question*, the first book by a U.S. legal academic to analyze men, masculinities, and feminist theory, offered an influential synthesis of masculinities in relation to feminist theory.[20] Dowd defined the most important principles of masculinities theory as follows:

1. Men are not universal or undifferentiated;
2. Men pay a price for privilege;
3. Intersections of manhood, particularly with race, class, and sexual orientation are critical to the interplay of privilege and disadvantage, to hierarchies among men, and to factors that may entirely trump male gender privilege;
4. Masculinity is a social construction, not a biological given;
5. Hegemonic masculinity recognizes that one masculinity norm dominates multiple masculinities...
6. The patriarchal dividend is the benefit that all men have from the dominance of men in the overall gender order...
7. The two most common pieces defining masculinity are, at all costs, not to be like a woman and not to be gay...
8. Masculinity is as much about relation to other men as it is about relation to women...
9. Men, although powerful, feel powerless...
10. Masculinities study exposes how structures and cultures are gendered male...
11. The spaces and places that men and women daily inhabit and work within are remarkably different...
12. The role of men in achieving feminist goals is uncertain and unclear...
13. The asymmetry of masculinities scholarship and feminist theory reflects the differences in the position of men and women.[21]

From first principles, feminist legal scholars next turned to consider how masculinities might influence their analytical methods. Dowd exhorted scholars to "ask the man question" in analyzing gender issues and in cases where gender issues may not be obvious, noting that in race-based cases, gender may also be a key factor. She urged asking the question especially in gender-segregated environments, where gender dominates but is often invisible. Dowd pointed to the juvenile justice system, in which boys predominate, and the welfare system in which women predominate, as examples.[22] Although we speak of these systems as gender-neutral, we must question why they are segregated by sex, Dowd argued.[23]

The early feminist legal scholars who engaged with masculinities laid out the case for what feminist theory has to gain from integrating masculinities theory. Dowd posited four reasons why masculinities research complements feminist theory. First, masculinities theory contributes to a better understanding of male power and the process of subordination; it therefore leads to the goal of women's equality.[24] Second, masculinities scholarship renders men's harms visible. Though men as a group exercise tremendous power, feminist theory should recognize that many men because of their position in society may themselves be subjugated to male power.[25] This subjugation may, in turn, lead men to engage in behaviors that are harmful to women, less-valued men on the hierarchy, gender-nonconforming men, and nonbinary individuals.[26] Third, masculinities theory helps us compare how gender operates in homosocial or male-dominant environments as well as mixed-gender environments.[27] Fourth, masculinities theory allows feminists to engage in a more nuanced, nonessentialist analysis because of masculinities' focus on men's differences due to their identities and locations in society.[28]

While highlighting this complementarity, feminist scholars stopped short of calling for feminism and masculinities to merge theories, recognizing that both groups of theorists have existed in different bunkers for too long. Instead, feminist scholars have urged feminism and masculinities to draw from one another, engage in integrative thinking, and reevaluate each discipline in light of the other.[29] Each discipline has much to offer the other. Masculinities theorists in social sciences have generally spent little time analyzing women, while feminist theorists have essentialized men.[30] An effort to expand each theory to analyze both men and women as gendered subjects while recognizing the superior power that men as a group hold would benefit both theories. Feminists have sounded a note of caution, however, that masculinities scholarship not be misused to shift the focus from women and gender minorities to how men are harmed by gendered expectations, nor to blame women for men's harms.[31] Such a misreading of masculinities theory, albeit one that was embraced by the earlier spin-off of the men's rights movement, has been resoundingly rejected by feminist scholars.

C. Applications of Masculinities to Male-Only Spaces

By the end of the second decade of the twenty-first century, masculinities theory had become a forceful influence on critical legal theory, including legal feminism. Legal scholars examined the role of law in reproducing and naturalizing concepts of men and masculinity, and they linked masculinities with divergent but complementary critical theories to generate practical legal applications. Relying on masculinities theory, often in combination with other legal theories, legal scholars have applied masculinities to a wide range of issues in many areas of law, including criminal law and the death penalty,[32] employment and family law,[33] juvenile justice,[34] education law,[35] immigration law,[36] and constitutional law.[37]

Masculinities theory has been particularly productive in illuminating the gender issues in male-only spaces that feminist legal theory alone might have missed. For example, much male-on-male bullying is invisible to sex discrimination law because it is often characterized as normal roughhousing or hazing.[38] Examining how men treat other men who are lower in the masculine hierarchy demonstrates the pressure imposed on men to conform to the accepted masculine norms. Recognizing this pressure may explain not only men's treatment of other men but also how men treat women as inferiors, especially in locations that have been reserved traditionally for men. The "weaker" men who are lower on the hierarchy are encouraged to demonstrate their masculinity by harassing women to assure their acceptance by their more traditionally masculine male peers. This insight enriches the analysis of male-on-female harassment and exclusion in workplaces and other settings. It demonstrates that much harassment even between men and women does not occur because of sexual attraction but rather can be attributed to hostility toward women in the workplace, a lack of confidence of male harassers in their own masculinity, and a need to police the environment as belonging to men.

Unfortunately, courts often conclude that harassment and bullying of men by men do not occur "because of sex" and are therefore not illegal under Title VII of the 1964 Civil Rights Act, which makes unwelcome sex harassment illegal if it is sufficiently severe or pervasive to alter the terms or conditions of one's employment. A failure to recognize that this behavior occurs because of sex—either because the victim is not sufficiently masculine or because the harassers confirm their own masculinity by policing masculine norms in the workplace—harms men, women, and nonbinary individuals because it creates a hierarchy with traditional masculinity at the top and other forms of masculinity and femininity at the bottom.[39] Greater acceptance of masculinities theory by courts should broaden legal understandings of harassment to recognize these gendered harms.

Masculinities theory can also help expose other harms to women in male-dominated settings. *Gender Outlaws: Challenging Masculinity in Traditionally Male Institutions*[40] demonstrates this insight. Valorie Vojdik describes Shannon Faulkner's lawsuit in Faulkner's quest for admission to The Citadel, a male-only public military-style college that had excluded women for 154 years. Faulkner was ultimately admitted, but she left to protect herself from death threats and excruciating hostility. Vojdik, Faulkner's counsel, soon recognized that formal equality—securing women's admission to The Citadel on equal terms as men—alone was insufficient to protect Faulkner and other women. Explaining that masculinity is an institution that requires men to engage in masculine practices to assure acceptance by other men, Vojdik concluded that The Citadel's purpose was, literally, to create men. In doing so, the college and its students engaged in traditional masculine practices that required cadets to conform to traditional masculinity. Assuming that these practices were gender-neutral, the college applied them with the court's agreement to their first female cadet—Shannon Faulkner. Vojdik demonstrated that, as applied to Faulkner, these practices (including the shaving of Faulkner's head) were not neutral but rendered her a gender "outlaw."

Vojdik's analysis showed that male-only spaces such as The Citadel are saturated in masculine behaviors and expectations, which are considered gender-neutral or at least "natural" in our society. Analogizing the situation for women's admission to the Citadel to earlier cases where persons of color challenged the whites-only admissions policies and courts not only struck down those policies but also barred racist practices and symbols, Vojdik concluded that the masculine policies and practices of a formerly all-male institution must be dismantled for women to gain equality.[41]

II. The "Multidimensional Turn" and the Future of Masculinities Research

Although the original masculinities theorists were mostly white men, masculinities theory in the social sciences matured to encompass a variety of perspectives from a diverse group of scholars, including those identifying as white women, men and women of color, and LGBTQ+ and nonbinary individuals. Legal scholars too have brought an intersectional lens to masculinities and have grappled with how best to theorize plural identities.

A. From Intersectionality to Multidimensionality

Influenced by critical race feminists' theorizing of intersectionality, legal scholars combined masculinities with intersectional analysis of race, class, gender identity, sexual orientation, and gender to produce a rich critique of gendered concepts in American law.[42] Legal theorists drew from feminist and masculinities theories as well as critical race theory to develop new understandings of masculinities in relation to law. For example, critical race and feminist legal scholars such as Angela Harris and Frank Rudy Cooper have applied masculinities to the study of police abuse, criticizing law for its failure to understand that both gender and race influence police confrontations with civilians.

In her influential article, *Gender, Violence, Race, and Criminal Justice*,[43] Angela Harris analyzed race, class, immigration status, and gender in the now-infamous New York City police brutality case of Haitian immigrant Abner Louima. Louima was brutally beaten and sodomized with a broomstick by police officers at a New York City precinct in 1997 after being arrested on charges of an altercation at a nightclub. Harris unpeeled the race and immigration issues apparent in Louima's abuse by police, and she also analyzed how the policemen engaged in masculine gender performances in their use of objects to sodomize Louima. These were actions of men *as men* marginalizing and abusing Louima *as a man*. As masculinities researchers have demonstrated, sodomy by groups of men or boys against other men or boys is not an uncommon method of demeaning the victims, forcing them to be regarded not as real men but as feminine in their receptive posture and inability to prevent their attacks.[44] This insight is one example of how masculinities theory enhances the analysis of feminist theory. Without Harris's integrated analysis of race, gender, and immigration, observers of Louima's torture would not fully understand the role this confluence of identities played in the humiliation imposed upon Louima.[45]

Frank Rudy Cooper has also charted an intersectional approach to the analysis of race and gender in discussing Black men and the law. In his article, *Against Bipolar Black Masculinity: Intersectionality, Assimilation, Identity Performance, and Hierarchy*,[46]

Cooper argued that representations of heterosexual Black men in our society are bipolar: the "Good Black Man" and the "Bad Black Man." The Good Black Man reduces white anxiety by assimilating into white society, whereas the Bad Black Man challenges white society and increases anxiety. Cooper employed this intersectional approach in *"Who's the Man?": Masculinities Studies, Terry Stops, and Police Training*,[47] positing that when police officers—the majority of them male and white—stop Black male citizens under *Terry v. Ohio*,[48] which permits officers to "stop and frisk" a suspect under a mere "reasonable suspicion" standard, they enact a "masculinity contest." In essence, not only race but also masculinity governs police behaviors, and those studying *Terry* and the legal framework governing police stops should understand the intersectional causes of the stops and the harms to the Black community.[49]

As masculinities scholarship has become increasingly intersectional, some scholars working in masculinities have advocated a shift from an intersectional approach to one that is better described as multidimensional. Multidimensional masculinities theory (MMT) is a critical theory of law that contends that law distributes power by

> relying upon assumptions of human behavior that reproduce preexisting social relations. The theoretical foundations of multidimensional masculinities theory are feminist and feminist legal theories, critical race theory (especially critical race feminism, as it is influenced by queer theory) and masculinities studies in social science disciplines. MMT sees law and culture as co-constitutive: cultural norms influence law and legal norms simultaneously influence culture.[50]

MMT posits that categories of identities are intertwined with one another and experienced and interpreted differently depending on the context of the situation.[51]

Multidimensionality is an offshoot of intersectionality theory, which was introduced in 1989 by legal scholar Kimberlé Crenshaw.[52] Crenshaw explained the experience of Black women as sitting at the intersection of race and gender oppression. Multidimensionality, on the other hand, implicitly signals more than two identities coming together at a particular intersection.[53] An early adopter of the term, legal scholar Darren Hutchinson, used "multidimensionality" to explicitly include sexual identities as well as racial identities, class, and gender, in analyzing subordination.[54] Athena Mutua later used the term in her edited collection, *Progressive Black Masculinities*.[55] Mutua invoked the "multidimensional turn" of intersectionality theory to argue that Black men who are racially subordinated by whites should consciously engage in progressive Black masculine behaviors that oppose the subjugation of Black women based on their race and gender.

Frank Rudy Cooper and I embraced multidimensionality and placed it at the center of masculinities theory in our edited collection of essays, *Masculinities and the Law: A Multidimensional Approach*.[56] Through our own analysis and contributions by other legal scholars, we sought to show how considering masculinities theory through a multidimensional lens complicates and enriches the study of masculinities.[57] At a metaphorical level, "multidimensionality" signals that rather than a two-dimensional "intersection," multiple identities can simultaneously affect the expectations that others have of the person and can also affect how the person responds to others' expectations.[58] The turn to MMT also emphasizes that both the context of the situation and the intersection of identities govern how people are viewed, and, ultimately, how they react.[59]

In its methodology, multidimensionality encourages scholars to relentlessly "shift the lens" to analyze situations in context and from different points of view.[60] For example, if a situation appears to be about women, multidimensionality invites scholars to shift the lens to consider the repercussions of their solutions if applied to men. If a situation is rife with gender issues, scholars should shift the lens to examine the problem through a racial lens. If race issues seem to dominate, scholars should shift to a gender lens to analyze the situation. Although this method at times requires only a one-way shift, in many situations, a scholar shifts the lens from a dominant aspect to one that is less obvious and then back, for example, from race to gender, and then back to race again, to deepen understanding.

Although many scholars use this method,[61] one example is the lens shift I used to analyze the bullying of Jonathan Martin, a Black former Miami Dolphins football player whose harassment by his male teammates was so severe that Martin was hospitalized for emotional distress.[62] Many understood that situation to be about race, so I shifted the lens to draw out the gender and class tensions between Martin and his teammates. The new focus emphasized that his teammates believed that Martin was insufficiently masculine and that this failure threatened them and the team. Looking at the Martin case through a gender lens, however, did not erase the racial lens. Instead, it deepened the understanding of Martin's situation. As I explained:

> [I]t enhances our consideration of race because it allows us to pinpoint the different stereotypes and expectations that society harbors regarding black men as opposed to black women. Black men are supposedly angry and tough, a stereotype that often works to their disadvantage. But in the NFL, anger and toughness are valued personality traits. Hence, Martin's coworkers may not have related to the soft-spoken black classics major from Stanford [Martin]. Unless the law considers race and gender, it presents an incomplete picture of the possible motivations for the harassers' behavior.[63]

I argued that this analysis demonstrated that the Miami Dolphins should have been liable for employment discrimination based on both race and gender if Martin had brought a lawsuit under Title VII of the 1964 Civil Rights Act.[64]

The multidimensional method also takes into account the situational dimension of masculinities. For example, although Black male firefighters may be more valued and dominant as workers than their Black female counterparts, Black men are considered more dangerous by many in society and may therefore be subject to fear and harsher treatment than Black women when they are on the street. A gay white lawyer may be treated differently in court than he would be in a gay bar; his treatment in court might also differ from that of a poor Black lesbian defendant in a criminal case. The same Black lesbian may expect different and better treatment in a grocery store near her home. The varying identities of the lawyer—male, gay, white, middle class—and of the criminal defendant—female, lesbian, Black, poor—will affect their treatment and their expectations of and reactions to that treatment. Moreover, the context such as a courtroom, a gay bar, and a local grocery store will affect how others judge the individuals' identities and how the individuals react.

Because law is a discipline that requires interpretation of human behaviors and motivations, attending to multidimensional masculinities invites judges and juries to look past their assumptions about human behavior and its causes.[65] It is important for legal actors to consider expertise in social sciences in order to understand human motivations and behaviors.[66] Deciding how "reasonable persons" respond to a certain situation requires not only a study of one's own responses but also a change of perspective, an understanding of the identities of the individuals involved, and attention to the context of the situation.[67] Multidimensional masculinities theory encourages legal decisionmakers to make this shift in perspective in order to gain the understanding necessary to make better legal decisions.

An example of how MMT can aid legal actors in challenging the stereotypes that affect how the law is applied can be found in the adage that "boys will be boys." Although this saying often excuses middle-class white boys of culpability in criminal cases, it does not excuse Black and Latino boys of similar behaviors.[68] Young boys of color are punished severely for the same behaviors that do not even lead to the arrest of white boys. Moreover, the "boys will be boys" rationale can also account for the difficulty women have in proving that sexual harassment by male colleagues and supervisors is unwelcome and severe or pervasive.[69] The maxim serves to minimize the significance of the harassment, blocking it from the threshold needed to be actionable. At the same time, masculinities theory has shown that the "boys will be boys" adage allows judges to assume that severely harassing sexualized behavior of men by other men at work is merely "horseplay" or "roughhousing" and not illegal sex-based conduct.[70] Masculinities theory can explain why these judges are incorrect, that the behavior *does* occur because of sex, both of the victim and of the perpetrators. The perpetrators attempt to prove and enhance their own masculinity and that of the job in question by engaging in the harassment, while the victims are harassed because of their failure to live up to conventional gender norms, or the perpetrators' fears that the victims will not join in the gender policing at work.[71]

Use of the term "multidimensional" rather than "intersectional" masculinities is not without controversy, however. Some highly regarded scholars have challenged the choice of the term "multidimensionality" because they argue that intersectionality already encompasses analysis of a broad array of different identity categories in different contexts.[72] Sumi Cho, in her thoughtful essay, *Post-Intersectionality: The Curious Reception of Intersectionality in Legal Scholarship*,[73] argued that multidimensionality reflects a post-intersectional movement that (erroneously) faults intersectionality for focusing primarily on intersectional issues of Black women. The critique sparked scholarly debate over whether "intersectional" or "multidimensional" masculinities better represents current work in the field, with both sides of the debate agreeing on the importance of drawing from intersectionality theory and antiessentialism, whichever terminology is used.[74] As Professor Cooper and I have explained, and I continue to emphasize, adopting multidimensionality as the guiding frame should not be understood as signaling "post-intersectionality" in the sense of trying to get beyond intersectionality.[75] Rather, multidimensionality embraces and builds upon intersectionality by more explicitly bringing in and situating multiple identities. While the concept and language of intersectionality remain foundational, the *term* "multidimensional" more accurately describes what masculinities scholars are doing.[76]

Much of the past decade of masculinities scholarship, including the contributions to Cooper's and my edited collection, *Masculinities and the Law*, places multidimensionality at the core of the analysis, showcasing MMT in action. One notable example is Lety Saucedo's interviews of male Mexican immigrants who worked in the Las Vegas home construction industry during the pre-2008 housing boom.[77] The interviews, which took place both in the United States and in Mexico, reveal masculine narratives emphasizing danger and risk to the subjects who came to the United States illegally. These men saw their border crossings as affirmations of their masculinity. This research raises the question of whether immigration policies that make border crossings more difficult have the unintended effect of encouraging crossings. Other scholars who contributed to the same volume also analyzed masculinities from a multidimensional perspective. David Cohen examines legal forms of sex segregation and how they reinforce both hegemonic masculinity—the notion that one particular masculine performance is more powerful than others—and the hegemony of men's power over women; he notes in particular the negative effects of sex segregation on gender-variant individuals.[78] Bob Chang analyzes popular culture's view of firefighters as heroes as dominated by misogyny and homophobia; he notes the absence of Asian American men, who are stereotypically considered either too feminine or hypermasculine, from cultural depictions of firefighting and discusses recent lawsuits that focus on discrimination against Black male firefighters but do not reckon with the issue of discrimination against Asian male applicants.[79] Val Vojdik uses the case study of Turkey's ban on headscarves to show that masculinities analysis also applies to the treatment of women. She demonstrates how the Turkish headscarf ban situated the state as the masculine protector of women against fundamentalism. By filing claims challenging the ban before the European Court of Human Rights, women fought back, rejecting both the misogynist tenets of their religion and the state's misogynist protectionism.[80]

These scholars and many others have applied multidimensional masculinities theory to explore the many factors and identities that influence human behavior and society's reactions to individuals. Their work showcases the variability of lenses through which we can observe identities and how the social context affects not only the viewers' judgments of individual behaviors but also the individuals' reactions themselves to the social cues.

B. The Next Generation of Masculinities Scholarship

As masculinities legal theory and MMT have emerged as a force in law and legal theory, masculinities studies in the social sciences have continued to evolve, representing increasingly diverse groups from different disciplines. Consequently, some of the original "tenets" of masculinities have faced challenges. British sociologist Jeff Hearn, for example, has questioned the concept of "hegemonic" masculinity—the idea that there is one preferred masculinity that dominates other masculinities. Like feminist theorists, he is more concerned that the "hegemony of men" subjugates women as a group.[81] This "turn" away from focusing on men's injuries that result from masculinities is welcome insofar as it broadens the lens to capture how masculinities harm women. And, yet, scholars in the field continue the important work to understand the hierarchy of gender performances and how men relate to other men in order to analyze how concepts of gender harm others.

Masculinities theorists have also come to recognize that groups of men respond to "hegemonic" masculinity differently, by adopting subversive forms of subordinated (or "reactive") masculinities in an effort to prove that their own forms of masculinity are more masculine and, therefore, superior to what has been considered the most powerful, "hegemonic" masculinity.[82] For example, some male blue-collar workers, in reaction to the power exerted over them by predominantly white, upper-middle-class male managers, ridicule their bosses for their lack of masculinity (such as by calling them "pansies" or other derogatory labels to feminize them) and enact hypermasculine performances that set powerful norms in shop culture.[83] Different masculinities, then, may dominate in their own minicultures. Yet, there is a risk in detailing variant forms of hegemonic and subordinated masculinities by subculture. Legal scholars' attempts to recognize diverse groups of men may inadvertently "essentialize" those people they are seeking to protect, using reductionist descriptors that trade on stereotypes and further marginalize them. Current and future research on reactive forms of masculinities may show us how to avoid essentializing groups of vulnerable people.

One example of a powerful alternative to the traditional valorized masculinity of the straight, upper-middle-class, white male who exemplifies the hegemonic ideal is revealed by the considerable recent social science research on the increasing power and acceptance of gay and transgender masculinities.[84] Legal scholars have begun to use this research on gay and transgender masculinities to push the envelope. In *Acting Gay, Acting Straight: Sexual Orientation Stereotyping*,[85] for example, Luke Boso combines stereotyping and masculinities theories to explain that feminine gay men are often treated differently at work than masculine gay men. He argues that to fulfill the promise of banning discrimination based on sexual orientation and to protect the most marginalized groups, the law must ban employment decisions based on all stereotypes about gay men and women.

Future work in masculinities should focus on transgender, bisexual, and nonbinary individuals' rights to be free from discrimination in employment and other areas. Feminist and masculinities scholars have long understood that gender, defined as a fixed set of expectations for persons based on the sex assigned to them at birth, is a problem not only for cisgender men and women but also for LGBTQ+ and nonbinary individuals. Many lauded the recent Supreme Court decision in *Bostock v. Clayton County, Georgia*,[86] which held that employers illegally discriminated against gay and transgender individuals under Title VII. For the first time, the Supreme Court recognized that "sex" discrimination also includes discrimination based on sexual orientation and transgender status. But the celebrated decision also raises some concerns. It does not clearly protect bisexual, pansexual, and other individuals with sexual orientations other than gay or lesbian.[87] Neither does it clearly protect nonbinary individuals from discrimination.[88] And, many condemn the opinion's failure to confirm a robust sex stereotyping theory of *Price Waterhouse v. Hopkins*.[89] Although sex stereotyping theory seemed to have a majority of the Court's support at the time *Bostock* was decided, subsequent changes in the composition of the Court, including the death of Justice Ruth Bader Ginsburg, could potentially lead to a future in which it is legal to discriminate based on an individual's failure to adhere to stereotypes of femininity or masculinity.[90] Masculinities legal theorists should work to strengthen and reinforce the stereotyping doctrine as they focus on how gender order harms LBGTQ+ and nonbinary individuals. Masculinities theory's insights on hierarchy based on individuals' adherence to preferred and accepted gender ideals should inform law and policy in this area in the future. Finally, it is important for future masculinities scholars to engage in gender analysis through a multidimensional, shifting lens so that all persons' rights are protected by the law.

III. Conclusion: Masculinities, Feminist Theory, and Law

In *Past as Prologue: Old and New Feminisms*, Martha Chamallas predicted that masculinities theory as applied to law would be an important influence on feminist thought.[91] As we have seen, Chamallas's prediction has come true. Not only feminist legal theory but also critical race feminism and queer theory have influenced and been influenced by MMT.[92]

The importation of masculinities theory into law and its interaction with other legal theories are important postmodern developments that urge changes in theory, policy, and doctrine, creating the possibility of new ways for legal decisionmakers to approach legal topics. With the tools of masculinities theory and MMT, lawyers, judges, juries, and legislators can encourage greater equality in our society.

Notes

1. *See* Nancy E. Dowd, The Man Question: Male Subordination and Privilege 63 (2010) [hereinafter The Man Question].
2. Nancy E. Dowd, Nancy Levit & Ann C. McGinley, *Feminist Legal Theory Meets Masculinities Theory*, in Masculinities and the Law: A Multidimensional Approach 25 (Frank Rudy Cooper & Ann C. McGinley eds., 2012) [hereinafter Masculinities and the Law].

3. Scholars from cultural anthropology and geography have also examined masculinities. See THE MAN QUESTION, *supra* note 1, at 34. Public health experts rely on masculinities theory. *See, e.g.*, Derek M. Griffith, Katie Gunter & Daphne Watkins, *Measuring Masculinity in Research on Men of Color: Findings and Future Directions*, 102 AM. J. PUB. HEALTH 187 (2012) (examining studies of nonbiological gender aspects and how they affect the health of men of color).
4. I use the terms "masculinities scholars" and "masculinities theorists" interchangeably.
5. THE MAN QUESTION, *supra* note 1, at 18–21 (noting that Joseph Pleck and Jack Sawyer edited MEN AND MASCULINITY in 1974 and that Pleck published THE MYTH OF MASCULINITY in 1981).
6. JAMES MESSERSCHMIDT, MASCULINITIES AND CRIME: CRITIQUE AND RECONCEPTUALIZATION OF THEORY (1993).
7. *See id.* at 79–80.
8. *See, e.g.*, R. W. CONNELL, MASCULINITIES (1995 & 2005); MICHAEL KIMMEL, GUYLAND: THE PERILOUS WORLD WHERE BOYS BECOME MEN (2008); Michael Kimmel, *Masculinity as Homophobia: Fear, Shame, and Silence in the Construction of Gender Identity*, in THEORIZING MASCULINITIES (M. Brod & M. Kauffman eds., 1994).
9. MEN AS MANAGERS; MANAGERS AS MEN: CRITICAL PERSPECTIVES ON MEN, MASCULINITIES AND MANAGEMENTS (David L. Collinson & Jeff Hearn eds., 1996).
10. *See* Patricia Yancey Martin, *"Said and Done" Versus "Saying and Doing": Gendering Practices, Practicing Gender at Work*, 17 GENDER & SOC'Y 342, 357 (2003) (stating that masculine practices allow powerful white men to define what work is while denying that the workplace is gendered).
11. Like the early feminist scholars, masculinities scholars originally seemed to accept the gender binary. As discussed infra in Section II.B, feminist and masculinities scholars now understand that the gender binary, not merely men and women, must be reanalyzed and have incorporated that analysis into their work.
12. *See, e.g.*, Bethany M. Coston & Michael Kimmel, *White Men as the New Victims: Reverse Discrimination Cases and the Men's Rights Movement*, 13 NEV. L.J. 368, 369–70 (2013).
13. *Id.* at 372.
14. *See id.*
15. *See, e.g.*, Kenneth L. Karst, *The Pursuit of Manhood and the Desegregation of the Armed Forces*, 38 UCLA L. REV. 499, 499–506, 509–10 (1991) (discussing laws prohibiting integration by sex, gender, sexuality, and race in the U.S. armed forces that reinforce the masculine ideal); Mary Anne Case, *Disaggregating Gender from Sex and Sexual Orientation: The Effeminate Man in the Law and Feminist Jurisprudence*, 105 YALE L.J. 1, 3, 68 (1995) (arguing that women will be equal only when the law protects feminine men from discrimination); Francisco Valdes, *Queers, Sissies, Dykes, and Tomboys: Deconstructing the Conflation of "Sex," "Gender," and "Sexual Orientation" in Euro-American Law and Society*, 83 CALIF. L. REV. 1, 8 (1995) (stating that our society engages in "conflation" of sex, gender, and sexual orientation, a practice that "validates heteropatriarchy"); Joan C. Williams, *Toward a Reconstructive Feminism: Reconstructing the Relationship of Market Work and Family Work*, 19 N. ILL. U. L. REV. 89, 93–95 (1998) (arguing that domesticity's division of labor into market and family work harms men).
16. Richard Collier, *"Waiting Till Father Gets Home": The Reconstruction of Fatherhood in Family Law*, 4 SOC. & LEGAL STUD. 5 (1995).

17. *See generally* Nancy E. Dowd, *Rethinking Fatherhood*, 48 FLA. L. REV. 523 (1996). Dowd's later works on masculinity and fatherhood include: Nancy E. Dowd, *From Genes, Marriage and Money to Nurture: Redefining Fatherhood*, 10 CARDOZO WOMEN'S L.J. 132 (2003) (defining fatherhood as nurturing rather than genetic), and Nancy E. Dowd, *Fathers and the Supreme Court: Founding Fathers and Nurturing Fathers*, 54 EMORY L.J. 1271 (2005) (criticizing Supreme Court's definition of fatherhood as genetic).

18. *See generally* Nancy Levit, *Feminism for Men: Legal Ideology and the Construction of Maleness*, 43 UCLA L. REV. 1037 (1996).

19. *Id.* at 1039–40.

20. Another key development connecting masculinities to feminist analysis occurred in 2009, when Martha Albertson Fineman and British Law professor Michael Thomson hosted a workshop dealing with masculinities, law, and feminism, resulting in publication of a collection of essays. *See* EXPLORING MASCULINITIES: FEMINIST LEGAL THEORY REFLECTIONS (Martha Albertson Fineman & Michael Thomson eds., 2013) (including essays by U.S. and European legal and social scientists Martha Alberston Fineman, Michael Thomson, Nancy E. Dowd, Roja Fazaeli, Camille A. Nelson, Frank Rudy Cooper, Marie Fox, Chris Beasley, Fionnuala Ni Aoláin, Naomi Cahn, Dina Hayes, Jamie R. Abrams, Juliet Williams, David S. Cohen, Ann C. McGinley, Leticia M. Saucedo, Maria Cristina Morales, Richard Collier, Jocelyn Elise Crowley, and Clifford J. Rosky).

21. THE MAN QUESTION, *supra* note 1, at 57–65.

22. Nancy E. Dowd, *Asking the Man Question: Masculinities Analysis and Feminist Theory*, 33 HARV. J. L. & GENDER 415, 416 (2010); Nancy E. Dowd, BOYS, *Masculinities and Juvenile Justice*, 8 J. KOREAN L. 115 (2008) (proposing masculinities theory to remedy the juvenile justice system's failure to consider boys as gendered subjects).

23. THE MAN QUESTION, *supra* note 1, at 416–17.

24. *Id.* at 419–20.

25. *Id.* at 420–22.

26. *See* ANN C. MCGINLEY, MASCULINITY AT WORK: EMPLOYMENT DISCRIMINATION THROUGH A DIFFERENT LENS 23 (2016) [hereinafter MASCULINITY AT WORK]. *See also* Nancy Ehrenreich, *Subordination & Symbiosis: Mechanisms of Mutual Support Between Subordinating Systems*, 71 UMKC L. REV. 251 (2002).

27. *See* Dowd, *Asking the Man Question*, *supra* note 22, at 422–23.

28. *Id.* at 423–24.

29. Dowd et al., *supra* note 2, at 34.

30. *Id.* at 32–34.

31. Dowd, *Asking the Man Question*, *supra* note 22, at 424. *See also* Dowd et al., *supra* note 2 (giving examples of how masculinities theory can complement feminist analysis).

32. *See, e.g.*, Kimberly D. Bailey, *Sex in a Masculinities World: Gender, Undesired Sex, and Rape*, 21 J. GENDER RACE & JUST. 281 (2018); Angela Harris, *Gender, Violence, Race, and Criminal Justice*, 52 Stan. L. Rev. 777 (2000); Frank Rudy Cooper, *Against Bipolar Black Masculinity: Intersectionality, Assimilation, Identity Performance, and Hierarchy*, 39 U.C. Davis L. Rev. 853 (2006); Leigh Goodmark, *Hands up at Home: Militarized Masculinity and Police Officers Who Commit Intimate Partner Abuse*, 2015 B.Y.U. L. REV. 1183 (2015); Joan W. Howarth, *Executing White Masculinities: Learning from Karla Faye Tucker*, 81 OR. L. REV. 183 (2002).

33. *See, e.g.*, Ann C. McGinley, *Reasonable Men*, 45 U. CONN. L. REV. 1 (2012); Keith Cunningham-Parmeter, *Men at Work, Fathers at Home: Uncovering the Masculine Face of Caregiver Discrimination*, 24 COLUM. J. GENDER & L. 253 (2013).

34. *See, e.g.*, Dowd, *Boys, Masculinities and Juvenile Justice, supra* note 22.
35. *See, e.g.*, Deborah L. Brake, Getting in the Game: Title IX and the Women's Sports Revolution (2010); Nancy Chi Cantalupo, *Masculinity and Title IX: Bullying and Sexual Harassment of Boys in the American Liberal State*, 73 Md. L. Rev. 887 (2014); David S. Cohen, *No Boy Left Behind? Single Sex Education and the Essentialist Myth of Masculinity*, 84 Ind. L.J. 135 (2009); Ann C. McGinley, *Schools as Training Grounds for Sexual Harassment*, 2019 U. Chi. Legal F. 171.
36. *See, e.g.*, Leticia M. Saucedo, *Border-Crossing Stories and Masculinities, in* Masculinities and the Law, *supra* note 2, at 146, 149–158, 162.
37. *See, e.g.*, Valorie Vojdik, *Gender Outlaws: Challenging Masculinity in Traditionally Male Institutions*, 17 Berkeley Women's L.J. 68 (2002); Marc R. Poirier, *Hastening the Kulturekampf:* Boy Scouts of American v. Dale *and the Politics of American Masculinity*, 12 Law & Sexuality 271 (2003); Keith Cunningham-Parmeter, *(Un)Equal Protection: Why Gender Equality Depends on Discrimination*, 109 Nw. U. L. Rev. 1 (2014).
38. *See generally* Ann C. McGinley, *Creating Masculine Identities: Bullying and Harassment "Because of Sex,"* 79 U. Colo. L. Rev. 1151 (2008).
39. *Id.*
40. Vojdik, *supra* note 37 at 74–75.
41. *See also* Poirier, *supra* note 37, at 306–10 (relying on Michael Kimmel's *Masculinity as Homophobia*, and explaining that the Boy Scouts' ban on gay scoutmasters reinforced the masculine identities of the organization and of individual boy scout members); Michael Kimmel, *Masculinity as Homophobia: Fear, Shame, and Silence in the Construction of Gender Identity, in* Theorizing Masculinities (M. Brod & M. Kauffman eds., 1994); *See also* Ann C. McGinley, *Masculinities at Work*, 83 Or. L. Rev. 359 (2004) (combining feminist and feminist legal theories with masculinities studies to demonstrate the prevalence of masculinities in workplaces and how those structures and practices deny women equality at work).
42. *See* Ann C. McGinley & Frank Rudy Cooper, *Introduction: Masculinities, Multidimensionality, and Law: Why They Need One Another, in* Masculinities and the Law, *supra* note 2, at 2–3, 6–7.
43. 52 Stan. L. Rev. 777 (2000).
44. *See* Ann C. McGinley, *The Masculinity Motivation*, 71 Stan. L. Rev. Online 99, 100, 102–06 (2018).
45. *See* Camille Gear Rich, *Angela Harris and the Racial Politics of Masculinity: Trayvon Martin, George Zimmerman, and the Dilemmas of Desiring Whiteness*, 102 Calif. L. Rev. 1027, 1031, 1044–45. (2014) (explaining the influence of Angela Harris's article on multidimensional masculinities theory and noting that Harris's article created a "conceptual toolbox" for scholars).
46. 39 U.C. Davis L. Rev. 853 (2006).
47. 18 Colum. J. Gender & L. 671 (2009).
48. 392 U.S. 1 (1968) (permitting police to stop citizens without probable cause if they have a reasonable suspicion that the citizens are engaged in criminal behavior).
49. *See also* Ann C. McGinley, *Policing and the Clash of Masculinities*, 59 How. L.J. 221 (2018).
50. McGinley & Cooper, *supra* note 42, at 1 (citations omitted).
51. *Id.* at 2.

52. *Demarginalizing the Intersection of Race and Sex: A Black Feminist Critique of Antidiscrimination Doctrine, Feminist Theory and Antiracist Politics*, 1989 U. CHI. L.F. 139 (arguing that antidiscrimination doctrine analyzes race and/or gender only along one axis—either race or gender—effectively ignoring Black women's experience that occurs at the intersection of both race and gender).
53. McGinley & Cooper, *supra* note 42, at 6–7.
54. *See* Darren Lenard Hutchinson, *Out yet Unseen: A Racial Critique of Gay and Lesbian Legal Theory and Political Discourse*, 29 CONN. L. REV. 561, 638–44 (1997) (proposing the adoption of "multidimensionality" theory, which draws from intersectionality theory and describes the multiple layers of racial, class, and sexual identities); *see also* Valdes, *supra* note 15.
55. PROGRESSIVE BLACK MASCULINITIES (Athena D. Mutua ed., 2006).
56. Cooper & McGinley, *supra* note 2.
57. Contributing authors include Michael Kimmel, Ann C. McGinley, Frank Rudy Cooper, Nancy E. Dowd; Nancy Levit, Devon W. Carbado, Athena D. Mutua, Robert Chang, John M. Kang, Leticia M. Saucedo, David S. Cohen, Kim Shayo Buchanan, Deborah L. Brake, Fionnuala Ni Aoláin, Naomi Cahn, Dina Haynes, Camille A. Nelson, and Valorie K. Vojdik.
58. *See* McGinley & Cooper, *supra* note 42, at 6–7.
59. *Id.* at 7.
60. *Id.* at 4–5; *see also* MASCULINITY AT WORK, *supra* note 26, at 17–19; Ann C. McGinley, *Ricci v. De Stefano: A Masculinities Analysis*, 33 HARV. J. L. & GENDER 581 (2010); Frank Rudy Cooper, *Masculinities, Post-Racialism and the Gates Controversy: The False Equivalence Between Officer and Civilian*, 11 NEV. L.J. 1 (2010).
61. *See, e.g.*, THE MAN QUESTION, *supra* note 1, at 1, 6; Dowd et al., *supra* note 2, at 35; Harris, *supra* note 32.
62. *See* MASCULINITY AT WORK, *supra* note 26.
63. *Id.* at 19.
64. *Id.* at 10–11. *See also* McGinley, *Creating Masculine Identities*, *supra* note 38 (challenging the prevailing view that bullying does not occur because of the sex of the victim, and arguing that many bullying behaviors are illegal under Title VII of the 1964 Civil Rights Act).
65. *See* McGinley & Cooper, *supra* note 42, at 8.
66. *Id.*
67. *Id.*
68. *Id.* at 8–11. *See also* Ann C. McGinley & Frank Rudy Cooper, *How Masculinities Distribute Power: The Influence of Ann Scales*, 91 DENV. U. L. REV. 187, 193–97, 198–200 (2015).
69. *See* McGinley & Cooper, *supra* note 42, at 9–10.
70. *See* MASCULINITY AT WORK, *supra* note 26, at 56–57.
71. *Id.* at 67–68.
72. *See* Ann C. McGinley & Frank Rudy Cooper, *Identities Cubed: Perspectives on Multidimensional Masculinities Theory*, 13 NEV. L.J. 326, 335 nn. 47–48 (referencing Juliet Williams's and Devon Carbado's grounds for arguing for the term "intersectionality").
73. 10 DU BOIS REV. 385, 397–99 (2013).
74. Participants discussed this controversy at a colloquium held at the University of Nevada, Las Vegas, Boyd School of Law in 2011. In 2013, the *Nevada Law Journal* published fourteen original essays based on papers presented at the colloquium, in a symposium issue titled

Men, Masculinities and Law: A Symposium on Multidimensional Masculinities Theory. Contributors include Ann C. McGinley, Frank Rudy Cooper, Athena D. Mutua, Bethany M. Coston, Michael Kimmel, June Carbone, Naomi Cahn, Richard Collier, Nancy E. Dowd, Zachary A. Kramer, John M. Kang, Deborah L. Brake, Juliet A. Williams, Leticia M. Saucedo, Jamie R. Abrams, Barbara Pozzo, and Martha Albertson Fineman.

75. *See id.*
76. *See* McGinley & Cooper, note 72, at 335. Subsequently, Cooper and I used the term "intersectionality" in an article on race, class, and (dis)abilities. *See* Ann C. McGinley & Frank Rudy Cooper, *Intersectional Cohorts, Dis/ability, and Class Actions*, 47 FORDHAM URB. L.J. 293 (2020), reflecting our understanding that the term "multidimensionality" has neither replaced nor pushed aside the term "intersectionality." Because that particular article dealt with children with disabilities who have a number of identities and did not discuss masculinities, intersectionality was a better fit than multidimensional masculinities.
77. *See* Saucedo, *supra* note 36, at 146, 149–158, 162.
78. *See* David S. Cohen, *Sex-Segregation, Masculinities, and Gender-Variant Individuals*, *in* MASCULINITIES AND THE LAW, *supra* note 2, at 167, 168, 182.
79. *See* Robert Chang, *Rescue Me*, *in* MASCULINITIES AND THE LAW, *supra* note 2, at 119, 123. *See* Ann C. McGinley, *Introduction: Men, Masculinities, and Law: A Symposium on Multidimensional Masculinities*, 13 NEV. L.J. 315 (2013).
80. *See* Valorie K. Vojdik, *Masculinities, Feminism, and the Turkish Headscarf Ban: Revisiting Sahin v. Turkey*, *in* MASCULINITIES AND THE LAW, *supra* note 2, at 270.
81. *See* Jeff Hearn, *From Hegemonic Masculinity to the Hegemony of Men*, 5 FEMINIST THEORY 49 (2004).
82. MASCULINITY AT WORK, *supra* note 26, at 24.
83. *See id.* at 5, 25–27.
84. *See, e.g.*, GAY MASCULINITIES (Peter M. Nardi ed., 2000); Tristan Bridges, *A Very "Gay" Straight: Hybrid Masculinities, Sexual Aesthetics, and the Changing Relationship Between Masculinity and Homophobia*, 28 Gender & Soc'y 58 (2014); Vasu Reddy, *Negotiating Gay Masculinities*, 14 AGENDA 65 (1998); Lucas Gottzén & Wibke Straub, *Trans Masculinities*, 11 NORMA 217 (2017).
85. 83 TENN. L. REV. 575 (2016); *see also* Luke Boso, *Real Men*, 37 U. HAW. L. REV. 107 (2015) (proposing that courts take context into account as well as identities to understand sex stereotyping).
86. 140 S. Ct. 1731 (2020).
87. *See* Ann C. McGinley et al., *Feminist Perspectives on Bostock v. Clayton County*, 53 CONN. L. REV. ONLINE 1 (2020).
88. *Id.*
89. 490 U.S. 228 (1989) (holding that discrimination against a woman for failure to live up to feminine gender stereotypes is discrimination because of sex).
90. *See* McGinley et al., *supra* note 87, at 2.
91. 17 MICH. J. GENDER & L. 157, 172 (2010).
92. *See also* Katherine T. Bartlett, *Gender Law: After Twenty-Five Years*, 27 DUKE J. GENDER L. & POL'Y 1, 16–18 (2019) (recognizing the importance of masculinities scholarship to gender analysis).

CHAPTER 11

GOVERNANCE FEMINISM AND DISTRIBUTIONAL ANALYSIS

AZIZA AHMED

QUESTIONS of distribution—who bears the various burdens and costs, and who reaps the benefits—are in the foreground or background of all legal reform projects. Various schools of legal scholarship implicitly or explicitly theorize how we might uncover the social and economic distributional consequences of proposed or implemented reforms. Some engage directly with broad-based questions of economic distribution, including law and economics,[1] critical legal studies,[2] and, more recently, law and political economy,[3] whereas others, such as critical race theory[4] and feminist legal theory,[5] are animated by the distributional concerns of particular groups.

A new body of work, situating itself in the lineage of critical legal studies, puts distributional analysis at the center of the study of law and critical theory.[6] Distributional analysis refers not just to an overall cost-benefit accounting but to an analysis of where the consequences fall, and along what social, economic, and cultural fault lines. This chapter considers the way feminist, gender, and queer legal scholarship, coming out of the critical legal studies tradition, takes on questions of distribution. It focuses on the work of Janet Halley, a Harvard law professor and critical legal scholar who contributed to the development of a theory of distribution in the context of critical legal studies (CLS) and then applied it to feminist theory.[7] Although many schools of feminist legal theory are concerned with distribution, Halley's work has made explicit the connections between distributional analysis and feminist legal reform. This chapter seeks to situate "governance feminism" and distributional analysis in its scholarly lineage and in relationship to other bodies of feminist writing. To trace the trajectory of this strand of thought in legal scholarship, I begin by describing the key analytic and theoretical frames that CLS has contributed to the understanding of law and distribution. I then turn to Halley's application of this work which offers a step-by-step way for feminist scholars and advocates to begin to think about distributional analysis and legal reform, which she calls "doing a distributional analysis."[8] Finally, I offer examples of scholars who have utilized distributional analysis to better understand the way feminist expertise and advocacy are mobilized with distributional consequences. The chapter explicates how distributional analysis offers feminist advocates and scholars a tool for evaluating legal and policy choices by shifting feminists away from advocacy based on identity and toward an approach that centers the full range and distribution of consequences.

I. The Emergence of Distributional Analysis: From Critical Legal Studies to Feminist Theory

Recent theorizing on distributional analysis in the feminist context can be traced to early ideas of law and distribution emerging from CLS. CLS scholars had a range of divergent goals though they largely saw themselves as writing from the left.[9] The work of Duncan Kennedy, an early and foundational CLS scholar, serves a particularly central role in animating questions of distribution.[10] For Kennedy, law plays an important role in the distribution, rationalization, and construction of wealth, power, and knowledge.[11] In turn, understanding distribution, and possibilities for redistribution, required theorizing the connections between law and politics. This was a direct challenge to mainstream legal scholarship which reified the idea that the adjudication of law is neutral and objective and can be devoid of politics as well as formal and predictable in its application. Kennedy argued that the connection between law and politics required seeing the indeterminacy of law; litigation produces indeterminate results based on the situated nature of how and where a legal claim is located and adjudicated.[12] The indeterminacy thesis provided an opening for understanding courts as sites of distribution where politics shapes outcomes.[13] This insight was not only important for understanding the gains made by conservatives but foreboding for progressives who turned to the law to generate just outcomes.

CLS scholars bore down on the question of the productive role of the law in creating and maintaining hierarchy. In an extended critique of law and economics, CLS scholars attacked the idea that people bargain in a free market. According to law and economics scholars, the freedom to bargain produced optimal outcomes.[14] This core law and economics core premise ignored the prior distribution of material goods and resources that embedded the aggregation of rights and entitlements. In their critique of the law and economics scholarship on bargaining, CLS scholars drew on the work of legal realist Robert Hale, who in his now famous article, *Coercion and Distribution in a Supposedly Non-Coercive State*, describes how legal rules, including those of property, contract, criminal law, and tort law, set the terrain of economic struggle.[15] These rules can be in the foreground or the background. In a labor struggle, for example, the foreground rules dictating labor and employment contracts impact the ability of a worker to demand different wages. Yet, Hale digs deeper to imagine that the probable outcomes of a wage negotiation are not simply set by constitutional norms upholding freedom of contract but also by property entitlements held by the bargaining parties that coerce parties to act in a particular way. According to Hale, the free-market is permeated with "coercive restrictions of individual freedom."[16] (For Hale, coercion applies to all parties in an arrangement, since all are subjected to the background rules.) Looking to the background rules requires paying attention to the "not-hidden-but-ignored" legal rules that coerce legal actors into their bargaining positions. Examining only labor rules would not explain the rich array of possibilities and constraints in a negotiation offered by one's legal position.[17]

Taking Hale's insights further, in his book *World of Struggle: How Power, Law, and Expertise Shape Global Political Economy*, legal scholar David Kennedy, writing in the tradition of critical legal studies, connects law and distribution by drawing on 19th-century political economist David Ricardo.[18] Kennedy describes how legal arrangements can produce conditions for parties in a contractual relationship, for example, where one is able to extract more economic gains than the other.[19] These relationships are exemplified in the contracts formed by landlord and lessee, employer and employee, or two countries trading with one another under the conditions of colonialism. Law is a terrain of struggle; groups leverage their power shaped by background legal and institutional structure. Yet the law also consolidates resources and power, making the imbalance in inequality that can be observed in the world seem natural. Understanding the role of law means seeing how it shapes the ability of individuals and groups to struggle and provides the terrain for doing so.

CLS scholars have developed a body of work showing that parties who aggregate power through legal ordering begin to negotiate with the state on their side. This impacts the bargaining endowments for both parties, as the actors in a negotiation understand who the state typically acts on behalf of. One party knows that there is a promise of enforcement in their favor. While these shadows of prior legal struggles structure negotiations, as power aggregates, the relationship between parties (landlords and tenants or capital and labor) becomes naturalized. As David Kennedy states, relative power becomes "a fact of the situation rather than the outcome of a prior struggle."[20] Through this process, the legal rules themselves become naturalized, as society begins to understand that the legal order favors certain parties. Societies begin to take for granted a maldistribution of goods and resources. Critical legal theory disrupts these settled understandings by arguing that these legal rules are not natural. It reminds us that the legal arrangements that produce inequality are the product of prior struggle, one that is ongoing.[21]

Duncan Kennedy has also theorized the symbolic and material productive effects of the law beyond those that we might see at first instance. In this work, Kennedy is engaging with the ideas of radical feminism, both taking seriously and challenging the idea that patriarchy and sexual abuse overdetermine heterosexual sexuality. He uses the example of "sexy dressing" as a site of conflict within the gender regime. Women, he argues, are able to engage in "symbolic play"[22] through exploiting a semiotic system that registers these sexual signals. Men eroticize women's subordination and some women eroticize this domination.

Yet, as Kennedy acknowledges, abuse does occur. And, some abuse is not punished due to underenforcement. This is what Kennedy calls the "tolerated residuum of abuse." The rules governing abuse are implemented in the context of a range of other legal rules which can, in turn, incentivize and disincentive the behavior of abusers and victims.[23] These legal arrangements have their own effects, creating feelings of desire, shame, and eroticism in unexpected ways that do not always map onto the structural understanding of power by radical feminists, whose ideas about sex and gender were increasingly gaining traction at the time he was writing the article. Kennedy challenges radical feminism by complicating the idea put forward by radical feminists that distribution only occurs along the lines of the "perpetrator-victim" dyad of sexual abuse.[24] Instead, Kennedy argues that even situations that seem not to involve sexual abuse may be related to the distribution of benefits and losses associated with sexual abuse.[25] In her piece, *Sexy Dressing, Gender, and Legal Theory*, legal scholar Vasuki Nesiah argues that Duncan Kennedy's focus in sexy dressing is on "technologies of distribution."[26] She describes Kennedy's theory as one of the background conditions, the legal rules and social norms, "against which male–female bargaining takes place to then assess the impact, from the bedroom to the boardroom."[27] With this challenge to radical feminism, Kennedy opens the door for queer theory in the law, new thinking on "pleasure/resistance," and integrating sex (and sexual abuse) into questions of distribution.

II. Feminism and Distributional Analysis

Distributional analysis in feminist legal theory has been pushed forward by Janet Halley. Halley takes these core insights from legal realism and critical legal studies and applies them to feminist ideas and feminist practice. By centering law and distribution in the context of feminism, Halley contends that there can be unexpected costs and benefits of legal reform projects, and understanding these may shift and change the types of laws one might support for progressive causes. Offering a technique for understanding legal reform means that advocates can better predict consequences of legal reform projects and guard against potential harms. A distributional analysis also helps tell us about the productive possibilities of law. The law, for example, can construct identity (e.g., woman or man) or feelings (such as shame and desire).

Along with coauthors Chantal Thomas, Rachel Rebouché, Hila Shamir, and Prabha Kotiswaran, Halley developed the idea of "governance feminism" in a book bearing that title.[28] In their work, they define governance feminism as "every form in which feminists and feminist ideas exert a governing will within human affairs: to follow Michel Foucault's definition of governmentality, every form in which feminists and feminist ideas 'conduct the conduct of men.' "[29] They show that some modes of feminists and feminism have achieved new heights of power and new influence.

In her chapter *Distribution and Decision: Assessing Governance Feminism*, Halley describes how feminists can, and why they should, do a distributional analysis. This flows from the idea that feminists have influence in the legal reform projects they design, advocate, and implement. Doing a distributional analysis is one way to assess legal reform projects and take up Max Weber's call for an ethic of responsibility which requires a greater acknowledgment of the consequences of one's actions. In order to enact this ethic, a feminist must understand the way law and legal institutions relate to the distribution, understood broadly to encompass material goods, money, cultural capital, symbolism, and more. A distributional analysis becomes profoundly important as feminists gain influence inside institutions.[30]

The idea that feminists can govern is controversial because it challenges the idea that feminist ideas and feminists are always in subordinate positions inside institutions. Halley and her coauthors also recognize, however, that feminism is not always powerful. In turn, a key question that animates scholarship on governance feminism is how and why some feminist ideas rise to the top while others fail to gain as much traction.[31] The explanation for why some feminist ideas rose is often a local story, documented in the work of many scholars writing in this vein. In some instances, feminists aligned themselves with powerful conservatives making feminist ideas more palatable. This occurred in the 1970s and 1980s, for example, when feminist advocates joined forces with the police to further domestic violence reforms and aligned with the growing victim right's movement.[32] In other cases, dominance feminist ideas aligned with neoliberal policy reforms in the global south from microfinance to property rights, making dominance feminism the primary ideological frame for understanding gender.[33]

Halley argues that wherever feminists have gained power, they should act with an ethic of responsibility. But how should a feminist inside an institution and with the power to make change act with an ethic of responsibility? Halley offers a step-by-step methodology for feminist scholars and advocates to take on an ethic of responsibility. At the risk of oversimplifying, I offer a summary below.

First, a distributional analysis would separate *is* from *ought*. Drawing on the work of Oliver Wendell Holmes and Karl Llewellyn, Halley invokes the tenets of legal realism, which teach the importance of understanding how a law will be applied and how an actor may act in a legal order. Yet, Halley continues, it is important to separate what the law *is* from what the law *ought* to be. This is necessary to consider both when mapping the world and in understanding the consequences. Too often, Halley contends, feminist advocates and scholars begin from the place of "ought." They have a vision of where they are headed and what the goal of a feminist reform project should be (e.g., women's liberation) but without a clear enough sense of the current distribution of rights and how it will affect the distributional consequences of reforms. Thus, in Halley's terminology, "carrying a brief for" women—prioritizing the advancement of the interests of women above all else—blocks the ability to see how a legal reform project might have consequences that are far-reaching and wide, and perhaps even harmful for some women, some genders, and some people who are not characterized by sex or gender at all.[34] Eradicating these blind spots requires first understanding the world as it is: What are the current legal frameworks in play? Who wins and who loses, given the ways laws exist and are being applied? Although describing the world as it "is" will always produce a situated perspective because describing the world is never value-neutral, in this exercise, a person describing the world as it is should try to cabin bias. After describing the world as it is, a feminist can begin to imagine what the world ought to be. This disaggregated process allows legal realism to lead: we understand how the legal rules will actually shape realities for parties touched by the reform.

Seeing the world as it is requires correctly identifying "the struggle and the players."[35] This is step two of a distributional analysis and contains two parts. First, identifying the surplus at stake, and second, seeing how players bargain in the shadow of the law. Answering these questions requires widening the lens by which we look at a particular legal problem. Who are the various stakeholders? Who might be touched by a legal transformation? This requires looking beyond a subset of women or girls that a feminist might imagine are impacted by a particular legal reform to other stakeholders, which could include any variety of people, including men, different types of women (e.g., poor women and women of color), and children. It could also include people acting in various capacities, such as landlords, tenants, brothel owners, and development experts. Examples abound. Lawyers and advocates for sex workers, for example, critique some feminist legal reforms for not considering the effects of laws seeking to abolish sex work, not only on the sex worker and her client but also on the client's family. Or, in a feminist reform project on ending domestic violence in the immigrant community, critics might ask how altering an immigration rule that would allow for the deportation of the abuser but not his wife could have unintended consequences. Will a woman move forward with her domestic violence case if she knows it will lead to economic instability or the deportation of extended family?

Then, we must identify the "surplus at stake," or the gains in human welfare that a particular legal rule might produce.[36] Halley roots the identification of surplus in a Marxian understanding of the production of surplus of value produced by labor. By starting with Marx, feminists are able to challenge the liberal and neoliberal idea that the distributions of the market are fair. Looking at surplus allows us to identify how stakeholders with greater social power are able to appropriate excess. As players consolidate power through aggregating surplus, and legal rules are naturalized to allow for the accumulation of gains from the law, we may begin to assess how proposed policy changes will impact the future.

Next, Halley urges the importance of acknowledging that the law conditions, rather than governs, by examining how people bargain in the shadow of "background rules."[37] As described earlier, understanding the role of background rules requires shifting away from the foreground principles to looking in the background to see how parties have the power to coerce one another in the context of a contract negotiation. For Hale, property laws coerce individuals and shape their capacity to bargain for labor contracts. From this, one can see how the law distributes, as the distribution of income from a labor contract is the product of the "relative power of coercion which different members of the community can exert against one another."[38] Understanding the way the law conditions through a set of foreground and background rules helps to show how distributive outcomes flow from legal arrangements.

Finally, once feminists have described the world as it *is*, Halley advises that it is finally time to consider the *ought*. What is the new legal order that we are imagining? How will it impact the range of players that we have now identified? How does shifting rules in the foreground or background shift our perspective on how legal reforms will impact our players? By doing a distributional analysis, we are better able to see the consequences of the legal reform projects we propose. The "ought" is crafted from this rich body of work and deeper understanding of the winners and losers of a reform project.

III. Applying a Distributional Analysis

From this methodology, Halley and other legal scholars have critiqued various modes of feminist intervention, exploring the dynamics of governance feminism and related questions of distribution on topics ranging from international human rights law[39] and anti-trafficking programs[40] to national security[41] and development.[42] These scholars share the premise that feminists and feminist ideas have left a significant imprint on global and national efforts for social, political, and economic change. Their examination of feminist expertise has generated new ways of thinking about power and identity in international institutions.[43] The emerging scholarship on governance feminism challenges the notion that feminists and feminism are always marginal by showing how feminist ideas influence governance efforts. Much of this work highlights how feminist expertise within institutions has produced underexamined distributional shifts.

A. The Case of Sex Work

Sex work provides an instructive example of how and why a distributional analysis as applied to feminist strategy and activism can be helpful. It also serves as a way to understand the concept of governance feminism because feminists have played a large role in influencing legal and institutional responses to sex work.

Halley and her coauthors pay particular attention to the rise of dominance feminism, which they describe as the melding of power feminism and cultural feminism.[44] They define dominance feminism as finding "male domination in two distinct forms: in the false superiority of male values and male *culture*, and in the domination of all things F [female] by all things M [male] *as sexuality*."[45] In "carrying a brief for women," dominance feminists prescribed a number of legal reforms to end pornography and prostitution, including criminalizing the purchase of sex (also called "ending demand"). The emphasis on criminal law by feminists is now called "carceral feminism," which describes the feminist turn to criminal law to effectuate legal reform goals.[46]

Some dominance feminists, whom I will call carceral anti-trafficking feminists (CAFs), have also connected prostitution to trafficking by promoting the idea that all prostitution (also known as sex work) is sex-trafficking.[47] This view is contrary to that taken by sex-positive feminists who believe that there is potential for sex workers' exercise of power and agency in sex work. The CAF perspective has undeniably entered the governance space on prostitution and trafficking. Adherents to this view argue that because there is no consent in prostitution, it is necessarily sex-trafficking. This proved to be a successful strategy. Feminists helped to successfully advocate for the view that the exchange of money for commercial sex is equivalent to sex-trafficking in U.S. law at the federal and state level.[48] They were also successful in pushing for the conflation of sex work and sex-trafficking in foreign policy (although imposing more severe forms of punishment for sex-trafficking still requires proof of coercion).[49] As this understanding gained adherents, many feminists increased their calls for criminal law solutions, a position that was advanced by casting trafficking as an issue of domestic and international crime.[50] While some antitrafficking feminists pushed back, seeking to distinguish between sex work and trafficking,[51] CAFs nevertheless had considerable global impact as they helped infuse U.S. foreign policy and bilateral assistance with a criminal law-oriented project to eradicate sex work.[52]

Sex-positive feminists and queer scholars concerned about the consequences of anti-trafficking laws, argued that this was a deadly cocktail. The CAF agenda presumably started with the "ought," assuming that criminal laws eradicating prostitution would universally benefit all women, but without careful consideration of the distributional effects of their policies, ended up harming poor women in the United States and around the world.[53] With criminal law amped up, and the definition of sex work and trafficking blurred, sex workers, their clients, and peer-educators were arrested in raids aimed at ending the sex industry.[54] The distributional consequences became even more clear as the CAF position—a conflation of sex work with trafficking—migrated into public health. In the legal and public health response to AIDS, CAFs exerted their influence in the crafting and implementation of the U.S. government's Leadership Act on HIV/AIDS, TB, and Malaria.[55] The legislation made the United States the largest bilateral donor to AIDS and aimed to end the spread of the epidemic through prevention and treatment of HIV. Although interventions led by sex workers, including peer-education programs, had been highly successful in furthering the AIDS response, CAFs mobilized to ensure that the Leadership Act did not fund sex workers because they saw projects that provided support to sex workers as furthering the traffic in women by making selling and buying sex safer. CAFs pushed for language in the legislation that came to be known as the anti-prostitution loyalty oath (APLO). The APLO mandated that organizations receiving U.S. funding endorse a policy opposing sex trafficking and prostitution and prohibited recipient organizations from advocating for the legalization of prostitution or sex trafficking.[56] This led to the closure of AIDS interventions for sex workers and to the arrest of sex workers organized in the context of those HIV interventions.[57] In sum, the APLO undermined the anticarceral harm-reduction approach favored by sex workers and sex-positive feminists.

The reliance on the criminal law led to a fierce feminist debate in the United States about how to address the harms faced by people in the sex industry. A distributional analysis, however, allows us to shift focus and get beyond opposing views. By revealing the background rules that alter the power and resources of various stakeholders that are a part of sex markets, one is able to see the myriad legal arrangements and possible legal levers that shift the bargaining positions of various players. In turn, a distributional analysis can help uncover the range of legal reform possibilities that can distribute the surplus born of the current legal regime.

Two examples from the literature on governance feminism and distribution are illustrative. First, legal scholar Prabha Kotiswaran, writing about India and the postcolonial context, moves beyond criminal law and focuses on the relational dynamics of the brothel, including labor and tenancy. The legal rules surrounding property and labor impact the ability of a sex worker to negotiate the sex market, from negotiating with clients to housing security and avoiding arrest.[58] By situating the sex worker within a web of "power relations," Kotiswaran describes how legal rules, informal norms, and market dynamics produce distributional effects and alter the way sex workers are able to bargain and negotiate security and livelihood. A sex worker who rents a room in a brothel, for example, may be better able to protect herself from arrest than a woman who is selling sex on the street. The ability to rent the room is controlled by the relevant laws impacting the legality of brothels and the landlord-tenant arrangements that flow from either a legal or illegal brothel. The landlord-tenant relationship could also be influenced by market dynamics: excessive room availability could mean a willingness to rent a room to a sex worker, room shortages could allow a landlord to exploit a sex worker or deny her housing. In turn, the sex worker's exposure to arrest could be dictated both by criminal laws on sex work but also the existence of market forces and laws on housing and tenancy related to brothels.[59]

In a second example, writing about Israel, Hila Shamir points to the shift in migration rules by the Israeli government in response to pressure from CAFs and the U.S. government.[60] Altering immigration rules to restrict migrant sex workers from entry altered the capacity of sex workers to bargain for a fair contract or prevent exploitation in ways unforeseen by antitrafficking feminists. The goal of the reformers was to end the exploitation faced by migrant sex workers through sex work. Although this was meant to shut down the sex industry, it instead had the effect of retaining the sex work market and merely purging it of migrant women. Sex workers were now mostly Israeli. While the specific forms of exploitation experienced by migrant women ended, Israeli sex workers now face a new set of opportunities and challenges, including the need for more attention to the needs of trafficked women and greater service provision paired with a strengthened border patrol. A background rules analysis deepens the reformers' capacity to understand the range of laws that shape the interactions between stakeholders impacted by the reform project.

A distributional analysis shows that each legal change brings a new group of stakeholders, a new set of interests, new outcomes, and new sites of struggle. Paying attention to the background legal and economic arrangements can also reveal opportunities for sex workers to exercise their own power. If feminists are carrying a brief for women, and in these examples, women who are sex workers, they have before them a new set of legal interventions that can distribute material resources, including access to public health services, housing laws, and immigration visas in a manner that distributes resources toward sex workers.

B. Governance Feminism and Distribution beyond Sex Work

Tracking the rise of feminist institutional power, often coupled with a distributional analysis, has been the focus of much scholarly work using the lens of governance feminism outside sex work. In the context of ending violence against women, for example, scholars have asked how and why some feminist positions, particularly those pushing carceral responses, gained traction. In the United States, Leigh Goodmark has mapped how the alignment of feminism with the carceral state, although intended as a way to get at the root of violence against women and break down the perceived public/private divide, ended up backfiring. Costs to communities grew as more men were incarcerated, as undocumented immigrant women began to fear the deportation of their spouses if they were to report violence, and as an expectation grew that mothers must report violence or risk losing custody of their children.[61] In a similar vein, Karen Engle has analyzed how carceral ideas were carried into the international sphere, diverting attention from the need to pressure governments and international agencies to pay attention to the broader economic and structural dimensions of transforming their nations, including addressing the legacy of imperialism and taking action to change the economic distribution.[62]

Accounts of governance feminism and distribution also go beyond carceral feminism and violence against women. Vasuki Nesiah's work shows how market-oriented empowerment discourse, the well-known celebration of microfinance programs, was aided by feminist interventions into law and development which helped to sell women as responsible borrowers.[63] These interventions dovetailed with neoliberal logics to create new forms of feminized debt burden in the postconflict setting. Borrowing from the influential critical theorist and American cultural critic Lauren Berlant, Nesiah identifies this type of empowerment discourse as "cruel optimism."[64]

The close relationship between feminist and queer theory has also meant that ideas about distribution, with its roots in CLS, have migrated into thinking about activism on lesbian, gay, bisexual, and transgender (LGBT) issues in our contemporary moment. The push to better understand the distributive, productive, and emotionally charged consequences of the law was not a purely theoretical exercise.[65] In her work, legal scholar Libby Adler brings together queer theory and core critical legal studies ideas to critique the mainstream LGBT movement. By using the legal realist insights generated by CLS and distributional analysis, Adler reimagines the types of legal reform project LGBT advocates should engage in. She draws on core CLS ideas to argue that turning away from antidiscrimination and equal marriage rights enabled legal reform projects to focus on what she calls "low-profile" legal rules, including laws ending the ban on sitting or lying on park benches or banning loitering, that can bring about a redistribution of resources to the most marginalized in the LGBT community. The turn to low-profile laws requires examining the often-neglected background rules that shape people's ability to bargain and construct their various identities, as Duncan Kennedy previously argued in his work, and as Adler describes in new detail.

IV. CONCLUSION

As feminists increasingly demonstrate that they have the power to govern and shape our world, documented in the growing literature on governance feminism, it becomes increasingly necessary for feminist activists and scholars to consider the range of distributional consequences that flow from legal reform projects. As explained in this chapter, many scholars have taken up the call to a distributional analysis as prescribed by Halley and rooted in the tradition of critical legal studies, representing a new path forward in feminist legal scholarship.

NOTES

1. *See generally* ROBERT COOTER & THOMAS ULEN, LAW AND ECONOMICS 1–10 (6th ed. 2016).
2. *See generally* Duncan Kennedy, *Law and Economics from the Perspective of Critical Legal Studies*, in THE NEW PALGRAVE DICTIONARY OF ECONOMICS AND THE LAW (Peter Newman ed., 1998) [hereinafter Kennedy, *Critical Legal Studies*]; DUNCAN KENNEDY, LAW DISTRIBUTES I: RICARDO AND MARX AND CLS (2021) [hereinafter KENNEDY, LAW DISTRIBUTES], https://papers.ssrn.com/sol3/papers.cfm?abstract_id=3813439.
3. *See generally* Amy Kapczynski et al., *Law and Political Economy: Toward a Manifesto, Law & Political Economy Project* (2017), https://lpeproject.org/blog/law-and-political-economy-toward-a-manifesto/.
4. *See generally* CRITICAL RACE THEORY: THE KEY WRITINGS THAT FORMED THE MOVEMENT (Kimberlé Crenshaw, Neil Gotanda, Gary Peller & Kendall Thomas eds., 1996).
5. *See generally*; MARTHA CHAMALLAS, INTRODUCTION TO FEMINIST LEGAL THEORY (2d ed. 2003).
6. *See, e.g.,* KENNEDY, LAW DISTRIBUTES, *supra* note 2; Paulo Barrozo, *Critical Legal Thought: The Case for a Jurisprudence of Distribution*, 92 U. COLO. L. REV. 1043 (2021).
7. *See generally* JANET HALLEY ET AL., GOVERNANCE FEMINISM: AN INTRODUCTION (2018).
8. *Id.*
9. For histories and readings about CLS, see Mark Tushnet, *Critical Legal Studies: A Political History*, 100 YALE L.J. 1515 (1991); Duncan Kennedy & Karl E. Klare, *A Bibliography of Critical Legal Studies*, 94 YALE L.J. 461 (1984).

10. *See generally* Duncan Kennedy, *The Stakes of Law, or Hale and Foucault!*, XV LEGAL STUD. FORUM 327 (1991) [hereinafter Kennedy, *Stakes of Law*]; DUNCAN KENNEDY, SEXY DRESSING ETC.: ESSAYS ON THE POWER AND POLITICS OF CULTURAL IDENTITY (1993); Kennedy, *Critical Legal Studies, supra* note 2.
11. *See* Kennedy, *Stakes of Law, supra* note 10.
12. Duncan Kennedy, *Freedom and Constraint in Adjudication: A Critical Phenomenology*, 36 J. LEGAL EDUC. 518 (1986); DUNCAN KENNEDY, A CRITIQUE OF ADJUDICATION (1998).
13. *See* Tor Krever, Carl Lisberger, & Max Utzschneider, *Law on the Left: A Conversation with Duncan Kennedy*, 10 UNBOUND 1 (2015).
14. *See* Kennedy, *Critical Legal Studies, supra* note 2.
15. *See* Robert L. Hale, *Coercion and Distribution in a Supposedly Non-Coercive State*, 38 POL. SCI. Q. 470 (1923).
16. *Id.* at 470.
17. As described in Janet Halley & Kerry Rittich, *Critical Directions in Comparative Family Law: Genealogies and Contemporary Studies of Family Law Exceptionalism*, 58 AM. J. COMP. L. 753 (2010).
18. *See* DAVID KENNEDY, A WORLD OF STRUGGLE: HOW POWER, LAW, AND EXPERTISE SHAPE GLOBAL POLITICAL ECONOMY (2018).
19. *Id.* at 11–12.
20. *Id.* at 199.
21. *See id.* at 134.
22. HALLEY, *supra* note 5, at 170.
23. *See* Duncan Kennedy, *Sexual Abuse, Sexy Dressing and the Eroticization of Domination*, 26 NEW ENG. L. REV. 1309, 1320 (1992).
24. As explained in Vasuki Nesiah, *Sexy Dressing, Gender, and Legal Theory: A Style of Political Engagement*, 5 TRANSNAT'L LEGAL THEORY 640, 643 (2014).
25. *Id.*
26. *Id.* at 642.
27. *Id.*
28. *See generally* HALLEY ET AL., *supra* note 7; Janet Halley et al., *From the International to the Local in Feminist Legal Responses to Rape, Prostitution/Sex Work, and Sex Trafficking: Four Studies in Contemporary Governance Feminism*, 29 HARV. J.L. & GENDER 335 (2006) [hereinafter, Halley et al., *From the International to the Local*]; GOVERNANCE FEMINISM: NOTES FROM THE FIELD (Janet Halley, Prabha Kotiswaran, Rachel Rebouché & Hila Shamir eds., 2019) [hereinafter NOTES FROM THE FIELD].
29. HALLEY ET AL., *supra* note 7, at ix.
30. *See* HALLEY ET AL., *supra* note 7, at xi.
31. Halley et al., *From the International to the Local, supra* note 29, at 44.
32. *See* AYA GRUBER, THE FEMINIST WAR ON CRIME: THE UNEXPECTED ROLE OF WOMEN'S LIBERATION IN MASS INCARCERATION (2020). For additional discussion on carceral feminism, see Leigh Goodmark, *The Unintended Consequences of Domestic Violence Criminalization: Reassessing a Governance Feminist Success Story*, in NOTES FROM THE FIELD, *supra* note 29, at 124–56.
33. *See* Vasuki Nesiah, *Indebted: The Cruel Optimism of Leaning in to Empowerment*, in NOTES FROM THE FIELD, *supra* note 29, at 505–54.

34. HALLEY, *supra* note 5, at 16–17.
35. HALLEY ET AL., *supra* note 7, at 254–62.
36. *Id.* at 256–59.
37. The term "bargaining in the shadow of the law" originated in Robert H. Mnookin & Lewis Kornhauser, *Bargaining in the Shadow of the Law: The Case of Divorce*, 88 YALE L.J. 950 (1979). For a discussion of "bargaining in the shadow of the law" as developed by Mnookin and Kornhauser, see Janet Halley, DOES LAW HAVE AN OUTSIDE? (Osgoode CLPE Research Paper No. 2, 2011).
38. HALLEY ET AL., *supra* note 7, at 260 (quoting Hale, *supra* note 15).
39. *See generally* KAREN ENGLE, THE GRIP OF SEXUAL VIOLENCE IN CONFLICT: FEMINIST INTERVENTIONS IN INTERNATIONAL LAW (2020).
40. *See generally* Amy J. Cohen & Aya Gruber, *Governance Feminism in New York's Human Trafficking Intervention Courts*, *in* NOTES FROM THE FIELD, *supra* note 29, at 83–112.
41. *See generally* Vasuki Nesiah, *Feminism as Counter-terrorism: The Seduction of Power*, *in* GENDER, NATIONAL SECURITY, AND COUNTER-TERRORISM: HUMAN RIGHTS PERSPECTIVES 127–51 (Margaret L. Satterthwaite & Jayne Huckerby eds., 2013); Vasuki Nesiah, *Uncomfortable Alliances: Women, Peace and Security in Sri Lanka*, *in* SOUTH ASIAN FEMINISMS 139–61 (Ania Loomba & Ritty A. Lukose eds., 2012).
42. *See generally* Kerry Rittich, *The Future of Law and Development: Second-Generation Reforms and the Incorporation of the Social*, *in* THE NEW LAW AND ECONOMIC DEVELOPMENT: A CRITICAL APPRAISAL (David Trubek & Alvaro Santos eds., 2006).
43. *See generally* HALLEY ET AL., *supra* note 7; NOTES FROM THE FIELD, *supra* note 29.
44. In her book *Split Decisions*, Halley describes the differences between power feminism and cultural feminism as the following:

> Though cultural feminism is roughly half of the time devoted to the cultural revaluation of women's distinctive relationship to care, the rest of the time it is concerned about women's distinctive engagement in sexuality. That part of cultural feminism agrees with power feminism in characterizing male sexuality as a vast social problem. But while MacKinnon focuses on the unjust male domination of women through power, cultural feminism emphasizes the unjust male derogation of women's traits or points of view through male-ascendant normative value judgments. And the early MacKinnon regarded male *and female* sex, gender, and sexuality to be fully constituted by the eroticization of male domination; whereas cultural feminism reserved a special place for the redemptive normative insights that women derive from their sexuality and their role as mothers. For all their differences, however, power feminism and cultural feminism turn strongly on m/f, they are subordination theories in which the problem is m > f, and they carry a brief for f, with a vengeance.

HALLEY, *supra* note 5, at 27–28.
45. HALLEY ET AL., *supra* note 7, at 34.
46. The term "carceral feminism" was coined by Elizabeth Bernstein in her article *The Sexual Politics of the "New Abolitionism,"* 18 DIFFERENCES 128 (2007).
47. *See generally* Halley et al., *From the International to the Local*, *supra* note 29.
48. *See generally* Victims of Trafficking and Violence Protection Act of 2000, Pub. L. No. 106-386, 114 Stat. 1464 (2000) (codified as amended at 22 U.S.C.A. §§7101–14); Organizational Integrity of Entities That Are Implementing Programs and Activities Under the Leadership Act, 45 C.F.R. §89 (2010).

49. *See* Victims of Trafficking and Violence Protection Act of 2000, *supra* note 49.
50. *See* Bernstein, *supra* note 47, at 130.
51. *See generally* ANNE T GALLAGHER, *The International Law of Human Trafficking* (2010); Jo Doezema, *Now You See Her, Now You Don't: Sex Workers at the UN Trafficking Protocol Negotiation*, 14 SOC. & LEGAL STUD. 61 (2005).
52. For a detailed account, see Janie A. Chuang, *Rescuing Trafficking from Ideological Capture: Prostitution Reform and Anti-Trafficking Law and Policy*, 158 U. PA. L. REV. 1655 (2010). Chuang documents how the Coalition Against Trafficking in Women and Equality Now were leaders in the feminist fight to conflate sex work and trafficking in the neoabolitionist mode.
53. KIMBERLY KAY HOANG, DEALING IN DESIRE (2015). *See* Noy Thrupkaew, *The Crusade Against Sex Trafficking*, THE NATION (September 16, 2009), https://www.thenation.com/article/archive/crusade-against-sex-trafficking/.
54. For two case studies showing the harms of antitrafficking laws, see Aziza Ahmed & Meena Seshu, *"We have the right not to be 'rescued' . . . ": When Anti-Trafficking Programmes Undermine the Health and Well-Being of Sex Workers*, 1 ANTI-TRAFFICKING REV. 149 (2012); Joanna Busza, *Having the Rug Pulled from Under Your Feet: One Project's Experience of the US Policy Reversal on Sex Work*, 21 HEALTH POL'Y & PLAN. 329 (2006).
55. United States Leadership Against HIV/AIDS, Tuberculosis, and Malaria Act of 2003, Pub. L. No. 108-25, 117 Stat. 711 (2003) (codified as amended at 22 U.S.C.A. §§7601 et seq. (West 2010)).
56. *Id.*
57. Ahmed & Seshu, *supra* note 55; Busza, *supra* note 55.
58. *See* Prabha Kotiswaran, *Born unto Brothels—Toward a Legal Ethnography of Sex Work in an Indian Red-Light Area*, 33 LAW & SOC. INQUIRY 579 (2008).
59. *Id.*
60. Hila Shamir, *Anti-Trafficking in Israel: Neo-Abolitionist Feminists, Markets, Borders, and the State, in* GOVERNANCE FEMINISM: AN INTRODUCTION (Janet Halley et al. eds., 2018)
61. *See* Goodmark, *supra* note 33, at 132–38.
62. *See* Karen Engle, *The Grip of Sexual Violence: Reading UN Security Council Resolutions on Human Security, in* RETHINKING PEACEKEEPING, GENDER EQUALITY, AND COLLECTIVE SECURITY 23–47 (Gina Heathcote & Dianne Otto eds., 2014).
63. *See* Nesiah, *supra* note 34, at 515.
64. *See* LAUREN BERLANT, CRUEL OPTIMISM (2011).
65. *See* LIBBY ADLER, GAY PRIORI: A QUEER CRITICAL LEGAL STUDIES APPROACH TO LAW REFORM (2018).

CHAPTER 12

THE EQUAL RIGHTS AMENDMENT, THEN AND NOW

JULIE C. SUK

IN many constitutional democracies around the world, feminism has changed the law through constitutional amendment.[1] In the United States, the Nineteenth Amendment to the Constitution prohibited the denial of the right to vote on account of sex in 1920. But feminist activists in the United States have struggled for generations with proposals to entrench gender equality beyond the right to vote in the text of the Constitution through an amendment.[2] The unique trajectory of the Equal Rights Amendment (ERA), recounted in this chapter, raises challenging questions about both the process of feminist constitutional change and the substance of feminist aspirations as they changed over time through many different legal paths.

The ERA that has been advancing through the constitutional amendment process since 1972, reads simply:

1. *Equality of rights under the law shall not be denied or abridged by the United States or by any State on account of sex.*
2. *Congress shall have the power to enforce, by appropriate legislation, the provisions of this Article.*
3. *This Amendment shall take effect two years after the date of ratification.*[3]

Although the ERA was first introduced with slightly different language in 1923,[4] Congress did not adopt it until nearly fifty years after its introduction, in 1972.[5] And although a majority of the states ratified it immediately, the U.S. Constitution requires a three-fourths supermajority of the states to ratify a constitutional amendment,[6] which the ERA did not achieve before the congressionally imposed deadlines on ratification had passed. Recent efforts to revive ratification in the states have raised new questions about the meaning of the ERA and the reasons for adding the amendment to the Constitution now.

Section I of this chapter provides an overview of the ERA and its history. The failure of the ERA has often been attributed to feminists' inability to convince the country of their vision of women's roles, but in fact the ERA was blocked by antidemocratic deadlines and procedural roadblocks that prevented a national referendum on gender equality from taking place. Section II explains the ERA's goals when it was introduced and later adopted and explores why it did not achieve the requisite number of ratifications within the deadlines. Although their arguments and emphasis changed over time in response to legal developments, ERA proponents throughout this era shared a common vision of supporting women's equality and ensuring that childbearing and childrearing did not impede the full exercise of women's economic and political citizenship. More than the force of opponents' arguments, legislative stonewalling and obstructionist tactics prevented this vision from taking root in the Constitution. Section III examines the significance of the ERA's resurgence from 2017 to 2020, when Nevada, Illinois, and Virginia ratified the amendment to bring the ratification count to thirty-eight states, arguably sufficient to add it to the Constitution. This latest push for ratification reflects a unifying theme among generations of ERA supporters to press for legislative action to secure meaningful equality for women, even as they added their own expansive understanding of what gender equality means. Section IV examines the ERA's future. Because of intervening legal developments during the decades that separated the adoption and final ratification of the amendment, legitimizing the ERA's transgenerational path poses important questions for how the twenty-first-century ERA should be implemented and interpreted. The ultimate significance of ratifying the ERA has as much to do with including women among our Constitution's framers and adopters and bolstering constitutional legitimacy as it does with mobilizing future legislative action to expand and secure gender equality for all.

I. A Brief History of the ERA

The Equal Rights Amendment was first introduced in Congress in December 1923. The initial proposal for the amendment read, "Men and women shall have equal rights throughout the United States and every place subject to its jurisdiction. Congress shall have the power to enforce this article by appropriate legislation."[7] It was the brainchild of the National Woman's Party, led by Alice Paul, who was known for her militant tactics in the suffrage movement.[8] Crystal Eastman, who had graduated at the top of her class at NYU Law School, worked with Paul on drafting the Amendment,[9] and Burnita Shelton Matthews, the chief lawyer of the National Woman's Party, defended the ERA in congressional hearings after it was introduced. They argued that a constitutional amendment was necessary because women were treated unequally under almost every law that affected women's economic and social status beyond suffrage.

Suffragists viewed the Nineteenth Amendment, empowering women to vote, as a beginning, not an endpoint, in securing women's equality.[10] The ERA was the inexorable next step, a constitutional guarantee to end women's exclusion from the good jobs and schools, which was essential to their prospects for economic independence. Equal rights would give women the same right to own their earnings that men had. The existing laws of some states treated married women's earnings from market work as the property of their husbands. The ERA would also give mothers the same legal authority as guardians of their own children as fathers. The National Woman's Party described their proposed constitutional amendment as a "blanket amendment" because it would invalidate every state and federal law that treated the sexes unequally.[11]

Although the ERA was introduced in Congress in 1923, with hearings from 1925 through the 1940s, it was not until 1972 that both houses of Congress adopted it by the two-thirds vote required under Article V. The Senate voted twice, in 1950 and 1953, to adopt the ERA, but only with a rider in place that would arguably weaken its protections by stating that the amendment would not impair any rights, benefits, or protections conferred by law on the female sex.[12] In the House, the Judiciary Committee, chaired by Emmanuel Celler, refused to hold hearings on the ERA and declined to report out the resolution throughout the 1950s and 1960s.[13]

In 1970, the entire body of the House debated and voted on the ERA, but only because Representative Martha Griffiths collected 218 representatives' signatures on a discharge petition to wrest the ERA resolution out of the control of the all-male Judiciary Committee. Once the entire House was able to debate the ERA on the floor, nine of the ten women who were in the House took the crucial opportunity to persuade their colleagues that the ERA was needed. The House voted by an overwhelming majority to adopt the ERA—352 to 15[14]—well over the two-thirds threshold required by the Constitution. But the Senate did not follow suit in that session. When the resolution reached the Senate floor in October, with less than a month before elections, opponents proposed several changes to the ERA, including a seven-year deadline on ratification.[15] In effect, this killed the ERA for that legislative session, because even if the Senate were to adopt this slightly different version of the ERA, there would not be sufficient time before elections to reconcile the House and Senate versions in conference committee, and the likelihood of a lame-duck Congress doing so after elections was low.

Both houses of Congress adopted the ERA in the next legislative session, in 1971–72. When Martha Griffiths reintroduced the ERA after the Senate opponents had sent it to the legislative graveyard the previous year, she inserted a seven-year ratification deadline into the resolution as a compromise strategy to calm the Senate opponents, who were small in number but fierce with tactics. The text of the proposed ERA remained unchanged, but the resolution introducing it proposed that it would be "valid to all intents and purposes as part of the Constitution when ratified by the legislatures of three-fourths of the several States within seven years from the date of its submission by Congress." It passed the House by an overwhelming majority again—354 to 24. This time the Senate followed, with eighty-four votes in favor and only eight opposed, well over the two-thirds required by Article V.

Initially, states were quick to ratify the ERA. Thirty states—the majority of them—ratified it by the end of 1973. Five additional states ratified by 1977. But the pace of ratification slowed in the mid-1970s in part due to the STOP-ERA campaign led by conservative icon Phyllis Schlafly. While a 2020 television miniseries dramatized Schlafly's undoubtedly significant role in defeating the ERA in the 1970s,[16] the STOP-ERA movement's success was enabled by the seven-year deadline and minority-empowering institutional features of Congress and state legislatures that are often taken for granted, even though they are undemocratic and easily abused. By 1978, women in Congress had formed a Women's Caucus, and they grew increasingly concerned that the ERA was three states shy of ratification, as it approached the seven-year deadline.[17] Representative Liz Holtzman, a founder of the Congressional Women's Caucus, successfully proposed a resolution to extend the ERA deadline by three additional years, to 1982. Congressional hearings and floor debates highlighted Congress's power to change the deadline, as well as the delay tactics by a small number of opponents in state legislatures who had prevented debates and votes on ratification during the 1970s.[18] Members of Congress acknowledged that several states had also taken votes to rescind their ratifications and suggested that a future Congress, convening at the time that thirty-eight ratifications were complete, could decide whether to count states that ratified and rescinded as among the ratified states.[19]

Despite the changed deadline, no additional states ratified the ERA prior to the extended deadline. The ERA was presumed dead in 1982. Proponents of the ERA reintroduced new ERA resolutions in Congress, on the assumption that the constitutional amendment would require a new two-thirds vote by both houses of Congress, and new ratification votes by thirty-eight states.[20] Although the House voted on the resolution in 1983, it fell six votes short of a two-thirds majority. Progress toward enacting the ERA stalled.

Meanwhile, another proposed amendment became the Twenty-Seventh Amendment in 1992. That amendment, which provides that any pay raises Congress votes to give its members take effect only in the next legislative session, was adopted by Congress in 1789. Ratification had stalled for centuries, but after debates about the ERA renewed public attention to the effects of time on the validity of constitutional amendments, a majority of state legislatures ratified the congressional pay amendment from 1983 to 1992.[21] The thirty-eighth state ratified the amendment in 1992, and both houses of Congress adopted resolutions recognizing it as a validly ratified part of the Constitution.[22]

The uncontroversial constitutionalization of the Twenty-Seventh Amendment led ERA proponents to argue that the 1972 ERA could still be ratified,[23] in what became known as the "three-state strategy." If three additional states ratified the ERA, bringing the total count to thirty-eight states, that could constitute a valid path to make the ERA part of the Constitution. Since Congress had voted to change the ERA deadline in 1978, proponents of the "three-state strategy" presumed that Congress could change the deadline again, including by removing the deadline altogether. In addition, proponents of the three-state strategy began to raise questions about whether the seven-year deadline had any binding legal effect on the states to begin with. ERA ratification resolutions were drafted and introduced in several state legislatures in the 1990s and 2000s.

In 2017, the Nevada legislature adopted an ERA ratification resolution, becoming the first state to ratify the ERA after the congressional deadlines. In 2018, Illinois followed. In 2020, Virginia became the thirty-eighth state.[24] In Congress, the House voted within two weeks of Virginia's ratification to lift the ratification deadline.[25] The Senate did not follow suit in 2020, and in the next legislative session, the House voted again to lift the deadline.[26] Although a bipartisan resolution has been introduced in the Senate[27] at the time of this writing, it remains to be seen whether the Senate resolution will attract the sixty votes necessary to defeat cloture as long as the Senate filibuster rule remains unchanged. As no Democratic member of Congress has opposed or voted against ERA deadline removal, it is assumed that if the resolution were to receive a floor vote in the Senate, it would be passed by a majority.

Meanwhile, the three states that ratified the ERA following the deadline immediately brought a lawsuit against the National Archivist, arguing that the thirty-eight ratifications are valid and thus require the Archivist to add the ERA to the Constitution.[28] These states argued that Congress's seven-year ratification deadline did not bind the states. Some states that never ratified the ERA joined with some states that rescinded their ratifications to intervene in the lawsuit, arguing that the ratification deadline expired in 1979, and that five states validly rescinded their ratifications before that deadline.[29] The district court dismissed the lawsuit, finding that the plaintiff states lacked standing to sue the Archivist, whose failure to act caused no direct injury to the states.[30] The district court also determined that the congressionally imposed ratification deadline was valid, and therefore the three most recent ratifications came too late.[31] As of this writing, the dismissal has been appealed.[32]

II. Uncovering the ERA's Meaning, from 1923 to the Present

Although the ERA's procedural validity is embattled, the key question for feminism is what the ERA would do if it became part of the Constitution. If the ERA is substantively empty or even harmful, then the procedural issues are not worth the fight. Understanding what's at stake in the amendment is critical to the ERA's future, as well as to the future of the amendment process under Article V.

On the surface, a constitutional guarantee of equal rights under the law, unabridged on account of sex by the federal or state government, seems simple to understand as a prohibition of governmental sex discrimination. Nonetheless, as the history of constitutional equal protection and statutory antidiscrimination jurisprudence shows, what constitutes sex discrimination is often a subject of disagreement, even among those committed to the general principle of gender equality.

As soon as the ERA was introduced in 1923, questions arose as to whether the ERA would eliminate sex-specific laws that guaranteed minimum wages for women and required safe working conditions for pregnant women and mothers. By 1917, at least twenty states had maximum-hours laws for women only, and several states also required employers to pay minimum wages to women, set by the state's minimum wage commission.[33] Women who worked in factories, often because they were poor and needed the income, relied on these laws to protect their means of survival.

These laws applied only to women, largely because the U.S. Supreme Court had struck down laws that regulated the hours that men could work since 1905. In *Lochner v. New York*, the Supreme Court struck down a New York state law that limited the working hours of (male) bakers, holding that the Fourteenth Amendment entitled workers and employers to decide for themselves—exercising the freedom of contract—the hours of work.[34] Under *Lochner* and other judicial decisions striking down labor laws on similar grounds, the labor protections that survived were those restricted to women. The Supreme Court upheld women-only labor protections against a similar constitutional challenge in *Muller v. Oregon* in 1908.[35] Acknowledging that its decision in *Lochner* upheld men's freedom of contract under the Due Process Clause, the Supreme Court held that the police power of the state could nevertheless reach the protection of working women and upheld a state law setting maximum hours for women factory workers. Women were vulnerable because of their childbearing functions, the Court reasoned, and therefore should be protected by law from exploitation.

However, the Nineteenth Amendment's ratification—and the proposal for an ERA that immediately followed—called the *Muller* doctrine into question. In 1923, the Supreme Court struck down a District of Columbia law requiring minimum wages for women workers, invoking the right to freedom of contract protected in *Lochner*. The Court held in *Adkins v. Children's Hospital* that the women's minimum wage law violated the Fifth Amendment's Due Process Clause, reasoning that women had the same freedom of contract as men. The Court cited the newly ratified Nineteenth Amendment to suggest that women now enjoyed equal status to men and therefore no longer needed the special labor protections upheld in *Muller*. "In view of the great—not to say revolutionary—changes which have taken place . . . in the contractual, political, and civil status of women, culminating in the Nineteenth Amendment, it is not unreasonable to say that these differences have now come almost, if not quite, to the vanishing point."[36]

The *Adkins* ruling divided suffragists who had united to advance the Nineteenth Amendment. That division became apparent in the first congressional hearings on the ERA. The Court's decision galvanized some suffragists—those who advanced the cause of working-class women—to oppose the ERA when it was proposed a few months later. Florence Kelley, a social reformer who had orchestrated the "Brandeis Brief" to protect women workers in the *Muller v. Oregon* case,[37] testified in 1929 ERA hearings before a subcommittee of the House Judiciary Committee:

> There are every year from 23,000 to 26,000 deaths of mothers consequent upon childbirth and the diseases and incidents connected with it. . . . Is there any answer

to the question, 'What corresponding dangers are there suffered by men?' How can it be said in the presence of these deaths that the resisting power of women is identical with the resisting power of men under the strains and hazards of industry?[38]

If men and women did not have equal bargaining power in the industrial workplace, an ERA potentially requiring men and women to be treated the same could lead to the judicial invalidation of protective labor laws. Kelley, on behalf of women workers, supported the principle of equal rights but opposed the ERA because the language of the so-called equal rights amendment was sufficiently vague as to empower judges hostile to labor to strike down all labor laws in the name of equal treatment. Other supporters of working women agreed. Dorothy Kenyon, a lawyer who went on to argue sex discrimination cases under the Fourteenth Amendment for the ACLU,[39] said, "The equal rights amendment would operate like a blind man with a shotgun. No lawyer can confidently state what it would hit,"[40] Kenyon said. In the hands of a conservative judiciary hostile to labor rights, the ERA could be weaponized to attack, rather than promote, policies that helped women workers.

But by the time the ERA gained enough support in Congress to advance in one chamber, the Supreme Court had switched course, abandoned *Lochner*, and upheld protective labor legislation in *West Coast Hotel v. Parrish*[41] and *United States v. Darby Lumber*.[42] With the Court now much less likely to strike down labor protections, replacing *Lochner* with a deferential stance toward state and federal laws regulating workplace conditions, ERA opposition from advocates of working women weakened. Furthermore, many constitutions around the world that were drafted after World War II included a provision guaranteeing equal rights for women and men, in accordance with the 1945 U.N. Charter. When the Senate voted favorably on the ERA in 1950 and 1953, it did so only after a provision was added that made it compatible with special protections for women. Although some ERA proponents feared that this rider would dilute the goals of the ERA, they still voted for the ERA in its modified form, preferring it to the absence of an ERA.[43]

From 1970 to 1972, opponents of the ERA in both chambers—Emanuel Celler in the House and Sam Ervin in the Senate—insisted on the ratification deadline, plotting a procedural derailment of the ERA. But their main objection to the ERA was substantive, not procedural. In the Senate floor debates where the ratification deadline was introduced in 1970, Senator Ervin insisted that the ERA "seeks to rob the wives, the homemakers, the mothers, the working women, and the widows of America."[44] Caricaturing the vision that the proponents of the ERA had advanced in the House, Ervin claimed that the ERA would require sex blindness under all circumstances, leading to many undesirable consequences, such as unisex bathrooms. He claimed that sex blindness would deprive mothers and homemakers of alimony or child custody in the event of divorce.

By 1972, Phyllis Schlafly, who had previously been uninterested in the ERA, embraced Ervin's motherhood-based anti-ERA stance. Schlafly had ignored the ERA when she ran unsuccessfully for Congress in 1970, as the women of the House advanced it on the floor. Ironically, Schlafly lost her bid to a man who said that she should "quit attacking my foreign aid votes and stay home with her husband and six kids."[45] But after the House adopted the ERA, Schlafly penned an anti-ERA tirade arguing that it would threaten "the most precious and important right of all," which only women in America, not men, possessed: "the right to keep her own baby and to be supported and protected in the enjoyment of watching her baby grow and develop."[46] She wrote, "Most women would rather cuddle a baby rather [sic] than a typewriter or a factory machine."[47] Schlafly argued that if the ERA treated husbands and wives equally in marriage and divorce, women would lose alimony and child custody. Women, like men, would be subject to the military draft. She accused the proponents of women's liberation of promoting "federal day care centers for babies instead of homes," and "abortions instead of families."[48]

Schlafly, building on congressional opponents' objections, proliferated exaggerated claims about what the ERA would do if it became law and stoked cultural anxieties about combining paid work and motherhood. Unlike the ERA that was proposed in 1923 and opposed by reformers on behalf of working mothers, which might have ended sex-based protective labor laws, the ERA that emerged from Congress in 1970 and 1972 intended to overcome the inequalities women faced because of their role in childbearing and childrearing, which made them economically dependent. Contrary to Schlafly's dystopian vision where women abandon their babies or have abortions to enter the labor force, the 1970s feminist vision for the ERA aimed to make motherhood and work compatible so that women could do both. The 1972 ERA had a vision to which a broad coalition of women lawmakers subscribed, including Patsy Takemoto Mink and Shirley Chisholm, the first women of color elected to Congress, and Florence Dwyer and Margaret Heckler, Republican women who emphasized how the ERA would help homemakers and mothers.[49]

Women in Congress made equality for working mothers a centerpiece of the ERA. Patsy Mink was a champion of working mothers. She drew Congress's attention to the inequalities faced by working mothers, not only in her floor speeches advancing the ERA but also in her other legislative activities. In judicial confirmation hearings in 1970, Patsy Mink sharply criticized a Fourth Circuit judge who declined to rehear *Phillips v. Martin Marietta*, which held that an employer's exclusion of mothers of preschool-age children was not sex discrimination.[50] Mink's testimony helped prevent Judge Carswell from being confirmed as a Supreme Court Justice. Mink took a leading role in committee hearings, at which Shirley Chisholm testified in 1970, on proposed legislation to establish federally funded comprehensive preschool education throughout the nation.[51] Chisholm framed the child care bill as an initiative to support working women.[52] Both congresswomen touted the ERA as a catalyst for legislative action on the policy issues that would help working mothers. When Mink testified in hearings about the ERA, she presented the amendment as a wake-up call to "our somnolent public servants," to remind them of "the lack of action by our executive, legislative and judicial bodies to put into effect the equal rights safeguards already in the Constitution."[53] The ERA would leave to legislators "the formidable task of seeking extensive legislation and judicial actions to implement it."[54]

The ERA would help working mothers and homemakers by breaking down barriers to women's education and employment, and by giving married women access to credit independent of their husbands. Establishing credit, even within marriage, would protect women from the economic risks that could materialize if their husbands died or divorced them. In the event of divorce, the ERA would require courts to evaluate the circumstances of the spouses in awarding alimony or custody without making presumptions based on stereotyped expectations of mothers and fathers. As for the military draft, Louise Hicks, a conservative Democrat, argued that the ERA was compatible with exemptions from military service for mothers of young children.[55] But the STOP-ERA movement distorted this vision and depicted the ERA as a dystopian attack on traditional motherhood. In actuality, the ERA's proponents sought to provide mothers who needed to work outside the home with a viable path to economic security.

By the end of 1973, thirty states had ratified the ERA, but with the increased efforts of the STOP-ERA movement, ratification stalled. Only five additional states ratified by 1977, and no additional state followed until 2017, by which time the original 1979 deadline, and three-year extension, had long lapsed.

The received wisdom about the ERA's failure is that Phyllis Schlafly stopped the ERA by turning the ratification process into a cultural referendum on American motherhood. But that account hides the distortions caused by the ratification process itself, as institutions and procedures prevented the meaningful legislative—and cultural—debate necessary to confront any confusion or disagreement about what the proposed amendment would or should do. Consider, for instance, the history of failed ratification in Virginia, which finally became the thirty-eighth state to ratify the ERA in 2020. In 1978, as Congress considered extending the deadline on ratification, Congresswoman Margaret Heckler (R-Mass.) pointed out that the ERA was not getting a real debate in the Virginia legislature because the state's House of Delegates' Privileges and Elections Committee, led by the most senior men, kept blocking it from being debated on the floor.[56] The U.S. Constitution does not require the state legislatures to consider amendments proposed by two thirds of Congress; state legislatures are free to make their own rules for the consideration of federal constitutional amendments.[57] The Virginia House of Delegates empowers a small committee to play gatekeeper, and the discharge petition process is not available for the ratification of federal constitutional amendments. Efforts to change these procedures failed from the mid-1970s to 2019.[58]

In Phyllis Schlafly's home state of Illinois, Schlafly went to the capitol with STOP-ERA brigades, bearing freshly baked bread marked "From the breadmakers to the breadwinners."[59] Legislators received such treats on days that they were to consider ERA ratification. But it was not the bread alone that stopped the ERA. Each chamber of the Illinois legislature, in full control of its own process by which to consider federal constitutional amendments, adopted rules requiring a three-fifths supermajority of the chamber to ratify such amendments.[60] Both houses of the Illinois legislature voted by a constitutional majority (51 percent majority of all its members) on two occasions to ratify the ERA, and in many states, that would have produced a valid ratification. But the supermajority rule in Illinois raised the bar that proponents would have to meet.

Even before the time-limited process of ratification began in the states, the amendment process that occurred in Congress involved undemocratic dynamics that empowered the minority who objected to the ERA. In the House, Emanuel Celler managed to shield the ERA from debate as chair of the House Judiciary Committee by preventing it from being reported. In the Senate, although the ultimate vote showed overwhelming support for the ERA, Sam Ervin managed to insert the deadline into the ERA by taking advantage of the Senate's unlimited time for debate. Ervin had participated in the filibuster of the Civil Rights Act of 1964, and it is clear that his efforts to insert a range of amendments to ERA proposals were a delay strategy that always threatened to send the ERA to the legislative graveyard. When ERA proponents agreed to the deadline in 1971, it was largely because they had already seen how a single powerful opponent, even while being in the minority, could manipulate the unique Senate rule on debate time to cause a measure to die without taking the political heat for killing it.[61] Parliamentary procedures in Congress and the state legislatures were institutional enablers of the STOP-ERA movement's cultural success in stalling the ERA. The ERA failed not because a majority of the country did not support its proponents' stance on women, work, and motherhood but because not enough of the men who controlled Congress and the state legislatures did.

III. The Twenty-First-Century ERA

When the Nevada legislature ratified the ERA on March 22, 2017, forty-five years to the date on which the Senate adopted it in 1972, state senator Pat Spearman, the sponsor of the resolution, invoked the ERA's 1970s goals to direct its twenty-first-century meaning. She began by quoting Ruth Bader Ginsburg's 1970s writings:

> This is what ratifying the ERA will do: In the words of Supreme Court Justice Ruth Bader Ginsburg, who wrote in the *Harvard Women's Law Journal*, and I quote, "With the Equal Rights Amendment, we may expect Congress and the state legislatures to undertake in earnest systematically and pervasively the law revision so long deferred and in the event of legislative default the courts will have an unassailable basis for applying the bedrock principle: All men and women are created equal.[62]

The vision of the ERA affirmed in the Nevada legislature in 2017 assigned primary responsibility for enforcing equal rights to Congress and the state legislatures rather than to courts. Section 2 of the ERA explicitly authorizes Congress to enforce it, and § 3, in providing for a two-year delay in the ERA's effective date, creates a period that ERA proponents in 1971–72 assumed would enable legislatures to revise existing laws to implement "equality of rights." Echoing Mink and Chisholm from decades ago, Spearman pointed out in the state's legislative debate over ratification that legislation on child care and paid parental leave would be necessary to address the persistence of unequal pay between women and men. Unequal pay results not only from intentionally paying women less than men but largely from the effects of childbearing and childrearing on women's market work.

After ratifying the ERA, the Nevada legislature adopted several laws designed to support working mothers, including the Pregnant Workers' Fairness Act,[63] the Nursing Mothers Accommodation Act,[64] and the Domestic Violence Leave Law,[65] which entitles employees who are victims of domestic violence to leave without risking termination. In the next election, Nevada voters elected historic numbers of women to the legislature, making Nevada the first and only state legislature in the nation to have more women (51 percent) serving as elected representatives than men.

In Illinois, the legislative history of the 2018 ratification of the ERA similarly reflects proponents' focus on its role as a catalyst of legislative action. Juliana Stratton, an ERA proponent in the Illinois House of Representatives, went on to be elected lieutenant governor of Illinois that year, becoming the first African American woman to hold that statewide office. When justifying ERA ratification on the House floor, she noted that Congress would have a sound constitutional basis for legislation effectively remedying gender violence. It would direct law enforcement to do more to prevent domestic violence and to support its victims.[66]

By the time 2020 arrived, Virginia's ratification of the ERA was nationally anticipated. Many women running for legislative seats in November 2019 had explicitly made it a campaign issue. A ratification effort led by women of color in both legislative chambers had failed in the previous legislative session, largely because a few opponents had prevented the resolution from reaching the floor of the House of Delegates. In Virginia, the ratification was as much about changing the face of Virginia politics, in light of the state's history of noninclusion of women and minorities, as it was about the specific policies that would support working mothers and achieve greater inclusion. Senator Jennifer McClellan, one of the first Virginia legislators to give birth while in office,[67] and Delegate Jennifer Carroll Foy, one of the first women to attend the Virginia Military Institute after the U.S. Supreme Court opened it to women in *United States v. Virginia*,[68] pushed the ERA forward. In a legislative session that began with ERA ratification, women lawmakers in Virginia—now constituting 30 percent of the legislature[69]—successfully spearheaded the enactment of a pregnant worker fairness law; a law easing abortion restrictions; and a law expanding antidiscrimination protections to include pregnancy, sexual orientation, and gender identity as grounds of discrimination.[70]

These three twenty-first-century ratifications updated the meaning of the ERA that was adopted by Congress in 1972, from a focus on judicial review of sex discriminatory laws to an emphasis on prompting state and federal legislation to facilitate women's equality. When the House of Representatives adopted the ERA in 1971, the Supreme Court had not yet decided *Reed v. Reed*,[71] the Court's first case to strike down a sex-discriminatory law as a violation of the Equal Protection Clause. In 1973, one year after the Senate completed Congress's adoption of the ERA, the Supreme Court decided *Frontiero v. Richardson*,[72] which struck down a federal regulation that treated male and female military employees differently for the purposes of benefits coverage for their spouses. That regulation, the Court reasoned, was premised on overbroad generalizations about the proper roles of men and women. Although a majority of the Justices did not agree on what the legal standard should be, a plurality of four Justices in the case recognized that congressional adoption of the ERA signaled a democratically legitimate move toward strictly scrutinizing sex classifications in the law.[73]

Subsequent Supreme Court decisions embracing a heightened scrutiny standard for sex discriminatory laws under the Fourteenth Amendment arguably achieved one of the goals of the 1972 ERA proponents. In an era when courts permitted sex classifications in the law to perpetuate women's second-class citizenship, some ERA proponents hoped that the amendment would furnish a new rule of decision for courts akin to the "strict scrutiny" that was in operation for racial classifications back then. Beginning in 1971, the Supreme Court used the Equal Protection Clause to strike down several laws that treated men and women differently when they were premised on stereotypes about men's and women's roles within the family, settling on an intermediate scrutiny standard of review.[74]

This trajectory culminated in *United States v. Virginia*,[75] which concluded that the male-only admissions policy of the Virginia Military Institute (VMI) violated the Equal Protection Clause. *United States v. Virginia* stopped short of adopting "strict scrutiny" for governmental sex classifications, recognizing that "strict scrutiny" by 1995 had come to mean something different in the race context from what it had meant in the early 1970s, when ERA proponents were demanding that standard for sex classifications. Writing for the Court, Justice Ginsburg dropped a footnote to *Adarand Constructors v. Peña*, a 1995 case that applied strict scrutiny to race-based affirmative action,[76] and explained that the Court was applying "skeptical scrutiny" to governmental sex classifications. In reasoning this way, the *United States v. Virginia* Court preserved the possibility that the Court's tough equal protection standard for sex discrimination would allow the government to treat the sexes differently "to compensate women 'for particular economic disabilities [they have] suffered,'" or "to 'promo[e] equal employment opportunity.'"[77] After *United States v. Virginia* was decided, Justice Ginsburg and some commentators suggested that the Fourteenth Amendment's sex equality jurisprudence had achieved the primary goals of the 1970s ERA.

In light of these intervening legal developments, an ERA adopted by Congress in 1972 but ratified by the full complement of thirty-eight states nearly fifty years later raises novel questions about the purpose and legal meaning of an amendment when it is made across generations. If such an amendment is added to the Constitution in the twenty-first century, what is its public meaning? The ERA's 1970s framers in Congress proposed a constitutional amendment in part to invalidate sex-discriminatory laws. But their purpose was not limited to courts scrutinizing sex classifications in the law, and they did not foresee the anti-affirmative action turn that "strict scrutiny" would later take. In floor debates and committee hearings, the ERA's congressional proponents demonstrated their intent for the ERA to catalyze and legitimize further legislation by Congress and the states to establish public policy regimes that would make equality real in the domains of education, employment, and child care.

Although courts closely scrutinized governmental sex distinctions under the Fifth and Fourteenth Amendments eventually in the 1970s, the legislative catalyst for proactive governmental policies to support working mothers and homemakers and to remove the root causes of disadvantage did not take hold. Decades later, the twenty-first-century ratifiers in Nevada, Illinois, and Virginia raised additional issues of gender inequality that the 1970s framers did not explicitly discuss, such as the rights of LGBTQ (lesbian, gay, bisexual, transgender, and queer or questioning) to be free of discrimination based on their sex or gender, sexual harassment and domestic violence, and reproductive healthcare, including abortion. The ERA that completed ratification in 2020 must speak to both the unrealized 1970s vision of the ERA as a legislative catalyst and the gender inequality issues that are more explicitly at the forefront of the twenty-first-century public attention.

The legislative histories created by the three twenty-first-century ratifications, like those created in Congress in the 1970s, focus on the role of legislatures, rather than courts, in realizing the promise of equal rights. These recent ratifiers have also explicitly taken the position that "on account of sex" should encompass a broad definition that includes gender, pregnancy, sexual orientation, and gender identity.[78] In Virginia, ERA ratification was driven by a critical mass of women in the legislature who concurrently worked on legislation lifting abortion restrictions and guaranteeing fairness to pregnant workers. The need for law to respond more effectively to sexual assault also animated the Illinois ratification debates.[79]

In Congress, the hearings, report, and floor debates leading to the House's vote to lift the ratification deadline have also updated the meaning of the ERA. Before the House voted to remove the ratification deadline in 2020, the Judiciary Committee held hearings and issued a written report affirming the continued importance of the ERA for the twenty-first century. The House report advanced the following account of what the ERA could do prospectively:

> Because the ERA would empower Congress to enforce its provisions through legislation, it could provide a basis for Congress to engage in affirmative efforts to support gender equality both at home and in the workplace. Additionally, under some theories, the ERA could provide a basis for plaintiffs to challenge laws or policies that have a disparate impact on women, or to support efforts to create gender balance in certain contexts. Additionally, the ERA's prohibition against discrimination "on account of sex" could be interpreted to prohibit discrimination on the basis of sexual orientation or gender identity.[80]

Taken together, the legislative histories of the three postdeadline ratifications along with the legislative history of the deadline removal in Congress put forth a coherent twenty-first-century vision of the ERA. The twenty-first-century ERA is a constitutional recognition of the principle that people of all genders have equal status as rights bearers, and that this principle must be made real as a matter of public policy by legislatures, not courts. Consistent with both the new legislative history as well as the history of the ERA from 1923 through 1972, the ERA would render it inappropriate for courts to interfere with legislative action to support gender equality at home or in the workplace, to rewrite policies that have a disparate impact on women, or to bring about gender balance in the exercise of public power.

IV. THE FUTURE OF THE ERA

There is no constitutional obstacle to adding the 1972 ERA to the Constitution. Congress has the power to remove the ratification deadline. In *Coleman v. Miller*,[81] the Supreme Court understood Congress's power over the timeline of amendment ratification as a political question, not subject to judicial second-guessing. Accordingly, if both houses of Congress were to act to lift the deadline, such action, if challenged in litigation, would be immune from judicial invalidation.

Although the three-state strategy is plausible without congressional action, the legitimacy and potential of the ERA depend on Congress removing the ratification deadline. Because precedents establish that determining the reasonable time for amendment ratification is a political question for Congress, the Supreme Court would more likely validate congressional action to lift the deadline than accept the ERA's postdeadline ratification in litigation by ERA proponents seeking to validate the three-state strategy. But that is not the only point in favor of a congressional path. Congressional action would also provide additional opportunities to develop the ERA's legislative history, and thereby establish the ERA's clear public meaning for the twenty-first century, particularly after a global pandemic has had devastating effects on women's economic security. Every committee hearing and floor debate in Congress is an opportunity to update the ERA's purposes and the meaning of its words in the twenty-first century. These public exchanges connect the ERA framers' goals, successful and deferred, to the problems that have most animated the twenty-first century's renewed press for ratification. An important through-line from early debates about the ERA in 1923 to the most recent ratifications in 2020 is the idea that the implementation of equal rights is a task primarily for legislators, rather than for courts. From labor legislation responsive to the needs of working women in the 1920s to child care and equal educational opportunity in the 1970s to sexual violence, reproductive justice, and the caregiving infrastructure needed to rebuild the postpandemic economy in the twenty-first century, a constitutional recognition of women's equal citizenship stature is only the beginning for the significant political work necessary to realizing women's equality. Throughout the movement for the ERA, its proponents have understood the amendment as a necessary political legitimizer of this work, but by no means sufficient to ensure success.

Pauli Murray, the African American civil rights lawyer whom Ruth Bader Ginsburg credited for pioneering the sex equality arguments that the Supreme Court embraced in the 1970s,[82] noted in her testimony at a 1970 ERA hearing in Congress: "I suggest that what the opponents of the Amendment most fear is not equal rights but equal power and responsibility. I further suggest that underlying the issue of equal rights for women is the more fundamental issue of equal power for women."[83] The ERA has become both the vehicle and the goal of this long, slow struggle for women's political and economic empowerment. That is how it differs from existing sex discrimination protections under the Fifth and Fourteenth Amendments. The ERA's main contribution to feminist jurisprudence is not limited to its ability to change the rules of decision that courts enforce; it has always been as concerned with who is making and implementing constitutional equality as with what constitutional equality should do as law. The ERA is an amendment that was made by women for women, but women have lacked the political power in Congress and the state legislatures to defeat the procedural tactics of delay and avoidance that men who opposed the ERA used to their advantage, even when ERA opposition did not represent the will of the American people. And even though ERA proponents had the ingenuity to change the law of equal protection to incorporate sex equality through litigation, that work remains invisible to nonlawyer citizens who get their constitutional law from looking at the text of their pocket constitutions rather than from reading the complex doctrinal explanations of the Supreme Court's sex equality precedents.

Notwithstanding nearly a century of concerted effort, a constitutional mandate for gender equality, achieved by women as Constitution makers, has yet to be adopted by a formal constitutional provision. The final step of adding the ERA to the Constitution's text is necessary to preserve the enduring legitimacy of the imperfect democracy that the Constitution established in 1789. Adding the ERA to the Constitution after this long and unprecedented trajectory would transform the women who fought for constitutional equality into constitutional framers and founders. In the twenty-first century, feminist jurisprudence must question whether any constitution with no female framers can maintain its legitimacy. And if it can't, the amendment process—even though, and perhaps especially because, it spanned generations—must be interpreted to provide a path of repair.

The process by which the ERA succeeded, failed, and returned shapes its twenty-first-century meaning and justification. Some commentators invoke the prevalence of women's equal rights guarantees in most constitutions around the world to conclude that the ERA is long overdue in the United States.[84] But a more compelling justification for constitutionalizing women's equality emerges from the ERA's distinctive trajectory in the United States. The ERA's path through the Article V amendment process enabled women's contributions to the democratic process and therefore helps legitimize a Constitution that operated unequally for most of its history and, many feminists believe, continues to do so. The ERA's failed ratification, if left unrectified due to the procedural time bar, reflects and may perpetuate the disproportionate power that legislative minorities can abuse to thwart democracy.

Notes

1. *See* Julie C. Suk, *An Equal Rights Amendment for the Twenty-First Century: Bringing Global Constitutionalism Home*, 28 Yale J. L. & Feminism 381 (2017).
2. For a book-length narrative of this century-long struggle, *see* Julie C. Suk, We the Women: The Unstoppable Mothers of the Equal Rights Amendment (2020).
3. H.R.J. Res. 208, 92d Cong. (1971).
4. *See* H.R.J. Res. 75, 68th Cong. (1923).
5. *See* 118 Cong. Rec. 9598 (1972).
6. *See* U.S. Const. art. V.
7. H.R.J. Res. 75, 68th Cong. (1923).
8. *See* Aileen Kraditor, The Ideas of the Woman Suffrage Movement, 1890-1920, 231–40 (1965).
9. On Crystal Eastman's involvement in drafting the ERA, *see* Amy Aronson, Crystal Eastman: A Revolutionary Life 234–35 n.64 (2020).
10. Shortly after the Nineteenth Amendment was ratified, Crystal Eastman wrote, "Now at last we can begin," in an article describing the next goals after suffrage, namely, occupational choice and economic independence. *See* Crystal Eastman, *Now We Can Begin*, The Liberator, Dec. 1920, *reprinted in* Crystal Eastman on Women and Revolution 52 (Blanche Wiesen Cook ed., 1978).
11. *See Equal Rights Amendment to the Constitution: Hearing on H.R.J. Res. 75 Before the H. Comm. on the Judiciary*, 68th Cong. 12 (1925) (statement of Burnita Matthews).
12. *See* 96 Cong. Rec. 870 (1950); 99 Cong. Rec. 8974 (1953).
13. *See* Susan D. Becker, The Origins of the Equal Rights Amendment: American Feminism Between the Wars 273 (1981).
14. 116 Cong. Rec. 28,036 to 28,037 (1970).
15. 116 Cong. Rec. 35,947, 36,478 to 36,479 (1970).
16. *See* Mrs. America (FX Hulu, 2020).
17. *See* Irwin Gertzog, Congressional Women: Their Recruitment, Treatment, and Behavior 183 (1984).
18. *See* 124 Cong. Rec. 26,201 (1978).
19. 124 Cong. Rec. 26,225 to 26,233 (1978).
20. For a thorough account of the ERA's reintroduction and debates in the early 1980s, *see* Serena Mayeri, *A New E.R.A. or a New Era?*, 103 Nw. U. L. Rev. 1223 (2009).
21. *See* Matt Largey, *The Bad Grade That Changed the U.S. Constitution*, NPR (May 5, 2017).
22. 138 Cong. Rec. 11,869 (1992); 138 Cong. Rec. 12,052 (1992).
23. *See* Allison L. Held, Sheryl L. Herndon & Danielle M. Stager, *The Equal Rights Amendment: Why the ERA Remains Legally Viable and Properly Before the States*, 3 Wm. & Mary J. Women & L. 113 (1997).
24. For a narrated account of the floor debates in these states leading to ratification, *see* Suk, *supra* note 2, at 129–71.
25. 166 Cong. Rec. H1142 (2020).
26. H.J. Res. 17 (2021).
27. S.J. Res. 1 (2021).
28. Virginia v. Ferriero, Case No. 20-242 (D.D.C. filed Jan. 30, 2020).
29. Virginia v. Ferriero, 466 F. Supp. 3d 253 (D.D.C. 2020).

30. Virginia v. Ferriero, Case No. 20-242 (RC), Memorandum Opinion, (D.D.C. Mar. 5, 2021), at 12–13, available at https://ecf.dcd.uscourts.gov/cgi-bin/show_public_doc?2020cv0242-117.
31. *Id.* at 36.
32. Virginia v. Ferriero, Case No. 20-242 (RC), Notice of Appeal, (D.D.C. May 3, 2021).
33. Nancy Woloch, A CLASS BY HERSELF 87 (2015).
34. Lochner v. New York, 198 U.S. 45 (1905).
35. 208 U.S. 412 (1908).
36. Adkins v. Children's Hosp., 261 U.S. 525, 553 (1923).
37. For a detailed account of Florence Kelley's collaboration with Louis Brandeis on the brief for the state of Oregon in *Muller v. Oregon*, *see* Josephine Goldmark, IMPATIENT CRUSADER: FLORENCE KELLEY'S LIFE STORY 150–59 (1953).
38. *Equal Rights Amendment: Hearing on S.J. Res. Before a Subcomm. of the S. Comm. on the Judiciary*, 71th Cong. 56–57 (1929) (statement of Florence Kelley).
39. Dorothy Kenyon represented Gwendolyn Hoyt in *Hoyt v. Florida*, in an unsuccessful challenge to a Florida law exempting women from jury service. Hoyt v. Florida, 368 U.S. 57 (1961).
40. *Equal Rights Amendment: Hearing on S.J. Res. 64 Before a Subcomm. of the S. Comm. on the Judiciary*, 70th Cong. 42 (1929) (statement of Dorothy Kenyon).
41. 300 U.S. 379 (1937) (upholding state law guaranteeing minimum wage for women).
42. 312 U.S. 100 (1941) (upholding the federal Fair Labor Standards Act).
43. Republican Senator Margaret Chase Smith, who had sponsored the ERA in 1945 as a member of the House, objected to the rider but then voted for the ERA with the rider in place. *See* 99 CONG. REC. 8974 (1953).
44. 116 CONG. REC. 35,935 (1970).
45. *See* CAROL FELSENTHAL, PHYLLIS SCHLAFLY: THE SWEETHEART OF THE SILENT MAJORITY 203–04 (1982).
46. Phyllis Schlafly, WHAT'S WRONG WITH EQUAL RIGHTS FOR WOMEN?, THE PHYLLIS SCHLAFLY REPORT (Feb. 1972).
47. *Id.*
48. *Id.*
49. *See* 116 CONG. REC. 28,004 (1970).
50. *See George Harrold Carswell: Hearings on the Nomination of George Harrold Carswell of Florida to Be Associate Justice of the Supreme Court of the United States Before the S. Comm. on the Judiciary*, 91st Cong. 81–88 (1970) (statement of Patsy Mink).
51. *Comprehensive Preschool Education and Child Day-Care Act of 1969: Hearings on H.R. Res. 13520 Before the Select Subcomm. on Educ. of the H. Comm. on Educ. and Lab.*, 91st Cong. 792 (1970) (statement of Shirley Chisholm).
52. *Id.* at 792.
53. 117 CONG. REC. 35,314 (1971).
54. *Id.*
55. *See* 117 CONG. REC. 35,324 (1971).
56. *See* 124 CONG. REC. 26,201 (1978).
57. *See* Dyer v. Blair, 390 F. Supp. 1291 (N.D. Ill. 1975).
58. *See* SUK, *supra* note 2, at 165–68.
59. *See* FELSENTHAL, *supra* note 45, at 242–66.
60. *See* interview by Mark DePue with Dawn Clark Netsch, Ill. State Sen., Abraham Lincoln Presidential Library, in Chicago, Ill. (Sept. 10, 2010), https://www2.illinois.gov/alplm/libr

ary/collections/oralhistory/illinoisstatecraft/legislators/Documents/NetschDawnClark/Netsch_Daw_4FNL_V2.pdf.
61. *See* David E. Kyvig, HISTORICAL MISUNDERSTANDINGS AND THE DEFEAT OF THE EQUAL RIGHTS AMENDMENT, 18 THE PUB. HIST. 45, 57 (1996).
62. NEV. LEG., S. Floor Sess. (Mar. 1, 2017) (quoting Ruth Bader Ginsburg, THE EQUAL RIGHTS AMENDMENT IS THE WAY, 1 HARV. WOMEN'S L.J. 19 (1978)) (statement of Pat Spearman).
63. S.B. 253, 2017 Leg., 79th Sess. (Nev. 2017).
64. Assemb. B. 113, 2017 Leg., 79th Sess. (Nev. 2017).
65. S.B. 361, 2017 Leg., 79th Sess. (Nev. 2017).
66. ILL. H. OF REP., 100th General Assemb., 141 TRANSCRIPTION DEB. 342 (May 30, 2018), https://www.ilga.gov/house/transcripts/htrans100/10000141.pdf.
67. *See* Jennifer McClellan, Plenary IV Speech at the National Organization for Women (NOW) Conference (July 20, 2019).
68. *See On a Point of Personal Privilege* before Va. H. Dels., Reg. Sess. (Va. 2019) (statement by Del. Carroll Foy). See United States v. Virginia, 518 U.S. 515 (1996).
69. Va. H. of Dels., Reg. Sess. (Va. 2020) (statement by Del. Vivian Watts).
70. *See generally* SUK, *supra* note 2, at 158–71. The legislation passed by the Virginia General Assembly in the 2020 session includes H.B. 827 Pregnant Worker Fairness Act (2020), S.B. 712, Virginia Human Rights Act (2020); S.B. 733, Abortion; Informed Consent (2020).
71. 404 U.S. 71 (1971) (striking down an Idaho statute giving preference to males over females in administration of estates).
72. 411 U.S. 677 (1973).
73. *Id.* at 687–88 (Brennan, J., concurring).
74. *See, e.g.*, Stanley v. Illinois, 405 U.S. 645 (1972); Weinberger v. Wiesenfeld, 420 U.S. 636 (1975); Craig v. Boren, 429 U.S. 190 (1976); and Taylor v. Louisiana, 419 U.S. 522 (1975).
75. 518 U.S. 515 (1996).
76. *Id.* at 532.
77. *Id.* at 533.
78. In Virginia, for instance, ratification debates in the House of Delegates included a speech by Danica Roem, Virginia's first transgender delegate, who said, "To single someone out based on sexual orientation and gender identity is to inherently single them out on account of sex." Va. H. of Dels., Reg. Sess. (2020).
79. For an account of the historical context of the #MeToo movement and its role in the Illinois legislature's 2018 ratification of the ERA, *see* SUK, *supra* note 2, at 142–157.
80. H.R. REP. No. 116-378, 6 (2020).
81. 307 U.S. 433, 454 (1939) ("The decision by the Congress . . . of the question whether the amendment had been adopted within a reasonable time would not be subject to review by the courts.").
82. *See* Brief for Appellant, Reed v. Reed, 404 U.S. 71 (1971) (No. 70-4). Ginsburg put Pauli Murray's name, as well as that of Dorothy Kenyon, on the cover page of the brief as coauthors, even though neither Murray nor Kenyon worked on this particular brief. Ginsburg included their names to recognize their authorship of the arguments that Ginsburg was making in the brief.
83. *Equal Rights 1970: Hearings on S.J. Res. 61 and S.J. Res. 231 Before the S. Comm. on the Judiciary*, 91st Cong. 427–33 (1970) (statement of Pauli Murray); *see also* Pauli Murray, *The Negro Woman's Stake in the Equal Rights Amendment*, 6 HARV. C.R.-C.L. L. REV. 253, 253–59 (1970–71).

84. Julie C. Suk, *An Equal Rights Amendment for the Twenty-First Century: Bringing Global Constitutionalism Home*, 28 YALE J. L. & FEMINISM 381 (2017). *See also* Catharine MacKinnon, *Towards a Renewed Equal Rights Amendment: Now, More Than Ever*, 37 HARV. J. L. & GENDER 569 (2014); *Equal Rights Amendment: Hearing on H.R.J. Res. 38 Before the Subcomm. on the Constitution, Civil Rights, and Civil Liberties of the H. Comm. on the Judiciary*, 116th Cong. 1–8 (2019) (statement of Kathleen M. Sullivan), https://www.congress.gov/116/meeting/house/109330/witnesses/HHRG-116-JU10-Wstate-SullivanK-20190430.pdf; Caroline Bettinger-Lopez & Delphi Cleaveland, *Constitutionalizing Equality: The Equal Rights Amendment as a Catalyst for Change*, COUNCIL ON FOREIGN REL. BLOG (Sept. 3, 2020, 8:00 AM), https://www.cfr.org/blog/constitutionalizing-equality-equal-rights-amendment-catalyst-change.

CHAPTER 13

THE ANTI-RAPE AND BATTERED WOMEN'S MOVEMENTS OF THE 1970S AND 1980S

LEIGH GOODMARK

THE anti-rape and battered women's movements of the 1970s and 1980s were a core component of the women's liberation movement that began in the late 1960s and early 1970s. Early grassroots organizing responding to rape and domestic violence relied heavily on community-based strategies including the creation of shelters, safe houses, and feminist self-defense classes. Using the language of the women's liberation movement, feminist advocates highlighted how existing rape and domestic violence law shored up the patriarchy, characterized women as the property of their fathers and husbands, and enabled the state to sidestep responsibility for violence. Reacting to a legal system whose responses to gender-based violence included official policies of non-interference, skepticism about women's credibility, and concern for family privacy above women's safety, some anti-violence advocates viewed the grassroots community-based strategies as insufficient. Instead, they pushed for greater state intervention, maintaining that taking gender-based violence seriously required criminal law reform.

But the anti-rape and anti–domestic violence movements were not united in embracing such strategies. Feminist organizing of the 1970s and 1980s reflected tensions between competing visions of the role of the state in addressing gender-based violence, visions shaped by race, class, and professional status. Women of color, in particular, voiced concern about the consequences of ceding so much power to the state. Notwithstanding these tensions within the movement, by the end of the 1980s, culminating in the passage of the Violence Against Women Act (VAWA) in 1994, feminists who favored state intervention had successfully codified and implemented a criminal legal strategy for responding to rape and intimate partner violence. Whereas the history of the gender violence movement is often presented as a linear progression from grassroots activism to reliance on the state, with most if not all advocates agreeing to state intervention, the reality is messier, revealing the origins of a debate that continues to the present.

I. THE ANTI-RAPE MOVEMENT

The anti-rape movement has long historical roots in the United States. Feminists organized to stop rape as early as the 1830s.[1] One of the central issues for the early civil rights movement was the need to protect Black women from rape by white men. In 1944, her first year with the Montgomery, Alabama, chapter of the NAACP (and eleven years before the Montgomery bus boycott), Rosa Parks led a campaign seeking justice for Recy Taylor, a Black woman raped by six white men.[2] Anti-rape organizing was also one of the priorities of the women's liberation movement of the 1970s. In addition to securing reproductive rights, workplace justice, and health care, confronting rape became one of the key issues for the feminist movement.[3] That organizing employed a variety of tactics: Feminists "stormed city halls and district attorneys' offices; they demonstrated in the streets and held speak-outs, conferences, and workshops; in cities and towns across the country they organized women against rape (WAR) groups; and they created the first rape crisis centers and hotlines to assist survivors of violence."[4] Their overarching project was to change the perception that rape was an isolated crime committed by a few sick men or the product of bad choices made by women.[5]

A. Early Organizing Efforts

Consciousness-raising groups contributed to the early momentum of feminist anti-rape efforts.[6] From those meetings came direct action. In July 1970, the Berkeley feminist newspaper *It Ain't Me Babe* ran "Anatomy of a Rape," a woman's account of her rape and experiences with her boyfriend, friends, police, and doctors in the aftermath. Articles titled "Fight!," urging women to fight back against rapists, and "Disarm Rapists," listing things women could do to protect themselves, ran in the same issue.[7] Feminist anti-rape organizers picketed the wedding of an alleged rapist in Berkeley in August 1970 and disrupted a Berkeley City Council meeting, demanding public hearings for rape victims, in December 1970.[8] In January 1971, the New York Radical Feminists held a speak-out on rape, creating space for women to share stories of their rapes and subsequent treatment by friends, family, professionals, and law enforcement.[9] In April 1971, the New York Radical Feminists held what the *New York Post* called the "world's first" conference on rape.[10]

National organizing increased following the April 1971 conference. Women Against Rape groups coalesced in a number of cities. Those groups sought both to draw attention to the issue of rape and to help individual victims "by publicly politicizing rape from a feminist perspective, holding speak-outs and workshops on rape, setting up legal and medical advocacy programs, escorting women to hospitals and police stations, or publishing rape handbooks and survival manuals."[11] In 1972, the first rape crisis center was established in the District of Columbia.[12] By the late 1970s, there were four hundred such centers in the United States. Anti-rape advocates from rape crisis centers and grassroots organizations joined to form the National Coalition Against Sexual Assault in 1979.[13]

The 1970s also saw the first organized federal governmental responses to rape, including the creation of the National Center for the Prevention and Control of Rape, which provided funding for research into the causes and consequences of sexual violence.[14] Federal legislation soon followed—the Rape Victim Services Act, enacted in 1980, provided funding for victims of rape.[15] According to the social work professor and anti-violence advocate Susan Schechter, "At the height of the anti-rape movement in 1976, there were approximately 1,500 separate projects—task forces, study groups, crisis centers, 'doing something about rape.'"[16] By the early 1980s, many projects had been bureaucratized or otherwise subjected to state control, largely as a condition of receiving funding. Grassroots feminists were replaced with professionals, and, as Schecter writes, "'Co-optation' happened before many women understood the meaning of the term."[17]

Other informal responses continued to flourish, however, with women coalescing in "antirape squads" to both prevent and avenge rapes and feminist self-defense classes being organized in community spaces.[18] Anti-rape activists formed "grassroots emergency services" in their neighborhoods. In the Boston area, for example, "feminists launched an all-volunteer Green Light Program, training neighborhood residents in self-defense and providing them with a green lightbulb for their front porch to signal that theirs was a 'safe home' for anyone under threat of violence on the street," and created a "street reps" system "responsible for coordinating telephone trees and block watches, as well as offering weekly self-defense classes."[19] In 1975, Philadelphia held the first Take Back the Night march in the United States.[20] Started in the 1960s in Belgium and England, Take Back the Night marchers protested women's inability to feel safe on the streets at night.[21] Marches soon sprung up around the United States.

The continued proliferation of informal responses reflected the ambivalence some rape victims felt about contacting law enforcement. Some women believed that law enforcement would not take their rapes seriously; others feared unfair treatment by courts, an experience described as a "second rape."[22] Some questioned whether calling law enforcement would lead to the kind of change in norms necessary to end violence. As the *Feminist Alliance Against Rape* newsletter asked, "How is this after-the-fact action helping women? . . . If all men who had ever raped were incarcerated tomorrow, rape would continue."[23] Feminists also noted the irony of asking police to assist, given regular accusations that police were, in fact, committing rapes.[24] Feminist anti-rape activists saw their grassroots work as providing an alternative to a male-dominated (and therefore untrustworthy) criminal legal system and empowering women to retain control over the responses to their rapes and their own lives.[25]

For women of color, concerns about engaging law enforcement grew not only from a general concern about the criminal legal system but also from stereotypes about Black women and concerns about the intrusion of the state into Black communities. Black feminists confronted specific rape myths: that Black women were more sexually active, unaffected by rape, and inured to violence.[26] A Black woman at a January 1971 New York Radical Feminists speak-out didn't report her rape to the police because "black women are supposed to be whores anyway. They [the police] would jeer and I would be humiliated."[27] And as another Black woman explained, "I didn't report this to the police. Nationalism was all mixed up in this. It was partly being a Nationalist and the police were white, I felt I would be guilty in turning in another Third World person who had raped me...."[28]

B. Rape Law Reform

But some in the feminist anti-rape movement saw criminal law as "an obvious target for activists who sought significant social change."[29] In the early 1970s, feminist legal scholars argued that rape myths (that rapists were "deranged sex maniacs" rather than "normal men," women wanted to be raped, and women often made false complaints of rape, for example) were responsible for low conviction rates and the legal system's mistreatment of rape victims.[30] In 1975, Susan Brownmiller's *Against Our Will: Men, Women, and Rape* made a similar case to a popular audience. The term "date rape" first appeared in print in Brownmiller's book, highlighting the distinction between stranger rapes and rapes by acquaintances. Scholars also noted how existing statutes and evidentiary rules made rape more difficult to prosecute.[31]

A gap emerged between feminists who continued to have concerns about state action and those who saw engagement with the legal system as the only avenue for guaranteeing justice for rape victims. In part, those concerns were philosophical. Feminist anti-rape activists saw rape as a product of sexism, male dominance, patriarchy, and gender roles; engaging the legal system could change the lens through which rape was seen to one of law and order, muting the feminist analysis.[32] For feminists of color, investment in the criminal legal response to rape meant engaging with a racist system.[33] Black feminists were concerned not only about how that system treated Black women (and ignored the rapes of Black women by white men). Black men had long been disproportionately and discriminatorily targeted in rape prosecutions, particularly for the rapes of white women. Black feminists such as Angela Davis called for an "intersectional politics of rape that supported victims while also working against historical racist tropes of the black beast rapist,"[34] and criticized the failure of *Against Our Will* to recognize the historical racism in rape law enforcement.[35] The Free Willie Sanders movement in Boston, organized to protest the prosecution of a falsely accused Black man for the rapes of several white women, highlighted how "[t]he State has historically tried to pit those who fight to end racism against those who fight to stop violence against women," and argued that their common enemy was "the racist and sexist criminal justice system."[36]

Greater state involvement would ultimately prevail. By the mid-1970s, "the state began dominating antirape efforts, favoring increased criminalization, co-opting key feminist interventions such as rape crisis centers, and ultimately dismissing the larger feminist analysis in favor of exclusively reform-oriented solutions."[37] That victory was likely the product of several factors. Narrow conceptions of justice fed the belief that justice could only be found through criminal punishment. Anti-rape activists may have also hoped that increasing the frequency of rape prosecutions would raise public awareness of the crime and public condemnation of the act.

Anti-rape feminists were not naïve about the limitations of the legal system, and "[f]ew, if any, activists believed that rape reform could solve the problem of rape" entirely.[38] Nonetheless, activists sought reforms to make prosecuting rape more likely and more productive. For example, in many states, rape victims were required to have corroboration of their testimony before such claims could be prosecuted. Rape law reform repealed such requirements.[39] Law reform also eliminated requirements that victims prove they had resisted "to the utmost" throughout a rape and that they promptly report rapes.[40] States created separate crimes for rape and sexual assault and distinguished between such crimes by factors including the use of weapons or the extent of injury.[41] States discontinued the use of cautionary jury instructions based on Chief Justice Lord Matthew Hale's 1680 admonition to juries that "rape is an accusation easily to be made, hard to be proved, and harder to be defended by the party accused, tho' never so innocent."[42] Some states repealed laws exempting rape within marriage from prosecution; others preserved such protections.[43] Rape shield legislation was enacted to prevent a victim's sexual history from being used to attack her credibility.[44] Anti-rape feminists and racial justice activists disagreed about the need for such legislation, however, with the latter expressing concern about the impact of such laws on those accused of rape, particularly Black men.[45]

Activist groups coalesced around proposals to eliminate the use of the death penalty as punishment for rape.[46] Feminists opposed making rape eligible for the death penalty for a number of reasons. Some were concerned that juries would be reluctant to convict because the penalty was so harsh.[47] Amici in *Coker v. Georgia*, in a brief authored by then-law professor Ruth Bader Ginsburg, argued that using the death penalty undergirded notions of women as "damaged goods" after rape.[48] Ginsburg wrote that imposing it was a "vestige of an ancient, patriarchal view of women as the property of men" and "a barrier to proper and vigorous enforcement of rape laws."[49] Others, particularly Black feminists, were concerned about the disproportionate impact on men of color.[50] As Ginsburg's brief noted, "the death penalty for rape has operated in a singularly uneven fashion: it has been applied overwhelmingly to condemn black men for 'violating' Southern white women."[51] The Supreme Court struck down the use of the death penalty for rape in *Coker v. Georgia* in 1977.[52]

Feminist rape law reform was remarkably successful, if success is measured by the numbers of laws passed and the numbers of jurisdictions in which they were passed. By 1980, virtually every state had made reforms.[53] The anti-rape movement is credited with fundamentally changing how the public views rape and sexual violence; the story of "feminist-inspired rape law reform" is, by most scholarly and popular accounts, a success story.[54] But critical scholars have questioned the effectiveness of these reforms.[55] Marital rape exemptions continue to exist in some states,[56] and prohibitions on requiring corroboration or prompt report have not kept defense attorneys from arguing that the failure to provide corroboration or to promptly report undermines a victim's credibility.[57] Rape law reform has produced only minor increases in prosecution.[58] Moreover, law reform failed to change the underlying attitudes toward rape and rape victims held by many in the criminal legal system.[59] For example, although in 1975, *Against Our Will* discussed the problem of date rape, in 1987, Susan Estrich condemned the legal system's continuing failure to treat seriously cases of "simple rape" (rape committed by people known to the victim, as opposed to "real rape" committed by strangers).[60] As the history and gender studies professor Catherine Jacquet concludes, "The lack of substantial change resulting from rape law reforms confirms the concerns that many feminists had about the ability of the legal system to produce meaningful results."[61] And, as the social work professor Rose Corrigan notes, reforms "play[ed] out on terrain 'owned' and controlled by state actors such as police and prosecutors."[62]

Feminist anti-rape activists also worked to support women prosecuted for defending themselves against rapists, demanding that women such as Joan Little and Inez García be recognized as victims by the criminal legal system.[63] Little, a twenty-year-old Black woman, faced trial in 1974 for killing sixty-two-year-old white correctional officer Clarence Alligood with an ice pick. Little argued that Alligood had tried to rape her and that she acted in self-defense; Alligood's defenders said he was far too racist to want to have sex with a Black woman and disparaged Little's chastity, cleanliness, and humanity. Little was acquitted by a jury in just over an hour.[64] Feminist anti-rape activists believed that supporting (even encouraging) women who acted to protect themselves from male violence could coexist with rape law reform. Self-defense, explains the gender and sexuality studies professor Emily Thuma, was seen as "a grassroots alternative to abusive men and an unresponsive state," not a rejection of law reform.[65] Anti-violence feminists used the Free Joan Little campaign to highlight women's vulnerability to sexual assault and the importance of self-defense. But Black feminists argued that, notwithstanding their advocacy for individual women who acted in self-defense, white feminist support for the criminal legal system jeopardized women like Joan Little, because it strengthened the system that not only targeted men who raped but also decided the fate of women who defended themselves from rape.[66] This criticism was initially apt in the case of Inez García, who shot and killed one of the two men who beat and raped her on March 19, 1974. The judge in García's case told the jury that García's rape prior to the shooting was irrelevant, precluding her from arguing self-defense. García was convicted and sentenced to five years to life, although that verdict was overturned in 1976. García was acquitted in a second trial in 1977.[67]

C. Assessing the Movement

By the mid-1980s, with the exception of attempts to end marital rape exemptions, the major work of the anti-rape movement had largely been completed. A national coalition and state coalitions were serving local rape crisis centers and engaging in state and national policy work, rape crisis centers were responding to victims across the country, and most law reforms had been enacted. The traditional narrative has pointed to the great success of the anti-rape movement in creating services for rape victims and changing antiquated and damaging laws. Although services and activism are still part of the anti-rape movement, the expectation for some time has been that victims of rape and sexual assault should seek assistance from the legal system; the failure to do so undermines victims' credibility.[68]

Anti-violence feminists succeeded in changing the law. Whether they achieved the goals underlying their desire for legal change—securing justice for rape victims and changing norms concerning sexual violence—is questionable. Resistance to taking rape seriously is still widespread. Victims of rape are still ambivalent about turning to the legal system. Rape is one of the least reported crimes; only 25% of rape and sexual assault victims reported to police in 2018.[69] Despite the recent spate of convictions in cases involving such public figures as Harvey Weinstein[70] and Bill Cosby,[71] conviction rates for rape remain quite low.[72] In the maelstrom created when Dr. Christine Blasey Ford made public her allegations against Supreme Court nominee Brett Kavanaugh, the hashtag #WhyIDidntReport trended on Twitter, with millions of sexual assault victims explaining why they did not call law enforcement—and what happened when they did report that made them wish they hadn't.[73] As Department of Justice investigations into gender-biased policing make clear, law enforcement in many jurisdictions continues to handle sexual violence with attitudes ranging from outright contempt to indifference. As one Baltimore Sex Offense Unit Detective said, "[A]ll our cases are bullshit." When challenged on that statement, the detective replied, "Ok, 90 percent."[74] The substantive law has changed since the 1970s, but many of the attitudes and biases that plagued victims at the start of the anti-rape movement remain.

II. THE BATTERED WOMEN'S MOVEMENT

The battered women's movement also grew out of the women's liberation movement of the 1970s, and "[a]lthough many activists in the battered women's movement never did rape crisis work, the battered women's movement maintains a striking and obvious resemblance to the anti-rape movement and owes it several debts."[75] Like the anti-rape movement, the anti–domestic violence movement initially focused on nonlegal responses to intimate partner violence (then called "spouse abuse") before turning to legal system reforms. Those reforms would come to dominate the movement and set the stage for the passage of the Violence Against Women Act, the premiere federal legislation regarding gender-based violence.

Before the battered women's movement of the 1970s and 1980s, intimate partner violence was not widely discussed. In the 1960s, psychologists and psychiatrists still attributed intimate partner violence to women's hostility, manipulative behavior, frigidity, and masochism.[76] "As late as 1974," Schechter notes, "the term 'battered woman' was not part of the vocabulary... even the founders of battered women's programs were unaware of the magnitude of the problem they had uncovered."[77]

A. Early Organizing Efforts

The first organized response to intimate partner violence involved one of the most pressing immediate needs of victims of violence: shelter. Early shelters grew out of community groups and feminist projects such as Al-Anon, consciousness-raising groups, and feminist women's centers.[78] The first shelters in the United States included Haven House in Pasadena, California, which opened in 1964 to provide respite for women with "alcoholic husbands." When it became clear that the need for temporary housing extended beyond women dealing with addicted spouses, Haven House opened its doors to all women subjected to abuse.[79] Other early shelters included Rainbow Retreat in Phoenix, which opened in 1973, and Women's Advocates in St. Paul, which started out as a consciousness-raising group in 1971 and added shelter in 1973.[80] Shelters for particular communities of women emerged shortly thereafter. Both Casa Myrna Vasquez, serving Boston's Latina population, and the White Buffalo Calf Women's Society, on the Sicangu Lakota Nation's Rosebud Reservation in South Dakota, opened in 1977.[81] In 1981, Everywoman's Shelter, the first to serve primarily Asian women, opened in Los Angeles.[82]

By the early 1980s, there were hundreds of shelters and safe houses across the country.[83] Shelters served not only as places to house women fleeing abuse but also as centers of political organizing and symbols of the larger movement to end violence against women.[84] But from their inception, they faced a number of challenges. The number of people seeking shelter has always outpaced the number of available beds.[85] In 1976, for example, New York, New York, population eight million, provided only forty-five beds for homeless women.[86] Funding was, and is, tenuous; in the early shelter movement, volunteers significantly outnumbered paid staff.[87] Legitimacy was an issue for shelters, which had to "convince sometimes skeptical communities and funding agencies that their shelter legitimately represented battered women."[88] Shelters had to navigate unhelpful bureaucracies and restrictive laws—including, in some places, laws that prohibited women from living communally.[89] Shelters found themselves providing services not only to women but also to traumatized children, raising issues regarding parenting, discipline, and child abuse and neglect.[90] Shelters grappled with racism among residents and staff and with questions about the division of authority between residents and staff, volunteer and professional staff, and workers who had experienced violence and those who had not.[91]

As in the anti-rape movement, organizations serving women subjected to abuse formed coalitions concerning their work. State coalitions performed a variety of functions, including setting standards for anti-violence programs, disseminating federal funding, and providing a feminist analysis of the work. The earliest state and local coalitions, including the Chicago Abused Women's Coalition and the Pennsylvania Coalition Against Domestic Violence, first formed in 1976.[92] The National Coalition Against Domestic Violence (NCADV) followed in 1978.[93] Not all women experienced the coalitions as welcoming spaces. The whiteness of the leadership at the first NCADV conference in 1980 prompted women of color to organize a Third World Women's Caucus (which later became the Women of Color Task Force).[94] Women of color used state coalition structures to organize, network, and share information while simultaneously critiquing coalitions for failing to understand domestic violence as an intersectional problem.[95]

B. Domestic Violence Legislation

Federal legislation provided modest support for the work of the feminist anti-violence movement in the 1970s and 1980s. The Law Enforcement Assistance Administration (LEAA) authorized the first federal funding specifically dedicated to domestic violence. In the 1970s, the LEAA's Family Violence Program provided a small but steadily increasing amount of funding to support the work of community-based organizations and social services agencies in preventing and responding to domestic violence, but the program was completely defunded in 1980.[96] Conservatives in Congress saw federal support for these programs as funding "missionaries who would war on the traditional family or on local values" and resented the intrusion on family privacy.[97] Nonetheless, in 1984, Congress enacted the Family Violence Prevention and Services Act, which initially funded prevention and direct services and which, in 1996, began supporting the National Domestic Violence Hotline. The Victims of Crime Act, also enacted in 1984, reimbursed victims of crime (including domestic violence) for costs directly related to crime and supported domestic violence victim services, including shelters and other direct service providers.[98]

C. Legal System Reform

Like the anti-rape movement, the battered women's movement saw the legal system's appalling treatment of victims of domestic violence as a significant impediment to securing safety for victims and holding those who used violence accountable. Women who called police for assistance were told that police could do nothing because it was a family matter. Some women were ordered to leave their homes because their husbands owned those homes. When police took action, it was often to tell the man to take a walk around the block or to actually walk him around the block, then send him home. "Arrest," Schechter explains, "generally occurred only if wounds required stitches or if the violent husband turned on the police, challenging their right to control the situation."[99] Women described equally problematic encounters with judges, who minimized the violence and suggested that women who stayed with violent partners must enjoy the abuse.[100] Anti-violence feminists sought to make remedies for victims of violence more widely available and ensure that those in the legal system acted to provide those remedies.

Advocates turned first to the civil system to expand the legal options available to women subjected to abuse. Using existing restraining order law as a framework, jurisdictions across the country developed civil protection orders designed specifically for victims of domestic violence. Pennsylvania passed the first such law in 1976. Other jurisdictions soon followed, and by the 1990s, all United States jurisdictions had enacted such laws.[101] The earliest protective orders provided only basic relief, requiring that those bound by them not assault, threaten, harass, or otherwise abuse and stay away from their partners.[102] These orders gave women a remedy that, in most jurisdictions, they could access without asking police or prosecutors to intercede.[103] Over time, the remedies available in protective orders have become more capacious, including provisions for custody of children, use and possession of family homes, economic relief, and the removal of firearms from those who use violence.[104] But in the 1970s and 1980s, even the provision of these basic remedies was groundbreaking.

Civil protection orders provided a significant benefit to battered women, who could bring their own cases and ask courts for the things they believed they needed in order to be safe. But many anti-violence advocates believed that for domestic violence to be taken seriously—for cultural mores regarding the acceptability of violence to change—intervention by the criminal legal system was required. Domestic violence had to be treated as a crime. Justice required criminal punishment.[105] To that end, the movement advocated for policies to change the criminal legal system's response to domestic violence.

Police inaction was the first problem the movement tackled. As noted, police were reluctant to intervene to stop domestic violence; indeed, the police training materials of the time told new officers to "[a]void arrest if possible. Appeal to their [women's] vanity."[106] Police regularly declined to use their discretion to take men who used violence into custody. But the dominant view in the battered women's movement was that "the best protection for both a woman and her husband [is] to have a police officer armed with a mandatory duty to arrest, intervene."[107] Anti-violence activists asserted that position in court. In 1976, feminist lawyers challenged police failures to arrest in two class-action lawsuits, *Bruno v. Codd*[108] and *Scott v. Hart*.[109] In *Bruno*, lawyers argued that police failed to intervene on behalf of women subjected to abuse in New York, New York, violating those women's rights to protection. They sought policies that compelled the police to make arrests. In Oakland, California, the plaintiffs in *Scott* made similar claims. The suits resulted in settlements requiring police in both jurisdictions to adopt pro-arrest policies.[110] In the same year, the International Association of Chiefs of Police adopted a pro-arrest position in domestic violence cases, arguing that arrest "promotes the well-being of the victim."[111] States began moving toward more stringent arrest policies around the same time, with Oregon enacting the first domestic violence mandatory arrest law in 1977.[112] Mandatory arrest laws required police to make an arrest in any domestic violence case where they had probable cause to do so. Preferred arrest laws, by contrast, presumed that arrest should be the police response in domestic violence cases but left individual officers with discretion to make case-by-case determinations.

The belief that intervention by the legal system would benefit all women subjected to abuse was not uniformly held, however. Women of color expressed concern from the beginning of the anti-violence movement about overreliance on the criminal legal system and were skeptical that system would protect all women subjected to abuse. As one legal advocate explained, "I think White women talked more as if the courts belonged to us [all women] and therefore should work for us where we [women of color] always saw it as belonging to someone else and talked more about how to keep it from hurting us."[113]

Two events in 1984 contributed to the widespread adoption of mandatory and preferred arrest laws in the United States. First, Tracy Thurman won a multi-million-dollar judgment against the city of Torrington, Connecticut, after police failed to intervene to restrain her husband, Charles, despite her repeated requests for assistance.[114] Concerned about incurring liability, jurisdictions nationally searched for innovative police practices that might insulate them from similar judgments. They found hope in research published in 1984 by the sociologists Lawrence Sherman and Richard Berk claiming that arrest deterred recidivist domestic violence.[115] Based on their research, Sherman and Berk explained that they "favor[ed] a *presumption* of arrest: an arrest should be made unless there are good, clear reasons why an arrest would be counterproductive. We do not, however, favor *requiring* arrests in all misdemeanor domestic violence cases."[116] They cautioned that the study should be replicated before states enacted preferred or mandatory arrest policies; when conducted, those replication studies found that arrest had effects on recidivism ranging from moderate to nonexistent to spurring violence.[117] Nonetheless, jurisdictions quickly moved to adopt such policies. By 1989, 89% of police departments had preferred or mandatory arrest policies.[118] As of 2014, twenty states and the District of Columbia had enacted mandatory arrest policies.[119] Mandatory and preferred arrest policies increased arrest rates but had serious unintended consequences, including a significant uptick in the numbers of women arrested for domestic violence.[120]

Having addressed the problem of police inaction, advocates in the battered women's movement next turned to prosecutors' failure to pursue cases against men who used violence. When asked why prosecution rates were so low, prosecutors cited victim reluctance to testify. Two innovations emerged as a result. First, prosecutors instituted evidence-based prosecution policies. With this method, prosecutors rely on evidence other than victim testimony—photographs, victim statements, hospital records, and physical evidence—to prove their cases.[121] Prosecutors' offices also adopted policies that made it clear that they would prosecute any case for which they had sufficient evidence, with or without the victim's consent. Known as no-drop prosecution policies, they came in two varieties: soft and hard. In soft no drop prosecution jurisdictions, prosecutors provided incentives for victims to testify—access to victim support services, for example. In hard no-drop jurisdictions, prosecutors used any tool that they had to compel victim testimony, including subpoenaing unwilling victims, asking that courts issue arrest warrants for victims who failed to comply with those subpoenas, and in some cases asking that victims be incarcerated using material witness warrants until they gave testimony. By 1996, about two-thirds of prosecutors' offices had adopted (primarily soft) no-drop prosecution policies.[122]

The battered women's movement also organized around women who had been convicted of killing their abusive partners. Studies found that substantial numbers of women convicted of murder or manslaughter had killed abusive partners.[123] Publications such as the National Communications Network for the Elimination of Violence Against Women told the stories of these women, including Roxanne Gay, who stabbed her husband to death, and Gloria Timmons, who shot her husband.[124] Feminists formed "defense committees," organized letter-writing campaigns, attended the trials of women accused of killing their partners, raised money to pay attorney's fees and costs, and developed and shared legal strategies to educate defense attorneys about domestic violence.[125]

New thinking about why battered women, thought to be meek and passive, resorted to killing their partners aided these efforts. Battered women had little success using self-defense law to justify their actions, particularly when they used weapons or acted during a break in the violence.[126] Lenore Walker addressed these concerns in a theory she called "battered woman syndrome," which purported to explain why women killed their partners. Walker's theory combined learned helplessness—the idea that over time women learned that no matter what strategies they used, they could never escape domestic violence, and therefore passively remained in relationships—with the cycle of violence that Walker found in the cases of the women she studied.[127] Walker argued that the cycle of violence repeated and escalated over time, leaving women with the belief that they had no choice but to kill in order to protect themselves.[128]

Battered woman syndrome was controversial from its inception.[129] Labeling the experiences of women who used force a syndrome created the impression that women subjected to abuse were mentally ill or unstable.[130] Social science researchers disputed victims' passivity, arguing that battered women were active survivors using a variety of strategies to free themselves.[131] Instead of testifying about "battered woman syndrome," advocates and experts talked instead about "battering and its consequences" or "the experience of domestic violence" to help judges and juries understand why battered women did not leave their abusive partners and why they employed force.[132]

By the late 1980s and early 1990s, advocates had organized mass clemency campaigns for incarcerated battered women in several states, arguing that if the women had been permitted to introduce evidence about the abuse they experienced during their trials, they would not have been convicted. These campaigns resulted in grants of clemency for twenty-five women in Ohio in December 1990 and eight women in Maryland in February 1991.[133]

III. THE MORE THINGS CHANGE...

With national and state coalitions firmly entrenched, rape crisis centers in every state, and the majority of states having updated their rape laws, the transformative work of the anti-rape movement had largely ended by the mid-to-late 1980s.[134] The high-water mark for the battered women's movement came in 1994 with the passage of the Violence Against Women Act. The Act's revolutionary civil rights remedy, permitting victims of gender-motivated violence to sue their attackers, was found unconstitutional by the United States Supreme Court in *United States v. Morrison* in 2000.[135] What was left after *Morrison* was primarily a funding bill, and that funding was, and is, significant. The Act allocates hundreds of millions of dollars annually to efforts to combat gender-based violence; as of fiscal year 2018, more than $8 billion in grants had been awarded through the Act.[136] The vast majority of that funding goes to the criminal legal system. In 1994, 62% of the Act's funds were allocated to courts, police, prosecutors, and community-based agencies supporting the work of law enforcement; by 2013, the percentage was 85%.[137] Much of the work of the national anti-violence movement involves seeking to expand the Act to create new programs and add protections for marginalized communities.[138] On the state level, law reform generally involves changes to protective order laws and increased criminalization—for example, at the urging of advocates, a number of states created independent crimes of strangulation in response to research showing that strangulation is highly correlated with lethality.[139]

The story most often told about the anti-rape and battered women's movements of the 1970s and 1980s centers the embrace of carceral feminism.[140] Like most stock stories, that narrative is oversimplified. In fact, there was real disagreement and debate within the anti-rape and battered women's movements about whether and how to engage with the criminal legal system to address gender-based violence.[141] In 1974, the Feminist Alliance Against Rape wrote, "What we are saying is that we don't believe increasing the conviction rate will lead to the elimination of rape. Therefore, we question whether we as feminists should devote our energy to winning individual convictions, or whether we should examine alternatives which may have a greater influence on society as a whole."[142] Similarly, in 1982, Susan Schechter asked how much the battered women's movement should rely on the criminal legal system (a system that many within the movement perceived as racist as well as sexist), cautioned that mandatory state intervention should not trump women's rights to self-determination, and asked what role battered women should have "within a movement that is called theirs."[143] Commentators also foresaw the disproportionate impact that criminalization would have on communities of color and the confluence of the anti-violence and prison abolitionist movements. As the law professor Mari

Matsuda wrote upon VAWA's passage in 1994, "For women of color, for feminists of all colors.... [w]e know that the police are a source of violence in our communities, not just a deterrent to it.... For now, feminists must deal with the devil, demanding that the existing criminal justice system protect women from violence, even while working to abolish that system."[144]

The work done by the anti-rape and anti-violence movements foreshadowed many of the challenges that anti-violence activists still confront. The calls to free Joan Little in the 1970s and the battered women's clemency campaigns of the late 1980s were the antecedents of the #SurvivedandPunished[145] movement and the calls to free Marissa Alexander,[146] Bresha Meadows,[147] Cyntoia Brown,[148] and other women incarcerated for crimes related to their own victimization. Concerns about the impact of criminalization in communities of color, particularly Black communities, are still relevant. Police killings of people of color, calls to defund the police,[149] and the continued overrepresentation of people of color in the criminal legal system[150] have forced anti-rape and anti-violence programs to consider whether and how they collaborate with and rely on carceral systems.[151] Although transformative justice advocates have long worked to develop community-based options for supporting victims of violence and holding those who use violence accountable, the devastating consequences of sending those who use violence to COVID-19-infested jails and prisons[152] has renewed a broader conversation about community-based interventions. The historical antecedents of these issues in the anti-rape and anti-violence movements of the 1970s and 1980s should inform the choices we make today.

Notes

1. Catherine O. Jacquet, The Injustices of Rape: How Activists Responded to Sexual Violence, 1950–1980 7–8 (2019).
2. Danielle L. McGuire, At The Dark End of the Street: Black Women, Rape, and Resistance—a New History of the Civil Rights Movement from Rosa Parks to the Rise of Black Power xvii (2011).
3. Jacquet, Injustices of Rape, *supra* note 1, at 3.
4. *Id.*
5. Jami Ake & Gretchen Arnold, *A Brief History of Anti-Violence Against Women Movements in the United States*, in Sourcebook on Violence Against Women 6 (Claire M. Renzetti, Jeffrey L. Edleson, & Raquel Kennedy Bergen eds., 3d ed. 2018).
6. *Id.*
7. Jacquet, Injustices of Rape, *supra* note 1, at 78–79.
8. *Id.* at 80.
9. *Id.* at 81.
10. *Id.*
11. *Id.* at 87.
12. Ake & Arnold, *Brief History*, *supra* note 5, at 6; Jacquet, Injustices of Rape, *supra* note 1, at 88.
13. Ake & Arnold, *Brief History*, *supra* note 5, at 6.
14. *Id.*

15. Jacquet, Injustices of Rape, *supra* note 1, at 12.
16. Susan Schechter, Women and Male Violence: The Visions and Struggles of the Battered Women's Movement 39 (1982).
17. *Id.* at 42; *see also* Jacquet, Injustices of Rape, *supra* note 1, at 154, 156.
18. Jacquet, Injustices of Rape, *supra* note 1, at 90, 92.
19. Emily L. Thuma, All Our Trials: Prisons, Policing, and the Feminist Fight to End Violence 132 (2019).
20. *TBTN History*, Take Back the Night Foundation, https://takebackthenight.org/history/ (last visited July 7, 2020).
21. *About Us*, Take Back the Night Foundation, https://takebackthenight.org/about-us/#:~:text=History%3A%20Take%20Back%20The%20Night,the%20street%20alone%20at%20night (last visited July 7, 2020).
22. Jacquet, Injustices of Rape, *supra* note 1, at 101; Thuma, All Our Trials, *supra* note 19, at 139.
23. Jacquet, Injustices of Rape, *supra* note 1, at 150 (quoting Jackie MacMillan and Freada Klein, *F.A.A.R. Editorial*, Feminist Alliance Against Rape Newsletter 1 (1974)).
24. *Id.* at 151. Police-perpetrated rape continues to be a concern today; *see generally* Andrea J. Ritchie, Invisible No more: Police Violence Against Black Women and Women of Color (2017).
25. Jacquet, Injustices of Rape, *supra* note 1, at 89.
26. *Id.* at 96–97.
27. *Id.* at 98 (quoting New York Radical Feminists, Rape: The First Sourcebook for Women 44 (Noreen Connell & Cassandra Wilson eds., 1974).
28. *Id.* at 85 (included in New York Radical Feminists, First Sourcebook, at 42–44).
29. *Id.* at 14.
30. *Id.* at 103–6.
31. *Id.* at 106–7.
32. *Id.* at 147, 149.
33. *Id.* at 152.
34. *Id.* at 143 (citing Angela Y. Davis, Women, Race & Class [1981]).
35. Alison Edwards, *Rape, Racism, and the White Women's Movement: An Answer to Susan Brownmiller* (1979), http://www.sojournertruth.net/rrwwm.html.
36. Thuma, All Our Trials, *supra* note 19, at 69, 136 (quoting Willie Sanders Defense Committee, From Scottsboro 1930 to Boston 1980: The Frame-Up Continues [1980]).
37. Jacquet, Injustices of Rape, *supra* note 1, at 136.
38. Rose Corrigan, Up Against a Wall: Rape Reform and the Failure of Success 29 (2013).
39. Susan Caringella, Addressing Rape Reform in Law and Practice 14 (2009).
40. *Id.* at 14, 16.
41. *Id.* at 15.
42. *Id.* at 16.
43. *Id.* at 20.
44. *Id.* at 15.
45. Jacquet, Injustices of Rape, *supra* note 1, at 167–73.
46. *Id.* at 179.
47. Caringella, Addressing Rape Reform, *supra* note 39, at 19.

48. Coker v. Georgia: *Ginsburg Revisits Her Brief*, LAW LIBRARY—AMERICAN LAW AND LEGAL INFORMATION, https://law.jrank.org/pages/23555/Coker-v-Georgia-Ginsburg-Revisits-Her-Brief.html.
49. Brief for ACLU, et al. as Amici Curiae, Coker v. Georgia, 433 U.S. 584 (1976) (No. 75-5444), 1976 WL 181482 at *9.
50. JACQUET, INJUSTICES OF RAPE, *supra* note 1, at 6.
51. Brief for ACLU, et al. as Amici Curiae, *supra* note 49, at 9.
52. 433 U.S. 584 (1977).
53. CARINGELLA, ADDRESSING RAPE REFORM, *supra* note 39, at 13.
54. *Id.* at 2–3.
55. *See* Katharine K. Baker & Michelle Oberman, chapter 26, *infra*.
56. CORRIGAN, UP AGAINST A WALL, *supra* note 38, at 43.
57. *See* CARINGELLA, ADDRESSING RAPE REFORM, *supra* note 39, at 29–34; JACQUET, INJUSTICES OF RAPE, *supra* note 1, at 184–85.
58. CARINGELLA, ADDRESSING RAPE REFORM, *supra* note 39, at 35–37; JACQUET, INJUSTICES OF RAPE, *supra* note 1, at 184–85.
59. JACQUET, INJUSTICES OF RAPE, *supra* note 1, at 184–85.
60. SUSAN ESTRICH, REAL RAPE: HOW THE LEGAL SYSTEM VICTIMIZES WOMEN WHO SAY NO 6 (1987).
61. JACQUET, INJUSTICES OF RAPE, *supra* note 1, at 185.
62. CORRIGAN, UP AGAINST A WALL, *supra* note 38, at 24.
63. JACQUET, INJUSTICES OF RAPE, *supra* note 1, at 126–27.
64. MCGUIRE, DARK END OF THE STREET, *supra* note 2, at 246–74.
65. THUMA, ALL OUR TRIALS, *supra* note 19, at 46.
66. *Id.* at 32.
67. *Id.* at 37–38.
68. LYNN HECHT SCHAFRAN, BARRIERS TO CREDIBILITY: UNDERSTANDING AND COUNTERING RAPE MYTHS 9–12, https://www.nationalguard.mil/Portals/31/Documents/J1/SAPR/SARCVATraining/Barriers_to_Credibility.pdf.
69. Rachel E. Morgan & Barbara A. Oudekerk, Bureau of Just. Stat., U.S. Dep't of Just., PUB. NO. NCJ 253043, CRIMINAL VICTIMIZATION, 2018 8 (2019).
70. Shayna Jacobs, *Harvey Weinstein Guilty on Two Charges, Acquitted on Others in New York Sexual Assault Case*, WASH. POST (Feb. 24, 2020, 5:25 PM), https://www.washingtonpost.com/lifestyle/harvey-weinstein-trial-verdict/2020/02/24/057b9f36-5284-11ea-b119-4faabac6674f_story.html.
71. Manuel Roig-Franzia, *Bill Cosby Convicted on Three Counts of Sexual Assault*, WASH. POST (Apr. 26, 2018, 9:12 PM), https://www.washingtonpost.com/lifestyle/style/bill-cosby-convicted-on-three-counts-of-sexual-assault/2018/04/26/d740ef22-4885-11e8-827e-190efaf1f1ee_story.html.
72. Andrew Van Dam, *Less Than 1% of Rapes Lead to Felony Convictions. At Least 89% of Victims Face Emotional and Physical Consequences*, WASH. POST (Oct. 6, 2018, 7:00 AM), https://www.washingtonpost.com/business/2018/10/06/less-than-percent-rapes-lead-felony-convictions-least-percent-victims-face-emotional-physical-consequences/.
73. Jacey Fortin, *#WhyIDidntReport: Survivors of Sexual Assault Share Their Stories After Trump Tweet*, N.Y. TIMES (Sept. 23, 2018), https://www.nytimes.com/2018/09/23/us/why-i-didnt-report-assault-stories.html.

74. U.S. Dep't of Justice Civil Rights Div., Investigation of the Baltimore City Police Department 122 (2016), https://www.justice.gov/crt/file/883296/download.
75. Schechter, Women and Male Violence, *supra* note 16, at 34.
76. *Id.* at 21.
77. *Id.* at 16.
78. *Id.* at 56–57.
79. Ake & Arnold, *Brief History*, *supra* note 5, at 7; Schechter, Women and MaleViolence, *supra* note 16, at 55–56.
80. Ake & Arnold, *Brief History*, *supra* note 5, at 7; Schechter, Women and Male Violence, *supra* note 16, at 33.
81. Ake & Arnold, *Brief History*, *supra* note 5, at 7.
82. *Id.*
83. Schechter, Women and Male Violence, *supra* note 16, at 83.
84. Ake & Arnold, *Brief History*, *supra* note 5, at 8.
85. Schechter, Women and Male Violence, *supra* note 16, at 81.
86. *Id.* at 11.
87. *Id.* at 82–83.
88. *Id.* at 84.
89. *Id.* at 86–87.
90. *Id.* at 88–90.
91. *Id.* at 90–91, 98–101.
92. *Id.* at 69, 113.
93. *Id.* at 137.
94. Ake & Arnold, *Brief History*, *supra* note 5, at 9.
95. *Id.*
96. Leigh Goodmark, A Troubled Marriage: Domestic Violence and the Legal System 18–19 (2012); Schechter, Women and Male Violence, *supra* note 16, at186–89.
97. Elizabeth Pleck, Domestic Tyranny: The Making of American Social Policy Against Family Violence from Colonial Times to the Present 197 (1987).
98. Njeri Mathis Rutledge, *Looking a Gift Horse in the Mouth: The Underutilization of Crime Victim Compensation Funds by Domestic Violence Victims*, 19 Duke J. Gender L. & Pol'y 223, 230–31 (2011).
99. Schechter, Women and Male Violence, *supra* note 16, at 24–25.
100. *Id.* at 25–26, 54.
101. Jane Aiken & Katherine Goldwasser, *The Perils of Empowerment*, 20 Cornell J.L. & Pub. Pol'y 139, 146 (2010).
102. Goodmark, A Troubled Marriage, *supra* note 96, at 17.
103. *Id.*
104. *Id.*; *see also* Catherine F. Klein & Leslye E. Orloff, *Providing Legal Protection for Battered Women: An Analysis of State Statutes and Case Law*, 21 Hofstra L. Rev. 801 (1993).
105. Leigh Goodmark, Decriminalizing Domestic Violence: A Balanced Policy Approach to Intimate Partner Violence 2 (2018).
106. Schechter, Women and Male Violence, *supra* note 16, at 157; *see also* Aya Gruber, The Feminist War on Crime: The Unexpected Role of Women's Liberation in Mass Incarceration 68 (2020).
107. Laurie Woods, *Litigation on Behalf of Battered Women*, 5 Women's Rts. L. Rep. 7, 29 (1978); *see also* Goodmark, Decriminalizing Domestic Violence, *supra* note 105, at 13.

108. Bruno v. Codd, 396 N.Y.S.2d 974 (Sup. Ct. 1977), *rev'd*, 64 A.D.2d 582, 407 N.Y.S.2d 165 (1978), *aff'd*, 47 N.Y.2d 582, 393 N.E.2d 976 (1979).
109. Scott v. Hart, No. C-76-2395 WWS (N.D. Cal. 1976).
110. GRUBER, FEMINIST WAR ON CRIME, *supra* note 106, at 68.
111. U.S. Comm'n on Civil Rights, UNDER THE RULE OF THUMB: BATTERED WOMEN AND THE ADMINISTRATION OF JUSTICE 16 (1982).
112. Oregon Coalition Against Domestic Violence, *Historical Timeline*, https://www.ocadsv.org/about-us/historical-timeline (last visited Mar. 22, 2020).
113. Melanie F. Shephard & Ellen L. Pence, *An Introduction: Developing a Coordinated Community Response*, in COORDINATING COMMUNITY RESPONSES TO DOMESTIC VIOLENCE: LESSONS FROM DULUTH AND BEYOND 7 (Melanie F. Shephard & Ellen L. Pence eds., 1999).
114. Thurman v. City of Torrington, 595 F. Supp. 1521 (D. Conn. 1984).
115. Lawrence W. Sherman & Richard A. Berk, THE SPECIFIC DETERRENT EFFECTS OF ARREST FOR DOMESTIC ASSAULT, 49 AM. SOC. REV. 261 (1984).
116. *Id.* at 270.
117. GOODMARK, DECRIMINALIZING DOMESTIC VIOLENCE, *supra* note 105, at 14.
118. GRUBER, FEMINIST WAR ON CRIME, *supra* note 106, at 82.
119. GOODMARK, DECRIMINALIZING DOMESTIC VIOLENCE, *supra* note 105, at 14.
120. GRUBER, FEMINIST WAR ON CRIME, *supra* note 106, at 88–89; *see also* ALESHA DURFEE, SITUATIONAL AMBIGUITY AND GENDERED PATTERNS OF ARREST FOR INTIMATE PARTNER VIOLENCE, 18 VIOLENCE AGAINST WOMEN 64 (2012) (finding that the operation of mandatory arrest policies rather than increased violence was responsible for part of the increase in women's arrests for domestic violence).
121. Erin Leigh Claypoole, *Evidence-Based Prosecution: Prosecuting Domestic Violence Cases Without a Victim*, 39 PROSECUTOR 18, 18 (2005). The use of victim statements became more difficult, but not impossible, after the Supreme Court's decision in Crawford v. Washington, 541 U.S. 36 (2004).
122. GOODMARK, DECRIMINALIZING DOMESTIC VIOLENCE, *supra* note 105, at 14–15.
123. SCHECHTER, WOMEN AND MALE VIOLENCE, *supra* note 16, at 171.
124. *Id.* at 170.
125. *Id.* at 172–73.
126. Joan H. Krause, *Of Merciful Justice and Justified Mercy: Commuting the Sentences of Battered Women Who Kill*, 46 FLA. L. REV. 699, 709–13 (1994); *see generally* Martha R. Mahoney, *Misunderstanding Judy Norman: Theory as Cause and Consequence*, 51 CONN. L. REV. 671 (2019).
127. LENORE E. WALKER, THE BATTERED WOMAN 59 (1979). *But see* David L. Faigman, *The Battered Woman Syndrome and Self-Defense: A Legal and Empirical Dissent*, 72 VA. L. REV. 619 (1986) (arguing that Walker's own data did not support the existence of a cycle of violence experienced by a majority of victims).
128. Lenore E. Walker, *Battered Women and Learned Helplessness*, 2 VICTIMOLOGY 525 (1977).
129. *See* Sarah Buel, chapter 24, *infra*.
130. *See, e.g.*, Elizabeth M. Schneider, *Describing and Changing: Women's Self-Defense Work and the Problem of Expert Testimony on Battering*, 14 WOMEN'S RTS. L. REP. 213 (1992).
131. EDWARD W. GONDOLF & ELLEN R. FISHER, BATTERED WOMEN AS SURVIVORS: AN ALTERNATIVE TO TREATING LEARNED HELPLESSNESS (1988).

132. *See, e.g.*, Sue Ostoff & Holly Maguigan, *Explaining Without Pathologizing: Testimony on Battering and Its Effects*, in CURRENT CONTROVERSIES ON FAMILY VIOLENCE (Donileen R. Loseke, Richard J. Gelles, & Mary M. Cavanaugh eds., 2d ed. 2005).
133. Allison M. Madden, *Clemency for Battered Women Who Kill Their Abusers: Finding a Just Reform*, 4 HASTINGS WOMEN'S L.J. 1, 4–5 (1993).
134. CORRIGAN, UP AGAINST A WALL, *supra* note 38, at 40.
135. United States v. Morrison, 529 U.S. 598 (2000); *see also* Julie Goldscheid, United States v. Morrison *and the Civil Rights Remedy of the Violence Against Women Act: A Civil Rights Law Struck Down in the Name of Federalism*, 86 CORNELL L. REV. 109 (2000).
136. Lisa N. Sacco, CONGRESSIONAL RESEARCH SERVICE, NO. R45410, THE VIOLENCE AGAINST WOMEN ACT (VAWA): HISTORICAL OVERVIEW, FUNDING, AND REAUTHORIZATION 1 (2019).
137. Jill Theresa Messing et al., *The State of Intimate Partner Violence Intervention: Progress and Continuing Challenges*, 60 SOC. WORK 305, 306 (2015).
138. *NTF/NCADV Statement on Bipartisan Senate VAWA Reauthorization Conversations*, NATIONAL TASK FORCE TO END SEXUAL AND DOMESTIC VIOLENCE & NATIONAL COALITION AGAINST DOMESTIC VIOLENCE (Nov. 11, 2019), https://ncadv.org/blog/posts/ntfncadv-statement-on-bipartisan-.
139. *See, e.g.*, Vickie Aldous, *Strangulation Elevated to Felony in More Cases*, Mail Tribune (Mar. 7, 2018), https://www.mailtribune.com/news/crime-courts-emergencies/strangulation-elevated-to-felony-in-more-cases/#:~:text=Strangulation%20can%20now%20be%20prosecuted,also%20now%20qualifies%20as%20strangulation.
140. THUMA, ALL OUR TRIALS, *supra* note 19, at 7.
141. *See, e.g.*, GRUBER, FEMINIST WAR ON CRIME, *supra* note 106; JACQUET, INJUSTICES OF RAPE, *supra* note 1; THUMA, ALL OUR TRIALS, *supra* note 19.
142. THUMA, ALL OUR TRIALS, *supra* note 19, at 46–47 (quoting San Francisco Women Against Rape and Feminist Alliance Against Rape, READERS RESPONSES, FAAR NEWS 7–8 (1974)).
143. SCHECHTER, WOMEN AND MALE VIOLENCE, *supra* note 16, at 174–82, 281.
144. NANCY WHITTIER, FRENEMIES: FEMINISTS, CONSERVATIVES, AND SEXUAL VIOLENCE 182 (2018) (quoting Mari Matsuda, *Crime and Punishment*, 5 MS. MAG. 86 [1994]).
145. Survived and Punished works to decriminalize the actions of survivors of sexual and domestic violence taken to protect themselves, support and free criminalized survivors, and abolish gender violence, prisons, and criminal interventions. *See End the Criminalization of Survival*, SURVIVED AND PUNISHED, https://survivedandpunished.org/ (last visited Mar. 22, 2020).
146. Marissa Alexander was sentenced to twenty years in prison after shooting into the wall of her home to scare her abusive ex-husband, Rico Gray. Alexander was freed on January 27, 2017. *See* FREE MARISSA NOW, https://www.freemarissanow.org/ (last visited Mar. 22, 2020).
147. Bresha Meadows killed her father after he repeatedly victimized her and her family. Meadows was released on February 4, 2018. #FREEBRESHA, https://freebresha.wordpress.com/ (last visited Mar. 22, 2020).
148. Mariame Kaba & Brit Schulte, *Not a Cardboard Cutout: Cyntoia Brown and the Framing of a Victim*, THE APPEAL (Dec. 6, 2017), https://theappeal.org/not-a-cardboard-cut-out-cyntoia-brown-and-the-framing-of-a-victim-aa61f80f9cbb/. On August 7, 2019, Cyntoia Brown, who was trafficked as a teenager, was freed after serving fifteen years of

a life sentence imposed for killing a man who bought her for sex at age sixteen. Christine Hauser, *Cyntoia Brown Is Freed From Prison in Tennessee*, N.Y. TIMES (Aug. 7, 2019), https://www.nytimes.com/2019/08/07/us/cyntoia-brown-release.html.

149. Melissa Jeltsen, *Don't Use Domestic Violence Victims to Derail Police Reform*, HUFFPOST (June 5, 2020), https://www.huffpost.com/entry/domestic-violence-defund-police_n_5eda8fe1c5b692d897d2de13.

150. THE SENTENCING PROJECT, REPORT OF THE SENTENCING PROJECT TO THE UNITED NATIONS SPECIAL RAPPORTEUR ON CONTEMPORARY FORMS OF RACISM, RACIAL DISCRIMINATION, XENOPHOBIA, AND RELATED INTOLERANCE REGARDING RACIAL DISPARITIES IN THE UNITED STATES CRIMINAL JUSTICE SYSTEM (2018).

151. Washington State Coalition Against Domestic Violence, MOMENT OF TRUTH: STATEMENT OF COMMITMENT TO BLACK LIVES (June 30, 2020), https://wscadv.org/news/moment-of-truth-statement-of-commitment-to-black-lives/.

152. Aya Gruber and Leigh Goodmark, *Domestic Violence Is Also a Virus: During the Coronavirus Crisis, We Need the Right Criminal Justice Response to the Crime*, N.Y. DAILY NEWS (Mar. 26, 2020), https://www.nydailynews.com/opinion/ny-20200326-gydiz22wcraptezg34wvyic3ma-story.html.

CHAPTER 14

THE TITLE IX MOVEMENT AGAINST CAMPUS SEXUAL HARASSMENT

How a Civil Rights Law and a Feminist Movement Inspired Each Other

NANCY CHI CANTALUPO

If the inauguration of our first Black president made 2009 a "big" (if complicated) year for progress on racial equality, 2009 also witnessed a significant marker for gender equality, as hundreds of thousands of students and their allies began to mobilize against campus sexual assault. Although at first focusing on that single issue, this movement quickly expanded its goals, organizing them around the groundbreaking civil rights statute, Title IX of the Education Amendments of 1972.

This chapter tells the story of how Title IX and the student movement, led primarily by campus sexual assault survivors, interacted from 2009 to 2020, and how the movement weathered backlash against it and influenced not only later feminist movements such as #MeToo but also nonfeminists' understandings of sexual harassment. It begins with the Title IX movement's genesis during the Obama administration and feminist insights about structural inequalities in the criminal legal system that animated the movement. It then discusses the backlash facing the movement, one that utilizes stereotypes of rape victims dating back centuries to ancient criminal law doctrine. It concludes by examining how the movement's direct-action protests and litigation challenging the regulations issued in May 2020 by then-Secretary of Education Betsy DeVos demonstrate the continued power and promise of both feminist law and feminist organizing.

I. The Birth of the Title IX Movement

The decade covered here saw campus survivor activists recognizing both the harassment they experienced and their schools' (mis)handling of it as violations of their rights to equal educational opportunity. Their movement would quickly identify the criminal legal system's inadequacies and look to Title IX for alternatives.

A. Campus Sexual Harassment as a Systemic Civil Rights Violation

Prior to the 2010s, sexual harassment led to frequent but intermittent campus protests, sometimes focused on the problem and its gendered impact and sometimes focused on a particular educational institution and its mishandling of a specific incident. In neither case did the attention typically lead to recognition that both harassment and its mishandling are *systemic* problems, and even when it did, the "system" was seen as confined to a single campus.

Title IX played a key role in breaking down this isolated view of the problem beginning in 2009. Because it applies to all educational programs that receive federal funds—and therefore almost all U.S. college campuses—Title IX provided a framework that illuminated commonalities and patterns in seemingly unrelated events on different campuses. It helped student survivor activists see what journalist Rebecca Traister would later articulate about #MeToo: that "the tie that bound [various forms of sexually harassing and violent conduct was] sexism, plain and simple. Sexism, and the systemic damage it did; sexism, as it mingled with class and race to create unequal opportunities and outcomes."[1]

Journalists played a key role in bringing student activists and Title IX together in ways that ultimately created a civil rights movement. Center for Public Integrity (CPI) reporters published a 2009–2010 series of articles on campus sexual assault, profiling multiple survivors at different campuses who faced similar difficulties getting their universities to take their victimization seriously.[2] These survivors' common experiences exposed a broad pattern: widespread toleration by most campuses of severe sexual harassment (i.e., sexual violence or abuse) and their failure to remedy—or even acknowledge—the "tidal wave" of educational harms that resulted.[3] In addition, schools were failing to investigate reports or to meaningfully sanction students found responsible for sexually harassing their classmates. Many survivors and their allies who read the CPI series undoubtedly saw similarities between those stories and their own experiences.

The CPI series also revealed federal law and policy's role in this pattern, including a piece focused on the historically lax approach to sexual harassment taken by the

Office for Civil Rights (OCR) of the U.S. Department of Education (ED), which is responsible for administratively enforcing Title IX. This article quoted President Obama's first Assistant Secretary for Civil Rights, Russlyn Ali, committing OCR to change course and use "all of the tools at our disposal... to ensure that women are free from sexual violence."[4]

B. The 2011 *Dear Colleague Letter* and the Rejection of a Criminal Law Model

OCR's now (in)famous *2011 Dear Colleague Letter* (*DCL*) on Title IX and sexual violence would prove that Ali was serious.[5] After consulting numerous experts and stakeholders, OCR addressed several long-standing problems with how campuses commonly mishandled sexual harassment, particularly peer sexual assault. First, some campuses actively covered up sexual harassment, while others passively discouraged victims from reporting through opaque and confusing policies and procedures. Common practices such as failing to protect victims' privacy, failing to investigate named harassers, and denying victims the services and accommodations necessary to continue their education tended to retraumatize victims and discourage reporting.

Whatever their underlying motivation, policies suppressing reporting enabled schools to claim, and even genuinely believe, that sexual abuse was not a problem for their campuses. This perception diverged significantly from that of students whose awareness of campus sexual harassment stemmed from having experienced it themselves, knowing classmates who were harassed, or hearing of such dangers through whisper networks or rumors. Moreover, students who enrolled in women's and gender studies or other feminist courses, who got involved in feminist student organizations, and/or who attended events such as Take Back the Night marches learned about long-standing and widespread gender-based violence on campus, in the nation, and around the world. As a result, with the exception of a few (mostly feminist) faculty and staff on some campuses, students were significantly more likely than school employees to know the statistic—documented and repeatedly confirmed in national studies beginning in 1988—that one in four or five women would be sexually assaulted during college.[6]

These data, which galvanized critical support for stronger Title IX enforcement when prominently cited in the *DCL*, were collected through key feminist social science innovations. Dr. Mary P. Koss and her research team's explicitly feminist Sexual Experiences Survey (SES) measured sexual victimization more accurately by asking survey respondents to describe the conduct experienced rather than fit it into criminal legal definitions.[7] This greater accuracy meant widespread adoption of the SES methodology, including by the study cited in the *DCL*,[8] and helped to establish that sexual assault is not limited to a few bad actors and institutions.

The *DCL* also addressed a second long-standing problem underlying school mishandling of sexual harassment: campuses imitating criminal court procedures instead of using processes appropriate for civil rights violations. It clarified that Title IX, unlike the criminal law, requires schools to give equal procedural rights to those involved in sexual harassment investigations. After observing that some schools were using criminal or quasi-criminal standards of evidence in such proceedings, the *DCL* stated that OCR expected schools to use the civil rights standard, preponderance of the evidence, for all sexual harassment investigations.

In clarifying OCR's expectations, the *DCL* recognized the structural inequalities inherent in the criminal law: Even if criminal laws, police, and prosecutors all worked perfectly 100 percent of the time, the criminal system still could not address sexual harassment as a matter of inequality. This incapacity stems from the wholly different purposes of civil rights versus criminal laws: criminal laws aim to keep society safe from violence, balancing incarceration of offenders with constitutional protections against incarcerating the innocent. The criminal system's focus is on the defendant's rights, with no mandate to focus equally, or indeed at all, on the victim's needs.

Because sexual harassment victims' needs are especially extensive and urgent, the criminal law's structural inability to address those needs exacerbates the harm victims experience. Sexual abuse causes serious health problems, including increased risk of substance abuse, eating disorders, unsafe sexual behaviors, pregnancy, self-harm, suicidality, and being victimized again, often resulting in economic losses that can contribute to lifelong impoverishment.[9] For students, such health problems require time off from school and can cause drops in grades and educational performance, financial aid and tuition dollar losses, transferring to a less desirable school, and/or dropping out.[10] These dynamics disproportionately impact certain, intersectionally disadvantaged student populations, such as first-generation college students, who often lack the resources to create the time and space for survivors to heal and earn their degrees.[11]

The criminal system does nothing to address such urgent needs, as its main "remedy" is punishing the perpetrator. In contrast, Title IX, as a civil rights law, can provide stay-away orders; living, working, transportation, and academic accommodations; and other relief designed to reestablish equal opportunities in the face of trauma. The criminal law's inadequacies partially explain why so many victims of sexual harassment, which also constitutes a crime, do not report to police.

Even more damaging than this lack of remedies, the criminal system can also actively harm victims by wresting control from them over their reporting of sexual harassment and their private information, and giving it to police and prosecutors. Because sexual assault involves a profound loss of control over one of life's most intimate decisions and one's bodily integrity, seizing control in this manner may cause victims to experience a "second rape" by the investigation itself. Decades of social sciences research has confirmed that avoiding this loss of control is a major reason for victims' nonreporting. Certain populations such as victims of color and immigrant victims often have additional reasons to avoid interacting with the police. As a result, the vast majority of victims use the "victim's veto," whereby "[t]he individual victim of crime . . . maintain[s] complete control over the process . . . by avoiding [it] altogether through non-reporting."[12]

The *DCL*'s important intervention embraced the civil rights model and insisted that Title IX investigations' procedural rules not imitate criminal laws and instead treat victims and accused students equally, including by using an equitable standard of proof. For instance, Title IX proceedings may not treat victims as mere "complaining witnesses," who, in the criminal system, would have neither the same party status nor the same procedural protections as defendants.[13] This imbalance between victims' and criminal defendants' rights is, theoretically, designed to serve criminal laws' goals of safeguarding against punishing innocent people.[14] Title IX's different, equal protection–based goals compel Title IX systems to give both accused harassers and victims equal party status and procedural rights.

A prominent feature of the "procedural equality" embraced by the *DCL* is the preponderance of the evidence standard of proof, which has long been recognized as the only evidentiary standard that treats the victim and the accused equally. By requiring fact-finders to determine whether it is "more likely than not" that victims' allegations are true (placing the burden of proof on victims to establish that the wrongful conduct occurred), the preponderance standard reflects the parties' presumptively equal credibility.[15] In contrast, requiring victims to prove their allegations by a significantly higher threshold of probability, as both the criminal standard ("beyond a reasonable doubt") and the quasi-criminal standard ("clear and convincing evidence") do, signals skepticism of victims' credibility alone and puts extra burdens on victims to convince the fact-finder of their truthfulness. Structurally signaling skepticism of only one side's account is arguably discriminatory on its face, at least in cases where both parties have an equal stake in the outcome. In sexual harassment and gender-based violence cases, such one-sided skepticism also draws from and compounds gender-based stereotypes and the myth that women lie about being raped, discussed more in Section II.

In addition to rejecting preconceived judgments about credibility, the preponderance standard reflects the parties' equal stakes in Title IX investigations' outcomes.[16] Evidentiary standards are not about accuracy, as no standard is more accurate than another. Instead, such standards are chosen based on the *kind* of *in*accuracy that they risk. The standard of proof reflects a decision about the appropriate balance between risking a "false positive" outcome (referred to as a "wrongful conviction" in the criminal context) versus a "false negative" (or "wrongful acquittal"). Criminal and quasi-criminal standards are structured to avoid wrongful convictions, even if that means risking many wrongful acquittals, thus reflecting the stakes of criminal proceedings, in which the defendant could go to jail or have to register as a sex offender. Although these safeguards are often insufficient to protect certain defendants, especially defendants of color accused of committing crimes against white victims, this is due to discriminatory application of the standard, not the standard itself.

In contrast to the stakes in a criminal proceeding, students in Title IX investigations both have equally high stakes in the outcome. Neither can be sent to jail by the school, but both risk potentially grave disruptions to their education if they lose. The accused harasser may be suspended or expelled, and an expulsion may affect that student's ability to go to school elsewhere. This risk is present even if, as the limited data available suggest, harassers are rarely expelled, and the few who are expelled have transferred to other schools.[17] In contrast, research shows that many victims will transfer or drop out of school if the named harasser remains at that institution.[18] Thus, the *DCL*'s endorsement of the preponderance standard accurately calibrated the equal stakes and potential harms from false positives and false negatives in Title IX cases.

C. The Response on Campus and the Nationalization of the Movement

Despite OCR's strengthened Title IX enforcement, campuses were slow to change. While the *DCL* moved the needle in steering schools toward more equitable processes for resolving sexual harassment complaints, it did almost nothing to fix another longstanding problem contributing to school mishandling of such cases: lack of training for school personnel in assisting victims or investigating complaints. The *DCL* gave lip service to the need for Title IX training, but offered little guidance on what content to include in the training, other than referencing schools' Title IX obligations.[19] The focus on compliance-based training fed into a preexisting "check-the-box" approach that led schools to bureaucratize their Title IX obligations. For most institutions, Title IX training failed to change campus cultures or instill an appreciation of why Title IX prohibits sexual harassment and abuse in the first place. Better training, grounded in the gendered realities of sexual assault, might have prevented much of the upheaval surrounding the ambiguity in the *DCL* regarding "mandatory reporting."

Although some schools did make an effort to strengthen their policies and improve their Title IX systems, many campuses made few or no changes in response to the *DCL*. Of those schools that took action, most did not approach Title IX as a feminist, civil rights law. At many campuses, Title IX compliance was foisted onto the existing school bureaucracy, with responsibility falling on persons with no awareness of sexual abuse's connection to gender inequality. At the rare campus with victim services and advocacy staff, these professionals were often not included in Title IX compliance efforts, despite their expertise. Instead, those involved in Title IX-related work began to report that ambiguous language in the *DCL* was being used to strip campus victim services professionals of their ability to keep victims' reports confidential. On these campuses, such professionals were told that unless the confidentiality of students' sexual harassment disclosures was protected by state privilege laws, the *DCL* required them to report those disclosures to other school officials, even without the student's permission. This prompted strenuous objections from these professionals, who understood that their inability to protect victims' privacy would further chill already low victim reporting rates. These disagreements led victim services professionals and other school staff to deluge OCR with questions about whether the *DCL* actually required such "mandatory reporting."

Meanwhile, the *DCL* did not end widespread sexual assault or institutional neglect on college campuses. It had raised expectations for improvements in Title IX compliance, however, and with social media facilitating connections among campuses, survivors and their allies increasingly organized on a national level. A wave of complaints about campus mishandling of sexual harassment began to be filed with OCR, including an early prominent complaint by Yale University survivors.[20] OCR's enforcement infrastructure quickly became strained, and activists expressed their dissatisfaction, demanding via national platforms that OCR enforce Title IX more effectively to protect survivors' civil rights. By early 2013, newspapers such as the *New York Times* began to prominently cover survivors' stories and organizing efforts. That summer, students organized a major protest at ED's headquarters and collected nearly 175,000 signatures in an online petition.[21]

By the time the 2013 protests occurred, Obama administration officials had committed to improving OCR's Title IX enforcement. Then-Vice President Biden lamented, as the Violence Against Women Act (VAWA) neared its twentieth anniversary, that gender-based violence targeting school-aged women and girls had uniquely not declined since VAWA's passage.[22] Against this backdrop, President Obama announced the White House Task Force to Protect Students from Sexual Assault (Task Force) in January 2014. White House Council on Women and Girls lead, Valerie Jarrett, and Lynn Rosenthal, the first White House advisor on violence against women, co-chaired it, immediately launching listening sessions with experts, survivors, and concerned members of the public.

The Task Force issued an influential report in April 2014, which OCR would soon follow with additional guidance, styled as a "Question and Answer" document (the *2014 Q&A*).[23] Both documents reflected the growing influence of the Title IX movement and the Obama administration's responsiveness to survivors' concerns. The *2014 Q&A* held fast to the *DCL*'s positions on equitable processes for survivors, including the preponderance of the evidence standard, and responded to the mandatory reporting controversy by endorsing a reporting system modeled after the U.S. military's "restricted and non-restricted" reporting.[24] This approach put maximum control into victims' hands, allowing them to choose between confidential and nonconfidential paths based on what was most important to them: initiating an investigation or accessing accommodations. The Task Force strongly recommended that schools make available confidential sources of support for survivors and provided reassurance that "on-campus counselors and advocates—like those who work or volunteer in sexual assault centers, victim advocacy offices, and women's and health centers as well as licensed and pastoral counselors—can talk to a survivor in confidence."[25] Additional recommendations encouraged schools to conduct climate surveys using feminist methodologies like the SES, develop prevention programs that engage men, and establish and improve systems for responding to sexual harassment.[26] The Task Force issued a checklist for schools to use to develop a comprehensive policy, deliberately refusing to provide a "model policy" so that schools would write policies appropriate for, and with buy-in from, their own communities. It would continue to produce best practice recommendations for the remainder of the Obama administration, many of which remain available via the website http://changingourcampus.org/.

During this period, two other developments contributed to an unprecedented level of administrative Title IX enforcement. First, the U.S. Department of Justice (DOJ) investigated the Universities of Montana and New Mexico, sending high-profile signals that the federal government would no longer leave Title IX enforcement exclusively to the weaker and less-resourced OCR. Second, in keeping with the Task Force's commitment to transparency and in direct response to Title IX movement activists' explicit demands, ED began publishing the names of schools under Title IX investigation by OCR. That publication encouraged more OCR complaints, ballooning the number of investigations from April 2014's 55 schools to more than 300 by the Obama administration's close.[27] Students also began filing lawsuits in large numbers, many of which attracted substantial media attention.[28]

Contemporaneously, showings of the documentary film *The Hunting Ground* further added to public awareness. The film followed several key movement-building Title IX activists and allies, highlighting their social media use to build national connections with other student survivors, and was shown widely across the country and eventually broadcast on CNN.[29] Lady Gaga co-wrote and performed the film's hit song, *'Till It Happens to You*, at the 2016 Academy Awards, with dozens of college survivors joining her on stage.[30] The movement had, quite literally, ascended to a national stage.

Title IX activists thus built a powerful national network that could disseminate information and strategies quickly and to activists thousands of miles apart. For instance, multiple survivors in Massachusetts were represented in internal Title IX investigations by attorneys from the Victim Rights Law Center in Boston, one of the earliest legal organizations to represent student survivors in such proceedings.[31] Their clients—who were, after all, also good students—learned about Title IX and how they could use it from those attorneys, then spread that information through the network. Activists collaborated to form organizations, including SurvJustice, End Rape on Campus, and Know Your IX, all seeking to use Title IX to address sexual assault as a form of gender discrimination, with a shared understanding that gender inequality is both a cause and a consequence of sexual violence. In these ways, the movement broke the silence and isolation that prevented previous generations from effectively organizing around Title IX's powerful protections. It drew attention to systemic patterns of victimization and institutional complicity, debunking any notion that a few "bad apples" caused this problem and properly situating it as matter of civil rights and equal educational opportunity.

II. Backlash to the Movement and to Title IX

Movement activists were not the only ones who understood Title IX's power. So, too, did those opposed to the movement and the direction taken by the Obama administration. They expressed their vehement disagreement using tactics that targeted individual survivors, sought legislative and policy changes, and promoted narratives that downplayed sexual harassment's harms and magnified the consequences of being accused of sexual harassment.[32]

The *DCL*'s endorsement of the preponderance of the evidence standard provided a particular rallying cry. This opposition did not come from educational institutions—most of which had long used the preponderance standard for all student conduct violations, including sexual misconduct[33]—but from an anti-civil rights coalition that included the Foundation for Individual Rights in Education (FIRE), several "men's rights" groups, and conservative funders such as the Koch brothers and Betsy DeVos (before she became President Trump's Secretary of Education).[34]

This backlash drew upon criminal law–based assumptions to counter the Title IX movement's insights about sexual violence as a form of gender inequality best addressed with civil rights laws. In contesting this framework, the opposition did not rely on the criminal law per se but on a stereotype deeply embedded in it: that victims—who the stereotype treats as synonymous with "women"—lie. This stereotype derives from what feminist legal scholar and now college president Michelle Anderson calls the six "special" rules of criminal rape.[35] Dating as far back as the 1200s, these rules place unique evidentiary burdens on victims alleging rape and reflect women's subordinated legal status, which feminists had only begun to dismantle when Title IX was enacted. They required that rape victims' testimony be corroborated by third-party evidence, that juries be given "cautionary instructions" warning them "to treat a rape complainant's testimony with suspicion," and that only chaste (meaning virginal) women could credibly allege rape. A marital rape exception meant that husbands could never rape their wives, reinforcing not only marriage's fundamental inequality but also the chastity rule, since wives' nonvirgin status meant that married women, even if fidelitous, could not be raped.

Even after feminist rape law reforms, these doctrines "continue to infect both statutory law and the way that . . . police, prosecutors, judges, and juries—see the crime of rape,"[36] an analysis borne out in countless examples. For instance, in both the Thomas and Kavanaugh Supreme Court nomination hearings, additional accusers were not allowed to corroborate sexual harassment allegations by Professors Anita Hill and Christine Blasey Ford, facilitating the dismissal of both women's allegations as "he said, she said," even though they were actually "he said, *they* said."[37]

These embedded stereotypes that "victims/women lie" make up the core of each backlash strategy used against the Title IX movement. In a first example showing this strategy's deployment, accused harassers have sought to exploit and increase jury distrust of victims' credibility by filing aggressive defamation lawsuits against survivors and hiring private investigators to follow and question victims and their families and friends. Claims of defamation, "[t]he offense of injuring a person's character, fame, or reputation by false and malicious statements," directly accuse defendant sexual harassment victims of lying.[38] Similarly, private investigators often search for "evidence" that taps into this stereotype, as with one survivor who was targeted by an investigator who attempted to exploit chastity stereotypes by getting her family and friends to say "how much of a whore [] this girl [is]."[39]

This trope is also at the heart of backlash assertions that Title IX sexual harassment complainants use those complaints to shut down free speech by and academic freedom of professors who defend accused harassers. This tactic was used most prominently by Professor Laura Kipnis, who established herself as an opposition poster child by alleging that her university subjected her to a Title IX "witch-hunt" because she vocally supported a colleague being investigated for sexually assaulting two students.[40] Kipnis made a public statement that the accused harasser had been dating the students who reported him for groping or sexually assaulting them while they were incapacitated by alcohol—a statement vehemently denied by the students. When asked to publicly clarify that her statement was based on the named harasser's claims, she refused, and the students filed a Title IX retaliation complaint against her for calling them liars.[41] Kipnis was ultimately cleared by the university and wrote another widely read essay and a book in which she continued to contest the truthfulness of the students' accounts.[42] Far from chilling her speech, the controversy Kipnis generated began and ended with accusations that a sexual assault victim was lying.[43]

A third deployment of the "victims/women lie" stereotype uses a narrative involving race and racial inequality to discredit the Title IX movement.[44] In its most extreme form, this narrative—advanced by individuals on the "left" and "right" of the political spectrum—links campus sexual harassment accusations to one of the Jim Crow era's most pernicious racist legacies: using white women's false sexual assault accusations to justify the white supremacist lynching of Black men and boys.[45] Unpacking this anti-Title IX narrative exposes how it strategically and disingenuously exploits this racist history.

First, although the narrative assumes that Black men are disproportionately accused of campus sexual assault, no empirical evidence, and very little anecdotal evidence, backs up this assumption. More important, those ostensibly concerned about racial disparities in Title IX discipline have actually opposed measures that would gather such evidence or address documented disparities in non-sexual harassment–related school discipline. Most campus investigations are not public, and schools are not legally required to disclose any information about them, including with regard to the racial demographics of those involved.[46] Title IX activists have pressed for greater transparency, including requiring schools to track such potential disparities.[47] Rather than supporting those efforts, however, the last Republican-controlled Congress proposed legislation seeking to make such data collection and disclosure more difficult.[48] The Trump administration also weakened schools' incentives to address documented racial disparities in school discipline.[49]

Second, this narrative blames survivors—incorrectly suggesting that survivors rather than schools have the power to discipline other students—for unconfirmed racial disparities in school-imposed discipline for sexual misconduct. Not only is there not even anecdotal evidence that accusers are collaborating with disciplinarians (as in the lynching era), but the little research that does exist points in the opposite direction, consistently showing that most sexual assault is *intra*- rather than *inter*racial.[50] Thus, the narrative that accusers of Black men are lying likely blames women accusers of color, Black women in particular, for using false rape allegations to launch racist attacks against Black men.

This nonsensical implication exposes not only the gender but also the racial stereotypes at the root of this narrative, intersectional stereotypes that ultimately cause the most harm to women of color. By combining well-known stereotypes depicting women of color as hypersexual and promiscuous with criminal law–based stereotypes that only chaste women can credibly allege rape, the narrative renders women of color fundamentally unrapable and therefore invisible as sexual harassment victims. This invisibility then makes women of color more vulnerable to sexual harassment because abusers are more likely to target those victims who are the least likely to be believed if they report. This reality is confirmed by evidence that women of color are sexually harassed both more and more severely than white women.[51]

Two university cases prominently used to support the racial-disparity narrative in fact illustrate this harmful erasure of women of color. The first case involved an African American Harvard Law student survivor who spoke in *The Hunting Ground* about being sexually assaulted by an African American male classmate who also assaulted the survivor's non-law student white friend.[52] The accused assailant was criminally charged only for assaulting the white woman. Yet when former *Dear Prudence* columnist Emily Yoffe wrote about the case, she foregrounded the race of "the accused, a young Black man with no previous record of criminal behavior" while later making only a glancing reference to the victims' races. She also made no mention of the prosecutor's decision to criminally charge an accused assailant for sexually assaulting a white woman but not a Black woman. A group of Harvard Law professors later seized on the case to criticize the university's Title IX process for allegedly inadequate due process protections, citing the risk of racial bias against Black men and giving tacit approval to Yoffe's misrepresentative suggestion that the law student accuser was white.

In the second case, a self-described feminist and Democrat wrote a lengthy op-ed piece discussing her representation of a Black male student in a university sexual assault investigation.[53] After foregrounding the races of her client and the white accuser, the op-ed waits until a parenthetical ten paragraphs later to mention a second, "unsubstantiated" accusation against the same student, which did not specify that survivor's race. That gap prompted the white survivor to explain in a responsive Letter to the Editor that "[t]he second accuser of my assailant . . . is my friend, a woman of color; in her case, she wasn't believed." As with Yoffe and the Harvard Law professors, the op-ed author either consciously or subconsciously dismissed—and thereby erased—the woman of color, but not the white woman, as a sexual harassment victim.

Pitting the civil rights of people of color (who such narratives assume to be all men) against those of women (assumed to be all white) is an old technique for disrupting both civil rights and feminism in this country, dating back at least to the nineteenth-century abolition and suffrage movements.[54] It is unsurprising, then, that the racial-disparity narrative would be included in the Trump administration's efforts to incorporate such backlash strategies directly into Title IX policy and administrative law, efforts to which the next section turns.

III. THE POLITICAL AND LEGAL BATTLE FOR THE FUTURE OF TITLE IX

Riding the backlash wave, the Trump administration immediately set about undoing Obama-era enforcement efforts and even waged war on older, long-standing Republican and Democrat administrations' Title IX interpretations. Within months, it rescinded the 2011 *DCL* and *2014 Q&A* and replaced them with "interim" guidance pending a full rulemaking.[55] Late in 2018, Secretary DeVos issued a Notice of Proposed Rulemaking (NPRM) planning extensive changes to Title IX's regulations relevant to sexual harassment, finalizing the new rules in May 2020 (2020 rules).[56]

The 2020 rules aimed for a sea change in OCR's enforcement, reversing ED's decades-long approach to Title IX enforcement in ways too numerous to discuss comprehensively here. However, the most significant changes include the criminal law–based principles, processes, and stereotypes that both first mobilized the Title IX movement and have been used to attack it, including (1) encouraging/compelling use of the quasi-criminal "clear and convincing evidence" standard in Title IX investigations, (2) requiring cross-examination in higher education sexual harassment investigations, (3) raising OCR's standard for a Title IX violation to the significantly harder to meet court enforcement standard of "actual notice" and "deliberate indifference," and (4) narrowing Title IX's definition of sexual harassment.[57]

These stark changes, as well as the Trump administration's policies generally, met with determined feminist protests, both organized and spontaneous. Some protests, like the 2017 Women's March (the largest single-day protest in world history), targeted sexual harassment and gender-based violence alongside other issues such as immigration, racist policing, and gun control.[58] Others, like the #MeToo movement, focused on sexual harassment and shared important commonalities with the Title IX movement, including relying on social media–based organizing and looking to a civil rights, equality-based framework—not the criminal law—for solutions. Critical reporting by journalists similarly fueled the #MeToo movement by connecting thousands and even millions of survivors and allies, regardless of whether their stories were published, to each other. Lady Gaga's Academy Awards performance with the college survivors may have also introduced many prominent Hollywood sexual harassment survivors to organizing strategies and successes pioneered by the Title IX movement.

Even as Title IX activists were linked to and participating in these other movements, their main focus remained on resisting—through both direct-action grass-roots protests and litigation—the Trump ED's undercutting of Title IX and stereotyping of sexual abuse victims as liars. Activists took full advantage of two calls for comment designed to solicit public input on, first, ED's regulations generally and, next, the proposed Title IX regulations, filing reams of comments demanding Obama administration–style Title IX enforcement and exposing the backlash strategies embedded in the government's proposed changes.[59]

As the movement led the charge, a broader, Title IX-supportive public followed suit, adding vast numbers of comments to movement-generated ones, responding to both calls for comments and demonstrating that the Trump administration's retreat from Obama-era Title IX enforcement had little popular support. Nevertheless, DeVos forged ahead, repeating the unsupported backlash refrain that Title IX was a "failed system" without "due process" and saving all condemnation in her speeches for purported discrimination against accused harassers, not even acknowledging the discrimination that Title IX was originally passed into law to prohibit.[60] Trump's ED also made filing public comments as difficult as possible, such as by scheduling the NPRM's mandatory comment period during college students' end-of-semester exams and winter break. Nevertheless, the NPRM generated over 124,000 comments, leading the magazine *Mother Jones* to exclaim, "There's A Quiet #MeToo Movement Unfolding in the Government's Comments Section."[61] A "crowd-research" effort to catalog the comments—ongoing at this writing—confirms that the NPRM's changes were overwhelmingly opposed by the public.

The reasons and explanations for opposition to the NPRM/2020 Rules, moreover, reflect the significant influence of the Title IX movement—an influence most apparent in comments filed by persons outside the movement, who do not necessarily identify as feminist. For instance, a joint comment by five higher education professional associations expressed concern that the proposed rules would chill sexual harassment reporting, a protest all the more notable because higher education institutions share an economic incentive to minimize such reporting.[62] Similarly, more than 900 mental health professionals specializing in trauma signed a comment stating that subjecting victims to cross-examination by an accused harasser's advisor (who could be, for example, the accused's fraternity brother or angry parent) would exacerbate victims' trauma, cause "serious harm" to those who came forward, and discourage reporting.[63]

Even more notably, many in law enforcement sided with the Title IX movement in opposing the regulations. The International Association of Campus Law Enforcement Administrators echoed feminist critiques of "rape exceptionalism" by criticizing the proposed regulations for singling out sexual assault as requiring a "presumption of innocence" and creating heightened procedural requirements only for disciplining sexual harassers.[64] Furthermore, in perhaps the most significant indication of the movement's influence, a joint comment by twenty state attorneys general, the top law enforcement officers in their states, condemned the inequality of this presumption as "inherently favor[ing] the respondent's denial over the complainant's allegation."[65]

When, despite the evidence of public opinion against it, the Trump administration finalized the regulations, the Title IX movement utilized yet another common civil rights and feminist movement tool to protect Title IX and its beneficiaries: It sued. Even before this point, a coalition of feminist and civil rights organizations had filed a lawsuit challenging the rescission of the Obama-era guidance as based on gender stereotypes about survivors.[66] After the 2020 Rules were finalized, these groups came together again to challenge the regulations in two lawsuits, echoing the 2018 lawsuit's charges that Trump's ED had written rules rife with gender stereotypes.[67]

As with the public comment process, the Title IX movement's influence is evident in the allies who stepped forward to support these legal challenges or bring their own, many of whom lacked an explicit feminist mission or identity. A broad cross-section of the educational establishment, including twenty-five higher education organizations (led by the American Council on Education, the association for college and university presidents) and three associations collectively representing most of the nation's K–12 public school districts, filed *amicus* briefs in support of the challengers.[68] Twenty state attorneys general filed two more lawsuits against the 2020 Rules.[69] Like the feminist organizations suing, they argued that the new regulations undermine Title IX's protections against sexual harassment as a form of sex discrimination and that the regulations' criminal law–inspired procedures are structurally incapable of protecting survivors' civil rights.[70] Also like the feminist challengers, the attorney general lawsuits called out the "pervasive stereotype" that victims lie as underlying changes such as those to the evidentiary standard.[71] Even more striking, they explicitly connected the regulations' gender ideology to that of the Trump administration itself, as expressed by Trump's first OCR head, Candice Jackson, quoted as stating that "90 percent [of sexual assault accusations] fall into the category of 'we were both drunk,' 'we broke up, and six months later I found myself under a Title IX investigation because she just decided that our last sleeping together was not quite right.'"[72] Thus, the Title IX movement's influence on advocacy and litigation strategies extended far beyond its own litigation challenging the 2020 Rules.

IV. Conclusion

In March 2021, the Biden–Harris administration issued an Executive Order stating its policy that "all students should be guaranteed an educational environment free from discrimination on the basis of sex, including discrimination in the form of sexual harassment, which encompasses sexual violence."[73] OCR later announced its plans to solicit public input on the 2020 Rules in anticipation of an NPRM to revise them.[74] Two lawsuits challenging the 2020 Rules remained active at that time.

Thus, the passions and tensions that fueled the Title IX movement have no end in sight. The movement's first decade has been tumultuous yet enormously influential, including on those not identifying as feminist, resulting in broad agreement on its two core teachings: first, that criminal law–based approaches are structurally incapable of fulfilling Title IX's gender equality goals, and second, that Title IX's proper functioning—as a civil rights law—requires a break from the gendered, and racialized, stereotypes entrenched in the criminal law. Moreover, the movement's success in resisting the backlash to it is now pushing feminist legal analysis to consider previously un- or undertheorized questions, such as whether sexual harassment survivors– not only accused students– also have "due process" rights.[75] Ultimately the inspiration that the Title IX movement has sparked in a new generation of feminist activists promises to be as strong and resilient as the most powerful of past feminist movements.

Notes

1. Rebecca Traister, Good and Mad: The Revolutionary Power of Women's Anger 39 (2018).
2. Kristine Villaneuva, *Q&A: Kristen Lombardi on the Legacy of Her Sexual Assault on Campus Series*, Ctr. for Pub. Integrity (Dec. 6, 2019), https://publicintegrity.org/inside-publici/qa-kristen-lombardi-on-the-legacy-of-her-sexual-assault-on-campus-series/.
3. Ilene Seidman & Susan Vickers, *The Second Wave: An Agenda for the Next Thirty Years of Rape Law Reform*, 38 Suffolk U. L. Rev. 467, 471 (2005).
4. Kristin Jones, *Lax Enforcement of Title IX in Campus Sexual Assault Cases*, Ctr. for Pub. Integrity (Feb. 25, 2010), https://publicintegrity.org/education/lax-enforcement-of-title-ix-in-campus-sexual-assault-cases/.
5. Office for Civil Rights, Dear Colleague Letter: Sexual Violence, U.S. Dep't Educ. (Apr. 4, 2011), https://www2.ed.gov/about/offices/list/ocr/letters/colleague-201104.html.
6. *See* Robin Warshaw, I Never Called It Rape (1988) (reporting findings from the Sexual Experiences Survey, a study by Dr. Mary P. Koss and her co-researchers); Bonnie S. Fisher, Francis T. Cullen & Michael T. Turner, The Sexual Victimization of College Women (2000); Bianca DiJulio & Miranorton Peytoncraighill, Survey of Current and Recent College Students on Sexual Assault, Kaiser Family Found. (June 12, 2015), https://www.kff.org/other/poll-finding/survey-of-current-and-recent-college-students-on-sexual-assault/.
7. *See* Mary P. Koss et al., Sexual Experiences Survey Long Form Victimization (SES-LFV), MIDSS (2007), https://www.midss.org/content/sexual-experiences-survey-long-form-victimization-ses-lfv.
8. *See* Christopher P. Krebs et al., U.S. Dep't of Justice, The Campus Sexual Assault Study: Final Report (Oct. 2007).
9. *See* Nicole Spector, *The Hidden Health Effects of Sexual Harassment*, NBC News (Oct. 13, 2017), https://www.nbcnews.com/better/health/hidden-health-effects-sexual-harassment-ncna810416.
10. *See* Kathryn M. Reardon, *Acquaintance Rape at Private Colleges and Universities: Providing for Victims' Educational and Civil Rights*, 38 Suffolk U. L. Rev. 395, 396 (2005); Katharine K. Baker et al., Title IX & the Preponderance of the Evidence: A White Paper (2016), http://www.feministlawprofessors.com/wp-content/uploads/2016/11/Title-IX-Preponderance-White-Paper-signed-11.29.16.pdf.
11. *See* Nancy Chi Cantalupo, *For the Title IX Civil Rights Movement: Congratulations and Cautions*, 125 Yale L.J. F. 281, 295–96 (2016)(citing Rebecca Marie Loya's Ph.D. dissertation).
12. Douglas Evan Beloof, *The Third Model of Criminal Process: The Victim Participation Model*, 1999 Utah L. Rev. 289, 306 (1999).
13. For instance, criminal trials deny victims equal evidentiary access and privacy protections, *see* Wayne R. LaFave, Principles of Criminal Law §§ 1.2(e), 1.3(a) (2d ed. 2010), and only the defendant has a right to appeal. 15A Charles Alan Wright, Arthur R. Miller, & Mary Kay Kane, Federal Practice and Procedure § 3902.1 (2d ed. 1991).
14. In application, however, the criminal legal system has led to such high levels of incarceration of people of color, especially African American men, that Professor Michelle Alexander named her book on mass incarceration The New Jim Crow (2020), and Professor Paul Butler has suggested, in Chokehold: Policing Black Men (2017), that the U.S. criminal legal system is *designed* to oppress and control Black men in particular.

15. For more details on the preponderance standard's incorporation of victims' and accused's equal credibility and stakes in sexual harassment investigations, *see* Nancy Chi Cantalupo, *Title IX Symposium Keynote Speech: Title IX & the Civil Rights Approach to Sexual Harassment in Education*, 25 ROGER WILLIAMS U. L. REV. 225, 234–35 (2020).
16. *Id.*
17. *See* Tara N. Richards, *No Evidence of "Weaponized Title IX" Here: An Empirical Assessment of Sexual Misconduct Reporting, Case Processing, and Outcomes*, 43 L. & HUM. BEHAV. 180 (2019); Tara N. Richards, Taylor Claxton & Lane Kirkland Gillespie, *Examining Incidents of Sexual Misconduct Reported to Title IX Coordinators: Results from New York's Institutions of Higher Education*, 20 J. OF SCH. VIOLENCE 374 (2021).
18. *See* Nancy Chi Cantalupo, *And Even More of Us Are Brave: Intersectionality & Sexual Harassment of Women Students of Color*, 42 HARV. J. L. & GENDER 1, 13–14 (2019).
19. *See* Office for Civil Rights, *supra* note 5, at 14.
20. *See Yale Is Subject of a Title IX Inquiry*, N.Y. TIMES, Mar. 31, 2011, https://www.nytimes.com/2011/04/01/us/01yale.html.
21. *See* Know Your IX, *Department of Education: Hold Colleges Accountable That Break the Law by Refusing to Protect Students from Sexual Assault*, CHANGE (2013), https://www.change.org/p/department-of-education-hold-colleges-accountable-that-break-the-law-by-refusing-to-protect-students-from-sexual-assault.
22. *See* The Obama White House, *President Obama Speaks at the Launch of the "It's On Us" Campaign*, YOUTUBE (Sept. 19, 2014), https://www.youtube.com/watch?v=VWzicOS0PqI&t=146s.
23. WHITE HOUSE TASK FORCE TO PROTECT STUDENTS FROM SEXUAL ASSAULT, NOT ALONE (2014), https://www.justice.gov/archives/ovw/page/file/905942/download; Office for Civil Rights, QUESTIONS AND ANSWERS ON TITLE IX AND SEXUAL VIOLENCE, U.S. DEP'T EDUC. (Apr. 29, 2014), http://www2.ed.gov/about/offices/list/ocr/docs/qa-201404-title-ix.pdf.
24. *See* DEP'T OF DEF., REPORT TO THE PRESIDENT OF THE UNITED STATES ON SEXUAL ASSAULT PREVENTION AND RESPONSE 9 (2014), https://sapr.mil/public/docs/reports/FY14_POTUS/FY14_DoD_Report_to_POTUS_Full_Report.pdf.
25. WHITE HOUSE TASK FORCE TO PROTECT STUDENTS FROM SEXUAL ASSAULT, *supra* note 23, at 2.
26. *Id.* at 3–5. I advised the Task Force to mandate climate surveys, based on my research showing how such surveys would create incentives for schools to prevent sexual harassment. *See* Nancy Chi Cantalupo, *Accurate Reporting of Sexual Assault on Campus Without Shame*, N.Y. TIMES, Jan. 3, 2017, https://www.nytimes.com/roomfordebate/2014/08/12/doing-enough-to-prevent-rape-on-campus/accurate-reporting-of-sexual-assault-on-campus-without-shame.
27. *See* Nick Anderson, *At First, 55 Schools Faced Sexual Violence Investigations. Now the List Has Quadrupled*, WASH. POST, Jan. 18, 2017, https://www.washingtonpost.com/news/grade-point/wp/2017/01/18/at-first-55-schools-faced-sexual-violence-investigations-now-the-list-has-quadrupled/.
28. *See, e.g.*, Anita Wadhwani, *Settling Sex Assault Lawsuits Costs Universities Millions*, THE TENNESSEAN, July 6, 2016, https://www.tennessean.com/story/news/2016/07/06/settling-sex-assault-lawsuits-costs-universities-millions/86756078/.
29. *See* David Folkenflik, *Acclaimed Documentary About Campus Rape Draws Critics Too*, NPR (Dec. 3, 2015), https://www.npr.org/2015/12/03/458031996/acclaimed-documentary-about-campus-rape-draws-critics-too.

30. *See* Alex Needham, *Lady Gaga Performs with Survivors of Sexual Assault at the Oscars*, THE GUARDIAN, Feb. 28, 2016, https://www.theguardian.com/film/2016/feb/29/lady-gaga-performs-with-survivors-of-sexual-assault-oscars-2016-joe-biden.
31. This organization has been engaged in such representation since at least the early 2000s. *See* Reardon, *supra* note 10.
32. *See* Cantalupo, *supra* note 18, at 10–11; Cantalupo, *supra* note 11, at 291–96.
33. *See* Nancy Chi Cantalupo, *Campus Violence: Understanding the Extraordinary Through the Ordinary*, 35 J.C. & U.L. 613 (2009) (showing OCR settlements requiring the preponderance standard as early as 1995); Nancy Chi Cantalupo, *Title IX's Civil Rights Approach and the Criminal Justice System*, in THE CRISIS OF CAMPUS SEXUAL VIOLENCE: CRITICAL PERSPECTIVES ON PREVENTION AND RESPONSE 125, 133–34 (Sara Carrigan Wooten & Roland W. Mitchell eds., 2016) (reviewing evidence that schools themselves viewed the preponderance standard as a best practice since at least the early 2000s).
34. *See* Nancy Chi Cantalupo, *Dog Whistles and Beachheads: The Trump Administration, Sexual Violence, and Student Discipline in Education*, 54 WAKE FOREST L. REV. 303, 343–47, 359 (2019).
35. Michelle J. Anderson, *Diminishing the Legal Impact of Negative Social Attitudes Toward Acquaintance Rape Victims*, 13 NEW CRIM. L. REV. 644, 645–47 (2010).
36. *Id.* at 645.
37. *See* Allison Leotta, *I Was a Sex-Crimes Prosecutor. Here's Why: "He Said, She Said" Is a Myth*, TIME (Oct. 3, 2018), http://time.com/5413814/he-said-she-said-kavanaugh-ford-mitchell/; TRAISTER, *supra* note 1, at 191.
38. *What Is Defamation?*, THE LAW DICTIONARY (2d ed.), https://thelawdictionary.org/defamation/. For coverage of such cases, *see* Tyler Kingkade, *As More College Students Say "Me Too," Accused Men Are Suing for Defamation*, BUZZFEED NEWS (Dec. 5, 2017), https://www.buzzfeed.com/tylerkingkade/as-more-college-students-say-me-too-accused-men-are-suing.
39. *See* Harry Shukman, *Male Students Charged with Rape Are Hiring Private Investigators to Follow Their Accusers*, BABE (Dec. 8, 2017), https://babe.net/2017/12/08/the-untold-story-of-how-private-investigators-are-set-on-the-women-who-speak-out-about-rape-24157.
40. *See* Doe v. HarperCollins Publishers, LLC, No. 17-cv-3688, 2018 WL 1174394 (N.D. Ill. Mar. 6, 2018).
41. *See* Tyler Kingkade, *How Laura Kipnis' "Sexual Paranoia" Essay Caused a Frenzy at Northwestern University*, HUFFINGTON POST (May 31, 2015), http://www.huffingtonpost.com/2015/05/31/laura-kipnis-essay-northwestern-title-ix_n_7470046.html.
42. This insistence eventually caused one student to file a defamation suit that the court refused to dismiss, stating that "the Book . . . provides numerous factual statements seemingly intended to paint [the student] as a liar, who falsely accused a professor of . . . forcing her to engage in nonconsensual sex." *Doe*, 2018 WL 1174394.
43. *See* Brian Leiter, Doe v. Kipnis, *HarperCollins Has Settled*, LEITER REPORTS: A PHILOSOPHY BLOG (Nov. 10, 2018).
44. For a comprehensive analysis of this narrative, *see* Cantalupo, *supra* note 18, at 10–24; Cantalupo, *supra* note 34, at 308, 319–22, 341–43.
45. *See* Antuan M. Johnson, *Title IX Narratives, Intersectionality, and Male-Biased Conceptions of Racism*, 9 GEO. J. L. & MOD. CRITICAL RACE PERSP. 57, 72–74 (2017).
46. The little bit of empirical data available regarding campus sexual harassment shows few expulsions and no demographic data. In two states where legislation has required greater transparency about school discipline, neither state requires disclosure of demographic

data, and criminologists found that suspensions and expulsions were rare. Richards, *supra* note 17; Richards et al., *supra* note 17. Anecdotal evidence is even weaker, with all assertions about a pattern of racial disparities appearing to derive from claims that two authors based on a single documented case and an unspecified number of asserted but undocumented cases. *See* Cantalupo, *supra* note 34, at 308 n.16, 342 n.198.

47. *See* Cantalupo, *supra* note 18, at 74–79.
48. The 115th Congress's H.R. 4508 forbade ED from instituting mandatory and ED-created climate surveys that might have required schools to report student disciplinary case demographic information. *See* Cantalupo, *supra* note 34, at 341.
49. The Trump administration rescinded Obama-era OCR guidance creating such incentives. *Id.* at 346–52.
50. *Id.* at 318–19.
51. *See* Cantalupo, *supra* note 18, at 41–54; Jamillah Bowman Williams, *Maximizing #MeToo: Intersectionality and the Movement*, B.C. L. Rev. (forthcoming 2021) (manuscript at 4–8), https://papers.ssrn.com/sol3/papers.cfm?abstract_id=3620439.
52. For a more detailed discussion of this case, *see* Cantalupo, *supra* note 34, at 319–21.
53. For a more detailed discussion of this case, *see id.* at 321–22.
54. Traister, *supra* note 1, at 113–33; Victoria Nourse, *Violence Against Women and Liberal Sexism*, in Research Handbook on Feminist Jurisprudence 213, 221–25 (Robin West & Cynthia Grant Bowman eds., 2019).
55. Office for Civil Rights, Q&A on Campus Sexual Misconduct, U.S. Dep't of Educ. (Sept. 2017), https://www2.ed.gov/about/offices/list/ocr/docs/qa-title-ix-201709.pdf.
56. Nondiscrimination on the Basis of Sex in Education Programs or Activities Receiving Federal Financial Assistance, 85 Fed. Reg. 30,026 (May 19, 2020) (codified at 34 C.F.R. pt. 106).
57. *See* 34 C.F.R. §§ 106.45(b)(1)(vii) (evidentiary standard), 106.45(b)(6)(i), 106.45(i)–(ii) (cross-examination), 106.30, 106.44(a) ("actual knowledge" and "deliberate indifference"), and 106.30(a) (definition of sexual harassment).
58. *See generally* Women's March Organizers & Conde Naste, Together We Rise: Behind The Scenes at the Protest Heard Around the World (2018).
59. When ED first invited comments on how it might "deregulate," it received nearly 61,000 comments for preserving a robust Title IX and only 137 comments opposed. *See* Tiffany Buffkin et al., *Widely Welcomed and Supported by the Public: A Report on the Title IX-Related Comments in the U.S. Department of Education's Executive Order 13777 Comment Call*, 9 Calif. L. Rev. Online 71 (2019).
60. Susan Svrluga, *Transcript: Betsy DeVos's Remarks on Campus Sexual Assault*, Wash. Post, Sept. 7, 2017, https://www.washingtonpost.com/news/grade-point/wp/2017/09/07/transcript-betsy.
61. Madison Pauly, *There's a Quiet #MeToo Movement Unfolding in the Government's Comments Section*, Mother Jones (Jan. 15, 2019), https://www.motherjones.com/politics/2019/01/betsy-devos-title-ix-sexual-assault-harassment-metoo/.
62. Letter from Five Student Affairs Associations to Kenneth L. Marcus, Ass't Sec'y for Civil Rights, Dep't of Educ. 7 (Jan. 29, 2019), https://www.regulations.gov/document?D=ED-2018-OCR-0064-11689; Nancy Chi Cantalupo, *Burying Our Heads in the Sand: Lack of Knowledge, Knowledge Avoidance, and the Persistent Problem of Campus Peer Sexual Violence*, 43 Loy. U. Chi. L.J. 205, 219 (2011).
63. Letter from 902 Mental Health Professionals and Trauma Specialists to Kenneth L. Marcus, Ass't Sec'y for Civil Rights, Dep't of Educ. (Jan. 30, 2019), https://assu.stanf

ord.edu/sites/g/files/sbiybj6236/f/student_body_presidents_comment_on_title_ix_proposal_1.pdf.
64. Letter from Int'l Ass'n of Campus Law Enforcement Administrators to Betsy DeVos, Sec'y, Dep't of Educ. 4–6 (Jan. 28, 2019), https://www.regulations.gov/document?D=ED-2018-OCR-0064-10515.
65. Letter from 20 Attorneys General to Betsy DeVos, Sec'y, Dep't of Educ. (July 19, 2017), https://www.attorneygeneral.gov/taking-action/press-releases/20-ags-call-on-secretary-devos-to-maintain-protections-for-survivors-of-campus-sexual-assault.
66. Democracy Forward, SurvJustice, Equal Rights Advocates & Victim Rights Law Center v. DeVos (July 25, 2019), https://democracyforward.org/lawsuits/survjustice-equal-rights-advocates-victim-rights-law-center-v-devos/.
67. American Civil Liberties Union, *ACLU Sues Betsy Devos for Allowing Schools to Ignore Sexual Harassment and Assault* (May 14, 2020), https://www.aclu.org/press-releases/aclu-sues-betsy-devos-allowing-schools-ignore-sexual-harassment-and-assault; National Women's Law Center, *NWLC Files Lawsuit Against Betsy DeVos, Trump Administration's Sexual Harassment Rules* (June 10, 2020), https://nwlc.org/press-releases/nwlc-files-lawsuit-against-betsy-devos-trump-administrations-sexual-harassment-rules/.
68. Brief of the American Council on Education and 24 Other Higher Education Organization as Amici Curiae in Support of Plaintiffs' Motion for Preliminary Injunction or 5 U.S.C. §705 Stay, *Victim Rights Law Center et al. v. Devos et al.*, No. 1:20-cv-11104-WGY (D. Mass. July 21, 2020).
69. Brief Amici Curiae of AASA, the School Superintendent's Association, The Council of the Great City Schools, and the National Association of Secondary School Principals in Support of Plaintiffs' Motion for Preliminary Injunction or Section 705 Stay, *Victim Rights Law Center et al. v. Devos et al.*, No. 1:20-cv-11104-WGY (D. Mass. July 29, 2020).
70. Compl. at 39, *Victim Rights Law Center et al. v. Devos et al.*, No. 1:20-cv-11104-WGY (D. Mass. June 10, 2020) [hereinafter *VRLC Compl.*].
71. Compl. at 49, *State of New York v. DeVos*, No. 1:20-cv-4260 (S.D.N.Y. Jun. 4, 2020) [hereinafter *NYAG Compl.*]
72. Compl. at 3, *Know Your IX et al. v. DeVos*, No. 1:20-cv-01224-RDB (D. Md. 2020); *NYAG Compl.*, supra note 71, at 28; *VRLC Compl.*, supra note 70, at 29.
73. Exec. Order No. 14021, 86 Fed. Reg. 13,803 (Mar. 11, 2021), https://www.govinfo.gov/content/pkg/FR-2021-03-11/pdf/2021-05200.pdf.
74. Office for Civil Rights, Letter to Students, Educators, and other Stakeholders re Executive Order 14021, U.S. Dep't Educ. (Apr. 6, 2021), https://www2.ed.gov/about/offices/list/ocr/correspondence/stakeholders/20210406-titleix-eo-14021.pdf.
75. *See generally* Ijeoma Oluo, *Due Process Is Needed for Sexual Harassment Accusations—But for Whom?*, The Establishment (Nov. 30, 2017), https://theestablishment.co/due-process-is-needed-for-sexual-harassment-accusations-but-for-whom-968e7c81e6d6/index.html; Sage Carson & Sarah Nesbitt, *Balancing the Scales: Student Survivors' Interests and the Mathews Analysis*, 43 Harv. J. L. & Gender 319 (2020), https://harvardjlg.com/wp-content/uploads/sites/19/2020/09/HLG204_crop.pdf.

CHAPTER 15

FEMINISM AND #METOO
The Power of the Collective

TRISTIN K. GREEN

THE ultimate power of #MeToo as an enduring feminist movement lies in its collective force. As one woman after another came forward as part of #MeToo, two things happened: (1) each woman's voice was made more credible and powerful by support from others, especially when it came to specific harassers, and (2) the breadth and sheer mass of shared experience translated into calls for change, making the broader problem of sex-based harassment in the workplace more difficult to ignore. Each of these things is important, but the second—the broader collective force driving the calls for change—is what marks #MeToo indelibly as a feminist movement that can have lasting impact through change in organizations, norms, and overarching narratives about women's place in society.

In this chapter, I situate #MeToo as a feminist movement, and I consider what it reveals about challenges for feminism, especially the challenges brought on by individualization and emerging antifeminist collective narratives. Both of these challenges are challenges to the collective force of feminism. Seeing them as such can help position a stronger feminist response and ultimately bolster the staying power and impact of the #MeToo movement.

The chapter is organized in two sections. The first section recounts the brief, yet still-unfolding history of #MeToo and situates it as a feminist movement by highlighting some of its feminist threads. The second emphasizes #MeToo's collective force, the movement's most powerful tool for long-term meaningful impact. I explore two ways that #MeToo's collective force might be undermined: through individualization and collective counternarrative. In doing so, I draw lessons from history, including the effort to combat sexual harassment through employment discrimination law, as well as from contemporary commentary. The chapter concludes with some suggestions for how a feminist movement such as #MeToo might retain its collective force in the face of these challenges.

One initial caveat: Because "feminism" can be a slippery term, I should say at the outset that I define feminism in this chapter as a position or belief that sex is a central category for analysis (even if nonbinary), that equality between men and women is a crucial social objective, and that equality cannot be achieved without fundamental social transformation.[1] Following a long line of feminists before me, I regard as feminist not just any theory or position involving or addressing women, but rather a theory or position that places women's subordination front and center and that seeks change aimed at reducing that subordination and inequality.

I. #MeToo as a Feminist Movement

We would be hard pressed to find someone who would say that #MeToo is not a feminist movement. Indeed, one of the beautiful things about the movement has been its capacity to bring feminism to the national stage in a way that is nonacademic and real to people's lives.[2] Clearly, #MeToo is a movement driven by women and a movement about women, but what exactly makes it a feminist movement? In this section, I situate #MeToo as a feminist movement, tracing its evolution and drawing out some of its feminist threads. My portrait supports my main contention: that it is the overarching collective force of the movement—its call for change in norms, systems, and practices—that gives #MeToo its feminist character and that will determine its significance over time.

A. The #MeToo Movement

#MeToo is a decidedly modern movement sparked primarily through social media, something unimaginable as few as two decades ago. The phrase was coined by Black civil rights activist Tarana Burke in 2006. Burke began using "Me Too" as a tool to raise consciousness about sexual violence inflicted against girls and women of color. Her call was aimed at using self-identification to build a community of healing for survivors.[3]

The term went viral on social media in October 2017 with the hashtag #MeToo when actress Alyssa Milano posted her tweet: "If you've been sexually harassed or assaulted write 'me too' as a reply to this tweet."[4] As one commentator recently described, "Within a day it had been retweeted 500,000 times, and within days, millions of women from 85 countries had taken to social media with the hashtag."[5] At around the same time, two mainstream media sources published stories detailing years of harassment and assault by media mogul Harvey Weinstein within his company.[6] With that revelation, #MeToo exploded as an "interlocking dynamic of mainstream and social media."[7]

Much of the immediate change fostered by #MeToo in the United States was extralegal in the sense that the sheer force of social movement pressured and shamed companies and other organizations to fire offenders and investigate abuses; indeed, #MeToo may have been born out of frustration with more traditional legal channels, in this sense something of a revolution.[8] #MeToo is credited with bringing down numerous powerful individual abusers, from Harvey Weinstein in Hollywood to Travis Kalanick at Uber in Silicon Valley. Some organizations also came under pressure to hire investigators, often law firms, to investigate complaints and identify broader sources of harassment in institutions.[9] Although sparked in its recent hashtag form by Hollywood actresses, the movement spread across the country and across the labor spectrum to workers in fast-food and high-end restaurants and hotels, as well as law firms, tech workplaces, courthouses, and capitol hills.[10]

#MeToo extended into the legal sphere with #TimesUp, a legal-funding, advocacy, and litigation branch of the #MeToo movement aimed at helping women of all kinds, especially low-income women and people of color, achieve justice.[11] It also sparked calls for changes in laws. For example, one campaign resulted in a change to federal law that made federal lawmakers personally liable for settlements reached in harassment and retaliation cases.[12] Legal reforms within state legislatures across the country followed as well,[13] with several states extending the statute of limitations for harassment claims and enacting laws that limit the use of nondisclosure and mandatory arbitration provisions in employment contracts and settlement agreements.[14] Other states, such as California, amended their employment discrimination statutes to alter the substantive law for individuals seeking redress.[15] For example, a new California law now makes clear that a single incident of harassment may create a triable issue of harassment under state law. The legislation expressly condemns an opinion by former Circuit Court of Appeals Judge Alex Kozinski (who resigned in the face of #MeToo allegations against him) that held that a forcible touching of the plaintiff's breast was not sufficient to constitute a violation of federal law, Title VII of the Civil Rights Act.[16] The California law also establishes that the legal standard for sexual harassment should not vary by type of workplace and rejects what is known as the "stray remarks doctrine," stating that "existence of a hostile work environment depends upon the totality of the circumstances and a discriminatory remark, even if not made directly in the context of an employment decision or uttered by a non-decisionmaker, may be relevant, circumstantial evidence of discrimination."[17]

B. Feminist Threads in #MeToo

The #MeToo movement is at its core a feminist movement in that women (and men) seek to combat the subordination of women by challenging norms, culture, structure, and overarching narratives about women's place in society and appropriate behavior regarding women and men. It is also a group-based effort. It is collective both in its generative dimension (many people acting together) and its outcome dimension (its call for change). As *New York Times* columnist Lindy West pointed out, "Unseating a couple (or a score, or even a generation) of powerful abusers is a start, but it's not an end, unless we also radically change the power structure that selects their replacements and the shared values that remain even when the movement wanes."[18]

#MeToo has provided women voice—it has, as one commentator put it, "amplified" the voices of the women who speak up.[19] Research shows that victims of harassment and discrimination who speak up about their experiences can suffer negative effects to their reputation[20] and are frequently targets of retaliation.[21] The threat of retaliation and a general fear of being disbelieved or ostracized can lead to silence. Even when complaints are made, those complaints are often buried within institutions or dismissed as mere personnel problems that can be resolved by a quick meeting or a minor alteration in job duties so that an identified few people cross paths less often.[22]

The more powerful the abuser, the more willing organizations are to bury and ignore complaints about the abuser.[23] Professor Rachel Arnow-Richman shows that although "top-level employees are able to exert superior market power to obtain job security as well as binding and desirable employment terms," there are rarely competing incentives to retain rank-and-file at-will employees, who have little to no contractual protections and can be fired for any reason (as long as it is not discriminatory or retaliatory).[24] For example, reporters Jodi Kantor and Megan Twohey described the typical response within The Weinstein Company when complaints arose about Harvey Weinstein as "this is his company. If you don't like it, you can leave."[25] Similarly, when Susan Fowler complained about Travis Kalanick, the CEO (chief executive officer) of Uber at the time, she was initially told by the chief technology officer that he would take care of her complaint, but she later heard that human resources didn't feel comfortable punishing Kalanick because he was a high performer.[26]

#MeToo changed this dynamic so that more women feel empowered to speak about their experiences. In this way, #MeToo is also feminist in its centering of women and in its listening to women as a source of truth and knowledge.[27] Men feature in many of the #MeToo stories, but the overall focus has been on the experiences of women: what it is like to work in a field or workplace dominated by men; what it is like to experience catcalls or constant requests for dates; what it is like to go to work every day with someone who groped you or sexually assaulted you.[28]

The #MeToo Movement is feminist in its capacity to embolden a range of diverse women and men to tell their distinct stories, and yet some would say that it is also feminist in its tendency to fall short of that goal. Feminist theorists have long faced criticism for placing white women at the forefront of discussion[29] and for equating queer experience to the experience of heterosexual women.[30] This same critique has been levied at #MeToo.[31] News outlets have tended to cover the most salacious stories involving powerful (white) men and beautiful (often white) women.[32] One study revealed that in the first twenty-four hours after #MeToo went viral, fewer than 1% of those posting #MeToo were Black.[33] As Professor Angela Onwuachi-Willig explains in her essay, *What About #UsToo?: The Invisibility of Race in the #MeToo Movement*, "[T]he unique form of racialized sexism that women of color face routinely gets marked as outside of the female experience."[34] She shows how the responses to the experiences of female Black actress Leslie Jones and female Black journalist and sportscaster Jemele Hill were both racialized and gendered, with tweets referring to Jones as a "Black dude" and Hill as an "angry Black woman." Yet these women did not receive the outpouring of #MeToo support that Rose McGowan, a white actress, received during the same time. This is a side of feminism that continues to need attention: Feminism is and should be about rising up all women, not just heterosexual, white women.

Beyond generating and empowering individual stories that show that the problem is real and widespread, #MeToo is also feminist in its collective call for change. As feminist legal theorists have long recognized, sexual harassment is usually about sexism, not sexual desire.[35] Reducing sexual harassment, then, requires the dismantling of systems, practices, and cultures that are sexist and that favor men over women, and certain men over others. Indeed, male victims of harassment, too, have spoken up as part of #MeToo, and the movement can and should be understood as a broader gender-based discrimination movement. Even men and women who may not have themselves experienced the forms of sexual harassment aired by #MeToo have spoken out for change, in solidarity for reducing the subordination and inequality of women.

In short, #MeToo is feminist in that it is a movement by and for women and women's equality. It is powerful because it provides space for individual stories about women's experiences and, importantly, because it demands change in broader systems, structures, practices, and cultures that keep women down, including those that facilitate or foster harassment. This is the collective force of #MeToo. The breadth and sheer mass of shared experience translates into calls for systemic change—not just punishment of individual harassers—making the broader problem of sex-based harassment in the workplace highly visible.

II. Challenges for #MeToo: Undermining the Collective Force

The collective, feminist force of a movement like #MeToo can be undermined in at least two ways. The first is by allowing the focus to fix mainly on individuals, whether an accused or a victim. The second is by failing to adequately respond to collective counternarratives that seek to protect existing cultures and systems. Although feminists have been relatively cognizant of the importance of keeping a systemic frame, there has been less discussion about the potential of counterfeminist collective narratives to stem the momentum of the feminist movements, including #MeToo.

A. Individualizing

An ongoing challenge for any antisubordination movement is to keep attention on the systemic nature of subordination, and especially on the role that context plays in driving individual actions and sustaining inequality. Context here refers to structures, systems, and cultures, usually within particular entity-influenced spheres, such as workplaces.

Without a sense of these broader causal forces of subordination, solutions can become overly narrow, aimed at individual stories, individual victims, and individual harassers to the exclusion of broader reform. Indeed, this was a concern of Tarana Burke's when she witnessed #MeToo take off ten years after she began using the term. She emphasized that her vision of #MeToo was not about "taking down powerful white men, but rather about solidarity, healing, and the systems that spur and enable sexual harassment." As she stressed, "It has to be a movement about how we dismantle the systems, not the individuals."[36]

We can see individualizing and its harms in the development of federal harassment law in the United States. By most accounts, the Supreme Court's 1986 declaration in *Meritor Savings Bank v. Vinson*[37] that sexual harassment may amount to discrimination under Title VII of the Civil Rights Act was a victory for sex-based equality.[38] However, the law since *Meritor* has tended to sustain a narrow focus on individual wrongdoers and victims to the exclusion of broader harms and sources of harassment and discrimination at work. In *Harris v. Forklift Systems*, for example, the Supreme Court adopted a subjective prong that must be met in order for a plaintiff to recover for a hostile work environment—she must show that she "subjectively perceive[d] the environment to be abusive."[39] This prong emphasizes the individual's reaction to the harassment and can pose difficulty for women who wish to pursue collective claims through the class action device. Although some courts have certified harassment classes of harassment victims in spite of *Harris*,[40] others have not, holding that the inherently "individualized" nature of plaintiffs' claims of harassment prevents class treatment.[41]

In a pair of cases decided in 1998, the Supreme Court further narrowed stories of harassment by requiring a plaintiff to identify a specific harasser, prove that he acted as her supervisor, and prove that he took a tangible employment action against her. Otherwise, the employer is entitled to assert an affirmative defense, escaping liability if it shows "(a) that the employer exercised reasonable care to prevent and correct promptly any sexually harassing behavior, and (b) that the plaintiff unreasonably failed to take advantage of any preventive or corrective opportunities provided by the employer or to avoid harm otherwise."[42] To avoid the defense, a plaintiff must individualize her claim. Moreover, both elements of the defense individualize: the first by focusing on the employer's treatment of the harasser and the second by focusing on how the victim reacted to the harassment, leading to questions about why she didn't complain sooner or through the right channels.

With this individualizing comes narrow calls for change. For decades now, reforms have been largely limited to training programs aimed at reducing individuals' biases and adoption of internal procedural systems of complaint and response.[43] This is true even as research increasingly shows that complaint systems and diversity and harassment training, especially when training is aimed at employees rather than managers, are not adequate to combat discrimination and can often be problematic.[44] Trainings can exacerbate stereotypes and generate backlash,[45] and internal investigations can lead to retaliation and are often skewed toward findings of personal conflict over harassment or discrimination that require broader, institutional solutions.

Similar individualizing moves have been in play in the media response to #MeToo. Emphasis in the media tends to be on the most salacious stories and the most egregious cases of assault in isolation rather than on the broader workplace environments in which the harassment or assault took place. We saw reporting, for example, about Harvey Weinstein, what he had done and how, including how he prevented women from speaking about their stories, but very little discussion about what the organization (or others within the organization) could have done to prevent the harassment in the first place.[46]

Given this tendency to focus on individual stories, it should not surprise us that the most common legal changes prompted so far by #MeToo have been to laws aimed at improved processes for individual complaints and limits on confidentiality agreements.[47] To be sure, these are positive and important developments. Better processes may protect those who speak up from retaliation and should result in more effective investigations. Limiting confidentiality agreements is also likely to result in greater institutional and societal knowledge about women's experiences. As important as these measures are, however, they focus on individual stories of the accused and victim rather than on solutions aimed at broader structural and cultural change.

The same is true of individualized punishment as the perceived remedy or solution to pervasive harassment. Individualizing the problem as one of microrelations leads to an individualized remedy—punishment of the harasser.[48] Such an overly narrow focus on punishing harassers as an end goal, however, limits the story of collective harm and undermines calls for broader change.

In addition to individualized measures, #MeToo as a feminist movement could harness its collective force by focusing on expanding opportunity for class actions[49] and combatting mandatory arbitration laws that prevent harassment victims from coming together to challenge practices and cultures that foster harassment.[50] The collective force of #MeToo might also require that employers enhance their complaint systems to amass data and to analyze complaints for more systemic patterns and causes.

Relatedly, a broader focus would connect individual complaints of abuse or harassment to sex-based segregation and discrimination. Although sometimes a single harasser uses sexual conduct as a weapon of personal power, often sex-based power is manifested through less sexually oriented but equally undermining conduct, such as "hostile behavior, physical assault, patronizing treatment, personal ridicule, social ostracism, exclusion or marginalization, denial of information, and work sabotage."[51] Research also suggests that although harassers sometimes act on their own, as rogues within a broader context of equality, they more often act within contexts in which women are devalued, including through lack of representation in positions of power.[52]

Some organizations have gone further than investigating individuals. In response to complaints about its CEO, the Board at Uber hired a team led by former U.S. Attorney General Eric Holder to investigate and make recommendations. Although many of the team's recommendations focused on individuals (e.g., mandatory training and improved complaint processes) and soft attempts to change culture (e.g., "valuing diversity"), several recommendations were more systemic. Specifically, Uber was counseled to clarify its promotion requirements, to remove barriers to employee transfer (and to involve an independent evaluator to monitor for patterns), to revamp its performance review process and pay practices, and to expand the representation of women and racial minorities in interview pools for key positions.[53] These are the kinds of structural and systemic changes that are likely to affect an organization's work culture and reduce harassment and discrimination across the board.

Driven by its collective force, #MeToo might also do more to target culture directly by consistently identifying it as a feature of work that can lead to harassment and discriminatory outcomes. In one recent case, the district court certified a class of women suing Goldman Sachs for discrimination in pay, performance reviews, and promotions, but denied class status to what it saw as an independent claim that a "boys club" atmosphere contributed to systemic disparate treatment of women at the firm.[54] In doing so, the judge set apart allegations and evidence related to the "boys club" atmosphere—including testimony of sexual harassment and assault, stereotyping, impunity for male misconduct, and retaliation—from the plaintiffs' discrimination claims. What the court missed was that the sexist culture at Goldman Sachs was an integral part of the plaintiffs' overarching case of systemic, sex-based discrimination and that evidence related to these allegations would buttress plaintiffs' argument that the disparities were the result of sex-based biases rather than some other cause. The culture of the organization is also crucial to plaintiffs' framing of the appropriate remedy in a discrimination case like this one. Individualizing each instance of harassment or assault will not achieve the same comprehensive systemic reform as an attack on the culture itself.[55]

Individualizing can also disempower the individual voices that call for such change. This phenomenon was apparent in Christine Blasey Ford's allegations of sexual assault levied at U.S. Supreme Court nominee Brett Kavanaugh during the Senate confirmation hearings. Blasey Ford testified that when they were teenagers Kavanaugh laughed with his male friend as he pushed her onto a bed, put his hand over her mouth, groped her, pinned her down, and tried to rip her clothes off.[56] Even though many senators—including Republicans—found Blasey Ford to be "credible,"[57] a majority in the Senate nonetheless dismissed her testimony and voted to confirm Kavanaugh (by a margin of 50–48). In doing so, those senators voting to confirm—even those who deemed her "credible"—isolated her individual charge from the broader charges of unfitness against Kavanaugh, charges that included lying under oath, heavy drinking (including in later years), and sexually harassing at least one other woman.[58] Deeming her "credible" in this way might be seen as a tool of individualizing, a way of minimizing an individual's complaint by listening to her story but ultimately disregarding it as merely one complaint by a confused victim.

Another individualizing turn has come from #MeToo critics (usually women) who portray those who complain about harassment and assault as overly sensitive, as one critic put it, "as frail as Victorian housewives."[59] There is often an ideological thread of neoliberal individualism underlying these claims, namely, the idea that calling out subordination and inequality compromises individual agency. This critique mirrors one levied against dominance feminism: that portraying sex in the workplace as sexual violence denies women's experience of sexual agency and choice.[60] Resolving this longstanding debate within feminism is beyond the scope of this chapter, but it is worth noting that ignoring the larger context for individual action—seeing any woman who complains as somehow undermining herself as a feminist—dilutes the feminist power of a movement like #MeToo by fixating on individual women and their agency.

Finally, the insistent call for due process for those accused of harassment and assault is another way of individualizing and thereby undermining the broader collective force of #MeToo. Due process is admittedly important. There is no question that we need systems in place that fairly determine guilt and innocence in resolving specific instances and allegations of harassment and discrimination. But focusing on due process as a response to #MeToo treats the movement solely as one aimed at individuals and their microrelations rather than as a collective action seeking equality for all women in workplaces dominated by men. For example, when Moira Donegan's Shitty Media Men list[61]—a compilation of women's complaints about men in journalism and publishing—hit social media, some commentators expressed concern that the list (or others like it) would result in damage to all men on the list, regardless of distinctions in the severity of their actions and without any consideration of whether the accusations were true with respect to any specific harasser.[62] According to Donegan, the list was designed as a "whisper network" wherein women could let each other know about their experiences and thereby empower others to protect themselves with that knowledge,[63] but it was the naming of men that took center stage. Similar critiques were launched more broadly at #MeToo, calling it a "witch-hunt" and "McCarthyism."[64] This, too, can be seen as a tactic of individualizing, picking apart the broader scope of the movement by emphasizing differences in severity of individual incidents and calling for due process for individual harassers.

B. Collective Counternarratives

Beyond individualizing, the other preeminent threat to the collective force of #MeToo lies in collective counternarratives that directly resist change in the very cultures, structures, and systems that the movement seeks to challenge. When culture and overarching structures or systems need to change, resistance to that change can build at a collective level. This resistance is sometimes framed as anger at changed rules or overly harsh policing of individuals, when in reality it is an effort to maintain a cultural, systemic status quo.

Here, too, lessons might be drawn from the Kavanaugh hearings. As we have seen, individualization isolated Blasey Ford and her complaints from Kavanaugh's broader history and may have made it easier to disregard her story. Individualization also focused on Kavanaugh as someone who was being treated unfairly. But the individualized story of Kavanaugh was intertwined with a collective story. Kavanaugh's anger and that of his supporters may have been less about individual due process and more about what some viewed as an unfair switch from lauding him for the culture he abided by—leadership in sports, high grades, whiteness, attendance at an elite prep school, and "working on my service projects"—to vilifying him for abiding by that same culture when it came to its other aspects, such as heavy binge drinking, male elitism, and hypermasculine displays, including the championing of sexual exploits and group-based mistreatment of women.[65] Notably, Kavanaugh did not deny the picture painted of him as a sometimes heavy-beer-drinking, prep school athlete who engaged in "locker room" behavior. Rather, he railed against the idea that what he did may have been wrong. This position maintains that it must be acceptable to perform according to culturally established norms of male elites, even when those norms include behavior that subjugates women.[66]

According to U.S. Senator Lindsey Graham, to challenge Kavanaugh on his record regarding mistreatment of women, including Blasey Ford, would "destroy the ability of good people to come forward" to present themselves for prominent positions like that of United States Supreme Court Justice.[67] This response protects the culture as much as it does the individual, and therein lies its force as a response to #MeToo. Indeed, at the close of his opening statement before the Senate, Kavanaugh called upon the senators and the American public to judge him "by the standard that you would want applied to your father, your husband, your brother or your son." In doing so, he invoked fear of a culture change and the specter of widespread condemnation of men across the country.

We have seen a similar move by judges applying sex discrimination law. Judges continue to personalize harassment by ignoring or downplaying those instances of harassment or discrimination that employees other than the specific plaintiff have suffered, sometimes disregarding a broader context that may involve multiple actors in the harassing behavior.[68] Some judges have also required that plaintiffs restrict their proof to targeted harassment directed at the plaintiff rather than document pervasive harassment more broadly in a workplace. Still others have deemed extreme sexually harassing behavior in male-only workplaces as somehow less problematic than in workplaces where women are present.[69] These judicial interpretations and glosses on antidiscrimination law in the harassment context work together to preserve subordinating cultures within white, male-dominated workplaces.

A related counternarrative also emerged in the commentary responding to the Shitty Media Men list. Some commentators created the counternarrative that those who speak out against #MeToo are themselves shunned by an emerging culture that is overly concerned with sex equality. Katie Roiphe's essay, *The Other Whisper Network*, described a world in which women are afraid to air their criticisms of #MeToo, that "many women . . . fear varieties of retribution (e.g., Twitter rage, damage to their reputations, professional repercussions, and vitriol from friends) for speaking out."[70] This complaint is framed as one of concern about individuals, emphasizing the harm that they suffer. But it targets beliefs about the culture more broadly. To accept that we should be concerned about normative pressure on the individuals whom Roiphe identifies, we must conclude that the cultural shift to combat harassment rather than accede to it is itself problematic. If, on the other hand, we adopt a cultural norm that rejects sexual harassment, then those who speak out against that norm *should* be made to feel uncomfortable.

The defense team in the Harvey Weinstein case traded on similar counternarratives. As *New Yorker* reporter Jia Tolentino described, the defense was framed "to pretend that [the #MeToo movement] has already won—to pretend that centuries of male domination have been swiftly reversed to make women the rulers of the land."[71] This is a collective culture turn—it is a claim that we have arrived at a culture that is worse than the one that came before it. Men are no longer positioned in powerful roles vis-à-vis women; structures are no longer built to advantage men. This collective counternarrative suggests that change has happened, indeed, has gone too far, and that we should now roll it back.

In her famous book, *Backlash,* feminist Susan Faludi declared that a "backlash" against feminism had eviscerated the women's rights movement of the 1970s.[72] So far, the #MeToo movement has managed to duck such a fatal backlash, but it may not in the long run. Meeting the force of these and other collective counternarratives is crucial if #MeToo is to have lasting impact as a feminist movement.

III. Conclusion

This chapter aims to situate #MeToo as a feminist movement and to expose its potential as well as its vulnerabilities. The law surfaces throughout this chapter as both a product of social norms and narratives—for example, judges resisting culture change in their application of civil rights laws or individualizing hostile work environment around sexualized, targeted action—and also as a tool for meaningful large-scale reform. Law can itself represent and disseminate powerful norms.[73] Moreover, law can provide a crucial space for collective action that carries across individual identities (e.g., race, class, and sexuality), and it can generate corresponding collective calls for change in the systems, structures, and cultures that perpetuate the subordination of women in U.S. organizations and society.

#MeToo may turn out to be the most powerful feminist movement of the twenty-first century. It brings to the forefront the depth and breadth of sexual abuse and harassment in our society and calls for meaningful change. It will only achieve that change, however, if its supporters can resist individualizing and respond adequately to competing collective counternarratives. To counter the tendency toward individualizing, feminists need to emphasize structural solutions, changes in culture and systems, and the expansion of space for collective action, including in legal actions.[74] To challenge collective counternarratives, feminists need to call out those narratives for what they are—and push back. On both of these fronts, being relentlessly inclusive and intersectional will be key. To maintain its force as a feminist movement, #MeToo must drive people to imagine new gender equality norms and to demand change, even when that change seems an uncomfortable or even frightening prospect.

Notes

1. See Katherine Bartlett, *Feminist Legal Methods*, 103 HARV. L. REV. 829, 833 (1990) (on meaning of the term "feminist"); *see also* Deborah L. Rhode, *Feminist Critical Theories*, 42 STAN. L. REV. 617 (1990) (describing feminist critical theories and methodologies); Clare Dalton, *Where We Stand: Observations on the Situation of Feminist Legal Thought*, 3 BERKELEY WOMEN'S L.J. 1, 2 (1988–89) (defining feminism as it relates to law); BELL HOOKS, FEMINISM IS FOR EVERYONE: PASSIONATE POLITICS xii (2015) ("Feminism is a movement to end sexism, sexist exploitation, and oppression.").
2. HOOKS, *supra* note 1 (lamenting feminism's difficulty in reaching "everyone").
3. Leslie Wexler, Jennifer K. Robbennolt & Colleen Murphy, *#MeToo, Time's Up, and Theories of Justice*, 2019 U. ILL. L. REV. 45, 51–52.
4. Alyssa Milano (@Alyssa_Milano), TWITTER (Oct. 15, 2017, 4:21 PM), https://twitter.com/Alyssa_Milano/status/919659438700670976.
5. Brenda Cossman, *#MeToo, Sex Wars 2.0 and the Power of Law*, in ASIAN YEARBOOK OF HUMAN RIGHTS AND HUMANITARIAN LAW 18 (Vol. 3, 2019).
6. Jodi Kantor & Megan Twohey, *Harvey Weinstein Paid Off Sexual Harassment Accusers for Decades*, N.Y. TIMES, Oct. 5, 2017, https://www.nytimes.com/2017/10/05/us/harvey-weinstein-harassment-allegations.html; Ronan Farrow, *From Aggressive Overtures to Sexual Assault: Harvey Weinstein's Accusers Tell Their Stories*, NEW YORKER (Oct. 10, 2017), https://www.newyorker.com/news/news-desk/from-aggressive-overtures-to-sexual-assault-harvey-weinsteins-accusers-tell-their-stories.
7. Deborah L. Rhode, *#MeToo: Why Now? What Next?*, 69 DUKE L.J. 377, 397 (2019); Jamillah Bowman Williams, Lisa Singh & Naomi Mezey, *#MeToo as Catalyst: A Glimpse into 21st Century Activism*, 2019 U. CHI. L.F. 371 (surveying legal changes post-#MeToo).
8. For consideration of the procedural "rules" guiding the extralegal process of #MeToo, see Jessica A. Clarke, *The Rules of #MeToo*, 2019 U. CHI. LEGAL F. 37. For consideration of some of the intersections and similarities as well as differences between Black Lives Matter and #MeToo, see Linda S. Greene et al., *Talking About Black Lives Matter & #MeToo*, 34 WIS. J. L. GENDER & SOC'Y 109 (2019).
9. *See, e.g., Uber Report: Eric Holder's Recommendations for Change*, N.Y. TIMES, June 13, 2017, https://www.nytimes.com/2017/06/13/technology/uber-report-eric-holders-recommendations-for-change.html.
10. *See generally* Rhode, *supra* note 7 (describing some of these impacts in various industries); *see also* Williams et al., *supra* note 7. For compelling critique of the limits of judicial discipline, see Veronica Root Martinez, *Avoiding Judicial Discipline*, 115 N.W. L. REV. 953 (2020).
11. *See Our Story*, TIME'S UP NOW, https://timesupnow.org/about/our-story/.
12. The Congressional Accountability Act of 1995 Reform Act, 2 U.S.C. § 1301 (2018).
13. *See* Jon Griffin, *Halting Harassment*, STATE LEGIS. MAG. (Sept/Oct. 2018).
14. *See* NATIONAL WOMEN'S LAW CENTER, PROGRESS IN ADVANCING ME TOO WORKPLACE REFORMS IN #20STATESBY2020 (July 2019) (describing states' laws).
15. California S.B. 1300. For discussion of the Fair Employment and Housing Act (FEHA) and other California law changes, some prior to passage, see Ramit Mizrahi, *Sexual Harassment After #MeToo: Looking to California as a Model*, 128 YALE L.J. F. 121 (2018); Morin I. Jacob & Paul D. Knothe, *After MeToo*, 42 L.A. LAW. 20 (Jan. 2020) (describing recent changes to FEHA, the California state fair employment act).

16. Cal. Gov't Code § 12923.
17. *Id.*
18. Lindy West, *We Got Rid of Some Bad Men. Now Let's Get Rid of Bad Movies*, N.Y. TIMES, Mar. 3, 2018, https://www.nytimes.com/2018/03/03/opinion/sunday/we-got-rid-of-some-bad-men-now-lets-get-rid-of-bad-movies.html.
19. Shelly Cavalieri, *On Amplification, Extralegal Acts of Feminist Resistance in the #MeToo Era*, 2019 WIS. L. REV. 1489.
20. *See* Anne Lawton, *Between Scylla and Charybdis: The Perils of Reporting Sexual Harassment*, 9 U. PA. J. LAB. & EMP. L. 603, 632 (2007)(discussing harm to professional reputation as a consequence of reporting harassment).
21. Deborah L. Brake, *Retaliation in an EEO World*, 89 IND. L.J. 115 (2014); Nicole Buonacore Porter, *Ending Harassment by Starting with Retaliation*, 71 STAN. L. REV. ONLINE 49 (2018).
22. *See* ELLEN BERREY, ROBERT L. NELSON & LAURA BETH NIELSEN, RIGHTS ON TRIAL: HOW WORKPLACE DISCRIMINATION LAW PERPETUATES INEQUALITY (2017); LAUREN B. EDELMAN, WORKING LAW: COURTS, CORPORATIONS, AND SYMBOLIC CIVIL RIGHTS (2016).
23. Rachel Arnow-Richman, *Of Power and Process: Handling Harassers in At-Will World*, 128 YALE L.J. F. 85 (2018); Joanna L. Grossman, *The Culture of Compliance: The Final Triumph of Form over Substance in Sexual Harassment Law*, 26 HARV. WOMEN'S L.J. 3, 60 (2003)(noting that women who are relatively powerless within an organization may be more likely to suffer retaliation if they complain).
24. Arnow-Richman, *supra* note 23.
25. Kantor & Twohey, *supra* note 6.
26. Amelia Tait, *Susan Fowler: "When the Time Came to Blow the Whistle on Uber, I Was Ready,"* THE GUARDIAN, Mar. 1, 2020, https://www.theguardian.com/world/2020/mar/01/susan-fowler-uber-whistleblower-interview-travis-kalanick.
27. Patricia Cain, *Feminist Legal Scholarship*, 77 IOWA L. REV. 19, 20 (1991) ("[L]egal scholarship is not feminist unless it is grounded in women's experience.").
28. Indeed, some commentators argue that #MeToo needs to do more to challenge men to acknowledge and reckon with their position, much as whites must do so with respect to race. *See* Mischa Haider, *The Next Step in #MeToo is for Men to Reckon with Their Male Fragility*, SLATE (Jan. 23, 2019) (drawing on ROBIN DIANGELO, WHITE FRAGILITY: WHY IT'S SO HARD FOR WHITE PEOPLE TO TALK ABOUT RACISM (2018)).
29. *See, e.g.,* Dorothy Roberts, *Spiritual and Menial Housework*, 9 YALE J.L. & FEMINISM 51 (1997).
30. *See, e.g.,* Patricia A. Cain, *Feminist Jurisprudence: Grounding the Theories*, 4 BERKELEY WOMEN'S L.J. 191 (1989-90); Maxine Eichner, *Feminism, Queer Theory, and Sexual Citizenship*, in GENDER EQUALITY: DIMENSIONS OF WOMEN'S EQUAL CITIZENSHIP 307 (Linda McClain & Joanna Grossman eds., 2009).
31. Kimberlé Crenshaw, *Opinion, We Still Haven't Learned from Anita Hill's Testimony*, N.Y. TIMES, Sept. 27, 2018; Trina Jones & Emma E. Wade, *MeToo?: Race, Gender, and Ending Workplace Sexual Harassment*, 27 DUKE J. OF GENDER & L. POL'Y, 203 (2020); Angela Onwuachi-Willig, *What About #UsToo?: The Invisibility of Race in the #MeToo Movement*, 128 YALE L.J. F. 105 (2018); Jamillah Bowman Williams, *Maximizing #MeToo: Intersectionality and the Movement*, 62 BOSTON C. L. REV. 1787 (2021).
32. Tarana Burke, *#MeToo Was Started for Black and Brown Women and Girls. They're Still Being Ignored*, WASH. POST, Nov. 9, 2017; Sandra E. Garcia, *The Woman Who Created*

#MeToo Long Before Hashtags, N.Y. TIMES, Oct. 2017. Scholars have worked to expand the lens. Onwuachi-Willig, *supra* note 31; Brian Soucek, *Queering Sexual Harassment Law*, 128 YALE L.J. F. 67 (2018).

33. *The #MeToo Research Collaboration*, MASSIVE DATA INST. & GENDER JUSTICE INITIATIVE, http://metoo.georgetown.domains/.
34. Onwuachi-Willig, *supra* note 31, at 118.
35. *See generally* Vicki Schultz, *Open Statement on Sexual Harassment by Employment Discrimination Law Scholars*, 71 STAN. L. REV. ONLINE 17 (2018).
36. Jennifer Smola, *Founder of "Me Too" Movement Fears Narrative Being Hijacked from Helping Survivors Heal*, COLUM. DISPATCH, Apr. 23, 2018("This is about systems. There were systems in place that allowed [perpetrators of sexual violence] to behave the way they behaved . . . . It has to be a movement about how we dismantle the systems, not the individuals."); *see generally* Wexler et al., *supra* note 3 (gathering news sources relaying Burke's vision and concerns).
37. 477 U.S. 57 (1986).
38. Feminists were influential in the Court's recognition of sexual harassment as a form of discrimination. *See* CATHARINE A. MACKINNON, SEXUAL HARASSMENT OF WORKING WOMEN: A CASE OF SEX DISCRIMINATION (1979) (developing a theory of sexual harassment as sex discrimination). For more on the law of sexual harassment and its erasure of broader context, see Tristin K. Green, *Was Sexual Harassment a Mistake?*, 128 YALE L.J. F. 152 (2018).
39. 510 U.S. 17, 20 (1993).
40. *See, e.g.*, Sellars v. CRST Expedited, Inc., 321 F.R.D. 578, 613 (N.D. Iowa 2017) (certifying class and modifying *Harris* for a two-stage process); Jenson v. Eveleth Taconite Co., 824 F. Supp. 847, 875-76 (D. Minn. 1993) (same).
41. *See, e.g.*, Elkins v. American Showa, Inc., 219 F.R.D. 414, 424 (S.D. Ohio 2002) (denying class certification on the ground of no commonality because of individualized variation among plaintiffs' complaints of harassment). When paired with another requirement (the objective prong) under which plaintiffs must show that the environment was objectively hostile or offensive, the doctrine becomes doubly troubling. It fosters decisions in which judges conclude that a plaintiff subjectively experienced harassment, but her subjective response was "unreasonable" because the harassment did not rise to the level of the objective standard as understood by the judge (who in the United States is often a white man). *See generally* THERESA M. BEINER, GENDER MYTHS V. WORKING REALITIES: USING SOCIAL SCIENCE TO REFORMULATE SEXUAL HARASSMENT LAW 17–32 (2005) (describing cases).
42. Burlington Indus. v. Ellerth, 524 U.S. 742 (1998); Faragher v. City of Boca Raton, 524 U.S. 775 (1998).
43. Tristin K. Green & Alexandra Kalev, *Discrimination-Reducing Measures at the Relational Level*, 59 HASTINGS L.J. 1435 (2008) (critiquing the individualized focus in solutions and calling for a relational lens).
44. *See* Frank Dobbin & Alexandra Kalev, *The Promise and Peril of Sexual Harassment Programs*, 116 PNAS 12255 (2019).
45. *See* Susan Bisom-Rapp, *Sex Harassment Training Must Change: The Case for Legal Incentives for Transformative Education and Prevention*, 71 STAN. L. REV. ONLINE 62, 70 (2018); Elizabeth C. Tippett, *Harassment Trainings: A Content Analysis*, 39 BERKELEY J. OF EMP. & LAB. L. 481 (2018).

46. Kantor & Twohey, *supra* note 6; Farrow, *supra* note 6.
47. *See supra* notes 11–13 and accompanying text (detailing changes).
48. For #MeToo, much of this punishment has been in the form of cancelled contracts and firings, and some of these narratives have turned quickly to questions about forgiveness.
49. The Supreme Court's narrow focus on individuals constrains class actions; it also risks altering the substantive law for systemic discrimination claims. Wal-Mart v. Dukes, 564 U.S. 338 (2011); *see generally* Tristin K. Green, *The Future of Systemic Disparate Treatment Law*, 32 BERKELEY J. OF EMP. & LAB. L. 395 (2011) (describing the danger of individualizing for class certification and for the substantive law of systemic disparate treatment).
50. In *Epic Systems Corp. v. Lewis*, a case involving claims under the National Labor Relations Act, the Supreme Court upheld an arbitration agreement that prevented collective actions. 138 S. Ct. 1612 (2018). The majority made no mention of collective actions to enforce antidiscrimination laws under Title VII of the Civil Rights Act, although Justice Ginsburg, in dissent, insisted that the Court's decision would not apply to collective claims under Title VII. *Id.* at 1648. On efforts to alter arbitration clauses, see Jean R. Sternlight, *Mandatory Arbitration Stymies Progress Toward Justice in Employment Law: Where to, #MeToo?*, 54 HARV. C.R.-C.L. L. REV. 155, 203–05 (2019) (describing social pressure placed on major U.S. companies like Uber, Microsoft, and Google to eliminate the practice of mandatory arbitration clauses for sexual harassment); *see also id.* at 205–07 (describing efforts to pass federal legislation banning arbitration clauses in employment contracts).
51. Vicki Schultz, *Reconceptualizing Sexual Harassment Again*, 128 YALE L.J. F. 22, 33–34 (2018).
52. Vicki Schultz, *Reconceptualizing Sexual Harassment*, 107 YALE L.J. 1683 (1998).
53. *Uber Report, supra* note 9.
54. Chen Oster et al. v. Goldman, Sachs & Co., 10 Civ. 6950 (S.D.NY. Mar. 3, 2018), at 47–49.
55. The reforms need not necessarily or exclusively require policing of culture directly, but they should take work culture into account as a source of harassment and discrimination and as a solution. *See* Tristin K. Green, *Work Culture and Discrimination*, 93 CALIF. L. REV. 623 (2005) (discussing practical concerns around regulating social relations directly through legal rights).
56. For transcript of the hearing, see *Washington Post*: https://www.washingtonpost.com/news/national/wp/2018/09/27/kavanaugh-hearing-transcript/.
57. Conservative Fox News anchor Chris Wallace declared Blasey Ford's testimony credible and a "disaster" for Kavanaugh's nomination. *See Fox News' Chris Wallace Calls Ford's Testimony a Disaster for the GOP*, NOW THIS (Sept. 27, 2018), https://www.thewrap.com/fox-news-chris-wallace-christine-fords-testimony-disaster-republicans/. During the afternoon of the hearing, Sen. John Cornyn (R-Tex.) told reporters, "I found no reason to find [Ford] not credible." *Id.* According to one reporter, "even Republicans were calling Ford 'credible' in a way that, for a moment, felt like a real sea change." *Kavanaugh, Kanye, Beyoncé, 'Black Panther': Washington on Pop Culture in 2018*, N.Y. TIMES, Dec. 31, 2018, https://www.nytimes.com/2018/12/30/arts/kavanaugh-kanye-beyonce-washington-pop-culture.html. Not all allowed that Blasey Ford could be credible. *See* Peter Baker, *In Risky Shift, Trump and G.O.P. Directly Assail Christine Blasey Ford*, N.Y. TIMES, Oct. 3, 2018, https://www.nytimes.com/2018/10/03/us/politics/blasey-ford-trump-republicans.html.
58. Even Kavanaugh did not say that Blasey Ford was lying, only that she was confused about who assaulted her. Transcript, *supra* note 56.

59. Daphne Merkin, *Publicly We Say #MeToo, Privately, We Have Misgivings*, N.Y. TIMES, Jan. 5, 2018, https://www.nytimes.com/2018/01/05/opinion/golden-globes-metoo.html.
60. For more on this critique and its link to critiques of dominance feminism, *see* Kathryn Abrams, *Songs of Innocence and Experience: Dominance Feminism in the University*, 103 YALE L.J. 1533, 1553–57 (1994).
61. Moira Donegan, *I Started the Media Men List: My Name Is Moira Donegan*, THE CUT (Jan. 2018), http://www.thecut.com/2018/01/moira-donegan-i-started-the-media-men-list.html.
62. The debate over the Shitty Media Men list and especially a subsequent article in Babe.net in January 2018 about a woman's sexual experience with actor Aziz Ansari sparked what some saw as a "feminist intergenerational feud." *See* Cossman, *supra* note 5 (arguing that rather than an intergenerational feud, the controversy unveiled long-standing disagreement among feminists about sexuality, consent, and the role of law).
63. *See* Donegan, *supra* note 61.
64. For discussion of the use of the term "witch-hunt" and the argument that more should be done to protect women's speech, see Mary Anne Franks, *Witch Hunts: Free Speech, #MeToo, and the Fear of Women's Words*, 2019 U. CHI. LEGAL F. 123.
65. I include "whiteness" in the description of the culture to which Kavanaugh belongs and adheres because race overlays judgments about the value of that culture and actions within it. *See* Stephanie Wildman, *Hearing Women: From Professor Hill to Dr. Ford*, 33 J. OF C.R. & ECON. DEV. 85 (2019).
66. As Kavanaugh once put it in a speech, "What happens at Georgetown Prep, stays at Georgetown Prep. That's been a good thing for all of us." *See* Moriah Balingit, *What Happens at Georgetown Prep Stays at Georgetown Prep: Kavanaugh Remarks in 2015 Get Renewed Scrutiny*, WASH. POST, Sept. 19, 2018; *see generally* Mary Ann Case, *Institutional Responses to #MeToo Claims: #VaticanToo, #KavanaughToo and the Stumbling Block of Scandal*, 2019 U. CHI. L. F. 1 (describing the institutional apparatus behind protection of Kavanaugh). Kavanaugh's behavior included use of the phrase "Renate Alumnius" on his senior high school yearbook page, referring to a girl who attended a school nearby Georgetown Prep. Jia Tolentino, *Brett Kavanaugh, Donald Trump, and the Things Men Do for Other Men*, NEW YORKER (Sept. 26, 2018). Camille Gear Rich, *What the Truth Looks Like: Race, Gender, and the Politics of Credibility at the Kavanaugh Confirmation Hearings* (unpublished draft on file with author) (noting that Blasey Ford's story "raised larger questions about the ethical and moral atmosphere of elite spaces like prep school and high school parties and elite college dorms," and that these questions resulted in new constructs to "deflect scrutiny of these elite areas").
67. Transcript, *supra* note 56.
68. Green, *supra* note 38. Ironically, some judges call evidence in the form of testimony by others who experienced harassment or discrimination "me too" evidence and exclude it unless a plaintiff can show that the same supervisor was involved in each of the instances. *See generally* Emma Pelkey, Comment, *The "Not Me Too" Evidence Doctrine in Employment Law: Courts' Disparate Treatment of "Me Too" Versus "Not Me Too" Evidence in Employment Discrimination Cases*, 92 OR. L. REV. 545 (2013) (citing cases involving "me too" evidence and "not me too" evidence). For discussion of how a focus on individuals leads to exclusion of evidence, see Tristin K. Green, *Insular Individual: Employment Law After* Ledbetter v. Goodyear, 43 HARV. C.R.-C.L. L. REV. 353 (2008).

69. *See* TRISTIN K. GREEN, DISCRIMINATION LAUNDERING: THE RISE OF ORGANIZATIONAL INNOCENCE AND THE CRISIS OF EQUAL OPPORTUNITY LAW 89–92 (2017) (discussing cases).
70. Katie Roiphe, *The Other Whisper Network: How Twitter Feminism Is Bad for Women*, HARPER'S MAGAZINE (Mar. 2018) (after describing her experience at *Harper's* in advance of the release of her essay, she asks: "With this level of thought policing, who in their right mind would try to say anything even mildly provocative or original?").
71. Jia Tolentino, *After the Kavanaugh Allegations, Republicans Offer a Shocking Defense: Sexual Assault Isn't a Big Deal*, NEW YORKER (Sept. 20, 2019), https://www.newyorker.com/news/our-columnists/after-the-kavanaugh-allegations-republicans-offer-a-shocking-defense-sexual-assault-isnt-a-big-deal.
72. SUSAN FALUDI, BACKLASH: THE UNDECLARED WAR AGAINST WOMEN (2006).
73. *See* Soohan Kim, Alexandra Kalev & Frank Dobbin, *Progressive Corporations at Work: The Case of Diversity at Work*, 36 N.Y.U. REV. L. & SOC. CHANGE 171, 182–88 (2012).
74. *See supra* notes 48–54 and accompanying text.

CHAPTER 16

FROM REPRODUCTIVE RIGHTS TO REPRODUCTIVE JUSTICE

Abortion in Constitutional Law and Politics

MARY ZIEGLER

REPRODUCTIVE justice involves "the human right to maintain personal bodily autonomy, have children, not have children, and parent ... children in safe and sustainable communities."[1] Since about 2010, calls for reproductive justice have energized feminist scholars and activists and captured broader public attention. Commentators have described it as a "model for progressive organizing"[2] and a "powerful vision for the future."[3] This movement has had a long and fraught relationship with the reproductive rights movement, however. The latter mobilized to guarantee the legal right to access such services as abortion and birth control. By tracing the history of these two parallel movements, this chapter illuminates the untapped potential of new reproductive justice strategies. Calls for reproductive justice can appeal to a broader and more diverse group of women, help destigmatize abortion, and improve public understanding of the complexity of decisions about reproduction.

But this history also exposes the potential obstacles facing the reproductive justice movement. Because abortion has become both a political wedge issue and a federal constitutional right, abortion rights advocates in the past dismissed reproductive justice claims as risky and unlikely to appeal to a broad enough audience. The constitutional trajectory of abortion rights also created obstacles to a productive partnership between reproductive rights and reproductive justice activists. Seeking to capitalize on existing legal precedent, the former favored a privacy-based framework that seemed most likely to work in the Supreme Court—a framework that made it harder to demand government support for patients and parents for whom freedom otherwise would be hollow.

Lessons from the history of these movements make a compelling case that these obstacles are not as daunting as they first appear. Reframing the abortion right as a matter of women's equality—a rationale that has gained prominence in recent decades—may eliminate some of the constitutional hurdles facing a reproductive justice approach. The political obstacles to such an approach may be just as surmountable, especially as demographic shifts and the evolution of the Democratic Party change the kinds of reproductive health demands play well at the polls. Understanding the history of the constitutional discourse concerning reproductive justice and reproductive rights may allow us to move beyond the impasse that has defined the relationship between the two for too long.

I. From Criminal Law to Reproductive Rights

In order to understand the movements for reproductive rights and reproductive justice, we must begin with the story of the American abortion debate. At the outset, the push to reform abortion laws had little to do with either rights or justice. In the early 1960s, state laws dating from the mid-to-late nineteenth century made it a crime to perform an abortion, with most states recognizing a narrow exception for when patients' lives would be at risk. For decades, despite periodic crackdowns and the looming threat of prosecution, doctors had still performed abortions. But by the 1960s, some physicians bridled at the legal status quo. As obstetric and gynecological care improved, it became harder for doctors to invoke the life-of-the-patient exception, and as a result, some doctors felt that there was a gap between what the law permitted and what good practice required.[4]

The early movement to change abortion laws, unsurprisingly, focused on patients' health. Physicians argued that some patients needed access to abortion to protect their mental, as well as physical, wellbeing. Indeed, one study of abortions performed at major hospitals found that physicians justified nearly half on psychiatric grounds.[5]

Health-based exceptions suggested that legal abortion should depend on the strength of the justification behind the woman's reason for needing an abortion. Reformers made similar arguments about abortion in cases of fetal abnormality. Reformers stressed that new abortion laws would prevent the births of severely disabled children. "Our present law prohibits abortion with the result that many infants are forced to suffer through their blighted lives, a burden to themselves, their parents, and society," argued Robert Force, the author of a proposed abortion-reform bill in Indiana.[6]

A movement to legalize abortion as a matter of reproductive rights took shape in part because of the shortcomings of reform. States began to pass laws based on the model introduced by the American Law Institute (ALI), which permitted abortions to be performed in licensed hospitals in cases of rape or incest, fetal abnormality, or to protect the woman's health, but the number of illegal abortions barely fell.[7] Those dissatisfied with the law demanded more meaningful change. At the same time, as feminists played a more prominent role in the reform movement, newly mobilized activists insisted that patients should have a right to abortion regardless of the woman's reasons for wanting one or the policy consequences of any single decision. Groups such as the National Organization for Women (NOW) and the Women's National Abortion Action Coalition framed abortion as a civil right for women—one that patients could exercise without having to justify themselves to anyone else. As Betty Friedan, a prominent member of the National Abortion Rights Action League (NARAL) and NOW, reasoned: "[T]here is no freedom, no equality, no full human dignity and personhood possible for women until we assert and demand the control over our own bodies, over our own reproductive process."[8]

Early calls for reproductive rights echoed ideas about what would later be called reproductive justice. Friedan, for example, positioned abortion as one of several choices that pregnant people should have in determining the course of their lives. "Am I saying that women must be liberated from motherhood? No, I am not," Friedan explained. "I am saying that motherhood will only be liberated to be a joyous and responsible human act when women are free to make with full conscious choice and full human responsibility the decision to be mothers."[9] Nevertheless, the movement for abortion rights focused overwhelmingly on a single issue—and on a strategy of securing constitutional rights.

This focus on rights intensified as the movement to change abortion law moved into the courts. Litigators took hope from a series of recent Supreme Court decisions on the right to privacy. In 1965, *Griswold v. Connecticut* struck down a law prohibiting married couples from using contraception.[10] And in 1972, the year before *Roe v. Wade*[11] was decided, the Court held in *Eisenstadt v. Baird* that "[i]f the right of privacy means anything, it is the right of the individual, married or single, to be free from unwarranted governmental intrusion into matters so fundamentally affecting a person as the decision whether to bear or beget a child."[12] State and federal courts in states from Connecticut to California recognized a privacy right that encompassed abortion as well as contraception.[13]

The Court's decision in *Roe* grounded reproductive rights in this newly recognized constitutional right to privacy. In *Roe*, the Court heard challenges to a Georgia version of the ALI model abortion reform law and a much more draconian Texas law banning all abortions unless a patient's life was at risk. By invalidating both laws, the Court wiped out most of the criminal abortion laws on the books. Under the Court's new framework, states could not regulate abortion at all in the first trimester; in the second trimester, the state could impose restrictions on abortion only if they advanced an interest in women's health; and by the third trimester, which the Court understood to coincide with viability, states could prohibit abortion altogether, with exceptions for the woman's life and health, in order to protect fetal life. In support of a constitutional right to abortion, the Court reasoned that the "right to privacy [was] broad enough to encompass a woman's decision whether or not to terminate her pregnancy."[14]

Although celebrated at the time by reproductive rights advocates, *Roe*'s framing created obstacles to later demands for reproductive justice. In defending an abortion right, the organized reproductive rights movement often borrowed from and reinforced

Roe's privacy rhetoric, both in litigation and in political engagement. But this idea of privacy made it harder for poor, often nonwhite women to be heard by those leading the fight to preserve *Roe*, especially when those women needed government support.

II. Early Calls for Reproductive Justice

To some women, including women of color, poor women, and socialist feminists, the existing reproductive rights framework increasingly appeared inadequate. By the mid-1970s, controversy about sterilization abuse fueled concerns that the idea of reproductive rights did not fully account for patients' needs and experiences. In earlier decades, compulsory eugenic sterilization laws had authorized forced surgery on patients deemed to be "feebleminded." In the South after World War II, these laws overwhelmingly affected poor Black women. A more subtle form of sterilization abuse also festered in Puerto Rico and the continental United States, where some patients were sterilized without informed consent and not knowing that tubal ligation was permanent. All lacked real alternatives, given that employers and bureaucrats neither funded nor destigmatized other options, including birth control. At the same time, wealthier, often white women who pursued sterilization found themselves refused.[15]

The tension between those who viewed sterilization as a right—who often prioritized access to the procedure—and victims of sterilization abuse came to the fore in the mid-1970s, when the Department of Health, Education, and Welfare proposed new regulations for informed consent to sterilization. Many champions of reproductive rights, including NOW and the Planned Parenthood Federation of America, opposed the regulations, arguing that they would deny patients autonomy. Other reproductive rights supporters worried that abortion foes would use the sterilization abuse scandal to demand more onerous restrictions on consent to abortion. Planned Parenthood's position was illustrative. Faye Wattleton, the group's new head, endorsed the proposed federal regulations but suggested that the pendulum might have swung too far in the direction of regulation. "People have the right to decide to be sterilized," she reasoned.[16]

Feminists of color bristled at this response. First, such activists as Helen Rodríguez-Trías blamed reproductive rights groups for prioritizing *Roe* over equally important reproductive issues, sterilization first among them. As important, the sterilization-abuse scandal suggested that a reproductive rights framework based on a theory of privacy and freedom of choice could not capture the needs of patients who required support and not merely liberty from the government. In 1974, Rodríguez-Trías and like-minded activists formed the Committee to End Sterilization Abuse to champion this perspective on reproductive justice.[17]

Skepticism of the reproductive rights agenda grew after the passage of the Hyde Amendment, a federal ban on Medicaid reimbursement for abortion. Abortion opponents had promoted bans on the use of public dollars and facilities since before *Roe*, but for such anti-abortion groups as the National Right to Life Committee (NRLC), these laws took on new importance in the 1970s. At first, opposition to *Roe* had focused on amending the Constitution to define a fetus as a person for the purpose of the Fourteenth Amendment. If the Constitution recognized fetal personhood, virtually all abortions would be criminal in every state, including those performed by private citizens. But the constitutional amendment campaign had stalled, and leading anti-abortion groups such as the NRLC looked for ways to make abortions harder to obtain in the near term. A Medicaid ban seemed to be an especially effective weapon: Roy White of the NRLC estimated that there would be nearly half a million fewer abortions if patients did not receive reimbursement for ending pregnancies.[18]

White may have underestimated the success that funding bans would have. States and cities passed their own measures before Congress introduced the Hyde Amendment in 1976 as a rider to an appropriations bill for the Department of Health, Education, and Welfare. The following year, the Supreme Court upheld a Connecticut funding ban in *Maher v. Roe*,[19] raising questions about the efficacy of reproductive rights as a framework for protecting women's reproductive choices. The regulations in dispute in *Maher* prohibited state Medicaid reimbursement for elective procedures. The feminist attorneys challenging the law did not argue that women had a right to funded abortions. *Roe* did not support such a demand, and in recent years the Court had not looked favorably on claims that the Constitution entitled anyone to government support for exercising their constitutional rights. Instead, those challenging the regulation argued that if the state chose to fund any reproductive services, such as childbirth, the Equal Protection Clause required that abortion, a fundamental right, be funded on an equal basis. Conspicuously absent from the brief was any reference to sex discrimination under the Equal Protection Clause, in part because *Roe* had not leaned on these ideas. Instead, these attorneys relied on the fundamental rights branch of equal protection analysis and argued that the Court should look below the surface of a law to its real-world effects. Lucy Katz and Catherine Roraback of the Planned Parenthood League of Connecticut suggested that such laws should be unconstitutional if they unduly burdened women's access to abortion.[20]

The Court rejected these arguments, adopting a very different definition of an undue burden. *Maher* reiterated that abortion was a privacy right, one that at most entitled patients to be left alone. If the government did not itself create an obstacle facing a patient, the Court explained, there was no constitutional problem. "An indigent woman who desires an abortion suffers no disadvantage as a consequence of Connecticut's decision to fund childbirth," the Court reasoned. "[S]he continues as before to be dependent on private sources for the service she desires." The Court later rejected a challenge to the Hyde Amendment in an even more draconian decision. Whereas Connecticut's law funded medically necessary abortions, the Hyde Amendment did not. The Supreme Court found no distinction. Patients who could not afford the cost had no right to access abortion.[21]

Despite the harsh impact of the Hyde Amendment and the Court's decision in *Maher*, abortion rights groups such as Planned Parenthood and NARAL prioritized the fight against a long-shot anti-abortion constitutional amendment over restoring funding of abortion services for low-income women. Movement leaders believed that the Supreme Court might still invalidate the Hyde rider, *Maher* aside. The reasons for de-emphasizing the Hyde Amendment were also tactical: Groups such as NARAL struggled to raise money to support broadening women's access to abortion, while threats of abortion bans easily got donors to open their pocketbooks. Poor women, women of color, and socialist feminists felt that abortion funding—an issue of more importance to them—had been given short shrift. Moreover, *Maher* showed that constitutional rights might have done little to help women who needed government support to have any meaningful right to choose.[22]

These two blows, the rift concerning sterilization regulation and the persistence of abortion funding restrictions, inspired the formation of the Committee for Abortion Rights and Against Sterilization Abuse (CARASA), a group founded in New York but later active nationwide. While emphasizing the Hyde Amendment, CARASA focused not only on abortion rights and sterilization abuse but also on birth control, workplace safety, childcare, and healthcare. Founded in 1975, the National Women's Health Network (NWHN) also placed abortion rights in the context of a broader agenda. In a 1978 position paper the group argued that abortion was "inextricably intertwined with a number of issues," including "sterilization abuse" and "childcare services and pregnancy disability rights."[23]

But the kind of reproductive justice framework defended by NWHN and CARASA did not catch on with established reproductive rights groups, especially those that viewed elective politics as their movement's future. In the late 1970s, anti-abortion groups boasted that they had made a difference in key midterm Senate races, unseating Democratic incumbents. The Life Amendment Political Action Committee, an anti-abortion PAC, claimed credit for the result, as did several state PACs affiliated with the NRLC. Leaders of NARAL and Planned Parenthood concluded that pro-lifers had cowed politicians into believing that they could not afford strong support for abortion rights.[24]

Consequently, NARAL settled on a message designed to appeal to ambivalent voters. Rather than advocating for a broad reproductive justice agenda or even mentioning the word "abortion," NARAL described itself as pro-choice and emphasized the evils of government interference. Other mainstream reproductive rights groups followed suit. Nevertheless, ideas about reproductive justice articulated by those in groups such as CARASA and the Reproductive Rights National Network continued to take root and inspire debate in the decades to come.[25]

III. THE PULL OF REPRODUCTIVE RIGHTS IN THE 1980S

By the mid-1980s, mainstream reproductive rights groups at times recognized the objections made by many nonwhite feminists to a framework centered on choice and privacy. But any efforts to broaden their agenda quickly faltered. First, when groups such as NARAL tried to focus on access to abortion—which disproportionately affected poor nonwhite, young, and rural women—fundraising streams dried up. Voters and donors seemed energized by the possibility that abortion would once again be criminalized, but apparently were unmoved by restrictions on access that hit poor women the hardest. And yet by 1983 the anti-abortion amendment pushed by opponents of *Roe* for nearly a decade seemed to be a lost cause.[26]

Reproductive rights groups reconsidered how to define their cause if there was no longer an imminent threat to the legality of abortion. Ideas tied to reproductive justice provided one compelling answer. These ideas gained in prominence as feminists of color launched new groups that explicitly demanded a more comprehensive reproductive justice agenda. In 1984, Lillie Allen and Byllye Avery founded the National Black Women's Health Project to advocate for a bolder vision of reproductive health activism. The early membership was divided about the abortion issue and continued to pursue a broader agenda even after participating in the 1986 March for Women's Lives, a pro-choice rally. The National Latina Health Organization, founded in 1986, similarly fought not only for legal abortion but also for "access to quality education [and] the right to jobs that are environmentally safe and afford us the economic means for good, safe housing."[27] The emergence of these new groups exposed a weakness of reproductive rights organizations, which remained overwhelmingly white. Such groups as NARAL and NOW recognized that they needed to do more to appeal to feminists of color and considered reframing their agenda to attract a more diverse base of support. At that time the reproductive rights movement felt comfortable pursuing a broader agenda because the threat to abortion seemed less immediate. Its rulings on abortion funding notwithstanding, the Supreme Court showed no interest in overturning *Roe*, and Congress had proved unable to pass an anti-abortion amendment.[28]

One indication of how a broader reproductive justice agenda was beginning to influence the reproductive rights movement was in its response to anti-abortion propaganda. The typical reproductive rights arguments had failed to defuse the opposition's arguments about a right to life, which were gaining cultural traction in a new, widely watched film. The NRLC and other pro-life groups rallied around a film called *The Silent Scream*, which claimed to depict ultrasound footage of a first-trimester abortion in real time. Bernard Nathanson, a former founder of NARAL who had converted to the pro-life cause, narrated the film, claiming that it provided evidence of fetal pain caused by abortion. At first, reproductive rights groups had focused on inaccuracies in the film, which they labeled misleading and emotionally manipulative. But these arguments did not appear to dent the momentum of the film. Instead, in a sign of the growing influence of the ideas pressed by reproductive justice activists, some reproductive rights supporters looked to illuminate the experiences of real women, many of whom wanted to speak to issues beyond abortion.[29]

In the mid-1980s, NARAL and Planned Parenthood launched Silent No More, a campaign that drew heavily on emerging ideas of reproductive justice. The vision for the campaign grew from a weekend of strategizing at which attendees agreed on the importance of finding a framework that went beyond *Roe v. Wade*. The framers of the campaign recognized that women cared not only about abortion access but also about "prenatal care, childcare, supportive services for the disabled, [and] education."[30] They realized that "different classes, races, and disabled women" had different needs when it came to reproductive health.[31] They invited letters from individuals and families who had benefited from abortion. The letters illustrated how abortion fit into a broader reproductive health agenda. Silent No More showcased the ways in which "choice" was an illusion for women who lacked the resources to raise the children they had (or the children they wanted). Nevertheless, because all of these issues were still packaged as arguments to support abortion rights, the campaign ultimately revealed the obstacles facing a reproductive justice approach. These arguments, albeit nominally looping in reproductive issues beyond abortion, still served primarily as a tool to preserve abortion rights. Although NARAL purported to make room for arguments about other issues, Silent No More still remained a primarily single-issue campaign.[32]

These tensions only deepened as the threat to abortion grew. As the decade advanced, concerns about voter preferences and the Supreme Court undermined any interest that reproductive rights leaders had in a broader justice framework. Abortion rights did not yet appear to be under an existential threat, but ominous signs loomed. In 1986, the Supreme Court struck down a major multi-restriction abortion law in *Thornburgh v. American Obstetricians and Gynecologists*, with four Justices dissenting—the most since the Court had decided *Roe*. The following year, Lewis Powell, one of the Justices who had joined the *Roe* majority, retired. Ronald Reagan, who defined himself as a strongly pro-life president, not only replaced Powell but also named several new Supreme Court Justices.

These nominations left their mark on the Court. By 1989 the existential threat had appeared: The Court openly questioned whether *Roe* should be overturned. In a closely watched case decided that year, *Webster v. Reproductive Health Services*, the Court upheld most of a disputed abortion law. The most revealing part of the Court's opinion addressed a measure that defined fetal viability and prescribed steps physicians needed to take if they suspected fetal viability. This provision conflicted with *Roe* because it did not allow physicians to decide for themselves when viability occurred. For the *Webster* Court, any tension with its present ruling exposed problems with *Roe*. Most ominously, a plurality of four Justices criticized *Roe*'s trimester framework for valuing the government's interest in fetal life only after viability—and for requiring legislators to keep up with ever-changing medical rules. Many Court watchers predicted that the Justices would reverse *Roe* within a matter of years.[33]

With the apparent loss of the Supreme Court, reproductive rights leaders set aside demands for reproductive justice in favor of what they believed to be a strategy with the broadest popular appeal. In part, such groups as NARAL believed that a broader agenda would alienate swing voters who did not care much about reproductive issues but resented the idea of big government, even when it came to abortion. Reproductive rights organizers, as NARAL leader Kate Michelman wrote, looked for "evidence of numbers and [a] potential pro-choice majority."[34] Armed with proof of a pro-choice majority, NARAL and others could pressure lawmakers to pass the federal Freedom of Choice Act, which would have codified a liberty right to end a pregnancy. And by proving that most Americans favored legal abortion, reproductive rights supporters hoped to create "a political climate in which it is unacceptable to erode or overrule *Roe*."[35] Reproductive justice claims, NARAL worried, would alienate the white moderate voters that they wanted to persuade. Hickman-Maslin Research, a consultant and pollster that worked with NARAL, explained: "Remember, there are millions of people who agree with us about the basic issue of CHOICE who may not agree on any other issue, including those we may assume are inter-related, i.e., civil rights, feminism, labor issues, etc."[36]

Further dimming the prospect of a convergence, the turn to politics to secure the constitutional right to abortion came at a time when reproductive rights groups sought to professionalize and coordinate their political operations. Focus groups, polls, and political consultants became a staple of this work. Top-down, election-centered organizing relied on strategies thought to appeal to wavering politicians. Reproductive justice strategies, which were more grassroots and seemed more ambitious and visionary, struck movement pragmatists as unwise. This calculation might have been right in the short term: Democrats would win both the White House and Congress in 1992. But these short-term gains came at considerable cost: the ongoing alienation of women of color and the further stigmatization of abortion itself.

IV. THE 1990S RESURGENCE OF REPRODUCTIVE JUSTICE AND A BROADER EMPHASIS ON WOMEN'S HEALTH

In 1992 in *Planned Parenthood of Southeastern Pennsylvania v. Casey*,[37] the Supreme Court defied expectations and declined to reverse *Roe*. With that landmark decision, the fortunes of the movements for reproductive justice and reproductive rights changed again. *Casey* seemed to put abortion rights on more secure footing, at least for the time being, allowing reproductive rights groups to consider a broader agenda. But *Casey* also produced additional roadblocks to arguments for reproductive justice. The Court set aside *Roe*'s trimester framework in favor of an undue burden test, which asked whether a law had the purpose or effect of creating a substantial obstacle for women pursuing abortion. Any restriction short of an undue burden is constitutional. *Casey* suggested that cost and travel distance—factors that could be insurmountable for poor women— did not count as undue burdens. The test, it seemed, adopted the perspective of privileged women.[38]

Yet reproductive rights groups had political as well as legal reasons to pursue a broader agenda. Following his successful run for the White House, Bill Clinton promoted national healthcare reform. Reproductive rights groups fought for inclusion of abortion in the healthcare bill, framing abortion as part of a comprehensive reproductive health agenda. At the same time, reproductive justice organizers pushed for a more comprehensive approach to supporting women's health. Following the 1994 United Nations Conference on World Population, Black feminists took issue with what they saw as reproductive rights groups' neglect of the interests of patients of color. In 1997, these groups formulated a new agenda, founding the SisterSong Reproductive Justice Collective. From the outset, SisterSong adopted a broad agenda, touching on issues from HIV/AIDS to cancer screenings, drug and alcohol treatment, contraception and abortion, and the treatment of sexually transmitted diseases.[39]

But a resurgent anti-abortion movement once again heightened tensions between the movements for reproductive rights and reproductive justice. It might have been hard to predict how quickly the anti-abortion movement would rebound after several devastating setbacks. When extremists murdered several abortion doctors in the mid-1990s, Americans questioned whether this movement as a whole was misogynistic or violent. At the same time, larger anti-abortion groups had hitched their wagon to the Republican Party, and that party was out of power. For the first time since *Roe* came down, a pro-choice president vowed to undo some of the steps taken by Ronald Reagan and George H.W. Bush. The anti-abortion movement was also reeling from the *Casey* decision, which dashed their hopes for the imminent overruling of *Roe*. In order to reestablish their relevance, such organizations as Americans United for Life and the NRLC changed their tactical plan: Rather than focusing on fetal rights, abortion foes would stress claims that abortion hurt women. Americans United for Life believed that these claims would undermine the foundation of abortion rights. After all, *Casey* had preserved those rights in part because the Justices believed that women relied on abortion to lead more equal lives. If abortion foes persuaded voters and the Court that abortion was bad for women, then the Justices might rethink their decision to preserve *Roe*.[40]

Arguments that abortion hurt women opened another front in the abortion wars. Reproductive rights groups found themselves on the defensive as they confronted laws requiring doctors to warn women about what abortion foes described as the risk of the procedure. Other new laws adopted targeted regulation of abortion providers (known as TRAP laws), making it expensive or impossible for clinics to operate. Recently founded anti-abortion groups such as the Elliott Institute published studies claiming to document harm done by abortion. Independent anti-abortion researchers such as Joel Brind publicized what they saw as compelling proof of a connection between abortion and breast cancer. When existing research did not support their findings, abortion opponents could simply assert that the matter was uncertain—or that the medical establishment buried the truth for political reasons. Battling these laws required reproductive rights groups to educate lawmakers and judges about technical or scientific questions. Reproductive rights leaders again prioritized abortion at the expense of a broader agenda.[41]

This narrow focus came into view during fights about a ban on a procedure that anti-abortion leaders labeled "partial-birth abortion." Abortion foes got hold of a paper given at the annual conference of the National Abortion Federation by Martin Haskell about a specific abortion technique, dilation and extraction (D&X), describing the procedure in graphic terms. Minnesota activists published a piece denouncing the technique, complete with line drawings of it. When Republicans took control of the House of Representatives in 1994, the NRLC championed a law banning the procedure. Debate about the ban dragged on for years before George W. Bush signed a prohibition into law in 2003.[42]

In their opposition to the law, reproductive rights organizers fell back on well-worn arguments about constitutional liberty. They had initially focused their arguments on the lack of an exception for patients' health. Drawing on their recent arguments about scientific uncertainty, however, anti-abortion groups insisted that D&X was never needed to protect patients' health or fertility, and in fact itself created health risks. In order to answer these objections, reproductive rights groups appealed to the kind of abstract ideas about privacy and choice that seemed likely to win over the same ambivalent voters who might otherwise favor a ban on the gruesome-sounding procedure. The National Abortion Rights Action League launched a media campaign, Choice for America, that labeled choice a fundamental value, like freedom of speech, that all Americans embraced. Reproductive rights groups had their hands full fighting a partial-birth abortion ban and did not commit resources to a broader reproductive justice agenda. At the same time, they worried that a broader agenda would distract from choice arguments that they believed could help defeat these laws.[43]

When the Supreme Court took up the D&X bans, it eventually signaled a weakened commitment to abortion rights that only deepened mainstream reproductive rights groups' commitment to a conventional strategy. Initially, the Court sided against supporters of a law banning the procedure. In 2000, the Court invalidated Nebraska's so-called partial-birth abortion law, emphasizing that it was impermissibly vague, swept in dilation and evacuation (the most common procedure performed after the first trimester), and lacked a necessary health exception.[44] But just seven years later, in *Gonzales v. Carhart*, the Court upheld the federal Partial-Birth Abortion Ban Act. The Court described D&X in graphic detail, quoting in full the testimony of an anti-abortion witness. *Gonzales* seemed to embrace new justifications for abortion restrictions, such as concerns about the dignity of human life, the reputation of abortion providers, and the regret women would presumably experience after choosing an abortion they did not fully understand.[45]

The Court sent a similarly unsettling message in its discussion of scientific uncertainty. Reproductive rights lawyers argued that the Act violated the Constitution because it lacked a health exception. Congress had responded with findings that claimed to show no medical need for D&X. The Court sided with Congress, giving "state and federal legislatures wide discretion to pass legislation in areas where there is medical and scientific uncertainty."[46] *Gonzales* did not explain how to define scientific uncertainty, but given the dubiousness of Congress' conclusions, establishing uncertainty did not seem very hard. *Gonzales* put abortion rights on a less firm foundation. The Court suggested that the undue-burden standard required legislators to defer to legislators—an approach likely to uphold most abortion restrictions. Supporters of reproductive rights once again felt compelled to prioritize abortion.[47]

Reproductive justice organizers, meanwhile, continued to pursue their own agenda. Groups including the Black Women's Health Imperative and the National Latina Institute for Reproductive Health organized the 2004 March for Women's Lives, rejecting the original framing of March for Choice. On the heels of the march, reproductive justice advocates published two compelling overviews of the theory and practice of their movement, seeking to convince reproductive rights activists to place a greater focus on the intersectional harms suffered by women of different races, income levels, disabilities, and experiences. In 2005, with the help of SisterSong, Asian Communities for Reproductive Justice published a position paper explaining the need for "comprehensive strategies that push against the structural and societal conditions that control our communities by regulating our bodies, sexuality, and reproduction."[48] The group mapped out a campaign to tackle not only abortion restrictions but also bias against queer and transgendered patients in the healthcare system, unsafe personal care products for women, violence against women, discrimination against immigrants, and substandard conditions for undocumented workers. The following year, working with the Center for American Progress, the Women's Health Leadership Network brought out More Than a Choice, an effort to introduce reproductive justice concepts more broadly and explain how to implement them. More Than a Choice explicitly tackled the shortcomings of liberty as an animating principle for the movement. "It is not sufficient for the government to simply acknowledge particular rights and then refrain from interfering with them," the report explained.[49] "The progressive view demands that the government remove regulatory obstacles, protect people from interference by private individuals and institutions, and provide concrete supports."[50]

As reproductive justice advocates realized, an equality framework might have made it easier to fuse their perspective with that of reproductive rights supporters. The latter had fought for decades to preserve *Roe* and *Casey*, decisions rooted in concerns about autonomy. Reproductive justice advocates recognized that arguments about equality made more sense as a tool to ask for more than freedom from the government. Had *Roe* relied on a different doctrinal framework, the tensions between reproductive rights and reproductive justice might not have run so high. But because the former was committed to defending *Roe*, they often pursued a narrower agenda.

V. Abortion, Justice, and the Affordable Care Act

Between 2008 and 2013, national political developments created new opportunities for reproductive rights groups to incorporate reproductive justice concepts into their agenda. Barack Obama's election in 2008, together with a new focus on national healthcare reform, drew fresh attention to the question of what an ideal healthcare agenda required. As had been the case in earlier decades, anti-abortion groups mobilized to argue that abortion was not a form of healthcare and should not be covered by any reform that Obama proposed. Reproductive justice organizers mobilized communities of color to support both healthcare reform and abortion coverage and conducted research to show that communities of color supported legal abortion as part of a comprehensive package of reproductive justice services and to devise strategies for how to talk about abortion with Black, Latinx, and younger respondents. While debate about the Affordable Care Act (ACA) raged on, reproductive justice groups branched off from established reproductive rights groups to undertake their own abortion campaigns, mobilizing the Latinx community against personhood proposals and taking the lead in fighting laws that banned abortions for reasons of race. For example, SisterSong spearheaded a campaign opposing anti-abortion billboards erected in Atlanta, Georgia, that portrayed abortion as a racist conspiracy to limit Black population growth. Loretta Ross of SisterSong insisted that Black women wanted access to abortion (and to other reproductive health services) to make the best decisions for themselves and their families. "Controlling our fertility was part of our uplift out of poverty strategy, and it still works," she explained.[51]

The ACA eventually passed following a compromise on the abortion issue. President Obama signed an executive order barring federal funding of abortion under the ACA but allowing women to purchase abortion coverage through the exchanges. The compromise did not satisfy hardcore abortion opponents and contributed to a backlash against the ACA. This time, the backlash would help bring reproductive justice and reproductive rights groups closer together.

Leading the backlash was a purportedly grassroots Tea Party consisting of older, white, middle-class Americans who resented what they saw as unfair advantages given to immigrants, people of color, and the young. The GOP leaders sponsored Tea Party protests in order to strengthen opposition to the ACA, though they had diametrically opposed preferences with regard to some issues, such as Social Security and Medicare. Despite their policy differences, the Tea Party's show of strength in the 2010 midterm elections bolstered its influence in the GOP leadership ranks. Tea party activists and GOP leaders did agree wholeheartedly on one issue: opposition to abortion. Although it had not been a central election issue, the new Tea Party Republicans almost universally favored abortion restrictions or outright bans. The first wave of new restrictions focused on laws that prohibited new insurance exchanges created by the ACA from covering abortion. In this political climate, reproductive rights groups recognized the importance of establishing that abortion was a valuable health service—and part of a comprehensive healthcare agenda rather than a standalone issue.[52]

The battle over a contraceptive mandate in the ACA likewise energized supporters of reproductive justice and created common ground with reproductive rights leaders. In 2011, the Obama administration added eighteen forms of female contraception to the list of preventative services made available under the ACA without a co-pay. Efforts to restrict contraceptive coverage quickly followed. Initially, the contraceptive mandate exempted churches but not religious nonprofit businesses. Citing faith-based objections, some religious employers pressed to broaden the exemption, refusing to subsidize what they saw as abortion-inducing drugs, including the birth control pill and the morning-after pill, as well as intrauterine devices. Reproductive justice activists resisted the move and illuminated connections between opposition to abortion and contraception.[53]

As with abortion, backlash to the contraceptive mandate centered on claims about conscience and religious liberty. Religious liberty arguments obviously had intersectional impact; religious conservatives invoked these claims not only in refusing to provide or pay for abortion or birth control but also in denying services to same-sex couples, LGBTQ+ individuals seeking healthcare, adoption, or other services.[54] The potential reach of religious objections united reproductive justice and reproductive rights leaders against a common enemy.

Nevertheless, tensions between the two movements remained. Conflict between them resurfaced in 2011, when Mississippi proposed a personhood amendment to its state constitution that would ban all abortions in the state and potentially criminalize certain contraceptives and assisted reproductive technologies. At the same time, the state also promoted a voter identification law opposed by SisterSong members, who saw the latter as a way to limit the electoral influence of Black voters, especially women. Planned Parenthood steered clear of any claimed connection between personhood and the voter identification bill, insisting that voters who backed the identification bill could be won over to the pro-choice side with regard to personhood. Whereas the personhood amendment did not prevail, voter identification passed. Feminists of color viewed it as a betrayal. By failing to see the issues in intersectional terms and not fighting for access to the vote for women of color, Planned Parenthood had made it easier for anti-abortion activists to pass new restrictions.[55]

Eventually, battles such as the personhood debacle began to convince Planned Parenthood, NOW, NARAL, and others to distance themselves from the language of choice. Persuaded by the demands of a new generation of activists, many in the reproductive rights movement now realized that a choice framework ignored the needs of poor women and inadvertently stigmatized abortion by making it seem private and shameful. It was becoming clear that the short-term gains made by sidelining reproductive justice demands had been costly, making abortion a dirty word and convincing many women of color that the movement did not represent them. Even after adopting the rhetoric of reproductive justice, groups such as Planned Parenthood did not initially credit women of color for developing a more comprehensive framework for reproductive health. Monica Simpson of SisterSong and other movement leaders wrote an open letter to Planned Parenthood criticizing the organization for adopting the language of reproductive justice without acknowledging their debt to women of color. The letter had a positive impact: Planned Parenthood and SisterSong leaders deepened their collaboration, with SisterSong leading trainings on reproductive justice at Planned Parenthood clinics while referring patients to Planned Parenthood for a range of services.[56]

This collaboration continued following the election of Donald Trump and the creation of what seemed to be a more conservative Supreme Court majority. In Georgia, for example, SisterSong worked with the Center for Reproductive Rights and similar groups to challenge a new law banning abortion at six weeks. The suit would spotlight the way abortion bans not only imposed special injuries on people of color and trans men but also undermined the ability of reproductive justice organizations to pursue other changes by consuming their already limited resources.[57]

At the time of this writing, reproductive justice organizations, arguments, and strategies enjoy unprecedented prominence, in traditional reproductive rights organizations and elsewhere. At law schools and on college campuses, the idea of reproductive justice serves as a prominent organizing principle for students seeking to change the way law and society treat both reproduction and social justice. Yet the history of the parallel movements for reproductive rights and reproductive justice shows the obstacles that may once again face those seeking the latter.

VI. Future Promise, Future Hurdles

Reproductive justice arguments hold great promise for expanding women's ability to control their reproductive lives. Limits on abortion, contraception, or other health services affect all women, and a rights-centered message has alienated those who require more than freedom from government to lead the lives they want. A reproductive justice framework can mobilize a much larger, more diverse group of activists. The long history of the reproductive rights movement shows that the women and pregnant people most affected by restrictions on abortion, limits on contraception, and lack of access to health services are the very people for whom ideas of rights, choice, and privacy seem the most hollow. Reproductive justice arguments illuminate the real-world effects of laws regulating reproduction.

At the same time, the history of these movements foreshadows future challenges that reproductive justice leaders may confront. Abortion is unique in that it has become a major (and at times defining) election issue. Historically, reproductive rights groups have bent to pressure to frame their cause in a way that would maximize either the support of voters or the commitment of wavering politicians. And reproductive rights supporters have often rallied around the Supreme Court's framing of the right, one based on privacy, in a bid to save *Roe*, rather than using an equality approach that might have allowed for a more productive conversation about reproductive justice.

Neither of these pressures need inevitably undermine the momentum of the reproductive justice movement. After all, some politicians understand the value of reproductive justice strategies and would support organizations that champion the cause. Their leaders have persuasively argued that voters care deeply about reproductive justice and may be more likely to turn out if the cause is framed in a more resonant way. Moreover, as the Supreme Court seemingly retreats from *Roe* and its progeny, reproductive rights lawyers can work with a fresher slate, promoting an equality framework and even weaving it into arguments under the undue burden test to highlight the greater burdens placed on some groups of women.[58] Scholars have also spotlighted the interplay between the Due Process and Equal Protection Clauses, suggesting that denying patients access to care involves a denial of autonomy, equality, and dignity. These claims speak to reproductive justice activists concerned about specific kinds of discrimination, such as bias based on race, gender identity, sexual orientation, or economic class. But challenges remain. Attorneys often anchor their claims in precedent, which tends to use more conventional ideas about reproductive rights. And when the courts move to the right, as they have since 2016, lawyers often search out arguments most likely to work with conservative judges. Reproductive justice arguments may once again strike some reproductive rights leaders as unrealistic and insufficiently pragmatic.

The reproductive justice movement has grown up at a time when abortion has upended American law and politics. For decades, the reproductive rights movement was at odds with proponents of reproductive justice, believing that a more comprehensive agenda would jeopardize wins in the Court and on election day. But the recent history of the abortion wars suggests that the dichotomy between a principled commitment to reproductive justice and pragmatism might have been a false one all along. A commitment to reproductive justice might help solidify the base that backs access to abortion—and to finally undo the stigma surrounding the procedure.

NOTES

1. SisterSong, REPRODUCTIVE JUSTICE, https://www.sistersong.net/reproductive-justice (last visited Oct. 19, 2020).
2. Elissa Slattery, *How Reproductive Justice Serves as Model for Progressive Organizing*, OPEN SOCIETY FOUNDATIONS (Jun. 23, 2017), https://www.opensocietyfoundations.org/voices/how-reproductive-justice-serves-model-progressive-organizing.
3. Kiersten Gillette-Pierce, *New Reproductive Justice Guide Is a Powerful Vision for the Future*, REWIRE NEWS GROUP (Apr. 3, 2017, 12:07 PM), https://rewirenewsgroup.com/article/2017/04/03/reproductive-justice-guide-powerful-vision-future/.
4. *See* LESLIE J. REAGAN, WHEN ABORTION WAS A CRIME: WOMEN, MEDICINE, AND THE LAW IN THE UNITED STATES, 1867–1973, 10–25 (1997); KRISTIN LUKER, ABORTION AND THE POLITICS OF MOTHERHOOD 192 (1984).
5. *See* Lawrence Lader, *The Scandal of Abortion Laws*, N.Y. TIMES (Apr. 25, 1965), at SM32; C. Lee Buxton, *One Doctor's Opinion of Abortion*, 68 AM. J. NURSING 1026, 1026–28 (1968); Herbert Packer & Ralph Gampell, *Therapeutic Abortion: A Problem in Law and Medicine*, 11 STAN. L. REV. 417, 417–59 (1959).
6. Robert Force, *Legal Problems of Abortion Reform*, 19 ADMIN. L. REV. 364, 371–72 (1967); *see also* LESLIE J. REAGAN, DANGEROUS PREGNANCIES: MOTHERS, DISABILITIES, AND ABORTION IN MODERN AMERICA 60–63 (2010).
7. *See*, e.g., Keith Monroe, *How California's Abortion Law Isn't Working*, N.Y. TIMES (Dec. 29, 1968), at SM10; *see also* Martin Tolchin, *Doctors Divided on Issue*, N.Y. TIMES (Feb. 27, 1967), at 1.
8. Betty Friedan, ADDRESS AT THE FIRST NATIONAL CONFERENCE ON ABORTION LAWS: ABORTION; A WOMAN'S CIVIL RIGHT (Feb. 1969) (on file with the author); *see also* Linda Greenhouse, *Constitutional Question: Is There a Right to Abortion?* N.Y. TIMES (Jan. 25, 1970), at SM30.
9. *See* Friedan, Address, *supra* note 8, at 1–4.

10. Griswold v. Connecticut, 381 U.S. 479, 485–86 (1965).
11. 410 U.S. 113 (1973).
12. Eisenstadt v. Baird, 405 U.S. 438, 446–55 (1972).
13. *See* DAVID GARROW, LIBERTY AND SEXUALITY: THE RIGHT TO PRIVACY AND THE MAKING OF *ROE V. WADE* 529–90 (1998).
14. Roe v. Wade, 410 U.S. 113, 153 (1973).
15. *See* LAURA BRIGGS, REPRODUCING EMPIRE: RACE, SEX, SCIENCE AND U.S. IMPERIALISM IN PUERTO RICO 147–50 (2003); REBECCA KLUCHIN, FIT TO BE TIED: STERILIZATION AND REPRODUCTIVE RIGHTS IN AMERICA, 1950–1980 90–94 (2011); JOHANNA SCHOEN, FROM CHOICE TO COERCION: BIRTH CONTROL, STERILIZATION, AND ABORTION IN PUBLIC HEALTH AND WELFARE (2005).
16. *See* Judy Klemesrud, *Planned Parenthood's New Head Takes a Fighting Stand*, N.Y. TIMES (Feb. 3, 1978), https://www.nytimes.com/1978/02/03/archives/planned-parenthoods-new-head-takes-a-fighting-stand-watchdog.html.
17. *See* KLUCHIN, FIT TO BE TIED, at *supra* note 15, 186–87.
18. *See* MARY ZIEGLER, AFTER ROE: THE LOST HISTORY OF THE ABORTION DEBATE 35–65 (2015).
19. Maher v. Roe, 432 U.S. 464 (1977).
20. *See* Brief of the Appellees, at 13–15, Maher v. Roe, 432 U.S. 464 (1977) (No. 75-1440).
21. Maher, 432 U.S., at 473–74. *See also* Harris v. McRae, 448 U.S. 297 (1980).
22. *See* MARY ZIEGLER, ABORTION AND THE LAW IN AMERICA: ROE V. WADE TO THE PRESENT 30–53 (2020).
23. Position Paper on Abortion Adopted by the National Women's Health Network Board (Jun. 4, 1978) (1–2, in THE BARBARA SEAMAN PAPERS, Box 3, Folder 142); *see also* JENNIFER NELSON, WOMEN OF COLOR AND THE REPRODUCTIVE RIGHTS MOVEMENT 138–47 (2003).
24. *See* Ziegler, After *Roe, supra* note 18, at 62–76.
25. *See id.* at 139-145.
26. *See id.* at 71–72.
27. JAEL SILLIMAN, MARLENE GERBER FRIED, ELENA GUTIÉRREZ, & LORETTA ROSS, UNDIVIDED RIGHTS: WOMEN OF COLOR ORGANIZE FOR REPRODUCTIVE JUSTICE 250 (2d ed., 2016).
28. *See id.* at 61-62.
29. *See* SARA DUBOW, OURSELVES UNBORN: A HISTORY OF THE FETUS IN MODERN AMERICA 156–61 (2010); JOHANNA SCHOEN, Abortion after *Roe* 145–51 (2015).
30. *See* NARAL Strategy Weekend Second Day Session (Mar. 1985) (on file with the Schlesinger Library, Harvard University, The NARAL Papers, Box 185, Folder 5).
31. *Id.*
32. *See* ZIEGLER, AFTER *ROE*, *supra* note 18, at 80–82.
33. *See* ZIEGLER, ABORTION AND THE LAW, *supra* note 22, at 100–110.
34. *See* NARAL Agenda (Mar. 8, 1989) (on file with the Schlesinger Library, Harvard University, The NARAL Papers, Box 204, Folder 8).
35. *See id.*
36. Letter from Hickman-Maslin Research to NARAL, *Re: Do's and Don'ts* (Mar. 22, 1989) (on file with the Schlesinger Library, Harvard University, The NARAL Papers, Box 204, Folder 9).
37. Planned Parenthood v. Casey, 505 U.S. 833 (1992) (plurality opinion).
38. *See id.* at 857–89.
39. *See* LORETTA ROSS & RICKIE SOLINGER, REPRODUCTIVE JUSTICE: AN INTRODUCTION 60 (2017).

40. *See* ZIEGLER, AFTER *ROE*, *supra* note 18, at 139–68.
41. For a sample of the Elliot Institute's work, *see Post-Abortion Trauma: Learning the Truth, Telling the Truth*, The Elliot Institute (n.d., ca. 1993) (on file with Bingham Library, Duke University, The National Coalition of Abortion Providers Papers, Box 3, Elliot Institute Folder); David C. Reardon, *The Abortion Suicide Connection*, THE POST-ABORTION REVIEW (Summer 1993) (*id.*); David C. Reardon, *JAMA Gymnastics: Jumping Through Hoops to Prove Abortion Is Safe*, THE POST-ABORTION REVIEW (Summer 1993) (*id.*).
42. *See* JOHN DOMBRINK & DANIEL HILLYARD, SIN NO MORE: FROM ABORTION TO STEM CELLS, UNDERSTANDING CRIME, LAW, AND MORALITY IN AMERICA 79–82 (2007); SHELDON EKLAND-OLSON, LIFE AND DEATH DECISIONS: THE QUEST FOR MORALITY AND JUSTICE IN HUMAN SOCIETIES 40–53 (2013).
43. *See* ZIEGLER, ABORTION AND THE LAW, *supra* note 22, at 166–88.
44. *See* Stenberg v. Carhart, 530 U.S. 914 (2000).
45. *See* Gonzales v. Carhart, 550 U.S. 124, 146–56 (2007).
46. *Id.* at 163.
47. *See id.*
48. *See* Asian Communities for Reproductive Justice, A NEW VISION FOR ADVANCING OUR MOVEMENT FOR REPRODUCTIVE RIGHTS AND REPRODUCTIVE JUSTICE (2005), https://forwardtogether.org/tools/a-new-vision/.
49. *See* Jessica Arons, CTR. FOR AM. PROGRESS, MORE THAN A CHOICE: A PROGRESSIVE VISION FOR REPRODUCTIVE HEALTH AND RIGHTS (2006), https://cdn.americanprogress.org/wp-content/uploads/issues/2006/09/more_than_a_choice.pdf.
50. *Id.*
51. *See* Shaila Dewan, *Anti-Abortion Billboards on Race Split Atlanta*, N.Y. TIMES (Feb. 6, 2010), at A9; Shaila Dewan, *To Court Blacks, Foes of Abortion Make Racial Case*, N.Y. TIMES (Feb. 27, 2010), at A1; *see also* SILLIMAN ET AL., UNDIVIDED RIGHTS, at *supra* note 27, 271–78.
52. On the Tea Party, *see* THEDA SKOCPOL & VANESSA WILLIAMSON, THE TEA PARTY AND THE REMAKING OF REPUBLICAN CONSERVATISM 3–19 (2013). On the abortion laws passed in the period, *see* John Leland, *Abortion Foes Advance Cause at State Level*, N.Y. TIMES (Jun. 2, 2010), at A10.
53. *See* Sarah Kliff, *Lawmakers Debate Contraceptive Mandate*, WASH. POST (Feb. 17, 2012), at A3.
54. SILLIMAN ET AL., UNDIVIDED RIGHTS, *supra* note 27, at 271–78.
55. *See* Frank James, *Mississippi Rejects Personhood Amendment*, NPR (Nov. 8, 2011), https://www.npr.org/sections/itsallpolitics/2011/11/08/142159280/mississippi-voters-reject-personhood-amendment.
56. Abigail Abrams, *We Are Grabbing Our Own Microphones: How Advocates of Reproductive Justice Stepped Into Their Spotlight*, TIME (Nov. 21, 2019), https://time.com/5735432/reproductive-justice-groups/.
57. *See id.*
58. After this Chapter was written, the Supreme Court overruled Roe and its progeny in Dobbs v. Jackson Women's Health Organization, 142 S. Ct. 2228 (2022). The tensions and contradictions between abortion rights and reproductive movements discussed in this Chapter, however, will likely continue.

CHAPTER 17

LAW AND ECONOMICS AGAINST FEMINISM

MARTHA T. MCCLUSKEY

THE rise of feminism in law in the late twentieth century overlapped with the rise of another influential framework for legal analysis, one identified as "law and economics." That overlap was not accidental. Despite, or because of, its widely credited claim to be a neutral tool for evaluating law, law and economics has been especially useful for mobilizing and rationalizing a backlash against legal feminism.

Looking back from the first decade of the twenty-first century, the American historian Daniel T. Rodgers concluded, "Equality ha[s] come and gone as a social idea with traction, even among liberal intellectuals."[1] The intellectual stage set by law and economics makes equality largely marginal or suspect to sound law and policy. The fundamental premise that economic gain can be separated from social and political values cuts deeply against meaningful gender equality, even while appearing to excise law's biases.

The first part of this article shows that law and economics developed its institutional power as part of a deliberate plan to counter egalitarian law and policy. A group of nonacademic organizations invested in law and economics as a seemingly neutral methodology that could build academic credibility for right-wing ideology and legal change. Their funding linked academic law and economics with a broader network of think tanks and organizations designed to implement and promote a rightward shift in law and to undermine feminist theory and policy in particular.

The second part turns to the substantive content of law and economics, focusing on how it constructs the economy as a sphere that law can and should insulate from contested morality and politics. Law and economics frames legal analysis with a conceptual division between seemingly objective economic maximizing and subjective social distribution. That binary frame puts feminist law in a double bind, naturalizing and legitimating a gendered moral and political baseline that generally makes feminist reforms appear costly, unfair, or ineffective. This core conceptual move closes off feminist legal efforts to question and redefine the assumptions and values that determine what counts as productive, legitimate economic gain.

The final part focuses on how this core division constructs an idea of liberty that makes feminist efforts to remedy gender-based harms appear illegitimate and oppressive. Law and economics identifies freedom with an economy in which individual self-interested choices are insulated from public support or social responsibility. That ideal of freedom as self-serving individual choice closes off analysis of how law's gendered assumptions and unequal protections pervasively limit individual agency and meaningful choice in the economy and in society.

I. Law and Economics as an Anti-Feminist Political Investment

Examining the rise and fall of different approaches to law, the prolific legal scholar Cass Sunstein asked, "Why has Law and Economics had such staying power?"[2] He describes both feminist legal theory and economic analysis of law as examples of how academic groups can create "informational cascades" in which irrational influences of habit, reputational pressures, mass psychology, and emotional ties may lead academics to adopt bad ideas about law.[3] By assuming that both feminism and law and economics deserve equivalent scrutiny for problems of "political correctness," Sunstein's analysis fails to consider whether the two approaches actually hold positions of similar power on the academic and political playing field.[4]

A. Legal Theory in Political Economic Context

Consistent with the law and economics orthodoxy, Sunstein's behavioral explanation of the way bad legal ideas can win unjustified influence does not take account of how the broader context of political, social, and economic power shapes behavior. Law and economics has received far more funding from private organizations outside academia than any other contemporary school of legal thought. Moreover, those funders deliberately designed their investments as a strategy for transforming the politics of law.

Omitting these dramatic differences from the picture obscures how the success of law and economics is related to feminism's comparatively marginal position. Feminism will appear to be on shaky ground compared to law and economics if, like Sunstein, we assume that intellectual merit is mainly threatened by insufficient scholarly detachment from emotions or moral commitments. Proponents of orthodox law and economics have attributed its success to its distinctly neutral, scientific method of legal analysis,[5] apparently stripped of the contested politics, sentiment, and value judgments of other approaches.

Although law and economics claims to depoliticize law, in contrast to legal feminism's explicit focus on contesting power, the law and economics movement itself is steeped in a political and economic context of its own that deserves attention. Law and economics owes its influence to its receipt of vast resources from organizations working to oppose movements for equality and social justice. And although this influential legal theory makes self-interested material gain a dominant lens through which to evaluate law, it is striking that this lens has distinctly closed off analysis of the material special interests shaping its own theory, application, and impact.

B. The Political Economics of Law and Economics

As the most prominent organization leading the movement to reshape legal thought in the late twentieth century, the Olin Foundation spent more than $68 million to develop and institutionalize the emerging approach known as law and economics.[6] The foundation viewed this strategic investment as its most significant and successful strategy for its success as a "venture capital fund for the conservative movement."[7] As its "premier project," Olin provided the "financial and moral support" for specialized seminars attended by hundreds of U.S. law professors and thousands of judges (along with many other government officials and legal professionals from around the world), with additional major funding from the Charles Koch Foundation, the Searle Freedom Trust, and major oil, insurance, and pharmaceutical corporations with direct interests in judicial rulings.[8] A recent empirical study found that judges tend to rule more conservatively on a number of issues after attending these seminars.[9]

Supplementing these seminars, Olin funding established law and economics centers within many U.S. law schools,[10] providing tens of millions of dollars for Olin programs at Harvard, Yale, and the University of Chicago, and many other schools.[11] To further embed the approach in legal academia, Olin gave "a long string of six-figure gifts"[12] solidified with ideological strings[13] to transform George Mason University (recently renamed the Antonin Scalia Law School) into a specialized base for its law and economics approach. In addition, Olin collaborated with other major conservative foundations, industries, and wealthy individuals to develop an interconnected network of think tanks, law firms, and publications geared toward implementing and reinforcing the ideas, law reforms, and policy arguments generated by this newly influential academic approach.[14] This ecosystem cultivated core law and economics ideas as widely recognized, credible, and firmly established principles of sound thinking. In contrast, despite significant student and faculty interest, feminist legal theory has remained more at the institutional margins, with far fewer law school centers, fellowships, career pipelines, or well-funded and well-connected ties to policy institutions.[15]

Though not exclusively targeting feminism, these institutional investments in law and economics were carefully designed to discredit support for egalitarian social change, especially targeting efforts to integrate economics with questions of race, gender, economic class, and power. In the early 1970s, a protest led by African American students at Cornell University triggered arms manufacturer John M. Olin's decision to transform his foundation into a leading producer of right-wing ideas building on his concerns that "socialist" policies of the New Deal and the 1960s threatened "free enterprise" and capitalism.[16] As Olin Foundation president William E. Simon explained, "[T]he power to shape our civilization" should "reside in the free market."[17]

Olin Foundation leaders chose law and economics as their primary project not from academic interest but rather for its strategic value in advancing and obscuring its right-wing political mission.[18] Olin's executive director explained that "you couldn't get into the law schools with programs targeted at constitutional law.... If you went in with constitutional law, you wouldn't want Larry Tribe constitutional law, you'd want Bob Bork constitutional law. But you couldn't go in and say that."[19] Law and economics "seems neutral but it isn't in fact," because it promotes a "philosophical thrust in the direction of free markets and limited government."[20]

The Olin Foundation structured its academic law and economics funding to preserve overall alignment with its overarching ideological goals.[21] For example, when the African American law faculty director of Duke University's Olin Center, Jerome M. Culp Jr., commented on white supremacy in contemporary Supreme Court rulings, the foundation stopped funding the program, denying that the decision was directly related to the comment but acknowledging that it was motivated by disapproval of Culp's "racial politics."[22]

Further, the foundation worked closely with other politically motivated funders to link the law and economics message of an apolitical, optimizing market to a right-wing moral, cultural, and social mission explicitly embraced by their larger web of grantees. In particular, the think tank and law firm networks developed by Olin and its philanthropic allies promoted the idea that legal feminism illegitimately usurps the market's superior protection of individual freedom, fundamental fairness, and societal well-being. For example, the Olin Foundation funded and shared leadership with the Center for Individual Rights,[23] a nonprofit law firm focused on "economic liberty" that litigated the successful case to overturn a portion of the Violence Against Women Act that was widely supported by feminists, on the grounds that it was an invalid regulation of commerce and illegitimately extended congressional civil rights powers to private behavior.[24] Olin also funded the Independent Women's Forum, a libertarian group with close ties to conservative activists that was originally formed to defend Supreme Court nominee Clarence Thomas against sexual harassment claims.[25] This organization went on to similarly take stands in other high-profile feminist legal efforts such as filing amicus briefs in opposition to the constitutional challenge to the exclusion of women from the Virginia Military Institute, a prestigious public undergraduate institution.[26]

Olin's active support for the conservative Manhattan Institute think tank further shows how leading funders of law and economics designed their institutional networks to actively disparage and marginalize legal feminism while advancing law and economics ideas. Heather Mac Donald, who long worked as the Manhattan Institute's John M. Olin Fellow, built an influential career challenging the legitimacy of legal initiatives for gender and racial justice. In response to growing interest in feminist legal theory in U.S. legal academia in the 1990s, for example, the Manhattan Institute promoted a series of commentaries by Mac Donald warning that feminist jurisprudence and critical race theory amount to a "dangerous flight from reason and logic,"[27] causing many law schools to become "the scene of a full-scale attack on Anglo-American law by a new generation of minority and female professors."[28]

Finally, the strategic and covert efforts to integrate orthodox law and economics with general right-wing moral and political ideology are perhaps most clearly represented today by the Federalist Society. The Olin Foundation's support was "indispensable" to developing that organization into a legal and political powerhouse.[29] Far outstripping the influence and resources of its more liberal or centrist counterpart, the American Constitution Society, the Federalist Society has chapters in virtually every U.S. law school, with more than seventy thousand members and annual revenues reaching $26 million in 2016, thanks to ample funding from other major right-wing foundations such as Mercer, Scaife, and Koch.[30]

The Federalist Society engages a broad audience of students and faculty by showcasing and normalizing conservative arguments on such hot-button constitutional issues as gun control, affirmative action, abortion, and freedom of speech.[31] Even while highlighting public law and "culture war" issues not directly associated with economic policy, these conservative arguments often share an underlying message of deference to unequal private power as the basis for moral and legal legitimacy. In particular, the Federalist Society organizes numerous lectures criticizing feminist legal protections as contrary to the fundamental freedom and rationality exemplified by individualized market choice.

Beneath its public face as an academic debating group, the Federalist Society has recently gained notoriety for its covert role in organizing and funding a political transformation of the federal judiciary.[32] The Federalist Society's longtime executive vice president, Leonard Leo, who was also a private advisor to President Donald Trump, has led a network of interrelated "dark money" organizations focused on raising hundreds of millions of dollars for right-wing political causes.[33] Leo played a major role in securing the Supreme Court nomination of longtime Federalist Society member Brett Kavanaugh,[34] who overcame allegations of sexual assault with a display of outrage and victimization at being held to account for a woman's concerns.

Expressing a view common among legal academics and policy experts, Leo responded to reports of the Federalist Society's role in politicizing and monetizing control of U.S. courts, "I don't waste my time on stories that involve money and politics because what I care about is ideas."[35] Indeed, Leo's actions show that he cares especially about organizing (and obscuring) money and political power for right-wing ideas about law and that the extensive time he devotes to money and politics is not wasted by assuming that legal ideas are best produced in impartial academic debates.[36]

The ideas of law and economics no doubt contribute to its broad appeal well beyond its conservative funding base. The point of situating law and economics in a larger context of institutional motives and money is not to establish guilt by association but rather to direct closer scrutiny toward the assumptions and consequences of these particularly well-funded ideas about law and economics, especially the claims to be providing a distinctly neutral and rational tool for law and policy. As Part II demonstrates, influential law and economics ideas operate to undermine feminism, regardless of the intent or sincerity of those who adopt or credit these ideas.

II. Framing the Economy in an Anti-Feminist Double Bind

Law and economics wields stealth ideological force through a master narrative that denies that the economy is inherently comprised of social and political institutions. The many technical variations of this core law and economics orthodoxy share an overarching conceptual frame positing two distinct goals for law: efficiency and distribution, or in other common terminology, "economic welfare" and fairness. That division is often presented metaphorically as the choice between maximizing or dividing the "economic pie."[37] This binary frame emerged not from rigorous, uncontested theory or falsifiable evidence but from historical and instrumental efforts to brand the neoclassical school of economics as distinctly scientific.[38]

On its surface, this division appears to reflect common sense: Producing more economic resources differs from giving someone a bigger slice of resources. But by staging law's core tension as one between more total gain for all and more relative gain for some, this fundamental division obscures and skews the core questions of justice. What gain represents an overall increase, rather than a transfer to partial interests? The frame provides a circular answer: Law can distinguish rules and procedures that advance overall net benefit by modeling its rules and procedures on a market defined by rules and processes that prioritize efficiency over distribution.

A. Efficiency Versus Equality as a Hierarchical Dualism

The efficiency-equality dualism echoes and amplifies the equality-difference double bind that confronted feminist anti-discrimination law. As Catharine MacKinnon observed, that liberal legal dualism offers feminists a losing choice: Women can be equal to men or different from men.[39] Either way, men are the standard by which women are measured.

If law requires formally equal treatment, then it will not protect against harms particularly likely to affect women, especially those most disadvantaged by systemic discrimination. If law requires special treatment in recognition of gender differences affecting women's bodies or social, economic, and historical position, then law will risk reinforcing the stereotypes, stigma, segregation, and marginalization that have long driven and rationalized systemic gender discrimination. In contrast, those who are most privileged by gender, race, class, and other status markers tend to get a double benefit. The dualism's inherently unequal substantive baseline enables those with privileged status to have it both ways, getting protection for their particular bodies and interests as a basic condition of equality and neutrality.[40]

Frances Olsen explained that law is shaped by hierarchical dualisms such as reason/emotion, objective/subjective, abstract/contextualized, and principled/personalized in which one side is implicitly defined as the essential quality and the other as the exception or supplement lacking that quality.[41] The male/female binary permeates and connects these hierarchical legal dualisms, so that the dominant traits are generally associated with normative masculinity.[42]

Feminism can resist law's losing choices by challenging these dualisms. The dominant trait is thoroughly dependent on its purported opposite, masking the normative and political questions of how law should define and shape what counts as equal, normal, rational, formal, and principled or otherwise superior.[43] For example, by challenging employment law's masculinized ideal of a worker who normally leaves childbearing and family care to feminized or racialized others, legal requirements for employers to accommodate family leave or breastfeeding can be viewed as normal, basic working conditions such as providing bathroom breaks or chairs, rather than special treatment.[44]

Like the sameness/difference division, any real-world application of the efficiency/equity binary deploys covert moral and political judgments. Deciding whether women and men are the same or different in any instance requires judging what substantive qualities are relevant, and why. Similarly, deciding whether a particular law or practice is maximizing or dividing the economic pie requires a prior moral judgment about what substantive qualities, and for whom, count as more pie, and why.

Moreover, like other formal legal dualisms, the efficiency/distribution distinction inherently casts the two functions in a hierarchical moral order. Efficiency (or economic welfare) is the dominant and defining norm, and equality (redistribution) is the deviation from that norm. By definition, efficiency (or welfare) maximizes productive gain for the whole, whereas distribution, by definition, transfers gain to some at the expense of others. This assumed division makes efficiency appear essential and primary, whereas distribution appears discretionary, secondary, and dependent, because we can only distribute resources that are first produced.[45]

The binary frame's skewed choice between efficiency and equality puts feminism in a double bind. Feminist law can promote efficiency, which would make women's (and others') well-being depend on the presumed productive value of their individual tastes, talents, and experiences, in an economy in which productivity need not account for unfairness or gender bias. Or, feminist law can promote redistribution to compensate for women's (or others') presumed lack of productive value, taking resources away from more economically valuable uses or users, with the result that society will have fewer resources to support those who are less productive. The binary rests on an implicitly biased assumption that the well-being of women (or others marked by non-normative gender) constitutes a special political interest or moral question of social distribution that is marginal to aggregate economic well-being.

In contrast, this framing division between economic production and social distribution sets up efficiency so as to provide a double benefit. By first assuming an efficient economy that normally and neutrally maximizes productivity, laws can rationalize extending greater protections and privileges to the existing economy's winners as a means of maximizing economic well-being overall. With the economic pie maximized, this theory presumes that more resources will be available to alleviate the harms borne by those with the smallest share of the economic pie.[46]

B. Law and Economics Puts Formal Equality on Shaky Ground

Although the binary frame might seem to support feminist law reforms as special corrections of economic inefficiencies,[47] it makes such arguments suspect. By presuming that efficiency is the economic norm, law and economics suggests that any particular harm to women (or others) generally represents individual failures to measure up to the demands of economic maximizing.

The prominent law and economics scholar Richard Epstein deploys the binary's master narrative to conclude that law should not prohibit even overt and irrational employment discrimination.[48] In the orthodox law and economics view, welfare maximizing is best determined without legal second-guessing or costly oversight, since it defines the overall economic good as the aggregation of individual preferences unmediated by substantive governance.[49] In addition, in the orthodox narrative, any deviations from this naturally maximizing system are likely to be more effectively corrected by that system itself, as part of its presumed impartial and invisible pressures toward optimal equilibrium. For example, if an employer fails to hire the most productive workers owing to irrational gender bias, then in this theory, market competition generally will force that employer to change or fail.[50]

Even when law and economics arguments do not push as far as Epstein does, efficiency arguments are a double-edged sword for feminism because they reinforce the idea that equality is normally a misguided and costly goal. Within this binary frame, anti-discrimination law will appear suspect when targeting the most egregiously irrational unequal treatment. That is because implementing and enforcing formal equality rules will appear to require shifting resources and power from purportedly efficient and impartial economic production to courts and administrative agencies that inevitably are dependent on partial, subjective judgments of fact and value.

C. Law and Economics Undermines Substantive Equality

Law and economics also sets up substantive equality to fail, though it appears to present redistribution as a legitimate alternative to efficiency. It posits a sphere of supposedly formally equal and neutral "private law" rules and institutions as the basis for maximizing economic gain, while constructing substantive equality primarily as a redistributive transfer of gain best relegated to a politicized taxing-and-spending process. This deceptively frames substantive equality as a contested, hierarchical "taking," detracting from a productive, consensual "making." For example, if law requires workplace accommodations for family responsibilities, in this view employers will have fewer resources for production, inducing firms to reduce jobs, decrease pay or benefits, or raise consumer prices—effects likely to especially burden the most disadvantaged families.

Contrary to the law and economics façade of an apolitical, natural economic order, however, the seemingly high societal costs of feminist substantive reforms are not dictated by natural or necessary economic laws, but instead reflect the contingent flaws of a legal structure taken as the neutral economic baseline. The law and economics orthodoxy fails to acknowledge that law could improve both general economic productivity and social justice by changing the underlying rules and institutions that make the current system and feminist reforms so costly to so many. For example, unpaid family care could count as valuable economic production in the gross national product or similar measures of aggregate gain.[51] The costs of family care could be shifted from parents (especially mothers) and employers to instead count as a public investment via public stipends to families and expanded public support for high-quality care outside the family for children, elders, and people with disabilities.[52] The federal government could use its extensive power over its currency to fund an expansive public jobs program with generous wages and family leave policies to compete with private employers unable or unwilling to provide family-friendly work, and these jobs could include expanding health, education, social services, and environmental quality to further reduce the private costs of family care.[53]

Such proposals for transformative public spending and public protection appear political and redistributive only by ignoring the gendered substance of the seemingly formal private and public law assumed to create the neutral market. Private-law rules of property, tort, contract, finance, and corporate governance pervasively distribute hierarchical substantive privileges and penalties.[54] Legal feminism has extensively shown how the market's unequal legal substance is deeply gendered. For example, contract law restricts enforcement of intrafamily contracts for domestic labor;[55] tort law discounts or excludes damages for women's reproductive injuries;[56] and criminal law has long failed to equally and effectively enforce laws against domestic violence and sexual assault.[57]

Moreover, private market opportunities are extensively shaped by public investments in such infrastructure as roads, utilities, and civil and criminal justice systems. Tax incentives and direct public spending targeted to attract and reward globally mobile corporate capital have become a necessary, normal, and openly politicized requirement for local economic development both in the United States and in developing regions around the world.[58] Central banking and monetary systems routinely design and allocate federal funds to support private gains from financial risk-taking under a myth of depoliticized independence.[59] In the United States, extensive public funding for private for-profit men's sports teams is promoted as valuable economic development despite evidence that they will not lead to measurable economic gains in the broader community, on the theory that their intangible effect on local morale counts toward productive value.[60]

In contrast, feminist proposals for expansive public support for feminized labor such as child care typically count as social redistribution and personal consumption rather than productive investment, regardless of evidence of larger, long-term economic (as well as social) benefits. The problem is not merely the failure to accurately analyze the economic benefits of social programs; it is also the underlying idea that the quality and equality of society and the economy is fundamentally separable from law's support for economic production. Without challenging that division of economy and society, correcting the economy's structural harms often will appear less rational and practical than the more limited forms of targeted redistribution more likely to leave feminist reforms in a double bind.

D. Law and Economics Revives Gendered Separate Spheres

The foundational law and economics division between economic productivity and social responsibility is thoroughly entangled with the longstanding ideology of separate gendered spheres (further structured by race, class, sexuality, geography and other status markers). That ideology centers the economy on private production by autonomous interest-maximizing actors, set apart from social "reproduction" associated with hierarchical private relationships of altruism, dependency, and moral authority. Law continually reshapes that separation by designating some labor and interests as components of valuable production deserving public support and authority, while constructing other labor and interests, particularly those associated with feminized domesticity, as non-economic personal qualities, private responsibilities, or costly dependency meriting private sacrifice and submission.[61]

Although the efficiency/redistribution binary does not explicitly assign its distinct spheres by gender, it draws on this gendered ideology and history for its narrative force.

Nancy Fraser analyzes how unjust and destructive power is mobilized and masked by defining and enforcing the boundaries of the economy, with those deemed inside it entitled to exploit and expend the people, resources, and activities relegated to the outer spheres of social reproduction and nature.[62] Similarly, Angela Harris explains that the American political economy "was built on ... [and] continues to reproduce relations of caste through property, race, kinship in the space marked 'the social.' "[63] The exclusion of agricultural and domestic workers from many U.S. labor law protections is one example of the way law sets the economy's boundaries to reinforce social caste. In order to instead direct the economy toward human flourishing, Harris urges law to challenge how the "social" determines "[t]he lives that matter and don't, the populations that are and are not 'native,' the poor who are and are not deserving."[64]

Law and economics reinforces this systemic, gendered subordination of the social with its core idea that well-being is inevitably dependent on and subordinate to an economy independent of social quality. During the Covid-19 pandemic, political pressures to support the U.S. economy by lifting public health restrictions regardless of human cost followed an ideal of economic well-being that assumes many people will need to sacrifice both their money and their lives to support wealth for a relatively privileged few.[65] As Lynn Parramore explains, the antisocial idea of economic welfare maximizes not real societal wealth but rather the inverse condition of societal "illth," the term coined by nineteenth-century political economist John Ruskin to describe the harmful effects of the emerging system of industrial capitalism.[66] From this perspective, rising contemporary economic insecurity among men does not represent a zero-sum loss resulting from women's gains. Instead, it reflects an antisocial economy designed to hold most people back from their potential for constructing a better world for themselves and others.

What the law and economics model fails to recognize is that the social trust built from political and legal systems designed to broadly provide and reward care and protection for diverse individuals, environments, and communities can produce resilience, adaptability, and solidarity vital to long-term economic strength.[67] Individualized gain-seeking cannot rationally provide meaningful personal security or freedom in the contemporary context of catastrophic global risks from multiple systemic threats of pandemic, climate disruption, economic inequality and instability, social division, and political authoritarianism. By changing the legal subject from the autonomous individual liberal subject to the embodied human who is universally but uniquely born into physical and social dependency and mortality, Martha Fineman draws on feminism to ground economic welfare in responsibility for social quality and equality, making substantive provisioning for universal human vulnerability the central measure of productivity and legitimacy.[68]

III. Framing Freedom as an Anti-Feminist Economic Value

Building on liberal political theory's focus on individual autonomy, the law and economics master narrative further undercuts feminism with a neoliberal ideal of freedom severed from public moral governance. It responds to liberalism's conundrum that advancing liberty through democracy and human rights means that individuals must submit to the contested substantive judgments of others by positing an efficient market of formally neutral legal rules wherein individuals freely pursue self-determined gain via consensual transactions. In this view, the private market fosters diversity and personal agency free from collective control, and so is seemingly compatible with feminist resistance to prescribed gender norms. But by grounding legitimate freedom in individualized, private self-interest, this narrative makes systemic gender-based subordination and violence appear to deserve legal deference or even fundamental legal protection.

A. Reducing Liberty to Individual Self-Interest

In her intellectual history of neoliberal "rational choice" theory, S. M. Amadae concludes that the ideal of freedom as calculated individual gain-seeking reduces consent to no more than the act of showing up in a system beyond individual control.[69] With a gun at your head, the choice to forfeit your money rather than your life is self-interested but is the opposite of meaningful freedom. A deeper understanding of liberty would turn not on the individual freedom to choose, but on the moral qualities of the collective conditions and processes governing our options.

Neither economics nor individualized choice can enable law to impartially settle the questions of justice necessary for meaningful freedom. What conditions, for whom, constitute consent free from force and fraud? What individual gains from imposing harm on others should be protected as legitimate private rights or excused as personal, social, or local discretion or indiscretion? Government inevitably distributes the power to use force by the way law defines, punishes, monetizes, and immunizes acts of violence.[70]

Contrary to the law and economics presumption of markets free of force, the recent #MeToo movement against sexual assault illustrates how the strong arm and insidious shadow of physical force are common, not marginal, to the everyday economic lives of many women, a factor to bargain with in the process of securing opportunities for education, work, housing, and health care.[71] The Black Lives Matter movement similarly shows that deadly public and private violence, tied to militarized policing, mass incarceration, and racial disenfranchisement, routinely looms over ordinary private activity to reinforce an economy of vastly unequal personal freedom and opportunity. Both of these movements are examples of how laws governing physical force are thoroughly gendered in ways that intersect with race, class, sexuality, nationality, and other status markers.[72]

The law and economics binary frame helps naturalize and legalize this unequal protection by identifying violence as a social or psychological problem or background fact outside an economic realm of self-interested rationality. Steeped in this view, the Supreme Court invalidated federal damage remedies for private gender-motivated violence despite voluminous evidence of its economic harm, claiming that "[g]ender-motivated crimes of violence are not, in any sense of the phrase, economic activity."[73] The philosopher Kate Manne analyzes misogynist violence as a "law enforcement" system aimed at defining and defending an economy structured to support an unequal masculine entitlement to gain from women's service, sexual or otherwise, as a non-mutual social duty.[74] Although most men don't assault women, privileged men can nonetheless gain from a system that makes it reasonable or legitimate to advance their own interests by commanding women's attention, bodies, and labor without mutual obligation or accountability.

The feminist legal scholar Robin West explains that sexual harassment continues to be normalized and excused in a legal and cultural context that covertly discounts and discredits women's freedom to control access to their bodies.[75] While tort law in theory assumes that bodies generally are not up for grabs, in practice it makes sexual harassment hard to remedy by assuming that some bodies are naturally or normally welcoming or tolerant of intrusion, so that being grabbed by privileged men tends not to be a cognizable injury.[76]

The idea that law protects individual freedom by insulating private self-interest from moral accountability reinforces gendered and unequal entitlements. The feminist legal scholar Anita Bernstein analyzes how seemingly formal laws pervasively distribute freedom by means of status-based stereotypes identifying some people's self-interested agency as presumptively unruly, deserving public and private constraint, while others' self-interested agency is presumptively productive, deserving legal discretion and deference despite its harmful impact on others.[77] As Bernstein explains, "If femaleness or blackness makes a person crazy or angry, then the absence of these traits makes him rational, or his behaviors reasonable and comprehensible."[78]

West explains that the law and economics goal of maximizing self-interest free from moral governance effectively justifies laws privileging the interests of those wielding the most private power, regardless of inequality, societal costs, or constraining effects on others.[79] According to the welfare-maximizing criterion, "might is innocent" as long it appears free from overt collective moral control, because self-interested action by economic winners is by definition productive rather than malicious, sadistic, irrational, or dangerous.[80] Furthermore, by identifying liberty with maximizing private interests, the law and economics orthodoxy justifies interpreting and adapting law to further privilege and protect those who can use private power to constrain others' self-interest. If a firm can increase profits by giving its workers the choice to lose their job or accept working conditions that pose a substantial risk to health or life,[81] then that choice can appear to advance personal liberty more than stricter government enforcement of workplace health and safety rules.

Indeed, this view of liberty as private interest-maximizing strips law of the moral authority to challenge those presumed to be the natural and normal winners,[82] so that unequal power to engage in arbitrary lawlessness is compatible with justice.[83] By legitimizing the self-interested power to harm others as deference to individual freedom, the law and economics binary undermines individual liberty overall, while reinforcing longstanding subordination based on gender, race, class, and other identities marked as morally suspect.

For example, the feminist legal theorists June Carbone, Naomi Cahn, and Nancy Levit explain the consequences of replacing the idea that corporate success requires cooperative teamwork and long-term institutional commitments with the theory that efficient corporations should reward amoral individualized maximizing of self-interest.[84] That management model has led to corporate "masculinities contests" that select leaders who are especially ruthless, narcissistic, and unprincipled.[85] The result is an economy in which competitive pressures steer businesses toward normalizing unproductive and unlawful practices, including sexual harassment and discrimination, wage theft, and fraud,[86] thereby eroding individual freedom and agency as well as societal well-being.

B. Constructing Legal Feminism as a Fundamental Threat to Individual Freedom

By framing individual liberty as private power separated from collective morality, the law and economics binary positions legal feminism as a threat to liberty. The idea that equality threatens freedom is a central precept of neoliberalism, melding the purported moral detachment of economic libertarians with the moral fundamentalism of social conservatives.[87] That view ignores the way legal rules governing the seemingly free market are "permeated with coercive restrictions on individual liberty," as the legal realist Robert Hale famously explained, so that state power routinely and inherently produces market inequalities that are neither natural, consensual, nor necessarily productive.[88]

The legal division between rational self-interested choice and collective morality is steeped in conventional gender ideologies. The references in popular culture to political correctness and the feminist thought police or "feminazis" represent feminist moral governance as an especially suspect public intrusion into an imagined preexisting realm of private individual freedom. Similarly, the term "nanny state"[89] disparages systems of care and protection as illegitimate disruptions of a more normal, natural, and independent masculine (and racialized and classed) authority.[90]

The moral assumptions and practical effects of feminist ideals and strategies should not be immune from careful scrutiny and critique. Yet criticisms of feminist aspirations for moral governance are suspect if assumed to represent tough-minded rationality freed from social and moral commitments. The feminist theorist Susan Fraiman links the stance of strenuous detachment from care and protection to a romantic vision of coolness and independence "epitomized by the modern adolescent boy in his anxious, self-conscious and theatricalized will to separate from the mother" who is imagined as controlling, moralistic, sentimental, and not sexy.[91]

Underneath its surface anti-moralism, the law and economics narrative of legal deference to individual maximizing of self-interest promotes a moralistic message that people should be individually responsible for advancing their own interests without substantive protection and support from government and law.[92] This naturalizes and moralizes the substantive legal rights and privileges that empower market winners, justifying their success not merely as superior self-serving power but also as productive contributions to a valuable societal "pie." In that narrative, feminist challenges to harmful private practices such as date rape and the failure to accommodate workers' family responsibilities, represent unproductive evasion of the risks and costs of personal choices or immoral domination of more productive and self-sufficient others.

Recent Supreme Court doctrine embraces this vision of liberty as narrow self-interest. A new constitutional paradigm advances what Robin West terms the right to exit.[93] Promoted by the Federalist Society, this paradigm grounds individual liberty in an idealized free market where people are governed not by public values and democratic processes but by individualized self-interest in a competition for private control and consumption of scarce resources free from collective obligations. West identifies this paradigm as the basis for newly proposed or established fundamental rights to opt out of public obligations such as the constitutional right to bear arms for individualized violent self-help, the right to opt out of public health insurance at the individual and state level, and workers' right to opt out of contributing to their workplace union.[94] West explains that these new constitutional rights to individualized self-interest undermine civil rights movements' efforts to expand democracy and equality by what she terms "rights to enter" systems of public power and protection.[95] In particular, First Amendment freedoms have been reconfigured as a constitutional right to refuse civil rights requirements such as employers' statutory obligation to cover contraceptives in their workers' health insurance policies.[96]

IV. Conclusion

Feminism challenges the core law and economics premise of a value-neutral yet value-perfecting formal sphere of individual freedom set against a social and political sphere of suspect substantive power. A feminist vision that integrates social and economic well-being can help resist the masculinized, antisocial ideas of freedom, rationality, and productivity that have fueled twenty-first-century crises in finance, climate, democracy, public health, and inequality. Law and economics cuts against legal feminism not because gender justice is a non-economic goal, but because law and economics promotes a misleading economic ideology steeped in gender and tilted toward those most willing and able to disregard and discount others' well-being.

Notes

1. Daniel T. Rodgers, Age of Fracture 271 (2011).
2. Cass R. Sunstein, *Foreword, On Academic Fads and Fashions*, 99 Mich. L. Rev. 1251, 1251 (2001).
3. *Id.* at 1251–52.
4. *Id.* at 1258.
5. George L. Priest, The Rise of Law and Economics: An Intellectual History 72–73 (2020).
6. John J. Miller, A Gift of Freedom: How the John M. Olin Foundation Changed America 62 (2006).
7. *Id.* at book jacket.
8. Jane Mayer, Dark Money: The Hidden History of the Billionaires Behind the Rise of the Radical Right 110 (2016); Nan Aron, Barbara Moulton, & Chris Owens, *Judicial Seminars: Economics, Academia, and Corporate Money in America*, 25 Antitrust L. & Econ. Rev. 33, 33–35 (1994).
9. Elliott Ash, Daniel L. Chen, & Suresh Naidu, *Ideas Have Consequences: The Impact of Law and Economics on American Justice* (Mar. 20, 2019) (unpublished manuscript) (available at SSRN: https://ssrn.com/abstract=2992782).

10. Steven M. Teles, The Rise of the Conservative Legal Movement 188–190, 200 (2008).
11. Martha T. McCluskey, *How Money for Legal Scholarship Disadvantages Feminism*, 9 Issues Legal Scholarship 25–39 (2011).
12. Miller, Gift of Freedom, *supra* note 6, at 69.
13. Teles, Rise of the Conservative Legal Movement, *supra* note 10, at 209–211.
14. Mark Dowie, American Foundations: An Investigative History 214–17 (2001).
15. McCluskey, *Money for Legal Scholarship*, *supra* note 11, at 27–30.
16. Miller, Gift of Freedom, *supra* note 6, at 29–33.
17. William E. Simon, A Time for Truth 194 (1978).
18. Teles, Rise of the Conservative Legal Movement, *supra* note 10, at 173, 188–89.
19. *Id.* at 191.
20. *Id.* at 189.
21. *Id.* at 190, 202.
22. Miller, Gift of Freedom, *supra* note 6, at 80.
23. CIR Board, Center for Individual Rights, https://www.cir-usa.org/board/ (last visited June 20, 2020) (listing longtime Olin Foundation executive director as board member); The Center for Media and Democracy, *Center for Individual Rights*, Sourcewatch, https://www.sourcewatch.org/index.php/Center_for_Individual_Rights (last visited June 20, 2020) (listing nearly $2 million in Olin funds).
24. United States v. Morrison, 529 U.S. 598 (2000); *see also* Martha McCluskey, *Toward a Law and Political Economy of Gender Violence*, Law and Political Economy Blog (Nov. 12, 2018) https://lpeblog.org/2018/11/12/toward-a-law-and-political-economy-of-gender-violence/ (critiquing the case's analysis of economics).
25. Barbara Spindel, *Conservativism as the "Sensible Middle": The Independent Women's Forum, Politics, and the Media*, 21 Soc. Text 99, 100 (2003).
26. *Id.*
27. Heather Mac Donald, *Law School Humbug*, City J. (Autumn 1995).
28. Heather Mac Donald, Beyond All Reason *by Daniel A. Farber and Suzanna Sherry*, Commentary (1997) (book review).
29. Miller, Gift of Freedom, *supra* note 6, at 93 (quoting Steven Calabresi).
30. Evan Mandery, *Why There's No Liberal Federalist Society*, Politico Mag. (Jan. 23, 2019), https://www.politico.com/magazine/story/2019/01/23/why-theres-no-liberal-federalist-society-224033.
31. Amanda Hollis-Brusky, Ideas With Consequences: The Federalist Society and the Conservative Counterrevolution (2015).
32. Robert O'Harrow Jr. & Shawn Boburg, *A Conservative Activist's Behind-the-Scenes Campaign to Remake the Nation's Courts*, Wash. Post (May 21, 2019), https://www.washingtonpost.com/graphics/2019/investigations/leonard-leo-federalists-society-courts/.
33. *Id.*
34. *Id.*
35. *Id.*
36. *Id.*
37. Martha T. McCluskey, *Defining the Economic Pie, Not Dividing or Maximizing It*, 5 Critical Analysis of L. 77, 77–80 (2018).
38. Mark Blaug, Economic Theory in Retrospect 575 (Cambridge Univ. Press, 5th ed. 1996) (1962).

39. Catherine MacKinnon, Toward a Feminist Theory of the State 221 (1989).
40. Martha T. McCluskey, *Defending and Developing Critical Feminist Theory as Law Leans Rightward*, in Transcending the Boundaries of Law: Generations of Feminism and Legal Theory 353 (Martha Albertson Fineman ed., 2011).
41. Frances E. Olsen, *Feminism and Critical Legal Theory: An American Perspective*, in Feminist Legal Theory I: Foundations and Outlooks 473-75 (Frances E. Olsen ed., 1995).
42. Id.
43. Id. at 482-85.
44. Joan Williams, *Do Women Need Special Treatment? Do Feminists Need Equality?*, 9 J. Contemp. Legal Issues 279, 318 (1998).
45. McCluskey, *Defining the Economic Pie, supra* note 37, at 88-96.
46. *See* Martha T. McCluskey, *Efficiency and Social Citizenship: Challenging the Neoliberal Attack on the Welfare State*, 78 Ind. L.J. 783, 805-8 (2003) (explaining how the efficiency/redistribution frame creates a double bind for defending welfare programs and advancing other social and economic rights).
47. *See* Gillian K. Hadfield, *Feminism, Fairness, and Welfare: An Invitation to Feminist Law and Economics*, 1 Ann. Rev. L. & Soc. Sci. 285, 292-95 (2005) (arguing that, with further attention to social values, the idea of efficiency can help inform and advance feminist goals).
48. Richard A. Epstein, Forbidden Grounds: The Case Against Employment Discrimination Laws 9-10 (1992).
49. Id. at 42-43.
50. Id.
51. *See* Nancy Folbre & James Heintz, *Investment, Consumption, or Public Good? Unpaid Work and Intra-Family Transfers in the Macro-Economy*, 91 Ekonomiaz 100, 109-114 (2017) (evaluating several accounting models for including unpaid domestic work).
52. *See, e.g.*, Washington Center for Equitable Growth, What Does the Research Say About Care Infrastructure, Factsheet: Families (April 2021), https://equitablegrowth.org/factsheet-what-does-the-research-say-about-care-infrastructure/ (summarizing the broad economic benefits of public care investments and noting President Biden's proposed steps toward that goal).
53. Pavlina R. Tcherneva, *The Job Guarantee: Design, Jobs, and Implementation* 17-19 (Levy Econ. Inst. of Bard Coll., Working Paper No. 902, 2018).
54. *See* Katharina Pistor, The Code of Capital: How the Law Creates Wealth and Inequality (2019) (analyzing the way law encodes seemingly formal private law principles into substantive hierarchies of capital).
55. Katherine Silbaugh, *Turning Labor Into Love*, 91 Nw. U. L. Rev. 1, 28-36 (1996-1997); *see also* Martha Ertman, chapter 39, *Feminism and Contract Law*, in this volume.
56. Martha Chamallas & Jennifer B. Wriggins, The Measure of Injury: Race, Gender, and Tort Law 172-183 (2010); *see also* Sarah Swan, chapter 38, *Feminism and Tort Law*, in this volume.
57. *See generally* Kate Manne, Down Girl: The Logic of Misogyny 177-219 (2018) (explaining the rationales and practices that often exonerate men who murder or assault women); Donna Coker, *Crime Control and Feminist Law Reform in Domestic Violence Law: A Critical Review*, 4 Buff. Crim. L. Rev. 801 (2001) (explaining the race and class

inequalities resulting from criminal law remedies and suggesting alternative legal solutions); *see also* Leigh Goodmark, chapter 14, *The Anti-Rape and Battered Women's Movements of the 1970s and 80s*, in this volume.
58. Martha T. McCluskey, *Subsidized Lives and the Ideology of Efficiency*, 8 AM. U.J. GENDER, SOC. POL'Y & L. 115, 139–142 (2000).
59. *Id.* at 135–36; Timothy A. Canova, *The New Global Dis/order in Central Banking and Public Finance*, in RESEARCH HANDBOOK ON POLITICAL ECONOMY AND LAW 44–51 (Ugo Mattei & John D. Haskell eds., 2015).
60. McCluskey, *Subsidized Lives*, *supra* note 58, at 143–44.
61. Martha T. McCluskey, *Are We Economic Engines Too? Precarity, Productivity, and Gender*, 49 U. TOL. L. REV. 631, 640–45 (2018).
62. Nancy Fraser & Rahel Jaeggi, *Capitalism: A Conversation in Critical Theory* 13–60 (Brian Milstein ed., 2018).
63. Angela P. Harris, *The App and the Operating System: Neoliberalism and "Social Reproduction,"* LAW AND POLITICAL ECONOMY BLOG (Feb. 18, 2019), https://lpeblog.org/2019/02/18/the-app-and-the-operating-system-neoliberalism-and-social-reproduction/.
64. *Id.*
65. *See* Matt Ford, *Trumpworld Embraces the Death Wish Economy*, THE NEW REPUBLIC: THE SOAPBOX (Mar. 25, 2020), https://newrepublic.com/article/157052/donald-trump-economic-nihilism (last visited June 28, 2020) (criticizing arguments that widespread deaths will rescue the economy from the pandemic); Martha T. McCluskey, *Personal Responsibility for Systemic Inequality*, in RESEARCH HANDBOOK ON POLITICAL ECONOMY AND LAW 227, 232–33 (Ugo Mattei & John D. Haskell eds., 2015) (criticizing the neoliberal economic logic promoting widespread, unequal individual sacrifice as the solution to the financial industry's destructive risk-taking).
66. Lynn Parramore & Jeffrey L. Spear, *America's Chilling Experiment in Human Sacrifice*, INSTITUTE FOR NEW ECONOMIC THINKING (May 14, 2020), https://www.ineteconomics.org/perspectives/blog/americas-chilling-experiment-in-human-sacrifice.
67. *See* SEVASTI CHATZOPOULOU, SOCIAL TRUST AND GOVERNMENT RESPONSES TO COVID-19, SOCIAL EUROPE (May 4, 2020), https://www.socialeurope.eu/social-trust-and-government-responses-to-covid-19 (last visited June 28, 2020) (discussing the value of co-operation in responding to crisis).
68. Martha Albertson Fineman, *The Vulnerable Subject: Anchoring Equality in the Human Condition*, 20 YALE J.L. & FEMINISM 1, 8–12 (2008).
69. S. M. AMADAE, PRISONERS OF REASON: GAME THEORY AND NEOLIBERAL POLITICAL ECONOMY 200 (2015).
70. Martha McCluskey, *Toward a Law and Political Economy of Gender Violence*, LAW AND POLITICAL ECONOMY BLOG (Nov. 12, 2018), https://lpeblog.org/2018/11/12/toward-a-law-and-political-economy-of-gender-violence/.
71. *See* Tristin Green, chapter 16, *The #MeToo Movement*, in this volume.
72. *See, e.g.*, Blanche Cook, *Citizenship Transmission Laws and a White Heteropatriarchal Property Right* IN PHILANDERING, SEXUAL EXPLOITATION, AND RAPE (THE "WHP") OR JOHNNY AND THE WHP, 31 YALE J.L. & FEMINISM 57 (2019) (showing how U.S. citizenship transmission law rests on an assumed entitlement to sexual domination of foreign women).
73. United States v. Morrison, 529 U.S. 598, 613 (2000).

74. Kate Manne, Down Girl, *supra* note 57, at 63.
75. Robin West, *Manufacturing Consent*, 39 The Baffler (May 2018), https://thebaffler.com/salvos/manufacturing-consent-west (last visited June 29, 2020).
76. *Id.*; *see also* Theresa Beiner, chapter 22, *The Claim for Sexual Harassment*, in this volume.
77. Anita Bernstein, *What's Wrong with Stereotyping*, 55 Ariz. L. Rev. 655, 665–71 (2013).
78. *Id.* at 690.
79. Robin West, *Law, Rights, and Other Totemic Illusions: Legal Liberalism and Freud's Theory of the Rule of Law*, 134 U. Pa. L. Rev. 817, 846–852 (1986).
80. *Id.* at 852.
81. *See* Thomas O. McGarity, Michael C. Duff, & Sidney Shapiro, Protecting Workers in a Pandemic: What the Federal Government Should Be Doing, The Center for Progressive Reform 4–13 (June 2020), http://progressivereform.org/our-work/workers-rights/protecting-workers-in-a-pandemic/#Intro (last visited June 29, 2020) (discussing examples of workers at risk of deadly Covid-19 infection on the job).
82. West, *Laws, Rights, and Other Totemic Illusions*, *supra* note 79, at 851–52.
83. Martha T. McCluskey, *Toward a Fundamental Right to Evade Law: The Rule of Power in* Shelby County *and* State Farm, 16 Berkeley J. Afr.-Am. L. & Pol'y. 216 (2014).
84. June Carbone, Naomi Cahn, & Nancy Levit, *Women, Rule-Breaking and the Triple Bind*, 87 Geo. Wash. L. Rev. 1105, 1113–15 (2019).
85. *Id.* at 1123–28.
86. *Id.* at 1127–29, 1159–62.
87. Martha T. McCluskey, *From the Welfare State to the Militarized Market: Losing Choices, Controlling Losers*, in Accumulating Insecurity: Violence and Dispossession in the Making of Everyday Life 27–29 (Shelley Feldman, Charles Geisler, & Gayatri A. Menon eds., 2011).
88. Robert L. Hale, *Coercion and Distribution in a Supposedly Non-Coercive State*, 38 Pol. Sci. Q. 470, 470–74 (1923).
89. *See, e.g.*, Cato Institute, The Nanny State, https://www.cato.org/research/nanny-state (last visited June 30, 2020) (website criticizing public health regulations); Paul Gattis, *Rep. Mo Brooks Calls Alabama a "Nanny State" Over Coronavirus Shelter-at-Home Order*, Al.com (Apr. 21, 2020), https://www.al.com/news/2020/04/rep-mo-brooks-calls-alabama-a-nanny-state-over-coronavirus-shelter-at-home-order.html (last visited June 30, 2020) (news of politician disparaging pandemic protections).
90. Martha T. McCluskey, *How Equality Became Elitist: The Cultural Politics of Economics from the Court to the "Nanny Wars,"* 35 Seton Hall L. Rev. 1291, 1299–1300 (2005).
91. Susan Fraiman, Cool Men and the Second Sex xii (2003).
92. McCluskey, *Defending and Developing Critical Feminist Theory*, *supra* note 40, at 353–55.
93. Robin West, *A Tale of Two Rights*, 94 B.U. L. Rev. 893, 897–905 (2014).
94. *Id.* at 902–3.
95. *Id.* at 895–97.
96. *See* Burwell v. Hobby Lobby Stores, Inc., 573 U.S. 682 (2014) (exempting private secular businesses from law requiring contraceptive coverage in employer-provided health insurance plans).

CHAPTER 18

BACKLASH AGAINST FEMINISM

Rethinking a Loaded Concept

SALLY J. KENNEY

THE *Oxford English Dictionary* defines backlash as the "jarring reaction or striking back of a wheel or set of connected wheels in a piece of mechanism, when the motion is not uniform or when sudden pressure is applied."[1] Like the snarl produced by the overcast fishing reel or cotton gin gears that misfire to dangerous effect,[2] the term denotes "a sudden violent movement backwards."[3] In politics, backlash is a conservative reaction to progressive social or political change.[4] The mere threat of change or even a false belief that one's group has lost ground can trigger a backlash.[5] More than mere opposition to a liberal or progressive agenda, the concept of backlash posits that real or perceived social change causes individuals to alter their opinions or take different action than if the backlash had not occurred.

Political analysts first used the term to refer to Southern and Northern whites' resistance to civil rights after Congress passed the 1964 Civil Rights Act.[6] In popular parlance, many use the term "backlash" to signify that social movements or policymakers have responded negatively to their opponents' successes or perceived gains. But social movement scholars would call this kind of response a countermobilization, which is not necessarily the same as backlash.[7] The term "backlash," by definition, means that the reaction to change must be different in kind or degree from mere opposition to change. For a countermovement to rise to the level of backlash would require that public opinion changed significantly or that those previously inactive have mobilized, increased their activity, or become more threatening in tone, or even violent. Backlash implies that the original efforts to bring about change, if not misguided, were counterproductive—that objectively measured progress has not just been slowed but reversed.

Susan Faludi's blockbuster book popularized the term.[8] Faludi's argument had three components. First, focusing on popular culture, she argued that women were losing ground—women wrote or produced fewer TV shows and films, and fewer of them had women main characters. Second, she exposed a primary narrative in public discourse and popular culture that claimed women had achieved equality but were miserable as a result, attempting to shame successful women into believing they were psychotic, workaholic spinsters with no love lives and barren wombs.[9] She dissected and refuted several so-called trend media stories, the most notorious being that women over forty are more likely to be killed by a terrorist than marry. Third, Faludi refuted this backlash narrative with extensive evidence that women were not objectively miserable and, most significantly, showed that to the extent that women did express discontent, they identified continuing or worsening *inequality*, not equality, as the culprit. By showing that antifeminists had reversed women's progress far short of the finish line, Faludi revealed the backlash narrative that women have achieved equality to be false. Faludi concluded, "the antifeminist backlash has been set off not by women's achievement of full equality but by the increased possibility that they might win it. It is a *preemptive strike* that stops women long before they reach the finish line."[10]

Implicit in the concept of backlash are theoretical and empirical propositions that answer fundamental questions about feminism, law, and social change. Can we measure progress empirically on a simple linear dimension or could things be both better and worse at the same time? Do changes lead to progress for all women, or does progress for some women come at the expense of others, or simply leave others behind? Does progress necessarily entail diminished opposition, or is opposition constant? Does progress cause increased opposition, or do certain mechanisms of progress—for example, judicial decisions—trigger increased opposition? Most writers who use the term, however, do not expressly take a position on these issues and fewer still offer empirical evidence to support their claims. In this chapter, I argue that labeling anything opponents do in response to actual or perceived progress of women or other subordinated groups a "backlash" is not analytically or politically helpful. Instead, we should reserve the term for the causal claim that people changed their views or acted differently by mobilizing or escalating threatening tones and behaviors leading to a reversal of progress. It is vital that feminists correctly gauge the strength of opposition, plot how opposition adapts discursively and pivots strategically in response to feminist successes, and understand progress to include quantitative measures (such as number of strong women characters on television or a reduced pay gap) as well as discursive elements like the belief that women have achieved equality, while disaggregating the category of "women" to allow for a more complex intersectional approach. Too much is at stake to simply assume that progress has been reversed or that certain kinds of progress trigger greater opposition. We may also need to abandon a simplistic linear view of progress where misogyny withers away and instead embrace what critical race theorists such as Derrick Bell call the permanence of racism and see, in our case misogyny, as constantly morphing as it is reinscribed.

At times, allies and presumptive supporters of feminism have been too quick to mistake a countermovement for a backlash. Their assertions of backlash have rested on unproven empirical claims about the relationship between feminist-inspired change and opposition to such change. For example, some feminist and progressive allies have claimed that by moving too far too fast, the Supreme Court created a backlash hurting the causes of racial integration, reproductive justice, or LGBTQI+ rights. But like the antifeminist claims that Faludi unmasks, these claims also lack empirical support. Rather than resting on solid evidence, such claims rely on assumptions about whether incremental social change is more sustainable than bold rights claims, whether courts uniquely rile up opponents, whether it is best to always avoid conflict, and whether some rights to equality are more important than others. The more we interrogate assertions of backlash and show that opposition to feminism is neither new nor strengthened, and the more we widen the field to take an intersectional approach to consider who has made progress and who faces new versus ongoing threats of violence, the more difficult it becomes to meaningfully distinguish backlash from preexisting opposition to feminism. Using the term "backlash" risks strengthening false propositions about social change.

Feminists *should* think deeply about and investigate empirically how social change works and how to counter both oppressive discourses and policy reversals. Identifying backlash behaviors (ridicule, exclusion, violence) and debunking backlash narratives (such as that women have already achieved equality) are important to this work. We should, however, be more cautious about the baggage that comes along with the term "backlash."

I. Anatomy of Backlash: Behaviors, Discourse, and Tone

To label a set of actions a backlash is to draw attention to a coherent pattern of practices and narratives, attribute motivation, recognize the affective response to the status threat, and posit an objective reversal of progress. This section sketches some key features and characteristics scholars have used to detect backlash.

A. Identifying Backlash Patterns and Practices

Scholarly work on backlash has gone beyond Faludi's emphasis on cultural narratives and media frames to explore how backlash functions in specific settings. In my work on gender and judges, I identified a repertoire of five hostile practices antifeminists used to reverse women's progress in gaining judicial office.[11] First is treating women differently than men in the judicial selection process, such as by asking intrusive personal questions, denying them a hearing, taking longer to schedule a vote, or disproportionately voting not to confirm; in short, discriminating. Second is when judicial colleagues deny women judges the professional courtesy that is routinely and heretofore universally extended to all sitting judges, independent of party, ideology, and ability, and even openly attack them. Third, lawyers and litigants challenge women's positional authority on the bench, ranging from interrupting them, making patronizing remarks, and addressing them in a way that denies their professional status to formally challenging their objectivity by filing motions to recuse. Fourth is directing attacks against them, such as bringing charges of misconduct for behaviors tolerated when men do them, actively seeking to remove them from office through retention elections and running opponents against them. Finally, replacing women with men when they retire or are removed from office is a backlash to women's increasing presence on the bench.[12] This hostility to women—and to minority men—serving in the judiciary continues.

Other scholars have explored backlash in a variety of settings. Legal scholar Deborah Brake deconstructs the mechanics of backlash in three different contexts: Title IX and sports, sexual assault on campus, and sexual harassment in employment retaliation claims under Title VII. In an example of backlash against girls competing against boys in the masculine sport of wrestling, individual boys gained notoriety by forfeiting their matches and refusing to wrestle girls. Like Faludi, Brake explores backlash as not just a behavior—refusing to wrestle—but a set of narratives and media practices. She shows four discursive moves those seeking to reverse gender equality use to counter the threat posed by girls wrestling boys: religion versus equality (wrestling girls violates the boy wrestler's religion), asymmetrical agency (journalists explore the boy's motives for not wanting to wrestle but do not consider why the girl wanted to wrestle), leveling down (he forfeits rather than wrestles her, so both lose), and appropriating feminist arguments (wrestling a girl constitutes violence against women). Brake shows how reporters accepted at face value the heroism of a boy who forfeited a match rather than wrestle a girl, valorizing him as the chivalrous rural male motivated by deeply held religious (and perhaps even feminist) beliefs. By ignoring the girl's courage, achievement, and agency as a champion, the media neutralized her equality claims. Brake demonstrates how this erasure deemphasized the homoerotic aspects of wrestling, shored up the masculinity-conferring qualities of sport, and reinforced the gender binary.

Legal scholar Mary Anne Case's work describes how one powerful institution, the Catholic Church, countermobilized against what it called feminism's gender ideology.[13] Case sees the Vatican's top-down campaign against gender ideology as a backlash against feminist successes in challenging the idea of essential sex differences and preordained social roles, LGBTQI+ activist's successes in challenging the notion of a gender binary, and feminist claims for reproductive justice. She identifies the key actors and institutions, follows the money, analyzes the discourse, and tracks the diffusion of ideas. By linking Catholic conservatives, evangelical Christians, and Mormons, the campaign to roll back what the conservative social movement calls gender ideology bore fruit.[14] The Catholic Bishop Conference reversed its support for the Violence Against Women Act, the Senate confirmed conservative Catholic and opponent of gender equality and reproductive freedom Amy Coney Barrett to the U.S. Supreme Court, and the Trump Administration eroded transgender rights. These and other examples highlight the significance of religion versus equality in resisting feminist gains. In liberal philosophy and in Western constitutional and human rights law, claims of religious freedom often trump gender equality claims.[15]

To claim backlash is to observe a pattern rather than individual random acts of sexist individuals, or what Cudd calls "anomalous fluctuations from a norm of civility."[16] Whether in documenting the playbook of making charges of sexual assault against athletes disappear[17] or revealing the unacknowledged patterns of misogyny that underlie mass shootings,[18] backlash theorists reveal a strategic, coordinated, and patterned set of behaviors and narratives.

B. Discourse

Backlash is not merely a set of actions opposing social progress but also a set of narratives and discourses. For Faludi, the main backlash narrative was to claim that women had already achieved equality. As Faludi knew, at the root of backlash is a fierce debate over reality. *New York Times* writer Cameron Tung describes the dynamic:

> One faction positions itself as a beleaguered voice of dissent, bravely pushing back against some draconian orthodoxy. The other sees itself as battling a society already suffused in this supposedly "dissenting" viewpoint. Each side looks at the world around it and sees, for the most part, the flourishing of the other. It's less a culture war than a war over who's already winning.[19]

As Faludi and subsequent researchers have shown, the backlash narrative that women have already attained equality is empirically false. Whether women are progressing toward or have already attained equality is an empirical question. Social scientists, journalists, and activists have bolstered Faludi's argument that women have failed to achieve equality well before they lost ground during the global COVID pandemic. They have developed more precise objective measures of the pay gap; counted the number of women murdered by intimates or holding leadership positions; and tracked the number of women's novels, films, or creative works winning prizes and garnering elite reviews.

Even though false, the narrative that women are already equal is powerful. Internalizing that narrative prevents women from recognizing and challenging discrimination. When sociologist Dana Britton studied women scientists, she found that even if they did not believe women had achieved equality in science, they mostly chose to act as if they had. When they encountered sexism, they would brush it aside as the unsavory acts of a few throwbacks and get on with their work. Later in their careers, they would encounter significant gendered expectations about service work and pervasive and significant resistance to their leadership that made it harder to dismiss sexism as a trait of a few exceptional individuals.[20]

Critical race theorist Derrick Bell identified the "racism is over" narrative that parallels Faludi's backlash narrative that women have achieved equality. Bell articulated how the mechanism of divide and conquer allows racism to persist—picking out some winners to advance the argument that the game is fair, but also keeping the have-nots from seeing their plight as shared.[21] The backlash narrative works by blaming individuals for their failure to advance rather than recognizing the racism and sexism holding groups of people back. When some individuals do advance, it is taken as proof that sexism and racism pose no barrier.

As we plumb the discursive strategies of feminist and antifeminist movements, social movement scholars remind us that discourse is not static; instead, movements constantly draw on the effective discursive strategies of their opponents, appropriating what they can to score points that resonate with activists, policymakers, and the wider public as norms change.[22] Sociologist Tina Fetner labels this relationship symbiotic.[23] Although the narrative that women's equality has arrived persists, feminists have identified other backlash narratives. For example, those who oppose abortion have pivoted from focusing on the sanctity of human life that begins at conception to arguing that abortion is bad for women or genocidal for minorities, hoping to appeal to feminists and antiracists.[24]

One component of the discursive pattern of backlash—the playbook, if you will—involves exaggerating feminist and equality advocates' claims to appear ridiculous. Rather than attack the new norm head on, opponents take an example that they argue goes too far and exaggerate it, lending it to ridicule in cartoons and late-night comedy. In order to portray the change as ridiculous, opponents must distort the facts (what feminist legal scholar Nancy Levit labels a salience error):[25] bra burning, Al Franken losing his Senate seat for one misunderstood squeeze or joke, getting millions of dollars in damages after spilling take-out coffee. As in Brake's case of the girl who wanted to wrestle, to show that the norm change has overtaken "common sense," opponents must omit key details from their depictions. More damaging than omitting one side of the story is the distortion of profoundly overstating the legal remedies victims receive. Opponents use a few selective examples to suggest that the mere invocation of a claim now secures a legal remedy, despite evidence to the contrary—such as that sexual harassment plaintiffs have the lowest rate of success of any plaintiffs, universities sanction few perpetrators of sexual assault, and courts routinely reduce or eliminate high jury awards on appeal. By showcasing exaggerated and outrageous examples, opponents of feminism hide their opposition: they do not oppose feminism, only that which is unreasonable.

Such narratives work by deception and subterfuge. Journalist Jia Tolentino captures the dynamic of ridicule, omission, and distortion in her *New Yorker* piece, "The Rising Pressure of the #MeToo Backlash."[26] She diagnoses the claim that the pendulum has swung too far in the direction of women at the expense of men and that fairness or common sense requires a correction, as a backlash narrative. The discourse overstates the power of the feminist movement and the actors seeking to advance that agenda. Most observers of the fall of sexual predators such as Bill Cosby, Harvey Weinstein, and Larry Nasser fail to appreciate just how precarious the efforts were to bring them to justice. If the judge in the second Bill Cosby trial had not allowed other victims to testify unlike the first judge (Cosby later won his appeal on a different legal issue), if Harvey Weinstein had once again succeeded in shutting down the investigation by the journalists who exposed his conduct, if Larry Nasser had not disposed of his hard drive with 37,000 pieces of child pornography on the curb outside his house just as police finally decided they had complaints worth investigating, and if journalists had not coaxed the first of two women (of the more than 350 girls he molested) to come forward,[27] each of these injustices might never have been exposed. To the #MeToo critics, the alleged harm of feminist overreach seems more dangerous than the molestation of hundreds of girls and the rape of many women.[28] The deception and subterfuge is the feigned appearance of sharing the new norm: that neither children nor adults should be sexually assaulted, when in fact, consciously or not, the #MeToo critics aim to diminish the ability of victims to hold their perpetrators accountable.

Legal scholars and commentators have identified a similar pattern of distortion in the discourse behind former Secretary of Education Betsy DeVos's issuance of regulations revoking the preponderance-of-evidence standard for campus adjudication of sexual assault allegations.[29] They show the exaggeration of unfair sanctions against perpetrators was not a mistake or a misunderstanding but a deliberate strategy to further conservative goals beyond campus sexual assault policy. Heuristics of false allegations (narratives of exceptional and anomalous cases posing as the norm) overpowered women's accounts of victimization.[30] Alleged concern with due process and the rights of the accused established a right-wing beachhead against civil rights, allowing Secretary DeVos and other opponents of public education to pose as champions for the due process rights of minorities and the free speech rights of students, despite having consistently defended neither.[31] Through such discursive strategies, antifeminist actors appear to champion progressive ideas, gaining a beachhead, but are really seeking to undermine the broader cause of the role of the federal government in enforcing civil rights.[32]

Psychologist Jennifer Freyd has identified and labeled a particular backlash narrative DARVO—deny, attack, reverse victim and offender—and analyzed it as a key strategy in the Trump playbook—so much so that it was featured on an episode of *South Park*.[33] This well-worn narrative against affirmative action (whites are the real victims) is now being effectively deployed to defend those the #MeToo movement has named, leading to campaigns post-Kavanaugh such as "fear for your sons."[34] The strategy may be working: 40 percent of Americans surveyed in 2018 thought that the #MeToo movement had gone too far.[35]

Whether calling such deceptive discourses "stalking horses" or "beachheads," backlash theorists expose opponents as not merely mistaken or hypocritical but as intentionally concealing their true objectives. I made such an argument in *Gender and Justice* about the campaign to unseat the first woman chief justice of the California Supreme Court, Rose Bird.[36] Conservative opponents of the rights of workers and consumers weaponized gender and the death penalty to turn voters against Bird. Opponents of Bird activated deeply rooted gender stereotypes and implicit biases about women lacking managerial competence, being soft on crime, and jumping the queue. A direct campaign to restrict the rights of civil litigants would not have generated sufficient emotional outrage to mobilize voters to turn her out of office.

C. The Emotional Register of Backlash

Social movement scholars, organizational sociologists, and gender scholars writing about backlash urge us to pay special attention to emotions. Backlash has an important emotional dimension: rage, characterized by a menacing tone. The mere threat of women's progress unleashes intense emotions on the part of those who feel they stand to lose. Those who are losing power experience that change more intensely than the powerless because they come to view their powerful status as the natural order.[37]

Philosophers Anita Superson and Ann Cudd and the contributors to their edited volume, *Theorizing Backlash*, distinguish what Martha Chamallas calls gender devaluation, the "laid-back smugness of most of the earlier responses" of sexism—the ridicule—from the "greater shrillness and tenacity of many of the later ones."[38] For them, backlash has a distinctively menacing bullying tone. Cudd writes, "The response to feminism is not argument but disdain, not rational disagreement but irrational resentment, not dispassionate debate but sexist attack."[39] It is the burbling up of these intense emotions that seem at first blush wildly inappropriate to the situation and different from other philosophical disagreements that cue analysts to perceive a backlash afoot.[40] Early second-wave feminists such as Dorothy Dinnerstein and Nancy Chodorow drew on psychoanalytic theory to explain the intense rage men felt when women threatened any incursion into their power as rooted in early childrearing practices. Other scholars have referred to backlash (e.g., over gender-neutral bathrooms) as a form of hysteria.[41]

The sense that less deserving others have jumped the queue and are garnering special treatment fuels the emotional pitch of backlash.[42] Backlash reveals "who should not, or cannot, have power, lest the 'natural' power hierarchy be disrupted."[43] As the number of women in nontraditional fields increases, detractors respond with increasing hostility to a feared "feminization."[44] Such hostility is well documented for women in nontraditional fields from firefighting to academia to soldiering.[45] Those seeking to understand Trumpism highlight the strong feeling that women, minority men, LGBTQI+ persons, immigrants, and city dwellers have jumped the queue, ahead of the deserving people who "work hard and play by the rules." Their belief that the mainstream media, Hollywood liberals, and academics look down on them and treat them with scorn drives them into the arms of Fox News.[46] Backlash functions as a constitutive exclusion which "solidifies the sense of belonging for those who are constructed as proper citizens."[47]

The menacing tone of backlash threatens violence and is not an idle threat. In my work identifying backlash practices against women judges, I would now add an additional behavior: violence—killing women judges or their children.[48] Violence as a centerpiece of backlash has a long pedigree. Lynching was a backlash response to emancipation and reconstruction. Both slavery and lynching are oppressive—but distinctive—practices. Slave owners committed violence against slaves with impunity, as property owners, but their use of violence could hurt their own interests, whereas lynching was a response to Black people's independence, which upended the social order when they ceased to perform unpaid labor or perform social deference.[49]

This section has traced the patterns, practices, and defining features of a backlash. The next section traces how supporters have used false claims of backlash to dampen demands for progress.

II. FALSE CLAIMS THAT PROGRESSIVES HAVE TRIGGERED BACKLASH BY MOVING TOO FAR TOO FAST

While opponents of progressive causes hide their opposition by claiming that the pendulum has swung into the sphere of the ridiculous, the unjust, or the nonsensical, supporters of social change have argued that change is occurring too swiftly and either the pace of change or the mechanism of change is generating opposition, whereas a slower approach would generate greater support. Martin Luther King famously recognized that those who do not suffer from oppression frequently counsel patience, whether they be opponents of integration, white liberals, or religious communities. In his 1963 *Letters from a Birmingham Jail*, he opined:

> We know through painful experience that freedom is never voluntarily given by the oppressor; it must be demanded by the oppressed. Frankly, I have yet to engage in a direct-action campaign that was "well timed" in the view of those who have not suffered unduly from the disease of segregation. For years now I have heard the word "Wait!" It rings in the ear of every Negro with piercing familiarity. This "Wait" has almost always meant "Never." We must come to see, with one of our distinguished jurists, that "justice too long delayed is justice denied."[50]

Such an argument, as King recognized, may be a strategy for feigning support for a new norm, such as ending sexual coercion, liberalizing abortion law, allowing gays to marry, or ending school segregation, while actually seeking to slow progress. But King also recognized that some supporters of racial justice, too, feared inciting violence and favored incremental change.

Fearing backlash, some social scientists, strategists, and even allies of feminist and antiracist causes have latched on to "too far too fast" in defense of a more cautious strategy for creating lasting change. For example, legal scholars Michael Klarman and Gerald Rosenberg argued that the Supreme Court's decision in *Brown v. Board of Education* failed to bring about change because it got too far ahead of public opinion.[51] Progress toward meaningful desegregation only occurred, Rosenberg argued, when Congress conditioned federal funding on integration and business elites used judicial decisions as cover for their desire to not have their communities appear backward. Scholars have fiercely contested these empirical and normative claims.

Like Klarman and Rosenberg, Ruth Bader Ginsburg famously championed the "too far too fast" argument in her criticism of *Roe v. Wade*.[52] Ginsburg argued that *Roe*'s bold rather than incremental change engendered a negative opinion cascade. She also claimed that when courts, rather than democratic institutions, declare rights that reflect shifting norms, it catalyzes opposition. According to this line of argumentation, Blacks seeking integration, gays seeking to marry, women seeking the power to terminate pregnancies, or disabled people who want to work should go more slowly and build more public support rather than turn to courts to vindicate their rights, lest they unleash a backlash. Historians have soundly refuted Ginsburg's empirical claim that the states were on a path to liberalize abortion law if only the Court had not mucked up the process by declaring a constitutional right.[53] Legal scholars Robert Post and Reva Siegel reject the argument that oppressed groups should turn to courts to vindicate only those rights not likely to trigger a backlash and contest the assumption that surfacing differences over minority rights is dangerous for democracy.

A similar controversy emerged over the Americans with Disabilities Act (ADA). In an edited volume, legal scholar Linda Krieger uses backlash as the frame for understanding judges' misinterpretation of the legislative history and creation of doctrine that thwarts the ADA's transformative purpose.[54] Krieger builds on the insights of other scholars who have shown that although new legislation may reflect a norm shift and call for a rupture with a previous legal regime, judges reinscribe old values into the doctrine of the new regime.[55] Reluctant to infer that the judges dismantling the ADA are substituting their own policy preferences against rights for those with disabilities, Krieger posits instead that the small number of Washington insiders who drafted the ADA failed to generate the shift in consciousness that the civil rights movement did before passing new laws.[56] Krieger thus applies the term "backlash" to mean judges' failure to understand, embrace, and apply new norms on disability rather than reserving it for opposition to those norms. Yet while arguing that drafters of the ADA got too far ahead of public opinion to explain why judges failed to give effect to the legislative intent, she fails to show that going "too far too fast" made those with disabilities worse off, like an overcast fishing reel, where one part of the mechanism gets too far ahead of the other and shifts violently backward. Legislating norms ahead of public consciousness may produce disappointing results, but Krieger has not shown that it generates opposition or sets back the cause. She might more fruitfully argue that the passage of the ADA created a false sense of "problem solved," akin to Faludi's backlash narrative that women have already achieved equality. If Ginsburg's "too far too fast" argument rests on faulty empirical evidence and may wrongly caution social change advocates to go slowly, Krieger's analysis shows how expanding the meaning of the term can muddle causal arguments about social change. Both Ginsburg and Krieger favor change, unlike opponents feigning support. But both muddle our diagnosis of the problem, responding to countermobilization or educating judges on the new conceptual regime, respectively.

Supporters of equality who use "too far too fast" as a way of navigating backlash fail to distinguish between opposition from those who were already opposed to the change (what social movement scholars call countermobilization) and a reversal of public opinion following an allegedly "too far too fast" change. In the case of gay marriage, where some gay rights supporters made "too far too fast" claims, those already opposed to gay rights made up the countermovement; favorable court decisions did not generate new or greater opposition to the movement.[57] Assertions that rights advances have caused or strengthened opposition often lack empirical support; more often than not, those who claim to have discovered a public opinion backlash are merely witnessing the preexisting opposition and not a change in opinion. The "go slow or risk harming your cause" argument is "more politically than empirically motivated."[58] Without empirical support that backlash is actually occurring, fretting over a backlash begins to look like obfuscation rather than a difference of opinion among strategists, an attempt to thwart progress while pretending to share underlying values.[59]

Mistakenly claiming backlash clouds our understanding of progressive social change. Even absent backlash, public opinion frequently fluctuates around cultural flashpoints.[60] Allies who fear backlash and opponents who seek to slow social change while falsely professing shared values share an overly simplistic understanding of norms and norm change. Rather than thinking courts should wait to recognize only those rights supported by public opinion (abdicating the constitutional role of the judiciary as protector of minority rights), we should recognize that courts are important institutions and arenas for norm contestation and development. Although the Supreme Court could not end white supremacy on its own in *Brown*, as "the arena of principle," it could strengthen an important new norm of racial equality, draw attention to the nation's failure to live up to constitutional values, provide institutional cover, and act as a catalyst for other institutions and actors. In similar fashion, legal recognition of gay marriage ultimately strengthened public opinion in favor of marriage equality.[61] Negative effects on public opinion generated by courts deciding the issue are mostly either short-lived or a function of preexisting policy preferences.[62]

Although I have concluded that in these four cases the arguments about backlash were wrongheaded, I cannot help thinking that in some cases, flying under the radar might be a good strategy. In *Silent Revolution*, Herb Jacob makes a convincing case that proponents of divorce reform fared better when they worked behind the scenes and framed the issue as legal integrity rather than feminist family reform.[63] My own experience, too, suggests that sometimes it is prudent not to draw one's enemies' fire.

III. BACKLASH VERSES OPPRESSION

As the previous discussion suggests, it is not always easy to distinguish backlash from oppression, "the always present and often violent policing of who belongs in the polity and the public space."[64] If backlash is motivated by the belief that feminists have made great strides, whereas misogyny is more constant,[65] the distinction depends on flimsy and contestable assumptions about the state of women's progress. More important than how to distinguish the two concepts is to ask why and how it helps, conceptually or politically, to do so.

In thinking about backlash against women judges, I identified a set of behaviors as well as a narrative. As I revisit the list of behaviors and add violence, I am now less convinced that one can distinguish backlash from discrimination by the tone or emotional "registers" and the threat and use of violence. At the root of backlash and oppression, which requires difference and hierarchy, is exclusion. Scholars who take a more intersectional approach to backlash argue that "backlash emanates from enduring exclusions regarding membership and status that are anti-intersectional."[66] Once we start to probe the effects of backlash and ask, rollback of progress for whom?, "[w]e would be less likely to think of backlash as a potentially rectifiable kink rather than a *condition of modernity.*"[67] And once we make visible the ongoing violence against marginalized groups, it becomes more difficult to see behaviors or narratives as distinctively *backlash*. Fundamentally, we must ask, what turns on seeing backlash as distinctive from opposition or countermobilization?

Those who question the conceptual utility of backlash challenge Faludi's assumption that history moves in only two directions and that we can measure all progress linearly.[68] Both the backlash narrative and Faludi's counternarrative rest on an overly simplistic assumption that progress is linear: women are progressing, staying the same, or falling further behind. Faludi did not consider how some women might be better off from certain measures of equality than others—for example, how stopping the sexual harassment of certain media kingpins might do little to reduce sexual harassment of women farmworkers, or how the increase in women CEOs might do little to reduce the poverty of women service workers. Nor did she consider that equality gains for some women might come at the expense of others.

Assessing progress toward gender equality in the realm of representation, popular culture, and discourse is particularly fraught. Representations are subject to simultaneous conservative or liberatory readings with different audiences. Norms might shift to see women as capable of exercising political power at the same time that they are regarded as unlikable for their political ambition. White women might be seen as more acceptable leaders than women of color who may be constructed as angry, biased, unpatriotic, or incapable. Rather than moving either toward a feminist future or backward toward patriarchy, the "[r]ight might advance toward a future that is both innovative and worse."[69] In this future, oppositional discourse can be simultaneously feminist and antifeminist. For example, the forfeiting male wrestler deployed feminist arguments to counter the girl's equality right to wrestle, saying he did not want to commit violence against women. Likewise, "the dynamics of contestation between pro-life and pro-choice movements are too complex to be captured by the concept of backlash."[70] Whether coming in the form of backlash or oppression, we need to be alert to and expose the constant inventiveness of exclusionary politics.[71]

Rather than spending our time debating whether backlash is distinctive from what came before it, and whether it is triggered by women's advances—advances that leave many behind—it would be more fruitful to think about specific behaviors we want to make visible—derision, trolling, and violence—and narratives we want to counter. In particular, feminists have much to gain from theorizing the role of gender-based violence. Kate Manne's insightful book *Down Girl*, for example, carefully analyzes the gender dynamics at play in mass shootings and the extensive lengths commentators go to deny that misogyny is the driving force.[72] By documenting the fierce and vitriolic hostility to women's gains, it becomes harder to believe that the path to equality is a gentle and incremental one where stereotypes wither away once women and minority men prove their abilities and people become accustomed to their presence, as social theorists once predicted.[73]

In the end, it may not matter whether violence amounts to backlash or the continuation of oppression. Whether animus against women legislators stems from their gender nonconformity,[74] their increasing numbers, or their increasing policy successes,[75] violence against women in politics is worrisome.[76] Is the kidnapping plot against Michigan Governor Gretchen Whitmer a backlash, but the plot against the first Minnesota Congresswoman Coya Knudson mere opposition?[77] How should we think about the large number of death threats against Muslim Congresswoman Ilhan Omar? Scholars who study violence against women in politics document the ever present aspect of violence against women, rather than carving off a time-bound period of backlash.[78] The foundation of the American constitutional system rests on white supremacy; so too, women's exclusion from the public sphere was (and remains) a constitutive feature of liberal democratic and republican polities, just as it is of authoritarian regimes and military dictatorships.[79]

Rather than split hairs over backlash, versus misogyny, we need to focus on the behaviors that perpetuate this constitutive exclusion, such as violence against women in public office, and strategize about how best to push back against discursive countermobilizations. We should resist thinking about change in a linear binary—sexism or backlash—and instead pay attention to how countermovements evolve and develop feminist discourse to use against them.

IV. COUNTERING BACKLASH WITH COUNTERNARRATIVES

Even before the ascendency of Donald Trump, social movement scholars warned progressives that they could not simply counter lies with facts.[80] Instead, activists need to deploy counternarratives that work at an emotional, not just a rational, level. For example, instead of debunking the facts behind the narrative of the greedy McDonald's customer, opponents of tort "reform" to limit personal injury suits should tell a story of the indifferent large corporation against the uninsured burn victim of fast-food coffee. Progressives need to better understand and use to our advantage media practices, narratives, and discourse.

Rather than focusing on the specifics of legal doctrine, advocates of strengthening sex discrimination law should consider how to disrupt and counter the tenacity of deep-seated and pervasive beliefs denying the existence of discrimination and faith in American meritocracy—that is, social facts.[81] Social science experiments have found that if people do not believe discrimination or sexual assault is widespread, if they think of those who discriminate or rape as bad people and do not see what looks like a bad person before them, or if they believe women often lie about sexual coercion, they are likely to conclude that no wrong has occurred, no matter how much researchers stacked the evidence in the plaintiff's favor. Law is not just a system of rules but an arena for norm contestation (albeit not a neutral one) and a discourse. Winning legal cases has material distributive consequences, but it also helps groups draw attention to a cause, shape discourse and norms, and educate the public about social facts.[82]

More so now than ever, feminists are able to influence discourse: to adduce evidence, expose faulty reasoning, describe mobilizations, and uncover lies and hypocrisy. We have a presence in the media, as part of law faculties, as academics and public intellectuals, as civil servants, as senior members of the legal profession, as legislators, and as judges. Changes in technology have also given women less mediated ways to communicate, such as #MeToo. Dedicated journalists in Steubenville and Missoula kept institutions from burying stories of sexual assault.[83] Damning video and text messages went viral: Chanel Miller's eloquent victim impact statement describing how Stanford swimmer Brock Turner's sexual assault affected her garnered millions of views. *New York Times* journalists Jodi Kantor and Megan Twohey's *She Said*[84] and Ronan Farrow's *Catch and Kill*,[85] breaking the Harvey Weinstein story, when read together, show the difference mainstream media gatekeepers make. Without the new gender beat at the *New York Times* and Jill Abramson as executive editor, and the sympathetic response of the *New Yorker*, NBC might have successfully buried the Harvey Weinstein story, just as Fox News managed to conceal the serial perpetration of Roger Ailes and others,[86] and the *Washington Post* tried to bury Amy Brittain's reporting on Charlie Rose. These journalists are now "players in position."[87] Even so, journalists such as Farrow and survivors such as Chanel Miller and Dr. Christine Blasey-Ford (who testified against Brett Kavanaugh) have faced a vicious response that includes death threats, litigation, threats of financial ruin, and public shaming, forcing some voices off of social media and others into hiding.

Faludi urges us to respond to backlash by "challeng[ing] its deluge of half-baked claims and myths by holding a bright spotlight up to its propagators' threadbare logic and fallacious data."[88] We need to expose and stop oppressive behaviors, disrupt countermobilization narratives, and deploy feminist narratives. Upon reflection, we cannot see backlash as distinctive from opposition and oppression. Falsely claiming backlash from either judicial action or moving too swiftly when the evidence does not support such claims clouds our understanding of social change and risks chilling legitimate demands for justice. Given its imprecision, the failure of those who assert it to offer evidence in support of their claims, the way both allies and opponents use it to caution against demanding change in or outside of courts, and its simplistic assumptions about progress and discourse, it is time to, if not jettison the term "backlash" altogether, recognize its political baggage and analytic shortcomings.

Notes

1. *Backlash*, Oxford English Dictionary (2nd ed., 1989).
2. Michelle V. Rowley, *Anything but Reactionary: Exploring the Mechanics of Backlash*, 45 Signs: J. Women in Culture & Soc'y 278, 282 (2020).
3. Felice A. Stern, *Backlash*, 40 Am. Speech 156 (1965).
4. Seymour Martin Lipset & Earl Raab, The Politics of Unreason: Right-Wing Extremism in America: 1790-1970 (1970); Jane Mansbridge & Shauna L. Shames, *Toward a Theory of Backlash: Dynamic Resistance and the Central Role of Power*, 4 Pol. & Gender 623, 624 (2008).
5. In *Symbolic Crusade*, Gusfield famously wrote about temperance as a response to the threat of Catholics, Southern Europeans, and city dwellers to rural the dominance of white Protestants. *See* Joseph R. Gusfield, Symbolic Crusade: Status Politics and the American Temperance Movement (1986). Beauvoir wrote about anticommunism as resistance to progress. *See* Brittany R. Leach, *Whose Backlash, Against Whom? Feminism and the American Pro-Life Movement's "Mother-Child Strategy,"* 45 Signs: J. Women in Culture & Soc'y 319, 321 (2020).
6. Robert C. Post & Reva B. Siegel, Roe *Rage: Democratic Constitutionalism and Backlash*, 42 Harv. C.R.-C.L. L. Rev. 373, 388 (2007); Reva B. Siegel, *Constitutional Culture, Social Movement Conflict and Constitutional Change: The Case of the De Facto Era*, 94 Calif. L. Rev. 1323, 1362–63 (2006). For a recent discussion of white backlash, *see* Robert D. Putnam & Shaylyn Romney Garrett, The Upswing: How America Came Together a Century Ago and How We Can Do It Again (2020).
7. Nancy L. Cohen, Delirium: The Politics of Sex in America (2012); Comparative Perspectives on Social Movements: Political Opportunities, Mobilizing Structures, and Cultural Framings (Doug McAdam et al. eds., 1996); David S. Meyer & Suzanne Staggenborg, *Movements, Countermovements, and the Structure of Political Opportunity*, 101 Am. J. Soc. 1628 (1996); Siegel, *supra* note 6; Mayer N. Zald & Bert Useem, *Movement and Countermovement Interaction: Mobilization, Tactics, and State Involvement*, in Social Movements in an Organizational Society (1987).
8. Susan Faludi, Backlash: The Undeclared War Against American Women (1991).
9. Susan Faludi et al., *A Conversation with Susan Faludi on Backlash, Trumpism, and #MeToo*, 45 Signs: J. Women in Culture & Soc'y 336, 341 (2020).
10. Faludi, *supra* note 8, at xx (emphasis added).
11. Sally J. Kenney, Gender and Justice: Why Women in the Judiciary *Really* Matter (2013). *See also* Rosemary Hunter, *The High Price of Success: The Backlash Against Women Judges in Australia*, in Calling for Change: Women, Law, and the Legal Profession 281 (E. Sheehy & S. McIntyre eds., 2006); Constance Backhouse, *Bias in Canadian Law: A Lopsided Precipice*, 10 Can. J. Women & L. 170 (1998).
12. Kathleen A. Bratton & Rorie L. Spill, *Existing Diversity and Judicial Selection: The Role of the Appointment Method in Establishing Gender Diversity in State Supreme Courts*, 83 Soc.

Sci. Q. 504 (2002); Beverly Blair Cook, *Women Judges: The End of Tokenism*, in WOMEN IN THE COURTS (Winifred Hepperle & Laura Crites eds., 1978).
13. Mary Ann Case, *Trans Formations in the Vatican's War on "Gender Ideology,"* 44 SIGNS: J. WOMEN IN CULTURE & SOC'Y 639 (2019).
14. Nancy L. Cohen, *Toward a Feminist Future: A Political Strategy for Fighting Backlash and Advancing Gender Equity*, 45 SIGNS: J. WOMEN IN CULTURE & SOC'Y 328, 332 (2020).
15. Mary Anne Case, *Feminist Fundamentalism as an Individual and Constitutional Commitment*, 19 AM. U. J. GENDER, SOC. POL'Y & L. 549 (2011).
16. Ann E. Cudd, *Analyzing Backlash to Progressive Social Movements*, in THEORIZING BACKLASH: PHILOSOPHICAL REFLECTIONS ON THE RESISTANCE TO FEMINISM 5 (Ann E. Cudd & Anita M. Superson eds., 2002).
17. JESSICA LUTHER, UNSPORTSMANLIKE CONDUCT: COLLEGE FOOTBALL AND THE POLITICS OF RAPE (2016).
18. KATE MANNE, DOWN GIRL: THE LOGIC OF MISOGYNY (2017).
19. Cameron Tung, *Chain Reaction*, N.Y. TIMES, Apr. 29, 2018, at 9–11.
20. Dana M. Britton, *Beyond the Chilly Climate: The Salience of Gender in Women's Academic Careers*, 31 GENDER & SOC'Y 5, 16 (2017). *See Nova: Picture a Scientist* (PBS television broadcast Apr. 14, 2021), https://www.pbs.org/wgbh/nova/video/picture-a-scientist/.
21. DERRICK A. BELL, FACES AT THE BOTTOM OF THE WELL: THE PERMANENCE OF RACISM (1992).
22. Siegel, *supra* note 6.
23. TINA FETNER, HOW THE RELIGIOUS RIGHT SHAPED LESBIAN AND GAY ACTIVISM (2008).
24. DIANA GREENE FOSTER, THE TURNAWAY STUDY (2020).
25. Nancy Levit, *Confronting Conventional Thinking: The Heuristics Problem in Feminist Legal Theory*, 28 CARDOZO L. REV. 391, 414 (2006).
26. Jia Tolentino, *The Rising Pressure of the #MeToo Backlash*, NEW YORKER (Jan. 24, 2018), https://www.newyorker.com/culture/culture-desk/the-rising-pressure-of-the-metoo-backlash.
27. RACHAEL DENHOLLANDER, WHAT IS A GIRL WORTH?: MY STORY OF BREAKING THE SILENCE AND EXPOSING THE TRUTH ABOUT LARRY NASSAR AND USA GYMNASTICS (2019).
28. Tolentino, *supra* note 26.
29. Deborah L Brake, *Fighting the Rape Culture Wars Through the Preponderance of the Evidence Standard*, 78 MONT. L. REV. 109 (2017); Nancy Chi Cantalupo, *Dog Whistles and Beachheads: The Trump Administration, Sexual Violence, and Student Discipline in Education*, 54 WAKE FOREST L. REV. 303 (2019); Anne McClintock, *Who's Afraid of Title IX?*, JACOBIN (Feb. 23, 2017), https://jacobinmag.com/2017/10/title-ix-betsy-devos-doe-colleges-assault-dear-colleague.
30. Sabrina Erdely, *A Rape on Campus*, ROLLING STONE (Nov. 19, 2014) (retracted Apr. 5, 2015). *See generally* Levit, *supra* note 25.
31. Cantalupo, *supra* note 29, at 325.
32. Brake, *supra* note 29, at 146.
33. Jennifer Freyd, *What Is Darvo?*, https://dynamic.uoregon.edu/jjf/defineDARVO.html.
34. Deborah L. Brake, *Coworker Retaliation in the #MeToo Era*, 49 U. BALT. L. REV. 1, 3 (2019).

35. Tovia Smith, *A Year Later, Americans Are Deeply Divided over the #MeToo Movement*, NPR (Oct. 31, 2018), https://www.npr.org/2018/10/31/662696717/a-year-later-americans-are-deeply-divided-over-the-metoo-movement.
36. KENNEY, *supra* note 11, at 149–59.
37. GUSFIELD, *supra* note 5; Mansbridge & Shames, *supra* note 4.
38. Linda A. Bell, *Women in Philosophy: A Forty-Year Perspective on Academic Backlash*, in THEORIZING BACKLASH: PHILOSOPHICAL REFLECTIONS ON THE RESISTANCE TO FEMINISM 247, xii (Anita M. Superson & Ann E. Cudd eds., 2002).
39. *Id* at xiii.
40. THEORIZING BACKLASH: PHILOSOPHICAL REFLECTIONS ON THE RESISTANCE TO FEMINISM xiii (Ann E. Cudd & Anita M. Superson eds., 2002).
41. COHEN, *supra* note 7.
42. KATHERINE J. CRAMER, THE POLITICS OF RESENTMENT: RURAL CONSCIOUSNESS IN WISCONSIN AND THE RISE OF SCOTT WALKER (2016); ARLIE RUSSELL HOCHSCHILD, STRANGERS IN THEIR OWN LAND: ANGER AND MOURNING ON THE AMERICAN RIGHT (2016); Tali Mendelberg, *Status Politics and Rural Consciousness*, 34 POL. COMM. 142 (2017); Daniel Kreiss et al., *Trump Gave Them Hope: Studying the Strangers in Their Own Land*, 34 POL. COMM. 470 (2017).
43. Erica Townsend-Bell, *Backlash as the Moment of Revelation*, 45 SIGNS: J. WOMEN IN CULTURE & SOC'Y 287, 291 (2020). *See also* Janice D. Yoder, *Rethinking Tokenism: Looking Beyond Numbers*, 5 GENDER & SOC'Y 178, 192 (1991) (documenting an "intrusiveness effect" perceived by opponents of women's gains).
44. Margaret Thornton, *"Otherness" on the Bench: How Merit Is Gendered*, 29 SYDNEY L. REV. 391, 411 (2007). *See also* CYNTHIA FUCHS EPSTEIN, WOMEN IN LAW 194 (2012).
45. CYNTHIA COCKBURN, IN THE WAY OF WOMEN: MEN'S RESISTANCE TO SEX EQUALITY IN ORGANIZATIONS (1991); Sally J. Kenney, *New Research on Gendered Political Institutions*, 49 POL. RES. Q. 445 (1996); Sally J. Kenney & Susan Sterett, *Tenure in a Chilly Climate*, 32 P/S: POL. SCI. & POL. 91 (1999); Yoder, *supra* note 43.
46. Hochschild, *supra* note 42; Kreiss et al., *supra* note 42.
47. Zein Murib, *Backlash, Intersectionality, and Trumpism*, 45 SIGNS: J. WOMEN IN CULTURE & SOC'Y 295, 296 (2020).
48. Tracy Tully, *Judge Whose Son Was Killed by Misogynistic Lawyer Speaks Out*, N.Y. TIMES (Aug. 3, 2020), https://www.nytimes.com/2020/08/03/nyregion/esther-salas-roy-den-hollander.html.
49. JENNY IRONS, RECONSTITUTING WHITENESS: THE MISSISSIPPI STATE SOVEREIGNTY COMMISSION (2010).
50. MARTIN LUTHER KING, JR., LETTERS FROM A BIRMINGHAM JAIL (1963).
51. Michael J. Klarman, *How* Brown *Changed Race Relations: The Backlash Thesis*, 81 J. AM. HIST. 81 (1994); GERALD N. ROSENBERG, THE HOLLOW HOPE: CAN COURTS BRING ABOUT SOCIAL CHANGE? (1991).
52. Post & Siegel, *supra* note 6.
53. Rosemary Nossiff, *Why Justice Ginsburg Is Wrong About States Expanding Abortion Rights*, 27 PS: POL. SCI. & POL. 227 (1994); Rosemary Nossiff, *Gendered Citizenship: Women, Equality, and Abortion Policy*, 29 NEW POL. SCI. 61 (2007).
54. LINDA HAMILTON KRIEGER, BACKLASH AGAINST THE ADA: REINTERPRETING DISABILITY RIGHTS (2003).

55. Kenney, *supra* note 45.
56. KRIEGER, *supra* note 54, at 341.
57. Thomas M. Keck, *Beyond Backlash: Assessing the Impact of Judicial Decisions on LGBT Rights*, 43 LAW & SOC'Y REV. 151 (2009).
58. Benjamin G. Bishin et al., *Opinion Backlash and Public Attitudes: Are Political Advances in Gay Rights Counterproductive?*, 60 AM. J. POL. SCI. 625, 639 (2016).
59. Linda Greenhouse & Reva Siegel, *The Unfinished Story of* Roe v. Wade, *in* REPRODUCTIVE RIGHTS AND JUSTICE STORIES 2086 (Melissa Murray et al. eds., 2018).
60. Tung, *supra* note 19.
61. Andrew R. Flores & Scott Barclay, *Backlash, Consensus, Legitimacy, or Polarization: The Effect of Same-Sex Marriage Policy on Mass Attitudes*, 69 POL. RES. Q. 43 (2016).
62. Scott Barclay & Andrew R. Flores, *Policy Backlash: Measuring the Effect of Policy Venues using Public Opinion*, 5 IND. J. L. & SOC. EQUALITY 391 (2017); David Fontana & Donald Braman, *Judicial Backlash or Just Backlash? Evidence from a National Experiment*, 112 COLUM. L. REV. 731 (2012).
63. HERBERT JACOB, SILENT REVOLUTION: THE TRANSFORMATION OF DIVORCE LAW IN THE UNITED STATES (1988).
64. Jennifer M. Piscopo & Denise M. Walsh, *Introduction: Backlash and the Future of Feminism*, 45 SIGNS: J. WOMEN IN CULTURE & SOC'Y 267 (2020). *See also* KRIEGER, *supra* note 54, at 380 (finding it difficult to distinguish backlash from sociolegal capture).
65. Townsend-Bell, *supra* note 43; Ana Jordan, *Conceptualizing Backlash: (UK) Men's Rights Groups, Anti-Feminism, and Postfeminism*, 28 CAN. J. L. & FEMINISM 18, 22 (2016) (analogizing antifeminism to a perpetual viral condition where backlash is the acute state when symptoms appear).
66. Murib, *supra* note 47, at 297.
67. Rowley, *supra* note 2, at 281; Mary Hawkesworth, *Visibility Politics: Theorizing Racialized Gendering, Homosociality, and the Feminicidal State*, 45 SIGNS: J. WOMEN IN CULTURE & SOC'Y 311, 312 (2020).
68. Ann Braithwaite, *Politics of/and Backlash*, 5 J. INT'L WOMEN'S STUD. 18 (2004).
69. Leach, *supra* note 5, at 321.
70. *Id.* at 324.
71. Murib, *supra* note 47, at 300 ("while the groups affected may remain the same, the tactics that are used to oppress them are always morphing. . . . [We should focus] on the potential connections between discourse and actions.").
72. MANNE, *supra* note 18.
73. ROSABETH MOSS KANTER, MEN AND WOMEN OF THE CORPORATION (1977).
74. Kira Sanbonmatsu, *Gender Backlash in American Politics?*, 4 POL. & GENDER 634 (2008).
75. Elaine Weiss urges us not to ignore the "rage and backlash unleashed by the [19th] amendment's expansion of voting rights and promise of a more inclusive democracy," but points out that the efforts of antisuffragists to nullify Tennessee's ratification of the Nineteenth Amendment using bribes, dirty tricks, blackmail, and threats were the same opposition tactics they used to oppose ratification. Elaine Weiss, *Women Would Abolish Child Labor (and Other Anti-Suffrage Excuses)*, N.Y. TIMES (Aug. 26, 2020), https://www.nytimes.com/2020/08/26/opinion/sunday/suffrage-19th-amendment.html; *see also* ELAINE WEISS, THE WOMAN'S HOUR (2018).

76. Donald P. Haider-Markel, *Representation and Backlash: The Positive and Negative Influence of Descriptive Representation*, 32 LEGISLATIVE STUD. Q. 107 (2007); Hawkesworth, *supra* note 67; Inter-Parliamentary Union, SEXISM, HARASSMENT AND VIOLENCE AGAINST WOMEN PARLIAMENTARIANS (2016), https://www.ipu.org/resources/publications/issue-briefs/2016-10/sexism-harassment-and-violence-against-women-parliamentarians; Juliana Restrepo Sanín, *Violence Against Women in Politics: Latin America in an Era of Backlash*, 45 SIGNS: J. WOMEN IN CULTURE & SOC'Y 302 (2020); Sanbonmatsu, *supra* note 74.
77. GRETCHEN URNES BEITO, COYA COME HOME: A CONGRESSWOMAN'S JOURNEY (1990).
78. Mona Lena Krook & Juliana Restrepo Sanín, *Violence Against Women in Politics: A Defense of the Concept*, 23 POLITICA Y GOBIERNO 459 (2016); Sanín, *supra* note 76; Hawkesworth, *supra* note 67, at 316.
79. JOAN B. LANDES, WOMEN AND THE PUBLIC SPHERE IN THE AGE OF THE FRENCH REVOLUTION (1988); CAROLE PATEMAN, THE DISORDER OF WOMEN: DEMOCRACY, FEMINISM, AND POLITICAL THEORY (1989).
80. WILLIAM HALTOM & MICHAEL MCCANN, DISTORTING THE LAW: POLITICS, MEDIA, AND THE LITIGATION CRISIS (2004).
81. Katie R. Eyer, *That's Not Discrimination: American Beliefs and the Limits of Anti-Discrimination Law*, 96 MINN. L. REV. 1275 (2012).
82. Post & Siegel, *supra* note 6, at 395.
83. JON KRAKAUER, MISSOULA: RAPE AND THE JUSTICE SYSTEM IN A COLLEGE TOWN (2015); ROLL RED ROLL (Nancy Schwartzman ed., 2019).
84. JODI KANTOR & MEGAN TWOHEY, SHE SAID: BREAKING THE SEXUAL HARASSMENT STORY THAT HELPED IGNITE A MOVEMENT (2019).
85. RONAN FARROW, CATCH AND KILL: LIES, SPIES, AND A CONSPIRACY TO PROTECT PREDATORS (2019).
86. Susan Faludi, *"She Said" Recounts How Two Times Reporters Broke the Harvey Weinstein Story*, N.Y. TIMES, Sept. 22, 2019, at BR14; BOMBSHELL (Jay Roach ed., 2019), https://bombshell.movie/; *The Morning Show* (Jay Carson); Deborah L. Rhode, *#MeToo: Why Now? What Next? 2019 Currie-Kenan Distinguished Lecture*, 69 DUKE L.J. 377, 398 (2019).
87. JOHN W. KINGDON, AGENDAS, ALTERNATIVES, AND PUBLIC POLICIES, UPDATE EDITION, WITH AN EPILOGUE ON HEALTH CARE (2nd ed. 2010).
88. Faludi et al., *supra* note 9, at 341.

CHAPTER 19

SEXUAL HARASSMENT

The Promise and Limits of a Feminist Cause of Action

THERESA M. BEINER

THE development of sexual harassment law has an interesting history, and one distinctively feminist in origin. Feminists won a significant legal victory in 1986 when the U.S. Supreme Court recognized sexual harassment in employment as actionable sex discrimination under Title VII of the Civil Rights Act of 1964 ("Title VII").[1] But the feminist push to recognize sexual harassment as a wrong began a decade earlier, outside the legal arena. Feminists first gave a name to sexual harassment and then started a grass-roots movement to address it. In 1978, feminist activist and former journalist Lin Farley published an influential book describing sexual harassment,[2] while other like-minded feminists and their organizations worked to raise awareness of this troubling workplace practice. Feminist lawyers and legal theorists then worked to develop legal claims and remedies. In 1979, Catharine MacKinnon conceptualized sexual harassment as a form of sex discrimination rather than a private moral wrong. At the time, workplace psychologists had not yet studied sexual harassment. Thus, the legal theory developed without a full understanding of how sexual harassment operated in the workplace.[3] As MacKinnon later noted: "Sometimes, even the law does something for the first time."[4]

This chapter begins by looking at the work of grass-roots feminists who raised awareness of sexual harassment, followed by the legal feminists who theorized sexual harassment as a form of actionable sex discrimination under Title VII. It then considers the development of that law after the Anita Hill/Clarence Thomas hearings, including some setbacks in the courts. Next, it examines feminist engagement with sexual harassment from a variety of perspectives, including critical race feminism, relational feminism, sex-positive feminism, and law and society-inspired legal realist/pragmatic feminism. Some of this work further developed the theoretical foundation for the claim, while much of it critiqued the court-developed standards, as well as the early feminist theory behind the claim, for falling short of fully addressing workplace sexual harassment. Finally, the chapter explores more recent suggestions to abandon discrimination law altogether and instead use tort law, healthy workplace law, and corporate law to attack sexual harassment in the workplace.

I. Feminists, Sexual Harassment, and the Courts

Apart from a few early lawsuits, sexual harassment law first took root in consciousness-raising and grass-roots activism. It eventually moved to the legal arena, where feminist legal theorists, the courts, and the Equal Employment Opportunity Commission (EEOC) set out the basics of the claim. Although lawyers ultimately took over the steering, it was feminist activists who set the wheels in motion.

Beginning in the early 1970s, federal trial courts acknowledged racial and ethnic harassment as a form of race discrimination under Title VII.[5] With respect to sexual harassment, however, trial courts initially held against plaintiffs.[6] Judges dismissed sexual harassment claims as nothing more than a "personal problem" between two individuals—not anything involving the terms or conditions of employment covered by Title VII.[7] In 1977, the first appellate court held that a quid pro quo claim—the conditioning of tangible employment benefits (including sometimes employment itself) on sexual favors—was actionable.[8] It took more time and work by feminist activists and scholars to gain broader recognition of sexual harassment as a legal claim.

In 1975, a group of feminist activists at Cornell University, including Farley, first coined the term "sexual harassment." These feminists began to raise awareness about this workplace wrong, experienced by mostly women, after receiving a complaint about sexual harassment from an administrative assistant, Carmita Wood, working at Cornell University.[9] Farley worked for Cornell's Human Affairs Program (HAP) at the time. As a result of Wood's complaint, the feminists working at HAP began talking to other women and realized that sexual harassment was an issue that the feminist movement needed to attack both politically and legally.[10] In 1978, Farley published *Sexual Shakedown: The Sexual Harassment of Women in the Working World*, detailing instances of sexual harassment of women and raising awareness of the problem.[11]

The following year, feminist legal scholar Catherine MacKinnon theorized sexual harassment as a form of actionable sex discrimination in her influential book, *Sexual Harassment of Working Women*.[12] Her work, along with the promulgation of EEOC Guidelines on sexual harassment the following year,[13] helped turn the corner in the case law. MacKinnon's legal analysis provided a much-needed theoretical framework to move judges from ruling that sexual harassment was a private moral wrong to a form of sex discrimination that was actionable under Title VII.

With a theory grounded in dominance feminism, MacKinnon explained that sexual harassment was not an issue of "bad manners" but instead about power. Men, who held positions of authority in the workplace, had the power to impose sexual conditions on working women.[14] As she explained, "[s]exual harassment is a clear social manifestation of male privilege incarnated in the male sex role that supports coercive sexuality reinforced by male power over the job."[15] Farley and other feminist activists likewise grounded their approach in dominance feminism, arguing that sexual harassment resulted from patriarchy, with Farley explaining that "the name of the game is dominance."[16] MacKinnon advanced two approaches to conceiving of sexual harassment as a form of sex discrimination: an inequality argument and a differences argument. With respect to inequality, she argued that sexual harassment "reinforce[s] the social inequality of women to men" and is a form of sex discrimination.[17] In her differences approach, she argued that sexual harassment also fit within disparate treatment—essentially a condition of women's employment to which men were not subjected.[18]

MacKinnon identified two forms of sexual harassment—what she termed quid pro quo and "conditions of work" harassment.[19] While "conditions of work" harassment lines up with what the Court later identified as "hostile environment" harassment, MacKinnon focused mostly on sexually oriented behavior rather than hostility directed at women.[20] Consistent with the language of Title VII, she explained that sexual harassment has an impact on both the privileges of employment (quid pro quo context) and the terms and conditions of employment (hostile environment context).[21] Analogizing to race, she contended that, similar to racial epithets, derogatory and insulting sexist comments directed at women at work were likewise sex discrimination.[22]

Critiquing the extant case law at the time as looking at the claim from the perspective of tort law, MacKinnon characterized sexual harassment as a group-based harm, not an individual harm.[23] She rejected any "natural" account of sexual harassment, asserting instead that women's work roles were socially constructed.[24] While suggesting that tort law had some potential for redress, she explained that tort, labor, and criminal laws had not helped women confronted by harassment.[25] Tort law also missed the "nexus between women's sexuality and women's employment."[26]

As MacKinnon worked on legal theory, second-wave feminists founded organizations that attacked sexual harassment publicly. Groups such as Working Women United (WWU) and the Alliance Against Sexual Coercion raised awareness, with the WWU eventually establishing an institute that tracked legal cases.[27] Along with relying on dominance feminism, these feminist groups incorporated elements of the Civil Rights movement's analysis of race discrimination and critiques based on the exploitation of labor.[28] They drew parallels between rape and sexual harassment.[29] The work of these groups, along with shifts in American culture and legal advocacy, led to recognition that sexual harassment was a significant workplace problem for women.[30]

The EEOC's promulgation of Guidelines on Sexual Harassment in 1980 also influenced the development of the case law. At the time the EEOC issued its interim Guidelines, Eleanor Holmes Norton was its chairperson.[31] Specifically acknowledging Farley's book as influencing the Guidelines,[32] the EEOC puzzled over the line between what it termed "acceptable social behavior" and harassment, reaching a compromise position that conduct that "has the purpose or effect of unreasonably interfering with an individual's work performance or creating an intimidating, hostile, or offensive working environment" would be actionable.[33]

The Guidelines also waffled over the standard for imputing liability to employers for such harassment. While the Guidelines adopted respondeat superior liability for supervisory harassment, employers were held liable for harassment by coworkers and third parties only when the employer knew or should have known about the harassment and failed to take "immediate and appropriate corrective action."[34] Yet, at the time, very little was known about what corrective or preventative actions would eliminate or even lessen sexual harassment.[35] Indeed, this dearth of knowledge spawned some counterproductive case law for targets of sexual harassment. For example, courts considered an employer's corrective action adequate even if the harassment persisted.[36]

Even with the Guidelines in place, whether and under what circumstances hostile environment sexual harassment was actionable remained an open issue. In 1982, the Eleventh Circuit in *Henson v. City of Dundee* became the first circuit court to hold hostile work environment sexual harassment actionable under Title VII.[37] In 1986, the U.S. Supreme Court, relying heavily on *Henson*, finally agreed in *Meritor Savings Bank, FSB v. Vinson*.[38] Catharine MacKinnon wrote the appellate brief in the case.[39] The EEOC, under the direction of then-chairperson Clarence Thomas, wrote a brief against plaintiff Mechelle Vinson's position.[40] Holding such harassment actionable, the Court emphasized that it must be "sufficiently severe or pervasive 'to alter the conditions of [the victim's] employment and create an abusive working environment.'"[41] While the ruling was a win for feminists, it came with strings attached that made it difficult for plaintiffs to succeed. For example, the Court explained that sexual advances must be "'unwelcome,'" placing the burden on the plaintiff to demonstrate this through her conduct.[42] Acknowledging that the determination of unwelcomeness presents "difficult problems of proof and turns largely on credibility determinations committed to the trier of fact,"[43] it also held that evidence related to Ms. Vinson's "dress and personal fantasies"[44] was "obviously relevant."[45] The Court's discussion of unwelcomeness appeared to invite lower courts to scrutinize—and fault—the plaintiff's behavior for not more clearly objecting to the harassment.

The Court's approach to imputing liability to employers caused confusion. The Court did not settle on a standard for holding an employer liable for a harasser's conduct. The bank had a grievance procedure and argued that Mechelle Vinson's failure to use it or to otherwise inform the company of her harasser's actions insulated it from liability.[46] Vinson, supported by the EEOC Guidelines, argued that, as with other forms of discrimination, the employer should be liable for the supervisor's harassment. Refusing to establish a "definitive rule," the Court instead held that employers are not automatically liable for supervisor sexual harassment, and that lower courts should instead follow agency principles in such cases.[47] Finally, the Court explained that the existence of a grievance process and policy against discrimination like that adopted by the bank, along with Vinson's refusal to use it, did not necessarily absolve the bank of its responsibility for the harasser's actions, pointing out major flaws in the bank's policy.[48] *Meritor* left a fair amount of ambiguity in the law, which the Court did not clarify for another decade.

Once the courts recognized sexual harassment as a form of sex discrimination under Title VII, it became actionable in other areas of the law that prohibited sex discrimination. Courts soon recognized sexual harassment claims under the Fair Housing Act (FHA),[49] which Congress amended in 1974 to add a prohibition of sex discrimination.[50] In 1985, the Sixth Circuit considered the first case relating to sexual harassment and housing in *Shellhammer v. Lewallen*,[51] upholding a magistrate's ruling that the Fair Housing Act's prohibition on sex discrimination parallels that of Title VII. Like the Court in *Meritor*, it cited *Henson v. City of Dundee* in addressing whether the magistrate had erred in ruling against the plaintiffs on the merits of their hostile environment claim. Although the court upheld the finding against the plaintiffs on the facts of that claim, the court opened the door to hostile environment claims under the FHA. Other circuits have similarly used Title VII case law to assess claims for sexual harassment in housing.[52]

Another natural extension of sexual harassment law took place in Title IX of the Civil Rights Act of 1972, which prohibits sex discrimination in any educational program or activity that receives federal funding.[53] Ironically, however, the Court created a more limited claim for students in the educational context than it did for employees under Title VII. In 1998, the Supreme Court held that schools were liable for teacher–student sexual harassment only if a school official with authority to address the harassment knew of it and responded with deliberate indifference.[54] *Gebser v. Lago Vista Independent School District* involved egregious sexual contact perpetrated by a teacher on a student.[55] The Court extended the reasoning of *Gebser* to student-on-student sexual harassment in *Davis v. Monroe County Board of Education*.[56] As long as the school's response was not "clearly unreasonable," it would not be liable.[57] Finally, the harassment had to be "so severe, pervasive, and objectively offensive that it effectively bars the victim's access to an educational opportunity or benefit."[58] The doctrinal hurdles under Title IX make sexual harassment suits even more difficult for students than the developing law of sexual harassment under Title VII.

II. The Hill/Thomas Hearings and the Court's 1990s Case Law Refinements

With the Supreme Court finally acknowledging sexual harassment as a form of sex discrimination in 1986, the EEOC received a marked increase in such charges by the end of the decade.[59] Meanwhile, academic research by psychologists such as Barbara Gutek improved understanding of workplace sexual harassment.[60] At the same time, a backlash began. The Reagan Administration tried to dilute the EEOC Guidelines and weaken the enforcement authority of the EEOC.[61] Men accused of harassment fought back by filing defamation lawsuits.[62] Employers began to resist, providing commentary on proposed EEOC Guidelines to limit their reach, and employer organizations began filing amici curiae briefs in sexual harassment cases.[63] Grass-roots organizations that had worked on the issue began losing funding in the 1980s as employer criticism of the claim increased.[64] As employers invested more heavily in training programs, some feminists began providing corporate training seminars on sexual harassment.[65] With grass-roots efforts floundering, women turned to law for solutions.[66] At the dawn of the new decade, the stage was set for a clash of interests over the developing law of sexual harassment.

This clash reached a fever pitch as a rapt public watched the Senate, on national television, examine Anita Hill's allegations of sexual harassment leveled at then Supreme Court nominee and former EEOC chairperson Clarence Thomas during his 1991 confirmation hearings.[67] The hearings, combined with the Tailhook scandal,[68] led to an even more dramatic increase in the number of sexual harassment charges filed with the EEOC.[69] As women's rights attorney Marcia Greenberger pointed out, "The issue of sexual harassment was out of the shadows. Before Hill's testimony, sexual harassment was viewed as a problem for victims, predominantly women, to solve on their own. Most women suffered in silence rather than jeopardize their careers by complaining."[70]

With more cases reaching the court system, the Court further refined the claim in the 1990s. In 1993, in *Harris v. Forklift System, Inc.*, the Court held that a plaintiff need not suffer psychological harm in order for hostile environment harassment to be actionable, reversing a lower court decision tossing the claim for want of serious injury.[71] However, the Court also adopted an objective and subjective test that would later prove to bar many claims from going forward, requiring that both the target and a hypothetical reasonable person would find the conduct sufficiently severe or pervasive enough to create a hostile work environment.[72] Recognizing that this was not a "mathematically precise test,"[73] the court explained that triers of fact should look "at all the circumstances."[74] The standard left much discretion for lower courts to gauge whether the harassing conduct was severe enough to be actionable.

After *Harris* and *Meritor*, the paradigmatic sexual harassment case remained based on sexual interest or attraction. For example, in *Meritor*, Mechelle Vinson's supervisor's ostensible pursuit of a sexual relationship formed the basis of her sexual harassment claim. Lower courts adopted a "sex *per se*" standard of causation, finding conduct of a sexual nature to satisfy the based-on sex standard.[75] Courts initially were confused, however, when harassment appeared to be based on something other than sexual attraction. Commentators referred to this form of harassment as "gender harassment," because it was not based on sexual interest but instead directed hostility at women (and gender nonconforming men) in the workplace.[76] Teresa Harris, the plaintiff in *Harris v. Forklift Systems*, for example, experienced a combination of sexual overtures and demeaning comments.[77] Courts likewise struggled when the harasser and the harassed employee were of the same sex, sometimes finding such conduct actionable only when the harasser was gay.[78]

The Supreme Court finally held same-sex sexual harassment actionable in 1998 in *Oncale v. Sundowner Offshore Services, Inc.*[79] Noting that this conduct went beyond the "principal evil" that Congress sought to address in Title VII, the Court explained that "'[t]he critical issue... is whether members of one sex are exposed to disadvantageous terms or conditions of employment to which members of the other sex are not exposed.'"[80] The Court provided examples of same-sex harassment that amount to sex discrimination, such as where members of the other sex are spared similar conduct or where the harassment evinces a general hostility toward members of that sex, but left it to lower courts to elaborate other theories of discrimination, such as sex stereotyping and gender nonconformity.[81] Noting that Title VII is not a "general civility code," the Court clarified that "genuine but innocuous differences in the ways men and women routinely interact with members of the same sex and of the opposite sex" were not actionable.[82] "Male-on-male horseplay" and "intersexual flirtation," for example, did not constitute discrimination based on sex for purposes of Title VII.[83]

The Court finally settled on the standard for imputing liability to employers for supervisor sexual harassment in two cases decided the same day in 1998: *Burlington Industries, Inc. v. Ellerth*[84] and *Faragher v. City of Boca Raton*.[85] Lower courts already had reached a consensus on a negligence standard in cases involving coworker harassment (and harassment by third persons, such as clients and customers): If the employer knew or should have known about the sexual harassment but failed to take corrective actions, it would be liable.[86] Similarly, courts agreed that employers were vicariously liable for supervisor quid pro quo harassment.[87] However, employer liability for hostile environment sexual harassment perpetrated by supervisors caused great debate in the lower courts, with courts adopting various standards, including straying from the vicarious liability standard applicable generally to supervisory discrimination under Title VII.[88] Courts asserted that sexual harassment fell outside the scope of employment, harkening back to early cases holding harassment not actionable because it was a "personal problem." The Supreme Court's ultimate standard contains vestiges of this approach.

In the *Ellerth* and *Faragher* decisions, the Court set a baseline of vicarious liability for supervisor sexual harassment, but with the following defense applicable in hostile environment cases in which no tangible employment action was taken:

> The defense comprises two necessary elements: (a) that the employer exercised reasonable care to prevent and correct promptly any sexually harassing behavior, and (b) that the plaintiff employee unreasonably failed to take advantage of any preventive or corrective opportunities provided by the employer or to avoid harm otherwise.[89]

While the Court explained that not every employer would need an antiharassment policy with a grievance process to establish the defense, such a policy would be relevant for proving the first element of the defense.[90] Additionally, the Court instructed, an employee's failure to use such a policy would "normally suffice to satisfy the employer's burden under the second element of the defense."[91]

As a result of the *Ellerth/Faragher* affirmative defense, employers could avoid liability for supervisor-created sexually hostile environments by adopting an anti-sexual harassment policy and grievance process. In addition, because courts imposed a negligence standard for employer liability for coworker sexual harassment,[92] employers could avoid liability for both supervisor and coworker harassment by putting in place and following an anti-sexual harassment policy that provided a means for a target of harassment to notify the employer. And, contrary to the *Ellerth* and *Faragher* Courts' statements that the defense could just limit damages,[93] lower courts used it to free employers from liability for acts of sexual harassment in the workplace.[94] Since the Supreme Court's decision in 1999 in *Kolstad v. American Dental Association*,[95] an employer also can point to its sexual harassment policies and training programs to show that it "engage[d] in good faith efforts to comply with Title VII," and thus shield itself from punitive damage awards.[96]

In the end, the sexual harassment claim became weighed down with legalistic doctrines providing employers with many ways to defeat plaintiffs' claims. Lower courts liberally granted summary judgment on a variety of grounds. Feminist legal scholars responded.

III. Feminist Responses to the Evolving Legal Claim

In the 1990s, feminist legal scholars began taking a hard look at the court-developed sexual harassment claim. Critical race feminists criticized the inaugural legal and feminist theories for failing to incorporate the experiences of women of color. Some feminist scholars struggled to create a theory that would encompass same-sex sexual harassment. Relational feminism played a role in the critique of the "reasonable person" standard. Law and society feminist scholars incorporated the studies of organizational psychologists in an effort to reform court-made standards. Other feminist legal scholars leveled a sex-positive critique at the law, arguing that the law had gone too far, resulting in attempts to eliminate all sexual expression in the workplace. With sexual harassment still common in American workplaces and courts routinely throwing plaintiffs' claims out of court based on legalistic reasoning, it was clear the work of feminist legal theorists was nowhere near finished.

Early in the continuing feminist discussions of sexual harassment law, law professor Kimberlé Crenshaw criticized sexual harassment theory for disregarding and marginalizing the experiences of African American women. She explained that, for Black women, racism and sexism intersect in their experiences.[97] Sexual harassment of Black women often has a racialized component that incorporates stereotypes regarding Black women's sexuality.[98] These stereotypes also have an impact on whether Black women are believed.[99] Harassment for Black women is especially problematic when the harasser is a Black man. This places Black women in a "double bind," whereby they risk harming an ally by speaking up and harming themselves by not doing so.[100] Black women were pivotal to the movement, bringing several of the early sexual harassment cases, two of which involved harassment by Black male bosses.[101] These early pioneers were among those unsuccessful plaintiffs in the trial courts. Yet, as Tanya Kateri

Hernández explained, courts ignored that these sexual harassment plaintiffs were Black women in many cases, including *Meritor*, and thereby engaged in "racial silencing"—essentially obscuring the experiences of minority women.[102]

Other critical race feminists likewise explored the implications of sexual harassment for Latinas, women of Asian descent, and gender-nonconforming women.[103] But while MacKinnon noted that "[a]pparently, sexual harassment can be both a sexist way to express racism and a racist way to express sexism," she still emphasized sex as the defining factor, explaining that "[a]lthough racism is deeply involved in sexual harassment, the element common to these incidents is that the perpetrators are male, the victims are female,"[104] which fueled the critique.

Consistent with the essentialism critique by critical race feminists, legal scholars raised the lack of economic diversity in perspectives on sexual harassment. While the movement was predominantly one of middle-class women, working-class women also played a role in grass-roots organizing as well as by bringing some of the early cases.[105] Indeed, women in traditionally male occupations, many of which are blue collar, experience high levels of sexual harassment. While feminists concentrated on sexually oriented harassment, many women also experienced gender-related hostility on the job that was not of a sexual nature.[106] Feminist legal scholars such as Vicki Shultz and Kathryn Abrams developed sexual harassment theories that encompassed the hostility-based harassment targeted at women, especially those working in traditionally male-dominated workplaces.[107]

One of the early criticisms of sexual harassment law from those opposed to the claim was that behaviors directed at both men and women or directed at members of the harasser's same sex did not seem to fit within the concept of sex discrimination as developed under Title VII, in part due to the limited manner that the Court conceptualized same-sex harassment claims in *Oncale*.[108] Several feminist legal scholars attempted to create theories that would encompass same-sex sexual harassment as well as sexual harassment of men. Difficulties doing so led to an interesting exchange between legal scholars Kathryn Abrams, Anita Bernstein, Katherine Franke, and Vicki Schultz. Referred to as sexual harassment's "second generation,"[109] these feminists labored to reconceptualize "the wrong" of sexual harassment—is it based on the institutionalization of women's subordination (Abram's theory[110]), a dignitary harm based on a lack of respect (Bernstein's position[111]), or perpetuation of heteropatriarchy (Franke's account[112])? Abrams criticized Bernstein's approach, arguing it was individualized and did not emphasize sexual harassment's role in the workplace as a tool used by the more powerful against the less powerful.[113] Franke, according to Abrams, in an effort to encompass same-sex sexual harassment, did not fully situate the problem of sexual harassment in the workplace.[114] Describing workplaces as "sites of resistance" for women, and that sexual harassment acts as a means of "preserving male control and masculine norms that have characterized the workplace,"[115] Abrams explained that "[a] distinctive feature of these control oriented forms of sexual harassment is that they operate against women as a group."[116] Abrams was concerned that, in an effort to create a theory that incorporates the oppression of nonconforming men, these other scholars lost the role of sexual harassment in the subordination of women.[117] While Abrams acknowledged the contribution of Schultz in extending sexual harassment to nonsexual acts, she criticized Schultz as "run[ning] a higher risk of replacing one unitary theory of sexual harassment for another."[118] In the end, Abrams eschewed creating a "one-size-fits-all" theory of sexual harassment.[119]

Feminist legal scholars also grappled with the "reasonable person" standard that courts applied to sexual harassment. Relational feminists argued that women viewed these situations differently than men, and a gender-neutral standard privileged a male perspective on what courts would consider sexually harassing.[120] While the work of psychology professor Barbara Gutek substantiated that men and women had different perceptions on what is sexually harassing, other feminists worried that using a "reasonable woman" standard reinforced stereotypes about women as "irrational" and in need of paternalistic protection.[121] They also raised concerns about essentialism—that this "reasonable woman" was white, heterosexual, and middle class.[122] While the Ninth Circuit adopted the reasonable woman standard in *Ellison v. Brady*, the Supreme Court avoided the issue in *Harris v. Forklift Systems*, a case in which feminists split on advocating for which standard—reasonable person or reasonable woman—the Court should apply.[123] Later, in *Oncale*, the Court retained the reasonable person terminology but directed triers of fact to judge the harassment "from the perspective of the reasonable person in the plaintiff's position, considering 'all the circumstances,'"[124] leaving open the question of whether the plaintiff's gender is such a circumstance. Subsequent scholarship using empirical methods has questioned how much the formulation matters, suggesting that judges and juries may be unable to dislodge their own gendered perspectives merely by changing the standard from reasonable person to reasonable woman.[125]

As workplace psychologists began to produce more academic work about how people perceived sexual harassment and how targets responded, another group of feminists began to criticize the Court's legal standards for not reflecting these realities. Coming from a legal realism or pragmatic feminism perspective, these feminist legal scholars challenged the Court's reliance on training programs and grievance processes by employers asserting the *Ellerth/Faragher* defense.[126] Studies showed that targets of harassment rarely complained due to reasonable fears of retaliation or because they thought nothing would be done; yet, employers easily met the affirmative defense by putting a grievance process in place that targets rarely used.[127] Legal scholars also criticized courts for finding that sexual harassment was not sufficiently severe or pervasive to be actionable in situations in which studies showed that both women and men agreed that the behaviors were harassing.[128]

With the rise of employer enforcement of anti-sexual harassment policies, Vicki Schultz took a sex-positive approach, criticizing both employers and feminists for taking sexual harassment law too far and encouraging asexual workplaces that were counterproductive to workers' agency. Reasoning that an emphasis on eliminating sexual conduct at work results in too broad an application of sexual harassment law, Schultz laid part of the blame at the feet of feminist scholars who argued that "[m]en's sexual overtures subverted gender equality."[129] Schultz previously had asserted that feminists' reliance on sexual harassment as sexual exploitation limited their opportunity to link sexual harassment to sex segregation and other inequities in the workplace.[130] Her new work went farther, detailing the costs, including to women, of a sexually sanitized workplace.

While Schultz criticized sexual harassment law for going too far, other scholars condemned the law for not doing enough to rectify the wrong of sexual harassment. As feminist legal scholars discussed and critiqued various aspects of the court-developed claim, it became increasingly clear that women (and some men) continued to have difficulties successfully pursuing these claims under Title VII.[131]

IV. OTHER LEGAL MEANS OF ADDRESSING WORKPLACE SEXUAL HARASSMENT

The failure of Title VII to adequately address workplace sexual harassment has led some feminist legal scholars to consider other claims that might prove more effective. Some of these scholars have returned to tort law, which a few plaintiffs had used successfully in some early cases. In a similar vein, corporate scholars have argued for using business law as a means of addressing sexual harassment. Both approaches reflect a turn to a more inclusive "universal" framework for addressing sexual harms and away from the explicitly gendered lens of sex discrimination law.

Katie Eyer has advocated for reducing reliance on discrimination law in favor of a more universal approach that uses what she terms "extradiscrimination remedies," including claims for violation of "just cause" laws, the Family and Medical Leave Act, and healthy workplace laws.[132] Eyer examined the psychological research on attributions of discrimination, concluding that "psychology scholars have found extensive support for the conclusion that people are reluctant to make attributions to discrimination, even in the presence of compelling 'direct' evidence, and even when given objective measures of the likelihood that discrimination has occurred."[133] Concerned that universalist approaches are "likely to dilute feminist workplace gains and mask inequality," Jessica Clarke countered that such a shift might lead to sexual harassment being seen "as no worse than personality conflicts."[134] The debate about universalist approaches continues among feminists.

Legal scholars have come full circle in suggesting that tort law may provide a means to compensate targets of sexual harassment and curb the behavior. Before Congress expanded Title VII remedies to include compensatory and punitive damages, and even after it did so, due to the caps Congress placed on damage awards under Title VII,[135] commentators suggested that tort law would offer a better means of making targets whole.[136] In addition, some commentators theorized that sexual harassment did not operate like a group harm but instead more like an individual wrong.[137] They argued that targets of harassment could use intentional infliction of emotional distress and other tort theories, such as assault and battery, to better address harassment.[138]

These arguments harken back to MacKinnon's initial rejection of tort law as an adequate remedy, and her advocacy for developing a distinctive legal theory that recognized the group-based nature of sexual harassment.[139] Farley, too, had observed that women had tried "nearly every imaginable form of civil legal action; this includes unemployment hearings, private suits, human rights complaints, and federal-law suits brought under Title VII jurisdiction,"[140] and they still found no consistent means of relief. But a new cohort of feminist scholars is revisiting these suppositions. As recently as 2020, one feminist legal scholar has advocated the application of dignitary tort law to workplace sexual harassment.[141] Yet it remains unclear whether tort law would work any better today than it did in the 1970s.

Like the proponents of tort law, scholars of corporate law argue that Title VII has fallen short in its failure to eliminate workplace sexual harassment.[142] They suggest using breach of fiduciary duty and duties of care and loyalty. Corporate fiduciaries, in theory, violate the duty of loyalty when they engage in sexual harassment.[143] This theory works for instances in which women have accused corporate executives of sexual harassment. Rampant sexual harassment at workplaces such as Uber and Signet Jewelers, as well as misconduct by executives such as Roger Ailes and Bill O'Reilly at Fox, provide examples.[144] Publicly traded companies also can be held liable for false statements under Rule 10b-5 of the Securities Exchange Act.[145] Not disclosing sexual harassment by top executives might qualify as actionable under this theory. Commentators note that shareholder suits have the advantage of a longer statute of limitations than Title VII and have no damage caps—distinct advantages in comparison to Title VII.[146] The advantages of this approach, too, remain to be seen.

V. Conclusion

The rise of the #MeToo movement raises the question of whether the grass-roots feminists who first attacked workplace sexual harassment in the 1970s were headed in the right direction when they complained that government solutions, in particular the EEOC Guidelines, were "bureaucratic and legalistic."[147] Indeed, some of the early feminists who took on sexual harassment preferred activist approaches, such as consciousness-raising and leafleting, to courtrooms.[148] The court-developed doctrines applied to sexual harassment became legalistic in a way that incentivized bulletproofing by employers and failed to provide many targets of harassment with relief. As MacKinnon herself noted, "[t]he [#MeToo] movement is surpassing the law in changing norms and providing relief that the law did not."[149] But perhaps legal action acts in synergy with such movements, resulting in better case outcomes. The Third Circuit's decision in *Minarsky v. Susquehanna County* shows some promise in this regard. In that case, the court explicitly acknowledged that it was informed by the #MeToo movement in overturning the trial court's granting summary judgment for the employer, reasoning that an issue of fact existed as to the reasonableness of the plaintiff's failure to report harassment based on fears of retaliation.[150] With the successful prosecution of Harvey Weinstein, sexually harassing behavior that powerful people long got away with is now having consequences for harassers.[151] In addition, corporations have become more active in addressing sexual harassment as a result of #MeToo.[152] This includes increasing board diversity, using "Weinstein" clauses in mergers and acquisitions and abandoning mandatory arbitration of sexual harassment claims.[153] The groundswell of support from women resulting from the #MeToo movement provides hope for increased success for sexual harassment plaintiffs in court.

NOTES

1. 42 U.S.C. §§ 2000e-1 et seq.; Meritor Sav. Bank, FSB v. Vinson, 477 U.S. 57 (1986).
2. LIN FARLEY, SEXUAL SHAKEDOWN: THE SEXUAL HARASSMENT OF WOMEN ON THE JOB (1978).
3. CATHARINE A. MACKINNON, SEXUAL HARASSMENT OF WORKING WOMEN: A CASE OF SEX DISCRIMINATION xii (1979).
4. Louise F. Fitzgerald, Suzanne Swan & Vicki J. Magley, *But Was It Really Sexual Harassment? Legal, Behavioral, and Psychological Definitions of the Workplace Victimization of Women*, in SEXUAL HARASSMENT: THEORY, RESEARCH, AND TREATMENT 5, 9 (William O' Donohue ed., 1997) (quoting MacKinnon).
5. *See, e.g.,* Rogers v. EEOC, 454 F.2d 234 (5th Cir. 1971) (discrimination based on Latina heritage), *cert. denied*, 406 U.S. 957 (1972).
6. *See, e.g.,* Corne v. Bausch & Lomb, Inc., 390 F. Supp. 161, 163 (D. Ariz. 1975), *rev'd*, 525 F.2d 55 (9th Cir. 1977); Miller v. Bank of Am., 418 F. Supp. 233, 236 (N.D. Cal. 1976), *rev'd*, 600 F.2d 211 (9th Cir. 1979); Tomkins v. Public Serv. Elec. & Gas Co., 422 F. Supp. 553 (D.N.J. 1976), *rev'd*, 568 F.2d 1044 (3d Cir. 1977); *cf.* Williams v. Saxbe, 413 F. Supp. 654 (D.D.C. 1976), *vacated sub nom.*, Williams v. Bell, 587 F.2d 1240 (D.C. Cir. 1978); *see also* CARRIE N. BAKER, THE WOMEN'S MOVEMENT AGAINST SEXUAL HARASSMENT 28–31(2008) (detailing cases in which plaintiffs lost).
7. *See, e.g., Corne*, 390 F. Supp. at 163, *vacated*, 562 F.2d 55 (9th Cir. 1977); *Tomkins*, 422 F. Supp. at 556, *rev'd*, 568 F.2d 1044 (3d Cir. 1977); Barnes v. Train, No. 1828-73, 1974 WL 10628 (D.D.C. Aug. 9, 1974), *rev'd sub nom.*, Barnes v. Costle, 561 F.2d 983 (D.C. Cir. 1977).
8. *See, e.g., Barnes*, 561 F.2d (stating the plaintiff-employee had an actionable claim under Title VII).
9. BAKER, *supra* note 6, at 28, 31.
10. *Id.* at 30.
11. FARLEY, *supra* note 2.
12. MACKINNON, *supra* note 3, at 4; Patti A. Giuffre & Christine L. Williams, *Boundary Lines: Labeling Sexual Harassment in Restaurants*, 8 GENDER & SOC'Y 378, 379 (1994) (noting significance of MacKinnon book).
13. EEOC 1980 Guidelines on Sexual Harassment, 29 C.F.R. § 1604.11 (1980).
14. MACKINNON, *supra* note 3, at 173.
15. *Id.* at 191–92.
16. FARLEY, *supra* note 2, at 34, 49, 260–61; *see also* BAKER, *supra* note 6, at 94.

17. MacKinnon, *supra* note 3, at 174.
18. *Id.* 193.
19. *Id.* at 32.
20. *Id.* at 40.
21. *Id.* at 208.
22. *Id.* at 210.
23. MacKinnon, *supra* note 3, at 172.
24. *Id.* at 220.
25. *Id.* at 158–59, 161–72.
26. *Id.* at 171.
27. Baker, *supra* note 6, at 31, 40–41.
28. *Id.* at 94.
29. *Id.* at 95; *see also* MacKinnon, *supra* note 3, at 218–20 (also discussing rape).
30. *See* Baker, *supra* note 6, at 63.
31. *See id.* at 116–19.
32. *See* J. Clay Smith, Jr., *Prologue to the EEOC Guidelines on Sexual Harassment*, 10 Capital U. L. Rev. 471, 471 (1981).
33. *See id.* at 472–73.
34. *See id.* at 475 (quoting interim guidelines).
35. *See* Theresa M. Beiner, *Sex, Science and Social Knowledge: The Implications of Social Science Research on Imputing Liability to Employers for Sexual Harassment*, 7 Wm. & Mary J. Women & L. 273 (2001); Susan Bisom-Rapp, *An Ounce of Prevention is a Poor Substitute for a Pound of Cure: Confronting the Developing Jurisprudence of Education and Prevention in Employment Discrimination Law*, 22 Berkeley J. Emp. & Lab. L. 1 (2001).
36. *See, e.g.,* Blankenship v. Parke Care Ctrs., Inc., 123 F.3d 868 (6th Cir. 1997), *abrogation recognized by* Collette v. Stein-Mart, Inc. 126 F. App'x. 678, 684 at n. 3 (6th Cir. 2005); Crenshaw v. Delray Farms, Inc., 968 F. Supp. 1300, 1306–07 (N.D. Ill. 1997).
37. Henson v. City of Dundee, 682 F.2d 897, 901 (11th Cir. 1982).
38. 477 U.S. at 66–67.
39. *See* Baker, *supra* note 6, at 154.
40. *See id.* at 164–65.
41. *Meritor*, 477 U.S. at 67 (quoting *Henson*, 682 F.2d at 904).
42. *Id.* (quoting 29 C.F.R. § 1604.11(a) (1985)).
43. *Id.*
44. *Id.* at 68 (quoting 743 F.2d at 146 n.36).
45. *Id.* at 69.
46. *Id.* at 70.
47. *Meritor*, 477 U.S. at 72.
48. *Id.* at 72–73.
49. *See* Shellhammer v. Lewallen, 770 F.2d 167 (6th Cir. 1985) (per curiam); DiCenso v. Cisneros, 96 F.3d 1004 (7th Cir. 1996).
50. 42 U.S.C.A. §§ 3604–06, 3617, 3631; *see* Braunstein v. Dwelling Managers, Inc., 476 F. Supp. 1323, 1326 (S.D.N.Y. 1979); United States v. Reece, 457 F. Supp. 43, 45 n.2 (D. Mont. 1978).
51. *Shellhammer*, 770 F.2d 167.
52. *See, e.g.,* Honce v. Vigil, 1 F.3d 1085, 1088 (10th Cir. 1993); Glover v. Jones, 522 F. Supp. 2d 496, 503 (W.D.N.Y. 2007).

53. 20 U.S.C. § 1681(a). *See* Franklin v. Gwinnett Cty. Pub. Schs., 503 U.S. 60 (1992); Gebser v. Lago Vista Indep. Sch. Dist., 542 U.S. 274 (1998); Davis v. Monroe Bd. of Educ., 526 U.S. 629 (1999).
54. *Gebser*, 524 U.S. at 290.
55. *Id.* at 277–78.
56. *Davis*, 526 U.S. at 633.
57. *Id.* at 649.
58. *Id.* at 647.
59. Baker, *supra* note 6, at 170 (increasing from 3,661 in 1981 to 5,557 in 1990).
60. *Id.* at 157–59; Barbara A. Gutek, Sex and the Workplace: The Impact of Sexual Behavior and Harassment on Women, Men, and Organizations (1985).
61. *See* Baker *supra* note 6, at 136–39.
62. *See id.* at 140–42.
63. *See id.* at 142–43.
64. *See id.* at 154.
65. *Id.* at 153–54.
66. *Id.* at 154–56.
67. *See, e.g.*, Don DeMaio, *Sexual Harassment Complaints Are Increasing in Rhode Island*, Providence Bus. News, Apr. 10, 1995, at 15; M.A. Stapleton, *Sexual Harassment Filings on Rise as Awareness Increases, Seminar Told*, Chi. Daily L. Bull., Dec. 8, 1994, at 1 (recounting the increase in sexual harassment suits after the hearings); Phil Willon, *EEOC Chief Faces Long Haul: America Mired in Decade of Anger, Confusion over Equal Rights*, Richmond Times-Dispatch, Dec. 24, 1995, at A1.
68. *See* Baker, *supra* note 6, at 171–73; Michael Winerip, *Revisiting the Military's Tailhook Scandal*, N.Y. Times Online, May 13, 2013, https://www.nytimes.com/2013/05/13/booming/revisiting-the-militarys-tailhook-scandal-video.html.
69. According to one news source, sexual harassment charges filed with the EEOC increased from 6,000 in 1990 to 15,300 in 1996. *See* Leslie Kaufman, *A Report from the Front: Why It Has Gotten Easier to Sue for Sexual Harassment*, Newsweek (Jan. 13, 1997), at 32.
70. *See* Marcia D. Greenberger, *What Anita Hill Did for America*, CNN (Oct. 22, 2010, 9:54 AM), https://www.cnn.com/2010/OPINION/10/21/greenberger.anita.hill/index.html.
71. 510 U.S. 17, 20–21 (1993).
72. *Id.* at 21–22.
73. *Id.*
74. *Id.* at 23.
75. *See* Linda Kelly Hill, *The Feminist Misspeak of Sexual Harassment*, 57 Fla. L. Rev. 133, 151–53 (2005) (describing the cases).
76. *See* L. Camille Hébert, *Sexual Harassment Is Gender Harassment*, 43 U. Kan. L. Rev. 565 (1995); Vicki Schultz, *Reconceptualizing Sexual Harassment*, 107 Yale L.J. 1683 (1998).
77. *Harris*, 510 U.S. at 19. For example, the president of the company referred to Harris as "a dumb ass woman" as well as suggested to her that they go to a hotel to negotiate her raise.
78. *See, e.g.*, Fredette v. BVP Mgmt. Ass'n, 112 F.3d 1503 (11th Cir. 1997) (holding harassment by homosexual male supervisor was actionable).
79. 523 U.S. 75 (1998).
80. *Id.* at 80 (quoting *Harris*, 510 U.S. at 25 (Ginsburg, J., concurring)).
81. *Id.* at 80–81.

82. *Id.* at 81.
83. *Id.*
84. 524 U.S. 742 (1998).
85. 524 U.S. 775 (1998).
86. *See, e.g.,* Fenton v. Hisan, Inc., 174 F.3d 827, 829–30 (6th Cir. 1999); Carter v. Chrysler Corp., 173 F.3d 693, 700 (8th Cir. 1999) (racial harassment context); Baty v. Willamette Indus., Inc., 172 F.3d 1232, 1241–42 (10th Cir. 1999); Burrell v. Star Nursery, Inc., 170 F.3d 951, 955 (9th Cir. 1999).
87. *See, e.g.,* Sauer v. Salt Lake City, 1 F.3d 1122, 1127 (10th Cir. 1993); Davis v. Sioux City, 115 F.3d 1365, 1367 (8th Cir. 1997); Steel v. Offshore Shipbuilding, Inc., 867 F.2d 1311, 1316 (11th Cir. 1989).
88. For a summary of this confusion, *see* Benjamin David Oppenheimer, *Exacerbating the Exasperating: Title VII Liability of Employers for Sexual Harassment Committed by Their Supervisors*, 81 CORNELL L. REV. 66, 71 (1995).
89. *Ellerth*, 524 U.S. at 765.
90. *Id.*
91. *Id.*
92. *See Faragher*, 524 U.S. at 799 (acknowledging that lower courts have been "uniformly judging employer liability for coworker harassment under a negligence standard").
93. *Ellerth*, 524 U.S. at 765; *Faragher*, 524 U.S. at 807.
94. *See* THERESA M. BEINER, GENDER MYTHS V. WORKING REALITIES: USING SOCIAL SCIENCE TO REFORMULATE SEXUAL HARASSMENT LAW 153 (2005); Beiner, *supra* note 35, at 290–91.
95. 527 U.S. 526, 527–28 (1999).
96. *See, e.g.,* Woodward v. Ameritech Mobile Commc'ns, Inc., No. IP 98–0744–C H/G, 2000 WL 680415, at *16 (S.D. Ind. Mar. 20, 2000); Hull v. APCOA/Standard Parking Corp., No. 99 C 2832, 2000 WL 198881, at *15 (N.D. Ill. Feb. 14, 2000).
97. Kimberlé Crenshaw, *Race, Gender, and Sexual Harassment*, 65 S. CALIF. L. REV. 1467, 1468 (1992).
98. *Id.* at 1469.
99. *Id.* at 1470.
100. *Id.* at 1472.
101. *See* BAKER, *supra* note 6, at 15–16, 180–84; Williams v. Saxbe, 413 F. Supp. 654 (D.D.C. 1976), *vacated sub nom.*, Williams v. Bell, 587 F.2d 1240 (D.C. Cir. 1978); Barnes v. Train, No. 1828-73, 1974 WL 10628 (D.D.C. 1974), *rev'd sub nom.*, Barnes v. Costle, 561 F.2d 983 (D.C. Cir. 1977).
102. Tanya Kateri Hernández, *"What Not to Wear"—Race and Unwelcomeness in Sexual Harassment Law: The Story of Meritor Savings Bank v. Vinson, in* WOMEN AND THE LAW STORIES 277, 279–80 (Elizabeth M. Schneider & Stephanie M. Wildman eds., 2011).
103. *See, e.g.,* Maria L. Ontiveros, *Three Perspectives on Workplace Harassment of Women of Color*, 23 GOLDEN GATE U. L. REV. 817 (1993); Tanya Katerí Hernández, *A Critical Race Feminism Empirical Research Project: Sexual Harassment & the Internal Complaints Black Box*, 39 U.C. DAVIS L. REV. 1235 (2006); Sumi Cho, *Converging Stereotypes in Racialized Sexual Harassment: Where the Model Minority Meets Suzie Wong*, 1 J. GENDER, RACE & JUST. 177 (1997).
104. MACKINNON, *supra* note 3, at 30–31.
105. BAKER, *supra* note 6, at 67–81.

106. *See id.* at 67–76.
107. *See* Schultz, *supra* note 76; Kathryn Abrams, *The New Jurisprudence of Sexual Harassment*, 83 CORNELL L. REV. 1169, 1196–98, 1206–07 (1998).
108. *Oncale*, 523 U.S. at 80–81; *see also* Hill, *supra* note 75, at 159–62.
109. *See* Hill, *supra* note 75, at 149.
110. Abrams, *supra* note 107.
111. Anita Bernstein, *Treating Sexual Harassment with Respect*, 111 HARV. L. REV. 445 (1997).
112. Katherine M. Franke, *What's Wrong with Sexual Harassment?*, 49 STAN. L. REV. 691 (1997).
113. *See* Abrams, *supra* note 107, at 1185.
114. *See id.* at 1193–94.
115. *See id.* at 1198.
116. *See id.* at 1208.
117. *Id.* at 1204.
118. *Id.* at 1215.
119. Abrams, *supra* note 107, at 1217.
120. *See* Naomi R. Cahn, *The Looseness of Legal Language: The Reasonable Woman Standard in Theory and in Practice*, 77 CORNELL L. REV. 1398, 1413–14 (1992) (contrasting cultural feminism with the reasonable woman standard).
121. *See, e.g.*, Kathryn Abrams, *The Reasonable Woman: Sense and Sensibility in Sexual Harassment Law*, DISSENT 48, 50 (Spring 1995); Erin M. Lehane, *Who Is the Reasonable Plaintiff and What Does She Mean for the Rest of Us? Feminist Theory and Hostile Work Environment*, 19 WOMEN'S RTS. L. REP. 229, 236 (1998); Bernstein, Bernstein, *supra* note 111, at 475.
122. *See* Bernstein, *supra* note 111, at 473–74; Cahn, *supra* note 120, at 1415–17.
123. *See* Abrams, *supra* note 121, at 51.
124. *Oncale*, 523 U.S. at 81 (quoting *Harris*, 510 U.S. at 23).
125. *See* BEINER, *supra* note 94, at 55–57 (detailing the findings of the empirical studies); Barbara A. Gutek et al., *The Utility of the Reasonable Woman Legal Standard in Hostile Environment Sexual harassment Cases: A Multimethod, Multistudy Examination*, 5 PSYCHOL. PUB. POL'Y & L. 596, 623 (1999).
126. *See, e.g.*, Joanna L. Grossman, *The Culture of Compliance: The Final Triumph of Form over Substance in Sexual Harassment Law*, 26 HARV. WOMEN'S L.J. 3, 21–23 (2003); Susan Bisom-Rapp, *Fixing Watches with Sledgehammers: The Questionable Embrace of Employee Sexual Harassment Training by the Legal Profession*, 24 U. ARK. LITTLE ROCK L. REV. 147 (2001); Bisom-Rapp, *supra* note 35; Beiner, *supra* note 35.
127. *See* Beiner, *supra* note 35, at 288–91; Grossman, *supra* note 126, at 23–26.
128. *See* Theresa M. Beiner, *Let the Jury Decide: The Gap Between What Judges and Reasonable People Believe Is Sexually Harassing*, 75 S. CALIF. L. REV. 791 (2002); *see also* Jill D. Weinberg & Laura Beth Nielsen, *What Is Sexual Harassment? An Empirical Study of Perceptions of Ordinary People and Judges*, 36 ST. LOUIS U. PUB. L REV. 39 (2017) (detailing a study which found that ordinary people have broader perceptions of what is sexually harassing than judges).
129. Vicki Schultz, *The Sanitized Workplace*, 112 YALE L.J. 2061, 2075 (2003).

130. *See* Schultz, *supra* note 76, at 1696–1701.
131. *See, e.g.,* Theresa M. Beiner, *The Misuse of Summary Judgment in Hostile Environment Cases*, 34 WAKE FOREST L. REV. 71 (1999); M. Isabel Medena, *A Matter of Fact: Hostile Environments and Summary Judgments*, 8 S. CALIF. REV. L. & WOMEN'S STUD. 311 (1999); Elizabeth M. Schneider, *The Dangers of Summary Judgment: Gender and Federal Civil Litigation*, 59 RUTGERS L. REV. 705 (2007).
132. Katie R. Eyer, *That's Not Discrimination: American Beliefs and the Limits of Anti-Discrimination Law*, 96 MINN. L. REV. 1275, 1341, 1343–44 (2012).
133. *Id.* at 1299.
134. Jessica A. Clarke, *Beyond Equality? Against the University Turn in Workplace Protections*, 86 IND. L.J. 1219, 1219–20 (2011).
135. *See* Civil Rights Act of 1991, 42 U.S.C. § 1981a(a)(1).
136. *See* Joanna Stromberg, *Sexual Harassment: Discrimination or Tort?*, 12 UCLA WOMEN'S L.J. 317, 348 (2003) (suggesting a tort approach to avoid damage caps); Krista J. Schoenheider, Comment, *A Theory of Tort Liability for Sexual Harassment in the Workplace*, 134 U. PA. L. REV. 1461, 1462 (1986).
137. *See* Ellen Frankel Paul. *Sexual Harassment as Sex Discrimination: A Defective Paradigm*, 8 YALE L. & POL'Y REV. 333, 349, 357, 361 (1990); Stromberg, *supra* note 136.
138. *See* Paul, *supra* note 137, at 361–62; Mark McLaughlin Hager, *Harassment as Tort: Why Title VII Hostile Environment Liability Should Be Curtailed*, 30 CONN. L. REV. 375, 376 (1998); Stromberg, *supra* note 136, at 337–41.
139. MACKINNON, *supra* note 3, at 220.
140. FARLEY, *supra* note 2, at 165.
141. L. Camille Hébert, *How Sexual Harassment Law Failed Its Feminist Roots*, 22 GEO. J. GENDER & L. (2021); *see also* L. Camille Hébert, *Conceptualizing Sexual Harassment in the Workplace as a Dignitary Tort*, 75 OHIO ST. L.J. 1345 (2014).
142. Daniel Hemel & Dorothy S. Lund, *Sexual Harassment and Corporate Law*, 118 COLUM. L. REV. 1583, 1603 (2018).
143. *See id.* at 1641.
144. *See* Amelia Miazad, *Sex, Power, and Corporate Governance*, 54 U.C. DAVIS L. REV. 52 (2021).
145. Hemel & Lund, *supra* note 142 at 1635–40.
146. *Id.* at 1666.
147. *See* BAKER, *supra* note 6, at 132.
148. *Id.* at 97.
149. Catharine A. MacKinnon, *Where #MeToo Came From, and Where It's Going*, THE ATLANTIC (March 24, 2019), https://www.theatlantic.com/ideas/archive/2019/03/catharine-mackinnon-what-metoo-has-changed/585313/.
150. 895 F.3d 303, 313 n.12 (3d Cir. 2018).
151. *See* Audrey Carlsen et al., *#MeToo Brought Down 201 Powerful Men. Nearly Half of Their Replacements Are Women*, N.Y. TIMES, Oct. 23, 2018, https://www.nytimes.com/interactive/2018/10/23/us/metoo-replacements.html; MacKinnon, *supra* note 149, at 8.
152. *See* Miazad, *supra* note 144, at 63–79.
153. *See id.* at 63–66, 74–75, 79–80.

CHAPTER 20

DEGENDERING THE LAW THROUGH STEREOTYPE THEORY

STEPHANIE BORNSTEIN

A foundational principle of feminist movements is that women should be able to live their lives free from stereotypical notions about what they can or should do. Inherent in this idea is a challenge to the gender hierarchy that such stereotypes reinforce: feminists seek not just equal opportunity to take on traditionally masculine roles but also to uproot the subordinated position that accompanies traditionally feminine roles. Beyond challenging the power structure supported by sex-role stereotypes lies the potential to dismantle binary notions of gender altogether, and to recognize the liberty of all individuals to live as they wish.

The development of gender stereotype theory in both feminism and in the law reflects these three interrelated ideas—antisubordination, dismantling the gender binary, and promoting individual liberty. Early challenges to sex-role stereotypes developed in response to the ideology of "separate spheres" of home and market: that women's biology made them better suited to caregiving and domestic work, while "breadwinning" should be left to men. As the fields of psychology and sociology advanced, social scientists began to develop a language for identifying biases based on classifications like race and sex, identifying the systemic ways in which stereotypes operate to disadvantage all women. Toward the end of the twentieth century, gender stereotype theory served as the foundation for LGBT+ advocates to challenge penalties for failing to conform to sex-role expectations.

It was within this context that feminist legal scholars and advocates developed the legal theory of gender stereotyping in antidiscrimination law. Throughout the 1970s and 1980s, advocates litigated a series of constitutional law cases under equal protection and statutory cases under Title VII of the Civil Rights Act of 1964 (Title VII) to establish that penalizing individuals based not only on their sex but also based on *stereotypes associated with* their sex constituted unlawful sex discrimination. Early cases took an anticlassification approach to challenge separate spheres ideology, while laying the groundwork for more fundamental attacks. In the 1990s and 2000s, social scientific knowledge on the operation of biases provided a framework for antisubordination approaches that challenged the structural nature of gender stereotypes in the workplace. In the 2010s and 2020s, advocates successfully framed discrimination on the basis of sexual orientation or gender identity as an unlawful penalty for failure to conform to gender stereotypes.

Gender stereotyping as a legal theory has evolved to become a primary concept in antidiscrimination law. Judicial recognition of the theory has broadened the lens of what constitutes discrimination "because of sex" and allowed a wider array of proof to support discrimination claims. The theory has also made its mark beyond antidiscrimination law, providing a useful critical lens to expose the gendered assumptions built into other areas of law.

Yet the reach of the theory is not without limits. Courts have readily adopted gender stereotyping arguments to support formal equality, anticlassification ends but have yet to fully embrace the more substantive, structural approach that the social science of stereotyping could support. The root of gender stereotyping in separate spheres ideology, designed to preserve the domesticity of middle-class white women, has also limited the theory's usefulness in redressing intersectional discrimination and the racialized gender stereotyping that women of color experience. Although discrimination on the basis of sexual orientation or gender identity now constitutes discrimination because of "sex," the formal textualist rationale for that legal rule complicates the role of stereotyping arguments around gender nonconformity and risks reifying a binary notion of gender. As with feminist legal theory itself, then, gender stereotype theory remains a work in progress.

I. THE FEMINIST MOVEMENT'S EMBRACE OF GENDER STEREOTYPING THEORY

Breaking free from women's proscribed social roles has long been a core goal of Western feminism. Feminist legal scholars have advanced a theory of gender stereotyping to explain and contest women's disadvantage.

A. Breaking Out of Domesticity

The concept of gender stereotyping dates back to the first wave of the women's movement in the mid-nineteenth century, with the rise in popularity of the "cult of domesticity."[1] As the economy moved from agrarian to industrial, Victorian notions of "separate spheres" from England gained popularity in the United States.[2] Despite the fact that women had always worked, particularly less affluent women and women of color, when work became separated from family farms, moving from a home-based to a factory-based economy, sex-role stereotypes gained influence among the middle class. Women, primarily white women, were perceived to be more properly suited to the domestic sphere, based on their roles as mothers and caregivers, and men for the market sphere, as breadwinners and providers.[3] While less affluent women and women of color were expected to work, they were still affected by assumptions about women's "primary" role, relegated to domestic labor or other jobs for which they were paid less than men.[4]

The stereotypes of domesticity can be seen in early legal decisions on workplace health and safety in the early industrial age, as more women moved into the "market" sphere. Prior to the passage of the Fair Labor Standards Act of 1935 (FLSA), labor rights reformers sought to improve working conditions by passing state laws that limited working hours.[5] In the 1905 Supreme Court case *Lochner v. New York*,[6] such limits were famously struck down for male workers as contrary to their constitutional right of freedom to contract. Yet working-hours limits were, for a period of time, upheld for women based on stereotypical assumptions of womanhood. In 1908's *Muller v. Oregon*,[7] when upholding a state law that limited women's maximum working hours, the Supreme Court concluded that such laws served the "public interest" because "woman's physical structure and the performance of maternal functions place her at a disadvantage in the struggle for subsistence," as is "especially true when the burdens of motherhood are upon her."[8] For the next decade and a half, most states passed laws limiting work hours or types of occupations for women, but not for men, based on the primacy of women's roles as mothers and related stereotypes about their feminine "nature."[9]

In 1923, in a return to *Lochner*ian principles, the Court struck down such restrictions on women,[10] leaving all workers without protection from excessive hours until the passage of the FLSA.[11] But despite placing women's hours on the same footing as men's, and despite the significant rise in women's labor force participation that followed when millions of working-age men were serving overseas during World War II,[12] the deeply held ideas of domesticity persevered. Separate spheres ideology continued to hold powerful sway over the organization of work and public life, used by those in power to support existing power structures and gender and racial hierarchies.

By 1970, women composed nearly 40 percent of the paid U.S. labor force,[13] yet there was little question that the workplace remained designed around men, and that women who participated were considered outsiders. Congress enacted Title VII in 1964, making it illegal under federal law to discriminate based on sex.[14] But the United States lacked—and still lacks—universal paid maternity leave,[15] relying on the assumption that women would or should leave the workforce during pregnancy to stay home with young children.

This persistent notion of separate spheres was at the heart of much of U.S. liberal feminism when it developed most robustly in the 1960s and 1970s. Women, especially women of color, had been working for decades, yet they remained marginal and powerless in most workplaces and could be forced out of work when they became pregnant. Efforts around reproductive freedom were linked not just with sexual freedom but also with economic freedom. As a result, liberal feminists focused their efforts on advocating for women to be treated equal to men in the market sphere and as individuals in society, a theoretical frame that would seed an anticlassification approach in law.

B. Building the Social Science of Gender Stereotypes

As the separate spheres ideology pervaded U.S. social and economic life during the early twentieth century, the burgeoning field of psychology began to trace the root and impact of such beliefs. Coined by writer Walter Lipmann in 1922 as an analogy to print typesetting,[16] the term "stereotype" was popularized in social psychology by Gordon Allport in his 1954 book *The Nature of Prejudice*. "Whether favorable or unfavorable," Allport explained, "a stereotype is an exaggerated belief associated with a category [that] function[s] to justify (rationalize) our conduct in relation to that category."[17] In the 1960s and 1970s, social psychologists challenged the biological nature of sex-role stereotypes, separating the concept of "gender" from "sex" and questioning the binary nature of male versus female traits.[18]

In the decades since, a rich and diverse body of social science research has documented widely held beliefs about sex roles and the resilient persistence of gender stereotypes that continue to impede equality. First, researchers have mapped an array of gender-based stereotypes that, while rooted in assumptions about biology and domesticity, go far beyond separate spheres. As sociologist Cecilia Ridgeway has explained, "[a] wide variety of research . . . has demonstrated that people . . . hold well-defined, largely consensual gender stereotypes"—that men are "agentic" or "instrumental," assumed to be "competent, assertive, independent, forceful, and dominant," while women are "communal" or "expressive," expected to be "emotional . . . nurturing, sensitive, kind, [and] responsive."[19] These categorizations lead to assumptions about what men and women can or should do or how they should look or behave. Although such stereotypes may be "descriptive" about how men and women "are," they also become "prescriptive" when individuals are penalized for deviating from expected sex roles or gender performance.[20] For example, legal scholar Joan Williams has identified common patterns of how gender stereotypes play out at work, reflecting that women must constantly prove their competence but balance it with demonstrations of warmth.[21]

Second, researchers have shown that stereotypes are both an individual and a systemic problem. In the early 2000s, legal scholar Linda Krieger and social psychologist Susan Fiske popularized research demonstrating that, due to our need to sort information and make decisions quickly, we often rely on stereotypes and engage in either explicit or implicit bias when making judgments.[22] Because cultural understandings or "schemas" of gender stereotypes are so pervasive, this may happen automatically, but it may also be controlled by the processes we use to make decisions.[23]

The development of the social science of stereotypes from the 1990s to the present provided a more robust picture of the array of gender stereotypes and their pervasiveness in society and its institutions. Both the social science evidence and the language of gender stereotypes that evolved during this period provided the theoretical basis for antisubordination approaches in law, paving the way for systemic and structural challenges.

Despite its modernization during this period, however, gender stereotype theory has been subject to criticism about its inherent limitations. Because early sex stereotype theory developed in response to the separate spheres ideology designed to protect the domesticity of primarily white, middle-class women, it bears remnants of essentialist views of "women" and "men." A number of scholars have worked to expose how gender stereotypes may be racialized,[24] yet the ability of gender stereotype theory to redress intersectional harms remains limited. Stereotypes around, for example, motherhood and sexuality are different for white and Black women, resulting in different expectations of behavior that a focus on gender alone fails to address.[25]

Likewise, challenges to sex stereotyping grew out of opposition to the constraints of binary sex-role differences rather than to the construct of gender as a whole. Another body of feminist theory focuses on identifying the performative nature of gender and the goal of greater freedom from all gender constraints.[26] While such theory seeded the idea of using law to protect gender nonconformers, whether this reaches as far as protecting those whose gender is nonbinary remains to be seen.

Both the promise of gender stereotype theory and its limitations appear in how the concept has been translated by courts and incorporated into the law.

II. Gender Stereotyping in Antidiscrimination Law

By the mid-twentieth century, feminist theorists and social scientists had established a framework for understanding the constraints of gender stereotypes. Legal advocates began to translate that understanding into antidiscrimination law, first through the constitutional law of equal protection and then through federal statutory law barring sex discrimination.

A. Constitutional Law: Equal Protection

Gender stereotyping as a legal theory developed from the foundational efforts of Ruth Bader Ginsburg in a series of cases she litigated as the head of the ACLU Women's Rights Project in the 1970s.[27] Drawing on the efforts of the liberal feminist movements in both the United States and Sweden, where she had spent time researching, Ginsburg sought to challenge the ways in which U.S. law codified domesticity's separate spheres.[28] As she conceived it, if the law reflected stereotypical views of the proper roles of men and women, this amounted to sex discrimination that hurt both genders. Embedded sex-role stereotypes constrained individuals, both men and women, from living their lives as they wished. Moreover, the law's reliance on sex-role stereotypes served to reinforce gender hierarchy, where feminine roles were subordinated to masculine roles.[29] In several cases, Ginsburg chose to represent male plaintiffs, understanding that masculine and feminine expectations were two sides of the same discriminatory coin that served to reinforce this dichotomy.[30] Ginsburg's legal strategy set out to remove "all overt gender-based classifications" and to "open all doors" for men and women alike[31]—a primarily anticlassification strategy that served an antisubordination goal.

To achieve this end, Ginsburg litigated a series of cases before the U.S. Supreme Court challenging laws that relied on gender stereotypes in a variety of areas of life. In doing so, she succeeded in both establishing a heightened level of scrutiny under the Constitution's guarantee of equal protection for government actions based on sex and exposing how classifications that rely on gender stereotypes constitute sex discrimination.[32] In a sequence of cases building upon one another, Ginsburg challenged laws that codified the stereotype that women, but not men, should be family caregivers in the domestic sphere, and that men, but not women, should be breadwinners in the market sphere. In 1971, in her first case before the Court, *Reed v. Reed*,[33] Ginsburg challenged an Idaho state probate law that preferred male to female estate administrators after a family member's death. The plaintiff, Sally Reed, sought to be named administrator of her teenage son's estate after he committed suicide. Under state law creating a preference for male estate administrators, however, her estranged ex-husband—who had only recently sought partial custody over their son—was appointed instead.[34] Even though Sally Reed did not work outside the home, Ginsburg argued, Reed was better suited than her ex-husband to administer their son's estate given her expertise with managing "the financial affairs of their family unit" as "a central part of [her] daily occupation."[35] Noting that "legislative judgments have frequently been based on inaccurate stereotypes of the capacities and sensibilities of women," Ginsburg challenged directly the codification of separate spheres ideology as "reinforced by diverse provisions of state law."[36] The Court agreed, striking down the Idaho statute as an "arbitrary legislative choice" that violated the Fourteenth Amendment.[37]

Ginsburg continued to prevail in several cases that followed over the next decade, building upon *Reed* to cement the Court's holding that laws that rely on sex stereotypes are unconstitutional. In *Weinberger v. Wiesenfeld*,[38] she successfully challenged federal social security law that provided "mother's insurance benefits" to children and surviving widows who cared for them, but not to widowers whose wives had died. In *Califano v. Goldfarb*,[39] she challenged a similar provision that entitled widows to social security survivor's benefits automatically, but only wid*owers* who could prove financial dependency on their deceased wives. The Court held in the plaintiff's favor, clearly identifying such "'archaic and overbroad' generalizations" as sex stereotypes that violated equal protection.[40] A handful of other cases in which Ginsburg participated as *amicus curiae* on behalf of the ACLU Women's Rights Project continued this trend, striking down, under equal protection, laws that limited work-related benefits to mothers but not fathers and financial support to husbands but not wives.[41]

Over the next decade, the Court extended stereotype theory beyond domesticity's division of work and home, invalidating a wide array of government action that reflected sex stereotyping. In two cases in 1975 and 1976, the Court struck down state laws setting different ages of majority for men and women based on gender stereotypes, and adopted an "intermediate" level of scrutiny for distinctions based on sex.[42] The Court also invalidated state policies assuming proper occupations for women and men, including a bar on admitting men to a Mississippi state nursing school,[43] and—in a decision authored by then Supreme Court Justice Ginsburg—a bar on admitting women to the Virginia Military Institute.[44] In a series of family law–related decisions, the Court held that both presumptions that husbands should control marital property[45] and presumptions that mothers' should bear custodial responsibility for children (in another opinion authored by Justice Ginsburg)[46] violated guarantees of equal protection.

Yet the string of wins was not unbroken, reflecting the challenge of using a gender stereotyping approach focused on facial classifications to dismantle sex discrimination that is structural in nature. In several cases, the Court refused to hold that sex-differentiated state action violated equal protection, finding that some rationales for treating men and women differently could satisfy intermediate scrutiny. In 1974, in *Kahn v. Shevin*,[47] the Court upheld a Florida law that provided a state property tax exemption for widows but not for widowers. Reasoning that "[t]here can be no dispute that the financial difficulties confronting the lone woman ... exceed those facing the [lone] man," the Court held that the statute was "reasonably designed to further the state policy of cushioning the financial impact of spousal loss upon the sex for which that loss imposes a disproportionately heavy burden."[48] In 1979, in *Personnel Administrator of Massachusetts v. Feeney*,[49] the Court upheld a Massachusetts law that gave veterans a preference in hiring for state jobs, despite its discriminatory effect on women. Disparate impact claims were not available under the Constitution, veteran status was a gender-neutral criteria, and the law was not adopted for a "discriminatory purpose" or to "keep[] women in a stereotypic and predefined place," the Court held.[50]

The gender stereotyping theory as applied to constitutional law was not without its critics. Some legal scholars, including Mary Becker and Catharine MacKinnon, viewed the Ginsburg approach as hollow, or worse—a formal "assimilationism" that, by casting the law's harms to men and women as equally pernicious, failed to adequately redress the subordinated status of women.[51] Although the theory worked well to address irrational or overbroad generalizations, it did not create true equality for women: a gender-neutral law that, for example, provided the same social security benefits or property tax credits to widowed men and women left women in a worse position due to their preexisting, subordinated status.

Ginsburg herself recognized that formal equality was a necessary first step, but she viewed the antistereotyping approach as offering the promise of uprooting the gender hierarchy enforced by separate spheres.[52] Indeed, as a jurist, Ginsburg took a more nuanced position that banned harmful gender stereotypes but left room for the law to allow helpful distinctions. Writing for the Court in 1996 in *United States v. Virginia*,[53] Ginsburg explained:

> "Inherent differences" between men and women ... remain cause for celebration, but not for denigration ... Sex classifications may be used to compensate women "for particular economic disabilities [they have] suffered," to "promot[e] equal employment opportunity," to advance full development of the talent and capacities of our Nation's people. But such classifications may not be used ... to create or perpetuate the legal, social, and economic inferiority of women.[54]

Separating classifications that compensate women from those resting on stereotypes has proven difficult, however, and the Court has not always offered persuasive justifications for where it has drawn this line.[55]

B. Statutory Law: Title VII of the Civil Rights Act of 1964

By 1980, the concept of gender stereotyping had been firmly established in constitutional law. Yet the Constitution applies to state actors only; to extend the legal concept of gender stereotyping to claims against private actors would require the Court to interpret federal statutes similarly. The primary relevant statute, Title VII of the Civil Rights Act of 1964,[56] prohibits discrimination in employment because of sex, race, and other protected characteristics. Within a short time after Title VII's enactment—and during the same period in which Ginsburg was litigating equal protection cases—plaintiffs' attorneys began using Title VII to challenge employer decisions that relied on gender stereotypes.[57]

Early cases laid the groundwork for the use of stereotype theory in statutory law. In 1971, in *Phillips v. Martin Marietta Corp.*,[58] the Court held that it was sex discrimination for an employer to refuse to hire women with preschool-age children when it hired men with young children and women without children. The employer could not rely on a stereotype about the "existence of such conflicting family obligations" for women but not for men without proof that it was directly related to a job requirement.[59] Likewise, in 1978, in *City of Los Angeles Department of Water & Power v. Manhart*,[60] the Court held that an employer could not require female employees to make larger contributions than male employees to the employer's pension fund based on statistics that women, on average, live longer than men. As the Court acknowledged, the employer's decision did not "involve a fictional difference between men and women"—that is, some female employees *would* predecease some male employees.[61] Nevertheless, relying on sex stereotypes, whether based on real differences or not, violates Title VII when individuals are assumed to comport with the behavior of their protected class group.[62]

Then, in 1989, the Court decided *Price Waterhouse v. Hopkins*,[63] the case now most associated with using sex stereotype theory to prove sex discrimination. Plaintiff Ann Hopkins sued for sex discrimination after being denied promotion to partner at national accounting firm Price Waterhouse. In 1982, the year Hopkins applied for promotion, only seven of the firm's 662 partners were women, and Hopkins was the only woman of eighty-eight employees proposed for partnership.[64] Hopkins had five years with the firm and a stellar record as senior manager, with accomplishments surpassing those of her peers.[65] Yet her evaluations for promotion were marked by the operation of gender stereotypes. Those critical of her application noted her "abrasiveness" and "brusqueness," making her "overly aggressive, unduly harsh, [and] difficult"—characteristics that would not have been viewed as negatively had she been a man.[66] They described her as "macho" and "overcompensat[ing] for being a woman," and told her that, to become partner, she should "take a course at charm school," "walk more femininely, talk more femininely, dress more femininely, wear make-up, [and] have her hair styled."[67]

To make out her case, Hopkins drew on social science, presenting expert testimony from social psychologist Susan Fiske. Fiske's role was to link the decisionmakers' stereotyped thoughts to their actions, to show how "the partnership selection process . . . was likely influenced by sex stereotyping."[68] The Court agreed, holding that the partners' criticism of Hopkins "stemmed from an impermissibly cabined view of the proper behavior of women" and noting that "[w]e are beyond the day when an employer could evaluate employees by assuming or insisting that they matched the stereotype associated with their group."[69] Moreover, Price Waterhouse put Hopkins, and all female employees, in an impossible bind: assertiveness was required to succeed on the job and valued in men, but assertive women were penalized.[70]

Engaging in stereotypical thinking alone, however, was not enough for liability, the Court cautioned; the employer must have "actually relied on [] gender in making its decision."[71] Hopkins had proven this, too: Price Waterhouse "[gave] . . . effect to . . . comments that resulted from sex stereotyping" when it factored her perceived failure to conform to feminine stereotypes into evaluation of her work performance.[72] Indeed, the plurality opinion explained, Fiske's expert testimony was unnecessary:

> It takes no special training to discern sex stereotyping in a description of an aggressive female employee as requiring "a course at charm school . . ." [I]f an employee's flawed "interpersonal skills" can be corrected by a soft-hued suit or a new shade of lipstick, . . . [the criticism is likely] motivated by stereotypical notions about women's proper deportment.[73]

With this decision, the Court recognized gender stereotyping as a form of sex discrimination under Title VII, parallel to that which it had recognized under equal protection. Just as state actions that penalize men and women who do not follow traditional sex roles violate the Constitution, employer actions that penalize employees for failing to conform to an expected gender stereotype of appearance or behavior at work constitutes unlawful sex discrimination under Title VII.

III. The Promise and Limitations of Advancing Gender Stereotype Theory in Law

Even as gender stereotyping arguments have taken root in foundational equal protection cases and expanded under Title VII since *Price Waterhouse,* the exact contours of the theory itself remain undefined. In recent works, legal scholars have responded by offering a rich variety of definitions, analyses, and even criticisms of the concept.[74] Anita Bernstein describes sex stereotyping as "a technology of actionable discrimination"—"a mode by which injustice gains effect" when stereotypes are applied to constrain individuals.[75] Kerri Stone focuses on the actionability of sex stereotypes, explaining that to be unlawful, a stereotype must be "voiced or somehow acted upon" and bear a "sufficient nexus" to an employer's adverse action.[76] More skeptical of its transformative potential, Meredith Render argues that a "sex stereotype" is "conceptually empty," a "heuristic" that fails to sort rules that are discriminatory from those that are not, focusing on the "descriptive accuracy" of gendered assumptions but ignoring their "prescriptive force."[77] And Kimberly Yuracko argues that recognition of sex stereotyping has failed to create true gender neutrality or freedom from the constraints of gender; while useful as a burden-shifting mechanism, it risks reinscribing binary gender differences.[78]

Scholars may debate its scope and transformative potential, but there is little doubt that gender stereotyping as a legal theory for alleging discrimination has helped federal courts expand the reach of actionable gender bias. Courts have now held that penalizing an individual for failing to conform to a stereotype associated with a protected class, even a well-meaning or positive stereotype, is discrimination based on that class.[79] It has also allowed some courts to recognize discrimination even without what is known as "comparator evidence"—proof that someone outside the protected class was treated better than the plaintiff.[80] Although stereotype theory has been most directly applied to the protected class of sex, it has opened the door to arguments about the harmful impacts of stereotypes based on other protected classes, such as race, religion, national origin, disability, and age.[81]

Gender stereotyping as a legal theory, then, has helped plaintiffs overcome the challenges of proving their Title VII cases, during a period in which the federal courts have become increasingly hostile to arguments based on implicit bias and disparate impact.[82] In particular, it has succeeded in strengthening protections under Title VII by broadening what constitutes discrimination "because of sex" in two significant areas: (1) caregiver discrimination and (2) sexual orientation and gender identity discrimination.

A. Caregiver Discrimination

In response to gender stereotyping arguments, federal courts have now recognized discrimination against employees because of their family caregiving responsibilities as a subset of sex discrimination under Title VII. Beginning in the 2000s, in a series of cases drawing on social science related to sex-role stereotypes lingering from domesticity, plaintiffs established that employment actions based on assumptions that a mother will be a less committed or less competent employee is unlawful sex discrimination.[83] Courts have so held even where a female plaintiff could not point to a male comparator who was treated better: an adverse employment action based on stereotypes about motherhood alone was enough evidence to infer sex discrimination.[84] Such stereotyping was unlawful even if well intentioned—for example, assuming that an employee who was a mother would rather not relocate for a promotion or take on important assignments that required travel.[85]

Based on a growing body of case law and legal scholarship, in 2007, the federal Equal Employment Opportunity Commission (EEOC) issued Enforcement Guidance on caregiver discrimination that detailed how the gender stereotype theory from *Price Waterhouse* paved the way for such cases.[86] Moreover, echoing Ginsburg's strategy in her equal protection cases, the guidance made clear that men were also protected: both penalizing women by assuming they will conform to caregiver stereotypes and penalizing men who failed to conform to breadwinner stereotypes violated Title VII.[87] This was a significant expansion of the interpretation of discrimination "because of sex" that has strengthened Title VII protections for countless working mothers and caregiving fathers and helped chip away at the remnants of domesticity's separate spheres.

Though it offers groundbreaking protection from workplace penalties stemming from stereotypes about caregivers, this approach has important limits. Courts may now recognize discriminatory sex stereotypes around caregiving that may, alone, establish an inference of sex discrimination, but courts are still far more likely to recognize stereotyping as discrimination when a plaintiff has evidence of either a man who was treated better or explicit expressions of stereotypes about motherhood.[88] And it is only penalties based on stereotyping about, not the reality of, work/family conflict that are unlawful. If workplace penalties are based on a caregiver's actual needs or behaviors—that is, a desire for reduced hours, greater flexibility, or pregnancy accommodation—stereotype theory offers little help.[89]

B. Sexual Orientation and Gender Identity Discrimination

Gender stereotype theory also laid the foundation for the Supreme Court's ruling that discrimination "because of sex" under Title VII includes discrimination because of homosexuality or transgender status.[90] In cases since the 1970s, LGBT+ advocates argued that, when employees were harassed or penalized at work because of their sexual orientation, it was for violating gender stereotypes, and so constituted sex discrimination. Most early federal courts,[91] and the EEOC,[92] disagreed, holding that "sexual orientation" was a separate protected class than "sex," beyond what Congress contemplated when it passed Title VII in 1964.

Then, in 1998, in *Oncale v. Sundowner Offshore Services, Inc.*,[93] the Supreme Court held that same-sex sexual harassment could be actionable under Title VII. In that case, where the plaintiff was a married heterosexual man on an all-male oil rig crew who was sexually assaulted by male coworkers, the fact that the victim and the harassers were men did not bar a sexual harassment claim.[94] Around the same time, the Seventh and Ninth Circuits, relying on *Price Waterhouse*, held that where gay men were sexually harassed for being effeminate, they experienced sex discrimination based on gender stereotyping.[95] Over the next two decades, the Second Circuit and a number district courts held similarly[96]; most other circuit courts disagreed, continuing to view this as sexual orientation discrimination beyond the scope of Title VII.[97]

A parallel line of cases pursued similar arguments on behalf of transgender employees, arguing that discrimination on the basis of gender identity was sex discrimination per se.[98] Advocates argued that to penalize an employee for their transgender status was to penalize them for failing to conform to the gender appearance and behavior associated with the plaintiff's sex assigned at birth. Such arguments also had mixed, though slightly greater, success for plaintiffs. A handful of federal district and circuit courts held that "sex" included transgender status based on a gender stereotype theory[99]; a few others disagreed, though most of those were decided prior to the Court's ruling in *Price Waterhouse*.[100]

In more recent years, the EEOC weighed in again, clarifying its view that gender stereotyping expanded the meaning of "because of sex" under Title VII. In 2012, the EEOC ruled that transgender status discrimination was sex discrimination under Title VII.[101] In 2015, in the wake of the U.S. Supreme Court's ruling in *Obergefell v. Hodges*[102] that the Constitution protects same-sex marriage, and reversing its earlier position, the EEOC ruled that sexual orientation discrimination is sex discrimination under Title VII.[103]

The orientation and gender identity lines of cases converged in June 2020, when the Supreme Court held, in *Bostock v. Clayton County, Georgia*,[104] that discrimination because of one's status as either gay or transgender constitutes discrimination "because of sex." Surprisingly, the majority opinion, authored by Justice Gorsuch, seemed to say little about the theory of gender stereotyping, despite its prominence in prior cases and in the parties' briefing.[105] The word "stereotype" appears only twice in the thirty-three-page opinion, and *Price Waterhouse* is cited only once. But it is hard to understand the Court's formal textualist interpretation of the word "sex" in Title VII to include homosexuality and transgender status without the inference that "sex" includes expected sex stereotypes. Indeed, the two references to "stereotypes" and the citation to *Price Waterhouse* appear in the core of the majority's holding:

> The statute . . . tells us three times . . . that our focus should be on individuals, not groups . . . [A]n employer who fires a woman . . . because she is insufficiently feminine

and also fires a man ... for being insufficiently masculine may treat men and women as groups more or less equally. But in both cases the employer fires an individual in part because of sex.[106]

Shortly thereafter, the opinion restates this idea, noting that "just as an employer who fires both [a man and a woman] for failing to fulfill traditional sex stereotypes doubles rather than eliminates Title VII liability, an employer who fires both ... for being gay or transgender does the same."[107] The Court's holding that sex is a "but-for" cause of such discrimination reflects Ruth Bader Ginsburg's framing five decades earlier: that gender stereotyping that constrains individuals from being treated as individuals, free from assumptions based on their membership in a particular sex group, is discrimination because of sex.

It is possible, then, to read the Court's opinion in *Bostock* as an endorsement of sex stereotype theory so complete that the word "stereotype" need not appear: it is no longer a unique or subset legal theory but instead sex discrimination itself.[108] But again, the reach of the theory has its limitations. Because the Court's textualist reasoning relies on the fact that you cannot identify someone as gay or transgender without knowing their assigned biological sex, the holding protects against gender nonconformity discrimination in a formal, binary way. As a result, a formalist *Bostock*-style approach that leaves binary gender intact may not protect an employee fired for being bisexual, pansexual, or nonbinary.[109]

IV. CONCLUSION

The legal theory of gender stereotyping was introduced and developed through antidiscrimination law. Yet it also applied social science to women's lived experiences, which helped unearth the gender stereotypes that shape many other areas of law. Any time a legal distinction is made based on assumptions related to gender, or an individual is held to expectations based on their group gender status, gender stereotyping has reared its head. The legal doctrine may not apply directly to prohibit the action (as it would in a sex discrimination claim), but the social science of stereotyping may still do some of the work.

A cursory glance at several other areas of law is instructive. In family law, sex stereotypes have played a role in the development of laws related to no-fault divorce and presumptions about alimony payments and child custody.[110] In tort law, the reasonable person standard and damages for "loss of consortium" may involve gendered expectations.[111] In criminal law, gender stereotypes may impact jury selection or defenses involving intimate partner violence.[112] And the broader definition of "sex" encompassed by *Bostock* has been applied to protect transgender students in their educational pursuits.[113] Indeed, while each of Ginsburg's foundational cases was premised on constitutional law, the state actions she challenged involved laws regulating a wide array of substantive fields, including trusts and estates, social security, military benefits, and tax.[114]

Gender stereotype theory as applied in law has greatly strengthened protections against an ever-widening notion of what constitutes discrimination because of "sex." Just as freedom from the constraints of separate spheres was a foundational concept in liberal feminism, freedom from the operation of gender stereotypes has become a foundational concept in feminist approaches to law. The social science of how gender stereotypes operate on both an individual and a systemic level has also advanced courts' abilities to recognize a greater array of discriminatory actions. But work remains if gender stereotype theory is to reach its full potential. Based on its origins to challenge laws meant to protect middle-class white women's domesticity, sex stereotype theory has yet to fully redress the intersectional gender stereotypes experienced by women of color. Although it has helped courts move beyond requiring comparator evidence, legal recognition of penalties for gender nonconformity remain comparative, reinforcing a binary notion of gender. Sex stereotyping arguments have worked well for facial classifications and have begun to chip away at gender hierarchy, but they have had limited purchase in redressing structural sex discrimination. Ironically, each of these challenges proves just how pervasive and sticky traditional sex-role stereotypes are, making the work of gender stereotype theory as important as ever.

Notes

1. *See* Stephanie Bornstein, *The Politics of Pregnancy Accommodation*, 14 HARV. L. & POL'Y REV. 293, 297–98 (2020); Cary Franklin, *Separate Spheres*, 123 YALE L.J. 2878, 2889–94 (2014); JOAN C. WILLIAMS, UNBENDING GENDER: WHY FAMILY AND WORK CONFLICT AND WHAT TO DO ABOUT IT 1–9, 14–39 (1999).
2. *See* Stephanie Bornstein, *The Law of Gender Stereotyping and the Work-Family Conflicts of Men*, 63 HASTINGS L. J. 1297, 1299–1302 (2012); Cary Franklin, *The Anti-Stereotyping Principle in Constitutional Sex Discrimination Law*, 85 N.Y.U. L. REV. 83, 92–97 (2010); WILLIAMS, *supra* note 1, at 1–9, 14–39.
3. *See* WILLIAMS, *supra* note 1, at 1–9, 14–39.
4. *See id.* at 162–63.
5. *See* Bornstein, *supra* note 1, at 297–99.
6. 198 U.S. 45 (1905).
7. 208 U.S. 412, 421 (1908).
8. *Id.*
9. *See, e.g.*, Bosley v. McLaughlin, 236 U.S. 385 (1915); Miller v. Wilson, 236 U.S. 373 (1915); *see also* Bornstein, *supra* note 1, at 298–99.
10. *See* Adkins v. Children's Hosp., 261 U.S. 525, 552–53 (1923).
11. Fair Labor Standards Act of 1938, 29 U.S.C. §§203 et seq.
12. *See* U.S. DEP'T OF VETERANS AFF., AMERICA'S WARS (2020), https://www.va.gov/opa/publications/factsheets/fs_americas_wars.pdf.
13. U.S. Dep't of Labor, WOMEN'S BUREAU, *Civilian Labor Force by Sex*, https://www.dol.gov/agencies/wb/data/facts-over-time/women-in-the-labor-force#civilian-labor-force-by-sex (last visited Aug. 1, 2021).
14. Title VII of the Civil Rights Act of 1964, 42 U.S.C. §§2000e et seq.

15. *See* Krystin Arneson, *Why Doesn't the US Have Mandated Paid Maternity Leave?*, BBC News (June 28, 2021), https://www.bbc.com/worklife/article/20210624-why-doesnt-the-us-have-mandated-paid-maternity-leave.
16. *See* Anita Bernstein, *What's Wrong With Stereotyping?*, 55 Ariz. L. Rev. 655, 658 (2013) (citing Walter Lippmann, Public Opinion 89–90 (1922)).
17. Gordon Allport, The Nature of Prejudice 191 (1954).
18. *See* Monica Biernat & Kay Deaux, *A History of Social Psychological Research on Gender, in* Handbook of the History of Social Psychology 475–97 (A. W. Kruglanski & W. Stroebe eds., 2011).
19. Cecilia L. Ridgeway, Framed by Gender: How Gender Inequality Persists in the Modern World 58–68 (2011) (describing studies).
20. *Id.* at 58.
21. Joan C. Williams & Rachel Dempsey, What Works for Women at Work: Four Patterns Working Women Need to Know (updated ed., 2018) (naming four patterns—"Prove it Again," "The Tightrope," "The Maternal Wall," and "The Tug of War"—and noting that women of color also experience "Double Jeopardy").
22. Linda Hamilton Krieger, *The Content of Our Categories: A Cognitive Bias Approach to Discrimination and Equal Employment Opportunity*, 47 Stan. L. Rev. 1161, 1219–20, 1229–37 (1995); Linda Hamilton Krieger & Susan T. Fiske, *Behavioral Realism in Employment Discrimination Law: Implicit Bias and Disparate Treatment*, 94 Calif. L. Rev. 997, 1003 n.21 (2006) (cataloging the literature on implicit bias).
23. *See, e.g.,* Krieger, *supra* note 22, at 1187–1218 (citing and summarizing in detail the social science on implicit bias). How this research should apply to employer liability for discrimination has been the subject of some debate. *Compare, e.g.,* Susan Sturm, *Second Generation Employment Discrimination: A Structural Approach*, 101 Colum. L. Rev. 458, 460–61 (2001), *and* Anthony G. Greenwald & Linda Hamilton Krieger, *Implicit Bias: Scientific Foundations*, 94 Calif. L. Rev. 945 (2006), *with* Gregory Mitchell & Philip E. Tetlock, *Antidiscrimination Law and the Perils of Mindreading*, 67 Ohio St. L.J. 1023 (2006), *and* Amy L. Wax, *Discrimination as Accident*, 74 Ind. L.J. 1129 (1999).
24. *See, e.g.,* Angela P. Harris, *Race and Essentialism in Feminist Legal Theory*, 42 Stan. L. Rev. 581 (1990); Kimberlé Crenshaw, *Demarginalizing the Intersection of Race and Sex: A Black Feminist Critique of Antidiscrimination Doctrine, Feminist Theory and Antiracist Politics*, 1989 U. Chi. Legal F. 139 (1989); *see also* Williams & Dempsey, *supra* note 21 (describing "Double Jeopardy" for women of color).
25. *See, e,g.,* Crenshaw, *supra* note 24, at 157–60, 163–66.
26. *See, e.g.,* Judith Butler, Gender Trouble: Feminism and the Subversion of Identity (1990); Katherine M. Franke, *The Central Mistake of Sex Discrimination Law: The Disaggregation of Sex From Gender*, 144 U. Pa. L. Rev. 1 (1995); *see also* Martha Chamallas, *Of Glass Ceilings, Sex Stereotypes and Mixed Motives: The Story of* Price Waterhouse v. Hopkins, *in* Women & the Law Stories 307–35 (Elizabeth M. Schneider & Stephanie M. Wildman eds., 2011).
27. *See* Ruth Bader Ginsburg, *Gender and the Constitution*, 44 U. Cinn. L. Rev. 1, 8–9, 37–38 (1975) (discussing Title VII and constitutional law together); *see also* Amy Leigh Campbell, *Raising the Bar: Ruth Bader Ginsburg and the ACLU Women's Rights Project*, 11 Tex. J. Women & L. 157 (2002).
28. *See* Franklin, *supra* note 2, at 87–88, 91–92, 104–06, 120–25.
29. *See* Ginsburg, *supra* note 27, at 28–29, 34–42.

30. Deborah Jones Merritt & Wendy Webster Williams, *Transcript of Interview of U.S. Supreme Court Associate Justice Ruth Bader Ginsburg, April 10, 2009*, 70 OHIO ST. L.J. 805, 814 (2009) (noting that, in numbers, she represented more men than women before the Supreme Court).
31. Interview by Joan C. Williams with Ruth Bader Ginsburg, Legally Speaking Series, Univ. of Cal., Hastings Coll. of the Law, in San Francisco, Cal. (Sept. 15, 2011).
32. *See* Bornstein, *supra* note 2, at 1301–12.
33. 404 U.S. 71 (1971).
34. *Id.* at 71–73.
35. Brief for Appellant at 66, Reed v. Reed, 404 U.S. 71 (1971) (No. 70-4).
36. *Id.* at 17, 34.
37. *Reed*, 404 U.S. at 76.
38. 420 U.S. 636, 640–41 (1975).
39. 430 U.S. 199 (1977).
40. *Id.* at 206–07.
41. *See, e.g.*, Frontiero v. Richardson, 411 U.S. 677 (1973) (striking down federal statute that provided an automatic increase in housing and medical benefits allowance when military men married, but required military women to provide proof of financial dependency of their new husbands); Cleveland Bd. of Educ. v. LaFleur, 414 U.S. 632 (1974) (striking down Ohio school board rule forcing women onto unpaid leave while pregnant, until three months after birth); Orr v. Orr, 440 U.S. 268 (1979) (striking down Alabama statute allowing ex-husbands to be required to pay alimony, but not ex-wives); Califano v. Westcott, 443 U.S. 76 (1979) (striking down federal program providing unemployment benefits for unemployed fathers but not mothers); Wengler v. Druggists Mut. Ins. Co., 446 U.S. 142 (1980) (striking down Missouri law providing widows with worker's compensation death benefits but only widowers if they prove dependency on their wives).
42. *See* Stanton v. Stanton, 421 U.S. 7 (1975) (striking down Illinois law that set age of majority of eighteen for women but twenty-one for men, based on a stereotype that women required less education than men); Craig v. Boren, 429 U.S. 190 (1976) (adopting "heightened scrutiny" review for state action distinctions by sex, and striking down difference in legal drinking age by gender for failing to bear a "substantial relationship" to an "important governmental interest").
43. Mississippi Univ. for Women v. Hogan, 458 U.S. 718 (1982).
44. United States v. Virginia, 518 U.S. 515 (1996).
45. Kirchberg v. Feenstra, 450 U.S. 455 (1981) (striking down Louisiana law giving husbands the right to control community marital property).
46. Sessions v. Morales-Santana, 137 S. Ct. 1678 (2017) (striking down section of federal immigration law requiring different standards for passing citizenship to children from mothers and fathers). *But see* Miller v. Albright, 523 U.S. 420 (1998) (where parents unmarried and child born outside United States, higher citizenship requirements for child whose citizen parent is father rather than mother did not violate equal protection; Justice Ginsburg dissented).
47. 416 U.S. 351 (1974).
48. *Id.* at 353, 355. The case was a rare loss for Ginsburg, who had argued before the Court that it was imposing an unnecessary all-or-nothing choice: rather than strike down the discriminatory credit, hurting widowed women, the Court could have instead held the law

49. unconstitutional and extended the credit to widowed men, too. Brief for Appellants, Kahn v. Shevin, 416 U.S. 351 (1974) (No. 73-78), 1973 WL 172384.
49. 442 U.S. 256 (1979).
50. *Id.* at 279 (applying Washington v. Davis, 426 U.S. 229 (1976)).
51. *See* Catharine A. MacKinnon, *Reflections on Sex Equality Under Law*, 100 YALE L.J. 1281, 1286–97 (1991); Mary Becker, *Patriarchy and Inequality: Towards a Substantive Feminism*, 1999 U. CHI. LEGAL F. 21, 22; *see also* Franklin, *supra* note 2, at 85–86.
52. Ruth Bader Ginsburg & Barbara Flagg, *Some Reflections on the Feminist Legal Thought of the 1970s*, 1989 U. CHI. LEGAL F. 9 (1989).
53. 518 U.S. 515 (1996).
54. *Id.* at 533–34.
55. *See, e.g.,* Michael M. v. Superior Ct. of Sonoma Cty., 450 U.S. 464 (1981) (upholding sex-differentiated state law on statutory rape); Rostker v. Goldberg, 453 U.S. 57 (1981) (upholding requirement that only men register for the military draft); Nguyen v. I.N.S., 533 U.S. 53 (2001) (upholding law that applied more restrictive citizenship requirements to foreign-born child of an American father than mother).
56. Title VII of the Civil Rights Act of 1964, 42 U.S.C. §§2000e et seq. (prohibiting discrimination because of sex, race, color, national origin, or religion).
57. *See* Bornstein, *supra* note 2, at 1312–20.
58. 400 U.S. 542 (1971).
59. *Id.* at 544.
60. 435 U.S. 702 (1978).
61. *Id.* at 707–08.
62. *Id.*
63. 490 U.S. 228 (1989).
64. *Id.* at 233.
65. *Id.* at 233–34.
66. *Id.* at 234–36, 251.
67. *Id.* at 235.
68. *Id.*
69. *Id.* at 236–37, 251.
70. *Id.* at 251 ("An employer who objects to aggressiveness in women but whose positions require this trait places women in an intolerable and impermissible catch 22: out of a job if they behave aggressively and out of a job if they do not. Title VII lifts women out of this bind."). This passage has led some to incorrectly limit gender stereotype theory to only situations including a Catch-22 double bind, though case law does not require this.
71. *Id.*
72. *Id.* at 237.
73. *Id.* at 256.
74. *See* Stephanie Bornstein, *Unifying Antidiscrimination Law Through Stereotype Theory*, 20 LEWIS & CLARK L. REV. 919, 940–941, nn. 112–116 (2016) (describing scholarship).
75. Bernstein, *supra* note 16, at 671, 687, 715–21.
76. Kerri Lynn Stone, *Clarifying Stereotyping*, 59 U. KAN. L. REV. 591, 594, 621, 634–56 (2011).
77. Meredith M. Render, *Gender Rules*, 22 YALE J.L. & FEMINISM 133, 142–43 (2010).
78. Kimberly A. Yuracko, *Soul of a Woman: The Sex Stereotyping Prohibition at Work*, 161 U. PA. L. REV. 757, 758–62, 770–71 (2013); *see also* KIMBERLY A. YURACKO, GENDER NONCONFORMITY & THE LAW 104–09, 137–49 (2016).

79. See Bornstein, *supra* note 74, at 959, 962–63.
80. See id. at 941–54.
81. See id. at 963–72.
82. See id. at 972–76.
83. See id. at 941–54.
84. See, e.g., Back v. Hastings on Hudson Union Free Sch. Dist., 365 F.3d 107, 126 (2d Cir. 2004).
85. See, e.g., Stern v. Cintas Corp., 319 F. Supp. 2d 841, 853, 862–65 (N.D. Ill. 2004) (travel); Lust v. Sealy, Inc., 383 F.3d 580, 583 (7th Cir. 2004) (relocation).
86. U.S. EEOC, ENFORCEMENT GUIDANCE: UNLAWFUL DISPARATE TREATMENT OF WORKERS WITH CAREGIVING RESPONSIBILITIES (2007), https://www.eeoc.gov/laws/guidance/enforcement-guidance-unlawful-disparate-treatment-workers-caregiving-responsibilities.
87. Id.
88. See Bornstein, *supra* note 74, at 943–44.
89. In the context of pregnancy, Judge Posner expressed this concept by stating that "[e]mployers can treat pregnant women as badly as they treat similar[] nonpregnant employees." Troupe v. May Dep't Stores Co., 20 F.3d 734, 738 (7th Cir. 1994). After Young v. UPS, 135 S. Ct. 1338 (2015), this is no longer a completely accurate statement of the law on pregnancy accommodation, but the concept remains for caregivers.
90. Bostock v. Clayton Cty., 140 S. Ct. 1731 (2020). This wording mirrors the Court's use of the terms "gay" or "homosexual" and "transgender"—reflecting the specific plaintiffs in the case—rather than "sexual orientation" or "gender identity." As discussed *infra*, it remains an open question whether *all* sexual orientation or gender identity discrimination is prohibited under *Bostock*. A significant body of legal scholarship has addressed gender stereotype theory in the context of sexual orientation or gender identity discrimination. For a sampling, see, e.g., William N. Eskridge, Jr., *Title VII's Statutory History and the Sex Discrimination Argument for LGBT Workplace Protections*, 127 YALE L.J. 322 (2017); Zachary R. Herz, *Price's Progress: Sex Stereotyping and Its Potential for Antidiscrimination Law*, 124 YALE L.J. 396 (2014); William C. Sung, *Taking the Fight Back to Title VII: A Case for Redefining "Because of Sex" to Include Gender Stereotypes, Sexual Orientation, and Gender Identity*, 84 S. CALIF. L. REV. 487 (2011); Ilona M. Turner, *Sex Stereotyping Per Se: Transgender Employees and Title VII*, 95 CALIF. L. REV. 561, 563 (2007); Mary Anne C. Case, *Disaggregating Gender From Sex and Sexual Orientation: The Effeminate Man in the Law and Feminist Jurisprudence*, 105 YALE L.J. 1, 2–3 (1995).
91. See, e.g., Blum v. Gulf Oil Corp., 597 F.2d 936 (5th Cir. 1979); DeSantis v. Pac. Tel. & Tel. Co., 608 F.2d 327 (9th Cir.1979); Berg v. Claytor, 436 F. Supp. 76 (D.D.C. 1977).
92. See, e.g., Morrison v. Dep't of the Navy, EEOC Appeal No. 01930778, 1994 WL 746296 (June 16, 1994); Freeman v. USPS, EEOC Appeal No. 01911814, 1991 WL 1186889 (July 11, 1991); Dillon v. Frank, EEOC Appeal No. 01900157, 1990 WL 1111074 (Feb. 14, 1990).
93. 523 U.S. 75 (1998).
94. *Id.* at 79, 81–82.
95. See Rene v. MGM Grand Hotel, Inc., 305 F.3d 1061, 1064–65 (9th Cir. 2002); Nichols v. Azteca Rest. Enters., Inc., 256 F.3d 864, 869, 874–75 (9th Cir. 2001); Doe v. City of Belleville, 119 F.3d 563, 566, 580–81 (7th Cir. 1997), *rev'd on other grounds*, 523 U.S. 1001 (1998).
96. See, e.g., Zarda v. Altitude Express, Inc., 883 F.3d 100 (2d Cir. 2018); Terveer v. Billington. 34 F. Supp. 3d 100 (D.D.C. 2014); Hall v. BNSF Ry. Co., No. C13-2160 RSM, 2014 WL 4719007

(W.D. Wash. Sept. 22, 2014); Heller v. Columbia Edgewater Country Club, 195 F. Supp. 2d 1212 (D. Or. 2002); *see also* Hively v. Ivy Tech Cmty. Coll. of Ind., 853 F.3d 339 (7th Cir. 2017).

97. *See, e.g.,* Higgins v. New Balance Athletic Shoe, Inc., 194 F.3d 252 (1st Cir. 1999); Prowel v. Wise Bus. Forms, Inc., 579 F.3d 285 (3d Cir. 2009); Kalich v. AT&T Mobility, LLC, 679 F.3d 464 (6th Cir. 2012); Williamson v. A.G. Edwards & Sons, Inc., 876 F.2d 69 (8th Cir. 1989); Medina v. Income Support Div., 413 F.3d 1131 (10th Cir. 2005); Evans v. Ga. Reg'l Hosp., 850 F.3d 1248 (11th Cir. 2017).

98. *See* Bornstein, *supra* note 74, at 950–54, 959–61.

99. *See, e.g.,* Smith v. City of Salem, 378 F.3d 566 (6th Cir. 2004); Schwenk v. Hartford, 204 F.3d 1187 (9th Cir. 2000); Glenn v. Brumby, 663 F.3d 1312 (11th Cir. 2011) (so holding and citing cases that agreed from district courts in Arizona, the District of Columbia, Pennsylvania, New York, and Texas); Schroer v. Billington, 424 F. Supp. 2d 203 (D.D.C. 2006).

100. *See, e.g.,* Ulane v. E. Airlines, Inc., 742 F.2d 1081 (7th Cir. 1984); Sommers v. Budget Mktg., Inc., 667 F.2d 748 (8th Cir. 1982); Holloway v. Arthur Andersen & Co., 566 F.2d 659 (9th Cir. 1977); *see also Smith*, 378 F.3d at 573 (discussing the abrogation of these cases by *Price Waterhouse*). *But see* Etsitty v. Utah Transit Auth., 502 F.3d 1215, 1221 (10th Cir. 2007) (refusing, in 2007, to hold that "transsexuals" as a class are protected under "sex").

101. *See* Macy v. Dep't of Justice, EEOC Appeal No. 0120120821, 2012 WL 1435995 (Apr. 20, 2012).

102. 576 U.S. 644 (2015).

103. *See* Baldwin v. Foxx, EEOC Appeal No. 0120133080, 2015 WL 4397641 (July 15, 2015).

104. 140 S. Ct. 1731 (2020).

105. *Id.* at 1763 (Alito, J., dissenting) (noting that gender stereotype theory "figure[d] prominently in the decisions of the lower courts and in [the Bostock] briefs" but "the Court apparently finds [the Price Waterhouse] argument[] unpersuasive").

106. *Id.* at 1741 (citing Price Waterhouse v. Hopkins, 490 U.S. 228, 239 (1989)).

107. *Id.* at 1742–43.

108. Justice Alito would disagree. *See supra* note 105. But Alito's conclusion that, because the Bostock employers would "apply [gender stereotypes] equally to men and women," there is no sex discrimination, reflects a fundamental misunderstanding: Title VII prohibits *individuals* from being punished by being compared to *any* stereotype related to the protected class of sex. *Bostock*, 140 S. Ct. at 1764 (Alito, J., dissenting).

109. *See* Naomi Schoenbaum, *The New Law of Gender Nonconformity*, 105 Minn. L. Rev. 831, 888–99 (2020); *see also* Jessica A. Clarke, *They, Them, and Theirs*, 132 Harv. L. Rev. 894 (2019). *But see* Katie R. Eyer, *The "But For" Theory of Anti-Discrimination Law*, 107 Va. L. Rev. 1621 (2021); Deborah A. Widiss, *Proving Discrimination by the Text*, 106 Minn. L. Rev. 353 (2021).

110. *See, e.g.,* Orr v. Orr, 440 U.S. 268, 268 (1979) (presumption of alimony by ex-husbands, but not ex-wives violates equal protection); Caban v. Mohammed, 441 U.S. 380 (1979) (allowing new spouse of birth mother, but not birth father, to adopt children without birth father's consent violates equal protection).

111. *See, e.g.,* Ellison v. Brady, 924 F.2d 872 (9th Cir. 1991) (adopting "reasonable woman" rather than "reasonable person standard" in sexual harassment claims); Benjamin v. Cleburne Truck & Body Sales, Inc., 424 F. Supp. 1294 (D.V.I. 1976) (allowing a husband but not a wife to bring loss of consortium claim violates equal protection).

112. *See, e.g.,* United States v. Dingwall, 6 F.4th 744 (7th Cir. 2021) (discussing circuit split on admissibility of evidence on the effects of domestic abuse for a female criminal

defendant's defense of duress); J.E.B. v. Alabama *ex rel.* T.B., 511 U.S. 127 (1994) (striking down use of peremptory challenges to dismiss jurors based on their sex).

113. *See* Adams v. Sch. Bd. of St. Johns Cnty., 3 F.4th 1299, 1304 (11th Cir. 2021) (bathroom policy barring transgender student from using male restroom violates equal protection); Grimm v. Gloucester Cnty. Sch. Bd., 972 F.3d 586, 593 (4th Cir. 2020) (same, and violates Title IX); Hecox v. Little, 479 F. Supp. 3d 930 (D. Idaho 2020) (barring transgender students from women's sports teams likely violates equal protection and Title IX); *see also* Enforcement of Title IX of the Education Amendments of 1972 With Respect to Discrimination Based on Sexual Orientation and Gender Identity in Light of *Bostock v. Clayton County*, 86 Fed. Reg. 32,637 (June 22, 2021).

114. *See infra* section II.A.

CHAPTER 21

BEYOND BATTERED WOMEN'S SYNDROME

SARAH M. BUEL

FEMINIST jurisprudence has been instrumental in developing and advancing legal protections for gender violence survivors.[1] Starting in 1868, with the Seneca Falls Declaration of Sentiments and Resolutions, early feminists denounced the tyrannical impact of legal sexism for promoting the subjugation of women.[2] Later feminist activists and scholars, as part of second-wave feminism beginning in the late 1960s, decried the continuing use of law as a mechanism to maintain the status quo of male dominion in all aspects of women's lives, including perpetration of gender violence (GV). In the 1970s, the rape crisis and battered women movements gained momentum as feminist advocates and GV survivors formed new alliances in their reform efforts. They focused on individual women's immediate safety needs when pursuing the seemingly modest goals of establishing emergency shelters and promulgating civil protection order statutes. Although successful in passing these laws in every state, advocates were dismayed by many courts' reluctance to issue protective orders and, even if granted, to enforce them.[3] State inaction emboldened batterers and placed victims and their children in continued danger—leaving many women with no option but self-defense.

Meanwhile, criminal law fell harshly on survivors who acted in self-defense, and feminist attention turned to the need for criminal law reform. Feminist legal scholars wrote foundational articles and books exposing bias in criminal law's treatment of survivors, and especially in the doctrine of self-defense.[4] In critiquing self-defense law's treatment of survivors, some feminists pressed for recognition of a distinctive set of characteristics purportedly associated with survivors, termed "battered woman syndrome" (BWS). Intended to ameliorate the harsh effects of criminal law on survivors, BWS sought to explain why battered women responded as they did in terms that judges and juries might better relate to the legal requirements for self-defense.

However, many feminists had reservations about the development of a doctrine positing a "syndrome" for battered women as an undifferentiated group, and the new reform sparked feminist critique and resistance just as it was gaining acceptance by courts. As the limitations and pitfalls of BWS became painfully apparent, illuminated by judicial applications of the doctrine, feminist scholars and activists pressed for a more nuanced recognition of the particular experiences and diversity of GV survivors.[5] At the present juncture, BWS remains influential in the case law, despite a growing chorus of feminist scholars and activists urging the legal system to jettison the terminology and theory of BWS as a misguided effort to impose a standardized experience on all survivors. A key lesson of feminist engagement with BWS is that legal professionals, expert witnesses, and courts should move beyond BWS and instead focus on the effects of battering and its relevance to survivors charged with crimes against their abusers.

I. The Development of BWS Theory

In criminal law, self-defense requires that a reasonable person fears life-threatening, imminent harm before engaging in an act of violence against another person.[6] Recognizing that the legal standard is a poor fit for a survivor acting against her abuser, feminists worked to unpack the gendered assumptions embedded in the law of self-defense. Feminists exposed the male bias in what was implicitly a "reasonable man" standard, which presumed a killing was rational only if a man would have perceived impending death in the GV survivor's position. The limits of self-defense law had long left survivors and their attorneys with few options. For at least the prior century, attorneys typically convinced GV survivors charged with crimes against their abusers to either plead guilty or use the excuse of insanity or diminished capacity, which might at best mitigate or reduce punishment but would not exonerate the person charged. This strategy left survivors with little hope of avoiding conviction.

This result was unsurprising given that unreserved victim-blaming, by judges, lawyers, and even scholars, was the norm. So widespread was this response that three male psychiatrists writing in the 1960s described their clinical observations of women who sought court protection in Massachusetts as follows:

> The periods of violent behavior by the husband served to release him momentarily from his anxiety about his ineffectiveness as a man, while, at the same time, giving his wife apparent masochistic gratification and helping probably to deal with the guilt arising from the intense hostility expressed in her controlling, castrating behavior.[7]

That victim-blaming could be expressed in such raw and unapologetic terms by professionals interfacing with survivors in the legal system spoke volumes about the steep path ahead for feminists seeking to make the law more responsive to survivors' experiences.

In 1978, feminist activists and lawyers started the Women's Self-Defense Law Project—a partnership of the Center for Constitutional Rights and the National Jury Project—to help attorneys improve their representation of GV survivors charged with harming their abusers. The group encouraged attorneys defending survivors to draw on, and introduce, expert testimony to help judges and juries better understand how the experiences of survivors shaped their beliefs and actions.

As feminist interventions gained strength, victim-blaming norms were increasingly being contested. For centuries, egregious GV cases persisted, but feminist activists succeeded in focusing media attention on the struggles facing survivors when, in the late 1970s, several high-profile cases came to light in which GV survivors who killed their abusers to protect themselves invoked the more apt justification of self-defense. In these cases, defendants' lawyers called on expert witnesses with a background in clinical psychology, such as Dr. Lenore Walker, to educate juries about the reasonableness of GV survivors' belief that force was needed to defend their lives.[8] As a student in the 1960s and 1970s, Dr. Walker credited feminist mentors who encouraged her interest in domestic violence research, enabling her to secure a National Institute of Mental Health grant to study battered women's experiences with abuse. Walker explained, "I named my work 'Battered Woman Syndrome' copying the child abuse work called 'Battered Child Syndrome.'"[9] In 1977, Walker first testified about BWS—and helped secure a "not guilty"—in the case of Miriam Grieg, a battered woman in Montana who claimed self-defense in the killing of her husband.[10]

Walker advanced BWS theory to explain a victim's behavior patterns within a violent relationship. In her first book on BWS, published in 1979, Walker described its two key components as (1) "learned helplessness" and (2) a three-stage cycle of increased tension, a violent incident, and a honeymoon or remorse phase. For the first component, Walker drew on the work of psychology professors Martin Seligman and Bruce Overmier, who coined the term "learned helplessness" in 1967, based on their experiments in which dogs were subjected to inescapable electric shocks, with the result that even when their cage door was later opened, they made no attempt to leave. Walker adopted the learned helplessness term and concept for BWS, analogizing to survivors who—just like the shocked dogs—stop attempting to flee even when doing so seems feasible to outsiders.[11]

In her subsequent books, Walker has adhered to her definition of BWS and further fleshed out what she viewed as the behavioral components of the syndrome. These consisted of six sets of characteristics exhibited by battered women, according to Walker's theory. The first three are consistent with posttraumatic stress disorder widely known as PTSD. The remaining three are specific to victims of violence by intimate partners. Walker identifies the six components as follows:

> 1) Intrusive recollections of the trauma event(s); 2) Hyperarousal and high levels of anxiety; 3) Avoidance behavior and emotional numbing usually expressed as depression, dissociation, minimization, repression and denial; 4) Disrupted interpersonal relationships from batterer's power and control measures; 5) Body image distortion and/or somatic or physical complaints; and 6) Sexual intimacy issues.[12]

Walker later expanded her definition of BWS to recognize the roles of coercive control and psychological abuse. With some modification, Walker has largely adhered to the core of her theory, including use of the terms "syndrome" and "mental disorder," along with the cycle theory and learned helplessness,[13] despite ongoing feminist criticism.

II. FEMINIST CRITIQUE OF BWS

Early on, lawyers for survivors generally welcomed BWS, as it expanded the field of forensic psychology by offering what appeared to be a plausible explanation of survivors' actions that could help mitigate their guilt. Over time, however, feminist activists and scholars increasingly voiced serious concerns about the theory's plausibility, lack of intersectional scope, application in courts, and consequences for survivors. Feminists were troubled by Walker's classifications of what behaviors GV survivors exhibit, which suggested survivors must report these behaviors in order to qualify as "real" victims. By the 1990s, skepticism of BWS had become widespread. As feminist law professor Myrna Raeder wrote in 1996, "BWS is being vigorously attacked by feminists who take affront at its characterization of victims as passive, by psychologists who disagree with its current theoretical conceptualization, and by academics who are distressed by the nature and quality of the empirical research supporting its validity."[14] The many problematic aspects of BWS were elaborated in feminist critiques demonstrating the harm to GV survivors long before court involvement with BWS amplified these concerns.

First, feminist scholars and activists lamented the ways in which BWS reinforces gender typecasting with its rigid descriptions of how "true" GV survivors behave. As Professor Elizabeth Schneider noted, "Indeed, the overall impact of the battered woman syndrome stereotype may be to limit rather than expand the legal options of women who cannot conform to these stereotypes."[15] Even for survivors who conformed to the expectations imposed by BWS, the theory could undermine rather than support survivor self-defense. Too often, legal stakeholders[16] view GV survivors as mentally ill if labeled with BWS, or as vicious women if their actions did not meet the BWS two-prong definition. The dichotomous approach to "real" victims created a double bind in which survivors meeting the criteria were positioned as lacking in the very rationality and agency presupposed in self-defense law, while nonconforming survivors were unworthy of whatever understanding and compassion BWS might provide.

Understanding the power of taxonomy, feminists were similarly troubled by BWS's characterization of survivors' responses to grievous abuse as a "syndrome," a clinical term that connotes mental deficiency. A 1996 National Institute of Justice Report by researchers and activists explained that BWS demeaned and pathologized survivors by presenting them as mentally defective—reinforced by a common understanding of "syndrome" as indicative of a psychological disorder or deviance.[17] The Report recognized that since a survivor must assert that she acted reasonably to claim self-defense, courts and juries were understandably confused as to how they should apply BWS evidence. Beyond criminal law, the stigma of a BWS label could further harm survivors' cases involving divorce, custody, clemency or parole, tort, or any matter in which their judgment was at issue.[18] Such harms prompted Professor Marina Angel to call for eradication of the words "syndrome" and "learned helplessness," arguing, "Women are not dogs. There is no scientific evidence that they act like dogs. There are studies that show that abused women increase, not decrease, their attempts to exit."[19]

GV expert Professor Kathleen Ferraro captured the shared skepticism of many feminist advocates when she asked, at the beginning of her 2003 article critiquing BWS, "Is it *so difficult* to understand why battered women fear for their lives without relying on a dubious psychological malady? Apparently it is."[20] Professor Ferraro joined other feminists in decrying the continued use of BWS for its false typecasting of how *true* abuse victims behave, which, though long debunked, still stubbornly holds sway with juries, lawyers, and judges.

A second component of the feminist critique is that BWS contributes to misplaced victim-blaming by making a survivor's failure to leave the abuser the focus, instead of explaining the reasonableness of her heightened fear and subsequent behavior. Conflating agency with autonomy, legal stakeholders persist in asking, "Why did she stay with an abuser?" which mistakenly presumes both that survivors choose to stay in the face of viable options and that leaving will achieve safety. In fact, empirical studies document prolific violence at the point of separation—long reported by GV survivors, yet generally ignored by the courts or excused as inherent in the severance process. Post-separation proves to be an especially dangerous time for the great majority of GV victims. A representative study of 161 survivors found that 76 percent faced ongoing harm from their abusers.[21] For 36 percent of these women, the abuse not only continued but intensified over time and thus created concomitant danger for them and their children. As legal stakeholders rarely help survivors create short- and long-term safety plans, victims are left to navigate the overwhelming, perilous next steps on their own.

Instead of directing attention to separation violence to explain why survivors stay with abusers, BWS offers only learned helplessness and the cycle theory, neither of which accurately reflects the full range of how victims cope. Survivor agency is evident in their strategizing how to evade, prevent, endure, and escape the abuse, as survivors must engage in a nuanced cost-benefit calculus with fluid, multilayered risks that force rapid reassessments.[22] GV experts, advocates, and scholars challenged the premise of "learned helplessness" by documenting that most survivors employ a range of help-seeking behaviors—frequently to no avail.[23] Yet legal stakeholders often expect survivors to make many attempts and, ultimately, to flee their abusers, regardless of overwhelming obstacles.

The ability to escape a batterer is typically a function of privilege, dependent on a safety net of family or friends, since domestic violence shelters turn away the majority of victims seeking refuge due to inadequate funding. The incidence and severity of GV have worsened during the COVID-19 pandemic with its attendant home confinement, layoffs, and reduced access to resources. Because informal social networks are a crucial means of support and escape for many GV survivors, forced isolation has further narrowed the path for exit. Feminists lament that mandatory quarantine with violent abusers may leave survivors little choice but to act in self-defense. Activists have urged state and community service providers to initiate creative outreach efforts, especially to the most vulnerable people, but worry that it will not be enough.[24]

Concerns about the differential effects of battering tie into a third and deeply problematic aspect highlighted in the feminist critique of BWS: the marginalization of survivors by race. Early on, Walker acknowledged that when battered defendants are white and present as docile, obedient wives, BWS testimony is more likely to result in a not guilty finding or a lesser prison term.[25] Likewise, a survivor's deviation from BWS's inflexible requirements of learned helplessness and three-stage cycle more frequently results in harsh sentences for victims from marginalized communities, such as those who are of color and/or low income.[26] These disparate outcomes are not surprising, given the absence of an intersectional approach guiding the development of BWS theory.

Professor Kimberlé Crenshaw's 1989 trailblazing article developed the theory of intersectionality and exposed how feminist legal theory and antidiscrimination law too often perpetuate gendered and raced subordination.[27] Embracing an intersectional lens to understand the oppression of Black women, she subsequently expanded this analysis by articulating the political and structural relationships of GV, race, class, and identity politics, while elucidating the profound impact of each on the other.[28] Further exploring intragroup variations, Crenshaw captured how different aspects of their identities—such as class, gender, and race—impact the way survivors of color view GV. She argued that "[r]ace, gender and other identity categories are most often treated in mainstream liberal discourse as vestiges of bias or domination-that is, as intrinsically negative frameworks ... [but] delineating difference ... can instead be the source of social empowerment and reconstruction."[29]

Building on Crenshaw's work, in her 1991 article, Sharon Angella Allard methodically explained how BWS promotes toxic racial tropes.[30] The theory implicitly presumes a stereotypically white woman, as Walker applied learned helplessness only to survivors who are dependent, docile, and passive. Allard persuasively argues that BWS is of little help to Black women, given persistent negative stereotypes defining them as aggressive, hostile, and domineering. Such bias makes judges and juries less likely to view Black women's actions as self-defense and less worthy of expert assistance. As Allard notes, Walker acknowledged as much, admitting that for BWS to be effective a survivor must not seem angry, since a jury will be sympathetic only if the survivor's self-defense was based solely on fear. Recognizing that Black women are stereotyped as "angry," Walker allowed that BWS would likely prove ineffective for them, adding, "[n]ot surprisingly, even expert testimony has been unable to overcome the double bias of racism and sexism when a minority woman is on trial."[31] In a later book, Walker stated, "[t]he ratio of Black women to white women convicted of killing their abusive husbands is nearly two to one in one of my studies."[32]

III. The Influence of BWS and Its Critique of the Law

Although these rich, provocative critiques from within feminism prompted much critical analysis and reconsideration in academic and theoretical realms, BWS has largely continued to aid those who are deemed "real" GV victims and to ferret out survivors regarded as undeserving. The intersectionality critique in particular, although acknowledged by Walker, has not resulted in meaningful change in how the theory is conceptualized or applied. Despite conceding the racial bias embedded in the theory, Walker has continued to hold fast to BWS, which has itself remained largely impervious to the intersectional critique.

The closest Walker has come to incorporating an intersectional lens is in the latest edition of her book on BWS, published in 2017. In it, she added a chapter, "Cross-Cultural and Cross-National Issues in Domestic Violence," which offers data on GV incidence within specific countries and some racial categories. However, Walker stopped short of using this information to revise or reconsider BWS. Instead, she offers an overly rosy assessment of the success of BWS, asserting that in the 1980s and 1990s, GV victims who killed their abusers in self-defense could "obtain a fair trial with expert witness testimony to educate lay juries and judges as to the reasonableness of their fear of imminent danger when they defended themselves against the often escalating aggression from the batterer."[33] Continuing her rendition of this success story, she further explains, "[s]tate by state, testimony on BWS was permitted, often after appellate decisions defined BWS as including both the signs and symptoms of the psychological effects from abuse as well as the dynamics of the abusive relationship that included the cycle theory of violence and the learned helplessness theory in some states."[34]

Walker's assertion that experts were available to help GV survivors get a fair trial fails to acknowledge the dearth of qualified, affordable appellate counsel and experts to assist survivors in such cases, and the race discrimination permeating every aspect of the criminal justice system (CJS). This success narrative also ignores that all too often, trial attorneys for survivors simply counsel their battered client to accept a plea—whether from ignorance about how to properly handle such cases or from their own unexamined biases. Throughout the book, Walker retains the BWS moniker and use of learned helplessness and the cycle paradigm without offering an analysis of the racial impact or how to remedy it. That Walker, who has been so closely associated with BWS, has remained steadfast in the face of critique has set the tone for other proponents of BWS to stay the course as well.

BWS is not entirely without success. It has helped some survivors avoid long sentences or be exonerated—primarily those who are white; have strong evidence of suffering horrific abuse (such as eye witnesses, photos, and medical records); and who present as docile, terrified, and law-abiding. But despite now-decades of feminist critique, BWS still lacks an explanation for the financial, cultural, legal, emotional, and social factors that overlap in ways that exacerbate survivor trauma. GV victims who come into conflict with the law are typically trying to raise their children while grappling with poverty, shame, low-self-esteem, religious dictates, tenuous immigration status, disabilities, language barriers, substance use, mental and physical illness, and many more compounding challenges. In the absence of an intersectional methodology, BWS fails to accommodate the broad range of survivor experience and perpetuates a cramped, racialized narrative. That BWS theory still lacks an intersectional approach means victims are further marginalized if their race, class, abilities, sexual orientation, and myriad relevant lived experiences and identities depart from the assumptions underlying the prototype of a BWS survivor. And yet, despite these failings, BWS theory has persisted largely unchanged from Walker's account.

Feminist critiques of BWS are gradually changing how the legal system responds to survivors charged with crime—but only in a seemingly unpredictable manner. Some courts and legal actors apply BWS in a way that resonates with, and gives life to, the feminist critique.

Courts have understood and applied BWS as a confining set of expectations by which victims are judged, often to the disadvantage of GV survivors. For example, an influential West Virginia appellate court opinion described the BWS expert's testimony as having "explained that 'a battered spouse syndrome is a cluster of types of thinking and feeling and acting by women, 99.9 percent of the time, in which they repeatedly get into bad relationships.'"[35] Without objection, the court admitted this testimony. As the West Virginia court's ruling illustrates, BWS lends itself to legal actors blaming women for making poor choices in relationships, and then excusing them from the consequences of their choices—an understanding that grossly distorts the experiences of GV survivors and does not encourage empathy.

GV survivors have fallen into the traps set by BWS. A recent example came on the heels of New York's enactment of the 2019 Domestic Violence Survivors Justice Act (DVSJA), praised by survivors' advocates, which permits judges to give a reduced sentence when a battered defendant was impacted by sexual, physical, or psychological abuse before the criminal offense. One of the first cases decided under the DVSJA, seemingly an ideal candidate for a reduced sentence, shows the limits of law reform when judges, lawyers, and other stakeholders continue to apply the stereotypes underlying BWS instead of recognizing even the most basic, long-recognized precepts of GV and trauma.

The case, *New York v. Addimando*,[36] involved compelling facts of extreme abuse by a ruthless, relentless batterer who repeatedly violated court-imposed restraining orders. Both parties were white, and the defendant, Nicole Addimando—a teacher with two young children—had numerous witnesses attest to her kind nature, help-seeking actions, and frequent, visible injuries at the hands of her intimate partner, Christopher Grover. Ms. Addimando testified as to years of physical and sexual abuse by Grover including his burning her vaginal area with a heated spoon, tying her up and taking compromising photos and videos which he then uploaded to a pornographic website, raping and gagging her with objects; whipping, strangling, and beating her; and repeatedly threatening to kill her—with no cessation during either of her two pregnancies.[37] Numerous witnesses corroborated Nicole's story, including her therapist, midwife, coworkers, and friends, who all said they saw frequent black eyes and bruises all over her body. Feeling trapped and terrified, Nicole shot Grover after eight years of horrific abuse. She was convicted of second-degree murder and second-degree criminal possession of a weapon, for which she received a sentence of nineteen years to life.[38]

Judge Edward McLaughlin, who presided over the case, claimed, "this Court supports the important goals and legal necessity of the battered women's syndrome defense, as well as the spirit and goal of Penal Law § 60.12," and further acknowledged, "[t]he defendant presents a compelling story of abuse, with horrific allegations that include repeated, sadistic sexual violence and physical abuse, complete with pictures and eyewitnesses viewing the results of her abuse."[39] In declining to apply DVSJA, however, Judge McLaughlin cited what he found to be the prosecutor's persuasive argument doubting Ms. Addimando's "alleged abuse" and finding that her behavior—and ultimately killing her batterer—indicate she is not a *real* battered woman.[40]

Discounting the realities faced by survivors fleeing abuse, Judge McLaughlin asserted that Nicole Addimando had "opportunities to escape her situation" before killing her abuser, noting that she was given information about shelters to which she could flee with her two young children.[41] The judge implied that knowledge of a local domestic violence shelter put the onus on Ms. Addimando to leave her home. Judge McLaughlin was apparently oblivious to the reality that because shelters are consistently full, Addimando likely would have had little chance of finding shelter space on demand. A survivor with children is even less likely to find room at a shelter, and even if she could, many shelters permit only four- to six-week stays. Post-shelter, Ms. Addimando would need first and last month's rent plus a security deposit to secure her own apartment, which she would have had to have saved from her part-time job—a job she likely would have lost from quitting or being fired in the chaos of flight and resettlement. Upon reading this case, GV expert and therapist Dr. Johanna Malaga observed, "This judge either lacks any knowledge of the manifestations of trauma or is blinded by his condemnation of her life and what he perceives as her poor choices."[42] The case illustrates that little has changed since feminists warned, decades ago, of the dangers of typecasting a set of stock criteria for how "true" victims behave.

Despite its drawbacks, BWS remains the term most often used by courts when experts offer testimony explaining the dynamics of domestic violence and the ways it impacts survivors.[43] As the New Jersey Supreme Court explained, "Battered Women's Syndrome is recognized as a collection of common behavioral and psychological characteristics exhibited in women who repeatedly are physically and emotionally abused over a prolonged length of time by the dominant male figure in their lives."[44] Both the terminology and substance of BWS persist, little changed, in the courts.

In addition to inviting judges to unfavorably compare survivors charged with a crime against some imagined ideal of a battered woman, BWS has also served to distract legal actors from addressing efforts by abusers to obstruct the ability of survivors to use the legal system to seek help. The emphasis on BWS has proven a distraction from courts' failure to address batterers' ubiquitous witness tampering intended to prevent survivors from leaving and accessing help.[45] Even if arrested, abusers frequently continue to intimidate their victims from jail—using a variety of tactics such as minimizing the injuries, characterizing themselves as the true victims, urging recantation to save the relationship, insisting the case will harm the children, blaming police for interfering in their private matter, and threatening further abuse if the victim does not retract the allegations.[46] Batterers also employ de facto witness tampering through financial sabotage, custodial and parental interference, false counterallegations, cyber tampering, bribery, and myriad tactics to manipulate GV survivors into compliance.[47] Since witness tampering compounds other challenges and oppressions, survivors may accurately decide they have no choice but to comply with the abuser's demands of silence. By focusing on whether the survivor adhered to a set of expected behaviors for battered women, BWS obscures the tactics used by abusers to control survivors' ability to seek help.

Continued adherence to BWS and the law's ongoing unresponsiveness to the stark realities survivors face have compromised victim safety and ignored the conditions contributing to some survivors' resort to crime, the subject of the next section.

IV. Survival Crime and the Broader Agenda for Survivor Justice

The singular emphasis on BWS as the remedy for survivors' unjust engagement with criminal law has left little room for addressing the underlying problem of too many GV victims being forced to engage in crime. Moreover, the narrow focus on self-defense eclipses and does nothing to address the broader criminal charges facing many survivors. Nor does BWS help channel resources toward altering the conditions that give survivors little recourse but to break the law.

BWS was developed as a way to enable survivors charged with a crime of violence against their abusers to bolster a legally cognizable claim of self-defense. However, the great majority of survivors accused of committing crimes are charged with nonviolent offenses.[48] Victim advocates use the term "survival crime" to capture the dire circumstances in which survivors resort to crime as a matter of survival. Many survivors are propelled along gendered trajectories to, among other offenses, shoplift essentials, write bad checks, sell drugs, engage in sex work, or kill their abuser in order to stay alive. Economic desperation is the fire that fuels survivor crime.[49]

Without financial resources, survivors cannot readily escape their abusers, and the lack of a government safety net leaves survivors to fend for themselves in the private market. Predatory consumer lending practices take advantage of survivors' desperate straits and further narrow their options for economic sufficiency. Numerous studies document that the great majority of payday debtors are women with children under seventeen in their care, and that women of color are disproportionately harmed by predatory lending practices.[50] Trapped in a cycle of debt from which it is difficult to extricate, GV survivors may be forced to take drastic measures to survive.

Economic and social conditions render some survivors particularly vulnerable to financial distress. For example, lower-income single mothers often must contend with wage theft, sexual harassment, on-demand schedules, a dearth of affordable child care, and lack of child support. This cascade of adversity—coupled with GV—means they are more likely to be evicted, homeless, fired, and, in desperation, forced to deal with loan sharks or payday lenders with planned debt traps. Other groups of marginalized GV survivors—including those who are undocumented, immigrant, exotic dancers, and sex workers or who have a criminal record, history of substance use, and mental health or other challenges—may have few options other than survival crime.

Survivors of color face a trifecta of compound constraints, as they frequently must deal with more acute economic conditions, greater levels of GV, and harsher treatment in the criminal justice system when they do commit crime. For example, Native American women—who are often omitted from data analysis—face dramatically disproportionate rates of poverty, overcrowding, substance use, homelessness, and mental illness that can trigger survival crime. Native women also suffer horrific GV levels; more than half of all Native American women are survivors of domestic violence and sexual assault.[51] The majority of these abuses are committed by non-Indian men, as has been the case since European colonization centuries ago.[52] When Native American survivors do commit a crime, the state's response is often disproportionately harsh: arrest, pretrial detention, prosecution, and sentencing; indeed, Native women are six times more likely to be imprisoned than white women.[53]

For many Latina, Asian/South Asian, African, Haitian/Caribbean, Middle Eastern, and other immigrant GV survivors, language barriers create an additional obstacle to seeking and obtaining help—especially since many abusers prevent their partners from learning English and obtaining jobs. In addition, undocumented survivors live with the persistent fear of Immigration Customs Enforcement (ICE) raids and deportation. Abusive husbands who have legal status often refuse to apply for a marriage-based green card for their undocumented wife as a means of psychological terror, leaving her subject to deportation, while her U.S.-born children would remain. Geographic isolation, patriarchal gender norms, religious dictates, and acculturative stress can also interfere with the social support networks and economic independence necessary for recent immigrants to escape an abuser.

Gender-nonconforming and gay and lesbian survivors also face distinct obstacles, leaving them especially vulnerable to abuse and economic desperation. A meta-analysis of studies on GV against LGBTQ+ people revealed abuse rates overall that are on par with or higher than that of other groups but specifically found that the rate of abuse against transgender individuals is by far greater than that of any other group, ranging from 31 percent to 50 percent. Since LGBTQ+ survivors often cannot turn to traditional community resources for help, they may be forced to remain with their abusers or face the twin dangers of homelessness and work within the fringe economy.[54] LGBTQ+ people, and especially those who are low income and of color, are far more likely to interact with the CJS due to the criminalization of homelessness, poverty, and survival sex work.[55]

Despite the precarious situations faced by so many GV survivors, BWS does nothing to illuminate how poverty and abuse combine to narrow survivors' options for breaking from an abuser. The key components of BWS ignore the effects of socioeconomic status on how race and gender are lived—and particularly how the structural feminization of poverty amplifies economic and social inequality. Structural correlates of poverty that disproportionately harm women include the institutionalized, discriminatory policies within housing, healthcare, banking, and labor markets.[56] Moreover, with its focus on crimes of violence against an abuser, BWS obscures the complex realities of survival crime that ensnare so many survivors in the criminal justice system.

But the problem is not simply that BWS is nonresponsive to survival crime that does not fit the paradigm of a survivor attacking her abuser in self-defense. As importantly, it drains attention and resources from a broader campaign to reduce the prosecution and incarceration of women, many of whom likely are survivors. Indeed, the great majority of female criminal suspects are GV survivors.[57] Historic increases in the incarceration of women mean that more survivors are being incarcerated than ever before. From 1980 to 2017, women's incarceration rate rose by 750 percent, a figure that does not include those not yet convicted. In most jails, 60 percent of the women held are awaiting trial—most often because they cannot make bail, which typically ranges from $500 to $1,200.[58] With BWS taking up so much oxygen in the legal system and discourse surrounding criminal law's response to survivor self-defense, less energy and resources remain to support a broader agenda to reduce the incarceration of survivors for crimes committed under desperate circumstances.

V. Feminist Support for "Battering and Its Effects"

As the critique of BWS gained force, feminists worked to replace BWS with an alternative approach to help women charged with criminal offenses against their abusers. In 1987, feminist activists Sue Osthoff and Barbara Hart established the National Clearinghouse for the Defense of Battered Women. Its staff have since helped countless lawyers and advocates with case strategy, use of experts, jury instructions, document review, and virtually every aspect of case handling, as well as with legislation and policy. That same year, they brought together advocates, expert witnesses, defense attorneys, and researchers to discuss problematic aspects of BWS and to consider instead using the term "battering and its effects" in expert testimony about abuse histories. This approach continued to gain support by feminists who had come to view BWS as deeply flawed.

In 1995, motivated by feminist scholarship on the topic, the Women Judges' Fund for Justice sponsored research, roundtable discussions, and publication of materials on GV expert testimony. From the outset, their position was that BWS should be replaced with a focus on "battering and its effects," since BWS has "served to stigmatize the battered woman defendant, or to create a false perception that she 'suffers from' a mental disease or defect (one court even referred to it as a 'malady')."[59] After providing examples of court opinions describing abuse survivors' "abnormal behavior" and "losing control of their faculties," a report by the Women Judges' Fund for Justice concluded, "Rather than perpetuate such inaccuracies, we use (and urge others to use) the generic, inclusive language utilized by many expert witnesses and in a number of state statutes on the admissibility of expert testimony on battering and its effects."[60] Their call to action echoed that made two years earlier by trauma expert, psychologist, and professor Dr. Mary Ann Dutton, who urged advocates to document the compound traumas within survivors' lives in order to identify experts who could explain these to fact-finders and help victims receive services most likely to engender healing.[61] Decades later, feminists have continued to urge judges and lawyers to embrace this approach.

Rather than codifying some version of BWS for use in self-defense cases, as many states have done, feminist advocates and scholars now support an expanded and more inclusive inquiry into the conditions and circumstances facing survivors, using the terminology of "battering and its effects." Feminists generally agree that the many deficiencies of the BWS construct require integrating an intersectional approach into some version of "battering and its effects," and have gradually succeeded in changing some state's evidence rules to reflect this more apt concept.[62]

In addition to jettisoning a problematic terminology that saddles survivors with a "syndrome" and suggests mental infirmity, the switch to "battering and its effects" marks a substantive departure from the theory of BWS. An approach based on evidence of battering and its effects could help decisionmakers better understand a GV survivor–suspect's state of mind and actions resulting from what batterer's treatment expert Dr. David Adams calls the abuser's ongoing, planned pattern of coercive control.[63] Unlike BWS, this inquiry centers the batterer's conduct and its effects on the survivor rather than scrutinizing the survivor's conduct for deviations from the "syndrome." "Battering and its effects" offers a more nuanced, individualized approach that is more accurate and respectful of survivors' experiences—and would likely be more beneficial when survivors are charged with offenses against their abusers or with other survival crime.

Feminist advocacy for such a shift has met with modest success. Some courts—albeit still clinging to the BWS moniker—have begun to provide more accurate explanations of survivors' experiences.[64] Still, the shift is far from complete, in part because too few lawyers adequately represent survivors charged with crime. Even though specific guidance for the ethical handling of GV matters has been readily available from experienced lawyers and advocates for decades, some lawyers still offer scant evidence of a defendant's history of abuse and its relevance to the survivor's commission of crimes.[65] And, as in the examples of cases discussed in Section III some judges continue to minimize or deny the relevance of this critical information, resulting in only those survivors with appellate counsel having a chance to educate decisionmakers. For example, one federal appellate court recently vacated a lower court's decision after finding that

"(1) expert testimony on Battered Woman Syndrome (BWS) and the effects of past abuse may be used by a defendant to support her duress defense and rehabilitate her credibility, and (2) [the court's] error in excluding defendant's expert evidence on Battered Woman Syndrome was not harmless."[66]

Since most of the problematic aspects of BWS—perpetuating negative stereotypes, blaming victims, minimizing race, ignoring witness tampering, and disregarding survival crime—persist, meaningful feminist reform will require judges, lawyers, experts, and other legal actors to fully abandon BWS as the guiding theory for understanding survivor crime. BWS theory was born of outrage at the systemic injustices resulting from frequent exclusion of critical evidence relevant to the victim's state of mind at the time she acted in self-defense. However well-intentioned, feminists now agree it is past time to omit "syndrome" from the lexicon about GV survivors' actions and to reconceptualize the relevant evidence for exonerating survivors and mitigating culpability by focusing the inquiry on "battering and its effects."

VI. NEXT STEPS

Since the 1970s, feminist activists have used education, public information campaigns, and litigation to convince legal stakeholders to lower their resistance to accepting evidence of the grave realities of GV, especially in the context of women's self-defense actions. As an amalgam of interdisciplinary scholarship, feminist jurisprudence has supplemented the work of activists to bring the essential perspectives of behavioral sciences (including neurology, psychology, and sociology), critical theory (including critical race, queer, and Latinx), and poverty law to the GV reform agenda. Feminists have long pleaded for people to *really listen* to women's stories—to hear difference, pain, inequality, and pleas for safety. By ignoring women's voices and imposing constricted stereotypes of how *real* GV victims should behave, BWS allows legal stakeholders to punish those women who have dared fight back in self-defense. In judging survivors who act to protect themselves as "other"—as crazy, bad, dangerous women—courts can justify punitive sentences.

But it is not enough to jettison BWS. Competent handling of GV-related matters requires familiarity with empirically sound legal and behavioral science evidence to change the narrative from "dangerous female criminal" to survivor whose conduct is reasonable within the context of relentless abuse and cumulative trauma. If made familiar with such knowledge, legal stakeholders could better understand how such conditions as the dearth of social supports and living wage jobs, punitive welfare rules, and the cumulative trauma of physical and sexual abuse constrain survivors' choices. By inviting consideration of evidence of battering and its effects, the criminal justice system could become more fair and responsive to survivors.

Even beyond recalibrating the law of self-defense to better suit survivors, legal stakeholders can learn much from activists and feminist legal theory about pursuing gender and racial justice, for fair dispositions can only result when diverse lenses are embraced to actually hear raced, classed, and gendered narratives of survivors' lives. Despite missteps with the development of BWS as the operative lens for survivor crime, feminist jurisprudence is gradually increasing understanding of, and empathy for, GV victims' survival crime.

Notes

1. Gender violence includes domestic violence, human trafficking, sexual assault, and stalking as defined in all state and federal criminal statutes, as well as psychological abuse and abuse directed toward pets and property. *Victim* and *survivor* are used interchangeably in this chapter, as "victim" is the legally recognized term for persons subjected to harm and "survivor" recognizes those who have at the minimum not been killed by their perpetrators.
2. Women, LGBTQ (lesbian, gay, bisexual, transgender, and queer or questioning), and nonbinary people constitute the great majority of survivors and they are the focus of this chapter, but men can also be targeted—especially if they are perceived as feminine. Herein, *female* and *women* are meant to be inclusive of those who were assigned female at birth and transgender or genderqueer people who do not identify with the gender they were assigned at birth and identify as women.
3. Sarah M. Buel, *Domestic Violence and the Law: An Impassioned Exploration for Family Peace*, 33 FAM. L.Q. 719 (1999).
4. Elizabeth M. Schneider, *Equal Rights to Trial for Women: Sex-Bias in the Law of Self-Defense*, 15 HARV. C.R.-C.L. L. REV. 623 (1980); MARY P. KOSS ET AL., NO SAFE HAVEN: MALE VIOLENCE AGAINST WOMEN AT HOME, AT WORK, AND IN THE COMMUNITY (1994); CAROLINE FORELL & DONNA MATTHEWS, A LAW OF HER OWN: THE REASONABLE WOMAN AS A MEASURE OF MAN (2000).
5. Kimberlé Crenshaw, *Demarginalizing the Intersection of Race and Sex: A Black Feminist Critique of Antidiscrimination Doctrine, Feminist Theory and Antiracist Politics*, 1989 U. CHI. LEGAL F. 139.
6. WAYNE R. LAFAVE, CRIMINAL LAW § 5.7(D) at 491–96 (3d ed. 2000).
7. John E. Snell et al., *The Wifebeater's Wife: A Study of Family Interaction*, 11 ARCHIVES OF GEN. PSYCHIATRY 107 (1964).
8. Sue Osthoff & Holly Maguigan, *Explaining Without Pathologizing: Testimony on Battering and Its Effects*, in CURRENT CONTROVERSIES ON FAMILY VIOLENCE 225, 228 (Donileen R. Loseke et al. eds., 2005) [hereinafter *Explaining Without Pathologizing*].
9. Giselle Gaviria et al., *Feminist Pioneer: Lenore E. A. Walker*, 40 WOMEN & THERAPY 442, 446–47 (2017).
10. *Id.* at 448.
11. LENORE E. WALKER, THE BATTERED WOMAN 55–70 (1979).
12. LENORE E. A. WALKER, THE BATTERED WOMAN SYNDROME 42 (2007).
13. LENORE E. A. WALKER, THE BATTERED WOMAN SYNDROME 529 (4th ed. 2016).
14. Myrna S. Raeder, *The Double-Edged Sword: Admissibility of Battered Woman Syndrome by and Against Batterers in Cases Implicating Domestic Violence*, 67 U. COLO. L. REV. 789, 796 (1996).

15. Elizabeth M. Schneider, *Describing and Changing: Women's Self-Defense Work and the Problem of Expert Testimony on Battering*, 9 WOMEN'S RTS. L. REP. 195, 198 (1986).
16. Legal stakeholders herein will include attorneys, prosecutors, judges, juries, law enforcement, corrections officers, probation and parole officers, and related criminal justice system professionals.
17. U.S. DEPARTMENT OF JUSTICE OFFICE OF JUSTICE PROGRAMS, NATIONAL INSTITUTE OF JUSTICE, THE VALIDITY AND USE OF EVIDENCE CONCERNING BATTERING AND ITS EFFECTS IN CRIMINAL TRIALS, REPORT RESPONDING TO SECTION 40507 OF THE VIOLENCE AGAINST WOMEN ACT 19 (1996).
18. Osthoff & Maguigan, *supra* note 8, at 229–30; Emily J. Sack, *From the Right of Chastisement to the Criminalization of Domestic Violence: A Study in Resistance to Effective Policy Reform*, 32 T. JEFFERSON L. REV. 31, 41 (2009).
19. Marina Angel, *The Myth of Battered Woman Syndrome*, 24 TEMP. POL. & CIV. RTS. L. REV. 301, 306 (2014).
20. Kathleen J. Ferraro, *The Words Change, but the Melody Lingers: The Persistence of the Battered Woman Syndrome in Criminal Cases Involving Battered Women*, 9 VIOLENCE AGAINST WOMEN 110 (2003).
21. Cathy Humphreys & Ravi K. Thiara, *Neither Justice nor Protection: Women's Experiences of Post-Separation Violence*, 25 J. OF SOC. WELFARE & FAM. L. 195 (2003).
22. Sarah M. Buel, *Fifty Obstacles to Leaving, a.k.a. Why Abuse Victims Stay*, 28 COLO. B.J. 19 (1999).
23. EDWARD W. GOLDOLF & ELLEN R. FISHER, BATTERED WOMEN AS SURVIVORS: AN ALTERNATIVE TO TREATING LEARNED HELPLESSNESS 11 (1988).
24. Amalesh Sharma & Sourav Bikash Borah, *Covid-19 and Domestic Violence: An Indirect Path to Social and Economic Crisis*, 37 J. FAM. VIOLENCE 759 (2022).
25. Lenore E. Walker, *A Response to Elizabeth M. Schneider's Describing and Changing: Women's Self-Defense Work and the Problem of Expert Testimony on Battering*, 9 WOMEN'S RTS. L. REP. 223, 224 (1986).
26. LISA YOUNG LARANCE ET AL., UNDERSTANDING AND ADDRESSING WOMEN'S USE OF FORCE IN INTIMATE RELATIONSHIPS: A RETROSPECTIVE, 25 VIOLENCE AGAINST WOMEN 56 (2019).
27. Crenshaw, *supra* note 5, at 149, 155–58.
28. Kimberlé Crenshaw, *Mapping the Margins: Intersectionality, Identity Politics, and Violence Against Women of Color*, 43 STAN. L. REV. 1241, 1245–46 (1991).
29. *Id.* at 1242.
30. Sharon Angella Allard, *Rethinking Battered Woman Syndrome: A Black Feminist Perspective*, 1 UCLA WOMEN'S L.J. 191, 197 (1991).
31. Walker, *supra* note 25.
32. LENORE E. WALKER, TERRIFYING LOVE: WHY BATTERED WOMEN KILL AND HOW SOCIETY RESPONDS 206 (1989).
33. WALKER, *supra* note 13, at 37–38.
34. *Id.*
35. State v. Riley, 201 W. Va. 708, 500 S.E.2d 524, 528 n.3 (1997).
36. People v. Addimando, 120 N.Y.S.3d 596 (2020).
37. *Id.* at 603–04.

38. Geoffrey Wilson, *Addimando Sentenced to 19 Years to Life in Murder of Boyfriend Grover in Poughkeepsie*, THE POUGHKEEPSIE J., Feb. 11, 2020, https://www.poughkeepsiejournal.com/story/news/local/2021/04/01/nicole-addimando-murder-conviction-sentencing-appeal-heard/4839771001/.
39. *Addimando*, 120 N.Y.S.3d at 618.
40. *Id.* at 619.
41. *Id.*
42. Interview with Dr. Johanna Malaga (June 10, 2020).
43. *See, e.g.*, Virger v. State, 824 S.E.2d 346 (2019) (explaining that in 1981 Georgia recognized BWS, but that their courts now use the updated term "battered person syndrome," as possibly relevant to help a jury assess a defendant's self-defense claim).
44. State v. Hess, 23 A.3d 373 (2011) (quoting State v. B.H., 870 A.2d 273 (2005), and cited in State v. Nobles, 2018 WL 3468085 (N.J. Super. App. Div. July 19, 2018)).
45. Sarah M. Buel, *Putting Forfeiture to Work*, 43 U.C. DAVIS L. REV. 1295 (2010).
46. Amy Bonomi & David Martin, *Jail Calls: What Do Kids Have to Do with It?*, 33 J. FAM. VIOLENCE 99 (2018).
47. Sarah M. Buel, *De Facto Witness Tampering*, 29 BERKELEY J. OF GENDER, L. & JUST. 72 (2014).
48. ELIZABETH SWAVOLA, KRISTINE RILEY & RAM SUBRAMANIAN, OVERLOOKED: WOMEN AND JAILS IN AN ERA OF REFORM 9 (2016).
49. *Id.* at 19.
50. Lara Sofia Romero et al., *Payday Lending Regulations and the Impact on Women of Color*, 11 ACCT. & TAX'N 83 (2019).
51. Sarah Deer, *Bystander No More? Improving the Federal Response to Sexual Violence in Indian Country*, 2017 UTAH L. REV. 771, 774 (2017).
52. *Id.* at 774.
53. André B. Rosay, *Violence Against American Indian and Alaska Native Women and Men*, 38 NAT'L INST. JUST. J. 1 (2016), available at http://nij.gov/journals/277/Pages/violence-againstamerican-indians-alaska-natives.aspx.
54. THE WILLIAMS INSTITUTE, UCLA SCHOOL OF LAW, INTIMATE PARTNER VIOLENCE AND SEXUAL ABUSE AMONG LGBT PEOPLE 2–3 (2015).
55. *Id.*
56. Nandini Gunewardena, *Pathologizing Poverty: Structural Forces Versus Personal Deficit Theories in the Feminization of Poverty*, 4 J. EDUC. CONTROVERSY 1–3 (2009).
57. Angela Browne et al., *Prevalence and Severity of Lifetime Physical and Sexual Victimization Among Incarcerated Women*, 22 INT'L J. L. & PSYCHIATRY 301, 304 (1999).
58. ALEKS KAJSTURA, WOMEN'S MASS INCARCERATION: THE WHOLE PIE 2019, REPORT OF THE ACLU PRISON POLICY INITIATIVE 1 (2019), https://www.prisonpolicy.org/reports/pie2019women.html.
59. Janet Parrish, *Trend Analysis: Expert Testimony on Battering and Its Effects in Criminal Cases*, 11 WIS. WOMEN'S L.J. 75, 82 (1996).
60. *Id.* at 82.
61. Mary Ann Dutton, *Understanding Women's Responses to Domestic Violence: A Redefinition of Battered Woman Syndrome*, 21 HOFSTRA L. REV. 1191, 1195 (1993).

62. For example, Cal. Evid. Code § 1107 (a) states: "In a criminal action, expert testimony is admissible by either the prosecution or the defense regarding intimate partner battering and its effects, including the nature and effect of physical, emotional, or mental abuse on the beliefs, perceptions, or behavior of victims of domestic violence, except when offered against a criminal defendant to prove the occurrence of the act or acts of abuse which form the basis of the criminal charge."
63. David Adams, *Treatment Models of Men Who Batter: A Pro-Feminist Analysis*, in FEMINIST PERSPECTIVE ON WIFE ABUSE (Kirsti Ylo & Michele Bograd eds., 1988).
64. For example, a 2021 decision from the Court of Appeals of Maryland used the terms "Battered Spouse Syndrome" or "Battered Women Syndrome," with no reference to the increasingly preferred terminology, "Battering and Its Effects." *See* Maryland v. Elzey, 244 A.3d 1068 (2021). *See also* Katie Fair, *Battered Spouse Syndrome: A Comparative Regional Look at Domestic Abuse and Self-Defense in Criminal Courts*, 5 LINCOLN MEM'L U. L. REV. 1 (2018) (discussing only "Battered Spouse Syndrome" in reviewing the laws and evidence rules of California, Georgia, Oregon, South Carolina, Tennessee, and Washington, even though "Battering and Its Effects" is the codified term).
65. *See, e.g.,* Sarah M. Buel, *Effective Assistance of Counsel for Battered Women Defendants*, 26 HARV. WOMEN'S L.J. 217 (2003); THE NATIONAL CLEARINGHOUSE FOR THE DEFENSE OF BATTERED WOMEN, www.ncdbw.org (last visited June 8, 2021).
66. United States v. Lopez, 913 F.3d 807 (9th Cir. 2019).

CHAPTER 22

TITLE IX

Separate but Equal for Girls and Women in Athletics

ERIN E. BUZUVIS

TITLE IX, the federal civil rights law that prohibits sex discrimination in education, is well known for transforming girls' and women's sports. Because the requirements it imposes on scholastic and collegiate athletics do not reflect a single unified theory of gender equality, it has been aptly dubbed a law of "many feminisms."[1] Since its early history, Title IX has embraced a system of sex segregation in sports, going against the grain of civil rights statutes that mandate gender integration and formal equality in other realms. Yet Title IX's "separate but equal" regime is increasingly being challenged by feminists who argue that it has not done enough to eliminate gender disparities and inequities in sports and is fundamentally incompatible with the inclusion and fair treatment of transgender and nonbinary athletes. The first two sections of this article trace the history of Title IX as it has been applied to sports and present evidence of the dramatic, but unfinished and racially uneven, impact it has had on increasing athletic opportunities for women and girls. The article then canvasses the feminist arguments for and against sex segregation in sports and makes the case that a regime of strict sex separation is no longer the best strategy for assuring girls' and women's success in sports and dislodging pernicious stereotypes of women's inferior athleticism.

I. THE ORIGINS OF TITLE IX AND ITS APPLICATION TO ATHLETICS

In 1972, Congress passed and President Nixon signed an omnibus education bill, the Education Amendment Acts of 1972.[2] Amid provisions allocating funds for student financial aid in higher education, support for vocational education, financial assistance to help school districts desegregate and to improve education opportunities for Native American students, and (most controversially) attempting to delay the effective date of certain desegregation orders, the provision enumerated as Title IX of this legislation quietly prohibited sex discrimination in educational programs receiving federal funds.[3] Modeled on Title VI of the Civil Rights Act of 1964, which banned discrimination on the basis of race in federally funded programs, Title IX harnessed Congress's power under the Constitution's spending clause to condition the receipt of federal funds on nondiscrimination.

In the United States, unlike many countries, schools were and are a major source of athletic opportunities for children and young adults. Yet Congress initially gave virtually no consideration to Title IX's effect on collegiate and scholastic sports.[4] Instead, Title IX's advocates and their allied legislators were primarily concerned about other areas of education where sex discrimination was rampant, such as gender-based admission caps in graduate and professional education and employment discrimination in the faculty ranks.[5] It wasn't until after the law's passage, and a move by the National Collegiate Athletics Association (NCAA) and major college athletic programs to block the law's application to men's revenue-producing sports, that Congress confirmed Title IX's application to athletics. Rather than enter into the fray itself, Congress directed the Department of Health, Education, and Welfare (HEW, the predecessor to the Department of Education) to issue regulations to fill in the details of what Title IX means for athletics.[6] In delegating this authority to HEW, Congress's instructions did not endorse any particular theory of equality, instead requiring only that the agency take into account "the nature of particular sports."[7]

When HEW's Office for Civil Rights (OCR) took up this directive, the first question it had to address was whether to allow separate teams for men and women. Civil rights laws in other contexts, including Title IX's application to other areas, such as admissions, use a formal equality principle in which similarly situated individuals must be treated the same without regard to their sex. For athletics, this would mean requiring schools to have gender-blind team tryouts using the same criteria of talent and skill for male and female athletes. The choice was mired in controversy.

Given a history of pseudoscientific beliefs that participation in athletics was harmful to women and to their fertility in particular,[8] it was not uncommon at the time for sporting organizations and educational institutions to categorically exclude women and girls from certain sports. In fact, feminists were already waging an integration campaign against sports that restricted membership to boys. By the mid-1970s, the National Organization for Women (NOW) had successfully challenged the exclusion of girls from such organizations as Little League by arguing that the liberal feminism reflected in the Constitution's Equal Protection Clause does not permit the exclusion of girls with interests and abilities similar to those of the boys who play.[9] Liberal feminists, along with NOW, defended integrated sports against arguments that girls would be better served by separate leagues, arguing that coed participation fostered a mutual respect between boys and girls that would lead to more cooperative adult relationships.[10]

But whereas OCR initially considered allowing schools to satisfy Title IX by simply selecting the "best athletes" in gender-neutral tryouts,[11] the agency ultimately decided against basing the athletics regulations on a theory of equality inspired by the Equal Protection Clause. The proposed regulations, circulated for public comment on June 20, 1974, instead permitted schools to separate men's and women's teams in competitive sports.[12] The agency proceeded to propose measures of nondiscrimination that would operate in a context of sports separated by sex. It rejected "equal aggregate expenditures" as the standard and instead banned sex-based discrimination in the provision of equipment and supplies "or in any other matter," and required "affirmative efforts" to expand women's athletic skills and interests.

The Office for Civil Rights received almost ten thousand comments on the proposed regulations.[13] Many were from stakeholders in men's sports who argued for excluding athletics from Title IX or for special rules protecting revenue-generating sports.[14] The NCAA bolstered the policy argument for this position with a legal one, namely, that Title IX does not apply to athletic departments on the grounds that they do not themselves receive federal funds.[15] Women's sports advocates countered by endorsing Title IX's application to athletics and arguing for stronger regulations to secure equal opportunity for women—though they did not necessarily agree on what theory of equality would best accomplish this goal. Some, such as the Association of Intercollegiate Athletics for Women (AIAW), wanted women's sports to remain separate in order to avoid exposing them to the corrupting commercial influences that men's sports had embraced.[16] They believed that college and university athletic programs should not exist solely to pursue wins but to support a student's education and personal growth. To this end, AIAW members objected to such mainstays in men's sports as recruiting, restrictions on transfers, athletic scholarships, and long-distance competition—all of which prioritized winning over students' academic and athletic experiences. They wanted separate programs with equal funding and the discretion to spend it as they wished, without having to replicate the practices of men's programs. In seeking to preserve the "different voice" of women's sports and assign it (literally) equal value, this position evokes the work of cultural feminists who, in opposition to liberal feminism, seek to accommodate gender differences and ensure that practices and values distinctive to women are not devalued as such.[17]

Other arguments for a separate-but-equal framework focused not on the philosophy of sports promoted by female educators but on other asserted differences between the sexes. A separate-but-equal model of sports appealed to those who believed in women's equal right to athletic opportunities notwithstanding their belief in women's inherent athletic inferiority.[18] Others substituted structural inequality for biological determinism as the reason for women's lesser athletic abilities and argued that because discrimination has artificially suppressed women's participation, a system that distributes opportunity based on gender-neutral athletic criteria would only perpetuate existing disparities.[19]

The final regulations, released in 1975, sided largely with the proponents of separate women's programs. The regulations retained the allowance of separate teams, but replaced the "affirmative efforts" mandate, which was criticized for being vague, with more specific requirements for measuring nondiscrimination in the distribution of athletic opportunities.[20] In response to requests by educational institutions for more guidance, and criticisms from women's groups about lax enforcement, OCR issued a clarifying interpretation in 1979, permitting schools to demonstrate compliance with the regulation's equal participation mandate in one of three ways.[21] First, schools could demonstrate that they offer women athletic opportunities substantially proportionate to female undergraduate enrollment. Even though women constituted a minority of college students at the time, OCR understood that compliance under this prong would not be achieved quickly, and so it offered two alternatives for demonstrating compliance.[22] The second option for complying is to show a "history and continuing practice" of expanding opportunities for the underrepresented sex, meaning women.[23] For schools that could not comply under either of these tests, the third option allowed schools to comply by demonstrating that their existing sports offerings "fully and effectively" satisfied the interests and abilities of the underrepresented sex (women). In order for that to occur, schools would have to show that their female students did not want any more sports than the ones already offered.[24]

Later, courts would affirm that the third test did not allow schools to merely track the "relative interests" of male and female students in structuring their sports programs. Even if a school could show that its female students expressed lower levels of interest in athletics than did its male students, it still had to fully provide for the athletic skills and interests of its female students.[25] As long as women remain underrepresented in athletics in relation to their enrollment, this three-pronged test protects women's teams from being eliminated for any reason other than diminished interest and puts pressure on schools to expand their offerings in women's sports.

The final regulations did allow for some slippage, however, in what schools must provide to their female athletes. As an accommodation to college athletics' concern about protecting resources for men's sports, the draft version's refusal to require equal aggregate expenditures was retained.[26] Instead, the regulations require equal treatment of the men's and women's respective programs by ensuring comparable quality of such amenities as facilities, equipment, coaching, and other dedicated staff, schedules for practice and competition, and publicity and promotion.[27] In addition, the regulations require athletic departments to allocate scholarship dollars to female athletes in proportion to women's share of athletic participation, and not their (likely higher) share of enrollment.[28]

Most of the Title IX athletic regulations adhere to a separate-but-equal framework, but there is a narrow exception for talented female athletes to cross over to play on the boys' (or men's) team. If a school offers only one team in a particular sport, it must allow members of the other sex to try out—but only if two conditions are met. First, the sport in question must not be a contact sport; second, opportunities for members of the otherwise-excluded sex must have "previously been limited."[29] This provision makes it possible for girls (whose athletic opportunities are typically the ones that have been "previously limited") to try out for what might otherwise be a boys-only team in such sports as golf, volleyball, swimming, and tennis. Owing to the limitation on contact sports, however, popular boys-only sports such as football and baseball are exempt from this requirement.[30] This limited provision offers small consolation to feminists like NOW's members, who sought to attain equality through integration. Perverting the argument of feminists who called for the separation of women's sport for reasons of difference, the contact sport exception reinforces prevailing stereotypes about female athletes' being unsuited for the most masculine of sports.[31]

II. Feminist Recognition of Persisting Inequality

In the near fifty years since Title IX's passage, girls' and women's sports have grown exponentially. High schools offered only about 300,000 athletic opportunities for girls in 1972, compared to 3.5 million today,[32] and college opportunities for women expanded from 30,000 to more than 218,000.[33] Despite relatively weak enforcement mechanisms,[34] the separate-but-equal framework has had the desired effect of promoting and protecting athletic opportunities for women and girls. Courts have relied on the three-part test as the basis for injunctive relief against schools that have provided too few athletic opportunities to female students,[35] or that have tried in the absence of proportionality to cut women's teams.[36] Enforcement by OCR has also produced settlement agreements that require school districts to add sports for girls.[37] Perhaps more important than the power of Title IX to motivate compliance through enforcement, the law's symbolic power has fueled the expansion of women's sports by normalizing the expectation of equality in the realm of athletics.[38]

Despite this progress, both the quantity and quality of women's athletic opportunities are far from equal to men's. At the vast majority of colleges and universities, the percentage of female athletes is disproportionately low.[39] Resources such as operating budgets and scholarship dollars still heavily favor men's sports.[40] Girls are also likely to be underrepresented in high school sports.[41] Finally, leadership in scholastic and collegiate sports is overwhelmingly male, with men holding the majority of head coach positions, even in women's sports, and women locked out of all but a tiny handful of positions coaching male athletes.[42]

Intersectional and critical race feminism have been particularly important to exposing the extent to which existing inequalities overburden girls and women of color, particularly those who are economically disadvantaged. For example, 40% of predominantly minority schools have proportionality gaps of 10 percentage points or more.[43] At the college level, white women receive 68% of the athletic opportunities in NCAA-sponsored women's sports, despite making up only 54% of the female undergraduate population. Underrepresentation of women of color still exists and is particularly acute for women whose race is reported as something other than white or Black, including Asian, Latina, and Native American. Black women are concentrated in just a handful of sports, namely, basketball, bowling, and track. In the vast majority of sports, Black women are underrepresented among athletes, coaches, and in other leadership positions of power. Title IX has done little to erase the barriers to entry posed by urban location and lower socioeconomic status that disproportionately disadvantage Black students[44] or the historical racial segregation of sport-related facilities such as swimming pools and country clubs.

Women of color also experience a unique version of the burden of apologetic behavior that the heteropatriarchy imposes on female athletes in general. Apologetic behavior refers to the invoked actions of female athletes to emphasize stereotypical female appearance and behavior in order to strategically manage society's policing of female athleticism by disparaging athletic women as mannish or as lesbians.[45] Yet the femininity deemed acceptable for this purpose is a white femininity, which is off-limits to many women of color. Female athletes of color, particularly Black women, have been targeted for exclusion and criticism because their hair, clothes, bodies, and general deportment transgress stereotypes of normative (implicitly white) femininity.[46]

III. Feminist Support for a Separate-but-Equal Standard

Much of the feminist support for Title IX accepts the separate-but-equal standard as a pragmatic solution for maximizing women's and girls' participation in sports. While acknowledging the law's failure to deliver on its promise of equality, supporters of Title IX maintain that both "separate" and "equal" are justified objectives. Compared with an equal-access rule (simply allowing female athletes an equal right to try out for an existing team), a system of separate girls' and women's sports takes into account the ways in which women and girls are differently situated from their male counterparts when it comes to athletics. An equal-access rule would have a disparate impact on female participation—not only because of group-based physical differences between sexes, but also because of the persistent inequality in access to opportunity and resources needed to develop talent. Having separate women's sports protects female athletes from losing ground to their male counterparts and from having their participation restricted in ways that often result in the establishment of coed sports.[47]

Feminist arguments have also been deployed in support of the equality principle in the separate-but-equal framework. Specifically, feminist scholars have addressed the critique that Title IX unfairly favors female athletes because it provides them, as a class, with more athletic opportunity than is justified by their collective interests and abilities. Because formal equality requires treating similarly situated groups in the same way, it does not justify offering the same quantity and quality of athletic opportunities to groups with different athletic interests. Some scholars,[48] as well as some colleges and universities that were sued for eliminating women's teams, have condemned this departure from formal equality, arguing that Title IX should allow schools to distribute athletic opportunities in proportion to men's and women's respective levels of interest in playing sports.

In a rare foray beyond the gender-blind liberal feminist model that dominates civil right discourse, courts have uniformly rejected this argument as incompatible with the language of the 1979 document clarifying the regulations and likely to reinforce the very disparities that gave rise to those gender-disparate interest levels in the first place.[49] Feminist scholars have offered theoretical justifications for proportionality to bolster it against continued attack. Kimberly Yurako, for example, argues that proportionality is best supported when athletic opportunities are regarded as tools that help students develop the skills they need to be successful in life, as opposed to rewards that students receive on the basis of talent.[50] In support of the tool-giving framework, she notes that beyond such physical and socioemotional skills as teamwork, leadership, and character development, athletic opportunities empower nonparticipants by ensuring that girls as well as boys have role models of strength, competence, and agency. Viewed as tools, the idea that athletic opportunities should be made equally available to members of each sex—without adjusting for relative interest and abilities—is compelling.[51] But beyond this liberal feminist application of formal equality, Yurako argues that proportionality finds still more justification in its capacity to support a cultural transformation that expands society's perceptions both of "athlete" and of "female" so that each is more compatible with the other.[52]

Deborah Brake offers a theoretical defense of Title IX that is rooted in antisubordination theory rather than formal equality.[53] She notes that structural inequality in scholastic and collegiate athletic programs has suppressed and continues to suppress the athletic interests and abilities of female students. Because interest and ability are flawed criteria for distributing opportunity, Title IX justifiably imposes an equality mandate to address structural inequality. Brake's analysis of structural inequality includes the widespread gender disparities in the allocation of scholastic and collegiate athletic opportunities, which suppress women's athletic interest by limiting the chances women and girls have to imagine themselves as athletes.

At the same time, the disparity in participation reinforces society's association of athleticism with masculinity by positioning female athleticism outside the norm. In addition to shortchanging female students in terms of the quality of athletic opportunities available to them, educational institutions reinforce the notion of male entitlement to sports and the anti-normalization of female athleticism in many other ways, as well. Examples include allocating the lion's share of resources to men's teams,[54] hiring predominantly men to serve as administrators and coaches of both men's and women's teams,[55] tolerating sexual misconduct committed by male coaches and athletes,[56] pressuring female athletes and coaches to maintain "culturally appropriate" femininity,[57] and tolerating or promoting practices that objectify, marginalize, and belittle female athleticism.[58] Because educational institutions construct female athleticism through such practices, Title IX should not use women's existing athletic skills and interests as the standard for measuring equal opportunity.

IV. Feminist Arguments for Alternatives to the Separate-but-Equal Standard

But feminist defenses of the equal participation test have not quelled the controversy among feminists concerning Title IX's baseline of sex segregation. The separate-but-equal framework remains subject to criticism by feminists for normalizing the practice of segregation and the generalizations and stereotypes that underlie it.[59] Civil rights laws do not accept gender-based classifications in other contexts,[60] and some feminist scholars have questioned whether it is any more appropriate to do so in the context of sports.

Separation invites an unequal distribution of resources.[61] Nearly fifty years into Title IX's separate-but-equal regime, inequalities persist.[62] Sports for boys and men were already established prior to Title IX's enactment, so equalizing opportunities for girls and women requires schools to make either the unpopular choice of diverting resources from their male athletic programs or the improbable choice of finding new funding sources and physical space to create new girls' and women's teams without disturbing men's.[63] The separate-but-equal standard is more likely to be an unrealized promise in schools that predominantly serve students of color because those schools are more likely to have fewer resources to expand opportunities.[64] External forces make it even harder for schools to dismantle gender-based resource inequality. For example, high school booster clubs are more enthusiastic about and successful at raising funds to support boys' sports,[65] and fans will pay more to watch men's college sports, both live and on television. Schools are unable to match for women's and girls' teams the funds generated by or on behalf of men's sports. These inequities not only undermine equality but also subvert cultural feminist objectives of using sports to empower women. Instead, the resulting disparities "link maleness with highly valued and visible skills" that sports put on display.[66] Inferior treatment constructs women's sports as less legitimate than men's, ensuring that society continues to ascribe the positive physical and character traits showcased in sports with men and not women. It also perpetuates the gender gap in performance by depriving female athletes of access to the same quality opportunities that male athletes have to cultivate athletic interest and ability.

Even if segregation was accompanied by equal resources and opportunities, the act of separation itself is inherently unequal because it constructs the stigmatizing stereotype that female athletes are inferior.[67] Notwithstanding generalized gender differences, there are plenty of examples of women competing successfully against men.[68] Segregation of sports keeps those examples from happening more frequently. Instead, it ensures that female athleticism is contextualized in the category regarded as inferior—inviting fans to discount female athletic performance because it takes place under modified rules ("Yeah, she's good, but she only had to play three sets").[69] The stereotypes constructed by separating women's sports affect not only society's view of women but also women's and girls' self-perception. The professed need for pervasive women's sports sends a strong message to girls that they should not expect themselves to compete as well as boys. As girls internalize the negative stereotypes about female athleticism, those stereotypes operate to constrain their performance.[70] Integrated sports give female athletes the freedom to strive for participation in the sporting contexts that receive the most resources and that are deemed most valuable by society.[71] They liberate them from the constraints imposed by the message sent by segregation that such success is not possible. And it fosters male athletes' positive impressions of their female teammates, potentially leading to reduced gender stereotyping in other realms as well.

Feminists who critique the separate-but-equal regime on these grounds generally refrain from calling for the elimination of women's sports.[72] Most recognize that, because society has yet to fully overcome the effects of past discrimination on women's participation, women's sports still play a role in remediating these effects. But, they argue, separation is employed with no persuasive rationale, uncritically, as a default and compulsory paradigm that provides no opportunity for female athletes and society at large to reap the benefits of integrated sports. Gender-inclusive athletic opportunities are difficult to find even at the margins and notwithstanding the limitations and downsides of separate-but-equal treatment.

This treatment has done no more to protect women's different voices in sports than an equal access rule would have accomplished. Formal equality may be critiqued for its simplistic approach to equality, which simply extends rather than upends existing privilege. But the separate-but-equal model simply replaces individually focused formal equality with a group-based version. By requiring institutions to treat women's sports like men's, Title IX has simply extended to women the version of sports created by men to showcase their traits and reflect their values.[73] Despite the aspirations of proponents of women's sports, nothing in the separate-but-equal standard allows women's "distinct contributions" to the meaning of sports to endure even for women's sports, let alone contribute to the meaning of sports as it applies to all.

One example of Title IX's limited transformative potential in this regard is the fact that the women's sports with the most growth have been those with male analogs, such as soccer.[74] It has been difficult for sports that are rooted in women's experience and that showcase distinctly female athleticism to be taken seriously.[75] Instead of transforming the male model, which values competitive outcomes over participation, women's sports have conformed to it.[76] One example of this conformity is found in the controversy concerning compensating college athletes, as warranted by the commercial value that they provide.[77] Title IX's equal treatment provision supports the argument that female athletes should receive compensation comparable to that of male athletes, but it obscures the feminist argument for decommercializing sports altogether.[78] Separate women's sports have also failed to protect women's coaching and athletic administration positions, as their conformity to the male model contributed to defining leadership in male terms and with the example of men in mind.

With these downsides to separation acknowledged, the feminist case against separate-but-equal treatment would accept separation only when narrowly tailored to the goal of remedying disparities in participation and past discrimination. Some sports could potentially have boys and girls together on a gender-inclusive team without decreasing girls' participation.[79]

One area of agreement among feminists on both sides of this debate bears noting: Whereas critics of the separate-but-equal standard acknowledge a limited role for women's sports, many advocates of the current framework also support girls' rights to try out for boys' teams. Feminists unanimously condemn the regulatory exception that allows schools to reserve contact sports for football exclusively for boys.[80] And though courts have so far rejected this view, some feminist supporters of separation as the default (though not all) would also expand girls' rights to try out for boys' teams to include situations where a girls' team is offered in that sport but that team provides a lesser competitive experience owing to unequal resources, status, or skill level.[81] This division of opinion concerning whether the most athletic girls should be able to "play up" on the better boys' teams reflects the tension between Title IX's emphasis on group-based versus individual rights. The female athlete who chooses the boys' team benefits at the expense of the girls' team, which misses the opportunity to benefit from her talent.

V. THE SEPARATE-BUT-EQUAL STANDARD AND GENDER DIVERSITY

Increasing awareness of gender diversity has added new urgency to the debate about the segregation of athletics by sex. The separate-but-equal framework in athletics is limited in its capacity to accommodate athletes who are transgender or intersex. The dominant practice of designating athletes as either male or female reinforces outdated notions of sex and gender that rely only on students' binary, birth-assigned designations as male or female. Here I use the label "transgender" to refer to students for whom the gender with which they identify corresponds to the sex other than the one they were assigned at birth, as well as those whose gender identity is nonbinary and is not reflected by either the male or the female label. Where separate women's and girls' sports are promoted as an essential accommodation of inferior female athleticism, the idea of including transgender girls (who identify as female, though assigned male at birth) is often met with skepticism, hostility, and exclusion. And the act of separating sports into only two categories, male and female, denies nonbinary students an opportunity to participate without experiencing dissonance between their gender identity and the gender label on their sport, even if they are given the opportunity to choose which one. As "nonbinary" increasingly becomes available as a legal gender, Title IX's endorsement of equal opportunity for "both sexes" must adapt to ensure that nonbinary athletes remain eligible for binary-gendered sports and that gender-inclusive athletic opportunities are supported and endorsed.[82]

Integrating more athletic opportunities would mitigate these problems and create more inclusive opportunities for gender-diverse students. In the meantime, however, state athletic associations as well as government bodies have taken various positions on the eligibility of transgender athletes to compete in separate girls' and women's sports.[83] Most college and some high school athletic associations require athletes wishing to compete as females to have medically curtailed their body's testosterone so that their physical characteristics align with their affirmed female gender. Such policies are aimed at ensuring that those similarly situated with respect to testosterone are treated similarly with respect to their eligibility for women's sports. Within a formal equality analysis, however, the tradeoff is that those whose gender identity is female are not all treated the same, since some transgender girls are excluded on the basis of hormones.

Feminists do not agree about whether eligibility for women's sports should be based on testosterone or on gender identity.[84] Proponents of the former, relying on a narrow definition of the term "women," argue that transgender inclusion threatens the fragile gains realized under Title IX. They believe that testosterone bestows athletic advantage and that eligibility for women's sports should be restricted in order to neutralize athletic advantage.[85] Because the population of transgender athletes is small, such a rationale is not rooted in the separate-but-equal objective of ensuring girls and women access to athletic opportunities. Rather, it is rooted in the objective of preventing a transgender girl from potentially depriving a cisgender girl of the opportunity to win. This objective reflects a narrow and essentialist definition of "female" that disregards intersectional feminists' emphasis on women's multiple, simultaneous, and diverse identities and fails to connect the gender oppression that creates discrimination against women's sports with the discrimination that transgender women face.

In addition, insisting that "the opportunity to win" must be distributed fairly conflicts not only with the educational value of sports but with other strands of feminist legal theory that are part of Title IX's story. For one, the focus on winning makes it harder to rationalize the separate-but-equal framework in the first place, which is on strongest footing when athletic opportunity is understood as a "tool-giving" experience instead of a reward for talent.[86] It also invites women and girls to see themselves as inherently and essentially inferior as a result of their comparatively diminished testosterone and invites men to take the opposite view of themselves.[87] Finally, it underscores the vast ideological distance from the 1970s-era feminists who argued for separate women's sports as a means of preserving their distinct values. Support for testosterone-based eligibility represents the worst of formal equality by establishing that women's sports are "equal" to men's in their emphasis on winning above all—the aspect of sports that is least compatible with its educational mission.[88] Given that arguments for transgender exclusion place the limitations and flaws of segregation in stark relief, the pursuit of transgender inclusion may eventually lead to the dismantling of the separate-but-equal model's hegemonic status.

VI. Conclusion

When Congress and OCR undertook the challenge of deploying Title IX to address gender inequality in athletics, they faced a thorny problem: an open tryout model, though consistent with the formal equality approach applied in other civil rights contexts, would freeze low levels of female participation because it does not account for gender differences that have created disparities in interest and ability. At the same time, creating separate sports for women and girls promotes opportunities but risks undermining female athleticism by constructing women and girls as inherently weak and inferior. Title IX makes a reasonable effort to navigate this dilemma by employing a variety of feminist theoretical approaches: separation to promote women's participation in sports in light of gender differences, equal treatment of those separate sports programs as a form of group-based formal equality, and some rights for individual girls to try out for boys' teams, a measure of formal equality for individuals. But the overarching concern behind Title IX's compromise, protecting female athletic opportunities, has diminished over time, necessitating a reevaluation of the competing interests at stake.

The courts have already provided one example of a more nuanced approach to the default of separation: the Eighth Circuit Court of Appeals recently enjoined a Minnesota state athletic association rule that prohibited boys from participating on high school girls' competitive dance teams.[89] In light of the state's overall equitable distribution of athletic opportunities, the court concluded that the association could not justify the boys' exclusion with a protectionist rationale. The court addressed the plaintiff's equal protection claim instead of its Title IX claim, but its effort to confine separation to its most persuasive justification, preserving opportunities for girls, resonates with the feminist reckoning with Title IX as well. Although the court's opinion is limited to one state and addresses a sport in which integration will not generate controversy with regard to competitive equity, it represents an initial step forward in a broader effort to critically evaluate the separate-but-equal regime and scale it back so that its feminist aspirations are not overshadowed by its costs.

Another opportunity to reconsider Title IX's default to separation is presented by the controversy regarding transgender inclusion. When feminists argue for exclusion as a means of preserving competitive balance, they contribute to negative stereotypes about female athleticism. And although the act of creating a girls' team in the first instance can be justified as a means of protecting and preserving opportunities that girls otherwise might not have, no such rationale justifies excluding transgender girls. First and foremost, they *are* girls. And second, the relatively small numbers of transgender girls pose no risk of displacing cisgender girls from sports. A gender-inclusive model of sports would not only reflect feminist solidarity with all those oppressed by heteropartriarchy but it would also empower cisgender girls to strive for athletic excellence in a field of competition that includes gender diversity. Whether feminists can unify around this issue will determine our commitment to resisting the negative stereotypes about female athleticism that construct women's sports as a perpetually inferior category.

Notes

1. Deborah L. Brake, Getting in the Game: Title IX and the Women's Sport Revolution 8 (2010).
2. 20 U.S.C. § 1681 *et seq.*
3. *Major Provisions of the Measure on Aid to Education and Limits on Pupil Busing*, N.Y. Times, Jun. 9, 1972, at 17.
4. Sarah K. Fields, Female Gladiators: Gender, Law, and Contact Sports in America 11 (2005) (noting that Title IX's application to sports was only minimally discussed in the context of football).
5. *See* Susan Ware, Title IX: A Brief History with Documents 3 (2007); Bernice R. Sandler, *"Too Strong for a Woman"—The Five Words That Created Title IX*, in Susan Ware, Title IX: A Brief History with Documents 35 (2007); *see also* Cohen v. Brown Univ., 101 F.3d 155, 165 (1st Cir. 1996) (citing 118 Cong. Rec. 5804 [1972] [statement of Sen. Bayh]).
6. *See* Gender and Athletics Act, Pub. L. No. 93-380, § 844, 88 Stat. 484, 612 (1974).
7. *See* Ware, Title IX, *supra* note 5, at 3 (explaining that Congress recognized that some sports would cost more than others for reasons other than discrimination).
8. *See*, e.g., Suzanne Sangree, *Title IX and the Contact Sports Exemption: Gender Stereotypes in a Civil Rights Statute*, 32 Conn. L. Rev. 381, 405–10 (2000).
9. *See*, e.g., Nat'l Org. for Women, Essex Cty. Chapter v. Little League Baseball, Inc., 318 A.2d 33, 39 (N.J. App. Div.), *aff'd sub nom.* 338 A.2d 198 (N.J. 1974) (rejecting Little League's argument that girls' exclusion was warranted by different safety risks and privacy concerns).
10. *See*, e.g., Joseph B. Treaster, *Girls a Hit in Debut on Diamond*, N.Y. Times, Mar. 25, 1974, at 67.
11. Fields, Female Gladiators, *supra* note 4, at 11.
12. Education Programs and Activities Receiving or Benefiting from Federal Financial Assistance, 39 Fed. Reg. 22236 (proposed Jun. 20, 1974) (to be codified at 45 C.F.R. pt. 86).
13. Brake, Getting in the Game, *supra* note 1, at 21.
14. Comment, *Implementing Title IX: The HEW Regulations*, 124 U. Pa. L. Rev. 806, 836 (1976).
15. The NCAA made this argument in litigation as well. *See*, e.g., Nat'l Collegiate Athletic Ass'n v. Califano, 444 F. Supp. 425, 429 (D. Kan. 1978), *rev'd*, 622 F.2d 1382 (10th Cir. 1980). The Supreme Court endorsed this program-specific limitation on the scope of Title IX's mandate in Grove City Coll. v. Bell, 465 U.S. 555 (1984). But Congress had the last word, amending Title IX to confirm that any program's receipt of federal funding obligates the entire institution (or school district) to comply. *See* 20 U.S.C. § 1687 (1988).
16. Ying Wushanley, Playing Nice and Losing: The Struggle for Control of Women's Intercollegiate Athletics, 1960–2000 (2004); *see also* Ware, Title IX, *supra* note 5, at 11–12.
17. *See*, e.g., Susan Birrell, *Separatism as an Issue in Women's Sports*, 8 Arena Rev. 21, 24 (1987).
18. Comment, *Implementing Title IX*, *supra* note 14, at 838–39.

19. See, e.g., Brenda Fasteau, *Giving Women a Sporting Chance*, Ms. MAG., July 1973, at 56; Ann Crittenden Scott, *Closing the Muscle Gap*, Ms. MAG., SEPT. 1974, at 49.
20. 34 C.F.R. § 106.41(c)(1) (2020).
21. Title IX of the Education Amendments of 1972; A Policy Interpretation; Title IX and Intercollegiate Athletics, 44 Fed. Reg. 71,413, 71,418 (Dec. 11, 1979) (to be codified at 45 C.F.R. pt. 86).
22. *Id.*
23. *Id.*
24. *Id.*
25. Pederson v. La. State Univ., 213 F.3d 858, 878–79 (5th Cir. 2000); Neal v. Bd. of Trs. of Cal. State Univs., 198 F.3d 763, 767–69 (9th Cir. 1999); Cohen v. Brown Univ., 101 F.3d 155, 176 (1st Cir. 1996); Kelley v. Bd. of Trs., 35 F.3d 265, 270 (7th Cir. 1994); Roberts v. Colo. State Bd. of Agric., 998 F.2d 824, 830 (10th Cir. 1993).
26. 34 C.F.R. § 106.41(c) (2020).
27. 34 C.F.R. §§ 106.41(c)(2)–(10) (2020).
28. 34 C.F.R. § 106.37(c) (2020).
29. 34 C.F.R. § 106.41(b) (2020).
30. The regulation broadly defines contact sports as "boxing, wrestling, rugby, ice hockey, football, basketball and other sports the purpose or major activity of which involves bodily contact." 34 C.F.R. § 106.41(b) (2020).
31. Sangree, *Title IX and the Contact Sports Exemption*, supra note 8, at 405–10.
32. National Federation of High Schools, *High School Sports Participation Increases for 29th Consecutive Year* (2018).
33. NCAA, SPORT SPONSORSHIP AND PARTICIPATION RATES REPORT (2018).
34. Title IX permits both government enforcement and private lawsuits. The Office of Civil Rights has the power to threaten the withholding of federal funding to motivate compliance, but the agency has never taken this step, preferring instead to resolve matters through resolution agreements. Private lawsuits are usually only filed when there are highly motivated plaintiffs such as disappointed members of an unlawfully terminated women's team or other cases of extreme or pervasive inequality. For these reasons, neither the threat of public enforcement nor private lawsuits motivate educational institutions to prospectively correct long-standing inequalities at great cost. On the limits of public enforcement, *see*, e.g., Julie A. Davies & Lisa M. Bohon, *Re-Imagining Public Enforcement of Title IX*, 2007 B.Y.U. EDUC. & L.J. 25, 50–54 (2007); Sudha Setty, *Leveling the Playing Field: Reforming the Office for Civil Rights to Achieve Better Title IX Enforcement*, 32 COLUM. J.L. & SOC. PROBS. 331, 340–42 (1999).
35. *See*, e.g., Ollier v. Sweetwater Union High Sch. Dist., 768 F.3d 843, 859 (9th Cir. 2014); Cruz by Cruz v. Alhambra Sch. Dist., No. CV 04-1460 ABC (MCX), 2012 WL 13167767, at *5 (C.D. Cal. Aug. 3, 2012).
36. *See*, e.g., Biediger v. Quinnipiac Univ., 691 F.3d 85 (2d Cir. 2012); Cohen, 101 F.3d 155; Roberts v. Colorado State Bd. of Agric., 998 F.2d 824 (10th Cir. 1993); Mayerova v. E. Mich. Univ., 346 F. Supp. 3d 983 (E.D. Mich. 2018), *appeal dismissed*, No. 18-2238, 2020 WL 1970535 (6th Cir. Apr. 20, 2020).
37. *See*, e.g., Resolution Agreement, Chicago Public School District #299, OCR Case Nos. 05-11-1034 and 05-89-1020 (July 1, 2015).
38. BRAKE, GETTING IN THE GAME, *supra* note 1, at 13, 228–29.

39. Compared to 218,000 or more opportunities for women, there are 281,000 for men in NCAA-sponsored sports. *See* NCAA, SPORT SPONSORSHIP AND PARTICIPATION RATES. Given that women are now a majority of the undergraduate student population overall, it is not surprising that only 4% of NCAA member institutions have attained proportionality compliance. ELLEN J. STAUROWSKY ET AL., WOMEN'S SPORTS FOUNDATION, CHASING EQUITY: THE TRIUMPHS, CHALLENGES, AND OPPORTUNITIES IN SPORTS FOR GIRLS AND WOMEN 47–48 (2020) (also reporting findings suggesting the absence of proportionality compliance among high schools). And while Title IX provides alternatives to proportionality, the alternative tests are virtually impossible to satisfy when schools cut existing women's teams or take seriously their obligation to assess female athletes' interests and abilities.
40. STAUROWSKY ET AL., CHASING EQUITY, *supra* note 39, at 48.
41. Alia Wong, *Where Girls Are Missing Out on High-School Sports*, THE ATLANTIC (Jun. 26, 2015), https://www.theatlantic.com/education/archive/2015/06/girls-high-school-sports-inequality/396782/.
42. Nefertiti Walker, *Cross-Gender Coaching: Women Coaching Men*, in WOMEN IN SPORT COACHING (Nicole M. LaVoi ed., 2016).
43. NATIONAL WOMEN'S LAW CENTER, FINISHING LAST: GIRLS AND COLOR AND SCHOOL SPORTS OPPORTUNITY (2015).
44. Tonya M. Evans, *In the Title IX Race Toward Gender Equity, the Black Female Athlete Is Left to Finish Last: The Lack of Access for the "Invisible Woman,"* 42 HOWARD L.J. 105 (1998); Alfred Dennis Mathewson, *Black Women, Gender Equity and the Function at the Junction*, 6 MARQ. SPORTS L.J. 239, 251–52 (1996).
45. MARY JO FESTLE, PLAYING NICE: POLITICS AND APOLOGIES IN WOMEN'S SPORTS (1996).
46. *See, e.g.,* Delia D. Douglas, *To Be Young, Gifted, Black and Female: A Meditation on the Cultural Politics at Play in Representations of Venus and Serena Williams*, 5 SOC. OF SPORT ONLINE 1 (2002); Kristine E. Newhall & Erin E. Buzuvis, *(e)Racing Jennifer Harris: Sexuality and Race, Law and Discourse in Harris v. Portland*, 32 J. SPORT & SOC. ISSUES 345 (2008); Jamie Schultz, *Reading the Catsuit: Serena Williams and the Production of Blackness at the 2002 U.S. OPEN*, 29 J. SPORT & SOC. ISSUES 338 (2005).
47. BRAKE, GETTING IN THE GAME, *supra* note 1, at 23–28.
48. *See, e.g.,* Michael Straubel, *Gender Equity, College Sports, Title IX and Group Rights: A Coach's View*, 62 BROOK. L. REV. 1039, 1041–42 (1996); Earl C. Dudley Jr. & George Rutherglen, *Ironies, Inconsistencies, and Intercollegiate Athletics: Title IX, Title VII, and Statistical Evidence of Discrimination*, 1 VA. J. SPORTS & L. 177, 179–80 (1999).
49. Pederson v. La. State Univ., 213 F.3d 858, 878–79 (5th Cir. 2000); Neal v. Bd. of Trs. of Cal. State Univs., 198 F.3d 763, 767–69 (9th Cir. 1999); Cohen v. Brown Univ., 101 F.3d 155, 176 (1st Cir. 1996); Kelley v. Bd. of Trs., 35 F.3d 265, 270 (7th Cir. 1994); Roberts v. Colo. State Bd. of Agric., 998 F.2d 824, 830 (10th Cir. 1993).
50. Kimberly A. Yuracko, *One for You and One for Me: Is Title IX's Sex-Based Proportionality Requirement for College Varsity Athletic Positions Defensible?*, 97 NW. U. L. REV. 731 (2003).
51. *Id.* at 778–88.
52. *Id.* at 795–98.

53. Deborah Brake, *The Struggle for Sex Equality in Sport and the Theory Behind Title IX*, 34 U. MICH. J.L. REFORM 13 (2000).
54. *Id.* at 75–80.
55. *Id.* at 83–92.
56. *Id.* at 95–107.
57. *Id.* at 113–15 (discussing how the "lesbian label" is used to control and regulate women's participation in sports).
58. *Id.* at 110–13, 116–20. Such practices include asymmetrical labeling ("basketball" and "women's basketball") and nicknaming ("Raiders" and "Lady Raiders"), marketing materials that portray female athletes in makeup and nonathletic poses, and using cheerleaders to reinforce the message that women's role in sport is to support men.
59. *See, e.g.*, EILEEN MCDONAGH & LAURA PAPPANO, PLAYING WITH THE BOYS: WHY SEPARATE IS NOT EQUAL IN SPORTS (2008); Nancy Leong, *Against Women's Sports*, 95 WASH. U. L. REV. 1249 (2018); Karen L. Tokarz, *Separate But Unequal Educational Sports Programs: The Need for a New Theory of Equality*, 1 BERKELEY WOMEN'S L.J. 201 (1985).
60. *See, e.g.*, United States v. Virginia, 518 U.S. 515, 553 (1996) (rejecting a sex-segregated state-sponsored military leadership school).
61. Note, *Cheering on Women and Girls in Sports: Using Title IX to Fight Gender Role Oppression*, 110 HARV. L. REV. 1627, 1630, 1633–35 (1997).
62. Postsecondary athletics Title IX complaints have risen in recent years. *See generally* Celene Reynolds, *The Mobilization of Title IX across U.S. Colleges and Universities, 1994–2014*, 66 SOC. PROBS. 245, 255–56 (2019). According to one recent study, "[c]omplaints citing three athletic issues—interests and abilities (106.41c1), equal opportunity (106.41c), and meeting the requirements of part three of the three-part test (106.41c1–3)—represent[ed] 74 percent of the total filings in 2014." *Id.* at 256.
63. *See generally* B. Glenn George, *Fifty/Fifty: Ending Sex Segregation in School Sports*, 63 OHIO ST. L.J. 1107, 1113–32. Two particularly challenging areas of inequality have been facilities, such as inadequate softball fields, and scheduling, such as putting girls' sports in the less favorable season, day of the week, or time of day. *See* Erin E. Buzuvis & Kristine E. Newhall, *Equality Beyond the Three-Part Test: Exploring and Explaining the Invisibility of Title IX's Equal Treatment Requirement*, 22 MARQ. SPORTS L. REV. 427, 441–47 (2012). As second-comers to athletics, female athletes get whatever space and time is yet unclaimed.
64. NATIONAL WOMEN'S LAW CENTER, FINISHING LAST: GIRLS AND COLOR AND SCHOOL SPORTS OPPORTUNITY (2015).
65. *See generally* Powell Latimer, *Title IX Compliance Sometimes Means Turning Down Money*, STARNEWS ONLINE (Nov. 28, 2010, 5:41 PM), https://perma.cc/6RX7-6H39.
66. Lori Bryson, *Sport and the Maintenance of Masculine Hegemony*, in WOMEN, SPORT AND POWER 47, 48 (Susan Birrell & Cheryl L. Cole eds., 1994); *see also* Nancy Theberge, *The Construction of Gender in Sport: Women, Coaching, and the Naturalization of Difference*, 40 SOC. PROBS. 301, 301 (1993) (Calling sports "[o]ne of the cultural practices of most significance in the construction of gender" because it has served, for men, as "a setting for the development and display of traits and abilities that signify masculine power and authority").
67. MCDONAGH & PAPPANO, PLAYING WITH THE BOYS, *supra* note 59, at 15–17.

68. For examples of female athletes succeeding in integrated competition see Leong, *Against Women's Sports*, at 1264–70; McDonagh and Pappano, Playing with the Boys, *supra* note 59, at 73–74.
69. Leong, *Against Women's Sports, supra* note 59, at 1275.
70. One study noted that "there are two main pathways in which sex stereotypes manifest in sporting contexts. First, as long as it is known by the individual, a stereotype can operate directly and affect his/her performance if it is activated in a valued situation. Stereotypes can also operate indirectly, through an internalization process." Julie Boiché et al., *Development of Sex Stereotypes Relative to Sport Competence and Value During Adolescence*, 15 Psychol. Sport & Exercise 212, 212 (2014) (citations omitted).
71. *See* Adam Cohen et al., *Investigating a Coed Sport's Ability to Encourage Inclusion and Equality*, 28 J. Sport Mgmt. 220 (2014) (noting examples of sex-specific rules that are common in coed football and coed softball); *see also* Catherine LeClair, *Why Co-Ed Sports Leagues Are Never Really Co-Ed*, Deadspin (July 25, 2018, 11:55 AM), https://deadspin.com/why-co-ed-sports-leagues-are-never-really-co-ed-1827699592.
72. McDonagh & Pappano, Playing with the Boys, *supra* note 59, at 7–8 (rejecting "coercive" segregation); Leong, *Against Women's Sports, supra* note 59, at 1249 (acknowledging that sex segregation in sport is sometimes "the best choice, or should be included as an option" and instead urging readers to think "carefully and critically about when and why we engage in such segregation"); Tokarz, *Separate But Unequal Educational Sports Programs*, *supra* note 59, at 206 (acknowledging the possibility that "sex-based affirmative action programs for females [e.g., all-female teams maintained parallel to programs open on a competitive bases to both sexes]" are not foreclosed by the equal protection analysis of segregation that she proposes).
73. *See, e.g.*, Catharine MacKinnon, Women Self-Possession and Sport (1982), *in* Feminism Unmodified: Discourses on Life and Law (1987); *see also* Christine A. Littleton, *Reconstructing Sexual Equality*, 75 Calif. L. Rev. 1279 (1987); Brake, Getting in the Game, at 63–64.
74. NCAA women's soccer had 1,855 participants in 1981, compared to 28,310 today. NCAA, Sport Sponsorship and Participation Rates. This is the highest growth rate of any women's sport.
75. Though it is problematic when college athletic departments count underdeveloped competitive cheer programs as a Title IX sport to avoid adding other opportunities, it is also possible that resistance to acceptance of competitive cheer as a sport stems from the fact that it wasn't first developed in the male model. As a sport that displays coordinated athleticism for the sake of its aesthetic value rather than in the service of defeating an on-field opponent, competitive cheer arguably speaks from a distinctly "different voice." Refusing to label competitive cheer as sport for this reason ensures that the label "sport" remains impervious to modification and influence by that different voice. *See generally* Erin E. Buzuvis, *The Feminist Case for the NCAA's Recognition of Competitive Cheer as an Emerging Sport for Women*, 52 B.C. L. Rev. 439 (2011).
76. One example is the present-day controversy regarding compensating college athletes, warranted by the commercial value that they provide. Title IX's equal treatment provision supports the argument that female athletes should also be compensated, but it obscures the argument for decommercializing sports altogether.

77. *See generally* Erin E. Buzuvis, *Athletic Compensation for Women Too? Title IX Implications of* Northwestern *and* O'Bannon, 41 J.C. & U.L. 297 (2015).
78. The AIAW made this argument as a justification for separation, as was noted in Part I of this article. Although the AIAW prevailed in its support for separate women's teams, the structure for college sports in general unified under the male model, erasing feminist sporting values.
79. Factors to consider include teams' existing capacity to add more players, inclusivity of the rules and structure of the sport, and whether consolidating to an all-gender team would allow everyone to play it in the sport's more favorable season. The author has proposed Massachusetts high school golf as an example of a sport where the benefits of segregation do not outweigh the costs. *See* Erin E. Buzuvis, Attorney General v. MIAA *at Forty Years: A Critical Examination of Gender Segregation in High School Athletics in Massachusetts*, 25 TEX. J. ON C.L. & C.R. 1 (2019).
80. Sangree, *Title IX and the Contact Sports Exemption*, *supra* note 8. BRAKE, GETTING IN THE GAME, *supra* note 1, at 64 (calling the contact sports exception "an embarrassment under any plausible theory of equality"). Fortunately, the contact sport exception's incompatibility with the Equal Protection Clause limits its operation to private colleges and universities.
81. BRAKE, GETTING IN THE GAME, *supra* note 1, at 51–52, 64. Although this suggestion maximizes individual right of girls, it is also vulnerable to criticism that it perpetuates the inferiority of women's sports by allowing talented female athletes to escape.
82. Jessica A. Clarke, *They, Them, and Theirs*, 132 HARV. L. REV. 894, 967 (2019) ("The best way to accommodate nonbinary athletes may be incremental moves toward eliminating sex classifications in sports").
83. *See, e.g.*, Erin Buzuvis, *"As Who They Really Are": Expanding Opportunities for Transgender Athletes to Participate in Youth and Scholastic Sports*, 34 L. & INEQ. 341 (2016); Scott Skinner-Thompson & Ilona M. Turner, *Title IX's Protections for Transgender Student Athletes*, 28 WIS. J.L. GENDER, & SOC'Y 271 (2013); PAT GRIFFIN & HELEN J. CARROLL, ON THE TEAM: EQUAL OPPORTUNITIES FOR TRANSGENDER STUDENT ATHLETES (2010).
84. Beyond the question of transgender girls' and women's eligibility for women's sports, this dispute also applies to the eligibility of female athletes with elevated endogenous testosterone (hyperandrogenism) resulting from an intersex condition. Although this question has vexed international sports, it has not yet caused controversy at the level of scholastic and collegiate sports, where Title IX applies.
85. *See* Doriane Lambelet Coleman, *Sex in Sport*, 80 L. & CONTEMP. PROBS. 63 (2017).
86. *See supra* discussion at Part II.
87. *See supra* discussion at Part IV.
88. *See supra* discussion at Part I.
89. D.M. by Bao Xiong v. Minn. State High Sch. League, 917 F.3d 994, 1003 (8th Cir. 2019).

CHAPTER 23

CONSENT, RAPE, AND THE CRIMINAL LAW

KATHARINE K. BAKER AND MICHELLE OBERMAN

IF one views the story of U.S. feminist rape reform as a criminal law story, one sees a period of rapid change—redefining centuries-old crimes, passing victim-protective evidence laws, developing special sex crimes units in both police and prosecutors' offices—followed by stagnation. Despite these changes to criminal laws, procedures, and reporting rates, prosecution rates and conviction rates for rape have increased only slightly since the 1970s. If the goal of rape reform was to put more rapists in jail, rape reform has not worked.

By contrast, if one views this history as a norm-shifting story—a change in the law as a central contribution to a change in attitudes about the importance of consent in sexual encounters—then the story is a much more positive one. This article tells both stories in brief and argues that if one looks beyond the criminal law, particularly at behavior on college campuses and in the workplace, one sees dramatic evidence of shifting attitudes and practices concerning what constitutes sexual consent and sexual misconduct alike.

The fundamental change brought about by the criminal rape law reforms of the 1970s to the 1990s was to reduce the job of proving rape to one of proving the lack of consent. Those who hoped the consent-based definition of rape would make it easy to secure convictions and lead to a rise in rates of prosecution have been disappointed. It remains very difficult to prove nonconsent beyond a reasonable doubt. Nor, as we discuss below, is that the only barrier hindering the enforcement of criminal rape laws. But rape law's consent-based definition of wrongdoing has been critically important in changing norms elsewhere.

This article discusses the forces impeding criminal rape law enforcement, while highlighting the success of rape law reform in fostering new understandings with regard to sexual consent. Part I gives a brief history of the rape reform movement in the United States. Part II considers the range of factors associated with the law's failure to bring about a significant change in law enforcement and prosecution patterns. Part III makes the case for the powerful expressive function served by contemporary rape laws.

It argues that the nonconsent standard has become the lynchpin of sexual harassment programming in the school and work settings. By insisting that we focus on the victim's meaningful ability to say no to sex she does not want, the law has helped dislodge entrenched scripts and facilitated significant reform in noncriminal domains.

Before proceeding, we caution that our analysis focuses mainly on heterosexual behavior between acquaintances. We adopt this frame because it was the notion that acquaintances, friends, and spouses could be held responsible for criminal rape—the insistence that rape was not just a stranger jumping out of the bushes with a knife—that initially made the question of consent so critical. In focusing on heterosexual, mostly intraracial,[1] and mostly young couples, we acknowledge that we are highlighting only one part of a much deeper problem. Contemporary reports suggest that acquaintance rape is just as much, if not more, of a problem in LGBTQ populations.[2] And historical evidence demonstrates the toxic ways in which rape laws have, in practice, been used to further racist ends.[3] The heterosexist and racist implementation of rape laws, both historically and in the rape reform movement, remain critical issues for analysis, and though we touch on them in passing, a full analysis of those issues is beyond the scope of this chapter.

I. The Rape Reform Story

Until the 1970s, the crime of rape in the United States was defined, almost everywhere, as "carnal knowledge of a woman, not the man's wife, forcibly and against her will."[4] This definition reflected what had been centuries of understanding rape as a crime as much against fathers and husbands as against rape victims. Indeed, rape originally was viewed as a violation of a family's property rights because the value of the woman to the family was damaged when the woman's chastity was compromised.[5] The traditional understanding of rape also required evidence that the perpetrator used force to overcome the woman's will. It was the woman's duty to fight men off. Failure to do so left her without recourse if men simply disregarded or overrode her refusal. Phrased differently, unless the woman fought the man off, it was not illegal for him to take the sex he wanted.

The rape reform movement of the 1970s and 1980s, fueled in part by feminists who documented the ubiquity of men taking the sex they wanted,[6] and by the growing influence of the women's movement generally, encouraged state legislatures to reevaluate their rape laws.[7] Eliminating the force requirement was the first major change.[8] No other crime required victim resistance in the manner traditional rape prosecutions did, and there was ample evidence that fighting back did women little good and often made the violence worse.[9] The requirement that the victim not be married to the perpetrator also disappeared in most states, though it took quite a while for this requirement to be removed everywhere.[10] The gravamen of rape, reformers emphasized, is the violation of women's sexual autonomy, the disregard of her desire to not have her body invaded and touched, not an insult to the men to whom she might be related.[11]

The standard they favored, now law in most states, is a definition of rape that relies exclusively on the notion of consent to delineate the difference between criminal and noncriminal sexual activity.[12] Nonconsensual sex or sexual touching is rape or sexual assault; consensual sex or sexual touching is sex.[13]

Rape law reform efforts did not end with changing the substantive definition of rape. Reformers emphasized that rape culture was reproduced by extralegal norms that blamed women—particularly those whose behavior deviated in any way from the stereotypically passive and chaste norms associated in the public mind with innocent (white) victims—and refused to blame men for male sexual aggression. Consider the comments of one community member coming to the defense of the men tried for the 1983 gang rape made famous in the movie *The Accused*: "I'm also a woman, but you don't see me getting raped. If you throw a dog a bone, he's gonna take it—if you walk around naked, men are just going to go for you."[14] This ethos led judges and jurors to blame rape victims, not the perpetrators, if those victims dressed provocatively, spoke provocatively, or simply left themselves defenseless. Ultimately it is jurors and judges who decide whether a perpetrator will be held accountable, and it was clear to reformers that many people were going to blame women for their own rapes, regardless of how the law defined the crime.

In order to help discourage jurors from this kind of victim blaming, reformers ushered in rape shield laws, such as Federal Rule of Evidence 412, that limit the extent to which defense counsel can introduce evidence of victims' sexual demeanor and past sexual behavior.[15] These rules bar the introduction of evidence regarding clothing or behavior if that evidence is offered to try to establish that the woman must have consented because she is a woman who easily consents or as evidence that the jury should not care whether she consented because she was asking for it.

That these rules were necessary highlights the magnitude of the problem criminal rape reformers faced. If clothing or behavior such as drinking or flirting will be viewed as a sign of consent not only by perpetrators but also by jurors, then the elimination of the force requirement in rape statutes will not matter very much. Making consent or the lack thereof the defining feature of rape will do little to curb rape culture if the culture blames women for getting raped.

Further complicating the problem of crafting a legal response to sexual assault were cultural norms that informed the ways in which those charged with enforcing the law viewed victims' claims. Historically, women—especially white women—were not expected to pursue sex. Nor were they expected to provide verbal consent to wanted sex. Indeed, saying yes too often might bring social censure in the form of slut shaming. Women were, however, responsible for saying no. And anything but an unequivocal no—including silence, fear, equivocation, confusion—could be interpreted as a yes, because after all, no one ever said yes.

Black women, by contrast, were perceived as hypersexualized.[16] As slaves, Black women were subjected to rape at every step of their journey and throughout the fabric of their daily lives. The law offered no protection, even defining rape as sexual assault against a white woman.[17] Sexual violence against Black slaves was rationalized away by white slave owners who characterized Black women as so sexually lascivious that they lured the men into having sex with them.[18] One particularly insidious legacy of that era is the persistence of the stereotype of Black women's innate hypersexuality. The result is a longstanding pattern of even greater underenforcement of rape crimes when the victims are Black women.[19]

What is true for Black and white women alike is that claims of rape will be evaluated against default norms and prejudices surrounding permissible sexual expression. Actual sexual expression, that is, women articulating what they want, is itself often viewed as deviant. Not surprisingly, this means that miscommunication and confusion permeate many sexual encounters. One comprehensive study from the mid-1990s found that 22% of women reported having been forced to do something sexual, but only 3% of men reported having forced women to do something sexual.[20] Men tend to interpret their female partners' nonverbal actions as indicia of consent when their partners mean nothing of the sort.[21] Studies of contemporary sexual activity on college campuses suggest that both men and women regularly are unsure about whether consent was given.[22]

It was in an attempt to clear up that kind of confusion that reformers advocated for what is the last significant rape reform measure: an affirmative consent standard. In the absence of yes, all parties should assume no. This innovation requires a party who wants to move forward to determine whether his or her partner feels the same way. This change flips the standard social script's embrace of male sexual prerogative, placing the burden of navigating that ambiguity on the pursuer, rather than on the pursued.

The affirmative consent standard is controversial. Critiques from the right see this standard as state-imposed thought and behavior control, an attempt to quash what is "natural" in the name of political correctness.[23] From the left, queer theorists argue that the potential danger in miscommunication, the risk of being harmed physically or emotionally, may be an essential part of the erotic. Katherine Franke writes, "It is precisely the proximity to danger, the lure of prohibition, the seamy side of shame that creates the heat that draws us toward our desires. . . . It is also what makes pleasure, not a contradiction of or haven from danger, but rather a close relation."[24] These critiques may explain why so many first-time sexual encounters still proceed without affirmative consent. Traditional scripts of male aggression and female passivity still often control sexual encounters among young people, even when the affirmative consent standard is supposed to govern.[25] Culturally, we appear to be a distance away from putting the burden of ambiguity on the sexual pursuer.

To date, a handful of states have adopted affirmative consent provisions, either legislatively or judicially. Some men have been convicted under them.[26] The proposed Model Penal Code's revised sexual assault laws include an affirmative consent–based sexual assault crime, although it allows consent to be inferred from some circumstances.[27]

Despite these ongoing legislative changes, rape reporting rates, prosecution rates and conviction rates have not increased since the 1970s.[28] Why have prosecution statistics changed so little given all of the success that reformers achieved? The answer, to which we turn in the following section, has much to do with the inherent limitations of the criminal law, particularly when it butts up against entrenched social norms.

II. Consent Meets the Criminal Law

At a theoretical level, rape law reform's signature success—changing the definition of rape to a consent-based standard—seems uncontroversial.[29] It is the natural outgrowth of fidelity to autonomy, a value that lies at the heart of Western culture. If women are individuals endowed with autonomy, then physically invading or touching a woman when she does not want to be invaded or touched should be a crime. It should not matter if she is a "good girl"; it should not matter if she was frozen in fear and therefore could not say no; it should not matter if the perpetrator had a gun or a knife. The perpetrator should not feel entitled to appropriate her body for his own desires.

In order to understand why changing the definition of rape to reflect that basic insight did not lead to an uptick in rape prosecutions, one must consider not the theoretical but, rather, the practical barriers to prosecuting rape crimes. In addition to the legal challenges associated with any effort to enforce criminal laws—for example, the burden of proof—there are residual challenges uniquely associated with sexual assault. These include practical barriers such as immigration status or fraught police relations among communities of color, along with persistent resistance to indicting as criminals young men who were "just" doing what had always been done in taking the sex they wanted. The decision to view oneself as a rape victim—and one's partner as a rapist—is one of consequence, especially as suspicion of the carceral state has grown. There are many compelling reasons why one might hesitate before invoking criminal law apparatus in response to nonconsensual sex.

A. The Challenge of Proving Nonconsent in Court

We live in an era when casual sexual encounters with relative strangers are commonplace. Hookups are the norm on college and high school campuses. Phone apps facilitate anonymous sex. Consensual nonmarital sex is celebrated. The old social script whereby women could not say yes has been swapped out for a script in which yes is almost always permissible—though still often unspoken.

This shift in sexual mores has unfolded in a context in which social norms continue to favor wordless sexual encounters. There is a surprisingly persistent view that stopping to ask permission is unsexy. Most people do not talk about the details of sex, what touch triggers which feeling, which sound conveys what emotion, what hurts, which movements relay which messages.[30] Indeed, critics of affirmative consent standards celebrate just how little we talk during sex; that wordlessness is thought to enhance the excitement of sex.[31]

It is no wonder that acquaintance rape is still prevalent. In a context in which parties who have just met attempt to discern consent from ambiguous gestures and body language, how could we expect otherwise? When consent marks the line between rape and sex, the ambiguity of these nonverbal signals intensifies the already uphill battle faced by prosecutors, who essentially must prove nonconsent in order to secure a conviction.

The feminist response to this dilemma has usually been simple: "Believe women."[32] Given the centuries of disbelieving and disregarding women's allegations of rape,[33] this response is understandable, but it is inconsistent with longstanding principles of criminal law. Criminal due process mandates a presumption of innocence in the defendant; his claim that she consented is entitled to deference, and in order to convict him, the state must prove his claim wrong. The Constitution enshrines a criminal defendant's right to confront his accuser—for the sole purpose of encouraging jurors to disbelieve her. In order to convict, the prosecution must not only overcome the presumption of innocence but it must persuade the jury that there can be no reasonable doubt about the victim's nonconsent.

The circumstances in which rapes occur and the content of the criminal trial make it likely that the victim's story will falter. Most acquaintance rapes occur after one or both parties have been drinking alcohol, thus impairing both parties' memories.[34] The incidents take place in private, with no witnesses and no physical evidence (unless there was force). Rape victims "tend to have less clear and vivid memories than people with other types of traumatic or unpleasant experiences,"[35] and the healthiest response to a rape is often to block the event from one's memory.[36]

When victims take the stand, they are asked to recount, in detail, in front of strangers, an act which most people have very little experience describing.[37] Yet a rape victim must find words to describe what happened, and with those words she must convince people that what she is saying is true, even though the people listening have no experience judging the veracity of stories like hers because no one talks about it.

When she is done describing this traumatic incident—the humiliation, shame, and pain surely intensified by a public airing[38]—defense counsel is entitled, if not ethically obliged, to attack everything she said through cross-examination. The defense does not have to convince a jury that the defendant's story is more plausible. The defendant does not even have to tell a story. Indeed, most rape defendants do not take the stand. All the defense has to do is create sufficient reason for a few jurors to question the victim's veracity—her claim that she did not consent in a situation in which consent is commonplace.

Given the toll this process takes on victims, it is hardly surprising that they do not often come forward. Even if they do recall what happened, even if they feel confident that they did not consent, many women do not want to submit to the ordeal of the criminal process. Even in clear-cut cases of nonconsent, such as in the prosecutions of Bill Cosby, who drugged his victims, attacking the victim's credibility and intentions is a standard defense strategy.[39] Indeed, one might view the Bill Cosby and Harvey Weinstein trials as proof that only when there are multiple victims, only when the power differential is so obvious, and thus only when some inaccuracies in the victims' accounts or inconsistencies in their behavior can be overwhelmed by the totality of the evidence, will it be worth it for women to come forward.

Professor Michelle Alexander explained it this way in her essay about her rape:

> I didn't call the police—not after he left my dorm room and not after I discovered I was pregnant. I never once imagined that calling the police could help my situation. It could only make things worse. I envisioned prosecutors, courtrooms and interrogations.... I know many women who've been raped; not one has called the cops.[40]

Professor Alexander is a Black woman and her essay helps demonstrate why the hesitance to come forward is all the more intense for rape victims who are women of color. Because the hypersexualized stereotypes led people to believe that Black women always said yes, and because the stereotype of a rape victim was a white woman, a Black woman faced enhanced difficulty in trying to convince the police, prosecutor, and jury that she did not consent.

A standard feminist explanation for why rape reform has failed to result in more convictions suggests that police and prosecutors "unfound" (decide not to move forward with) legitimate cases.[41] No doubt, some degree of unfounding is still attributable to police officers' and prosecutors' choosing not to believe women or blaming them for their own assaults. This is especially true for Black rape victims, who in addition to combating hypersexualized stereotypes also must face the criminal justice system's general lack of interest in any injuries inflicted against Black victims. But studies suggest that rape victims' decisions not to proceed account for a significant percentage of police and prosecutorial decisions to drop rape cases.[42] One does not have to be an expert on the criminal process or a member of a community victimized by the carceral state to appreciate the profound personal costs of proceeding criminally. If the crime took place under circumstances in which consent is perfectly plausible, if the victim is going to be rhetorically re-assaulted during a criminal trial, if the number of times a victim is going to have to relive the event is in itself injurious, and if there is not a strong chance that the process will lead to conviction, then it may not be in the victim's interest to proceed.

B. Calling It Rape

Empirical studies of sexual assault suggest another reason why more victims do not come forward: "Research has consistently found that a large percentage of women— typically over 50%—who have experienced vaginal, oral or anal intercourse against their will label their experience as something other than rape."[43] Regardless of how the law defines rape, women use their own understanding of what rape is to determine whether they have been victimized.[44] When asked whether they have ever experienced what most affirmative consent statutes describe as rape, women report a rate of victimization that is eleven times greater than when asked if they have been raped.[45] Many women reject the simplicity of the legal definition of rape.

This is not to say that women believe there was nothing wrong with the sexual encounters at issue. Women report feeling used, cajoled, and exploited by these encounters. They absolutely wish they had not happened. They blame the men for being careless and selfish and mean much more than they blame themselves.[46] But they are unwilling to call the men rapists.

To blame men criminally for just taking the sex they want requires condemning behavior that has been condoned as inevitable ("if you give a dog a bone...")[47] and celebrated as exciting ("the heat that draws us toward our desires").[48] Many women are hurt and angry about what happened, but they are not comfortable condemning their friends and acquaintances, the boys they grew up with or their doppelgangers, as rapists. They are unwilling, as a criminal matter, to blame men for failing to bear the burden of making sure their partner has consented before proceeding to have sex.

Feminists anticipated at least some of these problems. They understood the inherent difficulty in criminally prosecuting the commonplace. Catharine MacKinnon wrote: "[W]hen so many rapes involve honest men and violated women... is the woman raped, but not by a rapist?"[49] Susan Estrich recognized that "[i]t is easier to condemn date rape than it is to punish date rapists."[50] Lynne Henderson acknowledged that "[f]eminists are caught in a bind between the arguments for retributive justice... [and the tolerance for] imposition of heavy penalties on large numbers of men."[51] Using the criminal law to uproot entrenched social norms is notoriously difficult.[52]

Treating unwanted sex as a crime also requires a belief that the encounter—as terrible as it was—warrants the intervention of the carceral state. That is a weighty decision, especially for women in communities that have been disproportionately ravaged by the criminal law. Women who have brothers, fathers, husbands, and friends who are in jail because of raced constructions of criminal behavior may be particularly hesitant to invoke the criminal law on their own behalf.

Mariame Kaba, a Black woman and one of the country's leading anti-incarceration activists, voiced her rejection of the criminal legal system as an antidote to rape in a long interview with MSNBC's Chris Hayes:

> I'm a survivor of rape.... I was... incredibly hurt and harmed and... if you had put me right on a panel after that and said what should we do to rapists I would have said we should kill them.... [T]wo years after my situation they would have gotten a very different answer from me.... [A] lot of victim rights groups are now filled with people who are talking in very different ways about criminal punishment. This is true in New York State where people are now saying things like: "We don't want to be locking everybody up. This is not the way we're going to solve it." Because guess what, they've had years of seeing how that policy's actually not worked for anybody in a good way.[53]

Kaba's view is not an isolated one. Indeed, many of the leading voices in the prison abolition movement are women of color who are survivors of sexual assault.[54] Their lived experience teaches them that it is folly to rely on the carceral state to remedy the wrongs done to them at the hands of their rapists.

A refusal to blame men and invoke the carceral state helps explain why more men are not charged with rape. It is not only police, prosecutors, and jurors who reject the law's attempt to put the burden of consensual ambiguity on men; it is women themselves. It will take more than the occasional conviction of a high-profile rapist such as Bill Cosby or Harvey Weinstein to persuade women to place their faith in the criminal law's ability to respond to their victimization with the compassion, fairness, and sensitivity that both victim and perpetrator deserve.

As we argued at the outset, though, the impact of rape law reform ought not be measured simply in terms of an increased enforcement of rape crimes. We turn, in the following section, to a consideration of the ways in which rape reform has contributed to the ascendency of social norms enshrining consent.

III. The Quiet Revolution

In order to understand what rape law reform has accomplished, one must begin by noting the varied nature and purposes served by the criminal law. The criminal law is widely recognized as serving multiple functions. First, the law provides a vehicle for collective retribution, empowering us to exact punishment from those who violate its precepts. Second, laws can deter would-be criminals from acting in a manner that will hurt others. Third, the law serves an expressive function: It declares a particular act worthy of condemnation. The foregoing discussion suggests that much modern rape law is not serving a retributive function particularly well, but we think it is likely both deterring harmful behavior and helping shift norms concerning consent by declaring certain behavior off-limits.

It is hard to measure the impact of any given law's expressive function. As Professor Cass Sunstein notes, "The effect of any legal rule can be described in an infinite number of ways."[55] But the fact that it is hard to tease out the causal relationship between the law's message and a shift in attitudes does not mean it does not exist. Next, we explore two settings in which it is clear that rape law's consent-based definition has infused the evolving norms and practices regarding sexual encounters: schools and the workplace.

A. Sexual Assault Awareness Education and Training

The federal government began tracking rape statistics in 1973.[56] These surveys use the traditional common-law definition of rape, and even using that narrow definition, they demonstrate a consistently high prevalence of rape—on average one in six U.S. women has been the victim of attempted or completed rape.[57] Colleges and universities have conducted more recent surveys, most of which use capacious definitions of sexual assault (including questions about being too drunk or otherwise incapable of giving meaningful consent)—definitions that grew out of rape reform's focus on the importance of consent. Using those reformed definitions, the college and university surveys have consistently found higher incidence of nonconsensual sex (somewhere closer to one in four) than do studies tracking reports of criminal rape.[58]

It is probably impossible to know how prevalent rape is, but there is no disputing that many men continue to take the sex they want on college and high school campuses. The shifting regulatory landscape with regard to sexual misconduct on college campuses is explored elsewhere in this volume,[59] but regardless of what those regulations require, one point is clear: The schools themselves are embarrassed by the results of their surveys.[60] No administrator is willing to say publicly that it is permissible for 20% to 30% of the students to have sex expropriated from them, without their consent, while they are at school.[61] Schools beseeched the Trump Administration to allow them to continue the work they started in taking sexual misconduct more seriously.[62] These schools understand that they cannot rely on the criminal law to police the problem of nonconsensual sex. They want the freedom to sanction behavior that is technically criminal but that the criminal law has proved incapable of punishing.

Alongside these often controversial noncriminal regulatory responses to sexual assault on campuses is an educational response that is arguably more far-reaching, yet almost completely uncontroversial. Schools now view it as their duty to educate students about the line between sex and rape. This pedagogical approach has quickly become standard: At least 85% of colleges require mandatory sexual assault awareness and prevention training for all students. High schools are using these programs as well.[63]

The content of sexual assault awareness and prevention programs varies, but these trainings of necessity focus heavily on the issue of consent: how the law defines it, how to recognize the line between consensual and nonconsensual conduct, and what conduct is impermissible. The law is used as a way to send a message about the collective norms regarding sexual encounters.

Emerging research shows that this educational effort is having an impact. A 2016 review of the literature found that "blatant forms of victim blaming appear to have become socially unacceptable."[64] A study by the FrameWorks Institute—a think tank advancing public discourse about social science issues including sexual violence—studied the impact of sexual assault training and found that "none of the [participants] engaged in directly blaming victims for their attacks."[65] This result marks a major step forward from past public discourse, in which taking the sex one wanted was represented as a natural and therefore a noncriminal part of (hetero)sexual relationships and in which violent acts were assumed to be the sole responsibility of sexually "provocative" or "promiscuous" women.[66] A particularly effective form of sexual assault prevention involves bystander intervention training.[67] These programs have demonstrated that the use of distraction, a query about sobriety or preparation, or even just a check-in can interrupt the traditional script of active pursuer and passive recipient.[68] A growing body of research documents that these trainings are associated with a marked shift away from rape myths.[69]

These interventions work because they challenge the (male) pursuer's sense of entitlement and underline women's right to say no. By adopting consent as the sine qua non of sex and nonconsent as the sine qua non of sexual assault, the law has empowered educators to foster a culture in which women have the right to say no and men no longer have the right to take the sex they want. Of course, a bystander is not always there to interrupt, many women continue to let traditional scripts control, and a good deal of unwanted sex happens—especially if the parties have been drinking—but the ground has shifted. A growing class of young men and young women understand that consent is essential and that women have the right to withhold it.[70]

B. Workplace Responses to Sexual Harassment

During the same decades that saw widespread rape law reform, a parallel shift occurred in laws governing sexual harassment in the workplace. The shift began in the late 1970s with the publication of Catharine MacKinnon's pivotal work *The Sexual Harassment of Working Women*.[71] As with rape law reform, there was early success in changing the letter of the law of sexual harassment.[72] But also as with rape reform, there is evidence that many men did not alter their entitled behavior. The #MeToo movement that began in 2017 made clear that some men continued to take the sex they wanted in the workplace.[73]

The #MeToo movement is both a reflection and a product of the broader societal forces that have reshaped social norms so that unwanted, unwelcome sexual contact has come to be understood as morally and legally wrong.[74] Even before the #MeToo movement began, companies invested in sexual harassment training, understood they could be held accountable for male employees who took the sex they wanted, and felt the need to hide instances in which the behavior continued. It has taken decades, but the #MeToo era's dethroning of high-profile harassers formerly considered above the law suggests that we are entering a time in which no employer can defend the activity once it comes to light. It is increasingly clear that in the workplace, men no longer have the right to assault others even if, like many of the high-profile men who were felled by #MeToo, they do not go to jail for it.

One can readily observe the complementary and even synergistic effect that the movement to combat workplace sexual harassment has had on the notion of consent that was at the heart of rape law reform. Rather than turning on whether a victim consented to a particular sexual encounter, workplace sexual harassment law recognizes that consent can be coerced, owing to a function of hierarchy within work environments. Workplace sexual harassment training sends the message that no one has the right to expropriate "consent" from someone who is not in a position to freely say no. Women have the right to say no, and the law recognizes that this ability may be circumscribed by the hierarchical nature of the work environment. The work of naming and combating sexual harassment in the workplace has added depth and nuance to the notion of consent in the context of rape.

The success of the #MeToo movement indicates that, in the workplace, people are willing to place the burden of ambiguity and the responsibility for ascertaining genuine consent on the pursuer. The notion that consent must be genuine and the expectation that the pursuer bears the burden of clarifying consent both mark a profound shift in how society is coming to understand the meaning of sexual consent.

Survivors and advocates are quick to caution against complacency in response to the takedowns of powerful harassers. We don't mean to suggest that the structures that perpetuate harassment and insulate harassers have been shattered completely. But there is no doubt that the culture is changing in ways that forbid men from simply taking the sex they want. Rebecca Solnit thoughtfully reflects on the impact of that cultural shift:

> The most important change will be found in what we cannot measure — all the crimes that don't happen because would-be perpetrators fear the consequences, now that there are consequences. All the potential victims who know that if they speak up, someone might hear them and heed them.[75]

IV. Conclusion

For those of us who, like Solnit, want a world where "the desire and entitlement to commit sexual violence wither away, not out of fear but out of respect for the rights and humanity of victims,"[76] there is surely more work ahead. It is important to remain alert to the ways in which rape law, and university rules and the law of sexual harassment, fail to provide redress for the injuries women suffer when men take the sex they want. But there is ample evidence to suggest that in simplifying the definition of rape to the absence of consent, rape reform generated a widespread understanding that consent is both essential and complicated. That is progress.

Notes

1. This is not to say that race ceases to be a factor even if the rape is intraracial. Racial stereotypes have long played a critical role in constructing paradigms of a rapist and a rape victim. In this country, the paradigmatic rapist is an angry Black man, such that it is particularly hard for some to see a young, white, economically privileged man as a rapist. The paradigmatic rape victim is a young, innocent white woman, making it difficult for some people to even imagine a Black woman as a rape victim. *See* Katharine K. Baker, *Once a Rapist? Motivational Evidence and Relevancy in Rape Law*, 110 Harv. L. Rev. 563, 594–97 (1997). But there are, and always have been, victims and perpetrators of rape from all races. *See, e.g., Statistics on Violence Against API Women*, Asian Pac. Inst. on Gender-Based Violence, https://www.api-gbv.org/about-gbv/statistics-violence-against-api-women/ (last visited Oct. 16, 2020) (21% to 55% of Asian women in the United States report experiencing physical or sexual violence perpetrated by an intimate in their lifetime). Different cultural responses to rape can lead to varying kinds of hardships for victims. *See* Courtney Leiker Abar, *Rape Culture in Hispanic Communities*, Trauma & Crisis Intervention Blog (Apr. 25, 2019), http://sites.bu.edu/daniellerousseau/2019/04/25/rape-culture-in-hispanic-communities/ (discussing the prevalence of sexual violence and the tendency to ostracize rape victims in the Hispanic community).

2. Katharine K. Baker, *Campus Sexual Misconduct as Sexual Harassment: A Defense of DOE*, 64 Kan. L. Rev. 861, 872–73 (2016) (discussing reports of nonconsensual sexual activity in LGBTQ populations).
3. *See generally* Jennifer Wriggins, *Rape, Racism and the Law*, 6 Harv. Women's L.J. 103 (1983) (discussing racist execution of rape laws). *See also* Emily Yoffe, *The Question of Race in Campus Sexual Assault*, The Atlantic (Sept. 11, 2017) (questioning whether contemporary college enforcement of Title IX regulations disproportionately impacts men of color).
4. Wayne LaFave, Criminal Law 891–94 (5th ed. 2010).
5. Katharine K. Baker, *Why Rape Should Not (Always) Be a Crime*, 100 Minn. L.J. 221, 225–26 (2015) (describing the origins of rape law as a property crime perpetrated against fathers and husbands).
6. Susan Griffin, Rape: The All-American Crime (1971); Diana E. H. Russell, The Politics of Rape: The Victim's Perspective (1974); Susan Brownmiller, Against Our Will (1975).
7. Cassia Spohn, *The Rape Reform Movement: The Traditional Common Law and Rape Law Reforms*, 39 Jurimetrics 119, 122 (1999) (discussing when and how states reevaluate their laws pertaining to sexual assault). *See also* Leigh Goodmark, Chapter 13, this volume.
8. Spohn, *supra* note 7, *Rape Reform Movement*, at 124
9. *Id.* at 124. Traditionally, force and resistance were two separate elements. The assailant had to use force in addition to that required to accomplish intercourse, and the victim had to resist. *Id.*
10. Deborah C. England, *The History of Marital Rape Laws*, Crim. Def. Law., https://www.criminaldefenselawyer.com/resources/criminal-defense/crime-penalties/marital-rape.htm (last visited Oct. 15, 2020).
11. For a full account of rape as a violation of women's sexual autonomy, *see* Stephen J. Schulhofer, Unwanted Sex: The Culture of Intimidation and the Failure of Law (1998) (concluding chapter titled *Taking Sexual Autonomy Seriously*).
12. It bears noting that the reform is not yet complete. A minority of states still define rape to require proof of some degree of force, in addition to nonconsent. Stephen J. Schulhofer, *Reforming the Law of Rape*, 35 Law & Inequality 335, 342 (2017).
13. In an effort to secure more convictions, rape law reformers also encouraged legislatures to adopt gradations of sexual assault. Taking sex without consent is a crime, but the gravity of the crime depends on surrounding circumstances, including whether force was used, whether a weapon was used, and whether the victim was intoxicated. *See* Patricia J. Falk, *Not Logic, but Experience: Drawing on Lessons from the Real World in Thinking About the Riddle of Rape-by-Fraud*, 123 Yale L.J. Online 353, 357–58 (2013) (listing seven different "nonviolent" categories of behavior that are often criminalized).
14. Lynn S. Chancer, *New Bedford, Massachusetts, March 6, 1983–March 22, 1984: The Before and After of a Group Rape*, 1 Gender & Soc'y 239, 251 (1987).
15. *See Rape Shield Statutes as of March 2011*, Nat'l Ctr. for the Prosecution of Child Abuse (2011), https://ndaa.org/wp-content/uploads/NCPCA-Rape-Shield-2011.pdf (listing rape shield laws).
16. *See* C.M. West, *Mammy, Jezebel, Sapphire, and Their Home-Girls Developing an "Oppositional Gaze" Toward the Images of Black Women*, in Lectures on the Psychology of Women 286–299 (J. Chrisler, C. Golden, & P. Rozee eds., 2008) (exploring images of Black women as sexual Jezebels). J.B. Woodard & T. Mastin, *Black Womanhood: Essence and Its Treatment of Stereotypical Images of Black Women*, 36 J. Black Stud. 264–82 (2005) (exploring stereotype of Black woman as hypersexualized).

17. *See* George v. State, 37 Miss. 316 (Miss. Ct. App. 1859); *id.* at 317, 320 (holding that a Black man could not be convicted of raping a Black woman because it was not illegal). *See also* Erin Edmonds, *Mapping the Terrain of Our Resistance: A White Feminist Perspective on the Enforcement of Rape Law*, 9 HARV. BLACKLETTER L.J. 43, 49 (1992) ("The rape of a Black woman by any man was not a crime").
18. Jeffrey J. Pokorak, *Rape as a Badge of Slavery: The Legal History of, and Remedies for, Prosecutorial Race-of-Victim Charging Disparities*, 7 NEV. L.J. 1, 9 (2006).
19. For a powerful summary of the problem and indictment of the legal system's response, see Reema Sood, *Biases Behind Sexual Assault: A Thirteenth Amendment Solution to Under-Enforcement of the Rape of Black Women*, 18 U. MD. L.J. RACE RELIG. GENDER & CLASS 405 (2019).
20. ROBERT T. MICHAEL ET AL., SEX IN AMERICA: A DEFINITIVE STUDY 223 (1995).
21. Michelle Anderson, *Negotiating Sex*, 78 S. CAL. L. REV 1401, 1417 (2005) (citing studies).
22. Katharine K. Baker & Michelle Oberman, *Women's Sexual Agency and the Law of Rape in the 21st Century*, 69 STUD. IN L., POL. & SOC'Y, 63, 91–97 (2015) (discussing hookup culture).
23. *See* Neil Gilbert, *The Phantom Epidemic of Sexual Assault*, 103 PUB. INT. 54, 60 (1991); George F. Will, *Sex Amidst the Semicolons*, NEWSWEEK (Oct. 4, 1992), at 92.
24. Katharine Franke, *Theorizing Yes: An Essay on Feminism, Law and Desire*, 101 COL. L. REV. 181, 206–7 (2001).
25. *See* Baker & Oberman, *Women's Sexual Agency*, *supra* note 22, at 86–92 (discussing studies of sexual behavior on college campuses).
26. For a discussion of state prosecutions under these standards, see Baker, *Why Rape Should Not (Always) Be a Crime*, *supra* note 5, at 231–32.
27. MODEL PENAL CODE § 213.4 cmt. at 68 (2014). The American Law Institute's endeavor to revise its antiquated model rape law has occasioned a protracted, controversial struggle. The working formulation of affirmative consent, as Professor Aya Gruber notes, is relatively modest: "[S]ex must occur with consent, which the defendant may determine from the all the circumstances, including words, conduct, and overall context." Aya Gruber, *Not Affirmative Consent*, 47 U. OF THE PAC. 683, 684 (2016).
28. Studies suggest that only 41.4% of criminal rapes are reported to the police, only 39.5% of reported forcible rapes are followed by arrests, and conviction rates remain low. Cassia Spohn & Katharine Tellis, *The Criminal Justice System's Response to Sexual Violence*, 18 VIOLENCE AGAINST WOMEN, 169, 170 (2012). For a discussion of the inherent challenges of assessing rape's prevalence, see the section titled Sexual Assault Awareness Education and Training.
29. *But see* Jed Rubenfeld, *The Riddle of Rape-by-Deception and the Myth of Sexual Autonomy*, 12 YALE L.J. 1372 (2013) (rejecting an affirmative consent standard).
30. *See, e.g.*, Richard Perez-Pena & Kate Taylor, *Fight Against Sexual Assaults Holds Colleges to Account*, N.Y. TIMES (May 3, 2014) (one Columbia University student commented that when she had to testify about how she was raped anally, "she had to tell an embarrassing story and then teach them an embarrassing subject [which felt] really gross"); Walt Bogdanich, *Reporting Rape, and Wishing She Hadn't: Inside One College's Response When a Student Came Forward*, N.Y. TIMES (Jul. 13, 2014) ("It was one of the hardest things I have ever gone through.... I felt like I was talking to someone who knew nothing about any sort of social interaction; what happens at parties; what happens in sex.").
31. *See* Franke, *Theorizing Yes*, *supra* note 24, at 207.
32. *See* Morrison Torrey, *When Will We Be Believed?*, 24 U. C. DAVIS L. REV. 1013 (1991) (detailing ways in which police, prosecutors, and jurors refuse to believe women).

33. *Id.*
34. Meichun Mohler-Kuo et al., *Correlates of Rape While Intoxicated in a National Sample of College Women*, 65 J. STUD. ON ALCOHOL 37, 40 (2004) (72% of college rape victims reported being intoxicated during the rape).
35. Arthur Garrison, *Rape Trauma Syndrome: A Review of Behavioral Science Theory and Its Admissibility in Criminal Trials*, 23 AM. J. TRIAL ADVOC. 591, 625 (2000).
36. *Id.*
37. *See* Perez-Pena & Taylor, *Fight Against Sexual Assaults Holds Colleges to Account*; SUSAN ESTRICH, REAL RAPE 2 (1984) (describing how difficult it was to recount what happened to her to the police).
38. The victim impact statement of Chanel Miller illustrates these harms. Before divulging her name, Miller gained notoriety when her victim impact statement was read in full by Ashleigh Banfield on CNN. "I was pummeled with narrowed, pointed questions that dissected my personal life, love life, past life, my family life, inane questions accumulating trivial details to try and find an excuse . . . [the statement listed a sample of forty-two questions that the victim was asked by defense counsel]. . . . After a physical assault, I was assaulted with questions designed to attack me." Katie J. M. Baker, *Here's the Powerful Letter the Stanford Victim Read to Her Attacker*, BUZZFEED NEWS (Jun. 3, 2016), https://time.com/4357618/stanford-sexual-assault-victim-letter/.
39. Emily Crocket, *Why Bill Cosby's Defense Strategy Is a Problem for Rape Victims Everywhere*, Vox (May 25, 2016), https://www.vox.com/2016/5/25/11764448/bill-cosby-trial-rape-sexual-assault-defense-strategy.
40. Michelle Alexander, *My Rapist Apologized: I Still Needed an Abortion*, N.Y. TIMES (May 23, 2019), https://www.nytimes.com/2019/05/23/opinion/abortion-legislation-rape.html.
41. *See generally* ROSE CORRIGAN, UP AGAINST A WALL: RAPE REFORM AND THE FAILURE OF SUCCESS 80–100 (2014) (police and prosecutors often do not take rape claims seriously); Lynn Hecht Schafran, *Writing and Reading About Rape: A Primer*, 66 ST. JOHN'S L. REV. 979, 1010–11 (1993) (police and prosecutors "unfound" cases that do not fit into the stranger rape paradigm). *See generally* Torrey, *When Will We Be Believed?*, *supra* note 32.
42. Spohn & Tellis, *Criminal Justice System's Response*, *supra* note 28, at 178.
43. Arnold S. Kahn et al., *Calling It Rape: Differences in Experience of Women Who Do or Do Not Label Their Sexual Assault as Rape*, 27 PSCYHOL. WOMEN'S Q. 233, 233 (2003).
44. H. Littleton, H. Tabernick, E. Canales, & T. Backstrom, *Risky Situation or Harmless Fun? A Qualitative Examination of College Women's Bad Hook-up and Rape Scripts*, 60 SEX ROLES 793, 802 (2009).
45. Leah Adams-Curtis & Gordon Forbes, *College Women's Experiences of Sexual Coercion: A Review of Cultural Perpetrator, Victim and Situational Variables*, 5 TRAUMA, VIOLENCE AND ABUSE 91, 98 (2004).
46. *See* Baker & Oberman, *Women's Sexual Agency*, *supra* note 22, at 91.
47. *See* Chancer, *New Bedford, Massachusetts*, *supra* note 14.
48. *See* Franke, *Theorizing Yes*, *supra* note 24.
49. CATHARINE A. MACKINNON, TOWARD A FEMINIST THEORY OF THE STATE 183 (1989).
50. Susan Estrich, *Palm Beach Stories*, 11 LAW AND PHIL. 5, 32–33 (1992).
51. Lynne Henderson, *Rape and Responsibility*, 11 LAW AND PHIL. 127, 175–76 (1992).
52. Dan Kahan, *Gentle Nudges vs. Hard Shoves: Solving the Sticky Norms Problem*, 67 U. CHI. L. REV. 607 (2000) (explaining the problem of norms that stick despite their inconsistency with the criminal law).

53. *Thinking About How to Abolish Prisons with Mariame Kaba:* PODCAST & TRANSCRIPT, NBC NEWS (Apr. 10, 2019), https://www.nbcnews.com/think/opinion/thinking-about-how-abolish-prisons-mariame-kaba-podcast-transcript-ncna992721. *See also* Lara Bazelon & Aya Gruber, *#MeToo Doesn't Always Have to Mean Prison*, N.Y. TIMES (Mar. 2, 2020), https://www.nytimes.com/2020/03/02/opinion/metoo-doesnt-always-have-to-mean-prison.html (advocating a restorative justice approach to sex crimes and sexual harassment).

54. Consider, for example, Sujatha Baliga, founder of the Restorative Justice project at Impact Justice. A MacArthur genius and former public defender, she discusses her experience as a survivor of childhood sexual abuse, noting why the state would not have been able to respond meaningfully to her suffering, and advocates for a restorative justice response to all crimes, including her own. *The Ezra Klein Show: The Transformative Power of Restorative Justice*, STITCHER (Jun. 17, 2020), https://podcasts.apple.com/us/podcast/the-transformative-power-of-restorative-justice/id1081584611?i=1000478414868.

55. Cass R. Sunstein, *On the Expressive Function of Law*, 144 U. PA. L. REV. 2021, 2023 (1996).

56. *See* DATA COLLECTION: NATIONAL CRIME VICTIMIZATION SURVEY, BUREAU OF JUST. STAT. (2019), https://www.bjs.gov/index.cfm?ty=dcdetail&iid=245.

57. *See* VICTIMS OF SEXUAL VIOLENCE: STATISTICS, RAPE, ABUSE, & INCEST NATIONAL NETWORK (RAINN) https://www.rainn.org/statistics/victims-sexual-violence (last visited Oct. 16, 2020) (summarizing statistics from the National Crime Victimization Survey, 2018).

58. These studies are cited and described in American Association of Universities, AAU CLIMATE SURVEY ON SEXUAL ASSAULT AND SEXUAL MISCONDUCT EXECUTIVE SUMMARY, xiii–xv (2015), https://www.aau.edu/sites/default/files/%40%20Files/Climate%20Survey/Executive%20Summary%2012-14-15.pdf. The AAU surveyed a variety of schools—large, small, urban, and rural—and found 33% of women reporting incidents of nonconsensual sexual activity. The AAU survey did not find that the reporting rate differed depending on the kind of school, and it found that LGBTQ students reported the highest incidence of nonconsensual sexual activity. *Id.* at viii [hereinafter "*AAU Summary*"].

59. *See* NANCY CHI CANTALUPO, Chapter 14, this volume.

60. *See* Eric Isaacs, *Message About Sexual Misconduct from Provost Eric D. Isaacs*, U. Chi Announcements (Sept. 24, 2015), https://csl.uchicago.edu/get-involved/climate-survey-project/spring-2015-climate-survey-materials/message-on-sexual-misconduct (describing results from the University of Chicago's survey of its own population as "similar to the results of ... peer institutions ... [and] ... deeply troubling"); Letter from Steven Hyman, *Task Force on the Prevention of Sexual Assault, to Drew Faust*, President of Harvard University (Sept. 21, 2015), http://sexualassaulttaskforce.harvard.edu/files/taskforce/files/hyman_letter_final_9.21.2015.pdf?m=1442844014 (describing the results at Harvard as part of a "widespread and pervasive ... problem across universities" and suggesting that Harvard "must plan and put in place interventions potent enough to meet the serious challenges documented by the survey").

61. *See AAU Summary*, *supra* note 58 (studies showing nonconsensual sexual encounter rates of 20% to 35%).

62. *See* Letter from Pepper Hamilton LLP, et al. to Betsy DeVos, *Secretary of Education* (Jan. 30, 2019), https://www.pepperlaw.com/resource/35026/22G2.

63. A growing number of states are now mandating some sort of education regarding sexual assault in public schools. See Tovia Smith, *To Prevent Sexual Assault, Schools and Parents Start Lessons Early*, NPR (Aug. 9, 2016), https://www.npr.org/2016/08/09/487497208/to-prevent-sexual-assault-schools-and-parents-start-lessons-early#:~:text=To%20

Prevent%20Sexual%20Assault%2C%20Schools%20And%20Parents%20Start%20Lessons%20Early,-Listen%C2%B7%205%3A37&text=If%20colleges%20are%20a%20hunting,are%20too%20little%2C%20too%20late. (indicating that twenty-five states now have such laws).

64. See Sarah McMahon in consultation with Karen Baker, *Changing Perceptions of Sexual Violence Over Time*, VAWNET: NATIONAL RESOURCE CENTER ON DOMESTIC VIOLENCE (2011) at 7, http://citeseerx.ist.psu.edu/viewdoc/download?doi=10.1.1.229.909&rep=rep1&type=pdf. *See also* Lea Winerman, *Making Campuses Safer: Psychologist-Designed Programs Are Showing Some Success at Preventing Sexual Assault on College Campuses, but There Are No One-Size-Fits-All Solutions*, 49 AM. PSYCHOL. ASS'N. 54, 55–56 (2018) (discussing success of by-stander intervention programs).

65. Moira O'Neil & Pamela Morgan, *American Perceptions of Sexual Violence*, FRAMEWORKS INSTITUTE (2010) at 4.

66. *Id*. The report goes on to suggest that respondents still put considerable pressure on women to make "good choices" but that the willingness to blame women for their own rape has decreased significantly. *Id*. at 19–20.

67. *See, e.g.*, C. Gidycz, L. Orchowski, & A. Berkowitz, *Preventing Sexual Aggression Among College Men: An Evaluation of a Social Norms & Bystander Intervention Program*, 17 VIOL. AGAINST WOMEN 720 (2011).

68. *See* Nancy Cohen, *Training Men and Women on Campus to Speak up to Prevent Rape*, NPR (Apr. 30, 2014), https://www.npr.org/2014/04/30/308058438/training-men-and-women-on-campus-to-speak-up-to-prevent-rape.

69. Annika M. Johnson & Stephanie M. Hoover, *The Potential of Sexual Consent Interventions on College Campuses: A Literature Review on the Barriers to Establishing Affirmative Sexual Consent*, 4 PURE INSIGHTS 7 (2015) (discussing outcomes of sexual assault intervention studies).

70. Along these lines, one of us has been teaching rape as part of a first-year criminal law class for the past fifteen years. Using similar case studies over the course of time, she has noticed a profound increase in the students' willingness to blame the perpetrators for failing to ascertain consent. Indeed, class discussion in recent years typically focuses on the legal significance of consent and on the implausibility of the claim that the victim consented, rather than, as in earlier years, whether the defendant was legally entitled to infer consent. *See* Michelle Oberman, *Getting Past Legal Analysis . . . or How I Learned to Stop Worrying and Love Teaching Rape*, 45 CREIGHTON L. REV. 799 (2012).

71. CATHARINE MACKINNON, SEXUAL HARASSMENT OF WORKING WOMEN (1979).

72. For a detailed discussion of the origins and impact of sexual harassment law, see *Theresa Beiner*, Chapter 19, this volume.

73. E. Nicolaw & Courtney Smith, *A #MeToo Timeline to Show How Far We've Come—& How Far We Need to Go*, REFINERY 29 (Oct. 5, 2019), https://www.refinery29.com/en-us/2018/10/212801/me-too-movement-history-timeline-year-weinstein.

74. *See* Tristin Green, Chapter 15, this volume for a detailed discussion of this social movement and its impact on society.

75. Rebecca Solnit, *The Harvey Weinstein Verdict Is a Watershed—And a Warning*, N.Y. TIMES (Feb. 25, 2020), https://www.nytimes.com/2020/02/25/opinion/sunday/harvey-weinstein-verdict.html.

76. *Id*.

CHAPTER 24

PREGNANCY AND WORK

50 Years of Legal Theory, Litigation, and Legislation

DEBORAH A. WIDISS

How should the law regulate workplace responses to pregnancy, childbirth, and infant care? This subject has long been a focus of debate in feminist theory, and these debates have directly informed the development of law and policy. Is equality best served by treating men and women identically, notwithstanding evident biological differences in this context, or should women receive "special" supports for workplace needs related to pregnancy and childbirth? Should the law seek to accommodate or disrupt gendered norms around infant care? The subject also calls into question the proper role of the state relative to the private family, and the ways in which race, class, and other factors intersect with sex in the lived reality of policy choices. More recently, these questions have been complicated by advances in assisted reproductive technology, increasingly diverse family forms, and religiously affiliated employers seeking to impose moral beliefs related to these subjects that may not align with those of their employees.

This chapter explores the historical development and current state of American law and policies on these subjects, and it contrasts the American structure with the approach taken in most other countries. It begins by discussing research demonstrating that pregnant workers and new parents are often subject to unfounded assumptions of incapacity yet may also sometimes benefit from workplace accommodations or time off. It then shows how the interplay between discrimination and accommodation mandates—specifically the concern that mandating accommodations might increase discrimination—led to heated disagreements among feminists as to whether pregnancy should be treated like other medical conditions or addressed as a *sui generis* condition. This debate coincided with the emergence of neoliberalist ideologies that have also shaped policy in this area, by framing family formation as a private choice rather than a public good. An intersectional lens reveals how race, class, sexual orientation, gender identity, family structure, and other factors can interact with pregnancy and parenthood to compound disadvantage.

The chapter concludes by highlighting recent legislative developments in the United States—at the federal and state levels—that provide more robust support for pregnant workers and infant caregiving within legislation addressing health needs and caregiving more generally. Feminists continue to debate the merits of universalizing such protections, but research showing men as well as women claiming parental leave at relatively high rates suggests this approach may be beginning to bear fruit. The current patchwork of protections remains far from sufficient, however. Ensuring economic security for new parents will require bolder measures, such as federal legislation affirmatively requiring employers to provide workplace accommodations for pregnancy, guaranteeing a generous period of paid leave for new parents, and providing access to high-quality affordable child care.

I. Discrimination and Accommodation in the Context of Pregnancy and Infant Care

Many women[1] who work for pay seek to remain employed throughout a pregnancy.[2] Work provides essential income and serves as a key source of social citizenship.[3] Pregnant employees often face two distinct but interrelated challenges. The first is what is typically considered discrimination—pregnant women may be fired or otherwise face adverse actions at work as a result of their condition. The second is what is typically considered a need for accommodation—pregnant women may need support at work or modification of regular workplace policies to allow them to work safely through a pregnancy, or time off from work during pregnancy or to recover from childbirth. Furthermore, new parents more generally—both male and female, including new adoptive or foster parents as well as new biological parents—often seek time off from work to take care of a child. The basic challenges regarding discrimination and accommodation are relatively consistent across families and cultures. However, the structure of laws responding to these needs varies dramatically, reflecting distinctly different choices made by policymakers regarding conceptions of equality, privacy, and the role of the state.

Pregnancy discrimination reflects deeply embedded assumptions about women, work, and pregnancy. Employers may believe that pregnant women are incapable of performing their jobs, or that customers would be made uncomfortable by seeing a pregnant employee or being served by a pregnant employee. As a result of such beliefs, pregnant women may be fired, refused promotions, or otherwise denied workplace opportunities. Sometimes, employers openly discriminate against pregnant employees. For example, one recent study reported that women working in low-wage service positions, particularly food service and other customer-facing roles, were often fired as soon as they announced a pregnancy or as soon as the pregnancy began to show.[4]

Supervisors may also rely on biased assessments of capability, sometimes without even being aware that their judgment is being distorted. Sociological studies and significant anecdotal evidence confirm that such biases remain prevalent. In one leading study, researchers had participants assess the performance of an individual made to appear pregnant and an individual who did not appear pregnant.[5] Although the performance was identical, participants in the study consistently rated the woman who appeared pregnant to be less proficient. More recent studies confirm that such biases persist.[6] When supervisors hold such discriminatory attitudes, pregnant employees may face negative repercussions at work. This kind of discrimination is similar to the kind of discrimination that employees may face on the basis of race or other factors generally unrelated to the ability to do a job, and, as discussed in section IV, it may interact with race, sexual orientation, class, or other forms of bias to compound disadvantage.

Workplace decisionmakers may also assume—again, often inaccurately—that a pregnant woman who takes maternity leave will be unlikely to return to work or, if she does come back, will prioritize family needs over work obligations.[7] This may likewise lead to a pregnant employee being unfairly fired, denied a promotion, or otherwise denied workplace opportunities, or a mother who returns from maternity leave being sidelined or denied opportunities. Men who take leave to provide child care may likewise face discrimination; in fact, several studies find that men face greater risks of discrimination when they seek such workplace flexibility since their request is counter to gender norms.[8]

Accommodation, by contrast, refers to workplace supports that pregnant employees may need to help them perform their work without jeopardizing the health or safety of the pregnancy. Many such changes are relatively minor, such as the ability to sit on a stool, carry a water bottle, or take extra restroom breaks. Pregnant women are often advised by medical professionals to avoid heavy lifting and exposure to certain kinds of chemicals. In some jobs, it may be easy to accommodate such requests; in others, it could require a restructuring of responsibilities or transfer to a different position. In other words, some needed accommodations may be costly, but many are free or quite low cost.

Whether or not employees need accommodations during a pregnancy, most will need at least some time off from work for labor, delivery, and recovery from childbirth. And new parents more generally will often need or want to take some time off from work to provide infant care, even if ultimately the family will rely on nonparental caregivers. If a birth mother seeks to breastfeed, medical professionals typically advise that she should be physically accessible to the baby for at least the first several weeks of life, to stabilize her milk flow and to ensure the baby develops adequate ability to suckle before being introduced to a bottle. Both male and female parents (and other adults) can provide other aspects of infant care. However, in the United States, as in most other countries, long-standing social norms traditionally have placed primary responsibility for such care on mothers.

The discrimination experienced by some pregnant employees and new parents is a distinct concept from the need for accommodations. There are pregnant workers who face unwarranted bias when they are fully able to do their job without any modification, and there are some employers that hold no particular bias against pregnant women but deny requests for accommodations because they are unwilling to incur any extra workplace costs. But they may also be interconnected.[9] Some bias or discrimination against pregnant workers may be the result of employers that are unwilling to bear the costs associated with providing time off or other supports to a pregnant employee. And some employers may be unwilling to provide accommodations because they hold unwarranted beliefs that pregnant women are less capable or less committed than other workers.

That said, as is true in the disability context, the extent to which providing support to employees during pregnancy and for a period of newborn care requires "special" treatment in the form of an accommodation depends on the more general structures that define workplace expectations in a given society. In the United States, employees are guaranteed very little, and sometimes no, job-protected paid or unpaid leave. Mandatory overtime is also permissible. Furthermore, most workplaces in the United States were designed to meet the needs of an "ideal" worker, who is presumptively male and unencumbered with care-based responsibilities for dependents.[10] With such structures in place, even a few weeks of job-protected leave, or permission to forgo overtime, must be addressed through an accommodation mandate. By contrast, if generally applicable labor standards guaranteed annual leave or limited mandatory overtime, special treatment would not be necessary.

The interplay between discrimination and accommodation makes policymaking in this area particularly challenging, as there is a risk that enhanced accommodation mandates may spur greater discrimination. Relatedly, theorists, and ultimately policymakers, have grappled with the extent to which the law should seek to conform to or disrupt socially enforced gender norms around caretaking, again with the risk that mandates specifically for women will increase sex-based discrimination but a corollary risk that women will be disproportionately disadvantaged by inadequate supports.

II. Equality's Riddle: Sameness, Difference, and the Puzzle of Pregnancy

In the United States, as in most countries, it was once both common and lawful for employers to fire female employees when they became pregnant.[11] In fact, many companies had explicit or implicit policies of firing women as soon as they got married. It was also common for employment policies that provided employees with support for health-related needs, such as health insurance, short-term disability benefits, or job-protected time off, to either exclude pregnancy and maternity-related health conditions entirely or to offer less generous benefits than most other health conditions received. Such practices both expressed and supported a separate spheres ideology; new mothers were expected to focus on domestic responsibilities and new fathers were expected to take on primary breadwinning responsibility. That said, there were also some employers that provided special supports for pregnant employees, such as maternity leaves, while not providing a comparable leave for other kinds of health conditions. Both practices required feminist theorists, legislators, courts, and administrators to grapple with thorny questions regarding what "equality" means in the context of pregnancy and infant care.[12]

The heart of the question—famously characterized by academic and advocate Wendy Williams as "equality's riddle"[13]—directly implicates the interplay between antidiscrimination protections and accommodation mandates. Were pregnant women best served by a general mandate that simply treated pregnancy like other health conditions and provided men and women equal rights to child care–related leave, even if such protections might be minimal or nonexistent? Or by special supports that met their needs for time off and workplace accommodations?

Feminist theorists debated this question, generally mapping a larger divide between "sameness" feminists and "difference" feminists.[14] Proponents of the same-treatment approach argued that singling out women for what was characterized as "special" treatment would spur workplace discrimination against women more generally and reify assumptions that women should and would remain primarily responsible for family care; accordingly, they argued for a universal approach, even if this was less robust than maternity-specific policies.[15] By contrast, proponents of so-called special treatment argued that the absence of such supports would disproportionately disadvantage women as compared to men, and thus that enhanced supports were appropriate and necessary.[16] Some took this position based on a pragmatic assessment that it would be easier politically to achieve leave and other benefits for new mothers, but with the hope that job-protected leave might ultimately be expanded to fathers as well. Others embraced a difference approach more strongly, arguing that women's traditional role as caregivers should be affirmatively supported and valued, and often seeking benefits that would be universally available to new mothers rather than benefits tied to the workplace.

The theoretical debates had real-world consequences as they corresponded to positions that feminist activists and women's organizations took in litigation and legislative advocacy. As noted at the beginning of this section, it was once permissible and common to fire women who became pregnant, just as it was once permissible and common to specify certain positions as available only to women and others as available only to men. That began to change with the enactment of the Civil Rights Act of 1964. This landmark law prohibited discrimination on the basis of sex as well as race, color, religion, and national origin.[17]

The Equal Employment Opportunity Commission (EEOC), the federal agency charged with enforcing the new law, decided relatively quickly that Title VII precluded sex-segregated job postings and other employment-related decisions that were based on sex alone. However, it announced it was unsure how a prohibition on sex discrimination would apply to pregnancy. In its first report to Congress, it explained that although in other areas, it understood the legislative mandate to require "equality of treatment," the pregnant employee had "no analogous male counterpart."[18] The question, therefore, was whether discrimination on the basis of pregnancy was unlawful, and also whether special supports for pregnancy would be unlawful.

By the early 1970s, the agency, and most lower federal courts, had held that discrimination on the basis of pregnancy was a form of discrimination on the basis of sex. The U.S. Supreme Court, however, disagreed. It first faced the question in a constitutional challenge to a California state program that provided short-term disability benefits for most health conditions but excluded coverage for pregnancy. Four female employees challenged the policy, arguing that it violated the Constitution's guarantee of equal protection under the laws.[19] The threshold matter for the Court was to determine whether the exclusion should be considered a sex-based classification, such that heightened scrutiny would apply. The Court ruled it was not, reasoning that the policy divided employees into "pregnant persons" and "nonpregnant persons," and that since the latter group included men and women, it was not a classification on the basis of sex.[20] It then upheld the policy as a reasonable cost-saving choice, under the deferential "rational basis" review standard. A few years later, the Court faced the same question in a case involving a private employer's health plan under Title VII's statutory prohibition on sex discrimination. Relying on the earlier constitutional decision, the Court held that the policy was permissible.[21]

Advocates quickly organized a lobbying effort to supersede the Court's statutory holding. They were successful, and in 1978, Congress passed the Pregnancy Discrimination Act (PDA).[22] The PDA provides explicitly that the statute's prohibition on sex discrimination includes discrimination on the basis of "pregnancy, childbirth or related medical conditions" and further mandates that woman affected by pregnancy "shall be treated the same for all employment-related purposes" as other persons "similar in their ability or inability to work." Under the clear terms of the amended statute, it was no longer lawful for employers to fire employees simply because they were pregnant or to provide less support for pregnancy than for other kinds of medical conditions. In this respect, the PDA is generally considered to adopt a "same" treatment approach to pregnancy. However, it is important to recognize that in doing so, the law had the effect of generally enhancing the level of support provided pregnancy, as it came on the heels of a significant expansion in employer-provided benefits related to health conditions.

Feminist advocates and women's organizations across the spectrum supported the PDA. However, the second clause of the PDA, requiring that employees affected by pregnancy be treated the "same" as other employees with similar abilities, sparked a new controversy that more directly implicated the sameness/difference debate. At the time the PDA was enacted, there were a handful of state laws that required employers to provide maternity leave, even if they did not provide more general disability leave. Once the PDA was enacted, employers argued that the state laws were in tension with the PDA's same-treatment language, and thus were no longer enforceable.

In law review articles and litigation briefs (often authored by the same individuals), feminist theorists and women's rights organizations vigorously debated how the nondiscrimination language of Title VII and the PDA should be applied in the context of specific benefits for pregnant employees and new mothers.[23] The question gained particular urgency after the U.S. Supreme Court agreed to hear a challenge to California's law mandating maternity leave. Broadly speaking, California-based organizations and academics took the position that the law was permissible, distinguishing pregnancy-based supports from earlier protective labor legislation and emphasizing that pregnancy was a "real physical sex-based difference" that could, and should, be recognized to achieve substantive equality for women. East Coast–based organizations, by contrast, generally argued that the state law was preempted by Title VII. They took the position that even though a mandatory maternity leave might appear beneficial to women, it ultimately would work to their detriment as it would spur sex-based discrimination.[24] They suggested, however, that the appropriate remedy would be to expand the mandate to a more general disability leave.

In a 1986 decision, the Supreme Court approved of California's mandate for maternity leave, at least for the period of time when women are recovering from childbirth. The Court took the position that both the PDA and the California law were intended to promote equal opportunity, by allowing "women, as well as men, to have families without losing their jobs."[25] The EEOC and federal courts have interpreted the holding in this case narrowly, however. The accepted understanding of the decision is that it permits enhanced leave benefits for new mothers, as compared to new fathers, only during the limited period of time in which a birth mother is physically recovering from childbirth; in most instances, this is assumed to be six to eight weeks.[26]

Federal legislation likewise adopts a same-treatment approach to these questions. After the Supreme Court upheld the legality of the California law, the sponsor of that law, who had in the intervening years been elected to Congress, suggested there should be a similar federal law. Feminist leaders, however, lobbied for a gender-neutral structure. They suggested that Congress should allow both male and female parents to take time off to care for a new child, and that such parental leave should be bundled with a right for workers to also take time off to address their own medical conditions or to care for family members with a serious health condition. The advocates hoped this approach would help change gender norms around infant caregiving and reduce the likelihood that working women would face discrimination.

The resulting law, the Family and Medical Leave Act (FMLA), was adopted in 1993.[27] It provides twelve weeks unpaid leave to each parent as part of a more general leave right. However, significant concessions were required to enact the law. The FMLA applies only to relatively large employers—with at least fifty employees—and length of service and hour requirements exclude additional workers. Although as initially introduced, the FMLA would have provided separate entitlements for medical leave and for parenting time, the law as enacted combines these categories. This means that employees who need to take time off for pregnancy-related medical needs may exhaust their entire entitlement of leave benefits before a baby is even born.

Virtually every other country, by contrast, offers new mothers considerably more time off for pregnancy, childbirth, and early infant care than new fathers. Maternity leaves are standard around the world, while only about half of countries guarantee paternity leave.[28] Even where offered, paternity leaves tend to be much shorter than maternity leaves. The differential treatment of maternity versus paternity leaves is generally permitted under other countries' sex discrimination doctrine, as it is common to explicitly allow women to receive benefits related to pregnancy and childbirth that are not provided to men.[29] These leaves are also generally funded by either general taxes or payroll taxes. This approach reflects a quite different conception of private versus public responsibility than the U.S. model, as discussed in section III. In addition to sex-specific maternity and paternity leaves, many countries provide a supplemental gender-neutral parental leave (often at a lower pay rate or unpaid), allotted on a family basis and usable by either parent.

In other words, virtually every other country in the world has adopted a leave structure that American theorists would consider "special" treatment for women. That said, the questions that animated equality's riddle remain contested. Norms around caregiving remain quite gendered. Evidence from other countries suggests that women use the vast majority of shared "parental" leave,[30] as well as maternity leave, and that the extended period of time new mothers take away from work may contribute to gender-based pay gaps.[31] To respond to this gendered use pattern, countries are now beginning to designate a share of parental leave as usable only by fathers.[32] This approach is closer to that taken by the FMLA, in that it functionally makes a share of parental leave individual and nontransferable to each parent.

On the other hand, the limits of the formal equality embodied by the PDA and the FMLA are also well known. The PDA's same-treatment mandate is often inadequate to guarantee pregnant women will receive workplace supports they may need to work safely through the pregnancy, and the FMLA's leave is unpaid. Moreover, despite the FMLA's gender-neutral structure, women take considerably more time off under the law to care for new children than men do.[33] This gender gap in leave-taking has stubbornly persisted, although recently enacted state laws mandating *paid* leave, discussed in section V, have increased leave-taking by both mothers and fathers.

III. Neoliberalism and the Public/Private Debate

The sameness/difference debate is the most common feminist lens applied to workplace regulation of pregnancy, childbirth, and parental leave. It was highly influential to the litigation and legislative strategy that ultimately led to the PDA and the FMLA. But at the time those landmark laws were being debated, and in the years since they have been enacted, legal feminists have also used other theoretical frames that amplify both the possibilities and the limits of legal regulation in this area. The emergence of neoliberalism, and related debates over the appropriate scope of public versus private responsibilities in the context of pregnancy and childbirth, has also played a key role in shaping policy in this area.

During the 1970s and 1980s, simultaneous to, but somewhat distinct from, the sameness/difference debates, feminist socialists highlighted the extent to which capitalism rested on patriarchal structures, including a division of labor in which women provided child care and household work and received lower wages if they worked for pay.[34] One strand of this thinking sought to reframe child care as a public obligation rather than a private burden.[35] In 1971, Congress passed an ambitious program that would have provided universal public child care. President Nixon vetoed the project, concerned about accusations it was communist in nature, and Congress failed to muster sufficient votes to override the veto. In the half century since, there has never been another serious attempt to provide universal child care in the United States. Although families may claim a tax credit for a share of expenditures, and very poor parents are eligible for subsidies, the United States provides far less public support for child care costs than most other nations with developed economies.[36]

At the same time as these policy debates were occurring, emerging constitutional jurisprudence reinforced the conception of family-related choices as inherently private. A string of cases, beginning with landmark decisions relating to interracial marriage[37] and access to birth control,[38] and later encompassing the choice to terminate a pregnancy[39] and to engage in consensual sexual intimacy,[40] articulates a doctrine known as "substantive due process." This doctrine provides that choices regarding sexual intimacy, reproductive rights, and family formation implicate fundamental liberties and that government regulations are permissible only if they serve very compelling justifications. In a 1974 case, the Supreme Court cited this doctrine to hold that public schools could not require teachers to take unpaid leaves early in a pregnancy.[41]

Substantive due process doctrine doesn't preclude mandates on private employers to provide accommodations to pregnant workers or benefits such as parental leave. Nor does it preclude government spending to support leave or child care. However, the conceptualization of *choices* regarding family formation as "private" in the constitutional context worked in tandem with neoliberal and fiscally conservative arguments to conceptualize *costs* associated with family formation as also "private." For example, in debates over the PDA, opponents pointed to the legalization of abortion to argue that pregnancy was a "choice" unlike other health conditions, such that it was inappropriate to require employers to bear costs resulting from individual choices.[42] This framing also reinforced the arguments that Title VII required formal equality and that "special" supports for pregnancy and childbirth—at least any supports that went beyond clearly delineated physical needs—were equivalent to state-mandated conformity with traditional gender roles and thus impermissible.

Although this approach is helpful for women who remain able to work productively throughout a pregnancy, it arguably undermines efforts to require more general supports needed for pregnancy and childbirth, including recognition that virtually all women who bear children need at least some time off after childbirth.[43] Legal feminists have pointed to the public, as well as private, benefits that come from reproduction to argue for more robust public support for caregiving.[44] That said, there have also been legal feminists who questioned such proposals, arguing that mandating employers or the state to provide such benefits could reduce incentives for fathers to provide care; unfairly burden male and female workers without children; or perpetuate "repronormative" assumptions that frame motherhood as the defining characteristic of (at least white) female identity.[45]

Although feminists differ on the degree to which the state should subsidize pregnancy and maternity, all agree that the United States is relatively unusual in the extent to which it conceptualizes policies regarding pregnancy and leave as fundamentally private rather than public concerns. Healthy economies depend on maintaining a stable working population from generation to generation. In many countries, it is common to emphasize the public benefits served by supporting bearing and raising children as a justification for publicly financed paid maternity, paternity, and parental leave and public or publicly supported child care options. This is true even in other countries, such as the United Kingdom or Australia, that are generally categorized as sharing liberal welfare regimes that conceptualize most aspects of family-wellbeing as private responsibilities.

IV. Intersectionality and Diversity of Families

The sameness/difference debate articulates competing claims as to how best to advance "women's" equality, with relatively little consideration of how factors such as race, class, or sexual orientation interact with sex to create distinct forms of discrimination. The theory of intersectionality, as developed by Kimberlé Crenshaw and others, highlights the salience of assessing how multiple facets of identity may interact to compound disadvantage.[46] As with so many areas of law, the intersectional lens raises important questions about which women are centered in, and most helped by, a given feminist analysis.

Women who are pregnant may face discrimination on the basis not only of their pregnancy but also of other aspects of their identity. Although data are limited, studies suggest that African American women make up a disproportionate share of pregnancy discrimination claims.[47] Racial stereotypes and biases may also shape the extent to which employers are willing to provide necessary accommodations. Research suggests, for example, employers are more likely to deny Black women's requests for such supports, as they may (consciously or unconsciously) subscribe to stereotypes that Black women are less sensitive to pain and better able to withstand physical labor than white women.[48] This problem is compounded by the fact that accommodations are more frequently needed in low-wage service jobs, since these are often physically demanding and highly regulated work environments, and such jobs are disproportionately filled by women of color.

The structure of the FMLA also results in race and class-based inequities. As discussed in section II, advocates in the United States purposefully embedded maternity and parental leave rights in a more general "family and medical leave" structure. When the bill was being considered in Congress, many employers opposed the broad scope of this leave. To pass the law, the sponsors made significant concessions in terms of coverage, concessions that might not have been required for a law that simply required maternity or parental leave.[49] The FMLA's exclusions disproportionately disadvantage women and workers of color, as they are more likely to work part-time, work for smaller businesses, and change positions relatively frequently.[50] Such vulnerable workers are also far less likely to be able to afford to take unpaid leave, or to receive paid leave as a voluntary benefit from employers.[51]

Debates over parental leave policy and public support for child care have also been shaped in part by the charged racial dynamics of American welfare policy. Welfare benefits in America, as in many other countries, generally prioritize aid for a caregiving parent and for children. However, during the second half of the twentieth century, the popular conception of a welfare recipient evolved from a (presumptively white) mother deserving of public support after the death of a wage-earning husband to a (presumptively Black) mother taking advantage of taxpayers after giving birth to a child outside marriage. The welfare reform of the 1990s responded to this distorted racial conception of "welfare queens" by creating time-limited benefits and permitting states to deny benefits even to mothers with very young children. This undermined a system that had served as a de facto paid leave policy for many low-wage working mothers.[52] And although some of the savings were to be used to enhance public support for child care, such funding remains woefully inadequate to meet basic needs.

Sexual orientation may also be important in assessing the sufficiency of pregnancy protections and leave policies. Historically, many gay and lesbian couples faced challenges in both being recognized as legal parents to a child and, accordingly, being able to access supports such as parental leave. The legalization of same-sex marriage and the expanded scope of parentage laws have largely mitigated this problem. In fact, the individualized and non–sex-specific structure of American leave laws better serves same-sex couples than some other countries' policies that prioritize maternity leave over paternity leave.[53]

That said, although parental leave policy in the United States is generally gender-neutral, legislation relating specifically to protections and accommodations for pregnancy discrimination and lactation-related needs sometimes incorporates sex-specific language. Legislation that refers specifically to "women" or "mothers" has invited arguments that transmen who are pregnant, transwomen who are breastfeeding, or cisgender women who have served as a surrogate may be excluded from relevant protections.[54] Advocates have recently begun to argue that relevant legislation should be framed in sex-neutral terms. Some theorists have suggested that pregnancy more generally should be "de-sexed" to encourage sharing of pre-birth preparations for caregiving, just as parental leave laws in the United States have been de-sexed to encourage sharing of post-birth caretaking.[55]

The increasing diversity of family structures and choices around sexual intimacy and reproduction has also given rise to an increase in legal conflicts when employers seek to enforce moral beliefs that differ from those of their employees. Religiously affiliated employers, including for-profit companies owned and operating in accordance with their owners' religious beliefs, have sought an exemption from the general mandate that employer-provided healthcare must cover contraception.[56] There are also numerous examples of such employers discriminating against employees who utilized assisted reproductive technology; who are pregnant without being married; or who are lesbian, gay, or transpeople who become parents.[57]

Existing antidiscrimination paradigms have often been inadequate to address this kind of workplace discrimination. Constitutional law doctrine increasingly recognizes an interplay between fundamental liberties related to sexual intimacy and family formation and the antidiscrimination guarantees of the Equal Protection Clause. However, courts interpreting the statutory laws that govern discrimination in the private context have limited the scope of antidiscrimination protections with expansive conceptions of religious exemptions, or they have conceptualized such discriminatory actions as responding to *conduct*, and thus unprotected, rather than *status*.[58]

In sum, a myopic focus on "women's" equality without adequate consideration of how other factors—including race, class, sexual orientation, gender identity, family structure, and religion—interact with sex risks compounding other forms of structural disadvantage. Feminist theory and feminist advocacy in this area should incorporate a nuanced assessment of how multiple facets of identity intersect to shape the lived experience of pregnant persons and new parents.

V. Contemporary Moves Toward Universalism

Feminists in the 1970s and 1980s generally shared a hope that pregnant workers and new parents would receive support from their employers for needs related to pregnancy, childbirth, and infant care. They disagreed, however, as to whether such support should be provided specifically to pregnant women and new mothers or through more general support for health conditions and family needs. In large part, the United States adopted the latter approach. This structure, particularly in conjunction with neoliberal policies that imposed costs associated with pregnancy and child care on individual families, disproportionately disadvantaged poor and working-class women of color. That said, fifty years later, the same-treatment strategy has at least partially succeeded. Recently enacted federal laws provide more robust support for pregnancy and childbirth within universal structures addressing health needs more generally; these changes also have the effect of expanding the comparative mandate of the PDA. States have helped fill the gaps in federal policy by mandating specific accommodations for pregnancy and providing paid time off for new parents. While the current patchwork of protections remains inadequate, these new laws provide a helpful template for further reform.

One of the most important developments in this vein is the Americans with Disabilities Act (ADA), which requires employers to provide reasonable accommodations for qualifying disabilities. The ADA defines disability as an "impairment" that "substantially limits" an individual's ability to conduct a "major life activity," such as walking, lifting, or standing.[59] The law's implementing regulations interpret this language to preclude coverage of normal pregnancies, on the ground that pregnancy is not an "impairment."[60] In a series of early decisions issued shortly after the law was passed, the U.S. Supreme Court interpreted the ADA's "substantially limits" language quite stringently, further restricting the prospects for pregnancy, or pregnancy-related complications, to qualify as a disability. However, in 2008, Congress amended the law to supersede the narrow construction of disability in the early Court decisions.[61] The amended law broadens considerably the range of health conditions that may qualify, and the amended regulations now indicate explicitly that temporary conditions may be covered.[62] However, the agency's position that pregnancy itself is not covered has not changed. Nonetheless, in light of these amendments, theorists have argued that many pregnancy-related health conditions may now be covered[63] and, more provocatively, that even normal pregnancies should be covered.[64]

Other legislative changes have also expanded support for medical needs related to pregnancy and childbirth. At the time the PDA was enacted, many employer-provided health insurance policies excluded pregnancy and maternity entirely or provided less robust support for those conditions than for other health conditions. While the PDA made such carve-outs illegal, it did not require employers to provide health insurance or set minimum standards for coverage. The Affordable Care Act of 2010 (ACA) takes significant steps toward remedying those deficiencies. Pursuant to the ACA and guidance provided by the agency charged with its implementation, employer-provided health insurance must cover basic contraception and many maternity-related health needs.[65] Many employees who are breastfeeding are entitled to break time to express breast milk,[66] and insurance plans must help cover the costs of breast pumps and other lactation-related services.[67]

Recent developments under the PDA have also expanded access to workplace accommodations for pregnancy. In 2015, the U.S. Supreme Court held that, under the PDA's same-treatment mandate, if a pregnant employee shows that she was denied an accommodation that other employees with similar limitations were granted, the employer must articulate a "legitimate non-discriminatory rationale" for the distinction, and this rationale cannot simply be additional cost.[68] Courts must assess whether the employer's decision to deny the accommodation was infected by bias, such as stereotypical assumptions that pregnant women are less committed or capable than other employees.[69] Such scrutiny is required even if the accommodations for other health conditions were provided pursuant statutory mandates, such as the ADA or legislation concerning workplace injuries. Although the Court did not definitively decide whether such compliance might serve as a sufficient justification for different treatment, and other aspects of the standard remain contested, some employers have chosen to reduce liability exposure by simply granting accommodations to pregnant employees.[70]

There has also been a rapid growth in state laws, generally known as Pregnant Workers Fairness Acts (PWFA), explicitly requiring reasonable accommodations for pregnancy, childbirth, and related medical needs. As of 2021, more than half of the states have enacted such laws.[71] In May 2021, the U.S. House of Representatives passed a federal analogue, with broad bipartisan support.[72] As this chapter goes to press, the bill is pending in the U.S. Senate. Such legislation provides important supports for individual women and can help destabilize stereotypes regarding the presumed incapacity of pregnant women more generally.[73]

Finally, there has been a significant expansion in access to paid parental and family leave on the state and federal level. As of 2021, nine states and the District of Columbia have passed paid-leave laws.[74] Because several of these states have large populations, more than a quarter of the U.S. population is now covered by a paid-leave law. Additionally, in December 2019, Congress enacted paid parental leave for most federal workers.[75] The massive disruptions caused by the Coronavirus pandemic have further highlighted the need for paid leave. The relief bills passed by Congress in Spring 2020 provided temporary paid leave for some caretaking responsibilities but did not cover bonding with a new child.[76] However, there is growing support for passing a more comprehensive paid-leave bill at the federal level.[77]

Initial evidence from states that have passed paid-parental-leave laws suggest that both women and men are taking leave at relatively high rates.[78] However, men, even more than women, may face discrimination and stigma at work when they seek to take such leave, as it runs counter to expected gender norms.[79] The structure of the paid-leave laws, however, disadvantages single parents, as it provides benefits as independent benefits to each parent, with no mechanism to transfer or extend benefits even when custody is not shared. This is a significant problem, as almost 40 percent of new mothers in the United States are unmarried, a figure that includes disproportionately high numbers of poor and working-class women of color.[80]

One important factor to consider when assessing policies concerning employment-related health needs is the extent to which they serve the growing share of the workforce that engages in contingent work, including temporary workers, part-time workers, and the growing gig economy.[81] Recent paid-leave laws, for example, permit self-employed workers to opt into the system, providing an important model for how traditional employment-related benefits in the United States can be restructured to better serve the modern, factionalized workforce. Likewise, the ACA established healthcare exchanges that allow individuals to purchase private health insurance at relatively reasonable rates.

Universalist approaches offer some theoretical and pragmatic benefits. They can garner broader political support, they avoid essentializing identity, and they are less vulnerable to challenge as a discriminatory preference and less likely to stigmatize disadvantaged groups that receive benefits.[82] Also, in the particular context of family caregiving, eschewing sex-specific benefits can play an important role in disrupting gendered norms that tend to undermine women's equality more generally. If truly robust, policies that successfully support all individuals in addressing all health and all caregiving needs offer significant appeal. However, universalist policies also risk masking structural inequities or diluting support for those who are most in need.[83] Given the pervasiveness of sex-based stereotypes around pregnancy and parenting, and the reality of limited public resources, a combination of universal and identity-specific protections may be most effective.

VI. Looking Forward

The past half century has seen a considerable expansion in support in the United States for protections for pregnancy, childbirth, and child leave, but much more remains to be done. First, the laws on the books must be more adequately enforced. For more than four decades, the PDA has clearly prescribed discrimination based on pregnancy; nonetheless, it remains pervasive.[84] Complaints made to the EEOC remain common and the studies referenced throughout this chapter show the persistence of discrimination. As is true of employment discrimination cases generally, even when unlawful animus may have played a part in a decision, it can be quite difficult to prove in court.

Federal legislation is necessary to ensure that pregnant workers and new parents receive the workplace supports they need. Legislation and private policies must be assessed to ensure that they meet the needs of today's diverse families. And public investment is necessary to ensure that when parents go back to work, there is adequate, affordable, high-quality child care available. The questions that animated equality's riddle remain pressing, and only partially answered. Ultimately, further reform is necessary to make it possible for both men and women to start a family without jeopardizing their economic security.

Notes

1. The vast majority of persons who are pregnant, give birth, or seek support for lactation are cisgender women. Accordingly, the text generally refers to such persons as "women" and uses feminine pronouns. However, it is important to recognize that some transmen retain female reproductive capabilities and may become pregnant, give birth, and lactate, and some transwomen may take steps to stimulate lactation. The fourth section of this chapter discusses how relevant laws and policies may apply, or not apply, to transpeople.
2. This varies some by country, but in the United States it is common to work until the very end of a pregnancy. *See, e.g.*, Current Population Reports, U.S. Census Bureau, Maternity Leave and Employment Patterns of First-Time Mothers 1961–2008 (Oct. 2011), https://www.census.gov/prod/2011pubs/p70-128.pdf (reporting 82 percent of first-time mothers worked during the last month of their pregnancy).
3. *See generally* Joanna L. Grossman, *Pregnancy, Work, and the Promise of Equal Citizenship*, 98 Geo. L. Rev. 567 (2010).

4. *See* Stephanie Bornstein, *Work, Family, and Discrimination at the Bottom of the Ladder*, GEO. J. ON POVERTY L. & POL'Y 1 (2012); *see also* Michelle R. Hebl et al. *Hostile and Benevolent Reactions Toward Pregnant Women: Complementary Interpersonal Punishments and Rewards That Maintain Traditional Roles*, 92 J. APPLIED PSYCH. 1499 (2007) (describing lab-based experiment finding discrimination against pregnant applicants in retail setting).
5. Jane A. Halpert et al., *Pregnancy as a Source of Bias in Performance Appraisals*, 14 J. OF ORGANIZATIONAL BEHAV. 649, 562–63 (1993).
6. *See, e.g.*, Whitney Botsford Morgan et al., *A Field Experiment: Reducing Interpersonal Discrimination Toward Pregnant Job Applicants*, 98 J. APPLIED PSYCH. 799 (2013).
7. *See id.* This study also found that providing information that countered these stereotypes could decrease discrimination.
8. *See, e.g.*, Scott Coltrane et al., *Flexibility Stigma*, 69 J. SOC. ISSUES 279 (2013).
9. *See* Deborah A. Widiss, *Gilbert Redux: The Interaction of the Pregnancy Discrimination Act and the Amended Americans with Disabilities Act*, 46 U.C. DAVIS. L. REV. 961, 972–78 (2013).
10. *See generally* JOAN WILLIAMS, UNBENDING GENDER: WHY FAMILY AND WORK CONFLICT AND WHAT TO DO ABOUT IT (1999).
11. For a more extensive discussion of this history and the way in which theoretical debates informed litigation and legislation, *see* Widiss, *supra* note 9, at 978–1004; *see also* Deborah L. Brake & Joanna L. Grossman, *Unprotected Sex: The Pregnancy Discrimination Act at 35*, 21 DUKE J. OF L. & POL'Y 67, 71–82 (2013).
12. Other chapters in this volume describe with greater depth and nuance the various "strands" of feminist theory and feminist legal theory. *See also, e.g.*, MARTHA CHAMALLAS, INTRODUCTION TO FEMINIST LEGAL THEORY (3d ed. 2013); Martha Chamallas, *Past as Prologue: Old and New Feminisms*, 17 MICH. J. GENDER & L. 157 (2010); Deborah Rhode, *Feminist Critical Theories*, 42 STAN. L. REV. 617 (1990). My focus in this chapter is tracing specifically how some of these debates shaped the legal regulation of employment laws related to pregnancy, childbirth, and infant care.
13. Wendy W. Williams, *Equality's Riddle: Pregnancy and the Equal Treatment/Special Treatment Debate*, 13 N.Y.U. REV. OF L. & SOC. CHANGE 325 (1984).
14. *See, e.g.*, Lucinda M. Finley, *Transcending Equality Theory: A Way Out of the Maternity and the Workplace Debate*, 86 COLUM. L. REV. 1118, 1142–63 (1986).
15. *See, e.g.*, Williams, *supra* note 13, at 352–64; *see also* Katharine T. Bartlett, *Pregnancy and the Constitution: The Uniqueness Trap*, 62 CALIF. L. REV. 1532 (1974).
16. *See, e.g.*, Herma Hill Kay, *Equality and Difference: The Case of Pregnancy*, 1 BERKELEY WOMEN'S L.J. 1 (1985).
17. 42 U.S.C. § 2000e-2(a) (2018).
18. EQUAL EMP. OPPORTUNITY COMM'N, FIRST ANNUAL REPORT TO CONGRESS FOR FISCAL YEAR 1965–66 (1967).
19. *See* Geduldig v. Aeillo, 417 U.S. 484 (1974).
20. *Id.* at 496 n.20.
21. *See* General Elec. Co. v. Gilbert, 429 U.S. 125 (1976).
22. Pub. L. No. 95-555, 92 Stat. 2076 (1978) (codified at 42 U.S.C. § 2000e(k) (2018)).
23. *See* Widiss, *supra* note 9, at 999–1000 (collecting and discussing sources).
24. *See, e.g.*, Brief Amici Curiae of the Nat'l Org. for Women et al., *Cal. Fed. Sav. & Loan Ass'n v. Guerra*, 479 U.S. 272, 289 (1987) (making this argument and highlighting that the California law, as passed, had several provisions that disadvantaged pregnancy as compared to other health conditions).

25. California Fed. Sav. & Loan Ass'n v. Guerra, 479 U.S. 272, 289 (1987).
26. 29 C.F.R. § 1604.10.
27. Pub. L. 103-3, 107 Stat. 6 (1993) (codified at 29 U.S.C. §§ 2601 *et seq.* (2018)).
28. *See, e.g.,* LAURA ADDATI, NAOMI CASSIRER & KATHERINE GILCHRIST, INTERNATIONAL LABOUR ORGANIZATION, MATERNITY AND PATERNITY AT WORK: LAW AND PRACTICE ACROSS THE WORLD (2014).
29. *See* Deborah A. Widiss, *The Hidden Gender of Gender-Neutral Leave: Examining Recently-Enacted Laws in the United States and Australia*, 41 COMP. LAB. L. & POL'Y J. 723 (2021) (describing how different conceptions of sex discrimination law shape leave policies).
30. *See* ADDATI ET AL., *supra* note 28, at 61.
31. *See, e.g.*, DAMIAN GRIMSHAW & Jill Rubery, THE MOTHERHOOD PAY GAP: A REVIEW OF ISSUES, THEORY, AND INTERNATIONAL EXPERIENCE, INT'L LAB. ORG. (2015).
32. *See* INT'L NETWORK ON LEAVE POL'Y & RES., REPORT, 15TH INTERNATIONAL REVIEW OF LEAVE POLICIES AND RELATED RESEARCH 2019, at 22 (Aug. 2019), https://www.leavenetwork.org/fileadmin/user_upload/k_leavenetwork/annual_reviews/2019/2._2019_Compiled_Report_2019_0824-.pdf.
33. *See* ABT ASSOCIATES, INC., FAMILY AND MEDICAL LEAVE IN 2012: TECHNICAL REPORT 141 (2012), https://www.dol.gov/sites/dolgov/files/OASP/legacy/files/TECHNICAL_REPORT_family_medical_leave_act_survey.pdf (showing the vast majority of men using the FMLA for parental leave took none to ten days' leave, while the majority of women took at least forty-one days' leave); *id.* at 138 (showing higher percentage of female employees than male employees take FMLA leave for a new child).
34. Cynthia Grant Bowman, *Recovering Socialism for Feminist Legal Theory in the 21st Century*, 49 CONN. L. REV. 117 (2016).
35. MAXINE EICHNER, THE FREE-MARKET FAMILY: HOW THE MARKET CRUSHED THE AMERICAN DREAM (AND HOW IT CAN BE RESTORED) (2019).
36. *See* OECD Family Database, *Public Spending on Childcare and Early Education* (2019), available at https://www.oecd.org/els/soc/PF3_1_Public_spending_on_childcare_and_early_education.pdf.
37. Loving v. Virginia, 388 U.S. 1 (1967).
38. Griswold v. Connecticut, 381 U.S. 479 (1965); Eisenstadt v. Baird, 405 U.S. 438 (1972).
39. Roe v. Wade, 410 U.S. 113 (1973).
40. Lawrence v. Texas, 539 U.S. 558 (2003).
41. *See* Cleveland Bd. of Educ. v. LaFleur, 414 U.S. 632 (1974).
42. *See* Deborah Dinner, *Beyond "Best Practices": Employment-Discrimination Law in the Neoliberal Era*, 92 IND. L.J. 1059 (2017).
43. Julie C. Suk, *Are Gender Stereotypes Bad for Women? Rethinking Antidiscrimination Law and Work-Family Conflict*, 110 COLUM. L. REV. 1 (2010).
44. *See, e.g.*, MARTHA ALBERTSON FINEMAN, THE NEUTERED MOTHER, THE SEXUAL FAMILY, AND OTHER TWENTIETH CENTURY TRAGEDIES (1995); Mary Becker, *Patriarchy and Inequality: Towards a Substantive Feminism*, 1999 U. CHI. LEGAL F. 21; Linda C. McClain, *Care as a Public Value: Linking Responsibility, Resources, and Republicanism*, 76 CHI.-KENT L. REV. 1673 (2001).
45. *See, e.g.*, Mary Anne Case, *How High the Apple Pie? A Few Troubling Questions About Where, Why, and How the Burden of Care Should Be Shifted*, 76 CHI.-KENT L. REV. 1753 (2001); Katherine M. Franke, *Theorizing Yes: An Essay on Feminism, Law, and Desire*, 101 COLUM. L. REV. 181 (2001).

46. Kimberlé Crenshaw, *Mapping the Margins: Intersectionality, Identity Politics, and Violence Against Women of Color*, 43 STAN. L. REV. 1241 (1991).
47. Nora Ellmann & Jocelyn Frye, *Efforts to Combat Pregnancy Discrimination* (Ctr. for Am. Progress, Nov. 2 2018), https://www.americanprogress.org/issues/women/news/2018/11/02/460353/efforts-combat-pregnancy-discrimination/.
48. *See, e.g.*, Sophie Trawalter et al., *Racial Bias in Perceptions of Others' Pain*, 11(3) PLOS ONE e48546 (2012).
49. *See* Widiss, *supra* note 9, at 1002 (gathering sources making this point).
50. *See* Ann O'Leary, *How Family Leave Laws Left Out Low-Income Workers*, 28 BERKELEY J. EMP. & LAB. L. 1 (2007).
51. Figures, Bureau of Lab. Stats., Table 31, *Leave Benefits: Access Civilian Workers* (Mar. 2019), https://www.bls.gov/ncs/ebs/benefits/2019/ownership/civilian/table31a.pdf (reporting 19 percent of private civilian employees and 9 percent of lowest quartile of earners receive paid family or parental leave).
52. O'Leary, *supra* note 50 (describing how debates of the FMLA presumed welfare benefit scheme that was subsequently dismantled). For a discussion of the welfare queen trope more generally, *see, e.g.*, Camille Gear Rich, *Reclaiming the Welfare Queen: Feminist and Critical Race Theory Alternatives to Existing Anti-Poverty Discourse*, 25 S. CALIF. INTERDISC. L.J. 257 (2016).
53. *Cf.* NATALIE PICKEN & BARBARA JANTA, LEAVE POLICIES AND PRACTICE FOR NON-TRADITIONAL FAMILIES, EUR. PLATFORM FOR INVESTING IN CHILD. (Aug. 2019) (advocating for reform of European sex-specific policies to address needs of same-sex parents).
54. *See, e.g.*, David Fontana & Naomi Schoenbaum, *Unsexing Pregnancy*, 119 Colum. L. Rev. 309 (2019); Jessica A. Clarke, *They, Them, and Theirs*, 132 HARV. L. REV. 894 (2019); Meghan Boone, *Lactation Law*, 106 CALIF. L. REV. 1827 (2018).
55. *See generally* Fontana & Schoenbaum, *supra* note 54; *cf.* Darren Rosenblum, *Unsex Mothering: Toward a New Culture of Parenting*, 35 HARV. J. L. & GENDER 57 (2012)
56. Burwell v. Hobby Lobby Stores, Inc., 573 U.S. 682 (2014); *see also* Little Sisters of the Poor v. Pennsylvania, 140 S. Ct. 2367 (2020) (finding regulations providing opportunity to opt out on moral or religious grounds permissible).
57. *See, e.g.*, Deborah A. Widiss, *Intimate Liberties and Antidiscrimination Law*, 97 B.U. L. REV. 2083 (2017) (collecting and critiquing this case law).
58. *See id.* In the three years since that article was published, the Supreme Court has further expanded religious exemptions to antidiscrimination mandates. *See* Our Lady of Guadalupe Sch. v. Morrissey-Berru, 140 S. Ct. 2049 (2020).
59. 42 U.S.C. § 12102 (2018).
60. *See* 29 C.F.R. pt. 1630 app. § 1630.2(h).
61. *See* ADA Amendments Act of 2008, Pub. L. No. 110–325, 112 Stat. 3553 (2008) (codified at 42 U.S.C. §§ 12101 *et seq.*) (2018).
62. *See* 29 C.F.R. § 1630.2(j)(ix).
63. Joan C. Williams et al., *A Sip of Cool Water: Pregnancy Accommodation After the ADA Amendments Act*, 32 YALE L. & POL'Y REV. 97 (2013).
64. Jeannette Cox, *Pregnancy as "Disability" and the Amended Americans with Disabilities Act*, 53 B.C. L. REV. 443 (2012).
65. *See* 42 U.S.C. § 300gg-13(a) (requiring employer- and exchange-provided plans to cover "preventative" services); Health Resources & Servs. Admin., *Women's Preventive Services Guidelines*, https://www.hrsa.gov/womens-guidelines/index.html (last updated Dec.

2019). For a detailed discussion of these provisions, as well as legal challenges to them, *see* VICTORIA L. KILLION, CONG. RESEARCH SERV., R45928, THE FEDERAL CONTRACEPTIVE COVERAGE REQUIREMENT: PAST AND PENDING LEGAL CHALLENGES (2020); *see also* sources cited *supra* note 58.

66. *See* 29 U.S.C. § 207(r) (2018); *see also* U.S. Dep't of Lab., Fact Sheet #73: Break Time for Nursing Mothers (2018), https://www.dol.gov/agencies/whd/fact-sheets/73-flsa-break-time-nursing-mothers#:~:text=Employers%20are%20required%20to%20provide,from%20view%20and%20free%20from.
67. *See* sources cited *supra* note 65.
68. Young v. United Parcel Servs., Inc., 135 S. Ct. 1338, 1354 (2015).
69. *See id.* The Court indicated this assessment should also consider whether the employer accommodates a large percentage of nonpregnant employees, while denying accommodations to most pregnant employees. *Id.*
70. *See* Joanna L. Grossman & Gillian Thomas, *Making Sure Pregnancy Works: Accommodation Claims After* Young v. United Parcel Service, Inc., 14 HARV. L. & POL'Y REV. 319 (2020) (summarizing and critiquing post-*Young* case law).
71. *See* A Better Balance, *State and Local Pregnant Workers Fairness Laws* (Aug. 2021), available at https://www.abetterbalance.org/resources/fact-sheet-state-and-local-pregnant-worker-fairness-laws/.
72. *See* H.R. 1065, 117th Cong. (passed House 315–101). 99 Republicans and 216 Democrats voted in favor of the bill.
73. *See* Reva B. Siegel, *The Pregnant Citizen: From Suffrage to Present*, 108 GEO. L.J. 167 (2020).
74. A Better Balance, *Overview of Paid Family & Medical Leave Laws in the United States* (2021), available at https://www.abetterbalance.org/resources/paid-family-leave-laws-chart.
75. *See* Federal Employee Paid Leave Act, enacted as part of the National Defense Authorization Act for Fiscal Year 2020, Pub. L. No. 116-92, §§ 1121 et seq., 133 Stat. 1198 (2019).
76. *See* DEPARTMENT OF LABOR, FAMILY FIRST CORONAVIRUS RESPONSE ACT: EMPLOYEE PAID LEAVE RIGHTS (2020), available at https://www.dol.gov/agencies/whd/pandemic/ffcra-employee-paid-leave (explaining paid leave is available for specific COVID-related needs, such as quarantine orders or child care and school closures).
77. *See* Deborah A. Widiss, *Equalizing Parental Leave*, 105 MINN. L. REV. 2175 (2021) (discussing federal bills).
78. *See* Widiss, *supra* note 29.
79. *See* sources cited *supra* note 8.
80. *See* Widiss, *supra* note 77.
81. *See generally*, ARNE L. KALLEBERG, GOOD JOBS, BAD JOBS: THE RISE OF PRECARIOUS AND POLARIZED EMPLOYMENT SYSTEMS IN THE UNITED STATES, 1970S TO 2000S (2011).
82. *See, e.g.*, Samuel R. Bagenstos, *Universalism and Civil Rights (with Notes on Voting Rights After* Shelby), 123 YALE L.J. 2838 (2014) (articulating both strengths and weaknesses of a universalist approach to civil rights).
83. *See, e.g.*, Jessica A. Clarke, *Beyond Equality? Against the Universal Turn in Workplace Protections*, 86 IND. L.J. 1219 (2011).
84. For a review and critique of recent (albeit pre-*Young v. UPS*) PDA case law, *see, e.g.*, Brake & Grossman, *supra* note 11, at 98–117. For post-*Young* case law, *see, e.g.*, Grossman & Thomas, *supra* note 70.

CHAPTER 25

CONSTITUTIONALIZING REPRODUCTIVE RIGHTS (AND JUSTICE)

MELISSA MURRAY AND HILARIE MEYERS

THE conventional wisdom posits *Griswold v. Connecticut*, *Eisenstadt v. Baird*, and *Roe v. Wade* as the seminal cases in constitutional law's understanding of reproductive rights. According to this account, "the origin story" of reproductive rights is one that emphasizes privacy, the individual's right to be free from undue governmental interference in matters of intimate life, and, above all, "choice." This framing is unfortunate—and deeply ahistorical. As we explain in this chapter, at the time these foundational cases were litigated and decided, in fact, other frames through which to understand—and constitutionalize—reproductive rights were available and debated. Those litigating challenges to legal bans on contraception and abortion framed their claims in a variety of terms, including standard restraints on the state's use of criminal law and claims of class and sex equality.

Understanding the diversity of claims that once undergirded the effort to secure reproductive freedom helps to explain the critical response to the Court's more limited framing of reproductive rights. As this chapter demonstrates, many viewed the Court's articulation of reproductive rights—and some advocates' seemingly uncritical acceptance of it—as unduly narrow and limited. Mining an earlier vein of reproductive rights advocacy, these advocates and activists sought a more expansive understanding of reproductive freedom—one that centered questions of class, race, sexual orientation, and disability alongside broader institutional and systemic concerns. The resulting reproductive justice framework was intended as a counterpoint to the more limited understanding of reproductive rights. However, over time, some aspects of the logic and rhetoric of reproductive justice have made their way into the reproductive rights discourse. Mainstream reproductive rights advocacy now includes consideration of law's impact on marginalized communities and demands for greater access to reproductive healthcare. But tellingly, those opposed to reproductive rights have also begun to integrate features of reproductive justice into their appeals to constrain reproductive freedom. Specifically, those opposed to abortion have deployed the twin specters of discrimination and eugenics in their defense of trait-selection abortion restrictions.

This chapter proceeds in five sections. Section I considers the Court's decisions grounding reproductive rights in constitutional law. As that section suggests, the Court's understanding of reproductive rights focused narrowly on issues of privacy, individual choice, and freedom from undue government interference. Section II pivots to explain that the Court's limited understanding of reproductive freedom was not inevitable. As it explains, in litigation that preceded the Court's seminal reproductive rights cases, advocates and activists offered other frames and narratives to undergird a constitutional commitment to reproductive freedom. However, these alternative constitutional arguments never made their way into the Court's reproductive rights jurisprudence. Section III considers the response to the narrow constitutional framing of reproductive rights. In so doing, this section traces the emergence of the reproductive justice movement, which sought to integrate concerns about race, class, and government provision into the debate over reproductive rights. Section IV then discusses the ways in which the reproductive justice framework has influenced the broader fight for reproductive freedom. Section V explores the surprising ways in which reproductive justice themes of racism and systemic discrimination may become integrated into constitutional law.

I. Creating Reproductive Rights and Constitutional Privacy

On June 7, 1965, the Court announced its 7–2 decision in *Griswold v. Connecticut*,[1] invalidating two Connecticut statutes that criminalized the use and distribution of contraceptives. In so doing, the *Griswold* Court famously announced a right to privacy that emanated from the penumbras of the "specific guarantees in the Bill of Rights."[2] It was perhaps unsurprising that privacy figured so prominently in the decision. After all, advocates and activists eager to reform criminal morals offenses had long emphasized the idea of an inviolate space insulated from state encroachment.[3] Indeed, the notion of constitutional privacy had emerged in two cases, *Rochin v. California*[4] and *Mapp v. Ohio*,[5] involving the rights of criminal defendants.[6] Tentatively in *Rochin*, and then more emphatically in *Mapp*, the Court articulated a "freedom from unconscionable invasions of privacy" implicit in the Fourth and Fifth Amendments.[7] Thomas Emerson and Catherine Roraback, the lawyers representing Estelle Griswold and Lee Buxton, the defendants in *Griswold*, raised the privacy principle in their briefs—and did so in a manner that sounded in the register of criminal law reform. Specifically, they emphasized the idea of privacy as an essential feature of limited government—that is, that "governmental powers stopped short of certain intrusions into the personal and intimate life of the citizen."[8]

Although the majority opinion in *Griswold* embraced the notion of privacy as a bulwark against an over-encroaching state, it tethered the privacy right to the institution of marriage and the marital couple—an abrupt departure from the individual-focused conception of privacy cultivated in the criminal reform debate.[9] While Emerson and Roraback discussed marriage in their briefs, they did so to augment a broader argument about the right of all citizens to be secluded—in most places, but especially in the home—from the all-encompassing authority of the state.[10] On their rendering, privacy's protections were not reserved exclusively for married couples but were "a vital element" of the Constitution's efforts to "safeguard[] the private sector of the citizen's life," whether in or outside of marriage.[11]

For the *Griswold* majority, however, marriage provided a limiting principle for the newly announced right to privacy—a right that the Court likely realized could extend broadly to give constitutional shelter to a wide range of sexual conduct. According to the Court's logic, the Connecticut contraceptive ban was unconstitutional not because it demanded the individual's conformity with traditional mores about the use of contraception, but because it "operate[d] directly on an intimate relation of husband and wife and their physician's role in one aspect of that relation."[12]

The privacy right announced in *Griswold* underwrote the expansion of reproductive rights in the following years. In 1972's *Eisenstadt v. Baird*, the Court built upon *Griswold* to permit unmarried persons access to contraception.[13] Rather than focusing exclusively on the marital couple, the *Eisenstadt* Court instead emphasized "the right of the individual, married or single, to be free from unwarranted governmental intrusion into matters so fundamentally affecting a person as the decision whether to bear or beget a child."[14] In doing so, the Court recovered, at least in part, the understanding of privacy as an individual right against state encroachment that featured so prominently in the *Griswold* litigants' arguments. A year later, in *Roe v. Wade*, the Court again relied on *Griswold*, this time holding that the right of privacy was "broad enough to encompass a woman's decision whether or not to terminate her pregnancy."[15]

II. The Road(s) Not Taken—Constitutional Alternatives to Privacy

Griswold v. Connecticut and *Roe v. Wade* have come to stand as a kind of shorthand for constitutional protections for reproductive rights. Rooted in the language of privacy and individual choice, both cases reflect an understanding that the Constitution protects only negative rights as opposed to conferring positive entitlements.

But meaningfully, the association of reproductive rights with privacy and negative constitutional rights was not inevitable. In the period before *Griswold* and *Roe* were decided, advocates litigated other challenges to laws prohibiting contraception and abortion—and critically, in so doing, they offered a wide range of constitutional grounds in which to root reproductive freedom. Five cases in particular—*Poe v. Ullman*,[16] *Trubek v. Ullman*,[17] *Abramowicz v. Lefkowitz*,[18] *Abele v. Markle*,[19] and *Struck v. Secretary of Defense*[20]—provide a glimpse of what might have been. In these cases, advocates, informed by social movement activism, argued for a broader understanding of reproductive freedom within constitutional law.

A. *Poe v. Ullman* and *Trubek v. Ullman*—Litigating a Right to Contraception

Griswold v. Connecticut struck down Connecticut's ban on contraceptives on the ground that the laws violated the right of privacy, but it was not the Court's first confrontation with the challenged Connecticut statutes. In 1960, Yale law professor Fowler V. Harper and civil rights attorney Catherine Roraback challenged the laws in two related cases—*Poe v. Ullman*[21] and *Trubek v. Ullman*.[22] Although the two cases reached the Supreme Court, they were ultimately dismissed on jurisdictional grounds.[23] Today, these pre-*Griswold* cases receive little attention,[24] but they nonetheless shed light on the various doctrinal arguments that were available to the Court in determining the constitutionality of Connecticut's contraceptive ban.

In *Poe*, a physician and three married couples harnessed the logic of contemporaneous criminal reform efforts, which emphasized privacy as a bulwark against state interference, to argue that privacy secluded married couples and their intimate decisions, including the decision to use contraception, from the state's reach.[25] Notably, each couple's interest in contraception stemmed from the fact that a pregnancy would result in serious health challenges for the wife or child.[26] In their brief, Harper and Roraback explained that because Connecticut prohibited married couples from using contraception, the plaintiffs were forced to choose between marital abstinence, which was not only unrealistic but undesirable, or a potentially life-threatening pregnancy.[27] As such, the contraceptive ban infringed upon "a constitutionally protected right to marital intercourse."[28]

If the *Poe* plaintiffs relied squarely on privacy as a defense against undue state interference, the *Trubek* plaintiffs offered a different take on privacy, linking it to an interest in sex equality and egalitarian marriage.[29] For David and Louise Trubek, two recently married Yale Law students, the interest in contraception was rooted in their desire to plan their family in a manner that made sense for their marriage, and, as importantly, allowed both of them to establish and build careers as practicing lawyers.[30] In their complaint, the Trubeks argued that access to contraception would allow Louise to avoid an ill-timed pregnancy that would disrupt her professional education and career.[31] Access to contraception was not simply about stripping marriage of its procreative character; it was about restructuring marriage along more egalitarian lines, relieving wives of the obligations of domesticity and allowing them to participate in spheres traditionally reserved for husbands. Put differently, the Trubeks envisioned marital privacy—and, by extension, access to contraception—as a precondition for equal citizenship.

In the end, the Supreme Court declined to review *Trubek*, and dismissed *Poe* on the ground that it lacked the "immediacy which is an indispensable condition of constitutional adjudication."[32] Yet, despite the Court's decision to avoid ruling on the merits, a number of Justices noted another possible constitutional frame for reproductive rights—the Connecticut ban's disproportionate impact on the poor.[33] As some of the Justices in *Poe* observed, although the challenged laws were rarely enforced against private physicians, who often prescribed contraception to their patients, they were used to prevent the operation of birth control clinics that would make contraception accessible to those without the means to secure private medical care.[34]

Critically, however, when the next challenge to Connecticut's contraceptive ban came before the Court five years later in *Griswold*, the Court took little notice of these other constitutional frames. The equality arguments that had surfaced in *Poe* and *Trubek* and were advanced by those in the birth control movement were wholly absent in the *Griswold* Court's decision. Although the class-based concerns that fueled litigation over the contraceptive ban were discussed in briefs and at oral argument,[35] the fact that the laws disproportionately burdened low-income women was mentioned only briefly, in Justice White's concurrence.[36] Sex equality arguments were ignored entirely. Neither the *Griswold* appellants nor their amici raised the ban's impact on women or its prospects for democratizing marriage, as the Trubeks had. Instead, the *Griswold* appellants and their amici emphasized an individual right to privacy, the privacy of married couples, and the rights of physicians to appropriately advise their patients, but focused little on the dimensions of women's equality.

B. *Abramowicz v. Lefkowitz, Abele v. Markle,* and *Struck v. Secretary of Defense*—Litigating Abortion Rights

Just as *Griswold* was neither the first nor only challenge to Connecticut's contraceptive ban, *Roe v. Wade* was only one of many cases in the late 1960s and early 1970s that invoked the Constitution to challenge abortion laws.[37] The earliest of these lawsuits held criminal abortion laws to be unconstitutionally vague, violating the rights of physicians who lacked clear guidance about the circumstances under which abortions could be legally performed.[38] By 1969, however, feminist lawyers began to bring new constitutional claims that built on *Griswold*'s interest in marital privacy while also articulating new claims that sounded in the register of sex, race, and class equality.

In October 1969, advocates filed four separate lawsuits challenging New York's abortion ban, each featuring different plaintiffs—doctors, ministers, an antipoverty organization, and a class of women—with distinct interests and claims.[39] The women's suit, *Abramowicz v. Lefkowitz*, was brought by Nancy Stearns of the Center for Constitutional

Rights on behalf of 109 named women plaintiffs.[40] Whereas earlier lawsuits had primarily approached abortion through a medical perspective, the *Abramowicz* litigators framed the issue as a matter of women's rights, drafting a brief that catalogued women's experiences with the challenged New York abortion law. In their own voices, the women plaintiffs explained the real-life impact of abortion restrictions, as well as the class, sex, and race inequality that women routinely encountered—both in avoiding pregnancy and in motherhood. As the brief argued, the New York abortion law not only violated the right of privacy recognized in *Griswold*, it also constituted invidious discrimination under the Equal Protection Clause because it punished women for the act of sexual intercourse, but not men.[41] Not only did women shoulder the "threats and punishments"[42] associated with illegal abortion, but they also bore "the burdens of bearing and raising children"[43] when forced to continue a pregnancy. Critically, these burdens went well beyond the nine months of pregnancy, forcing women to endure "a whole range of de facto types of discrimination based on the status of motherhood."[44]

When the New York legislature repealed the offending statute, the legal challenge in *Abramowicz* was dismissed as moot.[45] Undeterred, movement lawyers brought similar challenges to abortion laws in other states. In Connecticut, Stearns worked with Catherine Roraback, who had helped litigate *Poe*, *Trubek*, and *Griswold*, to challenge the state's criminal abortion law on behalf of a class of 1,700 women plaintiffs.[46] In bringing the case, known as *Abele v. Markle* or *Women v. Connecticut*, feminist lawyers explicitly linked women's control over pregnancy and childrearing to their economic security and leveled critiques of the gendered division of labor in American society. A recruiting pamphlet for plaintiffs proclaimed, "Women must not be forced into personal and economic dependence on men or on degrading jobs in order to assure adequate care for the children they bear. Our decisions to bear children cannot be freely made if we know that aid in child care is not forthcoming and that we will be solely responsible for the daily care of our children."[47] Echoing *Trubek*'s call for women's equal citizenship, the recruiting materials explained that "the actuality of an unwanted pregnancy, or the possibility of such a pregnancy, severely limits a woman's liberty and freedom to engage in the political process, to choose her own profession, and to fulfill herself in any way which does not relate to the bearing and raising of children."[48]

Meaningfully, the *Abele* plaintiffs also raised a class-based equal protection claim, emphasizing the Connecticut abortion ban's disproportionate impact on poor women.[49] Women of means, they explained, could afford to travel elsewhere for abortion care.[50] Poor women, on the other hand, were doubly burdened, as they were least likely to be able to obtain abortion care and more likely to suffer from the economic consequences of an unwanted child.[51] Significantly, the *Abele* litigants also highlighted the social and economic forces that prevented certain women, namely, low-income women and women of color, from exercising their right to *have* children: "Those of us who are poor and live on welfare know that opponents of welfare want to limit the size of our families. We are pressured to use contraceptives or be sterilized; each time we have another child the meager allowance per child gets even smaller."[52]

Remarkably, the district court's opinion in *Abele*, which invalidated the ban on equal protection and Ninth Amendment grounds, invoked some of these themes. Writing for the three-judge panel, Judge J. Edmund Lumbard emphasized that "[t]he decision to carry and bear a child has extraordinary ramifications for a woman," not only because of physical risks and implications of pregnancy but also because of the economic and social consequences of having a child.[53]

Shortly after the district court's decision, Connecticut passed a new law prohibiting abortions except when necessary to save the life of the mother.[54] The new law was immediately challenged, and once again, the district court held the new statute unconstitutional, this time concluding that "a woman's right to decide whether to have an abortion cannot be completely abridged by a state statute imposing upon her the uniformity of thought about the nature of a fetus."[55] Connecticut appealed the decision, but before the appeal could be taken up, the Supreme Court issued its decision in *Roe*.[56]

Another abortion-related challenge, *Struck v. Secretary of Defense*,[57] raised a set of distinct, but related concerns about reproductive freedom. Susan Struck, the plaintiff, was an Air Force captain who became pregnant while serving in Vietnam. When she alerted her supervisors about her circumstances, she was told that military policy required her to either terminate her pregnancy or leave the Air Force.[58] A practicing Catholic, Struck was unwilling to seek an abortion.[59] But she was also unwilling to give up her career. Instead, she hoped to carry the pregnancy to term and then surrender the child for adoption. In her brief on behalf of Struck, the ACLU Women's Rights Project's Ruth Bader Ginsburg argued that the case implicated sex equality, personal autonomy and privacy, and religious liberty.[60] Not only was the Air Force *requiring* Struck to terminate her pregnancy in order to keep her position, in defiance of her religious beliefs, it imposed no similar choice on male military personnel.[61]

As Justice Ginsburg later explained, *Struck* was an appealing vehicle for advancing reproductive freedom because, unlike other challenges to contraceptive bans or abortion bans, it did not focus on the choice to *avoid* pregnancy but rather on the decision to *continue* a pregnancy on terms that honored the woman's religious beliefs and her desire to have a career.[62] It underscored that reproductive freedom was not confined to the "choice" of contraception and abortion, but instead included issues where women's "choices" were actively constrained by the state and by personal circumstances. Importantly, *Struck* also raised pregnancy discrimination as a species of sex-based inequality. As the facts of *Struck* made clear, one thing that conspicuously distinguishes women from men is that only women become pregnant, and if women are subjected to disadvantageous treatment on the basis of pregnancy, as Captain Struck was, this constituted a deprivation of equal protection under law.[63]

The Supreme Court never had the opportunity to consider the array of questions that *Struck* presented. Although the Court agreed to hear the case in 1972, the Air Force waived Struck's discharge, allowing her to remain in the Air Force and mooting the case.[64] *Roe v. Wade* was decided three months later in January 1973.

Notwithstanding the examples of *Abramowicz*, *Abele*, and *Struck*, *Roe* litigators Sarah Weddington and Linda Coffee avoided the issue of sex equality, arguing instead that the Texas abortion ban was unconstitutionally vague, violated the right to privacy, and discriminated against the poor.[65] By the time the case came before the Supreme Court, they had largely abandoned the class equality claim, fully embracing *Griswold*'s privacy framing. Still, concerns about the Texas law's impact on women, and low-income women in particular, lived on in amicus briefs.[66] Moreover, several amicus briefs, including one authored by Nancy Stearns, explicitly raised sex equality arguments against the Texas abortion law.[67] Reviving the claims articulated in *Abramowicz* and *Abele*, Stearns argued that abortion bans discriminated against women by reflecting and perpetuating gender biases and class inequality.[68]

Despite these valiant efforts, the Court's 7–2 decision in *Roe* prioritized privacy as the framework for its decision, ignoring these equality themes. Justice Blackmun's majority opinion in *Roe* framed pregnancy largely as medical issue—a decision to be made by the woman in consultation with her doctor—and recognized a state's interest in regulating abortion as a matter of health and safety.[69]

III. Responding to *Roe*—the Emergence of the Reproductive Justice Movement

Taken together, *Griswold*, *Eisenstadt*, and *Roe* rested on a series of assumptions. First, the cases assumed a certain degree of affluence and access—women seeking contraception or choosing an abortion ostensibly had access to medical care, and as such, made their decisions in consultation with medical professionals.[70] Relatedly, *Roe* framed abortion as the "choice" of whether or not to have a child, irrespective of the background conditions that might inform or shape such choices.[71] The trio of decisions offered no quarter to those women whose reproductive "choices" were shadowed by economic insecurity, the absence of healthcare, a dearth of safe and affordable child care options, and racial and gender injustice.[72] Nor did the three decisions venture beyond the issue of preventing or terminating a pregnancy to consider the conditions necessary to exercising the "choice" to bear and raise a child to adulthood.[73]

But it was not only that *Griswold*, *Eisenstadt*, and *Roe* framed the issue of reproductive freedom narrowly around contraception, abortion, and avoiding a pregnancy; the decisions also resolved the conflict by resorting to the constitutional discourse of negative rights.[74] *Griswold*, *Eisenstadt*, and *Roe* offered women the right to make the decision to use contraception or to have an abortion free from undue state interference and regulation.[75] But neither case offered, and later cases would emphatically reject,[76] positive constitutional entitlements that could *facilitate* the exercise of reproductive rights.[77]

As discussed in section II, advocates had advanced a broader range of concerns in which to situate claims for reproductive rights, but this more expansive vision was sacrificed in the Court's embrace of constitutional privacy. And critically, in the following years, as challenges to *Griswold*, *Eisenstadt*, and *Roe* mounted, the Court's narrow framing of reproductive rights seemed to constrain the legal imagination. As reproductive rights advocates sought to defend the rights to contraception and abortion, they reiterated the Court's narrow framing, further entrenching the rhetoric of privacy, individual choice, and negative rights.

Harris v. McRae is illustrative of this impulse. In *Harris*, the Court considered a challenge to the Hyde Amendment, an appropriations rider that prohibits the use of federal funds, including Medicaid funding, for abortion services, except in cases of rape or where necessary to save the woman's life.[78] As many recognized, the Hyde Amendment was legislated, in part, to blunt *Roe*'s impact by preventing women who relied on Medicaid and public assistance from accessing abortion. Predictably, the Hyde Amendment's force was keenly felt by poor women and women of color. Indeed, drawing connections between economic oppression, reproductive control, and women's subordination, the Committee for Abortion Rights and Against Sterilization Abuse (CARASA) argued that the restriction was not simply aimed at preventing poor women and women of color from accessing abortion but rather was part of an antinatalist effort to force poor women and women of color to submit to sterilization.[79]

Although groups like CARASA articulated the connections between race, class, and sex at issue in *Harris v. McRae*, more traditional mainstream reproductive rights groups were largely silent on the issue and Hyde's impact on poor women and women of color. More troublingly, the Court's disposition of the case was shaped by the negative rights framing that had prevailed in *Griswold*, *Eisenstadt*, and *Roe*. As the Court explained, "[t]he Hyde Amendment . . . places no governmental obstacle in the path of a woman who chooses to terminate her pregnancy, but rather, by means of unequal subsidization of abortion and other medical services, encourages alternative activity deemed in the public interest."[80] According to this logic, although the Constitution recognized a right to abortion, the state was under no obligation to facilitate—or in this case, to subsidize—an individual's exercise of that right.[81]

One member of the Court, however, recognized the race and class implications of the majority's decision. In a vehement dissent, Justice Thurgood Marshall, the first Black justice to sit on the Court, noted that "[t]he class burdened by the Hyde Amendment consists of indigent women, a substantial proportion of whom are members of minority races."[82] Further, because "nonwhite women obtain abortions at nearly double the rate of whites" and "the burden of the Hyde Amendment falls exclusively on financially destitute women," Justice Marshall believed the Court's review of the Hyde Amendment demanded a "more searching judicial inquiry."[83]

Because of the limits of the Court's privacy and disparate impact jurisprudence, this sort of searching judicial inquiry was unlikely to happen in the courts.[84] But on the ground, in grassroots organizing and activism, an effort was underway to recuperate the concerns of race, sex, and class inequality that had marked reproductive rights advocacy in the years before *Roe*, while also integrating concerns about health, access for marginalized communities, political power, and structural discrimination.

Combining the terms "reproductive rights" and "social justice," the reproductive justice movement emerged in the 1990s as a counterpoint to the reproductive rights framework that *Roe* and its progeny engendered.[85] In so doing, the movement recovered the equality themes that once underlay feminist lawyering for reproductive rights, but meaningfully went beyond the interest in sex equality to take a more intersectional approach to questions of reproductive freedom and oppression. Rooted in the work of groups like the Committee to End Sterilization Abuse (CESA), CARASA, and the Combahee River Collective, the reproductive justice movement explicitly centered the experiences of marginalized groups—women of color, the poor, queer communities, and people with disabilities.[86] Moreover, it purposefully looked beyond the Court's— and mainstream feminism's—cramped understanding of reproductive rights to consider a broad range of issues that impacted reproductive freedom, including sterilization, assisted reproductive technology, access to child care, pregnancy discrimination, community safety, food and housing insecurity, the criminalization of pregnancy, and access to reproductive healthcare.[87]

Instead of accepting uncritically the negative rights posture that underlay *Griswold*, *Eisenstadt*, and *Roe*, reproductive justice explicitly considers the prospect of positive entitlements to certain forms of government support. In this regard, reproductive justice advocates emphasize a tripartite framework that focuses on (1) the provision of more robust health services to historically underserved communities; (2) increased access to contraception and abortion and an end to coerced sterilization; and (3) greater attention to the social, political, and economic systemic inequalities that impact women's reproductive health and their ability to control their reproductive lives.[88] As activists explained, the reproductive justice framework was purposely holistic, "encompassing the various ways law shapes the decision 'whether to bear or beget a child' and the conditions under which families are created and sustained."[89]

IV. Integrating Reproductive Rights and Reproductive Justice

In the white paper "What Is Reproductive Justice," Loretta Ross, a leader of SisterSong Women of Color Reproductive Health Collective and an architect of the reproductive justice movement, noted that "[o]ne of the key problems addressed by Reproductive Justice is the isolation of abortion from other social justice issues that concern communities of color."[90] All too often, abortion rights were framed as issues of "choice," without regard to the ways in which, depending on one's circumstances, the notion of "choice" could be severely constrained.[91] As Ross explained, it was essential to understand abortion rights in concert with other issues that impacted communities of color, including "issues of economic justice, the environment, immigrants' rights, disability rights, discrimination based on race and sexual orientation, and a host of other community-centered concerns."[92] All these issues, whether individually or in concert, "directly affect an individual woman's decision-making process."[93]

The critique hit home. By the early 2000s, both Planned Parenthood and NARAL Pro-Choice America (formerly known as the National Abortion and Reproductive Rights Action League) expanded their reform agendas beyond abortion to include broader access to contraception and healthcare.[94] By 2010, the changes were even more profound, as mainstream reproductive rights groups began to embrace the vernacular and logic of the reproductive justice movement in earnest.[95] In 2004, the national conference of the National Organization of Women (NOW) featured programming that explicitly focused on reproductive justice.[96] By 2016, NOW's platform had a decidedly reproductive justice cast, as the organization demanded access not only to abortion but also to "birth control, pre-natal care, maternity leave, child care and other crucial health and family services."[97] In the same vein, Planned Parenthood also adjusted its messaging. Recognizing that the term "pro-choice" failed to capture a range of issues that mattered to women of reproductive age, the venerable reproductive rights organization sidelined choice-focused messaging in favor of arguments that spoke to a broader range of issues, including pay equity, access to healthcare, and broader contraceptive access for marginalized communities.[98] As Professor Mary Ziegler notes, the rhetorical shift allowed for "more in-depth discussion of reproductive justice" within these mainstream reproductive rights groups.[99]

Critically, reproductive justice's influence was not only felt in broadening the range of issues that traditional reproductive rights groups addressed. It was also keenly felt in their discussion of their bread-and-butter concern: abortion rights themselves. For example, once criticized as inattentive to the threat the Hyde Amendment,[100] traditional abortion rights groups had, by the 2000s, begun highlighting Hyde's impact on marginalized communities.[101]

Additionally, in their court-centered advocacy efforts, reproductive rights groups began to deploy reproductive justice's methods and messaging. For example, the Affordable Care Act's contraceptive mandate, which requires employers to provide contraceptive care to employees as part of preventative health coverage, was framed as a necessary measure to ensure consistent and cost-effective access to contraceptive care. Likewise, in various legal challenges to the contraceptive mandate and the various accommodation procedures available to objecting employers, reproductive rights groups have emphasized the mandate's impact in ensuring reliable, free contraceptive access to working women.[102]

And, in a recent Supreme Court abortion challenge, *June Medical Services v. Russo*,[103] both the petitioner's brief and related amicus briefs explicitly invoked reproductive justice themes,[104] including the impact of the challenged abortion restriction on marginalized communities throughout Louisiana and the state's disinterest in securing women's health beyond restricting abortion access.[105] In a move that echoed both the "women's voices" brief filed in *Abramowicz* and the reproductive justice movement's effort to center the narratives of those affected by reproductive policies, a brief filed in *Whole Woman's Health v. Hellerstedt*,[106] a 2016 challenge to two Texas abortion restrictions, reproduced statements from women lawyers who maintained that their ability to obtain an abortion had positively shaped their careers and economic lives.[107]

V. Cooptation and Contestation

As traditional reproductive rights groups came to frame their defense of abortion and contraception in terms that drew on reproductive justice discourse, in time, their anti-abortion opponents parried with their own vision of reproductive justice, trading heavily in familiar tropes of racial inequity, gender injustice, and disability rights. For example, in 2009, Life Dynamics, a predominantly white anti-abortion activist group, produced the documentary *Maafa 21: Black Genocide in 21st Century America*,[108] which linked abortion to an elaborate (alleged) conspiracy to eliminate "surplus" Black labor after emancipation.[109] Similarly, the Radiance Foundation, an anti-abortion group, placed billboards in predominately Black neighborhoods asserting, "Black children are an endangered species."[110] Life Always, another prominent anti-abortion group, orchestrated a billboard campaign in minority neighborhoods that proclaims, "The Most Dangerous Place for an African American Is in the Womb."[111] And recent calls for Black Lives Matter have been met with claims from anti-abortion groups that *unborn* Black lives matter.[112] Indeed, Reverend Clenard Childress, the creator of BlackGenocide.org and the president of Life Education and Resource Network (LEARN), a prominent Black anti-abortion organization, has suggested that the Black Lives Matter movement cannot advocate in favor of Black uplift as long as they continue to partner with abortion rights groups like Planned Parenthood.[113] As these anti-abortion groups maintain, they are calling attention to the disproportionate rate of abortions among Black women and countering the broader message of reproductive rights and reproductive justice groups that abortion rights serve Black women's autonomy and the interests of the Black community.[114]

Just as the reproductive justice movement considered reproductive regulation intersectionally, through multiple lenses of oppression and injustice, efforts to limit reproductive freedom have also taken on an intersectional approach. In recent years, abortion opponents have sought to link abortion with sex discrimination and the eugenic effort to eliminate cognitive and physical disabilities. Abortion legislation that prohibits abortion for the purpose of "trait selection" has proliferated across the country, including at the federal level.[115] These trait-selection laws prohibit abortion if undertaken for the purpose of sex or race selection or to avoid bearing a child with a disability. Likewise, in their litigation strategies to defend such laws, anti-abortion groups have framed their claims in terms that sound in the register of reproductive justice. For example, briefs defending trait-selection laws speak of extending antidiscrimination protections to the unborn, while also pointing to abortion as a modern-day version of the state-sponsored eugenics programs once aimed at persons with disabilities.[116]

Importantly, it is not just anti-abortion groups that have invoked these themes in their opposition to abortion. In June 2019, in a concurrence in *Box v. Planned Parenthood*,[117] Justice Clarence Thomas defended an Indiana trait-selection law in terms that echoed these themes.[118] According to Justice Thomas, the challenged trait-selection law was a modest attempt to prevent abortion "from becoming a tool of modern-day eugenics."[119] In making this claim, Justice Thomas invoked a selective history of reproductive rights. As he explained, the modern birth control movement "developed alongside the American eugenics movement,"[120] which was preoccupied with both "inhibiting reproduction of the unfit"[121] and preventing the white race from being "overtaken by inferior races."[122] And although Justice Thomas eventually conceded that the movement to legalize contraception was distinct from the movement to legalize abortion, he nonetheless maintained that the arguments lodged in favor of birth control "apply with even greater force to abortion, making it significantly more effective as a tool of eugenics."[123]

To be sure, the claim that abortion, contraception, and family planning more generally, are part of a broader effort to limit—or curb entirely—Black reproduction has long persisted within certain segments of the Black community.[124] In the 1930s, members of the Pan-African movement, including Marcus Garvey, condemned contraception as "race suicide."[125] And as the 1960s dawned, the strains of Black natalism that undergirded Garvey's Pan-African movement were reflected in the nascent Black Power movement and its opposition to contraception and abortion, which it viewed through the lens of racial genocide and political subordination.[126]

In this regard, Justice Thomas's concurrence and the efforts of anti-abortion groups to associate abortion with racial injustice are of a piece with some strands of opposition to reproductive rights from within the Black community. But despite these shared roots, the effort to associate reproductive rights with racial and disability injustice (and even deracination) also speak to the reproductive justice movement's success in centering questions of race, class, and disability in the debate over reproductive freedom. And the anti-abortion community's invocation of eugenics, with its race and disability connotations, makes clear that the reproductive justice movement's success has also made its arguments and rhetoric ripe for cooptation—and indeed, contestation.

VI. Conclusion

Today, more than fifty years after *Griswold v. Connecticut* recognized the right of privacy, the constitutional landscape for reproductive rights looks increasingly grim. *Roe*'s protections for abortion have been hobbled,[127] and states enjoy broad latitude to regulate abortion,[128] sharply limiting access.[129] As this chapter suggests, concerns about race, sex, and disability discrimination have also been marshalled in the effort to curtail abortion access.

With this forecast in mind, it is perhaps worthwhile to reflect upon the constitutional moorings on which we have anchored protections for reproductive freedom. At one point, our legal imagination was unbounded in its understanding of what constitutional claims might be made in service of reproductive freedom. The Court's choice of privacy as the legal home for reproductive rights has resulted in a more cabined understanding of reproductive freedom and those who claim it. The reproductive justice movement has resurfaced and recovered critical lenses through which we might understand the effort to regulate reproductive freedom. However, as this chapter suggests, some aspects of the reproductive justice movement's understanding of reproductive freedom may be making its way into the Court's abortion jurisprudence—albeit in ways that may be deleterious (if not devastating) to the entire project of reproductive rights.

NOTES

1. 381 U.S. 479 (1965).
2. *Id.* at 484.
3. Melissa Murray, Griswold's *Criminal Law*, 47 CONN. L. REV. 1045, 1052 (2015)("In seeking legislative reform of extant criminal laws regulating sex and sexuality, the MPC, the Wolfenden Report, and many of the state legislative reform efforts emphasized a sphere of private, intimate life secluded from the state and insulated from criminal regulation.").
4. 342 U.S. 165 (1952).
5. 367 U.S. 643 (1961).
6. Murray, *supra* note 3, at 1052.
7. *Mapp v. Ohio*, 367 U.S. at 657.
8. Brief for Appellants at 79, Griswold v. Connecticut, 381 U.S. 479 (1965) (No. 496).
9. *See* Melissa Murray, *Sexual Liberty and Criminal Law Reform: The Story of* Griswold v. Connecticut, *in* REPRODUCTIVE RIGHTS AND JUSTICE STORIES 11, 24 (Melissa Murray, Katherine Shaw & Reva B. Siegel eds., 2019) [hereinafter REPRODUCTIVE RIGHTS] (discussing privacy and criminal law reform arguments in *Griswold*'s briefing).
10. *Id.*
11. Brief for Appellants, *supra* note 8, at 79.
12. *Griswold*, 381 U.S. at 481.
13. 405 U.S. 438 (1972).
14. *Id.*
15. 410 U.S. 113 (1973). This chapter was written before the U.S. Supreme Court decided Dobbs v. Jackson Women's Health Organization, 142 S. Ct. 2228 (2022) overruling Roe v. Wade.
16. 367 U.S. 497 (1961).
17. 367 U.S. 907 (1961).
18. 305 F. Supp. 1030 (S.D.N.Y. 1969).
19. 342 F. Supp. 800 (D. Conn. 1972).
20. 409 U.S. 1071 (1972).
21. 367 U.S. 497 (1961).
22. 367 U.S. 907 (1961).
23. *Poe*, 367 U.S. 497 (1961); *Trubek*, 367 U.S. 907 (1961).
24. *See* Melissa Murray, *Overlooking Equality on the Road to* Griswold, 124 YALE L.J.F. 324, 325 n.8 (2015).
25. Brief for Appellants at 28, *Poe*, 367 U.S. 497 (1961) (No. 60) ("When the long arm of the law reaches into the bedroom and regulates the most sacred relations between a man and his wife, it is going too far. There must be a limit to the extent to which the moral scruples, of a substantial minority or, for that matter, of a majority, can be enacted into laws which regulate the private sex life of all married people.").

26. *Id.* at 5–7.
27. *Id.* at 28–33 (discussing "the harmful effects of abstinence on the individual" and on "family life").
28. *Id.* at 29.
29. *See* Murray, *supra* note 24, at 326.
30. Complaint at 3, Trubek v. Ullman, 367 U.S. 907 (1961) (No. 847).
31. Trubek v. Ullman, 165 A.2d 158, 159–60 (Conn. 1960).
32. *Poe*, 367 U.S. at 508.
33. For a discussion of the socioeconomic dimensions of the birth control movement, see Cary Franklin, *The New Class-Blindness*, 128 YALE L.J. 2, 19–35 (2018).
34. *E.g., Poe*, 367 U.S. at 511 (Douglas, J., dissenting) (noting that a "public clinic dispensing birth-control information" had already been closed as a result of the laws' enforcement); *id.* at 509 (Brennan, J., concurring).
35. Emerson emphasized the fact that because the bans were primarily enforced against public clinics meant "not only that contraceptive devices are not available to such persons who cannot afford to go to private doctors, but that the whole range of medical services which are supplied by a clinic are not available to those people." Transcript of Oral Argument at *16, Griswold v. Connecticut, 381 U.S. 479 (1965) (No. 496).
36. *Griswold*, 381 U.S. at 503 (White, J., concurring) ("And the clear effect of these statutes, as enforced, is to deny disadvantaged citizens of Connecticut, those without either adequate knowledge or resources to obtain private counseling, access to medical assistance and up-to-date information in respect to proper methods of birth control.").
37. *See, e.g.*, Crossen v. Breckenridge, 446 F.2d 833 (6th Cir. 1971); Doe v. Rampton, 366 F. Supp. 189 (D. Utah 1973); Doe v. Scott, 310 F. Supp. 688 (N.D. Ill. 1970).
38. People v. Belous, 458 P.2d 194 (Cal. 1969); United States v. Vuitch, 305 F. Supp. 1032, 1034–35 (D.D.C. 1969). For more discussion of vagueness challenges to abortion statutes, *see* Risa L. Goluboff, *Dispatch from the Supreme Court Archives: Vagrancy, Abortion, and What the Links Between Them Reveal About the History of Fundamental Rights*, 62 STAN. L. REV. 1361 (2010).
39. Linda Greenhouse & Reva B. Siegel, *The Unfinished Story of* Roe v. Wade, *in* REPRODUCTIVE RIGHTS AND JUSTICE STORIES, *supra* note 9, at 53, 63.
40. Reva B. Siegel, *Roe's Roots: The Women's Rights Claims that Engendered* Roe, 90 B.U. L. REV. 1875, 1885 (2010).
41. Plaintiffs' Brief, Abramowicz v. Lefkowitz, 305 F. Supp. 1030 (69 Civ. 4469), *reprinted in* LINDA GREENHOUSE & REVA SIEGEL, BEFORE ROE V. WADE: VOICES THAT SHAPED THE ABORTION DEBATE BEFORE THE SUPREME COURT'S RULING 140, 143 (2d ed. 2012), https://documents.law.yale.edu/sites/default/files/BeforeRoe2ndEd_1.pdf.
42. *Id.*
43. *Id.* ("It reaches to the heart of the unequal position of women with respect to the burdens of bearing and raising children and the fact that they are robbed of the ability to choose whether they wish to bear those burdens.").
44. *Id.* at 144.
45. Greenhouse & Siegel, *supra* note 39, at 64–65.
46. *Id.* at 65.
47. Women vs. Connecticut Organizing Pamphlet (1970), *reprinted in* GREENHOUSE & SIEGEL, *supra* note 41, at 163, 169.
48. *Id.* at 173.

49. Franklin, *supra* note 33, at 55–56.
50. Women vs. Connecticut Organizing Pamphlet, *supra* note 47, at 174.
51. *Id.* at 173–74.
52. *Id.* at 169.
53. Abele v. Markle, 342 F. Supp. 800, 801–02 (D. Conn. 1972).
54. Abele v. Markle, 351 F. Supp. 224 (D. Conn. 1972).
55. *Id.* at 231.
56. Siegel, *supra* note 40, at 1894.
57. 409 U.S. 1071 (1972).
58. Brief for Petitioner at 3–4, Struck v. Sec'y of Def., 409 U.S. 1071 (1972) (No. 72-178).
59. *Id.* at 56.
60. *Id.* at 3–4.
61. *Id.* at 23 ("Most conspicuously, the regulation discriminates against women by treating pregnancy, a temporary physical condition unique to the female sex, as the basis for involuntary discharge, while no other temporary physical condition occasions peremptory discharge.").
62. Neil S. Siegel, *The Pregnant Captain, the Notorious REG, and the Vision of RBG: The Story of* Struck v. Secretary of Defense, *in* Reproductive Rights and Justice Stories, *supra* note 9, at 33, 38.
63. Brief for Petitioner, *supra* note 58, at 36 ("[The policy] insures that a woman will not be 'an equal competitor with her brother,' for it deprives her of opportunity for training and work experience during pregnancy and, in many cases, for a prolonged period thereafter.").
64. *Struck*, 409 U.S. at 1071.
65. Brief for Plaintiffs Jane Roe, John Doe, & Mary Doe, *Roe*, 314 F. Supp. 1217 (Nos. 3-3690, 3-3691).
66. *E.g.*, Brief of State Cmtys. Aid Ass'n as Amicus Curiae at 4–5, *Roe*, 410 U.S. 113 (Nos. 70-18, 70-14).
67. Brief of New Women Lawyers et al. as Amici Curiae Supporting Petitioners at 6, 14, 25, *Roe*, 410 U.S. 113 (Nos. 70-18, 70-40) [hereinafter Brief on Behalf of New Women Lawyers]; *see also* Brief of Am. Ass'n of U. Women et al. as Amicus Curiae at 7, 24, *Roe*, 410 U.S. 113 (Nos. 70-18, 70-14) ("[T]he value of the present right to vote, to equal pay, to equal job opportunities, to choose one's marriage partner, to joint custody of children . . . can be sharply decreased by an unwanted pregnancy.").
68. Brief on Behalf of New Women Lawyers, *supra* note 67, at 27 ("[A] woman who has a child . . . may be suspended or expelled from school and thus robbed of her opportunity for education and self-development. She may be fired or suspended from her employment and thereby denied the right to earn a living and, if single and without independent income, forced into the degrading position of living on welfare.").
69. *Roe*, 410 U.S. at 163–65.
70. *Id.* at 166 (calling abortion "primarily, a medical decision" such that "basic responsibility for it must rest with the physician.").
71. *Id.* at 141, 153.
72. *See* Rebecca Rauch, *Reframing* Roe: *Property over Privacy*, 27 Berkeley J. Gender L. & Just. 28, 63 (2012) (noting the right announced in *Roe* "might provide the right woman with reproductive choice . . . but for the wrong woman—one with limited resources—the so-called 'choice' becomes nonexistent"); Erwin Chemerinsky & Michele Goodwin, *Pregnancy, Poverty and the State*, 127 Yale L.J. 1270, 1329–31 (2018)) (reviewing Khiara M. Bridges, The Poverty of Privacy Rights (2017)) (discussing how *Roe* helped provided "little solace to . . . poor wom[e]n" seeking abortion access).

73. *See* Linda C. McClain, *The Poverty of Privacy,* 3 COLUM. J. GENDER & L. 119, 125–26 (1992) (discussing how reproductive choices for certain women are often burdened by "circumstance and constraint").
74. *See* Rauch, *supra* note 72, at 63 (noting "the right to privacy . . . is relegated to the land of negative rights").
75. *Roe,* 410 U.S. at 163.
76. Harris v. McRae, 448 U.S. 297 (1980); Maher v. Roe, 432 U.S. 464 (1977).
77. Rachel Rebouché, *The Limits of Reproductive Rights in Improving Women's Health,* 63 ALA. L. REV. 1, 24 (2011)("*Roe* has not been a ready platform for thinking about abortion in terms of women's right to health care.").
78. *Harris,* 448 U.S. at 300.
79. Khiara M. Bridges, *Elision and Erasure: Race, Class, and Gender in* Harris v. McRae, *in* REPRODUCTIVE RIGHTS AND JUSTICE STORIES, *supra* note 9, at 117, 120.
80. *Harris,* 448 U.S. at 315.
81. *Id.* at 316 ("[I]t simply does not follow that a woman's freedom of choice carries with it a constitutional entitlement to the financial resources to avail herself of the full range of protected choices.").
82. *Id.* at 344 (Marshall, J., dissenting).
83. *Id.* at 343–44 (quoting United States v. Carolene Prods. Co., 304 U.S. 144, 153, n.4 (1938)).
84. Bridges, *supra* note 79, at 118.
85. *See* Mary Ziegler, *Roe's Race: The Supreme Court, Population Control, and Reproductive Justice,* 25 YALE J. L. & FEMINISM 1, 38–40 (2013) [hereinafter "Roe's Race"]; Zakiya Luna & Kristin Luker, REPRODUCTIVE JUSTICE, 2013 ANN. REV. L. & SOC. SCI. 327, 334–40 (2013).
86. *See Roe's Race, supra* note 85, at 38–40; Luna & Luker, *supra* note 85, at 333–37; Cynthia Grant Bowman, *Recovering Socialism for Feminist Legal Theory in the 21st Century,* 49 CONN. L. REV. 117, 126–33 (2016); Human Rights Program at Justice Now, PRISONS AS A TOOL OF REPRODUCTIVE OPPRESSION, 5 STAN. J. C.R. & C.L. 309, 312 (2009).
87. *See, e.g., Roe's Race, supra* note 85, at 39.
88. *E.g.,* Rachel Rebouché, *How Radical Is Reproductive Justice? Remarks for the FIU Law Review Symposium,* 12 FIU L. REV. 9, 16–19 (2016).
89. Melissa Murray, Katherine Shaw & Reva B. Siegel, *Introduction, in* REPRODUCTIVE RIGHTS AND JUSTICE STORIES, *supra* note 9, at 1 (footnote omitted) (quoting Eisenstadt v. Baird, 405 U.S. 438, 453 (1972)).
90. Loretta Ross, *What Is Reproductive Justice?, in* REPRODUCTIVE JUSTICE BRIEFING BOOK: A PRIMER ON REPRODUCTIVE JUSTICE AND SOCIAL CHANGE 4, 4 (SisterSong ed., 2007).
91. *Id.*
92. *Id.*
93. *Id.*
94. *See* Charles Babington, *Abortion-Rights Group Broadens Focus,* WASH. POST, Dec. 24, 1992, at A1 (discussing the shift in NARAL's agenda); Shari Roan, *Moving Beyond Abortion,* L.A. TIMES, Nov. 4, 1993, at 1 (discussing the change in Planned Parenthood's agenda).
95. Mary Ziegler, *Reproducing Rights: Reconsidering the Costs of Constitutional Discourse,* 28 YALE J. L. & FEMINISM 103, 142 (2016).
96. *Id.*

97. *Id.*
98. *See* Jackie Calmes, *Activists Shun "Pro-Choice" to Expand Message*, N.Y. TIMES, July 28, 2014, http://www.nytimes.com/2014/07/29/us/politics/advocates-shun-pro-cho ice-to-expand-message.html; Dawn Laguens, *We're Fighting for Access, Not Choice*, HUFFINGTON POST (July 30, 2014), http://www.huffingtonpost.com/dawn-laguens/ were-fighting-for-access_b_5635999.html.
99. Ziegler, *Reproducing Rights, supra* note 95, at 142.
100. Consolidated Appropriations Act, Pub. L. No. 113-76, §§ 506–07, 128 Stat. 5, 409 (2013).
101. PUBLIC FUNDING FOR ABORTION, ACLU, https://www.aclu.org/other/public-fund ing-abortion?redirect=public-funding-abortion) (last visited Dec. 27, 2020); *Hyde Amendment*, PLANNED PARENTHOOD, https://www.plannedparenthoodaction.org/iss ues/abortion/hyde-amendment (last visited Dec. 27, 2020).
102. *E.g.*, Brief of ACLU et al. as Amici Curiae at 14, Little Sisters of the Poor v. Pennsylvania, 140 S. Ct. 2367 (2020) (Nos. 19-431, 19-454).
103. 140 S. Ct. 2103 (2020).
104. *See, e.g.*, Brief for Petitioner at 30, June Med. Servs. v. Russo, 140 S. Ct. 2103 (2020) (No. 18-1323) (discussing the impact of the challenged abortion restriction on low-income women); Brief of Amici Curiae for National Health Law Program and National Network of Abortion Funds Supporting Petitioners-Cross-Respondents, *June Med. Servs.*, 140 S. Ct. 2103 (No. 18-1323) (discussing the impact of the challenged abortion restriction on low-income people, people of color, LGBTQ-GNC people, and people experiencing intimate partner violence); Brief for Women with a Vision et al. as Amici Curiae, *June Med. Servs.*, 140 S. Ct. 2103 (No. 18-1323) (discussing the impact of the challenged abortion restriction on people of color and "other" marginalized individuals and communities).
105. *See, e.g.*, Brief for Women with a Vision, *supra* note 104; Brief of African-American Pro-Life Organizations as Amici Curiae in Support of Rebekah Gee, *June Med. Servs.*, 140 S. Ct. 2103 (Nos. 18-1323, 18-1460); Brief for Petitioners, *June Med. Servs.*, 140 S. Ct. 2103 (Nos. 18-1323, 18-1460); Brief in Opposition, *June Med. Servs.*, 140 S. Ct. 2103 (Nos. 18-1323, 18-1460).
106. 136 S. Ct. 2292 (2016).
107. Brief of Janice MacAvoy, et al. as Amicus Curiae in Support of Petitioners, Whole Woman's Health v. Hellerstedt, 136 S. Ct. 2292 (2016) (No. 15-274); *see also* Brief for Michele Coleman Mayes, et al. as Amici Curiae Supporting Petitioners, *June Med. Servs.*, 140 S. Ct. 2103 (2020) (No. 18-1323), 2019 WL 6650222.
108. MARK CRUTCHER, MAAFA 21: BLACK GENOCIDE IN 21ST CENTURY AMERICA (Life Dynamics 2009), https://www.maafa21.com/ (2012).
109. *Id.*
110. *See* DOROTHY ROBERTS, KILLING THE BLACK BODY: RACE, REPRODUCTION, AND THE MEANING OF LIBERTY xiv–xv (2d ed. 2017); *see also* Jill C. Morrison, *Resuscitating the Black Body: Reproductive Justice as Resistance to the State's Property Interest in Black Women's Reproductive Capacity*, 31 YALE J. L. & FEMINISM 35, 40 (2019) (citing Radiance Found., *Black Children Are an Endangered Species* (Feb. 4, 2010), http://toomanyaborted. com/black-children-are-an-endangered-species/).
111. ROBERTS, *supra* note 110, at xiv; Morrison, *supra* note 110, at 40 (citing *"The Most Dangerous Place for an African-American Is in the Womb": Black Politician Criticises* [sic] ANTI-ABORTION BILLBOARD, DAILY MAIL (Feb. 24, 2011), https://www.dailymail.co.uk/

news/article-1360125/The-dangerous-place-African-American-womb-Black-politician-criticises-anti-abortion-billboard.html).

112. *Black Preborn Lives Matter*, PRO LIFE AM. (last visited Aug. 11, 2020), https://prolifeamerica.org/preborn-black-lives-matter/; Opinion, *Planned Parenthood Claims "Black Lives Matter," But Kills 247 Black Babies in Abortion Every Day*, LIFE NEWS (June 4, 2020), https://www.lifenews.com/2020/06/04/planned-parenthood-claims-black-lives-matter-but-kills-247-black-babies-in-abortion-every-day/.

113. Rev. Clenard Childress, *John Leaps Evangelicization Livestream*, YOUTUBE (June 26, 2020), https://www.youtube.com/watch?v=hvforA4A_gM.

114. *See, e.g.*, James L. Sherley, *Preborn Black Lives Matter, Too*, WASH. TIMES (Aug. 2, 2020), https://www.washingtontimes.com/news/2020/aug/2/preborn-black-lives-matter-too/. To be sure, the messages espoused by these antiabortion groups has been countered by others in the Black community who have offered a more nuanced message. Although some Black evangelicals reject abortion, they nonetheless recognize "a contradiction in the great concern some lawmakers and activists show toward the fetus versus the limited focus on policies that uplift the black community." John Eligon, *When "Black Lives Matter" Is Invoked in the Abortion Debate*, N.Y. TIMES (July 6, 2019), https://www.nytimes.com/2019/07/06/us/black-abortion-missouri.html.

115. BANNING ABORTIONS IN CASES OF RACE OR SEX SELECTION OR FETAL ANOMALY, GUTTMACHER INST. (Jan. 2020), https://www.guttmacher.org/evidence-you-can-use/banning-abortions-cases-race-or-sex-selection-or-fetal-anomaly.

116. *E.g.*, Brief of Susan B. Anthony List as Amicus Curiae, Box v. Planned Parenthood of Ind. & Ky., 139 S. Ct. 1780 (2019) (No. 18-483).

117. 139 S. Ct. 1780 (2019).

118. *Id.* at 1792–93.

119. *Id.* at 1783.

120. *Id.*

121. *Id.* at 1784.

122. *Id.* at 1785.

123. *Id.* at 1784.

124. Regina Austin, *Beyond Black Demons & While Devils: Antiblack Conspiracy Theorizing & the Black Public Sphere*, 22 FLA. ST. U. L. REV. 1021, 1026 (1995).

125. *See* ROBERTS, *supra* note 110, at 84; Dorothy Roberts, *Black Women and the Pill*, 32 FAM. PLAN. PERSPS. 92, 93 (2000). *See also* Morrison, *supra* note 110, at 38; Beryl Satter, *Marcus Garvey, Father Divine and the Gender Politics of Race Difference and Race Neutrality*, 48 AM. Q. 43, 43 (1996).

126. Melissa Murray, *Race-ing Roe: Reproductive Justice, Racial Justice, and the Battle for* Roe v. Wade, 134 HARV. L. REV. 2025 (2021).

127. *See* Whole Woman's Health v. Jackson, 2021 WL 3910722 (Sept. 1, 2021) (per curiam) (allowing a Texas ban on abortion at 6 weeks to go into effect).

128. Planned Parenthood of Se. Pa. v. Casey, 505 U.S. 833 (1992).

129. Melissa Murray, *The Symbiosis of Abortion and Precedent*, 134 HARV. L. REV. 308 (2020).

CHAPTER 26

DISPUTED CONCEPTIONS OF MOTHERHOOD

JENNIFER S. HENDRICKS

A principal project of American legal feminism has been the conceptual disentanglement of biological motherhood from social motherhood and the separation of both from womanhood. Distinguishing between biological and social motherhood has contributed to progress in obtaining legal protections for nonbiological parents, especially lesbian partners of birth mothers, in transforming the ideal of fathering into something more like mothering, and in articulating the rights to use contraception and abortion to avoid motherhood. At the same time, these projects have left legal feminism with little to offer in support of political claims that are grounded in motherhood, whether biological, social, or both. The gender-neutral sensibilities of U.S. law are as uncomfortable with political campaigns that claim moral authority from motherhood (e.g., Mothers Against Drunk Drivers, Moms Demand Action for Gun Sense) as they are with legal arguments that attribute social importance to biological motherhood.[1] As a result, the law in key realms, in which power is contested in gendered terms, remains relatively untouched by feminist analysis.[2] During pregnancy, the default legal framework used by courts is that of "maternal-fetal conflict," a disentangled concept tailor-made for criminalizing pregnancy and mothering.[3] The claims of birth mothers in the contexts of adoption, surrogacy, and reproductive technology are framed through the lens of neoliberal market ideology rather than feminism. In order to move forward with the current activist agenda for reproductive justice, feminists need to offer courts a positive theory of motherhood that goes beyond mere disentanglement.

The interplay between individual identities and legal, social, and political systems of gender presents linguistic challenges in discussing the entanglement and disentanglement of biological and social motherhood. By "biological motherhood" I mean primarily gestation and birth, regardless of the gender identity of the person who performs these tasks. I use the term "birth mother" in this biological sense to include anyone who gives birth: cis women, trans men, and others. By "social motherhood" I mean legal and social status as one of the child's primary caregivers. Usually, this term is used when the caregiver identifies as a woman, though some may use it to distinguish a more-involved parent (like a traditional mother) from a less-involved parent (like a traditional father).[4] In disentangling these categories, the overlap between them is often overlooked. This omission leaves the law without a feminist perspective on the ways in which biological motherhood and social parenthood overlap—and thus cannot be fully disentangled because the process of gestation and birth is itself social and a form of caretaking.

I. The Feminist Disentanglement Project

The feminist disentanglement project—the project of separating, first, the categories of "woman" and "mother"—started in the law of the workplace and has had its greatest legal successes there. Pregnancy discrimination is illegal, and although discrimination on the basis of family responsibilities is not yet broadly illegal, it is at least viable as a theory of liability for some claims under Title VII of the Civil Rights Act of 1964.[5] Feminists and the law agree that "family friendly" workplace policies should apply equally to caregivers regardless of sex or gender identity. The principal remaining problem has been seen as one of policy rather than law: how to get men to step up and complete their half of the stalled revolution.[6]

This disentanglement project has two valences, one that resonates primarily with liberal feminism, and one that is more culturally feminist. First, liberal feminism seeks to induce men to participate equally with women in families. That would mean that, even if discrimination on the basis of family responsibilities continued, the burden of that discrimination would be shared equally according to gender. In such a world, family-responsibilities discrimination might still be a problem, but it would no longer be a sex-equality problem, as sex equality has been defined in the law. Second, though, many feminists also hope that more men participating as caregivers will raise the value of caregiving and strengthen the movement to make work and family more compatible. This aspiration has a more cultural feminist tinge because it implicitly adopts a premise that either (1) the liberal aspiration of equality may never be fully achieved—women will remain disproportionately entangled with parenthood—and so sex equality will continue to depend on fighting family-responsibilities discrimination or (2) caregiving itself is a feminist value, regardless of the sex or gender identity of those who perform it. Premise (1) is that of more traditional cultural feminism, with its acceptance of at least some persistent sex differences.[7] Premise (2) undergirds the vulnerability feminism pioneered by Martha Fineman and aptly described by Marc Spindelman as "feminism without feminism."[8] Vulnerability theory recognizes that the needs of women identified by cultural feminism, such as support for caregiving, are "universal and ... inherent in the human condition."[9] It is a feminism in which theories about caregiving, vulnerability, and power are freed from the tethers of personal identity.

A. Maternity Leave

A remaining stumbling block in discrimination law is the question of maternity leave. Women mostly become parents by giving birth, and men mostly become parents without giving birth. Behind those "mostlys" stands not only a huge numerical disparity but the law's very understanding of what constitutes the sex difference.[10] Feminists are divided about whether those who give birth should receive *extra* accommodation beyond what everyone receives for family responsibilities.[11] But contrary to policy in many other countries, in the United States that extra must be limited to what is physically necessary for gestation, birth, and recovery.[12] For example, women who adopt children can—and indeed, must—be treated as fathers for purposes of the employers' leave policies. When an employer offers six weeks of leave for mothers but three days for fathers, the policy must be based on the real difference of birth, not on a conception of "mother" that assumes the female parent is always the primary caregiver after birth.

Except for this issue of accommodating the actual birth, the disentanglement of "woman" and "mother" is conceptually complete in employment law. Some feminists, echoing Shulamith Firestone, look forward to finishing the project via technology or the market: surrogacy markets could disentangle gestational motherhood even further from womanhood, or the two could be fully separated with *Brave New World*-style artificial wombs.[13] Neither will be a widespread practical option any time soon, but even imagining them does substantial ideological work within the law.[14] The legal imagination has come a long way in its ability to conjure the concept of "woman" without reference to her potential motherhood.

B. Abortion Rights

Feminists have also sought to disentangle biological motherhood (meaning pregnancy and birth) and social motherhood. This has been a primary strategy when it comes to abortion rights. For example, feminists scrupulously avoid using the word "mother" to refer to a pregnant woman. Some courts, however, have not been won over to this terminology. In particular, Justice Kennedy, who served as the pivot point for abortion rights from *Planned Parenthood v. Casey*[15] until his retirement, persisted in describing women seeking abortions, and even women who had already had abortions, as "mothers."[16] But he nevertheless accepted the feminist argument that avoiding motherhood—and thus, having access to abortion—was necessary for women's equality. In *Casey*, he joined the Joint Opinion arguing that women had "define[d] their views of themselves and their places in society, in reliance on the availability of abortion in the event that contraception should fail. The ability of women to participate equally in the economic and social life of the Nation has been facilitated by their ability to control their reproductive lives."[17]

Abortion rights thus prevent biological motherhood from becoming social motherhood. The equality thereby achieved is a derivative, consequentialist sort of equality.

It recognizes the social reality that the burden of caring for children falls disproportionately on women and argues that women cannot achieve professional and economic equality without control over childbearing.[18] The same social reality that employment equality law insists we ignore is thus the basis for *Casey*'s equality argument for abortion rights. This seems like a contradiction, but it makes sense from the perspective of disentanglement. The goal in employment law is for women to be equal to men; in order to achieve that, the women must avoid being turned into mothers. That means that, if they become pregnant, they must either (1) get through the childbirth wrinkle but then become gender-neutral parents or (2) avoid parenthood entirely. Either way, they have avoided social motherhood in its most traditional sense.

C. Presumptions of Parenthood

A similar disentanglement between biological and social motherhood has also made headway in the definition of the legal relationship of parent and child. The word "mother" historically meant "the person who gives birth to the child and is a parent with rights and responsibilities." We can now also use "mother" as the feminine of "father" to mean "a person who does not give birth to the child but has a connection that makes her a parent with rights and responsibilities." Of course, the law has long recognized adoptive mothers as legal parents, but adoption carried social stigma that the law did little to alleviate. By shrouding adoption in secrecy and encouraging adoptive families to attempt to pass as biological families, the law's institutions reinforced the link between biological and social motherhood even as it allowed for the exception of adoption.[19]

Feminist and LGBTQ advocacy has helped challenge that link, most notably in the emerging trend of what Susan Appleton has elegantly called "presuming women": applying family law's marital presumption of parenthood to female married couples.[20] The traditional marital presumption held that a man was presumed to be the father of any child borne by his wife. It was always ambiguous whether this was a true evidentiary presumption (the law *assumes* he is the biological father unless proven otherwise) or a more substantive policy disguised as presumption (the law *declares* that the husband is the father, biology be damned). With the advent of same-sex marriage, the trend is toward the latter: to hold that when a married person gives birth, her spouse is the child's default second parent, regardless of the spouse's sex or biological link to the child.[21] Women can thus become social mothers regardless of biology[22] and without necessarily going through the still-cumbersome procedures required to adopt.

D. Surrogacy and Technology

Finally, the disentanglement of biological from social motherhood works in the other direction, too. Just as a nonbirthing woman can be a mother, the birthing woman can be not-a-mother. This development is clearest in the increasing embrace in the United

States of enforceable surrogacy contracts. In order to justify enforcing contracts for the creation of children, U.S. courts have described pregnant women as "hosts" and "foster mothers," and, in another context, the Supreme Court has dismissed gestation and childbirth as amounting to merely being "present at the birth" of the child.[23] Although feminism, broadly speaking, has no consensus position on surrogacy, liberal legal feminism has provided courts with the language of autonomy and market-oriented sex equality that helps cast surrogacy as liberatory for both the birth mother and her client.

The law of surrogacy, however, has not proceeded solely through the realm of contract doctrine. In the early years, courts were confronted with statutory definitions of "mother" that did not anticipate surrogacy contracts. In particular, they did not anticipate gestational surrogacy, in which the birth mother is not a genetic parent. Courts framed their task as determining who was the real mother, and they chose intent—a euphemism for the contract—as their guide.[24] These early moves are now being replicated in state statutes and the Uniform Parentage Act.[25] The result is to separate social and legal motherhood from *birth* motherhood, but not necessarily from genetic motherhood (and fatherhood). The emerging surrogacy regime depends not only on separating birth motherhood from social motherhood but also on downgrading birth motherhood relative to genetic parenthood.

This downgrade has ripple effects beyond surrogacy contracts. Once the law went beyond the contract and redefined "parenthood" to mean "genetic parenthood," it began applying that definition to the other main type of situation where genetic and gestational motherhood diverge: when fertility clinics mix up genetic material in derogation of the contractual intent of all involved.[26] Multiple women have now gone public—or gone to court—after giving birth to children who were the genetic offspring of different customers of their fertility clinics. In each case I can identify, the outcome has been to declare that the child is not hers and must be "given back" to the genetic progenitors.[27] Although there is no contract, and thus no intent, in this situation, social and legal motherhood have been so disentangled from biological motherhood—again, in the sense of gestation—that the law is blind to the gestational mother's relationship to the child.

It may seem strange to find this emphasis on genes in the law of reproductive technology, which also allows eggs and sperm to be bought and sold; a woman who becomes pregnant with a purchased ovum can still become a legal mother by giving birth. This seeming contradiction is part of the manipulability of genetic ideology as it intersects with hierarchies of gender, race, and class.[28] In neoliberal culture, market value is equated with moral value, and ownership supersedes human relationships. People own their genes, but a pregnant woman does not own her fetus, which means the genes are more important. In surrogacy disputes, courts invoked intent, meaning contract, as the supposed tiebreaker when genes and gestation conflict, but in embryo mix-up cases, there is no contract, and no relevant intent. These cases reveal that the actual rule courts are applying is that the child belongs to whoever produced the genes *or* paid for them.

E. Adoption

The shift in the law's treatment of birth mothers has taken a different path in the area of adoption. The law has long used adoption to separate biological from social motherhood. The secrecy and stigma that surrounded adoption were a sign of how taboo that separation was. In recent years, contrary to the general project of disentanglement, women who place newborns for adoption have achieved more recognition as mothers in two ways. First, they are much more likely to participate in choosing the child's adoptive parents. Second, many birth mothers and adoptive parents make agreements about continuing contact with or about the child—for example, the birth mother might be entitled to periodic updates and photos of the child, or the adoptive parents might have the right to give the birth mother's contact information to the child at some point.[29] Courts initially resisted the latter development by refusing to enforce those agreements, but that resistance has faded in most places.[30] Both changes recognize that the birth mother is acting *as a mother* when she places the child for adoption and that she has a claim to be something more than a legal stranger. Birth mothers in adoption are thus at the vanguard of the possible recognition of a quasi-parental status: people who are not legal parents but also not legal strangers and who have some set of parent-like rights regarding the child.[31] Others in this category include many unwed fathers—who have what the Supreme Court has called an "inchoate interest" in their newborn biological children—and egg and sperm donors in non-anonymous transactions; non-anonymity in this context signals that the biological connection cannot be completely severed.[32] This increased, quasi-parental status for birth mothers in adoption runs counter to the main current of the feminist project of disentangling biological and social motherhood.

Other than the enhanced status of birth mothers in adoption, all of these shifts have been in the direction of disentanglement. Not all, however, have been specifically feminist projects in the law. Employment law bears the heaviest mark of feminist influence toward gender neutrality that seeks to minimize any consequences of sex differences—it frowns both on treating women as presumptive mothers and on treating biological mothers as naturally suited for a caregiving rather than a breadwinning role. Recognition of lesbian couples as parents has also been an activist priority. On the most bitterly contested terrain—abortion—the attempt to separate "pregnant women" from "mothers" has been less successful and may have backfired, since it supports the anti-abortion framing of the woman and fetus as separate entities with opposing interests.[33] It may also have contributed to courts' willingness to construct the pregnant woman as not-a-mother in surrogacy disputes and fertility clinic error cases.

As with adoption, the surrogacy cases have not been notably influenced by feminist legal theory, in part because feminist opinion is more deeply divided than it is with regard to questions of employment discrimination, lesbian parenting, and abortion. Disagreement about the latter subjects tends to focus on details and tactics, not such fundamental questions as whether women should engage in paid work, raise children with other women, or have the right to abortion.[34] When it comes to surrogacy, however, feminists split on the fundamental question of whether commercial surrogacy should exist, and this split roughly tracks the divide between liberal and cultural feminism.[35] Feminists can agree about some aspects of how legal surrogacy, if it is to exist, should be regulated,[36] but they split over whether we should disentangle biological and social motherhood in this way at all.

II. Missing Threads

As with any project of legal reform, the disentanglement project has made ripples that interact with and affect areas of law beyond those that feminists specifically targeted. Disentanglement has combined with other ideas and forces such as the market and the marriage equality movement to create new ways of defining motherhood. But by promising that sex equality lies in disentangling biological and social motherhood—and both from womanhood—feminism has failed to influence the law in areas where women's interests are bound up with their motherhood, both biological and social.

Feminism has not labored alone in the disentanglement effort. In addition to other branches of critical theory, most especially queer theory, feminism has also had a few less savory bedfellows. The most notable of those is the institution of marriage, which has grabbed the leading role in protecting parental rights for lesbian couples. Before same-sex marriage was available nationally, nonbiological mothers were starting to win parental rights in some states on the theory of de facto parenthood.[37] Many feminists supported this development not only because it recognized lesbian partners as parents but also because it offered an alternative to the patriarchal institution of marriage itself.[38] In spite of some concern about stepfathers acquiring de facto parental rights against their wives, feminism overall welcomed the turn away from marriage. That turn, however, has now been reversed, which is a mixed result for feminism. On one hand, marriage has the potential to protect lesbian parenthood more robustly and sooner than the de facto parenthood rule would have, with less exposure of straight women to latecomer claims from stepfathers. But on the other, the cost may be giving up, for now, on organizing family law around something other than marriage. Rather than continuing to develop ways to place value on nonmarital relationships, the law strongly steers couples toward marriage if they want to have protected parental rights.

Another bedfellow with which legal feminism has an ambivalent relationship is free-market capitalism. Liberal feminism, which has made so much progress in employment law, fits most comfortably with the market. The liberal theory of sex equality and the market's demand to extract more of the value of women's labor have combined to change employment law. But the market has also been a principal driver in the disentanglement of biological and social motherhood in family law, where feminist influence is much less apparent. Perhaps owing to the absence of unified feminist advocacy, the law of surrogacy and reproductive technology has become the domain of contract law, not family law and certainly not sex-equality law. And the changes in the status of birth mothers in adoption, especially the growth of open adoption, seem to have more to do with market forces than with principled efforts to better theorize family relationships. Birth mothers now have increased bargaining power, largely because there are fewer babies to adopt, thanks to the greater availability of contraception and abortion and the decreased stigma of single motherhood.[39] Thus, while liberal feminism and the market have combined to drive changes in employment law, the market has been the principal driver in the disentanglement of biological and social motherhood in family law.

Perhaps it is the absence of a supporting bedfellow in some important areas that has left a gaping hole in feminist influence on the law of motherhood.[40] In addition to sanctioning marital presumptions, adoption, surrogacy, and reproductive technology, the law also disentangles biological motherhood from social motherhood by declaring some women to be failed mothers. This can happen during pregnancy, with pregnant women prosecuted, detained, or deprived of parental rights for allegedly endangering their fetuses.[41] In much greater numbers, it happens after the birth. In the majority of these cases, the allegations against the parent constitute neglect rather than abuse, and the neglect often boils down to being poor.[42] The parents who lose their children for being poor are mainly female and nonwhite. Although legal actors are aware of this disparity and sometimes aware of how race and sex stereotypes infect child protection proceedings, the disproportionate impact of neglect prosecutions is generally understood to have its origin outside the legal system, in the fact that poverty itself is disproportionately female and nonwhite. It is therefore not surprising that, since the system targets poor parents, it punishes women of color disproportionately.

Feminist theory has had little influence on how courts view this problem. For example, feminist theory has not made inroads against the Supreme Court's holding in 1981 that losing one's children is a categorically lesser harm than even the briefest term of imprisonment.[43] For that reason, the threat of losing a child does not trigger a presumptive constitutional right to counsel for indigent parents accused of abuse or neglect. This ruling is, of course, formally gender-neutral but does little to ameliorate the racial and gender impact of neglect law. A limiting factor is that feminism has had the most influence on courts when it promotes equality in the form of gender neutrality. The disentanglement project is an important component of that influence and helps explain why areas of the law that are of great practical concern to women show few signs of impact from feminist theory.

The primary exception to the rule of feminism-as-gender-neutrality in the law concerns not questions of motherhood but questions of sexual abuse, especially sexual harassment in the workplace. Thanks in great part to the efforts of Catharine MacKinnon, U.S. law was able to incorporate the proposition that sexual harassment was not merely something that disproportionately affected women but was itself a form of discrimination and subordination.[44] This project owed at least some of its success to another strange bedfellow of feminism: sexual puritanism. There remains a fair bit of confusion, especially in human resources departments, about why, exactly, sexual harassment is wrong,[45] but doctrinally it is clear that it is wrong because it is discriminatory. Feminist legal theory was thus successful in identifying a mechanism of subordination intimately bound up with sex differences and convincing the legal system to target that mechanism as a matter of sex equality. There is, therefore, at least a nascent theory in the law about how sexual exploitation is used to subordinate women.

Why can the law see the sex discrimination in sexual harassment (even the harassment of men) but not in attacks on parenthood (including fatherhood)? In part, it is because there is not a similar feminist legal theory of pregnancy and motherhood, and their relation to sex equality, that has successfully been embedded in the law.[46] Abortion is probably the motherhood-related issue most frequently discussed in terms of sex equality outside of employment law, but in that discussion, the metric for equality remains equality in the public realm of employment. In other words, abortion is a matter of sex equality because pregnancy and motherhood interfere with women's pursuit of equality at work. That is not a theory about what female reproductive biology means for equality; it is a theory for circumventing female reproductive biology in order to make progress elsewhere. Such an approach has helped bolster the arguments of men's rights advocates who want their own "right to abortion," by which they mean the right not to pay child support if they asked the mother to have an abortion and she refused.[47] Legal feminism needs a theory of pregnancy that can explain why growing and giving birth to a new human being is not analogous to incurring a monthly child support obligation. That requires accounting for the social as well as the physical aspects of pregnancy.

Pregnancy is treated in a similarly transactional way in the law of reproductive technology, where it is not an obstacle to career success but a service in demand. In both contexts, the law has much to say about control over pregnancy and its consequences, but feminism has done little to influence the law's theorizing of pregnancy itself. This failure to grapple directly with sex difference threatens even the careful gender neutrality that the disentanglement project has supported in employment law. Employment law carved out the typically brief period of actual disability due to pregnancy and childbirth as the only exception to gender neutrality—the time when "special treatment" for women who become mothers that way might be acceptable. This accommodation is under strain for two reasons.

First, the idea of a neat separation between recovering from childbirth and caring for the baby does not match reality.[48] If we imagine, for example, that birth mothers generally receive six weeks off from work for childbirth and recovery and that all new parents receive six weeks' caregiving leave, the effect in most cases will be that birth mothers will spend twelve weeks recovering from childbirth *and* serving as primary caregiver. It is also very likely that those will be the first twelve weeks of the child's life. Other parents will have six weeks as caregivers, usually later on, after the birth mother has already become established as the "expert" in caring for the child.

This problem (from some perspectives) of early emphasis on the birth mother as primary parent is exacerbated by the current policy emphasis on breastfeeding. Initially, courts flat-out denied that lactation had anything to do with pregnancy and treated it merely as a caregiving preference that happened to be incompatible with most employment.[49] A political backlash by feminists has failed to produce any legal mandates to accommodate breastfeeding, save for accommodations for pumping breast milk at work.[50] This failure to support the practice of breastfeeding may have occurred because breastfeeding is inconsistent with the sharp division between biology and caregiving on which the disentanglement of biological and social motherhood depends.

Although the disentanglement project has contributed to important legal advances for women, it is less suited to improving the law in areas that disproportionately or uniquely affect birth mothers and primary caregivers. The accepted strategy within the law remains gender neutrality: that is, to reduce the imbalance by increasing men's involvement with caregiving. This strategy is inadequate, however, when disproportionate caregiving is entwined with biology, either inextricably, via the caregiving of gestation, birth, and breastfeeding, or consequentially, via the bonds formed by those activities.

III. Tying Things Together

In some ways, feminist theories of gender just keep getting more and more disentangled. Our understanding of how sex and gender *as systems* relate to body parts, reproduction, and individual identity is still a work in progress, but it has become more nuanced and complex in recent years. With even pregnancy and childbirth no longer quite so closely tied to sex or gender as they had been, the time is again ripe for reconsidering the connection between social and biological motherhood.

In separating the two, the law's focus has been on de-emphasizing the aspects of biological motherhood that it considers characteristic of women—gestation, birth, and nursing—in favor of genetics. This means, first, that feminism has not challenged the growing primacy of genes in defining parenthood. This can be seen most widely in the growing legal acceptance of gestational surrogacy and the ease with which its principles have been transferred to the involuntary surrogacy cases created by fertility clinic mistakes. Although critical race feminists, most notably Dorothy Roberts, have chronicled how the law uses genetic ideology to promote racist and patriarchal norms, many feminists have embraced genetics as a sex-neutral, scientific definition of parenthood.[51] This is a superficial form of sex neutrality that serves to devalue other biological bonds that are specific to gestation and birth.

Second, disentangling biological from social motherhood ignores the fact that gestation is both biological and social. Although genes have been invested with an almost spiritual level of connection between parents and children, the legal vision of sex neutrality is so insistent on superficial neutrality that it is taboo to suggest that a social or emotional bond could arise from pregnancy and childbirth. For example, in *Nguyen v. INS*, the Supreme Court considered whether the federal government could adopt different citizenship rules for children born abroad to U.S. citizens, depending on whether the citizen parent was the mother or the father.[52] When the parents are unmarried, the mother's U.S. citizenship passes automatically to the child, but the father can transmit citizenship only by taking legal steps to establish his paternity. The government argued that the distinction was justified because it wanted to ensure that an actual parental relationship existed, which was necessarily true of mothers, while a father might not even know that the child exists.

The Supreme Court steered clear of this argument, seemingly wary of being accused of stereotyping women as mothers—that is, of failing to disentangle social and biological motherhood. The majority refused to assume an automatic relationship between mother and child. Instead, the Court upheld the law by saying that it ensured an "opportunity" for a meaningful relationship, which the mother had by her necessary "presence at the birth."[53] The additional requirement of acknowledging paternity was imposed because fathers were not necessarily present at birth. Thus was the process of growing a fetus, laboring, and delivering a child reduced to being present at the child's arrival. The same reduction has allowed courts in both voluntary and involuntary surrogacy cases to characterize birth mothers as "hosts" or foster mothers and to criticize them for forming unauthorized emotional attachments.[54]

The superficial approach to sex equality is in part a reaction to some of the early excesses of cultural feminism, which embraced some of the sex stereotypes that most legal feminists were trying to fight. Cultural feminism recognizes the relational nature of pregnancy and childbirth, but too often, it has used that as a starting point for generalizations that lead to essentialist claims about women and men. For example, some cultural feminist scholarship can be read to claim that the relational nature of pregnancy and childbirth causes all women to be more relationship-oriented.[55] This sort of causal claim has rightly been discredited, tarnishing cultural feminism in the process.[56] But it was the overgeneralizing, not the initial insight about pregnancy, that was the problem.

Biological and social motherhood are inherently intertwined in pregnancy. That does not have to mean that women are specially destined to perform other, nonbiological parenting, nor must it mean that the social relationship between a birth mother and her child is all that different from other human bonds. But the relationship does exist, and minimizing it contributes to minimizing caregiving-based bonds wherever they are found. For example, in *Nguyen*, the father who sought to give his son U.S. citizenship was not only present at the birth but in fact raised the child alone after the mother walked out of the hospital and disappeared a few days later. But having minimized pregnancy as a technicality rather than a relationship, the Supreme Court was able to gloss over the father's caregiving relationship as well.

Feminist theory today is better equipped to provide a nuanced approach to motherhood. With the help of the transgender movement, feminism has come to recognize additional possibilities for disentangling sex, gender, body parts, and reproductive functions.[57] These possibilities make it easier to analyze the gendered hierarchies that structure legal ideology distinct from individual identities. We can see more clearly how law devalues *the feminine*, apart from any identity characteristics of the person in whom it is embodied in a particular circumstance. Traditional ideologies point to the caregiving that pregnancy entails in order to associate women with caregiving in ways that devalue both women and caregiving in general. The cultural feminist project sought to maintain the association but reverse the valuation. The disentanglement project sought to break the association, and in many ways it succeeded. The best of both projects would have been to value caregiving wherever and by whomever performed, including the caregiving performed during pregnancy. But in rejecting cultural feminism's loyalty to the link between women and care, legal feminism embraced a too-extreme version of the disentanglement project that denied not just an inherent link between women and care but the link between pregnancy and care.

To return to the *Nguyen* example: In that case, the law assumed that a bond automatically exists between a birth mother and her child. It refused to make that assumption about the genetic father. If we assume that it is legitimate to require some bond in order to transmit citizenship, then these assumptions are reasonable starting points. Assuming the existence of a mother-child relationship of some sort does not stereotype women as inherently nurturing or caregiving. It merely reflects the fact of their having shared not merely a life but also a body, until the time of birth. In childbirth one person becomes two, and it seems absurd to deny that the connection between them matters. Acknowledging this connection does not require that the relationship between mother and child be good, healthy, or desired by the mother; in *Nguyen*, something about it appears to have been undesired, because the mother walked away.

The problem with the law in *Nguyen* was not, as the Justices thought, that it assumed a connection between mother and child but that it denigrated the possibility of a similar connection between father and child. The only way for a father to prove a connection to the child was to file a legal document acknowledging paternity—eighteen years' caregiving labor as a single father counted for nothing. This rule wrongly treated the mother-child caregiving bond as unique. Although pregnancy may be unique in blending biology with caregiving in a particular way, there is no basis for treating the relationship that results as categorically different from other parental caregiving relationships. Neither, however, should it be devalued because of the way in which it is unique and linked to gender.

Legal feminists rightly remain uncomfortable with political claims by women that are rooted in their status as mothers. The names of such organizations as Mothers Against Drunk Driving, Moms Demand Action, and Lawyer Moms of America suggest that motherhood uniquely entitles women to make political claims about morality and the welfare of children. To the contrary, caregiving and relationship bonds are universal human experiences, and so are the moral sensibilities that can arise from these experiences. The project of disentangling women from biological motherhood serves two vital purposes for feminism: It emphasizes the equal value of relationships formed in other kinds of caregiving, and it resists the traditional ideology that defines womanhood in terms of pregnancy.

At the same time, pregnancy and childbirth are a unique context for caregiving and the development of a relationship—a context that consists of a biological process rather than a purely social one. Legal actors go too far when they conclude that sex equality requires them to ignore the social aspects of this biological process. In matters of family law and reproduction, the law has yet to settle on a theory of pregnancy, motherhood, and their relation to sex equality, a gap that leaves the field open to values other than feminism's, such as those of the free market.

Notes

1. *See, e.g.,* Naomi Mezey & Cornelia T.L. Pillard, *Against the New Maternalism*, 18 MICH. J. GENDER & L. 229 (2012) (criticizing political activism under the banner of motherhood); Courtney Megan Cahill, *The New Maternity*, 133 HARV. L. REV. 2221 (2020) (criticizing the assumption that birth mothers are differently situated toward children than are biological fathers).
2. Susan Frelich Appleton, *How Feminism Remade American Family Law (And How It Did Not)*, in RESEARCH HANDBOOK ON FEMINIST JURISPRUDENCE (Cynthia Grant Bowmand & Robin West eds., 2019).
3. Many scholars have critiqued the framing of legal and medical issues as conflicts between the pregnant woman and her fetus, including Michelle Oberman, *Mothers and Doctors' Orders: Unmasking the Doctor's Fiduciary Role in Maternal-Fetal Conflicts*, 94 Nw. U. L. REV. 451 (2000); April Cherry, *Maternal-Fetal Conflicts, the Social Construction of Maternal Deviance, and Some Thoughts About Love and Justice*, 8 TEX. J. WOMEN & L. 245 (1999); DOROTHY ROBERTS, KILLING THE BLACK BODY: RACE, REPRODUCTION, AND THE MEANING OF LIBERTY 40 (1999).
4. *See* Darren Rosenblum, *Unsex Motherhood: Toward a New Culture of Parenting*, 35 HARV. J.L. & GENDER 57 (2012).
5. *See* Phillips v. Martin Marietta Corp., 400 U.S. 542 (1971); U.S. Equal Emp't Opportunity Comm'n, No. 915.002, Enforcement Guidance: Unlawful Disparate Treatment of Workers with Caregiving Responsibilities (2007). *See generally* Joan C. Williams & Nancy Segal, *Beyond the Maternal Wall: Relief for Family Caregivers Who Are Discriminated Against on the Job*, 26 HARV. WOMEN'S L.J. 77 (2003).
6. ARLIE HOCHSCHILD, THE SECOND SHIFT: WORKING PARENTS AND THE REVOLUTION AT HOME 12 (1989) (coining the term "stalled revolution"); Karen Czapanskiy, *Volunteers and Draftees: The Struggle for Parental Equality*, 38 UCLA L. REV. 1415, 1415 (1991) ("Women's entry into the paid workforce has been aided by legal changes promoting equal treatment of male and female workers. No equivalent legal movement has promoted men's entry into the unpaid workforce of the home").
7. *See* Robin West, *Jurisprudence and Gender*, 55 U. CHI. L. REV. 1 (1988).
8. Marc Spindelman, *Feminism Without Feminism*, 9 ISSUES IN LEGAL SCHOLARSHIP [i] (Dec. 2011).
9. Martha Albertson Fineman, *The Vulnerable Subject: Anchoring Equality in the Human Condition*, 20 YALE J.L. & FEMINISM 1, 1 (2008).
10. *See* Ann E. Freedman, *Sex Equality, Sex Differences, and the Supreme Court*, 92 YALE L.J. 913, 920–21 (1983) (identifying the "real differences" cases as those in which the Supreme Court invokes natural sex differences to justify different legal treatment of men and women); Sylvia A. Law, *Rethinking Sex and the Constitution*, 132 U. PA. L. REV. 955 (1984) (same).
11. *Compare* Wendy W. Williams, *Equality's Riddle: Pregnancy and the Equal Treatment/ Special Treatment Debate*, 13 REV. OF L. & SOC. CHANGE 325 (1984) (arguing for formally

equal treatment), *with* Herma Hill Kay, *Equality and Difference: The Case of Pregnancy*, 1 Berkeley Women's L.J. 2 (1985) (arguing for unique treatment of pregnancy).
12. *See, e.g.*, Nev. Dept. of Human Resources v. Hibbs, 538 U.S. 721, 731 (2003) (criticizing as discriminatory the practice of giving women and men different amounts of leave "not attributable to any differential physical needs of men and women, but rather to the pervasive sex-role stereotype that caring for family members is women's work").
13. Shulamith Firestone, The Dialectic of Sex: The Case for Feminist Revolution 226–28 (1970) (calling pregnancy "barbaric" and looking forward to the day when technology would free women from the physical demands of reproduction).
14. *See* Jennifer S. Hendricks, *Not of Woman Born: A Scientific Fantasy*, 62 Case W. Res. L. Rev. 399 (2012) (discussing the effect that the fantasy of artificial gestation has on legal discourse about pregnancy and reproduction).
15. Planned Parenthood of Southeastern Pa. v. Casey, 505 U.S. 833 (1992).
16. *See, e.g.*, Gonzales v. Carhart, 550 U.S. 124, 159 (2007) (describing a woman who was previously pregnant and who had an abortion as a mother: "a mother who comes to regret her choice to abort"). *See also* Beth Burkstrand-Reid, *From Sex for Pleasure to Sex for Parenthood: How the Law Manufactures Mothers*, 62 Hastings L.J. 211, 211 (2013) (arguing that the law uses "desexualization" and "ritualization" to cast women as mothers as soon as they are "even thinking about having sex").
17. Casey, 505 U.S. at 856.
18. I criticized this approach to abortion rights in Jennifer S. Hendricks, *Body and Soul: Pregnancy, Equality, and the Unitary Right to Abortion*, 45 Harv. Civil Rights–Civil Liberties L. Rev. 329 (2010).
19. Ellen Herman, Kinship by Design: A History of Adoption in the Modern United States 121–23 (2008).
20. Susan Frelich Appleton, *Presuming Women: Revisiting the Presumption of Legitimacy in the Same-Sex Couples Era*, 86 B.U. L. Rev. 227 (2006). *See* Nancy Polikoff, *This Child Does Have Two Mothers: Redefining Parenthood to Meet the Needs of Children in Lesbian-Mother and Other Nontraditional Families*, 78 Geo. L.J. 459 (1990).
21. Pavan v. Smith, 137 S.Ct. 2075 (2017) (holding that where a state listed birth mothers' husbands on birth certificates, regardless of biology, it had to do the same for birth mothers' wives).
22. In female couples, one woman may provide the ovum while the other gestates the child, so in that sense both are biological mothers.
23. *See, e.g.*, In re Roberto d.B., 923 A.2d 115, 117 (Md. App. 2007) ("host"); Johnson v. Calvert, 851 P.2d 776, 786 n.13 (1993) (noting with approval the lower court's analogy of a surrogate mother to a foster mother); Nguyen v. INS, 533 U.S. 53, 64 (2001) ("present at the birth").
24. *See, e.g.*, Johnson, 851 P.2d, at 782.
25. Unif. Parentage Act §§ 703, 801–18 (2017).
26. E.g., Perry-Rogers v. Fasano, 715 N.Y.S.2d 19, 26 (2000) (holding that genetic parents were the sole legal parents of a child born after their embryo was mistakenly implanted in another woman who was a client of the same fertility clinic). *See* Leslie Bender, *Genes, Parents, and Assisted Reproductive Technologies: ARTs, Mistakes, Sex, Race, and Law*, 12 Colum. J. Gender & L. 1, 25 (2003).
27. *Compare* Barbara Katz Rothman, Recreating Motherhood: Ideology and Technology in a Patriarchal Society 80 (1989) (describing a surrogacy broker who characterizes the surrogate mother as giving the baby "'back to the father,' as if it came

from him in the first place"); *see also* Bender, *Genes*, *supra* note 26, at 23 (noting differences between a baby and a fertilized embryo in the context of Perry-Rogers v. Fasano).

28. *See, e.g.,* ROTHMAN, RECREATING MOTHERHOOD, *supra* note 27, at 34–40 ("The new procreative technology being developed is based on the patriarchal focus on the seed"), 232 ("What makes a man a father is not his relationship to the mother, we are told, but that it is his sperm and his money"); Dorothy E. Roberts, *The Genetic Tie*, 1995 U. CHI. L. REV. 209 ("The genetic tie's value is not determined by biology. Rather, it systematically varies in a way that promotes racist and patriarchal norms."); Julie Shapiro, *A Lesbian Centered Critique of "Genetic Parenthood,"* 591 J. GENDER, RACE & JUSTICE 9 (2006); Libby Adler, *Inconceivable: Status, Contract, and the Search for a Legal Basis for Gay Lesbian Parenthood*, 123 PENN. ST. L. REV. 1 (2018) (exploring class differences in access to parenthood).

29. Carol Sanger, *Bargaining for Motherhood: Postadoption Visitation Agreements*, 41 HOFSTRA L. REV. 309, 314–15 (2012).

30. *Id.* at 315–19.

31. *See* ARTHUR D. SOROSKY, Annette Baran, & REUBEN PANNOR, THE ADOPTION TRIANGLE: THE EFFECTS OF THE SEALED RECORD ON ADOPTEES, BIRTH PARENTS, AND ADOPTIVE PARENTS 210–14 (1978) (describing the roles and relationships formed as part of the first legal open adoptions between the birth mother, the child, and the adoptive families); *see generally* Michael Higdon, *The Quasi-Parent Conundrum*, 90 U. COLO. L. REV. 941 (2019).

32. I discuss anonymity bans as a form of recognizing quasi-parenthood in Jennifer S. Hendricks, *Schrödinger's Child: Non-Identity and Probabilities in Reproductive Decision-Making*, 69 STUD. L. POL. & SOC'Y 221 (2016).

33. *See* Joan Williams, *Gender Wars: Selfish Women in the Republic of Choice*, 66 N.Y.U. L. REV. 1559 (1991) (arguing that advocates for abortion rights should put less emphasis on the rhetoric of choice and more on shared reverence for motherhood).

34. Joan Williams, *"It's Snowing Down South": How to Help Mothers and Avoid Recycling the Sameness/Difference Debate*, 102 COLUM. L. REV. 812, 816–17 (2002) ("The agenda of empowering the ponytails is quite simply different—not better, not worse, just different—from the agenda of allowing women crewcuts. If we insist on sanctifying the 'One True Way,' we will only deflect our energy away from achieving gender change into the sameness/difference debate and other fights among feminists.").

35. *See* Joan C. Callahan & Dorothy E. Roberts, *A Feminist Social Justice Approach to Reproduction-Assisting Technologies: A Case Study on the Limits of Liberal Theory*, 84 KY. L.J. 1197 (1995–96).

36. On the liberal and cultural feminist split concerning whether to permit surrogacy, *see* Sara Ainsworth, *Bearing Children, Bearing Risks: Feminist Leadership for Progressive Regulation of Compensated Surrogacy in the United States*, 89 WASH. L. REV. 1077 (2014) (discussing how the split can leave a void in feminist input on the regulation of surrogacy); June Carbone & Jody Lyneé Madeira, *The Role of Agency: Compensated Surrogacy and the Institutionalization of Assisted Reproduction Practices*, 90 WASH. L. REV. ONLINE 7 (2015) (proposing a framework for regulation). Especially in the international context, feminists tend to debate how to regulate surrogacy, focusing on its potential for exploiting women who work as surrogates. *See, e.g.,* Cyra Akila Choudhury, *The Political Economy and Legal Regulation of Transnational Commercial Surrogate Labor*, 48 VAND. J. TRANSNAT'L L. 1 (2015); Seema Mohapatra, *Achieving Reproductive Justice in the International Surrogacy Market*, 21 ANNALS OF HEALTH L. 191 (2012); Barbara Stark,

Transnational Surrogacy and International Human Rights Law, 18 ILSA J. INT'L & COMP. L. 369 (2012).

37. *See* Melanie B. Jacobs, *Micah Has One Mommy and One Legal Stranger: Adjudicating Maternity for Nonbiological Lesbian Coparents*, 50 BUFF. L. REV. 131 (2002).
38. *See* Katherine Franke, *Longing for Loving*, 76 FORDHAM L. REV. 2685, 2686 (2008) (arguing that advocacy for same-sex marriage should be done "in a way that is compatible with efforts to dislodge marriage from its normatively superior status as compared with other forms of human attachment, commitment, and desire"); *see also* Melissa Murray, *Obergefell v. Hodges and Nonmarriage Inequality*, 104 CAL. L. REV. 1207 (2016).
39. Sanger, *Bargaining*, at 314–15.
40. Feminists have sometimes allied with the family-values Right in order to support motherhood. *See* Deborah Dinner, *Strange Bedfellows at Work: Neomaternalism in the Making of Sex Discrimination Law*, 91 WASH. U. L. REV. 453 (2014).
41. Dorothy E. Roberts, *Punishing Drug Addicts Who Have Babies: Women of Color, Equality, and the Right of Privacy*, 104 HARV. L. REV. 1419 (1991); Dawn Johnsen, *Shared Interests: Promoting Healthy Births Without Sacrificing Women's Liberty*, 43 HASTINGS L.J. 569 (1992).
42. David Pimentel, *Punishing Families for Being Poor: How Child Protection Interventions Threaten the Right to Parent While Impoverished*, 71 OKLA. L. REV. 885 (2019); *see generally* DOROTHY E. ROBERTS, SHATTERED BONDS: THE COLOR OF CHILD WELFARE (2002); Janet L. Wallace & Lisa R. Pruitt, Judging Parents, Judging Place: Poverty, Rurality, and Termination of Parental Rights 77 MO. L. REV. 95 (2012).
43. Lassiter v. Dept. of Soc. Servs., 452 U.S. 18 (1981).
44. Reva B. Siegel, *A Short History of Sexual Harassment*, in DIRECTIONS IN SEXUAL HARASSMENT LAW 9 (Catharine A. MacKinnon & Reva B. Siegel eds., 2003) ("During the 1970s, lawyers, advocates, and theorists had to persuade the American judiciary that sexual harassment is 'discrimination on the basis of sex.' . . . Catharine MacKinnon's analysis in *Sexual Harassment of Working Women[: A Case of Sex Discrimination* (1979)]—a stunningly brilliant synthesis of lawyering and legal theory—played a crucial role in this process.").
45. When a presidential candidate talked about grabbing women "by the pussy," about one-third of the country was angry that he was bragging about sexual assault. Another third was offended that he used a crude word. (The other third cheered.)
46. Theoretical efforts do exist, but they have not achieved the sort of influence in the law attained by feminist theories about sexual harassment. *See, e.g.*, Annette Ruth Appel, *Virtual Mothers and the Meaning of Parenthood*, 34 U. MICH. J. L. REFORM 683 (2001); Katharine K. Baker, *The DNA Default and Its Discontents: Establishing Modern Parenthood*, 96 B.U. L. REV. 2037 (2016); Sarudzayi M. Matambanadzo, *Reconstructing Pregnancy*, 69 S.M.U. L. REV. 187 (2016).
47. Ethan J. Leib, *A Man's Right to Choose: Men Deserve a Voice in the Abortion Decision*, 28 LEGAL TIMES 1, 61 (2005).
48. Sarudzayi M. Matambanadzo, *The Fourth Trimester*, 48 U. MICH. J. L. REFORM 117 (2014) (drawing on obstetrics and midwifery literature to reconceptualize pregnancy for legal purposes, defining the "fourth trimester" as the period of transition and recovery for a postpartum woman and as a period of intense vulnerability for newborns).
49. E.g., Puente v. Ridge, No. Civ.A. M-04-267, 2005 WL 1653017 (S.D. Tex. July 6, 2005) (holding that lactation was not a "medical condition related to pregnancy" for purposes of the Pregnancy Discrimination Act, and thus there was no recourse for a woman denied

lactation breaks even though the employer liberally permitted other employees to take smoking breaks).
50. Patient Protection and Affordable Care Act of 2010, 29 U.S.C. 207(7)(r).
51. Roberts, *Genetic Tie*, supra note 28; e.g., Courtney Megan Cahill, *The New Maternity*, 133 Harv. L. Rev. 2221 (2020) (criticizing the assumption that birth mothers are differently situated toward children than biological fathers); Naomi Schoenbaum & David Fontana, *Unsexing Pregnancy*, 119 Colum. L. Rev. 309 (2019) (proposing to redefine "pregnancy" to include all activities undertaken in preparation for parenthood); Marjorie Maguire Shultz, *Reproductive Technology and Intent-Based Parenthood: An Opportunity for Gender Neutrality*, 1990 Wis. L. Rev. 297; Melanie B. Jacobs, *Parental Parity: Intentional Parenthood's Promise*, 64 Buff. L. Rev. 465 (2016); Dara E. Purvis, *Intended Parents and the Problem of Perspective*, 24 Yale J.L. & Feminism 210 (2012). I include "intent" standards as based on genetics because the contracts to which "intent" refers assign parenthood to the people who own the genetic material that is used to create the child, whether as original owners who produced the egg or sperm or as purchasers.
52. Nguyen v. INS, 533 U.S. 53 (2001).
53. Nguyen, 533 U.S., at 64–68.
54. See Perry-Rogers v. Fasano, 715 N.Y.S.2d 19, 26 (2000) (criticizing a woman for "purposefully" creating a bond with the child she gave birth to, although her fertility clinic informed her during the pregnancy that it might not be genetically hers).
55. See West, *Jurisprudence and Gender*, supra note 7, at 14, 20–21.
56. See Angela Harris, *Race and Essentialism in Feminist Legal Theory*, 42 Stan. L. Rev. 581, 602–5 (1990).
57. See Spindelman, *Feminism Without Feminism*, supra note 8 (describing how, instead of seeking universality by ascribing to all women a core, essential experience of gender, feminism now aspires to universality through multifacetedness and intersectionality); Jessica Clarke, *They, Them, Theirs*, 132 Harv. L Rev. 894 (2019) (setting out a feminist legal theory agenda in regard to nonbinary identity); Paisley Currah, *The Transgender Rights Imaginary*, in Feminist and Queer Legal Theory: Intimate Encounters, Uncomfortable Conversations (Martha Albertson Fineman, Jack E. Jackson, & Adam P. Romero eds., 2009) (discussing the treatment of gender categories in feminist and queer and trans theory).

CHAPTER 27

APPLYING INTERNATIONAL FEMINIST INSIGHTS TO GENDERED VIOLENCE IN THE UNITED STATES

TRACY E. HIGGINS

FEMINISTS in the United States have had a significant and sometimes controversial impact on the way that international human rights law defines and regulates gender-specific harm. This has been the case since the beginning of the modern international human rights movement. Early formulations of international human rights reflected the argument of liberal feminists in the United States that women's equal capacity for citizenship entitled them to rights on par with men.[1] According to this view, gender-neutral articulations of rights were made sufficiently inclusive by language prohibiting discrimination based on sex. During the Cold War, U.S. feminists working internationally navigated between advocating for an expansion of human rights to include women more fully and embracing a leftist critique of the liberal rights paradigm altogether, a debate that echoed that of liberal and radical feminists at home.[2] Perhaps forgetting the difficult lessons of race and cultural difference learned at home, some U.S. feminists also pushed for the globalization of human rights guarantees while paying too little attention to issues of power.[3] The work of U.S. feminists on women's human rights has thus triggered a sometimes contentious but also constructive engagement among feminists globally. The resulting theoretical advances have, in turn, informed many of the developments discussed in this chapter.

The focus here, however, is not on the oft-considered ways that U.S. feminists have influenced international human rights theorizing but instead on the ways that feminist international human rights theorists have influenced and might continue to inform the legal regulation of gender, and especially gender-motivated violence, in the United States. The chapter asks: What have feminists working on these issues in the United

States learned from international human rights law and advocacy, and what might they learn in the future? Answering this question requires, first, consideration of some of the key insights of feminist legal theorists working within the international human rights framework. How have feminists challenged, tested, reworked, and reconsidered the international human rights paradigm? Rather than attempt to comprehensively synthesize the enormous and varied literature on feminism and international human rights, this chapter instead explores several foundational insights that are particularly useful for thinking about gender hierarchy, especially gendered violence, within the framework of U.S. law.

After reviewing some of the central elements of feminists' critique of the human rights project, the chapter surveys feminist efforts to expand the traditional focus of international human rights law—state power—to encompass the unique ways that state-sponsored violence is deployed against women. It then turns to feminist arguments that state responsibility for gender violence must not be limited to state-sponsored violence, even broadly defined, but must encompass "state-tolerated violence" and include an obligation on the part of states to eliminate private violence. It also examines feminist arguments that state policy choices often create power structures that make women more vulnerable to violence and discrimination. Feminists have insisted that this state-enabled violence must also be part of the analysis of state responsibility under international human rights law. Finally, this section ends with a look at how international human rights instruments have evolved over time to reflect these arguments.

The chapter's final section turns to the question of how these insights have and might bear on U.S. domestic law and policy, despite U.S. reluctance to sign, ratify, and implement important treaties, including the Convention on the Elimination of all forms of Discrimination Against Women (CEDAW). It examines each category of violence, state-sponsored, state-tolerated, and state-enabled, and offers examples of their treatment under both domestic and international human rights paradigms. The aim is to demonstrate how feminist arguments derived from international law have or could inform responses to gender violence and gender hierarchy in the United States. Finally, the chapter concludes with an examination of the possible pitfalls of feminist strategies that depend on an expansion of state power.

I. How Does International Human Rights Law Address Gendered Violence and Discrimination?

From the outset, international human rights law has largely focused on the way a state uses its power against or, to a more limited degree, on behalf of its citizens.[4] Thus, human rights instruments prohibit extrajudicial killing, religious persecution, and the imprisonment of dissidents.[5] They also oblige states to promote the well-being of their citizens by working to secure education, medical care, and housing.[6] Insofar as women and men are equal in their capacity for citizenship, international human rights law has always, formally anyway, included women in its mandate. The Universal Declaration of Human Rights, drafted in 1948, reflects this liberal conception of women as formally equal citizens by simply providing that the rights identified in the Declaration would be guaranteed "without distinction of any kind, such as race, colour, sex, language, religion, political or other opinion, national or social origin, property, birth or other status."[7]

Even those instruments that were directed toward the status of women, such as the Convention on the Political Rights of Women, emphasized formal equality and adopted a male standard against which those rights would be measured.[8] Treating gender inequality as a product of gender bias or discrimination, these instruments did not account for or even acknowledge the profound ways that women's experiences differed from men's and how those differences reflected systemic gender hierarchy.[9] This embrace of gender neutrality and formal equality might be understood as an attempt at inclusion, rejecting gender distinctions and adopting an even-handed antidiscrimination standard emphasizing "sameness" across gender categories. Or, it might be accounted for simply as an inevitable by-product of women's lack of participation in the process. As Hilary Charlesworth, an early advocate of applying feminist legal insights to international law, argued in 1995, "because the law-making institutions of the international legal order have always been, and continue to be, dominated by men, international human rights law has developed to reflect the experiences of men and largely to exclude those of women, rendering suspect the claim of objectivity and universality in human rights law."[10] More specifically, men created international human rights law to protect themselves from the power they feared most, that of the state. Although facially gender-neutral and guaranteed to all, these early instruments did not reflect women's priorities. Rather, as Elisabeth Friedman—a political scientist who studies gender and transnational movements—has observed, "[They] protected a male subject, who experienced violations primarily directed at men, in largely male spaces."[11]

Beginning in the 1970s, feminists began to think more systematically about what it would mean for the human rights paradigm to take gender seriously and expressly account for the circumstances of women. Feminist critics began to highlight the ways in which the existing international framework failed to do so and explored the implications of that failure. With respect to gender violence, two important insights emerged. First, the specific limitations on state power instantiated in human rights instruments reflected the priorities of the (powerful, mostly male) drafters, leaving out important gendered harms. And second, by defining the family as a place for exercising autonomy outside the reach of the state, the framework not only failed to protect women but also reinforced gender hierarchy.

A. Expanding the Understanding of State-Sponsored Violence

The implications of these insights have been far-reaching, giving rise to a nuanced understanding of state responsibility for gender violence. Although theorizing gendered violence has proceeded both in the domestic and in the international spheres, the arc of the development has differed in important ways. In domestic law, because the state's jurisdiction to regulate private violence is presumed, feminist theorists have focused on how state power might best be used to respond to and prevent such violence. In contrast, because the relationship between private violence and state obligation under international law could not be taken for granted, international human rights scholars have paid less attention to the specifics of policymaking around gender violence and instead have focused, by necessity, on the nature and scope of state responsibility.

Accepting the premise that international human rights law regulates state power and defines state obligation, feminist human rights theorists sometimes divide gender-motivated violence into two categories, state-sponsored and state-tolerated. In theory at least, the former falls within the scope of first-generation human rights guarantees. The latter does not. Beginning in the 1990s, feminists set about enlarging the scope of international human rights frameworks both to reflect a more comprehensive understanding of state sponsored violence and to extend state responsibility for "private" violence.

As noted above, insofar as the focus of first-generation human rights was on the threat posed by the state itself to the life and liberty of its citizens, those rights were protected without regard to gender. Citizens were protected from torture, extrajudicial killings, and restrictions on their speech. Further, the early human rights framework included express nondiscrimination principles that addressed gender as one of several protected categories. This meant that rights were not only guaranteed but that they must be protected on a nondiscriminatory basis. Of critical importance, of course, was that the definition of rights was premised, as Charlesworth observed, on the experiences of men, not women.[12] This meant that, to the extent that women experience the same kind of violence or discrimination as men, they might be protected, at least in theory. At the same time, as feminist human rights scholar Christine Chinkin has argued, the very fact that the target is a woman can make the violence more likely to be seen as personal rather than official, even when perpetrated by a state actor.[13] Even more important, defining rights based on men's experience also meant that violations that were primarily, if not uniquely, experienced by women, such as rape in conflict zones or forced pregnancy, were often not included within the proscribed categories at all.[14]

In response, feminists argued for an expanded definition of state-perpetrated violence that accounted for the experiences of women. For example, advocates have paid particular attention to gender-specific issues such as rape in wartime.[15] As a result, international law no longer treats rape during armed conflict as a matter of family honor.[16] Turning attention to peacekeeping, feminists have also drawn attention to the problem of sexual violence committed by humanitarian actors under the sponsorship of the United Nations.[17] More recently, feminist advocates have argued that the denial of abortion services to women raped in conflict situations is a violation of humanitarian law.[18] Each of these examples illustrates the impact of feminist theorizing on the traditional understanding of international human rights law, expanding the definition of state harm to reflect the gendered aspects of state power and the experiences of women.

B. Private Violence as a Human Rights Concern

The second category of violence comprehended by international human rights law includes violence perpetrated by private actors. This category might be labeled "state-tolerated" to emphasize the feminist insight that the state is responsible for the boundaries placed on private violence and that state policy determines the impunity enjoyed by perpetrators of that violence. This is one of the most powerful insights of feminist legal theory developed in the context of international human rights, and it has brought within the scope of human rights a category of gender-based harm that was entirely omitted by traditional conceptions. Taking for granted power hierarchies within the "private" sphere, the traditional liberal view of state power is one in which that power must be circumscribed in ways that promote individual freedom and autonomy. Embracing this liberal paradigm, the human rights guarantee of formal equality in the public sphere coupled with limitations on state interference in the private sphere allowed the state to appear ungendered even while reinforcing and protecting hierarchies of private power.[19] As a result, acts of gender violence committed by private actors were seen as beyond the reach of international human rights.[20]

For decades, feminists have insisted on the necessity of a broader definition of gender violence. As early as 1990, Charlotte Bunch, one of the first feminist legal scholars to examine gender in a global framework, argued that a framework that held states accountable only for the acts they perpetrated, and not for the acts they permitted and enabled, could never fully address a basic source of women's inequality: private violence.[21] Indeed, international human rights standards that include torture but not domestic violence fail to address the central source of violence in women's lives.[22] The point is not merely that regulating only the affirmative acts of the state leaves women underprotected, though that is true. Rather, it is that the "inaction" of the state is altogether illusory. The state is fully implicated in creating and maintaining the social structure and institutions that leave women vulnerable.[23] Catharine MacKinnon famously made this argument with respect to both domestic violence and rape, noting that "the state actually is typically deeply and actively complicit in the abuses."[24] She argues that the state's response to these crimes—whether the police take them seriously or not—and the law's definition of them together constitute the boundaries of private power in a way that is highly gendered.[25] When police decline to respond to a domestic violence complaint or when intimate violence is not defined as a crime, the state sanctions the exercise of private power.[26] Human rights law must therefore regard the creation and maintenance of this legal regime as an affirmative act by the state to the same degree as torture of detainees by military police.

C. State-Enabled Violence

To the categories of state-sponsored violence and state-tolerated violence, feminist scholars would add a third category, state-enabled violence. The inclusion of this category would expand the focus beyond how states respond or not to acts of violence by nonstate actors to encompass an examination of the broad range of ways that state policy increases women's vulnerability by reinforcing private power. Examples range from tax law to housing policy to property and inheritance laws.[27] Although perhaps facially neutral, legal regulation in each of these areas can undermine the protection of women's economic power and thereby limit their ability to exit abusive relationships.

In human rights theorizing, this attention to the socioeconomic structures reinforced by the state reflects a broader inversion of thinking about the relationship between civil and political rights and economic, social, and cultural rights. Early conceptions of human rights were often premised on the assumption that the protection of women's right to political participation and equal citizenship, guarantees of equality in the public sphere, would eventually translate into socioeconomic equality for women through their exercise of political power. Feminists have argued instead that economic, social, and cultural rights (food, healthcare, housing, education) are necessary to the exercise of civil and political rights.[28] Put differently, the failure of the state to ensure, for example, women's basic economic rights, undermines women's political rights regardless of any formal guarantees of equality in that domain.

Extending this observation about the foundational nature of economic, social, and cultural rights to the context of gendered violence, feminists have argued that the state enables violence when it normalizes social structures that reinforce gender hierarchy, whether or not these structures are the direct products of state action. An important example is state policy regarding market regulation in a globalized economy. Within a human rights paradigm premised on state responsibility, the enjoyment of economic, social, and cultural rights depends, in significant measure, upon a redistributive state. The state must simultaneously have both the resources and the capacity to reallocate them in a way that promotes the realization of rights. Indeed, state obligations to fulfill economic, social, and cultural rights "to the maximum of their available resources" are expressly contingent on this capacity. Although a perhaps necessary recognition of the limits on state capacity, this language may be invoked to justify the prioritization of economic growth over redistribution. Within neoliberal orthodoxy, the demand to fulfill economic rights thus provides a rationale for minimizing state intervention to promote the required economic productivity.[29]

Although the elimination of gender discrimination is not subject to the progressive realization clause, the retrenchment of the state often entails shrinking the social safety net and deregulating labor markets, both of which tend to reduce women's economic power and increase their dependency, even absent overt discrimination. As care work is (further) privatized and supplied by women at home, women often become more marginalized workers in the formal labor force or drop out of the formal work force entirely. Their informal labor increases as does their dependence on a family wage earner, often a male. This dynamic, in turn, further entrenches women within the confines of the family and makes it more difficult for them to exit a violent situation. Emphasizing the indivisibility of civil and political rights and economic, social, and cultural rights within the international human rights framework has thus allowed international feminist theorists to attend more closely to the power implications of social and economic structures and to expose state responsibility for their creation and reinforcement.

D. Feminist Theory's Impact on International Human Rights Law

The international human rights legal framework addressing gender equality, including gendered violence, has been informed, indeed transformed, by these feminist insights. As the feminist critique took hold, advocates and power brokers began to rethink the traditional human rights framework. One of the bedrocks of this framework, firmly rooted in the superficial gender neutrality of liberalism, the Universal Declaration of Human Rights (UDHR) provides that "all are equal before the law" and that everyone is entitled to the rights and freedoms described in the instrument "without distinction of any kind," including sex.[30] Yet the UDHR situates and protects women within the traditional, heteronormative nuclear family, reifying this highly patriarchal structure.[31] Similarly, the two major, broad-based human rights treaties, the International Covenant on Economic, Social, and Cultural Rights (ICESCR) and the International Covenant on Civil and Political Rights (ICCPR), reflect a concern for gender only in the form of traditional nondiscrimination provisions.[32] Even CEDAW embraces, at many points, a concept of equality that is dependent on a male-defined metric, guaranteeing rights to women on an equal basis with men.[33] Remarkably, the text of CEDAW contains no provisions regarding violence against women.

By the dawn of the 1990s, however, the core insights of the feminist critique had gone mainstream. In 1993, the United Nations acknowledged that human rights must be understood in a gender-specific way and explicitly recognized gendered violence as a violation of international human rights. Going beyond a male-centered nondiscrimination obligation, the Vienna Declaration states: "The full and equal participation of women in political, civil, economic, social and cultural life, at the national, regional and international levels, and the eradication of all forms of discrimination on grounds of sex are priority objectives of the international community."[34] The Declaration urged the General Assembly to adopt the Declaration on the Elimination of Violence Against Women (DEVAW), which it did in December of that year.[35]

The language of DEVAW clearly reflects many of the key insights and critiques that feminist theorists had developed in response to earlier instruments. For example, DEVAW notes that violence against women is a distinct violation of human rights:

"violence against women constitutes a violation of the rights and fundamental freedoms of women."[36] It also acknowledges that gender violence both contributes to and results from other forms of discrimination against women:

> Violence against women is a manifestation of historically unequal power relations between men and women, which have led to domination over and discrimination against women by men and to the prevention of the full advancement of women, and that violence against women is one of the crucial social mechanisms by which women are forced into a subordinate position compared to men.[37]

This language reflects the argument of feminists that the threat of violence is tightly interwoven with patriarchal social structures.

Outlining state obligations, Article IV of DEVAW responds, to varying degrees, to the three categories of gender violence noted above. With respect to state-sponsored violence, it urges states to refrain from committing acts of gender violence.[38] It also addresses state-tolerated violence, insisting that states "exercise due diligence to prevent, investigate and, in accordance with national legislation, punish acts of violence against women, whether those acts are perpetrated by the State or by private persons."[39] It urges states to take affirmative steps to "modify social and cultural patterns of conduct of men and women and to eliminate prejudices, customary practices and all other practices based on the idea of the inferiority or superiority of either of the sexes and on stereotyped roles for men and women."[40] This language, although limited by its presumption of the gender binary, nevertheless looks to states to be proactive in addressing manifestations of gender hierarchy in the "private" sphere.

With respect to the third category, state-enabled violence, DEVAW stops somewhat short of fully embracing the feminist critique. Notwithstanding the language that gender violence is "a manifestation of historically unequal power relations between men and women," DEVAW does not draw an express link between those unequal power relations and state policies creating and reinforcing them. Nevertheless, despite some limitations, the language of international human rights instruments has come to reflect the insights of feminist legal theorists and, as a result, embrace a much more nuanced understanding of both the causes and consequences of that violence than did earlier human rights instruments or, as discussed below, U.S. law.

II. How Are Those Insights and Lessons Relevant to Domestic Law in the United States?

The insights of feminist legal theory on the international level can be readily translated and applied to gendered violence in the United States both as a model for legal reform and as a critical lens to expose the limitations of domestic law. The application of these concepts to U.S. law is powerful for several reasons. First, it reveals the lacunae in domestic law that often remain invisible even to feminist advocates who work primarily within the United States. The scope of international guarantees, particularly the emphasis on positive rights, reveals the striking limitations of U.S. constitutional rights, constrained as they are to negative rights against the state. Second, by focusing on the failures of even a wealthy nation to ensure basic economic, social, and cultural rights to much of its population, such an analysis reveals how policy choices rather than a lack of resources drive gender hierarchy. Finally, the analysis helps to displace the deeply problematic assumption that states in the Global North, particularly the United States, exemplify the gold standard in terms of gender equality.

A. How State-Sponsored Violence Affects Women in the United States

Feminist legal insights can be applied to U.S. law in the same three contexts as outlined above: violence directly perpetrated by the state, violence tolerated by the state and violence enabled by the state. First, examining state-sponsored violence in the United States from the standpoint of women reveals the ways that such violence is deeply gendered. For example, one of the most important targets of research, advocacy, and legal reform over the past two decades in the United States has been the carceral state. This important work has ranged from examining the racist origins and effects of mass incarceration to exposing the economic and political power of the prison-industrial complex.[41] Applying a feminist human rights lens to the issue can help expand this work to address the particular ways in which state violence toward incarcerated people reflects and reinforces gender hierarchy.

The work of scholar and political activist Angela Davis and prison abolitionist Cassandra Shaylor provides an example of the value of a multifaceted human rights approach to violence against women in prison. They note that despite increased attention to violence against women as a violation of human rights, "the violence linked to women's prisons remains obscured by the social invisibility of the prison."[42] They apply a contextualized and expansive human rights-based approach to gendered violence in prisons, noting that it "takes the form of medical neglect, sexual abuse, lack of reproductive control, loss of parental rights, the denial of legal rights and remedies, the devastating effects of isolation, and, of course, arbitrary discipline."[43] Focusing solely on the last of these, arbitrary discipline, obscures the many ways that women's experiences in prison are informed by gender hierarchy. Instead, as Davis and Shaylor argue, incidents of violence against women in prison must be seen on a spectrum that runs from prisons to the battering relationships between intimate partners.[44]

The power of their analysis extends beyond the circumstances of women who are incarcerated and can help to elucidate the relationship between gender violence more broadly and the abuse of women in prisons. For example, women who are incarcerated are disproportionately more likely to have been victims of gender violence prior to their incarceration.[45] A 2011 study found that the rate of past physical or sexual abuse among the female prison population was over 90 percent.[46] This observation, although important, is often underanalyzed. As Davis and Shaylor note, the statistic itself implies that violence perpetrated by nonstate actors might have been a contributing factor, or even the determinative cause of the behavior that resulted in incarceration. This assumption, however, obscures the degree to which the state is often directly responsible for the root cause of women's incarceration. Indeed, research indicates that reforms in domestic violence policy, including mandatory arrest laws, have increased the likelihood that survivors of abuse will be drawn into the criminal legal system.[47]

Analyzed from the standpoint of international human rights law, violence suffered by women in prison is clearly a violation of state obligations under the ICCPR. A *feminist* human rights lens on this issue offers a broader conception of the scope of the violence, revealing the gendered nature of much of that violence. It also entails a much wider search for and theorizing of state responsibility.

B. How Private Power Leaves Women Vulnerable

In the context of domestic violence, a pair of decisions based on the same set of facts offers a powerful illustration of the difference a feminist international human rights approach can make. The case of Jessica Lenahan (formerly Gonzales), a survivor of domestic violence, was adjudicated first in the U.S. federal court system[48] and then decided by the InterAmerican Commission on Human Rights.[49] The facts of the case, while tragic, are not unique. Lenahan, the mother of three young girls, had separated from her abusive husband and obtained a permanent restraining order.[50] Coupled with the mandatory arrest law, the restraining order included language that constrained the discretion of the police in handling domestic violence cases.[51] Although the order limited Gonzales's midweek contact with his daughters to one dinner visit prearranged by the parties, he abducted the three girls and their friend from in front of Lenahan's home.[52] Despite her multiple calls to the police and requests that they enforce the order, the police declined to take action. Approximately ten hours after Lenahan's first call to the police, the father drove to the police station, opened fire, and was killed when officers returned fire.[53] The bodies of the three daughters, who had apparently been shot at point-blank range, were found in the trunk of his car.[54]

As is well-known to students of U.S. constitutional law, the Supreme Court eventually heard arguments in Lenahan's case against the Castle Rock Police Department. The Court rejected her due process claim, holding that, notwithstanding the clear language of the restraining order and Colorado's mandatory arrest policy, Lenahan had no entitlement to the protection implied by these provisions and thus had not been deprived of any constitutional cognizable property interest without due process of law.[55] Essentially, the indifference of the police to private violence might have tragic consequences, but under U.S. law, the state has no constitutional obligation to protect its citizens even in the face of an apparent commitment to do so. The Court's majority opinion, written by Justice Scalia, focused not on the question of whether Lenahan had a right to be protected from her abuser but whether, under state law, she had a property right to the protection of the police.[56] Only if this were the case would that right then trigger the further protection of the due process clause. The Court did not address the question of whether the state had a broader obligation to exercise reasonable care in protecting its citizens from acts of violence that were both illegal and foreseeable. Instead, Justice Scalia observed obliquely, "The benefit that a third party may receive from having someone else arrested for a crime generally does not trigger protections under the Due Process Clause."[57] Of course, a "benefit," as Justice Scalia refers to the protection Lenahan sought, is not something to which one is normally entitled but rather a matter of state largesse.

In stark contrast to the Supreme Court's reasoning, the InterAmerican Commission found in favor of Lenahan based on the state's failure to "act with due diligence to protect [her and her daughters] from domestic violence, which violated the state's obligation not to discriminate and to provide equal protection before the law."[58] Beyond this duty of care, the Commission noted that a state's duty "to address violence against women also involves measures to prevent and respond to the discrimination that perpetuates this problem."[59] States must not only react to protect women within existing structures of gender hierarchy but must "adopt the required measures to modify the social and cultural patterns of conduct of men and women and to eliminate prejudices, customary practices and other practices based on the idea of the inferiority or superiority of either of the sexes, and on stereotyped roles for men and women."[60]

Although the language taken from CEDAW is rooted in a somewhat outdated conception of comparative equality, the larger idea that the Commission embraces is premised on a state obligation to dismantle gender hierarchy proactively. Rather than answer differently the narrow question posed by the U.S. Supreme Court, whether the state's actions had given rise to a protectable property right on the part of Lenahan, the Commission identified a much broader responsibility for the state not only to respond to the threat of gender violence but to work affirmatively to dismantle the patriarchal structure that enables it.

C. How State Structures Leave Women Vulnerable: Positive Rights/Caregiving and the State

In the case of Jessica Lenahan, the Inter-American Commission invoked the state's obligation to address women's structural inequality as a contributing factor to gender violence. The case offers several examples: the normalizing and downplaying of the perpetrator's aggression toward Lenahan and her daughters over time; the dismissive attitude of the police toward Lenahan when she called repeatedly to express her concern; and the assumption that, despite his history of violence, Gonzales was still entitled, as a father, to unsupervised visitation with his young daughters. Unstated norms about masculinity, femininity, and the nature of the family all contributed to render Jessica Lenahan and her daughters more vulnerable.

Broadening the lens on the relationship between structural inequality and gender violence brings into focus examples of not just the state-tolerated violence perpetrated by Gonzales but of state-enabled violence as well. For example, a feminist human rights framework can offer insights into the increase in women's economic and physical vulnerability during the global COVID-19 pandemic.[61] During the pandemic, rates of unemployment and poverty increased across the board but especially for women.[62] This impact was particularly significant for women workers who were already marginalized, including women of color and immigrant women.[63] At the same time, early evidence indicates that gender-motivated violence also increased during the course of the pandemic, especially domestic violence.[64] The reasons for these patterns are complex and not yet altogether clear; however, experts suggest that economic and social isolation coupled with the dramatic increase in women's caregiving responsibilities made women even more vulnerable to abuse.[65] The pandemic resulted in job losses that often reduced the numbers of earners and thus increased financial interdependence within families, and, at the same time, quarantine restrictions reduced access to alternative housing such as shelters.[66] There was literally nowhere to flee, and the bonds of family obligation were even stronger than before.

A feminist human rights approach is especially useful because it foregrounds state responsibility for women's preexisting vulnerability. Focusing on structural inequality—social and economic rights in human rights terminology—reveals that public policy choices regulating how care is provided and by whom have a profound impact on gender hierarchy. A recent study by Brookings found that, before COVID-19, nearly 20 percent of all working women relied on child care outside the home (schools or commercial centers) to care for children while they worked.[67] The closing of schools and daycare centers shifted, almost overnight, the responsibility of providing care to the family and the site of that care to the home. It is therefore not surprising that four times as many women as men had dropped out of the labor force by September 2020.[68]

For low-wage working women, the pandemic further destabilized their already fragile economic circumstances. In 2018, nearly half of all working women were working in such jobs, with a median wage only about $10 per hour.[69] Rather than supplementing the earnings of another family member, many of these women were supporting their families on their low wages, with more than half of working women working full-time throughout the year.[70] Moreover, more than 40 percent of working women live in households defined as "working poor."[71] These women were among the most likely to become unemployed as a result of the crisis and, if they kept their jobs, were among the least likely to be able to shift to at-home work.[72]

Of course, the pandemic did not create the caregiving crisis. Rather, it exacerbated it and expanded its reach to middle-class families who, in the past, were better able to purchase caregiving in the marketplace. The destruction of the already thin and fraying social safety net meant that families, and primarily women, had to immediately and directly provide an enormous amount of caregiving. From a human rights standpoint, it perfectly illustrates the argument that international feminists have been making for a very long time: gender equality and the enjoyment of full and equal citizenship depends on the realization of economic, social, and cultural rights. Issues such as free or subsidized child care, after-school programs and reforming the school calendar, quality eldercare, raising the minimum wage, and universal healthcare are all profoundly impactful along gender lines. The policy choices of a state that are reflected in the strength or weakness of its social safety net are directly determinant of women's economic status and therefore their vulnerability to violence. The inadequate social safety net in the United States, in other words, reflects an affirmative policy choice that directly and predictably leads to higher levels of gender violence.

D. Thinking About the State

Finally, a further development in feminist theory on the international level worth noting here is the critique of the turn to state power inherent in many of the legal reforms described above. International human rights law importantly pierces state sovereignty and regulates the relationship between the state and its citizens. States are no longer regarded as reliable guardians of the well-being of their own citizens. As anthropologist and human rights scholar Sally Engle Merry has observed, though much of human rights law imposes limitations on the state, "social and economic rights, such as the right to development or the right to adequate housing, require state action as does the provision of many civil and political rights. . . . Thus, human rights activism ends up demanding more state regulation and services."[73] Feminists have pressed for an expansion of state obligations not only to provide for the needs of its citizens but also, in the case of antidiscrimination principles and especially gender violence, to intervene and regulate the relationship among citizens.

As feminists have begun to argue, this turn to the state can be problematic on various levels. First, it depends upon a particular conception of the modern state, one that is stable, characterized by a professional bureaucracy, and adequately resourced. To the extent that states do not meet this description, for example because their economies are underdeveloped, the reliance of human rights law on the state to secure rights to education, housing, and healthcare will be more impactful in some regions than others, and may direct international attention to the failures of poor states rather than the obligations of wealthy ones.

Second, the turn to the state enlarges state power in a way that is likely to have unintended consequences. This is especially true when feminists rely on the criminal legal system, whether domestic or international, as the key source of violence prevention. For example, as the foregoing analysis of women in prison shows, many women are incarcerated as a direct result of their interaction with the criminal legal system as victims rather than perpetrators of violence. In addition to making women themselves directly vulnerable to police, policies that rely on criminalization may deter women from accessing them. As feminist legal scholar Julie Goldscheid notes, "Many survivors who live in communities subject to mass incarceration will not seek out additional criminal justice interventions."[74] Finally, law enforcement itself exhibits gender bias and may not be regarded by women as working in their interests, as was the case for Jessica Lenahan. In humanitarian law, feminists' successful campaign to include sexual violence in conflict has also been the subject of feminist reexamination. For example, Karen Engle, a legal scholar who writes on feminism, international law, and human rights, has recently argued that prioritizing this category of harm has diverted resources from other issues such as the feminist peace movement and the impact of globalization on women in developing economies.[75]

Though not susceptible to easy resolution, these ongoing debates illustrate the way that international law, because it operates at the supranational level and across all states, necessarily foregrounds the issue of the role of the state in a way that can be useful for feminists thinking about law reform on the domestic level. Rather than focusing on a particular problem to which law may be one solution, feminist legal theorists and reformers might usefully think about the broader implications of what they should expect the state to do and the unintended consequences of enlarging state power to accomplish feminist ends.

III. Conclusion

The development of feminist theory in the context of international human rights has benefited from the work that feminists everywhere have done domestically, carefully researching and reflecting on the ways that gender hierarchy is created and maintained. Translating those insights to the international level necessarily entails the sometimes-perilous work of theorizing cross-culturally to fashion principles that can address challenges with almost infinite local variations. Yet, despite its difficulty, this work can function as a lens through which feminist theorists and activists can view their local context in a new way, creating opportunities not only for collaboration but for transformation.

Notes

1. An early proponent of this view was Eleanor Roosevelt, who worked to include in the Universal Declaration of Human Rights protection of those rights "without distinction of any kind," including "sex." G.A. Res. 217 (III) A, Universal Declaration of Human Rights, at art. 2 (Dec. 10, 1948). For an overview of Roosevelt's work, see Allida M. Black, *Eleanor Roosevelt and the Universal Declaration of Human Rights*, 22 OAH Mag. Hist. 34–37 (2008).
2. For a discussion of liberal feminist engagement with international human rights, see Karen Engle, *International Human Rights and Feminism: When Discourses Meet*, 13 Mich. J. Int'l L. 517 (1992). For an early and important example of a critique of international law from outside the liberal paradigm, see Hilary Charlesworth, Christine Chinkin & Shelley Wright, *Feminist Approaches to International Law*, 85 Am. J. Int'l L. 613 (1991).

3. An enormously influential example of the critical scholarship that emerged is Chandra Talpade Mohanty, Ann Russo & Lourdes Torres, Third World Women and the Politics of Feminism (1991), and especially Chandra Mohanty, *Under Western Eyes: Feminist Scholarship and Colonial Discourses*, 30 Feminist Rev. 61 (1988).
4. *See* Louis Henkin, *Rights: American and Human*, 79 Colum. L. Rev. 405, 409–10 (1979) (locating the foundation of international human rights law in protection of an individual's "natural rights" from the state). *See, e.g.*, 45 Am. Jur. 2d International Law §44 (2006) (noting the responsibility of states under international law); Riane Eisler, *Human Rights: Toward an Integrated Theory for Action*, 9 Hum. Rts. Q. 287 (1987) (discussing the implications of the emphasis in international law on state responsibility).
5. *See, e.g.*, G.A. Res. 2200 (XXI) A, International Covenant on Civil and Political Rights, at art. 6, sec. 1 (Dec. 16, 1966) (right to life); G.A. Res. 2200 (XXI) A, International Covenant on Civil and Political Rights, at Art. 18 (Dec. 16, 1966) (freedom of religion); G.A. Res. 2200 (XXI) A, International Covenant on Civil and Political Rights, at Art. 19, Sec. 1 (Dec. 16, 1966) (freedom of thought).
6. *See, e.g.*, International Covenant on Economic, Social and Cultural Rights, Dec. 16, 1966, 993 U.N.T.S. 3, at Art. 11, Sec. 1 (housing); Art. 12, Sec. 2 (medical care); Art. 13, Sec. 1 (education).
7. Universal Declaration of Human Rights, *supra* note 1.
8. Convention on the Political Rights of Women, Dec. 20, 1952, A/RES/640 (VII).
9. For a more comprehensive overview of this historical evolution, see Laura Parisi, *Feminist Perspectives on Human Rights*, *in* Oxford Research Encyclopedia of International Studies 2 (2010), http://internationalstudies.oxfordre.com/view/10.1093/acrefore/978019 0846626.001.0001/acrefore-9780190846626-e-48 (last visited June 28, 2021).
10. Hilary Charlesworth, *Human Rights as Men's Rights*, *in* Women's Rights, Human Rights: International Feminist Perspectives 103, 103 (Julie Peters & Andrea Wolper eds., 1995).
11. Elisabeth Friedman, *Bringing Women to International Human Rights*, 18 Peace Rev. 479, 480–81 (2006).
12. Charlesworth, *Human Rights as Men's Rights*, *supra* note 10, at 103.
13. Christine Chinkin, Violence Against Women: The International Legal Response, 3 Gender & Dev. 23 (1995).
14. Kelly D. Askin, Prosecuting Wartime Rape and Other Gender-Related Crimes Under International Law: Extraordinary Advances, Enduring Obstacles, 21 Berkeley J. Int'l L. 288, 395 (2003) (reviewing examples in humanitarian law of silence on violence against women and gender-motivated violence).
15. *See, e.g.*, Barbara Bedont & Katherine Hall-Martinez, *Ending Impunity for Gender Crimes Under the International Criminal Court Implementing the International Criminal Court*, 6 Brown J. World Aff. 65 (1999) (discussing the process of including gender specific crimes within the jurisdiction of the International Criminal Court).
16. *See id.* at 70–71. (discussing this transition).
17. *See, e.g*, Muna Ndulo, *The United Nations Responses to the Sexual Abuse and Exploitation of Women and Girls by Peacekeepers During Peacekeeping Missions*, 27 Berkeley J. Int'l Law 127 (2009) (examining the problem of sexual abuse and exploitation in peacekeeping operations).

18. See, e.g., Akila Radhakrishnan, Elena Sarver & Grant Shubin, *Protecting Safe Abortion in Humanitarian Settings: Overcoming Legal and Policy Barriers*, 25 REPRO. HEALTH MATTERS 40 (2017) (arguing that "properly construed, abortion services fall within the purview of the universal and non-derogable protections granted under international humanitarian and human rights law").
19. Donna Sullivan, *The Public/Private Distinction in International Human Rights Law*, in WOMEN'S RIGHTS, HUMAN RIGHTS: INTERNATIONAL FEMINIST PERSPECTIVES 126, 127 (Julie Peters & Andrea Wolper eds., 1995).
20. *See* Chinkin, *Violence Against Women*, *supra* note 13, at 24.
21. Charlotte Bunch, *Women's Rights as Human Rights: Toward a Re-Vision of Human Rights*, 12 HUM. RTS. Q. 486 (1990) (explaining how the structure of the public/private divide in human rights law relieves states of responsibility for private violence).
22. *See* Rhonda Copelon, *Intimate Terror: Understanding Domestic Violence as Torture*, in HUMAN RIGHTS OF WOMEN: NATIONAL AND INTERNATIONAL PERSPECTIVES 116 (Rebecca Cook ed., 1994) (arguing that domestic violence should be treated as torture under international human rights law).
23. *See* Frances E. Olsen, *The Family and the Market: A Study of Ideology and Legal Reform*, 96 HARV. L. REV. 1497, 1524 (1983) (noting that "once the state undertakes to define the marriage relation, it is impossible for the state to refuse to engage in some enforcement of the individual will of the parties"); Frances E. Olsen, *The Myth of State Intervention in the Family*, 18 U. MICH. J.L. REFORM 835, 837 (1985) (arguing that "because the state is deeply implicated in the formation and functioning of families, it is nonsense to talk about whether the state does or does not intervene in the family").
24. CATHARINE A. MACKINNON, ARE WOMEN HUMAN? AND OTHER INTERNATIONAL DIALOGUES 23 (First Harvard Univ. Press Paperback ed. 2007).
25. *Id.*
26. *See* Bunch, *Women's Rights as Human Rights*, *supra* note 21, at 491.
27. *See, e.g.*, Helen Hodgson & Kerrie Sadiq, *Gender Equality and a Rights-Based Approach to Tax Reform*, in TAX, SOCIAL POLICY AND GENDER 99 (Miranda Stewart ed., 2017) (applying a human rights framework to tax reform to remedy gender inequality); Anne L. Alstott, *Tax Policy and Feminism: Competing Goals and Institutional Choices*, 96 COLUM. L. REV. 2001 (1996) (analyzing the gender specific implications of tax policy in the U.S.); Kaori Izumi, *Gender-Based Violence and Property Grabbing in Africa: A Denial of Women's Liberty and Security*, 15 GENDER & DEV. 11 (2007) (exploring ways that property and housing insecurity contribute to violence against women in Africa); Poonam Pradhan Saxena, *Matrimonial Laws and Gender Justice*, 45 J. INDIAN L. INST. 335 (2003) (examining the ways that customary marriage norms, including those governing property rights, undermine women's power in marriage in India).
28. Laura Parisi, *Feminist Praxis and Women's Human Rights*, 1 J. HUM. RTS. 571 (2002).
29. *See* Parisi, *Feminist Perspectives*, *supra* note 9, at 12–13 (noting that "implicit in this design is the assumption of an economically prosperous, democratic state or, at the very least, an effectual one that subscribes to a neoliberal economic agenda").
30. Universal Declaration of Human Rights, *supra* note 1, Art. 2.
31. *Id.*, Art. 16 (noting that "the family is the natural and fundamental group unit of society and is entitled to protection by society and the State").

32. International Covenant on Economic, Social and Cultural Rights, Dec. 16, 1966, 993 U.N.T.S. 3, at Art. 2, Sec. 2 ("without discrimination of any kind"); G.A. Res. 2200 (XXI) A, International Covenant on Civil and Political Rights (Dec. 16, 1966).
33. Convention on the Elimination of All Forms of Discrimination Against Women, Dec. 18, 1979, A/RES/34/180 Art. 2, Sec. c (obliging states to "establish legal protection of the rights of women on an equal basis with men").
34. Vienna Declaration and Programme of Action, G.A. Res. 48/121, ¶ 18 (Jun. 25, 1993).
35. The U.N. Declaration on the Elimination of Violence Against Women, G.A. Res. 48/104 (Dec. 20, 1993).
36. Id.
37. Id.
38. Id., Art. 4(b).
39. Id., Art. 4(c).
40. Id., Art. 4(j).
41. Important works of this vast scholarship include Kelly Lytle Hernández, Khalil Gibran Muhammad & Heather Ann Thompson, *Introduction: Constructing the Carceral State*, 102 J. AM. HIST. 18 (2015); MICHELLE ALEXANDER, THE NEW JIM CROW: MASS INCARCERATION IN THE AGE OF COLORBLINDNESS (10th anniversary ed. 2020); JAMES FORMAN, LOCKING UP OUR OWN: CRIME AND PUNISHMENT IN BLACK AMERICA (1st ed. 2017); KHALIL GIBRAN MUHAMMAD, THE CONDEMNATION OF BLACKNESS: RACE, CRIME, AND THE MAKING OF MODERN URBAN AMERICA (2010).
42. Angela Y. Davis & Cassandra Shaylor, *Race, Gender, and the Prison Industrial Complex: California and Beyond*, 2 MERIDIANS 1 (2001).
43. Id. at 15.
44. Id. at 7.
45. ASHA DUMONTHIER, CHANDRA CHILDERS & JESSICA MILLI, THE STATUS OF BLACK WOMEN IN THE UNITED STATES 118 (Institute for Women's Policy Research, 2017).
46. Id. (citing 2011 study published by the American Civil Liberties Union).
47. DUMONTHIER ET AL., STATUS OF BLACK WOMEN, *supra* note 45; MALIKA SAADA SAAR ET AL., THE SEXUAL ABUSE TO PRISON PIPELINE: THE GIRLS' STORY 48.
48. Castle Rock v. Gonzales, 545 U.S. 748 (2005).
49. Jessica Lenahan (Gonzales) v. U.S.A., Case 12.626, Inter-Am. Comm'n H.R., Report No. 80/11 (2011).
50. Castle Rock, 545 U.S. at 152.
51. Id. at 752.
52. Id. at 753.
53. Id. at 754.
54. Id.
55. Id. at 766.
56. Id. at 760.
57. Id. at 768.
58. Jessica Lenahan (Gonzales) v. U.S.A., Case 12.626, Inter-Am. Comm'n H.R., Report No. 80/11, 52-3 (2011).
59. Id. at 2.
60. Id. at 35.
61. Megan L. Evans, Margo Lindauer & Maureen E. Farrell, *A Pandemic Within a Pandemic— Intimate Partner Violence During COVID-19*, 383 N. ENGL. J. MED. 2302 (2020).

62. Nicole Bateman & Martha Ross, *Why Has COVID-19 Been Especially Harmful for Working Women?*, BROOKINGS (2020), https://www.brookings.edu/essay/why-has-covid-19-been-especially-harmful-for-working-women (last visited June 28, 2021).
63. Evans et al., *A Pandemic Within a Pandemic*, supra note 62.
64. *Id.*
65. Karen Michele Nikos-Rose, *COVID-19 Isolation Linked to Increased Domestic Violence, Researchers Suggest*, U.C. DAVIS (2021), https://www.ucdavis.edu/news/covid-19-isolation-linked-increased-domestic-violence-researchers-suggest (last visited June 28, 2021).
66. Evans et al., *A Pandemic Within a Pandemic*, supra note 62.
67. Bateman & Ross, *Why Has COVID-19 Been Especially Harmful*, supra note 63.
68. Julie Kashen et al., *How COVID-19 Sent Women's Workforce Progress Backward*, Center for American Progress, https://www.americanprogress.org/issues/women/reports/2020/10/30/492582/covid-19-sent-womens-workforce-progress-backward (last visited Jun 28, 2021).
69. Bateman & Ross, *Why Has COVID-19 Been Especially Harmful*, supra note 63.
70. *Id.*
71. *Id.*
72. Kashen et al., *How COVID-19 Sent Women's Workforce Progress Backward*, supra note 69.
73. SALLY ENGLE MERRY, HUMAN RIGHTS AND GENDER VIOLENCE: TRANSLATING INTERNATIONAL LAW INTO LOCAL JUSTICE (2006).
74. Julie Goldscheid, *Considering the Role of the State: Comment on "Criminalizing Sexual Violence Against Women in Intimate Relationships,"* 109 AJIL UNBOUND 202 (2015).
75. KAREN ENGLE, THE GRIP OF SEXUAL VIOLENCE IN CONFLICT: FEMINIST INTERVENTIONS IN INTERNATIONAL LAW (2020).

CHAPTER 28

FEMINISM'S TRANSFORMATION OF LEGAL EDUCATION AND UNFINISHED AGENDA

JAMIE R. ABRAMS

FEMINISM has powerfully influenced legal education over more than a century of critical engagement. Yet, the feminist agenda remains unfinished as it adapts to contest modern manifestations of century-old challenges. This chapter traces and evaluates the influences of feminism in legal education. It explores how feminist critiques challenged the substance of legal rules, the methods of law teaching, and the culture of legal education. Following decades of advocacy, feminist pedagogical reforms have generated new fields, new courses, new laws, new leaders, and new feminist spaces.

This chapter also examines feminism's unfinished agenda in legal education. While notable changes have endured and flourished, legal education today still looks more similar than different to law school a century ago.[1] Legal education remains largely standardized with only soft innovation and differentiation among schools.[2] The Socratic method still fosters a competitive, adversarial, and marginalizing classroom. Women faculty remain disproportionately burdened by service obligations, caregiving in the workplace and the home, and bias in hiring, promotion, and evaluation. Doctrinal areas of study and hierarchies within law school institutions continue to privilege a traditional model of legal education built by and for men.

In part, the limits of the feminist legal education revolution reflect that law schools cannot adapt and reform in isolation. They interface with powerful institutions, systems, and norms. The legal profession, law school accreditors, and regulators remain deeply influential in legal education.[3] As law schools prepare lawyers for the bar exam and the modern practice of law in a competitive, regulated market, these external and interconnected forces demand that the feminist agenda examine larger structural changes to secure lasting reforms.

I. Early Feminist Efforts: Access to Legal Education

Early liberal feminist activism focused on removing formal barriers to legal education and bar admission. The University of Iowa and Washington University in St. Louis became the first law schools to admit women in 1869, followed in 1870 by the University of Michigan.[4] While educating women lawyers was considered radical at the time, formal legal education was *itself* a new innovation. Most lawyers at the time trained through apprenticeships, but these too were unavailable to women or restricted to fields like family law.[5]

In 1896, Ellen Spencer Mussey and Emma Gillett made history by establishing the Washington College of Law (WCL) in Washington, D.C. for the purpose of educating women lawyers.[6] WCL incorporated some unique structural protections to support its women students, such as night classes and low tuition, and even allowed one student to attend under a pseudonym to protect her identity.[7] But aside from the radical move of seeking legitimacy as a women-run law school for women students, its legal education pedagogy was entirely conventional.[8] And even as a law school for "women," the radicalness of Mussey and Gillett's fledgling feminist institution was severely undercut by the exclusion of African Americans for fifty more years.[9]

Entry to law school was only one of many barriers facing women in the legal profession. When women could not vote or serve on juries, it was common for local bar associations to exclude women. These external barriers led Mussey and Gillett to establish the D.C. Women's Bar Association in 1917,[10] an important foreshadowing of the external work feminists would need to accomplish to advance women in law schools.

Despite these early institutional pioneers, many law schools resisted the admission of women well into the twentieth century. Harvard did not admit women law students until 1950 and Washington & Lee until 1972.[11] Women's law school enrollment remained statistically low for decades, at only 6.35 percent in 1972.[12]

Legal education hit a milestone in 2016 when women's enrollment exceeded men's,[13] an achievement that has now held for four years.[14] But national numbers shroud a less rosy picture, as women are disproportionately enrolled in certain (mostly lower ranked) law schools and remain well below the 50 percent mark in many others.[15]

Women of color report complex and multidimensional experiences in law school. Today, 31 percent of enrolled law students are students of color, reflecting a steady upward trajectory when examined in the aggregate.[16] These aggregate numbers obscure vast differences when examined further by gender, race, and region. Notably, enrollment of women of color vastly *exceeds* men of color.[17] Black women's enrollment doubles Black male enrollment.[18] In fact, enrollment for African American/Black students has trended downward for four consecutive years, even as the aggregate number of students of color has risen.[19] These aggregate numbers also obscure vast differences when examined by race and by region, with states such as Texas, Arizona, California, Florida, and Hawaii reporting enrollment rates closer to 45 percent, while other states remain in the 10–20 percent range.[20] Despite their statistical advantage, women of color report more negative *experiences* in law school than male peers when measured by their overall satisfaction.[21] Women of color disproportionately contemplate withdrawing from law school compared to all other categories of students, and attrition rates for students of color are indeed disproportionately higher.[22]

Law school gains have not held in the legal profession, reflecting equity concerns in advancement and retention. Women, and especially women of color, are still dramatically underrepresented in law practice, law faculties, law school administration, the judiciary, and law review authors.[23]

The number of women faculty has grown mightily over the decades. In 1977, there were 391 women law professors nationwide,[24] comprising 8.6 percent of all tenure and tenure-track faculty.[25] By the mid-1980s, this percentage had doubled to 15.9 percent.[26] Today, women comprise nearly 40 percent of law school faculty, and faculty of color comprise 16.7 percent of law school faculty,[27] reflecting strong trajectories in the aggregate. Women of color remain dramatically underrepresented and even more so in the tenure/tenure-track ranks.[28] Women of color were just 7 percent of law faculty in 2009, when such data were last released.[29]

A closer look at aggregate numbers also reveals entrenched hierarchies and segmentation. Female faculty occupy lower-status and lesser-paid jobs while more male faculty hold full professorships at more prestigious schools.[30] Women faculty are saddled with disproportionate institutional service and support, described as the school's "housework."[31] The paradox of more work for less status is even starker for women of color.[32] These uneven gains point to the unfinished business of even a liberal feminist agenda.

In addition to growth in law student and faculty representation, women have risen in the leadership ranks. In April 2018, 31 percent of American Association of Law School (AALS) member schools had women deans, 6.7 percent of whom were women of color.[33] And yet, careful observers watch these numbers warily for their long-term predictive power. Skeptics observe that the rise in women deans has notably coincided with nationwide law school budget cuts, admissions declines, and job placement challenges.[34]

Despite their historic significance, all these gains remain fraught, vulnerable, and segmented. Deep struggles remain to preserve feminist gains in access to legal education and the legal profession. The global coronavirus (COVID-19) pandemic both reminds feminists that historic gains need to be protected and reveals a norm-shattering moment in legal education to advance the feminist agenda, as explored in section "II. Developing a Feminist Pedagogy."

Although the liberal feminist agenda succeeded in getting women in the door, at the podium, and in the Dean's Suite of law schools, it did little to *integrate* women into the curriculum.[35] Ironically, after centuries of women's exclusion on the basis of presumed differences from men, once admitted, women were assumed to be the same.[36] Women endured sexism,[37] tokenism,[38] and sexual harassment.[39] Women's initial law school presence compelled them "to simply join the academic procession, not to question its direction."[40] The next challenge feminists faced was thus transforming legal education itself, following in the footsteps of feminist pedagogical reforms across other disciplines.

II. Developing a Feminist Pedagogy

Before legal education reforms, feminist educators challenged the masculinist styles that dominated in all academic disciplines and developed specialized spaces for the study of sex and gender. Women's studies courses and programs emerged in the late 1960s and 1970s as a stand-alone academic study, drawing upon feminist methods; centrally examining women's lives and experiences; questioning constructs of gender; interrogating systems of privilege and power; and exploring the intersections of gender, race, sexual orientation, class, and disability.[41] These courses, materials, and programs grew rapidly, along with newly emerging feminist journals and a feminist press.[42]

Women's studies programs and courses inseparably transformed both *what* was studied and *how* learning was structured by reconfiguring classrooms, reenvisioning assignments, and leveling power imbalances.[43] Faculty in women's studies courses sought to create spaces that were nonauthoritarian and egalitarian without any one voice dominating the conversation, fostering a spirit of cooperation instead of competition.[44]

Early women's studies programs wrestled with how to interface and integrate with the largely unaltered power structures of the larger university,[45] a challenge feminist law faculty would soon face as well.[46] These programs also struggled to give full voice to the experiences of women of color, lesbian women, and any women outside the cisgender heterosexual white able-bodied women who typically founded and directed these programs.[47]

Over time, specialized women's courses expanded to the humanities and the social sciences, where women faculty were present in strong numbers, then later to the arts, sciences, and professional fields.[48] These courses sought to address the "virtual absence" and invisibility of women from substantive fields, often relegating women to an appendix or a footnote, positioned as an exception to the field as a whole.[49]

Emerging courses and specialized content shaping *what* was taught across disciplines continued to transform *how* material was taught, challenging teaching styles that privileged and marginalized.[50] Across disciplines, feminist pedagogy came to demand that multiple perspectives be considered, that all voices be valued, that experiences be contextualized, and that fields be reoriented from the notion of one absolute, objective truth.[51] Feminist pedagogy also directed learning toward achieving transformative changes in society through action.[52]

Notably, these principles of feminist pedagogy are not about the narrow question of advancing *women*. Rather, they stand to improve the experiences of *all* learners and communities. These feminist pedagogical influences eventually took root in legal education.

III. Feminist Methods Transform Legal Education

As women took their place in the legal academy as students, faculty, and administrators, feminists sought greater transformations. Feminists' victories in institutional access were the starting point, not the finish line.[53] Feminists began creating communities and spaces to convene and to collaborate.[54] They challenged core doctrinal premises, problematic legal rules, and ineffective teaching methods through their teaching, scholarship, and advocacy.

A. Creating Feminist Spaces and Building Feminist Communities

Feminist action begins with building community and experience-sharing in the consciousness-raising tradition. Women's early presence in law schools presented "a vexing combination of presence and absence."[55] Women experienced "exaggerated attention combined with near-total invisibility, seldom seen but always center stage."[56] These realities were and remain even starker for women of color, who report feeling both hypervisible and invisible.[57] Accordingly, community-building was and remains a critical component of feminist legal education pedagogy.

In the 1960s, feminist law faculty began creating spaces for conversation, community-building, scholarship, and advocacy. These spaces were more inclusive than the mainstream and nonhierarchal, thus bringing feminism to both "method and practice."[58] This mobilization also brought faculty out of the law school and into the community in scholarly discourse and activism. In the late 1960s, for example, a group of New York scholars organized a Women and the Law Conference to discuss topics such as family law, criminal law, discrimination law, reproductive rights, and constitutional law.[59] Law reform efforts targeted substantive areas like sexual harassment, rape, domestic violence, employment, the family, and reproduction. These public feminist reforms inevitably transformed learning inside the classroom. For example, reforms to rape laws led professors to reenvision the doctrine's place in the law school curriculum.[60]

Pioneering scholars began to publish casebooks on Women and the Law and Sex-Based Discrimination.[61] These materials, born out of scholarly faculty communities, created opportunity for specialized study and community-building at the student level. Over time, these specialized survey classes led to courses like Feminist Jurisprudence, bringing a feminist methodological lens.[62]

As powerful feminist spaces and academic materials emerged to deepen discourse within select pockets and courses, questions of the scalability and transferability of feminist methods emerged. Were there risks that specialized courses and programs would marginalize women's issues in ways that reinforced the myth of law's neutrality throughout *the rest* of the law school curriculum?[63] While urging these courses to continue, Catharine MacKinnon and other contemporaries boldly called for the "mainstreaming" of gender issues across legal education.[64] Feminism was not something to be done in fragments in select spots of courses or books but, rather, required a wholesale effort to rethink the curriculum holistically.[65]

Courses on women and the law, sex discrimination, and feminist jurisprudence have withstood the test of time as mainstays in the curriculum, even as the feminist agenda marched on to challenge deeper presumptions and norms dominating legal education.

B. Challenging the Foundational Assumptions Underlying Law and Pedagogy

Feminists pushed for a transformation of legal education and its threshold assumptions, approaches, and methodologies. They contested the "add woman and stir"[66] model and refused to limit feminism to a "narrow, one-dimensional, one-note, geographically limited, thin set of problems, questions, and people."[67] Instead, they marched forward challenging the unstated assumptions that shaped legal education and the law itself.

Feminists challenged the notion that long-standing legal rules were "given, static, and almost immutable."[68] For example, they challenged the premise of a gender-neutral person positioned at the law's center "for whose protection and honour the laws are written, and for whom the system is designed."[69] This perceived neutrality, feminists argued, rendered gender invisible, while exalting a system designed around privileged male norms.[70]

Feminists challenged the unidirectional process of professors transmitting knowledge through objective discussion.[71] They challenged the method of teaching with appellate cases because it obscured factual context and lawyering strategy.[72]

Feminists aligned with other critical communities in challenging legal education's structural and pedagogical premises. Critical legal studies converged with feminist pedagogies in seeking to dismantle law school hierarchies.[73] Critical race theorists and critical race feminists particularly revealed the invisibility of race and gender in law. Beginning from an unstated white male perspective positioned whiteness and masculinity as the norm, ushering in a "race-based system of rights and privileges."[74]

Feminist reforms would later coalesce with those urged by the LatCrit community and queer theorists, respectively advocating for the interests of the Latinx community and the LGBTQI (lesbian, gay, bisexual, transgender, queer, and intersex) community. These communities had their own pains, oppressions, and marginalizations that they saw magnified and exacerbated in legal education pedagogy and in the legal profession. Together, these critical perspectives aligned in demanding law and pedagogy reforms exposing and upending unstated hierarchies within the law and legal institutions.

C. Identifying Law's Gendered Harms and Exposing False Dichotomies

Feminists did not just contest the underlying doctrinal norms of law and legal study. They also exposed the *harms* that these norms caused.[75] The false dichotomies of rational–irrational, public–private, intellectual–emotional did not just *exist*, they reinforced gendered stereotypes and marginalized women.[76]

Dominance feminists particularly critiqued the neutrality and objectivity of the law, and the public–private dichotomy embedded in it, as the *source* of women's subordination. The dominance feminist lens found the objective, rational neutrality of the law "flawed" and distortive.[77] Male patriarchal norms, masquerading as normal and neutral, harm and discredit women.[78] For example, purportedly neutral standards like the "reasonable person" in tort law are framed around male wage-earning power, which compromises women's claims and depresses their damage recoveries.[79]

These harms are even more searing for women of color. Law school's "perspectiveless" approach marginalizes students of color. It discounts any particular perspective by pretending to hold "no specific cultural, political, or class characteristics."[80] This framing forces students of color to abandon their identities and instead adopt a perspective that is actually infused with a white, middle-class worldview. Students of color are left to provide marginalized "testimony" to challenge the dominant norms.[81] Students of color are then perceived as presenting "biased, self-interested, or subjective opinions" when they voice their experiences, creating "twin problems of objectification and subjectification."[82] Mari Matsuda describes this vacillating between a student's lived consciousness and "the white consciousness required for survival in elite educational institutions" as "multiple consciousness."[83]

D. Questioning the Socratic Method

Feminist reforms particularly challenged the Socratic method's positioning as the dominant paradigm for delivering legal education. The Socratic method is an inquisitive method of teaching whereby faculty lead students through rules and cases using a fluid question-and-answer dialogue to develop reasoning and argumentation skills. Feminist faculty excoriated the Socratic method for failing in both teaching and learning. It sits at a "level of abstraction" that is "both too theoretical and not theoretical enough" in that it fails to examine the foundations of legal rules and fails to teach students how to use the rules.[84]

Gendered double standards pervade the Socratic method. The iconic Professor Kingsfield personifies the archetype of the Socratic professor. Kingsfield domineered the Socratic classroom to great reverence, even as his students arrived in fear and left confused and demoralized.[85] Yet, women teachers do not easily fit within this model. Students leaving women faculty's classrooms confused and demeaned would more likely leave the faculty perceived as incompetent than deeply respected.[86] Fitting into this Socratic model is even more complicated for women faculty of color.[87]

Traditional performances of the Socratic method embed a teacher–student hierarchy and the hierarchy *is the point*.[88] Catherine MacKinnon elaborated:

> At its worst, the process embodies all the voices of inequality. Students are motivated by fear; infantilized, they learn the opposite of respect for their own thoughts ... law students are schooled in hierarchy, taught deference to power, and rewarded for mastering codes for belonging and fitting in. By initiation, they learn to inflict the same when their chance comes.[89]

Beginning in the 1980s and continuing into the 1990s, feminist scholars documented disparities in women's Socratic class participation. These studies revealed gendered discrepancies in class participation.[90] Male students were more willing to "take up space" while women remained silent in ways that compromised academic and professional success.[91] The 1994 publication of *Becoming Gentlemen: Women's Experiences at One Ivy League Law School* highlighted how similarly qualified male and female candidates diverge as they move from their first year of law school to their third.[92] Coauthored by Professor Lani Guinier, who would go on to become the first woman of color granted tenure at Harvard Law School,[93] the study revealed that women students received relatively lower grades, class ranks, and honors than their male peers.[94]

Although prior studies had documented women's reduced classroom participation,[95] *Becoming Gentlemen* exposed women's alienation resulting from the Socratic method, even as this pedagogy dominated (then and now) across all first-year instruction and much of the upper-level curriculum. Women described their first year as "a radical, painful, or repressive experience" with psychological and employment consequences.[96] The Socratic method represented legal education more broadly in which there were "few winners and many losers."[97] It turned differences among students into disadvantage.[98]

Becoming Gentlemen issued law schools a powerful call to action to change their structure and content. This call to action shifted the focus from adapting women *to* legal education toward examining law school's "institutional design."[99] The authors concluded that institutions have a "professional and educational obligation" to meet the needs of all its students and to "minimize the gendered differences in academic performance, whatever the source."[100] These Socratic method critiques brought the experiences of women and students of color to the forefront, revealing the importance of systemic legal education reforms. Yet, the Socratic method still endures in many large, doctrinal classes, a point explored more at the closing of this chapter.

E. Incorporating Women's Values, Experiences, and Perspectives

In reframing *how* legal education was delivered, feminists sought to inject women's perspectives and experiences into law study. Difference strands of feminist theory particularly explored how values traditionally associated with women were marginalized in legal education and needed to be pedagogically centered.[101] This marked a transformative pedagogical move away from trying to assimilate women *into* law schools toward aligning the culture of legal education *with* women's learning styles.

Historically, law school included little emphasis on practical lawyering skills, such as problem-solving and client counseling. This left legal education emphasizing competition and individualism.[102] Law schools rewarded students "making any argument for any point of view without cultivating empathy or connection to either side of the case," yielding a "kind of zeal that blinds rather than enlightens."[103] This approach left a narrow bandwidth for dialogue and suppressed critiques of the gender and race implications of rules and arguments.[104] Feminists sought less abstract exchanges centered on doctrinal analysis and more feedback, discussion, and simulations grounded in client-centered lawyering.[105]

Difference feminism celebrates a relational ethic of care that values collaboration, community, and cooperation as critical values in law beyond abstraction and competition.[106] Carol Gilligan notably described how women's approaches to justice embodied an ethic of care framed around context and relationships.[107] Designing law schools around women's learning styles would more centrally position "care, context, cooperation, and relationships" within law study and lawyering.[108] Feminists advocated that *all* law classes, not just gender-focused ones, could be more participatory, inclusive, and nonhierarchal. All classrooms might use a model of shared leadership valuing "personal experience as a valid source of knowledge."[109]

Valuing these relational skills might, in turn, improve the quality, depth, and breadth of *lawyering*.[110] Cultural approaches offered promise to transform the legal profession by rethinking long-standing formally gender-neutral obstacles to women's success, such as billable hour requirements and the absence of family leave.[111] Core values in the legal system, such as protecting individual rights and privacy over relationships and community, sparked cultural feminists' call for a turn toward relational values in law too.[112]

But not all feminists signed on to a cultural feminist agenda. An important critique of relational approaches is that there is no one singular approach or learning style that is inclusive of all women. Indeed, to suggest otherwise is to ignore rich variations across diverse cultures, classes, races, ages, and sexual identities.[113] Embracing a "women's perspective" risks engaging in a type of essentialism that erases differences, privileges dominant voices, and reinforces exclusionary hierarchies, repeating the exact same mistakes feminists sought to overcome.[114] Still, feminists could broadly agree on the need to expand the repertoire of skills and values traditionally valued in legal education. Feminists aligned in moving beyond a model designed by and for men, even as they differed in what model best responded to the critiques.

IV. THE FEMINIST-INSPIRED *EVOLUTION* OF LEGAL EDUCATION AND A *REVOLUTION* DEFERRED

For decades, feminists have developed a bold pedagogical vision for legal education. Feminist reforms have achieved many lasting changes. Feminists broke barriers gaining access to legal education and rising to the highest ranks of the profession. Specialized courses and materials have trained countless lawyers in feminist theory and method. Feminists have also cultivated and retained cherished convening spaces to discuss structural and substantive challenges in legal education and the law. A strong evolutionary drumbeat of feminist progress has beat for decades louder and rapider at times, quieter and slower at others.

Yet, it would surely go too far to conclude that the feminist agenda has *revolutionized* legal education or that the agenda is complete.[115] Rather, the core power systems, substance, and method of delivering legal education remain remarkably unchanged. The Socratic method still dominates legal education. Hierarchical, adversarial, and competitive classrooms still shape most required first-year and upper-level courses. Women faculty remain segmented in particular areas of law, including clinical teaching, legal writing, and family law, often with lesser pay, status, and security. At nearly every step of the academic career trajectory, persistent barriers still impede women's success. From the highly competitive faculty hiring process to bias embedded in student course evaluations to peer faculty hostility to vague and secretive tenure processes to disproportionate service and emotional labor, the feminist agenda to create and cultivate inclusive law schools remains unfinished.[116]

From a cultural standpoint, strong headwinds still afflict the careers of women faculty, students, and staff. A demoralizing and harmful "presumption of incompetence" painfully governs the careers of women and faculty of color, reminding these communities that they have yet to attain a sense of meaningful belonging in spaces they have occupied for over half a century. Many women and faculty of color describe suffering from an imposter syndrome, a "sense of fraudulence," and a lack of belonging.[117] Women continue to shoulder disproportionate amounts of service and emotional labor in the academe.[118] They are also still saddled with the "second shift," performing disproportionate caregiving and household management at home.[119] COVID-19 powerfully reminded legal educators how tenuous and fraught even liberal feminist progress is as child care providers and K–12 schools closed and professional work shifted to the home, placing unprecedented strain on professional caregiving.[120]

The legal profession is likewise still plagued with bias, discrimination, and harassment even as these issues morph and manifest in new ways. New terms have emerged to describe these harms such as microaggressions, mansplaining, hepeating, sidelining, whitesplaining, tokenism, and more. In 2016, the American Bar Association (ABA) added a new subsection to its rules on professional responsibility prohibiting attorneys from engaging in conduct that "the lawyer knows or reasonably should know is harassment or discrimination on the basis of race, sex, religion, national origin, ethnicity, disability, age, sexual orientation, gender identity, marital status or socioeconomic status in conduct related to the practice of law."[121] This reflects a recognition that such bias persists, an important normative commitment to equality, and a meaningful path to enforce these norms.

While the public displays of discrimination in legal education pedagogy (e.g., "Ladies Day") have ceased, harassing and predatory behavior still exist in law schools, albeit in more subtle and entrenched forms that are difficult to ferret out.[122] Just as the "Shitty Men" list broke open the #MeToo movement in media, so too has a list emerged detailing sexual misconduct of faculty at universities.[123] The #MeToo movement exposed several incidents of long-standing systemic sexual harassment in legal education.[124] Festering issues of harassment, bullying, and incivility are especially stubborn and complex for women of color in law teaching.

Any honest assessment of feminist influence in legal education and the profession must also acknowledge the ongoing work needed for white women to engage fully in meaningful, lasting, and serious inclusion efforts. Feminists of color have called on white women to shed habits of "defensiveness and emotional manipulation" and to work toward "acknowledging and working through the depths of White women's complicity in the oppression narrative."[125] This is hard work that white feminists cannot afford to defer.

Feminism changed legal education in ways that are evolutionary but not revolutionary. Yet, in fairness, no reforms have revolutionized law school. The powerful winds of competition and regulatory forces push against revolutionary changes in ways that perpetuate the status quo, even when the status quo is ineffective and harmful. The change, and inertia, reflected in the ABA's most recent accreditation changes, demonstrate this.

The ABA oversees accreditation standards to improve the competence of new lawyers entering law practice. The dominant approach for law school accreditation traditionally focused on the input and output of law schools, both the resources invested and the bar passage and job placement rates.[126] A handful of iconic publications in prior decades had nudged law schools toward considerable curricular reform, but the ABA had not formally modified the correlating accreditation standards to facilitate such reform.[127]

Eventually, the ABA's Section of Legal Education and Admissions to the Bar decided to revisit its accreditation standards and spent six years reviewing proposed changes until approved in 2014.[128] These revisions purportedly reflected a "fundamental shift" in the delivery of legal education and curricular design,[129] called a "renaissance" of sorts.[130] They communicated a "quantum shift" in educational delivery, from an emphasis on teaching to an emphasis on learning, and from an emphasis on inputs to an emphasis on outcomes.[131]

These reforms were overdue in legal education, coming well after accreditation reform in other disciplines in recent decades.[132] The historical model of teaching content and testing at the end was outdated and ineffective.[133] These reforms place pressure on law schools to modernize their curriculum toward preparing students for practice.[134] Law schools now must set goals for specific learning outcomes, gather information about how well students are achieving those designated learning outcomes, and work to improve student learning toward competency.[135]

These reforms are student-centered and have the *potential* to support all learners in ways that address feminist critiques. If measured outcomes must ensure that *all* students are meeting learning objectives, then obstacles impeding the success of whole populations of students should be promptly corrected. These reforms *aspire* to more effectively integrate theory and practice, moving away from learning abstract concepts.

This goal corresponds to some of the cultural feminist critiques of the administration of legal education and it addresses the tension between difference feminism and essentialist critiques by requiring faculty to support all learners in achieving competence in the stated learning objectives.

These reforms—in concept—seem consistent with feminist critiques of *what* is taught and *how* it is taught. Ultimately though, any convergence with feminism is more haphazard than organic. The ABA's reforms were driven more by market forces than philosophy and emerged as a response to pressure from universities and the legal profession to bring legal education in line with other accreditation processes and educational programs.

In practice, the reforms have turned out to be less sweeping than observers might have predicted. The new ABA standards have been implemented around the existing architecture of the large Socratic classroom dominating the 1L curriculum and upper-level courses. Innovations and experimentation have been segmented in corners of the curriculum without contesting the status quo of the dominant pedagogy.

Bringing some consistency and standardization, ABA Standard 302 requires all schools to meet learning outcomes that establish competency in *at least* these four highly conventional areas:

(a) Knowledge and understanding of substantive and procedural law;
(b) Legal analysis and reasoning, legal research, problem-solving, and written and oral communication in the legal context;
(c) Exercise of proper professional and ethical responsibilities to clients and the legal system; and
(d) Other professional skills needed for competent and ethical participation as a member of the legal profession.[136]

All law schools share these learning outcomes. Individual schools *can* add additional innovative learning outcomes, such as diversity and inclusion, cultural competence, client counseling, or client-centered lawyering. But while the ABA standard identifies cultural competency as a *possible* additional learning outcome, it would be to differentiate, not to align with, the stated objectives of legal education.

When measuring outcomes and competencies, law schools have marched ahead with traditional teaching methods despite decades of feminist advocacy revealing that these methods have not worked as effectively for women and students of color. With its latest reforms, the ABA acknowledged candidly that the traditional legal education curriculum, "teaching students to think like a lawyer," remains centrally positioned in J.D. programs. While the standards require law schools to make changes to the curriculum if learning outcomes are not met, it remains to be seen whether law schools will proactively undertake deeper pedagogical change to achieve equitable and inclusive outcomes.

Transformative change in legal education cannot happen around the margins. It needs to happen in the structural center of the curriculum. This includes finally reenvisioning Socratic-style classes, which likely requires meaningful, enduring, and consistent training, support, and accountability for faculty to facilitate inclusive classrooms. COVID-19 notably imposed unprecedented demands on faculty to reform and adapt in ways that months earlier seemed unthinkable. Schools mobilized with trainings, infrastructure, and collaboration, strengthening teaching and assessment to support students. Faculty keenly understood that our students needed their schools and teachers to rise to the challenge and produce a product that was adaptive and responsive. Faculty harnessed a "growth-mindset" for technology, teaching techniques, and assessment methods. Likewise, we need the same moment of reflection, community, and collaboration in lasting inclusive teaching pedagogies.

V. A CALL TO ACTION

Feminists have critiqued and influenced legal education for decades. Feminism has made surges of progress, but its mission is not yet complete. New challenges emerge on the path to progress, such as modern backlashes to critical theorists[137] and COVID-19 disparities and disruptions. The global COVID-19 pandemic presents a paradoxical opportunity to catapult the feminist agenda forward. COVID-19 upended many existing norms in legal education, from how legal education is delivered to professional licensure. In the tragedy of these disruptions and vulnerabilities sits hope and opportunity. This chapter captures many reasons to celebrate the accomplishments of our feminist pioneers and champions. It also serves as a critical call to action to modern faculty, administrators, and students to carry the work forward with a vigilant purpose and determination.

NOTES

1. Lucinda Finley, *A Break in the Silence: Including Women's Issues in a Torts Course*, 1 YALE J. L. & FEMINISM 41 (1989) (concluding that "U.S. law school looks remarkably like it did in [the late 1800s]" and that "the needs and concerns of women remain largely invisible or unexplored in mainstream law school classes").
2. See, e.g., BENJAMIN H. BARTON, FIXING LAW SCHOOLS: FROM COLLAPSE TO THE TRUMP BUMP AND BEYOND 28 (2019) ("[T]he most basic DNA of current law schools, including their structure and educational program, came from Harvard in the nineteenth century.").
3. See, e.g., Katharine T. Bartlett, *Feminist Perspective on the Ideological Impact of Legal Education upon the Profession*, 72 N.C. L. REV. 1259 (1994) (suggesting that progress "cannot be made by law schools alone, without corresponding changes in the legal profession").
4. Mary L. Clark, *The Founding of the Washington College of Law: The First Law School Established by Women for Women*, 47 AM. U. L. REV. 613, n.42 (1998).

5. Virginia G. Drachman, Sisters in Law: Women Lawyers in Modern American History 152 (1998).
6. Washington College of Law, Articles of Incorporation (1898). *See generally* Clark, *supra* note 4, at 672.
7. Grace Hathaway, Fate Rides a Tortoise: A Biography of Ellen Spencer Mussey 130 (1937).
8. Jamie R. Abrams & Daniela Kraiem, *Banding Together: Reflections on the Role of the Women's Bar Association of the District of Columbia and the Washington College of Law in Promoting Women's Rights*, 4 Mod. Am. 2 (2008).
9. Clark, *supra* note 4, at 656.
10. Letter from the WCL Alumni Ass'n (1917) (on file with the WBA Archives).
11. David Garner, *Socratic Misogyny?—Analyzing Feminist Criticism of Socratic Teaching in Legal Education*, 2000 BYU L. Rev. 1597, 1613 (2000).
12. *Id.*
13. *See* Elizabeth Olson, *Women Make Up Majority of U.S. Law Students for First Time*, N.Y. Times, Dec. 16, 2016.
14. *Law School Rankings by Female Enrollment (2019)*, Enjuris, https://www.enjuris.com/students/law-school-female-enrollment-2019.html.
15. *Id.* (noting disproportionately high rates of women at these law schools: District of Columbia (68.18 percent), North Carolina Central (67.86 percent), Atlanta's John Marshall (65.69 percent), Howard (64.18 percent), Texas Southern (63.78 percent), and over a dozen other schools exceeding 60 percent enrollment).
16. 2019 *Law School Diversity Report: JD Enrollment by Race & Ethnicity*, The Buzz (Oct. 5, 2020), https://equalopportunitytoday.com/2019-law-school-diversity-report-jd-enrollment-by-race-ethnicity/.
17. *Various Statistics on ABA-Approved Law Schools*, American Bar Association, https://www.americanbar.org/groups/legal_education/resources/statistics/ (citing 2020 enrollment data that 7,598 women of color enrolled, compared to 4,825 men of color, of 38,202 total 1L students).
18. *Law School Enrollment by Race & Ethnicity (2019)*, Enjuris, https://www.enjuris.com/students/law-school-race-2019.html.
19. *Id.*
20. *Id.*
21. The NALP Foundation for Law Career Research and Education & The Center for Women in Law, Women of Color: A Study of Law School Experiences (2020), https://utexas.app.box.com/s/kvn7dezec99khii6ely9cve368q4gj9o.
22. Kylie Thomas & Tiffane Cochran, *ABA Data Reveals Minority Students Are Disproportionately Represented in Attrition Features*, AccessLex (Sept. 18, 2018), https://www.accesslex.org/xblog/aba-data-reveals-minority-students-are-disproportionately-represented-in-attrition-figures.
23. American Bar Ass'n, A Current Glance at Women in the Law 4 (2019), https://www.nyipla.org/images/nyipla/Programs/2018December6/acurrentglanceatwomeninthelawjan2018.pdf. [hereinafter Women in the Law].
24. Nancy C. Jurik & Susan Ehrlich Martin, Doing Justice, Doing Gender: Women in Legal and Criminal Justice Occupations 124 (2006).
25. *Id.*

26. Richard H. Chused, *The Hiring and Retention of Minorities and Women on American Law School Faculties*, 137 U. PA. L. REV. 537, 548 (1988).
27. WOMEN IN THE LAW, *supra* note 23.
28. *See, e.g.*, YOLANDA FLORES NIEMANN, GABRIELLA GUTIÉRREZ Y MUHS, & Carmen G. GONZÁLEZ, eds., PRESUMED INCOMPETENT II: RACE, CLASS, POWER, AND RESISTANCE OF WOMEN IN ACADEMIA 3 (2020) [hereinafter PRESUMED INCOMPETENT II] (citing 2016 data from the National Center for Education Statistics published in 2018).
29. Meera E. Deo, *Trajectory of a Law Professor*, 20 MICH. J. RACE & LAW 441, 445-46 (2015) (citing 2009 numbers before AALS stopped releasing data).
30. *See* Paula Monopoli, *Gender and the Crisis in Legal Education: Remaking the Academy in Our Image*, 2012 MICH. ST. L. REV. 1745 (2012); Ann C. McGinley, *Reproducing Gender on Law School Faculties*, 2009 BYU L. REV. 99 (2009).
31. McGinley, *supra* note 30.
32. Deo, *supra* note 29.
33. Laura M. Padilla, *Presumptions of Incompetence, Gender Sidelining, and Women Law Deans*, in PRESUMED INCOMPETENT II, *supra* note 28, at 117-19 (noting that women have led many top-ten law schools and further analyzing the data of first Latina, Native, and Asian American deans).
34. *Id.* at 119 (explaining that current deans are doing "housekeeping, rather than growth").
35. Deborah L. Rhode, *Missing Questions: Feminist Perspectives on Legal Education*, 45 STAN. L. REV. 1547, 1547 (1993) (quoting the Dean of Harvard Law School reassuring alumni that women's presents in law school was unlikely to "change the character of the School or even its atmosphere to any detractable extent").
36. *Id.*
37. *Id.*
38. Stephanie Wildman, *The Question of Silence: Techniques to Ensure Full Class Participation*, 38 J. LEGAL EDUC. 147, 149 (1988) (describing class participation "Ladies Day").
39. Garner, *supra* note 11, at 1613.
40. *Id.* at 1614.
41. Marilyn J. Boxer, *For and About Women: The Theory and Practice of Women's Studies in the United States*, 7 SIGNS: J. OF WOMEN IN CULTURE & SOC'Y 661, 662-63 (1982).
42. *Id.* at 665 (documenting how 150 new women's studies programs emerged from 1970 to 1975 and 150 new programs from 1975 to 1980 along with 30,000 new courses offered at colleges and universities).
43. *Id.* at 667 (describing techniques such as "circular arrangement of chairs, periodic small-group sessions, use of first names for instructors as well as students, assignments that required journal keeping, 'reflection papers,' cooperative projects, and collective modes of teaching with student participation").
44. LORA H. ROBINSON, THE EMERGENCE OF WOMEN'S COURSES IN HIGHER EDUCATION 2-3 (ERIC Clearinghouse on Higher Educ., 1972).
45. Catherine M. Orr, *Tellings of Our Activist Pasts: Tracing the Emergence of Women's Studies at San Diego State College*, 27 WOMEN'S STUD. Q. 212 (1999).
46. Boxer, *supra* note 41, at 670.
47. *Id.* at 677, 679-80.
48. ROBINSON, *supra* note 44, at 1.
49. *Id.* at 2.

50. See, e.g., Elisabeth Hayes, *Insights from Women's Experiences for Teaching and Learning*, in 43 New Directions for Adult & Continuing Educ. 55, 56–57 (1989).
51. *Id.* at 58.
52. *Id.*
53. See Christine Boyle, *Teaching Law as If Women Really Mattered, or, What About the Washrooms?* 2 CAN. J. WOMEN & L. 96, 108–09 (1986).
54. *See generally* Linda K. Kerber, *Writing Our Own Rare Books*, 14 YALE J. L. & FEMINISM, 429 (2002) (chronicling early women and the law gatherings and casebook manuscripts).
55. Catharine A. MacKinnon, *Mainstreaming Feminism in Legal Education*, 53 J. LEGAL EDUC. 199, 211 (2003) [hereinafter *Mainstreaming Feminism in Legal Education*].
56. *Id.*
57. See Jessica Lavariega Monforti & Melissa R. Michelson, *They See Us, but They Don't Really See Us*, in PRESUMED INCOMPETENT II, *supra* note 28, at 59.
58. Carrie Menkel-Meadow, *Feminist Legal Theory, Critical Legal Studies, and Legal Education or "The Fem-Crits Go to Law School,"* 38 J. LEGAL EDUC. 61, 65 (1988).
59. Carrie Menkel-Meadow, Martha Minow & David Vernon, *From the Editors*, 38 J. LEGAL EDUC. 1 (1988).
60. *See generally* Kate E. Bloch, *A Rape Law Pedagogy*, 7 YALE J. L. & FEMINISM (1995) (noting that many criminal law instructors do not teach rape or they it teach it different from other rules).
61. See, e.g., BARBARA ALLEN BABCOCK, A. FREEDMAN, E. NORTON, S. ROSS, EDS., SEX DISCRIMINATION AND THE LAW: CAUSES AND REMEDIES (1975); KENNETH DAVIDSON, RUTH BADER GINSBURG & HERMA HILL KAY, TEXT, CASES, AND MATERIALS ON SEX-BASED DISCRIMINATION (1st ed. 1974). *See generally* Kerber, *supra* note 54.
62. See, e.g., Morrison Torrey, Jackie Casey & Karin Olson, *Teaching Law in a Feminist Manner: A Commentary from Experience*, 13 HARV. WOMEN'S L.J. 87 (1990).
63. See, e.g., Boyle, *supra* note 53, at 108.
64. Catharine MacKinnon, *Feminism in Legal Education*, 1 LEGAL EDUC. REV. 85, 93 (1989) [hereinafter *Feminism in Legal Education*].
65. *Id.* (providing examples of how this would work across other doctrinal courses).
66. Bartlett, *supra* note 3.
67. *Mainstreaming Feminism in Legal Education*, *supra* note 55, at 200.
68. Menkel-Meadow, *supra* note 58, at 68.
69. *Feminism in Legal Education*, *supra* note 64, at 88.
70. *Id.*
71. See, e.g., Susan H. Williams, *Legal Education, Feminist Epistemology, and the Socratic Method*, 45 STAN. L. REV. 1571 (1993).
72. See Rhode, *supra* note 35, at 1558.
73. DUNCAN KENNEDY, LEGAL EDUCATION AND THE REPRODUCTION OF HIERARCHY: A POLEMIC AGAINST THE SYSTEM (2007) (republishing 1983 work).
74. See, e.g., Emily A. Bishop, *Avoiding "Ally Theater" in Legal Writing Assignments*, 26 PERSP.: TEACHING LEGAL RES. & WRITING 1 (2018); Erin C. Lain, *Racialized Interactions in the Law School Classroom: Pedagogical Approaches to Creating a Safe Learning Environment*, 67 J. LEGAL EDUC. 780, 781–82 (2018).
75. See, e.g., Lucinda M. Finley, *The Nature of Domination and the Nature of Women: Reflections on Feminism Unmodified*, 82 NW. U. L. REV. 352, 384 (1988) [hereinafter *The Nature of Domination*].

76. Menkel-Meadow, *supra* note 58, at 71, 74.
77. Bartlett, *supra* note 3, at 1266.
78. *The Nature of Domination*, *supra* note 75, at 384; Margaret E. Montoya, *Silence and Silencing: Their Centripetal and Centrifugal Forces in Legal Communication, Pedagogy and Discourse*, 5 MICH. J. RACE & L. 847, 893 (2000).
79. Lucinda Finley, *Women's Experiences in Legal Education: Silencing and Alienation*, 9 LEGAL EDUC. REV. 101 (1989).
80. Kimberlé Crenshaw, *Foreward: Toward a Race-Conscious Pedagogy in Legal Education*, 11 NAT'L BLACK L.J. 1, 2 (1988).
81. *Id.*
82. *Id.* at 35–36.
83. Mari J. Matsuda, *When the First Quail Calls: Multiple Consciousness as Jurisprudential Method*, 14 WOMEN'S RTS L. REP. 297 (1992).
84. *See* Rhode, *supra* note 35, at 1558.
85. Catharine P. Wells, *Kingsfield and Kennedy: Reappraising the Male Models of Law School Teaching*, 38 J. LEGAL EDUC. 155, 156 (1988).
86. *Id.*
87. *See generally* GABRIELLA GUTIÉRREZ Y MUHS ET AL., EDS., PRESUMED INCOMPETENT: THE INTERSECTIONS OF RACE AND CLASS FOR WOMEN IN ACADEMIA (2012).
88. Duncan Kennedy, *Legal Education and the Reproduction of Hierarchy*, 32 J. LEGAL EDUC. 591 (1982).
89. *Mainstreaming Feminism in Legal Education*, *supra* note 55, at 201–02.
90. Garner, *supra* note 11, at 1627.
91. Stephanie Wildman, *The Question of Silence: Techniques to Ensure Full Class Participation*, 38 J. LEGAL EDUC. 147, 151 (1988).
92. Lani Guinier, Michelle Fine & Jane Balin, *Becoming Gentlemen: Women's Experiences at One Ivy League Law School*, 143 U. PA. L. REV. 1 (1994).
93. Harvard Law School, *Lani Guinier*, https://hls.harvard.edu/faculty/directory/10344/Guinier. Renowned Harvard Law School Professor Derrick Bell had previously taken an extended unpaid leave of absence, leading to his termination, in protest over Harvard's refusal to hire a single woman of color on its law faculty. *Harvard Law Notifies Bell of Dismissal for Absence*, N.Y. TIMES, July 1, 1992, at A19.
94. Guinier et al., *supra* note 92, at 21–32.
95. *See, e.g.*, Taunya Lovell Banks, *Gender Bias in the Classroom*, 38 J. LEGAL EDUC. 137 (1989).
96. Guinier et al., *supra* note 92, at 6, 42.
97. *Id.* at 68.
98. *Id.* at 81.
99. *Id.* at 45.
100. *Id.* at 88.
101. *See, e.g.*, Garner, *supra* note 11, at 1630.
102. Rhode, *supra* note 35, at 1205–06.
103. Bartlett, *supra* note 3, at 1264.
104. Crenshaw, *supra* note 80, at 43.
105. Rhode, *supra* note 35, at 1563. These feminist reform goals aligned synergistically with a larger progressive movement within legal education toward clinical teaching.
106. Bartlett, *supra* note 3, at 1267.

107. Carol Gilligan, In a Different Voice: Psychological Theory and Women's Development 1–2 (1982).
108. Rhode, *supra* note 35, at 1205–06.
109. Menkel-Meadow, *supra* note 58, at 80.
110. *Id.* at 78.
111. Bartlett, *supra* note 3, at 1267.
112. *Id.* at 1263.
113. Rhode, *supra* note 35, at 1551.
114. Martha Minow, *Feminist Reason: Getting It and Losing It*, 38 J. Legal Educ. 47 (1988).
115. *See, e.g.,* Nel Noddings, *Feminist Critiques in the Professions, in* Review of Research in Education 393, 401 (1990) ("[T]he impact on legal education seems so far to be minimal. The odd parody of Socratic teaching (the model is Professor Kingsfield) continues, abated here and there by . . . feminist teachers.").
116. *See generally* Meera E. Deo, Unequal Profession: Race and Gender in Legal Academia (2019).
117. Julia H. Chang, *Spectacular Bodies, in* Presumed Incompetent II, *supra* note 28, at 259, 261.
118. *See generally* Deo, *supra* note 29, at 58–59.
119. Arlie Russell Hochschild, The Second Shift: Working Parents and the Revolution at Home (1989).
120. *See, e.g.,* Helen Lewis, *The Coronavirus Is a Disaster for Feminism*, The Atlantic (Mar. 19, 2020), https://www.theatlantic.com/international/archive/2020/03/feminism-womens-rights-coronavirus-covid19/608302/.
121. Model Rules of Pro. Conduct § 8.4(g) (American Bar Association, 2016). *See generally* Kristen A. Kubes, Cara D. Davis & Mary E. Schwind, *The Evolution of Model Rule 8.4(g): Working to Eliminate Bias, Discrimination, and Harassment in the Practice of Law* (American Bar Association, Mar. 12, 2019), https://www.americanbar.org/groups/construction_industry/publications/under_construction/2019/spring/model-rule-8-4/.
122. *See, e.g.,* Dahlia Litwick & Susan Matthews, *Investigation at Yale Law School*, Slate (Oct. 5, 2018), https://slate.com/news-and-politics/2018/10/jed-rubenfeld-amy-chua-yale-law-school.html; Marilyn Odendahl, *Title IX Investigation Ends with IU Maurer Professor's Departure*, The Ind. Lawyer, May 15, 2019, https://www.theindianalawyer.com/articles/50313-title-ix-investigation-ends-with-iu-maurer-professors-departure.
123. Prachi Gupta, *Academia's "Shitty Men" List Has Around 2,000 Entries Detailing Sexual Misconduct at Universities*, Jezebel (Jan. 11, 2018), https://jezebel.com/academias-shitty-men-list-has-around-2-000-entries-deta-1821991028 (asking respondents to detail the nature and timing of the abuse and identify any recourse pursued).
124. *See* Gregory Yang, *Law Professors Facing Consequences of #MeToo Movement*, Tipping the Scales (Dec. 12, 2018), https://tippingthescales.com/2018/12/law-professors-facing-consequences-of-metoo-movement/.
125. Rachelle A.C. Joplin, *Through a White Woman's Tears, in* Presumed Incompetent II, *supra* note 28, at 215, 217 (explaining how women of color have to "attend[] to the fragile emotions and defense mechanisms of White women, all while already existing in a system that wants nothing more than their silence").
126. *See generally* A. Benjamin Spencer, *The Law School Critique in Historical Perspective*, 69 Wash. & Lee L. Rev. 1949, 1961–2015 (2012) (chronicling the historic legal education shifts from apprenticeships to the Langdell model to the ABA's centralized regulation).

127. *See generally* AMERICAN BAR ASSOCIATION, LEGAL EDUCATION AND PROFESSIONAL DEVELOPMENT—AN EDUCATIONAL CONTINUUM, REPORT OF THE TASK FORCE ON LAW SCHOOLS AND THE PROFESSION: NARROWING THE GAP (1992); WILLIAM M. SULLIVAN ET AL., EDUCATING LAWYERS: PREPARATION FOR THE PROFESSION OF LAW (2007); ROY STUCKEY ET AL., BEST PRACTICES FOR LEGAL EDUCATION: A VISION AND A ROAD MAP (2007).
128. STANDARDS AND RULES OF PROCEDURE FOR APPROVAL OF LAW SCHOOLS 2014–2015 (American Bar Association 2014), https://www.americanbar.org/content/dam/aba/publications/misc/legal_education/Standards/2014_2015_aba_standards_and_rules_of_procedure_for_approval_of_law_schools_bookmarked.pdf.
129. Anthony Niedwiecki, *Prepared for Practice? Developing a Comprehensive Assessment Plan for a Law School Professional Skills Program*, 50 U.S.F. L. REV. 245, 247 (2016).
130. David I. C. Thomson, *Defining Experiential Legal Education*, 1 J. EXPERIENTIAL LEARNING 1 (2015).
131. Cara Cunningham Warren, *Achieving the American Bar Association's Pedagogy Mandate: Empowerment in the Midst of a "Perfect Storm,"* 14 CONN. PUB. INT'L L.J. 67, 68 (2014).
132. *See, e.g.* Sarah Valentine, *Flourish or Founder: The New Regulatory Regime in Legal Education*, 44 J. L. & EDUC. 1, 4 (2015) (noting law schools historically distanced themselves from reforms in other sectors of undergraduate and higher education).
133. Niedwiecki, *supra* note 129, at 255–57.
134. Valentine, *supra* note 132, at 484–93.
135. *See* Warren, *supra* note 131, at 71.
136. ABA Standard 302, American Bar Association, Managing Director's Guidance Memo (2015), https://www.americanbar.org/content/dam/aba/administrative/legal_education_and_admissions_to_the_bar/governancedocuments/2015_learning_outcomes_guidance.pdf.
137. *See, e.g.*, Nathan M. Greenfield, *So Is Critical Race Theory Poisonous or Illuminating?*, U. WORLD NEWS, Jan. 9, 2021, https://www.universityworldnews.com/post.php?story=2021010810452697.

CHAPTER 29

FEMINIST JUDGING
Theories and Practices

KRISTIN KALSEM

JUDGES are powerful state actors, deciding matters that affect every aspect of our lives, whether on a societal scale or an individual basis. Judicial decisions literally can mean life or death, from the question of whether to grant a stay of execution or issue a protection order against an abusive spouse. In the United States, this power is wielded disproportionately by men. Women make up less than one third of federal[1] and state judges.[2]

Given the enormity and scope of judicial power, it is no wonder that, since the 1980s, feminists have been theorizing about what feminism should mean in the context of judging. Different feminist philosophies have informed scholarly and advocacy efforts to address institutional gender bias in the court system, with priorities and strategies shifting over time to include new insights, empirical data, and feminist methods. The scope of these initiatives has gradually expanded beyond efforts at gender integration to more broadly encompass social justice goals that relate not only to the makeup of the legal actors but to the process of dispensing justice. This chapter highlights questions, concerns, aspirations, and hopes that emerge when gender, social justice, and judging are considered together.

This chapter begins by examining the original liberal feminist goal of increasing the number of women judges to attain equal gender representation. Section I canvasses multiple reasons why greater gender diversity on the bench is desirable, from its symbolic value to its potential for reducing and counteracting implicit bias of legal actors. It also charts how scholarship has grown to encompass "outsider" judges, marked by race, ethnicity, and other marginalized identities, with particular attention to the experiences of female judges of color.

Section II then turns to analyzing scholarship that focuses on the ideal of "feminist judging." It recounts how, borrowing from cultural feminism, feminist scholars have applied the concept of an "ethic of care" and discussed the possibilities and impacts of empathetic judging. Finally, it explores how feminist judging takes into consideration the racial and gender dimensions of controversies and brings context to the forefront, employing an intersectional and social justice lens.

Moving from theory to practice, section III discusses two recent scholarly projects that integrate feminist judging into the real-world practices of judges. One such project applies the methods of legal participatory action research (legal PAR) to design and implement state-wide judicial training on best practices in intimate partner abuse cases. Using a community-based research and problem-solving paradigm, legal PAR effectuates a bottom-up approach to law and policymaking. The second project—the Feminist Judgments project—critiques the idea of judicial objectivity and reimagines landmark legal cases through the rewriting of judicial opinions from feminist perspectives. Inspired in the United States by similar projects in Canada and Great Britain, it has grown from a volume of twenty-five rewritten U.S. Supreme Court opinions to multiple volumes devoted to specific areas of law like employment discrimination and reproductive justice.

Section IV concludes with considerations for future feminist agendas in reaching the end goal of achieving social justice in the process and outcomes of judging. Throughout, this chapter is guided by the belief that what judges decide, as well as the process through which they reason and explain their decisions, matters.

I. The Value of Greater Diversity on the Bench

As always, in law, the liberal feminist goal of formal equality looms large. During the 1980s and 1990s, task forces on bias in the courts studied and produced reports on institutional gender bias in both state and federal court systems. The Gender Bias task force reports documented disparities in the treatment of women at all levels, whether plaintiffs, defendants, witnesses, court personnel, lawyers, or judges.[3] They revealed recurring instances of sexual harassment of female participants in the judicial process, documented pay inequities between male and female court employees, and reported egregious instances of disrespect toward female judges and attorneys. Many reports suggested that the paucity of women judges was both a cause and effect of such discriminatory treatment. In describing her situation and aspirations as a member of an underrepresented group in the judiciary, one woman judge remarked: "Of course being a woman makes a difference. How could it not? But, I don't want to be known as a "female" judge. I want to be known as a fair and just judge and looked up to for my intellect and skills."[4]

Although the task forces were also formed to address bias based on race and ethnicity in the courts, they did not take an intersectional approach. As Judith Resnik lamented, "[Task forces] are no longer oblivious to differences among women but remain fearful that incorporation, inclusion, and joint venturing will obstruct the attention paid either to gender or to race and ethnicity."[5] Just as single-axis constitutional analysis—discrimination based on race *or* gender—fails to account for harms that women of color face *as* women of color, these reports failed to capture their qualitatively different experiences of bias in the courts.

Since the publication of the initial task force reports,[6] researchers have performed numerous empirical studies to see *if* and *how* having more female judges on the bench would make a difference, specifically in case outcome. Some of the studies explored possible differences in outcomes in civil and criminal cases, including: Are female judges more likely to find for plaintiffs? If so, in what types of cases? Do female judges impose harsher sentences in criminal cases? Does the presence of a female judge on a federal appellate panel affect the outcome?

While studies have offered conflicting conclusions, many scholars agree with Sally Kenney that "the evidence provides little empirical support for the proposition that women as a group decide cases differently than men."[7] In her book *Gender and Justice*, Kenney argues that studies focusing on essential sex differences have "found few striking or consistent differences, with the exception of a greater propensity of women appellate judges to find more often for the plaintiff in sex discrimination cases and to persuade men colleagues on panels to vote with them."[8] Australian scholar Rosemary Hunter goes further and characterizes the assumptions that women judges would "make a difference simply by *being* there" as "at best naïve and at worst essentialist."[9] Specifically, she raises the following provocative questions:

> Why did we think women would transform institutions without simultaneously—or alternatively—being transformed by them? Why did we believe that women appointed to positions of power would be "representative" of women as a group, rather than being those who most resemble the traditional incumbents and are thus considered least likely to disturb the status quo? Why did we assume that women appointed to these positions would have the capacity to represent the whole, diverse, range of women's perspectives and experiences? And why did we imagine that individual women would want potentially to risk their newly-acquired status by taking a stand on behalf of other women, when it would be much safer for them to keep their heads down and attempt to gain some legitimacy amongst their skeptical peers and jealous subordinates?[10]

In the United States, the impassioned feminist opposition to the appointment of Justice Amy Coney Barrett to the U.S. Supreme Court to replace Justice Ruth Bader Ginsburg spoke to this concern that not all women will "stand on behalf of other women," or pursue a feminist agenda.[11]

Despite empirical evidence that gender does not lead directly to different case outcomes and the realization that some appointed women might hold decidedly unfeminist views, the lack of diversity on the bench remains consequential. For five interlocking reasons focusing on the harms of underrepresentation and the potential benefits of having a more inclusive judiciary, feminist scholars, including Kenney and

Hunter, have updated the case for a diverse judiciary, employing reasoning that draws from intersectional feminist theory.[12]

First, feminist scholars see symbolic value in a judiciary that is representative of the population it serves. A more diverse judiciary looks fairer, so that "justice is not merely done, but seen to be done."[13] It also is important for women and people of color to see that such positions of power are open to them, as well as to normalize the idea of historical "outsiders" wielding power in law. More diversity "at the top" also helps promote a more inclusive atmosphere generally.[14]

Second, beyond symbolism is the injustice to women and people of color who suffer employment discrimination in this realm. As with every profession, the judiciary should be free of discriminatory selection procedures and practices. This argument is central to Kenney's efforts to make "a nonessentialist case for more women judges."[15] Rather than focusing on how men and women might judge differently, Kenney asserts that the question should be why is it acceptable to exclude anyone on the basis of gender, race, ethnicity, or sexuality. She analogizes the opportunity to hold judicial office to that of serving on a jury, viewing it as "a component of citizenship and a marker of equal status."[16]

Research has provided explanations for why our judiciary fails to reflect the makeup of our society. Maya Sen's work, for example, shows that the American Bar Association gives lower ratings to women and people of color than to white, male nominees.[17] Another study by Christina Boyd and co-researchers pointed to substantively different questioning of Supreme Court nominees during confirmation hearings, with race and gender playing a role in questions relating to a nominee's competence for the job.[18] Such discriminatory treatment does not end once judges are on the bench. The Boyd study observed that "[p]ublic displays of bias against women and people of color" in confirmation hearings can "foster a culture of incivility in which advocates and other justices demonstrate disrespect for and call into question the credibility of their nontraditional colleagues."[19] As evidence, they cite other studies finding that female justices on the U.S. Supreme Court are interrupted more often than their male colleagues by both other justices and by male attorneys,[20] with Justice Sotomayor—the lone woman of color— the most interrupted Supreme Court justice.[21] Serious issues also have been raised concerning bias in judicial performance evaluations.[22] Eliminating such discriminatory practices is necessary to ensure, for judges, equal treatment, and for society, a more representative judiciary.

Third, scholars have noted that a more diverse bench would help to dismantle negative stereotypes and lessen the impacts of implicit bias. Task forces and numerous studies have documented that stereotypes and biases that disadvantage litigants, witnesses, attorneys, and others based on their gender, race, and ethnicity are ubiquitous throughout the court system. For example, a study conducted by Patricia Yancey Martin and others found that male judges were more likely than female judges to agree with the following biased statements: "(1) 'By and large female attorneys lack the competence of their male colleagues'; (2) 'Generally speaking men are more credible than women'; and (3) 'A woman who is outspoken or strongly adversarial is obnoxious.'"[23]

Not only would female judges be less likely to perpetuate these harmful stereotypes, but a critical mass of women judges would be in a position to call out problematic behaviors and decisions based upon them. Similarly, having a more representative judiciary could counter implicit biases in the profession. As Rosalind Dixon reports:

> [I]n an experimental setting, psychologists have shown that exposure to individuals from a stigmatized group can have a substantial capacity to curtail implicit bias. Even more importantly, they have shown that, when placed in a subordinate position to an individual from a stigmatized group, individuals who would otherwise exhibit implicit biases are less likely to express those biases. In a legal setting, this suggests that if male attorneys appear routinely before female judges sitting either alone or in an apparent position of influence on a panel, male attorneys will gradually begin to show less gender bias.[24]

In these ways, a more diverse judiciary would help address deeply ingrained, widespread systemic inequalities in the courts.

A fourth argument for increasing the number of diverse judges is to move the judiciary toward greater impartiality and fairness. A central premise of critical feminist legal theory is that no judge can be completely "objective" and that such a claim only serves to make a white, male perspective appear to be neutral.[25] Indeed, the very concept of judicial "objectivity" teems with gender, race, and ethnicity bias because, for centuries, only white men were judges, with their experiences, perspectives, and values taken as the norm. Against this backdrop, "objectivity" has allowed the perspectives of "outsiders" to this system to be characterized as "biased," "political," and "emotional." The case of *Blank v. Sullivan & Cromwell*[26] provides a stark example.

In *Blank*, several women alleged sex discrimination in employment. Presiding over the case was Judge Constance Baker Motley, the first African American woman appointed to a federal court. The defendant's lawyer made a formal motion for Judge Motley to recuse herself, arguing that her identities as a woman and an African American would make her unduly favorable toward the plaintiffs. Judge Motley refused, firmly denouncing the idea that her sex, race, or background as a civil rights lawyer in any way compromised her ability to hear and rule on a case fairly. Her opinion emphasized that *all* judges have a sex, race, and background and that if these "were, by definition, sufficient grounds for removal, no judge on this court could hear this case."[27]

Indeed, Kenney identifies the fear of heightened scrutiny of the conventional view of judicial impartiality as one of the greatest threats that "outsider" judges pose to the status quo. Criticizing the ability of a judge to be impartial shines a spotlight on the (im) possibility of judicial objectivity generally:

> The social location of white, upper-middle class, and largely Protestant men, of course, is never called into question or associated with potential bias. Only those marked as "other" are viewed as imbued with a social location that renders them unable to be objective or open-minded. Non-dominant groups must be excluded, in

part, because their entry into the field brings up the question of all judges' social location in ways that threaten the narrative of impartial judgment.[28]

Feminist scholars have recognized that the impossibility of objectivity makes diversity all the more urgent. For example, Carla Pratt argues that "[d]iversity operates as a diffusive mechanism that ensures that not all jurists will have a particular set of biases that cut only one way."[29] Pressing the argument further, Sherrilyn Ifill claims that the Fourteenth Amendment requires diversity in the courts to achieve what she terms "structural impartiality." For Ifill, structural impartiality will exist only when the judiciary as a whole is composed of judges from diverse backgrounds and the "interaction of these diverse viewpoints fosters impartiality by diminishing the possibility that one perspective dominates adjudication."[30] The idea that objectivity can be fostered through considered debate of different perspectives, rather than achieved by cloaking the ideas of the powerful in the guise of neutrality, has transformative potential.

Not only do outsiders bring a different set of views and experiences, but they also bring the ability, honed by necessity, of seeing the world from multiple perspectives. Judge Sotomayor made this point in her 2002 essay, *A Latina Judge's Voice*, when she opined that "a wise Latina woman with the richness of her experiences would more often than not reach a better conclusion than a white male who hasn't lived that life."[31] She was not suggesting by this remark that a Latina woman inherently possessed superior judicial capacities but rather that her experience of living a life as a subordinated minority and working in a white, male-dominated profession gave her a capacity to view the world from more inclusive perspectives.

During her confirmation hearing for the U.S. Supreme Court, however, Sotomayor's statement was used against her as presaging unjudicial bias on her part. Feminist scholarship clarifies how this outsider stance does not evidence bias but instead is necessary to create a more just judiciary. Carla Pratt specifically contextualizes the "wise Latina" comment, drawing on what Patricia Hill Collins has described as the "outsider within" phenomenon:

> Women and people of color on the bench are outsiders in that their presence on the bench is not the norm. Yet they are "within" because they have been placed in a position of power within an existing institutional power structure dominated by white males. According to Dr. Collins, when you are an outsider within, you learn to see the world from multiple perspectives, while those who are insiders are part of the dominant culture and do not necessarily have to learn to see the world from other perspectives.[32]

The wider the view, the greater the opportunity to reach a just result.

Fifth and finally, with more diverse voices, the "idea" of what judging should look like might change. Without a critical mass, women judges may feel compelled to fit in or at least not to stand out.[33] There is concern that being "a female judge" will make them less respected or less "judge-like." With greater numbers, however, "outsider" judges may feel freer to judge differently, including in a more feminist manner. In the next section, I examine what that might entail.

II. Features of "Feminist Judging"

In 1988, Judith Resnik published *On the Bias: Feminist Reconsiderations of the Aspirations for Our Judges* to "enable a dialogue between two traditions—the law of judges and feminist theory—that have not, heretofore, spoken with each other."[34] In this pathbreaking article, Resnik sparked a conversation that continues today about what feminist legal theory can tell us about the aspirations we should have for our judges. In this section, I focus on three aspects of feminist judging frequently discussed in the scholarship: (1) exercising an ethic of care; (2) examining the gender, race, and ethnicity implications of laws and decisions ("asking the Other question"); and (3) understanding and documenting how context matters.

At the time that Resnik wrote her article, cultural feminism was finding its way into legal scholarship, and the work of developmental psychologist Carol Gilligan was very influential.[35] In a series of studies, Gilligan identified what she termed "a different voice" between men and women.[36] Specifically, she characterized women and girls as approaching moral conflicts and problem-solving from the perspective of an "ethic of care."[37] This was in contrast to the "ethic of justice" more typical of men and boys.[38] Thus, rather than seeing issues as win-lose or either-or, Gilligan's research argued that women strove to preserve relationships and solve problems with an emphasis on responsibility and care.

When it comes to desirable attributes for judges, one can see the value in judges exercising an ethic of care, without accepting that this is a quality that only women can possess or put into practice. Kenney, for example, does not agree that women judges speak in a different voice; however, she argues that emotional intelligence, an aspect of an ethic of care, is an important aspiration for all judges.[39] Feminist judging recognizes the value of care and empathy and does not see these qualities as inappropriately "unobjective." Rather, being empathic signals listening attentively, showing respect, putting oneself in the shoes of the other, and considering how that change in perspective matters. In a qualitative study involving in-depth interviews of thirteen female family court judges from one Eastern state, researchers presented examples of judges exercising an ethic of care.[40] While the study also claimed that women judges bring "a different voice" to the bench because of their experiences of being women in a patriarchal society,[41] the examples show what an ethic of care looks like in feminist judging practiced by judges of any gender. For instance, one judge reported her judicial philosophy as follows:

> My whole approach to the law is to create community versus creating division. I don't want people to be pulling apart. I want people to be pulling together and so you have that sense of community and obligation to community.[42]

Other judges in this study believed that, as women, they were "more in touch with the reality of family life and responsibilities"[43] and "sensitive to... parents' needs."[44] This translated into judicial practices, such as making certain that court was let out on time to allow parents to pick up their children from school or from care providers.[45] Although some women, based on personal experiences, might be more readily in tune to these kinds of issues, feminist judges would be open to learning about these realities and responding to them with an ethic of care.

A second key aspect of feminist judging involves paying attention to and considering the roles that subordinating legal and societal structures may be playing in a given situation—centering gender, race, ethnicity, and other factors that are overlooked or deemed irrelevant. In her 1990 article on feminist legal methods, Katharine Bartlett articulated the importance of "asking the woman question."[46] While her article focuses on a single-axis analysis centered on gender, Bartlett also advised using this kind of questioning "as a model for deeper inquiry into the consequences of overlapping forms of oppression":[47]

> What assumptions are made by law (or practice or analysis) about those whom it affects? Whose point of view do these assumptions reflect? Whose interests are invisible or peripheral? How might excluded viewpoints be identified and taken into account? Extended beyond efforts to identify oppression based only on gender, the woman question can reach forms of oppression made invisible not only by the dominant structures of power but also by the efforts to discover bias on behalf of women alone.[48]

Mari Matsuda explicitly moves away from the gender primacy of Bartlett's method, employing the feminist method of asking "the Other question."[49] As an antidote to single-axis thinking, Matsuda explains, "When I see something that looks racist, I ask 'Where is the patriarchy in this?' When I see something that looks sexist, I ask, 'Where is the heterosexism in this?'"[50]

In taking subordinating structures into account, feminist judging must be concerned not only with specific outcomes but with process and broader societal impacts. As Hunter argues, feminist judging aims to achieve "gender justice in the outcomes of cases as well as in the process of judging, and to consider the effects of decisions on broader social relationships."[51] Hunter suggests that one of ways judges can seek to have impacts beyond the case at hand is to document important social realities in the judicial opinions themselves.[52] For example, Justice Souter's dissent in *United States v. Morrison*[53] includes a lengthy list of facts and statistics that Congress collected and considered in using its power under the Commerce Clause to enact a civil remedy for violence against women. Challenging the majority's blunt conclusion that Congress did not have the power to regulate this "noneconomic" conduct and was constitutionally bound to distinguish "what is truly national and what is truly local,"[54] Justice Souter made sure that real-life harms to women were not lost in the abstract language of the Commerce Clause and federalism. He was careful to include statistics such as that more than one million women seek medical help for injuries they sustain from an abusive partner and that 75 percent of women don't go to the movies alone after dark because they fear they will be raped.[55] His dissent also emphasized violence against women as a national scourge worthy of federal attention and constitutional analysis.

Finally, feminist judging involves having a sophisticated understanding of how and why context matters. As Patricia Cain points out, "[c]ontextualization may include considering the specific situation of the parties, the circumstances in which particular legislation was enacted, and/or the broader social context within and upon which the legal rules in question operate."[56] It is important to have sufficient facts about a particular situation to understand the reality of the parties' lives rather than to rely on abstract principles, stereotypes, or stock stories which can lead to unjust, often discriminatory, results.

The ultimate goal of feminist judging is putting theory into action. In the next section, I discuss two recent judging projects that have focused on the action part, on making feminist judging a practical possibility.

III. A Practical Approach to Feminist Judging

With feminist judging as a goal, how can we make it the practice of the judges we have, as well as the more diverse and feminist judiciary we aspire to have? In this section, I first discuss a judicial training program—developed by taking a legal PAR approach—that provided judges with data-based best practices in cases involving intimate partner abuse. The second part of this section describes an ongoing scholarly project—the Feminist Judgments project—which involves rewriting judicial opinions from a feminist perspective. In a concrete and creative way, the rewritten opinions illustrate how to translate feminist theory into judicial reasoning, language, and outcomes.

A. Legal Participatory Action Research: Training Judges in Feminist Practices

Feminist judging, Patricia Cain argues, is only possible when judges listen to the parties and judge with "the good bias [good connection], but not the bad one."[57] Central to this prescription is for judges to listen with engagement and without prejudgment. One judicial education project that fits well with Cain's vision of feminist judging aims to take into account those aspects of controversies that may not have been considered, to reject stock stories and myths that lead to misunderstanding, and to learn from experts and each other how to make more informed and just decisions in intimate partner abuse cases.

Guided by the legal PAR method,[58] a community-based team in Cincinnati, Ohio has developed an all-day training program for judges and magistrates on best practices in intimate partner abuse cases, reaching more than 400 judges and magistrates. The program was intentionally designed to employ a critical race/feminist method by following the process of legal PAR.

Legal PAR is distinctive in that it engages with community stakeholders as co-researchers rather than objects of study. In legal PAR, researchers bring their specific skill sets to a community and work with members to improve issues that the community itself has prioritized. In a prior article, my colleague Emily Houh and I explored the synergies between legal PAR and critical race/feminist theories. Specifically, like critical race/feminist theory, legal PAR critiques objectivity, breaks down traditional hierarchies and empowers community stakeholders, values lived experiences, and analyzes interlocking oppressions. It also bridges the gap between theory and practice. Legal PAR is inherently action-oriented: in interactive discussions the community identifies the issues to be addressed, as well as generates solutions to be explored.[59] Moreover, it is by definition a "bottom-up approach."[60]

Through the legal PAR methods, a representative group of community stakeholders in Cincinnati identified as its top priority instituting a system for more and better judicial training on intimate partner abuse. For two years, a group of community members actively researched best practices, performing literature searches and reviews of national and state training programs and materials, and engaging in broad outreach to their individual networks. The group solicited input from a wide variety of stakeholders, among others, prosecutors, defense attorneys, judges, magistrates, survivors, child services organizations, social workers, police officers, victim advocates, immigration services organizations, sheriffs' departments, and probation officers. A question posed to all was: "If you could have anything you wanted included in a judges' training on best practices in intimate partner abuses, what would that be and why?"

Based on the results of this research, the community researchers compiled a list of what judges should know and understand about intimate partner abuse and then developed a set of judicial trainings to achieve those learning outcomes.[61] Feminist judging was encouraged in various ways, including the use of narratives. For example, judges were presented with video clips of actual courtroom participants explaining how the exercise of an ethic of care had made or could make a significant difference in their willingness to participate in a prosecution or could impact their perceptions of their access to justice. Specifically, segments of video interviews with survivors were incorporated into the trainings (with their faces blurred to protect anonymity). The survivors talked about their courtroom experiences, including what judges did that was helpful, as well as problematic. For example, judges heard directly from survivors that "Explanations from the judge or magistrate on the possibilities of what can and can't happen is extremely helpful to the victim,"[62] and "To know that the judge understood me... was a weight lifted off my shoulders."[63]

In their course evaluations, judges emphasized how meaningful it was to hear directly from the survivors, for example, about how terrifying it was to be in the same room with their abusers, let alone to describe what that person had done to them. Judges also heard, many for the first time, how common it was for an abuser, in a show of intimidation, deliberately to park his vehicle right next to the survivor's car in the courthouse parking lot and how afraid survivors were to leave the courthouse for fear of being accosted by the abuser. In the trainings, judges discussed among themselves how easy it would be to start having bailiffs escort prosecuting witnesses to their cars.

Intersectionality, integral to legal PAR, influenced each stage of the project. For example, the trainings included the voices of immigrant survivors discussing the risks and challenges that made them afraid to report abuse. Topics ranged from the reluctance of communities of color to bring in the police to the lack of access to shelter for members of the LGBTQ community. Results from this community-based research made clear that assumptions and myths about intimate partner abuse, as well as stereotypes based on gender, race, ethnicity, and sexuality, were all too prevalent in Ohio courtrooms. The trainings shed light on the devastating impacts of these prejudgments and debunked them with counternarratives and research illuminating often-excluded perspectives and explanations.

Finally, the trainings demonstrated how and why context was key to understanding and making informed decisions. Attention was paid to what survivors might be experiencing when they appeared (or failed to appear) in court. The first session of the day, tellingly, was titled "Understanding Cases That Don't Make Sense," responding to the judges' request for such a session. They wanted to better understand cases that for them often were very frustrating. Uppermost in their minds was: What were they missing? How could they act differently? What did they need to know to really listen?

While a formal study of the impacts of these trainings has not been conducted, the evaluations of the sessions indicated that judges were learning about research, issues, and solutions they had never considered before. This judicial training project is a case study of how we might train judges now—the judges we have—in feminist judging.

B. The Feminist Judgments Project

The second project—the Feminist Judgments project—originated in Canada when, dismayed by several decisions of the Canadian Supreme Court, feminists decided that the courts' opinions needed to be rewritten to demonstrate in a concrete way the difference feminism and feminist judging could have in that nation. In 2010, Canada's Women's Legal Education and Action Fund (LEAF) started publishing opinions of a fictional Women's Court of Canada, "conceived as a 'higher' court that would 'review' the Supreme Court decisions."[64] The rewritten decisions showed the possibilities that opened up when arguments for women's substantive equality were taken into account. Similarly, in England, *Feminist Judgments: From Theory to Practice* was published "to demonstrate how feminist legal theory could be given practical effect in judgment form."[65] Both of these projects were meant to have real-world impacts, to be "a new and different kind of feminist intervention in law—a kind of hybrid form of critique and law reform project."[66] The projects were designed to influence the thinking of law students, as they studied the rewritten opinions alongside the originals, as well as to provide examples to practicing attorneys and judges. Together, the opinions represent a form of applied feminist scholarship that puts on display the paradigm-changing potential of feminist judging.

In 2016, Kathryn Stanchi, Linda L. Berger, and Bridget Crawford edited a U.S. version of feminist judgments in which legal academics rewrote twenty-five U.S. Supreme Court opinions.[67] In the U.S. collection, key opinions of the Supreme Court were rewritten "to demonstrate how the use of feminist theories, methods, and perspectives might have changed the reasoning, the result, or both."[68] Particularly because the authors of the rewritten opinions were limited to citing the laws and precedents in place at the time of the original decision, the revised opinions poignantly illustrated that there is not just one "objective" determination in any given case. They revealed that feminist outcomes and reasoning have long been possible and that a shift in perspective and emphasis can make an eye-opening difference. For example, Lisa Pruitt's rewriting of *Planned Parenthood of Southeastern. Pennsylvania v. Casey*,[69] the Court's major abortion case, centers the experiences of poor, rural, and Native American women. Pruitt's opinion shows that the "undue burden" for these women caused by a twenty-four-hour waiting period for an abortion is patently obvious in a way that is obscured in the original opinion. Likewise, Ilene Durst's rewritten opinion in *Nguyen v. INS*[70] highlights how a provision in the Immigration and Nationality Act that treats unmarried citizen fathers differently than unmarried citizen mothers was based on gender stereotypes, as well as historical discrimination against people of color and children born to unmarried parents, a dimension overlooked in the original opinion. Under her analysis, such a gender distinction could not stand up to heightened scrutiny under the Fourteenth Amendment.

This first U.S. volume, focusing on Supreme Court opinions as far back as *Bradwell v. Illinois*,[71] has been followed by rewritten opinions in tax,[72] employment discrimination,[73] family law,[74] reproductive justice,[75] torts,[76] and trusts and estates.[77] These opinions illustrate how the insights of feminist legal theory are relevant to all substantive areas of law, not just those directly dealing with issues of gender.

This body of rewritten opinions "construct[s] a feminist judicial language."[78] Some through the feminist method of narrative, bringing "to the surface untold, ignored, and suppressed alternative narratives of those conflicts."[79] Others through detailing how context matters, as well as situating an individual's circumstances within a larger system of inequality. As Crawford et al. explain, "A feminist judge is more likely to make decisions within context, to take into account detailed individual facts about a case, and to consider more broadly how the decision will impact women and other historically disadvantaged groups."[80]

The rewritten opinions educate by drawing on the multiplicity of ideas that fall within the purview of feminist legal theory. As feminists do, they "question everything": What does objectivity cover up? What power hierarchies exist and how are they being maintained? What assumptions or stereotypes are impacting the decisionmakers? What is not being said? What role(s) are gender, race, class, sexuality, and other characteristics of the parties involved playing? They also "open up a small vista on what law might look like if feminists were able to contribute, in a meaningful way."[81] For many, the Feminist Judgments project is empowering because it lifts feminist theory and reasoning out from under the academic realm. The judgments themselves are translations of "feminist theory into the language of law practice and judging."[82] They educate by showing *how* to do it. For the law students to whom I have introduced these rewritten opinions, they hold out the promise that feminist judging and outcomes are, indeed, possible—even given the built-in patriarchal structures of our legal system.

IV. Conclusion: Feminist Agendas for Gender and Judging

The scholarship on gender and judging has evolved and deepened since its early "numbers counting" days to embrace diverse theories of feminist judging with implications for activism and agenda setting. It has the capacity to fuel numerous feminist agendas—and the plural is key. My experience with legal PAR and judicial training has taught me that there need not be one feminist agenda on gender and judging. Some groups of feminist advocates might be better located than others (geographically, institutionally, within communities of color) to take on certain issues. Some might prefer to work on the local level, and others nationally. Some activists might have experience organizing, while others are familiar with the workings of the legislature.

Despite this multiplicity, there now seems to be widespread agreement that, at the very least, feminist agendas should prioritize getting more women and people of color on the bench. Even those who put more emphasis on feminist judging than numbers argue that there should be greater diversity in the judiciary. This effort must include an end to discriminatory practices in the nominating process, as well as making sure that judges are not treated and evaluated in a discriminatory manner. Other feminist agendas could explore opportunities to teach, promote, and reward feminist judging.

In the judicial training project described above, it became clear to me that a critical feminist process was key to achieving feminist goals. In setting feminist agendas to impact the judiciary, legal PAR offers methods to build effective coalitions and to move forward productively and intentionally. One method, known as "asset mapping," which encourages groups first to take stock of the individual and collective knowledge, experiences, perspectives, resources, and abilities they bring to bear on an issue, is especially helpful in ensuring that a group is representative of all the stakeholders. If certain voices are missing, solutions might not work, or worse, be counterproductive. Laying this groundwork helps to work through conflicting priorities, differences in approaches, and allocations of resources.

Judges make decisions that affect every aspect of life—work, family, economics, safety, health. Who does the judging and how matters. There is no denying that there is much to be done to make all judgments feminist—and just for all. To work toward this goal, feminists can put into practice the listening skills, attention to power dynamics, and intersectional perspective that we know are necessary to make fair judgments.

Notes

1. Forster-Long, *Gender Diversity Survey*, THE AMERICAN BENCH (2021), https://www.nawj.org/uploads/statistics/americanbench_genderdatadata_2020vs2021_nawj.pdf (survey charts show that women comprise: 2/8 Supreme Court Justices; 105/357 US Circuit Court judges; 546/1,669 US District Court judges; 106/300 Bankruptcy Court judges; and 30/103 Other Federal Court judges for a total of 789/2,437 federal judges).
2. TRACEY E. GEORGE & ALBERT H. YOON, AMERICAN CONSTITUTION SOCIETY, THE GAVEL GAP: WHO SITS IN JUDGMENT ON STATE COURTS (2018), https://www.acslaw.org/wp-content/uploads/2018/02/gavel-gap-report.pdf. This report concludes that although women represent half of the US population and half of American law students, "less than one-third of state judges are women. In some states, women are underrepresented on the bench by a ratio of one woman on the bench for every four women in the state. Not a single state has as many women judges as it does men." *Id.* at 2.
3. MARTHA CHAMALLAS, INTRODUCTION TO FEMINIST LEGAL THEORY 84–89 (3d ed. 2012).
4. Susan L. Miller & Shana L. Maier, *Moving beyond Numbers: What Female Judges Say about Different Judicial Voices*, 29 J. WOMEN, POL. & POL'Y 527, 546 (2008).
5. Judith Resnik, *Asking about Gender in Courts*, 21 SIGNS 952, 975 (1996).
6. Not surprisingly, there was backlash against these reports, with critics claiming that they problematically called into question the integrity and objectivity of the courts. As Resnik explained, "[o]bjectors accuse task forces that mark differences of *making* differences by seeking special favor and undermining the impartiality of law." Judith Resnik, *Changing the Topic*, 8 CARDOZO STUD. L. & LITERATURE 339, 347 (1996).
7. Sally J. Kenney, *Wise Latinas, Strategic Minnesotans, and the Feminist Standpoint: The Backlash against Women Judges*, 36 T. JEFFERSON L. REV. 43, 58 (2013) [hereinafter Kenney, *Wise Latinas*].
8. SALLY J. KENNEY, *Gender and Justice: Why Women in the Judiciary Really Matter* 3 (2012) [hereinafter KENNEY, GENDER AND JUSTICE]. Todd Collins and Laura Moyer, however, critique the studies that have found no measurable differences in outcomes based on race *or* gender for their single-axis analysis. Todd Collins & Laura Moyer, *Gender, Race, and Intersectionality on the Federal Appellate Bench*, 61 POL. RES. Q. 219, 219 (2008) (arguing that "the intersection of individual characteristics may provide an alternative approach for evaluating the effects of diversity on the federal appellate bench").
9. Rosemary Hunter, *Can Feminist Judges Make a Difference?*, 15 INT'L J. LEGAL PROF. 7, 8 (2008) [hereinafter Hunter, *Feminist Judges*].
10. *Id.* at 7–8.
11. Barrett has been characterized as "America's most powerful anti-feminist." Sophie McBain, *Amy Coney Barrett: The US Judge Poised to Undo Ginsburg's Legacy*, NEW STATESMAN (Oct. 12, 2020), https://www.newstatesman.com/world/2020/10/amy-coney-barrett-us-judge-poised-undo-ginsburg-s-legacy. Feminist organizations described Barrett as someone who was "groomed to overturn many of the important equality gains of the last 60 years." *NOW Denounces Amy Coney Barrett's Confirmation to SCOTUS*, NOW.ORG

(Oct. 26, 2020), https://now.org/media-center/press-release/now-denounces-amy-coney-barretts-confirmation-to-scotus. The National Women's Law Center, in a letter to the Senate Judiciary Committee opposing Barrett's nomination, stated that "[b]ased on our careful analysis of Judge Barrett's record on key gender justice issues, she would not only eviscerate reproductive rights and dismantle health care access, but also turn back protections for survivors of sexual harassment and reverse decades of progress and equality for communities of color, LGBTQ+ people, and anyone who experiences discrimination." Letter from Fatima Goss Graves to the U.S. Senate Committee on the Judiciary (Oct. 10, 2020), https://nwlc.org/wp-content/uploads/2020/10/NWLC-Opposition-Letter-to-Amy-Coney-Barrett-1.pdf.

12. While Hunter advocates for more "feminists" on the bench, she posits (and acknowledges as controversial) that women are more likely than men to be feminist. Hunter, *Feminist Judges, supra* note 9, at 8.
13. Kenney, *Wise Latinas, supra* note 7, at 66.
14. Sherrilyn A. Ifill, *Judging the Judges: Racial Diversity, Impartiality and Representation on State Trial Courts*, 39 B.C. L. REV. 95, 101 (1997) (arguing that the absence of minority judges "contributes to an atmosphere of racial exclusion which, at the very least, marginalizes African American lawyers, litigants and courtroom personnel in many jurisdictions").
15. KENNEY, GENDER AND JUSTICE, *supra* note 8, at 2. Kenney argues that the emphasis on differences based on sex misses the mark and deflects from what comes to light when gender is analyzed as a social process. Examining state and federal courts in the United States, as well as courts in the United Kingdom and the European Court of Justice, Kenney presents examples of ways in which "a gender analysis can help us more fully understand policy diffusion and emotions and social movement mobilization, backlash, policy implementation, agenda-setting, and representation." *Id.*
16. *Id.*
17. Maya Sen, *How Judicial Qualification Ratings May Disadvantage Minority and Female Candidates*, 2 J. L. & COURTS 33, 63 (2014).
18. Christina L. Boyd, Paul M. Collins, Jr. & Lori A. Ringhand, *The Role of Nominee Gender and Race at U.S. Supreme Court Confirmation Hearings*, 52 LAW & SOC'Y REV. 871, 895 (2018).
19. *Id.* at 872–873.
20. *Id.* at 876.
21. *Id.* at 893.
22. Rebecca D. Gill, *Implicit Bias in Judicial Performance Evaluations: We Must Do Better Than This*, 35 JUST. SYS. J. 301 (2014).
23. Patricia Yancey Martin, John R. Reynolds & Shelley Keith, *Gender Bias and Feminist Consciousness among Judges and Attorneys: A Standpoint Theory Analysis*, 27 SIGNS 665, 693 (2002).
24. Rosalind Dixon, *Female Justices, Feminism, and the Politics of Judicial Appointment: A Re-Examination*, 21 YALE J.L. & FEMINISM 297, 335 (2010).
25. CHAMALLAS, *supra* note 3, at 60.
26. 418 F. Supp. 1 (S.D.N.Y. 1975).
27. *Id.* at 4.
28. Kenney, *Wise Latinas, supra* note 7, at 51.
29. Carla D. Pratt, *Judging Identity*, 36 T. JEFFERSON L. REV. 83, 86 (2013).

30. Ifill, *supra* note 14, at 99.
31. Hon. Sonia Sotomayor, *A Latina Judge's Voice*, 13 BERKELEY LA RAZA L.J. 87, 92 (2002).
32. Pratt, *supra* note 29, at 84.
33. Similarly, in the field of employment discrimination, sociologist Rosabeth Moss Kanter has argued that underrepresented groups in an organization need to reach a critical mass before they are able to challenge structures of the organization that perpetuate stereotypes, determine what qualities define success, and limit opportunities. *See* ROSABETH MOSS KANTER, MEN AND WOMEN OF THE CORPORATION 206–242 (1977).
34. Judith Resnik, *On the Bias: Feminist Reconsiderations of the Aspirations for Our Judges*, 61 S. CALIF. L. REV. 1877, 1881 (1988).
35. Resnik detailed the work of four feminists from different disciplines whose ideas were prominent at the time her article was published: Carol Gilligan (psychology), Robin West (law), Sara Ruddick (philosophy), and Rosemary Ruether (theology). *Id.* at 1911–1921. I focus on the scholarship of Gilligan which has played a continuing role in the thinking about feminism and judging.
36. CAROL GILLIGAN, IN A DIFFERENT VOICE (1982).
37. *Id.* at 174.
38. *Id.*
39. Kenney, *Wise Latinas*, *supra* note 7, at 70–71 (arguing that Justice Sotomayor's "wise Latina" comment "situated her as a participant in an ongoing discussion about the nature of judging and... one who is deeply reflective and has a keen emotional intelligence").
40. Miller & Maier, *supra* note 4.
41. *Id.* at 536.
42. *Id.* at 542.
43. *Id.* at 544.
44. *Id.*
45. *Id.*
46. Katharine T. Bartlett, *Feminist Legal Methods*, 103 HARV. L. REV. 829 (1990).
47. *Id.* at 848.
48. *Id.*
49. Mari J. Matsuda, *Beside My Sister, Facing the Enemy: Legal Theory out of Coalition*, 43 STAN. L. REV. 1183, 1189 (1991).
50. *Id.*
51. Rosemary Hunter, Sharyn Roach Anleu, & Kathy Mack, *Judging in Lower Courts: Conventional, Procedural, Therapeutic and Feminist Approaches*, 12 INT'L J.L. CONTEXT 337, 347 (2016).
52. Hunter, *Feminist Judges*, *supra* note 9, at 11.
53. 529 U.S. 598 (2000) (Souter, J., dissenting).
54. *Id.* at 617–618.
55. Justice Souter's dissent included eleven such factual findings related to domestic violence and nine related to rape. *See id.* at 631–634.
56. Hunter, *Feminist Judges*, *supra* note 9, at 12.
57. Patricia A. Cain, *Good and Bad Bias: A Comment on Feminist Theory and Judging*, 61 S. CALIF. L. REV. 1945, 1946 (1987).
58. *See* Emily M. S. Houh & Kristin Kalsem, *It's Critical: Legal Participatory Action Research*, 19 MICH. J. RACE & L. 287 (2014) (analyzing what the principles and methods of participatory action research offer critical legal scholarship and activism).

59. The methods used in PAR are particularly effective for action-oriented social justice feminist work. *See* Kristin Kalsem & Verna L. Williams, *Social Justice Feminism*, 18 UCLA WOMEN'S L.J. 131, 183 (2010) ("social justice feminism is committed to making material changes to people's lives, not merely to theorizing").
60. Mari J. Matsuda, *Looking to the Bottom: Critical Legal Studies and Reparations*, 22 HARV. C.R.-C.L. L. REV. 323, 326 (1987) ("The method of looking to the bottom can lead to concepts of law radically different from those generated at the top").
61. For a full description of this legal PAR project, including the methodologies that were used, *see* Kristin Kalsem, *Judicial Education, Private Violence, and Community Action: A Case Study in Legal Participatory Action Research*, 22 J. GENDER, RACE & JUST. 41 (2019).
62. Interview with survivor 4 of intimate partner abuse (2017) (on file with author).
63. Interview with survivor 2 of intimate partner abuse (2017) (on file with author).
64. Rosemary Hunter, *The Power of Feminist Judgments?*, 20 FEM. LEG. STUD. 135, 136 (2012).
65. *Id.* at 137.
66. *Id.*
67. FEMINIST JUDGMENTS: REWRITTEN OPINIONS OF THE UNITED STATES SUPREME COURT (Kathryn M. Stanchi, Linda L. Berger & Bridget J. Crawford eds., 2016).
68. Linda L. Berger, Kathryn M. Stanchi & Bridget J. Crawford, *Learning from Feminist Judgments: Lessons in Language and Advocacy*, 98 TEX. L. REV. ONLINE 40, 44 (2019).
69. 505 U.S. 833 (1992).
70. 533 U.S. 53 (2001).
71. 83 U.S. 130 (1872).
72. FEMINIST JUDGMENTS: REWRITTEN TAX OPINIONS (Bridget J. Crawford & Anthony C. Infanti eds., 2017).
73. FEMINIST JUDGMENTS: REWRITTEN EMPLOYMENT DISCRIMINATION OPINIONS (Ann C. McGinley & Nicole Buonocore Porter eds., 2020).
74. FEMINIST JUDGMENTS: FAMILY LAW OPINIONS REWRITTEN (Rachel Rebouché ed., 2020).
75. FEMINIST JUDGMENTS: REPRODUCTIVE JUSTICE REWRITTEN (Kimberly M. Mutcherson ed., 2020).
76. FEMINIST JUDGMENTS: REWRITTEN TORT OPINIONS (Martha Chamallas & Lucinda M. Finley eds., 2020).
77. FEMINIST JUDGMENTS: REWRITTEN TRUSTS AND ESTATES OPINIONS (Deborah S. Gordon, Browne C. Lewis, & Carla Spivack eds., 2020).
78. Bridget J. Crawford, Kathryn M. Stanchi & Linda L. Berger, *Feminist Judging Matters: How Feminist Theory and Methods Affect the Process of Judgment*, 47 U. BALT. L. REV. 167, 181 (2018) [hereinafter Crawford et al., *Feminist Judging Matters*].
79. Margaret E. Johnson, *Feminist Judgments & #MeToo*, 94 NOTRE DAME L. REV. ONLINE 51, 52 (2018).
80. Crawford et al., *Feminist Judging Matters*, *supra* note 78, at 181.
81. FEMINIST JUDGMENTS, *supra* note 67, at 6.
82. Crawford et al., *Feminist Judging Matters*, *supra* note 78, at 168.

CHAPTER 30

CONTRACT'S INFLUENCE ON FEMINISM AND VICE VERSA

MARTHA M. ERTMAN

FEMINIST legal theory and contract theory have a long and complex relationship. On the upside, conceptual and doctrinal tools imported from contract have upgraded women's status from doormats to fuller citizenship, especially in families. But a number of feminists express concern that contract-based reforms do less good than the procontract camp acknowledges, and indeed inflict harm.

This tension between pro- and anticontract views likewise appears in the more abstract discussions of legal, social, and economic hierarchies. Political theorists and philosophers have long hypothesized that a mythical social contract established the civil state. Traditional social contract theory justifies law—state power over individuals—on the grounds that the regulated individuals were party to these hypothetical contract negotiations that gave the state the power to make and enforce laws in exchange for people's health, safety, and welfare. Feminist theorist Carole Pateman's highly influential 1988 book challenged this conventional wisdom. She argued that the social contract only masquerades as a deal made by everyone, for everyone, when it actually constitutes and continues to justify patriarchal rule of men over women.[1]

Philosopher Charles Mills extended Pateman's analysis of the social contract's faux neutrality to encompass race, arguing that the social contract actually created and sustains white supremacy.[2] His logic, however, leads to a different destination, one that sees contractual thinking as a vehicle for reform and reparations. Where Pateman and others would scrap the whole social contract metaphor—and presumably reforms that rest on contract—Mills would retain contract's liberal promise of equal opportunity for all. He built a compelling case for reparations for people of color who have been and continue to be systemically harmed by racial breaches of the social contract.

The combination of Pateman's distrust of contractual rhetoric and Mills's embrace of its progressive potential reflects the range of feminist positions regarding contract. Feminists have voiced both enthusiasm and serious concerns about contracts in, for example, marital and reproductive technology contracts. This chapter echoes that focus on family law since many contract-related reforms seek to improve women's economic and other interests in adult relationships and parenthood.[3]

First- and second-wave feminists used contract as a tool to remedy the status-based strictures grounded in gender that define traditional marriage. Status-based rules of coverture deprived wives of the right to enter contracts, enjoy an equal share of household wealth accumulation, and say "no" to their husbands' sexual advances. Feminist reforms to remedy those injustices included Married Women's Property Acts in the nineteenth century, repeal of the marital rape exception in the 1970s, and today's continuing struggles to gain adequate respect and pay for housework and other care work. Another feminist reform based on contractual thinking is the still-evolving advocacy for law to recognize alternatives to marriage such as cohabitation and expand ways to relinquish and attain legal parenthood via reproductive technologies and adoption. These feminists note that contract can reflect how families actually function, in contrast to status-based notions that designate only one type of family as "real" or "natural"—a heterosexual married couple raising kids to whom they are genetically related.

In contrast, anticontract feminists flag the dangers of gender, race, and class subordination in contract-based reforms. For example, attempts to protect wives in prenuptial agreements overlook lower rates of marriage among African-American women, race-related patterns of wealth accumulation that make prenups more likely in marriages of white people, that many if not most divorcing couples have more debts than property to divide, and continuing power disparities between spouses.[4] Likewise, contract skeptics see reproductive technology contracts as protecting white, propertied motherhood while courting eugenics and commodifying children.[5]

This chapter charts influential work on both sides of the contract debate and identifies a third approach that sees contract as a mechanism for law to move away from a hierarchal regime by stopping at a contractual way station en route to a more equal system of public ordering.[6] One example of such an innovation is known as collaborative family law, in which disputing couples essentially contract out of using traditional litigation-focused dispute resolution and into a system that honors the role of emotions and integrates social workers or other therapists into dispute resolution.[7]

The first section of this chapter sets out examples of feminist theory that portray contract as a route to gender equality. Section II discusses feminist scholarship that cautions against colluding with gender subordination. Section III introduces the view of contract as a private law laboratory of sorts to try out new forms of relation that can mature to public law rules that recognize gender equality. Finally, section IV identifies ways that feminist legal theorists have injected feminist insights into traditional contract law via doctrines such as good faith in employment contracts, debtor rights in lending relationships, and defenses such as unconscionability and duress.

I. Contracts as Instruments of Gender Equality

Some feminists disagree with poet and essayist Audre Lorde that "the master's tools will never dismantle the master's house."[8] They point to the crucial role that contract played in dismantling foundational elements of the patriarchal master's house by chipping away at coverture's refusal to recognize women's independent legal identities. Those modifications to the marriage contract allowed law to finally recognize and remedy intimate partner violence, marital rape, and women's economic subordination.[9] In addition, the framework of contract paved the way for law to expand the definition of family beyond marriage to include cohabitation, polyamory, living-apart-together, and relations of dependency,[10] and also to recognize a range of parent-child relationships made possible by reproductive technologies.[11]

A. Contract as an Upgrade from Status

One benefit of a contractual framework is that it presupposes the possibility of modification. Thus, family law can change, evolving to recognize new family forms such as same-sex marriages and nonmarital cohabitation. Cohabitation and other alternative family forms often take shape via contracts, such as living-together, surrogacy, and sperm donation agreements. Status is the alternative to a range of legally recognized families structured by contracts and legal rules that reflect their particular situations. A status-based view of family asserts that God or biology has designated only one form of family as natural and worthy of legal protection and social respect—married, heterosexual couples, raising genetically related kids.

Many feminist legal reforms have prompted a shift away from status and toward contract. For example, the nineteenth-century Married Women's Property Acts displaced elements of common-law coverture rules and gave wives the power to make contracts and own property. Along the same lines, the 1866 Civil Rights Act provided—and still provides—that "[a]ll persons . . . have the same right . . . to make and enforce contracts . . . as is enjoyed by white citizens."[12] Yet even contract enthusiasts acknowledge that contract was hardly a silver bullet that eradicated race and gender subordination. As historian Amy Dru Stanley pointed out regarding the nineteenth-century Married Women's Property Acts, wives of all races had the right to their own labor and person, yet the reforms left intact a husband's legal title to his wife's service at home.[13] Along the same lines the post-Reconstruction South reinstated debt peonage and sharecropping systems—within larger Jim Crow limits on African Americans' participation in civil and economic life—that mimicked enslavement in many respects.[14] Still, the turn to contract and away from status has revamped the strictures of marriage.

B. Marriage and Beyond

Marriage has long been a mix of status and contract, in different proportions at different times and contexts. Even the status-focused coverture framework presupposed that a woman entered a civil contract by which she subsumed her legal identity under that of her husband. Gradually, reforms eroded much of the status elements of the marriage contract to make it more of a formally equal partnership. Those modifications contributed to legal recognition of sexual assault within marriage and intimate partner violence more generally, as well as proposals to better value homemaking labor.

Contract requires genuine consent, and conversely rape involves the lack of consent. Catharine MacKinnon, in her signature brand of take-no-prisoners prose, excoriated the law for treating "[u]nvirtuous women, like *wives* and prostitutes, [as] consenting, whores, *unrapable.*"[15] The myth that marriage vows constituted a blanket consent every time the husband sought sex fell under this feminist challenge. By the late twentieth century, men no longer could rape their wives with impunity, though the punishments for rape often treat rape within marriage as less serious than stranger rape.[16]

Contracts also feature prominently in feminist legal theory addressing the persistent devaluation of homemaking labor and other care work.[17] The wages-for-housework movement dates back to the first wave of feminism,[18] but its modern incarnation came out of socialist feminists' engagement in Marxist thought. Advocacy and academic discourse coalesced in movements such as the 1970s International Wages for Housework Campaign and a Global Women's Strike in 2000, which aimed to show the value of caregiving work by going a day without it.[19] "Wages for housework" became a rallying cry that morphed into an avalanche of law review articles seeking to commodify homemaking labor through a theory justifying alimony as a payment to which divorced wives were entitled instead of charity that terminated when a woman remarried.[20]

Legal reforms altered not just the terms of the marital contract but also the outdated status-based limits on who can marry. Landmark cases that allowed interracial and same-sex couples to marry dramatically modified the marriage contract.[21] A crucial step in extending marriage equality to same-sex couples occurred when law and culture first recognized that a heterosexual couple living together outside of marriage were not criminals and thus entitled to enter into cohabitation contracts.

Living together has increased over 1000 percent since 1960. Fully 10 percent of American households included a cohabiting couple as of the 2010 Census, and by 2019 more Americans ages eighteen to forty-four had lived together than had been married.[22]

Prior to the mid-1970s, the law refused to recognize cohabitation agreements, labeling them "meretricious," or akin to prostitution. A California case changed that view. In the mid-1960s, actor Lee Marvin and aspiring singer Michelle Triola moved in together. Michelle took his name, as many cohabiting women do. They agreed that he would support her for life in exchange for her giving up her singing career to become his full-time "companion, homemaker, housekeeper, and cook."[23] After they split up, Michelle sued for breach of contract. In 1976, the California Supreme Court recognized her right—and other cohabitants—to sue for breach of this contract. That decision brought the term "palimony" into popular speech, or "galimony" when the cohabitants were both women. This new terminology helped family law and the public see cohabitation as an alternative to marriage instead of a crime. Other states quickly followed suit and today, live-ins can contract with each other nearly everywhere in the United States, though they often have to also satisfy procedural requirements such as getting the agreement in writing.[24]

Marvin played a key role in the LGBT rights movement's progress toward marriage equality and other legal rights. Between the 1970s and 2000, same-sex couples increasingly used contracts such as cohabitation agreements, wills, and powers of attorney to make the law at least partly recognize that they saw themselves as family. By the 1990s, domestic partnership employment policies in employment contracts and some municipalities, which gave couples more recognition and a measure of protection, further paved the way for same-sex couples to enjoy marriage equality.[25]

This expansion of contract within family law led scholars in the 1990s and early twenty-first century to debate whether the law ought to go all the way, abolishing civil marriage and replacing it with contracts.[26] Martha Fineman was among the first feminists to champion contract as an improvement over status-based understandings of adult relationships, finding it "a useful tool with which to examine family relationships—relationships that have their roots in the more ancient realms of status and hierarchy."[27] Fineman touted the value of giving individuals "the means to voluntarily and willingly assume obligations and gain entitlements," so as to bring stability to relationships while remaining open to the potential for change.[28] Fineman's highly influential body of work—and that of the many scholars who follow her lead—seeks to redefine "family" as parent-child and other relationships of dependency and vulnerability, instead of the current definition that centers on a sexual dyad in marriage. The core problem with having marriage define family, for Fineman, was that it privatizes responsibility for care and its costs. Fineman would instead demote marriage to a private, perhaps religious status and "collapse all sexual relationships into the same category-private-not sanctioned, privileged, or preferred by law."[29] Law would instead provide rights and responsibilities to support the inevitable dependency of children and others requiring care, and the derivative dependency of the caregivers (often mothers).

But not all feminists agreed with Fineman's push to replace marriage with contract. Anita Bernstein predicted that an explicit transition from status to contract would mean that

> All domestic relations between adult individuals would be formed by issue-specific agreements. Family law would survive in order to regulate the care of children, but two would no longer become one in any legal sense. The law would intervene in a couple's life just as it now uses the law of contracts, torts, crimes, and property to moderate relations between any other adults.[30]

Bernstein concluded that abolishing marriage-as-a-status would do more harm than good, since the role played by marriage would be replaced by "either the state or capital, an unrelenting press of the market."[31] With "[n]o blithe, freeing, choice-affirming alternative to this extraordinary institution ... available," she concluded that marriage should be mended, not ended.[32]

C. Expanding Parent-Child Relationships

Contracts also played a crucial role in creating and supporting families beyond the traditional mold of one man and one woman and their biological children. The law and a multi-billion-dollar reproductive technology sector allow gamete "donors" to contract out of legal parenthood when they sell their eggs or sperm to an egg or sperm bank, making room for "intended parents" who can step in as the legal parents of children born through alternative insemination or surrogacy. This reproductive labor provides new ways for women to earn money in work they deem fulfilling.[33] Increasingly, law recognizes three-parent families, such as a lesbian couple that contracts with a gay man for him to provide the sperm and all three of them to be legal parents.[34] So many gay men, lesbians, and single women became parents via this route that it's jokingly called a "gayby boom."[35]

One prominent case served as a pivot point. In 1988, the New Jersey Supreme Court case *Baby M* refused to enforce a surrogacy contract on the grounds that it violated public policy and perhaps even state law criminalizing baby selling.[36] That opinion—and the worldwide press coverage of the case—unleashed a deluge of debate about evolving methods of family formation and whether contracts—and contractual thinking—were good for women, children, and society more broadly. New Jersey's Supreme Court declared that "there are, in a civilized society, some things that money can't buy."[37] Yet the court used family law doctrine to achieve much of what the surrogacy contract contemplated: the intended parents had legal custody of the child, and the genetic mother and surrogate was allowed occasional visits.[38]

Just five years later, the California Supreme Court opened the golden state's doors to the reproductive technology industry via *Johnson v. Calvert*, which validated a surrogacy contract that differed from the one in *Baby M* in one crucial aspect.[39] By the 1990s, advances in in vitro fertilization (IVF) allowed a surrogate to bear a child to whom she had no genetic relationship because the egg was provided by another woman. The sperm typically came from the intended father. IVF, in short, enabled intentional parents and surrogates to "contract around" the legal and ethical specter of surrogate mothers relinquishing children to whom they are genetically related. Today more than nine of ten surrogacies are gestational, a method that, as of 2014, brought more than 1,600 children into the world each year.[40]

While California's willingness to enforce gestational surrogacy contracts made that state the center of the multi-billion-dollar reproductive technologies industry, other states also enforce commercial surrogacy agreements, though some others ban or sharply curtail the terms of those agreements. Liberal feminists whose work has supported that recognition include Marjorie McGuire Shultz and Carmen Shalev.[41]

II. Contract as an Instrument of Gender Subordination

Some feminists contend that contract is an unsuitable tool to dismantle the master's house. These scholars highlight how neoliberal principles radiating from the ideal of "freedom of contract" ignore that many people lack the socioeconomic resources to get to the bargaining table.[42]

A. Limited Benefit of Modified Marriage Contract

Scholars such as Robin Lenhardt and Nancy Polikoff warn against using marriage reform to serve feminist ends because marriage has long benefited white, middle-class Americans more than everyone else.[43] Most of this literature aims for intersectionality, with some scholars focusing more on racial inequalities and others seeing marriage as hopelessly heteropatriarchal and thus antithetical to feminist and LGBTQ interests.

For much of U.S. history, enslaved people were legally banned from marrying, and the post-Civil War expansion of marriage equality that purported to be part of the freed-people's newly equal status failed to deliver on that promise. Instead, in Lenhardt's words, "marriage regulation—not unlike Jim Crow segregation in public schools or housing—has been instrumental in locking African America into a second-class citizenship from which it has not yet fully emerged."[44] For example, extravagant government support for families such as the GI Bill and Social Security largely denied African Americans that social and economic capital. Instead of a new deal, African Americans were subjected to the same old deal via welfare regulations predicated on purported failures of personal responsibility that disrupted relationships, compromised autonomy, and exacerbated racial disadvantage and stigma.[45]

Today, marriage continues to benefit haves more than have-nots. White Americans are much more likely to marry than African Americans, and college graduates are more likely to marry than those with less education and thus more modest socioeconomic resources.[46] Those data, coupled with declining marriage rates across demographic groups, strengthen contract-skeptics' contention that we should abandon the marriage contract altogether.[47]

Nancy Polikoff's book *Beyond (Gay and Straight) Marriage* made perhaps the most comprehensive case for moving beyond conjugality. Where Martha Fineman focused on fragile economic circumstances of dependents and those who care for them, Polikoff would also recognize as "family" sexual adult relationships. She proposed a postconjugal legal regime in which law allocates rights and duties based on how intimate relationships function, whether they are between adults, caretaking relationships, between adults and children, or adult dependents. Instead of requiring marriage to trigger a person's rights and duties, Polikoff would use households or a similar reflection of who functions as a person's family.[48]

B. Dangers of Contractual Parenthood

Feminists also flag dangers in contracting for parenthood through surrogacy and other reproductive technologies, raising objections about limited access and market-inflicted harms. Regarding access, Libby Adler pointed out that these methods of family formation require advance planning, which "may be a class-based, racially, and regionally selective luxury."[49] Procedures can also be expensive, particularly surrogacy, in which intended parents pay as much as $150,000 - $200,000 to bring genetically related children into their families.[50]

The market is structured for white, middle-class women to access reproductive technologies, instead of facilitating access for everyone, including women of color. For example, intended parents order eggs or sperm off the internet through banks that stock genetic material from "donors" with sought-after traits such as height, education, health, and markers of whiteness such as skin color and hair texture. By stocking their shelves with much more genetic material from white donors than from donors of color, they essentially retail whiteness.[51]

On the seller side of reproductive technology contracts, surrogate mothers and egg donors usually have fewer resources than intended parents. Those power disparities take on international dimensions when fertility tourists travel to countries such as India to cut costs and take advantage of more lax regulatory environments.[52]

Surrogacy contracts have attracted substantial criticism.[53] Philosopher Elizabeth Anderson contended that surrogacy treats children and women's reproductive capacities as commodities, what she regarded as an "unconscionable commodification."[54] Along the same lines, Nancy Ehrenreich questions whether surrogates really exercise freedom of contract, since they are often low-income women with children who need a job that does not require them to leave their homes.[55]

Additional objections are that surrogacy contracts exploit women and collude with eugenics in ways that harm gamete donors, surrogates, and, more generally, people of color, women, people with disabilities, and the wider culture. As Anita Allen reminds us, legal rules commodified enslaved African American women's reproductive capacity by tracing children's status as slave or free to their mothers.[56] That single rule delivered a zero-sum bonanza to white men at the expense of Black women by exponentially increasing white male economic, social, and psychological power over African American women, men, and children.[57] Khiara Bridges tied this history to today's surrogacy law and practices, noting that legalized surrogacy has the potential to "magnify racial inequalities inasmuch as wealthy white people will look to poor women of color to carry and give birth to the white babies that the couples covet."[58]

Dorothy Roberts's work in this vein may well be the most influential, in particular her 1997 book *Killing the Black Body*.[59] Roberts tied that history to today's reproductive technology practices and regulation.[60] Through this lens, (largely) white women's freedom of contract to hire surrogates matters less than continued reproductive race injustices such as involuntary sterilization, mandatory birth control for public assistance recipients, incarcerated pregnant women being forced to give birth in shackles, and racial disparities in child-removal decisions.[61] Roberts also flagged the dangers of discrimination against people with disabilities, exacerbated by surrogacy.[62]

Finally, Naomi Cahn's influential critiques of contractual views of parenthood focused on the sale of gametes used in IVF and alternative insemination. *Test Tube Families* argued for increased state regulation of families created through assisted reproduction such as surrogacy and alternative insemination. She decried the current laissez-faire system in which would-be mothers may purchase sperm from anonymous donors via sperm banks, expressing concern that this practice denies children the right to know their origins. Cahn's proposed solutions included sperm donor registries and "donor-conceived" stamps on birth certificates of children conceived via contract instead of coitus.[63]

III. Contracts as an Instrument of Transitional Justice

A third group of feminist legal theorists see the benefits and burdens of contract in a more nuanced way.[64] In Peggy Radin's pragmatic formulation, which she called "incomplete commodification," contracts can provide some but not all of the regulation for a given transaction. As such, they serve as a way station between "ideal justice" and "nonideal justice," helping law and society "transition from where we are to a better world."[65] An example of this approach is Adrienne Davis's historical analysis of antebellum agreements to transfer property between white men and Black women with whom they cohabited.[66] While these concubinage agreements were hardly paragons of an idealized contractualist relationship among equal bargaining partners, they—and the law's willingness to enforce a surprising number of them—show that contract can provide a second-best solution when first-best is not an option.

In the family law context, Jana Singer is a leading proponent of the view that contract can provide a private law transition point between a publicly ordered system of gender subordination to a public law rule that more fairly allocates the benefits and burdens of family life.[67] She catalogued trends of increased privatization in the late twentieth century such as spouses' ability to contractually alter the state-supplied rules regarding property division and alimony, the shift to no-fault divorce, and contracting for parenthood through private adoptions and reproductive technology contracts. On the pro side, she noted that privatization of family law can facilitate alternative ways to form families that respect people's choice, autonomy, and diversity of family forms more than the old status-based models. However, downsides for families include the common tendency of marital and cohabitation contracts to deprive women of access to a household's economic assets, and the loss of shared values about the nature of families and what society owes them. Rather than champion particular reforms, Singer voiced appreciation for law's progression from privately ordered domestic partnership to same-sex marriage, gradually "recogniz[ing] and affirm[ing] family relationships as both a haven for individual self-expression and a vehicle for expressing our most cherished public values."[68] Along the same lines, Singer and Jane Murphy's 2015 book *Divorced from Reality* applies this framework to analyze contract-based reforms to dispute resolution such as collaborative lawyering, especially in parenting disputes.[69]

Empirical evidence supports this balanced approach. Sociologists Rosana Hertz and Margaret Nelson's comprehensive data collection and analysis told a complex story about positive, negative, and neutral ways that gamete markets shape relationships.[70] Likewise, sociologist, lawyer, and former family law practitioner Hillary Berk documented the actual terms in surrogacy contracts and the social dynamics among intended parents, surrogates, egg donors, and agencies. Her data set of 115 interviews with the parties, agency personnel, and lawyers about their surrogacy arrangements showed that contractualized reproduction can be simultaneously "empowering" and "oppressive" as reproductive labor is both commodified and legitimized.[71] This view acknowledges power imbalances while valuing contractual pregnancy's ability to provide surrogates with needed income and meaningful work.

Recent articles on surrogacy accept its continued existence—and thus its contractual framework—and focus on how to regulate it to empower women and broaden the range of family creation while avoiding exploitation.[72] For example, Rachel Rebouché mapped gaps between actual surrogacy contracts and surrogacy legislation on topics such as prenatal behaviors from alcohol consumption to manicures to who decides whether and when to terminate a pregnancy. Contract law and family law, together, may strike a balance between the freedom of choice and protecting against overreach when moneyed intended parents, agencies, and attorneys control much of the transactions.[73]

Although most contract-focused feminist legal theory imports contractualism into family law and related doctrines, some scholars instead transport feminist insights into traditional contract doctrines.

IV. Feminist Improvements to Traditional Contract Doctrines

Feminist proposals to right wrongs in contract doctrine draw on cultural feminism's centering of relationships and connection to others. These scholars challenge contract law's traditional assumptions that people are self-interested rational actors intent on maximizing their own welfare. Instead, they propose an alternative, relational contract theory, which presumes equality of the parties and recognizes that their intent reflects their commercial and personal relationships.[74] As Debora Threedy explained, relational contract theory shifts our focus from "the things contracted for to the relationship between the contracting parties," which allows contract doctrine to better respond to different kinds of contracts and to differences among contracting parties.[75]

Influential contributions in this literature address employment law; debtor-creditor relationships; and the defenses of duress, misrepresentation, and unconscionability that apply to any kind of contract.

A. Employment Law

Employment law evolved out of the common law rules governing households, which reflected and enforced hierarchies of men over women, adults over children, and masters over servants.[76] It involves a mix of contract and status, and as it has moved toward contractualization, feminists have argued for a relational understanding of contractual intent. These proposals tend to advocate for worker protections, perhaps because women's socioeconomic situation is more likely to put them in the position of employee than employer.

For example, Emily Houh has shown how the duty of good faith and fair dealing that exists in every contract could modify the general rule that workers are employed-at-will. Houh's approach would use this common law doctrine to protect employees from employers' subordinating conduct based on race, gender, and other identity categories when statutes fail to recognize those harms.[77] Houh also proposed expanding the duty of good faith to police conduct between employers and employees before a contract is formed. Traditionally, the duty of good faith arises out of the contract itself, so it does not exist prior to contract formation. Houh reasoned that employment law should start applying good faith duties in hiring and negotiation to protect employees from discrimination in the preemployment stage. Other uses of common law contract rules might provide protection for characteristics, such as obesity, or from harmful conduct, such as bullying, which employment discrimination statutes do not (yet) cover.[78] An expansive interpretation of good faith could fill those gaps.

Another example of feminist influence on employment contracts incorporates substantive fairness to temper harsh noncompete agreements. Rachel Arnow-Richman would recognize the relational components of employment by importing the family law requirement of substantive fairness in marital contracts.[79] She reasoned that because "noncompetes [and] premarital agreements are an attempt to control in advance the financial consequences of the dissolution of a legal relationship," courts should evaluate their validity by the marital contracting tests regarding "the quality of the spouse's consent and the fairness of the agreement at the time it was drafted."[80]

B. Debtor-Creditor Relationships

Traditional contract doctrine erases identity categories by assuming away peoples' gender, race, and class, all in the name of formal equality. Granted, formal equality is an upgrade from the bad old days of coverture and enslavement when the law deprived married women and enslaved Americans of the power to enter contracts. Still, law's supposed neutrality too often masks the law taking the perspective of more powerful parties. In the debt context, that faux neutrality can interfere with women's access to capital—and thus life choices—and ignore or exacerbate gendered vulnerabilities to sexual assault and responsibility to care for children and other dependents.

For example, Elizabeth Warren and others have long flagged the higher price of debt for women.[81] Two feminist proposals import relational contract insights to prevent creditors from taking advantage of debtors' gendered vulnerability.

Spousal surety cases—in which wives personally guarantee their spouses' business debts—provide fertile ground to plant feminist insights.[82] Gillian Hadfield used spousal surety agreements as a platform to propose a reliance-based, relational theory of contract that she called an "expressive theory of contract."[83] Spousal-guarantee cases have outsized effects on the lives of women and their families because the surety agreement allows a bank to sell the family home to collect a loan that it extended to cover a husband's business debts. That outcome is particularly unjust when the husband has misinformed the wife about the amount of the debt, a religious wife faces lifelong pressure to "accept a position of subservience and obedience to her husband," or the wife signed under duress.[84]

Because these circumstances raise serious questions about the genuineness of wives' consent, English courts have presumed undue influence or misrepresentation in cases where the surety and debtor are spouses or cohabitants. However, creditors can rebut this presumption by establishing that the surety fully understood the nature and consequences of the transaction: namely, that she could lose her home. Consequently, British lenders give special notice to each wife/surety of the amount of her potential liability and its risks, and also advise her to get independent legal advice. U.S. courts, in contrast, generally let spousal sureties defeat creditors' claims only if they can show that the creditor knew of or participated in the husband's duress, misrepresentation, undue influence, or fraud.[85]

Hadfield proposed a third path. She critiqued notice as insufficient to transform a surety under gendered constraints into a rational self-interest maximizer. Instead, she contended, contract law should balance gendered constraints against the danger of paternalist assumptions that women are unable to think for themselves. In Hadfield's view, the dominant contractarian "will" theory of contract should remain the rule for commercial contracts but be supplemented with a relational or reliance-based theory of contract in special cases such as spousal guarantees, surrogacy, and marital separation agreements.[86]

Another commercial context in which legal scholars have sought to import feminism to better balance debtor-creditor relations arises out of a statute, UCC Article 9. Article 9 governs secured transactions, in which debtors give creditors a "security interest" in collateral so that when a debtor defaults by, for example, failing to pay down the loan, the creditor can repossess the collateral to satisfy the debt.[87] The most remarkable thing about Article 9 is that creditors' repossession rights are entirely private; courts are not involved. Upon a debtor's default, a secured creditor can hire a private repo person to seize collateral and sell it at a private sale to satisfy the debt. Car loans are such a common—and familiar—instance of Article 9's application that an entire genre of TV shows features those repossessions.[88]

Jean Braucher and Debora Threedy have both proposed that the Article 9 standards for what repo people can and cannot do consider the perspective of female debtors. For example, Jean Braucher proposed a "repo code" that would supplement the current standard that repossessions cannot "breach the peace" with a set of more specific rules.[89] Following the federal Fair Debt Collection Practices Act, Braucher's repo code would prevent creditors from taking advantage of female debtors' fear of sexual assault and desire to protect their children by, for example, prohibiting: middle-of-the-night repossession at a debtor's home; entering a residence or garage of commercial building without contemporaneous permission; and "breaking, opening, or removing any lock gate, or other barrier."[90]

Where Jean Braucher's "repo code" implicitly protects the expectations of female debtors, Debora Threedy argued for something more like a "reasonable woman" standard in judging whether a repossession violated Article 9.[91] According to this view, the traditional standard that a threat of violence impermissibly breaches the peace is not enough. Instead, Threedy contended, judges deciding Article 9 cases should acknowledge that the mere fact of men showing up in the middle of the night could constitute a threat of violence. For example, one case involved a mother living with her two young children in a trailer home. Repo men woke her up at 4:30 A.M. to repossess her car.[92] She told them to stop and insisted that she needed to get personal items out of the car, yet the two repo men refused to comply and asserted their control by stepping between her and the car. Although UCC Article 9 formally says that repossession over debtor objection breaches the peace, the court concluded that the facts did not constitute an impermissible threat of force or risk of violence.[93] Threedy, in contrast, asserted that "perhaps standing in her nightclothes before two strangers in the middle of a winter night, with her two small children alone in the trailer, was intimidation enough."[94]

C. Defenses

Scholars such as Threedy have also examined how feminist interpretations of common law defenses of duress and misrepresentation could help contract law reflect the perspectives of women who assert them, instead of the people and institutions against whom they are asserted. Threedy grounded her approach in relational contract theory, urging us to question contract law's preferences for "objectivity over subjectivity [and] for abstraction over contextualization."[95] One influential application of this view is Threedy's archaeological excavation of the canonical contract case *Vokes v. Arthur Murray*, in which the plaintiff claimed she was induced on false premises to enter into expensive contracts with a dancing school that misrepresented her dancing ability.[96]

Threedy noted the tension between autonomy and fairness that runs throughout contract law and suggested Hadfield's expressive choice theory of contract could better justify Audrey Vokes being able to avoid the monumental bill racked up by the dance studio via its misrepresentations.[97]

V. Conclusion

Contract plays a prominent role in feminist legal theory. Contract has played a crucial role in overturning systemic structures of subordination such as coverture and the exclusion of same-sex couples from marriage. However, the presumptions of market access and equal bargaining power ignore or downplay systemic hierarchies of race, class, and gender in ways that can render contracts unsuitable to achieve foundational feminist goals. Perhaps the most nuanced view of contract within feminist legal theory situates it as a private law mechanism for law to transition from outdated public status-based rules to new public rules that more justly distribute resources.

Just as some feminists have used contract to improve family law, others have transported feminist insights to improve defects in traditional contract law. Often grounded in relational contract theory, these proposals would expand the duty of good faith in employment law, recognize gendered power differences in debtor-creditor relations, and reconstruct equitable defenses such as duress that apply in all contractual contexts. Although feminism has yet to radically reshape contract doctrine, feminist scholars' deep engagement with contract law has opened new possibilities for future developments in the law.

Notes

1. Carole Pateman, The Sexual Contract (1988).
2. Charles Mills, The Racial Contract (1997).
3. Contracts and not legally binding exchanges in the intimate sphere pack a strong gender punch. Lenore J. Weitzman, The Marriage Contract: Spouses, Lovers and the Law (1981); Lenore J. Weitzman, The Divorce Revolution: The Unexpected Social and Economic Consequences for Women and Children in America (1985); Arlie Russell Hochschild, The Second Shift: Working Families and the Revolution at Home (1989); Hila Keren, *Feminism and Contract Law*, in Research Handbook on Feminist Jurisprudence 406 (Robin West & Cynthia Grant Bowman eds., 2019).
4. Ralph Richard Banks, Is Marriage for White People? (2011); Dorothy Roberts, Killing the Black Body (1997); Twila L. Perry, *Alimony: Race, Privilege, and Dependency in the Search for Theory*, 82 Geo. L.J. 2481 (1994); Cynthia Grant Bowman, Unmarried Couples, Law, and Public Policy (2010).
5. Margaret Jane Radin, Contested Commodities (1996); Roberts, *supra* note 4.
6. *See, e.g.*, Jana B. Singer, *The Privatization of Family Law*, 1992 Wis. L. Rev. 1443.

7. *See, e.g.*, Jane C. Murphy & Jana B. Singer, Divorced from Reality: Rethinking Family Dispute Resolution (2015).
8. Audre Lorde, Sister Outsider 110 (rev. ed. 2007).
9. *See, e.g.*, Jill Elaine Hasday, *Contest and Consent: A Legal History of Marital Rape*, 88 Calif. L. Rev. 1373 (2000); Reva B. Siegel, *"The Rule of Love": Wife Beating as Prerogative and Privacy*, 105 Yale L.J. 2117, 2147 (1996); Reva B. Siegel, *The Modernization of Marital Status Law: Adjudicating Wives' Rights to Earnings, 1860-1930*, 82 Geo. L.J. 2127 (1994); Elizabeth S. Scott & Robert E. Scott, *Marriage as Relational Contract*, 84 Va. L. Rev. 1225, 1243 (1998); Marjorie Maguire Shultz, *Contractual Ordering of Marriage: A New Model for State Policy*, 70 Calif. L. Rev. 204, 211 (1982); Martha M. Ertman, *Marriage as a Trade: Bridging the Private/Private Distinction*, 36 Harv. C.R.-C.L. L. Rev. 79 (2001); Barbara A. Atwood, *Marital Contracts and the Meaning of Marriage*, 54 Ariz. L. Rev. 11 (2012).
10. Bowman, *supra* note 4; Nancy Polikoff, Beyond (Straight and Gay) Marriage: Valuing All Families under the Law (2008); Laura A. Rosenbury, *Friends with Benefits*, 106 Mich. L. Rev. 189 (2007). Adrienne D. Davis, *Regulating Polygamy: Intimacy, Default Rules, and Bargaining for Equality*, 110 Colum. L. Rev. 1955 (2010); Martha M. Ertman, *Race Treason: The Untold Story of America's Ban on Polygamy*, 19 Colum. J. Gender & L. 287, 291, 334–338 (2010); William N. Eskridge Jr., *Family Law Pluralism: The Guided-Choice Regime of Menus, Default Rules, and Override Rules*, 100 Geo. L.J. 1881 (2012); Cynthia Grant Bowman, *Living Apart Together, Women, and Family Law*, 24 Cardozo J. Equal Rts. & Soc. Just. 47 (2017); June Carbone & Naomi Cahn, *Nonmarriage*, 76 Md. L. Rev. 55 (2016); Judith Stacey, Unhitched: Love, Marriage, and Family Values from West Hollywood to Western China 151 (2011); Gillian Calder & Lori G. Beaman, Polygamy's Rights and Wrongs: Perspectives on Harm, Family, and Law (2014); Melissa Murray, *Accommodating Nonmarriage*, 88 S. Calif. L. Rev. 661 (2015); Martha Albertson Fineman, The Neutered Mother, The Sexual Family and Other Twentieth Century Tragedies (1995).
11. *See, e.g.*, Marjorie Maguire Shultz, *Reproductive Technology and Intent-Based Parenthood: An Opportunity for Gender Neutrality*, 1990 Wis. L. Rev. 297; Courtney Meghan Cahill, *Reproduction Reconceived*, 101 Minn. L. Rev. 617 (2016); April L. Cherry, *Choosing Substantive Justice: A Discussion of "Choice," "Rights" and the New Reproductive Technologies*, 11 Wis. Women's L.J. 431 (1997); Kimberly D. Krawiec, *A Woman's Worth*, 88 N.C. L. Rev. 1739 (2010); Kimberly M. Mutcherson, *Procreative Pluralism*, 30 Berkeley J. Gender, L. & Just. 22 (2015); Carol Sanger, *Separating from Children*, 96 Colum. L. Rev. 375 (1996); Courtney G. Joslin, *Protecting Children(?): Marriage, Gender, and Assisted Reproductive Technology*, 83 S. Calif. L. Rev. 1177 (2010); Baby Markets: Money and the New Politics of Creating Families (Michele Bratcher Goodwin ed., 2010).
12. 42 U.S.C. § 1981; Amy Dru Stanley, From Bondage to Contract: Wage Labor, Marriage, and the Market in the Age of Slave Emancipation (1998).
13. Stanley, *supra* note 12, at 175.
14. Eric Foner, Reconstruction: America's Unfinished Revolution (1988); Guyora Binder, *The Slavery of Emancipation*, 17 Cardozo L. Rev. 2063 (1996).
15. Catharine A. MacKinnon, Toward a Feminist Theory of the State 175 (1989) (emphasis added).
16. *See, e.g.*, Hasday, *supra* note 9; Leigh Goodmark, A Troubled Marriage: Domestic Violence and the Legal System (2012).

17. Katharine B. Silbaugh, *Marriage Contracts and the Family Economy*, 93 Nw. U. L. Rev. 65 (1998); Martha M. Ertman, *Commercializing Marriage: A Proposal for Valuing Women's Work through Premarital Security Agreements*, 77 Tex. L. Rev. 17 (1998). Martha M. Ertman, Love's Promises: How Formal & Informal Contracts Shape All Kinds of Families (2015) [hereinafter Ertman, Love's Promises].
18. *See, e.g.*, Cicely Hamilton, Marriage as a Trade (1912).
19. Silvia Federici, Wages for Housework (2d ed. 2017); Selma James & Maria Dalla Costa, The Power of Women and the Subversion of Community (1972); Selma James, Women, the Unions and Work: Or What Is Not to Be Done (1972); Global Women's Strike, https://globalwomenstrike.net/2000/03 (last visited Apr. 7, 2021).
20. Cynthia Starnes, *Divorce and the Displaced Homemaker: A Discourse on Playing with Dolls, Partnership Buyouts and Dissociation Under No-Fault*, 60 U. Chi. L. Rev. 67 (1993); Ann Laquer Estin, *Maintenance, Alimony, and the Rehabilitation of Family Care*, 71 N.C. L. Rev. 721 (1993); Joan C. Williams, *Is Coverture Dead? Beyond a New Theory of Alimony*, 82 Geo. L.J. 2227 (1994); Jana B. Singer, *Alimony & Efficiency: The Gendered Costs and Benefits of the Economic Justification of Alimony*, 82 Geo. L.J. 2423 (1994); Katharine B. Silbaugh, *Commodification and Women's Household Labor*, 9 Yale J.L. & Feminism 81 (1997); Ertman, *Commercializing Marriage*, supra note 17.
21. Legitimizing interracial marriage required a century of struggle, culminating with *Loving v. Virginia*, 388 U.S. 1 (1967). Marriage equality for same sex couples followed a few decades later, first in reforms to state law, then in federal cases that worked their way up to the U.S. Supreme Court. *See, e.g.*, Goodridge v. Dep't of Pub. Health, 798 N.E.2d 941 (Mass. 2003); United States v. Windsor, 570 U.S. 744 (2013); Obergefell v. Hodges, 576 U.S. 644 (2015).
22. Ertman, Love's Promises, *supra* note 17, at 118; Nikki Graf, *Key Findings on Marriage and Cohabitation in the U.S.*, Fact Tank (Nov. 6, 2019), https://www.pewresearch.org/fact-tank/2019/11/06/key-findings-on-marriage-and-cohabitation-in-the-u-s/.
23. Marvin v. Marvin, 557 P.2d 106, 110 (Cal. 1976).
24. Despite the utility of these agreements, most unmarried couples do not enter them. For an analysis of that phenomenon, *see, e.g.*, Helen Reece, *Leaping without Looking*, *in* Robert Leckey, After Legal Equality: Family, Sex, Kinship 115 (2015).
25. Martha M. Ertman, *Contractual Purgatory for Marginorities: Not Heaven, but Not Hell Either*, 73 Denv. U. L. Rev. 1107 (1996); Scott L. Cummings & Douglas NeJaime, *Lawyering for Marriage Equality*, 57 UCLA L. Rev. 1235 (2010).
26. *See, e.g.*, Fineman, *supra* note 10; Mary Lyndon Shanley, Just Marriage (Joshua Cohen & Deborah Chasman eds., 2004); Katherine Franke, Wedlocked: The Perils of Marriage Equality (2015); Polikoff, *supra* note 10; Summer L. Nastich, *Questioning the Marriage Assumptions: The Justifications for "Opposite-Sex Only" Marriage as Support for the Abolition of Marriage*, 21 Law & Ineq. 114 (2003).
27. Martha Albertson Fineman, *Contract and Care*, 76 Chi.-Kent L. Rev. 1403, 1408 (2001).
28. *Id.*
29. Fineman, *supra* note 10, at 5.
30. Anita Bernstein, *For and against Marriage: A Revision*, 102 Mich. L. Rev. 129, 135 (2003).
31. *Id.* at 212.
32. *Id.*
33. Heather Jacobson, Labor of Love: Gestational Surrogacy and the Work of Making Babies (2016); Joshua Gamson, Modern Families: Stories of Extraordinary Journeys to Kinship (2015); Rene Almeling, Sex Cells: The

MEDICAL MARKET FOR EGGS AND SPERM (2011). Works documenting and critiquing dehumanizing and exploitative elements of this work include JULIA DEREK, CONFESSIONS OF A SERIAL EGG DONOR (2004), and RADIN, *supra* note 5, at 150.

34. *See* ERTMAN, LOVE'S PROMISES, *supra* note 17, at 45–66. California and the District of Columbia allow a man who is the genetic father of a child to contractually agree to be the third legal parent along with a lesbian couple. CAL. FAM. CODE § 7613(b) (2012); D.C. CODE § 16-909 (2009). Progressive developments have also moved from contract to status. For example, until the 1970s, a man was a legal stranger to children born out of wedlock and had no duty to support them. Paula A. Monopoli, *Nonmarital Children and Post-Death Parentage: A Different Path for Inheritance Law?* 48 SANTA CLARA L. REV. 857, 860–861 (2008).
35. Tosca Langbert, *The Gayby Boom Is Here to Stay*, HARV. POL. REV. (Feb. 14, 2020), https://harvardpolitics.com/the-gayby-boom/.
36. In re Baby M, 537 A.2d 1227 (N.J. 1988).
37. *Id.* at 1249.
38. Carol Sanger, *Developing Markets in Baby-Making*, in CONTRACTS STORIES 127–159 (Douglas G. Baird ed., Foundation Press 2007).
39. Johnson v. Calvert, 851 P.2d 776 (Cal. 1993).
40. Sanger, *supra* note 38, at 144–145; Tamar Lewin, *Coming to U.S. for Baby, and Womb to Carry It*, N.Y. TIMES, July 5, 2014, at 1.
41. Shultz, *supra* note 11; CARMEN SHALEV, BIRTH POWER: THE CASE FOR SURROGACY (1991).
42. BRENDA COSSMAN & JUDY FUDGE, PRIVATIZATION, LAW, AND THE CHALLENGE TO FEMINISM (2002).
43. Robin A. Lenhardt, *Marriage as Black Citizenship*, 66 HASTINGS L.J. 1317 (2015); BOWMAN, *supra* note 4; POLIKOFF, *supra* note 10; MAXINE EICHNER, THE SUPPORTIVE STATE: FAMILIES, GOVERNMENT, AND AMERICA'S POLITICAL IDEALS (2010); FRANKE, *supra* note 26.
44. Lenhardt, *supra* note 43, at 1319; *see also* FRANKE, *supra* note 26.
45. Lenhardt, *supra* note 43, at 1323. *See also* Michele Estrin Gilman, *Welfare, Privacy, and Feminism*, 39 U. BALT. L.F. 1 (2008).
46. BANKS, *supra* note 4; NAOMI CAHN & JUNE CARBONE, RED FAMILIES V. BLUE FAMILIES: LEGAL POLARIZATION AND THE CREATION OF CULTURE (2010).
47. POLIKOFF, *supra* note 10.
48. *See also* CLARE HUNTINGTON, FAILURE TO FLOURISH: HOW LAW UNDERMINES FAMILY RELATIONSHIPS (2014) (proposing a legal regime with rules to disrupt bias against nonmarital families).
49. Libby Adler, *Inconceivable: Status, Contract, and the Search for a Legal Basis for Gay & Lesbian Parenthood*, 123 PENN. ST. L. REV. 1, 36 (2018); *see also* Kimberly M. Mutcherson, *Transformative Reproduction*, 16 J. GENDER RACE & JUST. 187 (2013).
50. Devon Quinn, *Her Belly, Their Baby: A Contract Solution for Surrogacy Agreements*, 26 J.L. & POL'Y 805, 814 (2018).
51. *See* Cheryl I. Harris, *Whiteness as Property*, 106 HARV. L. REV. 1707 (1993).
52. Jennifer Rimm, *Booming Baby Business: Regulating Commercial Surrogacy in India*, 30 U. PA. J. INT'L L. 1429, 1430 (2009); Seema Mohapatra, *Stateless Babies and Adoption Scams: A Bioethical Analysis of International Commercial Surrogacy*, 30 BERKELEY J. INT'L L. 412 (2012). Many of the same inequalities define adoption, which despite bans on child-selling is also structured by payments for the transfer of parental rights and

duties. Martha M. Ertman, *What's Wrong with a Parenthood Market? A New and Improved Theory of Commodification*, 82 N.C. L. REV. 1, 8–10 (2003); Martha M. Ertman, *Adoption*, in ENCYCLOPEDIA OF LAW AND ECONOMICS (Alain Marciano & Giovanni B. Ramello eds., 2019)

53. *See, e.g.,* DEBRA SATZ, WHY SOME THINGS SHOULD NOT BE FOR SALE: THE MORAL LIMITS OF MARKETS (2010); RADIN, *supra* note 5.
54. *See, e.g.,* Elizabeth S. Anderson, *Is Women's Labor a Commodity?*, 19 PHIL. & PUB. AFF. 71, 71 (1990); ELIZABETH S. ANDERSON, VALUE IN ETHICS AND ECONOMICS (1995). For a discussion of commodification more generally—the discussion of what is and should be in or excluded from market-based transactions, *see* MARTHA M. ERTMAN & JOAN C. WILLIAMS, RETHINKING COMMODIFICATION: CASES AND READINGS IN LAW & CULTURE (2005).
55. Nancy Ehrenreich, *Surrogacy as Resistance? The Misplaced Focus on Choice in the Surrogacy and Abortion Funding Contexts*, 41 DEPAUL L. REV. 1369, 1379–1380 (1992) (reviewing SHALEV, *supra* note 41).
56. Anita L. Allen, *The Black Surrogate Mother*, 8 HARV. BLACKLETTER J. 17, 17–19 (1991).
57. *Id.*
58. Khiara Bridges, *Windsor, Surrogacy, and Race*, 89 WASH. L. REV. 1125 (2014).
59. ROBERTS, *supra* note 4.
60. Dorothy E. Roberts, *The Genetic Tie*, 62 U. CHI. L. REV. 209 (1995); Dorothy E. Roberts, *Punishing Drug Addicts Who Have Babies: Women of Color, Equality, and the Right of Privacy*, 104 HARV. L. REV. 1419 (1991); Dorothy E. Roberts, *Rust v. Sullivan and the Control of Knowledge*, 61 GEO. WASH. L. REV. 587 (1993); Dorothy E. Roberts, *Crime, Race, and Reproduction*, 67 TUL. L. REV. 1945, 1961–1969 (1993). Dorothy E. Roberts, *Race and the New Reproduction*, 47 HASTINGS L.J. 935 (1996)].
61. In addition to Roberts's extensive writings, *see also* MICHELE GOODWIN, POLICING THE WOMB: INVISIBLE WOMEN AND THE CRIMINALIZATION OF MOTHERHOOD (2020); April L. Cherry, *Nurturing in the Service of White Culture: Racial Subordination, Gestational Surrogacy, and the Ideology of Motherhood*, 10 TEX. J. WOMEN & L. 83 (2001); Beverly Horsburgh, *Jewish Women, Black Women: Guarding against the Oppression of Surrogacy*, 8 BERKELEY WOMEN'S L.J. 29 (1993); Lisa C. Ikemoto, *Destabilizing Thoughts on Surrogacy Legislation*, 28 U. SAN FRANCISCO L. REV. 633 (1994); Isabel Marcus et al., *Looking Toward the Future: Feminism and Reproductive Technologies*, 37 BUFF. L. REV. 203 (1989); Patricia J. Williams, *Spare Parts, Family Values, Old Children, Cheap*, 28 NEW ENG. L. REV. 913 (1994).
62. Dorothy E. Roberts, *Privatization and Punishment in the New Age of Reprogenetics*, 54 EMORY L.J. 1343 (2005).
63. NAOMI CAHN, TEST TUBE FAMILIES: WHY THE FERTILITY MARKET NEEDS LEGAL REGULATION 27, 189–200, 230–231 (2009).
64. Singer, *supra* note 6. *See also* Adrienne Hunter Jules & Fernanda Nicola, *The Contractualization of Family Law in the United States*, 62 AM. J. COMP. L. 151 (2014); Jill Elaine Hasday, *Intimacy and Economic Exchange*, 119 HARV. L. REV. 491 (2005); Hila Keren, *Can Separate Be Equal?: Intimate Exchange and the Cost of Being Special*, 119 HARV. L. REV. F. 19 (2006); Laura Weinrib, *Reconstructing the Family: Constructive Trust at Relational Dissolution*, 37 HARV. C.R.-C.L. L. REV. 207 (2002); Sara L. Ainsworth, *Bearing Children, Bearing Risk: Feminist Leadership for Progressive Regulation of Compensated Surrogacy in the United States*, 89 WASH. L. REV. 1077, 1084–1086 (2014); Robert Leckey, *Contracting*

Claims and Family Law Feuds, 57 U. TORONTO L.J. 1 (2007); ÉLODIE BERTRAND ET AL., COMMODIFICATION OF NATURE AND BODY (2020).

65. RADIN, *supra* note 5, at 123.
66. Adrienne D. Davis, *The Private Law of Race and Sex: An Antebellum Perspective*, 51 STAN. L. REV. 221 (1999).
67. Singer, *supra* note 6.
68. *Id.* at 1567.
69. MURPHY & SINGER, *supra* note 7.
70. ROSANNA HERTZ & MARGARET NELSON, RANDOM FAMILIES: GENETIC STRANGERS, SPERM DONOR SIBLINGS, AND THE CREATION OF NEW KIN (2018).
71. Hillary L. Berk, *Savvy Surrogates and Rock Star Parents: Compensation Provisions, Contracting Practices, and the Value of Womb Work*, 45 LAW & SOC. INQUIRY 398, 400 (2020).
72. *See, e.g.*, Courtney Joslin, *Surrogacy and the Politics of Pregnancy*, 14 HARV. L. & POL'Y REV. 365 (2020); Douglas NeJaime, Reva Siegel & Daphne Barak-Erez, *Surrogacy, Autonomy and Equality*, in 2020 GLOBAL CONSTITUTIONALISM SEMINAR VOLUME, YALE LAW SCHOOL (2020), https://papers.ssrn.com/sol3/papers.cfm?abstract_id=3732265.
73. Rachel Rebouché, *Contracting Pregnancy*, 105 IOWA L. REV. 1591 (2020).
74. *See, e.g.*, Ian R. Macneil, *Values in Contract: Internal and External*, 78 Nw. U. L. REV. 340 (1983); Robert Leckey, *Relational Contract and Other Models of Marriage*, 40 OSGOODE HALL L.J. 1 (2002).
75. Debora L. Threedy, *Feminists & Contract Doctrine*, 32 IND. L. REV. 1247, 1264 (1999) [hereinafter *Feminists*].
76. Franklin G. Synder, *The Pernicious Effect of Employment Relationships on the Law of Contracts*, 10 TEX. WESLEYAN L. REV. 33, 37 (2003).
77. Emily M. S. Houh, *Critical Interventions: Toward an Expansive Equality Approach to the Doctrine of Good Faith in Contract Law*, 88 CORNELL L. REV. 1025, 1087–1088 (2003); Emily M. S. Houh, *The Doctrine of Good Faith in Contract Law: A (Nearly) Empty Vessel?*, 2005 UTAH L. REV. 1 (2005).
78. Yofi Tirosh, *The Right to Be Fat*, 12 YALE J. HEALTH POL'Y, L. & ETHICS 264 (2012); *see also* ROXANE GAY, HUNGER: A MEMOIR OF (MY) BODY (2017). Anne M. Payne, *Proof of Workplace Bullying That Does Not Involve Class-Based Discrimination*, 164 AM. JUR. PROOF OF FACTS 3d 109, §§ 1–2 & 11 (2017; updated 2021).
79. Rachel S. Arnow-Richman, *Bargaining for Loyalty in the Information Age: A Reconsideration of the Role of Substantive Fairness in Enforcing Employee Noncompetes*, 80 OR. L. REV. 1163 (2001).
80. *Id.* at 1167–1168.
81. Elizabeth Warren, *What Is a Women's Issue?: Bankruptcy, Commercial Law, & Other Gender-Neutral Topics*, 25 HARV. WOMEN'S L.J. 19 (2002); Amy J. Schmitz, *Sex Matters: Considering Gender in Consumer Contracting*, 19 CARDOZO J. L. & GENDER 437 (2013); Kristin Brandser Kalsem, *Bankruptcy Reform & the Financial Well-Being of Women: How Intersectionality Matters in Money Matters*, 71 BROOK. L. REV. 1181 (2006); Abbye Atkinson, *Race, Educational Loans & Bankruptcy*, 16 MICH. J. RACE & L. 1 (2010).
82. In one collection of essays by British legal scholars on feminism and contract law, spousal surety cases attracted more attention than any other context. LINDA MULCAHY & SALLY WHEELER, EDS., FEMINIST PERSPECTIVES ON CONTRACT LAW (2005).

83. Gillian K. Hadfield, *An Expressive Theory of Contract: From Feminist Dilemmas to a Reconceptualization of Rational Choice in Contract Law*, 146 U. PA. L. REV. 1235, 1247 (1998).
84. Rosemary Auchmuty, *The Rhetoric of Equality and the Problem of Heterosexuality*, in FEMINIST PERSPECTIVES ON CONTRACT LAW 51, 66–70 (Linda Mulcahy & Sally Wheeler eds., 2002).
85. *See, e.g.*, Sun Forest Corp. v. Shvili, 152 F. Supp. 2d 367, 393 (S.D.N.Y. 2001).
86. Hadfield, *supra* note 83, at 1266, 1268.
87. U.C.C. §§ 9-102, 9-203, 9-609, 9-610.
88. *See, e.g., Operation Repo* (EGA Prods., 2006–2014); *South Beach Tow* (Bodega Pictures and Nuyorican Prods., 2011–2014); *Repo Games* (495 Prods., 2011–2012).
89. Jean Braucher, *The Repo Code: A Study of Adjustment to Uncertainty in Commercial Law*, 75 WASH. U. L.Q. 549 (1997).
90. *Id.* at 587, 608.
91. Debora L. Threedy, *"Breach of the Peace" in Self-Help Repossession: Adopting a Gendered Perspective*, 7 COMMERCIAL DAMAGES REP. 245, 245 (1992).
92. Williams v. Ford Motor Credit Co., 674 F.2d 717 (8th Cir. 1982).
93. *Id.* at 719.
94. Threedy, *supra* note 91, at 249.
95. Threedy, *Feminists*, *supra* note 75, at 1249, 1257.
96. Debora L. Threedy, *Dancing around Gender: Lessons from Arthur Murray on Gender and Contracts*, 45 WAKE FOREST L. REV. 749 (2010) (citing and discussing Vokes v. Arthur Murray, Inc., 212 So. 2d 906 (Fla. Dist. Ct. App. 1968)).
97. *Id.* at 775. *See also* Orit Gan, *Contractual Duress and Relations of Power*, 36 HARV. J.L. & GENDER 171 (2013); Orit Gan, *Promissory Estoppel: A Call for a More Inclusive Contract Law*, 16 J. GENDER RACE & JUST. 47 (2013); Orit Gan, *Anti-Stereotyping Theory and Contract Law*, 42 HARV. J.L. & GENDER 83 (2018).

CHAPTER 31

FEMINISM, PRIVACY, AND LAW IN CYBERSPACE

MICHELE ESTRIN GILMAN

In 1999, Scott McNealy, chief executive officer (CEO) of the computer manufacturing company Sun Microsystems, reportedly remarked, "Privacy is dead. Get over it."[1] Presumably, he was commenting on how networked, digital technologies have reached into and transformed every aspect of modern life. This statement—and its ongoing echoes—embodies a commodified, static, and neoliberal view of privacy, in which old-fashioned privacy expectations are subsumed by technologies' benefits. In contrast, a feminist might counter: Privacy is a constantly negotiated and shifting dispute over power with individual and collective consequences.[2] Indeed, the value and meaning of privacy have been central feminist concerns since the organized movement for gender justice began.[3]

Cyberspace dramatically limits personal privacy by giving businesses, government, and individual Internet users access to massive troves of personal data generated from online interactions. Women face multiple, gendered harms in cyberspace, including online harassment, digital discrimination, and sexual surveillance. Although law has not kept up with these privacy losses, privacy is not dead, and it is nothing to "get over." Privacy may be on life support, but it is worth fighting for.

This chapter presents an overview of the oppression women and other marginalized people suffer through a loss of privacy in the digital age and the efforts that activists have taken to ameliorate the harms of cyberspace and to shape privacy norms in a feminist and inclusive manner. It describes the meaning of privacy through four waves of feminist theorizing and activism, analyzes how American privacy law responds to major gender equity challenges in cyberspace, and highlights current feminist theories and models of resistance.

I. WHAT IS PRIVACY?

In order to understand feminists' engagement with privacy, some general discussion of the meaning of privacy in the legal context is in order. Scholars generally agree that privacy is an amorphous concept tied to both individual and relational needs.[4] At an individual level, theorists have described privacy as the ability to control personal information, to be anonymous, to be secluded, and to limit access to the self. This is the concept of privacy that first emerged in American law in a pivotal law review article by Samuel Warren and Louis Brandeis in 1890, in which they identified and articulated a common law "right to be let alone."[5] Within feminist theory, feminist scholars from different schools of thought have viewed this individual conception of privacy as essential to women's self-development and self-determination. Privacy interests also extend beyond the individual.

At a relational level, privacy is recognized as a precondition to intimate relationships, the development of community, and democratic government.[6] In this vein, relational feminists recognize the norms of care and interdependence that mark women's lives, and thus relational concepts of privacy align with feminist commitments to human flourishing within social relationships. Privacy is also considered foundational to other human values, such as dignity and autonomy, which are central to multiple feminist legal theories and rights-based advocacy strategies. The various meanings attached to privacy underscore that privacy has no fixed meaning but is historically and culturally embedded, shaped by the surrounding social, cultural, political, and material environment.

In lieu of a unified theory of privacy, Jerry Kang describes three "clusters" of privacy interests: physical, decisional, and informational.[7] This categorization is helpful for legal analysis because each cluster triggers different legal regimes. First, physical privacy concerns the ability to keep one's bodily integrity and home free from outside intrusions. The Fourth Amendment, with its restriction on warrantless, governmental searches, is designed to protect physical privacy, as do tort doctrines such as invasion of privacy and intrusion upon seclusion.

Second, decisional privacy is related to autonomy; it preserves an individual's ability to make personal, reproductive, and familial choices without external interference. The U.S. Supreme Court has interpreted a constitutional right to decisional privacy in a line of cases including *Griswold v. Connecticut*,[8] guaranteeing the right to contraception; *Roe v. Wade*,[9] securing the right to abortion; and *Lawrence v. Texas*,[10] striking down antisodomy laws.

Third, informational privacy involves the ability to control personal data and limit access to such information by others. This is the privacy interest most impacted by cyberspace. Although the Supreme Court has not recognized a constitutional right to informational privacy, there are sectoral privacy statutes at the federal and state levels aimed at limiting harmful uses of sensitive personal data, such as the Health Insurance Portability and Accountability Act of 1996,[11] or HIPAA (protecting health data held by medical providers), and the Children's Online Privacy and Protection Act of 1998,[12] or COPPA (protecting children's data).

Despite these various legal regimes, it is widely recognized that American privacy law—consisting of constitutional, statutory, and common law at federal and state levels—fails to secure privacy in today's datafied society. Privacy law is too narrow and riddled with exceptions; it is shaped around middle-class and male norms, thereby excluding the interests of marginalized groups;[13] its neoliberal orientation puts the onus on individuals to protect their privacy; and it is outpaced by new technologies. Feminists have engaged with the various dimensions of privacy, as well as these failings of privacy law. For decades, they have been fighting to obtain "good privacy," which enriches autonomy and interpersonal relationships, such as the right to control one's body, while rejecting "bad privacy," which isolates and oppresses women, such as intimate violence. Cyberspace—or the networked communication technologies that facilitate and include the Internet[14]—raises new tensions between "good" and "bad" privacy. Just as privacy has multiple meanings, it calls for differing frames of feminist legal theory to strike this privacy balance.

II. Feminism's Waves and Privacy

Feminism has long centered on breaking down the public and private divide that traditionally organized social relations and "perpetuate[d] the subordination of women."[15] Under separate spheres ideology, men dominated the public sphere, which encompassed work, governance, and civil society, while women were relegated to the private sphere of the family and home. This was a form of "sexual constitutionalism, a separation of powers designed to avoid competition and conflict between the sexes while affirming and molding gender identity."[16] Each "wave" of feminism has challenged this public–private dichotomy with its own theoretical grounding and activism.[17]

In their fight for suffrage, first-wave feminists of the mid-nineteenth century to the 1920s successfully breached the public–private divide by securing the right to vote in 1920 and gaining access to the public square. Then, during second-wave feminism, from roughly the 1960s to the 1980s, feminists challenged the power structures upheld by the public–private divide and, in so doing, achieved significant legal and policy reforms, including passage of antidiscrimination laws and the recognition of a constitutional right to abortion. Along with these policy advances, however, came the realization that "[p]rivacy is most enjoyed by those with power. To the powerless, the private realm is frequently a sphere not of freedom but of uncertainty and insecurity."[18] With regard to gender violence, Catharine MacKinnon raised a dominance feminist critique of privacy, arguing that privacy could never be a basis for claiming rights because it is a tool of gender subordination that leaves men alone "to oppress women one at a time."[19]

By contrast, liberal feminists, such as Anita Allen and Linda McClain, defended privacy, cautioning against tossing out the privacy "baby ... with the bath water."[20] While acknowledging the abuses done to women under the cover of "privacy," they argued that privacy is nevertheless essential for women to "live out their disparate, nonconforming preferences," because it gives women space to develop and carry out their own ends.[21] Critical race feminists offered yet another perspective, contending that feminists had essentialized privacy and ignored the experiences of women of color. For example, Dorothy Roberts explained how poor women, and particularly Black women, have long worked outside the private "sanctity" of the home, providing a cheap source of labor, while also bearing higher levels of state intrusion in their own homes.[22] This variety of feminist views upholding, critiquing, and reframing privacy was characteristic of second-wave tensions, at the same time laying the groundwork for future feminist theorizing around the impact of cyberspace. Overall, second-wave feminism contested the value of privacy, shed light on its prismatic meanings, and implicitly tied its boundaries to power relations.

Third-wave feminism arose in the 1990s, tied to the rise of the digital age.[23] Third-wave feminists embraced Kimberlé Crenshaw's theory of intersectionality, which recognizes how different aspects of identity, including and beyond gender, can result in layered forms of oppression. Third-wavers thus honored diverse and multicultural narratives, including sharing personal confessions through online mediums. They claimed and celebrated their femininity and sexual empowerment, rejecting a "sex as oppression" narrative they associated with their mothers' generation, which was rooted in dominance feminism.[24] Third-wavers threw off the mantle of privacy and embraced online forms of expression such as videos, blogs, and webzines. They upended the feminist slogan, "the personal is political," seeing the personal not as political but as fodder for public consumption. Not every feminist agreed with this embrace of technology and public exposure of personal lives. Anita Allen, for example, suggested a need to "coerce" privacy by adopting policies that would ensure people retain private spaces free from governmental and corporate surveillance as a way of retaining liberal values of "human dignity, personhood, moral autonomy, workable community life, and tolerant democratic political and legal institutions."[25]

The fourth wave of feminism, emerging around the mid-2000s, blended the second-wavers' political analysis of power structures with the third-wavers' intersectional understandings and online tools. It was even more centered in cyberspace. As explained by Constance Grady, "[o]nline is where activists meet and plan their activism, and it's where feminist discourse and debate takes place."[26] Spurred by online organizing, fourth-wave feminists have rallied against sexual harassment through the #MeToo and #TimesUp online movements, marched by the millions against the sexist policies and prejudices of former President Donald Trump, and voted a record number of women into political office.

However, mimicking the society at large, fourth-wave feminism also has a more tempered relationship to cyberspace than did the third wave. Early enthusiasm about the Internet's capacity for democratization and liberation has been replaced with the sober realization that personal data are being monetized for the benefit of businesses and compiled for government surveillance—all without knowledge or control by individuals. Scandals such as Cambridge Analytica's data scraping of Facebook users for political purposes, massive data breaches at major companies, and Russian use of social media to interfere with elections have all spurred a "techlash" against Silicon Valley.[27] Indeed, despite its empowering potential, cyberspace threatens informational privacy with damaging ripple effects for women's decisional and physical privacy. Fourth-wave feminism is thus preoccupied with effecting a delicate balance—grappling with the perils of cyberspace while harnessing its potential.

III. Privacy in Cyberspace

In cyberspace, nothing is private. This section focuses on three major areas where the loss of informational privacy has particularly gendered impacts, in roughly the order in which they have emerged: online harassment, digital discrimination, and sexual surveillance. Each triggers a different feminist legal theory as a possible ground for reclaiming privacy. These sections explore distinct harms arising from privacy deprivations in the digital age and offer a feminist theory lens through which the harm is best explained and addressed. The first section deals with online harassment in its myriad and expanding forms, using the prism of dominance feminism to illustrate how online abuse operates but also to explore possible remedies. The next section explains how the digital extraction economy leads to gender-based discrimination that can be countered by an intersectional feminist approach. The final section exposes the ways in which the emerging Femtech industry engages in sexual surveillance and, in response, proposes a feminist autonomy approach as a path to claim control over personal data.

A. Online Harassment

Dominance feminism exposes the ways in which men oppress women through sexual, physical, and social domination.[28] To this mix, we can add technological domination. Men not only disproportionately design and build technology, but they also use it as a tool to control and belittle women. Technology magnifies gender violence, as it can be wielded anonymously, lives online permanently, and can be accessed and shared by millions of people. Thus, a dominance feminist frame is essential to understanding, and ultimately remedying, online harassment.

Online harassment takes myriad forms. In cyberspace, women have been subject to hateful speech, online threats, and unwelcome sexual requests; threatened by cyber mobs; cyberstalked; and sextorted (blackmailed by demanding sexual activity in exchange for not releasing sexual images). Harassers have posted nonconsensual pornography (also called revenge porn[29]); covertly recorded women's intimate activities and revealed women's personal information online; created deep fakes of their victims (i.e., inserting a victim's face into preexisting pornographic images); impersonated women; and hacked feminist websites. Within intimate relationships, abusers coerce victims to assume debt or steal their identities for the same purpose, saddling victims with harmful debt that gets embedded in their digital profiles.[30] In addition to these digital abuses, there is also a sprawling "manosphere" of "blogs, forums, and websites" that "often adopts liberal tropes of oppression to portray men as the victims of feminism gone too far."[31]

Online harassment is pervasive,[32] disproportionately experienced by women, and its consequences are often severe. It can lead victims—and even nonvictims who view harassing treatment—to retreat from their online life; to shut down blogs, email accounts, and social media, thus losing the online benefits of communication, expression, networking, and political organizing. Victims also report suffering depression and anxiety, and some have committed suicide. They have dropped out of school, been forced to move, and lost jobs. Some victims have been stalked, assaulted, and murdered by their online harassers. At a societal level, online harassment reinforces the idea that sexual victimization of women is "an acceptable form of entertainment or punishment."[33] As Mary Ann Franks explains, "The aggregate result of sex-based online harassment is to (re)make women into a marginalized class, using sexual objectification and gender stereotyping to make women feel unwelcome, subordinated, or altogether excluded from socially meaningful activities."[34]

Online harassment in all its forms strips women of their informational privacy, which in turn leaks into their physical privacy when they face offline threats to their personal safety. For instance, Gamergate was a high-profile incident of online misogyny, in which female video game developers and media critics were subjected to relentless, violent threats after the ex-boyfriend of Zoe Quinn, a female game designer, claimed she cheated on him with a video game reviewer to advance her career.[35] Anonymous hackers soon spread Quinn's address, nude pictures, and other personal information across the Internet, and she received death and rape threats that drove her from her home. Similar attacks spread to countless other women in the gaming industry, who also had to flee their homes for their safety.[36] Gamergaters sought to attack "effectively anyone who has ever questioned the patriarchal nature of the games industry, or the limited, often objectifying depiction of women."[37]

Digital technologies can also hinder women's decisional privacy. One example involves antiabortion activists who have used geofencing technology (i.e., using GPS location tracking to send messages to a mobile device) to target women at abortion clinics with antichoice announcements.[38] Technology also undermines women's sexual privacy, which Danielle Citron conceptualizes as essential to the values of "sexual autonomy, self-determination, and dignity secured when people can manage the boundaries around their bodies, intimate information, and intimate activities."[39] For instance, within intimate relationships, some abusers use technological tools to control and intimidate their partners, such as by gaining access to texts, social media, emails, and smart home technology and by placing geolocation trackers on cell phones and other devices.[40]

This reality is a far cry from the cyberutopia many technologists and feminists predicted. In its early days, the Internet promised women freedom from gendered restraints through the combination of anonymity and free expression.[41] In her 1985 *Cyborg Manifesto*, Donna Haraway envisioned a world in which human–machine hybrids break down oppressive binaries, including the "polarity of public and private," in ways that restructure social relations.[42] To be sure, many people have found the Internet a valuable place to explore their sexuality, try on other identities, and join communities unconstrained by gender binaries. However, cyberspace has not lived up to its utopian promise. Like so many institutions and systems created before it, cyberspace is fundamentally male dominated. It is built by men and shaped around male experiences.

Indeed, in the United States, women hold only about a quarter of tech industry jobs, usually in nonengineering roles. Given the male norms that rule cyberspace, women cannot escape gender online. As Sara Wachter-Boettcher states, "every digital product bears the fingerprints of its creators."[43]

Legal remedies for online harassment remain woefully insufficient. As dominance feminists have warned, law operates as a tool that perpetuates male power. Technology overwhelmingly serves male perspectives, and law is shaped to uphold patriarchy's preferences. Technology has also proved to be a tool to maintain white supremacy[44] and to reinforce rigid sex roles, making the lives and experiences of LGBTQ (lesbian, gay, bisexual, transgender, and queer or questioning) individuals invisible and marginalized.[45] Gender can combine with these and multiple other identities to generate intersectional harms.

In terms of civil remedies for online harassment, the key barrier is § 230 of the Communications Decency Act, a federal law which has been interpreted to insulate online platforms such as Facebook and Google for liability for content posted by users.[46] To go after harassers directly, state tort law claims such as defamation can provide some relief, yet litigation is costly, and it can be hard to identify and serve anonymous perpetrators, many of whom lack the ability to pay damages even if held liable. In addition, litigation requires plaintiffs to publicly reveal their identity, tell their stories, and confront their abusers in person, all of which strip women of privacy and can result in further stigma and emotional harm. A victim who was the photographer (and thus owner) of a sexually intimate picture that is nonconsensually posted can theoretically bring a copyright action, but even a successful case will usually not capture all the sites where a photo has migrated.[47] Sexual harassment statutes are likewise ill-fit for cyber harassment, because harassment often occurs outside legally protected settings such as the workplace and schools.[48]

On the criminal law side, a majority of states outlaw nonconsensual pornography and/or cyberharassment, but existing laws are too narrow in the conduct they proscribe and tend to have light penalties. For instance, the majority of states do not prohibit the dissemination of revenge porn if the images were initially filmed with the victim's consent.[49] Further, many statutes require the state to prove an intent to harm on the part of the perpetrator, diminishing the privacy violation that victims often suffer regardless of the harasser's intent.[50] Moreover, law enforcement agencies often do not take such cases seriously and can lack the technological savvy and resources to investigate and prosecute these cases. When police dismiss women who complain and tell them to simply turn off their computers, or describe the conduct as no more than "boys being boys," they trivialize this form of abuse, similar to the way in which workplace harassment was treated in the 1970s.[51]

Employing a dominance feminist approach, the feminist movement against online harassment has catalogued the ways online harassment oppresses women; aggressively litigated existing laws; and crafted new laws that recognize law's expressive character.[52] For instance, the Cyber Civil Rights Initiative (CCRI) is a group dedicated to combatting online abuses that threaten civil rights and civil liberties.[53] CCRI uses multiple strategies, including law reform and litigation, to fight against nonconsensual pornography, recorded sexual assault, and sextortion. For victims, CCRI provides a crisis hotline, information about image documentation and takedown, and referrals to pro bono legal help. CCRI also works with researchers to study the extent and effects of online sexual harassment, and that research, in turn, supports advocacy for legislative reform and technical solutions. CCRI has been instrumental in drafting model criminal laws against nonconsensual pornography that many states have adopted in some form, and in successfully defending some state laws against First Amendment challenges.[54] CCRI has assisted in drafting a proposed federal law introduced by Rep. Jackie Speier in Congress and worked collaboratively with the tech industry to develop and implement policies against nonconsensual pornography.[55]

As CCRI recognizes, law is not the only tool for combatting online harassment. Technology companies also bear responsibility for reigning in the abuses their platforms have unleashed. After years of downplaying and dismissing gendered harms,[56] large tech companies are taking steps to limit online abuse by allowing victims to file takedown requests. Some large tech platforms companies also use algorithmic analysis of content, images, and text to identify and remove nonconsensual pornography preventatively, without a takedown request, but these tools can be both overbroad (removing consensual sexual imagery) and underbroad (such as not recognizing cultural variations in gender-based harassment). Overall, tech companies' stated policies regarding online harassment are "varied and inconsistent."[57] And, even when content is taken down, harmful images may have already gone viral and remain on the screens of thousands of users. Further, victims differ in the forms of justice they are seeking as remedies for online harassment, making one-size-fits-all solutions problematic.[58] Online harassment must be fought on multiple fronts, with a variety of legal and preventative nonlegal tools, linked by a commitment to shifting power from abusers and toward enhancing the dignity and free expression of women.

B. Digital Discrimination

The second kind of gendered harm in cyberspace—described here as digital discrimination—inflicts injuries through corporate and governmental use and appropriation of personal information. A vast network of businesses and government agencies collect, aggregate, analyze, and sell personal data without the user's knowledge, resulting in permanent losses of informational privacy that feed algorithmic systems of sorting and segregation. Through the use of digital profiles and automated decisionmaking systems, individuals are subjected to new forms of bias that deprive them of access to opportunities and enjoyment of human and civil rights.

Women and other marginalized groups suffer the most serious harms of this digital discrimination. This new genre of digital discrimination is particularly resistant to feminist strategies that guided policy reforms in the past. For example, second-wave feminists wielded formal equality as a theory to combat gender discrimination, demanding to be treated equally to men. This theoretical frame may help to highlight the winners and losers of the big data economy but will ultimately fail in combatting digital discrimination because women do not need to be treated equally to men in a game in which for-profit businesses are the only winners. Likewise, difference feminism is also ill-suited to this problem. Women do not need more precise profiling tools that recognize their inherent differences; in an algorithmic universe, such differential treatment will only lead to more targeted discrimination. Rather, women need a societal commitment to identify and ban subordinating digital practices that reinforce existing biases and create new ones. Not only is digital discrimination gendered, but it also oppresses people across identities of race, ethnicity, class, sexual orientation, ability, age, and other characteristics. Thus, within feminist legal theory, intersectional approaches are best suited to counter digital discrimination.

At all hours of the day and throughout the night, individuals' data are gathered from sources such as Internet searches, social media sites, purchase history, emails, app usage, geolocation tracking, public records, and Internet-connected devices. Data brokers combine millions of data points to create and sell individualized digital profiles that various industries use for marketing, as they deploy sophisticated algorithms that attempt to predict and shape consumer behavior.[59] Shoshana Zuboff labels these systems "surveillance capitalism," which "unilaterally claims human experience as free raw material for translation into behavioral data."[60] Marketing, however, is just the tip of the iceberg. Digital profiles increasingly determine people's access to jobs, public benefits, housing, healthcare, education, insurance, credit, and other life necessities.[61]

These automated systems raise issues of digital discrimination on the basis of gender (as well as other identities). For example, until it was sued in 2019, Facebook allowed advertisers to target job-wanted ads at men and to exclude women. Amazon tested (and abandoned) a hiring algorithm for technical jobs that recommended men over equally qualified women.[62] In the area of credit, when Apple rolled out a new credit card, a prominent software developer tweeted in protest that his credit limit was twenty times that of his wife, despite her higher credit score and their joint tax returns and accounts.[63]

Gender discrimination is also rife in other data-centric technological systems. Facial recognition technology, used to match images of unknown people with existing photos, is notoriously inaccurate for women of color.[64] These inaccuracies can lead to mistaken identification, which in turn can result in entanglement with the criminal justice system and evictions from federally subsidized housing (where tenants are predominantly women of color). With regard to Google searches, Safiya Noble uncovered that searches for terms such as "Black girls" or "Asian girls" immediately linked to pornography, while the term "beautiful" resulted in photos of white women.[65] She demonstrated that search engines are not neutral as many people believe but, rather, operate through "decisionmaking protocols that favor corporate elites and the powerful." Natural language processing, which helps computers understand and interpret language, also contains gender biases. Researchers have shown that computers "learn" to identify relationships between words in ways that are gendered; thus, a computer will conclude man is to woman as computer programmer is to homemaker.[66] Even the fact that digital assistants such as Siri and Alexa are programmed to speak with female voices reinforces stereotypes of women as servants and can influence how users relate to real women.[67]

How do these gendered outcomes occur? Automated decisionmaking systems rely on algorithms, or computerized instructions, for problem-solving. Discrimination can result when the data sets that algorithms are trained on contain baked-in structural biases. For instance, the Amazon hiring disparity for technical jobs occurred because the algorithm was trained on data culled from the résumés of successful hires over the previous ten years. Because the tech industry and Amazon's workforce is dominated by men, the algorithm learned to prefer male candidates. Likewise, facial recognition systems are based on training data sets that disproportionately consist of men and white people, making those systems less accurate for people outside those categories. The same is true for natural language processing systems that are built from data sets aggregating past news stories, which inevitably contain the gendered biases of their authors.

Disparities can also result when the algorithms themselves favorably weigh factors that benefit men over women due to deeply embedded structural features of our economy. Catherine D'Ignazio and Lauren F. Klein explain that the extractive systems of big data create "a profound asymmetry between who is collecting, storing, and analyzing data and whose data are collected, stored, and analyzed. The goals that drive this process are those of the corporations, governments, and well-resourced universities that are dominated by elite white men."[68]

In the digital world, these institutions are able to replicate the patterns of domination through their monopoly on data and technical infrastructures, substituting this new kind of power for more personalized practices of the past.

Despite these gendered outcomes, digital discrimination can be hard to identify and challenge. To begin with, many algorithms deployed by businesses and government lack transparency. They are "black boxes" whose inner workings are invisible to the public.[69] For instance, in the case of the Apple credit card and its disparate impact on wives versus husbands, the bank issuing the card either could not or would not explain the mechanism that led to the disparity. Moreover, machine learning systems, which use algorithmic analysis of massive data sets to attempt to mimic human thought processes, can be so complex that even their developers cannot always explain how they arrive at certain outcomes. Further, many companies claim that their algorithmic systems are proprietary, making it difficult for the public to peer inside the black box. Even apart from the black box problem, many victims of digital discrimination never know that an algorithm was responsible for denying them access to housing or a job or the like. As a result, these victims never have the opportunity to view or correct any inaccurate, incomplete, or outdated data or to challenge a biased or erroneous model.

Algorithmic systems also lack legal accountability. At a statutory level, the United States lacks a comprehensive privacy law regulating personal data. Instead, American privacy law is fragmented and sectoral, governing only certain industries, in narrow circumstances, and leaving the data broker industry largely unregulated. The Federal Trade Commission is the primary privacy enforcer in the United States and can adjudicate against companies whose data practices are "unfair or deceptive." Yet the agency is understaffed and underresourced. Moreover, its enforcement authority is circumscribed because its powers are limited to enforcing corporate promises set forth in privacy policies; it cannot establish privacy requirements.

In lieu of regulation, our privacy system relies largely on notice and consent, which puts the onus on individuals to protect their own privacy rather than placing responsibility on the entities that gather and use data. However, the idea of consent is a myth, both because users do not—and practically cannot—read lengthy, legalistic, and boilerplate privacy policies and because they have no ability to negotiate its terms. Moreover, the corporate authors of privacy policies retain the power to revise their policies at whim and to disclaim responsibility for downstream uses of personal data. Civil rights statutes are also limited in their ability to fight digital discrimination because they were based on theories of human (rather than machine) behavior, and they are thus ill-fit to counter the statistical correlations generated by algorithms.[70] Using the doctrine of disparate impact to prove discrimination in the analog world is already challenging; scholars and civil rights advocates fear it is even harder in the digital world due to the opacity and complexity of algorithmic systems.

Opting out of cyberspace is not an option for securing privacy. Cutting off the Internet and disavowing a smartphone is simply not practical in modern society, nor does it constrain data mining. Whether they know it or not, people are surveilled and monitored when they move through public spaces and as their public records are electronically sold and traded. For example, when Princeton sociologist Janet Vertesi attempted to keep information related to her pregnancy out of the big data ecosystem, she discovered that it was not easy.[71] She stayed off social media and told family and friends not to post their congratulations; she used gift cards to buy a stroller; purchased all prenatal vitamins and maternity wear in cash; set up an Amazon account via a private server and had items delivered to a locker; and conducted research on a private browser that routes Internet traffic through foreign servers. Far from shielding her from negative consequences, the extreme actions she took to elude the digitized dragnet marked her as a potential criminal when retailers tagged her purchases as irregular. Her story exemplifies that individualized solutions for securing privacy do not work and that only collective and political action will ultimately preserve privacy.[72]

The feminist approach best suited to addressing the new digital discrimination is intersectional feminist legal theory. It has the advantage of identifying how structural systems of oppression impact people across their multiple identities and thus can respond to the diverse ways that the compilation and sale of data negatively affect a wide array of marginal individuals. Intersectional feminism also has the capacity to mobilize coalitions resisting patriarchy, white supremacy, and bias against other marginal groups, as these groups seek to understand and push back against digitized bias.

Such an intersectional approach is exemplified by Our Data Bodies (ODB), a grassroots research justice project that works with marginalized communities in Detroit, Charlotte, and Los Angeles to examine the impact of data collection and data-centric systems within a human rights framework.[73] ODB researchers interview residents, and together they engage in community organizing and capacity building on digital justice issues. ODB's methods look similar to the "revolutionary feminist consciousness-raising" approach that marked second-wave feminist organizing in its consideration of the structures of patriarchy and capitalism.[74] While ODB does not use legal tools, it generates insights that could help develop data privacy law in a more inclusive and less subordinating direction.

ODB organizes around the concept of "data bodies," which are "discrete parts of our whole selves that are collected; stored in databases, the cloud, and other spaces of digitally networked flows; and used to make decisions or determinations about us. They are a manifestation of our relationships with our communities and institutions, including institutions of privilege, oppression, and domination."[75]

In light of this framing, ODB interrogates how marginalized adults make sense of data-based systems, how they connect their ability to meet their basic needs to these systems, and the tactics they deploy to protect their privacy and self-determination. To continue these conversations in multiple settings, ODB has created a Digital Defense Playbook containing strategies for marginalized communities to "build community knowledge, defense, health and wellness, and collective organizing" around digital justice issues.[76] As one ODB participant stated, "The changes I would make would be to have data that is intentional and targeted and centering people in the middle of those decisions. So, data would be created for the people and with people as opposed to on people and against people."[77] ODB centers the experiences of marginalized people to help them and others understand how data extraction and surveillance systems "impact re-entry, fair housing, public assistance, community development, and people's overall ability to meet their basic human needs."[78] It uses intersectional theory to unveil the mechanisms and impacts of digital discrimination in order to lay a groundwork for resistance, organizing, and reform. As ODB recognizes, the needs and perspectives of marginalized people are essential to future lawmaking around digital privacy.

C. Sexual Surveillance

The third and final type of privacy invasion occurring in cyberspace targets women's reproductive health and sexuality and comes wrapped in rhetoric of feminist empowerment. Women's reproductive health is now a subject of intensive corporate surveillance. The privacy invasion arises as a by-product of the rise of Femtech, a new industry that has developed technological tools ostensibly to serve women's health needs. In this way, Femtech hitches its wagon to difference feminism, recognizing the gendered needs of women, particularly around reproduction and health, and creating online tools to meet that need. However, this framing is more symbolic than substantive because Femtech largely serves the for-profit goals of businesses more than the interests of women.

The term "Femtech" was coined by Ida Tin, CEO of CLUE, one of many apps that allows menstruators to track their cycles. In addition to period-tracking apps, the Femtech sector includes a "smart" birth control case designed to improve pill-taking habits, a fertility tracking app that measures basal temperature to predict fertility and is approved by the Food and Drug Administration (FDA) as a digital contraceptive, a digital sensor that tracks pregnancy contractions, a breast pump that digitally measures and records milk production, a pelvic floor trainer that sends biofeedback data to a mobile app when women perform kegel exercises, and an app for menopausal symptom management. Femtech is expected to be a $50 billion industry by 2025; period-tracking apps alone are used by one third of American women.[79]

Investors tout Femtech's attention to women's health issues, which have long been sidelined, underfunded, and understudied by the mainstream health industry. Femtech promises to give women greater knowledge about and control over their bodies while reducing the stigma around women's health issues. This marketing pitch syncs with fourth-wave feminism's goals and values in that it envisions technology as a tool for self-empowerment. However, Femtech diminishes privacy because most of these companies are harvesting and monetizing women's personal data for profit while granting users inadequate knowledge or control over the use of their information. To access the various apps and devices, users typically must provide not only demographic data but also deeply personal information, such as their sexual practices and positions, moods and feelings, and indicators such as the physical characteristics of menstrual flow or the quality of cervical mucus.[80]

Consumer Reports studied five popular period-tracking apps and found that users "have no guarantee that their information won't be shared in some way with third parties for marketing and other purposes."[81] Moreover, the profit model of many Femtech apps hinges on selling users' personal data to other businesses, including major online platforms such as Facebook and Google, and these data are then circulated and folded into user's digital profiles, which are bought and sold in a robust digital marketplace, as discussed above.[82] Advertisers are particularly interested in identifying pregnant women because of the opportunity to generate brand loyalty at the start of a major life change. Thus, in the United States, a pregnant woman's data are worth fifteen times that of the average person.[83] Digital profiling results not only in relentless marketing but also possibly in increased interest charges on loans or inability to obtain life insurance, depending on the consumer's health indicators.[84] Yet these harms are generally invisible to consumers, who are unable to trace the path of their personal data.

The law provides an inadequate restraint against these data flows and resulting harms.[85] Although HIPAA (the Health Insurance Portability and Accountability Act of 1996) protects health information given to medical providers such as doctors and hospitals, Femtech products fall outside the statutory definition of covered entities. In theory, the Federal Trade Commission protects consumers against "unfair and deceptive" practices, and thus could enforce violations of a Femtech company's privacy policies, but these policies are drafted to give companies leeway in the sale and use of consumer information and, like most privacy policies, are not read by users, who have no leverage to negotiate the terms in any event.

Femtech is also invading the workplace. Many employers are incentivizing workers to adopt Femtech as part of workplace wellness programs, which are one form of expanding worker surveillance fueled by new technologies that "evinces an ostensibly participatory character."[86] The *Washington Post* reported on Ovia, a fertility, pregnancy, and parenting app that has been adopted by employers who collectively have ten million employees.[87] Through tools such as Ovia, employers and their health insurers can access aggregate data such as the numbers of workers giving birth prematurely or facing high-risk pregnancies, as well as workers' anticipated dates for returning to work.

For employers, Femtech apps offer a way to minimize healthcare spending and engage in workforce planning. However, these workplace apps also raise the specter of pregnancy discrimination, reduced healthcare benefits, and data breaches. As Karen Levy, an information science professor, told the *Washington Post*, "The real benefit of self-tracking is always to the company. People are being asked to do this at a time when they're incredibly vulnerable and may not have any sense where that data is being passed."[88] Indeed, Ovia's terms of service grant the company "a royalty-free, perpetual, and irrevocable license, throughout the universe" to "utilize and exploit" the user's personal data for research and marketing.[89] Ovia makes money not only from employers who purchase the service but also from selling access to user profiles to advertisers. Here, too, law is no bulwark. There is currently no federal law regulating worker surveillance, and state laws generally only bar the most extreme privacy intrusions, such as cameras placed in a locker room. Outside those limited restrictions, the bulk of American employees work at will and have little choice but to "consent" to employer surveillance regimes for fear of losing their jobs.

Thus, in the Femtech space, privacy advocates urge users to carefully select apps with greater privacy controls, use two-factor authentication to access apps, turn on ad blockers, and turn off geolocation tracking.[90] These are important steps, but they represent only limited self-defense measures. They do not constitute consent, which must be freely given, reversible, informed, enthusiastic, and specific.[91] As the activists of the Latin American organization Coding Rights have stated, "The principle of consent is directly related to physical and psychic protection in queer and feminist circles."[92] When it is informed and voluntary, it is an "exercise of self-determination and liberty." However, the neoliberal concept of notice and consent in privacy law "tends to diminish the concept of consent to simple, non-active resistance, making excuses that tend to legitimize abuses."[93] To compound the injury, when users "consent" in order to access a service, they are often agreeing to a service with inaccurate information and/or lax security. Numerous medical researchers have concluded that the majority of period-tracking apps fail to accurately predict women's fertility window, and some women have had unintended pregnancies as a result.[94]

At bottom, Femtech apps and devices are highly gendered tools of surveillance. These apps flatten users' experiences and push them into rigid gendered categories. Maggie Delano, an engineering professor, wrote about her experience with Glow, a period-tracking app (created by four men), which offered users three "journeys": avoiding pregnancy, trying to conceive, or fertility treatment. She reflected that the app is designed for "straight, sexually active, partnered, cis women with enough money for a smartphone to run the app," while telling "queer, unpartnered, infertile, and/or women uninterested in procreating that they aren't even women."[95] The messaging of these apps also reinforces gendered offline behaviors. For instance, at one point, the Glow app reminded women who were trying to get pregnant to wear nice underwear on a fertile day, while sending notices to their partners to bring home flowers.[96] Given these design choices, the question arises, "How do these messages and incessant ads reinforce patterns of beauty, behavior and sexuality that are a far cry from freedom that they promise, especially considering their popularity among young people?"[97] Feminists value privacy for its autonomy-enhancing capacity. Femtech promises autonomy but often delivers the opposite.

To counteract the privacy-invading aspects of Femtech, feminists need to enlist a theory that reimagines and redefines consent and focuses squarely on women's agency. Autonomy feminism holds promise here. Although initially theorized in the domestic violence context to understand and support battered women,[98] its insight that autonomy is essential to empowerment can help give meaning to the distorted and impoverished notions of consent that are embedded in current privacy law. Autonomy feminism developed to combat the excesses of dominance feminism by emphasizing the agency that women exercise, even within subordinating structures.[99] Autonomy feminism aims to enhance women's ability to make choices that suit their needs and objectives with full knowledge of their options and constraints. It resists viewing women as victims or objects and provides a framework for centering women's needs and enabling women to engage in that discussion. Although notions of autonomy can sound overly individualistic, autonomy feminists recognize "such agency as emerging through collective action as well as individual self-reflection."[100]

An autonomy feminist perspective could displace Femtech surveillance with nonsubordinating, health-oriented technology that serves women's health and wellbeing, rather than corporate profits. For Femtech to enhance autonomy, the industry requires radical reenvisioning.[101] In this vision, medical professionals would be integral to Femtech design processes, ensuring that these tools are based on sound medical research and clinical practice. A diverse array of users would provide input on their expectations and interactions with Femtech in order to avoid stereotyping and biases in these tools. The algorithms that fuel Femtech would be tested for bias and accuracy before deployment and audited regularly thereafter. Femtech products would provide accurate and destigmatizing information about reproductive health and advise users about the tools' limitations. Rigorous data privacy norms would be enforced. Data sharing with for-profit third parties would be banned, data would be collected only to the extent necessary to deliver the services sought, data retention would be time-limited, and users could demand erasure of their data at any time. Data security features would be baked into Femtech tools, with legal and financial consequences for breaches. With these changes, Femtech would align with a rich conception of autonomy feminism.

A commitment to autonomy in both its individualistic and collective dimensions underwrites the Feminist Manifest-No, a platform issued in 2019 by a group of female data science professors. Autonomy in the service of empowerment is central to the Feminist Manifest-No with its declarations of refusal and commitment—refusing harmful data regimes and committing to new data futures.[102] Among its thirty-two "refusals," designed as a "powerful tool to open up and insist on radical and alternate futures," the Manifest-No declares:

1. We refuse to operate under the assumption that risk and harm associated with data practices can be bounded to mean the same thing for everyone, everywhere, at every time. We commit to acknowledging how historical and systemic patterns of violence and exploitation produce differential vulnerabilities for communities.
2. We refuse to be disciplined by data, devices, and practices that seek to shape and normalize racialized, gendered, and differently abled bodies in ways that make us available to be tracked, monitored, and surveilled. We commit to taking back control over the ways we behave, live, and engage with data and its technologies.

The Manifest-No has been collectively read in a variety of settings and shared through social media. It provides a rich, intersectional vision of resistance to the gendered harms of cyberspace by drawing firm lines against disempowering data practices and shifting power toward users. It embodies a collaborative, generative vision of autonomy that defies data determinism. It reconceptualizes data as a tool for justice rather than for oppression. These professor/activists are not "getting over" privacy; they are fighting to retain and regain it.

IV. Conclusion

Before the rise of the digital age, feminists recognized that women had too much bad privacy (entrapment in the home) and too little good privacy (opportunities for seclusion that allow for moral and self-development). Accordingly, feminists worked to shift public–private boundaries in ways that empower rather than oppress. Cyberspace is replicating similar privacy dilemmas. Women have too much "bad" privacy in cyberspace—they are silenced and pushed offline by threats and harassment, their personal and intimate information is shared across the Internet without their consent, their data are collected and monetized for corporate profits and purposes, and their values and experiences are not reflected within online environments. At the same time, they lack enough "good" privacy, or the autonomy to determine how much to share or withhold of themselves online. This is ripe terrain for feminist legal theory and activism in all its forms. Feminists know that privacy is ultimately about power—who gets to control the boundary between public and private in ways that can empower or oppress. Privacy is not dead, but it will take all our collective will to resuscitate it.

Notes

1. Judith Rauhofer, *Privacy Is Dead, Get Over It! Information Privacy and the Dream of a Risk-Free Society*, 3 INFO. & COMMC'N TECH. L. 185 (2008).

2. *See* Danah Boyd, *Why Privacy Is Not Dead*, MIT TECH. REV. (Aug. 25, 2010), https://www.technologyreview.com/2010/08/25/121116/why-privacy-is-not-dead/.
3. *See, e.g.,* Ruth Gavison, *Feminism and the Public/Private Distinction*, 45 STAN. L. REV. 1 (1992).
4. For discussion of various and overlapping attempts to define privacy, *see generally* DANIEL SOLOVE, UNDERSTANDING PRIVACY (2008).
5. Samuel Warren & Louis Brandeis, *The Right to Privacy*, 4 HARV. L. REV. 193 (1890).
6. *See* Ari Ezra Waldman, *Privacy as Trust: Sharing Personal Information in a Networked World*, 69 U. MIAMI L. REV. 559, 591–95 (2015) (describing social theories of privacy); *see also* JULIE C. INNESS, PRIVACY, INTIMACY, AND ISOLATION 56 (1992) (describing intimacy as the "common denominator" of privacy); Ruth Gavison, *Privacy and the Limits of Law*, 89 YALE L.J. 421, 455 (1980) (privacy "is also essential to democratic government because it fosters and encourages the moral autonomy of the citizen.").
7. *See* Jerry Kang, *Information Privacy in Cyberspace Transactions*, 50 STAN. L. REV. 1193, 1202–03 (1998).
8. 381 U.S. 479 (1965).
9. 410 U.S. 113 (1973).
10. 539 U.S. 558 (2003).
11. Pub. L. No. 104-191, 110 Stat. 1936 (codified as amended in scattered sections of 18, 26, 29, and 42 U.S.C.).
12. 15 U.S.C. §§ 6501–05 (2018).
13. *See generally* Michele Estrin Gilman, *The Class Differential in Privacy Law*, 77 BROOK. L. REV. 1389 (2012).
14. Julie Cohen explains that cyberspace "is part of lived space, and it is through its connections to lived space that cyberspace must be comprehended and, as necessary, regulated." Julie Cohen, *Cyberspace as/and Space*, 107 COLUM. L. REV. 210, 213 (2007).
15. Frances Olsen, *From False Paternalism to False Equality: Judicial Assaults on Feminist Community, Illinois 1869-1895*, 84 MICH. L. REV. 1518, 1522 (1986). *See also* CAROLE PATEMAN, THE DISORDER OF WOMEN: DEMOCRACY, FEMINISM, AND POLITICAL THEORY 118 (1989) ("The dichotomy between the private and the public is central to almost two centuries of feminist writing and political struggle; it is, ultimately, what the feminist movement is about.").
16. JEAN V. MATTHEWS, WOMEN'S STRUGGLE FOR EQUALITY: THE FIRST PHASE, 1828-1876, 7 (1997).
17. The wave metaphor is widely used, but also controversial because some feminists consider it reductionist. *See* Linda Nicholson, *Feminism in "Waves": Useful or Not?*, NEW POL. (Winter 2010), https://newpol.org/issue_post/feminism-waves-useful-metaphor-or-not/.
18. Olsen, *supra* note 15, at 325.
19. CATHARINE A. MACKINNON, FEMINISM UNMODIFIED 102 (1987).
20. ANITA L. ALLEN, UNEASY ACCESS: PRIVACY FOR WOMEN IN A FREE SOCIETY 71, 81 (1988); *see also* Linda C. McClain, *Reconstructive Tasks for a Liberal Feminist Conception of Privacy*, 40 WM. & MARY L. REV. 759, 765 (1999).
21. ALLEN, *supra* note 20, at 86–87.
22. Dorothy E. Roberts, *Punishing Drug Addicts Who Have Babies: Women of Color, Equality, and the Right to Privacy*, 104 HARV. L. REV. 1419, 1471 (1991).

23. *See* Bridget J. Crawford, *Toward a Third-Wave Feminist Legal Theory: Young Women, Pornography and the Praxis of Pleasure*, 14 MICH. J. GENDER & L. 99, 127–29 (2007).
24. *Id.* at 140.
25. Anita L. Allen, *Coercing Privacy*, 40 WM. & MARY L. REV. 723, 739, 756 (1999).
26. Constance Grady, *The Waves of Feminism, and Why People Keep Fighting over Them, Explained*, VOX, July 20, 2018; *see also* Ealasaid Muro, *Feminism: A Fourth Wave?*, 4 POL. INSIGHT 22 (2013) ("[I]t is increasingly clear that the Internet has facilitated the creation of a global community of feminists who use the Internet both for discussion and activism.").
27. *See, e.g.,* Ben Zimmer, *'Techlash': Whipping Up Criticism of the Top Tech Companies*, WALL ST. J., Jan. 10, 2019, https://www.wsj.com/articles/techlash-whipping-up-criticism-of-the-top-tech-companies-11547146279 [https://perma.cc/5G42-GL2G].
28. *See* MACKINNON, *supra* note 19, at 40.
29. The term "revenge porn" is disfavored by activists because it implies a particular intent on the part of the perpetrator, when in fact, nonconsensual pornography can have multiple motivations. *See* Yanet Ruvalcaba & Asia A. Eaton, *Nonconsensual Pornography Among U.S. Adults: A Sexual Scripts Framework on Victimization, Perpetration, and Health Correlates for Women and Men*, 10 PSYCH. OF VIOLENCE 68, 68 (2019).
30. *See* Angela Littwin, *Coerced Debt: The Role of Consumer Credit in Domestic Violence*, 100 CALIF. L. REV. 951 (2012).
31. *See* Alice Marwick & Rebecca Lewis, *Media Manipulation and Disinformation Online*, DATA & SOC'Y 14, https://datasociety.net/pubs/oh/DataAndSociety_MediaManipulationAndDisinformationOnline.pdf.
32. MAEVE DUGGAN, ONLINE HARASSMENT 2017 PEW RES. CTR. (July 11, 2017), http://assets.pewresearch.org/wp-content/uploads/sites/14/2017/07/10151519/PI_2017.07.11_Online-Harassment_FINAL.pdf.
33. Mary Anne Franks, *"Revenge Porn" Reform: A View from the Front Lines*, 69 FLA. L. REV. 1251, 1259 (2017).
34. Mary Anne Franks, *Sexual Harassment 2.0*, 71 MD. L. REV. 655, 658 (2012).
35. *See* Marwick & Lewis, *supra* note 31, at 8.
36. *See* Caitlin Dewey, *The Only Guide to Gamergate You Will Ever Need to Read*, WASH. POST, Oct. 14, 2014, https://www.washingtonpost.com/news/the-intersect/wp/2014/10/14/the-only-guide-to-gamergate-you-will-ever-need-to-read/.
37. Jenn Frank, *How to Attack a Woman Who Works in Video Gaming*, THE GUARDIAN (Sept. 1, 2014), https://www.theguardian.com/technology/2014/sep/01/how-to-attack-a-woman-who-works-in-video-games.
38. Lauren Rankin, *How an Online Search for Abortion Pills Landed This Woman in Jail*, FAST COMPANY (Feb. 26, 2020), https://www.fastcompany.com/90468030/how-an-online-search-for-abortion-pills-landed-this-woman-in-jail (also discussing ways that technological data trails are used to criminalize abortion).
39. Danielle Keats Citron, *Sexual Privacy*, 128 YALE L.J. 1870, 1898 (2019).
40. Twelve percent of people report digital abuse within intimate relationships. MICHELE YBARRA ET AL., INTIMATE PARTNER ABUSE, DATA & SOC'Y & CTR. FOR INNOVATIVE PUB. HEALTH RES. 3 (Jan. 18, 2017), https://datasociety.net/pubs/oh/Intimate_Partner_Digital_Abuse_2017.pdf.
41. Mary Ann Franks, *Unwilling Avatars: Idealism and Discrimination in Cyberspace*, 20 COLUM. J. GENDER & L. 224, 231–34 (2011).

42. Donna Haraway, *Manifesto for Cyborgs: Science, Technology, and Socialist Feminism in the 1980s*, 80 SOCIALIST REV. 65 (1985).
43. SARA WACHTER-BOETTCHER, TECHNICALLY WRONG: SEXIST APPS, BIASED ALGORITHMS, AND OTHER THREATS OF TOXIC TECH 149 (2017).
44. RUHA BENJAMIN, RACE AFTER TECHNOLOGY: ABOLITIONIST TOOLS FOR THE NEW JIM CODE (2019).
45. SASHA COSTANZA-CHOCK, DESIGN JUSTICE: COMMUNITY-LED PRACTICES TO BUILD THE WORLDS WE NEED (2020).
46. 47 U.S.C. § 230 (2018). *See* Danielle Keats Citron & Mary Anne Franks, *The Internet as a Speech Machine and Other Myths Confounding Section 230 Reform*, 2020 U. CHI. L. F. 45, 49–50 (2020) (arguing that courts have interpreted § 230 overly broadly, and that the courts' interpretation does not align with the drafters' intent).
47. Danielle Keats Citron & Mary Anne Franks, *Criminalizing Revenge Porn*, 49 WAKE FOREST L. REV. 345, 360 (2014).
48. *Id.* at 359–60.
49. Cynthia J. Najdowski, *Legal Responses to Nonconsensual Pornography: Current Policy in the United States and Future Directions for Research*, 23 PSYCH. PUB. POL'Y & L. 154, 159 (2017).
50. Franks, *"Revenge Porn," supra* note 33, at 1282.
51. Danielle Keats Citron, *Law's Expressive Value in Combating Cyber Gender Harassment*, 108 MICH. L. REV. 373, 393 (2009).
52. *See generally id.*
53. CYBER CIVIL RIGHTS INITIATIVE, https://www.cybercivilrights.org/ (last visited Feb. 18, 2021).
54. Franks, *"Revenge Porn," supra* note 33, at 1280–81. Not all state laws follow the recommendations of the CCRI and instead "suffer from overly burdensome requirements, narrow applicability, or constitutional infirmities." *Id.* at 1282.
55. *Id.* at 1256, 1270–77.
56. WACHTER-BOETTCHER, *supra* note 43, ch. 8.
57. JESSICA A. PATER ET AL., CHARACTERIZATIONS OF ONLINE HARASSMENT: COMPARING POLICIES ACROSS SOCIAL MEDIA PLATFORMS, PROC. OF THE 19TH ACM INT'L CONF. ON SUPPORTING GRP. WORK, GRP. 2016, 369 (2016).
58. Sarita Schoenebeck, Oliver L. Haimson & Lisa Nakamura, *Drawing from Justice Theories to Support Targets of Online Harassment*, NEW MEDIA & SOC'Y 1, 19 (2020), https://doi.org/10.1177/1461444820913122.
59. *See* AARON RIEKE ET AL., DATA BROKERS IN AN OPEN SOCIETY 5–12 Upturn: Open Society Foundations (2016) (describing the data broker industry).
60. SHOSHANA ZUBOFF, THE AGE OF SURVEILLANCE CAPITALISM: THE FIGHT FOR A HUMAN FUTURE AT THE NEW FRONTIER OF POWER 8 (2019).
61. Mary Madden et al., *Privacy, Poverty, and Big Data: A Matrix of Vulnerabilities for Poor Americans*, 95 WASH. U. L. REV. 53, 55–57 (2017).
62. Jeffrey Dastin, *Amazon Scraps Secret AI Recruiting Tool That Showed Bias Against Women*, REUTERS (Oct. 9, 2018), https://www.reuters.com/article/us-amazon-com-jobs-automation-insight/amazon-scraps-secret-ai-recruiting-tool-that-showed-bias-against-women-idUSKCN1MK08G.

63. Michael Hiltzik, *Apple Gets in Trouble Over the "Sexism" of Its New Apple Card*, L.A. Times, Nov. 11, 2019, https://www.latimes.com/business/story/2019-11-11/apple-sexism-apple-card.
64. Joy Buolamwini & Timnit Gebru, *Gender Shades: Intersectional Accuracy Disparities in Commercial Gender Classification*, 81 Proc. of Mach. Learning Res. 1 (2018).
65. Safiya Umoja Noble, Algorithms of Oppression: How Search Engines Reinforce Racism (2018).
66. *Emerging Technology from the arXiv, How Vector Space Mathematics Reveals the Hidden Sexism in Language*, MIT Tech. Rev. (July 27, 2016), https://www.technologyreview.com/2016/07/27/158634/how-vector-space-mathematics-reveals-the-hidden-sexism-in-language/.
67. Megan Specia, *Siri and Alexa Reinforce Gender Bias, U.N. Finds*, N.Y. Times, May 22, 2019, https://www.nytimes.com/2019/05/22/world/siri-alexa-ai-gender-bias.html.
68. Catherine D'Ignazio & Lauren F. Klein, Data Feminism 45 (2020).
69. Frank Pasquale, The Black Box Society: The Secret Algorithms That Control Money and Information (2015).
70. Pauline Kim, *Data-Driven Discrimination at Work*, 58 Wm. & Mary L. Rev. 857, 866–67 (2017); *see also* Solon Barocas & Andrew D. Selbst, *Big Data's Disparate Impact*, 104 Calif. L. Rev. 671, 701–02 (2016).
71. Janet Vertesi, *My Experiment Opting Out of Big Data Made Me Look Like a Criminal*, Time (May 1, 2014), https://time.com/83200/privacy-internet-big-data-opt-out/.
72. *See* Anita Allen, *Protecting One's Own Privacy in a Big Data Economy*, 130 Harv. L. Rev. F. 71, 78 (2016).
73. Our Data Bodies, https://www.odbproject.org/ (last visited Feb. 18, 2021).
74. bell hooks, Feminism Is for Everybody: Passionate Politics 7 (2000).
75. Our Data Bodies, *supra* note 73.
76. Tamika Lewis et al., *Digital Defense Playbook: Community Power Tools for Reclaiming Data*, *in* Our Data Bodies (2018), https://www.odbproject.org/wp-content/uploads/2019/03/ODB_DDP_HighRes_Single.pdf.
77. Tawana Petty et al., *Our Data Bodies: Reclaiming Our Data*, *in* Our Data Bodies 15 (June 15, 2018), https://www.odbproject.org/wp-content/uploads/2016/12/ODB.InterimReport.FINAL_.7.16.2018.pdf.
78. Digital Defense Playbook, *supra* note 76, at 7.
79. *See* Donna Rosato, *What Your Period Tracker App Knows About You*, Consumer Rep. (Jan. 28, 2020), https://www.consumerreports.org/health-privacy/what-your-period-tracker-app-knows-about-you.
80. *See* Karen Levy, *Intimate Surveillance*, 51 Idaho L. Rev. 679, 684 (2015).
81. Rosato, *supra* note 79.
82. *See* Levy, *supra* note 80, at 690–91.
83. No Body's Business But Mine: How Menstruation Apps Are Sharing Your Data, Priv. Int'l, (Sept. 9, 2019), https://privacyinternational.org/long-read/3196/no-bodys-business-mine-how-menstruations-apps-are-sharing-your-data.
84. Rosato, *supra* note 79.
85. Celia Rosas, *The Future Is Femtech: Privacy and Data Security Issues Surrounding Femtech Applications*, 15 Hastings Bus. L.J. 319 (2019).
86. *See* Ifeoma Ajunwa, Kate Crawford & Jason Schultz, *Limitless Worker Surveillance*, 105 Calif. L. Rev. 735, 739 (2017).

87. Drew Harwell, *Is Your Pregnancy App Sharing Your Intimate Data with Your Boss*, WASH. POST, Apr. 10, 2019, https://www.washingtonpost.com/technology/2019/04/10/tracking-your-pregnancy-an-app-may-be-more-public-than-you-think/?arc404=true.
88. *Id.*
89. *Id.* (quoting the privacy policy).
90. *See* Rosato, *supra* note 79.
91. UNA LEE & DANN TOLIVER, BUILDING CONSENTFUL TECH, ALLIED MEDIA PROJECTS (2017), https://www.andalsotoo.net/wp-content/uploads/2018/10/Building-Consentful-Tech-Zine-SPREADS.pdf.
92. NATASHA FELIZI & JOANA VARON, MENSTRUAPPS—HOW TO TURN YOUR PERIOD INTO MONEY [FOR OTHERS], https://chupadados.codingrights.org/en/menstruapps-como-transformar-sua-menstruacao-em-dinheiro-para-os-outros/.
93. *Id.*
94. *See, e.g.,* MICHELLE L. MOGLIA ET AL., EVALUATION OF SMARTPHONE MENSTRUAL CYCLE TRACKING APPLICATIONS USING AN ADAPTED APPLICATIONS SCORING SYSTEM, 127 OBSTETRICS & GYNECOLOGY 1153 (June 2019).
95. Maggie Delano, *I Tried Tracking My Period and It Was Even Worse Than I Could Have Imagined*, MEDIUM (Feb. 23, 2015), https://medium.com/@maggied/i-tried-tracking-my-period-and-it-was-even-worse-than-i-could-have-imagined-bb46f869f45.
96. Kaitlyn Tiffany, *Period-Tracking Apps Are Not for Women*, Vox (Nov, 16, 2018), https://www.vox.com/the-goods/2018/11/13/18079458/menstrual-tracking-surveillance-glow-clue-apple-health.
97. Felizi & Varon, *supra* note 92.
98. *See generally* Leigh Goodmark, *Autonomy Feminism: An Anti-Essentialist Critique of Mandatory Interventions in Domestic Violence Cases*, 37 FLA. ST. U. L. REV. (2009).
99. Kathryn Abrams, *From Autonomy to Agency: Feminist Perspectives on Self-Direction*, 40 WM. & MARY L. REV. 805, 831 (1999).
100. *Id.* at 807.
101. *See* Michele Gilman, *Periods for Profit and the Rise of Menstrual Surveillance*, 41 COLUM. J. GENDER & L. 100 (2021).
102. MARIKA CIFOR ET AL., FEMINIST DATA MANIFEST-NO (2019), https://www.manifestno.com/.

CHAPTER 32

ENVIRONMENTAL LAW AND FEMINISM

CINNAMON P. CARLARNE

ENVIRONMENTAL degradation and gender-based discrimination date back millennia.[1] The modern legal movements to curb these two forms of human behavior, however, are still young and emergent. Contemporary environmentalism and feminism developed side by side in the 1960s and 1970s, prompting growth in legal architecture in both areas. Environmentalism and feminism both respond to harms brought about by systemic failures that enable or even advance patterns of subordination. For environmentalism, the focus is on constraining unbridled ecosystem destruction. For feminism, the focus is on discovering and unraveling the systems and hierarchies that subordinate women.

The drivers of environmental degradation and the subordination of women overlap and interact. Yet as the fields of environmental law and feminism and the law matured, little was done to cultivate conversations and coalitions, and the intellectual and legal voids created by this silence have expanded over time. The onset of climate change and the maturing of climate law, however, are catalyzing new thinking and renewed exploration of the intersection of environmental law and feminist legal theory.

This chapter explores the important but poorly understood historic and contemporary relationship between environmental law and legal feminism. It first traces the emergence of the two fields, showing how environmental law quickly lost sight of its holistic ecosystem roots and became increasingly fragmented, technocratic, and efficiency-oriented as it sought to survive within a conventional legal framework. It then introduces ecofeminism as an early and still-evolving bridge attempting to span the chasm between the environmentalist and feminist movements. The chapter goes on to explore how, through initiatives such as the Green Belt Movement and the environmental justice movement, activists worldwide have begun to identify and respond to the intersections among environmental degradation, gender inequality, poverty, and racial discrimination.

After a brief introduction to the accelerating climate crisis, the chapter examines how climate law and the swelling climate justice movement create opportunities for rethinking the role of law in limiting the negative effects of climate change and refashioning social, political, and economic relationships along the way. At the same time, a "new more diverse feminist movement" is emerging that embraces an intersectional social justice paradigm.[2] Here, the chapter suggests that as both environmental law and feminist legal theory seek to situate ongoing challenges within larger structures of power and inequality, they draw closer together, creating opportunities for intellectual exchange and coalition building. It concludes by arguing that now, more than ever, environmental law and feminist legal theory scholars must deepen their engagement in order to better understand and advance mutual, often overlapping objectives.

It is worth noting at the outset that, in seeking to engage with feminism and the law, this chapter embraces an anthropocentric (human-centered) vision of environmentalism and the environmental law project. This viewpoint, in keeping with mainstream legal scholarship and practice, situates human interests at the center of environmental objectives. This is not, however, the only form of environmental consciousness, activism, and legal thinking. In fact, while most legal scholars continue to "hew closely to anthropocentric justifications"[3] to advance environmental protection, other scholars reject anthropocentrism in favor of ecocentric (nature-centered) perspectives that contend that nature possesses intrinsic value independent of humans. This approach informed early environmentalism[4] and continues to permeate modern environmental legal thinking.[5] Anthropogenic climate change, however, is an intrinsically human problem—in cause and consequence—with devastating and inequitable effects on humans both individually and collectively. Likewise, feminism and feminist legal theory have been anthropocentric undertakings, set up in counterpoint to naturalist ideologies that historically underwrote the material conditions of women's lived experiences. This chapter thus brackets for now the philosophical debate about the intrinsic value of nature and what it might mean not only for environmental and climate law but also for feminism and feminist legal theory and treats contemporary environmental and climate law, as well as feminism, as demanding "people first" platforms.[6]

I. It's All Connected

"It's all connected."[7] This insight informs the fields of ecology and conservation biology[8] and, by extension, much of environmental law. From its earliest days, ecology has taught us that living things are interdependent and form component parts of complex ecosystems.[9] In his ecological masterpiece, *On the Origin of Species*, Charles Darwin described this interdependence as flora and fauna coexisting and depending on each other in a "tangled bank."[10] The vision of species and systemic interdependence that ecology offers depicts a world where humans are not only component parts of complex ecosystems but also central actors influencing the health and stability of those systems and the species (human and non-human) that rely on them. We are at once part of, shaped by, and, increasingly, reshaping the ecosystems within which we exist.

In 1962, in her pioneering book *Silent Spring*,[11] renowned scientist Rachel Carson offered an alarming view of what can happen when humans acquire power to alter nature and use this power in ways that permanently disrupt the harmony of ecosystems.[12] In the case of *Silent Spring*, the disruptive force that blanketed the mythical town with a "strange blight" that silenced birds, sickened animals, and killed humans was the widely used pesticide DDT.[13] Carson's fictionalized depiction of the pervasive negative effects that one synthetic chemical can have on the environment portrayed to the public a vision of environmental pollution that instilled fear, but also prompted change. *Silent Spring*, alongside televised images of oil-slicked birds on the beaches of Santa Barbara, the Cuyahoga River on fire, and hydrogen bomb clouds over the Pacific Ocean, helped launch the environmental movement of the 1960s, which culminated in the first Earth Day in 1970 and, ultimately, helped catalyze the development of environmental law as we know it today.

A. The Beginnings of Environmental Law

Modern environmental law burst forth in 1969 with an optimistic and ambitious vision of harmonious coexistence. The first modern environmental law, the National Environmental Policy Act (NEPA) of 1969, declared it to be national policy

> [to] encourage productive and enjoyable harmony between man and his environment; to promote efforts which will prevent or eliminate damage to the environment and biosphere and stimulate the health and welfare of man; to enrich the understanding of the ecological systems and natural resources important to the Nation.[14]

Notably, NEPA embraced and responded to the interconnectedness of "*man* and *his* environment," reflecting the lessons of Darwin's and Carson's ecosystem vision. Yet this optimistic vision of harmony neither saw nor responded to the equity and distributive issues that the civil rights and feminist movements of the 1960s and 1970s were framing and that were embedded in existing systems of law. Nevertheless, it initiated a new era in lawmaking in which environmental considerations would form an essential part of governmental decision-making processes, at least in theory. While NEPA signaled the beginning of modern environmental law, the legal developments that followed failed to respond to ecology's core insight about humans' complex, systemic interconnectedness with nature, and speak to the systemic social and economic inequalities that the feminist and civil rights movements sought to address. From the outset, environmental law shut itself off from these other law reform projects, creating its own closed, increasingly scientific and technocratic lawmaking system.

As the field of environmental law grew through the creation of the Environmental Protection Agency (EPA) in 1970 and the adoption of laws such as the Clean Air Act

(1970), the Clean Water Act (1972), and the Endangered Species Act (1973), it evolved to focus on discrete causal pathways between human health and environmental degradation and between economic and environmental interests. Environmental law emerged in a fragmented manner, with each new law creating an insular, media-specific regime. Such laws were characterized by their ambition and their sophisticated efforts to engage with science, prompt technological innovation, and promote human health and economic well-being. They were also, however, characterized by their narrow focus on particular environmental challenges and technological solutions to these challenges.

None of these new legal regimes adopted approaches that would enable lawmakers to see or respond to the connections among air, water, waste, and chemical pollution or realize how controls in one area might have spillover effects in other areas. Moreover, the emerging legal frameworks created very little space for conceptualizing or responding to the inequitable distribution of environmental degradation. Instead, these regimes increasingly reflected the predominantly white, male, middle-class roots and interests of the environmental organizations and lawmakers pushing for action.[15] According to Dorceta Taylor, an environmental sociologist and environmental justice advocate, these organizations "grew increasingly big, bureaucratic, hierarchical, and distant from local concerns and politics," with "men dominat[ing] the top leadership positions in reform environmental organizations."[16] This demographic held sway in the legal arena, as well: The first seven administrators of the EPA were men and, until President Biden appointed Michael Regan in 2021,[17] only one African American, Lisa Jackson (2009–2013), had ever held this leadership role.[18] Equally, white male voices dominated the development of environmental legal theory, a field frequently described as originating with the help of its "founding fathers."[19] Buoyed by mainstream voices, environmentalism and environmental law thrived, but did so in isolation from the increasingly tangled web of social justice challenges ushered in by parallel social movements and law reform projects, including the women's liberation movement of the 1960s and 1970s.

B. Ecofeminism Emerges

At the intersection of environmentalism and second-wave feminism—but far outside the law and the legal academy—the ecofeminist movement began to emerge. Drawing insight from ecology and feminism, ecofeminism emphasizes the deep physical and conceptual linkages between the human world and the natural world and offers an expansive perspective on the interconnectedness between environmental exploitation and the subordination of women. As Mary Mellor describes it:

> Ecofeminism brings together elements of the feminist and green movements, while at the same time offering a challenge to both. It takes from the green movement a concern about the impact of human activities on the non-human world and from feminism the view of humanity as gendered in ways that subordinate, exploit and oppress women.[20]

Ecofeminism took up and deepened Simone de Beauvoir's insight that patriarchal societies "other" both women and nature.[21] In its early emanations in the 1970s and 1980s, ecofeminism drew heavily on intertwined theories of cultural and dominance feminism. The culturally inflected version of ecofeminism viewed women and nature as "connected in morally significant ways because both are identified with femininity (or traits labeled 'feminine')"[22] and suggested that "women's experiences (biological or cultural) give them a different natural mindset, a special knowledge that will enable them to save the planet and a tendency to protect the environment."[23] This relational view envisioned a connection between women and nature grounded in shared characteristics such as fecundity, vulnerability, and creativity. At the same time, ecofeminists also echoed dominance feminists by recognizing that shared feminine characteristics, in turn, made women and nature especially vulnerable to domination in a patriarchal society. Thus, as early as 1975, ecofeminism began sounding the warning that "[w]omen must see that there can be no liberation for them and no solution to ecological crisis within a society whose fundamental model of relationships continues to be one of domination."[24] Early ecofeminist voices offered mainstream environmentalism and environmental law one of the earliest reflections of their capacity for subordination, operating as they did (and still do) comfortably within the existing hierarchy.

By the 1990s, however, ecofeminism—which never found any firm base within feminist legal theory—was under fire and was pressured to evolve. It faced charges of gender essentialism[25] and allegations that the theory amounted to retrograde "glorifications of femaleness" that only reinscribed traditional norms of sex and gender.[26] Particularly because of its early failure to address racial and cultural differences,[27] ecofeminism began to migrate away from its roots in cultural feminism and from reductionist theories of oppression toward more pluralistic and intersectional ways of thinking about the complex relationships between gender, nature, and society. Still embracing as its starting point the view that "the dominations of women, other human Others, and nonhuman nature are interconnected, are wrong, and ought to be eliminated,"[28] ecofeminist thinking began to integrate lessons from critical race theory,[29] intersectional feminism,[30] and, eventually, social justice feminism.[31] The theme of the new ecofeminism was that "boundary conditions specify that an ecofeminist ethic must be anti-sexist, anti-racist, anti-classist, anti-naturist, and opposed to any 'ism' that presupposes or advances a logic of domination."[32] With this expansion, ecofeminist approaches began to offer not merely critiques of oppressive hierarchies but also visions of a more compassionate and inclusive world "within, beneath, and beyond domination."[33]

At its core and across internal divides, ecofeminism offers a vision of the world that imagines the fight for, and future of, women's equality and well-being as deeply intertwined with the objectives of achieving a more just and ecologically flourishing world. It draws from ecology an appreciation of complexity, and it embraces the comforts and discomforts of acknowledging the inevitability of change and the vast array of unknowns that define the evolving operations of any ecosystem. As such, even as it seeks to eliminate all forms of domination, ecofeminism offers a canvas for doing so that does not pretend to be complete but, instead, recognizes the challenges of navigating "complex social, ecological and eco-social truths"[34] on the pathway to effecting positive change.

Despite its relevance, ecofeminism failed to cross the divide into law and failed to infiltrate feminist legal theory or the emerging field of environmental law. Moreover, as the scale of the political, economic, and scientific challenges associated with combating environmental degradation became apparent, environmental law turned progressively inward. Laws and regulations became increasingly issue-specific, economically oriented, and highly technical in order to survive judicial scrutiny and make progress toward solving complex problems. Any vision of ecosystem interconnectedness that had informed the origins of environmental law was quickly lost amid the challenges of constructing a system of law that could survive in a rigid legal system that struggled to conceptualize environmental injuries. There was little space and inclination to search for and respond to the intersections among environmental injuries, ecosystem disruption, and social and economic injustice.

The optimism and visions of harmony that shaped environmental law's auspicious birth in the United States quickly faded amid the social and political realities of the hypercapitalism 1980s and 1990s. The field became a terrain of scrappy backroom bureaucratic fighting where every effort to reduce air and water pollution, to protect individual species, or to clean up abandoned waste sites involved years of effort, litigation, and concessions. Little thought, not to mention legal attention, was given to the racial, gender, or social justice implications of environmental degradation or to the potentially subordinating impacts of environmental law itself. As, piece by piece, Rachel Carson's vision of the intimate links between ecological health and human health and well-being was chopped up and drowned out, domestic environmental law walled itself off from its ecological roots, from the lessons of ecofeminism and, above all, from the complex relationship between humans and nature.

C. International Environmental Law

Meanwhile, environmental concerns were driving legal and social change around the world. At the global level, the field of international environmental law emerged at the crossroads of North-South relations within a frame closely focused on economic development that elided questions of sex difference and women's inequality. From the field's earliest days, international relations were defined by efforts to balance environmental goals, which frequently were advanced by developed countries, with the economic development and poverty alleviation objectives dominating the agendas of developing countries. While international environmental law nominally bore witness to the disparate needs of developed and developing countries and even future generations,[35] it did little to conceptualize or respond to the correlations between gender, poverty, marginalization, and the environment.[36] Like U.S. environmental law, international environmental law perpetuated existing paradigms of power and control, both horizontally (across states) and vertically (within them).[37] Yet below these superstructures of power, change was taking place, largely driven from the ground up and often led by women.

II. The Roots of Environmental and Feminist Intertwining

Because the environmental and second-wave feminist movements matured side by side but not arm in arm, it is not surprising that the "history of the legal literature is most striking for the scarcity of the literature on ecofeminism."[38] For at least the first two decades of modern environmental law's existence, gender considerations were largely absent from the narrative. Gradually, however, the threads of environmental and feminist legal theory are at last intertwining as the dire climate crisis and the maturing environmental and climate justice movements have sent environmental law into a midlife crisis.[39] Faced with the greatest existential challenge of our time—climate change—environmental law is coming full circle to remember that, in the end, it truly is all connected. At least for anthropocentrically minded environmentalists, this comes with the recognition that responding to the climate crisis requires responding to deep systemic inequities including gender inequalities; for feminists, likewise, this means recognizing that responding to deep systemic inequalities requires responding to the climate crisis.[40]

A. The Green Belt Movement

Before turning to climate change, it is important to appreciate that the current interweaving of environmental and feminist thought has roots in the African feminist activism that preceded the current crisis and forged a link between social justice and environmental degradation. In the 1960s, while patterns of environmental degradation intensified worldwide, ecological decline in Kenya was visible throughout the country, with "watersheds drying up, streams disappearing, and the desert expanding south from the Sahara."[41] Shortly after Kenya achieved independence from Great Britain (1963), a young woman named Wangari Maathai returned home from studying abroad in the United States and Germany. On reaching Kenya, she discovered that the lands where she had grown up were barely recognizable. Where vast forests used to be, land had been cleared for "plantations of fast-growing exotic trees that drained the ecosystem of water and degraded the soil."[42] The quickly changing landscape was reshaping the local communities in visible and invisible ways. As Maathai witnessed these transformations, she observed the connections between the health of the environment and the health and well-being of those who depended on it, particularly women. She began to see that the erosion of natural resources also resulted in the erosion of women's rights. Even as she witnessed the ongoing environmental and social change, Maathai was fighting to have a voice in a still deeply patriarchal society.

Maathai became one of the first women in East or Central Africa to earn her Ph.D. Along the way, she encountered layers of institutionalized gender bias, which she responded to by campaigning for equal rights and benefits for female staff and attempting to unionize the staff in order to advance gender equality. By the early 1970s, fighting gender barriers at every step, Maathai had carved out leadership roles for herself in the academic and civic communities.[43] As Maathai worked to advance social and economic development in Kenya, she became increasingly convinced that environmental degradation was the root cause of many of the country's most pervasive problems, including gender inequality. In what would become a turning point both for Maathai's own activism and for the global environmental movement, in 1977 Maathai initiated a tree-planting event to celebrate World Environment Day. The simple yet pathbreaking goal of the event, which emerged from Maathai's work with the National Council of Women of Kenya, was to "respond to the needs of rural Kenyan women who reported that their streams were drying up, their food supply was less secure, and they had to walk further and further to get firewood for fuel and fencing."[44]

The tree planting marked the inception of the global "Green Belt Movement,"[45] which encourages "women to work together to grow seedlings and plant trees to bind the soil, store rainwater, provide food and firewood, and receive a small monetary token for their work."[46] In the beginning, women questioned their knowledge and their ability to access the resources they needed to make their efforts meaningful, but once the women began to see that the project was possible and that their efforts were effecting change, the tree-planting process became "a wonderful symbol of hope.... They could, by their own actions, improve the quality of their lives."[47] The event became the first of many initiatives by Maathai that sought to weave together efforts to advance women's rights, environmental conservation, and economic development.

The effects of Maathai's work rippled outward, leading to the planting of more than fifty million trees worldwide and advancing understanding of the connections between environmental quality and women's rights, as well as the larger relationships between social and economic justice, human rights, and the environment. By concretely demonstrating the connections between environmentalism and feminism, Maathai created a roadmap for advancing women's rights, alleviating poverty, and enhancing democracy through local environmentalism. In 2004, in recognition of her "contribution[s] to sustainable development, democracy and peace," Maathai was awarded the Nobel Peace Prize,[48] the first African woman to receive this recognition.

B. The Environmental Justice Movement

As Maathai spent years cultivating gender- and social justice-oriented environmentalism in Kenya, a complementary justice-focused movement was developing in the United States. The modern environmental justice (EJ) movement emerged in 1982, when more than five hundred environmental and civil rights activists came together to protest the dumping of more than six thousand truckloads of PCB-laced soil in a landfill in Acton, North Carolina, a small, predominantly African American community.[49] Prompted by growing awareness of "the interplay of race, poverty, and environmental risk" and spurred by "[f]indings that poor and of-color communities suffer from pollution more frequently and severely than their white counterparts,"[50] the EJ movement in the United States sought to advance social and racial justice and to push back against environment-based inequities.[51]

As the movement evolved, women began taking on increasingly important leadership roles within it. In much the same way that Maathai perceived the disparate impacts of environmental degradation on women in Kenya, these same patterns have prompted U.S. women to become leaders in the domestic EJ movement. Robert Verchick claims that by the mid-1990s it had become a women's movement because

> many of the most visible and effective environmental justice organizations in the country are led by and consist mainly of *women*. As a result, while the environmental justice movement is certainly an environmental movement, a civil rights movement, and a public health movement, it is also, quite literally, a *women's* movement, and, I suggest, a *feminist* movement as well.[52]

These women leaders are responding not only to the disparate impacts of environmental pollution and degradation on their lives, but also to the distributional impacts of environmental rules themselves. Persistent patterns of inequitable enforcement have revealed the capacity of environmental law to perpetuate racism and other forms of discrimination.[53] A 1992 *National Law Journal* study, for example, found that environmental penalties assessed in minority areas were lower than those imposed for violations in largely white areas, that it takes longer for the government to address known environmental hazards in minority communities, and that the government frequently accepts solutions to environmental hazards in these communities that are less stringent than scientifically recommended.[54] Such racially imbalanced implementation and enforcement of environmental law leave minority communities to "feel they are victims three times over—first by polluters, then the government, and finally the legal system."[55]

The 2014–2015 Flint, Michigan, water crisis demonstrates the persistence of these patterns. In one of the worst domestic environmental crises of modern times, a series of governmental failures, including the failure to step in to enforce the Safe Drinking Water Act for months after being made aware of violations, led to the contamination of Flint's drinking water supply by lead and bacteria.[56] Flint is a community where 50% of the population is African American and more than 40% of the residents live below the poverty line. The long-term health impacts from the contaminated water are not yet known, but it is clear that they are extensive and disproportionately borne by already vulnerable populations. Notably, women leaders have played pivotal roles in exposing and responding to the Flint water crisis.[57]

Feminist and social-justice oriented perspectives such as those represented within the EJ movement and by Wangari Maathai increasingly are infused into environmental movements worldwide, reminding us that everything and everyone is connected.[58] Now, finally, the mounting climate crisis is reviving dialogue at the intersection of feminism, environmentalism, and social justice and creating the space and momentum for ecofeminist ideas to flourish.

III. THE CLIMATE CHANGE INTERVENTION

These budding intersectional conversations intervene at a critical moment in the history of interactions between humans and the Earth. Although humans have been transforming the planet for thousands of years,[59] the extent and scale of these changes have grown over time, so much so that human influence is now the principal driver of change to the Earth's ecosystem, prompting the onset of a new geological epoch, the Anthropocene.[60] This new era is one in which we are forced to confront the deep interconnections between human and natural systems and the possibility that our collective human behavior is hurtling us toward a series of planetary boundaries.

Because these planetary boundaries "define the safe operating space for humanity with respect to the Earth system,"[61] crossing these boundaries could lead to devastating, nonlinear change that undermines not only ecological but also social, cultural, and economic stability. The climate system represents one of these planetary boundaries, and we now find ourselves pushing up against the edges of this boundary and, consequently, confronting a climate crisis. Far more than an environmental challenge,[62] climate change is one of the most intractable and destabilizing dilemmas of our time. It exposes the depth of social and economic inequality both within the United States and across the international community and, ultimately, poses a moment of reckoning for efforts to advance not only gender equality but, ultimately, a safer and more just world.[63]

Since the early 1990s, growing appreciation of the magnitude of the problem has prompted a period of rapid lawmaking and policymaking. In fact, at all levels, "from cities through the international sphere," laws, regulations, and court decisions relating to climate change have proliferated.[64] The emerging body of laws and policies is extensive but fragmented and reliant on conventional systems of environmental law that embed existing systemic inequities and only address questions of justice at the margins.[65]

A. Links Between Gender and Climate Change

The links between gender and the climate crisis are apparent, if still underappreciated. There is little doubt that climate change poses one of the greatest threats to ongoing efforts to address poverty and facilitate equitable and sustainable development worldwide.[66] There is also abundant evidence highlighting the negative correlations between gender and climate change. Women continue to constitute the majority of the world's poor and are more dependent than are men on climate-vulnerable natural resources for their livelihoods.[67] Climate change multiplies the risks that women face because of the increasing risk of both slow-onset and sudden-onset disasters that undermine natural resources and that "hit poor communities first and worst."[68] Women's vulnerability worldwide is compounded by persistent patterns of gender inequality,[69] especially because they continue to face social, economic, and political barriers that limit their "coping capacity."[70] In particular, women lack access to basic human rights. Overall, continuing patterns of social and economic marginalization undermine women's basic human security, reduce resiliency, and impede their ability to participate in decision-making processes about climate change, despite evidence that women have valuable knowledge and expertise to bring to these discussions.[71]

Admittedly, both the negative connections between gender inequality and climate impacts and the positive contributions that women can make to addressing climate change are nominally recognized in international climate law.[72] Adopting a largely liberal feminist approach focused on "mak[ing] room for women,"[73] the parties to the United Nations Framework Convention on Climate Change (UNFCCC) in 2001 adopted a decision promoting gender balance, advancing the participation of women in UNFCCC negotiations, and prioritizing gender equality in national adaptation planning.[74] In the ensuing years, however, the UNFCCC struggled to achieve greater gender balance within its internal operations,[75] and the number of women represented in the decision-making UNFCCC continued to remained disproportionately low, even sliding backwards in the wake of the adoption of the Paris Agreement.[76]

In 2015, the landmark Paris Climate Change Agreement called on parties to the UNFCCC to "respect, promote and consider . . . gender equality [and] empowerment of women"[77] and to develop gender-responsive adaptation and capacity-building programs.[78] The integration of gender considerations into the Paris Agreement began the process of shifting the dominant paradigm of climate law, at least formally, to be more responsive to the pervasive connections between gender equality and climate change and to the voices and concerns of women. As yet, however, this "political commitment remains to be translated into action."[79] States and the UNFCCC continue to lag in efforts to incorporate women into decision-making processes and to systematically incorporate gender considerations into everything from adaptation planning to climate finance. Thus, even as world leaders caution that "to deal with climate change we must simultaneously address the underlying injustice in our world and work to eradicate poverty, exclusion, and inequality,"[80] questions of justice, equity, and fairness remain bracketed at the margins of international climate law.[81]

There is evidence that a growing base of global citizens no longer accepts this justice-blind approach to climate change. In the words of Mary Robinson, the former president of Ireland and author of the book *Climate Justice* (2018), people from all over the world who have "endured the drastic effects of global warming and are striving to help their communities adapt" are "finding common ground in their climate change experiences, personal stories, and solutions."[82] On the basis of these shared experiences and shared stories, they are mobilizing a "quest for climate justice,"[83] seeking not merely action on climate change, but *just* action on climate change. Together, these "women and men from Kiribati to Uganda to Mississippi"[84] are challenging mainstream climate leaders and offering a new vision of climate action and climate leadership that, collectively, constitutes the climate justice movement.

B. The Climate Justice Movement

The new climate justice movement responds to "the direct kinship between social inequality and environmental degradation."[85] Drawing from the EJ movement, it exposes not only how social and economic inequality has led to and perpetuates patterns of climate change, but also how climate change deepens inequality by disproportionately affecting the members of society who already are more vulnerable. Climate justice advocates seek greater emphasis on and involvement on the part of those most affected by climate change. This includes women and girls, who "are and have always been at the forefront of the climate justice movement."[86] Across generations and across the globe, female leaders are springing up. In addition to Mary Robinson, on the list are Greta Thunberg, the teenage founder and heart behind the Fridays for Future movement;[87] India Logan-Riley, a young Maori activist working for climate justice with the International Indigenous Peoples Forum;[88] Isra Hirsi, the teenage co-founder of youth climate strike in the United States;[89] and Oladosu Adenike, the Nigerian ecofeminist activist fighting for an intersectional approach to climate change. The movement they represent envisions a world where we simultaneously limit the negative effects of climate change and reshape existing social, political, and economic relationships along the way. It is a way of thinking and being that builds on the work of Wangari Maathai with a focus on tackling the root causes of inequality.

In this way, the climate justice movement mirrors a turn in feminism toward a model of social justice feminism that draws on lessons from intersectional and critical race feminism to recognize and respond to the intersections among gender, "race, class, sexual orientation, and other realities of experience."[90] As Kristin Kalsem and Verna L. Williams note in their 2010 article *Social Justice Feminism*, "[a]ctivists concerned about what women want in the twenty-first century want to do social justice feminism."[91] Equally, climate activists concerned about the interface between environment and equity want to do climate justice. At the intersection of the climate justice movement and the social justice turn in feminism is a shared concern that, whether the focus is on limiting environmental degradation or advancing women's rights, these efforts must be situated as part of a much wider movement to construct "a framework for transforming society and how its institutions allocate resources, rights, and the capacity to exercise rights."[92]

Social justice feminism seeks to advance understanding of how multiple, overlapping subordinating structures in society came into existence and persist. Climate justice advocates draw on this work to understand how such systems do the dual work of enabling both environmental degradation and the resulting human subordination. For social justice feminists, the focus is on deconstructing the myriad forms of inequality affecting historically subordinated groups such as women, children, and minorities.[93] Climate justice advocates share these commitments but add to them the insight that inequality is connected to environmental quality and the commitment to addressing the two together. Climate justice activists and social justice feminists offer a shared vision of change premised on fairness and social transformation. For the former, this vision is simply more expansive. It centers and makes visible the relationship between the subordination of humans and nature.

A multivocal, justice-oriented approach to climate change draws on long-standing ideas in feminist legal theory offered by Angela Harris,[94] Kimberlé Crenshaw,[95] Mari Matsuda,[96] and many others that seek to situate gender within multiple overlapping structures of power, authority, and inequality in order to better understand and respond to the causes and consequences of systemic inequities. In the context of climate change, this encourages policies that situate it within its broader social context and create opportunities for minimizing its disparate harms while maximizing the social and economic opportunities associated with transitioning justly to a low-carbon economy.[97]

The Green New Deal exemplifies this approach.[98] Proposed in 2019 by U.S. Representative Alexandria Ocasio-Cortez, the Green New Deal frames climate change as a crisis that exacerbates systemic injustice and intersects with the related crises of economic inequality, declining life expectancy, wage stagnation, deindustrialization, and antilabor policies. It proposes a sweeping new national, social, industrial, and economic response along the lines of the New Deal.[99] The Green New Deal would advance programs to achieve net-zero greenhouse gas emissions through a fair and just transition for all communities and workers, including the creation of new jobs, investment in sustainable infrastructure, the provision of a clean environment, and the promotion of justice and equity.

IV. Environmental and Feminist Legal Theory at the Crossroads

To return full circle to where environmental law began, climate change demonstrates that everything—and everyone—is connected. Even as these interdependencies are laid bare and the academic literature concerning climate law and ecofeminism deepens, legal academia has been slow to respond. This failure undermines both the scholarly analysis in environmental law and the ability of this body of scholarship to inform critical decision-making processes. Now, however, climate change provides a catalyst for drawing the disciplines of environmental law and feminist legal theory together to "reframe old controversies and spark coalitions among progressive scholars and activists."[100]

At a moment in time when global phenomena as varied as the "#MeToo" and "#TimesUp!" movements, the COVID-19 pandemic, the Black Lives Matter movement, and the climate crisis are bringing renewed attention to persistent patterns of gender, social, racial, and economic inequality and environmental degradation—and the intersections among them—the ability of feminist legal theorists and environmental law scholars to deepen their mutual engagement is more important than ever. A feminist imbued, social justice-oriented system of environmental law is essential to counteracting environmental law's subordinating tendencies and increasing its ability to respond to the intrinsic relationships between environmental degradation and inequality. As Jane Goodall has observed, "[W]hen nature suffers, we suffer. And when nature flourishes, we all flourish." In order to get there, however, all of us must do "our part to make that world a reality."[101]

Notes

1. *See, e.g.*, GERDA LERNER, THE CREATION OF PATRIARCHY (1987); Lucas Stephens et al., *Archaeological Assessment Reveals Earth's Early Transformation Through Land Use*, 365 SCIENCE 897 (2019); Marta Cintas-Peña & Leonardo García Sanjuán, *Gender Inequalities in Neolithic Iberia: A Multi-Proxy Approach*, 22 EUR. J. OF ARCHAEOLOGY 499 (2019).
2. MARTHA CHAMALLAS, INTRODUCTION TO FEMINIST LEGAL THEORY 107 (3d ed. 2013).
3. *See* Sarah Krakoff, *Mountains Without Handrails . . . Wilderness Without Cellphones*, 27 HARV. ENVTL. L. REV. 417, 458 (2003).
4. *Id.* at 454–59.
5. *See generally* Katherine Sanders, *"Beyond Human Ownership"? Property, Power and Legal Personality for Nature in Aotearoa New Zealand*, 30 J. OF ENVTL. L. 207 (2018); Christopher Stone, *Should Trees Have Standing? Towards Legal Rights of Natural Objects*, 45 S. CAL. L. REV. 450 (1972).
6. MARY ROBINSON, CLIMATE JUSTICE: HOPE, RESILIENCE, AND THE FIGHT FOR A SUSTAINABLE FUTURE 8 (2018).
7. Chris Cuomo, *On Ecofeminist Philosophy*, 7(2) ETHICS & THE ENV'T 1 (2002) (referencing Karren Warren's influential book ECOFEMINIST PHILOSOPHY [2000]).
8. *See, e.g.*, Michael E. Soulé, *What Is Conservation Biology?*, 35 BIOSCIENCE 727 (1985).
9. *See* Carl F. Jordan, *What Is Ecology?*, 56 BULL. OF THE ECOLOGICAL SOC'Y OF AM. 2, 2–3 (1975).
10. CHARLES DARWIN, ON THE ORIGIN OF SPECIES BY MEANS OF NATURAL SELECTION 489 (1859).
11. RACHEL CARSON, SILENT SPRING (1962).
12. For an overview of shifting theories of ecology, *see, e.g.*, Carl Folke et al., *Regime Shifts, Resilience, and Biodiversity in Ecosystem Management*, in FOUNDATIONS OF ECOLOGICAL RESILIENCE 119, 142 (Lance H. Gunderson et al. eds., 2009).
13. CARSON, SILENT SPRING, *supra* note 11, at 1–2.
14. 42 U.S.C. §§ 4321–70a (1982 & Supp. V 1987).
15. *See* DORCETA E. TAYLOR, THE RISE OF THE AMERICAN CONSERVATION MOVEMENT: POWER, PRIVILEGE, AND ENVIRONMENTAL PROTECTION (2016).

16. Dorceta E. Taylor, *Race, Class, Gender, and American Environmentalism*, 9–11, USDA, Gen. Tech. Rep. PNW-GTR-534, https://www.fs.fed.us/pnw/pubs/gtr534.pdf (2002). *See also* Jeremy P. Jacobs, Nick Sobczyk, & Timothy Cama, *"Overwhelmingly White" Green Groups Forced to Confront Past*, E&E News, June 5, 2020, https://www.eenews.net/stories/1063327335; Jedediah Purdy, *Environmentalism's Racist History*, THE NEW YORKER, Aug. 13, 2015, https://www.newyorker.com/news/news-desk/environmentalisms-racist-history.
17. Jeff Tolleson, *Biden's Pick to Head US Environment Agency Heartens Scientists*, Nature. (Dec. 18, 2020), https://www.nature.com/articles/d41586-020-03621-6.
18. U.S. EPA, CHRONOLOGY OF ADMINISTRATORS, https://www.epa.gov/history/chronology-epa-administrators.
19. *See, e.g.*, Eric A. Goldstein, *David Sive and Joe Sax, Titans of Environmental Law: An Appreciation*, NRDC, Mar. 14, 2014, https://www.nrdc.org/experts/eric-goldstein/david-sive-and-joe-sax-titans-environmental-law-appreciation.
20. MARY MELLOR, FEMINISM AND ECOLOGY 1 (1997).
21. SIMONE DE BEAUVOIR, THE SECOND SEX (2011).
22. *Id.* at 7.
23. Itzá Castañeda, Cintia Aguilar, & Allison Rand, *Measurement and Reporting: Important Elements of Gender Mainstreaming in Environmental Policies*, 22 CORNELL J.L. & PUB. POL'Y 667, 670 (2013).
24. Trish Glazebrook, *Karen Warren's Ecofeminism*, 7 ETHICS & THE ENV'T 12, 13 (2002) (quoting ROSEMARY RADFORD RUETHER, NEW WOMAN, NEW EARTH: SEXIST IDEOLOGIES AND HUMAN LIBERATION [1975]).
25. Greta Gaard, *Ecofeminism Revisited: Rejecting Essentialism and Re-Placing Species in a Material Feminist Environmentalism*, 23 FEMINIST FORMATIONS 26 (2011); Noël Sturgeon, ECOFEMINIST APPROPRIATIONS AND TRANSNATIONAL ENVIRONMENTALISMS, 6 IDENTITIES 255, 260–62 (1999).
26. Cuomo, *On Ecofeminist Philosophy*, *supra* note 7, at 8.
27. *See* A.E. Kings, *Intersectionality and the Changing Face of Ecofeminism*, 22 ETHICS & THE ENV'T 63, 63 (2017).
28. KAREN J. WARREN, ECOFEMINIST PHILOSOPHY: A WESTERN PERSPECTIVE ON WHAT IT IS AND WHY IT MATTERS 155 (2000).
29. Angela P. Harris, *Race and Essentialism in Feminist Legal Theory*, 42 STAN. L. REV. 581, 585 (1990).
30. Kimberlé Crenshaw, *Demarginalizing the Intersection of Race and Sex: A Black Feminist Critique of Antidiscrimination Doctrine, Feminist Theory and Antiracist Politics*, 1989 U. CHI. LEGAL F. 139 (1989).
31. Kristin Kalsem & Verna L. Williams, *Social Justice Feminism*, 18 UCLA WOMEN'S L.J. 131 (2010).
32. WARREN, ECOFEMINIST PHILOSOPHY, *supra* note 28, at 99.
33. Cuomo, *On Ecofeminist Philosophy*, *supra* note 7, at 7.
34. *Id.* at 10.
35. *See* DECLARATION OF THE UNITED NATIONS CONFERENCE ON THE HUMAN ENV'T, U.N. Doc. A/CONF.48/14, reprinted in 11 I.L.M. 1416, Principle 1 (June 16, 1972).
36. For example, the Stockholm Declaration makes no mention of gender, poverty, justice, fairness, or equity. *Id.* By 1992, the principles of international environmental law evolved to acknowledge the interests and role of women, indigenous peoples, and "people under oppression, domination and occupation." RIO DECLARATION ON ENV'T

AND DEVELOPMENT, U.N. Doc. A/CONF.151/26 (vol. 1), reprinted in 31 I.L.M. 874 (June 14, 1992).

37. See Phillipa Norman, *Surfacing the Silent Others: Women and the Environment*, 19 N.Z. J. ENVTL. L. 1 (2015); Carmen G. Gonzalez, *Bridging the North–South Divide: International Environmental Law in the Anthropocene*, 32 PACE ENVTL. L. REV. 407 (2015); Christopher C. Joyner & George E. Little, *It's Not Nice to Fool Mother Nature! The Mystique of Feminist Approaches to International Environmental Law*, 14 B.U. INT'L L.J. 223 (1996).

38. Linda A. Malone, *Environmental Justice Reimagined Through Human Security and Post-Modern Ecological Feminism: A Neglected Perspective on Climate Change*, 38 FORDHAM INT'L L.J. 1445 (2015). As Angela Harris similarly notes, "[w]ith a few notable exceptions, critical legal theorists have concentrated on 'social justice' and environmental scholars have concentrated on 'sustainability,' with few overlaps in these distinct conversations." Angela P. Harris, *Vulnerability and Power in the Age of the Anthropocene*, 6 WASH. & LEE J. ENERGY, CLIMATE & ENV'T 98, 104–5 (2015).

39. See Linda A. Malone, *Looking Beyond Environmental Law's Mid-Life Crisis*, 23 PACE ENVTL. L. REV. 679 (2006).

40. This is in addition to ongoing patterns of environmental degradation. See, e.g., Kate Darling, *A Weight for Water: An Ecological Feminist Critique of Emerging Norms and Trends in Global Water Governance*, 13 MELB. J. INT'L L. 368 (2012).

41. Mia MacDonald, *The Green Belt Movement, and the Story of Wangari Maathai*, YES! MAGAZINE, Mar. 26, 2005, https://www.yesmagazine.org/issue/media/2005/03/26/the-green-belt-movement-the-story-of-wangari-maathai/.

42. See *The Queen of Trees: Wangari Maathai Risked Her Own Life for Restoration*, BIOS, https://urnabios.com/the-queen-of-trees-wangari-maathai-risked-her-life-for-refore station/.

43. By the mid-1970s Maathai was the director of the Kenyan Red Cross Society, a member of the Kenyan Association of University Women, and a board member of the newly formed Environmental Liaison Center. *Id.*

44. The Green Belt Movement, *Our History*, THE GREEN BELT MOVEMENT, https://www.greenbeltmovement.org/who-we-are/our-history.

45. See WANGARI MAATHAI, THE GREEN BELT MOVEMENT: SHARING THE APPROACH AND THE EXPERIENCE (2003).

46. The Green Belt Movement, *Our History*, supra note 44.

47. Wangari Maathai, *Speak Truth to Power*, The Green Belt Movement, May 4, 2000, https://www.greenbeltmovement.org/wangari-maathai/key-speeches-and-articles/speak-truth-to-power.

48. THE NOBEL PRIZE, WANGARI MAATHAI: NOBEL LECTURE (2004), https://www.nobelprize.org/prizes/peace/2004/maathai/facts/.

49. However, the early roots of the U.S. environmental justice movement date back to the 1960s. One example is the Memphis Sanitation Strike of 1968. See U.S. Department of Energy, *Environmental Justice History*, OFF. OF LEGACY MGMT., https://www.energy.gov/lm/services/environmental-justice/environmental-justice-history.

50. Maxine Burkett, *Just Solutions to Climate Change: A Climate Justice Proposal for a Domestic Clean Development Mechanism*, 56 BUFF. L. REV. 169, 188 (2008). See also ROBERT D. BULLARD, DUMPING IN DIXIE: RACE, CLASS, AND ENVIRONMENTAL QUALITY 116 (2d ed. 1994); Rebecca Tsosie, *Indigenous People and Environmental Justice: The Impact of Climate Change*, 78 U. COLO. L. REV. 1625, 1629 (2007); Robert R. Kuehn, *A Taxonomy*

of Environmental Justice, 30 ENVTL. L. REP. NEWS & ANALYSIS 10681, 10688, 10693–94 (2000).

51. *See Toxic Wastes and Race in the United States: A National Report on the Racial and Socio-Economic Characteristics of Communities with Hazardous Waste Sites*, COMMISSION FOR RACIAL JUSTICE, UNITED CHURCH OF CHRIST (1987), http://d3n8a8pro7vhmx.cloudfront.net/unitedchurchofchrist/legacy_url/13567/toxwrace87.pdf?1418439935.

52. Robert R.M. Verchick, *In a Greener Voice: Feminist Theory and Environmental Justice*, 19 HARV. WOMEN'S L.J. 23, 24–25 (2006) (emphasis in original).

53. *See* Gerald Torres, *Introduction: Understanding Environmental Racism*, 63 U. COLO. L. REV. 839, 840 (1992); Keith Hirokawa, *Some Pragmatic Observations About Radical Critique in Environmental Law*, 21 STAN. ENVTL. L.J. 225, 237–38 (2002). *See also* Angela P. Harris, *Criminal Justice as Environmental Justice*, 1 J. GENDER RACE & JUST. 1, 23 (1997) (describing environmental justice analysis as seeking to "make visible the connections between local social ills such as pollution, ill health, and crime and larger patterns of economic and social injustice").

54. Marianne Lavelle & Marcia Coyle, *Unequal Protection: The Racial Divide in Environmental Law*, 15 NAT'L L.J., at S1–S12 (1992), https://www.ejnet.org/ej/nlj.pdf.

55. *Id.* For a recent illustration of this problem, *see* Jean Chemnick, SOOT RULE THRUSTS EPA INTO SPOTLIGHT ON RACE, E&E NEWS (June 12, 2020), https://www.scientificamerican.com/article/soot-rule-thrusts-epa-into-spotlight-on-race/.

56. *See* Lillian Gabreski ed., *The Safe Drinking Water Act and Flint, Michigan: How We Can Update Our Standards for Safe Drinking Water*, CORNELL POL'Y REV., May 31, 2018, http://www.cornellpolicyreview.com/sdwa-flint-michigan/; Lindsey J. Butler, Madeleine K. Scammell, & Eugene B. Benson, *The Flint, Michigan Water Crisis: A Case Study in Regulatory Failure and Environmental Injustice*, 9 ENVTL. JUST. 93 (2016).

57. *See, e.g.*, Jennifer Hammonds, *Clean Water Champions: The Women of the Flint Water Crisis*, NAT'L WILDLIFE FED'N BLOG, Mar. 20, 2019, https://blog.nwf.org/2019/03/clean-water-champions-the-women-of-the-flint-water-crisis/.

58. *See, e.g.*, Carmen G. Gonzalez, *Beyond Eco-Imperialism: An Environmental Justice Critique of Free Trade*, 32 DENV. U. L. REV. 1001, 1014 (2001) ("Environmental injustice cannot be separated from economic inequality, race and gender subordination, and the colonial and post-colonial domination of the global South").

59. Stephens et al., *Archaeological Assessment*, *supra* note 1.

60. *See* Paul J. Crutzen & Eugene F. Stoermer, *The "Anthropocene,"* 41 GLOBAL CHANGE NEWS 17, 17–18 (2000), http://www.igbp.net/download/18.316f18321323470177580001401/1376383088452/NL41.pdf; Will Steffen et al., *The Anthropocene: From Global Change to Planetary Stewardship*, 40 AMBIO 7 (2011).

61. *See* Johan Rockström et al., *A Safe Operating Space for Humanity*, 461 NATURE 472, 472 (2009).

62. *See, e.g.*, Cinnamon Carlarne, *Delinking International Environmental Law & Climate Change*, 4 MICH. J. ENVTL. & ADMIN. L. 1, 6 (2014).

63. *See* Noah S. Diffenbaugh & Marshall Burke, *Global Warming Has Increased Global Inequality*, 116 PNAS 9808 (2019).

64. *See* DANIEL A. FARBER & CINNAMON P. CARLARNE, CLIMATE CHANGE LAW 1 (2018).

65. *See generally* Cinnamon P. Carlarne & J.D. Colavecchio, *Balancing Equity and Effectiveness: The Paris Agreement and the Future of International Climate Change Law*, 27 N.Y.U. ENVTL. L.J. 107 (2019).

66. Sustainable development is a core principle in international environmental law, but it has been critiqued as "fundamentally at odds with the ecofeminist perspective" for failing to "sufficiently address the marginalization of the poor and women in developing countries" and perpetuating "essentially male-centered or androcentric views, of human beings as separate and above nature." Malone, *Environmental Justice Reimagined, supra* note 38, at 1457–58.
67. SUMUDU ATAPATTU, HUMAN RIGHTS APPROACHES TO CLIMATE CHANGE: CHALLENGES AND OPPORTUNITIES 198–217 (2016).
68. FACT SHEET: CLIMATE CHANGE AND WOMEN, OXFAM AMERICA (2008), https://www.oxfamamerica.org/static/media/files/climatechangewomen-factsheet.pdf ("women make up an estimated 70 percent of those living below the poverty line").
69. *See* Harris, *Vulnerability and Power, supra* note 38, at 99 (suggesting that "ecological vulnerability can serve as an important conceptual bridge between critical legal theory and the emerging 'green' legal theory, helping to close the gap between projects of social justice on one hand and environmental sustainability on the other").
70. WOMEN, GENDER EQUALITY AND CLIMATE CHANGE, UN WOMEN WATCH (2009), https://www.un.org/womenwatch/feature/climate_change/downloads/Women_and_Climate_Change_Factsheet.pdf.
71. *Id.*
72. *See* United Nations Framework Convention on Climate Change, GENDER AND CLIMATE CHANGE—DOCUMENTS, https://unfccc.int/topics/gender/resources/documentation-on-gender-and-climate-change.
73. *See* CHAMALLAS, INTRODUCTION TO FEMINIST LEGAL THEORY, *supra* note 2, at 20.
74. United Nations Framework Convention on Climate Change, IMPROVING THE PARTICIPATION OF WOMEN IN THE REPRESENTATION OF PARTIES IN BODIES ESTABLISHED UNDER THE UNITED NATIONS FRAMEWORK CONVENTION ON CLIMATE CHANGE OR THE KYOTO PROTOCOL, Decision 36/CP.7 at 27, U.N. Doc. FCCC/CP/2001/13/Add.4, Jan. 21, 2002.
75. *See* United Nations Framework Convention on Climate Change, GENDER AND CLIMATE CHANGE, U.N. Doc. FCCC/SBI/2013/L.16, Nov. 16, 2013; United Nations Framework Convention on Climate Change, REP. OF THE CONF. OF THE PARTIES ON ITS TWENTIETH SESSION, HELD IN LIMA FROM 1 TO 14 DECEMBER 2014: LIMA WORK PROGRAMME ON GENDER, 18/CP.20 at 35–36, U.N. Doc. UFCCC/CP/2014/10/Add.3, Feb. 2, 2015.
76. United Nations Framework Convention on Climate Change, WOMEN STILL UNDERREPRESENTED IN DECISION-MAKING ON CLIMATE ISSUES UNDER THE UN, Nov. 27, 2019, https://unfccc.int/news/women-still-underrepresented-in-decision-making-on-climate-issues-under-the-un.
77. United Nations Framework Convention on Climate Change, REP. OF THE CONF. OF THE PARTIES ON ITS TWENTY-FIRST SESSION, HELD IN PARIS FROM 30 NOVEMBER TO 13 DECEMBER 2015, U.N. Doc. FCCC/CP/2015/10/Add.1, pmbl (Jan. 29, 2016).
78. *Id.* arts 7.5 and 11.2.
79. *See* UN Women, LEVERAGING CO-BENEFITS BETWEEN GENDER EQUALITY AND CLIMATE ACTION FOR SUSTAINABLE DEVELOPMENT: MAINSTREAMING GENDER CONSIDERATIONS IN CLIMATE CHANGE PROJECTS, 15–16 (Oct. 2016), https://unfccc.int/files/gender_and_climate_change/application/pdf/leveraging_cobenefits.pdf. For a summary of the different measures the UNFCCC has taken see United Nations Framework Convention on Climate Change, COMPILATION OF DECISIONS, SUBSIDIARY

BODY REPORTS RELATED TO GENDER AND CLIMATE CHANGE, GCC/DRC/2017/1 (May 9, 2017).
80. ROBINSON, CLIMATE JUSTICE, *supra* note 6, at 8.
81. As with gender equality, the concept of climate justice was finally integrated into international climate law in the Paris Agreement, which observes "the importance *for some* of the concept of 'climate justice,' when taking action to address climate change." Paris Agreement, *supra* note 77, at pmbl (emphasis added).
82. ROBINSON, CLIMATE JUSTICE, *supra* note 6, at 12.
83. *Id.* at 12–13.
84. *Id.*
85. Burkett, *Just Solutions, supra* note 50, at 170.
86. Lucina Di-Meco, *Why Female Leadership Is What the Climate Justice Movement Needs*, Ms., July 2019, https://msmagazine.com/2019/07/19/why-female-leadership-is-what-the-climate-justice-movement-needs/.
87. FRIDAYS FOR FUTURE, https://fridaysforfuture.org/what-we-do/who-we-are/.
88. TE ARA WHATU, INDIA LOGAN-RILEY, https://tearawhatu.org/india.
89. Leila Ettachfini, *Isra Hirsi is 16, Unbothered, and Saving the Planet*, VICE, Sept. 18, 2019, https://www.vice.com/en_us/article/a357wp/isra-hirsi-ilhan-omar-daughter-climate-strike-profile.
90. Harris, *Race and Essentialism, supra* note 29, at 585.
91. Kalsem & Williams, *Social Justice Feminism, supra* note 31, at 192.
92. *Id.* at 150–51.
93. *Id.* at 158.
94. *See* Harris, *Race and Essentialism, supra* note 29.
95. *See* Crenshaw, *Demarginalizing the Intersection of Race and Sex, supra* note 30.
96. *See* Mari J. Matsuda, *Looking to the Bottom: Critical Legal Studies and Reparations*, 22 HARV. C.R.-C.L. L. REV. 323 (1987).
97. *See, e.g.,* Anna Kaijser & Annica Kronsell, *Climate Change Through the Lens of Intersectionality*, 23 ENVTL. POL. 417, 417 (2014).
98. H.R. Res. 109, 116th Cong. (2019). *See also* EUROPEAN COMMISSION, A EUROPEAN GREEN DEAL, https://ec.europa.eu/info/strategy/priorities-2019-2024/european-green-deal_en.
99. *See, e.g.,* Lisa Friedman, *What Is the Green New Deal? A Climate Proposal, Explained*, N.Y. TIMES, Feb. 21, 2019, https://www.nytimes.com/2019/02/21/climate/green-new-deal-questions-answers.html (reporting that the goal of the Green New Deal is to "reduce greenhouse gas emissions ... while also trying to fix societal problems like economic inequality and racial injustice").
100. CHAMALLAS, INTRODUCTION TO FEMINIST LEGAL THEORY, *supra* note 2, at 111.
101. Sally Blundell, *Jane Goodall: We Can Live in Harmony With Nature*, NOTED, July 24, 2017, http://newstoryhub.com/2019/08/we-can-all-make-a-difference-jane-goodall/.

CHAPTER 33

RECONCEPTUALIZING THE TERMS AND CONDITIONS OF ENTRY TO THE UNITED STATES

A Feminist Reimagining of Immigration Law

MARIA L. ONTIVEROS

THE U.S. immigration system controls the terms and conditions under which an individual from a foreign country may enter and remain in the United States. It is common wisdom that the main objectives of the immigration system are to encourage immigration by those who can provide necessary labor, to allow immigration by family members of U.S. residents, and to offer a safe haven for refugees who are fleeing persecution. In each of these situations, however, immigrants find themselves in a position of weakness because of their strong desire to move to the United States and the limitations imposed by the system. This places all immigrants, but especially female immigrants, in a precarious situation. In setting the terms and conditions of work-based immigration, the system maximizes the ability of employers to exploit immigrant workers and saddles female immigrant workers with additional, unique disadvantages. The immigration system also makes choices of which family members and refugees are worthy of entry because it limits the number of people who can immigrate each year. These choices, evidenced in the terms and conditions for entry, systematically ignore the unique persecution faced by women and often deny them the agency to determine whether to stay in the United States, instead vesting control in their male partners. A feminist reimagining of immigration law would fundamentally reconceptualize and change the terms and conditions of entry to the United States to provide better protection for female immigrants.

The U.S. immigration system regulates who may lawfully be in the United States and the activities in which they may participate. Within this system, U.S. citizens are relatively unencumbered in their ability to live, work, access social services, receive licenses, and participate in civil society. Noncitizens, however, do not have the same rights. In the United States, individuals become citizens either by being born in the United States (a structure referred to as "birth right citizenship"[1]) or by going through a naturalization process. For most individuals, the naturalization process begins with an application for a "green card," which indicates their status as a "lawful permanent resident." After holding a green card for a certain number of years, the individual may apply for citizenship. Traditionally, individuals qualify for a green card in one of three different categories: employment, humanitarian concerns, or family ties.[2] In addition to naturalization, the immigration system regulates individuals who come to the United States for a limited period of time, either to work, to study, or for tourism. Such limited authorizations are governed by a temporary visa system which ties the worker's authorization to remain in the United States to a specific employer. Finally, the immigration system must also concern itself with the approximately eleven million individuals who are physically present in the United States without legal authorization, most often by overseeing their deportation from the country.[3]

This chapter surveys feminist concerns relating to the four key areas of immigration law: employment-based immigration, humanitarian-based immigration, family-based immigration, and the treatment of unauthorized immigrants. It reveals a system that has ignored the problems faced both by women seeking to immigrate to the United States and female immigrants already in the United States, in many cases, erecting a structure that furthers their exploitation, injury, and subordination. Although feminist activists have responded in each of these areas, they have managed to make only modest, incremental reforms. For the most part, more fundamental change has been stymied by entrenched views regarding the purposes of the immigration system and hierarchical notions of patriarchy and white supremacy embedded in laws governing work and family life.

This chapter contends that solutions to these problems lie in sustained critical race and feminist analysis and critique of immigration issues and persistent advocacy to remake the system. It starts from the premise that the type of labor done by female immigrant workers must be more appropriately valued, and that the safety of such workers must be protected. It makes the basic point that when reforming the work visa system, the immigrant worker, not her employer, should be given the power to control her ability to remain in the United States. With respect to humanitarian-based immigration and provision of protective visas, it urges a change in perspective that would make the immigration system more attuned to and appreciative of the systemic dangers and oppression that women face, instead of requiring proof of a specific set of facts that apply only to a subset of women. With respect to reform of immigration rules governing family unification, it argues for policies grounded on the realities of domestic violence that afford immigrant women themselves—not their husbands—the power to control their ability to remain in the United States. The chapter concludes by examining the treatment of unauthorized immigrants and advocating for their human rights and rights as workers.

I. Employment-Based Immigration

Traditionally, most immigration scholars cite the Immigration Act of 1924 as the first formal piece of immigration law.[4] That law established maximum immigration quotas based on race and ancestry and set the stage for subsequent race-conscious immigration policies. Although such policies have been appropriately criticized by critical race scholars because of their preference for white, European immigrants,[5] the critiques have tended not to focus on the effects of the immigration rules on women of color. More recently, critical race and immigration scholars have argued that the laws authorizing and regulating slavery should be considered the true beginning of U.S. immigration policy.[6] Within this view, slavery is regarded as a system of forced immigration that brought millions of workers to the United States to labor under the ownership and control of slave masters, primarily performing domestic and agricultural work. An array of federal, state, and local laws supported and regulated the system of slavery, affecting the conditions of entry and terms of the use of labor, much like modern immigration laws.[7] So viewing the system of chattel slavery as the start of immigration law broadens the immigration law lens and allows us to see how race, gender, and employment-based immigration rules combine to oppress immigrant workers, including female immigrants.

The need for workers continues to drive the immigration system.[8] Employment-based immigration typically starts when an employer applies to sponsor an immigrant worker in one of several different visa categories.[9] Some employers bring workers over for a specified short period of employment, while others sponsor workers on a short-term visa with the intention that they will eventually convert to legal permanent resident status.[10] Significant numbers of women are employed in the temporary visa categories that cover agricultural workers (H-2A visas) and domestic workers. Those hired on short-term status with plans to convert to permanent resident status include nurses, home healthcare aides and women working in high-tech companies (H-1B visas).[11] Female immigrant workers are disadvantaged both because of their racial and gender identity and because of the structure of the visa system.

Employees engaged in agriculture and domestic work receive low pay and labor in substandard work conditions in part because of their race and gender. Historically, agriculture and domestic work were the two primary services performed by slaves.[12] As a direct result of this history, these two occupations were excluded from various protective labor laws, including minimum wage protection and the right to organize into unions.[13] These exclusions persist to this day, preventing these workers from insisting on being paid the legal minimum wage or an overtime premium, as well as allowing employers to fire them if they try to form a union or engage in concerted activity which would be protected for workers in other industries.

In addition, domestic work has traditionally been performed by women and especially by women of color.[14] The domestic work performed by women has been systematically devalued because it is in the private sphere, often performed by women without compensation, and considered to be so easy that "anybody can do it."[15] As a result, domestic work is not considered real work deserving of pay and traditional work benefits. Further, because of the so-called "private" nature of the work, the women who perform this work are also often seen as outside the reach of legal protection.

Outside the institution of chattel slavery, agricultural work has historically been performed primarily by immigrant workers, including Mexican slaves conscripted by California missionaries in the late 1700s; Chinese farmworkers in the 1800s; Japanese immigrants in the first half of the twentieth century; and, more recently, Mexican immigrants.[16] Currently, the majority of agricultural workers are foreign-born, mainly from Mexico; 25 percent are female; and approximately half lack legal authorization to work in the United States.[17] From slaves sold in slave markets to Filipinos found on Hawaiian plantation manifests "between fertilizer and fuel,"[18] agricultural workers have historically been dehumanized, being viewed as commodities and inputs rather than human beings.[19] When workers are viewed as commodities, rather than human beings, it is easier to deny them workplace rights and protections because "[a] commodity does not have a body, so it does not need health insurance ... does not have a family, so it does not need paid vacation or family leave ... does not have a future, so it does not need a pension, job security, training, or promotional opportunities ... does not have a heart, soul or brain, so it does not need to participate in the workplace community or decision making [and] does not live, so it does not need a living wage."[20]

In addition to these historical inequities linked to race and gender, the structure of the visa system also places such workers in a precarious situation. The central feature of all temporary workplace visas is that the employer "owns" the work authorization and controls whether the immigrant may remain in the United States. An employer applies for a visa from the government, and, once the visa is granted, selects an immigrant who matches their needs. The immigrant enters the United States on this specific visa, and the worker has no legal right to remain in the United States unless they remain attached to that specific employer.[21] This creates a dynamic, similar to that found in antebellum slave codes, where the employer completely owns and controls the labor of another human being.[22] It also means that an immigrant woman's ability to stay in the United States is controlled by her employer and is not under her own control.[23] If the employee quits or is fired, she is subject to deportation. As a result, immigrants on temporary work visas are highly constrained in their ability to leave a job or to complain about abusive situations out of fear that their employers will discharge and deport them.[24] Both the employer and the immigrant recognize the power dynamic created by this situation, resulting in visa workers experiencing a wide variety of workplace abuses.

Both agricultural workers and domestic workers experience wage insecurity and other forms of economic abuse. Since they are excluded from minimum wage protection, their earnings are far below that of other workers.[25] In addition, domestic workers brought in on au pair visas fare even worse because they have a statutorily set pay rate that is far below market rate.[26] Farmworkers, in particular, are routinely the victims of wage theft, where employers unlawfully withhold some amount of their wages or illegally charge them exorbitant amounts of money for goods and services.[27]

Many visa workers also end up indebted to the visa sponsor for costs associated with visa procurement and travel, and workers are prohibited from leaving employment until they pay off these debts.[28] Additionally, some visa workers are unable to quit their employment and go home because of large liquidated damages provisions found in the visa contracts.[29]

The experiences of a group of teachers, contracted under a visa program to teach for a school district in Louisiana, illustrate how these practices work together to oppress visa workers. The teachers were required, in contravention of the statute, to pay $5,000 for their visas. They then had to pay an additional $10,000 plus the cost of relocation to the United States or forfeit the $5,000 (an amount equal to 18 months' salary in their home country). Once in the United States, they could not quit because of their need to pay off the $15,000 debt; they knew they could not complain and risk termination because they would be deported with no way to pay back the money owed. A federal district judge ruled that the practices constituted forced labor through threats of serious financial harm and aptly described the predicament of the immigrants in this way: "The worker is therefore faced with a choice of forfeiting the first payment, knowing that repayment of the debt may be impossible, or paying the additional money.... Knowing that working in this program is the only way to repay the initial debt, the worker pays the additional sum and continues working in the program. Once the worker begins employment, complaints about the payments and working conditions are met with continued threats of termination and deportation. Knowing that this job is the only way to repay the debt, the worker remains silent and continues working."[30]

It is now widely known that domestic and agricultural workers are forced to endure abusive working conditions, including substandard housing, excessive hours, and sexual harassment and assault. For example, domestic workers may be given only a tiny room or dirty closet in which to live; agricultural workers often live in crowded, unsanitary work camps. Both groups work exceptionally long hours, unprotected by overtime laws. Domestic workers are often expected to be on call most any time of day or night, seven days a week, if their duties include child care. Finally, both groups are subjected to a high incidence of sexual harassment, including sexual assault. For domestic workers, this usually take place at the hands of the male head of the household in which she works.[31] Female farmworkers routinely suffer rape by supervisors in order to keep their jobs. In addition, they face sexual comments, offensive touching, and verbal and physical threats from their coworkers.[32]

When confronting workplace abuses, immigrant women face obstacles in reporting that go beyond the threat of discharge and deportation. They lack knowledge of the U.S. legal system, a problem exacerbated by language barriers.[33] Female Asian immigrants come from cultures where they have been taught not to openly complain. The machismo culture, prevalent for Mexican female immigrants, teaches women not to challenge the authority of male supervisors or bosses.[34] Finally, these women may have been taught that pursuing claims of sexual harassment brings shame upon themselves and their communities.[35] The sum total of these obstacles means that female immigrants who enter the United States to work end up laboring in abusive situations with little hope of improvement.

A feminist vision of employment-based immigration would change the system on several fronts. The most important change would be to take away the control employers possess over whether a visa worker may remain in the United States. Thus, once a visa worker enters the United States, she should be able to stay for the length of the visa, regardless of whether she remains employed by the employer who initially sponsored her. Visas should be portable, at the very least, to other qualifying employers or employers in the same industry or occupation. Working conditions for immigrants would be improved even more dramatically if the visa worker had full mobility within the U.S. economy to work at any job, even if the employer did not have authorization to employ a visa worker. Such a change would give the immigrant control over her own labor, rather than vesting ownership of her labor in the hands of someone else.

In addition, the work done by agricultural and domestic workers must be more fully valued. There is a need to increase advocacy and education about the real value of typically unpaid domestic work. The contributions of agricultural workers should also be highlighted and made more visible to the general public. Once such a revaluation and education take place, a compelling case can be made that such workers should be protected by the same wage and hour protections covering to the rest of the U.S. labor force.[36] Regulations regarding the health or safety of living conditions must also be revised and updated.

Finally, measures should be taken to make enforcement mechanisms more widely available to these workers. Culturally appropriate, gender-specific education should be delivered in the native language of the immigrant workers. Those tasked with enforcing the law must also be educated about the barriers presented by culture and gender so that their investigations and advocacy can be more effective. It is noteworthy that when such educational efforts are undertaken, immigrant women have been able to receive a measure of justice. For example, under the leadership of immigrant advocate William Tamayo, the office of the northern California Equal Employment Opportunity Commission began to investigate and bring cases on behalf of female farmworkers who had been victims of workplace harassment and sexual assault, using a culturally sensitive, gender-focused approach.[37] Members of the Equal Employment Opportunity Commission (EEOC) received training from rape crisis personnel about how to properly interpret witness credibility for victims of sexual assault; learned from agricultural worker advocates about the structure of the agricultural industry and the daily realities of farm workers; and focused on dispelling fears of deportation for those bringing complaints.[38] As a result, the EEOC has secured million-dollar settlements for female farmworkers and has overseen the creation of programs to educate farmworkers and agricultural employers with the goal of ending workplace harassment and sexual assault.

II. Humanitarian-Based Immigration

Some individuals enter the United States as refugees through a grant of asylum. Under the current law, such entry is available to those who are persecuted or who have a well-founded fear of persecution based on race, religion, nationality, membership in a particular social group, or political opinion.[39] Originally, refugee status focused on victims of state-sponsored violence or political violence and failed to reach gender-based violence, especially when carried out in private sphere.[40] Under this traditional approach, gender by itself was not found to constitute a "particular social group,"[41] and many types of gender-based violence did not rise to the level of a well-founded fear of persecution based on membership in that group. In the past twenty-five years, as a result of immigration attorneys bringing cases grounded in a feminist understanding of gender-based violence, asylum status has been extended to include female victims of certain types of persecution carried out in the private sphere. Litigation has focused on women threatened by female genital mutilation (FGM), forced marriage, and domestic violence.[42] Although some women have found refuge due to these reforms, the continued use of restrictive definitions given to a "particular social group" and "persecution" based on such membership, means many other women are still denied the opportunity to flee gender-based violence and safely immigrate to the United States.

Women threatened with FGM, defined as the removal or alteration of a woman's external genitalia for nonmedical reasons, have been the most successful when seeking asylum.[43] Beginning in 1996, the Board of Immigration Appeals and Circuit Courts began to grant asylum to women who faced the threat of female genital mutilation in the future. They were able to claim membership in a tribe that practiced FGM as their particular social group, and courts readily recognized this as an acceptable subgroup of women. Further, the physical nature of FGM was easily understood as persecution. Women who had already been victimized by FGM, however, fared less well because of the requirement that there be "threat" of persecution, and some courts concluded, erroneously, that FGM could not happen again or ignored the possibility of other threats.[44] Currently, advocates are arguing for grants of asylum to mothers whose daughters are facing the threat of FGM on the basis of the extreme psychological trauma associated with their child being mutilated or because they may be forced to abandon their daughter.[45] These FGM cases provide the opportunity for immigration law to expand the definition of persecution to reflect and respect injuries done to women.

Victims of domestic violence, however, have encountered considerable difficulty in meeting the requirement of being a member of a "particular social group."[46] Successful domestic violence asylum cases typically require the applicant to adopt a narrative that she is a helpless victim because decision makers define the particular social group as "victims of abuse who are unable to leave,"[47] as opposed to all victims of domestic violence. Victims must also show that that they are unable or unwilling to obtain protection from their home country.[48] This narrow definition excludes many victims of domestic violence, in particular women of color and lesbians who often react differently to such violence and thus are penalized for not playing the role of victim.[49]

Additionally, women threatened with forced marriage have trouble proving that they face persecution because of membership in a particular social group. Successful applicants have generally had to show either that they will be victims of violent retaliation for refusing a forced marriage (a so-called honor crime) or must allege that they are being forced into a polygamous marriage to an abusive older man.[50] Asylum status has generally not been granted if a woman is "merely" being forced into a marriage against her will. The reluctance stems from the perceived difficulty in distinguishing arranged marriages (which are not seen as persecution) from forced marriage (which is considered persecution).[51] Decision makers require a powerful "plus" factor to make clear that the marriage is not an arranged marriage where the woman theoretically has the ability to refuse the marriage. This is why claims tied to honor crimes or physical abuse at the hands of an elderly polygamist are the most likely to succeed.[52] Thus, women who were forced to marry under threat of imprisonment, or whose homes were vandalized, or who had family members assaulted were not found to have suffered persecution but merely nonactionable harassment.[53] Finally, some courts have found that the persecution in such cases is not based on membership in the protected category of gender but rather is attributable to "personal reasons," seen as something independent from a gender-based reason. For example, a woman who was forced into marriage to pay off a family debt was found to have been persecuted for personal reasons (i.e., repayment of the debt) and not because of her gender.[54] These requirements all run counter to the feminist arguments that being the victim of forced marriage should be sufficient to qualify as persecution based on social group status.[55]

A feminist reimagining of humanitarian-based immigration law would center on fundamentally changing the understanding of the requirement that persecution be based on membership in a particular social group. At its core, the social group status requirement within asylum law moves attention away from larger issues of systemic persecution confronting women, especially women of color,[56] to focus on specific subgroups of persecuted women. If the definition of particular social group were expanded to include women generally, however, an important legal obstacle placed on women fleeing FGM, forced marriage, and domestic violence would vanish.[57] From a feminist perspective, this reading makes sense because such victims are oppressed because they are women. Further, in reimagining the meaning of "persecution based on membership in the particular group," the new definition would need to recognize the ongoing nature of violence aimed at women, whether it is FGM or domestic violence. It would require elimination of the distinction between violence based on personal reasons and violence based on gender, when the victim is targeted with gender-based violence that can only be targeted at a woman.

III. Family-Based Immigration

The U.S. immigration system has always prioritized "family ties," and it is the primary basis for legal immigration into the United States. Under this program, U.S. citizens and legal permanent residents may sponsor their spouses, children, and parents on an immigrant visa that may turn into a green card.[58] Although the program serves important purposes of family formation and reunification, from the feminist viewpoint, the amount of control given to the sponsoring spouse can create serious problems for women entering as wives or fiancées. After entry and before becoming a legal permanent resident, such women remain in the category of conditional permanent residents for approximately two years. When this waiting period is over, the couple works together to certify the validity of the marriage and to complete the green card process. In this situation, the resident spouse (typically a man) has control over whether the certification will be approved and whether the woman will be able to stay in the United States.[59]

As a result, women who want to enter the United States and naturalize through this program need to stay with their husbands at all costs. Tragically, many of these women are victims of domestic violence. One survey of immigrant women in San Francisco revealed that 24 percent of Latinas and 20 percent of Filipinas suffered domestic violence; further, "for 42% of the Latinas and 20% of the Filipinas, dependence on their husbands for legal status was a major problem."[60] Many immigrant women feel compelled to stay with an abusive spouse because leaving the relationship could result in visa revocation and deportation.[61] Reported cases include an abused Filipina repeatedly cut with a meat cleaver by her U.S. citizen spouse, after she stayed with him because he threatened to have her deported if she left; a Polish woman married to an American citizen who was subjected to beatings but who felt unable to go to the police because she feared deportation; and a woman from China who fled an abusive relationship and fell into undocumented status because her husband refused to file a petition in support of her permanent residency.[62]

This systematic vesting of control over a woman's future into the hands of her spouse echoes the common law doctrine of coverture. The doctrine of coverture placed the wife under the total control of her spouse because she was not viewed as a separate legal person, and also gave the husband the right to "chastise" his wife to correct any misbehavior to enforce his control.[63] The overturning of some of the harshest aspects of coverture, such as the inability of women to independently own property—through Married Women's Property Acts—and recognition of women as independent legal actors, has been hailed as a key step to ensure women's equality. Critical race feminists, however, have critiqued this simplistic view of women's political and economic gains by noting that the overturning of coverture benefited only a certain subgroup of women and specifically did not benefit enslaved Black women.[64] Arguably, women seeking to immigrate through family formation still suffer under a regime resembling coverture because of the prevalence of domestic violence in such marriages and the legal rule that the resident spouse controls whether his spouse will gain resident status.[65]

One subset of family-based immigrants who suffer severe forms of sexual subjugation are mail-order brides. Using international marriage brokers, some individuals (primarily men) find a prospective spouse who is living abroad. They "shop" for brides, viewing photographs and descriptions of personality and physical attributes on websites. Women chosen through these programs then enter the United States on a "K" fiancé visa or on a tourist visa.[66] Once they arrive, the couple must marry within ninety days or the woman faces deportation.[67] After two years in conditional status, they may file for legal permanent resident status.[68] For generations, mail-order brides were primarily recruited from Asia.[69] More recently, women from the Russian federation have entered the realm of mail-order brides.[70]

Mail-order brides are particularly at risk of exploitation, domestic violence, and other forms of abuse because they have very little power to assert themselves and because the system is structured to ensure their subordination. Most women only seek the role of mail-order bride because their lives in their home country are marked by poverty, subordination, and gender inequality, giving them few satisfying life choices and leaving them little bargaining power when entering a foreign marriage.[71] Additionally, to attract American husbands, these women are marketed as submissive, docile, subservient, and willing to fulfill traditional feminine roles; once here, if they do not fit that role, they may be rejected by their husband and face deportation.[72] Finally, to successfully petition at the end of the two-year period, the couple has to show that their marriage was valid, a showing that generally requires that the wife engage in sex with the husband and perform domestic services.[73] The confluence of these factors results in a system that encourages a dynamic of control practiced by the male spouse, which can result in domination, psychological and emotional abuse, and domestic violence.[74] As a result, mail-order brides are three to six times more likely to experience domestic violence than other women in the United States.[75]

In addition to the fear of deportation and family separation, all categories of female immigrants face barriers to reporting abuse and violence due to language barriers, lack of familiarity with the legal system, lack of financial independence, lack of culturally sensitive social services, and culture-based notions of traditional gender roles.[76] To address this problem, at the behest of feminist activists, in 1994 Congress amended the program to allow women to self-petition for residency in certain circumstances.[77] Although this seemingly removed one barrier for abused women seeking residency, women have had difficulty qualifying for self-certification because of the limited ways they are allowed to prove that they have been battered or subjected to extreme cruelty perpetrated by their spouse.[78] Only applicants who have established a record of domestic violence in the relationship are the most likely to prevail, yet many immigrant women do not call the police to report abuse because of their fear of getting involved with authorities, lack of language skills, religious beliefs about marriage, and other cultural constraints based on expected gender roles.[79] Reforms to the mail-order bride system, in particular, have also been only marginally effective because the main legislative approach has focused on providing additional information to women before accepting an offer of marriage.[80]

This approach fails to deal with the realities of why women enter foreign marriages and their inability to escape abusive ones.

The laudable goals of family unification and family formation in U.S. law are undermined by vesting control over a woman's ability to immigrate in the hands of her husband. As a result, immigrant wives qualifying for residency on the basis of their spousal status are easy targets for subordination, abuse, and domestic violence. In the short term, some minor reforms to the system could begin to alleviate some of the harshest problems of the system. For example, for foreign-based spouses seeking to enter the United States to reunite with an established spouse, the removal of the two-year waiting period in which a woman is a conditional permanent resident would make her less vulnerable and dependent on staying with her husband. In addition, for mail-order brides, eliminating the requirement that a fiancée visa holder must marry within ninety days would put less pressure on the immigrant woman to enter into an abusive marriage, while also giving her more time to learn about her husband and to acclimate to living in a new country.

However, to truly remedy the situation, a feminist reimagining of family-based immigration would start by recognizing the presence of the twin ghosts of coverture and slavery embedded in the system. Vesting control over a woman's future in her spouse, while turning a blind eye to physical abuse, echoes key features of the doctrine of coverture. The ghost of slavery haunts the mail-order bride system, present in the idea that brides can be ordered, essentially purchased from a catalog or website. To conquer these ghosts, agency needs to be returned to these women. Only by doing so will women not find themselves at the mercy of an abusive spouse.

Agency requires both the right to make a choice and the ability or freedom to do so. For established spouses seeking to join someone to whom they are already married, the woman should be able to immigrate and become a permanent resident, without any contingencies. Concerns of fraudulent marriages can be overcome by requiring proof of an established marriage (exceeding a certain time period) or the presence of children. The system of mail-order brides, while problematic, should not be banned because banning the practice would rob women of the very agency they lack and deserve. Instead, for mail-order brides, increasing the information given to women about prospective spouses, including criminal records and prior marriages, would allow for a more informed choice, as would more information about their legal rights and protections. Most importantly, once an agreement is made for a woman to immigrate as a fiancée, the ability to stay should not be vested in the hands of the U.S.-based spouse-to-be. Although concerns about fraud exist, given that the total number of women entering in this category is relatively small, it is an acceptable risk to take, relative to the physical peril in which the current system places mail-order brides. From a larger perspective, women will only truly have agency in making decisions about becoming a mail-order bride if economic, political, and social conditions abroad improve so that they do not feel forced to enter into a marriage with a total stranger.

IV. Unauthorized Immigrants

Immigrants without legal authorization to be in the United States confront many of the same problems described above, but their lack of authorization makes their problems even worse. Without legal authorization to be present or work in the United States, they are subject to deportation at any time. Deportation of even law-abiding unauthorized immigrants has been steadily increasing in recent years.[81] For several reasons, deportation is a devastating event. First, many unauthorized immigrants have children who are U.S. citizens, as a result of birthright citizenship. When facing deportation, these women must choose between separation from their children or removing them from the United States and moving them into living situations which are dangerous and lack basic opportunities. In addition, some immigrants, especially those who immigrated at an early age, may not have a "home" in their country of origin and may find themselves deported to a country where they have no contacts and may not even speak the native language. As a result of these factors, many deported women will try to return to the United States, even though an illegal trip across the border is expensive and dangerous.[82] In 2019, approximately five hundred people died trying to cross the border, either from exposure, drowning, or violence.[83] In addition, women are often sexually assaulted during the trip across the border.[84] For all these reasons, unauthorized immigrants do everything they can to avoid detection. This reality impacts unauthorized victims of domestic violence and unauthorized workers in ways that make them even more vulnerable to exploitation and abuse than their visa-authorized sisters.

Unauthorized victims of domestic violence have fewer options than victims who are trying to immigrate via asylum or through family sponsorship. Since they are not already engaged in the naturalization process, they do not have the ability to self-petition for permanent residency. More important, if they call the police to report abuse or seek medical care, they know that they may be subject to deportation if their unauthorized status is discovered. To address this issue, feminist advocates pushed for the creation of a new visa category for victims of domestic violence.[85] The U-visa now allows unauthorized victims of crimes, including domestic violence, to stay in the United States under certain circumstances and then naturalize.[86] Although this is a helpful development, to qualify for a U-visa, victims must prove "law enforcement cooperation," a difficult task requiring that women not only be willing to report abuse and work with authorities but also be fortunate enough to find an agency willing to listen to their story and issue a certificate of cooperation.[87] The requirement of law enforcement cooperation has proven to be particularly problematic because some law enforcement officers are unwilling to respond to domestic violence complaints in immigrant communities and some jurisdictions even refuse to issue law enforcement cooperation certifications.[88] Finally, those who do qualify for a U-visa may still be denied because the number of such visas is capped at 10,000, which accommodates less than one-sixth of pending applications.[89]

Unauthorized status also makes unauthorized workers especially vulnerable to abuse. They are even more likely than visa-authorized domestic workers to live in squalid conditions and to be victimized by sexual assault and physical violence.[90] Many of these women are further constrained in their ability to leave because their employers confiscate their passports or other immigration documents.[91]

Similar vulnerabilities affect unauthorized agricultural workers who make up approximately 50 percent of the workforce.[92] As they labor in the same poor conditions as authorized workers, their being unauthorized makes them feel unable to complain about wage theft, sexual assault, and deplorable living conditions.[93] Many such workers feel trapped because of the need to repay debts incurred in coming to the United States, as well as shouldering living expenses while here. They also sometimes face threats by employers to call the police or inflict violence on workers or their families if they leave.[94]

In some cases, the treatment of unauthorized workers may be so severe that it constitutes forced labor or involuntary servitude under federal statutes that prohibit human trafficking for the procurement of labor. In these situations, a special visa (the T-visa) may be used by an individual to stay in the country. Like the U-visa, the number of T-visas has a cap, but, unlike the U-visa, the T-visa has been underutilized with fewer visas being granted than are authorized.[95] Like other immigrant protections, T-visas come with onerous evidentiary requirements, including proof that they are victims of a severe form of human trafficking, that they cooperated with law enforcement, and that hardship would result from deportation.[96] Enforcement of the protection that exists is stymied because victims distrust and fear law enforcement, so are unlikely to approach them for help,[97] and because legal representation is often unavailable or too expensive for victims to afford.[98] Until these barriers are addressed, the T-visa will remain an ineffective solution to the problems faced by unauthorized workers.

A feminist vision of immigration law would start with recognition of the reality that millions of unauthorized women live and work in the United States while living in fear of discovery and deportation. As immigration advocates have long urged, those who have established lives and families should be given a path to permanent residency and citizenship. Such a path would decrease the fear of deportation and enable workers to speak up and protest abuse. It would improve the economic and social conditions for this group of female workers. In the meantime, immigration enforcement should be severed from enforcement of criminal laws. Law enforcement and healthcare providers should be prohibited from inquiring into a person's immigration status and from reporting unauthorized individuals to immigration authorities. The T- and U-visa programs should be strengthened by eliminating numerical caps and assuring that individuals have culturally sensitive, language-accessible, low-cost legal help.

V. Conclusion

The U.S. immigration system imposes hardships on women seeking to immigrate to the United States, as well as those who are already here without legal authorization.

A feminist vision of the immigration system—centered on curbing gender abuse and fostering women's agency—would look very different than today's reality. Workers entering the United States on short-term work visas would be able to stay in the United States for the entire length of the visa, even if they separate from the employer, allowing them to seek other employment and escape abusive conditions. Women fleeing gender-based persecution, broadly defined, would be able find humanitarian-based asylum, and legal authorities would recognize the types of systemic persecution faced by women as women, such as domestic violence and forced marriage, rather than focusing on particularly horrific instances of individual persecution. Women who immigrate for the purpose of family formation or family reunification would immediately be granted permanent resident status, without waiting periods or later certification, allowing them agency over their actions, free of fear of retribution from their spouse. Finally, unauthorized workers who are already in the United States should have an ability to change their status and become legal permanent residents, enabling them to protest poor work conditions, to report sexual assault, and to freely seek other employment. As long as the threat of deportation hangs over the head of immigrant women, the system will constrain their ability to act as free human beings, to escape abuse, and to seek justice in the workplace. A feminist vision of the immigration system would recognize the humanity of women and place control of their lives in their own hands.

Notes

1. In certain situations, individuals born outside the United States may also become citizens at birth if one or both of their parents is a U.S. citizen.
2. Jeanne Batalova, Mary Hanna & Christopher Levesque, *Frequently Requested Statistics on Immigrants and Immigration in the United States*, MIGRATION POLICY INSTITUTE (Feb. 11, 2021), https://www.migrationpolicy.org/article/frequently-requested-statistics-immigrants-and-immigration-united-states-2020. A small number of individuals also enter the green card process through the diversity visa lottery.
3. *Id.*
4. Gabriel J. Chin, *The Civil Rights Revolution Comes to Immigration Law: A New Look at the Immigration and Nationality Act of 1965*, 75 N.C. L. REV. 273, 279 (1996).
5. *See, e.g.*, Kevin R. Johnson, *Race Matters: Immigration Law and Policy Scholarship, Law in the Ivory Tower, and the Legal Indifference of the Race Critique*, 2000 U. ILL. L. REV. 525 (2000); George A. Martinez, *Arizona, Immigration, and Latinos: The Epistemology of Whiteness, the Geography of Race, Interest Convergence, and the View From the Perspective of Critical Theory*, 44 ARIZ. ST. L.J. 175 (2012).
6. Rhonda V. Magee, *Slavery as Immigration?*, 44 U.S.F. L. REV. 273 (2009).
7. Gabriel J. Chin & Paul Finkelman, *Birthright Citizenship, Slave Trade Legislation, and the Origins of Federal Immigration Regulation*, 54 U.C. DAVIS L. REV. 2215, 2227–2250 (2021); Maria L. Ontiveros, *Is Modern Day Slavery a Private Act or a Public System of Oppression?*, 39 SEATTLE U. L. REV. 665, 687–91 (2016) [hereinafter Ontiveros, *Is Modern Day Slavery a Private Act*].
8. This section focuses on women who have authorization to enter the U.S. to work through visa programs; women who have entered without authorization often face similar issues. Their particular circumstances are discussed below.

9. U.S. Dept. of State, *Employment-based Immigrant Visas*, https://travel.state.gov/content/travel/en/us-visas/immigrate/employment-based-immigrant-visas.html (last visited Sept. 1, 2021).
10. Maria L. Ontiveros, *H-1B Visas, Outsourcing and Body Shops: A Continuum of Exploitation for High-Tech Workers*, 38 BERKELEY J. EMP. & LAB. L. 1, 9, 25–26 (2017) [hereinafter "Ontiveros, *H-1B Visas*"].
11. *Id.*; Maria L. Ontiveros, *"Liquidated Damages" in Guest Worker Contracts: Involuntary Servitude, Debt Peonage or Valid Contract Clause*, 19 NEV. L.J. 413, 429–31 (2018) [hereinafter Ontiveros, *Liquidated Damages*].
12. Ontiveros, *Is Modern Day Slavery a Private Act*, *supra* note 7, at 665, 683–86.
13. Juan Perea, *The Echoes of Slavery: Recognizing the Racist Origins of the Agricultural and Domestic Worker Exclusion From the National Labor Relations Act*, 72 OHIO ST. L. J. 95, 114–26 (2011); Maria L. Ontiveros, *Immigrant Workers' Rights in a Post-Hoffman World—Organizing Around the Thirteenth Amendment*, 18 GEO. IMMIGR. L.J. 651, 673–74 (2004); Marc Linder, *Farm Workers and the Fair Labor Standards Act: Racial Discrimination in the New Deal*, 65 TEX. L. REV. 1335 (1987).
14. Janie A. Chuang, *The U.S. Au Pair Program: Labor Exploitation and the Myth of Cultural Exchange*, 36 HARV. J. OF L. & GENDER 269, 278–79 (2013).
15. *Id.* at 308–18.
16. Maria L. Ontiveros, *Noncitizen Immigrant Labor and the Thirteenth Amendment: Challenging Guest Worker Programs*, 38 U. TOL. L. REV. 923, 930–38 (2007) [hereinafter Ontiveros, *Noncitizen Immigrant Labor*].
17. *Farm Labor*, USDA, https://www.ers.usda.gov/topics/farm-economy/farm-labor/#h2a (last updated Aug. 18, 2021) [hereinafter *Farm Labor*, USDA].
18. RONALD TAKAKI & PAU HANA, PLANTATION LIFE AND LABOR IN HAWAII 23–34 (1983).
19. Guadalupe T. Luna, *An Infinite Distance? Agricultural Exceptionalism and Agricultural Labor*, 1 U. PA. J. LAB. & EMP. LAW 487, 489–91 (1998); *see also* Gerald P. Lopez, *Don't We Like Them Illegal?*, 45 U.C. DAVIS L. REV. 1711, 1742–73 (discussing these waves of immigration and how the immigration system and nativist sentiment worked to disadvantage such immigrants).
20. Maria L. Ontiveros, *A Vision of Global Capitalism that Puts Women and People of Color at the Center*, 3 J. SMALL & EMERGING BUS. L. 27, 31 (1999).
21. Chuang, *supra* note 14, at 330–32.
22. Ontiveros, *H-1B Visas*, *supra* note 10, at 25–26.
23. *Id.* at 9, 25–26.
24. Briana Beltran, *The Hidden Benefits of the TVPA's Expanded Provision for Temporary Workers*, 41 BERKELEY J. EMP. & LAB. L. 229, 237–29 (2020).
25. The official wage rate is approximately 60 percent of nonfarm labor. *Farm Labor*, USDA, *supra* note 17.
26. Chuang, *supra* at note 14, at 278–81.
27. Beltran, *supra* note 24, at 24–42; Camil A. Sanchez-Palumbo, *Humberto in the Field: The Racialization of H-2A Migrant Farmworkers and a Dual Solution to its Resulting Abuses*, 94 NYU L. REV. 1019, 1043–44 (2019).
28. Ontiveros, *H-1B Visas*, *supra* note 10, at 33–35.
29. Ontiveros, *Liquidated Damages*, *supra* note 11, at 429–31 (discussing a group of teachers).
30. Nuang-Tanedo v. E. Baton Rouge Par. Sch. Bd., 790 F. Supp. 2d 1134, 1137 (C.D. Cal. 2011).
31. Chuang, *supra* note 14, at 306–07.

32. Sarah M. Block, *Invisible Survivors: Female Farmworkers in the United States and the Systemic Failure to Report Workplace Harassment and Abuse*, 24 TEX. J. WOMEN, GENDER & L. 127, 133–35 (2014); HUMAN RIGHTS WATCH, CULTIVATING FEAR: THE VULNERABILITY OF IMMIGRANT FARMWORKERS IN THE U.S. TO SEXUAL VIOLENCE AND SEXUAL HARASSMENT (May 2012), https://www.hrw.org/sites/default/files/reports/us0512ForUpload_1.pdf; SOUTHERN POVERTY LAW CENTER, INJUSTICE ON OUR PLATES (Nov. 8, 2010), https://www.splcenter.org/20101107/injustice-our-plates; Maria L. Ontiveros, LESSONS FROM THE FIELDS: FEMALE FARMWORKERS AND THE LAW, 55 ME. L. REV. 157 (2003) [hereinafter Ontiveros, *Lessons From the Fields*]. Both agricultural visa workers and unauthorized farm workers experience similar treatment.
33. Ontiveros, *Lessons from the Fields*, supra note 32, at 178–79.
34. *Id.* at 171.
35. *Id.* at 179.
36. They should also have the same protected right to form unions as other workers.
37. William R. Tamayo, *The EEOC and Immigrant Workers*, 44 U.S.F.L. REV. 253 (2009) [hereinafter Tamayo, *EEOC and Immigrant Workers*]; William R. Tamayo, *The Role of the EEOC in Protecting the Civil Rights of Farm Workers*, 33 U.C. DAVIS L. REV. 1075 (2000) [hereinafter Tamayo, *Role of the EEOC*]. They worked in conjunction with farm worker advocates, such as California Rural Legal Assistance, the Southern Poverty Law Center, Northwest Justice Project, and Lideres Campensinas.
38. Tamayo, *Role of the EEOC*, supra note 37, at 1075, 1080–83.
39. Immigration and Nationality Act (INA) § 241(b)(3)(A), 8 U.S.C.S. § 1231(b)(3).
40. Hope Lewis, *Universal Mother: Transnational Migration and the Human Rights of Black Women in the Americas*, 5 J. GENDER RACE & JUSTICE 197, 198 (2001).
41. Lori Nessel, *Willful Blindness to Gender-based Violence*, 89 MINN. L. REV. 71, 76 (2004).
42. Zsaleh E. Harivandi, *Invisible and Involuntary: Female Genital Mutilation as a Basis for Asylum*, 95 CORNELL L. REV. 599, 607–10 (2010) (protection had already been extended to women threatened with forced sterilization or forced abortion).
43. Stacey Kounelias, *Asylum Law and Female Genital Mutilation: "Membership in a Particular Social Group" Inadequately Protecting Persecuted Women*, 11 SCHOLAR 577, 578–79 (2009).
44. *Id.* at 591-96. Some courts have found the opposite and granted asylum.
45. Melanie A. Conroy, *Refugees Themselves: The Asylum Case for Parents of Children at Risk of Female Genital Mutilation*, 22 HARV. HUM. RTS. J. 109 (2009).
46. Kounelias, supra note 43, at 600–03.
47. Natalie Nanasi, *Are Domestic Abusers Terrorists? Rhetoric, Reality and Asylum Law*, 91 TEMP. L. REV. 215, 236–38 (2019) [hereinafter Nanasi, *Are Domestic Abusers Terrorists?*]; Natalie Nanasi, *Domestic Violence Asylum and the Perpetuation of the Victim Narrative*, 78 OHIO ST. L. J. 733, 743–52 (2017) [hereinafter Nanasi, *Domestic Violence Asylum*].
48. Nanasi, *Are Domestic Abusers Terrorists?*, supra note 47, at 243–44.
49. Nanasi, *Domestic Violence Asylum*, supra note 48, at 743–52 (2017).
50. Natalie Nanasi, *An "I Do" I Choose: How the Fight for Marriage Access Support a Per Se Finding of Persecution based on Forced Marriage*, 28 COLUM. J. GENDER & L. 48, 50 (2014) [hereinafter Nanasi, *An "I Do" I Choose*].
51. *Id.* at 53–56.
52. *Id.* at 90–94.
53. *Id.* at 63.
54. *Id.* at 66–67.

55. *Id.* at 51–52.
56. Lewis, *supra* note 40, at 197, 198.
57. Nanasi, *Domestic Violence Asylum, supra* note 47, at 767–68 (2017); Valena Elizabeth Beety, *Reframing Asylum Standards for Mutilated Women*, 11 J. GENDER RACE & JUST., 239, 264–65 (2008).
58. U.S. DEP'T OF STATE, BUREAU OF CONSULAR AFFAIRS, FAMILY IMMIGRATION, https://travel.state.gov/content/travel/en/us-visas/immigrate/family-immigration.html (last visited Sept. 1, 2021).
59. This section focuses on women who have authorization to enter, as part of family-based immigration; women who have entered without authorization often face similar issues, and they are discussed below.
60. Janet M. Calvo, *Spouse-Based Immigration Laws: The Legacies of Coverture*, 28 SAN DIEGO L. REV. 593, 618. (1991).
61. Mariela Olivares, *Battered by Law: The Political Subordination of Immigrant Women*, 64 AM. U. L. REV. 231, 241–42 (2014).
62. Calvo, *supra* note 60, at 593.
63. *Id.* at 596–98.
64. Diane Klein, *Their Slavery Was Her Freedom: Racism and the Beginning of the End of Coverture*, 59 DUQ. L. REV. 106 (2021).
65. Calvo, *supra* note 60, at 622–23.
66. Christina L. Pollard, *Here Comes Many More Mail-Order Brides: Why IMBRA Fails Women Escaping the Russian Federation*, 46 CAP. U. L. REV. 609, 644 (2018).
67. Olga Grosh, *Foreign Wives, Domestic Violence: U.S. Law Stigmatizes and Fails to Protect "Mail-Order Brides,"* 22 HASTINGS WOMEN'S L.J. 81, 106 (2011).
68. Pollard, *supra* note 66, at 649.
69. Eddy Meng, *Mail-Order Brides: Gilded Prostitution and the Legal Response*, 28 U. MICH. J.L. REFORM, 197 (1994).
70. Pollard, *supra* note 66, at 612–14.
71. Meng, *supra* note 69, at 226–28 (discussing Asian mail-order brides); Pollard, *supra* note 66, at 614–29 (mail-order brides from the Russian federation); Kate O'Rourke, *To Have and To Hold: A Postmodern Feminist Response to the Mail-Order Bride Industry*, 30 DENV. J. INT'L L. & POL'Y 476, 480.
72. Meng, *supra* note 69, at 205–09 (discussing Asian mail-order brides); Pollard, *supra* note 66, at 631–32 (discussing mail-order brides from the Russian federation).
73. *Id.* at 224–25.
74. Pollard, *supra* note at 66, at 658–59.
75. Grosh, *supra* note 67, at 82.
76. Monika Batra Kashyap, *Heartless Immigration Law: Rubbing Salt Into the Wounds of Immigrant Survivors of Domestic Violence*, 95 TUL. L. REV. 51 (2020).
77. Olivares, *supra* note 61, at 244.
78. Meng, *supra* note 69, at 214.
79. Meng, *supra* note 69, at 220–21.
80. Pollard, *supra* note 66, at 667 (discussing the International Marriage Broker Regulation Act).
81. Priscilla Alvarez, *Deportations of Migrant Families Continues to Jump under the Trump Administration*, CNN (Oct. 3, 2019), https://www.cnn.com/2019/10/03/politics/deportation-migrant-families/index.html (reporting a 171 percent increase in the number of

noncriminal individuals arrested between 2016 and 2019 and an increase in deportations of family groups).

82. Ontiveros, *Noncitizen Immigrant Labor, supra* note 16, at 928.

83. *2019: A Deadly Year for Migrants Crossing the Americas*, U.N. NEWS (Jan. 28, 2020), https://news.un.org/en/story/2020/01/1056202 (Between 2014 and 2019, almost 2,500 people died trying to cross the border. The 2019 number represents an approximate 10% in increase over the previous year).

84. Ontiveros, *Noncitizen Immigrant Labor, supra* note 16, at 928.

85. Advocates have also argued for the importance of preventing immigration status from affecting the provision of medical care or deterring immigrants from entering hospitals or clinics.

86. Rachel Gonzalez Settlage, *Uniquely Unhelpful: The U Visa's Disparate Treatment of Immigrant Victims of Domestic Violence*, 69 RUTGERS L. REV. 1747 (2016).

87. *Id.* at 1772–87.

88. *Id.* at 1776–86.

89. *Id.* at 1787–89. The U-Visa could also be used for victims of workplace harassment as well. Juliana Garcia, *Invisible Behind a Bandana: U-Visa Solution for Sexual Harassment of Female Farmworkers*, 46 U.S.F. L. REV. 855 (2012).

90. Nancy Zarate-Byrd, *The Dirty Side of Domestic Work: An Underground Economy and the Exploitation of Undocumented Workers*, 3 DEPAUL J. SOC. JUST. 245, 262–66 (2010).

91. Samantha Malone, *Domestic Work in the United States: Gender, Immigration and Personhood*, 10 GEO. J. L. & MOD. CRITICAL RACE PERSP. 65, 74 (2018) (62 percent report that employers confiscated immigration documents).

92. *Farm Labor*, USDA, *supra* note 17.

93. Because many of the workers are hired using false documents (either forgeries or those of a different person) and often work side by side with visa-authorized workers, it is difficult to determine whether their working conditions are different or worse than all agricultural workers.

94. Efthimia Barbagiannis, *Protecting Victims of Human Trafficking: Creating Better Residency Visas*, 25 CARDOZO J. INT'L & COMP. L. 561, 589 (2017); Cherish Adams, *Re-Trafficked Victims: How a Human Rights Approach Can Stop the Cycle of Re-Victimization of Sex Trafficking Victims*, 43 GEO. WASH. INT'L L. REV. 201, 206–07 (2011).

95. Barbagiannis, *supra* note 94, at 587.

96. *Id.* at 586–88.

97. *Id.* at 588.

98. Ivy Lee, *An Appeal of a T Visa Denial*, 14 GEO. J. ON POVERTY L. & POL'Y 455, 457–58 (2007).

CHAPTER 34

INVISIBLE WOMEN AND INTANGIBLE PROPERTY

A Feminist Consciousness Raising for Authors and Inventors

ANN BARTOW

MEN overwhelmingly control the most heavily commodified of the creative arts. One does not even need to footnote that assertion because it happens everywhere and in plain sight. The upper echelon of any creative industry—music, television, theater, movies, computer games and software, the visual arts, professional sports, architecture or publishing—is primarily comprised of men. These men are wealthy and powerful individuals who can shape rules, including intellectual property laws, to suit and enrich themselves.

Inventors are also disproportionately male, but their dominance tends to be less visible. Inventors rarely have ownership interests in their patentable ideas and are far less likely to be personally identified with their innovations than successful authors are with their creative output. People like to know who wrote the novel, who painted the painting or who is singing the song, but they pay less attention to who invented their mousetrap or electric toothbrush. Although there is some societal awareness that women are underrepresented in the STEM (science, technology, engineering, and math) professions, the negative impact this disparity has on the ability of women to develop patentable inventions in numbers comparable to men is not fully recognized.

This chapter focuses on the ways that gender and feminism intersect with intellectual property laws and policies. It begins by asserting two basic claims: first, that gender itself can be property, and is exploited as such in several intellectual property contexts, and second, that gender can affect the creation, distribution and consumption of works protected by intellectual property laws. The chapter then turns to examine issues of gender and gender inequality in the three core areas of intellectual property: patents, copyrights and trademarks. The final section discusses two legal areas adjacent to intellectual property, naming rights and artificial intelligence in the form of robots. Recognizing the significant gender disparities promulgated by intellectual property laws requires a feminist gaze.[1]

I. Gender as Property

Feminist legal theorists owe a tremendous debt to critical race scholars for the crucial insight that identity can constitute a kind of intangible property. In 1993, Cheryl Harris published a groundbreaking piece of legal scholarship, *Whiteness as Property*, which explains how whiteness, initially constructed as a form of racial identity, evolved into a form of property that is embedded in and protected by U.S. law.[2] Nancy Leong drew upon this insight to analyze what she calls "racial capitalism," acts by which white individuals and predominantly white institutions use nonwhite people to acquire social and economic value in response to demands for racial diversity. According to Leong, racial capitalism is "the process of deriving social or economic value from the racial identity of another person."[3] This concept explains why white people are so keen to tell you about their Black friends. It explains why white people are so anxious to tell you about the diverse neighborhood they live in. And, more generally, it "explains the intensity of the drive to acquire the capitol associated with nonwhiteness through affiliation."[4]

One example is the practice of some majority white universities to photoshop stock images of Black people into their catalogs and brochures to make their institutions look more racially diverse than they are.[5] Building on critical race scholarship, feminist legal theorists have also explored the ways in which gender—used here to encompass the personal, societal and cultural perceptions of femaleness and maleness, femininity and masculinity and a fluid, nonbinary concept of gender—is property that is commodified and exploited.

Throughout history and across cultures, women of all races have been treated as possessable objects, albeit in starkly varying ways depending on their racial and class positions. Black women enslaved under chattel slavery were the property of white slaveholders. For white women and other women whose class and/or race privilege protected them from chattel slavery, freedom did not mean full personhood. Almost two centuries following its founding, as the U.S. justice system evolved, "free" women were the legal property of their fathers and husbands. Under the doctrine of coverture, a married woman did not exist as an individual but was included in her husband's legal identity, "covered" by her husband. This meant that a married woman could not own property because she herself was property. Her personal belongings, her children, and even her own body were the legal possessions of the man she married. In the eyes of early post-Revolutionary law, a married woman, as a freely determined individual, simply did not exist.[6] Accordingly, in the eyes of the civil law, enslaved women, who were already the property of slaveholders, could not legally marry; civil marriage, which vested husbands with rights of control and possession over wives, was incompatible with the status of slavery.[7] Generally speaking, free single women fared no better than married women because they had few opportunities to support themselves and were often dependent upon their fathers and brothers.[8] It was not until the 1970s that women could open bank accounts or get credit cards in their own names, serve on juries in all fifty states,[9] or buy a house without a male co-signer.[10]

Although the Constitution and laws no longer treat women as property, and women can now own property on our own, remnants of the treatment of women as objects for the possession of others, rather than subjects of ownership rights, persist. One poignant example is the vulnerability of women in the performing arts to sexual exploitation. It is now widely known that former Hollywood producer Harvey Weinstein effectively made sexual contact a job requirement for women who were interested in working with him creatively. Securing roles in Weinstein's productions left many talented female actors feeling that they literally had to barter their bodies to get work in movies.[11] Although Weinstein was convicted of sexual assault and rape, many men accused of similar behavior have not been punished. In addition to actors, dancers[12] and musicians[13] are at risk of being forced to perform sex acts, simply to practice their craft. So are female athletes, who also provide entertainment to the public.[14]

Another way in which we as women are denied the full possession of our talents is when our intellectual accomplishments are expropriated by powerful men, who claim credit for women's creative works and their inventions. Consider the theft of Rosalind Franklin's research by Watson and Crick during the race to discover the structure of DNA.[15] Without her involuntary contribution to their work, it is unlikely they would have won a Nobel Prize. Another example is provided by Margaret Keane, an American artist now famous for her "Big Eye" paintings. For many years, Margaret's husband sold her paintings as his own and convinced Margaret not to reveal the lie, even threatening her life if she told the truth.[16]

History is filled with examples of women's creative labors being appropriated by men, but that is not the only way in which gender and property collide. Gender itself constructs property, shaping its character, use and value. What codes as male or masculine is valued differently than what codes as female or feminine. This process of gendering depends on a sharp differentiation between male and female, masculine and feminine.

Societal gender conventions draw sharp distinctions between males and females. Research has shown for decades that adults will treat babies differently depending on which gender they assume the child to be.[17] Because infants lack secondary sex characteristics, parents often inscribe gender onto the bodies of their babies. Hair length, hair style, and whether a baby is wearing hair accessories such as barrettes and headbands create strong assumptions about gender. To dispel the discomfort that many people feel when faced with gender ambiguity, some parents will literally glue hair accessories to the bald heads of their female infants.

Clothing choices also signal gender, and clothing is gendered by its color and other markers. In the United States, pink has been instantiated as a "girl" color, while boyhood is coded blue.[18] It is probably not a coincidence that blue is the most popular color, while pink is among the least favorite. One study that asked people to name their favorite color found:

> The overwhelming majority of people answered blue—42 percent for men and 29 percent for women. . . . For women, blue narrowly nudged out purple, which got 27 percent of the votes. It also turns out that pink isn't much of a favorite color anywhere, with only 1 percent of men answering that this was their favorite color, along with 7 percent of women.[19]

Although gender differentiation runs deep, what codes as masculine or feminine is not fixed but fluid, as cultural connotations change. Some historians believe that color coding and other signifiers of gender have changed markedly over time.[20] In addition to the color pink, current markers associated with the female gender include "high heels, makeup, wigs . . .—all of which were originally or primarily associated with masculinity and the 'male' gender."[21] One observer asserted:

> The origin of high heels, for example, can be traced back to the 16th century where soldiers wore them to help secure their feet in stirrups. High heels had found their place on the feet of not only the male soldiers, but also aristocrats and royals in many parts of the globe who wore them to look taller and more formidable, and to keep their robes out of the muck.[22]

Such shifts over time demonstrate that gender is a fluid social construct and that there is nothing inherently female about the color pink or high heels.[23] At this moment, in the United States and some other parts of the world, pink functions as a trademark writ large for the female gender. As such, all too often it is a signifier for products that cost more, are of lesser quality, or are shunned by the male gender, or all three combined.[24] It is also the color of commodified breast cancer.[25] Precisely because of its gender association, pink is the color that is used to denigrate femininity and shame men.[26] So, for example, when male athletes voluntarily wear pink or use pink equipment, it is usually a gesture intended and understood to draw attention to breast cancer.[27]

In addition to color-coding objects as a gendering device, there other mechanisms by which property can become marked by gender. Products consumed by women, in actuality or presumptively, can become gendered as feminine. Such is the case with "chick flicks," movies that are gendered feminine and marketed accordingly. Similarly, "chick lit," books trading in stereotypically feminine plot lines and characters, are marked as gendered based on their predominantly female audience. These labels are not only descriptive, they function to delegitimize the work as serious film or literature, and contribute to the message that art produced for women's consumption is mediocre or "fluff." Works that are gendered feminine are marked as low value, not worthy of awards or critical acclaim.

These examples are only some of the ways that property is gendered. The next section examines gender inequalities in the ownership of intellectual property and the role of law in constructing and reinforcing these inequalities.

II. Women and Intellectual Property

Much of the literature about women and wealth decries the lack of real property that women own or control, and with good reason: because women earn significantly less than men,[28] it is harder for them to purchase real estate, or to profit from it.[29]

When it comes to intellectual property as well, women own or control only a small fraction of what men do.[30] What is surprisingly murky and undertheorized is whether women produce less intellectual property, or whether they are just as energetically productive but disadvantaged by an intellectual property law framework that does not recognize or serve women as well. Innovations in areas like clothing, cooking, interior decorating, make-up and hair design are not generally rewarded with copyright or patent protections. This may be a good thing for society generally, but it raises questions about why some kinds of creativity are treated differently than others.[31] Perhaps because women are expected to share knowledge rather than commodify it, neither recipes nor food is copyrightable.[32] The same was also true for clothing for most of history,[33] despite efforts by some designers to have their works protected by intellectual property in some way.[34] Recently, however, a U.S. Supreme Court case suggests copyright laws may be bent or stretched to "protect" fairly basic clothing design features.[35]

Women inventors, authors, and creators are underrepresented in every area of traditional intellectual property.[36] Whether one considers patentable inventions or copyrightable works, the vast majority of the very profitable ones originated and are controlled by men. This causes a host of negative consequences for women, who control only a tiny portion of the world's wealth at a time when intellectual property rights are creating fortunes. Women lack access to ownership of valuable inventions or works of authorship which facilitate the starting or growing of businesses, enhanced employment opportunities, and the accumulation of capital generally. Following is an overview of the gender imbalances in the core areas of intellectual property: patents, copyright and trademark.

A. Patents

Patents signal innovation.[37] A utility patent is a bundle of monopolistic rights granted to the inventor of a process, machine, article of manufacture or composition of matter that is new, useful and nonobvious. It gives the patent holder the right to exclude others for a limited time (typically about seventeen years) from making, using or selling a patented product or process without the consent of the patent holder. Patent law is intended to provide incentives for inventors to make new things and disclose their inventions to the public in exchange for the limited-time monopoly over them provided by a patent. In the common imagination, inventors can be world-changing heroes,[38] and most of these inventions are claimed by men.[39]

Many people contribute to research that leads to patents without being credited as inventors, and a lot of them are women.[40] Statistics from the U.S. Patent & Trademark Office reveal that women apply for patents at much lower rates than men.[41] Whether that means there are fewer women inventors than men inventors, however, is unclear. When an invention results from the work of a group, decisions about who gets credit, and who is publicly identified as an inventor, can be impacted by sexism and racism. Official authorship of group work often downplays the contributions of women. For example, women's names appear less frequently at the tops of final papers, regardless of significant contributions they may have made to research projects.[42]

Women are underrepresented in every aspect of the patent system.[43] Empirical research shows that fewer women than men are named inventors on patents; fewer women than men are patent holders; fewer women than men are patent agents or patent lawyers; and fewer women than men are patent examiners,[44] patent litigators, district court judges, or federal circuit judges.[45] Women inventors account for just under 13 percent of patent applications globally and the percentage in the United States is similar.[46] The gender disparity among inventors is actually even starker because most female inventorship takes the form of a lone female on a male-dominated team of inventors.[47] One study found that "[m]ore than two-thirds of all patents come from all-male teams or individual male inventors—and just 6% from individual female inventors. All-female teams are nearly non-existent, making up just 0.3% of applications."[48]

Fewer women who apply for patents are successful and when women's applications are rejected, they are less likely to appeal.[49] When applications are granted, women's patents are more likely to have additional words added to their claims that reduce the scopes of their patents,[50] usually decreasing the value of the associated patented inventions. Patents on inventions by women fare poorly even after they issue. Women's patents are less likely to be maintained by their assignees (the patent owners, typically corporations) and receive fewer citations to their patents from other inventors and from patent examiners.[51] They probably also generate less licensing revenue, but that information is usually not publicly available.

The barriers facing women inventors are myriad. Often there is a pipeline problem that begins in college or earlier. Even when women enter a STEM profession pipeline in significant numbers, they get diverted from this path for more reasons and in larger numbers than men do.[52] There is little reason for optimism that the number of women inventors or the opportunities that are available to them will increase significantly in the immediate future.

B. Copyrights

Copyright law establishes monopoly rights that serve as incentives for authors to create new works and to make those works available to the public. The theory is that by granting certain exclusive rights, authors receive the benefit of economic rewards, and the public receives the benefit of the creative works that might not otherwise be created or disseminated. Copyright law does not impose obligations upon authors to make their copyrighted works publicly available and does not link the scope of copyright protection to the perceived quality of the works. Section 102(a) of the Copyright Act presents a nonexclusive list of categories of copyrightable works, including literary works, musical works, dramatic works, pantomimes and choreographic works, pictorial, graphic and sculptural works, motion pictures and other audiovisual works, sound recordings, and architectural works.[53]

Commercially valuable copyrightable works follow the same pattern as valuable patents; men originate and control most of the commercially valuable ones. Even in disciplines where there are appreciable numbers of women in the pipeline, the "authors" who have the most business-related and critical success are overwhelmingly male, even though the "small pool of women" problem of many STEM fields is absent. In fact, significantly more women than men enter and work in the creative fields for which copyright law is designed and assertively deployed, excepting computer software and spectator sports. Yet a series of factors other than low pipeline numbers cause gender disparities at the top levels of the commercial creative industries, and the primary factor is gender discrimination.

When creative efforts are associated with women, they are devalued. Implicit bias prevents people from judging performers from a gender-neutral baseline. To illustrate: female musicians who audition behind screens so that their gender is unknown are more likely to be rated positively. When all musicians audition behind screens, female musicians succeed at approximately the same rate as male musicians. Even in a competition in which a screen was used only for preliminary auditions, this intervention alone made it 50 percent more likely that a woman would advance to the finals.[54] From these data, one is forced to conclude that to succeed, women should hide their gender while men should flaunt theirs.

In most sectors of the performing arts, auditioning from behind screens is not an option. You can often tell the genders of singers by their voices, and you cannot judge the skills of dancers without seeing their bodies. Actors also usually audition with their genders on display, just like many of the rest of us do when we interview for jobs. Employers and audience members may be so uncomfortable with gender ambiguity that it interferes with the ability of a performer to get and retain a job,[55] putting considerable pressure on creative artists to declare and display their gender.

Authors of textual works have the option of hiding their gender by staying out of sight and using initials instead of first names to label their works. Joanne Rowling intentionally published her Harry Potter series as J. K. Rowling so that her gender would not put off potential readers. When her books became famous, she did as well, and the Harry Potter series stayed popular even after the public realized the author of the popular novels was a woman.[56] Nevertheless, when she secretly published her first murder mystery novel written for adults, it was under the masculine moniker Robert Galbraith,[57] and she continues to use it for the book series.

Visual artists often need to establish compelling public personas if they want to be successful. Although women visual artists can attempt to obfuscate their gender, as

Rowling managed to do temporarily, there is no evidence that doing so has been a sure path to fame or financial rewards. The monetary value of an artwork is linked in complicated ways to the identity, history, reputation and fame of the artist. Disguising one's gender would likely make landing an agent or developing a client base far more difficult or might be perceived as an attention-seeking gimmick and unlikely to boost sales.

When authors' gender is known, women are discriminated against. In her article *Let's Have a Year of Publishing Only Women—A Provocation*, Kamila Shamsie wrote:

> Several years ago, Martin Amis chaired a literary festival panel on "The Crisis of American Fiction" with Richard Ford, Jay McInerney and Junot Díaz. I was in the audience, and halfway through the discussion leaned over to the person sitting next to me and said: "Clearly the crisis of American fiction is that there are no women in it." It's not just that there weren't any women on the stage. In the entire discussion, which lasted nearly an hour, there was no mention of Toni Morrison, Marilynne Robinson, Annie Proulx, Anne Tyler, Donna Tartt, Jhumpa Lahiri or any other contemporary female writer. A single reference to Eudora Welty was the only acknowledgment that women in the US have ever had anything to do with the world of letters. Díaz, near the end of the hour, made the point that the conversation had centred on white American males, but it was too little, too late.[58]

Another observer of gender discrimination in fiction publishing revealed that submitting her manuscript to agents under a male pseudonym brought more than eight times the number of responses. She wrote: "My novel wasn't the problem, it was me, Catherine."[59] As with patents, there is no evidence that the significance of gender in copyrighted works will diminish anytime soon.

C. Trademarks

Trademarks are integrally related to branding activities. Women's bodies are frequently used as trademarks or in conjunction with selling and branding goods and services. Women are objectified in commercial advertising, often depicted in sexualized manners, dressed in revealing clothing and assuming bodily postures and facial expressions that imply sexual readiness.[60] Trademarks themselves can be racially and sexually exploitive as well. Notorious examples of exploitive trademarks include the mark for St. Pauli Girl beer, the Hooters mark and the now retired[61] Land O'Lakes "Indian Princess" and "Aunt Jemima" marks.

Trademarks are words, phrases, pictures, symbols, sounds or other signifiers that are used in connection with specific products or businesses. Trademarks allow companies to indicate the source of their goods or services, and to distinguish them from others in the industry. Trademark owners have the exclusive right to use their marks and can prevent others from using similar marks that could cause confusion among the public. Trademark rights can be established through use of the mark in a commercial or business setting. Registration of trademarks with the U.S. Patent and Trademark Office

(USPTO) is not required, but offers mark holders significant advantages. The registration process is the point at which the federal government gets involved in examining and regulating trademarks directly.

The Lanham Act [aka the Trademark Act] is focused on protecting trademark rights, but it is not intended to incentivize the adoption of multiple trademarks for every good or service on the market.[62] In that sense, trademarks are not actually "intellectual" property. Instead, they are intangible commercial property, used to identify and differentiate goods and services. Trademarks do not add to the store of knowledge or otherwise benefit society in the ways that patentable inventions and copyrightable works do. Trademarks add no value to a good or service other than the information they offer related to consumer perceptions or associations.

For more than fifty years the USPTO relied on language in Section 2(a) of the Lanham Act to prevent people from obtaining federal registrations on trademarks that would be offensive or disparaging to some cohort of the general public.[63] This served a bureaucratic inclination to protect people from objectionable trademarks that bear the imprimatur and protection of the federal government. Two recent U.S. Supreme Court cases, however, have held that content-based denials of trademark registrations are a violation of the free speech rights guaranteed by the First Amendment.

In *Matal v. Tam*,[64] the plaintiff, a musician, successfully contested the denial of a federal trademark registration for "The Slants," the name of a band whose members were all Asian.[65] The USPTO had refused to register "The Slants" based on the view that Slants was a term which was culturally understood to disparage Asian people. In a unanimous opinion, the U.S. Supreme Court ruled that prohibiting racially offensive trademark names that disparage others was unconstitutional, reasoning that "speech may not be banned on the grounds that it expresses ideas that offend."[66] Rejecting the government's argument that federal trademarks were a form of government speech and therefore immune from First Amendment review, the Court concluded that trademarks were private speech that is subject to First Amendment protection.[67] As Lisa Ramsey explained: "In *Tam*, the ... Justices ... unanimously agreed that the disparagement clause violates the First Amendment because it targets derogatory expression with an intent to discourage its use, while allowing registration of words and other marks that are positive or benign."[68]

In the follow up case of *Iancu v. Brunetti*,[69] the plaintiff persuaded the Supreme Court that "FUCT" should also be registrable, even if the public might be offended by this word. The Court struck down another provision of Section 2 of the Lanham Act that prohibited "immoral or scandalous" marks from obtaining federal registration. It held that the "immoral or scandalous" marks provision facilitated impermissible viewpoint discrimination just like the prohibition on disparaging marks, and was therefore also unconstitutional.

In the wake of these decisions it has become clear that there was a lot of pent-up interest in registering offensive and disparaging trademarks. The holdings in *Tam* and *Brunetti* opened the door for a deluge of racist, sexist and otherwise dehumanizing trademark registrations that the justice system will be bound to protect and enforce going forward. This change puts the government in the position of propertizing hate speech so that someone can commercialize it through trademark law. Even word marks such as racial epithets, including the n-word, can now obtain federal registration, making them valuable as trademarks and brands.[70] With help from the First Amendment, Trademark law now protects the commercial value of sexism, racism and other subordinating messages targeting marginalized persons.

III. IP-Adjacent Intangible Property

In addition to the gender disparities that pervade traditional intellectual property (IP) rights, women are also disadvantaged with respect to intangible interests that resemble or are adjacent to intellectual property. This section addresses two such IP-adjacent areas, naming rights and the gendering of robots.

A. Naming Rights and the Physical Public Domain

For many years women who married were required to give up their surnames.[71] As the Superior Court of the State of New York held in an 1881 opinion: "For several centuries, by the common law among all English-speaking people, a woman, upon her marriage, takes her husband's surname. That becomes her legal name, and she ceases to be known by her maiden name . . . her maiden surname is absolutely lost, and she ceases to be known thereby."[72] After marrying, a woman was legally labeled with her husband's identity, almost like a trademark. This rule persisted well into the twentieth century. In 1971, the U.S. Supreme Court affirmed, without opinion, an Alabama requirement that a woman adopt her husband's surname when applying for and receiving a driver's license.[73] Until fairly recently, many state name-change statutes expressly excluded married women. Missouri still permits name changes only where a court "is satisfied that the desired change would be proper and not detrimental to the interests of any other person." Missouri courts have interpreted this statute to require that the interests of a married woman's husband be considered before granting her name-change petition,[74] supporting women who take their husbands' names after marriage, and making it difficult for them to change their minds afterward. Transgender individuals and nonbinary persons also face barriers to securing legal name changes consistent with their identity.[75] Because people's names are their brands in many contexts, forcing or preventing name changes can result in the loss of an important aspect of personhood.

In addition to their personal importance to individuals, names have a public dimension. Publicly accessible portions of the built environment often bear the names of humans. The names become appended to buildings and other public spaces in a variety of ways, for example, because the privilege was purchased directly as a sponsorship, indirectly as the reward for a sizable gift, or resulted from a male-dominated political process. Whatever the mechanism, there is an obvious paucity of women being honored with naming rights. Women's names are grossly underrepresented on buildings, streets, parks, stadiums, law schools, bridges and other structures that facilitate naming rights. At a time when freighted monuments such as memorials to the Confederacy are rightfully being challenged, the lack of memorials to women is being addressed more slowly and less visibly.

Private naming acts are problematically dominated by white male beneficiaries but are largely beyond the reach of the law. They are customarily driven by money, and sometimes undone by scandal, without much transparency. The naming of public assets, however, can and should be interrogated. The Lanham Act conceptualizes the names of goods and services as forms of intangible commercial property and allows these names to be bought, sold and licensed. A trademark's value is related to how recognizable it is, and how many positive associations it carries among consumers.

When public assets are named, however, this phenomenon is completely reversed. Public parks, schools, roads, buildings and related amenities are valuable because they are visible and useful. When names or trademarks are appended to these public assets, the honoree or mark holder personally reaps some measure of the positive social value that the public associates with these resources. Commercial entities generally compensate the public for this usurpation of public goodwill by proffering payment for "naming rights." Private individuals, however, often claim public domain naming privileges for themselves, wielding power and exercising privileges that are available only to a small cohort of the population, and doing so outside the boundaries of democratic processes. Powerful white men in this nation embed their names and marks into the public domain at every opportunity. Women and People of Color have far fewer chances to do so.[76]

B. Artificial Intelligence: Robots, Algorithms, and Gender

Robots run on patented hardware inventions and copyrighted computer code. They use algorithms and data sets, and bear trademarks. When they can walk, robots are walking collections of cutting-edge intellectual property. Robots rely on algorithms, which decide the directions that computerized innovations will take and can negatively impact distinct social groups, including women. That algorithms can be biased has become a topic of great interest to researchers.[77] Algorithms are written by humans, and humans code their biases onto them.

In *Invisible Women: Data Bias in a World Designed for Men*, Caroline Criado Perez explains the impact that gender bias has on product design.[78] She recounts how pianos are designed for people with larger hands, who are disproportionately men. The same is true for many smart phones. Top-of-the-line voice recognition software was found in one study to be 70 percent more likely to accurately recognize male speech than female speech. Gender bias in smart phones and voice recognition software is due to gender bias in algorithms, reflecting the overrepresentation of men in most data sets, while women are both underrepresented and misrepresented.

Although the word "robot" is sometimes understood as limited to machines that possess anthropomorphic characteristics, "robots" can refer broadly to mechanical devices that perform a variety of tasks on command or according to instructions programmed in advance, or even through computer programs.[79] There is a specific subset of robots, however, which are made to look or sound like living beings, such as humans or dogs. They are designed that way because it is reassuring to have machines that perform human or pet-like tasks look and sound at least somewhat like the living creatures they supplant. But rarely is it functionally necessary that robots appear in corpus to be female or male.

Nevertheless robots are often highly gendered. In part, this is because research has shown that robots with human characteristics are more reassuring. Even if humanoid robots do not need gender as a functional matter, as explained earlier, androgyny makes people very uncomfortable. Gender policing, by which people are pressured to conform to the norms of their perceived sex, is a common phenomenon.[80] Sometimes it leads to violence.[81] At other times it is simply confusing, such as an incident in which this author was roundly chastised by otherwise seemingly rational people for walking a male dog in a pink harness. Obviously, the dog did not care, but the humans involved seemed to feel this was deceptive and offensive.

Like humans, robots are subject to gender policing, by which gender norms are enforced with respect to attributes such as appearance, name, design, function and potentially even clothing. If the robot is represented as "male," then many consumers do not want it called Susie or to see it in a dress. A study of people's reactions to avatars online has purportedly shown that androgynous avatars are trusted less than ones that are clearly either male or female.[82] Given the extreme anxiety that androgyny provokes among observers, it is not surprising that robots have become gendered. Even robots that lack body facsimiles usually have an intentional gender, and even when they do not, one is likely to be informally assigned to them. Sometimes a gender may be assumed because the robot is pink and rounded, versus blue and angular. At other times, a robot may have a gender-neutral design but be perceived to have a gender based on the cultural associations embedded in the tasks it performs. In still other instances, an assignment of gender may seem unrelated to the jobs a robot performs but nonetheless affects the way the robot is perceived.[83]

Humanoid robots can reinforce sexist stereotypes. Robots that perform domestic chores are usually assigned a female gender, while robots used in combat are generally depicted as male. Even when a robot is designed to look like an animal rather than a human, it is likely to be assigned a gender.[84] The gendering of robots both reflects gender-based assumptions and stereotypes and further instantiates them.[85]

Depictions of gendered robots are common in mainstream entertainment products. Consider the Transformers. It wasn't until Windblade, who was unambiguously coded female, joined the Transformers lineup that some fans realized that almost all the other Transformers were male.[86] Even though "[t]hey don't have sex (copious fanfic notwithstanding), they don't need sexes. They are forged or constructed cold, whole. There are no baby Transformers."[87]

The movie *Wall-E* is a love story between two robots, one depicted as male and the other as female. Perhaps Disney feared that a romance between two ungendered robots would be interpreted by the audience as a same-sex romance and was not prepared to ride out any negative reactions to that interpretation. In fairness, as a commentator observed:

> [E]ven though the physical elements of "Eve" and "Wall-E" were drawn to clearly indicate specific genders (Eve being more smooth, curved, and having a higher-pitched computerized voice), many of their personality characteristics reversed conventional gender expectations. Wall-E was the naive one, the hopeless romantic, and the one who was portrayed as having something "missing" in his life without love. Prior to meeting Wall-E, Eve seemed to be doing just fine independently. As the story progresses, Wall-E is the one who most often needs saving, and Eve is frequently the one to rescue him.[88]

Nevertheless, Disney is a company with a long history of aggressively gendering its characters and the related tie-in products it markets, including objects like teapots, clocks and candlesticks.[89] Even when it allows female characters to be tough or male characters to be sensitive, all of them have relentlessly obvious genders,[90] reflecting the hold that gender and the baggage it carries has on society. As one observer noted, "It would be good to imagine a future in which gender stereotyping no longer limited the aspirations of either men or women. But it seems even when we are able to hand over some of the arduous chores to robots, there will still be a clear distinction between the roles appropriate for a 'male' robot and those that should be carried out by a 'female' robot."[91]

Biologically inspired robots are designed to be lifelike so that humans can better understand and relate to them.[92] Even then, reactions may be highly correlated with the gender of the human interacting with the robot and their status in an organization. One study conducted at a hospital, for example, considered the importance of gender segregation in jobs in determining how employees related to robots and found:

> [S]ex segregation structures may have had an impact on how men and women, segregated into distinct jobs at the hospital, made sense of a new technology—a mobile autonomous robot. Male and female workers seemed to engage in sense-making around the robot according to their positions in the hospital: engineers and male administrators generally saw it as a machine that they could control; female administrators and low-level female staff workers anthropomorphized it as a human male that acted with agency, and nurses, predominantly female, saw it as a technology with no work utility and perhaps as further evidence of the low value placed on their jobs and work needs.[93]

A robot with autonomy over its own gender selection would have a lot of different variables to balance. If the robot's prime directive were to maximize its benefits to the humans it interacted with, and the expectations of these humans varied across context, androgyny might seem like an attractive option, but only if the antagonism toward androgyny could be overcome by making the robot appear very machinelike. That, however, would take away the human reassuring benefits of a humanoid appearance. The prospect of a robot routinely changing its external gender characteristics so that it could perform the appropriate gender for the particular audience it happened to be servicing would further instantiate gender norms and stereotypes. But gender switching might be the best choice that a smart and productive autonomous robot could make to maximize its value to humans.

Male robots are perceived as smarter, while female robots are perceived as more caring. When an IBM robot famously beat human contestants on the game show Jeopardy! in 2011,[94] it had a male name, Watson, and a male voice. Male robots are employed as soldiers, and associated with war machines, drones, weapons and automobiles. Female robots are deployed for caretaking, assisting in the kitchen, helping with cooking and cleaning the house. Female robots are not associated with safety or security, and most people probably do not assume that their Roomba would back them up in a fight with an intruder. Instead, female robots provide the voices of Apple voice assistant Siri, Amazon smart speaker assistant Alexa and many other electronic devices. Rather than showcasing women as spokespeople for useful technology, however, the default to women's voices is due to the strong association of females with secretarial and assistant job positions. Female voices for smart speakers relay the message that women are wonderful assistants, always there to help, but never to lead.

Finally, female robots are also designed to be mechanical sex partners. Sex robots are designed strictly for human pleasure and are completely controllable. They can perform in ways that human bodies cannot, and there are no consent issues. These robots can even fake "autonomy" if that is what the human who is programming it wishes. Sex robots currently on the market have settings from "wild" to "frigid." A sex robot with a frigid setting sounds counterintuitive, but it is very popular for rape role playing.

How engaging physically with sex robots affects people is unknown. It is possible that they create safe and useful outlets for legally or culturally deviant sex acts. It is conceivable that if pedophiles could be satisfied restricting their sex partners to childlike robots, that might be a benefit to society. However, it is more likely that sex robots lead to unrealistic performance expectations from human sex partners, and to changes in consent norms. There may be overarching positive outcomes arising from people having sex with robots, but experiences with pornography make it hard to be optimistic.

IV. Conclusion

This chapter highlights select gender disparities in the intellectual property law areas of patents, copyrights and trademarks that negatively affect women's economic and social status. It also examines the ways in which women are disadvantaged by practices and technological developments related to naming rights and gendered practices in robotics.

Accurately mapping these disparities can be thwarted by bad data sets that amplify bias, suggesting that we need better, more inclusive data as well as feminist insights. Both intellectual property laws and social policies related to innovation and creativity need to be reshaped to improve women's participation in creative and inventive pursuits, so that women can obtain a fair share of the wealth generated by intellectual property-based assets and enterprises.

Notes

1. Laura Mulvey, *Visual Pleasure and Narrative Cinema*, in FILM MANIFESTOS AND GLOBAL CINEMA CULTURES: A CRITICAL ANTHOLOGY 359–70 (Scott MacKenzie ed., 2014). This is an indirect reference to Laura Mulvey's theory of the male gaze. Filmmaker and theorist Laura Mulvey first coined the term "the male gaze" in her germinal 1973 paper, Visual Pleasure and Narrative Cinema.
2. Cheryl I. Harris, *Whiteness as Property*, 106 HARV. L. REV. 1707 (1993).
3. Nancy Leong, *Racial Capitalism*, 126 HARV. L. REV. 2153, 2153 (2013).
4. *Id.* at 2179.
5. *Id.*
6. *See* ANDREA DWORKIN & CATHARINE MACKINNON, PORNOGRAPHY AND CIVIL RIGHTS: A NEW DAY FOR WOMEN'S EQUALITY 12 (1988).
7. *See* Lea VanderVelde & Sandhya Subramanian, *Mrs. Dred Scott*, 106 YALE L.J. 1033 (1997). This did not stop slaveholders from encouraging social marriage when it opportunistically suited them to promote enslaved women's fertility and the stability of enslaved populations. *Id.* at 1041.
8. Sir WILLIAM BLACKSTONE, COMMENTARIES ON THE LAWS OF ENGLAND IN FOUR BOOKS, VOL. 1, 421 (2009) (e-book).
9. Katie McLaughlin, *5 Things Women Couldn't Do in the 1960s*, CNN (Aug. 25, 2014), https://www.cnn.com/2014/08/07/living/sixties-women-5-things/index.html; Trista, *40 Basic Rights Women Did Not Have Until the 1970s*, HISTORY COLLECTION (June 26, 2019), https://historycollection.com/40-basic-rights-women-did-not-have-until-the-1970s/34/.
10. Women's Business Ownership Act of 1988, Pub. L. No. 100-533, 102 Stat 2689 (1988) (codified at 15 U.S.C. § 631).
11. *See* Ronan Farrow, *From Aggressive Overtures to Sexual Assault: Harvey Weinstein's Accusers Tell Their Stories*, THE NEW YORKER (Oct. 10, 2017), https://www.newyorker.com/news/news-desk/from-aggressive-overtures-to-sexual-assault-harvey-weinsteins-accusers-tell-their-stories.
12. *See, e.g.*, Lucy Campbell & Agency, *Ballet Dancer Used His Fame to Abuse Students, London Court Told*, THE GUARDIAN (Apr. 26, 2021), https://www.theguardian.com/uk-news/2021/apr/26/ballet-dancer-used-his-fame-to-abuse-students-london-court-told.
13. Daniel Sanchez, *A List of Every Musician and Music Executive Facing Abuse Allegations in 2018*, DIGITAL MUSIC NEWS (Dec. 26, 2018), https://www.digitalmusicnews.com/2018/12/26/musicians-music-executives-abuse-allegations/.
14. *See, e.g.*, Kevin Draper, *Accusations of Abuse Shake U.S. Women's Soccer League*, N.Y. TIMES (Sept, 30, 2021), https://www.nytimes.com/2021/09/30/sports/soccer/nwsl-abuse-paul-riley.html; Juliet Macur, *Former Athletes File Sex Abuse Lawsuits Against U.S.A. Swimming*, N.Y. TIMES (June 10, 2020), https://www.nytimes.com/2020/06/10/sports/olympics/swimming-abuse-coaches-lawsuit.html.

15. Robin Lloyd, *Rosalind Franklin and DNA: How Wronged Was She?*, SCIENTIFIC AMERICAN (Nov. 3, 2010), blogs.scientificamerican.com/observations/rosalind-franklin-and-dna-how-wronged-was-she/. *But see* Matthew Cobb, *Sexism in Science: Did Watson and Crick Really Steal Rosalind Franklin's Data*, THE GUARDIAN (June 23, 2015), https://www.theguardian.com/science/2015/jun/23/sexism-in-science-did-watson-and-crick-really-steal-rosalind-franklins-data.

16. Lara Rutherford-Morrison, *9 Times Men Were Given Credit for Women's Work*, BUSTLE (Mar. 1, 2017), https://www.bustle.com/p/9-times-men-were-given-credit-for-womens-historic-accomplishments-41120; *see also* Jon Ronson, *The Big-Eyed Children: The Extraordinary Story of an Epic Art Fraud*, THE GUARDIAN (Oct. 26, 2014), https://www.theguardian.com/artanddesign/2014/oct/26/art-fraud-margaret-walter-keane-tim-burton-biopic.

17. Claudia Hammond, *The "Pink vs Blue" Gender Myth*, BBC FUTURE (Nov. 17, 2014), https://www.bbc.com/future/article/20141117-the-pink-vs-blue-gender-myth; Caroline Smith & Barbara Lloyd, *Maternal Behavior and Perceived Sex of Infant: Revisited*, 49 CHILD DEV. 1263, 1264–65 (1978). *See generally* Carol Lynn Martin & Diane N. Ruble, *Patterns of Gender Development*, 61 ANN. REV. PSYCH. 353 (2010); Leslie A. Zebrowitz & Joann M. Montepare, *Social Psychological Face Perception: Why Appearance Matters*, 2 SOC. PERSONALITY PSYCH. COMPASS 1497 (2008).

18. JO B. PAOLETTI, PINK AND BLUE: TELLING THE BOYS FROM THE GIRLS IN AMERICA (2012).

19. Debra Kelly, *The Real Reason Behind Blue for Boys and Pink for Girls*, THE LIST (Jan. 5, 2017), https://www.thelist.com/32342/real-reasons-behind-blue-boys-pink-girls/.

20. *Id.*; Shelley Zalis, *Busting Gender Stereotypes: The Pink Versus Blue Phenomenon*, FORBES (Sept. 5, 2019), https://www.forbes.com/sites/shelleyzalis/2019/09/05/busting-gender-stereotypes-the-pink-versus-blue-phenomenon/?sh=7426aa5c2764.

21. John Staughton, *What Is the Difference Between Sex and Gender?*, SCIENCE ABC: EYE OPENERS (Jan. 14, 2021), https://www.scienceabc.com/eyeopeners/what-is-the-difference-between-sex-and-gender.html.

22. *Id.* (citing Beth Potier, *These Shoes Were Made for Walking?: Peabody Museum Has High-Stepping New Exhibit*, HARV. GAZETTE (Feb. 6, 2003), https://news.harvard.edu/gazette/story/2003/02/these-shoes-were-made-for-walking/).

23. *See* Jeanne Maglaty, *When Did Girls Start Wearing Pink?*, SMITHSONIAN MAG. (Apr. 7, 2011), https://www.smithsonianmag.com/arts-culture/when-did-girls-start-wearing-pink-1370097/; Puja Bhattacharjee, *The Complicated Gender History of Pink*, CNN HEALTH (Jan. 12, 2018), https://www.cnn.com/2018/01/12/health/colorscope-pink-boy-girl-gender/index.html.

24. *See, e.g.*, Casey Johnston, *Does This Smartphone Make Me Look Stupid? Meet the "Ladyphones,"* ARSTECHNICA (Mar. 12, 2012), https://arstechnica.com/gadgets/2012/03/does-this-smartphone-make-me-look-stupid-meet-the-ladyphones/.

25. Barbara Ehrenreich, *Welcome to Cancerland: A Mammogram Leads to a Cult of Pink Kitsch*, HARPER'S MAG. (Nov. 2001), https://archive.harpers.org/2001/11/pdf/HarpersMagazine-2001-11-0075358.pdf?AWSAccessKeyId=AKIAJUM7PFZHQ4PMJ4LA&Expires=1568333045&Signature=HWjBLPajQSIfCgZFDl1dhshivZc%3D.

26. *See, e.g.*, Erin Buzuvis, *Reading the Pink Locker Room: On Football Culture and Title IX*, 14 WM. & MARY J. WOMEN & L. 1 (2007) (analyzing the University of Iowa history of painting the visiting locker room pink to insult the masculinity and shame opposing football teams).

27. *See, e.g.*, *MLB Whiffs by Banning Competitors' Pink Bats on Mother's Day*, YAHOO SPORTS (May 10, 2013), https://sports.yahoo.com/news/mlb-whiffs-by-banning-competitors--pink-bats-on-mother-s-day-013725273.html; *NFL Kicks Off Breast Cancer Awareness*

Month in October, NFL (Oct. 2, 2011), https://www.nfl.com/news/nfl-kicks-off-breast-cancer-awareness-month-in-october-09000d5d822caee6; *cf. Cavs Host "Breast Cancer Awareness Night*, NBA (Oct. 20, 2017), https://www.nba.com/cavaliers/releases/breast-cancer-awareness-171021.

28. U.S. DEP'T OF LAB., *Gender Earnings Ratios by Week and Annual Earnings*, https://www.dol.gov/agencies/wb/data/earnings/gender-ratio-weekly-annual.
29. PAUL GOLDSMITH-PINKHAM & KELLY SUE, THE GENDER GAP IN HOUSING RETURNS (Nat'l Bureau of Econ. Res. Working Paper No. 26914, 2020).
30. *See generally* Ann Bartow, *Patent Law, Copyright Law, and the Girl Germs Effect*, 90 ST. JOHN'S L. REV. 579 (2016); *see also* U.S. PATENT AND TRADEMARK OFFICE, OFFICE OF THE CHIEF ECONOMIST, PROGRESS AND POTENTIAL: 2020 UPDATE ON U.S. WOMEN INVENTOR-PATENTEES (July. 2020), https://www.uspto.gov/sites/default/files/documents/OCE-DH-Progress-Potential-2020.pdf; Dan L. Burk, BRIDGING THE GENDER GAP IN INTELLECTUAL PROPERTY, WIPO MAG. (Apr. 2018), https://www.wipo.int/wipo_magazine/en/2018/02/article_0001.html.
31. *See* Debora Halbert, *Feminist Interpretations of Intellectual Property*, 14 AM. U. J. GENDER SOC. POL'Y & L. 431 (2006).
32. Susan Spann, *Are Recipes Copyrightable?*, (Nov. 7, 2014), http://www.susanspann.com/ask-publaw-are-recipes-copyrightable/.
33. *Can You Copyright Clothing Designs?*, NEW MEDIA RIGHTS (Oct. 27, 2020), https://www.newmediarights.org/business_models/artist/can_you_copyright_clothing_designs.
34. PROTECTION FOR FASHION DESIGN: STATEMENT BEFORE THE SUBCOMM. ON CTS., THE INTERNET, AND INTELLECTUAL PROPERTY OF THE H. COMM. ON THE JUDICIARY, 109th Cong. (2006) (statement of the U.S. Copyright Office).
35. Star Athletica, L.L.C. v. Varsity Brands, Inc., 137 S. Ct. 1002 (2017).
36. *See* Bartow, *Patent Law, supra* note 30, at 583–88; Burk, *supra* note 30.
37. Ann Bartow, *Separating Innovation from Actual Invention: A Proposal for a New, Improved, Lighter, and Better-Tasting Form of Patent Protection*, 4 J. SMALL & EMERGING BUS. L. 1 (2004).
38. Jay Bennett, *15 Patents That Changed the World*, POPULAR MECHANICS (Apr. 27, 2018), https://www.popularmechanics.com/technology/design/g20051677/patents-changed-the-world/; Alana Horowitz, *The Fascinating Stories Behind 5 Inventions You Use All The Time*, READER'S DIGEST (June 10, 2021), https://www.rd.com/article/invention-stories/.
39. PROGRESS AND POTENTIAL: 2020 UPDATE ON U.S. WOMEN INVENTOR-PATENTEES, USPTO (2020), https://www.uspto.gov/ip-policy/economic-research/publications/reports/progress-potential; Erin Meyer & Na Hye Kim, *Patent Diversity Project: Addressing Racial and Gender Disparities in the U.S. Patent System*, PROSKAUER FOR GOOD (Mar. 22, 2021), https://www.proskauerforgood.com/2021/03/patent-diversity-project-addressing-racial-and-gender-disparities-in-the-u-s-patent-system/.
40. *See generally* Jennifer Hunt, Jean-Philippe Garant, Hannah Herman & David J. Munroe, *Why Don't Women Patent?* (IZA Discussion Paper No. 6886, 2012), https://www.research.uky.edu/uploads/why-dont-women-patent.
41. Nicole D. Galli & Jessica Stauring, *Closing the Patenting Gender Gap Requires More Women Patent Attorneys*, LAW.COM (Feb. 17, 2021), https://www.law.com/thelegalintelligencer/2021/02/17/closing-the-patenting-gender-gap-requires-more-women-patent-attorneys/?slreturn=20210119130528; Jyoti Madhusoodanan, *Why Do Women Inventors Win Fewer Patents?*, YALE INSIGHTS (Apr. 9, 2018), https://insights.som.yale.edu/insig

hts/why-do-women-inventors-win-fewer-patents; Kyle Jensen, Balázs Kovács & Olav Sorenson, *Gender Differences in Obtaining and Maintaining Patent Rights*, 36 NATURE BIOTECH. 307 (2018); Dennis Crouch, *Women as Patentees*, PATENTLYO (Dec. 21, 2006), https://patentlyo.com/patent/2006/12/women_as_patent.html. *But see* Kevin Fryling-Indiana, *Women at Universities File Patents at Higher Rate*, FUTURITY (July 10, 2015), https://www.futurity.org/patents-women-957642/.

42. *See, e.g.*, Jens Peter Andersen et al., *COVID-19 Medical Papers Have Fewer Women First Authors Than Expected*, 9 ELIFE (June 15, 2020), https://www.ncbi.nlm.nih.gov/pmc/articles/PMC7304994/.

43. *See, e.g.*, Alexander M. Bell et al., *Who Becomes an Inventor in America? The Importance of Exposure to Innovation* (Nat'l Bureau of Econ. Res. Working Paper No. 24062, revised 2019) (discussing the underrepresentation of women as inventors and contributing factors). *See generally* Rosa Monteiro, *Gender in the Portugal Research Arena: A Case Study in European Leadership*, ELSEVIER (June 7, 2021), https://www.elsevier.com/connect/gender-report.

44. *See* Galli & Stauring, *supra* note 41; Jensen et al., *supra* note 41.

45. *See* Kathryn Rubino, *Is There Gender Bias in Patent Litigation?*, ABOVE THE LAW (Jan. 25, 2018), https://abovethelaw.com/2018/01/is-there-gender-bias-in-patent-litigation/; Danielle Root, *Women Judges in the Federal Judiciary*, CENTER FOR AM. PROGRESS (Oct. 17, 2019), https://cdn.americanprogress.org/content/uploads/2019/10/16123531/JudicialDiversityFactsheet-women.pdf.

46. Clara Guibourg & Nassos Stylianou, *Why Are So Few Women Inventors Named on Patents?*, BBC NEWS (Oct. 2, 2019), https://www.bbc.com/news/technology-49843990.

47. *Id.*

48. Fryling-Indiana, *supra* note 41.

49. Madhusoodanan, *supra* note 41. *See generally* Guibourg & Stylianou, *supra* note 46.

50. Madhusoodanan, *supra* note 41.

51. *Id.*

52. *See* Guibourg & Stylianou, *supra* note 46.

53. 17 U.S.C. § 102.

54. Bartow, *Patent Law*, *supra* note 30, at 595.

55. *See generally* Lauren Windle, *These Parents Refuse to Tell People If Their "Theyby" Two-Year-Old Is a Boy or a Girl*, THE SUN (Apr. 15, 2018), https://www.thesun.co.uk/fabulous/6052816/parents-refuse-tell-people-theyby-boy-or-girl/.

56. Rowling's recent political statements about transgender people are soundly rejected by this author and have quite appropriately had a negative impact on the market for Harry Potter goods and services. *See* Antonio Miguel Aguila, *The Author Who Angered the Nation: How J.K. Rowling's Trans-phobic Opinions Ended Her Universal Popularity*, REDBRICK (Jan. 31, 2021), https://www.redbrick.me/the-author-who-angered-the-nation-how-j-k-rowlings-trans-phobic-opinions-ended-her-universal-popularity/; *see also* Adam B. Vary, *J.K. Rowling Defends Speaking Out on Trans Issues*, VARIETY (June 10, 2020), https://variety.com/2020/biz/news/j-k-rowling-trans-issues-sexual-assault-survivor-1234630367/; Abby Gardner, *A Complete Breakdown of the J.K. Rowling Transgender-Comments Controversy*, GLAMOUR (July 20, 2021), https://www.glamour.com/story/a-complete-breakdown-of-the-jk-rowling-transgender-comments-controversy.

57. *J.K. Rowling Suspected BBC of Revealing Robert Galbraith Pseudonym*, BBC NEWS (Oct. 6, 2018), https://www.bbc.com/news/entertainment-arts-45763539.

58. Kamila Shamsie, *Kamila Shamsie: Let's Have a Year of Publishing Only Women—A Provocation*, THE GUARDIAN (June 5, 2015), https://www.theguardian.com/books/2015/jun/05/kamila-shamsie-2018-year-publishing-women-no-new-books-men.
59. Alison Flood, *Sexism in Publishing: "My Novel Wasn't the Problem, It Was Me, Catherine,"* THE GUARDIAN (Aug. 6, 2015), https://www.theguardian.com/books/2015/aug/06/catherine-nichols-female-author-male-pseudonym; Catherine Nichols, *Homme de Plume: What I Learned Sending My Novel Out Under a Male Name*, JEZEBEL (Aug. 4, 2015), https://jezebel.com/homme-de-plume-what-i-learned-sending-my-novel-out-und-1720637627.
60. *See generally* Ozlem Sandikci, *Images of Women in Advertising: A Critical-Cultural Perspective*, 3 EUROPEAN ADVANCES IN CONSUMER RES. 76 (1998).
61. Kayla Ruble, *Land O'Lakes Drops Controversial Native American Logo From Butter Products*, TODAY (Apr. 17, 2020), https://www.today.com/food/land-o-lakes-drops-controversial-native-american-logo-butter-products-t179154.
62. Trademark Act of 1946, Pub. L. No. 79-489, 60 Stat. 427, as amended through 2020 (codified at 15 U.S.C. §§ 1051 et seq.).
63. Section 2 of the Lanham Act states that a mark will be ineligible for federal registration if it "consists of or comprises immoral, deceptive, or scandalous matter; or matter which may disparage or falsely suggest a connection with persons, living or dead, institutions, beliefs, or national symbols, or bring them into contempt, or disrepute." 15 U.S.C. § 1052(a). It is this statutory provision that grounds the conflict with the First Amendment's guarantee of freedom of speech.
64. 137 S. Ct. 1744 (2017).
65. *Id.* at 1747.
66. *Id.* at 1751.
67. *Id.* at 1748.
68. Lisa P. Ramsey, *The First Amendment Protects Offensive Trademarks*, THE REGULATORY REV. (July 25, 2017), https://www.theregreview.org/2017/07/25/ramsey-first-amendment-protects-offensive-trademarks/.
69. 139 S. Ct. 2294 (2019).
70. *See generally* Ned Snow, *Immoral Trademarks After* Brunetti, 58 HOUS. L. REV. 401 (2020).
71. For this observation and many related ones, I thank Kevin C. Paul, *Private/Property: A Discourse on Gender Inequality in American Law*, 7 MINN. J. LAW & INEQUAL. 399 (1989).
72. Chapman v. Phoenix Nat'l Bank of N.Y., 85 N.Y. 437, 449 (1881).
73. Forbush v. Wallace, 341 F. Supp. 217 (M.D. Ala. 1971), *aff'd*, 405 U.S. 970 (1971).
74. Mo. Rev. Stat. Ann. § 527.270 (West); In re Natale, 527 S.W.2d 402 (Mo. Ct. App. 1975).
75. *See* Dean Spade, *Documenting Gender*, 59 HASTINGS L.J. 731 (2008).
76. For an expanded take on these issues, *see* Ann Bartow, *Trademarks of Privilege: Naming Rights and the Physical Public Domain*, 40 U.C. DAVIS L. REV. 919 (2007).
77. Pauline T. Kim, *Data-Driven Discrimination at Work*, 58 WM. & MARY L. REV. 857 (2017); Ifeoma Ajunwa, *Age Discrimination by Platforms*, 40 BERKELEY J. EMP. & LAB. L. 1 (2019); Ignacio N. Cofone, *Algorithmic Discrimination is an Information Problem*, 70 HASTINGS L.J. 1389 (2019); Pauline T. Kim & Sharion Scott, *Discrimination in Online Employment Recruiting*, 63 ST. LOUIS U. L.J. 93 (2018); Ifeoma Ajunwa, *The Paradox of Automation as Anti-Bias Intervention*, 41 CARDOZO L. REV. 1671 (2020).
78. CAROLINE CRIADO PEREZ, INVISIBLE WOMEN: DATA BIAS IN A WORLD DESIGNATED FOR MEN 157–58 (2019).

79. *See generally* M. Ryan Calo, *Robots and Privacy*, in ROBOT ETHICS: THE ETHICAL AND SOCIAL IMPLICATIONS OF ROBOTICS (Patrick Lin, George Bekey & Keith Abney eds., 2011); M. Ryan Calo, *Open Robotics*, 70 MD. L. REV. 571 (2011).
80. *See, e.g.*, PAOLETTI, *supra* note 18.
81. *See* Ivette Feliciano, *When Enforcing Gender Norms Turns Violent*, PBS NEWS HOUR (May 31, 2015), https://www.pbs.org/newshour/nation/enforcing-gender-destroys-individual-identity-todays-youth.
82. Kristine L. Nowak & Christian Rauh, *The Influence of the Avatar on Online Perceptions of Anthromorphism, Androgyny, Credibility, Homophily, and Attraction*, 11 J. COMPUTER-MEDIATED COMMC'N 153, 173 (2006).
83. *See generally* Jenay M. Beer, Akanksha Prakash, Tracy L. Mitzner & Wendy A. Rogers, *Understanding Robot Acceptance* (Georgia Inst. of Tech. School of Psych., Human Factors and Aging Lab. Technical Report HFA-TR-1103, 2011).
84. *See* Roger Andre Soraa, *Mechanical Genders: How do Humans Gender Robots?*, 21 GENDER TECH. & DEV. 99 (2017), https://www.tandfonline.com/doi/full/10.1080/09718524.2017.1385320?scroll=top&needAccess=true.
85. *See, e.g.*, Friederike Eyssel & Frank Hegel, *(S)he's Got the Look: Gender Stereotyping of Robots*, 42 J. APPLIED SOC. PSYCH. 2213 (2012); Mikey Siegel, Cynthia Breazeal & Michael I. Norton, *Persuasive Robotics: The Influence of Robot Gender on Human Behavior*, IEEE/RSJ INT'L CONF. ON INTELLIGENT ROBOTS & SYSTEMS (2009); Jennifer Robertson, *Gendering Humanoid Robots: Robo-Sexism in Japan*, 16 BODY & SOC'Y 1 (2010).
86. Jaydot Sloane, *Meet Windblade, A Female Character Joining the Transformers Comic Canon*, THE MARY SUE (Jan. 20, 2014), http://www.themarysue.com/idw-windblade-comic/; Patrick Stinson, *Otheredbots: Windblade and the Issue of Gender Representation in The Transformers*, DEADSHIRT.NET (July 29, 2014), http://deadshirt.net/2014/07/29/otheredbots-windblade-issue-gender-representation-transformers/.
87. *I have 9 Grandparents: Transformers and Trinal Gender*, TUMBLR (May 26, 2012), http://obfuscobble.tumblr.com/post/23813075922.
88. Purtek, *The Gender-fication of Robots*, THE HATHOR LEGACY (July 11, 2008), https://web.archive.org/web/20080924141832/http://thehathorlegacy.com/wall-e-the-gender-fication-of-robots/.
89. FROM MOUSE TO MERMAID: THE POLITICS OF FILM, GENDER, AND CULTURE (Elizabeth Bell, Lynda Haas & Laura Sells eds., 1995).
90. *See* Gwendolyn Limbach, *"You the Man, Well Sorta": Gender Binaries and Liminality in Mulan*, in DIVERSITY IN DISNEY FILMS: CRITICAL ESSAYS ON RACE, ETHNICITY, GENDER, SEXUALITY AND DISABILITY 115–28 (Johnson Cheu ed., 2013); *Looking at Gender and Phallocentric Identity in Disney Films Blog*, WORD PRESS (Apr. 2, 2010), https://melimeloboivin.wordpress.com/.
91. Eyssel & Hegel, *supra* note 85.
92. Terrence Fong, Illah Nourbakhsh & Kerstin Dautenhahn, *A Survey of Socially Interactive Robots*, 42 ROBOTICS & AUTONOMOUS SYS. 143 (2003).
93. Rosanne M. Siino & Pamela Hinds, *Robots, Gender & Sensemaking: Sex Segregation's Impact on Workers Making Sense of a Mobile Autonomous Robot*, in PROCEEDINGS OF THE 2005 IEEE INTERNATIONAL CONFERENCE ON ROBOTICS AND AUTOMATION 2773–78 (2005).
94. IBM'S WATSON SUPERCOMPUTER CROWNED JEOPARDY KING, BBC NEWS (Feb. 17, 2011), https://www.bbc.com/news/technology-12491688.

CHAPTER 35

A TAXING FEMINISM

ANTHONY C. INFANTI AND BRIDGET J. CRAWFORD

TAXATION has always been a feminist issue. In 1848, women's rights advocates gathered at Seneca Falls, New York, and issued a Declaration of Sentiments against the laws and ideologies that contributed to women's subordinate status.[1] "We hold these truths to be self-evident: that all men and women are created equal," the Declaration began.[2] It then denounced laws that prohibited women from voting, owning property, or being treated as separate legal persons from their husbands. To add further injury, the drafters wrote, "After depriving her of all rights as a married woman, if single, and the owner of property, he has taxed her to support a government which recognizes her only when her property can be made profitable to it."[3] With this rhetoric, the early women's rights advocates borrowed from the colonial slogan "No taxation without representation" in an effort to highlight the injustices that women faced.[4]

In the years after the gathering at Seneca Falls, many prominent woman suffragists refused to pay their taxes in order to protest the ongoing denial of the franchise to women.[5] Some protestors forfeited property or went to jail for their failure to pay; they believed that tax laws were the powerful, tangible symbol of women's political, social, and economic status in an unfair society.[6]

I. ATTACKING FACIALLY DISCRIMINATORY LAWS

From the nineteenth century to the present, tax cases have had a special ability to illuminate injustice; they have a way of reducing inequality to dollars and cents. Consider, for example, that almost fifty years after women won the right to vote, the tax law again became a focal point of advocates for women's rights. In 1968, an unmarried Colorado man named Charles Moritz took a $600 deduction on his federal income tax return for expenses paid in connection with the care of his elderly mother who lived with him.[7] At the time, § 214 of the Internal Revenue Code permitted taxpayers who were gainfully employed to deduct expenses associated with the care of certain dependents, but the deduction was available only to "a taxpayer who is a woman or widower, or is a husband whose wife is incapacitated or is institutionalized, for the care of one or more dependents."[8] The U.S. Tax Court upheld the Internal Revenue Service's denial of the deduction to Moritz on the ground that "deductions are solely matters of legislative grace" and the statute, by its terms, afforded relief only to single persons who were widowers or women, but not single, never-married men like him.[9] Thus, the Tax Court ruled that Moritz owed an additional $296.70 in tax that he would not have had to pay had he been female.[10]

Luckily for Moritz, tax attorney Martin Ginsburg happened to be reading the Tax Court's advance sheets and persuaded his wife—also an attorney, but not typically a fan of tax cases—to read the decision.[11] Five minutes later, Ruth Bader Ginsburg and Martin Ginsburg had decided to represent Moritz on a pro bono basis and appeal his case to the U.S. Court of Appeals for the Tenth Circuit.[12] At least in part because of the impressive brief, which Martin Ginsburg later said was "90% Ruth's,"[13] the Tenth Circuit reversed the Tax Court, finding that disallowing Moritz's claimed deduction based on his sex was "an invidious discrimination and invalid under due process principles."[14]

The Ginsburgs' work on *Moritz* led to Ruth Bader Ginsburg's work writing the brief in *Reed v. Reed*, the first successful sex discrimination challenge decided by the U.S. Supreme Court on equal protection grounds.[15] (*Reed* was briefed after, but actually argued and decided before *Moritz*, which languished for more than a year in the Tenth Circuit after argument.)[16] In fact, the Tenth Circuit in *Moritz* relied on the decision in *Reed* when deciding in Moritz's favor.[17] The Supreme Court's decision in *Reed* was the first to articulate a heightened level of scrutiny (however unspecified) for sex-based classifications in the law.[18] In her capacity as director of the ACLU Women's Rights Project, Ruth Bader Ginsburg went on to represent plaintiffs in six sex discrimination cases before the Supreme Court.[19] Both *Moritz* and *Reed* are representative of Ginsburg's liberal feminist approach, which propelled these early cases: Challenge laws that treat women and men differently by exposing the way the law relies on gender stereotypes. *Moritz*, *Reed*, and other cases ultimately led to the establishment of an intermediate scrutiny standard for cases involving discrimination on the basis of sex.[20] The road to greater gender equality thus was paved with a tax case. In 1993, Ruth Bader Ginsburg was appointed as an Associate Justice of the Supreme Court.[21]

II. Examining Disparate Impact of Tax Laws

At the same time the *Moritz* case was working its way through the appeals process, Grace Blumberg, then a recent law school graduate, published a law review article critiquing the Internal Revenue Code's bias against working women.[22] In the context of a comparative study of the income taxation of working wives and mothers, Blumberg showed how the joint federal income tax return created a disincentive from working for a wife—who, as a matter of "contemporary social reality," was considered the secondary earner in a marriage—by effectively "stacking" the wife's income on top of her husband's and thus taxing her income beginning with her husband's marginal (i.e., highest) rate of tax.[23] Blumberg also drew attention to how the joint return, by aggregating a married couple's income and effectively splitting it between them for tax purposes, rewarded one-earner couples with a lighter tax burden and increasingly penalized two-earner couples (with the maximum tax penalty being visited on couples in which the husband and wife had equal earnings).[24] She further critiqued the lack of adequate deductions for childcare and housework as disincentives for women's paid labor.[25]

"If the right to work is understood as a fundamental individual right," Blumberg wrote, "every individual should be afforded a neutral context in which to make a decision about work."[26] The problem with the tax law, she pointed out, was that it was not gender-neutral in operation. To the contrary, the tax laws "inequitably and insensitively treated working wives" and gave voice to a social policy that "a married woman ought to stay at home unless her family is virtually destitute, that is, in danger of becoming or presently a public charge. The apparent basis for this policy is the belief that the family is better off, that is, more stable or cohesive, and, perhaps, that the wife also benefits from enforced domesticity."[27] Married women were making tax-influenced decisions about whether to work outside the home, and thus their behavior was being distorted by the tax law. Blumberg's arguments were designed to appeal to traditional tax scholars who believe that tax laws should not distort labor choices.[28]

III. The Development of Feminist Tax Scholarship

Although tax matters remained in the background of the feminist agenda throughout the 1970s and 1980s,[29] a critical mass of feminist scholarship in taxation began to emerge in the 1990s. The concerns raised in this scholarship tended to cluster in several areas: (1) the tax law's structural incentives against women's participation in the paid labor force; (2) specific provisions of the tax law that appear neutral on their face but have a disproportionately negative impact on women; and (3) tax policies that are consistent with or challenge feminist theories of justice. It is not possible to name all of the legal scholars who contributed to the growing body of feminist tax scholarship, and so this chapter necessarily is limited to citing only representative samples of the work from this period.[30]

A. *The Emergence of a Critical Voice*

Two books published in the late 1990s helped shape the next decade of feminist tax scholarship. Mary Louise Fellows and Karen Brown's *Taxing America* (1996) assembled a group of authors to examine race and gender dimensions of the income tax law.[31] Notable contributions to this book include Lily Kahng's chapter, *Fiction in Tax*, which explores the history of the joint income tax return and the legal fiction on which it relies, namely, the notion that husbands and wives are one for tax purposes.[32] Dorothy Brown's chapter, *The Marriage Bonus/Penalty in Black and White*, exposed how black couples and white couples experience the tax implications of marriage differently, finding that black couples were likely to experience the marriage penalty more frequently than white couples did.[33] Brown found this to be due to a combination of (1) employment discrimination that brought the earnings of black men and black women closer to parity than the earnings of white men and white women and (2) differences in wage labor participation that resulted in the wife's wages constituting a greater percentage of the average black couple's income than of the average white couple's income.[34]

The following year, Edward McCaffery's *Taxing Women* explored how federal tax policy decisions from the 1930s and 1940s that favored "traditional" family structures—a working husband with a stay-at-home wife—have persisted even as society has changed.[35] McCaffery built on his prior work exploring how gender bias in the tax code manifests not only in the joint return but also in the earned income tax credit, the disaggregation of spousal income for Social Security purposes, the tax treatment of childcare, and fringe benefit rules that favor full-time employees.[36] As he put it in the introduction to *Taxing Women*:

> Tax law changes were put in place to foster and reward this single-earner household. These changes were left in place, all but unexamined, as the system kept growing. The tax system's strong bias in favor of single-earner families now sits uneasily under modern conditions. It pushes against stable families at the lower-income levels, against working wives at the upper-income ones, and, by limiting satisfactory options, against the many families in between....
>
> Meanwhile, ... [t]he mainstream tax policy academy legitimated the structure of tax with a rhetoric of fairness, neutrality, and common sense. An emergent feminist voice was barely heard, even when its cries were consistent with basic economic principles.[37]

Nancy Staudt's article *Taxing Housework*, published just before McCaffery's book, analyzed the tax policy decision to exempt household labor from the income tax base.[38] Staudt proposed including the value of that labor in income both to affirm the value of labor provided in the home and to provide women who work in the home with economic security in retirement, tempering the impact of her proposal by suggesting the creation of a household income tax credit to offset the resulting tax burden on low-income households.[39] Echoing cultural feminists' emphasis on the value of women's caretaking work,[40] Staudt offered a sophisticated and practically oriented proposal to offset the bias she identified, while taking into account class-based differences among taxpayers.

Extending the investigation of structural tax policy choices on women's market participation, Mary Louise Fellows examined the tax law's treatment of childcare expenses in *Rocking the Tax Code*, demonstrating how the "tax law facilitates class, gender, and race subordination and how it could be designed to disrupt it."[41] She expanded the focus beyond traditional tax policy goals and concepts and, more important, beyond the purchaser of childcare (who is usually the focus in debates about the tax treatment of childcare) to the wages and working conditions of those who supply childcare services (who normally remain invisible in these debates).[42] Fellows put forward policy options that aimed to simultaneously erase the public-private divide in tax law and disrupt both the economic exploitation and the class, gender, and race hierarchies in the market for childcare services.[43]

Unique among tax scholars writing at the time, Wendy Gerzog used feminist legal theory to illuminate the otherwise hidden gendered aspects of the estate and gift tax marital deduction.[44] In *The Marital Deduction QTIP Provisions: Illogical and Degrading to Women*, Gerzog criticized the wealth transfer tax laws' reliance on the concept of "qualified terminable interest property," which allows the wealthier spouse (typically the man) to receive a full marital deduction (and thus tax-free treatment) for transfers to the less wealthy spouse (typically the woman), even for transfers that remain fully under the husband's control.[45] In other words, the law favors male interests by allowing a full marital deduction—usually available only for outright transfers to a spouse—for transfers in trust that the husband continues to control, "based on the fallacy that decisions by the husband are decisions of the marital unit."[46] Gerzog observed that the statute was gender-neutral on its face, but the law itself "can only be explained as a gender-biased, paternalistic, and degrading treatment of women."[47]

In 1997, building on her earlier work on the language of tax policy, Marjorie Kornhauser continued her work on anti–progressive tax rhetoric.[48] A year earlier, a group of scholars had argued that the views of theorists purporting to speak for marginalized communities should be empirically tested to determine whether they were truly representative of community views. In part, this was because a survey that those scholars had created showed that women did not support progressive taxation at rates significantly higher than men did, which, in their eyes, undermined Kornhauser's earlier reliance on "a feminist 'ethos of care'" in arguing in support of progressivity.[49] In responding to this empirical study, Kornhauser emphasized that feminist theories are valuable tools for critiquing the tax laws.[50] She warned against overreliance on empirical work, emphasizing that quantification might add a veneer of neutrality but that it also has its own inherent methodological flaws, particularly when studying taxpayers' self-reported views of a concept such as progressivity in the tax laws.[51] "Science," she wrote, "is not the only truth, nor even an absolute truth; rather, like all areas of human knowledge, it is tentative and evolving."[52] For that reason, feminist theory is a touchstone for tax analysis as illuminating as history, economics, or empirical work, according to Kornhauser.[53]

While other feminist scholars pursued questions about the structure, bias, and rhetoric of the tax laws as applied to women, tax scholar Patricia Cain began drawing attention to the tax discrimination faced by same-sex couples. In the 1990s, same-sex couples were not permitted to marry in any state, and even had they been, they would not have been recognized as married for federal income tax purposes.[54] Cain, already the author of a robust body of feminist scholarship, brought that expertise to her analysis of the tax treatment of same-sex couples as a form of gender discrimination.[55] This topic is one to which Cain and other scholars would devote significant attention in the following decade as the battle for marriage equality heated up.

B. *Expanding What Counts as "Feminist" Issues*

In the 1990s, the contours of the campaign for the right of same sex-couples to marry began to take shape—albeit haltingly—in several states. Challenges met with varying success, until Massachusetts became the first state to recognize same-sex marriage following the 2003 decision in *Goodridge v. Department of Public Health*.[56] When at least one mainstream tax scholar expressed doubt that the failure to recognize same-sex couples harmed them for federal income tax purposes,[57] scholars such as Anthony Infanti responded with a robust critique of the Internal Revenue Code's "unequal and discriminatory treatment" of same-sex couples and its adoption of society's "revulsion" toward lesbian and gay people.[58] Cain, Infanti, and Nancy Knauer all worked (and, even after the advent of marriage equality throughout the United States, continue to work) to expose the heteronormative underpinnings of the tax laws.[59] All of their work is undergirded by the belief that "the most effective and inclusive feminism takes into account the way that many intersecting identities can make the quest for justice more complex and elusive, given the structure of both the law itself as well as the meaning of equal protection as interpreted by twenty-first-century courts."[60] In other words, feminist tax scholarship is not only about women but about justice for all people.

In the second decade of the twenty-first century, tax scholars who self-identify as feminists have broadened their inquiry beyond areas of traditional interest to feminist scholars. There is now a vibrant body of feminist tax scholarship concerning wide-ranging subjects such as reproductive technology,[61] gender identity,[62] student loan indebtedness,[63] health care,[64] human rights,[65] and even tax-exempt organizations.[66] Again, the trend in feminist tax scholarship is to recognize the interconnectedness of gender equality with other social justice movements.[67]

IV. "A Critique from the Margin"

As the discussion thus far demonstrates, feminist analysis is far from new to tax law.[68] The rich history of feminist contributions to the tax literature might seem to call into question tax law's placement among the "emerging areas" of feminist engagement identified by this handbook's editors. Yet, this long history should not be confused with wide acceptance or embrace of those contributions, either in academic discourse or in the everyday drafting of tax legislation and regulations. It is in this sense that tax law might be considered an emerging area of feminist influence on the law.

A. *A Blinkered Worldview*

Conventional (also referred to as "traditional" or "mainstream") tax scholarship adopts a predominantly economic perspective on tax law and policy that imbues the work of tax scholars with "the hard, 'scientific' character of economic analysis."[69] In *Who Cooked Adam Smith's Dinner?*, Katrine Marçal accurately (if unintentionally) summed up the general attitude of mainstream U.S. tax academics when she described the "crux of economics": "When we participate in the market, we're all assumed to be anonymous. That's why the market can set us free. It doesn't matter who you are. Personal traits and emotional ties don't have a place here. The only thing that matters is your ability to pay."[70] With such a narrow focus on the economic dimension of individuals,[71] there is little room in conventional tax scholarship for feminist or other critical perspectives that explore the impact of tax law on individuals marginalized on the basis of, for example, gender or gender identity, race or ethnicity, sexual orientation, class, disability, or immigration status.

Like economists who "isolate a single variable within an economic model that encompasses several variables ... to simplify the world to be able to predict it,"[72] mainstream tax academics reduce complicated human beings and their interactions with each other to a single economic variable—income in income tax analyses or wealth in transfer tax analyses. As Nancy Knauer explains with implicit reference to the income tax:

> The three classic pillars of tax policy—equity, efficiency, and ease of administration—aim to design a system of taxation that fairly apportions the burdens of citizenship, minimizes tax distortions in economic behavior, and simplifies the task of compliance and administration. These organizing principles reflect widely-held equality and autonomy norms but proceed from a very strong presumption of taxpayer neutrality where the only salient distinction among taxpayers is that of income level. In other words, U.S. tax policy does not take into account demographic differences among taxpayers, such as race, ethnicity, gender, sexual orientation, or gender identity, nor does it attempt to evaluate the potentially disparate impact of taxation on the members of these groups.[73]

The conventional approach to tax scholarship thus simplifies the world in order that its tax rules might be reformed, replaced, or abandoned through tidy academic analyses—analyses that lack any real consideration of how existing or proposed tax rules might affect the multidimensional, flesh-and-blood people on whom those rules are intended to operate. Conveniently (for those with power and privilege), this singular focus on the economic dimension of individuals has a sanitizing effect, because it not only expurgates "uncomfortable discussions of racism, sexism, heterosexism, and disability discrimination"[74] from mainstream academic tax analysis but also, more insidiously, operates to "render[] any mention of these subjects in a tax context immediately suspect."[75]

In this way, the work of mainstream tax academics normalizes the discrimination that is embedded in tax law and renders it "more generally and widely acceptable by making it seem as if the tax laws are unconnected with social concerns and merely dictated by the play of impersonal market and economic forces that are beyond our control."[76] In turn, politicians of all stripes "pick up on this rhetorical thread and weave it into the tapestry of popular political discourse when they focus tax reform discussions on encouraging economic growth."[77] Taken together, the conventional academic and political fixations on economics have served to "reinforce[] the tax laws' privileging of the already privileged"[78] and have left little space for feminist or other critical contributions to take hold and effect positive change in the law.

B. *A Marginalized Scholarship*

Given the narrow worldview that shapes and influences conventional tax discourse, it should come as no surprise that mainstream tax academics' reception of feminist and other critical tax scholarship has been described as "contentious,"[79] characterized by a "stiff and sustained resistance"[80] or even "a visceral reaction that in some cases blocks intellectual engagement."[81] Some mainstream tax scholars seem to have taken critical tax scholarship as "a radical affront,"[82] with the body of critical tax scholarship having been "derided by mainstream tax scholars for being trendy, divisive, and less than rigorous."[83] Even so, "the largest numbers [of tax academics—not to mention those outside the academy] have simply ignored the critical tax endeavor, leaving women's and minorities' concerns somewhat peripheral to the broader tax subject."[84] In these ways, critical tax scholarship has been both "dismissed as 'mere critique' "[85] and itself subjected to "scathing critiques."[86]

Around the time the *North Carolina Law Review* devoted an entire issue to (at times, openly hostile) critiques of critical tax theory,[87] like-minded tax scholars began to hold a Critical Tax Conference, at first sporadically and then annually starting in 2000.[88] Despite its name, the conference "intentionally encouraged a focus beyond the antisubordination principle that initially drove critical tax theory. Its organizers have encouraged attendance of all tax scholars who are interested in cross-disciplinary work and in the identification of a broad range of hidden biases, influences, and unintended effects of the law or proposed reforms to it."[89] This capacious view of the contributions that should be welcomed at the conference provided an ostensibly salutary opportunity for conversation between critical and mainstream tax scholars. Over the years, however, the conference increasingly became just another opportunity for mainstream tax scholars to present their work, and the occasional critical tax presentation made at the conference too often generated negative responses.[90]

In the face of hostility to critical tax scholarship, Marjorie Kornhauser was given some pause when she was labeled a "feminist tax scholar"—despite her self-identification as both a tax scholar and a feminist.[91] This pause spurred self-reflection on Kornhauser's part that led to an examination of a critical tax article that she had written. She compared the citation pattern of that article, which "explicitly applie[d] feminist theory to the issue of progressive income tax,"[92] with that of a more traditional law review article published in the same year, on the same general topic (i.e., progressivity of the income tax), by similarly well-established tax scholars, and in a similarly ranked journal.[93] She found that although both articles had been cited a similar number of times, the pattern of citations differed markedly: "On the positive side, the perceived feminist aspect of [Kornhauser's] article made it a much more widely cited article outside the tax area. On the other hand, [Kornhauser] believe[d] that this very aspect is the reason it was less likely to be cited within the tax field, and when it was cited it was sometimes cited more for these feminist aspects than for its traditional tax aspects."[94] This led Kornhauser to conclude that "[t]he term feminist tax scholarship is a double-edged sword. . . . Its power to enrich both tax and other disciplines is limited by a potential for marginalization—of being read only for its feminist angle, or worse, being dismissed because of its feminist angle."[95] Despite being based on an unscientific analysis of citation patterns in an extremely limited data set, Kornhauser's speculation is fully in keeping with the general marginalization of critical tax scholarship that continues to this day.[96]

V. Emerging from the Academic Shadows

Reflecting at the turn of the twenty-first century on the role that tax law and scholarship might play in addressing the feminization of poverty at a conference organized by the University of Iowa College of Law's *Journal of Gender, Race & Justice*, Michael Livingston noted: "It is also important to remember that many of today's conservative policies originated in academic discussions and that future choices will likewise be circumscribed by today's theoretical debates. These factors suggest that there is at least something to be gained from an academic reconsideration of women's and poverty issues in the tax arena. Progress in the intellectual area might have real impact on the policy process, if not immediately then several years or decades down the road."[97] This message reminds us that change—even when it seems to come quickly—typically is preceded by much time and toil laying the groundwork for that change to occur. It appears that we are now beginning to see the fruits of the labor, patience, and perseverance of the critical tax scholars who have spent the past several decades laying the groundwork for creating a more just tax system that furthers the shared enterprise of permitting all members of our society to lead full and rewarding lives.

It is encouraging that critical tax perspectives have begun to find resonance outside academia. As Nancy Knauer has observed:

> Despite [its] inauspicious reception, many of the insights of critical tax theory now find support in international practices such as gender mainstreaming and gender-sensitive budgeting. Moreover, the prime assertion of critical tax theorists that tax is political has received widespread national attention in connection with *United States v. Windsor*, the groundbreaking U.S. Supreme Court case that challenged the constitutionality of the Defense of Marriage Act (DOMA). As it turns out, one of the most important civil rights cases of this generation was a tax case involving the exclusion of same-sex married couples from the marital deduction provisions under the federal estate tax.[98]

Critical tax perspectives have also begun, albeit slowly, to seep into the general tax policy discourse in the United States. For instance, under the leadership of its managing director Caroline Bruckner, the Tax Policy Center at American University's Kogod School of Business produced an important report in 2017 regarding the impact of tax law on women-owned businesses.[99] The report, *Billion Dollar Blind Spot: How the U.S. Tax Code's Small Business Expenditures Impact Women Business Owners*, demonstrated the misalignment between several small-business tax expenditures and the types of businesses that women own and operate.[100] The report found that "Congress and stakeholders have a billion dollar blind spot when it comes to understanding how effective small business tax expenditures are with respect to women-owned firms. This blind spot is primarily attributable to an absence of existing tax research on women-owned firms and indicates Congress doesn't have the information necessary to make evidence-based tax policy decisions with respect to women-owned firms."[101]

The results of this research reached the halls of Congress. Bruckner testified regarding the report's findings before the House Committee on Small Business in 2017 and before the Senate Committee on Small Business and Entrepreneurship in 2018.[102] Then, in 2019, Bruckner testified before the House Budget Committee on the report's findings as part of that committee's review of the impact of the 2017 Tax Cuts and Jobs Act.[103] The staff of the House Budget Committee then included a summary of Bruckner's testimony in a report on the hearing that was posted on the committee's website for wider dissemination.[104] Although this may seem like a very small step, the fact that legislators did not simply ignore or dismiss out of hand research illuminating the gendered dimensions of business-related tax reforms is an important indication that lawmakers are finally beginning to open their minds to the gendered dimensions of tax law.

Nongovernmental organizations in the United States also seem to be waking up to the importance of tax law in discussions of gender inequality. In November 2019, the National Women's Law Center (NWLC) produced a series of reports with the theme "Tax Justice Is Gender Justice" (but with the far catchier tagline "Tax the Patriarchy").[105] The three reports—*The Faulty Foundations of the Code*,[106] *Reckoning with the Hidden Rules of Gender in the Tax Code*,[107] and *A Tax Code for the Rest of Us*[108]—were the product of a truly collaborative effort. In the early stages of planning this project, NWLC contacted critical tax scholars (including both of the authors of this chapter) to gauge their receptivity to the project and to obtain their advice and expertise as the contours of the project were brought into focus. Then, draft reports were written by teams of authors that included NWLC staff, representatives from other policy organizations, and academics. Before finalizing the reports, NWLC brought together the authors of the reports along with a broader group of policy researchers and critical tax scholars for a day-long meeting to provide feedback on the drafts and to help shape the final reports. As of this writing, just months after the release of the reports, any judgment regarding their influence would be premature; however, it is worth noting that the reports have already garnered significant attention from the press.[109]

The intersection of taxation and gender issues has also taken on an unprecedented salience in public discourse. For example, *Cosmopolitan* proclaimed 2015 as "The Year the Period Went Public,"[110] at least in part because of the popular "Stop Taxing Our Periods! Period." online petition against the "tampon tax"—the sales tax imposed on menstrual products in more than thirty states.[111] In 2019, the ACLU issued a legislative toolkit and briefing paper on menstrual equity, both of which are designed to assist advocates in efforts to repeal the tampon tax.[112] The tampon tax is a constituent part of what the popular press now calls the "pink tax": taxes on menstrual products, gender-based pricing discrimination for substantially similar items (think blue razors versus pink razors), and the wage gap.[113] In 2019, New York Governor Andrew Cuomo announced his intention to eliminate gender-based priced differences in services and goods; that legislation took effect on September 30, 2020.[114] Although it is too soon to predict the trajectory of either the tampon tax in particular or the pink tax in general, taxation is a current focal point for gender-equality activism and legal reform.

The nascent recognition that tax law is an important contributor to gender discrimination in the United States is simultaneously long overdue and a welcome development. Of course, a few decades of critical tax scholarship cannot, by itself, successfully loosen the grip of patriarchy on the tax code. Tax law is closely tied to the society that creates it.[115] As a result, uprooting and eradicating deeply embedded gender discrimination— for example, and perhaps most prominently, the heteropatriarchal joint federal income tax return based in and on the privileging of marriage in U.S. tax law and society—can only be successfully accomplished as part of a broader movement for social change. That feminist tax work is beginning to have influence on policy matters and even public discourse—phrases such as "pink tax" and "tampon tax" are now well understood when only a few years ago they were not—demonstrates the continued vitality and importance of feminist tax perspectives, not to mention the need for feminist scholars outside tax law to actively engage with and understand these perspectives.

VI. Conclusion

The halls of tax academia have proved less than hospitable to the work of critical tax scholars because of mainstream tax scholars' tendency to view taxpayers as the sum of their economic transactions. Whereas mainstream tax scholars see taxpayers as one-dimensional balance sheets, critical tax scholars see them as multidimensional people with identities that may give rise to privilege or subordination, both inside and outside the tax system. Although there is still hope that critical perspectives will seep more broadly into both mainstream tax scholarship and feminist scholarship, the influence that critical tax perspectives have begun to have outside academia—for instance, in think tanks and policy organizations that are better positioned to disseminate this work to legislators and the public at large—may prove to be far more consequential in achieving positive changes in our tax system in the long run. An observation made by Michael Livingston in closing his remarks at the *Journal of Gender, Race & Justice* conference on women and poverty provides context for, and an important lesson in support of, this contention now:

> A bit of history may be relevant at this point. Thirty years ago, conservative think tanks began to think about public policy in a detailed but unified way. They began to consider how various aspects of the liberal state, including tax, welfare, and various other policies, interacted to undermine traditional values and replace them with a state-centered, liberal creed. By developing expertise in numerous areas, but with a unifying philosophy, conservative think tanks were able to affect public policy in a more extensive manner than anyone had deemed possible. I suspect that most participants in this symposium would prefer that the conservatives had just stayed home. But in procedure, if not substance, there is much to be gleaned from them. Those who wish to reverse the feminization of poverty, together with other relics of the past two generations, would do well to learn from their example.[116]

There is a long and rich history of feminist tax scholarship, despite the frustratingly difficult time that feminist and other critical tax perspectives have had in penetrating the mainstream of legal thought. Fortunately, it seems that others outside academia have been paying attention to the work being done by critical tax scholars who have patiently laid the intellectual foundation for a fundamental shift in how we all see and interact with our tax system. If there is to be any hope for making inroads in the shaping and reshaping of tax policy by bringing feminist and other critical tax perspectives to bear, it is through the emerging partnerships between critical tax scholars and those working in think tanks and the public policy sphere who, together, might just be "able to affect public policy in a more extensive manner than anyone had deemed possible."[117]

Notes

1. *The Declaration of Sentiments, Seneca Falls Conference, 1848*, Mod. Hist. Sourcebook, https://sourcebooks.fordham.edu/mod/senecafalls.asp (last updated Nov. 1998).
2. *Id.*
3. *Id.*
4. *See* Carolyn C. Jones, *Dollars and Selves: Women's Tax Criticism and Resistance in the 1870s*, 1994 U. Ill. L. Rev. 265, 267.
5. *Id.* at 268, 275–80.

6. *Id.* at 268–69, 275–80.
7. Moritz v. Comm'r, 55 T.C. 113 (1970), *rev'd*, 469 F.2d 466 (10th Cir. 1972), *cert. denied*, 412 U.S. 906 (1973).
8. I.R.C. § 214 (1968); *see* Revenue Act of 1964, Pub. L. No. 88-272, § 212, 78 Stat. 19, 49.
9. *Moritz*, 55 T.C. at 114–15.
10. *See* Brief for Petitioner-Appellant at 2, *Moritz*, 469 F.2d 466 (No. 71-1127).
11. Martin D. Ginsburg, ABA Tax Section Distinguished Service Award Presentation 1–2 (May 5, 2006), https://www.americanbar.org/content/dam/aba/administrative/taxation/awards/dsa/ginsburgremarks.pdf.
12. *Id.* at 2 ("I went next door, handed the advance sheets to my wife, and said, 'Read this.' Ruth replied with a warm and friendly snarl, 'I don't read tax cases.' I said, 'Read this one,' and returned to my room. No more than 5 minutes later—it was a short opinion—Ruth stepped into my room and, with the broadest smile you can imagine, said, 'Let's take it[.]' And we did.").
13. *Id.*
14. *Moritz*, 469 F.2d at 470.
15. *See* Reed v. Reed, 404 U.S. 71 (1971) (finding unconstitutional an Idaho statutory preference for a male administrator of a decedent's estate); Wendy Webster Williams, *Justice Ruth Bader Ginsburg's Rutgers Years: 1963–1972*, 31 Women's Rts. L. Rep. 229, 249–50 (2010); Lila Thulin, *The True Story of the Case Ruth Bader Ginsburg Argues in "On the Basis of Sex,"* Smithsonian Mag. (Dec. 24, 2018), https://www.smithsonianmag.com/history/true-story-case-center-basis-sex-180971110/.
16. Williams, *Ginsburg's Rutgers Years*, *supra* note 15, at 247 n.127; Thulin, *True Story*, *supra* note 15.
17. *Moritz*, 469 F.2d at 470.
18. *Reed*, 404 U.S. at 76–77.
19. *See* Duren v. Missouri, 439 U.S. 357 (1979) (challenging sex-based exemptions from jury service); Califano v. Goldfarb, 430 U.S. 199 (1977) (finding unconstitutional a law permitting widows but not widowers certain Social Security survivor benefits); Edwards v. Healy, 421 U.S. 772 (1975) (challenging sex-based exemptions from jury service); Weinberger v. Wiesenfeld, 420 U.S. 636 (1975) (finding unconstitutional a law that only allowed surviving children but not widowers to obtain Social Security survivor benefits); Kahn v. Shevin, 416 U.S. 351 (1974) (property tax exemption for widows but not widowers held constitutional); Frontiero v. Richardson, 411 U.S. 677 (1973) (invalidating the Air Force's policy of automatically granting spousal benefits to married male service members but requiring married female service members to prove the financial dependency of their spouses).
20. Craig v. Boren, 429 U.S. 190 (1976).
21. About the Court: Justices 1789 to Present, U.S. Supreme Ct., https://www.supremecourt.gov/about/members_text.aspx (last visited Oct. 29, 2020).
22. Grace Blumberg, *Sexism in the Code: A Comparative Study of Income Taxation of Working Wives and Mothers*, 21 Buff. L. Rev. 49 (1971).
23. *Id.* at 49; *see id.* at 50–54.
24. *Id.* at 54–59.
25. *Id.* at 62–74.
26. *Id.* at 90.
27. *Id.* at 91, 92–93.

28. For a more recent articulation of these concerns about distortion, see Louis Kaplow & Steven Shavell, *Why the Legal System Is Less Efficient Than the Income Tax in Redistributing Income*, 23 J. LEGAL STUD. 667 (1994).
29. For examples of feminist tax scholarship from this period, see Pamela B. Gann, *Abandoning Marital Status as a Factor in Allocating Income Tax Burdens*, 59 Tex. L. Rev. 1 (1980); Marjorie E. Kornhauser, *The Rhetoric of the Anti-Progressive Income Tax Movement: A Typical Male Reaction*, 86 MICH. L. REV. 465 (1987).
30. For a further sampling, see CRITICAL TAX THEORY: AN INTRODUCTION (Anthony C. Infanti & Bridget J. Crawford eds., 2009).
31. TAXING AMERICA (Karen B. Brown & Mary Louise Fellows eds., 1996).
32. Lily Kahng, *Fiction in Tax*, in TAXING AMERICA, at 25–44.
33. Dorothy A. Brown, *The Marriage Bonus/Penalty in Black and White*, in TAXING AMERICA, at 45–57.
34. *Id.* at 49–53.
35. EDWARD J. MCCAFFERY, TAXING WOMEN: HOW THE MARRIAGE PENALTY AFFECTS YOUR TAXES (1997).
36. *See, e.g.*, Edward J. McCaffery, *Taxation and the Family: A Fresh Look at Behavioral Gender Biases in the Code*, 40 UCLA L. REV. 983 (1993); Edward J. McCaffery, *Slouching Towards Equality: Gender Discrimination, Market Efficiency, and Social Change*, 103 YALE L.J. 595 (1993).
37. MCCAFFERY, TAXING WOMEN, *supra* note 35, at 1.
38. Nancy C. Staudt, *Taxing Housework*, 84 GEO. L.J. 1571 (1996).
39. *Id.* at 1618–40.
40. *See, e.g.*, ROBIN WEST, CARING FOR JUSTICE (1997).
41. Mary Louise Fellows, *Rocking the Tax Code: A Case Study of Employment-Related Child-Care Expenditures*, 10 YALE J.L. & FEMINISM 307, 308 (1998).
42. *Id.* at 312–55.
43. *Id.* at 385–93.
44. Wendy C. Gerzog, *The Marital Deduction QTIP Provisions: Illogical and Degrading to Women*, 5 UCLA WOMEN'S L.J. 301 (1995).
45. *Id.* at 301.
46. *Id.* at 310.
47. *Id.* at 305.
48. Marjorie E. Kornhauser, *What Do Women Want: Feminism and the Progressive Income Tax*, 47 AM. U. L. REV. 151 (1997); *see* Kornhauser, *Rhetoric of the Anti-Progressive Income Tax Movement*, *supra* note 29.
49. Kornhauser, *What Do Women Want*, *supra* note 49, at 153; William J. Turnier et al., *Redistributive Justice and Cultural Feminism*, 45 AM. U. L. REV. 1275 (1996).
50. Kornhauser, *What Do Women Want*, *supra* note 49, at 161–62.
51. *Id.* at 154–59.
52. *Id.* at 160.
53. *Id.*
54. *See* Boyter v. Comm'r, 668 F.2d 1382, 1385 (4th Cir. 1981) (deferring to state law in determining who is married for federal tax purposes); 1 U.S.C. § 7 (1996) (defining "marriage" for purposes of federal law as "only a legal union between one man and one woman as husband and wife").

55. *E.g.*, Patricia A. Cain, *Same-Sex Couples and the Federal Tax Law*, 1 Law & Sexuality 97 (1991); Patricia A. Cain, *Taxing Lesbians*, 6 S. Cal. Rev. L. & Women's Stud. 471 (1997).
56. Goodridge v. Dep't of Pub. Health, 798 N.E.2d 941 (Mass. 2003); *see* Opinions of the Justices to the Senate, 802 N.E.2d 565 (Mass. 2004). Although Hawaii was on the path to be the first state to recognize same-sex marriage after a landmark 1993 decision from the Hawaii Supreme Court, Baehr v. Lewin, 852 P.2d 44 (Haw. 1993), an amendment was later added to the Hawaii Constitution that placed the power to define marriage in the hands of the state legislature and effectively validated the challenged marriage law before a final decision could be reached in the case. Baehr v. Miike, No. 20371, 1999 WL 35643448 (Haw. Dec. 9, 1999).
57. Steve R. Johnson, *Targets Missed and Targets Hit: Critical Tax Studies and Effective Tax Reform*, 76 N.C. L. Rev. 1771, 1779 (1998).
58. Anthony C. Infanti, *The Internal Revenue Code as Sodomy Statute*, 44 Santa Clara L. Rev. 763, 765, 779 (2004).
59. *E.g.*, Patricia A. Cain, *The New York Marriage Equality Act and the Income Tax*, 5 Alb. Gov't L. Rev. 634 (2012); Anthony C. Infanti, *The House of* Windsor: *Accentuating the Heteronormativity in the Tax Incentives for Procreation*, 89 Wash. L. Rev. 1185 (2014); Nancy J. Knauer, *Heteronormativity and Federal Tax Policy*, 101 W. Va. L. Rev. 129 (1998).
60. Bridget J. Crawford & Anthony C. Infanti, *Introduction*, in Feminist Judgments: Rewritten Tax Opinions 3, 9 (Bridget J. Crawford & Anthony C. Infanti eds., 2017).
61. Katherine Pratt, *Deducting the Costs of Fertility Treatment: Implications of* Magdalin v. Commissioner *for Opposite-Sex Couples, Gay and Lesbian Same-Sex Couples, and Single Women and Men*, 2009 Wis. L. Rev. 1283.
62. *E.g.*, Anthony C. Infanti, *LGBT Taxpayers: A Collision of "Others,"* 13 Geo. J. Gender & L. 1 (2012); Katherine Pratt, *The Tax Definition of "Medical Care": A Critique of the Startling IRS Arguments in* O'Donnabhain v. Commissioner, 23 Mich. J. Gender & L. 313 (2016).
63. Victoria J. Haneman, *The Collision of Student Loan Debt and Joint Marital Taxation*, 35 Va. Tax Rev. 223 (2016).
64. Francine J. Lipman & James Owens, *Irresponsibly Taxing Irresponsibility: The Individual Tax Penalty Under the Affordable Care Act*, 23 Geo. J. on Poverty L. & Pol'y 463 (2016).
65. *E.g.*, Bridget J. Crawford & Carla Spivack, *Tampon Taxes, Discrimination and Human Rights*, 2017 Wis. L. Rev. 491; Tax, Inequality, and Human Rights (Philip Alston & Nikki Reisch eds., 2019).
66. *See* David A. Brennen, *Bob Jones University v. United States*, in Feminist Judgments: Rewritten Tax Opinions, at 150; Elaine Waterhouse Wilson, *Commentary on* Bob Jones University v. United States, in Feminist Judgments: Rewritten Tax Opinions, at 140.
67. *E.g.*, Kristin Kalsem & Verna Williams, *Social Justice Feminism*, 18 UCLA Women's L.J. 131 (2010); *see* Bridget J. Crawford, Toward a Third-Wave Feminist Legal Theory: Young Women, *Pornography and the Praxis of Pleasure*, 14 Mich. J. Gender & L. 99, 127 (2007) (describing coalition building as a hallmark of third-wave feminism).
68. This section takes its name from Patricia A. Cain, *Death Taxes: A Critique from the Margin*, 48 Clev. St. L. Rev. 677 (2000).

69. Michael A. Livingston, *Radical Scholars, Conservative Field: Putting "Critical Tax Scholarship" in Perspective*, 76 N.C. L. Rev. 1791, 1795–96 (1998); *see id.* at 1794; Nancy J. Knauer, *Critical Tax Policy: A Pathway to Reform?*, 9 Nw. J.L. & Soc. Pol'y 206, 226 (2014).
70. Katrine Marçal, Who Cooked Adam Smith's Dinner? A Story About Women and Economics 19 (Saskia Vogel trans., 2016).
71. Anthony C. Infanti, *Tax Equity*, 55 Buff. L. Rev. 1191, 1200–3 (2008); Knauer, *Critical Tax Policy, supra* note 69, at 208, 209–10.
72. Marçal, Who Cooked Adam Smith's Dinner?, *supra* note 70, at 21–22.
73. Knauer, *Critical Tax Policy, supra* note 69, at 209–10 (footnotes omitted).
74. Infanti, *Tax Equity, supra* note 71, at 1201.
75. *Id.* at 1253.
76. Anthony C. Infanti, Our Selfish Tax Laws: Toward Tax Reform That Mirrors Our Better Selves 141 (2018).
77. *Id.*
78. *Id.* at 143.
79. Livingston, *Radical Scholars, Conservative Field, supra* note 69, at 1815.
80. Knauer, *Critical Tax Policy, supra* note 69, at 226; *see also* Alice G. Abreu, *Tax Counts: Bringing Money-Law to LatCrit*, 78 Denv. U. L. Rev. 575, 590 (2001) ("substantial resistance"); Nancy E. Shurtz, *Critical Tax Theory: Still Not Taken Seriously*, 76 N.C. L. Rev. 1837, 1846 (1998) ("open resistance").
81. Karen B. Brown et al., *The Past, Present, and Future of Critical Tax Theory: A Conversation*, 10 Pitt. Tax Rev. 59, 64 (2012).
82. *Id.* at 63.
83. Knauer, *Critical Tax Policy, supra* note 69, at 227.
84. Michael A. Livingston, *Women, Poverty, and the Tax Code: A Tale of Theory and Practice*, 5 J. Gender Race & Just. 327, 330 (2002).
85. Knauer, *Critical Tax Policy, supra* note 69, at 228 (quoting Lawrence Zelenak, *Taking Critical Tax Theory Seriously*, 76 N.C. L. Rev. 1521, 1524 [1998]).
86. Abreu, *Tax Counts, supra* note 80, at 591 n.41.
87. Symposium, *Critical Tax Theory: Criticism and Response*, 76 N.C. L. Rev. 1519 (1998).
88. Brown et al., *Past, Present, and Future, supra* note 81, at 65.
89. *Id.* at 65–66.
90. *See* Dorothy A. Brown, *Tales from a Tax Crit*, 10 Pitt. Tax Rev. 47, 47 (2012).
91. Marjorie E. Kornhauser, *A Taxing Woman: The Relationship of Feminist Scholarship to Tax*, 6 S. Cal. Rev. L. & Women's Stud. 301, 301 (1997).
92. *Id.* at 302; *see* Kornhauser, *Rhetoric of the Anti-Progressive Income Tax Movement*, *supra* note 29.
93. Joseph Bankman & Thomas Griffith, *Social Welfare and the Rate Structure: A New Look at Progressive Taxation*, 75 Calif. L. Rev. 1905 (1987).
94. Kornhauser, *Taxing Woman, supra* note 91, at 317.
95. *Id.* at 321–22.
96. *E.g.*, Edward Kleinbard, Critical Tax Thinking, at slides 3–4 (Univ. S. Cal. Legal Studies Research Paper No. 19-10, 2019), https://papers.ssrn.com/sol3/papers.cfm?abstract_id=3373965; *see* Leo P. Martinez, *A Critique of Critical Tax Policy Critiques (Or, You've Got to Speak out Against the Madness)*, 28 Berkeley La Raza L.J. 49 (2018).
97. Livingston, *Women, Poverty, and the Tax Code, supra* note 69, at 335.
98. Knauer, *Critical Tax Policy, supra* note 69, at 229–30 (footnotes omitted).

99. It is worth noting that the Kogod Tax Policy Center's mission is not particularly focused on marginalized groups, as critical tax theory is; rather, the Center more broadly "seeks to increase public understanding of the nation's tax laws, and to spur balanced, productive dialogue on the status of current tax law, the challenges of tax compliance and planning, and the potential impact of tax reform, with a focus on 'average' Americans and small and mid-size businesses." KOGOD TAX POL'Y CTR., https://www.american.edu/kogod/research/taxpolicy/ (last visited Oct. 29, 2020).
100. CAROLINE BRUCKNER, KOGOD SCH. OF BUS. TAX POLICY CTR., *Billion Dollar Blind Spot: How the U.S. Tax Code's Small Business Expenditures Impact Women Business Owners* 7 (2017), https://www.american.edu/kogod/research/upload/blind_spot_accessible.pdf.
101. *Id.*
102. *Expanding Opportunities for Small Businesses Through the Tax Code: Hearing Before the S. Comm. on Small Bus. & Entrepreneurship*, 115th Cong. 26–36 (2018) (statement of Caroline Bruckner, Managing Director, Kogod Tax Policy Center); *Small Business Tax Reform: Modernizing the Code for the Nation's Job Creators: Hearing Before the H. Comm. on Small Bus.*, 115th Cong. 10–12, 13–14, 36–43 (2017) (statement of Caroline Bruckner, Managing Director, Kogod Tax Policy Center).
103. *Hearing on 2017 Tax Law: Impact on the Budget and American Families: Hearing Before the H. Comm. on Budget*, 116th Cong. 42–50 (2019) (statement of Caroline Bruckner, Managing Director, Kogod Tax Policy Center).
104. *Real-World Effects Prove the GOP Tax Law Was the Wrong Policy at the Wrong Time*, House Comm. on Budget (Mar. 6, 2019), https://budget.house.gov/publications/report/real-world-effects-prove-gop-tax-law-was-wrong-policy-wrong-time.
105. *Resource: Gender and the Tax Code*, NATIONAL WOMEN'S LAW CENTER (Nov. 13, 2019), https://nwlc.org/resources/gender-and-the-tax-code/; Melissa Boteach, *Five Reasons We Need to Tax the Patriarchy*, NATIONAL WOMEN'S LAW CENTER (Dec. 20, 2019), https://nwlc.org/blog/five-reasons-we-need-to-tax-the-patriarchy/.
106. ARIEL JUROW KLEIMAN ET AL., *The Faulty Foundations of the Code: Gender and Racial Bias in Our Tax Laws* (2019), https://nwlc-ciw49tixgw5lbab.stackpathdns.com/wp-content/uploads/2019/11/NWLC-The-Faulty-Foundations-of-the-Tax-Code-Accessible-FINAL.pdf.
107. KATY MILANI ET AL., *Reckoning with the Hidden Rules of Gender in the Tax Code: How Low Taxes on Corporations and the Wealthy Impact Women's Economic Opportunity and Security* (2019), https://nwlc.org/wp-content/uploads/2020/06/FINAL-NWLC-Reckoning_FactSheet.pdf.
108. MELISSA BOTEACH ET AL., *A Tax Code for the Rest of Us: A Framework and Recommendations for Advancing Gender and Racial Equality Through Tax Credits* (2019), https://nwlc.org/wp-content/uploads/2019/11/NWLC-GCPI-Tax-Code-for-the-Rest-of-Us-Nov14.pdf.
109. Andrew Keshner, *Tax Rules Have Been Largely Written by Rich, White Men—And It Shows, Researchers Say*, MARKETWATCH (Nov. 18, 2019), https://www.marketwatch.com/story/3-ways-the-tax-code-can-burden-women-and-the-poor-while-helping-out-wealthy-men-2019-11-15; Annie Lowrey, *Tax the Patriarchy*, ATLANTIC (Nov. 13, 2019), https://www.theatlantic.com/ideas/archive/2019/11/tax-patriarchy/601864/; Maura Quint, *Taxes Are a "Women's Issue," Too*, Ms. (Nov. 21, 2019), https://msmagazine.com/2019/11/21/taxes-are-a-womens-issue-too/.

110. Anna Maltby, *The 8 Greatest Menstrual Moments of 2015*, COSMOPOLITAN (Oct. 13, 2015), https://www.cosmopolitan.com/health-fitness/news/a47609/2015-the-year-the-period-went-public.
111. *No Tax on Tampons: Stop Taxing Our Periods! Period.*, CHANGE.ORG (Oct. 10, 2015), https://www.change.org/p/u-s-state-legislators-stop-taxing-our-periods-period [https://perma.cc/D38W-DR4G]. For a discussion of state sales tax regimes, see Bridget J. Crawford & Emily Gold Waldman, *The Unconstitutional Tampon Tax*, 53 U. RICH. L. REV. 439, 449–56 (2019).
112. ACLU & PERIOD EQUITY, *The Unequal Price of Periods: Menstrual Equity in the United States* (2019), https://www.aclu.org/report/unequal-price-periods; ACLU NATIONAL PRISON PROJECT & PERIOD EQUITY, *Menstrual Equity: A Legislative Toolkit* (2019), https://www.aclu.org/report/menstrual-equity.
113. *See, e.g.*, Ewan Palmer, *What Is the "Pink Tax"? New York Lawmakers Could Soon End Discriminatory Pricing of Women's Products*, NEWSWEEK (June 10, 2019), https://www.newsweek.com/new-york-pink-tax-pricing-women-products-1443149; Press Release, Congresswoman Carolyn B. Maloney, *Earn Less, Pay More: The State of the Gender Pay Gap and "Pink Tax" in 2018*, https://maloney.house.gov/sites/maloney.house.gov/files/Pink%20Tax%20report%20FINAL.pdf.
114. Press Release, Governor Andrew M. Cuomo, *Governor Cuomo Unveils Tenth Proposal of 2020, State of the State: Eliminating the Pink Tax* (Dec. 22, 2019), https://www.governor.ny.gov/news/governor-cuomo-unveils-10th-proposal-2020-state-state-eliminating-pink-tax; *see* N.Y. GEN. BUS. LAW § 391-u (McKinney 2021).
115. *See generally* INFANTI, OUR SELFISH TAX LAWS, *supra* note 76.
116. Livingston, *Women, Poverty, and the Tax Code*, *supra* note 69, at 336–37.
117. *Id.* at 337.

CHAPTER 36

TORT LAW AND FEMINISM

SARAH L. SWAN

TORT is often described as "a battleground of social theory" where the broad goals that should govern it are constantly contested and renegotiated.[1] Law and economics insists that tort should focus on minimizing social costs and maximizing wealth.[2] Compensation-deterrence contends that tort must seek only to "compensate and deter."[3] Corrective justice maintains that tort's focus should be solely on forcing "wrongdoer[s] to repair wrongful losses."[4] Legal feminism, which argues that tort should pursue goals of equality and social justice, is mostly fighting to just get on the field.[5] Despite the success of feminist advocacy in numerous other areas of law, decades of compelling feminist scholarship and advocacy have yet to take root to a substantial degree in tort law.[6] Some inroads have been made—often through statutory intervention—but by and large tort has resisted purposefully advancing the goals of gender, racial, and social equality. Instead, tort law continues to devalue injuries to women and other marginalized plaintiffs.

Part of tort's resistance to progressive change comes from its receptivity to another force: the "tort reform" movement. As the various schools of thought fight about the main goal of tort law, the business and corporate interests that come together under the tort reform banner are busily trying to eliminate the role of tort altogether.[7] Tort reform exerts a constant downward pressure on tort law, compacting tort and decreasing the size of the field entirely. Two main techniques accomplish this. First, the tort reform lobby aims to reduce the role of tort by simply making it more difficult or costly for plaintiffs to bring claims. To this end, tort reform has successfully lobbied for state legislation that puts caps on damages, immunizes various actors from liability, adds extra procedural hurdles to bringing lawsuits, and imposes numerous other miscellaneous measures that make it more difficult for plaintiffs to bring tort claims. Second, tort reformists have perpetuated a now widely held myth that America is an overly litigious society, awash in frivolous and nonmeritorious lawsuits that unfairly burden businesses and increase costs to society generally.[8]

These tactics have been remarkably successful, and at least thirty-three states have implemented tort reform provisions.[9] The desired drop in tort case filings is occurring:

In the early 1990s there were approximately ten tort suits for every one thousand people in the United States (which placed the country approximately fifth in the number of lawsuits filed per capita vis-à-vis comparable countries.)[10] By 2015, though, that number was down to less than two suits per thousand residents.[11] This decrease occurred not because wrongful injuries are occurring less often; instead, injured people are simply being pushed to bear the costs of the injuries that others inflict.

Impaired access to compensation and vindication works to the detriment of all who suffer injury, but it has particularly deleterious consequences for women and marginalized groups.[12] Accordingly, a feminist tort system would seek to reverse this trend and reestablish tort as a viable path to remedy for those who are wrongfully injured. Within an overall framework of promoting social justice and equality, a feminist tort law would aim to dismantle existing hierarchies of harm, center as critically important parts of tort law the injuries that women and minority plaintiffs tend to suffer, and craft a system that incorporates, reflects, and creates capacious notions of equality.[13]

This article imagines what such a feminist tort law might look like.[14] Focusing on four foundational concepts in tort law—duty, third-party liability, harm, and damages—it incorporates the insights and suggested reforms of feminist tort scholarship to map the theoretical contours of a tort law rooted in social justice and equality. First, with regard to duty, a feminist tort law would restructure the parameters of the general duty of care to encompass a more robust, relational form of duty that would offer broader accountability both in private relationships (by creating a general duty to rescue) and in relationships between individuals and the state (by curtailing the public duty doctrine).[15] Second, it would impose broader liability for third-party actors via the doctrinal paths of negligence, aiding and abetting, and vicarious liability. Third, a feminist tort law would recognize a range of sexual, reproductive, and harassment harms that are largely excluded from tort law. Finally, such a system would eliminate gender, racial, and other biases from the calculation of damage awards. Although tort law has not yet widely embraced these reforms, feminist incursions are constantly and quietly being made on these four fronts, setting in place the fault lines for the necessary change to occur.

I. Duty

Duty would look dramatically different in a feminist tort system. Currently, tort imposes a duty of care when an "actor's conduct creates a risk of physical harm."[16] Key, here, is that "conduct" means *active* conduct: The rule does not cover actors who cause harm by *failing* to act. Instead, these non-actors fall under the "no-duty-to-rescue" rule, which permits defendants to ignore other people in peril. So, as the standard law school trope goes, an Olympic swimmer who notices a small child drowning in the shallow end of a swimming pool will face no civil liability if he or she decides not to rescue the dying child.[17]

A feminist tort system would impose a duty on the Olympian.[18] Joining the chorus of utilitarian and moral critiques against the no-duty-to-rescue rule, feminist tort scholars have argued that allowing individuals to ignore other people in peril furthers a societal vision of people as fundamentally "individualistic, autonomous, and self-interested."[19] If tort were instead built on a relational conception of people as "social beings who must interact with one another," the duty to rescue would expand to require the "conscious care and concern of a responsible neighbor or social acquaintance."[20] Whereas the no-duty-to-rescue rule has stymied the growth of doctrinal developments that could be more responsive to gendered harms, this expanded notion of duty would buttress additional doctrinal reforms.

Subtle strides toward this feminist version of duty have already been made First, feminist tort scholarship has shown that the core "canonical" cases that allegedly support the no-duty-to-rescue rule plausibly support a much narrower reading.[21] Second, courts continue to expand the exceptions to the rule.[22] Third, often in response to high-profile, brutal sexual assaults, many states now have statutory duties to rescue.[23] Technically, most of these statutory duties form part of the criminal law because they attach criminal consequences (usually a small fine) to a violation. But these statutory duties interact with tort law in two important ways. Although these statutes are rarely enforced, they may help establish a broader cultural norm of rescue, which tort might ultimately come to reflect.[24] In addition, because statutory duties are one of the exceptions to the no-duty-to rescue rule, they can *themselves* form the basis for a tort duty to rescue.[25]

Retooling the duty to rescue would impact not only relations between private parties but also those between women and the state. Like private entities, the state does not currently have a general duty to rescue or protect people from harms inflicted by third parties.[26] In accordance with the "public duty doctrine," the police can egregiously fail to protect an individual from a known, obvious, and easily preventable threat and face no civil consequences. This issue frequently arises in the context of intimate partner violence: Much of the case law in this area involves women who are killed or seriously injured following pleas for police intervention and protection. One well-known example is *Riss v. City of New York*, where the public duty doctrine insulated the police after the plaintiff was burned in an acid attack arranged by her ex-boyfriend, who stalked her and from whom she had repeatedly and unsuccessfully sought police protection.[27] Similar outcomes occurred in *Barillari v. City of Milwaukee* and *Kircher v. City of Jamestown*.[28] In *Barillari*, the city was not liable when a woman was murdered by her ex-boyfriend after she relied on "concrete assurances of protection" from the police, and in *Kircher*, a police officer was not liable for the injuries the plaintiff suffered following her violent abduction from a parking lot, although the officer had assured concerned witnesses that he would take care of the matter and then took no action at all.[29]

A feminist duty of care would see liability in these public duty doctrine cases. Duty, like tort law in general, is about what we owe to each other. Part of the feminist torts project lies in revealing the inherent political power of tort in structuring the terms of our relations to each other and to the state.[30] Doctrines like no-duty-to-rescue and the public duty doctrine not only deny remedies to women and marginalized plaintiffs who are harmed by the wrongful actions of others but they also reflect, reify, and perpetuate existing gendered and social hierarchies and patterns of subordination.

II. THIRD-PARTY LIABILITY

A revised duty to rescue would shore up the second area of feminist reform: third-party liability. Often, the occurrence of a wrong is not the sole result of a single actor behaving badly; secondary actors who facilitate, encourage, or fail to prevent the wrong also contribute to it. For example, as tort suits helped show, the Catholic Church enabled the systemic sexual abuse of children by burying complaints and moving offending priests between parishes.[31] Because of the potential of third-party liability to create significant change in physical and social environments, a feminist vision of tort law would see such third-party liability doctrines as negligence, civil aiding and abetting, and vicarious liability grow to encircle a larger swath of activities.

A. Third-Party Liability in Negligence

Initially, narrow notions of duty act impeded the development of third-party liability.[32] But as tort law slowly became more comfortable with the idea of imposing liability on entities who facilitated or failed to prevent harm, third-party liability has emerged as a relatively successful way of imposing liability and achieving remedy for harms of sexual and gender violence.[33] In the early 1970s, courts saw very few claims brought by women harmed by sexual violence; by the first decade of the twentieth century that number had increased enormously, with the vast majority of that swell involving claims against third parties who facilitated or failed to prevent those harms. Duties to take reasonable care to prevent sexual assault have been imposed on landlords, corporations, cruise ships, businesses, schools, hospitals, fraternities, and other entities responsible for a physical or social environment, thereby establishing as a normative baseline that these spaces must be equally safe for women and men.[34] Further, duties to warn potentially vulnerable parties (often women) about the dangers posed by others have been imposed on psychologists, social workers, and therapists.[35] And employers and other entities can now be held responsible in negligence when their employees assault or abuse others.

Third-party negligence has provided many plaintiffs with a path to compensation and vindication, but it is not a panacea. Plaintiffs have sometimes been unable to establish that the third party owes them a duty of care. For purported policy reasons, such as the belief that civil courts are the wrong venue for a remedy or that imposing a duty would create a landslide of litigation, some courts have been unwilling to impose duties on third-party actors.[36] A feminist tort system would challenge these policy determinations and continue to harness the power of third-party liability to change physical and social environments.

B. Civil Aiding and Abetting

The liability gap in third-party negligence can sometimes be bridged by civil aiding and abetting claims.[37] Civil aiding and abetting occurs when someone knowingly substantially assists or encourages tortious conduct. Civil aiding and abetting is rooted in scienter, not duty, and thus can avoid the pitfalls of a duty analysis. For example, in *Solis v. S.V.Z.*, the court held that a supervisor owed no duty when he lied to the mother of a young teenage employee in an effort to cover up the sexual relationship between the daughter and a much older adult co-worker. Yet the court found that even in the absence of a duty, the supervisor could still be civilly liable for aiding and abetting the statutory rape.[38]

Although it often is overlooked as a basis for liability, civil aiding and abetting has significant feminist potential. Indeed, the history of the concept shows a perhaps unique doctrinal sensitivity to gender dynamics. Until the 1980s, misbehaving groups of boys constituted a major portion of the case law. The decisions read as prescient of a social dynamic that would later be explicitly recognized by masculinities studies: that because masculinities are relational, the presence of other men can sometimes have heightened influence on how men behave.[39] The homosocial bonds and group dynamics that exist between bands of men and boys encourage and facilitate risk-taking and wrongdoing, and courts have been sensitive to the particular kind of complicity and aiding and abetting that occurs within such groups.

In part because of this judicial receptivity, civil aiding and abetting could emerge as a potent means of finding civil liability when sexual assaults involve groups or audiences. Often, the third parties who serve as audience members for sexual assaults are not captured by other forms of liability (for instance, neither the men at the now infamous Massachusetts bar who watched a patron get gang raped in the 1980s, nor the approximately twenty people in Richmond, California, who observed the similar abuse of a high school student faced any legal consequences). Courts have already been willing to hold that spectating can constitute substantial assistance or encouragement for the purposes of civil aiding and abetting, suggesting that liability for this kind of participation is an area that can and should be pushed toward further feminist development.

C. Vicarious Liability

The third doctrinal avenue for increased third-party liability is vicarious liability, which reflects the common belief that business entities should pay when their employees engage in wrongdoing. This form of liability holds employers "automatically liable" for their employee's tortious acts when those acts are performed "in the course and scope of their employment."[40] In most contexts, the test for vicarious liability is applied quite broadly, but courts have been chronically reluctant to impose vicarious liability for sexual misconduct. In *Lisa M v. Henry Mayo Newhall Mem'l Hosp*, for example, the court found that a hospital was not vicariously liable when an ultrasound technician sexually abused a nineteen-year-old pregnant woman during an ultrasound.[41] Intimate contact with patients was on its face an inherent part of the employment, but the court held that the assault was driven by "propinquity and lust," thus placing it outside the course and scope of employment.

A feminist tort system would prevent such dodges and "sexual exceptionalism" by adopting a more nuanced, contextual test.[42] Following the lead of courts in Canada and the United Kingdom, this contextual test would impose vicarious liability whenever employers substantially increase the risk of tortious wrongdoing by either regularly requiring close contact with others as part of employment or by giving employees power over vulnerable persons. This test would capture scenarios like that in *Lisa M*, offering a path to vicarious liability in a wider variety of circumstances.

III. Harm

Sexual exceptionalism plagues tort law beyond the vicarious liability context. It also impacts the third major area of feminist reform: harm. Tort law's existing hierarchy of harms currently elevates property damage and physical injuries high above dignitary, relational, and emotional harm and often places harms involving sexual relationships, privacy, or reproduction outside its purview.[43] The general duty of care applies only to physical injury and property damages; there is "no general duty to protect against emotional harm or relational loss."[44] Instead, in order to recover for these kinds of harms, a plaintiff generally must squeeze into the elements of negligent infliction of emotional distress (which are notoriously narrow) or intentional infliction of emotional distress (a cause of action which by definition is limited to only the most outrageously egregious cases).[45]

A feminist vision of tort law would explode the current hierarchy and cover all forms of systemic sexualized harms. Note that initially classifying an injury as "physical" or "emotional" in the first place is not an objective process. Social framings and constructions of gender imbue the categorizations. Injuries connected to maternity and reproduction have long been legally coded as emotional rather than physical, which contorts the nature of the underlying harm and makes recovery difficult. For instance, if a doctor's negligence causes a woman to miscarry, she will often have to fit that harm into a negligent infliction of emotional distress claim, because tort law categorizes that injury as nonphysical.[46]

Feminist tort law would abolish such categorizations and prioritizations of physical harm over emotional harm. It would center both tangible and intangible harms within the same sphere and ensure that gendered harms are acknowledged. This would render such harms as intimate partner violence, harassment and discrimination, sexual privacy injuries, reproductive injuries, and acts of intimate deception legible to tort law.

This slate of harm-based reforms would provide increased redress for women and other marginalized plaintiffs, including disabled and trans plaintiffs.[47]

A. Intimate Partner Violence

The starkest example of tort's failure to address gendered harms is the jarring disconnect between the extremely high rate of intimate partner violence and the extremely low rate of tort suits related to that form of injury. Intimate partner violence is responsible for an estimated two million injuries each year, most inflicted on women, "making it a leading cause of death for women age 15–44 and a leading cause of death of pregnant women."[48] Yet in the approximately thirty-year period from 1985 to 2017—in which there would have been literally tens of millions of these injuries—a mere 163 tort claims were filed on this basis.[49]

Some statutory interventions have attempted to boost this dismal ratio. In 1994 Congress passed the Violence Against Women Act, which allowed civil suits for gender-motivated violence (including domestic violence). Though the Act was later struck down as unconstitutional, localities such as New York City and several states have created specific torts for domestic violence victims.[50] And some courts have expanded common-law claims to more explicitly include intimate partner violence.

These interventions indicate some feminist advancements in this area, but unfortunately they are unlikely to have significant impact. This is because the monumental mismatch between the prevalence of abuse, on one hand, and the lack of corresponding tort suits, on the other, is due to a number of legal obstacles unresolved by the statutory or common-law changes. Broadly, tort is often viewed as relevant mostly for accidents, not for intentional harms or harms involving "aggression or abuse of power," such as intimate violence.[51] And plaintiffs are often blocked by procedural hurdles such as miserly statutes of limitations, joinder rules that sometimes require filing claims in conjunction with a divorce action, and limits on the activities that legal service organizations can perform in relation to such suits. The most important obstacle, though, is that liability insurance currently will not cover such harms.

Liability insurance relies on two mechanisms to exclude intimate partner violence from coverage. The first is family member exclusions. A version of interspousal immunity, these exclusions prevent family members from recovering under the policy when they sue one another. Second, intentional act exclusions, rooted in the idea of moral hazard, also deny coverage. They are premised on the belief that being uninsured for these actions deters potential abusers from committing them (an obviously false assumption given the staggering number of injuries related to intimate violence that continue to occur).

Feminist tort law would close this insurance gap. Insurance exclusions are mutable, and insurance has often adapted to provide coverage for serious social problems.[52] Further, state legislatures have significant control over the products that insurers in this heavily regulated market must provide. Insurance companies can become "'remarkably creative" when they are required to be so.[53]

B. Harassment and Discrimination

Like intimate partner violence, workplace harassment is an extremely pervasive occurrence that receives little acknowledgement in tort law. Approximately 40% of working women state that they have experienced gender discrimination,[54] and approximately 40% of all workers report experiencing or witnessing incidents of racial discrimination in the workplace.[55] The Equal Employment Opportunity Commission indicates that almost 85% of the complaints of sexual harassment it receives each year involve men harassing women, and there is evidence that women of color and women in economically vulnerable positions are the most common targets.[56]

The tort system sees very few of these claims. Instead, the Equal Employment Opportunity Commission, exercising its authority to administer Title VII statutory civil rights claims, handles the vast majority of workplace harassment and bias suits. Although the Title VII statutory regime allows claimants to receive damages when employers do not respond appropriately to harassment complaints, this statutory framework offers a far more limited remedial regime than would be possible via tort law, leaving some plaintiffs without a remedy entirely.[57] Nevertheless, "special judge-made rules of preemption and heavy threshold requirements of proof... cordon off these suits from the domain of torts."[58]

A feminist tort system would reclaim these harms for tort law. Harassment could often meet the elements of intentional torts such as intentional infliction of emotional distress.[59] When courts nevertheless insist that workplace wrongs are outside of tort law, they offer an anemic vision of what torts are and can do and participate in "artificially shrinking the concept of 'outrageous' conduct and minimizing the importance of civil rights to individuals and society as a whole."[60] A feminist tort system would re-situate these often "gendered and racialized" harms squarely within the domain of tort.[61]

This system would not only embrace these harms as tortious but refine the tort of outrage to better account for them. Specifically, it would use the dual concepts of equality and dignity to inform the outrage tort. American tort law currently decouples the two, assigning civil rights to deal with equality and tort to deal with dignitary concerns. A feminist tort system would reunite equality and dignity, pushing the outrage tort past its traditional "honor-based" mode and into one that draws from dignity discourse and civil rights.[62] Once infused with dignity and equality in equal measure, the outrage tort would offer remedy for the workplace harms described by Regina Austin wherein "members of groups historically subject to multiple oppressions" experience "not isolated and sporadic rudeness" but "a pervasive phenomenon [of abusive supervision] that causes and perpetuates economic and social harm as well as emotional injury."[63] A remodeled outrage tort would remedy such a harm.

C. Sexual Autonomy and Privacy Rights

Another harm that feminist tort law would protect is sexual privacy rights.[64] With the Internet's ability to disseminate materials on a scale unimaginable thirty years ago, sexual privacy—defined as "the behaviors, expectations, and choices that manage access to and information about the human body, sex, sexuality, gender, and intimate activities"—has become increasingly important.[65] Future technologies will almost certainly continue to exacerbate the problem, the harms of which tend to fall most heavily on women, teens, and sexual and racial minorities.[66]

Although tort law does not currently provide much protection from sexual privacy violations, at one point mainstream tort law was actually poised to provide such relief. In the very first privacy case, *De May v. Roberts*,[67] a doctor attending a plaintiff who was giving birth brought a friend to watch, without disclosing that the friend was not a medical professional.[68] The court found that the doctor and his voyeur friend had violated the plaintiff's right to privacy because she was entitled to decide who could witness her "exposed laboring body."[69]

In fact, the majority of the early privacy plaintiffs were women, who often used privacy tort law to object to unwelcome "optical violation of their exposed bodies."[70] Although their claims were rooted in notions of bodily autonomy and self-determination, courts tended to reframe them into claims of female modesty. Courts were highly amenable to these privacy claims, and an alternate world in which privacy torts could have developed to rigorously protect intimate information and activities is apparent in these early historical moments.[71]

Privacy ended up evolving into the four limited and narrowly defined privacy torts that currently dominate tort law,[72] but feminist tort law would reinvigorate this early strand of privacy torts and flexibly respond to the privacy harms perpetrated in the modern technological era. Incorporating a more capacious notion of duty, feminist tort law would see "courts impose a duty of due care to protect against emotional distress in cases that implicate a plaintiff's interest in sexual integrity."[73] As part and parcel of this, it would offer remedy when private images are made public as in the increasingly widespread practice of revenge porn or when such intimate information as a person's private sexual proclivities or transgender status is wrongfully publicized.[74] Some advances are being made in this area—feminist advocacy has prompted a handful of states to adopt a model Civil Remedies for Unauthorized Disclosure of Intimate Images Act, for instance—and a feminist tort law would continue to expand this movement.[75]

D. Reproductive Harm

As the example of miscarriage described earlier suggests,[76] tort law currently offers little to no redress for reproductive injuries. Because of women's "biological and socially-assigned role in bearing and caring for children," this lack of redress has significant gendered impacts.[77] Regardless of whether wrongful acts thwart, preclude, or force procreation, tort law offers claimants only scant relief when there is no tangible physical injury.[78] Whereas courts accept that specialists are to blame for negligent acts such as botching vasectomies or mis-implanting embryos, they often categorize those injuries as merely emotional or relational, placing them generally outside the scope of recovery.[79]

Under a feminist tort system, these harms would warrant recompense. Feminist tort law would provide a path to full compensation for reproductive injuries relating to pregnancy, childbirth, and fertility and offer recognition to relational losses causing damage to or destruction of intimate family relationships.[80] Borrowing from constitutional law's long tradition of offering robust protection for procreation and familial relationships, feminist tort law would assign the same duty of care to reproduction and family relationships as applies to physical harm.

E. Intimate Deception

Sometimes, reproductive harm occurs by means of deception, as when a woman's male partner pokes holes in a condom or swaps out birth control pills for a placebo.[81] In keeping with the overall approach to sexually related harms, courts have been generally hostile to recovery for these kinds of claims as well. Similar to sexual exceptionalism, tort law currently draws a sharp distinction between deception that occurs in an intimate or familial context and deception that occurs in the commercial context: Acts that would clearly constitute fraud or other torts in a commercial context are not recognized as such when they occur in the intimate one,[82] for example, a wife whose husband "secretly sold the family business," a husband whose wife "surreptitiously siphoned money from the marital coffers to fund her affairs," and three sons who lost their share in a family home after their father lied to them about the paperwork they were signing were all denied recovery by the courts.[83]

Feminist tort law would require that courts approach cases of deception similarly, regardless of whether the deception occurs between people who are family members or intimates. Instead of marginalizing a harm most often associated with women, courts could apply a "rebuttable presumption" that plaintiffs alleging deception involving intimates can avail themselves of the same causes of action as those alleging non-intimate deception.[84] So, if fraud or misrepresentation would be available if the defendant were a stranger, the same legal tests should apply to a plaintiff suing an intimate for causing a similar harm. Erasing the exceptionalism usually applied to cases involving intimates would further goals of compensation and deterrence and promote unbiased recognition of harm.[85]

IV. Damages

Finally, a feminist vision of tort law would reconfigure non-economic and economic damages to reflect principles of equality. Feminist tort law would undo the damage caps that many states have statutorily set on non-economic damages as a result of tort reform and eliminate the use of gender- and race-specific tables when calculating economic damages.

Caps on non-economic damages, which are in place in approximately thirty states,[86] have the most significant impact on "persons whose injuries defy monetization and who are unable to prove the value of their loss in market-based terms," a category that includes women, the elderly, and trans and minority plaintiffs.[87] A recent Ohio case, *Simpkins v. Grace Brethren Church of Delaware*, illustrates the impact of non-economic damage caps on particularly vulnerable plaintiffs.[88] After a young female plaintiff successfully proved that she was raped by her pastor when she was fifteen and that the church knew that the pastor had been accused of rape two times before the incident occurred, the jury awarded her $3.5 million in non-economic pain and suffering damages. The damage cap, however, reduced that award to $250,000. Despite two furious dissenting opinions, one of which specifically assailed tort reform for "ensur[ing] that rapists and those who enable them will not have to pay the full measure of damages they cause—even if they rape a child," the Ohio Supreme Court affirmed the cap.

When non-economic caps such as this are in place, they make it less likely that plaintiffs will be able to bring a case forward in the first place. Without the possibility that the cases will bring in enough to cover a contingency fee, attorneys simply will not pursue them.[89] For cases that do make it through, non-economic caps undercompensate women and other marginalized plaintiffs and "blunt the more egalitarian effects of jury awards at a moment in history when juries represent the most diverse site of decision making in the torts system."[90] A feminist tort system would eliminate these caps and allow plaintiffs to recover the amount that would make them whole.

A feminist tort system would also eliminate the use of gender- and race-specific tables when calculating economic damages. Currently, when considering what a plaintiff would have earned in the future had he or she not been injured, courts rely on actuarial tables that calculate the plaintiff's anticipated wages, life expectancy, and how many years of that life expectancy would have been working years.[91] These tables are race- and gender-specific and use a statistical measure of the "past working experience of all people in a plaintiff's gender and racial group."[92] Given the realities of structural discrimination and racism, these statistics reflect such past inequities as women exiting paid employment and providing unpaid childcare and men of color facing incarceration and unemployment at disproportionate rates. The net result is that the tables assign a thirty-year-old white man a work-life expectancy of almost five years more than a thirty-year-old man of color and approximately nine years more than a woman of any race.

Feminist scholarship has rallied against these damage tables, charging that they are biased and likely unconstitutional.[93] The tables are based on the premise that the inequities of the past will continue into the future. Reliance on them turns that premise into reality. The tables foreground race and gender, while backgrounding numerous other factors such as marital status and religion that also are known to impact future earning power. They also skew incentives. By making it cheaper for a defendant to harm minority plaintiffs, these tables indirectly "create[] public and private incentives to allocate risk disproportionately to racial minority communities so as to minimize future liability."[94]

Driven by feminist scholarship, a number of courtrooms, compensation funds, and legislatures have begun banning or refusing to use these tables.[95] Judge Jack Weinstein on the court of the Eastern District of New York has been particularly receptive to the criticism of these tables. Citing the feminist scholar Martha Chamallas, in *McMillan v. City of New York* Judge Weinstein denied the defendant's invitation to use racially based tables to determine the damage award for a Black male who suffered a catastrophic injury in a negligent ferry crash, rendering him a quadriplegic.[96] Judge Weinstein reiterated this position in a later case, *G.M.M. v. Kimpson*, when he declined to use race-based tables which suggested that a three-year-old Hispanic child poisoned by the lead paint in his apartment would not have achieved a significant level of higher education and its associated earnings without the injury.[97] Instead, applying a contextual and more individualized analysis, Weinstein reasoned that the plaintiff child had a "high probability of superior educational attainment" and was entitled to recover an award keyed to the earnings of persons with post-college degrees.

Compensation funds, too, have been influenced by feminist criticism of these tables. After receiving numerous complaints from advocacy groups like the National Organization of Women that the tables being proposed for administering the September 11th Victim Compensation Fund to victims of the Twin Towers terrorist attack in New York City reflected gender bias, fund administrator Kenneth Feinberg applied the same expectancy table to all recipients.[98]

Finally, California recently implemented a statutory solution. Noting that the tables skew incentives and "perpetuate[] systemic inequity," the legislature in early 2019 passed a bill prohibiting "the estimation, measure, or calculation of past, present, or future damages for lost earnings or impaired earning capacity resulting from personal injury or wrongful death from being reduced based on race, ethnicity, or gender."[99] A similar federal bill has been proposed, but as of this writing, its fate remains uncertain.[100] A feminist tort law would see this trend toward eliminating the use of these tables continue and would require egalitarian calculation of compensation when awarding damages.

V. Conclusion

Feminist advances in the areas of damages, third-party liability, emotional and relational harm, and duty have not yet achieved the broad scale necessary to fundamentally transform tort law. But they are, at least, a beginning. Perhaps reinforced by rising social movements,[101] the headways and paths that feminism has already forged in tort law may grow and deepen. If legislatures begin to respond to feminist concerns, judges explicitly incorporate feminist analysis into their decisions,[102] and scholars continue to push for feminist reform, tort law may move toward a new version of itself, aimed toward social justice and equality, and offering recompense and remedy to all who are wrongfully injured.

Notes

1. William L. Prosser, Handbook of the Law of Torts § 3 (3d ed. 1964), also discussed in Michael L. Rustad & Thomas H. Koenig, *Taming the Tort Monster: The American Civil Justice System as a Battleground of Social Theory*, 68 Brook. L. Rev. 1, 8 (2002).
2. John C.P. Goldberg, *Twentieth Century Tort Theory*, 91 Geo. L.J. 513 at 11, 42 (2002).
3. *Id.*
4. John Fabian Witt & Karen M. Tani, Torts: Cases, Principles, and Institutions 3 (2019).
5. Feminism and other forms of critical legal scholarship, including the new law and political economy movement, are mainly sidelined on the fringe. *See* Martha Chamallas & Jennifer B. Wriggins, The Measure of Injury: Race, Gender, and Tort Law 29 (2010).
6. *See* Katharine K. Baker & Michelle Oberman, "Consent, Rape and Criminal Law," chapter 23 in this volume, and Leigh Goodmark, "The Anti-Rape and Battered Women's Movements of the 1970s and 80s," chapter 13 in this volume.
7. Stephen D. Sugarman, *United States Tort Reform War*, 25 U. New South Wales L. J. 51, 51 (2002).
8. David M. Engel, The Myth of the Litigious Society: Why We Don't Sue 1 (2016).
9. Doug Bennett, What to Know About Tort Reform in the U.S., Merritt Hawkins (Jan. 17, 2018).
10. *Risk Management: The Most Litigious Countries in the World*, Clements, https://perma.cc/E87N-ESR2.
11. Joe Palazzolo, *We Won't See You in Court: The Era of Tort Lawsuits Is Waning*, Wall St. J. (Jul. 24, 2017, 5:09 PM), https://www.wsj.com/articles/we-wont-see-you-in-court-the-era-of-tort-lawsuits-is-waning-1500930572.
12. *See* Lucinda M. Finley, *The Hidden Victims of Tort Reform: Women, Children, and the Elderly*, 53 Emory L. Rev. 1263, 1265 (2004) and Emily Gottlieb et al., Ctr. for Just. & Democracy, *Tort Reform and Racial Prejudice: A Troublesome Connection* (2004), https://centerjd.org/system/files/race/pdf.
13. Chamallas & Wriggins, Measure of Injury, *supra* note 5, at 6.
14. The Feminist Judgments Project was motivated by a similar question: "How would U.S. Supreme Court opinions change if the justices used feminist methods and perspectives when deciding cases?" Feminist Judgments: Rewritten Torts Opinions (Martha Chamallas & Lucinda M. Finley eds., 2020).
15. The public duty doctrine dictates that a government's duty is owed to the public at large, not to individuals, so individuals may not sue for breaches of that duty unless they can meet one of the exceptions to this rule. *See*, e.g., Anita R. Brown-Graham, *Local Governments and the Public Duty Doctrine After* Wood v. Guilford County, 81 N.C.L. Rev. 2291, 2292 (2003).
16. Restatement (Third) of Torts § 37. For a feminist critique of the restatement project itself, see Anita Bernstein, *Restatement (Third) of Torts: General Principles and the Prescription of Masculine Order*, 54 Vand. L. Rev. 1367 (2001).
17. Amelia J. Uelmen, *The Kindness of Strangers and the Limits of the Law: The Moral and Legal Obligations of Bystanders to a Vulnerable Person in Need of Emergency Assistance*

1 (2015) (S.J.D. diss., Georgetown University Law Center), https://repository.library.georget own.edu/bitstream/handle/10822/1060423/uelmen_amelia_j_sjd.pdf.
18. To be sure, in this and other reforms, not all feminist tort scholars agree. Anita Bernstein, for example, supports a no-duty-to-rescue rule and believes that its retention can further other feminist goals. *See* ANITA BERNSTEIN, THE COMMON LAW INSIDE THE FEMALE BODY (2018).
19. Leslie Bender, *An Overview of Feminist Torts Scholarship*, 78 CORNELL L. REV. 575, 580 (1993).
20. *Id.*
21. *See* Uelmen, *Kindness of Strangers*, *supra* note 17, at 18–44, suggesting that Prosser used "sleight of hand" to create a "distortion" in the law that is unmoored from the actual reasoning and holdings in these canonical cases. *See also* Peter F. Lake, *Bad Boys, Bad Men, and Bad Case Law: Re-Examining the Historical Foundations of No-Duty-to-Rescue Rules*, 43 N.Y.L. SCH. REV. 385 (1999).
22. RESTATEMENT (THIRD) OF TORTS, § 37, stating in the accompanying notes that courts can expand affirmative duties "just as courts may decide, for reasons of policy or principle, that additional no-duty rules should be recognized."
23. These duties are sometimes limited to the context of sexual assault or other violent crimes. For a list of states imposing statutory duties to rescue and/or report, see Zachary D. Kaufman, *Protectors of Predators or Prey: Bystanders and Upstanders Amid Sexual Crimes*, 92 SO. CAL. L. REV. 1317 (2019).
24. *See* Christine Carmody Tilley, *Tort Law Inside Out*, 126 YALE L.J. 1321 (2017) for a discussion of how tort law floats with community standards.
25. The RESTATEMENT (THIRD) OF TORTS § 38 notes that "[w]hen a statute requires an actor to act for the protection of another, the court may rely on the statute to decide that an affirmative duty exists and to determine the scope of the duty." Duty to *report* statutes, however, are often not a viable path to civil liability, because they "are frequently held neither to create a private right of action nor to set the standard of care in a tort case." DAN B. DOBBS, THE LAW OF TORTS § 405.
26. *See* Sarah L. Swan, *Bystander Interventions*, 2015 WIS. L. REV. 975, 1003 (2015).
27. 240 N.E.2d 860 (N.Y. 1968).
28. Barillari v. City of Milwaukee, 533 N.W.2d 759 (Wis. 1995) and Kircher v. City of Jamestown, 543 N.E.2d 443 (N.Y. 1989).
29. Barillari v. City of Milwaukee, 533 N.W.2d 759 (Wis. 1995) and Kircher v. City of Jamestown, 543 N.E.2d 443 (N.Y. 1989).
30. *See* Leslie Bender, *Tort Law's Role as a Tool for Social Justice Struggle*, 37 WASHBURN L.J. 249 (1998).
31. Martha Chamallas, *Vicarious Liability in Torts: The Sex Exception*, 48 VAL. U. L. REV. 133 (2013).
32. Yifat Bitton, *Transformative Feminist Approach to Tort Law: Exposing, Changing, Expanding—The Israeli Case*, 25 HASTINGS WOMEN'S L.J. 221, 247 (2014), noting that "it was through [duty] that common law courts objected to the expansion of tort liability to include peripheral tortfeasors."
33. Ellen M. Bublick, *Tort Suits Filed by Rape and Sexual Assault Victims in Civil Courts: Lessons for Courts, Classrooms and Constituencies*, 59 SMU L. Rev. 55 (2006).
34. Martha Chamallas, *Gaining Some Perspective in Tort Law: A New Take on Third-Party Criminal Attack Cases*, 14 LEWIS & CLARK L. REV. 1351 (2010).

35. *See, e.g.*, Tarasoff v. Regents of the University of California, 17 Cal. 3d 425 (1976), and Sharmila Lodhia & Stephanie M. Wildman, *Tarasoff v. Regents of the University of California*, in FEMINIST JUDGMENTS: REWRITTEN TORT OPINIONS (Martha Chamallas & Lucinda M. Finley eds., 2020).
36. Sarah L. Swan, *Aiding and Abetting Matters*, 12 J. TORT L. 255 (2019).
37. *Id.*
38. 566 S.W.3d 82 (Tex. App. 2018). However, the court went on to hold that Texas did not actually recognize civil aiding and abetting as a general font of liability, so this particular supervisor was not ultimately held liable.
39. *See* Ann McGinley, "Masculinities Theory as Impetus for Change in Feminism and Law," chapter 10, this volume.
40. Chamallas, *Vicarious Liability*, *supra* note 31, at 1360.
41. 907 P.2d 358, 359, 367 (Cal. 1995).
42. Chamallas, *Vicarious Liability*, *supra* note 31, at 137.
43. *Id.* Initially, the proffered justification for this hierarchy was "the greater seriousness and importance" of physical injury and the ease of faking emotional injury. Neither justification withstood scrutiny as it became more widely recognized that the social determinants of health and "the state of a person's emotional and relational life" are as significant as physical injury and emotional injuries became more verifiable through neuroscience. *See* Erica Goldberg, *Emotional Duties*, 47 CONN. L. REV. 809, 813–14 (2015). The modern justification is "pragmatic concerns about imposing disproportionate liability of [on] defendants and providing a clear stopping point for liability." CHAMALLAS & WRIGGINS, MEASURE OF INJURY, *supra* note 5, at 91.
44. CHAMALLAS & WRIGGINS, MEASURE OF INJURY, *supra* note 5, at 89: "Although also intangible, relational injury is distinct from emotional injury; it is centered on the damage or destruction done to important human relationships. For example, relational claims for wrongful death and loss of consortium compensate for the severing of ties between spouses or for the severe impairment of the parent/child relationship."
45. Martha Chamallas, *Feminist Legal Theory and Tort Law*, in RESEARCH HANDBOOK ON FEMINIST JURISPRUDENCE 386 (Robin West & Cynthia Grant Bowman eds., 2018).
46. Martha Chamallas & Linda K. Kerber, *Women, Mothers, and the Law of Fright: A History*, 88 MICH. L. REV. 814, 814 (1990).
47. *See* Courtney Sirwatka, *Unlikely Partners: Tort Law as a Tool for Trans Activism*, 20 CARDOZO J. OF L. & GENDER 111, 134–35 (2020), noting that issues of "sexual exploitation or the ability of women to control their own sexuality [. . .] also plague the trans community" and that "[t]rans people experience sexual violence at a much higher percentage than cisgender individuals. If sexual autonomy and integrity become special interests that trigger a duty of care in negligence law, it will be much easier to recover in these situations."
48. Martha Chamallas, *Will Tort Law Have Its #MeToo Moment?*, 11 J. TORT L. 39, 46 (2018).
49. *Id.*, citing Camille Carey, *infra* note 50.
50. Camille Carey, *Domestic Violence Torts: Righting a Civil Wrong*, 62 KANSAS L. REV. 695, 709 (2014).
51. Chamallas, *Will Tort Law Have Its #MeToo Moment?*, *supra* note 48, at 49.
52. *Id.* For example, Chubb now offers insurance coverage for parents whose children are victims of or perpetuate cyberbullying. *See* Chubb.com/us-en-individuals-families/products/cyber/cyberbullying.aspx.

53. CHAMALLAS & WRIGGINS, MEASURE OF INJURY, *supra* note 5, at 72, quoting KENNETH S. ABRAHAM, THE LIABILITY CENTURY: INSURANCE AND TORT LAW FROM THE PROGRESSIVE ERA TO 9/11 186 (2008). For the proposal that automobile insurance could cover domestic violence, see Jennifer Wriggins, *Domestic Violence Torts*, 75 S. CAL. L. REV. 121 (2001).
54. Kim Parker & Cary Funk, *Gender Discrimination Comes in Many Forms for Today's Working Women*, PEW RESEARCH CTR. (Dec. 14, 2017), https://www.pewresearch.org/fact-tank/2017/12/14/gender-discrimination-comes-in-many-forms-for-todays-working-women/.
55. Allana Akhtar, *42% of US Employees Have Experienced or Seen Racism at Work*, BUS. INSIDER (Feb. 10, 2020, 9:37 AM), https://www.businessinsider.com/glassdoor-42-of-us-employees-have-witnessed-or-experienced-racism-2019-10.
56. Minority men are also popular targets of harassment. *Id.*
57. Jarod S. Gonzalez, *State Antidiscrimination Statutes and Implied Preemption of Common Law Torts: Valuing the Common Law*, 59 S.C.L. REV. 115, 116 (2007).
58. CHAMALLAS & WRIGGINS, MEASURE OF INJURY, *supra* note 5, at 3.
59. "In a recent study of successful sexual harassment cases from 1982 to 2004 in which plaintiffs won damages, Catherine Sharkey found that fewer than half the cases (98 out of 232) contained a state tort claim. Even when tort claims are asserted, moreover, they are often treated as secondary by courts and litigators, as evidenced by the term 'collateral tort,' commonly used to refer to intentional infliction claims alleged in the employment context." *Id.* at 67.
60. *Id.*
61. *Id.* at 6. *See also* Richard Delgado, *Words That Wound: A Tort Action for Racial Insults, Epithets, and Name-Calling*, 17 HARV. C.R.-C.L. L. REV. 133 (1982).
62. Martha Chamallas, *Discrimination and Outrage: The Migration from Civil Rights to Tort Law*, 48 WM. & MARY L. REV. 2115 (2017).
63. Regina Austin, *Employer Abuse, Worker Resistance, and the Tort of Intentional Infliction of Emotional Distress*, 41 STAN. L. REV. 1, 4 (1988).
64. These rights are particularly important to individuals with disabilities. *See* Sagit Mor & Rina B. Pikkel, *Disability, Rights, and the Construction of Sexuality in Tort Claims*, 53 LAW & SOC'Y REV. 1016 (2019).
65. This section on sexual autonomy and privacy rights draws heavily from Danielle Keats Citron, *Sexual Privacy*, 128 YALE L. J. 1870 (2019).
66. For an exploration of the impact of sexual privacy harms on LBGT plaintiffs, *see* Anita Allen, *Privacy Torts: Unreliable Remedies for LGBT Plaintiffs*, 98 CALIF. L. REV. 1711 (2010).
67. 9 N.W. 146 (1881).
68. 46 Mich. 160 (1881). *See also* Alberto Bernabe, *Giving Credit Where Credit Is Due: A Comment on the Theoretical Foundation and Historical Origin of the Tort Remedy for Invasion of Privacy*, 29 J. MARSHALL J. COMPUTER & INFO L. 493, 506–7 (2012).
69. Citron, *Sexual Privacy*, *supra* note 65.
70. *Id.*, noting the work of the historian Jessica Lake.
71. *Id.*
72. William L. Prosser identified four distinct privacy torts in his article *Privacy*, 48 CALIF. L. REV. 383 (1960), a structure that still governs contemporary privacy tort law.
73. Martha Chamallas, *Critical Torts Theory and the Measure of Injury*, NYU PRESS BLOG (Oct. 19, 2009), https://www.fromthesquare.org/critical-torts-theory-and-the-measure-of-injury/. For a more cautionary view, *see* JANET HALLEY, SPLIT DECISIONS: HOW AND WHY TO TAKE A BREAK FROM FEMINISM 348 (2006).

74. Citron, *Sexual Privacy, supra* note 65.
75. Currently, three states (South Dakota, Nebraska, and Colorado) have adopted the model Civil Remedies for Unauthorized Disclosure of Intimate Images Act from the Uniform Law Commission. https://www.uniformlaws.org/viewdocument/final-act-no-comments-99?CommunityKey=668f6afa-f7b5-444b-9f0a-6873fb617ebb&tab=librarydocuments.
76. *See* Chamallas & Kerber, *Women, Mothers, and the Law of Fright, supra* note 46.
77. *Id. See also* Carol Sanger, *The Lop-sided Harms of Reproductive Negligence*, 117 COLUM. L. REV. ONLINE 1 (2017).
78. Dov Fox, *Reproductive Negligence*, 117 COLUM. L. REV. 149, 149 (2017).
79. *Id.*
80. Chamallas, *Critical Torts Theory, supra* note 73. *See also* Jamie R. Abrams, *Distorted and Diminished Tort Claims for Women*, 34 CARDOZO L. REV. 1955 (2013).
81. *See* JILL ELAINE HASDAY, INTIMATE LIES AND THE LAW 12 (2019).
82. Deanna Pollard Sacks, *Intentional Sex Torts*, 77 FORDHAM L. REV. 1051 (2008); Jane Larson, *Women Understand So Little, They Call My Good Nature Deceit: A Feminist Rethinking of Seduction*, 93 COLUM. L. REV. 374 (1993).
83. HASDAY, INTIMATE LIES AND THE LAW, *supra* note 81, at 1, citing Whelan v. Whelan, 56 Va. Cir. 362, 362–65 (2001), Smith v. Smith, 438 S.E.2d 457, 458–60 (N.C. Ct. App. 1994), and Collins v. Huculak, 783 N.E.2d 834, 836–41 (Mass. App. Ct. 2003), respectively. Hasday notes that "[p]opular culture routinely assumes that men are more likely to deceive their intimates and women are more likely to be deceived. . . . This conventional wisdom notwithstanding, the available evidence cannot establish whether women are more likely to be deceived within intimacy and men are more likely to deceive." *Id.* at 3.
84. *Id.* at 22.
85. *Id.*
86. Bennett, *What to Know About Tort Reform, supra* note 9.
87. CHAMALLAS & WRIGGINS, MEASURE OF INJURY, at 5. *See also* Finley, *Hidden Victims of Tort Reform*, and Thomas Koenig & Michael Rustad, *His and Her Tort Reform: Gender Injustice in Disguise*, 70 WASH. L. REV. 1 (1995).
88. Simpkins v. Grace Brethren Church of Delaware, 149 Ohio St. 3d 307 (2016). *See also* Shaakirrah Sanders, *Simkins v. Grace Brethren Church of Delaware Rewritten*, in FEMINIST JUDGMENTS: REWRITTEN TORT OPINIONS (Martha Chamallas & Lucinda M. Finley eds., 2020).
89. CHAMALLAS & WRIGGINS, MEASURE OF INJURY, *supra* note 5, at 70.
90. *Id.* at 6.
91. Kimberley A. Yuracko & Ronen Avraham, *Valuing Black Lives: A Constitutional Challenge to the Use of Race-Based Tables in Calculating Tort Damages*, 106 CALIF. L. REV. 325, 327 (2018).
92. Martha Chamallas, *The Architecture of Bias: Deep Structures in Tort Law*, 146 U. PA. L. REV. 463, 481 (1998).
93. Yuracko & Avraham, *Valuing Black Lives, supra* note 91, at 369. *See also* Martha Chamallas, *Civil Rights in Ordinary Tort Cases: Race, Gender, and the Calculation of Economic Loss*, 38 LOY. L. A. L. REV. 1435 (2005).
94. Yuracko & Avraham, *Valuing Black Lives, supra* note 91, at 334.
95. The impact has also been felt abroad: The Israeli Supreme Court has also rejected the use of biased tables. *See* CHAMALLAS & WRIGGINS, MEASURE OF INJURY, *supra* note 5, at 162–63.

96. 253 F.R.D. 247, 256 (E.D.N.Y.).
97. 116 F.Supp. 3d 126 (2015). *See also* Jennifer Wriggins, *G.M.M. v. Kimpson Rewritten*, in FEMINIST JUDGMENTS: REWRITTEN TORT OPINIONS (Martha Chamallas & Lucinda M. Finley eds., 2020).
98. Chamallas, *Architecture of Bias, supra* note 92, at 1444–45.
99. *See* Jesse Schwab, *The Problem with Defining Tort Damages in Terms of Race and Gender*, HARV. CIVIL RIGHTS–CIVIL LIBERTIES LAW REVIEW BLOG (Nov. 25, 2019). Notably, the bill passed with a vote of 78–0. Nora Freeman Engstrom & Robert L. Rabin, *California Bars the Calculation of Tort Damages Based on Race, Gender and Ethnicity*, THE RECORDER (Nov. 13, 2019, 4:40 PM), https://www.law.com/therecorder/2019/11/12/calif-bars-the-calculation-of-tort-damages-based-on-race-gender-and-ethnicity/.
100. The Fair Calculations in Civil Damages Act would prohibit federal courts from using calculations of projected future earning potential that relied on "race, ethnicity, gender, religion, or actual or perceived sexual orientation" when awarding damages. The bill was referred out to the Committee on the Judiciary on September 19, 2019.
101. For example, in 2020 the Black Lives Matter social movement achieved significant size and efficacy. *See* Larry Buchanan et al., *Black Lives Matter May Be the Largest Movement in U.S. History*, N.Y. TIMES (July 3, 2020), https://www.nytimes.com/interactive/2020/07/03/us/george-floyd-protests-crowd-size.htmls.
102. As with the old adage that justice must not only be done, it must be seen to be done, a feminist tort law would see judges make explicit the feminist analysis and insight undergirding their opinions. *See* Bitton, *Transformative Feminist Approach to Tort Law, supra* note 32, (arguing that courts must engage in "open recognition" of feminist contributions), and CHAMALLAS & WRIGGINS, MEASURE OF INJURY, *supra* note 5 (arguing that "the gender and racial contexts of tort cases [should] be made more visible").

Index

Note: Endnote content is indicated by the page number followed by "n" and the note number(s).

A

Abbey, Ruth, 21
Abele v. Markle, 445, 447–48, 449
Aberrations in Black (Ferguson), 155
abolitionist movement
   parallels with women's rights, 21–22
   on universal suffrage, 7
abortion
   ALI model abortion reform law, 277, 278
   conceptions of motherhood and, 463–64, 469
   Medicaid funding of, 279–80, 450
   NOW on abortion rights, 278, 289
   oppositional rhetoric, 318
   partial birth abortion ban, 285–86
   privacy rights, 278–80
   trait-selection laws, 453–54
   use of identity terminology, 98
   U.S. Supreme Court on, 278–79, 280, 282, 283, 284, 286–87
   women of color, 282, 284, 285, 289–90
abortion rights, as matter of women's equality, 276–93. *See also* reproductive rights and justice, constitutionalizing of
   Affordable Care Act and, 287–90
   from criminal law to reproductive rights, 277–79
   early calls for reproductive justice, 279–81
   future trends, 290–91
   reproductive rights groups during 1980s, 281–84
   women's health and reproductive justice during 1990s, 284–87
Abramowicz v. Lefkowitz, 445, 446–47, 449, 452
Abrams, Kathryn, 340–41

Abramson, Jill, 326
abstinence programs, 101–2
abuse/neglect of children, 468
Accused, The (film), 408
acquaintance rape, 410–11
Acting Gay, Acting Straight (Boso), 180
Acton, North Carolina landfill protests, 579–80
ActUp, 154
Adams, David, 382
Adams, John, 21
Adarand Constructors v. Peña, 212
Addimando, Nicole, 377–78
Adenike, Oladosu, 584
Adkins v. Children's Hospital, 13, 206
Adler, Libby, 196–97, 539
adoption of children, 464, 466–68
affirmative consent, 47, 55n91
affirmative consent standard, 409, 410. *See also* consent, rape, and criminal law
Affordable Care Act (ACA) (2010), 435, 436
   abortion, justice and, 287–90
   contraceptive mandate, 452
African American Policy Forum (AAPF), 87–88
African Americans. *See also* Black men; Black women; race and racism
   welfare policies and, 538
Against Bipolar Black Masculinity (Cooper), 175–76
Against Our Will (Brownmiller), 151, 223, 225
agriculture and domestic work, lack of labor protections for, 594–96, 604
AIDS crisis
   carceral anti-trafficking feminist impact on, 194–95
   queer theory and, 154–55

Ailes, Roger, 326, 343
Ain't I A Woman speech (Truth), 80, 90n34
Alexa, female voice of, 561, 623
Alexander, Marissa, 233, 238n146
Alexander, Michelle, 412
algorithmic systems, 560–62, 620–23
Ali, Russlyn, 242
Allard, Sharon Angella, 375
Allen, Anita L., 539, 554, 555
   Uneasy Access, 30
Allen, Florence, 13
Allen, Lillie, 282
Alliance Against Sexual Coercion, 334
Allport, Gordon
   The Nature of Prejudice, 353
Amadae, S. M., 305
Amazon.com
   use of gender targeted hiring algorithm, 560, 561
American Association of Law School (AALS), 498
American Bar Association (ABA), 505, 518
   Section of Legal Education and Admissions to the Bar, 506–7
American Booksellers Association, Inc. v. Hudnut, 43
American Civil Liberties Union (ACLU), 13. *See also* Women's Rights Project (WRP)
   legislative toolkit on menstrual equity, 640
American Constitution Society, 298
American Council on Education, 253
American Law Institute (ALI)
   model abortion reform law, 277, 278
   Model Penal Code, 55n91, 100, 409, 419n27
Americans United for Life, 285
Americans with Disabilities Act (ADA) (1990), 322, 435
American University, Tax Policy Center
   Billion Dollar Blind Spot report, 639, 646n99
American Woman Suffrage Association (AWSA), 7
Anderson, Elizabeth S., 539
Anderson, Michelle J., 248
androgyny, 621, 623
Angel, Marina, 374
Ansari, Aziz, 47

Anthony, Susan B., 2, 114
   convicted for illegal voting, 8
   as founder of NWSA, 7
Anthropocene era, 582
anti-abortion movement. *See* abortion rights, as matter of women's equality
antidiscrimination jurisprudence, 554
   critique of intent requirement, 84
   gender stereotype theory and, 351
   law and economics on, 301
anti-domestic violence movement. *See* battered women's movement
Anti-Pornography Civil Rights Ordinance, Indiana, 43, 49n22
anti-prostitution loyalty oath (APLO), 194–95
anti-rape movement, 220–26, 232–33. *See also* rape law
   accomplishments of, 232–33
   assessment of, 226
   early organizing efforts, 221–23
   rape law reform, 223–25
anti-sexual harassment policies, 338–39
antisocial ideas of freedom. *See* law and economics, against legal feminism
antisubordination theories (Colker), 45
antisubordination theory
   Brake on defense of Title IX and, 394
Anzaldúa, Gloria
   This Bridge Called My Back, 81
Apple, Inc.
   gendered credit card limits, 560, 561
Appleton, Susan F., 464
Arbery, Ahmaud, 87
Arnow-Richman, Rachel S., 262, 542
artificial intelligence, 620–23
Asian American women
   voting rights for, 10
Asian Communities for Reproductive Justice, 287
asset mapping, 527
Association of Intercollegiate Athletics for Women (AIAW), 390
asylum, for refugees, 598–99
athletics. *See* Title IX, separate but equal in athletics
Auclert, Hubertine, 1
"Aunt Jemima" trademark, 617

Austin, Regina, 117, 655
Australia
   child care during COVID-19 pandemic, 139
   publicly supported parent leave/child care options, 432
   residential schools for Indigenous children as colonial violence, 64
autonomy. *See also* relational feminism, self, autonomy, and law
   privacy and, 30–31, 553–54, 656
autonomy feminism, principles of, 566–67
Avery, Byllye, 282

B

Baby M case, 537
background rules, in distributional analysis, 192–93, 195–96, 197
Backlash (Faludi), 269, 313–14, 317
backlash against feminism, 313–31
   backlash patterns and practices in judicial selection, 315–17
   countering with counternarratives, 325–27
   emotional register of, 320–21
   false claims against progressives, 312–23
   narratives and discourse of, 317–19
   oppression vs., 323–25
backlash violence, 320
Bahn, Kate, 141
Barillari v. City of Milwaukee, 650
Barnard College conference (1982), 96
Barrett, Amy Coney, 316, 517, 528n11
Bartlett, Katharine T., 522
Bartow, Ann, 118
battered woman syndrome (BWS). *See also* gender violence (GV) survivors
   development of theory, 371–73
   female immigrants and, 601
   self-defense doctrine and, 370
   Walker on, 231, 372–73, 375–76
battered women's movement, 226–33. *See also* gender violence (GV) survivors
   accomplishments of, 232–33
   domestic violence legislation, 228
   early organizing efforts, 227–28
   legal system reform, 228–32
battering and its effects, use of term, 381–83

BDSM (bondage and discipline, domination and submission, and sadism and masochism), 98, 100, 104, 160–61, 167n71
Becker, Mary, 356
Becoming Gentlemen (Guinier, Fine, and Balen), 503
Bell, Derrick A., Jr., 314, 317–18
   Serving Two Masters, 76–78
Ben-Asher, Noa, 155, 159
Berger, Linda L., 526
   Feminist Judgments, 525–26
Berk, Hillary L., 541
Berk, Richard A., 230
Berlant, Lauren, 150, 196
Bernstein, Anita, 306, 340, 359, 536–37
Beyond (Gay and Straight) Marriage (Polikoff), 538–39
bias, 353
   against men who take leave to do child care, 425, 436
   against pregnant employees, 425–26
Biden, Joe, 88, 246, 253
big data, and gender discrimination, 559–63
Billion Dollar Blind Spot report (American University), 639, 649n99
Bill of Rights, 443–44
biological motherhood, defined, 461. *See also* motherhood, disputed conceptions of
BIPOC (Black, indigenous, women of color). *See* Black women; Native American women; women of color
Bird, Rose, 319
birth control. *See also Griswold v. Connecticut*; reproductive rights and justice, constitutionalizing of
   under ACA, 288–89
   legalization efforts, 12
   religiously affiliated employers and, 434
   smart technology and surveillance, 563–66
   sterilization and, 279, 281
bisexuality. *See* transgender, bisexual, and nonbinary identity
Blackett, Adelle, 62
Black feminist thought, 81–82, 83
Black Feminist Thought (Collins), 81
BlackGenocide.org, 453

Black Lives Matter movement, 61, 86–87, 141, 305, 453
Black men
   Cooper's intersectional critique of representation of, 175–76
   false accusations of sex offenses against, 44, 51n41, 223, 224, 249–50
   mass incarceration of, 47, 51n41
   MMT lens on, 177–78
   voting rights, 9
Blackmun, Harry A., 449
Black Power movement, 454
Black suffrage, 7
Blackwell, Henry, 7
Black women
   anti-abortion movement targeting of, 453–54
   anti-rape movement and, 221
   athletic opportunities under Title IX, 392–93
   Crenshaw's intersectionality critique and, 32, 176
   exclusion by Fifteenth Amendment, 9
   hypersexualized stereotype, 408–9, 412
   involvement in church and club organizations, 6, 10
   as law school students, 497–98
   mistrust of law enforcement, 223
   pregnancy discrimination claims, 432
   privacy and, 554
   racialized sexual harassment of, 339
   rape myths, 223
   as slaves, 539, 611–12
   sterilization laws and, 279
   welfare queen stereotype, 433
Black Women's Health Imperative, 287
Blanchett, Cate, 103
Blank v. Sullivan & Cromwell, 519
Blasey Ford, Christine, 226, 248, 266, 267–68, 274n66, 326
Blumberg, Grace, 631–32
Board of Immigration Appeals, 598
Bond, Kathryn Stockton, 154
Boso, Luke
   Acting Gay, Acting Straight, 180
Bostock v. Clayton County, Georgia, 28, 181, 361, 362, 367n90

Bowers v. Hardwick, 156, 157
Box v. Planned Parenthood, 453–54
Boyd, Christina L., 518
boys will be boys rationale, 178
Bradley, Joseph P., 5
Bradwell v. Illinois, 3, 5
Brake, Deborah L., 316, 318, 394
Brandeis, Louis, 13, 553
Braucher, Jean, 544
breastfeeding, 469–70
Brennan, William J., 27
Bridges, Khiara, 539
Brind, Joel, 285
Brionna Taylor, 87
Brittain, Amy, 326
Britton, Dana, 317
brominated flame retardants (BFR) toxicity, 66
Brown, Cyntoia, 233, 238n148
Brown, Dorothy A., 633
Brown, Karen
   Taxing America, 632–33
Brownmiller, Susan
   Against Our Will, 151, 223, 225
Brown v. Board of Education, 321, 323
Bruckner, Caroline
   Billion Dollar Blind Spot, 639
Bruno v. Codd, 229–30
Bunch, Charlotte, 482
Burke, Tarana, 46, 260, 264
Burlington Industries, Inc. v. Ellerth, 338–39, 341
Bush, George H.W., 285
Bush, George W., 286
business owners, tax law impacts on women, 639
Butler, Judith, 97, 163
   Gender Trouble, 152–53
Buxton, Lee, 443
BWS (battered woman syndrome). *See* battered woman syndrome (BWS); gender violence (GV) survivors
bystander intervention training, 415–16

C

Cable Act (1922), 10
Cady, Daniel, 3

Cahn, Naomi, 306
Test Tube Families, 540
Cain, Patricia A., 523, 634–35
Califano v. Goldfarb, 355
Califia, Patrick, 96
California Equal Employment Opportunity Commission, 597
Cambridge Analytica scandal, 555
campus sexual harassment. *See* Title IX, movement against campus sexual harassment
Canada
  denigration of Indigenous peoples, 64
Canada's Women's Legal Education and Action Fund (LEAF), 525
capitalism
  Leong on racial capitalism, 611
  liberal feminism and family law, 467–68
  Zuboff on surveillance capitalism, 560
Carbone, June, 306
carceral anti-trafficking feminists (CAFs), 194–95
carceral feminism, 46–47, 193–94, 232
carceral state, 486
caregiver discrimination, 360
care work, 483–84
Carlson, Daniel L., 141
Carmon, Irin, 27
Carson, Rachel, 578
  Silent Spring, 575
Carvalho Pinto de Sousa Morais v. Portugal (ECHR), 101, 109n72, 109n77
Cary, Mary Ann Shadd, 6
Casa Myrna Vasquez, Massachusetts, 227
Case, Mary Anne, 316
Catch and Kill (Farrow), 326
Catholic Bishop Conference, 316
Catholic Church
  campaign against gender ideology, 316
  systemic sexual abuse of children in, 651
Celler, Emmanuel, 203, 207, 210
Center for American Progress, 287
Center for Constitutional Rights, 371–72, 446–47
Center for Individual Rights, 297
Center for Public Integrity (CPI)
  on campus sexual assault, 241–42

Center for Reproductive Rights, 290
Chamallas, Martha, 96, 320, 659
  Past as Prologue: Old and New Feminisms, 181
Chang, Bob, 179
Changingourcampus.org, 246
Charles Koch Foundation, 296, 298
Charlesworth, Hilary, 480, 481
Chicago Abused Women's Coalition, 228
child care
  bias against men who take leave for, 425, 436
  during COVID-19, 139, 489–90
  as public obligation, 431
children, born abroad to U.S. citizens, 470–71, 526
Children's Online Privacy and Protection Act (COPPA) (1998), 553
Childress, Clenard, 453
child support, 469
Chinese Exclusion Repeal Act (1943), 10
Chinkin, Christine, 481
Chisholm, Shirley, 208
Cho, Sumi
  Post-Intersectionality, 178–79
Chodorow, Nancy, 320
Choice for America campaign, 286, 287
Citadel, The, 174
Citron, Danielle K., 30–31, 557
City of Los Angeles Department of Water & Power v. Manhart, 357
civil aiding and abetting, 652
civil protection orders, 229, 370
Civil Remedies for Unauthorized Disclosure of Intimate Images Act (model state law), 656
Civil Rights Act (1866), 534
Civil Rights Act, Title VII (1964), 313, 335
  caps on damage awards, 342
  formal equality and, 431
  Guidelines on Sexual Harassment, 333, 334–35, 336–37, 343
  harassment of men not illegal under, 174
  pregnancy discrimination, 462
  race discrimination under, 333
  sex discrimination as illegal, 352, 359, 427–28
  sexual harassment as sex discrimination, 264, 332–34, 336

Civil Rights Act, Title VII (1964) (cont.)
   sexual orientation and gender identity discrimination, 181, 360–62
   state legal reforms superseding, 261
   statutory law and, 357–59
   Title IX modeled after, 389
Clarke, Jessica A., 342
Clean Air Act (1970), 575–76
Clean Water Act (1972), 576
client-centered lawyering, 504
Climate Justice (M. Robinson), 583–84
climate justice movement, 584–85
Clinton, Bill, 284, 285
clothing, gendered by color, 612–13
CLUE (app), 563–64
Coasten, Jane, 75
Coding Rights, 565
Coercion and Distribution in a Supposedly Non-Coercive State (Hale), 188–89
Coffee, Linda, 448–49
cohabitation, 534, 535–36, 540–41
Cohen, Cathy, 154, 155
Cohen, David S., 179
Cohen, Jennifer, 141
Coker v. Georgia, 224
Coleman v. Miller, 214
Colker, Ruth, 45
collaborative family law, 533
Collier, Richard, 171
Collins, Patricia Hill, 81, 520
   Black Feminist Thought, 81
Collinson, David, 170
color coding, and gender, 612–13
Combahee River Collective, 451
Committee for Abortion Rights and Against Sterilization Abuse (CARASA), 281, 450, 451
Committee to End Sterilization Abuse (CESA), 279, 451
Communications Decency Act, § 230 (1996), 558
comparator evidence, 359, 360
competitive cheer, 404n75
Congressional Women's Caucus, 204
Connell, Raewyn, 170
consent, rape, and criminal law, 406–22. *See also* rape law

definition of rape, 408, 412–14
history of rape reform movement, 407–9
proving nonconsent in court, 410–12
sexual assault awareness education and training, 414–16
workplace responses to sexual harassment, 416–17
conservatism. *See also* backlash against feminism; culture wars, in U.S.; law and economics, against legal feminism
   viewpoint on sexual harassment, 124
contraception. *See* birth control
contract, in feminist legal theory, 532–51
   feminist improvements to contract doctrines
      debtor-creditor relationships, 542–44
      defenses of duress and misrepresentation, 544–45
      employment law, 542
   as instruments of gender equality
      marriage and beyond, 535–37
      parent-child relationships, 537
      as upgrade from status, 534
   as instruments of gender subordination
      dangers of contractual parenthood, 539–40
      limited benefit of modified marriage contract, 538–39
   as instruments of transitional justice, 540–41
Convention for the Protection of Human Rights and Fundamental Freedoms (U.N.), 101
Convention on the Elimination of all forms of Discrimination Against Women (CEDAW) (U.N.), 479, 484, 488
Convention on the Political Rights of Women (U.N.), 480
Cooper, Frank Rudy
   Against Bipolar Black Masculinity, 175–76
   Masculinities and the Law, 179
   Who's the Man? 176
Copyright Act (1976), 616
copyrights, 558
   by women authors, 614, 615–17
Corrigan, Rose, 225
Cosby, Bill, 226, 318, 411

Cosmopolitan
  Stop Taxing Our Periods! Period petition against tampon tax, 640
Coston, Bethany M., 171
coverture marriage, 21, 534, 535, 600, 602, 611
COVID-19 pandemic
  child care during, 139, 489–90
  gendered impacts of, 138–42
  gender gap, 138, 139–40
  increase in GV, 374–75, 489
  international welfare schemes, 139
  legal education and, 498, 505, 508
  temporary paid leave legislation during, 436
Craig, Lynn, 141
Craig v. Boren, 27
Crawford, Bridget J., 526
  Feminist Judgments, 525–26
creative industry. *See* intellectual property law, and gender disparities
Crenshaw, Kimberlé W., 585. *See also* intersectionality, genealogy of
  as co-founder of AAPF, 87
  critiques of sexual harassment theory, 339
  Demarginalizing the Intersection of Race and Sex, 78–79
  on intersectionality of Black women, 176
  Mapping the Margins, 78, 79
  theory of intersectionality, 32
  Theory of intersectionality, 55n94
  theory of intersectionality, 75, 81, 176, 375, 555
Crick, Francis, 612
Crimp, Douglas, 154–55
critical legal studies (CLS) movement, 76–77, 187–89, 196–97. *See also* governance feminism, and distributional analysis
critical race feminism
  on genetic ideology and racist/patriarchal norms, 470
  limits on overturning of coverture rules, 600
  on privacy, 554
  race-conscious immigration policies, 594
critical race theory (CRT), 76–78. *See also* intersectionality, genealogy of
Critical Tax Conference, 637
critical tax scholarship, 630–47

development of feminist tax scholarship
  emergence of critical voice, 632–35
  expansion of feminist areas of interest, 635
  disparate impact of tax laws, 631–32
  facially discriminatory laws, 630–31
  marginalization of, 637–38
  tax law and gender discrimination, 631–32, 638–40
  worldview of conventional tax scholarship, 636–37
Cudd, Ann, 317
  Theorizing Backlash, 320
Cullers, Patrice, 86
Culp, Jerome M., Jr., 297
cult of domesticity, 351–53
cultural feminism. *See* relational feminism; relational feminism, self, autonomy, and law
culture wars, in U.S. *See also* abortion rights, as matter of women's equality
  ERA Amendment, 204, 208, 209
  federal funding of domestic violence programs, 228
  sex education, 101
Cuomo, Andrew, 640
Cyber Civil Rights Initiative (CCRI), 558–59
cyberspace. *See* Internet; privacy and law in cyberspace
Cyborg Manifesto (Haraway), 557

D

Dailey, Anne, 32
Dalton, Harlon, 77
damages, equality, and tort law, 657–59
Darby Lumber; United States v., 207
DARVO (deny, attack, reverse victim and offender), 319
Darwin, Charles
  On the Origin of Species, 574
Darwinism, 5, 11
Davies, Margarite, 69
Davis, Adrienne D., 540
Davis, Angela Y., 81, 223, 486–87
Davis v. Monroe County Board of Education, 336
D.C. Women's Bar Association, 497

Dear Colleague Letter (DCL) (OCR), 242–45, 251
death penalty, for rape, 224
de Beauvoir, Simone, 82, 577
debtor-creditor relationships, 542–44
deception, and tort law, 657
decisional privacy, 30–31, 553, 557
Declaration of Sentiments, 2–3, 12, 22, 114, 370, 630
Declaration on the Elimination of Violence Against Women (DEVAW), 484–85
de facto parenthood theory, 467
defamation lawsuits, 248
Defense of Marriage Act (DOMA) (1996), 639
degendering the law, through stereotype theory, 350–69
  breaking out of domesticity, 351–53
  building gender stereotypes in social science, 353–54
  caregiver discrimination, 360
  constitutional law and equal protection, 354–57
  development of gender stereotype theory, 350–51
  promise and limitations of advancing gender stereotype theory in law, 359–62
  sexual orientation and gender identity discrimination, 360–62
  statutory law and Title VII, 357–59
DeGraffenreid v. General Motors, 78
Delano, Maggie, 565–66
de Lauretis, Teresa, 152
Delgado, Richard, 77
Demarginalizing the Intersection of Race and Sex (Crenshaw), 78–79
De May v. Roberts, 656
deportation, of unauthorized immigrants, 602–4
DeVos, Betsy, 240, 248, 251–52, 319
dialectics, as poststructuralist analytical tool, 121–22, 123–24
difference feminism. *See* relational feminism; relational feminism, self, autonomy, and law
Digital Defense Playbook (ODB), 563
digital discrimination, 559–63

D'Ignazio, Catherine, 561
dignitary tort law, and sexual harassment, 343
diminished capacity defense, 371
Dinnerstein, Dorothy, 320
disability, defined, 435
discursive analysis, defined, 116
Disney Corporation, 621
disparate effects, 83–85
distributional analysis. *See* governance feminism, and distributional analysis
Distribution and Decision: Assessing Governance Feminism (Halley), 191
Divorced from Reality (J. Singer and Murphy), 541
divorce reform, 323
Dixon, Rosalind, 131–33, 519. *See also* gender disruption, amelioration, and transformation
domestic violence. *See also* battered women's movement; intimate partner violence (IPV)
  family-based immigration and, 600–602
  law enforcement role in, 228–30, 487–88
  legislation, 211, 228, 377–78
  refugee status and, 598–99
  unauthorized immigrants and, 603–4
  women of color, 228, 230
Domestic Violence Leave Law (Nevada), 211
Domestic Violence Survivors Justice Act (New York), 377–78
domestic work. *See also* agriculture and domestic work, lack of labor protections for
  Blackett on, 62
dominance feminism, 31
  ecofeminism and, 577
  on flawed rational neutrality of law, 502
  on gender justice, 134, 136–37
  rise of, 193–94
  on technological domination, 556–59
dominance feminism theory (MacKinnon), 39–56, 82, 95, 96, 115
  #MeToo and dominance theory, 39, 46–48
  critiques of, 43–45, 266–67
  law as remedy of choice, 41–42
  legal claims for sexual harassment and pornography, 42–43

relational feminism vs., 57, 199n44
sexual harassment and male privilege, 333–34
sexualized domination, 40–41, 52nn63–64
shift to international sphere, 45, 50n25
Donegan, Moira, 267, 268, 274n62
Douglass, Frederick, 2
Dowd, Nancy, 169, 171
  The Man Question, 172
Down Girl (Manne), 325
duress and misrepresentation defenses (Threedy), 544–45
Durst, Ilene, 526
Dutton, Mary Ann, 382
duty of care, 649–51, 656–57
  in judicial decisions, 521–24
  and tort law, 649–51
duty of good faith, 542
Dworkin, Andrea, 39
  Woman Hating, 151
Dwyer, Florence, 208

E
Eastman, Crystal, 12–13, 202
ecofeminism, 576–78
economic production-social distribution dualism, 299–301
Education Amendments Acts (1972), 240, 388. *See also* Title IX; Title IX, movement against campus sexual harassment; Title IX, separate but equal in athletics
efficiency-equality dualism, 299–301
Ehrenreich, Nancy, 539
Eichner, Maxine, 30, 117
Eisenstadt v. Baird, 278, 442, 444, 449–50, 451
Elkins v. American Showa, Inc., 272n41
Elliott Institute, 285
Ellison v. Brady, 341
Emerson, Thomas, 443–44
emotional intelligence, 521
employer liability, for sexual harassment, 338–39
employment-based immigration, 594–97
employment law, 542, 594–97
Endangered Species Act (1973), 576
End Rape on Campus, 247
Engle, Karen, 196, 491

environmental justice (EJ) movement, 580–82
environmental law and legal feminism, 573–91
  climate change intervention
    climate justice movement, 584–85
    links between gender and climate change, 582–84
  environmental and feminist intertwining
    environmental justice movement, 580–82
    Green Belt movement, 579–80
  future trends, 585–86
  interconnected ecosystems, 574–79
    early environment law, 575–76
    ecofemnism emerges, 576–78
    international laws, 578–79
Epic Systems Corp. v. Lewis, 273n50
Epistemology of the Closet, The (Sedgwick), 152–53
Epstein, Richard A., 301
Equal Employment Opportunity Commission (EEOC)
  discrimination on basis of pregnancy, 427–28, 429, 437
  Enforcement Guidelines on caregiver discrimination, 360
  failure to enforce Title VII, 24
  Guidelines on Sexual Harassment, 333, 334–35
  rate of sexual harassment cases, 346n69, 655
  on sexual orientation, 361
  training to interpret witness credibility for victims of sexual assault, 597
  on transgender status discrimination as sex discrimination, 361
equality's riddle (W. Williams), 427, 430
Equal Rights Amendment (ERA), 201–19
  congressional votes on, 202–5, 207, 210, 213
  debates over benefits of, 23, 205–10
  early drafts of, 12–13
  future of, 214–15
  organizations supportive of, 24
  state ratification of, 204–5, 209, 210–11, 212, 213
  twenty-first-century ratifications, 210–14
Equity Gag Order (Trump), 88
erotic pleasure. *See* sex-positive feminism, and law of pleasure
Ervin, Sam, 207, 210
Estrich, Susan, 225, 413

ethic of responsibility (Weber), 191
eugenics, 12, 443, 453–54, 533, 539
European Court of Human Rights (ECHR)
    on age and sex discrimination, 101, 109n72, 109n77
    Turkish ban on headscarves cases, 179
Everywoman's Shelter, California, 227
evidence-based prosecution policies, 230–31
exclusionary politics, 323–25
extradiscrimination remedies (Eyer), 342
Eyer, Katie R., 342

F
Facebook
    § 230 protection from liability, 558
    Cambridge Analytica scandal, 555
    gender targeted job ads lawsuit against, 560
    purchases data of Femtech app users, 564
facial recognition technology, 560, 561
Fair Calculations in Civil Damages Act, proposed, 665n100
Fair Debt Collection Practices Act (1977), 544
Fair Housing Act (FHA) (1968), 336
Fair Labor Standards Act (1938), 13, 352
false consciousness (Marx), 4
Faludi, Susan, 315, 324, 326
    Backlash, 269, 313–14, 317
Family and Medical Leave Act (FMLA) (1993), 114–15, 342, 429–30, 433
family-based immigration, 600–602
family formation, 431, 434, 533, 537. *See also* contract, in feminist legal theory
Family Violence Prevention and Services Act (1984), 228
Family Violence Program (LEAA), 228
Faragher v. City of Boca Raton, 338–39, 341
Farley, Lin, 332, 334, 343
    Sexual Shakedown, 333
Farrow, Ronan
    Catch and Kill, 326
Faulkner, Shannon, 174
Faulty Foundations of the Code, The (NWLC), 639–40
Fay, Daniel L., 141–42
Federalist Society, 298, 307–8
Federal Rule of Evidence 412, 408
Federal Trade Commission (FTC), 561–62, 564

Fellows, Mary Louise
    Rocking the Tax Code, 633–34
    Taxing America, 632–33
female body, in law, 116–17
female genital mutilation (FGM), 598, 599
feminism and #MeToo, 259–75. *See also* #MeToo movement
    collective counternarratives, 267–69
    feminist threads in #MeToo, 261–63
    legal reforms, 261, 264, 265
    #MeToo movement as feminist movement, 260–61
    undermining collective force via individualization, 263–67
feminist, use of term, 1
Feminist Alliance, 11
Feminist Alliance Against Rape (newsletter), 222, 232
feminist judges and judicial decisions, 515–31
    features of, 521–23
    feminist agendas for gender and judging, 527–28
    Feminist Judgments project, 525–27
    legal participatory action research, 523–25
    value of diversity on the bench, 516–21
Feminist Judgments (Stanchi, Berger, and Crawford), 525–26
Feminist Judgments project, 525–27
Feminist Manifest-No, 566–67
feminist sex radicals. *See* sex-positive feminism
Femtech, 563–66
Ferguson, Roderick, 162
    Aberrations in Black, 155, 161
Ferraro, Kathleen J., 374
fetal personhood, 280
Fetner, Tina, 318
fiancée immigrants, 600–602
Fifteenth Amendment, 6, 7, 9
Fifth Amendment, 213, 215, 443
    Due Process Clause, 206, 290–91, 488
Fineman, Martha A., 304, 462, 536, 538
firefighter stereotypes, 179
Firestone, Shulamith, 463
First Amendment, 42–43, 308, 559, 618–19
first wave feminism, history of, 113–14
Fiske, Susan, 353, 358

Flint, Michigan water crisis, 581
Floyd, George, 87
Force, Robert, 277
forced labor, 596, 604
forced marriage, 598, 599
formal equality, 542–43
formal legal equality principle (Stanton), 4–5
Foucault, Michel, 97, 163
   on governmentality, 190–91
   The History of Sexuality Volume 1, 150–51
Foundation for Individual Rights in Education (FIRE), 248
Fourteenth Amendment, 6, 45, 207, 212, 213, 215, 280, 520, 526
   Due Process Clause, 158
   Equal Protection Clause, 25–26, 95, 158–59, 280, 290–91, 355, 389–90, 434, 447
   Privileges or Immunities Clause, 7–8, 9
Fourth Amendment, 443, 553
fourth wave feminism, 555
Fowler, Susan, 262
Fox News, 320, 326, 343
Foy, Jennifer Carroll, 211
Fraiman, Susan, 307
Framework Convention on Climate Change (UNFCCC), 583
FrameWorks Institute, 415
Franke, Katherine M., 99, 157, 340, 409
   Wedlocked, 158
Franklin, Rosalind, 612
Franks, Mary Anne, 45, 557
Fraser, Nancy, 303
Freedom of Choice Act, proposed, 284
Free Joan Little campaign, 225, 233
Freeman, Alan David, 84
free-market capitalism
   liberal feminism and family law, 467–68
Free Willie Sanders movement, 223
Freyd, Jennifer, 319
Fridays for Future move-, 584
Friedan, Betty, 24, 278
Friedman, Elisabeth, 480
Frontiero v. Richardson, 26–27, 211–12
Frug, Mary Joe, 116–18
   A Postmodern Legal Feminist Manifesto, 116–17
Fuller, Margaret, 3

G

Gamergate, 557
García, Inez, 225
Garvey, Marcus, 454
Garza, Alicia, 86
gay and transgender masculinities, legal research on, 180
Gebser v. Lago Vista Independent School District, 336
gender
   discrimination based on, 360–62
   as social construct, 612–13
   as unified class, 4
Gender, Violence, Race, and Criminal Justice (A. Harris), 175
Gender and Justice (Kenney), 319, 517
gender devaluation (Chamallas), 320
gender differences principle (Stanton), 5–6, 9
gender disruption, amelioration, and transformation, 131–49
   ameliorative and transformative approach to gender justice, 136–37
   disruptive approach to gender justice, 135–36
   feminist theoretical disagreement, 133–35
   framework in practice during COVID-19, 138–42
gender fluidity, 118
gender gap
   among female athletes, 395
   during COVID-19 pandemic, 138, 139–40
   parental leave and, 430
gender harassment, 337
gender neutrality (MacKinnon), 48n5
Gender Outlaws (Vojdik), 174
gender performativity (Butler), 97
gender policing, 621
gender stereotype theory. *See* degendering the law, through stereotype theory
Gender Trouble (Butler), 152–53
gender violence. *See also* international feminism, and gendered violence in U.S.
   defined, 384n1
   A. Harris on, 65
   immigration policies and, 380
   law enforcement officers as perpetrators of, 48, 65

gender violence (*cont.*)
   LGBTQ+ and, 380–81
   Native American women and, 380
   sex work and, 381
   technology and, 556–59
gender violence (GV) survivors, 370–87
   development of BWS theory, 371–73
   feminist critique of BWS, 370–71, 373–75
   feminist support for battering and its effects, 381–83
   future trends, 383–84
   influence of BWS and its critique on law, 376–79
   survival crime and survivor justice, 379–84
genealogy, as poststructuralist analytical tool, 122–23, 125
genetic parenthood, 464–65
geofencing technology, 557, 565
George Mason University, Antonin Scalia Law School, 296
Gerzog, Wendy C.
   The Marital Deduction QTIP Provisions, 634
Ghosh, Cyril, 159
Gillett, Emma, 497
Gilligan, Carol, 114, 504, 521
   In a Different Voice, 57–58, 521
Gilman, Charlotte Perkins
   Women and Economics, 11
Ginsburg, Martin D., 25, 631
Ginsburg, Ruth Bader
   death of, 181
   equality theory and, 14
   on ERA, 210, 212
   as head of ACLU Women's Rights Project, 24–29, 114, 354–55, 360, 362, 448, 631
   on rape law, 224
   recognition of Murray and Kenyon, 215, 218n82
   on *Roe v. Wade*, 322
   on sex classifications, 212
   on *VMI* case, 356–57
Glow (app), 565–66
G.M.M. v. Kimpson, 659
Golder, Ben, 118
Goldman Sachs, 266
Goldmark, Josephine, 13
Goldscheid, Julie, 490–91

Gonzales, Jessica. *See* Lenahan, Jessica
Gonzales v. Carhart, 286–87
Goodall, Jane, 586
good faith, duty of, 542
Goodmark, Leigh, 196
Goodridge v. Department of Public Health, 635
Google
   § 230 protection from liability, 558
   as purchaser of Femtech app user data, 564
Gorsuch, Neil, 28
governance feminism (Halley), 190–96
governance feminism, and distributional analysis
   application in sex work case, 193–96
   distribution beyond sex work, 196–97
   emergence of distributional analysis, 188–90
   feminism and distributional analysis, 190–93
Grady, Constance, 555
Graham, Lindsey, 268
Graham, Nicole, 69
Green Belt movement, 579–80
Greenberger, Marcia D., 337
Green Light Program, 222
Green New Deal, 585
Grieg, Miriam, 372
Griffiths, Martha, 203
Grimké, Angelina, 2, 22
Grimké, Sarah, 2, 22
   Letters on the Equality of the Sexes, 3
Griswold, Erwin, 25–26
Griswold, Estelle, 443
Griswold v. Connecticut, 278, 442, 443–45, 446–47, 449–50, 451, 553
Grover, Christopher, 377–78
Guinier, Lani, 78, 503
Gutek, Barbara A., 336, 341
GV survivors. *See* gender violence (GV) survivors

H
H-1B visas, 594
H-2A visas, 594
Hadfield, Gillian K., 543, 545
Hale, Matthew, 224
Hale, Robert L., 192, 307

Coercion and Distribution in a Supposedly Non-Coercive State, 188–89
Halley, Janet, 115
　on brain drain in feminism, 120
　contributions to distributional analysis and legal reform, 187, 190–96
　Distribution and Decision: Assessing Governance Feminism, 191
　queer legal studies lens on BDSM, 160–61
　as queer legal theorist, 45
　on sexuality and equality, 52nn57–58, 54n83
　on sodomy, 156
　Split Decisions, 117–18, 199n44
　on study of governance structures, 122
　on women's agency, 47
Halperin, David, 154
Haraway, Donna
　Cyborg Manifesto, 557
harms, hierarchy of in tort law, 653, 662n43
Harper, Fowler V., 445
Harris, Angela P., 32, 115, 585
　critique of MacKinnon's dominance theory, 43–45, 80, 90n32
　Gender, Violence, Race, and Criminal Justice, 175
　on gender violence, 65
　on U.S. political economy, 303
Harris, Cheryl I.
　Whiteness as Property, 611
Harris, Heather Brydie, 161–62
Harris, Jeremy O., 104–5
Harris, Luke, 87
Harris, Teresa, 337
Harris v. Forklift System, Inc., 264, 337, 341
Harris v. McRae, 450
Hart, Barbara, 381
Hart, Ericka, 97
Harvard University, 296
　Law School, 77–78, 497, 503
Haskell, Martin, 286
hate speech, 619
Haven House, California, 227
headscarf bans, 179
Health Insurance Portability and Accountability Act (HIPAA) (1996), 553, 564
Hearn, Jeff, 170, 180

Heckler, Margaret, 208, 209
hegemonic masculinity, 180
hegemony, defined, 119–20
Henderson, Lynne, 413
Henson v. City of Dundee, 335, 336
Hernández, Tanya Kateri, 339–40
Hertz, Rosana, 541
Hickman-Maslin Research, 284
Hicks, Louise, 209
high heels, origins of, 613
Hill, Anita, 43, 248, 337
Hill, Jemele, 262–63
Hirsi, Isra, 584
History of Sexuality Volume 1, The (Foucault), 150–51
Holder, Eric, 265–66
Holmes, Oliver Wendell, 191
Holtzman, Liz, 204
honor crimes, 599
hooks, bell, 81
Hooters trademark, 617
Hopkins, Ann, 357–58
hostile environment harassment, 334–35, 337, 338
Houh, Emily M. S., 524, 542
Hull, Gloria, 81
humanitarian-based immigration, 598–99
human rights law, 479–85
　impact of feminist theory on, 484–85
　state-enabled violence, 483–84, 485
　state-tolerated private violence as human rights concern, 482–83
　understanding state-sponsored violence, 481–82
human trafficking, 604
Hunter, Nan, 98
Hunter, Rosemary, 517–18, 522
Hunting Ground, The (documentary), 247, 250
Hutchinson, Darren L., 162–63, 176
Hyde Amendment (1976), 279–81, 450, 452

I

Iancu v. Brunetti, 618–19
"Id, The Ego, and Equal Protection, The" (Lawrence), 84
Ifill, Sherrilyn A., 520
Immigration Act (1924), 594

Immigration and Nationality Act (1952), 10, 526
immigration law, feminist reimagining of, 592–609
  citizenship and, 593
  employment-based immigration, 594–97
  family-based immigration, 600–602
  humanitarian-based immigration, 598–99
  treatment of unauthorized immigrants, 603–4
immigration policies, 179
  gender violence and, 380
implicit bias, 616
imposter syndrome, 505
In a Different Voice (Gilligan), 57–58, 521
incarceration, of women, 381
incomplete commodification (Radin), 540
Independent Women's Forum, 297
indeterminacy thesis, 188
India, sex work in, 195
Indian Citizenship Act (1924), 10
Indigenous self-determination, 64
infant care, 425–30
Infanti, Anthony C., 635
infants, gender ascribed to, 612
informational cascades (Sunstein), 295
informational privacy, 553, 555–59
Innocence Project, 51n41
insanity defense, 371
intellectual property law, and gender disparities, 610–29
  artificial intelligence, 620–23
  copyrights, 615–16
  gender as property, 611–13
  naming rights and physical public domain, 619–20
  patents, 614–15
  trademarks, 617–19
InterAmerican Commission on Human Rights, 487–88
intergenerational justice, 65–67
intermediate scrutiny, 19, 27
International Association of Campus Law Enforcement Administrators, 252
International Association of Chiefs of Police, 230
International Covenant on Civil and Political Rights (ICCPR), 484, 487

International Covenant on Economic, Social, and Cultural Rights (ICESCR), 484
international environmental law, 578–79
international feminism, and gendered violence in U.S., 477–95
  human rights law and, 479–85
    impact of feminist theory on, 484–85
    state-enabled violence, 483–84, 485
    state-tolerated private violence as human rights concern, 482–83
    understanding state-sponsored violence, 481–82
  relevancy to domestic U.S. law, 485–91
    positive rights, caregiving and the state, 488–90
    private power and vulnerability of women, 487–88
    state-sponsored violence effects on women, 486–87
    turn to state power, 490–91
International Indigenous Peoples Forum, 584
International Wages for Housework Campaign and a Global Women's Strike (2000), 535
Internet. *See also* privacy and law in cyberspace
  effects of porn on youth, 103
  gendered and intersectional harms due to, 31
intersectional feminism
  digital discrimination, 562–63
  diversity of families, 432–34
  ecofeminism and, 577
  on gender justice, 135, 136, 137, 141
  identity categories, 116–17
  legal PAR approach and, 525
  as origin of #MeToo movement, 123
  political and structural relationships of GV and, 375–77
  sex-role differences, 354
  surrogacy and, 539–40
  in Title IX athletics, 397–98
intersectionality, genealogy of, 75–93, 97
  features of intersectional analysis
    disparate effects and substantive equality, 83–85
    narrative as methodology, 83

social constructionism of race, gender, and sex, 82–83
origins of critical race theory, 76–78
roots in critical race theory, 78–80
roots in women-of-color-centered feminisms, 80–82
social movements and activism, 85–88
intimate deception, and tort law, 657
intimate partner violence (IPV). *See also* battered women's movement; domestic violence; Violence Against Women Act (VAWA) (1994)
    legal PAR approach and, 523–24
    private power and vulnerability of women, 487–89
    private violence as human rights concern, 482–83
    public duty doctrine and, 650
    relational feminism on, 61
    tort law reforms and, 654–55
inventors. *See* intellectual property law, and gender disparities
Invisible Women: Data Bias in a World Designed for Men (Perez), 620
in vitro fertilization (IVF), 537, 540. *See also* surrogacy and technology
Israel, migrant sex workers in, 195
It Ain't Me Babe (newspaper)
    "Anatomy of a Rape," 221
    "Disarm Rapists," 221
    "Fight!" 221

J

Jackson, Candice, 253
Jackson, Lisa, 576
Jacob, Herb
    Silent Revolution, 323
Jacquet, Catherine, 225
Jane Crow and the Law (Murray), 26
Jarrett, Valerie, 246
Jim Crow era
    passage of laws, 9
    reinstatement of debt peonage and sharecropping, 534
    sexualized injury during, 44
Johnson v. Calvert, 537
Jones, Leslie, 262–63

Journal of Gender, Race & Justice
    conference on women and poverty, 638, 641
judicial selection, backlash patterns in, 315–16, 320, 324
June Medical Services v. Russo, 452
Justice, Gender, and the Family (Okin), 23

K

Kaba, Mariame, 413
Kahng, Lily, 633
Kahn v. Shevin, 356
Kalanick, Travis, 261, 262
Kalsem, Kristin, 86
    Social Justice Feminism, 584
Kang, Jerry, 553
Kantor, Jodi, 262, 326
Katri, Ido, 163
Katz, Lucy, 280
Kavanaugh, Brett, 226, 248, 266, 267–68, 274n66, 298
Keane, Margaret, 612
Kelley, Florence, 10, 13, 206–7
Kennedy, Anthony, 156–57, 158–59, 463
Kennedy, David
    World of Struggle, 189
Kennedy, Duncan, 188, 189–90, 197
Kenney, Sally J., 519–20, 521
    Gender and Justice, 319, 517–18
Kenya, ecological decline and gender equality, 579–80
Kenyon, Dorothy, 26, 207, 218n82
Killing the Black Body (Roberts), 539–40
Kimmel, Michael, 170, 171
King, Martin Luther, Jr.
    Letters from a Birmingham Jail, 321
King, Tania, 140
Kipnis, Laura, 249
Kircher v. City of Jamestown, 650
Klarman, Michael, 321
Klein, Lauren F., 561
Knauer, Nancy, 635, 636, 639
Knizhnik, Shana, 27
Know Your IX, 247
Knudson, Coya, 325
Koch brothers, 248
Kolstad v. American Dental Association, 339
Kornhauser, Marjorie E., 634, 638

Koss, Mary P., 242
Kotiswaran, Prabha, 190–96
Kozinski, Alex, 261
Krieger, Linda H., 322, 353
Kuokkanen, Rauna J., 64

L

labor laws
   during cult of domesticity era, 352
   for pregnant workers, 426
Lady Gaga, 247, 251
Lamble, Sarah, 150, 155
Land O Lakes "Indian Princess" trademark, 617
Lanham Act (1946), 618, 620
Latina Judge's Voice, A (Sotomayor), 520
law and economics, against legal feminism, 294–312
   constructing legal feminism as threat to individual freedom, 307–8
   efficiency-equality dualism as double bind, 299–301
   instability of formal equality, 301
   legal theory in political economic context, 295–96
   political economics of law and economics, 296–99
   reducing liberty to individual self-interest, 305–6
   revival of gendered separate spheres, 303–4
   undermining of substantive equality, 301–3
law enforcement
   adoption of pro-arrest policies for domestic violence, 229–30
   gender bias of, 491
   mistreatment of domestic violence victims, 228–29
   mistreatment of rape victims, 223, 226
   officers as perpetrators of gendered/sexualized violence, 48, 65
   public duty doctrine, 650–51
   role in domestic violence situations, 487–88
   treatment of online harassment, 558
Law Enforcement Assistance Administration (LEAA)
   Family Violence Program, 228
Lawrence, Charles R., III
   "The Id, The Ego, and Equal Protection," 84

Lawrence v. Texas, 99–100, 156–57, 166n49, 553
law schools. *See* legal education, feminist influences in
Lawyer Moms of America, 472
Leadership Against HIV/AIDS, Tuberculosis, and Malaria Act (2003), 194
League of Women Voters, 10
learned helplessness, 231, 372–73, 374
legal education, feminist influences in, 496–514
   call to action, 508
   challenging assumptions underlying law and pedagogy, 501
   creating feminist spaces and communities for faculty, 500–501
   development of feminist pedagogy, 499
   feminist-inspired evolution of, 504–8
   history of access to, 497–99
   identifying law's gendered harms and exposing false dichotomies, 502
   incorporating women's values, experiences, and perspectives, 503–4
   questioning the Socratic method, 502–3, 505
legal feminism. *See* law and economics, against legal feminism
legal feminism theory, history of, 1–18
   during 1880-1920 and women's suffrage movement, 7–10
   emergence of during 1848-1880, 2–6
   liberal formalism during 1920-1970, 12–14
   progressive feminism during 1890-1930, 10–12
legal PAR approach, 523–25
legal realism, 14, 191–92
legal reform, and distributional analysis, 190–96
Lenahan, Jessica, 487–89
Lenhardt, Robin A., 538
Leo, Leonard, 298
Leong, Nancy, 611
Let's Have a Year of Publishing Only Women (Shamsie), 617
Letters from a Birmingham Jail (King), 321
Letters on the Equality of the Sexes (S. Grimké), 3
Levine, James, 47
Levine, Judith, 102

Levit, Nancy, 169, 171, 306, 318
Levy, Karen, 565
LGBTQ+. *See also* intersectional feminism
   Adler critique of, 196–97
   family law contracts, 536
   gender violence and, 380–81
   pornography and dominance theory, 42–43
   presumptions of parenthood, 464, 467
   three-parent families, 537
liability insurance, 654–55
liberal feminism
   family-responsibilities discrimination, 462
   on gender justice, 134, 135–36
   principles of, 8–9
liberal feminist jurisprudence, 19–38
   antiessentialist and intersectional critiques, 32
   dominance and relational feminism, 31
   early history of, 20–23
   formal equality through courts vs. legislatures, 29
   Ginsburg and WRP, 24–27
   Ginsburg as Supreme Court justice, 27–29
   on surrogacy, 465
   twentieth century liberalism, 23–24
   value of autonomy and privacy, 30–31
liberal formalism, during 1920–1970, 12–14
Life Always, 453
Life Amendment Political Action Committee, 281
Life Dynamics, 453
Life Education and Resource Network (LEARN), 453
Lipmann, Walter, 353
Lisa M v. Henry Mayo Newhall Mem'l Hosp, 652–53
Little, Joan, 225
Little League, 389
Livingston, Michael A., 638, 641
Llewellyn, Karl, 191
Lochner v. New York, 13, 206, 352
Locke, John, 4, 21–22
Logan-Riley, India, 584
Lorde, Audre, 81, 97, 534
Loughnan, Claire, 64
Louima, Abner, 175
Louis C K, 47

Lumbard, J. Edmund, 448
lynching, 320

M

Maafa 21: Black Genocide in 21st Century America (documentary), 453
Maathai, Wangari, 579–80, 582, 584, 588n43
Mac Donald, Heather, 297–98
machine learning systems, 561
MacKinnon, Catharine A. *See also* dominance feminism theory (MacKinnon)
   critique of Ginsburg's approach, 356
   on efficiency-equality dualism, 299
   on hierarchy in Socratic method, 503
   as lawyer in *Meritor* case, 335
   on #MeToo movement, 343
   on privacy and power, 31, 554
   on rape, 413, 482, 535
   on sexual harassment, 332, 333–34, 343, 468
   Sexual Harassment of Working Women, 333, 416
   on sexuality, 199n44
Maher v. Roe, 280–81
Mahoney, Antron D., 161–62
Mahoney, Martha, 44
mail-order brides, 601, 602
Malaga, Johanna, 378
Manhattan Institute, 297–98
man marriage, defined, 3
Manne, Kate, 305
   Down Girl, 325
Man Question, The (Dowd), 172
Mapping the Margins (Crenshaw), 78, 79
Mapp v. Ohio, 443
Marçal, Katrine
   Who Cooked Adam Smith's Dinner? 636
March for Women's Lives
   during 1986, 282
   during 2004, 287
Marital Deduction QTIP Provisions, The (Gerzog), 634
marriage. *See also* same-sex marriage
   coverture rules on, 21, 534, 535, 600, 602, 611
   forms of forced and refugee asylum, 598, 599
   mail-order brides, 601, 602
   naming rights, 619–20

marriage (*cont.*)
   prenuptial agreements, 533, 542
   privacy rights and, 444
   rape within, 224, 225, 226, 535
   spousal control in family-based immigration, 600–602
   spousal surety agreements, 543
   status vs. contract basis for, 534–39
Married Women's Property Acts, 533, 534, 600
Marshall, Thurgood, 450
Martin, Jonathan, 177
Martin, Patricia Yancy, 170, 518–19
Marvin, Lee, 535–36
Marxism, 4, 192, 535
Masculinities and the Law (Cooper and McGinley), 176–77, 179
masculinities theory, influence on legal feminism, 169–86
   applications of masculinities to male-only spaces, 173–74
   Dowd's listing of principles, 172
   engagement between theories, 171–73
   future trends in masculinities scholarship, 180–81
   intersectionality to multidimensionality research, 175–79
   masculinities' origins outside of law, 170–71
mass clemency campaigns, for incarcerated battered women, 231–32, 233
mass incarceration, 486, 490–91
   of Black men, 47, 51n41
mass shootings
   misogyny and, 317, 325
Matal v. Tam, 618–19
maternity leave. *See also* pregnancy and work, history of
   absence of universal paid, 352
Matsuda, Mari J., 115, 585
   call to ask the other question, 86, 522
   on multiple consciousness, 502
   race intervention into CLS and, 77, 79, 81–82
   on VAWA, 232–33
Matthews, Burnita Shelton, 12, 202
McCaffery, Edward J., 633
McClain, Linda C., 30, 554
McClellan, Jennifer, 211

McGinley, Ann C.
   Masculinities and the Law, 176–77
McGowan, Rose, 263
McLaughlin, Edward, 378
McMillan v. City of New York, 659
McNealy, Scott, 552
Meadows, Bresha, 233, 238n147
Medicaid, funding of abortions, 279–80, 450
Mellor, Mary, 576
men's rights activism, 171
menstrual equity, 640
Mercer Family Foundation, 298
Meritor Savings Bank v. Vinson, 42, 264, 335–36, 337, 340
Merry, Sally Engle, 490
Messerschmidt, James, 170
#MeToo movement, 96. *See also* feminism and #MeToo
   critiques of, 318–19
   dominance theory and, 39, 46–48
   influence of Title IX on, 240, 241, 251
   legacy of, 343–44, 416
   legal education and, 506
   online mobilization, 555
   physical force and economic lives of women, 305
   use of technology in evidence of assaults, 326
   women of color and, 123–24, 260, 262–63
Michelman, Kate, 283–84
microfinance programs, 196
Milano, Alyssa, 260
Mill, Harriet Taylor, 20, 21
Mill, John Stuart, 4, 20, 21, 25
   On Liberty, 22
   The Subjugation of Women, 22
Miller, Chanel, 326, 420n38
Mills, Charles, 532–33
Minarsky v. Susquehanna County, 343–44
Mink, Patsy Takemoto, 208
Minofou, Kevin, 75
Minor, Virginia, 8
Minor v. Happerset, 8
Minow, Martha, 57, 58, 118
misogyny
   mass shootings and, 317, 325
Moms Demand Action, 472

Montoya, Margaret E., 79, 80, 82
Moore v. Hughes Helicopter, 78
Moraga, Cherríe
  This Bridge Called My Back, 81
Morehead v. New York ex rel. Tipaldo, 13
More Than a Choice campaign, 287
Moritz, Charles, 630–31
Moritz v. Commissioner of Internal Revenue, 25–26, 630–31
Morrison; United States v., 232, 522
motherhood, disputed conceptions of, 461–77
  caregiving and biology, 463
  connection between social and biological motherhood, 470–73
  feminist disentanglement project, 462–67
    abortion rights, 463–64, 469
    adoption, 464, 466–67
    maternity leave, 463
    presumptions of parenthood, 464
    surrogacy and technology, 464–65, 467, 470, 471
  strange bedfellows and lack of influence on law, 467–70
Mother Jones
  "There's A Quiet #MeToo Movement Unfolding in the Government's Comments Section," 252
Mothers Against Drunk Driving, 472
Motley, Constance Baker, 519
Mott, Lucretia, 2–3, 21
Muller v. Oregon, 13, 206, 352
multidimensional masculinities theory (MMT), 176–79, 181
multiple consciousness (Matsuda), 502
Munoz, Jose Esteban, 155, 162
Murphy, Jane C.
  Divorced from Reality, 541
Murray, Pauli, 14, 24, 215, 218n82
  Jane Crow and the Law, 26
Musser, Amber J., 98
Mussey, Ellen Spencer, 497
Mutua, Athena D.
  Progressive Black Masculinities, 176

N

NAACP Legal Defense Fund, 76–77
naming rights, 619–20

NARAL Pro-Choice America, 452
narrative as methodology, in CRT, 83
Nasser, Larry, 318
Nathanson, Bernard, 282
National Abortion Federation, 286
National Abortion Rights Action League (NARAL), 278, 280–81, 282–84, 286, 289. *See also* NARAL Pro-Choice America
National American Woman Suffrage Association (NAWSA), 8–9, 10
National Black Women's Health Project, 282
National Center for the Prevention and Control of Rape, 222
National Clearinghouse for the Defense of Battered Women, 381
National Coalition Against Domestic Violence (NCADV), 228
National Coalition Against Sexual Assault, 222
National Coalition for Sexual Freedom, 100
National Collegiate Athletics Association (NCAA), 389, 390, 400n15
National Communications Network for the Elimination of Violence Against Women, 231
National Consumers League, 10
National Council of Women of Kenya, 580
National Domestic Violence Hotline, 228
National Environmental Policy Act (NEPA) (1969), 575
National Institute of Justice Report, on BWS, 373–75
National Institute of Mental Health, 372
National Jury Project, 371–72
National Latina Health Organization, 282
National Latina Institute for Reproductive Health, 287
National Law Journal, on environmental hazards in minority communities, 581
National Organization for Women (NOW)
  on abortion rights, 278, 289
  feminists of color and, 282
  on gender bias in compensation tables, 659
  on integrated sports, 389, 392
  as opposed to informed consent to sterilization, 279
  on reproductive justice, 452
  supportive of ERA Amendment, 24

National Right to Life Committee (NRLC), 280, 281, 282, 285, 286
National Woman's Party (NWP), 9, 10, 12–13, 203
National Woman Suffrage Association (NWSA), 7
National Women's Health Network (NWHN), 281
National Women's Law Center (NWLC), 528n11
   Tax Justice Is Gender Justice reports, 639–40
Native American women
   gender violence and, 380
   voting rights for, 10
natural language processing, 560–61
Nature of Prejudice, The (Allport), 353
negligence, third-party liability in, 651
Nelson, Margaret, 541
neoliberalism. *See also* law and economics, against legal feminism
   emphasis on individualism, 266–67, 307–8
   Leong on racial capitalism, 611
   liberal feminism and family law, 467–68
   notice and consent in privacy law, 565
   public/private debate and, 430–32
   Zuboff on surveillance capitalism, 560
Nesiah, Vasuki, 196
   Sexy Dressing, Gender, and Legal Theory, 190
New York Radical Feminists, 221, 223
New York v. Addimando, 377–78
Nguyen v. INS, 470–71, 472, 526
Nineteenth Amendment, 9–10, 13, 201, 203, 206
Ninth Amendment, 448
Nixon, Richard, 388, 431
Nobel Peace Prize recipients
   Watson and Crick, 612
   W. Maathai, 580
Noble, Safiya U., 560
no-drop prosecution policies, 230–31
no-duty-to-rescue doctrine, 649–51
nonbinary. *See* transgender, bisexual, and nonbinary identity
noncompete agreements, 542
nonconsensual pornography, 556, 558–59, 569n29

nonconsensual sex. *See* consent, rape, and criminal law
non-economic damage caps, 657–58
normative masculinity, hierarchical dualism in law and, 300
Norton, Eleanor Holmes, 334–35
Nursing Mothers Accommodation Act (Nevada), 211
Nussbaum, Martha C., 23–24

O

Obama, Barack, 246, 287–89
Obergefell v. Hodges, 156, 158–59, 361
Ocasio-Cortez, Alexandria, 585
Office for Civil Rights (OCR)
   CPI on lax approach to sexual harassment, 241–42
   Dear Colleague Letter (2011), 242–45, 251
   publication of names of schools under Title IX investigation, 247
   Q&A (2014), 246, 251
   Title IX athletic regulations, 389–92, 401n34
   Trump administration rule changes, 251–53
Okin, Susan Moller, 20, 30
   Justice, Gender, and the Family, 23
Olin, John M., 296–97
Olin Foundation, 296–98
Olsen, Frances, 300
Omar, Ilhan, 325
Omi, Michael, 82
Oncale v. Sundowner Offshore Services, Inc., 337–38, 340, 361
On Liberty (J.S. Mill), 22
online harassment, 556–59
On the Bias (Resnik), 521
On the Origin of Species (Darwin), 574
Onwuachi-Willig, Angela, 262
   What About #UsToo? 262
O'Reilly, Bill, 343
Orenstein, Peggy, 103
Osthoff, Sue, 381
Other Whisper Network, The (Roiphe), 268–69
Our Data Bodies (ODB), 562–63
outrage tort, 655
outsider within phenomenon (Collins), 520
Overmier, Bruce, 372
Ovia (app), 565

P

Pan-African movement, 454
parental leave, 462. *See also* Family and Medical Leave Act (FMLA) (1993); pregnancy and work, history of; Pregnancy Discrimination Act (PDA) (1978)
parent-child relationships, 537
Paris Climate Change Agreement (2015), 583, 591n81
Parks, Rosa, 221
Parramore, Lynn, 304
partial birth abortion ban, 285–86
Partial-Birth Abortion Ban Act (2003), 286
Past as Prologue: Old and New Feminisms (Chamallas), 181
Pateman, Carole, 532–33
patents, by women, 614–15
paternity leave. *See* pregnancy and work, history of
patriarchy. *See also* dominance feminism theory (MacKinnon)
   de Beauvoir on women and nature as "other," 577
   in naming of public assets, 620
   social contract theory and, 532–33
   systemic oppression of, 6
Paul, Alice, 9, 10, 12–13, 202
Payne v. Travenol, 78
Pennsylvania Coalition Against Domestic Violence, 228
people first platforms. *See* environmental law and legal feminism
Perez, Caroline Criado
   Invisible Women: Data Bias in a World Designed for Men, 620
Perkins, Frances, 13
Personnel Administrator of Massachusetts v. Feeney, 356
persons with disabilities, supported decisionmaking, 67–68
Phillips v. Martin Marietta Corp., 208, 357
physical privacy, 553
pink tax, 640
Planned Parenthood Federation of America, 279, 280–81, 282–83, 289, 452, 453–54

Planned Parenthood League of Connecticut, 280
Planned Parenthood of Southeastern Pennsylvania v. Casey, 31, 37n119, 284, 285, 287, 463–64, 526
Pleck, Joseph, 170
Plummer, Ken, 97
Poe v. Ullman, 445–46, 455n25
Polikoff, Nancy
   Beyond (Gay and Straight) Marriage, 538–39
Polischuk, Luciana, 141–42
Political Liberalism (Rawls), 23
Politics of Rape, The (Russell), 151
pornography
   dominance theory and, 42–43, 134
   nonconsensual, 556, 558–59, 569n29
   online access effects on youth, 103
   revenge porn, 31, 556, 558, 569n29, 656
   sex-positive feminism on, 42, 52n57
Post, Robert C., 322
Post-Intersectionality (Cho), 178–79
postmodern legal feminism, 112–30
   fourth wave of feminisms, 123–25
      #MeToo movement, 123–24
      reproductive rights, 124–25
   on gender justice, 135, 136
   poststructuralist analytical tools, 119–24
      dialectics, 121–22
      genealogy, 122–23, 125
      power of hegemony, 119–20
      strategic essentialism, 120–21
   transition to third wave feminism, 113–19
Postmodern Legal Feminist Manifesto, A (Frug), 116–17
poststructuralist analytical tools, 119–24
   dialectics, 121–22
   genealogy, 122–23, 125
   power of hegemony, 119–20
   strategic essentialism, 120–21
poverty
   environmental justice movement, 580–84
   impacts during COVID-19, 489–90
   parental neglect and, 468
   privacy and, 554
   rising inequality and, 63
Powell, Catherine, 141
Powell, Lewis, 283

power
  Foucault on sexuality and, 150–51, 160–61
  of hegemony as poststructuralist analytical tool, 119–20, 124
Pratt, Carla D., 520
predatory consumer lending, 379–80
pregnancy, and corporate surveillance, 564
pregnancy and work, history of, 29, 423–41, 469. *See also* Family and Medical Leave Act (FMLA) (1993); Pregnancy Discrimination Act (PDA) (1978)
  discrimination and accommodation in infant care and, 424–26
  future trends, 437
  intersectionality and diversity of families, 432–34
  movement toward universalism, 434–37
  neoliberalism and public/private debate, 430–32
  sameness/difference and equality, 426–30
Pregnancy Discrimination Act (PDA) (1978), 428–29, 430, 431, 434, 435, 437
pregnancy in the workplace, 29
Pregnant Workers' Fairness Act (Nevada), 211
Pregnant Workers Fairness Acts (PWFA) (2022), 436
prenuptial agreements, 533, 542
preponderance standard, under Title IX, 244–45, 248, 319
presuming women (Appleton), 464
Price Waterhouse v. Hopkins, 181, 357–58, 360, 361–62
prison abolition movement, 413
prison-industrial complex, 486
privacy and law in cyberspace, 552–72
  explanation of privacy, 552–54
  history of feminism and privacy, 554–55
  privacy in cyberspace
    digital discrimination, 559–63
    online harassment, 556–59
    sexual surveillance, 563–67
privacy rights. *See also* reproductive rights and justice, constitutionalizing of
  abortion and, 278–80
  Franke on, 157
  Kang on clusters of, 553
  as right to be let alone, 553
  sterilization and, 279

product design, and gender bias, 620
Progressive Black Masculinities (Mutua), 176
progressive feminism
  during 1890–1930, 10–12
prostitution. *See* sex work
Pruitt, Lisa, 526
PTSD (posttraumatic stress disorder), 372
public assets, gendered naming of, 620
public duty doctrine, 650–51, 660n15
public-private dichotomy. *See* privacy and law in cyberspace; separate spheres ideology

Q

Queer Nation, 154
queer of color critique (QOCC)
  on anti-LGBT law and policy, 161–63
  origins of term, 155
queer theory
  critical legal studies and, 196–97
  the personal is political slogan, 97
  as sex-positive, 96
queer theory, as a sensibility, 150–68
  anti-identitarian turn in law, 156
  beyond LGBT subject in law, 160–61
  break from gay and lesbian studies, 152–54
  connections to feminism, 151–52
  critique of the "normal," 154–55
  development of theory, 150–51
  offshoots of, 155
  queer of color critique (QOCC), 161–63
  same-sex marriage challenges, 158–60
  sodomy challenge, 151, 156–57
  trans legal studies, 163
quid pro quo sexual harassment, 334, 338
Quinn, Zoe, 557

R

race and racism. *See also* mass incarceration
  in campus sexual harassment, 249–50
  in early legal feminism, 6
  in flawed rational neutrality of law, 502
  Jim Crow laws, 9
  in Paul's suffrage efforts, 9
  as social construction, 82–83
  social contract theory and, 532–33
  in tax laws, 633–34
  in workplace, 655

racial capitalism (Leong), 611
racial formation theory (Omi and Winant), 82
racism is over myth (Bell), 314, 317–18
Radiance Foundation, 453
radical feminism. *See* dominance feminism theory (MacKinnon)
Radice v. New York, 13
Radin, Margaret J. "Peggy," 540
Raeder, Myrna S., 373
Rainbow Retreat, Arizona, 227
Ramsey, Lisa P., 618
rape crisis centers, 222, 226, 232
rape law. *See also* anti-rape movement; consent, rape, and criminal law
  civil aiding and abetting claims, 652
  in international conflict zones, 481
  lack of protections for female agricultural workers, 596–97
  married persons and, 224, 225, 226, 535
  non-economic damage caps, 658
  rape shield legislation, 224, 408
  reforms, 223–25
rape reform movement, 407–9
Rape Victim Services Act (1980), 222
rational basis review standard, 428
rational choice theory, 305
Rawls, John, 20, 30
  Political Liberalism, 23
  A Theory of Justice, 23
Reagan, Ronald, 283, 285, 336
reasonable accommodation, under ADA, 435–36
reasonable person standard, 341, 502
reasonable woman standard (Threedy), 544
Rebouché, Rachel, 190–96, 541
Reckoning with the Hidden Rules of Gender in the Tax Code (NWLC), 639–40
Reed, Sally, 355
Reed v. Reed, 25–26, 27, 211, 355, 631
Regan, Michael S., 576
relational feminism
  contract law and, 541–42, 544–45
  dominance and, 31
  ecofeminism and, 577
  family-responsibilities discrimination, 462
  on gender justice, 134, 137, 141
  Halley on drawbacks of, 199n44

history of, 114–15, 339, 471–72
influences on law schools, 504
principles of, 5–6, 8–9
on privacy, 553
relational feminism, self, autonomy, and law, 57–74
  autonomy and mental health and supported decisionmaking, 67–68
  law and rights, 61–63
  relational autonomy, 60–61
  relational insights on law and hierarchy, 63–65
  the relational self, 58–60
  self and intergenerational justice, 65–67
  Van Wagner on rights and relational property, 68–70
Render, Meredith M., 359
reparations, for people of color, 532
repo code (Braucher), 544
reproductive harm, and tort law, 656–57
reproductive health, and corporate surveillance, 563–67
reproductive justice, defined, 276. *See also* abortion rights, as matter of women's equality
reproductive justice movement, 449–51
reproductive rights, 124–25. *See also* abortion rights, as matter of women's equality
reproductive rights and justice, constitutionalizing of, 442–60
  Abele v. Markle, 445, 447–48, 449
  Abramowicz v. Lefkowitz, 445, 446–47, 449, 452
  constitutional alternatives to privacy, 444–49
  constitutional privacy and, 443–44
  cooptation and contestation, 453–54
  integration of reproductive rights and justice, 451–52
  Poe v. Ullman, 445–46, 455n25
  response to *Roe* and reproductive justice movement, 449–51
  Struck v. Secretary of Defense, 445, 448
  Trubek v. Ullman, 445–46, 447
Reproductive Rights National Network, 281
Republican Motherhood concept, 4–5, 8
Republican Party
  Tea Party protests on ACA, 288

690 INDEX

residential schools, state operated, 64
Resnik, Judith, 516–17
   On the Bias, 521
restraining orders, 487–88
revenge porn, 31, 556, 558, 569n29, 656
Ricardo, David, 189
Ridgeway, Cecilia, 353
right-wing ideology. *See* conservatism; culture wars, in U.S.
Rising Pressure of the #MeToo Backlash, The" (Tolentino), 318
Riss v. City of New York, 650
Roberts, Dorothy E., 125, 470, 554
   Killing the Black Body, 539–40
Robinson, Mary
   Climate Justice, 583–84
Robinson, Russell, 162–63
robots, algorithms and gender, 620–23
Rochin v. California, 443
Rocking the Tax Code (Fellows), 633–34
Rodgers, Daniel T., 294
Rodgers, Yana van der Meulen, 141
Rodríguez-Trías, Helen, 279
Roe v. Wade, 278–80, 283–85, 287, 290, 322, 442, 444–45, 446, 448–51, 553
Roiphe, Katie
   The Other Whisper Network, 268–69
Roraback, Catherine, 280, 443–44, 445, 447
Rose, Charlie, 326
Rosenberg, Gerald, 321
Rosenbury, Laura A., 98, 117
Rosenthal, Lynn, 246
Ross, Loretta, 288
   "What Is Reproductive Justice," 451
Rothman, Jennifer, 98, 108n56
Rowling, J. K., 616, 627n56
Rubin, Gayle
   Thinking Sex, 151–52
Ruskin, John, 304
Ruskola, Teemu, 157, 161
Russell, Diana
   The Politics of Rape, 151

S

Safe Drinking Water Act (1974), 581
safe houses, for women, 227
same-sex couples
   backlash to ACA services and, 289
   parental leave and, 433
   tax laws and, 634–35
   use of contracts, 536
same-sex marriage
   de facto parenthood theory, 467
   parental leave and, 433
   presumptions of parenthood, 464
   queer theory and, 158–60
   role of court decisions in, 323, 635
   Thomas on, 167n67
same-sex sexual harassment, 337–38, 340, 361
Sanger, Margaret, 12, 124–25
Saucedo, Leticia M., 179
#SayHerName campaign (AAPF), 87
Scaife Foundations, 298
Scalia, Antonin, 488
Schechter, Susan, 222, 227, 229, 232
Schlafly, Phyllis, 204, 207–8, 209
Schneider, Elizabeth M., 117, 373
Schultz, Vicki, 340, 341–42
Scott v. Hart, 229–30
search engines, and gender discrimination, 560–61
Searle Freedom Trust, 296
Seck, Sara L., 66
second wave feminism
   Halley on drawbacks of, 117–18
   history of, 114
   liberal legal feminism in, 24–29
Securities Exchange Act (1934)
   Rule 10b-5 and sexual harassment, 343
Sedgwick, Eve K., 152
   The Epistemology of the Closet, 152–53
self-defense doctrine, 370. *See also* gender violence (GV) survivors
Seligman, Martin, 372
Sen, Maya, 518
Seneca Falls convention (1848), 2–3, 22, 114, 370, 630
separate spheres ideology, 351–54, 554. *See also* degendering the law, through stereotype theory; pregnancy and work, history of
separation violence, 374
September 11th Victim Compensation Fund, 659

service industry
  tipped employees, 124
  treatment of pregnant workers, 424, 432
Serving Two Masters (Bell), 76–77
Sessions v. Morales-Santana, 28
sex-based power, 265
sex discrimination. *See* Civil Rights Act, Title VII (1964); Equal Employment Opportunity Commission (EEOC); European Court of Human Rights (ECHR)
sex education, 101–3
Sex Education (tv show), 104
sex/gender binary, 117, 135. *See also* queer theory, as a sensibility
sex offenders, registry requirement, 99
sex *per se* standard of causation, 337
sex-positive feminism
  on anti-trafficking laws, 194
  critique of dominance feminism, 39, 44
  on gender justice, 134, 136
  on pornography, 42, 52n57
  on sexual harassment, 339, 341–42
sex-positive feminism, and law of pleasure, 44, 94–111
  beyond gender binary, 98–99
  law's sex negativity, 99
  liberty and privacy reforms, 99–100
  popular culture and, 103–5
  power and BDSM test, 97–98
  set of values and women's agency, 94–97
  sex education as supportive, 101–3
  tort and anti-discrimination law as supportive, 100–101
sex radicals. *See* sex-positive feminism
sex rights, in progressive feminism, 12
sex robots, 623
  sex segregation, legal, 179. *See also* Title IX, separate but equal in athletics
sex stereotyping theory, 181, 359. *See also* degendering the law, through stereotype theory
sexual abuse, among female prison population, 487
sexual agency, 43–45, 47–48
sexual assault
  distinguished from rape, 224
  of female immigrants, 603
  third-party liability, 651
sexual assault awareness and prevention programs, 415–16
sexual autonomy and privacy rights, 656
sexual constitutionalism, 554
sexual exceptionalism, 108n56, 652–53, 657
Sexual Experiences Survey (SES), 242, 246
sexual harassment. *See also* Title IX, movement against campus sexual harassment
  class action cases, 264, 265
  conservative viewpoint on, 124
  domestic workers and, 596–97
  dominance theory and, 42–43, 468
  legal reforms, 261, 264, 265
  MacKinnon on, 332, 333, 339, 416, 468
  masculinities theory and, 173–74
  online harassment, 556–59
  proof of unwelcomeness, 335
  quid pro quo, 334, 338
  rate of successful claims, 318
  reasonable person standard, 341
  same-sex harassment, 337–38, 340, 361
  in service industry, 124
  tort law and, 306, 342–43
  training of workplace personnel, 245, 264, 337, 339
  women of color, 249–50, 665
sexual harassment, in the workplace, 332–49, 468–69
  in educational settings, 336
  employer liability, 338–39
  feminist activism, the courts and, 333–36
  feminist response to evolving legal claim, 339–42
  Hill/Thomas hearings and case law refinements, 336–39
  other legal means of addressing, 342–43
  workplace responses, 416–17
Sexual Harassment of Working Women (MacKinnon), 333, 416
sexualized domination, 40–41
sexual orientation. *See also* LGBTQ+
  discrimination and, 360–62
  parental leave and, 433
sexual privacy (Citron), 30–31

sexual puritanism, 468–69
Sexual Shakedown (Farley), 333
sexual surveillance, 563–67
sex wars, 44, 98, 151–52
sex work
    gender violence and, 381
    governance feminism and, 193–96
Sexy Dressing, Gender, and Legal Theory (Nesiah), 190
Shalev, Carmen, 537
Shamir, Hila, 190–96
Shamsie, Kamila
    Let's Have a Year of Publishing Only Women, 617
Shaylor, Cassandra, 486–87
Shellhammer v. Lewallen, 336
shelters, for women, 227–28, 374, 378
Sheppard-Towner Act (1921), 10
Sherman, Lawrence W., 230
She Said (Twohey), 326
Shitty Media Men (Donegan), 267, 268, 274n62
Shultz, Marjorie McGuire, 537
Siegel, Reva B., 322
Signet Jewelers, 343
Silent No More campaign, 282–83
Silent Revolution (Jacob), 323
Silent Scream, The (film), 282
Silent Spring (Carson), 575
Simon, William E., 297
Simpkins v. Grace Brethren Church of Delaware, 658
Simpson, Monica, 289
Sims, James Marion, 125
Singer, Jana B., 540–41
    Divorced from Reality, 541
Singer, Samuel, 163
Siri, female voice of, 561, 623
SisterSong Women of Color Reproductive Justice Collective, 285, 287, 288, 289–90, 451
Slants, The (band), 618
Slave Play, 104–5
slavery, 408–9, 538, 539, 594, 595, 611–12
Slutwalks, 47, 51n51
Smith, Barbara, 81, 155
social caste, in U.S. political economy, 303
social constructionism
    masculinities and, 170

race, gender, and sex, 82–83
sexuality and, 97
social contract theory, 532–33
Social Justice Feminism (Kalsem and V. Williams), 584
social justice feminism (SJF)
    climate justice movement and, 584–85
    ecofeminism and, 577
    intersectional activism and, 85–86
social motherhood, defined, 461–62. *See also* motherhood, disputed conceptions of
Social Security benefits, 355
Socratic method, 502–3, 505
sodomy, 151, 156–57, 175
Solis v. S.V.Z., 652
Solnit, Rebecca, 417
Sotomayor, Sonia, 518
    A Latina Judge's Voice, 520
Souter, David H., 522–23
Spacey, Kevin, 47
Spade, Dean, 163
Spearman, Pat, 210–11
special rules of criminal rape (M. Anderson), 248
spectators of crimes, and tort liability, 652
Spindelman, Marc, 462
Spivak, Gayatri, 120–21
Split Decisions (Halley), 117–18, 199n44
sports. *See* Title IX, separate but equal in athletics
spousal abuse. *See* battered women's movement; intimate partner violence (IPV)
spousal surety agreements, 543
Stanchi, Kathryn M., 526
    Feminist Judgments, 525–26
Stanley, Amy Dru, 534
Stanton, Elizabeth Cady, 21, 114
    feminist theory of, 2–6
    as founder of NWSA, 7
    legal training of, 3
    origin of legal feminism theory and, 2
    at Seneca Falls Convention, 2–3
    views on voting rights, 7
state-enabled violence, 483–84, 485
state-sponsored violence, 481–82, 486–87
state-tolerated private violence, 482–83

Staudt, Nancy C.
  Taxing Housework, 633
Stearns, Nancy, 446–47, 449
stereotype, defined, 353
stereotype theory. *See* degendering the law, through stereotype theory
sterilization, 279, 281
Stevens, Aimee, 28
Stone, Kerri L., 359
Stone, Lucy, 2, 7
STOP-ERA campaign, 204, 208, 209
Stop Taxing Our Periods! Period petition against tampon tax (*Cosmopolitan*), 640
St. Pauli Girl beer trademark, 617
strategic essentialism
  critique of, 132
  as poststructuralist analytical tool, 120–21, 124
Stratton, Juliana, 211
stray remarks doctrine, 261
Struck, Susan, 448
Struck v. Secretary of Defense, 445, 448
structural impartiality (Ifill), 520
Subjugation of Women, The (J.S. Mill), 22
substantive due process doctrine, 431
substantive equality, law and economics as undermining of, 301–3
substantive fairness, 542
suffrage. *See* voting rights; women's suffrage movement
Sunstein, Cass R., 295, 414
Superson, Anita
  Theorizing Backlash, 320
supported decisionmaking, 67–68
surplus at stake, in distributional analysis, 192
surrogacy and technology
  biological vs. social motherhood and, 464–65, 467, 470, 471
  contract vs. status view of family, 533
  expansion of parent-child relationships, 537
  intersectional feminism on, 539–41
surveillance capitalism (Zuboff), 560
survival crime and survivor justice, 379–84
#SurvivedandPunished movement, 233
SurvJustice, 247
systemic oppression (Stanton), 6

T

Tailhook scandal, 337
Take Back the Night marches, 222, 242
takedown requests, for online harassment, 559
Tamayo, William R., 597
tampon tax, 640
Taub, Nadine, 29
Tax Code for the Rest of Us, A (NWLC), 639–40
Tax Cuts and Jobs Act (2017), 639
Taxing America (Fellows and K. Brown), 632–33
Taxing Housework (Staudt), 633
Taxing Women (McCaffery), 633
Taylor, Dorceta E., 576
Taylor, Recy, 221
teacher work visas, in Louisiana schools, 596
Tea Party movement, 288
technological domination, 556–59
temporary work visas, 594–97
Terrell, Mary Church, 6, 10
Terry v. Ohio, 176–77
Test Tube Families (Cahn), 540
Theorizing Backlash (Superson and Cudd), 320
Theory of Justice, A (Rawls), 23
Thinking Sex (Rubin), 151
third-party liability in negligence, 651
third wave feminism
  critique of MacKinnon's dominance theory, 44, 51n51
Third World feminism, 81–82, 83
Third World Women's Caucus, 228
This Bridge Called My Back (Moraga and Anzaldúa), 81
Thomas, Chantal, 190–96
Thomas, Clarence, 43, 248, 297, 335, 337, 453–54
Thomas, Kendall, 159, 167n67
Thornburgh v. American Obstetricians and Gynecologists, 283
Threedy, Debora, 541–42, 544–45
Thuma, Emily L., 225
Thunberg, Greta, 584
Thurman, Tracy, 230
'Till It Happens to You (song), 247
#TimesUp movement, 54n80, 261, 555
Tin, Ida, 563

Title IX
  backlash in wrestling, 316, 318, 324
  Halley critique on, 47
  prohibition of sex-based discrimination, 102–3
Title IX, movement against campus sexual harassment, 240–48, 336
  backlash to movement, 247–50, 319
  comparison to criminal law remedies, 243–45
  impacts of *2011 Dear Colleague Letter*, 242–45
  nationalization of movement, 245–47
  political and legal battle for future of, 251–53
  system civil rights violations, 241–42
  training of school personnel, 245
Title IX, separate but equal in athletics, 388–405
  feminism on persisting inequality, 392–93, 401n34
  feminist alternatives to, 395–97, 404n75
  feminist support for separate-but-equal standard, 393–94
  gender diversity and separate-but-equal standard, 397–98
  origins of and applicability to athletics, 388–92
Tolentino, Jia, 269, 318
tolerated residuum of abuse (D. Kennedy), 190
Tometi, Opal, 86
too far too fast argument, 321–23
tort law, and sexual harassment, 306, 342–43
tort law and feminism, 648–65
  civil aiding and abetting, 652
  damages and equality
    compensation funds, 659
    elimination of race/gender tables, 658–59
    non-economic damage caps, 657–58
  duty of care, 649–51, 656–57
  harm-based reforms, 653–57
    intimate deception, 657
    intimate partner violence (IPV), 654–55
    reproductive harm, 656–57
    sexual autonomy and privacy rights, 656
    workplace harassment and discrimination, 655
  third-party liability in negligence, 651
  vicarious liability, 652–53

tort reform movement, 648–49
Trademark Act. *See* Lanham Act (1946)
trademarks, and gender discrimination, 617–19
trafficking of persons. *See* carceral anti-trafficking feminists (CAFs)
Traister, Rebecca, 241
trait-selection laws, 453–54
Transformers, 621
transgender, bisexual, and nonbinary identity
  discrimination lawsuits and, 361
  future masculinities research on, 180–81
  gender violence and, 380
  naming rights, 619
  parental leave and, 433
  sports inclusion, 397–98
  in Title IX athletics, 397–98
trans legal studies, 163
Triola, Michele, 535–36
Trubek, David, 445–46
Trubek, Louise, 445–46
Trubek v. Ullman, 445–46, 447
Trump, Donald, 88, 249, 250–51, 298, 316, 320, 555
Truth, Sojourner, 2
  Ain't I A Woman speech, 80, 90n34
#TruthBeTold campaign (AAPF), 88
Tuana, Nancy, 102
Tung, Cameron, 317
Turner, Brock, 326
T-visas, 604
Twenty-Seventh Amendment, 204
2 Live Crew, 79
Twohey, Megan, 262
  She Said, 326
Twyman v. Twyman, 160–61, 167n71

U

Uber, 262, 265–66, 343
unauthorized immigrants, and immigration law, 603–4
unconscionable commodification (E. Anderson), 539
unconscious bias, 84
Under the Blacklight initiative (AAPF), 87
Uneasy Access (A. Allen), 30
unified class concept, 4

Uniform Commercial Code (UCC), Article 9, 543–44
Uniform Parentage Act (2017), 465
United Kingdom (U.K.)
  child care tax reform during COVID-19 pandemic, 139
  publicly supported parent leave/child care options, 432
United Nations (U.N.)
  Convention for the Protection of Human Rights and Fundamental Freedoms, 101
  Convention on the Elimination of all forms of Discrimination Against Women (CEDAW), 479, 484, 488
  Convention on the Political Rights of Women, 480
  Declaration on the Elimination of Violence Against Women (DEVAW), 484–85
  Declaration on the Rights of Indigenous Peoples, 66
  Educational, Scientific, and Cultural Organization (UNESCO), 102
  Framework Convention on Climate Change (UNFCCC), 583
United States v. Darby Lumber, 207
United States v. Morrison, 232, 522
United States v. Virginia, 27–28, 211, 212, 356–57
United States v. Windsor, 639
universal child care, 431
Universal Declaration of Human Right (UDHR), 480, 484
University of Chicago, 296
University of Montana, 247
University of New Mexico, 247
U.S. Congress
  committee hearings on small business, 639
U.S. Education Department
  Office for Civil Rights, 241–42
U.S. Environmental Protection Agency (EPA), 575
U.S. Food and Drug Administration (FDA), 564
U.S. Health, Education, and Welfare Department (HEW), 279
  Office for Civil Rights, 389–90
U.S. Immigration Customs Enforcement (ICE), 380
U.S. Justice Department (DOJ)
  Title IX investigations, 247
U.S. Patent & Trademark Office (USPTO), 615, 617–18
U.S. Supreme Court
  on abortion, 278–79, 280, 282, 283, 284, 286–87
  denied women right to practice law, 3
  invalidation of federal damage remedies for private gender-motivated violence, 305
  nominee confirmation hearings, 518, 520
  rewritten opinions based on feminist methods, 526–27
  on same-sex sexual harassment, 361
  on sex discrimination, 181, 355–56
  on trademark law, 618
  on women as federal citizens, 8
  on workplace laws, 13, 206–7
U-visas, 603

V

Van Wagner, Estair, 68–70
Verchick, Robert R.M., 581
Vertesi, Janet, 562
vicarious liability, 652–53
victim-blaming norms, 371–72, 374, 408, 415
Victim Rights Law Center, Boston, 247
Victims of Crime Act (1984), 228
victims/women lie stereotype, 248–53
Vienna Declaration, 484
Vinson, Mechelle, 335, 337
violence. *See also* domestic violence; gender violence (GV) survivors; international feminism, and gendered violence in U.S.; intimate partner violence (IPV)
  against women in politics, 325
  women prison inmates as victims of, 490
Violence Against Women Act (VAWA) (1994), 220, 227, 232–33, 246, 297, 316, 654
Virginia Military Institute (VMI), 27–28, 211, 212, 297, 356–57
Virginia; United States v., 27–28, 211, 212, 356–57
visual arts, and gender discrimination, 616–17
VMI case. *See United States v. Virginia*
voice recognition software, and gender bias, 620

Vojdik, Valorie K., 179
   Gender Outlaws, 174
Vokes, Audrey, 544–45
Vokes v. Arthur Murray, 544–45
voting rights, 554. *See also* Black suffrage;
   women's suffrage movement
voter identification laws, 289
Voting Rights Act (1965), 10
vulnerability theory (Fineman and
   Spindelman), 462

W

Wachter-Boettcher, Sara, 558
wages-for-housework movement, 535
Walker, Lenore E., 231, 372–73, 375, 376–77
Wall-E (film), 621
Warner, Michael, 150
Warren, Elizabeth, 543
Warren, Samuel, 553
Washington and Lee University, 497
Washington College of Law (WCL), 497
Watson, James D., 612
Wattleton, Faye, 279
Way, Katie, 47
wealth transfer tax laws, 634
Weber, Max, 191
Webster v. Reproductive Health Services, 283
Weddington, Sarah, 448–49
Wedlocked (Franke), 158
Weeks, Jeffrey, 97
Weinberger v. Wiesenfeld, 355
Weinstein, Harvey, 46, 47, 226, 260, 261, 262,
   265, 269, 318–19, 326, 344, 411, 612
Weinstein, Jack, 659
Weinstein Company, The, 262
welfare policies, 125, 433, 447
welfare queen stereotype, 433
Wells-Barnett, Ida B., 10
West, Lindy, 261
West, Robin, 80, 96–97, 305–6, 307–8
West Coast Hotel Co. v. Parrish, 13, 207
What About #UsToo? (Onwauchi-Willig), 262
"What Is Reproductive Justice" (Ross), 451
White, Byron R., 446
White, Roy, 280
White Buffalo Calf Women's Society, South
   Dakota, 227

white femininity, 393
White House Council on Women and Girls, 246
White House Task Force to Protect Students
   from Sexual Assault (Task Force)
   (2014), 246, 247
Whiteness as Property (C. Harris), 611
white supremacy, 325
Whitmer, Gretchen, 325
Who Cooked Adam Smith's Dinner? (Marçal),
   636
WHO Expert Advisory Panels, 139
Whole Woman's Health v. Hellerstedt, 452–53
Who's the Man? (Cooper), 176
#WhyIDidntReport, 226
Williams, Joan, 353
Williams, Patricia J., 77, 79–80, 116
Williams, Verna L., 86
   Social Justice Feminism, 584
Williams, Wendy W., 29, 427
Wilson, Woodrow, 9
Winant, Howard, 82
Windsor; United States v., 639
Wollstonecraft, Mary, 3, 21
Woman Hating (Dworkin), 151
Woman's Christian Temperance Union
   (WCTU), 5, 8
Women Against Rape groups, 221–22
Women and Economics (Gilman), 11
Women and the Law Conference, 500
women as equal myth. *See* backlash against
   feminism
women in prison
   gendered violence within, 486–87
   as victims of violence, 490
Women Judges' Fund for Justice, 381–82
women of color. *See also* Black women; Native
   American women
   abortion rights, 282, 284, 285, 289–90
   athletic opportunities under Title IX,
      392–93
   convictions for killing abusive husbands, 375
   during cult of domesticity era, 352
   on domestic violence as intersectional
      problem, 228, 230
   in early legal feminism, 6
   facial recognition technology
      inaccuracies, 560

FMLA's exclusions and, 433
gendered impacts of COVID-19 pandemic on, 139
impacts of Hyde Amendment on, 450
incidence of campus sexual harassment, 249–50
intersectionality critique and, 32, 176
as law school faculty, 498, 502
as law school students, 497–98, 503
#MeToo movement and, 123–24, 260, 262–63
in service industry, 124
sexual harassment of, 655
sexualized injury of, 43–45
voting rights for, 10
welfare law and reproductive rights, 125
Women of Color Task Force, 228
Women's Advocates, Minnesota, 227
women scientists, 317
Women's Health Leadership Network, 287
Women's Joint Congressional Committee, 10
women's liberation movement. *See also* anti-rape movement
battered women's movement, 232–33
Women's March (2017), 251
Women's National Abortion Action Coalition, 278

Women's Rights Project (WRP), 19, 24–27, 354–55, 448
Women's Self-Defense Law Project, 371–72
women's studies programs, 499, 500–501
women's suffrage movement, 22
legal feminism theory and, 7–10
Wood, Carmita, 333
worker surveillance, 564–65
workforce demographics, women in (1970), 352
work from home (WFH), 140
working-class women, need for #MeToo movement, 48
Working Women United (WWU), 334
workplace sexual harassment. *See* sexual harassment, in the workplace
World of Struggle (D. Kennedy), 189
Wright, Frances, 3

Y

Yale University, 296
Yoffe, Emily, 250
Yuracko, Kimberly A., 359, 394

Z

Ziegler, Mary, 452
Zuboff, Shoshana, 560